The Borzoi College Reader

FIFTH EDITION

The Borzoi College Reader

FIFTH EDITION

Charles Muscatine
University of California, Berkeley

Marlene Griffith
Laney College

Alfred A. Knopf 🐕 *New York*

Fifth Edition
98765432
Copyright © 1966, 1971, 1976, 1980, 1984 by Charles Muscatine and
Marlene Griffith

Library of Congress Cataloging in Publication Data
Main entry under title:

The Borzoi college reader.

  Includes indexes.
  1. College readers. I. Muscatine, Charles.
II. Griffith, Marlene.
PE1122.B595   1983   808'.0427   83–23884
ISBN 0–394–33261–X

Acknowledgments

GORDON ALLPORT, "Prejudice and the Individual," from *The Black American Reference Book*, edited by Mabel M. Smythe. Copyright © by Prentice-Hall, Inc. Published by Prentice-Hall, Inc., Englewood Cliffs, New Jersey 07632. Reprinted by permission of the publisher.

HANNAH ARENDT, "Anton Schmidt," from *Eichmann in Jerusalem*, by Hannah Arendt. Copyright © 1963, 1964 by Hannah Arendt. Reprinted by permission of Viking Penguin Inc.

ISAAC ASIMOV, "The Nightmare Life Without Fuel," from *Time*. Copyright © 1977 by Time Inc. All rights reserved. Reprinted by permission.

BEN H. BAGDIKIAN, "The Gentle Suppression," from *The Effete Conspiracy and Other Crimes by the Press*, by Ben H. Bagdikian, pp. 40–46. Copyright © 1972 by Ben H. Bagdikian. Reprinted by permission of Harper & Row, Publishers, Inc.

JAMES BALDWIN, "Notes of a Native Son," from *Notes of a Native Son*, by James Baldwin. Copyright © 1955 by James Baldwin. Reprinted by permission of Beacon Press.

IMAMU AMIRI BARAKA (LeRoi Jones), "Young Soul," from *Black Magic: Poetry 1961–1967*. Copyright © 1969 by LeRoi Jones. Reprinted by permission of the Sterling Lord Agency.

WALTER W. BENJAMIN, "A Challenge to the Eco-Doomsters." Copyright 1979 Christian Century Foundation. Reprinted by permission from the March 21, 1979, issue of *The Christian Century*.

PETER BERGER, "A Tale of Two Moralities," from *Pyramids of Sacrifice: Political Ethics and Social Change*, by Peter L. Berger. Copyright © 1974 by Peter L. Berger. Reprinted by permission of Basic Books, Inc., Publishers, New York.

WENDELL BERRY, "The Reactor and the Garden," "Home of the Free," and "Horse-Drawn Tools and the Doctrine of Labor Saving." Excerpted from *The Gift of Good Land: Further Essays Cultural and Agricultural*. Copyright © 1981 by Wendell Berry. Published by North Point Press. All rights reserved.

PAUL BOHANNAN, "The Stranger," from *Science 81*, April 1981. Reprinted by permission of Science 83 Magazine, copyright the American Association for the Advancement of Science.

SISSELA BOK, "Lies for the Public Good," from *Lying: Moral Choice in Public and Private Life*, by Sissela Bok. Copyright © 1978 by Sissela Bok. Reprinted by permission of Pantheon Books, a Division of Random House, Inc.

DANIEL J. BOORSTIN, "The Rhetoric of Democracy," from *Democracy and Its Discontents*, by Daniel J. Boorstin. Copyright © 1971, 1972, 1973, 1974 by Daniel J. Boorstin. Reprinted by permission of Random House, Inc.

HAIG. A. BOSMAJIAN, from *The Language of Oppression*, pp. 1–9. Reprinted by permission of Public Affairs Press.

JOHN H. BROOMFIELD, "High Technology: The Construction of Disaster," from *Alternative Futures*, Vol. 3, No. 2 (Spring 1980), pp. 31–44. Copyright 1980 Merritt Abrash and Alexandra Aldridge, co-editors, *Alternative Futures*. Reprinted by permission.

JOSEPH CAMPBELL, "Mythic Images," from *Myths to Live By*, by Joseph Campbell. Copyright © 1972 by Joseph Campbell. Reprinted by permission of Viking Penguin Inc.

ALBERT CAMUS, "The Guest," from *Exile and the Kingdom*, by Albert Camus, translated

Review #15, Fall/Winter 1980. Reprinted by permission of the author and The Chowder Review.

WILLIAM GOLDING, "Thinking as a Hobby," from *Holiday*, August 1961. Reprinted by permission of Travel Magazine, Inc., Floral Park, New York 11001.

ROBERT GRAVES, "The Cool Web," from *The Collected Poems*, 1975, published by Cassells Limited. Reprinted by permission of Robert Graves.

DICK GREGORY, "Shame," from *Nigger: An Autobiography*, by Dick Gregory with Robert Lipsyte. Copyright © 1964 by Dick Gregory Enterprises, Inc. Reprinted by permission of the publisher, E. P. Dutton, Inc.

ANDREW GRIFFIN, "Sympathy for the Werewolf," from *University Publishing*, Winter 1979. Reprinted by permission of the author.

GERALD GROW, "How to Write 'Official,' " *Simply Stated*, No. 25. Copyright © 1982 by Gerald O. Grow. Reprinted by permission of the author and the publisher, the Document Design Center of the American Institute for Research, Washington, D.C.

GARRETT HARDIN, "Lifeboat Ethics: The Case Against Helping the Poor," from *Psychology Today Magazine*, September 1974, pp. 38–43, 123–126. Copyright © 1974, American Psychological Association. Reprinted by permission.

ROBERT HAYDEN, "Aunt Jemima of the Ocean Waves," from *Words in the Mourning Time*, by Robert Hayden. Copyright © 1970 by Robert Hayden. Reprinted by permission of October House.

JAMES HERRIOT, from *All Things Bright and Beautiful*, Chapter 3. Copyright © 1973, 1974 by James Herriot. Reprinted by permission of St. Martin's Press, Inc., New York, and Harold Ober Associates, Incorporated.

ADOLF HITLER, "Nation and Race," from *Mein Kampf*, by Adolf Hitler, translated by Ralph Manheim. Copyright 1943 and © renewed 1971 by Houghton Mifflin Company. Reprinted by permission of Houghton Mifflin Company and the Hutchinson Publishing Group Ltd.

MERLE HODGE, "The Shadow of the Whip," from *Is Massa Dead?*, edited by Orde Coombs. Copyright © 1974, by Doubleday & Company, Inc. Reprinted by permission of the author.

MATINA HORNER, "Fail: Bright Women," from *Psychology Today Magazine*, November 1969, pp. 37–38, 62. Copyright © 1969, American Psychological Association. Reprinted by permission.

JEANNE WAKATSUKI HOUSTON, "Beyond Manzanar: A Personal View of Asian-American Womanhood," from *Asian-Americans: Social and Psychological Perspectives*, Vol. II, edited by Russell Endo, Stanley Sue, and Nathaniel N. Wagner. Copyright © 1980 by Science and Behavior Books, Inc. Reprinted by permission of the author and the publisher.

ALDOUS HUXLEY, "Propaganda Under a Dictatorship" and "The Arts of Selling," from *Brave New World Revisited*, by Aldous Huxley. Copyright © 1958 by Aldous Huxley. Reprinted by permission of Harper & Row Publishers, Inc.; Mrs. Laura Huxley; and Chatto & Windus Ltd.

THOMAS H. HUXLEY, "The Method of Scientific Investigation," from *Darwiniana: Essays by Thomas H. Huxley*, originally published in 1896. Reprinted by permission of AMS Press, Inc.

PAUL JACOBS, "The Most Cheerful Graveyard in the World," from *The Reporter*, September 18, 1958, pp. 26–30. Reprinted by permission.

ROBERT M. KAUS, "What's Wrong with Roots," reprinted with permission from *The Washington Monthly*, March 1979, pp. 22–29. Copyright 1979 by The Washington Monthly Co., 2712 Ontario Road, N.W., Washington, D.C. 20009.

GARRISON KEILLOR, "Re The Tower Project," from *Happy to Be Here*, by Garrison Keillor. Copyright © 1971, 1982 by Garrison Keillor. Reprinted by permission of Atheneum Publishers. "Re The Tower Project" was first published in *The New Yorker*.

WILLIAM KILPATRICK, "Identity in a Temporary Society," from *Identity and Intimacy*,

Development and Josephine Miles. Copyright 1962 by the Association for Supervision and Curriculum Development. All rights reserved.

JAMES E. MILLER, JR., "Thought and Feeling," from *Word, Self, Reality: The Rhetoric of Imagination,* by James E. Miller, Jr. (Dodd, Mead), pp. 50–56. Copyright © 1972 by Harper & Row, Publishers, Inc. Reprinted by permission of the publisher.

N. SCOTT MOMADAY, Introduction to *The Way to Rainy Mountain.* Copyright © 1969 by the University of New Mexico Press. Reprinted by permission of the author. Originally published in *The Reporter* (January 26, 1967).

WILLIAM LEAST HEAT MOON, from *Blue Highways,* by William Least Heat Moon, pp. 7–11. Copyright © 1982 by William Least Heat Moon. Reprinted by permission of Little, Brown and Company.

HAROLD J. MOROWITZ, "Women's Lib and the Battle Against Entropy" and "Drinking Hemlock and Other Nutritional Matters," from *The Wine of Life and Other Essays on Societies, Energy and Living Things,* by Harold J. Morowitz. Copyright © 1979 by Harold J. Morowitz. Reprinted by permission of St. Martin's Press, Inc., New York.

TONI MORRISON, "A Slow Walk of Trees (as Grandmother Would Say) Hopeless (as Grandfather Would Say)," *New York Times Magazine,* July 4, 1976. Copyright © 1976 by the New York Times Company. Reprinted by permission.

MALCOLM MUGGERIDGE, "Credo," from *Jesus Rediscovered,* by Malcolm Muggeridge. Copyright © 1969 by Malcolm Muggeridge. Originally published in *The Observer.* Reprinted by permission of Doubleday & Company, Inc., and William Collins Sons & Company Ltd.

THE NEW YORKER, "The Wisdom of the Worm," from "The Talk of the Town," August 29, 1970. Copyright © 1970 The New Yorker Magazine, Inc. Reprinted by permission.

WILLIAM NICHOLS, "The Burden of Imagination: Stanley Milgram's *Obedience to Authority,*" from *Writing from Experience,* edited by William Nichols. Copyright © 1975 by Harcourt Brace Jovanovich, Inc. Reprinted by permission of Harcourt Brace Jovanovich.

JOYCE CAROL OATES, "Where Are You Going, Where Have You Been?" from *The Wheel of Love,* by Joyce Carol Oates. Copyright © 1970, 1969, 1968, 1967, 1966, 1965, by Joyce Carol Oates. Reprinted by permission of the publisher, Vanguard Press, Inc.

GEORGE ORWELL, "Politics and the English Language" and "Shooting an Elephant," from *Shooting an Elephant and Other Essays* by George Orwell. "Politics and the English Language" copyright 1946 by Sonia Brownell Orwell; renewed 1974 by Sonia Orwell. "Shooting an Elephant" copyright 1950 by Sonia Brownell Orwell; renewed 1978 by Sonia Pitt-Rivers. Both reprinted by permission of Harcourt Brace Jovanovich, Inc.; the estate of the late Sonia Brownell Orwell; and Martin Secker & Warburg Ltd.

MARGE PIERCY, "To Be of Use," from *Circles on the Water,* by Marge Piercy. Copyright © 1973 by Marge Piercy. Reprinted by permission of Alfred A. Knopf, Inc.

J. H. PLUMB, "De Mortuis," from *In the Light of History,* by J. H. Plumb. Copyright © 1972 by J. H. Plumb. Reprinted by permission of Houghton Mifflin Company and Penguin Books Ltd.

NEIL POSTMAN, "The Day Our Children Disappear: Predictions of a Media Ecologist," from *Phi Delta Kappan,* January 1981. Reprinted by permission of the author.

MARCEL PROUST, "Prologue," from *By Way of Sainte-Beuve,* by Marcel Proust, translated by Sylvia Townsend Warner. Copyright © 1958 by Meridian Books, Inc. Reprinted by arrangement with World Publishing Company, Cleveland and New York. Translation copyright © Chatto and Windus, Ltd., 1957. Reprinted by permission of the Translator's Literary Estate and Chatto & Windus Ltd. Originally published in French by Librairie Gallimard, Paris, 1954, under the title *Contre Sainte-Beuve.*

MICHAEL ROBERTS, "The Vicarious Heroism of the Sports Spectator," from *The New Republic,* November 24, 1974, pp. 17–20. Copyright © 1974 by The New Republic, Inc. Reprinted by permission of the publisher.

JAMES HARVEY ROBINSON, "On Various Kinds of Thinking," from *The Mind in the Making,* by James Harvey Robinson. Copyright 1921 by Harper & Row, Publishers, Inc.;

renewed 1949 by Bankers Trust Company. Reprinted by permission of Harper & Row, Publishers, Inc.

THEODORE ROETHKE, "Dolor," copyright 1943 by Modern Poetry Association, Inc., from *The Collected Poems of Theodore Roethke*. Reprinted by permission of Doubleday & Company, Inc.

HAROLD ROSENBERG, "Masculinity: Style and Cult," from *Vogue*, November 15, 1967, p. 106. Reprinted by permission of *Vogue*.

CARL SAGAN, "In Defense of Robots" and "A Sunday Sermon," from *Broca's Brain*, by Carl Sagan, pp. 239–249 and 281–291. Copyright © 1974, 1975, 1976, 1977, 1978, 1979 by Carl Sagan. Reprinted by permission of Random House, Inc.

E. F. SCHUMACHER, "A Culture of Poverty," from *Voices for Life: Reflections on the Human Condition*, edited by Dom Moraes. Copyright © 1975 by United Nations Fund for Population Activities. Reprinted by permission of Holt, Rinehart and Winston, Publishers. "Prologue" (pp. 1–4), from *Good Work*, by E. F. Schumacher. Copyright © 1979 by Verena Schumacher. Reprinted by permission of Harper & Row Publishers, Inc.

THOMAS B. SHERIDAN, "Seven Factors in Alienation," from "Computer Control and Human Alienation," *Technology Review*, October 1980, pp. 66–67, 71–73. Copyright 1980 by Technology Review. Reprinted by permission.

ISAAC BASHEVIS SINGER, "The Son from America," from *A Crown of Feathers*, by Isaac Bashevis Singer. Copyright © 1970, 1971, 1972, 1973 by Isaac Bashevis Singer. Reprinted by permission of Farrar, Straus & Giroux, Inc. "The Son from America" originally appeared in *The New Yorker*.

PHILLIP SLATER, "Community and Competition: Getting Together," from *The Pursuit of Loneliness: American Culture at the Breaking Point*, by Phillip Slater. Copyright © 1976 by Phillip Slater. Reprinted by permission of Beacon Press.

WILLIAM STAFFORD, "A Way of Writing," from *Writing the Australian Crawl: Views on the Writer's Vocation*, by William Stafford. Copyright © 1978 by the University of Michigan Press. Reprinted by permission of the publisher.

LINCOLN STEFFENS, "I Go to College" and "I Become a Student," from *The Autobiography of Lincoln Steffens*. Copyright 1931 by Harcourt Brace Jovanovich, Inc.; renewed 1959 by Peter Steffens. Reprinted by permission of the publisher.

JUDY SYFERS, "I Want a Wife," from *Ms. Magazine* (December 1971). Copyright © 1971 by Judy Syfers. Reprinted by permission of the author.

RABINDRANATH TAGORE, "Fruit Gathering," from *Collected Poems and Plays*, by Rabindranath Tagore. Copyright 1916 by Macmillan Publishing, Co., Inc.; renewed 1944 by Rabindranath Tagore. Reprinted by permission of Macmillan Publishing Co., Inc., and Macmillan, London and Basingstoke.

STUDS TERKEL, "The Stream: Leonel I. Castillo," "Carol and Tony Danlow," and "William Gothard," from *American Dreams: Lost and Found*, by Studs Terkel. Copyright © 1980 by Studs Terkel. Reprinted by permission of Pantheon Books, a Division of Random House, Inc. "Carl Murray Bates, Mason," "Nora Watson, Editor," and "Mike LeFevre, Steelworker," from *Working: People Talk About What They Do All Day and How They Feel About What They Do*, by Studs Terkel. Copyright © 1972, 1974 by Studs Terkel. Reprinted by permission of Pantheon Books, a Division of Random House, Inc.

LEWIS THOMAS, "Altruism," from the *New York Times Magazine*, July 4, 1976, p. 109. Copyright © 1976 by the New York Times Company. Reprinted by permission.

PAUL TILLICH, "The Lost Dimension in Religion," from *The Saturday Evening Post*, June 14, 1958. Copyright © 1958 by The Curtis Publishing Company. Reprinted by permission of *The Saturday Evening Post*.

ALEXIS DE TOCQUEVILLE, "Of Individualism in Democratic Countries," from *Democracy in America*, Vol. II, by Alexis de Tocqueville, translated by Henry Reeve, revised by Francis Bowen, and edited by Phillips Bradley. Copyright 1945 and renewed 1973 by Alfred A. Knopf, Inc. Reprinted by permission of the publisher.

ESTHER VILAR, "What Is Woman?" from *The Manipulated Man*, by Esther Vilar. Copyright © 1972 by Farrar, Straus & Giroux, Inc. Reprinted by permission of Farrar, Straus & Giroux, Inc.

ALICE WALKER, "To Hell with Dying." Copyright © 1967 by Alice Walker. Reprinted from her volume *In Love and in Trouble* by permission of Harcourt Brace Jovanovich, Inc.

JOSEPH WEIZENBAUM, from *Computer Power and Human Reason*, pp. 1–16. Copyright © 1976 by W. H. Freeman and Company. Reprinted by permission of the publisher.

JUDITH LEE WELLS, "Daddy's Girl," from *Libra* #1 (Winter 1972), pp. 43–45. Reprinted by permission of the author.

E. B. WHITE, "The Morning of the Day They Did It," from *The Second Tree from the Corner*, by E. B. White. Originally published in *The New Yorker*, (February 25, 1950). Reprinted by permission of Harper & Row Publishers, Inc.

VIRGINIA WOOLF, "Professions for Women," from *The Death of the Moth and Other Essays*, by Virginia Woolf. Copyright 1942 by Harcourt Brace Jovanovich, Inc.; renewed 1970 by Marjorie T. Parsons, Executrix. Reprinted by permission of Harcourt Brace Jovanovich, Inc.; The Author's Literary Estate; and The Hogarth Press. "Shakespeare's Sister," an extract from *A Room of One's Own*, by Virginia Woolf. Copyright 1929 by Harcourt Brace Jovanovich, Inc.; renewed 1957 by Leonard Woolf. Reprinted by permission of Harcourt Brace Jovanovich, Inc.; The Author's Literary Estate; and The Hogarth Press.

WILLIAM BUTLER YEATS, "Leda and the Swan," from *Collected Poems*, by William Butler Yeats. Copyright 1928 by Macmillan Publishing Co., Inc.; renewed 1956 by Georgie Yeats. Reprinted by permission of Macmillan Publishing Co., Inc., Michael B. Yeats, Anne Yeats, and Macmillan London Ltd.

WILLIAM K. ZINSSER, "Simplicity," from *On Writing Well*, by William K. Zinsser (Harper & Row). Copyright © 1976 by William K. Zinsser. Reprinted by permission of the author.

Preface

In presenting this fifth edition of our book, we want to affirm its character not only as a source of models of composition, but also as a source of ideas, ideas that are immediate occasions for critical thinking and writing.

Human values and ethical choice continue to be the underlying theme of the book. This edition contains five new groups of essays (College and Education, The Problem of Identity, Race and Prejudice, Television and Reality, and Computers and People). In addition, several of the old sections have been substantially rethought and refocused. The book is larger by twenty-five selections and contains sixty new ones. As with the earlier editions, we have done no silent editing, and most of the pieces are either complete works in themselves or coherent sections (usually chapters) of longer works. Allusions and references that cannot be found in a standard college dictionary are glossed at the foot of each page.

We have again provided headnotes that give background and other information about each piece and its writer, not only to show that significant writing comes out of real lives and careers but also to show that these lives and careers are the kind open to all college students.

In preparing this edition, we have ourselves been surprised to find how interconnected the readings are. Martin Luther King's "Letter from Birmingham Jail," for example, is a key piece in the section titled On Civil Disobedience, but it applies equally well to thinking about Race and Prejudice and about Right and Wrong. Robin Lakoff's essay, "You Are What You Say," a document on The Right Use of Language, applies equally well in the sections on The Problem of Identity, and On Women and Men. Steven Levy's article "Hackers in Paradise" in Computers and People can also be read in relation to The Good Life. The whole subsection On the Meaning of Work can be read as one facet of The Problem of Identity.

What this suggests is that ideas of sufficient importance always relate to other ideas. A collection such as this, then, introduces college students to the world of serious discourse as an interconnected structure. It shows that the subjects and ideas that lie before them do not exist in isolation but have sources, ramifications, and consequences in very different reaches of experience and knowledge.

We provide at the end of the book a rhetorical index, an index of genres, and a table of cross-references showing which essays are particularly well related to sections other than the ones in which they appear.

A Teacher's Guide is available from the publisher.

We owe particular thanks for help with this edition to the following friends and colleagues: Ann Connor, Gertrude Fator, Katherine Fulton, Sandra Gilbert, Bob Heilbroner, Christine Hilary, Christopher Hipkin, Bruce Jacobs, Susan McCallister, Quinto Pugliese, Susan Schacher, Sondra Shair, Marie Wilson, and Smokey Wilson.

As before, colleagues from other colleges and universities agreed to write detailed analyses and suggestions based on their experience with previous editions; our appreciation and thanks go to Lucien L. Agosta of Kansas State University; Barbara Benjamini of Sacred Heart University; Ruth Bryant of Sam Houston State University; Valerie Ann Bystrom of Seattle Central Community College; Amelia Canaday of Louisiana State University; Jim Meyers of the University of California at Berkeley; Barbara Munson Goff of Rutgers University, Cook College; John Pahl of Northwestern Michigan College; Charles Poston of Fairmont State College; Dennis Rygiel of Auburn University; Emily Seelbinder of The University of North Carolina at Chapel Hill; Mary Steussy Shanahan of Cameron University; and Cameron D. Webster of Bowling Green State University.

The manuscript was prepared with the expert bibliographical assistance of Susan McCallister, Susan Charlip, and Laurie Bagley. We were extraordinarily fortunate, too, with our editors at A. A. Knopf. Steve Pensinger and Elisa Turner shepherded the whole project from start to finish; Carolyn Viola-John handled the manuscript with elegant precision; and the presence of June Smith gave us, as ever, the sense that all's right with the publishing world at Knopf.

Jean O'Meara became more a collaborator than editorial assistant. The benefit of her scholarship, judgment, and teaching experience informs the whole book.

Contents

The Right Use of Language 73

College and Education 137

On Right and Wrong 159

The Social Contract   207

Community and Self   277

The Good Life 351

Race, Racism and Culture 437

Cultures in Tension

On Women and Men   531

Barriers, Visible and Invisible

On Women and Men

Toward Men's Liberation

The Media and Popular Culture   589

Journalism with a Human Voice

Technology and Human Values
667

Religion and the Search for Meaning   *761*

On Death and Dying   *809*

Advice to the Student: On Reading an Essay

In offering here some practical advice on how to read an essay, we do not mean to imply that there is just one way to go at it. Essays differ, and readers differ even more, and how a given reader comes to an understanding of an author's message may be a very individual process indeed. But for our present purpose—which is to offer some initial guidance to the comparatively inexperienced reader of essays—it will be safe to assume that if you have no settled way of starting out on your own, a good way to learn is to use standard moves that have worked well for others. The method we will offer, indeed, corresponds closely to what many college teachers do when an essay is being discussed in class. Thus students who follow our suggestions in the order given will often find that they have not only read an essay critically, but have prepared themselves for active class discussion and for writing about it.

First of all, you must be prepared—and leave time—to read the essay more than once. The first reading, which may be comparatively rapid, is to get a preliminary overview. This overview—a sense of how the essay goes from beginning to end—is essential to getting a good general sense of the essay's purpose and point. That is, the two main questions one asks oneself on first reading are: What is this essay trying to do? and What is its "main idea"?

What is the essay trying to do? Why is the writer telling us what he or she is telling us? A preliminary answer is essential to appreciating the essay, to coming to a secure conclusion about what it means. Most essays are prose statements that make some kind of a point, but within that rough definition they vary as much as the motives behind any human communication can vary. The writer may be trying, as one human being to another, to share an experience; or helpfully to explain something that might be interesting or puzzling to the reader; or to persuade the reader to an opinion about something, to move him or her to action, perhaps political. Some writers may even have selfish or questionable motives: to promote themselves or to deceive the reader. In any case, you need some general idea of what the writer is up to in order to ask the right questions and to come to secure conclusions about the meaning and value of the essay in all its details. In the present volume, the essays are marshaled around a number of important issues in our culture, and most of them will be found to be expository—that is, written to set out, explain, or prove to the reader the truth of an idea. Yet many essays, however they may involve ideas, are principally narratives. They tell us—share with us—some important experiences in the authors' lives. (See, for instance, Dick Gregory's "Shame," p. 160; the piece by James Herriot, p. 395; and Thomas Merton's "First Mass," p. 797). Other essays seem to move, as we read them, from narrative of this kind to an explicit idea that is drawn, finally, from the events narrated. (Such, for instance, are Hannah Arendt's "Anton Schmidt," p. 178; George Orwell's "Shooting an Elephant," p. 164; and Paul Bohannan's "The Stranger," p. 347).

Many others announce right off that they are about ideas. Alexis de Tocqueville tells us this in the first sentence of his essay titled "Of Individualism in Democratic Countries," when he writes: "I have shown how it is that in ages of equality every man seeks for his opinions within himself; I am now to show how it is that in the same ages all his feelings are turned towards himself alone" (p. 315). Still others let us know, earlier or later, that they want us to take sides in an ongoing controversy. (See Martin Luther King, Jr., on the civil rights movement, p. 254; Esther Vilar on the status of women, p. 564; Clarence Darrow on believing in God, p. 764).

While we are coming to a rough idea of what the essay is for, we will already be working on the second question, What is the essay's main idea? The two questions are related, but they are not the same. It is important to have read an essay right to the end before deciding what the main idea is, for quite often the idea with which an essay begins is not the principal idea of the essay. The opening sections of the essay may be introducing the topic, laying the groundwork, perhaps getting the reader into a frame of mind for accepting the main idea, which may itself be reserved for the end. Thus Orwell's "Politics and the English Language" starts out with the idea that "the English language is in a bad way" (p. 97), and in the second paragraph, that the badness of our language "makes it easier for us to have foolish thoughts" and that clear thinking may have something to do with our "political regeneration." He then spends some nine pages beautifully elaborating these preliminary ideas, not coming again to a full expression of what turns out to be his main idea—each aspect of which he has already argued in some detail—until his last paragraph: "The present political chaos is connected with the decay of language, and . . . one can probably bring about some improvement by starting at the verbal end." In "The Indispensable Opposition," Walter Lippmann gives us his main idea at the end of the fourth paragraph: "We must protect the right of our opponents to speak because we must hear what they have to say" (p. 221). We know that this *is* the main idea because by the end of the essay nothing else tops it; the rest of the essay is devoted to expounding and defending it. Of course, many essays will announce their main idea quite early, as does Haig Bosmajian's at the end of the first paragraph: ". . . the power which comes from naming and defining people has had positive as well as negative effects on entire populations" (p. 110). His essay emphasizes the negative effects. Marc Feigen Fasteau's main idea in "Friendships Among Men" comes at the end of the second paragraph, when he writes: "Despite the time men spend together, their contact rarely goes beyond the external, a limitation which tends to make their friendships shallow and unsatisfying" (p. 579). Both of these essays, like many others, by ending on an upbeat or corrective note, seem to have not one but two main ideas—the one that occupies the body of the essay and the one that follows it at the end. Be that as it may, you will have done your reading well if the first time through you can put your finger on a statement that all or most of the essay seems to be supporting. Notice that a main idea *is* an idea: It says something *about* something. You can test whether you are identifying an *idea* as opposed, merely, to a *topic* like "sex roles" or "politics and language" by whether you can express it in a sentence.

Sometimes the main idea is not stated anywhere by the author in so many words, and sometimes, as in poetry or fiction, it is not reducible to simple terms; in these cases the reader can supply only an approximation of it. The "main idea" of Dick Gregory's narrative, a narrative that freely mingles ideas and feelings, is something about the way shame can get in the way of human sympathy. James Herriot's account of his rounds as a veterinarian includes some uncomfortable incidents, yet the total effect is to show how satisfying such work can be.

The reason that it is useful to start with a notion of the purpose and the main idea of an essay is that most good essays are *organized* or *unified* around their purpose and main idea, and so can be understood most handily in those terms. Much of an appreciative, critical reading comes from being able to explain the various parts or features of the essay and relate them to the essay's purpose and main idea. The main features that a good reader will be on the alert for by the second reading will be organization or argument, the kinds of evidence presented, and any elements of technique, tone or style that contribute to its full meaning. By this time the reader should be well past the "receptive" stage of just sitting there and letting the words come. Try to take an active role, working along with the writer step by step, or standing behind the writer and watching and appreciating how it is done.

There are many ways to organize an essay, but in general, in the essay that tries to establish an idea, the main parts will be the steps used to get the reader to accept the idea. As we have said, the author's strategy may lead to announcing the idea at the beginning or to withholding it until the end, but the body of the essay will have to consist, in one way or another, of some organized combination of argument and evidence.

One of the simplest and best ways for a writer to make a point is to mention one by one all the things in personal experience or reading that make one feel the idea is true, organizing them by groups and subgroups in order to avoid diffuseness. Thus Marc Feigen Fasteau, after stating his main idea about the quality of friendships among men, starts in paragraph 3 (p. 579) with a group of observations about uncommunicativeness among men. He talks first about the general quality of male conversations, then in the next paragraph about the use of games as a substitute for conversation; in the next paragraph comes some evidence from his experience with a college friend and with his father; in the next comes an example from popular literature; then, after dealing with some exceptions, he lets us know, with the adverb *finally,* that his last piece of evidence for uncommunicativeness "is the way men depend on women to facilitate certain conversations" (p. 581). The next paragraph sees him summarizing for us the meaning of this subsection of his essay and announcing that he is now going to turn to "the reasons why men hide from each other," which "lie in the taboos and imperatives of the masculine stereotype" (p. 582). The alert reader will expect then, in the ensuing paragraphs, a list of cultural prohibitions or commands that make men behave the way they do, with some discussion of each. And sure enough, that is what he gives us, with due attention to some exceptions, and with a brief, constructive conclusion. Notice that a writer will often use adverbs and transitional phrases —*first of all, finally, however, furthermore,* and the like—to let the reader know continuously what is going on.

Your acceptance of the main idea of this kind of essay depends on your acceptance of the evidence presented. Is it true to your experience? Or, if it is not within your experience, do you believe it? What is the author's reliability? Is the author the kind of person who should be believed on this subject?

Sometimes the author will try to persuade by using some form of logic, a chain of argument. Thus Garrett Hardin (p. 289) argues that since the poor multiply many times faster than the rich, simply feeding the poor creates that much more of a surplus of poor people and makes the problem of world poverty ultimately greater, not less. In dealing with arguments based on logic, the experienced reader will want to test perhaps with the aid of further research or wider reading whether all the parts of the argument are true, whether the conclusions really do follow from the facts given, and whether anywhere in the argument the reader is being asked to accept a hidden assumption—something that is quietly assumed by the writer and intended to stand without proof. (The essay by Thomas H. Huxley, p. 25, will give you a good idea of two major forms of logic.)

Writers use many other means to help them make their meanings clear. Sometimes they offer contrasting definitions or comparisons, which help clarify each other. (See William Golding, p. 31, and James Harvey Robinson, p. 37, on kinds of thinking; Martin Luther King, Jr., on just and unjust laws, p. 260; Alexis de Tocqueville on egoism and individualism, p. 315). Sometimes they use analogy, that is, a reference to something familiar to the reader that is comparable to the idea being presented. (Hardin, p. 290, starts with the idea of the lifeboat to clarify his view of the situation of rich nations; and Walter Lippmann, p. 221, uses our tolerance of our doctor's diagnosis as an analogy to what he means by political tolerance.) Sometimes the writer relies heavily on a simple incident or anecdote or a few vivid pieces of evidence that seem to sum up or symbolize the whole meaning all at once. (Marcel Proust, p. 65, uses the remembered taste of a piece of toast in this way; Wendell Berry, p. 372, uses a few phrases from two advertisements.) Sometimes, as with James Baldwin, the writer seems to take us through the actual network of experiences that led him to his final conclusions. As you encounter these various devices, your appreciation of them will deepen if you continually ask yourself how and why they work to support or embody the author's main purpose and idea.

Of course, much that a writer does in an essay will go beyond the requirements of simply making ideas clear. The writer will, quite legitimately, want to appeal to the reader's feelings, to share feelings, or to suggest a proper emotional response to the topic. You should be sensitively aware of this aspect of the essay, not only to be on guard against improper manipulation of feelings—as, for instance, in appeals to sentimentality or prejudice—but also to enhance your understanding and enjoyment of the feelings themselves.

Feelings are powerfully generated by the techniques that the essay writer shares with the poet and novelist—the choice of particular words, sounds, and rhythms, the setting of scenes, telling of stories, creation of atmosphere—and by the particular tone of voice that the writer seems to adopt. An adequate account of all these would require volumes. Here we must be content to point briefly to some easily noticed effects of literary style in the essays usually read in college.

Some writers—often professors and scientists—write in an impersonal style that seems calculated to keep feelings neutral or at a distance. The kind of words they use seems to be saying: Let the ideas or facts speak for themselves. (Robinson, p. 37, writes like this, and so do Murray Edelman, p. 121; John Hope Franklin, p. 442; Joseph Campbell, p. 779; and Matina Horner, p. 552.) Other writers have more personal styles, as if they had found their own unique voices, and seem to be addressing us personally. (This is the way Wendell Berry sounds, pp. 269, 371, 706, and Toni Morrison, p. 519; James Baldwin, p. 462; Henry David Thoreau, p. 236; and Jeanne Wakatsuki Houston, p. 500). The personal relationship and directness implied by the way they write may have an important effect on the reader, often suggesting that the reader return the confidence and relative intimacy offered by the writer.

Some writers—Orwell is among the greatest of them—try for a plain style, in which the writing, like a pane of glass, rarely calls attention to itself, rarely interposes itself between the reader and what there is to be seen and felt. This style is much admired nowadays; it has an economy that harmonizes with the pace of modern life, and it suggests an attractive modesty on the part of the writer. Other authors seem almost intoxicated with words; they write a highly colored prose, with heavily distinctive word choice and rhythms, which can be very moving indeed, but more often gives the effect of excessiveness or self-display.

Some writers of essays use techniques characteristic of fiction. Thus the descriptions in Joan Didion's "Some Dreamers of the Golden Dream" are used less to give us the facts than to create artistically a certain atmosphere or tone. For instance, her opening description (p. 358), the choice and sequencing of details in the description of the funeral (p. 360), and the vivid characterization she gives to even the minor actors in her story, all suggest the talents of a fiction writer and all contribute to what she wants to say about the culture she is describing. The same can be said of the way N. Scott Momaday creates atmosphere through description in his "Introduction" to *The Way to Rainy Mountain* (p. 457). Indeed most good essay writers have some sensitivity to scene, atmosphere, character, word choice, and tone, and you should try to appreciate how any of these aspects adds to the meaning of the piece you are reading. Finally, you should be alert to the great devices of irony and humor, which often convey their meanings indirectly through some implied reversal of what they seem to say, often for the sake of satire. (The classic example of this is Jonathan Swift's "A Modest Proposal," p. 307; other, lighter examples are Paul Jacobs's "The Most Cheerful Graveyard in the World," p. 816; E. B. White's "The Morning of the Day They Did It," p. 669; and Garrison Keillor's "Re the Tower Project," p. 712.)

Because you are in a college classroom situation, you may well have started out to read an essay because of compulsion or on faith—on someone else's say so. It is wise to start out with a certain humility or faith or optimism that an essay someone wrote, and that was published and perhaps republished and then recommended or assigned—that such an essay must have a message of value. It is well to have started out with some receptiveness and some respect for the writer; but in the end, reading is for yourself, and once a couple of careful readings have given you an idea of the essay's meaning for the author, the final question to ask is: What does it mean for me? The words on the page will not take on their deepest meaning until you have come to terms with the essay, as if you had just had (what deep reading really is) a personal encounter with the writer. How does the message fit with what you already knew, wanted to know, or needed to know? How does the essay relate to others you have read; to ideas and experiences you have already had? If it challenges or disturbs you, where are the points of conflict? If it confirms your ideas, does it merely tell you what you already knew, or make you feel surer of yourself? Is it true to your experience, or false? If new to you, does it enlarge your experience or fail to find a place there; and if it fails, why so? What has it changed in your ideas or feelings? How, in fact, does it make you feel? Even your response to the writer's tone, or to the writer's own degree of involvement with the subject, is a legitimate part of the meaning of the essay for you.

The answers to any of these questions, besides capping your sense of the essay's meaning, will begin to move you from the role of reader to that of thinker, discussant, and writer. Even before you have clearly formulated ideas about the essay, your first emotional response to it will be useful; but you must try to follow out the line of that response, staying on its trail. It may lead you to finding its source in a significant complex of ideas about the essay, about the world, or about yourself. That experience is just what William Nichols describes in his essay, "The Burden of Imagination" (p. 170). He talks of having read a book, experiencing "raging disappointment" as he read it. Tracing this feeling, Nichols found that it was not only a reaction to the book's ideas but to its assumptions, some of which remained hidden. He read the book critically, trying to uncover these hidden assumptions, analyze them, and understand them. In the course of this process, he not only found out why he was angry, but came up with his own main idea, the thought-provoking one with which his essay ends.

The Borzoi
College Reader
FIFTH EDITION

On Writing

Few of us would feel offended if a friend or teacher returned a math problem marked "wrong." Yet almost all of us would feel at least hurt if something we had written were returned to us marked "wrong." Words are more intimately connected to our sense of self than numbers are. When we try to express an idea or a feeling, we risk not being understood. And writing is riskier than talking. We cannot follow our listeners' responses by watching their faces. We cannot interject "What I mean is . . ." or simply change direction or even subjects if we see or sense that we are being misunderstood. Not knowing how our reader will read us (as partner? as judge? as editor? as critic?) can cramp even our sense of how to begin.

The five writers in this section present us with different perspectives on writing and, by implication, they offer advice on what we may ask of—or hope for—from our readers. William Stafford sees writing as a way to help uncover what it is we want to say. A writer, he says, "is not so much someone who has something to say as he is someone who has found a process that will bring about new things he would not have thought of if he had not started to say them." Clearly, there is no "wrong" here, and equally clearly, the writer must simply have the courage to begin. Lawrence Langer thinks the fear of being judged keeps many students from saying anything that means very much to them—and thus to others. They avoid language that could break down barriers between reader and writer and lead to genuine understanding. In fact, they build barriers of "abstract diction and technical jargon" to protect themselves from their readers. Langer also reminds us of the responsibility of the reader, especially of a first reader, by citing a poignant example of a student who risked a very personal essay and an instructor who responded only by correcting it. Pat D'Arcy approaches risk-taking from a different angle. She recommends writing as a means of learning, a way of discovering

1

questions and confusions, of figuring out difficult ideas on our own. She recommends the use of a "learning log," a daily journal in which students can reflect on the material covered in class. Her aim is clearly stated by one student whom she quotes: "I wrote not because I wanted to get all the ideas clear and correct on paper but because I wanted to get all the ideas clear and correct in my head."

These first three essays focus on language as a means of formulating or clarifying what we think, feel, and know. The next two essays, by William Zinsser and Josephine Miles, are more concerned with how we express and communicate our thoughts, feelings, and knowledge.

Concerned as she is with teaching the student writer "how to make responsible statements," Josephine Miles shows how the structure of the argument depends on the thesis statement. The next writer seems to contradict what Stafford and D'Arcy have recommended. "Clear thinking becomes clear writing," says William Zinsser. "It is impossible for a muddy thinker to write good English." He then gives some excellent advice on fighting clutter, echoing the great William Strunk's admonition to "omit needless words." Both Miles and Zinsser seem to say that we need to know what we think in order to know what to say and how to say it. But what does this do to the advice to write, and so discover what we think or what we know?

Actually, what seems to be a contradiction may not be. Different people do, of course, write in different ways. There have always been those who work through several drafts before they are able to get a good handle on their thought or idea, while others have a clear idea in mind, perhaps even an outline, before they begin to put words on paper. You will want to discover your own best way of getting started.

It may also be that, whatever the individual style or emphasis, the two ways just described are actually different parts of the same process. Writers who simply begin to write as Stafford recommends may come to discover ideas, but this discovery may also bring the need to start again, to compose the ideas in a form that will be clear to someone else.

William Stafford

William Stafford is a poet who now lives in Washington, D.C., where he works as a Consultant in Poetry to the Library of Congress. He was born and raised in Kansas. During his school years, he writes, "we moved from one little town to another. . . . Our lives were quiet and the land was very steady. Our teachers were good. Not till I finished my BA degree at the University of Kansas and went on to graduate school in another state did I see an adult drunk or enraged or seriously menacing. Higher education and the coming of World War II supplied a new aspect of experience." A pacifist, he spent the war years in camps for conscientious objectors, fighting forest fires, building trails, and terracing eroding land. After the war he taught at Lewis and Clark College in Oregon, left to study in the creative writing program at the State University of Iowa, and then returned to Lewis and Clark until he moved to Washington.

Stafford has been published widely. Among his collections are *Traveling Through the Dark* (1962), for which he won the 1963 National Book Award in Poetry; *The Rescued Year* (1966), which includes an autobiographical account of his Kansas childhood; *Allegiances* (1970); *Someday, Maybe* (1973); *All About Light* (1978); *Two About Music* (1978); *Around You, Your House and a Catechism* (1979); and *The Quiet of the Land: Poems* (1979). His work also includes criticism and a collection of personal and autobiographical pieces on writing published in 1978 as *Writing the Australian Crawl*. From this comes the chapter printed below.

A Way of Writing

A writer is not so much someone who has something to say as he is someone who has found a process that will bring about new things he would not have thought of if he had not started to say them. That is, he does not draw on a reservoir; instead, he engages in an activity that brings to him a whole succession of unforeseen stories, poems, essays, plays, laws, philosophies, religions, or—but wait!

Back in school, from the first when I began to try to write things, I felt this richness. One thing would lead to another; the world would give and give. Now, after twenty years or so of trying, I live by that certain richness, an idea hard to pin, difficult to say, and perhaps offensive to some. For there are strange implications in it.

One implication is the importance of just plain receptivity. When I write, I like to have an interval before me when I am not likely to be interrupted. For me, this means usually the early morning, before others are awake. I get pen and paper, take a glance out of the window (often it is dark out there), and wait. It is like fishing. But I do not wait very long, for there is always a nibble—and this is where receptivity comes in. To get started I will accept anything that occurs to me. Something always occurs, of course, to any of us. We can't keep from thinking. Maybe I have to settle for an immediate impression: it's cold, or hot, or dark, or bright, or in between! Or—well, the possibilities are endless. If I put down something, that thing will help the next thing come, and I'm off. If I let the process go on, things will occur to me that were not at all in my mind when I started. These things, odd or trivial as they may be, are somehow connected. And if I let them string out, surprising things will happen.

If I let them string out. . . . Along with initial receptivity, then, there is another readiness: I must be willing to fail. If I am to keep on writing, I cannot bother to insist on high standards. I must get into action and not let anything stop me, or even slow me much. By "standards" I do not mean "correctness"—spelling, punctuation, and so on. These details become mechanical for anyone who writes for a while. I am thinking about such matters as social significance, positive values, consistency, etc. I resolutely disregard these. Something better, greater, is happening! I am following a process that leads so wildly and originally into new territory that no judgment can at the moment be made about values, significance, and so on. I am making something new, something that has not been judged before. Later others—and maybe I myself—will make judgments. Now, I am headlong to discover. Any distraction may harm the creating.

So, receptive, careless of failure, I spin out things on the page. And a wonderful freedom comes. If something occurs to me, it is all right to accept it. It has one justification: it occurs to me. No one else can guide me. I must follow my own weak, wandering, diffident impulses.

A strange bonus happens. At times, without my insisting on it, my writings become coherent; the successive elements that occur to me are clearly related. They lead by themselves to new connections. Sometimes the language, even the syllables that happen along, may start a trend. Sometimes the materials alert me to something waiting in my mind, ready for sustained attention. At such times, I allow myself to be eloquent, or intentional, or for great swoops (Treacherous! Not to be trusted!) reasonable. But I do not insist on any of that; for I know that back of my activity there will be the coherence of my self, and that indulgence of my impulses will bring recurrent patterns and meanings again.

This attitude toward the process of writing creatively suggests a problem for me, in terms of what others say. They talk about "skills" in writing. Without denying that I do have experience, wide reading, automatic orthodoxies and maneuvers of various kinds, I still must insist that I am often baffled about what "skill" has to do with the precious little area of confusion when I do not know what I am going to say and then I find out what I am going to say. That precious interval I am unable to bridge by skill. What can I witness about it? It remains mysterious, just as all of us must feel puzzled about how we are so inventive as to be able to talk along through complexities with our friends, not needing to plan what we are going to say, but never stalled for long in our confident forward progress. Skill? If so, it is the skill we all have, something we must have learned before the age of three or four.

A writer is one who has become accustomed to trusting that grace, or luck, or—skill.

Yet another attitude I find necessary: most of what I write, like most of what I say in casual conversation, will not amount to much. Even I will realize, and even at the time, that it is not negotiable. It will be like practice. In conversation I allow myself random remarks—in fact, as I recall, that is the way I learned to talk—so in writing I launch many expendable efforts. A result of this free way of writing is that I am not writing for others, mostly; they will not see the product at all unless the activity eventuates in something that later appears to be worthy. My guide is the self, and its adventuring in the language brings about communication.

This process-rather-than-substance view of writing invites a final, dual reflection:

1. Writers may not be special—sensitive or talented in any usual sense. They are simply engaged in sustained use of a language skill we all have. Their "creations" come about through confident reliance on stray impulses that will, with trust, find occasional patterns that are satisfying.

2. But writing itself is one of the great, free human activities. There is scope for individuality, and elation, and discovery, in writing. For the person who follows with trust and forgiveness what occurs to him, the world remains always ready and deep, an inexhaustible environment, with the combined vividness of an actuality and flexibility of a dream. Working back and forth between experience and thought, writers have more than space and time can offer. They have the whole unexplored realm of human vision.

Lawrence Langer

Lawrence Langer, born in New York City in 1929, is a professor of English at Simmons College in Boston. His books, which are based on his research in the literature of the Holocaust, include *The Holocaust and the Literary Imagination* (1975), *The Age of Atrocity: Death in Modern Literature* (1978), and *Versions of Survival: The Holocaust and the Human Spirit* (1982). The article reprinted below first appeared in January 1977 in *The Chronicle of Higher Education.*

The Human Use of Language

A friend of mine recently turned in a paper to a course on behavior modification.° She had tried to express in simple English some of her reservations about this increasingly popular approach to education. She

behavior modification Use of conditioning techniques, usually a system of reward and punishment, to change behavior by encouraging desirable actions and discouraging undesirable actions.

received it back with the comment: "Please rewrite this in behavioral terms."

It is little wonder that human beings have so much trouble saying what they feel, when they are told that there is a specialized vocabulary for saying what they think. The language of simplicity and spontaneity is forced to retreat behind the barricades of an official prose developed by a few experts who believe that jargon is the most precise means of communication. The results would be comic, if they were not so poisonous; unfortunately, there is an attitude toward the use of language that is impervious to human need and drives some people back into silence when they realize the folly of risking human words on insensitive ears.

The comedy is easy to come by. Glancing through my friend's textbook on behavior modification, I happened on a chapter beginning with the following challenging statement: "Many of the problems encountered by teachers in the daily management of their classes could be resolved if . . . ." Although I was a little wary of the phrase "daily management," I was encouraged to plunge ahead, because as an educator I have always been interested in ideas for improving learning. So I plunged. The entire sentence reads: "Many of the problems encountered by teachers in the daily management of their classes could be resolved if the emission of desirable student behaviors was increased."

Emission? At first I thought it was a misprint for "omission," but the omission of desirable student behaviors (note the plural) hardly seemed an appropriate goal for educators. Then I considered the possibility of metaphor, both erotic and automotive, but these didn't seem to fit, either. A footnote clarified the matter: " 'Emission' is a technical term used in behavioral analysis. The verb, 'to emit,' is used specifically with a certain category of behavior called 'operant behavior.' Operant behaviors are modified by their consequences. Operant behaviors correspond closely to the behavior colloquially referred to as voluntary." Voluntary? Is jargon then an attack on freedom of the will?

Of course, this kind of abuse of language goes on all the time—within the academic world, one regrets to say, as well as outside it. Why couldn't the author of this text simply say that we need to motivate students to learn willingly? The more I read such non-human prose, and try to avoid writing it myself, the more I am convinced that we must be in touch with ourselves before we can use words to touch others.

Using language meaningfully requires risk; the sentence I have just quoted takes no risks at all. Much of the discourse that poses as communication in our society is really a decoy to divert our audience (and often ourselves) from that shadowy plateau where our real life hovers on the precipice of expression. How many people, for example, have the courage to walk up to someone they like and actually *say* to them: "I'm very fond of you, you know"?

Such honesty reflects the use of language as revelation, and that sort of revelation, brimming with human possibilities, is risky precisely because it invites judgment and rebuff. Perhaps this is one reason why, especially in academe, we are confronted daily with so much neutral prose: Our students are not yet in touch with themselves; not especially encouraged by us, their instructors, to move in that direction; they are encouraged indeed to expect judgment and hence perhaps rebuff, too, in our evaluation of them. Thus they instinctively retreat behind the anonymity of abstract diction and technical jargon to protect themselves against us—but also, as I have suggested, against themselves.

This problem was crystallized for me recently by an encounter only peripherally related to the issue. As part of my current research, I have been interviewing children of concentration-camp survivors. One girl I have been meeting with says that her mother does not like to talk about the experience, *except with other survivors.* Risk is diminished when we know in advance that our audience shares with us a sympathy for our theme. The nakedness of pain *and* the nakedness of love require gentle responses. So this survivor is reticent, except with fellow victims.

But one day a situation arose which tempted her to the human use of language although she could not be sure, in advance, of the reception her words would receive. We all recognize it. This particular woman, at the age of 40, decided to return to school to get a college degree. Her first assignment in freshman composition was to write a paper on something that was of great importance to her personally. The challenge was immense; the risk was even greater. For the first time in 20 years, she resolved to confront a silence in her life that she obviously needed to rouse to speech.

She was 14 when the Germans invaded Poland. When the roundup of the Jews began a year later, some Christian friends sent their young daughter to "call for her" one day, so that they might hide her. A half hour later, the friends went themselves to pick up her parents, but during that interval, a truck had arrived, loaded aboard the Jewish mother and father —and the daughter never saw them or heard from them again. Their fate we can imagine. The girl herself was eventually arrested, survived several camps, and after the war came to America. She married, had children of her own, and except for occasional reminiscences with fellow survivors, managed to live adequately without diving into her buried personal past. Until one day her instructor in English composition touched a well-insulated nerve, and it began to throb with a painful impulse to express. I present verbatim the result of that impulse, a paper called "People I Have Forgotten":

"Can you forget your own Father and Mother? If so—how or why?

"I thought I did. To mention their names, for me is a great emotional struggle. The brutal force of this reality shakes my whole body and mind, wrecking me into ugly splinters; each crying to be mended anew. So the silence I maintain about their memory is only physical and valid as such but not true. I could never forget my parents, nor do I want to do it. True, I seldom talk about them with my husband or my children. How they looked, who they were, why they perished during the war. The love and sacrifices they have made for me during their lifetime, never get told.

"The cultural heritage to which each generation is entitled to have access seems to be nonexistent [*sic*], since I dare not talk about anything relating to my past, my parents.

"This awful, awesome power of not-remembering, this heart-breaking sensation of the conspiracy of silence is my dilemma.

"Often, I have tried to break through my imprisoning wall of irrational silence, but failed: now I hope to be able to do it.

"Until now, I was not able to face up to the loss of my parents, much less talk about them. The smallest reminder of them would set off a chain reaction of results that I could anticipate but never direct. The destructive force of sadness, horror, fright would then become my master. And it was this subconscious knowledge that kept me paralyzed with silence, not a conscious desire to forget my parents.

"My silent wall, my locked shell existed only of real necessity; I needed time.

"I needed time to forget the tragic loss of my loved ones, time to heal my emotional wound so that there shall come a time when I can again remember the people I have forgotten."

The essay is not a confrontation, only a prelude, yet it reveals qualities which are necessary for the human use of language: In trying to reach her audience, the author must touch the deepest part of herself. She risks self-exposure—when we see the instructor's comment, we will realize how great was her risk—and she is prepared for judgment and perhaps even rebuff, although I doubt whether she was prepared for the form they took. This kind of prose, for all its hesitant phraseology, throws down a gauntlet to the reader, a challenge asking him to understand that life is pain as well as plenty, chaos as well as form. Its imagery of locked shells and imprisoning walls hints at a silent world of horror and sadness far less enchanting than the more familiar landscape of love where most of us dwell. Language is a two-edged tool, to pierce the wall which hides that world, or build high abstract barriers to protect us from its threats.

The instructor who graded the paper I have just read preferred walls to honest words. At the bottom of the last page she scrawled a large "D-minus," emphatically surrounded by a circle. Her only comment was: "Your theme is not clear—you should have developed your 1st paragraph. You talk around your subject." At this moment, two realms collide: a universe of unarticulated feeling seeking expression (and the courage and encouragement to express) and a nature made so immune to feeling by heaven-knows-what that she hides behind the tired, tired language of the professional theme-corrector.

Suddenly we realize that reading as well as writing requires risks, and that the metaphor of insulation, so central to the efforts of the Polish woman survivor to re-establish contact with her past, is a metaphor governing the response of readers, too. Some writing, like "the emission of desirable student behaviors," thickens the insulation that already separates the reader from the words that throw darts at his armor of indifference. But even when language unashamedly reveals the feeling that is hidden behind the words, it must contend with a different kind of barrier, the one behind which our instructor lies concealed, unwilling or unable to hear a human voice and return a human echo of her own.

Ironically, the victor in this melancholy failure at communication is the villain of the piece, behavior modification. For the Polish survivor wrote her next theme on an innocuous topic, received a satisfactory grade, and never returned to the subject of her parents. The instructor, who had encountered a problem in the daily management of her class in the form of an essay which she could not respond to in a human way, altered the attitude of her student by responding in a non-human way, thus resolving her problem by increasing the emission of desirable student behavior. The student now knows how vital it is to develop her first paragraph, and how futile it is to reveal her first grief.

Even more, she has learned the danger of talking around her subject: She not only refuses to talk *around* it now, she refuses to talk *about* it. Thus the human use of language leads back to silence—where perhaps it should have remained in the first place.

Pat D'Arcy

Pat D'Arcy was educated at Bedford College and King's College, London University, and then became a teacher of English at the secondary level in grammar, secondary modern, and comprehensive schools. At present she is an adviser in English with the Wiltshire County Council.

From 1973 to 1976 she participated in the Writing Across the Curriculum Project at the London Institute of Education, and became a co-author of *Writing Across the Curriculum 11–16*, (published in 1976). A goal of the Project was to explore the relationships between language and growth—intellectual and personal—as reflected in the writing skills acquired in the course of secondary schooling. An ardent advocate of writing as a tool for learning, D'Arcy says that what ultimately matters is that teachers help students "in a way that enables them to perceive some meaning and significance in their studies which will remain with them long after their schooling is finished." She has written *The Examination Years: Writing in Geography, History and Social Studies* (1978), as well as articles on learning and writing. She also works with many teachers' groups in courses and at conferences, in the United States and in England. The piece printed here first appeared in *Forum for the Discussion of New Trends in Education,* Spring 1981.

Putting Your Own Mind to It

There is an ICI[0] advertisement which appeared in The Guardian earlier this year, the opening sentences of which read as follows:

INSIDE YOUR HEAD IS A SUBSTANCE THAT'S FAR MORE VALUABLE THAN NORTH SEA OIL. It's called grey matter. And that, not oil is our greatest natural asset. After all, it's going to have to solve the problems that will remain when the oil runs out. Fortunately brain power is one commodity that Britain isn't short of.

I wish more teachers, parents, employers, politicians—and above all pupils, believed the truth of those statements. What a pity that we feel more inclined to dismiss them as nothing more than an advertising con trick—what a waste!

It is not of course a new idea that the best way to encourage people of any age to learn is to begin with the assumption that they *can.* Most parents begin with that belief about their own children and it is interesting to observe that children under school age learn more—and learn more effectively than at any other time in their lives. Educationists past and present—Tolstoy, Dewey, Illich, Bruner, Britton—have similarly testified to the belief that human beings are natural learners, particularly children. And yet, and yet . . . whichever national system of state education we care to consider, what seems to happen is a movement *away from* a confirmation of that truth towards quite the opposite assumption: that there are a small number who can learn effectively but a much greater number whose learning is limited or for whom learning is at best a struggle and at worst a dead loss! The 'pass' rate of our external examinations[0] in this country is decided beforehand on precisely this premise. The teaching profession accepts, apparently without any unease or sense of affront, that only a small percentage of students are capable of passing an 'ordinary' level examination at the age of sixteen after eleven years of full-time schooling and that grade 4 on a five point scale of a *sub*-ordi-

ICI   Imperial Chemical Industries

external examinations   National examinations in Great Britain, given by subject, for the award of General Certificates of Education at Ordinary (O) level or Advanced (A) level; these examinations are particularly important to those students who hope to study at any of the universities.

nary level examination is the highest grade that most sixteen year olds can expect to gain! It is hardly surprising, when our expectations as teachers are so low, that students become disheartened, disillusioned and fail to prove us wrong. All too often self-fulfillment is really self-abasement and our response to that is the arrogant one of believing that our assumptions have been confirmed.

I do not want to speculate here about the reasons for this strange reversal from having confidence in the powers of the child's mind to a perverse undermining of the child's own confidence through our present methods of streaming, setting and examining. I want, instead, to ask how we can keep more steadily to a course which gives every student a sense of direction and purpose. How can we enable *all* of them to become increasingly confident that inside their heads they *do* have 'a substance that's far more valuable than North Sea oil'?

I am convinced that one thing we need to do as teachers is to interest children much more directly in the actual process of learning. All of us, whatever our age, or background, or ability, engage continually in processes of thinking, feeling, verbalising, communicating, observing and doing. They are functions of being human that we cannot avoid from the day we are born to the day we die. Increasingly, it has seemed logical to me that I should draw the attention of my pupils to this whole range of learning processes and that I should ask them, regularly, to consider their own thoughts, feelings, intentions, acts, observations, formulations and efforts to communicate. My objective has been to make them more aware of how they could operate successfully as learners. I have wanted them to be able to reflect consciously on how these processes have helped them to gain new insights and thus a clearer understanding of themselves and of their world. In pursuit of this objective I stopped focusing primarily on content and on product (what books had been read, what essays written, what exercises completed), and started focusing instead on process—what problems were being encountered, what insights achieved from day to day. This meant that I had to offer strategies, ways of looking at their work, that would help my students also to focus on what was happening inside their own heads. The most successful strategy and therefore the one that I want to describe here, chiefly through the work of a colleague who has been able to extend my original concept, is the daily use of a diary in which the pupil reflects back over whatever she has been doing inside the classroom that day. Such a 'learning log' differs from personal journal writing in that its central focus is on the school work that the student has been confronted with and on the questions that she needs to raise as a result of thinking further about her intentions, observations, thoughts and feelings during the school working day.

Anne Wotring is an English teacher in an American High School who joined a class of 15–16 year old students to study chemistry as a learner with no more experience than theirs for a whole year. She joined the class (in her own school) to find out whether writing logs in the way that I have described, could become an effective part of the learning process.

Here are some of the comments that she made later, in her dissertation, as a result of that experience:[1]

> I often felt that had I not been writing while I learned chemistry, I would not have worked with difficult ideas as long as I did without getting help. I often rely on others for help when I think something is too difficult for me to do on my own or when I need to hear myself talk so I can know what I know. My urge to talk about anything I learn is very strong. I believed that chemistry was difficult so it would have been natural for me to seek out a willing helper and a willing ear. But when I did the writing, I no longer felt the need of another person. The writing enabled me to know what I knew and to figure out the difficult ideas on my own. I realised that I could listen to myself think while I wrote my ideas on the paper. I wrote down whatever I thought as if I were trying to capture the flow of ideas in my brain on the paper. Sometimes I captured tangential thoughts which always proved to be useful and interesting. Frequently I captured ideas which didn't make sense, or sounded silly, or were wrong. When this happened, my internal critic or common sense, for lack of a better word, interrupted the idea with an evaluative comment. I would write the evaluative comments on the paper as well. If the internal critic remarked 'that doesn't seem right', I'd write 'that doesn't seem right'. I learned quickly to trust my internal critic's intuition. And my internal critic didn't only tell me when I was wrong. She often made comments of encouragement, such as 'I think I'm getting it' which kept me going when I was on the right track.
>
> I didn't cross out the silly, nonsensical or wrong things that I wrote. I also didn't cross out the internal critic's comments. I just went on writing. Crossing out wasn't necessary. I wrote not because I wanted to get all the ideas clear and correct on *paper* but because I wanted to get all the ideas clear and correct *in my head.* It wasn't important that no-one else would be able to read my writing and understand what I was saying about chemistry. What was important was that I understood what I was saying by the time I had completed my writing. The writing was for *now,* at the time I was doing it, not for later, and the writing was for me, not someone else.

The sense that first and foremost the student is writing for herself, in order to discover the picture that has been forming inside her own head, is an extremely important feature of the learning log strategy. The *act* of writing enables the student to develop that picture more fully—and to learn to trust her own ability to make sense of new information and unfamiliar concepts. At the same time, the student can sort out confusion from certainty and go back to the teacher with questions that, for her, need to be clarified further. One of the 16 year old students in the same chemistry class said:

[1] *Writing to Think about High School Chemistry.* M.A. Thesis—Anne Miller Wotring.

I just started writing the things I didn't understand . . . I started writing questions which were all specific . . . then I brought them up to the teacher and she could answer them for me . . . that way all my questions were cleared up.

She went on to say that she would never even have thought of some of the questions if she hadn't been keeping a learning log and writing down her thoughts about the day's lesson *as they occurred to her in retrospect.*

Two points interest me here—that the logs help students to formulate their own questions, often closely related to what they need in the way of further explanation from an expert; and that their requests for help are much more likely to meet with success than if the teacher is guessing in the dark about the needs of the class. The reversal from most school situations, where the teacher presents to a passive audience and then tests by asking *his* questions, is marked. In this instance, it is the student who questions, freely admitting to 'weaknesses' in order to learn more. The teacher is thus involved by the student as a partner in her learning, an involvement which leads to further insights and a growing sense of confidence and satisfaction.

Moreover, the confidence is well founded. Anne Wotring and the other students who kept learning logs, all found that when it came to a test, they no longer needed to make a desperate effort the night before to 'memorise' the teacher's notes—what was on the page was already inside their heads in a way that made sense because they had used their logs to clarify and reformulate as they went along:

I found that writing eliminated all my need to study the night before a test. I knew and understood everything already. I didn't need to memorise anything or cram anything into my head; and, because I didn't have any information precariously and hurriedly jammed into my head, I knew that I couldn't forget it in the middle of the test. I knew I had it all there in order, so it made sense, and I could call upon it and find it when I needed it. It was all neatly filed, not just thrown in. I was confident in this knowledge—in my knowledge. All the pressure I'd always associated with tests vanished.

Remember though, that 'write-thinking' will not fulfil many of the traditional expectations that we have about writing. It will not be orderly and sequential because the writer is finding out *as she writes;* it is process not product writing, expressive in the freedom that the writer has to voice thoughts, feelings, puzzlements, frustrations, satisfactions, as they arise. Here are four brief excerpts from learning logs or thinking diaries which I hope will illustrate these differences from conventional writing. The first three are from students in English comprehensive schools, while the last is taken from the thinking diary of an American 12 year old.[2]

[2]*When Children Think.* Gabriel Jacobs. Teachers College Press, Columbia University, New York.

The first comes from the notebook of an 11 year old. The class had spent several lessons on reproduction, starting with plants and culminating with a film that showed the birth of a human baby. After discussion the class had been asked by their teacher to spend 20–30 minutes concentrating on their own picture of how a baby grows inside the mother and is then born. The teacher made it clear to the class that he knew that all their pictures would be different and that they would be bound to miss some things out and probably make some mistakes. In other words, the teacher did his best to make it clear that this was more of a finding-out operation than a test and that he was interested in what their writing could tell him about their *developing* understanding of embryonic growth and birth.

This is what I think I know about the birth of a baby. The birth of the baby starts where the lady becomes pregnant. When her tummy gets very big this means that the baby is nearly ready to be born. The baby is kept inside the uterus which has a wall around it that is quite soft and is like a kind of cushion for the baby to move around in. The lady is brought to the hospital where she starts to feel pain because this means that the baby is going to be born. The lady has to put all her pressure on to help the baby coming out of the opening of the vagina. The baby's head comes out first, because this is the biggest part of his/her body. After the baby comes out the placenta wears away, because there is not a baby there to feed on it.

The baby has to be washed very carefully so as not to hurt it. I'm not really all that sure if the cord comes out as well. Does it? You can't really be sure. The baby has to stay in the hospital with its mother to find out whether it is a boy or a girl. You can tell the difference because the boy has a sack of skin with (I'm not sure) the testis in the middle. When you start to get to the age of about one the baby might even just about start to talk. The baby can either be fed by the breasts or by a bottle. When it is fed by the bottle it should never be too hot. The most common one of the two is the breasts. How does the milk get to the breasts to feed the baby?

In the next two pieces a group of 5th year students studying 'O' level Physics were invited by their teacher to write a Learning Log for homework. He found the information that the writing produced for him so useful that this year he is going to ask his 4th year groups to keep Learning Logs regularly.

6th March

After knowing what everything was about last week I am totally lost this week. I know how to use $\lambda = d \sin \theta$ to work out a sum (although I've probably got the homework wrong). I get a kind of (?) about the second ordering. What I don't know is where the first ends and the second begins and how you know? At the beginning of the lesson I kind of got kinetic theory, I got it all right but I had to use a book. I managed question 111 and 112 but I couldn't do the rest on change of states.

Another student just wrote down his own questions:

Questions
1. In destructive interference does the crest sink into the rough?
2. Can one measure out where the calm and rough areas are going to be, and if so how? (Do you use the wavelength and speed of the waves?)
3. What happens when one dipper produces waves with a greater wavelength? How would one get it to do that?
4. If the dipper goes faster or slower than the other what happens?
5. What happens if one dipper is bigger than the other?

As a final example here is an entry from Bonnie's thinking diary:

> Why is it that when kids teach a subject in class it is less confusing than if a teacher taught it? I think that a child who has gone through an experience in which something was confusing would know how and where it was confusing and then be able to teach it with less confusion. I am going to cite such an example.
>
> We are doing map skills, and a lot of the time when Mr Jacobs tells us directions kids get lost. I think if one of these kids taught the subject they may be able to teach kids and have them less confused. The reason I say this is that the child that is teaching will have had the experience of being confused and be able to avoid more confusion.
>
> On the other hand like Mr Jacobs says, 'Confusion is the beginning of learning'. In this case the kids would get confused and be continuously getting confused and finding out their mistakes they would probably learn better.

Logs certainly provide many opportunities for learners to learn from each other by sharing ideas, questions and suggestions, sometimes in pairs, sometimes in small self-chosen groups. The teacher is no longer in the lonely position of being the only learning resource for the class; write-thinking can be pooled and reflected on further by a group who are all engaged in the business of learning together, including the teacher. But most important of all, learning logs, as Anne Wotring discovered, are able to reveal to any student who is willing to take her own learning seriously, the exciting, astonishing and immensely reassuring fact that to anyone who pays attention, the mind inside the head will reveal all sorts of thoughts which appear already to be there, waiting to be noticed by their owners so that they can evolve a verbal shape for themselves. As Berthoff says:

> You don't have to philosophise or master psychological theories in order to learn to write, but it's important and I think comforting to know that the means of making meaning which you depend on when you make sense of the world and when you write are in part made for you by your brain and by language itself.[3]

In conclusion, although it didn't appear in his learning log, here is what one of my 5th year secondary modern school students[0] wrote after he had

[3]*Forming, Thinking, Writing.* Ann Berthoff. Hayden Press, New Jersey.

5th year secondary modern school student A student about sixteen years old. For those not planning to study for the advanced level examinations in order to prepare for the universities, the fifth year would probably be the last.

been working in this way for a couple of terms. It is the final paragraph of an eight page piece in which he reflects on his own writing and on the growing sense of confidence and power to shape his own meanings in his own way that the process of writing has given him:

> The following and concluding quotation is by Albert Einstein; I have only recently encountered a minute fraction of his work but I was completely amazed by its perceptiveness. 'The most beautiful things in the world are the mysterious for they are the only source of true art and beauty; he who cannot pause and wonder or stand in awe at these mysteries is already half dead.' My reply to that quotation is: the mind must surely be one of the most mysterious things in the world and I am definitely not yet half dead—on the contrary, I am wholly alive and kicking furiously and my writing takes the blows.

William Zinsser

William Zinsser has been a writer for most of his life. Born in New York in 1922, he graduated from Princeton in 1944 and served in the army for two years. He then joined the *New York Herald Tribune,* where he stayed until 1959, first as a feature editor, then as drama editor and film critic, and finally as an editorial writer. For the next ten years, he worked as a free-lance writer, published a number of books, and contributed to many magazines, including *Look* and *Life.* He was a member of the English faculty of Yale University from 1971 to 1979. A course he taught there in writing nonfiction led to the book *On Writing Well* (1976), from which the second chapter is reprinted here. In the first chapter, Zinsser says that there isn't any "right" way to write, but he adds that all good writing "has an aliveness that keeps the reader reading from one paragraph to the next, and it's not a question of gimmicks to 'personalize' the author. It's a question of using the English language in a way that will achieve the greatest strength and the least clutter." Such principles can be learned, he concludes, although perhaps they cannot be taught.

Zinsser's most recent book is *Writing with a Word Processor* (1983).

Simplicity

Clutter is the disease of American writing. We are a society strangling in unnecessary words, circular constructions, pompous frills and meaningless jargon.

Who really knows what the average businessman is trying to say in the average business letter? What member of an insurance or medical plan can decipher the brochure that tells him what his costs and benefits are? What father or mother can put together a child's toy—on Christmas Eve or any other eve—from the instructions on the box? Our national tendency is to inflate and thereby sound important. The airline pilot who wakes us to announce that he is presently anticipating experiencing considerable weather wouldn't dream of saying that there's a storm ahead and it may get bumpy. The sentence is too simple—there must be something wrong with it.

But the secret of good writing is to strip every sentence to its cleanest components. Every word that serves no function, every long word that could be a short word, every adverb that carries the same meaning that is already in the verb, every passive construction that leaves the reader unsure of who is doing what—these are the thousand and one adulterants that weaken the strength of a sentence. And they usually occur, ironically, in proportion to education and rank.

During the late 1960's the president of Princeton University wrote a letter to mollify the alumni after a spell of campus unrest. "You are probably aware," he began, "that we have been experiencing very considerable potentially explosive expressions of dissatisfaction on issues only partially related." He meant that the students had been hassling them about different things. As an alumnus I was far more upset by the president's syntax than by the students' potentially explosive expressions of dissatisfaction. I would have preferred the presidential approach taken by Franklin D. Roosevelt when he tried to convert into English his own government's memos, such as this blackout order of 1942:

> Such preparations shall be made as will completely obscure all Federal buildings and non-Federal buildings occupied by the Federal government during an air raid for any period of time from visibility by reason of internal or external illumination.

"Tell them," Roosevelt said, "that in buildings where they have to keep the work going to put something across the windows."

Simplify, simplify. Thoreau said it, as we are so often reminded, and no American writer more consistently practiced what he preached. Open *Walden* to any page and you will find a man saying in a plain and orderly way what is on his mind:

> I love to be alone. I never found the companion that was so companionable as solitude. We are for the most part more lonely when we go abroad among men than when we stay in our chambers. A man thinking or working is always alone, let him be where he will. Solitude is not measured by the miles of space that intervene between a man and his fellows. The really diligent student in one of the crowded hives of Cambridge College is as solitary as a dervish in the desert.

How can the rest of us achieve such enviable freedom from clutter? The answer is to clear our heads of clutter. Clear thinking becomes clear writing: one can't exist without the other. It is impossible for a muddy thinker to write good English. He may get away with it for a paragraph or two, but soon the reader will be lost, and there is no sin so grave, for he will not easily be lured back.

Who is this elusive creature, the reader? He is a person with an attention span of about twenty seconds. He is assailed on every side by forces competing for his time: by newspapers and magazines, by television and radio and stereo, by his wife and children and pets, by his house and his yard and all the gadgets that he has bought to keep them spruce, and by that most potent of competitors, sleep. The man snoozing in his chair with an unfinished magazine open on his lap is a man who was being given too much unnecessary trouble by the writer.

It won't do to say that the snoozing reader is too dumb or too lazy to keep pace with the train of thought. My sympathies are with him. If a reader is lost, it is generally because the writer has not been careful enough to keep him on the path.

This carelessness can take any number of forms. Perhaps a sentence is so excessively cluttered that the reader, hacking his way through the verbiage, simply doesn't know what it means. Perhaps a sentence has been so shoddily constructed that the reader could read it in any of several ways. Perhaps the writer has switched pronouns in mid-sentence, or has switched tenses, so the reader loses track of who is talking or when the action took place. Perhaps Sentence B is not a logical sequel to Sentence A—the writer, in whose head the connection is clear, has not bothered to provide the missing link. Perhaps the writer has used an important word incorrectly by not taking the trouble to look it up. He may think that "sanguine" and "sanguinary" mean the same thing, but the difference is a bloody big one. The reader can only infer (speaking of big differences) what the writer is trying to imply.

Faced with these obstacles, the reader is at first a remarkably tenacious bird. He blames himself—he obviously missed something, and he goes back over the mystifying sentence, or over the whole paragraph, piecing it out like an ancient rune, making guesses and moving on. But he won't do this for long. The writer is making him work too hard, and the reader will look for one who is better at his craft.

The writer must therefore constantly ask himself: What am I trying to say? Surprisingly often, he doesn't know. Then he must look at what he has written and ask: Have I said it? Is it clear to someone encountering the subject for the first time? If it's not, it is because some fuzz has worked its way into the machinery. The clear writer is a person clear-headed enough to see this stuff for what it is: fuzz.

I don't mean that some people are born clear-headed and are therefore natural writers, whereas others are naturally fuzzy and will never write well. Thinking clearly is a conscious act that the writer must force upon himself, just as if he were embarking on any other project that requires logic: adding up a laundry list or doing an algebra problem. Good writing doesn't come naturally, though most people obviously think it does. The professional writer is forever being bearded by strangers who say that they'd like to "try a little writing some time" when they retire from their real profession. Good writing takes self-discipline and, very often, self-knowledge.

Many writers, for instance, can't stand to throw anything away. Their sentences are littered with words that mean essentially the same thing and with phrases which make a point that is implicit in what they have already said. When students give me these littered sentences I beg them to select from the surfeit of words the few that most precisely fit what they want to say. Choose one, I plead, from among the three almost identical adjectives. Get rid of the unnecessary adverbs. Eliminate "in a funny sort of way" and other such qualifiers—they do no useful work.

The students look stricken—I am taking all their wonderful words away. I am only taking their superfluous words away, leaving what is organic and strong.

"But," one of my worst offenders confessed, "I never can get rid of anything—you should see my room." (I didn't take him up on the offer.) "I have two lamps where I only need one, but I can't decide which one I like better, so I keep them both." He went on to enumerate his duplicated or unnecessary objects, and over the weeks ahead I went on throwing away his duplicated and unnecessary words. By the end of the term—a term that he found acutely painful—his sentences were clean.

"I've had to change my whole approach to writing," he told me. "Now I have to *think* before I start every sentence and I have to *think* about every word." The very idea amazed him. Whether his room also looked better I never found out. I suspect that it did.

Josephine Miles

Josephine Miles is a teacher, a scholar, and a poet. Born in Chicago in 1911, she was educated at the University of California at Los Angeles (B.A., 1932) and at Berkeley (M.A., 1934; Ph.D., 1938). In 1940 she began teaching in the English Department at Berkeley, became a full professor in 1952, was honored as one of seven University Professors in 1973, and is now Professor Emeritus. She has published widely and won prizes both for her poetry and scholarship. Among her books are several collections of poems, including *Poems 1930–1960* (1960), *Kinds of Affection* (1967), *To All Appearances: New and Selected Poems* (1974), and *Coming to Terms* (1979). *Poetry and Change: Donne, Milton, Wordsworth and the Equilibrium of the Present* (1974) won the Modern Language Association Lowell Award for literary scholarship. Throughout her teaching career her interest in style, structure, and language has been demonstrated not only in print but also in many talks to teachers' groups and in a commitment to the teaching of freshman English. The essay that follows first appeared in *Educational Leadership* in February 1962; it has been edited by the author for inclusion in this book. (A slightly different version of the essay has been included in Josephine Miles' *Working Out Ideas: Predication and Other Uses of Language,* published in 1979 under the auspices of the Bay Area Writing Project.)

Essay in Reason

Prose essay like prose narrative or prose drama is an art of prose, and as an art it works in basic patterns. Rather than a sequence of events, it is a sequence of ideas, and it shapes up in certain ways, depending upon its main idea, its attempt or "essay." It makes a leading statement, that is, predicates its subject, and then unfolds, develops, substantiates both subject and predicate in the specific relation it has proposed for them.

Students in California have usually read widely and well in books of essays in ideas. The first week of the Fall term of 1961, 30 freshmen, my teaching assistant, and I talked about ideas we had met with during the past year. We were able to range from Thoreau to Jung and Freud, from Milton to Edith Hamilton, from Plato to Riesman. There were enough ideas for months of talking and writing.

Then I asked the students each to make a statement of one idea which particularly interested him, to suggest two or three different ways in which it might be developed into an essay. Blockade. Few associated the concept of an *idea* with the concept of a *statement* or a *sentence.* For many, ideas were at best abstract words or phrases; at worst, as one student suggested, "opinions or untrue facts." Inasmuch as a fact or topic assumes no responsibility for predication, no pattern of organization is obvious for it, and the student is at a loss to know what development may mean for it. Therefore the most typical response to the assignment is something like: "The importance of music: (a) development by examples, (b) general development." Or "The necessity for world government: (a) subjective, (b) objective." Not many aids to reason here!

First need then is to talk about ideas as sentences, that is, predicating the subjects, saying something about something, establishing relations. The student hopefully proposes, "Music is important" or "World government is necessary," and then goes on: "First I'll write a paragraph saying what I mean by *music* or *world government.* Then I'll develop my point in the predicate about important or necessary." But can importance or necessity be shown without showing possible alternatives? "Sure," says the student triumphantly. "Here's where I switch from objective to subjective!"

After some time discussing these terms as well as *general* and *particular,* demonstrating the need for both pairs and for the clarity of their relations, we come back to develop the useful structural implications of a good leading sentence. Here is one of the few really organizable ones achieved in the first week. Please ignore the horrors of its wordiness. These problems are secondary to sheer understanding of the point, and will mostly clear up when the writer's thought clears up. And he is on the right track: "A prevalent disease, mental retardation has received a minimum of public attention and this neglect has hampered any progress toward alleviating the problems of the disease."

What is the main point here? "Well, that lack of public interest in the disease has hampered progress in understanding it." Cheers. The subject is *lack;* the predicate, *has hampered;* so what will the basic organization be? "Chronological—stages of hampering, development of the verb. But now I see I don't want that kind of organization. I want to talk about ways of studying retardation and how they need public support." So? So: "Most ways of studying and improving mental retardation depend on public understanding and support." Then you'll have to demonstrate the predicate *depend,* and talk about *how* and *why.* "That's what I want to talk about—three *hows* and one *why.*" Now we are beginning to work out the development of an idea.

Chronology, spatial description, sequences work mainly with additive connectives: *and-and-and; then-then-then; also; moreover*—"Here are the main states in the study of retardation: such and such and such." Alternatives strive to separate, sometimes to compare: *either-or; on the one hand-on the other; not this, but that*—"Either we get public interest, or we give up." Conditional shows interdependent causal relations: *if-then; because-therefore*—"If public interest improves, our study of retardation will be aided in the following ways." This is the structure which, it turned out, our student intended to establish. Each of these procedures has its negatives. For example, *but* is a negative for *and; nor* for *or;* and concessional *though* for *if.*

The first help we can give the student writer then is to make him see whether the predication he has chosen to make, the verb he has chosen to apply to the subject, is really supportable by what he knows or can discover; and then, second, to see whether he has arranged the elements of support in the order and connection best for his purposes. A syllogism, the classic unit of reasoning, is in itself a small paragraph of substantiation. "I want to say something about Socrates, and what I want to say about him is that despite his great wisdom he is still mortal. Why is he mortal? Because all men are mortal, and Socrates is a man, as I can show in a paragraph of characteristics." Most of our thought concerns *some,* rather than the *all* referred to in this syllogism, but the pattern may be adapted to *some* by using recognition of negative as well as positive evidence: "Though two specific authorities deny it, public interest in retardation does help, and by public interest I mean not press-publicity, but active individual concern."

Reasoning means giving reasons: that is, it deals with the relations between statements, and these relations as we have said are of a few basic kinds: of cause or purpose—*if* this, therefore this, or this is so *because;* or of choice—this *or* this—both are impossible at once; or of association—this *and* this go along with this. Once a student recognizes that his own thought moves in these basic relations, he will be apt to enjoy both the art and the social force of the simple reasoning process of the paragraph. His planning or outlining will show first what main point or predication he is planning to make about his subject; then the main blocks of material he will use to support it, guided by such *pro* connections as *and, or, if* (and such *con* connections as *but, nor, though*); and finally a new main point, revised from the first hypothesis in the light of the evidence as it has developed. It is the predicate, not the subject, which is planned to be thus supported and modified. There is no such thing as too large or unwieldy a subject; what the student wants to say about the subject is what needs estimation. A student who tries to outline his material rather than his idea is trying, as one student has put it, to eat sardines without opening the can.

Man does not receive raw materials through the senses and then try to make meanings of them through the mind. Rather, the meanings that he makes, tentative and provisional as they may be at every stage, lead him to look for materials of experience which will test his meanings. So the writer does not need to stuff his mind with so-called "facts" before he can be responsible for a tentative statement; and so, on the other hand, for *any* statement he makes he can be held responsible. If we do not teach the student writer how to make responsible statements, we give in to the myths of "raw fact" or of individual autonomy, and make him the victim either of the outer world or of the inner. Thus we see the dangers on the one hand of the so-called "report" in composition-writing, which leads to an inert sort of copying, and on the other hand the dangers of journal writing or of so-called "creative" writing in which anything goes because there seems to be no valid outer check.

Why should we allow ourselves to be pulled between two extremes, when what we share is that very human power which philosophers have always spoken of, the power to agree on basic issues and to subordinate minor issues to major? For the Renaissance humanist, such reasonable powers served to mediate between man's sense and his spirit: so today it may mediate between man's psyche and his society. Robert Nisbet's *The Quest for Community* warns that so-called individual autonomy at one extreme and totalitarianism at the other tend to create a vacuum in between, where men actually live; and that men, to prevent this vacuum, need to strengthen the working categories of their own activities—their church, their club, their voting precinct, their job, to build a solid structure of human community between the forces of the personal and impersonal. So, I think, we need also to compose our thoughts: to learn to get from where we have been, to where we are, to where we want to go.

Thinking and Feeling

Almost all the selections in this book are records of men and women deliberately using their capacities to think and to feel in an effort to comprehend experience—either their own experience or that of other people and other times. It is fitting, then, that we present here a group of essays about thinking and feeling, activities that, however unavoidably and characteristically human, seem to have taken on a more problematic character than ever in recent times.

In the post-atomic age, indeed, thinking has become a matter of survival. The eminent biochemist Albert Szent-Gyorgyi, with the possibility of atomic war in mind, has put it plainly: "If it is our intelligence which led us into trouble, it may be our intelligence which can lead us out of it." Although we cannot yet be certain what intelligence is, there has been general agreement since Plato and Aristotle's time that logical thought is one—though only one—of its components. The piece by Thomas Huxley, which begins this section, is the clearest explanation we know of two of the most common processes of logical thinking: induction and deduction.

But for trained thinking, simply knowing the rules of logic is not enough. Thinking is a discipline, but it is also an art. Too often, though, our thoughts are subverted rather than energized by our feelings. What we accept rationally we often find hard to put into practice. Within us, what we understand rationally may be unsettling and sometimes in unconscious conflict with what we feel. Recognition of this fact gives persuasiveness to the next three essays.

William Golding's essay arises out of his awareness of the need to distinguish between thought and feeling; its theme is developed by a witty account of three different kinds of thinking. James Harvey Robinson's fuller and more philosophical treatment of kinds of thinking rests similarly on his recognition of the unconscious and of the need to distinguish rational thought from emotional prejudice. Aldous Huxley contrasts the intellectual's taste for rationality with the crowd's incapacity for moral choice; he shows how "exploiting the secret fears and hopes, the cravings, anxieties and frustrations" of people can lead to their political enslavement. (The reader may wish to consider whether "intellectuals" and "masses" are really two different groups, as Huxley seems to imply, or whether the difference comes about in our own minds depending upon the occasion or issue.)

But thinking is itself never enough. Threatened as we seem to be today by an impersonal, bureaucratic world, by a mechanized, standardized, alienating environment, we need more and more to be concerned with our capacity to feel: to love, to sympathize, to imagine, to appreciate.

The last three essays take up the need for feeling. James E. Miller, Jr., observes that the mind is neither a logic-machine nor "a great emotional sponge," but rather, it is a mixture of the two. Thought and feeling inevitably color each other and in such a way that even "to know what we think, we must know how we feel." Robertson Davies warns that "it is very much easier to think sensibly than to feel sensibly" and offers some advice on cultivating the capacity to feel. Marcel Proust describes the occasion in which for him feeling properly dominates thinking: feeling comes before intellect at the moment when the artist tries to reach back to the impressions that are "the only material of art."

For expressing feeling in words, poetry is best, and so we present last a group of four poems that were written largely in appreciation of feeling.

The Importance of Thinking

Thomas Huxley

Thomas Huxley (1825–1895)—British anatomist, embryologist, essayist, and lecturer—is one of the most memorable figures in nineteenth-century science. He studied medicine at the University of London. His researches on marine animals, made while serving as assistant surgeon on a naval vessel in the waters off Australia, earned him an early reputation as a first-class scientific investigator. He continued to publish technical scientific papers all his life, but he also became engrossed in advocating the scientific method and its findings to a wide audience. The publication of Charles Darwin's *Origin of Species* in 1859, and the controversy it aroused, brought Huxley to Darwin's defense. Huxley's lectures and writings on evolution, and on the place of humans in the universe, did much to establish a new freedom of debate and expression about matters of religion.

  Huxley also made notable contributions to elementary, technical, and medical education and was a strong advocate of higher education for women. Although he spent much of his career as a college teacher and administrator, his educational fervor embraced all kinds of people. In 1855 he began giving lectures addressed to laborers. Six of the lectures given in 1862, entitled "On Our Knowledge of the Causes of the Phenomena of Organic Nature," were devoted to Darwin's theories. The passage excerpted below is from the third lecture in the series and comes from the second volume of Huxley's *Collected Essays* (9 vols., 1893–1894). For Huxley, "the method of scientific investigation" was by no means limited to science. And though a great believer in liberal education and in literature and the arts, he maintained that "a perfect culture . . . could not be acquired without training in the methods of physical science."

The Method of Scientific Investigation

The method of scientific investigation is nothing but the expression of the necessary mode of working of the human mind. It is simply the mode at which all phenomena are reasoned about, rendered precise and exact. There is no more difference, but there is just the same kind of difference, between the mental operations of a man of science and those of an ordinary person, as there is between the operations and methods of a baker or of a butcher weighing out his goods in common scales, and the operations of a chemist in performing a difficult and complex analysis by means of his balance and finely-graduated weights. It is not that the action of the scales in the one case, and the balance in the other, differ in the principles of their construction or manner of working; but the beam of one is set on an infinitely finer axis than the other, and of course turns by the addition of a much smaller weight.

You will understand this better, perhaps, if I give you some familiar example. You have all heard it repeated, I dare say, that men of science work by means of induction and deduction, and that by the help of these operations, they, in a sort of sense, wring from Nature certain other things, which are called natural laws, and causes, and that out of these, by some cunning skill of their own, they build up hypotheses and theories. And it is imagined by many, that the operations of the common mind can be by no means compared with these processes, and that they have to be acquired by a sort of special apprenticeship to the craft. To hear all these large words, you would think that the mind of a man of science must be constituted differently from that of his fellow men; but if you will not be frightened by terms, you will discover that you are quite wrong, and that all these terrible apparatus are being used by yourselves every day and every hour of your lives.

There is a well-known incident in one of Molière's plays,[0] where the author makes the hero express unbounded delight on being told that he had been talking prose during the whole of his life. In the same way, I trust, that you will take comfort, and be delighted with yourselves, on the discovery that you have been acting on the principles of inductive and deductive philosophy during the same period. Probably there is not one here who has not in the course of the day had occasion to set in motion a complex train of reasoning, of the very same kind, though differing of course in degree, as that which a scientific man goes through in tracing the causes of natural phenomena.

A very trivial circumstance will serve to exemplify this. Suppose you go into a fruiterer's shop, wanting an apple,—you take up one, and, on biting it, you find it is sour; you look at it, and see that it is hard and green. You take up another one, and that too is hard, green, and sour. The shopman offers you a third; but, before biting it, you examine it, and find that it is hard and green, and you immediately say that you will not have it, as it must be sour, like those that you have already tried.

Nothing can be more simple than that, you think; but if you will take the trouble to analyse and trace out into its logical elements what has been done by the mind, you will be greatly surprised. In the first place, you have performed the operation of induction. You found that, in two experiences, hardness and greenness in apples went together with sourness. It was so in the first case, and it was confirmed by the second. True, it is a very small basis, but still it is enough to make an induction from; you generalise the

one of Molière's plays   *Le Bourgeois Gentilhomme,* written in 1670.

facts, and you expect to find sourness in apples where you get hardness and greenness. You found upon that a general law, that all hard and green apples are sour; and that, so far as it goes, is a perfect induction. Well, having got your natural law in this way, when you are offered another apple which you find is hard and green, you say, "All hard and green apples are sour; this apple is hard and green, therefore this apple is sour." That train of reasoning is what logicians call a syllogism, and has all its various parts and terms,—its major premiss, its minor premiss, and its conclusion. And, by the help of further reasoning, which, if drawn out, would have to be exhibited in two or three other syllogisms, you arrive at your final determination, "I will not have that apple." So that, you see, you have, in the first place, established a law by induction, and upon that you have founded a deduction, and reasoned out the special conclusion of the particular case. Well now, suppose, having got your law, that at some time afterwards, you are discussing the qualities of apples with a friend: you will say to him, "It is a very curious thing,—but I find that all hard and green apples are sour!" Your friend says to you, "But how do you know that?" You at once reply, "Oh, because I have tried them over and over again, and have always found them to be so." Well, if we were talking science instead of common sense, we should call that an experimental verification. And, if still opposed, you go further, and say, "I have heard from the people in Somersetshire and Devonshire, where a large number of apples are grown, that they have observed the same thing. It is also found to be the case in Normandy, and in North America. In short, I find it to be the universal experience of mankind wherever attention has been directed to the subject." Whereupon, your friend, unless he is a very unreasonable man, agrees with you, and is convinced that you are quite right in the conclusion you have drawn. He believes, although perhaps he does not know he believes it, that the more extensive verifications are,—that the more frequently experiments have been made, and results of the same kind arrived at,—that the more varied the conditions under which the same results are attained, the more certain is the ultimate conclusion, and he disputes the question no further. He sees that the experiment has been tried under all sorts of conditions, as to time, place, and people, with the same result; and he says with you, therefore, that the law you have laid down must be a good one, and he must believe it.

In science we do the same thing;—the philosopher exercises precisely the same faculties, though in a much more delicate manner. In scientific inquiry it becomes a matter of duty to expose a supposed law to every possible kind of verification, and to take care, moreover, that this is done intentionally, and not left to a mere accident, as in the case of the apples. And in science, as in common life, our confidence in a law is in exact proportion to the absence of variation in the result of our experimental verifications. For instance, if you let go your grasp of an article you may have in your hand, it will immediately fall to the ground. That is a very common verification of one of the best established laws of nature—that of gravitation. The method by which men of science establish the existence of that law is exactly the same as that by which we have established the trivial proposition about the sourness of hard and green apples. But we believe it in such an extensive, thorough, and unhesitating manner because the universal experience of mankind verifies it, and we can verify it ourselves at any time; and that is the strongest possible foundation on which any natural law can rest.

So much, then, by way of proof that the method of establishing laws in science is exactly the same as that pursued in common life. Let us now turn to another matter (though really it is but another phase of the same question), and that is, the method by which, from the relations of certain phenomena, we prove that some stand in the position of causes towards the others.

I want to put the case clearly before you, and I will therefore show you what I mean by another familiar example. I will suppose that one of you, on coming down in the morning to the parlour of your house, finds that a tea-pot and some spoons which had been left in the room on the previous evening are gone,—the window is open, and you observe the mark of a dirty hand on the window-frame, and perhaps, in addition to that, you notice the impress of a hob-nailed shoe on the gravel outside. All these phenomena have struck your attention instantly, and before two seconds have passed you say, "Oh somebody has broken open the window, entered the room, and run off with the spoons and the tea-pot!" That speech is out of your mouth in a moment. And you will probably add, "I know there has; I am quite sure of it!" You mean to say exactly what you know; but in reality you are giving expression to what is, in all essential particulars, an hypothesis. You do not *know* it at all; it is nothing but an hypothesis rapidly framed in your own mind. And it is an hypothesis founded on a long train of inductions and deductions.

What are those inductions and deductions, and how have you got at this hypothesis? You have observed, in the first place, that the window is open; but by a train of reasoning involving many inductions and deductions, you have probably arrived long before at the general law—and a very good one it is—that windows do not open of themselves; and you therefore conclude that something has opened the window. A second general law that you have arrived at in the same way is, that tea-pots and spoons do not go out of a window spontaneously, and you are satisfied that, as they are not now where you left them, they have been removed. In the third place, you look at the marks on the window-sill, and the shoe-marks outside, and you say that in all previous experience the former kind of mark has never been produced by anything else but the hand of a human being; and the same experience shows that no other animal but man at present wears shoes with hob-nails in them such as would produce the marks in the gravel. I do not know, even if we could discover any of those "missing links"⁰ that are talked about, that they would help us to any other conclusion! At any rate the law which states our present experience is strong enough for my present purpose. You next reach the conclusion, that as these kinds of marks have not been left by any other animals than men, or are liable to be formed in any other way than by a man's hand and shoe, the marks in question have been formed by a man in that way. You have, further, a general law, founded on observation and experience, and that, too, is, I am sorry to say, a very universal and unimpeachable one,—that some men are thieves; and you assume at once from all these premises —and that is what constitutes your hypothesis—that the man who made the marks outside and on the window-sill, opened the window, got into the room, and stole your tea-pot and spoons. You have now arrived at a *vera causa;* ⁰—you have assumed a cause which, it is plain, is competent to produce all the phenomena you have observed. You can explain all these phenomena only by the hypothesis of a thief. But that is a hypothetical conclusion, of the justice of which you have no absolute proof at all; it is only rendered highly probable by a series of inductive and deductive reasonings.

I suppose your first action, assuming that you are a man of ordinary common sense, and that you have established this hypothesis to your own satisfaction, will very likely be to go off for the police, and set them on the track of the burglar, with the view to the recovery of your property. But just as you are starting with this object, some person comes in, and on learning what you are about, says, "My good friend, you are going on a great deal too fast. How do you know that the man who really made the marks took the spoons? It might have been a monkey that took them, and the man may have merely looked in afterwards." You would probably reply, "Well, that is all very well, but you see it is contrary to all experience of the way tea-pots and spoons are abstracted; so that, at any rate, your hypothesis is less probable than mine." While you are talking the thing over in this way, another friend arrives, one of that good kind of people that I was talking of a little while ago. And he might say, "Oh, my dear sir, you are certainly going on a great deal too fast. You are most presumptuous. You admit that all these occurrences took place when you were fast asleep, at a time when you could not possibly have known anything about what was taking place. How do you know that the laws of Nature are not suspended during the night? It may be that there has been some kind of supernatural interference in this case." In point of fact, he declares that your hypothesis is one of which you cannot at all demonstrate the truth, and that you are by no means sure that the laws of Nature are the same when you are asleep as when you are awake.

missing links Hypothetical primates once thought to be a bridge between apes and humans in the evolutionary chain.
vera causa cause in accordance with fact (Latin).

Well, now, you cannot at the moment answer that kind of reasoning. You feel that your worthy friend has you somewhat at a disadvantage. You will feel perfectly convinced in your own mind, however, that you are quite right, and you say to him, "My good friend, I can only be guided by the natural probabilities of the case, and if you will be kind enough to stand aside and permit me to pass, I will go and fetch the police." Well, we will suppose that your journey is successful, and that by good luck you meet with a policeman; that eventually the burglar is found with your property on his person, and the marks correspond to his hand and to his boots. Probably any jury would consider those facts a very good experimental verification of your hypothesis, touching the cause of the abnormal phenomena observed in your parlour, and would act accordingly.

Now, in this suppositious case, I have taken phenomena of a very common kind, in order that you might see what are the different steps in an ordinary process of reasoning, if you will only take the trouble to analyse it carefully. All the operations I have described, you will see, are involved in the mind of any man of sense in leading him to a conclusion as to the course he should take in order to make good a robbery and punish the offender. I say that you are led, in that case, to your conclusion by exactly the same train of reasoning as that which a man of science pursues when he is endeavouring to discover the origin and laws of the most occult phenomena. The process is, and always must be, the same; and precisely the same mode of reasoning was employed by Newton and Laplace in their endeavours to discover and define the causes of the movements of the heavenly bodies, as you, with your own common sense, would employ to detect a burglar. The only difference is, that the nature of the inquiry being more abstruse, every step has to be most carefully watched, so that there may not be a single crack or flaw in your hypothesis. A flaw or crack in many of the hypotheses of daily life may be of little or no moment as affecting the general correctness of the conclusions at which we may arrive; but, in a scientific inquiry, a fallacy, great or small, is always of importance, and is sure to be in the long run constantly productive of mischievous, if not fatal results.

Do not allow yourselves to be misled by the common notion that an hypothesis is untrustworthy simply because it is an hypothesis. It is often urged, in respect to some scientific conclusion, that, after all, it is only an hypothesis. But what more have we to guide us in nine-tenths of the most important affairs of daily life than hypotheses, and often very ill-based ones? So that in science, where the evidence of an hypothesis is subjected to the most rigid examination, we may rightly pursue the same course. You may have hypotheses and hypotheses. A man may say, if he likes, that the moon is made of green cheese: that is an hypothesis. But another man, who has devoted a great deal of time and attention to the subject, and availed himself of the most powerful telescopes and the results of the observations of others, declares that in his opinion it is probably composed of materials very similar to those of which our own earth is made up: and that is also only an hypothesis. But I need not tell you that there is an enormous difference in the value of the two hypotheses. That one which is based on sound scientific knowledge is sure to have a corresponding value; and that which is a mere hasty random guess is likely to have but little value. Every great step in our progress in discovering causes has been made in exactly the same way as that which I have detailed to you. A person observing the occurrence of certain facts and phenomena asks, naturally enough, what process, what kind of operation known to occur in Nature applied to the particular case, will unravel and explain the mystery? Hence you have the scientific hypothesis; and its value will be proportionate to the care and completeness with which its basis had been tested and verified. It is in these matters as in the commonest affairs of practical life: the guess of the fool will be folly, while the guess of the wise man will contain wisdom. In all cases, you see that the value of the result depends on the patience and faithfulness with which the investigator applies to his hypothesis every possible kind of verification.

William Golding

William Golding, a British author born in Cornwall in 1911, was educated at Marlborough grammar school and at Oxford. During World War II he served in the Royal Navy, rising to the command of a rocket-launching ship. Since the war he has devoted himself to teaching and writing and to his hobbies, which he once described as "thinking, classical Greek, sailing, and archaeology." He is widely known for his strikingly original novels, of which the most famous is *Lord of the Flies* (1954), an account of a group of schoolboys marooned on an island who revert to savagery. Other novels include *The Inheritors* (1955), *Pincher Martin* (1956), *The Spire* (1964), *The Pyramid* (1967), *The Scorpion God* (1971), and more recently, *Darkness Visible* (1979), and *Rites of Passage* (1980). This essay first appeared in the August 1961 issue of *Holiday*.

Thinking as a Hobby

While I was still a boy, I came to the conclusion that there were three grades of thinking; and since I was later to claim thinking as my hobby, I came to an even stranger conclusion—namely, that I myself could not think at all.

I must have been an unsatisfactory child for grownups to deal with. I remember how incomprehensible they appeared to me at first, but not, of course, how I appeared to them. It was the headmaster of my grammar school⁰ who first brought the subject of thinking before me—though neither in the way, nor with the result he intended. He had some statuettes in his study. They stood on a high cupboard behind his desk. One was a lady wearing nothing but a bath towel. She seemed frozen in an eternal panic lest the bath towel slip down any farther; and since she had no arms, she was in an unfortunate position to pull the towel up again. Next to her, crouched the statuette of a leopard, ready to spring down at the top drawer of a filing cabinet labeled A–AH. My innocence interpreted this as the victim's last, despairing cry. Beyond the leopard was a naked, muscular gentleman, who sat, looking down, with his chin on his fist and his elbow on his knee. He seemed utterly miserable.

Some time later, I learned about these statuettes. The headmaster had placed them where they would face delinquent children, because they symbolized to him the whole of life. The naked lady was the Venus of Milo. She was Love. She was not worried about the towel. She was just busy being beautiful. The leopard was Nature, and he was being natural. The naked, muscular gentleman was not miserable. He was Rodin's Thinker, an image of pure thought. It is easy to buy small plaster models of what you think life is like.

I had better explain that I was a frequent visitor to the headmaster's study, because of the latest thing I had done or left undone. As we now say, I was not integrated. I was, if anything, disintegrated; and I was puzzled. Grownups never made sense. Whenever I found myself in a penal position before the headmaster's desk, with the statuettes glimmering whitely above him, I would sink my head, clasp my hands behind my back and writhe one shoe over the other.

The headmaster would look opaquely at me through flashing spectacles.

"What are we going to do with you?"

Well, what *were* they going to do with me? I would writhe my shoe some more and stare down at the worn rug.

"Look up, boy! Can't you look up?"

Then I would look up at the cupboard, where the naked lady was frozen in her panic and the muscular gentleman contemplated the hindquarters of the leopard in endless gloom. I had nothing to say to the headmaster. His spectacles caught the light so that you could see nothing human behind them. There was no possibility of communication.

"Don't you ever think at all?"

No, I didn't think, wasn't thinking, couldn't think—I was simply waiting in anguish for the interview to stop.

"Then you'd better learn—hadn't you?"

grammar school In Great Britain, the academic secondary school for those preparing for the university or the professions; students enter at about age eleven.

On one occasion the headmaster leaped to his feet, reached up and plonked Rodin's masterpiece on the desk before me.

"That's what a man looks like when he's really thinking."

I surveyed the gentleman without interest or comprehension.

"Go back to your class."

Clearly there was something missing in me. Nature had endowed the rest of the human race with a sixth sense and left me out. This must be so, I mused, on my way back to the class, since whether I had broken a window, or failed to remember Boyle's Law, or been late for school, my teachers produced me one, adult answer: "Why can't you think?"

As I saw the case, I had broken the window because I had tried to hit Jack Arney with a cricket ball and missed him; I could not remember Boyle's Law because I had never bothered to learn it; and I was late for school because I preferred looking over the bridge into the river. In fact, I was wicked. Were my teachers, perhaps, so good that they could not understand the depths of my depravity? Were they clear, untormented people who could direct their every action by this mysterious business of thinking? The whole thing was incomprehensible. In my earlier years, I found even the statuette of the Thinker confusing. I did not believe any of my teachers were naked, ever. Like someone born deaf, but bitterly determined to find out about sound, I watched my teachers to find out about thought.

There was Mr. Houghton. He was always telling me to think. With a modest satisfaction, he would tell me that he had thought a bit himself. Then why did he spend so much time drinking? Or was there more sense in drinking than there appeared to be? But if not, and if drinking were in fact ruinous to health—and Mr. Houghton was ruined, there was no doubt about that—why was he always talking about the clean life and the virtues of fresh air? He would spread his arms wide with the action of a man who habitually spent his time striding along mountain ridges.

"Open air does me good, boys—I know it!"

Sometimes, exalted by his own oratory, he would leap from his desk and hustle us outside into a hideous wind.

"Now boys! Deep breaths! Feel it right down inside you—huge draughts of God's good air!"

He would stand before us, rejoicing in his perfect health, an open-air man. He would put his hands on his waist and take a tremendous breath. You could hear the wind, trapped in the cavern of his chest and struggling with all the unnatural impediments. His body would reel with shock and his ruined face go white at the unaccustomed visitation. He would stagger back to his desk and collapse there, useless for the rest of the morning.

Mr. Houghton was given to high-minded monologues about the good life, sexless and full of duty. Yet in the middle of one of these monologues, if a girl passed the window, tapping along on her neat little feet, he would interrupt his discourse, his neck would turn of itself and he would watch her out of sight. In this instance, he seemed to me ruled not by thought but by an invisible and irresistible spring in his nape.

His neck was an object of great interest to me. Normally it bulged a bit over his collar. But Mr. Houghton had fought in the First World War alongside both Americans and French, and had come—by who knows what illogic?—to a settled detestation of both countries. If either country happened to be prominent in current affairs, no argument could make Mr. Houghton think well of it. He would bang the desk, his neck would bulge still further and go red. "You can say what you like," he would cry, "but I've thought about this—and I know what I think!"

Mr. Houghton thought with his neck.

There was Miss Parsons. She assured us that her dearest wish was our welfare, but I knew even then, with the mysterious clairvoyance of childhood, that what she wanted most was the husband she never got. There was Mr. Hands—and so on.

I have dealt at length with my teachers because this was my introduction to the nature of what is commonly called thought. Through them I discovered that thought is often full of unconscious prejudice, ignorance and hypocrisy. It will lecture on disinterested purity while its neck is being remorselessly twisted toward a skirt. Technically, it is about as proficient as most businessmen's golf, as honest as most politicians' intentions, or—to come near my own preoccupation—as coherent as most books that get written. It is what I came to call grade-three thinking, though more properly, it is feeling, rather than thought.

True, often there is a kind of innocence in prejudices, but in those days I viewed grade-three thinking with an intolerant contempt and an incautious mockery. I delighted to confront a pious lady who hated the Germans with the proposition that we should love our enemies. She taught me a great truth in dealing with grade-three thinkers; because of her, I no longer dismiss lightly a mental process which for nine-tenths of the population is the nearest they will ever get to thought. They have immense solidarity. We had better respect them, for we are outnumbered and surrounded. A crowd of grade-three thinkers, all shouting the same thing, all warming their hands at the fire of their own prejudices, will not thank you for pointing out the contradictions in their beliefs. Man is a gregarious animal, and enjoys agreement as cows will graze all the same way on the side of a hill.

Grade-two thinking is the detection of contradictions. I reached grade two when I trapped the poor, pious lady. Grade-two thinkers do not stampede easily, though often they fall into the other fault and lag behind. Grade-two thinking is a withdrawal, with eyes and ears open. It became my hobby and brought satisfaction and loneliness in either hand. For grade-two thinking destroys without having the power to create. It set me watching the crowds cheering His Majesty the King and asking myself what all the fuss was about, without giving me anything positive to put in the place of that heady patriotism. But there were compensations. To hear people justify their habit of hunting foxes and tearing them to pieces by claiming that the foxes liked it. To hear our Prime Minister talk about the great benefit we conferred on India by jailing people like Pandit Nehru and Gandhi. To hear American politicians talk about peace in one sentence and refuse to join the League of Nations in the next. Yes, there were moments of delight.

But I was growing toward adolescence and had to admit that Mr. Houghton was not the only one with an irresistible spring in his neck. I, too, felt the compulsive hand of nature and began to find that pointing out contradiction could be costly as well as fun. There was Ruth, for example, a serious and attractive girl. I was an atheist at the time. Grade-two thinking is a menace to religion and knocks down sects like skittles. I put myself in a position to be converted by her with an hypocrisy worthy of grade three. She was a Methodist—or at least, her parents were, and Ruth had to follow suit. But, alas, instead of relying on the Holy Spirit to convert me, Ruth was foolish enough to open her pretty mouth in argument. She claimed that the Bible (King James Version) was literally inspired. I countered by saying that the Catholics believed in the literal inspiration of Saint Jerome's *Vulgate,* and the two books were different. Argument flagged.

At last she remarked that there were an awful lot of Methodists, and they couldn't be wrong, could they—not all those millions? That was too easy, said I restively (for the nearer you were to Ruth, the nicer she was to be near to) since there were more Roman Catholics than Methodists anyway; and they couldn't be wrong, could they—not all those hundreds of millions? An awful flicker of doubt appeared in her eyes. I slid my arm round her waist and murmured breathlessly that if we were counting heads, the Buddhists were the boys for my money. But Ruth had *really* wanted to do me good, because I was so nice. She fled. The combination of my arm and those countless Buddhists was too much for her.

That night her father visited my father and left, red-cheeked and indignant. I was given the third degree to find out what had happened. It was lucky we were both of us only fourteen. I lost Ruth and gained an undeserved reputation as a potential libertine.

So grade-two thinking could be dangerous. It was in this knowledge, at the age of fifteen, that I remember making a comment from the heights of grade two, on the limitations of grade three. One evening I found myself alone in the schoolhall, preparing it for a party. The door of the headmaster's study was open. I went in. The headmaster had ceased to thump Rodin's Thinker down on the desk as an example to the young. Perhaps he had not found any more candidates, but the statuettes were still there, glimmering and gathering dust on top of the cupboard. I stood on a chair and rearranged them. I stood Venus in her bath towel on the filing cabinet, so that now the top drawer caught its breath in a gasp of sexy excitement. "A-ah!" The portentous Thinker I placed on the edge of the cupboard so that he looked down at the bath towel and waited for it to slip.

Grade-two thinking, though it filled life with fun and excitement, did not make for content. To find out the deficiencies of our elders bolsters the young ego but does not make for personal security. I found that grade two was not only the power to point out contradictions. It took the swimmer some distance from the shore and left him there, out of his depth. I decided that Pontius Pilate was a typical grade-two thinker. "What is truth?" he said, a very common grade-two thought, but one that is used always as the end of an argument instead of the beginning. There is a still higher grade of thought which says, "What is truth?" and sets out to find it.

But these grade-one thinkers were few and far between. They did not visit my grammar school in the flesh though they were there in books. I aspired to them, partly because I was ambitious and partly because I now saw my hobby as an unsatisfactory thing if it went no further. If you set out to climb a mountain, however high you climb, you have failed if you cannot reach the top.

I *did* meet an undeniably grade-one thinker in my first year at Oxford. I was looking over a small bridge in Magdalen Deer Park, and a tiny mustached and hatted figure came and stood by my side. He was a German who had just fled from the Nazis to Oxford as a temporary refuge. His name was Einstein.

But Professor Einstein knew no English at that time and I knew only two words of German. I beamed at him, trying wordlessly to convey by my bearing all the affection and respect that the English felt for him. It is possible—and I have to make the admission—that I felt here were two grade-one thinkers standing side by side; yet I doubt if my face conveyed more than a formless awe. I would have given my Greek and Latin and French and a good slice of my English for enough German to communicate. But we were divided; he was as inscrutable as my headmaster. For perhaps five minutes we stood together on the bridge, undeniable grade-one thinker and breathless aspirant. With true greatness, Professor Einstein realized that any contact was better than none. He pointed to a trout wavering in midstream.

He spoke: *"Fisch."*

My brain reeled. Here I was, mingling with the great, and yet helpless as the veriest grade-three thinker. Desperately I sought for some sign by which I might convey that I, too, revered pure reason. I nodded vehemently. In a brilliant flash I used up half of my German vocabulary. *"Fisch. Ja. Ja."*

For perhaps another five minutes we stood side by side. Then Professor Einstein, his whole figure still conveying good will and amiability, drifted away out of sight.

I, too, would be a grade-one thinker. I was irreverent at the best of times. Political and religious systems, social customs, loyalties and traditions, they all came tumbling down like so many rotten apples off a tree. This was a fine hobby and a sensible substitute for cricket, since you could play it all the year round. I came up in the end with what must always remain the justification for grade-one thinking, its sign, seal and charter. I devised a coherent system for living. It was a moral system, which was wholly logical. Of course, as I readily admitted, conversion of the world to my way of thinking might be difficult, since my system did away with a number of trifles, such as big business, centralized government, armies, marriage. . . .

It was Ruth all over again. I had some very good friends who stood by me, and still do. But my acquaintances vanished, taking the girls with them. Young women seemed oddly contented with the world as it was. They valued the meaningless ceremony with a ring. Young men, while willing to concede the chaining sordidness of marriage, were hesitant about abandoning the organizations which they hoped would give them a career. A young man on the first rung of the Royal Navy, while perfectly agreeable to doing away with big business and marriage, got as red-necked as Mr. Houghton when I proposed a world without any battleships in it.

Had the game gone too far? Was it a game any longer? In those prewar days, I stood to lose a great deal, for the sake of a hobby.

Now you are expecting me to describe how I saw the folly of my ways and came back to the warm nest, where prejudices are so often called loyalties, where pointless actions are hallowed into custom by repetition, where we are content to say we think when all we do is feel.

But you would be wrong. I dropped my hobby and turned professional.

If I were to go back to the headmaster's study and find the dusty statuettes still there, I would arrange them differently. I would dust Venus and put her aside, for I have come to love her and know her for the fair thing she is. But I would put the Thinker, sunk in his desperate thought, where there were shadows before him—and at his back, I would put the leopard, crouched and ready to spring.

James Harvey Robinson

James Harvey Robinson (1863–1936), an American historian, taught at the University of Pennsylvania and at Columbia. He resigned from Columbia in 1919 in protest against the expulsion of a group of professors for their opposition to World War I, at which time he attacked Columbia president Nicholas Murray Butler for his alleged attempts to suppress freedom of expression at the university. Robinson then helped to found the New School for Social Research in New York City and taught there until 1921, when he retired to devote the rest of his life to writing. Among his dozen volumes of historical and philosophical writing, perhaps the best known to the general public is *The Mind in the Making* (1921), subtitled *The Relation of Intelligence to Social Reform*. Chapter 2 of this book has been often excerpted and reprinted, but familiarity has not reduced its value. We reprint the chapter here in full, using the heading of its first section as title for the whole.

On Various Kinds of Thinking

Good sense is, of all things among men, the most equally distributed; for everyone thinks himself so abundantly provided with it that those even who are the most difficult to satisfy in everything else do not usually desire a larger measure of this quality than they already possess.

—DESCARTES

We see man to-day, instead of the frank and courageous recognition of his status, the docile attention to his biological history, the determination to let nothing stand in the way of the security and permanence of his future, which alone can establish the safety and happiness of the race, substituting blind confidence in his destiny, unclouded faith in the essentially respectful attitude of the universe toward his moral code, and a belief no less firm that his traditions and laws and institutions necessarily contain permanent qualities of reality.

—WILLIAM TROTTER

1. On Various Kinds of Thinking

The truest and most profound observations on Intelligence have in the past been made by the poets and, in recent times, by story-writers. They have been keen observers and recorders and reckoned freely with the emotions and sentiments. Most philosophers, on the other hand, have exhibited a grotesque ignorance of man's life and have built up systems that are elaborate and imposing, but quite unrelated to actual human affairs. They have almost consistently neglected the actual process of thought and have set the mind off as something apart to be studied by itself. *But no such mind, exempt from bodily processes, animal impulses, savage traditions, infantile impressions, conventional reactions, and traditional knowledge, ever existed,* even in the case of the most abstract of metaphysicians. Kant entitled his great work *A Critique of Pure Reason.* But to the modern student of mind pure reason seems as mythical as the pure gold, transparent as glass, with which the celestial city is paved.

Formerly philosophers thought of mind as having to do exclusively with conscious thought. It was that within man which perceived, remembered, judged, reasoned, understood, believed, willed. But of late it has been shown that we are unaware of a great part of what we perceive, remember, will, and infer; and that a great part of the thinking of which we are aware is determined by that of which we are not conscious. It has indeed been demonstrated that our unconscious psychic life far outruns our conscious. This seems perfectly natural to anyone who considers the following facts:

The sharp distinction between the mind and the body is, as we shall find, a very ancient and spontaneous uncritical savage prepossession. What we think of as "mind" is so intimately associated with what we call "body" that we are coming to realize that the one cannot be understood without the other. Every thought reverberates through the body, and, on the other hand, alterations in our physical condition affect our whole attitude of mind. The insufficient elimination of the foul and decaying products of digestion may plunge us into deep melancholy, whereas a few whiffs of nitrous monoxide may exalt us to the seventh heaven of supernal knowledge and godlike complacency. And *vice versa,* a sudden word or thought may cause our heart to jump, check our breathing, or make our knees as water. There is a whole new literature growing up which studies the effects of our bodily secretions and our muscular tensions and their relation to our emotions and our thinking.

Then there are hidden impulses and desires and secret longings of which we can only with the greatest difficulty take account. They influence our conscious thought in the most bewildering fashion. Many of these unconscious influences appear to originate in our very early years. The older philosophers seem to have forgotten that even they were infants and children at their most impressionable age and never could by any possibility get over it.

The term "unconscious," now so familiar to all readers of modern works on psychology, gives offense to some adherents of the past. There should, however, be no special mystery about it. It is not a new animistic abstraction, but simply a collective word to include all the physiological changes which escape our notice, all the forgotten experiences and impressions of the past which continue to influence our desires and reflections and conduct, even if we cannot remember them. What we can remember at any time is indeed an infinitesimal part of what has happened to us. We could not remember anything unless we forgot almost everything. As Bergson says, the brain is the organ of forgetfulness as well as of memory. Moreover, we tend, of course, to become oblivious to things to which we are thoroughly accustomed, for habit blinds us to their existence. So the forgotten and the habitual make up a great part of the so-called "unconscious."

If we are ever to understand man, his conduct and reasoning, and if we aspire to learn to guide his life and his relations with his fellows more happily than heretofore, we cannot neglect the great discoveries briefly noted above. We must reconcile ourselves to novel and revolutionary conceptions of the mind, for it is clear that the older philosophers, whose works still determine our current views, had a very superficial notion of the subject with which they dealt. But for our purposes, with due regard to what has just been said and to much that has necessarily been left unsaid (and with the indulgence of those who will at first be inclined to dissent), *we shall consider mind chiefly as conscious knowledge and intelligence, as what we know and our attitude toward it—our disposition to increase our information, classify it, and apply it.*

We do not think enough about thinking, and much of our confusion is the result of current illusions in regard to it. Let us forget for the moment any impressions we may have derived from the philosophers, and see what seems to happen in ourselves. The first thing that we notice is that our thought moves with such incredible rapidity that it is almost impossible to arrest any specimen of it long enough to have a look at it. When we are offered a penny for our thoughts we always find that we have recently had so many things in mind that we can easily make a selection which will not compromise us too nakedly. On inspection we shall find that even if we are not downright ashamed of a great part of our spontaneous thinking, it is far too intimate, personal, ignoble or trivial to permit us to reveal more than a small part of it. I believe this must be true of everyone. We do not, of course, know what goes on in other people's heads. They tell us very little and we tell them very little. The spigot of speech, rarely fully opened, could never emit more than driblets of the ever renewed hogshead of thought—*noch grösser wie's Heidelberger Fass.* [0] We find it hard to believe that other people's thoughts are as silly as our own, but they probably are.

We all appear to ourselves to be thinking all the time during our waking hours, and most of us are aware that we go on thinking while we are asleep, even more foolishly than when awake. When uninterrupted by some practical issue we are engaged in what is now known as a *reverie.* This is our spontaneous and favorite kind of thinking. We allow our ideas to take their own course and this course is determined by our hopes and fears, our spontaneous desires, their fulfillment or frustration; by our likes and dislikes, our loves and hates and resentments. There is nothing else anything like so interesting to ourselves as ourselves. All thought that is not more or less laboriously controlled and directed will inevitably circle about the beloved Ego. It is amusing and pathetic to observe this tendency in ourselves and in others. We learn politely and generously to overlook this truth, but if we dare to think of it, it blazes forth like the noontide sun.

The reverie or "free association of ideas" has of late become the subject of scientific research. While investigators are not yet agreed on the results, or at least on the proper interpretation to be given to them, there can be no doubt that our reveries form the chief index to our fundamental character. They are a reflection of our nature as modified by often hidden and forgotten experiences. We need not go into the matter further here, for

noch . . . Fass "even bigger than the Heidelberg barrel," a barrel famous for its size, located in the cellar of the castle at Heidelberg, Germany.

it is only necessary to observe that the reverie is at all times a potent and in many cases an omnipotent rival to every other kind of thinking. It doubtless influences all our speculations in its persistent tendency to self-magnification and self-justification, which are its chief preoccupations, but it is the last thing to make directly or indirectly for honest increase of knowledge.[1] Philosophers usually talk as if such thinking did not exist or were in some way negligible. This is what makes their speculations so unreal and often worthless.

The reverie, as any of us can see for himself, is frequently broken and interrupted by the necessity of a second kind of thinking. We have to make practical decisions. Shall we write a letter or no? Shall we take the subway or a bus? Shall we have dinner at seven or half past? Shall we buy U.S. Rubber or a Liberty Bond? Decisions are easily distinguishable from the free flow of the reverie. Sometimes they demand a good deal of careful pondering and the recollection of pertinent facts; often, however, they are made impulsively. They are a more difficult and laborious thing than the reverie, and we resent having to "make up our mind" when we are tired, or absorbed in a congenial reverie. Weighing a decision, it should be noted, does not necessarily add anything to our knowledge, although we may, of course, seek further information before making it.

2. Rationalizing

A third kind of thinking is stimulated when anyone questions our belief and opinions. We sometimes find ourselves changing our minds without any resistance or heavy emotion, but if we are told that we are wrong we resent the imputation and harden our hearts. We are incredibly heedless in the formation of our beliefs, but find ourselves filled with an illicit passion for them when anyone proposes to rob us of their companionship. It is obviously not the ideas themselves that are dear to us, but our self-esteem, which is threatened. We are by nature stubbornly pledged to defend our own from attack, whether it be our person, our family, our property, or our opinion. A United States Senator once remarked to a

[1]The poet-clergyman, John Donne, who lived in the time of James I, has given a beautifully honest picture of the doings of a saint's mind: "I throw myself down in my chamber and call in and invite God and His angels thither, and when they are there I neglect God and His angels for the noise of a fly, for the rattling of a coach, for the whining of a door. I talk on in the same posture of praying, eyes lifted up, knees bowed down, as though I prayed to God, and if God or His angels should ask me when I thought last of God in that prayer I cannot tell. Sometimes I find that I had forgot what I was about, but when I began to forget it I cannot tell. A memory of yesterday's pleasures, a fear of to-morrow's dangers, a straw under my knee, a noise in mine ear, a light in mine eye, an anything, a nothing, a fancy, a chimera in my brain troubles me in my prayer."—Quoted by Robert Lynd, *The Art of Letters*, pp. 46–47.

friend of mine that God Almighty could not make him change his mind on our Latin-America policy. We may surrender, but rarely confess ourselves vanquished. In the intellectual world at least peace is without victory.

Few of us take the pains to study the origin of our cherished convictions; indeed, we have a natural repugnance to so doing. We like to continue to believe what we have been accustomed to accept as true, and the resentment aroused when doubt is cast upon any of our assumptions leads us to seek every manner of excuse for clinging to them. *The result is that most of our so-called reasoning consists in finding arguments for going on believing as we already do.*

I remember years ago attending a public dinner to which the Governor of the state was bidden. The chairman explained that His Excellency could not be present for certain "good" reasons; what the "real" reasons were the presiding officer said he would leave us to conjecture. This distinction between "good" and "real" reasons is one of the most clarifying and essential in the whole realm of thought. We can readily give what seem to us "good" reasons for being a Catholic or a Mason, a Republican or a Democrat, an adherent or opponent of the League of Nations. But the "real" reasons are usually on quite a different plane. Of course the importance of this distinction is popularly, if somewhat obscurely, recognized. The Baptist missionary is ready enough to see that the Buddhist is not such because his doctrines would bear careful inspection, but because he happened to be born in a Buddhist family in Tokio. But it would be treason to his faith to acknowledge that his own partiality for certain doctrines is due to the fact that his mother was a member of the First Baptist church of Oak Ridge. A savage can give all sorts of reasons for his belief that it is dangerous to step on a man's shadow, and a newspaper editor can advance plenty of arguments against the Bolsheviki. But neither of them may realize why he happens to be defending his particular opinion.

The "real" reasons for our beliefs are concealed from ourselves as well as from others. As we grow up we simply adopt the ideas presented to us in regard to such matters as religion, family relations, property, business, our country, and the state. We unconsciously absorb them from our environment. They are persistently whispered in our ear by the group in which we happen to live. Moreover, as Mr. Trotter has pointed out, these judgments, being the product of suggestion and not of reasoning, have the quality of perfect obviousness, so that to question them

> . . . is to the believer to carry skepticism to an insane degree, and will be met by contempt, disapproval, or condemnation, according to the nature of the belief in question. When, therefore, we find ourselves entertaining an opinion about the basis of which there is a quality of feeling which tells us that to inquire into it would be absurd, obviously unnecessary, unprofitable, undesirable, bad

form, or wicked, we may know that that opinion is a nonrational one, and probably, therefore, founded upon inadequate evidence.[2]

Opinions, on the other hand, which are the result of experience or of honest reasoning do not have this quality of "primary certitude." I remember when as a youth I heard a group of business men discussing the question of the immortality of the soul, I was outraged by the sentiment of doubt expressed by one of the party. As I look back now I see that I had at the time no interest in the matter, and certainly no least argument to urge in favor of the belief in which I had been reared. But neither my personal indifference to the issue, nor the fact that I had previously given it no attention, served to prevent an angry resentment when I heard *my* ideas questioned.

This spontaneous and loyal support of our preconceptions—this process of finding "good" reasons to justify our routine beliefs—is known to modern psychologists as "rationalizing"—clearly only a new name for a very ancient thing. Our "good" reasons ordinarily have no value in promoting honest enlightenment, because, no matter how solemnly they may be marshaled, they are at bottom the result of personal preference or prejudice, and not of an honest desire to seek or accept new knowledge.

In our reveries we are frequently engaged in self-justification, for we cannot bear to think ourselves wrong, and yet have constant illustrations of our weaknesses and mistakes. So we spend much time finding fault with circumstances and the conduct of others, and shifting on to them with great ingenuity the onus of our own failures and disappointments. *Rationalizing is the self-exculpation which occurs when we feel ourselves, or our group, accused of misapprehension or error.*

The little word *my* is the most important one in all human affairs, and properly to reckon with it is the beginning of wisdom. It has the same force whether it is *my* dinner, *my* dog, and *my* house, or *my* faith, *my* country, and *my* God. We not only resent the imputation that our watch is wrong, or our car shabby, but that our conception of the canals of Mars, of the pronunciation of "Epictetus," of the medicinal value of salicine, or the date of Sargon I, are subject to revision.

Philosophers, scholars, and men of science exhibit a common sensitiveness in all decisions in which their *amour propre*[0] is involved. Thousands of argumentative works have been written to vent a grudge. However stately their reasoning, it may be nothing but rationalizing, stimulated by the most commonplace of all motives. A history of philosophy and theology could be written in terms of grouches, wounded pride, and aversions, and it would be far more instructive than the usual treatments of these themes. Sometimes, under Providence, the lowly impulse of resentment

[2]*Instincts of the Herd*, p. 44.

amour propre   self-respect (French).

leads to great achievements. Milton wrote his treatise on divorce as a result of his troubles with his seventeen-year-old wife, and when he was accused of being the leading spirit in a new sect, the Divorcers, he wrote his noble *Areopagitica* to prove his right to say what he thought fit, and incidentally to establish the advantage of a free press in the promotion of Truth.

All mankind, high and low, thinks in all the ways which have been described. The reverie goes on all the time not only in the mind of the mill hand and the Broadway flapper, but equally in weighty judges and godly bishops. It has gone on in all the philosophers, scientists, poets, and theologians that have ever lived. Aristotle's most abstruse speculations were doubtless tempered by highly irrelevant reflections. He is reported to have had very thin legs and small eyes, for which he doubtless had to find excuses, and he was wont to indulge in very conspicuous dress and rings and was accustomed to arrange his hair carefully.[3] Diogenes the Cynic° exhibited the impudence of a touchy soul. His tub was his distinction. Tennyson in beginning his "Maud" could not forget his chagrin over losing his patrimony years before as the result of an unhappy investment in the Patent Decorative Carving Company. These facts are not recalled here as a gratuitous disparagement of the truly great, but to insure a full realization of the tremendous competition which all really exacting thought has to face, even in the minds of the most highly endowed mortals.

And now the astonishing and perturbing suspicion emerges that perhaps almost all that had passed for social science, political economy, politics, and ethics in the past may be brushed aside by future generations as mainly rationalizing. John Dewey has already reached this conclusion in regard to philosophy.[4] Veblen[5] ° and other writers have revealed the various unperceived presuppositions of the traditional political economy, and now comes an Italian sociologist, Vilfredo Pareto, who, in his huge treatise on general sociology, devotes hundreds of pages to substantiating a similar thesis affecting all the social sciences.[6] This conclusion may be ranked by students of a hundred years hence as one of the several great

[3]Diogenes Laertius, book v.
[4]*Reconstruction in Philosophy.*
[5]*The Place of Science in Modern Civilization.*
[6]*Traité de Sociologie Générale, passim.* The author's term *"dérivations"* seems to be his precise way of expressing what we have called the "good" reasons, and his *"résidus"* correspond to the "real" reasons. He well says, *"L'homme éprouve le besoin de raisonner, et en outre d'étendre un voile sur ses instincts et sur ses sentiments"*—hence, rationalization. (P. 788.) His aim is to reduce sociology to the "real" reasons. (P. 791.)

Diogenes the Cynic   Greek philosopher (fourth century B.C.) who is known for his search to find an honest man. He lived in a tub to show his freedom from material needs.
Veblen   Thorstein Veblen (1857–1929), American economist and social critic.

discoveries of our age. It is by no means fully worked out, and it is so opposed to nature that it will be very slowly accepted by the great mass of those who consider themselves thoughtful. As a historical student I am personally fully reconciled to this newer view. Indeed, it seems to me inevitable that just as the various sciences of nature were, before the opening of the seventeenth century, largely masses of rationalizations to suit the religious sentiments of the period, so the social sciences have continued even to our own day to be rationalizations of uncritically accepted beliefs and customs.

It will become apparent as we proceed that the fact that an idea is ancient and that it has been widely received is no argument in its favor, but should immediately suggest the necessity of carefully testing it as a probable instance of rationalization.

3. How Creative Thought Transforms the World

This brings us to another kind of thought which can fairly easily be distinguished from the three kinds described above. It has not the usual qualities of the reverie, for it does not hover about our personal complacencies and humiliations. It is not made up of the homely decisions forced upon us by everyday needs, when we review our little stock of existing information, consult our conventional preferences and obligations, and make a choice of action. It is not the defense of our own cherished beliefs and prejudices just because they are our own—mere plausible excuses for remaining of the same mind. On the contrary, it is that peculiar species of thought which leads us to *change* our mind.

It is this kind of thought that has raised man from his pristine, subsavage ignorance and squalor to the degree of knowledge and comfort which he now possesses. On his capacity to continue and greatly extend this kind of thinking depends his chance of groping his way out of the plight in which the most highly civilized peoples of the world now find themselves. In the past this type of thinking has been called Reason. But so many misapprehensions have grown up around the word that some of us have become very suspicious of it. I suggest, therefore, that we substitute a recent name and speak of "creative thought" rather than of Reason. *For this kind of meditation begets knowledge, and knowledge is really creative in as much as it makes things look different from what they seemed before and may indeed work for their reconstruction.*

In certain moods some of us realize that we are observing things or making reflections with a seeming disregard of our personal preoccupations. We are not preening or defending ourselves; we are not faced by the necessity of any practical decision, nor are we apologizing for believing this or that. We are just wondering and looking and mayhap seeing what we never perceived before.

Curiosity is as clear and definite as any of our urges. We wonder what is in a sealed telegram or in a letter in which some one else is absorbed, or what is being said in the telephone booth or in low conversation. This inquisitiveness is vastly stimulated by jealousy, suspicion, or any hint that we ourselves are directly or indirectly involved. But there appears to be a fair amount of personal interest in other people's affairs even when they do not concern us except as a mystery to be unraveled or a tale to be told. The reports of a divorce suit will have "news value" for many weeks. They constitute a story, like a novel or play or moving picture. This is not an example of pure curiosity, however, since we readily identify ourselves with others, and their joys and despair then become our own.

We also take note of, or "observe," as Sherlock Holmes says, things which have nothing to do with our personal interests and make no personal appeal either direct or by way of sympathy. This is what Veblen so well calls "idle curiosity." And it is usually idle enough. Some of us when we face the line of people opposite us in a subway train impulsively consider them in detail and engage in rapid inferences and form theories in regard to them. On entering a room there are those who will perceive at a glance the degree of preciousness of the rugs, the character of the pictures, and the personality revealed by the books. But there are many, it would seem, who are so absorbed in their personal reverie or in some definite purpose that they have no bright-eyed energy for idle curiosity. The tendency to miscellaneous observation we come by honestly enough, for we note it in many of our animal relatives.

Veblen, however, uses the term "idle curiosity" somewhat ironically, as is his wont. It is idle only to those who fail to realize that it may be a very rare and indispensable thing from which almost all distinguished human achievement proceeds, since it may lead to systematic examination and seeking for things hitherto undiscovered. For research is but diligent search which enjoys the high flavor of primitive hunting. Occasionally and fitfully idle curiosity thus leads to creative thought, which alters and broadens our own views and aspirations and may in turn, under highly favorable circumstances, affect the views and lives of others, even for generations to follow. An example or two will make this unique human process clear.

Galileo was a thoughtful youth and doubtless carried on a rich and varied reverie. He had artistic ability and might have turned out to be a musician or painter. When he had dwelt among the monks at Valambrosa he had been tempted to lead the life of a religious. As a boy he busied himself with toy machines and he inherited a fondness for mathematics. All these facts are of record. We may safely assume also that, along with many other subjects of contemplation, the Pisan maidens found a vivid place in his thoughts.

One day when seventeen years old he wandered into the cathedral of his native town. In the midst of his reverie he looked up at the lamps hanging by long chains from the high ceiling of the church. Then something very difficult to explain occurred. He found himself no longer thinking of the building, worshipers, or the services; of his artistic or religious interests; of his reluctance to become a physician as his father wished. He forgot the question of a career and even the *graziosissime donne.*° As he watched the swinging lamps he was suddenly wondering if mayhap their oscillations, whether long or short, did not occupy the same time. Then he tested his hypothesis by counting his pulse, for that was the only timepiece he had with him.

This observation, however remarkable in itself, was not enough to produce a really creative thought. Others may have noticed the same thing and yet nothing came of it. Most of our observations have no assignable results. Galileo may have seen that the warts on a peasant's face formed a perfect isosceles triangle, or he may have noticed with boyish glee that just as the officiating priest was uttering the solemn words, *ecce agnus Dei,*° a fly lit on the end of his nose. To be really creative, ideas have to be worked up and then "put over," so that they become a part of man's social heritage. The highly accurate pendulum clock was one of the later results of Galileo's discovery. He himself was led to reconsider and successfully to refute the old notions of falling bodies. It remained for Newton to prove that the moon was falling, and presumably all the heavenly bodies. This quite upset all the consecrated views of the heavens as managed by angelic engineers. The universality of the laws of gravitation stimulated the attempt to seek other and equally important natural laws and cast grave doubts on the miracles in which mankind had hitherto believed. In short, those who dared to include in their thought the discoveries of Galileo and his successors found themselves in a new earth surrounded by new heavens.

On the 28th of October, 1831, two hundred and fifty years after Galileo had noticed the isochronous vibrations of the lamps, creative thought and its currency had so far increased that Faraday was wondering what would happen if he mounted a disk of copper between the poles of a horseshoe magnet. As the disk revolved an electric current was produced. This would doubtless have seemed the idlest kind of an experiment to the staunch business men of the time, who, it happened, were just then denouncing the child-labor bills in their anxiety to avail themselves to the full of the results of earlier idle curiosity. But should the dynamos and motors which have come into being as the outcome of Faraday's experiment be stopped this evening, the business man of to-day, agitated over labor troubles, might, as he trudged home past lines of "dead" cars, through dark streets to an unlighted house, engage in a little creative thought of his own and perceive that he and his laborers would have no

graziosissime donne   most gracious ladies (Italian).
ecce agnus Dei   behold the Lamb of God (Latin). In a Catholic Mass said in Latin, this is the opening phrase of a prayer recited by the priest as he lifts up the consecrated host.

modern factories and mines to quarrel about had it not been for the strange practical effects of the idle curiosity of scientists, inventors, and engineers.

The examples of creative intelligence given above belong to the realm of modern scientific achievement, which furnishes the most striking instances of the effects of scrupulous, objective thinking. But there are, of course, other great realms in which the recording and embodiment of acute observation and insight have wrought themselves into the higher life of man. The great poets and dramatists and our modern story-tellers have found themselves engaged in productive reveries, noting and artistically presenting their discoveries for the delight and instruction of those who have the ability to appreciate them.

The process by which a fresh and original poem or drama comes into being is doubtless analogous to that which originates and elaborates so-called scientific discoveries; but there is clearly a temperamental difference. The genesis and advance of painting, sculpture, and music offer still other problems. We really as yet know shockingly little about these matters, and indeed very few people have the least curiosity about them.[7] Nevertheless, creative intelligence in its various forms and activities is what makes man. Were it not for its slow, painful, and constantly discouraged operations through the ages man would be no more than a species of primate living on seeds, fruit, roots, and uncooked flesh, and wandering naked through the woods and over the plains like a chimpanzee.

The origin and progress and future promotion of civilization are ill understood and misconceived. These should be made the chief theme of education, but much hard work is necessary before we can reconstruct our ideas of man and his capacities and free ourselves from innumerable persistent misapprehensions. There have been obstructionists in all times, not merely the lethargic masses, but the moralists, the rationalizing theologians, and most of the philosophers, all busily if unconsciously engaged in ratifying existing ignorance and mistakes and discouraging creative thought. Naturally, those who reassure us seem worthy of honor and respect. Equally naturally those who puzzle us with disturbing criticisms and invite us to change our ways are objects of suspicion and readily discredited. Our personal discontent does not ordinarily extend to any critical questioning of the general situation in which we find ourselves. In

---

[7]Recently a re-examination of creative thought has begun as a result of new knowledge which discredits many of the notions formerly held about "reason." See, for example, *Creative Intelligence,* by a group of American philosophic thinkers; John Dewey, *Essays in Experimental Logic* (both pretty hard books); and Veblen, *The Place of Science in Modern Civilization.* Easier than these and very stimulating are Dewey, *Reconstruction in Philosophy,* and Woodworth, *Dynamic Psychology.*

every age the prevailing conditions of civilization have appeared quite natural and inevitable to those who grew up in them. The cow asks no questions as to how it happens to have a dry stall and a supply of hay. The kitten laps its warm milk from a china saucer, without knowing anything about porcelain; the dog nestles in the corner of a divan with no sense of obligation to the inventors of upholstery and the manufacturers of down pillows. So we humans accept our breakfasts, our trains and telephones and orchestras and movies, our national Constitution, our moral code and standards of manners, with the simplicity and innocence of a pet rabbit. We have absolutely inexhaustible capacities for appropriating what others do for us with no thought of a "thank you." We do not feel called upon to make any least contribution to the merry game ourselves. Indeed, we are usually quite unaware that a game is being played at all.

We have now examined the various classes of thinking which we can readily observe in ourselves and which we have plenty of reasons to believe go on, and always have been going on, in our fellow-men. We can sometimes get quite pure and sparkling examples of all four kinds, but commonly they are so confused and intermingled in our reverie as not to be readily distinguishable. The reverie is a reflection of our longings, exultations, and complacencies, our fears, suspicions, and disappoint-ments. We are chiefly engaged in struggling to maintain our self-respect and in asserting that supremacy which we all crave and which seems to us our natural prerogative. It is not strange, but rather quite inevitable, that our beliefs about what is true and false, good and bad, right and wrong, should be mixed up with the reverie and be influenced by the same considerations which determine its character and course. We resent criti-cisms of our views exactly as we do of anything else connected with ourselves. Our notions of life and its ideals seem to us to be *our own* and as such necessarily true and right, to be defended at all costs.

We very rarely consider, however, the process by which we gained our convictions. If we did so, we could hardly fail to see that there was usually little ground for our confidence in them. Here and there, in this depart-ment of knowledge or that, some one of us might make a fair claim to have taken some trouble to get correct ideas of, let us say, the situation in Russia, the sources of our food supply, the origin of the Constitution, the revision of the tariff, the policy of the Holy Roman Apostolic Church, modern business organization, trade unions, birth control, socialism, the League of Nations, the excess-profits tax, preparedness, advertising in its social bear-ings; but only a very exceptional person would be entitled to opinions on all of even these few matters. And yet most of us have opinions on all these, and on many other questions of equal importance, of which we may know even less. We feel compelled, as self-respecting persons, to take sides when they come up for discussion. We even surprise ourselves by our omniscience. Without taking thought we see in a flash that it is most

righteous and expedient to discourage birth control by legislative enact-
ment, or that one who decries intervention in Mexico is clearly wrong, or
that big advertising is essential to big business and that big business is the
pride of the land. As godlike beings why should we not rejoice in our
omniscience?

It is clear, in any case, that our convictions on important matters are not
the result of knowledge or critical thought, nor, it may be added, are they
often dictated by supposed self-interest. Most of them are *pure prejudices*
in the proper sense of that word. We do not form them ourselves. They
are the whisperings of "the voice of the herd." We have in the last analysis
no responsibility for them and need assume none. They are not really our
own ideas, but those of others no more well informed or inspired than
ourselves, who have got them in the same careless and humiliating manner as we. It should be our pride to revise our ideas and not to adhere to
what passes for respectable opinion, for such opinion can frequently be
shown to be not respectable at all. We should, in view of the considerations
that have been mentioned, resent our supine credulity. As an English
writer has remarked:

"If we feared the entertaining of an unverifiable opinion with the
warmth with which we fear using the wrong implement at the dinner
table, if the thought of holding a prejudice disgusted us as does a foul
disease, then the dangers of man's suggestibility would be turned into
advantages."[8]

The purpose of this essay is to set forth briefly the way in which the
notions of the herd have been accumulated. This seems to me the best,
easiest, and least invidious educational device for cultivating a proper
distrust for the older notions on which we still continue to rely.

The "real" reasons, which explain how it is we happen to hold a particular belief, are chiefly historical. Our most important opinions—those, for
example, having to do with traditional, religious, and moral convictions,
property rights, patriotism, national honor, the state, and indeed all the
assumed foundations of society—are, as I have already suggested, rarely
the result of reasoned consideration, but of unthinking absorption from
the social environment in which we live. Consequently, they have about
them a quality of "elemental certitude," and we especially resent doubt
or criticism cast upon them. So long, however, as we revere the whisperings of the herd, we are obviously unable to examine them dispassionately
and to consider to what extent they are suited to the novel conditions and
social exigencies in which we find ourselves to-day.

The "real" reasons for our beliefs, by making clear their origins and
history, can do much to dissipate this emotional blockade and rid us of our
prejudices and preconceptions. Once this is done and we come critically
to examine our traditional beliefs, we may well find some of them sus-

[8]Trotter, *op. cit.*, p. 45. The first part of this little volume is excellent.

tained by experience and honest reasoning, while others must be revised to meet new conditions and our more extended knowledge. But only after we have undertaken such a critical examination in the light of experience and modern knowledge, freed from any feeling of "primary certitude," can we claim that the "good" are also the "real" reasons for our opinions.

I do not flatter myself that this general show-up of man's thought through the ages will cure myself or others of carelessness in adopting ideas, or of unseemly heat in defending them just because we have adopted them. But if the considerations which I propose to recall are really incorporated into our thinking and are permitted to establish our general outlook on human affairs, they will do much to relieve the imaginary obligation we feel in regard to traditional sentiments and ideals. Few of us are capable of engaging in creative thought, but some of us can at least come to distinguish it from other and inferior kinds of thought and accord to it the esteem that it merits as the greatest treasure of the past and the only hope of the future.

Aldous Huxley

Aldous Huxley (1894–1963), one of the most well known of modern English novelists and essayists, came from a family celebrated for its intellectual achievement. He was the son of author and editor Leonard Huxley; the grandson of the naturalist Thomas Huxley (see p. 25); and the grandnephew of poet and critic Matthew Arnold. His brother Sir Julian was a distinguished biologist, and his half-brother David won the 1963 Nobel Prize for his work in physiology. Huxley studied at Eton and Oxford, despite a serious eye disease that made him almost totally blind for three years. Reading with the aid of a magnifying glass, he graduated from Oxford in 1915 with honors in English literature. In 1919 he joined the staff of *Athenaeum,* a London literary magazine, and began a steady production of writings in all genres.

The success of his early novels allowed Huxley to move to Italy in 1923 and thence to France; in 1934 he traveled in the United States and finally settled in southern California near Los Angeles. He continued to write books, articles, and an occasional screenplay. He studied Vedanta and other Eastern religions and became interested in the effects of drugs on the mind.

Huxley wrote eleven novels, of which the most famous is *Brave New World* (1932); others include *Antic Hay* (1923), *Point Counter Point* (1928), and *After Many a Summer Dies the Swan* (1939). His literary reputation rests equally on his over twenty volumes of essays and belles-lettres.

Huxley's *Brave New World* has turned out to be devastatingly accurate as a piece of futuristic science fiction and as a satire on modern technological mass-produced civilization. It became so widely known that in 1958 Huxley could safely give the title *Brave New World Revisited* to a study of the progress of dehumanization and mental tyranny in the intervening quarter century. Both Huxley essays in this book come from *Brave New World Revisited*. The following is Chapter 5.

Propaganda Under a Dictatorship

At his trial after the Second World War, Hitler's Minister for Armaments, Albert Speer, delivered a long speech in which, with remarkable acuteness, he described the Nazi tyranny and analyzed its methods. "Hitler's dictatorship," he said, "differed in one fundamental point from all its predecessors in history. It was the first dictatorship in the present period of modern technical development, a dictatorship which made complete use of all technical means for the domination of its own country. Through technical devices like the radio and the loud-speaker, eighty million people were deprived of independent thought. It was thereby possible to subject them to the will of one man. . . . Earlier dictators needed highly qualified assistants even at the lowest level—men who could think and act independently. The totalitarian system in the period of modern technical development can dispense with such men; thanks to modern methods of communication, it is possible to mechanize the lower leadership. As a result of this there has arisen the new type of the uncritical recipient of orders."

In the Brave New World of my prophetic fable technology had advanced far beyond the point it had reached in Hitler's day; consequently the recipients of orders were far less critical than their Nazi counterparts, far more obedient to the order-giving elite. Moreover, they had been genetically standardized and postnatally conditioned to perform their subordinate functions, and could therefore be depended upon to behave almost as predictably as machines. As we shall see in a later chapter, this conditioning of "the lower leadership" is already going on under the Communist dictatorships. The Chinese and the Russians are not relying merely on the indirect effects of advancing technology; they are working directly on the psychophysical organisms of their lower leaders, subjecting minds and bodies to a system of ruthless and, from all accounts, highly effective conditioning. "Many a man," said Speer, "has been haunted by the nightmare that one day nations might be dominated by technical means. That nightmare was almost realized in Hitler's totalitarian system." Almost, but not quite. The Nazis did not have time—and perhaps did not have the intelligence and the necessary knowledge—to brainwash and condition their lower leadership. This, it may be, is one of the reasons why they failed.

Since Hitler's day the armory of technical devices at the disposal of the would-be dictator has been considerably enlarged. As well as the radio, the loud-speaker, the moving picture camera and the rotary press, the contemporary propagandist can make use of television to broadcast the image as well as the voice of his client, and can record both image and voice on spools of magnetic tape. Thanks to technological progress, Big Brother[0] can now be almost as omnipresent as God. Nor is it only on the technical front that the hand of the would-be dictator has been strengthened. Since Hitler's day a great deal of work has been carried out in those fields of applied psychology and neurology which are the special province of the propagandist, the indoctrinator and the brainwasher. In the past these specialists in the art of changing people's minds were empiricists. By a method of trial and error they had worked out a number of techniques and procedures, which they used very effectively without, however, knowing precisely why they were effective. Today the art of mind-control is in process of becoming a science. The practitioners of this science know what they are doing and why. They are guided in their work by theories and hypotheses solidly established on a massive foundation of experimental evidence. Thanks to the new insights and the new techniques made possible by these insights, the nightmare that was "all but realized in Hitler's totalitarian system" may soon be completely realizable.

But before we discuss these new insights and techniques let us take a look at the nightmare that so nearly came true in Nazi Germany. What were the methods used by Hitler and Goebbels[0] for "depriving eighty million people of independent thought and subjecting them to the will of one man"? And what was the theory of human nature upon which those terrifyingly successful methods were based? These questions can be answered, for the most part, in Hitler's own words. And what remarkably clear and astute words they are! When he writes about such vast abstractions as Race and History and Providence, Hitler is strictly unreadable. But when he writes about the German masses and the methods he used for dominating and directing them, his style changes. Nonsense gives place to sense, bombast to a hardboiled and cynical lucidity. In his philosophical lucubrations Hitler was either cloudily daydreaming or reproducing other people's half-baked notions. In his comments on crowds and propaganda he was writing of things he knew by firsthand experience. In the words of his ablest biographer, Mr. Alan Bullock, "Hitler was the greatest demagogue in history." Those who add, "only a demagogue," fail to appreciate the nature of political power in an age of mass politics. As he himself said, "To be a leader means to be able to move the masses." Hitler's aim was first to move the masses and then, having pried them loose from their traditional loyalties and moralities, to impose upon them (with the hypno-

Big Brother   Head of the totalitarian state in George Orwell's antiutopian novel *Nineteen Eighty-Four.*
Goebbels   Joseph Goebbels, minister of propaganda under Hitler.

tized consent of the majority) a new authoritarian order of his own devising. "Hitler," wrote Hermann Rauschning[0] in 1939, "has a deep respect for the Catholic church and the Jesuit order; not because of their Christian doctrine, but because of the 'machinery' they have elaborated and controlled, their hierarchical system, their extremely clever tactics, their knowledge of human nature and their wise use of human weaknesses in ruling over believers." Ecclesiasticism without Christianity, the discipline of a monastic rule, not for God's sake or in order to achieve personal salvation, but for the sake of the State and for the greater glory and power of the demagogue turned Leader—this was the goal toward which the systematic moving of the masses was to lead.

Let us see what Hitler thought of the masses he moved and how he did the moving. The first principle from which he started was a value judgment: the masses are utterly contemptible. They are incapable of abstract thinking and uninterested in any fact outside the circle of their immediate experience. Their behavior is determined, not by knowledge and reason, but by feelings and unconscious drives. It is in these drives and feelings that "the roots of their positive as well as their negative attitudes are implanted." To be successful a propagandist must learn how to manipulate these instincts and emotions. "The driving force which has brought about the most tremendous revolutions on this earth has never been a body of scientific teaching which has gained power over the masses, but always a devotion which has inspired them, and often a kind of hysteria which has urged them into action. Whoever wishes to win over the masses must know the key that will open the door of their hearts." . . . In post-Freudian jargon, of their unconscious.

Hitler made his strongest appeal to those members of the lower middle classes who had been ruined by the inflation of 1923, and then ruined all over again by the depression of 1929 and the following years. "The masses" of whom he speaks were these bewildered, frustrated and chronically anxious millions. To make them more masslike, more homogeneously subhuman, he assembled them, by the thousands and the tens of thousands, in vast halls and arenas, where individuals could lose their personal identity, even their elementary humanity, and be merged with the crowd. A man or woman makes direct contact with society in two ways: as a member of some familial, professional or religious group, or as a member of a crowd. Groups are capable of being as moral and intelligent as the individuals who form them; a crowd is chaotic, has no purpose of its own and is capable of anything except intelligent action and realistic thinking. Assembled in a crowd, people lose their powers of reasoning and their

Hermann Rauschning Former high-ranking member of the Nazi party, who criticized its anti-Semitism and resigned and fled Germany in 1935. His 1939 book, *The Revolution of Nihilism,* was a report and analysis of Adolf Hitler and the Nazi movement.

capacity for moral choice. Their suggestibility is increased to the point where they cease to have any judgment or will of their own. They become very excitable, they lose all sense of individual or collective responsibility, they are subject to sudden accesses of rage, enthusiasm and panic. In a word, a man in a crowd behaves as though he had swallowed a large dose of some powerful intoxicant. He is a victim of what I have called "herd-poisoning." Like alcohol, herd-poison is an active, extraverted drug. The crowd-intoxicated individual escapes from responsibility, intelligence and morality into a kind of frantic, animal mindlessness.

During his long career as an agitator, Hitler had studied the effects of herd-poison and had learned how to exploit them for his own purposes. He had discovered that the orator can appeal to those "hidden forces" which motivate men's actions, much more effectively than can the writer. Reading is a private, not a collective activity. The writer speaks only to individuals, sitting by themselves in a state of normal sobriety. The orator speaks to masses of individuals, already well primed with herd-poison. They are at his mercy and, if he knows his business, he can do what he likes with them. As an orator, Hitler knew his business supremely well. He was able, in his own words, "to follow the lead of the great mass in such a way that from the living emotion of his hearers the apt word which he needed would be suggested to him and in its turn this would go straight to the heart of his hearers." Otto Strasser called him a "loud-speaker, proclaiming the most secret desires, the least admissible instincts, the sufferings and personal revolts of a whole nation." Twenty years before Madison Avenue embarked upon "Motivational Research," Hitler was systematically exploring and exploiting the secret fears and hopes, the cravings, anxieties and frustrations of the German masses. It is by manipulating "hidden forces" that the advertising experts induce us to buy their wares—a toothpaste, a brand of cigarettes, a political candidate. And it is by appealing to the same hidden forces—and to others too dangerous for Madison Avenue to meddle with—that Hitler induced the German masses to buy themselves a Fuehrer, an insane philosophy and the Second World War.

Unlike the masses, intellectuals have a taste for rationality and an interest in facts. Their critical habit of mind makes them resistant to the kind of propaganda that works so well on the majority. Among the masses "instinct is supreme, and from instinct comes faith. . . . While the healthy common folk instinctively close their ranks to form a community of the people" (under a Leader, it goes without saying) "intellectuals run this way and that, like hens in a poultry yard. With them one cannot make history; they cannot be used as elements composing a community." Intellectuals are the kind of people who demand evidence and are shocked by logical inconsistencies and fallacies. They regard over-simplification as the original sin of the mind and have no use for the slogans, the unqualified assertions and sweeping generalizations which are the propagandist's stock in trade. "All effective propaganda," Hitler wrote, "must be confined to a few bare necessities and then must be expressed in a few stereotyped formulas." These stereotyped formulas must be constantly repeated, for "only constant repetition will finally succeed in imprinting an idea upon the memory of a crowd." Philosophy teaches us to feel uncertain about the things that seem to us self-evident. Propaganda, on the other hand, teaches us to accept as self-evident matters about which it would be reasonable to suspend our judgment or to feel doubt. The aim of the demagogue is to create social coherence under his own leadership. But, as Bertrand Russell has pointed out, "systems of dogma without empirical foundations, such as scholasticism, Marxism and fascism, have the advantage of producing a great deal of social coherence among their disciples." The demagogic propagandist must therefore be consistently dogmatic. All his statements are made without qualification. There are no grays in his picture of the world; everything is either diabolically black or celestially white. In Hitler's words, the propagandist should adopt "a systematically one-sided attitude towards every problem that has to be dealt with." He must never admit that he might be wrong or that people with a different point of view might be even partially right. Opponents should not be argued with; they should be attacked, shouted down, or, if they become too much of a nuisance, liquidated. The morally squeamish intellectual may be shocked by this kind of thing. But the masses are always convinced that "right is on the side of the active aggressor."

Such, then, was Hitler's opinion of humanity in the mass. It was a very low opinion. Was it also an incorrect opinion? The tree is known by its fruits, and a theory of human nature which inspired the kind of techniques that proved so horribly effective must contain at least an element of truth. Virtue and intelligence belong to human beings as individuals freely associating with other individuals in small groups. So do sin and stupidity. But the subhuman mindlessness to which the demagogue makes his appeal, the moral imbecility on which he relies when he goads his victims into action, are characteristic not of men and women as individuals, but of men and women in masses. Mindlessness and moral idiocy are not characteristically human attributes; they are symptoms of herd-poisoning. In all the world's higher religions, salvation and enlightenment are for individuals. The kingdom of heaven is within the mind of a person, not within the collective mindlessness of a crowd. Christ promised to be present where two or three are gathered together. He did not say anything about being present where thousands are intoxicating one another with herd-poison. Under the Nazis enormous numbers of people were compelled to spend an enormous amount of time marching in serried ranks from point A to point B and back again to point A. "This keeping of the whole population on the march seemed to be a senseless waste of time and energy. Only much later," adds Hermann Rauschning, "was there revealed in it a subtle intention based on a well-judged adjustment of ends and means. Marching diverts men's thoughts. Marching kills thought.

Marching makes an end of individuality. Marching is the indispensable magic stroke performed in order to accustom the people to a mechanical, quasi-ritualistic activity until it becomes second nature."

From his point of view and at the level where he had chosen to do his dreadful work, Hitler was perfectly correct in his estimate of human nature. To those of us who look at men and women as individuals rather than as members of crowds, or of regimented collectives, he seems hideously wrong. In an age of accelerating over-population, of accelerating over-organization and ever more efficient means of mass communication, how can we preserve the integrity and reassert the value of the human individual? This is a question that can still be asked and perhaps effectively answered. A generation from now it may be too late to find an answer and perhaps impossible, in the stifling collective climate of that future time, even to ask the question.

The Need for Feeling

James E. Miller, Jr.

James E. Miller, Jr., was born in Oklahoma in 1920. He received his Ph.D. in 1949 from the University of Chicago and returned there as Professor of English in 1962. Miller is distinguished as a teacher and scholar, with a particular interest in American literature. The selection printed below is taken from Chapter 2 of *Word, Self, Reality: The Rhetoric of Imagination* (1972).

Thought and Feeling

The mind works in mysterious ways, and thoughts are not so easily summoned or marshalled in ranks as some rhetoricians have said. If thoughts were little soldiers, well-disciplined and obedient, we would have the orderly, intellectual world which has been more frequently described than actually experienced. But thoughts for most of mankind are not soldiers but rowdy children, capricious and undisciplined. They romp into view and quickly vanish around dark corners. They peer from behind decaying tree stumps, make grotesque faces, and fade from sight. Some of the timid ones remain in the distance, almost out of sight, and scurry into underbrush when approached. Some have idiot faces and emit shrill moronic laughter. Some are sober, somber, and slightly pompous, puffed up with self-importance. Still others are pale and ghostly, sleepless, sad-eyed, dragging themselves slowly across the horizon.

These and many more crowd our poor brains, and to put them in order requires boundless patience and energy. Outlines are of little avail. It is good, of course, to see a subject divide into a sequence of parts, but the most detailed outline is of little use if the language flow cannot be started. To seize some of these random thoughts and plant them on paper—this may be the key to inspiration. For there is a strange phenomenon about the flow of thoughts and language that every writer must soon learn: the more thoughts are summoned, seized, and put to use, the more others swarm into the brain as replacements. Every writer who has gotten over his initial panic has at some time experienced this feeling of interior proliferation, this feeling of an abundance so great that it must of its own will burst forth. Putting some of the crowding thoughts down on paper may have the same effect as priming the pump: to begin with a trickle that will lead to full flow.

However much is put down on paper initially to prime the pump or to bring some semblance of order out of the jumble of tumbling thoughts, whenever the act of writing actually begins it is likely not to be a smooth and continual movement through an orderly arrangement of parts, but rather a series of spurts, side-movements, weird reversals—a jerky movement of stop and go that makes for a rather rocky ride. It is in this process that surprises lurk and discoveries are made. We discover thoughts we never suspected we had or could have, and we are surprised by attitudes that we didn't know existed within us. Most experienced writers agree that it is best to drive through to the end, even when the end seems some kind of contradiction of the beginning—and this happens more frequently than has been revealed. A first draft will have its rough spots, lapses, paradoxes, outright conflicts—but it will also represent a thinking and muddling through that is invaluable. Run through the mind again with the thought-processes turned on and testing throughout, it can become the basis of a good piece of writing.

When they finally begin to swarm, where do the thoughts come from on which writing is entirely dependent? Is there a logic-machine that manufactures them when the right buttons are pushed? Or is there a great emotional sponge that, when squeezed, oozes views and attitudes that come sighing and seething to the surface?

It is astonishing how little is known about the working of the mind. But however little or much is known, it is fairly clear that the model of the logic-machine is not only wrong but mischievous. There are people who profess to believe that man can live by logic alone. If only, they say, men developed their reason, looked at all situations and dilemmas logically, and proceeded to devise rational solutions, all human problems would be solved. Be reasonable. Think logically. Act rationally. This line of thought is very persuasive, not to say seductive. It is astonishing, however, how frequently the people most fanatically devoted to logic and reason, to a cold review of the "facts" and a calculated construction of the truth, turn out not only to be terribly emotional in argumentation, but opinionated before any "truth" is "proved"—deeply committed to emotional positions that prove rock-resistible to the most massive accumulation of unsympathetic facts and proofs.

If man's mind cannot be turned into a logic-machine, neither can it function properly as a great emotional sponge, to be squeezed at will. All of us have known people who gush as a general response to life—who gush in seeing a sunset, who gush in reading a book, who gush in meeting a friend. They may seem to live by emotion alone, but their constant gushing is a disguise for absence of genuine feeling, a torrent rushing to fill a vacuum. It is not uncommon to find beneath the gush a cold, analytic mind that is astonishing in its meticulousness and ruthless in its calculation.

Somewhere between machine and sponge lies the reality of the mind —an amalgam of reason and emotion, of actuality and imagination, of fact and feeling. The entanglement is so complete, the mixture so thoroughly mixed, that it is probably impossible to achieve pure reason or pure emotion, at least for any sustained period of time.

It is probably best to assume that all our reasoning is alloyed with our emotional commitments and beliefs, all our thoughts colored by feelings that lie deep within our psyches. Moreover, it is probably best to assume that this stream of emotion is not a poison, not even a taint, but is a positive life-source, a stream of psychic energy that animates and vitalizes our entire thought process. The roots of reason are embedded in feelings— feelings that have formed and accumulated and developed over a lifetime of personality-shaping. These feelings are not a source of weakness but a resource of strength. They are not there for occasional using but are inescapable. To know what we think, we must know how we feel. It is feeling that shapes belief and forms opinion. It is feeling that directs the strategy of argument. It is our feelings, then, with which we must come to honorable terms.

Robertson Davies

Robertson Davies, a Canadian, is the author of six novels and many plays and volumes of criticism. Born in 1913 in Ontario, he attended Queens University there, and then received a degree from Balliol College in Oxford, England. Davies has been a journalist, actor, editor, and teacher, and since 1963 master of Massey College at the University of Toronto.

The "Deptford Trilogy" established Davies' reputation in the United States. These three novels, *Fifth Business* (1970), *The Manticore* (1972), and *World of Wonders* (1975), abound with rich, almost Dickensian characters. His theme, he says, is the isolation of the human spirit; it is "worked out in terms of characters who are trying to escape from early influences and find their own place in the world but who are reluctant to do so in a way that will bring pain and disappointment to others." A masterful plotter and storyteller, he is knowledgeably and comfortably at home with myth and magic. He re-creates for his readers many varied worlds: a rural Canadian town, a European Jesuit retreat, a traveling freak show.

The selection printed here is from *One Half of Robertson Davies* (1977), a book "composed of pieces written to be spoken." The selection is a talk he gave at Queens University when he accepted an honorary degree. We omit the opening remarks on his personal relationships to the university.

The Deadliest of the Sins

What shall we talk about, you and I, who are getting our first degrees from Queen's today? The problem is a little easier than is usually the case, because we are both going into new jobs. I have been an author for many years, and I intend to go on being one. But being an author isn't a job— it is a state of mind; also, it is not a gainful occupation except in a rather restricted sense. I have been earning my living as a journalist for twenty years, and now I am giving up that sort of work to take a different sort of job in a university. I shall be very green at it, and I expect I shall do a lot of things the wrong way. Perhaps I shall be a failure, but I have failed at several things already, and somehow I have lived through it. Failure at a specific task is always disagreeable and sometimes it is humiliating. But there is only one kind of failure that really breaks the spirit, and that is failure in the art of life itself. That is the failure that one does well to fear.

What is it like, this failure in the art of life? It is the failure which manifests itself in a loss of interest in really important things. It does not come suddenly; there is nothing dramatic about it, and thus it works with a dreadful advantage; it creeps upon us, and once it has us in its grip, it is hard for us to recognize what ails us.

It is not for nothing that this failure was reckoned by medieval theologians as one of the Seven Deadly Sins. I suppose you know what they were. Wrath, Gluttony, Envy, Avarice, and Lechery are not very hard to recognize and are perilously easy to justify, by one means or another. Pride is an extremely subtle sin because it is so clever at disguising itself as something else, and those astute men St. Ambrose and St. Augustine thought it the most dangerous of all the sins. But it is the seventh which I think is particularly prevalent in our day; medieval theologians called it Sloth.

Sloth is not really a suitable name for it now, because the word has come to mean a sluggishness and inactivity which is chiefly physical. But the sloth the theologians meant, the sloth which can damn you in this world and perhaps in the next, is spiritual. There was a better name, a Latin name, for it; it was also called Accidie, and it meant intellectual and spiritual torpor, indifference, and lethargy.

To be guilty of Acedia it is not necessary to be physically sluggish at all. You can be as busy as a bee. You can fill your days with activity, bustling from meeting to meeting, sitting on committees, running from one party to another in a perfect whirlwind of movement. But if, meanwhile, your feelings and sensibilities are withering, if your relationships with people near to you are becoming more and more superficial, if you are losing touch even with yourself, it is Acedia which has claimed you for its own.

How can it be recognized? Anatole France[o] said that the great danger of increasing age was that the feelings atrophied, and we mistook the sensation for the growth of wisdom. It is true that as one grows older, one's sense of proportion may become greater, and things which troubled us or wounded us deeply in our youth seem less significant. But that is a different thing from feeling nothing deeply, and leaping to the conclusion that therefore nothing is really very important. As one grows older, one learns how to spare oneself many kinds of unnecessary pain, but one is in great danger if one ceases to feel pain of any kind. If you cannot feel pain at some of the harsh circumstances of life, it is very likely that you have ceased to feel joy at some of the satisfactions and delights of life. When that happens, one lives at all times under a mental and spiritual cloud; it is always wet weather in the soul. That is Acedia, and it was called a Deadly Sin because it dimmed and discouraged the spirit, and at last killed it.

I am sure that all of you know some people who have yielded to Acedia. They are the dampers, the wet blankets of life. Unfortunately some of them have a great attraction for the young. Their chronic lack of enthusiasm looks so much like sophistication. They are often clever people, who are adept at putting a chilly finger on the weak spot in whatever attracts their friends. They seldom make mistakes, because they never put themselves in a position where they are not complete masters of the situation. They take a sly pleasure in the failure of others, and they are always ready to say 'I told you so'. They have made just one great—indeed monstrous —mistake: they have died to joy and pain, and thus to feeling.

The opposites of these people are not, of course, those who allow every enthusiasm to run away with them, whose hearts always rule their heads, who go a-whoring after everything that is new. They are, on the contrary, people who take pains to keep their common sense in repair, and who keep their intelligence bright, but who also make daily efforts to meet

Anatole France French novelist, poet, and political satirist (1844–1924) who was awarded the 1921 Nobel Prize in Literature.

experience with a fresh vision, and to give to everything that comes their way the measure of feeling, of emotion, of charity and understanding—yes, and also of pain—that it needs in order to understand it.

Because you are university people, I assume that you are people in whom mind is more prominent and better trained than is feeling. If you had not had some intellectual bias—even of quite a mild sort—it is unlikely that you would be here today to receive a degree. Therefore you must take special care that, in the years ahead of you, feeling is not neglected.

The temptation to neglect feeling is strong. You see—I say this knowing that it is blasphemy within university walls—it is really very much easier to think sensibly than it is to feel sensibly. We all know what messes people get into when they feel too much and think too little; but those people do not compel my pity so much as the hundreds of thousands whose lives are cast in a mould of midget tragedy because they think a good deal, in a strangulated, ill-nourished fashion, but hardly feel at all. These are the victims of Acedia.

Therefore I charge you, whether you are struggling under the burden of a mighty intellect, or perhaps just shuffling along with a pretty well-trained mediocre brain, to take pains not to lose your capacity to feel.

How is it to be done? I have some practical advice for you in this struggle, which is one of the great battles of life. Take some time every day—*every* day—to examine what you have been doing in the light of feeling, rather than of intelligence. It may be before you fall asleep at night; it may be while you are walking to your work; it may be at any time when you can withdraw your attention from external matters: that is the time to ask yourself—What do I really feel about all this? Not, what should I feel about it, what does the world expect me to feel, but what do I truly feel about it? You must be honest with yourself, because self-deception is one of the commonest roads to Acedia.

Now it may happen that you will find that you are committed to some course of action which you do not like—which you may positively hate. And yet, for good reasons, it may be necessary to continue with it. We all have to do things we detest, at one time or another, because we are not free to consult our own wishes only. But if you know the truth, you are protected from Acedia.

Nor is it only the detestable things that should be carefully examined. You must look clearly at the things which make your life happy and enviable, and you must give yourself up to a grateful contemplation of them. Never take such things for granted. I have seen many a promising marriage shrivel and dry up because one or both of the parties to it assumed that happiness was something that came by right, and could never be diminished. Consciously summoning up, and consciously enjoying, the good things that life brings us is a way of preserving them. It is not in their nature to last forever; they will change, and if you cherish them gratefully, the change is much more likely to be a change for the better than if you accept them as gifts which a grateful providence has showered upon you as a recognition of your magnanimity in condescending to inhabit the earth.

I have never been able to make up my mind which it is that people fear to feel most—pain or joy. Life will bring you both. You will not be able to escape the pain completely, though Acedia will dull it a little. But unfortunately it lies in your power to reject the joy utterly. Because we are afraid that great exultation may betray us into some actions, some words, which may make us look a little foolish to people who are not sharing our experience, we very often stifle our moments of joy, thinking that we shall give them their outlet later. But alas, after a few years of that kind of thing, joy ceases to visit us. I seem to be quoting theologians this afternoon. There is an old saying of medieval teachers which I recommend to your special notice:

Time Jesum transeuntem et non revertentem.

I shall translate it thus: 'Dread the passing of Jesus, for He does not return.' And thus it is with all great revelations, be they religious or not. Seize them, embrace them, let them engulf you, draw from them the uttermost of what they have to give, for if you rebuff them, they will not come again. We live in a world where too many people are pitifully afraid of joy. Because I wish you well, I beg you not to add yourself to their number.

Do not put off the moment of decision. Begin now. This is your hour. You are shortly to receive one of the great distinctions of your lifetime. Don't worry about looking dignified; don't be afraid that your pleasure may betray you into some lapse from that nullity of demeanour which we so pathetically accept as a substitute for true dignity. Don't accept your BA as if it were one more padlock on the inmost chamber of your heart. Education, if it is real and not a sham, is a releasing, not an imprisoning, thing. If you wish it to be so, the achievement of your degree is a step toward a new freedom. What is the word in your heart as you accept your diploma? Is it No—or is it Yes?

Marcel Proust

Marcel Proust's literary fame comes from his long novel *À la Recherche du temps perdu (Remembrance of Things Past).* He published the first volume in 1913 and was dictating passages of the eighth the night before he died in 1922. Although the novel is not autobiographical, it does record the life of a Paris dilettante, wealthy and purposeless until one day when he realizes that the memories of his own life, relived and reshaped into art, will provide the subject for a great novel.

Proust, asthmatic and nervous from earliest childhood, lived in his family home in Paris from his birth in 1871 until his mother's death in 1905. While in school he wrote essays and poems that show his early interest in the Decadent movement—a school of French writers who stressed the abnormal and artificial in their works. At the Sorbonne he enrolled as a student of law and political science, but his only academic interest was in philosophy. He spent most of his time widening his circle of acquaintances in the literary and artistic society of Paris and sporadically composing novels and shorter works. Though only a few were printed, he later worked parts of them into his major novel.

His mother's death grieved Proust excessively, for she had given his life a continuity and a portion of her own strict discipline. Her death did enable Proust to stop hiding his homosexuality—though none of his series of affairs lasted long, and the most intense ended tragically when his lover died in a plane crash in 1914.

In 1907 Proust moved to a flat, which he had made soundproof and from which, in later years, he almost never stirred. By 1909 he had begun steady work on *Remembrance of Things Past.* He saw less and less of aristocratic Paris society; because of his asthma he often worked on his novel all night and slept during the day. He became progressively weaker and more nervous, took large amounts of drugs for his asthma, and died of pneumonia in 1922.

Contre Sainte-Beuve (By Way of Sainte-Beuve), written between 1908 and 1910, was the only major interruption to the work on his novel. It began as a critical study but soon turned into an account of Proust's own processes of memory, thought, and feeling. The present essay, which opens the book, is celebrated as a description of how his masterpiece may have originated. The translation is by Sylvia Townsend Warner (1958). "Sainte-Beuve's Method," referred to in the final paragraph, is described elsewhere by Proust as "not separating the man and his work," "to surround oneself with every possible piece of information about a writer" before making a judgment on his writings. Proust did not admire this method.

Prologue

Every day I set less store on intellect. Every day I see more clearly that if the writer is to repossess himself of some part of his impressions, reach something personal, that is, and the only material of art, he must put it aside. What intellect restores to us under the name of the past, is not the past. In reality, as soon as each hour of one's life has died, it embodies itself in some material object, as do the souls of the dead in certain folk-stories, and hides there. There it remains captive, captive forever, unless we should happen on the object, recognise what lies within, call it by its name, and so set it free. Very likely we may never happen on the object (or the sensation, since we apprehend every object as sensation) that it hides in; and thus there are hours of our life that will never be resuscitated: for this object is so tiny, so lost in the world, and there is so little likelihood that we shall come across it.

Several summers of my life were spent in a house in the country. I thought of those summers from time to time, but they were not themselves. They were dead, and in all probability they would always remain so. Their resurrection, like all these resurrections, hung on a mere chance. One snowy evening, not long ago, I came in half frozen, and had sat down in my room to read by lamplight, and as I could not get warm my old cook offered to make me a cup of tea, a thing I never drink. And as chance would have it, she brought me some slices of dry toast. I dipped the toast in the cup of tea and as soon as I put it in my mouth, and felt its softened texture, all flavoured with tea, against my palate, something came over me —the smell of geraniums and orange-blossom, a sensation of extraordinary radiance and happiness. I sat quite still, afraid that the slightest movement might cut short this incomprehensible process which was taking place in me, and concentrated on the bit of sopped toast which seemed responsible for all these marvels; then suddenly the shaken partitions in my memory gave way, and into my conscious mind there rushed the summers I had spent in the aforesaid house in the country, with their early mornings, and the succession, the ceaseless onset, of happy hours in their train. And then I remembered. Every morning, when I was dressed, I went down to my grandfather in his bedroom, where he had just woken up and was drinking his tea. He soaked a rusk in it, and gave me the rusk to eat. And when those summers were past and gone, the taste of a rusk soaked in tea was one of the shelters where the dead hours—dead as far as intellect knew—hid themselves away, and where I should certainly never have found them again if, on that winter's evening when I came in frozen from the snow, my cook had not offered me the potion to which, by virtue of a magic past I knew nothing about, their resurrection was plighted.

But as soon as I had tasted the rusk, a whole garden, up till then vague and dim, mirrored itself, with its forgotten walks and all their urns with all their flowers, in the little cup of tea, like those Japanese flowers which do not reopen as flowers until one drops them into water. In the same way, many days in Venice, which intellect had not been able to give back, were dead for me until last year, when crossing a courtyard I came to a standstill among the glittering uneven paving-stones. The friends I was with were afraid that I might have slipped, but I waved to them to go on, and that I would catch up with them. Something of greater importance engaged me, I still did not know what it was, but in the depth of my being I felt the flutter of a past that I did not recognise; it was just as I set foot on a certain paving-stone that this feeling of perplexity came over me. I felt an invading happiness, I knew that I was going to be enriched by that purely personal thing, a past impression, a fragment of life in unsullied preservation (something we can only know in preservation, for while we live in it, it is not present in the memory, since other sensations accompany and smother it) which asked only that it might be set free, that it might come and augment my stores of life and poetry. But I did not feel that I had the power to free it. No, intellect could have done nothing for me at such a moment! Trying to put myself back into the same state, I retraced my steps a little so that I might come afresh to those uneven shining paving-stones. It was the same sensation underfoot that I had felt on the smooth, slightly uneven pavement of the baptistry of Saint Mark's. The shadow which had lain that day on the canal, where a gondola waited for me, and all the happiness, all the wealth of those hours—this recognized sensation brought them hurrying after it, and that very day came alive for me.

It is not merely that intellect can lend no hand in these resurrections; these past hours will only hide themselves away in objects where intellect has not tried to embody them. The objects which you have consciously tried to connect with certain hours of your life, these they can never take shelter in. What is more, if something else should resuscitate those hours, the objects called back with them will be stripped of their poetry.

I remember how once when I was travelling by train I strove to draw impressions from the passing landscape. I wrote about the little country churchyard while it was still passing before my eyes, I noted down the bright bars of sunlight on the trees, the wayside flowers like those in *Le Lys dans la Vallée.*° Since then, calling to mind those trees streaked with light and that little churchyard, I have often tried to conjure up that day, that day *itself,* I mean, not its pallid ghost. I could never manage it, and I had lost all hope of doing so, when at lunch, not long ago, I let my spoon fall on my plate. And then it made the same noise as the hammers of the linesmen did that day, tapping on the wheels when the train halted at stations. The burning blinded hour when that noise rang out instantly came back to me, and all that day in its poetry—except for the country churchyard, the trees streaked with light, and the Balzacian flowers, gained by deliberate observation and lost from the poetic resurrection.

Now and again, alas, we happen on the object, and the lost sensation thrills in us, but the time is too remote, we cannot give a name to the sensation, or call on it, and it does not come alive. As I was walking through a pantry the other day, a piece of green canvas plugging a broken window-pane made me stop dead and listen inwardly. A gleam of summer crossed my mind. Why? I tried to remember. I saw wasps in a shaft of sunlight, a smell of cherries came from the table—I could not remember. For a moment I was like those sleepers who wake up in the dark and do not know where they are, who ask their bodies to give them a bearing as to their whereabouts, not knowing what bed, what house, what part of the world, which year of their life they are in. For a moment I hesitated like

Le Lys dans la Vallée   *The Lily of the Valley,* by Honoré de Balzac.

this, groping round the square of green canvas to discover the time and the place where my scarcely awakened memory would find itself at home. All the sensations of my life, confused, or known, or forgotten, I was hesitating among all of them at once. This only lasted a minute. Soon I saw nothing more; my memory had fallen asleep again forever.

How often during our walks have not my friends known me halt like this at the turning-off of an avenue, or beside a clump of trees, and ask them to leave me alone for a minute. Nothing came of it. I shut my eyes and made my mind a blank to recruit fresh energies for my pursuit of the past, then suddenly reopened them, all in an attempt to see those same trees as if for the first time. I could not tell where I had seen them. I could recognise their shapes and their grouping, their outline seemed to have been traced from some beloved drawing that trembled in my heart. But I could tell no more of them, and they themselves seemed by their artless passionate attitude to say how sorry they felt not to be able to make themselves clear, not to be able to tell me the secret that they well knew I could not unriddle. Ghosts of a dear past, so dear that my heart beat to bursting, they held out powerless arms to me, like the ghosts that Aeneas met in the underworld. Was it in the walks near the town of my happy childhood, was it only in that imagined country where, later on, I dreamed that Mamma was so ill, close to a lake and in a forest where it was light all night long, a dream country only but almost as real as the country of my childhood which was already no more than a dream? I should never know more of it. And I had to rejoin my friends who were waiting for me at the turn of the road, with the anguish of turning my back forever on a past I might see no more, of disowning the dead who held out their powerless fond arms to me, and seemed to say, Recall us to life. And before I fell into step and into conversation with my friends, I again turned round for a moment to cast a less and less discerning glance towards the crooked, receding line of mutely expressive trees still undulating before my eyes.

Compared with this past, this private essence of ourselves, the truths of intellect seem scarcely real at all. So, and above all from the time when our vitality begins to dwindle, it is to whatever may help us to recover this past that we resort, even though this should entail being very ill-understood by intellectual people who do not know that the artist lives to himself, that the absolute value of what he sees means nothing to him and that his scale of values is wholly subjective. A nauseating musical show put on by a provincial company, or a ball that people of taste would laugh at, may be far more quickening to his memories, far more relevant to the nature of what he dreams of and dwells on, than a brilliant performance at the Opera House or an ultra-elegant evening party in the Faubourg Saint-Germain. A railway time-table with its names of stations where he loves to fancy himself getting out of the train on an autumn evening when the trees are already stripped of their leaves and the bracing air is full of their rough scent, or a book that means nothing to people of discrimination but is full of names he has not heard since he was a child, can be worth incommensurably more to him than admirable philosophical treatises, so that people of discrimination will remark that for a man of talent he has very stupid likings.

Perhaps it will cause surprise that I, who make light of the intellect, should have devoted the following few pages precisely to some of these considerations that intellect, in contradiction to the platitudes that we hear said or read in books, suggests to us. At a time when my days may be numbered (and besides, are we not all in the same case?) it is perhaps very frivolous of me to undertake an intellectual exercise. But if the truths of intellect are less precious than those secrets of feeling that I was talking about just now, yet in one way they too have their interest. A writer is not only a poet; in our imperfect world where masterpieces are no more than the shipwrecked flotsam of great minds, even the greatest writers of our century have spun a web of intellect round jewels of feeling which only here or there show through it. And if one believes that on this important point one hears the best among one's contemporaries making mistakes, there comes a time when one shakes off one's indolence and feels the need to speak out. Sainte-Beuve's Method is not, at first sight, such an important affair. But perhaps in the course of these pages we may be led to realise that it touches on very important intellectual problems, and on what is perhaps for an artist the greatest of all: this relative inferiority of the intellect which I spoke of at the beginning. Yet all the same, it is intellect we must call on to establish this inferiority. Because if intellect does not deserve the crown of crowns, only intellect is able to award it. And if intellect ranks only second in the hierarchy of virtues, intellect alone is able to proclaim that the first place must be given to instinct.

William Wordsworth
(1770–1850)

I Wandered Lonely as a Cloud

I wandered lonely as a cloud
That floats on high o'er vales and hills,
When all at once I saw a crowd,
A host, of golden daffodils;
Beside the lake, beneath the trees,
Fluttering and dancing in the breeze.

Continuous as the stars that shine
And twinkle on the milky way,
They stretched in never-ending line
Along the margin of a bay:
Ten thousand saw I at a glance,
Tossing their heads in sprightly dance.

The waves beside them danced; but they
Out-did the sparkling waves in glee:
A poet could not but be gay,
In such a jocund company:
I gazed—and gazed—but little thought
What wealth the show to me had brought:

For oft, when on my couch I lie
In vacant or in pensive mood,
They flash upon that inward eye
Which is the bliss of solitude;
And then my heart with pleasure fills,
And dances with the daffodils.

(1804)

William Butler Yeats
(1865–1939)

Leda and the Swan⁰

A sudden blow: the great wings beating still
Above the staggering girl, her thighs caressed
By the dark webs, her nape caught in his bill,
He holds her helpless breast upon his breast.
How can those terrified vague fingers push
The feathered glory from her loosening thighs?
And how can body, laid in that white rush,
But feel the strange heart beating where it lies?

Leda and the Swan   Reference to the Greek myth of the god Zeus, who, in the form of a swan, made love to Queen Leda. Their union resulted in the birth of the beautiful and legendary Helen, whose abduction started the Trojan War.

A shudder in the loins engenders there
The broken wall, the burning roof and tower
And Agamemnon dead.

                    Being so caught up,
So mastered by the brute blood of the air,
Did she put on his knowledge with his power
Before the indifferent beak could let her drop?

                                      (1923)

---

e. e. cummings
(1894–1962)

since feeling is first

since feeling is first
who pays any attention
to the syntax of things
will never wholly kiss you;

wholly to be a fool
while Spring is in the world

my blood approves,
and kisses are a better fate
than wisdom
lady i swear by all flowers. Don't cry
—the best gesture of my brain is less than
your eyelids' flutter which says

we are for each other: then
laugh, leaning back in my arms
for life's not a paragraph

And death i think is no parenthesis

                                      (1926)

Imamu Amiri Baraka
(LeRoi Jones)
(1934–)

Young Soul

First, feel, then feel, then
read, or read, then feel, then
fall, or stand, where you
already are. Think
of your self, and the other
selves . . . think
of your parents, your mothers
and sisters, your bentslick
father, then feel, or
fall, on your knees
if nothing else will move you,

then read
and look deeply
into all matters
come close to you
city boys—
country men

Make some muscle
in your head, but
use the muscle
in yr heart

The Right Use of Language

The subject of this section is an ancient one that goes back at least to the first rhetoricians and philosophers—Plato and Aristotle among them—who were deeply concerned with the distinction between eloquence devoted to good ends and eloquence devoted to bad. This distinction was crucial in a culture in which speech was the chief means of communication, and a capacity to speak, argue, and answer well was the sole protection of a person's rights.

In the intervening centuries the ethics of rhetoric has lost none of its importance. If anything, readers, writers, listeners, and viewers in today's age of mass communication—of public relations, advertising, and image manufacturing—need to be especially aware of the differences between honest language and deceit. Beneath the issue of "the right use of language" lie the profoundest matters of our psychic, political, and moral welfare.

The section begins with three very different pieces on how we use language and how it works. Paule Marshall's description of the talk in her mother's kitchen amiably illustrates the many ways language is used other than as the communication of information; she touches, too, on the ways in which ordinary people unselfconsciously create language, using it as poetry, so that it expresses the deepest traits of their culture. In contrast, Robert Graves' poem evokes people using language as limitation and protection—to shelter themselves from the dangerous reach of their deepest feelings. Susanne Langer's essay deals with language as symbolism and with the use of symbols as the activity most characteristic of humans. She stresses our unique capacity to *manipulate* symbols (with its paradoxical gifts of both reason and lunacy) and so opens the political and moral questions in their broadest terms: "The envisagements of good and evil, which make man a moral agent, make him also a conscript, a prisoner, and a slave. His constant problem is to escape the tyrannies he has created." She notes, too, "We control our inferiors by setting up symbols of our power, and the mere idea that words or images convey stands there to hold our fellows in subjection even when we cannot lay our hands on them."

Each of the remaining essays follows out some of the implications of the idea of language as power. George Orwell's essay shows how bad thinking and bad writing propagate each other and how they are related to badness in political life. Haig Bosmajian dwells on the importance of names and labels in the language of oppression: "The power which comes from names and naming is related directly to the power to define others—individuals, races, sexes, ethnic groups." Robin Lakoff illustrates this point precisely as regards the language used by women and the language used to describe them. Murray Edelman investigates the network of status, power, and authority propagated by the professional language of doctors, nurses, social workers, prison authorities, teachers, and other members of the "helping professions."

How Language Means

Paule Marshall

Paule Marshall was born in Brooklyn, N.Y., in 1929, of parents who had come from the Caribbean island of Barbados. After graduating from Brooklyn College, she worked as a librarian, as a staff writer for *Our World* magazine, and as a free-lance writer. She has lectured on black literature at Oxford, Columbia, and other universities. Marshall is best known, however, as a writer of fiction. She began writing before her tenth birthday and is noted for the range and originality of her treatment of the black experience. Her novels are *Brown Girl, Brownstones* (1959), *The Chosen Place, the Timeless People* (1969), and *Praisesong for the Widow* (1983). *Soul Clap Hands and Sing,* a collection of four short novels, appeared in 1961. This essay appeared in the *New York Times Book Review* on January 9, 1983.

From the Poets in the Kitchen

Some years ago, when I was teaching a graduate seminar in fiction at Columbia University, a well-known male novelist visited my class to speak on his development as a writer. In discussing his formative years, he didn't realize it but he seriously endangered his life by remarking that women writers are luckier than those of his sex because they usually spend so much time as children around their mothers and their mothers' friends in the kitchen.

What did he say that for? The women students immediately forgot about being in awe of him and began readying their attack for the question and answer period later on. Even I bristled. There again was that awful image of women locked away from the world in the kitchen with only each other to talk to, and their daughters locked in with them.

But my guest wasn't really being sexist or trying to be provocative or even spoiling for a fight. What he meant—when he got around to examining himself more fully—was that, given the way children are (or were) raised in our society, with little girls kept closer to home and their mothers, the woman writer stands a better chance of being exposed, while growing up, to the kind of talk that goes on among women, more often than not in the kitchen; and that this experience gives her an edge over her male counterpart by instilling in her an appreciation for ordinary speech.

It was clear that my guest lecturer attached great importance to this, which is understandable. Common speech and the plain, workaday words that make it up are, after all, the stock in trade of some of the best fiction writers. They are the principal means by which a character in a novel or story reveals himself and gives voice sometimes to profound feelings and complex ideas about himself and the world. Perhaps the proper measure of a writer's talent is his skill in rendering everyday speech—when it is appropriate to his story—as well as his ability to tap, to exploit, the beauty, poetry and wisdom it often contains.

"If you say what's on your mind in the language that comes to you from your parents and your street and friends you'll probably say something beautiful." Grace Paley tells this, she says, to her students at the beginning of every writing course.

It's all a matter of exposure and a training of the ear for the would-be writer in those early years of his or her apprenticeship. And, according to my guest lecturer, this training, the best of it, often takes place in as unglamorous a setting as the kitchen.

He didn't know it, but he was essentially describing my experience as a little girl. I grew up among poets. Now they didn't look like poets—whatever that breed is supposed to look like. Nothing about them suggested that poetry was their calling. They were just a group of ordinary housewives and mothers, my mother included, who dressed in a way (shapeless housedresses, dowdy felt hats and long, dark, solemn coats) that made it impossible for me to imagine they had ever been young.

Nor did they do what poets were supposed to do—spend their days in an attic room writing verses. They never put pen to paper except to write occasionally to their relatives in Barbados. "I take my pen in hand hoping these few lines will find you in health as they leave me fair for the time being," was the way their letters invariably began. Rather, their day was spent "scrubbing floor," as they described the work they did.

Several mornings a week these unknown bards would put an apron and a pair of old house shoes in a shopping bag and take the train or streetcar from our section of Brooklyn out to Flatbush. There, those who didn't have steady jobs would wait on certain designated corners for the white housewives in the neighborhood to come along and bargain with them over pay for a day's work cleaning their houses. This was the ritual even in the winter.

Later, armed with the few dollars they had earned, which in their vocabulary became "a few raw-mouth pennies," they made their way back to our neighborhood, where they would sometimes stop off to have a cup of tea or cocoa together before going home to cook dinner for their husbands and children.

The basement kitchen of the brownstone house where my family lived was the usual gathering place. Once inside the warm safety of its walls the women threw off the drab coats and hats, seated themselves at the large center table, drank their cups of tea or cocoa, and talked. While my sister and I sat at a smaller table over in a corner doing our homework, they talked—endlessly, passionately, poetically, and with impressive range. No subject was beyond them. True, they would indulge in the usual gossip: whose husband was running with whom, whose daughter looked slightly "in the way" (pregnant) under her bridal gown as she walked down the aisle. That sort of thing. But they also tackled the great issues of the time. They were always, for example, discussing the state of the economy. It was the mid and late 30's then, and the aftershock of the Depression, with its soup lines and suicides on Wall Street, was still being felt.

Some people, they declared, didn't know how to deal with adversity. They didn't know that you had to "tie up your belly" (hold in the pain, that is) when things got rough and go on with life. They took their image from the bellyband that is tied around the stomach of a newborn baby to keep the navel pressed in.

They talked politics. Roosevelt was their hero. He had come along and rescued the country with relief and jobs, and in gratitude they christened their sons Franklin and Delano and hoped they would live up to the names.

If F.D.R. was their hero, Marcus Garvey was their God. The name of the fiery, Jamaican-born black nationalist of the 20's was constantly invoked around the table. For he had been their leader when they first came to the United States from the West Indies shortly after World War I. They had contributed to his organization, the United Negro Improvement Association (UNIA), out of their meager salaries, bought shares in his ill-fated Black Star Shipping Line, and at the height of the movement they had marched as members of his "nurses' brigade" in their white uniforms up Seventh Avenue in Harlem during the great Garvey Day parades. Garvey: He lived on through the power of their memories.

And their talk was of war and rumors of wars. They raged against World War II when it broke out in Europe, blaming it on the politicians. "It's these politicians. They're the ones always starting up all this lot of war. But what they care? It's the poor people got to suffer and mothers with their sons." If it was *their* sons, they swore they would keep them out of the Army by giving them soap to eat each day to make their hearts sound defective. Hitler? He was for them "the devil incarnate."

Then there was home. They reminisced often and at length about home. The old country. Barbados—or Bimshire, as they affectionately called it. The little Caribbean island in the sun they loved but had to leave. "Poor —poor but sweet" was the way they remembered it.

And naturally they discussed their adopted home. America came in for both good and bad marks. They lashed out at it for the racism they encountered. They took to task some of the people they worked for, especially those who gave them only a hard-boiled egg and a few spoonfuls of cottage cheese for lunch. "As if anybody can scrub floor on an egg and some cheese that don't have no taste to it!"

Yet although they caught H in "this man country," as they called America, it was nonetheless a place where "you could at least see your way to make a dollar." That much they acknowledged. They might even one day accumulate enough dollars, with both them and their husbands working, to buy the brownstone houses which, like my family, they were only leasing at that period. This was their consuming ambition: to "buy house" and to see the children through.

There was no way for me to understand it at the time, but the talk that filled the kitchen those afternoons was highly functional. It served as therapy, the cheapest kind available to my mother and her friends. Not only did it help them recover from the long wait on the corner that morning and the bargaining over their labor, it restored them to a sense of themselves and reaffirmed their self-worth. Through language they were able to overcome the humiliations of the work-day.

But more than therapy, that freewheeling, wide-ranging, exuberant talk functioned as an outlet for the tremendous creative energy they possessed. They were women in whom the need for self-expression was strong, and since language was the only vehicle readily available to them they made of it an art form that—in keeping with the African tradition in which art and life are one—was an integral part of their lives.

And their talk was a refuge. They never really ceased being baffled and overwhelmed by America—its vastness, complexity and power. Its strange customs and laws. At a level beyond words they remained fearful and in awe. Their uneasiness and fear were even reflected in their attitude toward the children they had given birth to in this country. They referred to those like myself, the little Brooklyn-born Bajans (Barbadians), as "these New York children" and complained that they couldn't discipline us properly because of the laws here. "You can't beat these children as you would like, you know, because the authorities in this place will dash you in jail for them. After all, these is New York children." Not only were we different, American, we had, as they saw it, escaped their ultimate authority.

Confronted therefore by a world they could not encompass, which even limited their rights as parents, and at the same time finding themselves permanently separated from the world they had known, they took refuge in language. "Language is the only homeland," Czeslaw Milosz, the emigré Polish writer and Nobel Laureate, has said. This is what it became for the women at the kitchen table.

It served another purpose also, I suspect. My mother and her friends were after all the female counterpart of Ralph Ellison's invisible man. Indeed, you might say they suffered a triple invisibility, being black, female and foreigners. They really didn't count in American society except as a source of cheap labor. But given the kind of women they were, they couldn't tolerate the fact of their invisibility, their powerlessness. And they fought back, using the only weapon at their command: the spoken word.

Those late afternoon conversations on a wide range of topics were a way for them to feel they exercised some measure of control over their lives and the events that shaped them. "Soully-gal, talk yuh talk!" they were always exhorting each other. "In this man world you got to take yuh mouth and make a gun!" They were in control, if only verbally and if only for the two hours or so that they remained in our house.

For me, sitting over in the corner, being seen but not heard, which was the rule for children in those days, it wasn't only what the women talked about—the content—but the way they put things—their style. The insight, irony, wit and humor they brought to their stories and discussions and their poet's inventiveness and daring with language—which of course I could only sense but not define back then.

They had taken the standard English taught them in the primary schools of Barbados and transformed it into an idiom, an instrument that more adequately described them—changing around the syntax and imposing their own rhythm and accent so that the sentences were more pleasing to their ears. They added the few African sounds and words that had survived, such as the derisive suck-teeth sound and the word "yam," meaning to eat. And to make it more vivid, more in keeping with their expressive quality, they brought to bear a raft of metaphors, parables, Biblical quotations, sayings and the like:

"The sea ain' got no back door," they would say, meaning that it wasn't like a house where if there was a fire you could run out the back. Meaning that it was not to be trifled with. And meaning perhaps in a larger sense that man should treat all of nature with caution and respect.

"I has read hell by heart and called every generation blessed!" They sometimes went in for hyperbole.

A woman expecting a baby was never said to be pregnant. They never used that word. Rather, she was "in the way" or, better yet, "tumbling big." "Guess who I butt up on in the market the other day tumbling big again!"

And a woman with a reputation of being too free with her sexual favors was known in their book as a "thoroughfare"—the sense of men like a steady stream of cars moving up and down the road of her life. Or she might be dubbed "a free-bee," which was my favorite of the two. I liked the image it conjured up of a woman scandalous perhaps but independent, who flitted from one flower to another in a garden of male beauties, sampling their nectar, taking her pleasure at will, the roles reversed.

And nothing, no matter how beautiful, was ever described as simply beautiful. It was always "beautiful-ugly": the beautiful-ugly dress, the beautiful-ugly house, the beautiful-ugly car. Why the word "ugly," I used to wonder, when the thing they were referring to was beautiful, and they knew it. Why the antonym, the contradiction, the linking of opposites? It used to puzzle me greatly as a child.

There is the theory in linguistics which states that the idiom of a people, the way they use language, reflects not only the most fundamental views they hold of themselves and the world but their very conception of reality. Perhaps in using the term "beautiful-ugly" to describe nearly everything, my mother and her friends were expressing what they believed to be a fundamental dualism in life: the idea that a thing is at the same time its opposite, and that these opposites, these contradictions make up the whole. But theirs was not a Manichaean brand of dualism that sees matter, flesh, the body, as inherently evil, because they constantly addressed each other as "soully-gal"—soul: spirit; gal: the body, flesh, the visible self. And it was clear from their tone that they gave one as much weight and importance as the other. They had never heard of the mind/body split.

As for God, they summed up His essential attitude in a phrase. "God," they would say, "don' love ugly and He ain' stuck on pretty."

Using everyday speech, the simple commonplace words—but always with imagination and skill—they gave voice to the most complex ideas. Flannery O'Connor would have approved of how they made ordinary language work, as she put it, "double-time," stretching, shading, deepening its meaning. Like Joseph Conrad they were always trying to infuse new life in the "old old words worn thin . . . by . . . careless usage." And the goals of their oral art were the same as his: "to make you hear, to make you feel . . . to make you *see.*" This was their guiding esthetic.

By the time I was 8 or 9, I graduated from the corner of the kitchen to the neighborhood library, and thus from the spoken to the written word. The Macon Street Branch of the Brooklyn Public Library was an imposing half block long edifice of heavy gray masonry, with glass-paneled doors at the front and two tall metal torches symbolizing the light that comes of learning flanking the wide steps outside.

The inside was just as impressive. More steps—of pale marble with gleaming brass railings at the center and sides—led up to the circulation desk, and a great pendulum clock gazed down from the balcony stacks that faced the entrance. Usually stationed at the top of the steps like the guards outside Buckingham Palace was the custodian, a stern-faced West Indian type who for years, until I was old enough to obtain an adult card, would immediately shoo me with one hand into the Children's Room and with the other threaten me into silence, a finger to his lips. You would have thought he was the chief librarian and not just someone whose job it was to keep the brass polished and the clock wound. I put him in a story called "Barbados" years later and had terrible things happen to him at the end.

I was sheltered from the storm of adolescence in the Macon Street library, reading voraciously, indiscriminately, everything from Jane Austen to Zane Grey, but with a special passion for the long, full-blown, richly detailed 18th- and 19th-century picaresque tales: *Tom Jones. Great Expectations. Vanity Fair.*

But although I loved nearly everything I read and would enter fully into the lives of the characters—indeed, would cease being myself and become them—I sensed a lack after a time. Something I couldn't quite define was missing. And then one day, browsing in the poetry section, I came across a book by someone called Paul Laurence Dunbar, and opening it I found the photograph of a wistful, sad-eyed poet who to my surprise was black. I turned to a poem at random. "Little brown-baby wif spa'klin'/eyes/Come to yo' pappy an' set on his knee." Although I had a little difficulty at first with the words in dialect, the poem spoke to me as nothing I had read before of the closeness, the special relationship I had had with my father, who by then had become an ardent believer in Father Divine and gone to live in Father's "kingdom" in Harlem. Reading it helped to ease somewhat the tight knot of sorrow and longing I carried around in my chest that refused to go away. I read another poem. "Lias! Lias! Bless de Lawd!/Don' you know de day's/erbroad?/Ef you don' get up, you scamp/Dey'll be trouble in dis camp." I laughed. It reminded me of the way my mother sometimes yelled at my sister and me to get out of bed in the mornings.

And another: "Seen my lady home las' night/Jump back, honey, jump back./Hel' huh han' an' sque'z it tight . . . " About love between a black man and a black woman. I had never seen that written about before and it roused in me all kinds of delicious feelings and hopes.

And I began to search then for books and stories and poems about "The Race" (as it was put back then), about my people. While not abandoning

Thackeray, Fielding, Dickens and the others, I started asking the reference librarian, who was white, for books by Negro writers, although I must admit I did so at first with a feeling of shame—the shame I and many others used to experience in those days whenever the word "Negro" or "colored" came up.

No grade school literature teacher of mine had ever mentioned Dunbar or James Weldon Johnson or Langston Hughes. I didn't know that Zora Neale Hurston existed and was busy writing and being published during those years. Nor was I made aware of people like Frederick Douglass and Harriet Tubman—their spirit and example—or the great 19th-century abolitionist and feminist Sojourner Truth. There wasn't even Negro History Week when I attended P.S. 35 on Decatur Street!

What I needed, what all the kids—West Indian and native black American alike—with whom I grew up needed, was an equivalent of the Jewish shul, someplace where we could go after school—the schools that were shortchanging us—and read works by those like ourselves and learn about our history.

It was around that time also that I began harboring the dangerous thought of someday trying to write myself. Perhaps a poem about an apple tree, although I had never seen one. Or the story of a girl who could magically transplant herself to wherever she wanted to be in the world—such as Father Divine's kingdom in Harlem. Dunbar—his dark, eloquent face, his large volume of poems—permitted me to dream that I might someday write, and with something of the power with words my mother and her friends possessed.

When people at readings and writers' conferences ask me who my major influences were, they are sometimes a little disappointed when I don't immediately name the usual literary giants. True, I am indebted to those writers, white and black, whom I read during my formative years and still read for instruction and pleasure. But they were preceded in my life by another set of giants whom I always acknowledge before all others: the group of women around the table long ago. They taught me my first lesson in the narrative art. They trained my ear. They set a standard of excellence. This is why the best of my work must be attributed to them; it stands as testimony to the rich legacy of language and culture they so freely passed on to me in the wordshop of the kitchen.

Susanne K. Langer

Susanne K. Langer was born in New York City in 1895. She was educated at Radcliffe College, where she earned her doctorate in 1926. As a teacher and research scholar pursuing investigations in the philosophy of art, expression, and meaning, Professor Langer has reached a large audience and has had great influence on recent thought, particularly about the arts. Her best-known book is *Philosophy in a New Key* (1942), in which she investigates "the symbolism of reason, rite, and art." The present essay, clearly deriving from her interest in symbolism, appeared in *Fortune* in January 1944, at the height of World War II.

The Prince of Creation

The world is aflame with man-made public disasters, artificial rains of brimstone and fire, planned earthquakes, cleverly staged famines and floods. The Prince of Creation is destroying himself. He is throwing down the cities he has built, the works of his own hand, the wealth of many thousand years in his frenzy of destruction, as a child knocks down its own handiwork, the whole day's achievement, in a tantrum of tears and rage.

What has displeased the royal child? What has incurred his world-shattering tantrum?

The bafflement of the magnificent game he is playing. Its rules and its symbols, his divine toys, have taken possession of the player. For this global war is not the old, hard, personal fight for the means of life, *bellum omnium contra omnes,*° which animals perpetually wage; this is a war of monsters. Not mere men but great superpersonal giants, the national states, are met in combat. They do not hate and attack and wrestle as injured physical creatures do; they move heavily, inexorably, by strategy and necessity, to each other's destruction. The game of national states has come to this pass, and the desperate players ride their careening animated toys to a furious suicide.

These moloch gods, these monstrous states, are not natural beings; they are man's own work, products of the power that makes him lord over all other living things—his mind. They are not of the earth, earthy, as families and herds, hives and colonies are, whose members move and fight as one by instinct and habit until a physical disturbance splits them and the severed parts reconstitute themselves as new organized groups. The national states are not physical groups; they are social symbols, profound and terrible.

They are symbols of the new way of life, which the past two centuries have given us. For thousands of years, the pattern of daily life—working, praying, building, fighting, and raising new generations—repeated itself with only slow or unessential changes. The social symbols expressive of this life were ancient and familiar. Tribal gods or local saints, patriarchs,

bellum omnium contra omnes: war of all against all (Latin).

squires, or feudal lords, princes and bishops, raised to the highest power in the persons of emperors and popes—they were all expressions of needs and duties and opinions grounded in an immemorial way of life. The average man's horizon was not much greater than his valley, his town, or whatever geographical ramparts bounded his community. Economic areas were small, and economic problems essentially local. Naturally in his conception the powers governing the world were local, patriarchal, and reverently familiar.

Then suddenly, within some two hundred years, and for many places far less than that, the whole world has been transformed. Communities of different tongues and faiths and physiognomies have mingled; not as of old in wars of conquest, invading lords and conquered population gradually mixing their two stocks, but by a new process of foot-loose travel and trade, dominated by great centers of activity that bring individuals from near and far promiscuously together as a magnet draws filings from many heaps into close but quite accidental contact. Technology has made old horizons meaningless and localities indefinite. For goods and their destinies determine the structure of human societies. This is a new world, a world of persons, not of families and clans, or parishes and manors. The proletarian order is not founded on a hearth and its history. It does not express itself in a dialect, a local costume, a rite, a patron saint. All such traditions by mingling have canceled each other, and disappeared.

Most of us feel that since the old controlling ideas of faith and custom are gone, mankind is left without anchorage of any sort. None of the old social symbols fit this modern reality, this shrunken and undifferentiated world in which we lead a purely economic, secular, essentially homeless life.

But mankind is never without its social symbols; when old ones die, new ones are already in process of birth; and the new gods that have superseded all faiths are the great national states. The conception of them is mystical and moral, personal and devotional; they conjure with names and emblems, and demand our constant profession and practice of the new orthodoxy called "Patriotism."

Of all born creatures, man is the only one that cannot live by bread alone. He lives as much by symbols as by sense report, in a realm compounded of tangible things and virtual images, of actual events and ominous portents, always between fact and fiction. For he sees not only actualities but meanings. He has, indeed, all the impulses and interests of animal nature; he eats, sleeps, mates, seeks comfort and safety, flees pain, falls sick and dies, just as cats and bears and fishes and butterflies do. But he has something more in his repertoire, too—he has laws and religions, theories and dogmas, because he lives not only through sense but through symbols. That is the special asset of his mind, which makes him the master of earth and all its progeny.

By the agency of symbols—marks, words, mental images, and icons of all sorts—he can hold his ideas for contemplation long after their original causes have passed away. Therefore, he can think of things that are not presented or even suggested by his actual environment. By associating symbols in his mind, he combines things and events that were never together in the real world. This gives him the power we call imagination. Further, he can symbolize only part of an idea and let the rest go out of consciousness; this gives him the faculty that has been his pride throughout the ages—the power of abstraction. The combined effect of these two powers is inestimable. They are the roots of his supreme talent, the gift of reason.

In the war of each against all, which is the course of nature, man has an unfair advantage over his animal brethren; for he can see what is not yet there to be seen, know events that happened before his birth, and take possession of more than he actually eats; he can kill at a distance; and by rational design he can enslave other creatures to live and act for him instead of for themselves.

Yet this mastermind has strange aberrations. For in the whole animal kingdom there is no such unreason, no such folly and impracticality as man displays. He alone is hounded by imaginary fears, beset by ghosts and devils, frightened by mere images of things. No other creature wastes time in unprofitable ritual or builds nests for dead specimens of its race. Animals are always realists. They have intelligence in varying degrees—chickens are stupid, elephants are said to be very clever—but, bright or foolish, animals react only to reality. They may be fooled by appearance, by pictures or reflections, but once they know them as such, they promptly lose interest. Distance and darkness and silence are not fearful to them, filled with voices or forms, or invisible presences. Sheep in the pasture do not seem to fear phantom sheep beyond the fence, mice don't look for mouse goblins in the clock, birds do not worship a divine thunderbird.

But oddly enough, men do. They think of all these things and guard against them, worshiping animals and monsters even before they conceive of divinities in their own image. Men are essentially unrealistic. With all their extraordinary intelligence, they alone go in for patently impractical actions—magic and exorcism and holocausts—rites that have no connection with common-sense methods of self-preservation, such as a highly intelligent animal might use. In fact, the rites and sacrifices by which primitive man claims to control nature are sometimes fatal to the performers. Indian puberty rites are almost always intensely painful, and African natives have sometimes died during initiations into honorary societies.

We usually assume that very primitive tribes of men are closer to animal estate than highly civilized races; but in respect of practical attitudes, this is not true. The more primitive man's mind, the more fantastic it seems to be; only with high intellectual discipline do we gradually approach the realistic outlook of intelligent animals.

Yet this human mind, so beclouded by phantoms and superstitions, is probably the only mind on earth that can reach out to an awareness of things beyond its practical environment and can also conceive of such notions as truth, beauty, justice, majesty, space and time and creation.

There is another paradox in man's relationship with other creatures: namely, that those very qualities he calls animalian—"brutal," "bestial," "inhuman"—are peculiarly his own. No other animal is so deliberately cruel as man. No other creature intentionally imprisons its own kind, or invents special instruments of torture such as racks and thumbscrews for the sole purpose of punishment. No other animal keeps its own brethren in slavery; so far as we know, the lower animals do not commit anything like the acts of pure sadism that figure rather largely in our newspapers. There is no torment, spite, or cruelty for its own sake among beasts, as there is among men. A cat plays with its prey, but does not conquer and torture smaller cats. But man, who knows good and evil, is cruel for cruelty's sake; he who has a moral law is more brutal than the brutes, who have none; he alone inflicts suffering on his fellows with malice afore-thought.

If man's mind is really a higher form of the animal mind, his morality a specialized form of herd instinct, then where in the course of evolution did he lose the realism of a clever animal and fall prey to subjective fears? And why should he take pleasure in torturing helpless members of his own race?

The answer is, I think, that man's mind is *not* a direct evolution from the beast's mind, but is a unique variant and therefore has had a meteoric and startling career very different from any other animal history. The trait that sets human mentality apart from every other is its preoccupation with symbols, with images and names that *mean* things, rather than with things themselves. This trait may have been a mere sport of nature once upon a time. Certain creatures do develop tricks and interests that seem biologi-cally unimportant. Pack rats, for instance, and some birds of the crow family take a capricious pleasure in bright objects and carry away such things for which they have, presumably, no earthly use. Perhaps man's tendency to see certain forms as *images,* to hear certain sounds not only as signals but as expressive tones, and to be excited by sunset colors or starlight, was originally just a peculiar sensitivity in a rather highly devel-oped brain. But whatever its cause, the ultimate destiny of this trait was momentous; for all human activity is based on the appreciation and use of symbols. Language, religion, mathematics, all learning, all science and superstition, even right and wrong, are products of symbolic expression rather than direct experience. Our commonest words, such as "house" and "red" and "walking," are symbols; the pyramids of Egypt and the mysteri-ous circles of Stonehenge are symbols; so are dominions and empires and astronomical universes. We live in a mind-made world, where the things of prime importance are images or words that embody ideas and feelings and attitudes.

The animal mind is like a telephone exchange; it receives stimuli from outside through the sense organs and sends out appropriate responses through the nerves that govern muscles, glands, and other parts of the body. The organism is constantly interacting with its surroundings, receiving messages and acting on the new state of affairs that the messages signify.

But the human mind is not a simple transmitter like a telephone exchange. It is more like a great projector; for instead of merely mediating between an event in the outer world and a creature's responsive action, it transforms or, if you will, distorts the event into an image to be looked at, retained, and contemplated. For the images of things that we remember are not exact and faithful transcriptions even of our actual sense impressions. They are made as much by what we think as by what we see. It is a well-known fact that if you ask several people the size of the moon's disk as they look at it, their estimates will vary from the area of a dime to that of a barrel top. Like a magic lantern, the mind projects its ideas of things on the screen of what we call "memory"; but like all projections, these ideas are transformations of actual things. They are, in fact, *symbols* of reality, not pieces of it.

A symbol is not the same thing as a sign; that is a fact that psychologists and philosophers often overlook. All intelligent animals use signs; as do we. To them as well as to us sounds and smells and motions are signs of food, danger, the presence of other beings, or of rain or storm. Furthermore, some animals not only attend to signs but produce them for the benefit of others. Dogs bark at the door to be let in; rabbits thump to call each other; the cooing of doves and the growl of a wolf defending his kill are unequivocal signs of feelings and intentions to be reckoned with by other creatures.

We use signs just as animals do, though with considerably more elaboration. We stop at red lights and go on green; we answer calls and bells, watch the sky for coming storms, read trouble or promise or anger in each other's eyes. That is animal intelligence raised to the human level. Those of us who are dog lovers can probably all tell wonderful stories of how high our dogs have sometimes risen in the scale of clever sign interpretation and sign using.

A sign is anything that announces the existence or the imminence of some event, the presence of a thing or a person, or a change in a state of affairs. There are signs of the weather, signs of danger, signs of future good or evil, signs of what the past has been. In every case a sign is closely bound up with something to be noted or expected in experience. It is always a part of the situation to which it refers, though the reference may be remote in space and time. In so far as we are led to note or expect the signified event we are making correct use of a sign. This is the essence of rational behavior, which animals show in varying degrees. It is entirely realistic, being closely bound up with the actual objective course of history

—learned by experience, and cashed in or voided by further experience.

If man had kept to the straight and narrow path of sign using, he would be like the other animals, though perhaps a little brighter. He would not talk, but grunt and gesticulate and point. He would make his wishes known, give warnings, perhaps develop a social system like that of bees and ants, with such a wonderful efficiency of communal enterprise that all men would have plenty to eat, warm apartments—all exactly alike and perfectly convenient—to live in, and everybody could and would sit in the sun or by the fire, as the climate demanded, not talking but just basking, with every want satisfied, most of his life. The young would romp and make love, the old would sleep, the middle-aged would do the routine work almost unconsciously and eat a great deal. But that would be the life of a social, superintelligent, purely sign-using animal.

To us who are human, it does not sound very glorious. We want to go places and do things, own all sorts of gadgets that we do not absolutely need, and when we sit down to take it easy we want to talk. Rights and property, social position, special talents and virtues, and above all our ideas, are what we live for. We have gone off on a tangent that takes us far away from the mere biological cycle that animal generations accomplish; and that is because we can use not only signs but symbols.

A symbol differs from a sign in that it does not announce the presence of the object, the being, condition, or whatnot, which is its meaning, but merely *brings this thing to mind.* It is not a mere "substitute sign" to which we react as though it were the object itself. The fact is that our reaction to hearing a person's name is quite different from our reaction to the person himself. There are certain rare cases where a symbol stands directly for its meaning: in religious experience, for instance, the Host° is not only a symbol but a Presence. But symbols in the ordinary sense are not mystic. They are the same sort of thing that ordinary signs are; only they do not call our attention to something necessarily present or to be physically dealt with—they call up merely a conception of the thing they "mean."

The difference between a sign and a symbol is, in brief, that a sign causes us to think or act *in face of* the thing signified, whereas a symbol causes us to think *about* the thing symbolized. Therein lies the great importance of symbolism for human life, its power to make this life so different from any other animal biography that generations of men have found it incredible to suppose that they were of purely zoological origin. A sign is always embedded in reality, in a present that emerges from the actual past and stretches to the future; but a symbol may be divorced from reality altogether. It serves, therefore, to liberate thought from the immediate stimuli of a physically present world; and that liberation marks the essen-

---

Host Bread, usually in the form of a wafer, that, having been consecrated during Mass, is believed by Roman Catholics to be the body of Christ.

tial difference between human and nonhuman mentality. Animals think, but they think *of* and *at* things; men think primarily *about* things. Words, pictures, and memory images are symbols that may be combined and varied in a thousand ways. The result is a symbolic structure whose meaning is a complex of all their respective meanings, and this kaleidoscope of *ideas* is the typical product of the human brain that we call the "stream of thought."

The process of transforming all direct experience into imagery or into that supreme mode of symbolic expression, language, has so completely taken possession of the human mind that it is not only a special talent but a dominant, organic need. All our sense impressions leave their traces in our memory not only as signs disposing our practical reactions in the future but also as symbols, images representing our *ideas* of things; and the tendency to manipulate ideas, to combine and abstract, mix and extend them by playing with symbols, is man's outstanding characteristic. It seems to be what his brain most naturally and spontaneously does. Therefore his primitive mental function is not judging reality, but *dreaming his desires.*

Dreaming is apparently a basic function of human brains, for it is free and unexhausting like our metabolism, heartbeat, and breath. It is easier to dream than not to dream, as it is easier to breathe than to refrain from breathing. The symbolic character of dreams is fairly well established. Symbol mongering, on this ineffectual, uncritical level, seems to be instinctive, the fulfillment of an elementary need rather than the purposeful exercise of a high and difficult talent.

The special power of man's mind rests on the evolution of this special activity, not on any transcendently high development of animal intelligence. We are not immeasurably higher than other animals; we are different. We have a biological need and with it a biological gift that they do not share.

Because man has not only the ability but the constant need of *conceiving* what has happened to him, what surrounds him, what is demanded of him —in short, of symbolizing nature, himself, and his hopes and fears—he has a constant and crying need of *expression.* What he cannot express, he cannot conceive; what he cannot conceive is chaos, and fills him with terror.

If we bear in mind this all-important craving for expression we get a new picture of man's behavior; for from this trait spring his powers and his weaknesses. The process of symbolic transformation that all our experiences undergo is nothing more nor less than the process of *conception*, which underlies the human faculties of abstraction and imagination.

When we are faced with a strange or difficult situation, we cannot react directly, as other creatures do, with flight, aggression, or any such simple instinctive pattern. Our whole reaction depends on how we manage to conceive the situation—whether we cast it in a definite dramatic form, whether we see it as a disaster, a challenge, a fulfillment of doom, or a fiat of the Divine Will. In words or dreamlike images, in artistic or religious or even in cynical form, we must *construe* the events of life. There is great virtue in the figure of speech, "I can *make* nothing of it," to express a failure to understand something. Thought and memory are processes of *making* the thought content and the memory image; the pattern of our ideas is given by the symbols through which we express them. And in the course of manipulating those symbols we inevitably distort the original experience, as we abstract certain features of it, embroider and reinforce those features with other ideas, until the conception we project on the screen of memory is quite different from anything in our real history.

Conception is a necessary and elementary process; what we do with our conceptions is another story. That is the entire history of human culture —of intelligence and morality, folly and superstition, ritual, language, and the arts—all the phenomena that set man apart from, and above, the rest of the animal kingdom. As the religious mind has to make all human history a drama of sin and salvation in order to define its own moral attitudes, so a scientist wrestles with the mere presentation of "the facts" before he can reason about them. The process of *envisaging* facts, values, hopes, and fears underlies our whole behavior pattern; and this process is reflected in the evolution of an extraordinary phenomenon found always, and only, in human societies—the phenomenon of language.

Language is the highest and most amazing achievement of the symbolistic human mind. The power it bestows is almost inestimable, for without it anything properly called "thought" is impossible. The birth of language is the dawn of humanity. The line between man and beast—between the highest ape and the lowest savage—is the language line. Whether the primitive Neanderthal man was anthropoid or human depends less on his cranial capacity, his upright posture, or even his use of tools and fire, than on one issue we shall probably never be able to settle—whether or not he spoke.

In all physical traits and practical responses, such as skills and visual judgments, we can find a certain continuity between animal and human mentality. Sign using is an ever evolving, ever improving function throughout the whole animal kingdom, from the lowly worm that shrinks into his hole at the sound of an approaching foot, to the dog obeying his master's command, and even to the learned scientist who watches the movements of an index needle.

This continuity of the sign-using talent has led psychologists to the belief that language is evolved from the vocal expressions, grunts and coos and cries, whereby animals vent their feelings or signal their fellows; that man has elaborated this sort of communion to the point where it makes a perfect exchange of ideas possible.

I do not believe that this doctrine of the origin of language is correct. The essence of language is symbolic, not signific; we use it first and most vitally to formulate and hold ideas in our own minds. Conception, not social control, is its first and foremost benefit.

Watch a young child that is just learning to speak play with a toy; he says the name of the object, e.g.: "Horsey! horsey! horsey!" over and over again, looks at the object, moves it, always saying the name to himself or to the world at large. It is quite a time before he talks to anyone in particular; he talks first of all to himself. This is his way of forming and fixing the *conception* of the object in his mind, and around this conception all his knowledge of it grows. *Names* are the essence of language; for the *name* is what abstracts the conception of the horse from the horse itself, and lets the mere idea recur at the speaking of the name. This permits the conception gathered from one horse experience to be exemplified again by another instance of a horse, so that the notion embodied in the name is a general notion.

To this end, the baby uses a word long before he *asks for* the object; when he wants his horsey he is likely to cry and fret, because he is reacting to an actual environment, not forming ideas. He uses the animal language of *signs* for his wants; talking is still a purely symbolic process—its practical value has not really impressed him yet.

Language need not be vocal; it may be purely visual, like written language, or even tactual, like the deaf-mute system of speech; but it *must be denotative*. The sounds, intended or unintended, whereby animals communicate do not constitute a language, because they are signs, not names. They never fall into an organic pattern, a meaningful syntax of even the most rudimentary sort, as all language seems to do with a sort of driving necessity. That is because signs refer to actual situations, in which things have obvious relations to each other that require only to be noted; but symbols refer to ideas, which are not physically there for inspection, so their connections and features have to be represented. This gives all true language a natural tendency toward growth and development, which seems almost like a life of its own. Languages are not invented; they grow with our need for expression.

In contrast, animal "speech" never has a structure. It is merely an emotional response. Apes may greet their ration of yams with a shout of "Nga!" But they do not say "Nga" between meals. If they could *talk about* their yams instead of just saluting them, they would be the most primitive men instead of the most anthropoid of beasts. They would have ideas, and tell each other things true or false, rational or irrational; they would make plans and invent laws and sing their own praises, as men do.

The history of speech is the history of our human descent. Yet the habit of transforming reality into symbols, of contemplating and combining and distorting symbols, goes beyond the confines of language. All *images* are symbols, which make us think about the things they mean.

This is the source of man's great interest in "graven images," and in *mere appearances* like the face of the moon or the human profiles he sees in rocks and trees. There is no limit to the meanings he can read into natural phenomena. As long as this power is undisciplined, the sheer enjoyment of finding meanings in everything, the elaboration of concepts without any regard to truth and usefulness, seems to run riot; superstition and ritual in their pristine strength go through what some anthropologists have called a "vegetative" stage, when dreamlike symbols, gods and ghouls and rites, multiply like the overgrown masses of life in a jungle. From this welter of symbolic forms emerge the images that finally govern a civilization; the great symbols of religion, society, and selfhood.

What does an image "mean"? Anything it is thought to resemble. It is only because we can abstract quite unobvious forms from the actual appearance of things that we see line drawings in two dimensions as images of colored, three-dimensional objects, find the likeness of a dipper in a constellation of seven stars, or see a face on a pansy. Any circle may represent the sun or moon; an upright monolith may be a man.

Wherever we can fancy a similarity we tend to see something represented. The first thing we do, upon seeing a new shape, is to assimilate it to our own idea of something that it resembles, something that is known and important to us. Our most elementary concepts are of our own actions, and the limbs or organs that perform them; other things are named by comparison with them. The opening of a cave is its mouth, the divisions of a river its arms. Language, and with it all articulate thought, grows by this process of unconscious metaphor. Every new idea urgently demands a word; if we lack a name for it, we call it after the first namable thing seen to bear even a remote analogy to it. Thus all the subtle and variegated vocabulary of a living language grows up from a few roots of very general application; words as various in meaning as "gentle" and "ingenious" and "general" spring from the one root "ge" meaning "to give life."

Yet there are conceptions that language is constitutionally unfit to express. The reason for this limitation of our verbal powers is a subject for logicians and need not concern us here. The point of interest to us is that, just as rational, discursive thought is bound up with language, so the life of feeling, of direct personal and social consciousness, the emotional stability of man and his sense of orientation in the world are bound up with images directly given to his senses: fire and water, noise and silence, high mountains and deep caverns, the brief beauty of flowers, the persistent grin of a skull. There seem to be irresistible parallels between the expressive forms we find in nature and the forms of our inner life; thus the use of light to represent all things good, joyful, comforting, and of darkness to express all sorts of sorrow, despair, or horror, is so primitive as to be well-nigh unconscious.

A flame is a soul; a star is a hope; the silence of winter is death. All such images, which serve the purpose of metaphorical thinking, are *natural symbols.* They have not conventionally assigned meanings, like words, but recommend themselves even to a perfectly untutored mind, a child's or a savage's, because they are definitely articulated *forms,* and to see something expressed in such forms is a universal human talent. We do not have to learn to use natural symbols; it is one of our primitive activities.

The fact that sensuous forms of natural processes have a significance beyond themselves makes the range of our symbolism, and with it the horizon of our consciousness, much wider and deeper than language. This is the source of ritual, mythology, and art. Ritual is a symbolic rendering of certain emotional *attitudes,* which have become articulate and fixed by being constantly expressed. Mythology is man's image of his world, and of himself in the world. Art is the exposition of his own subjective history, the life of feeling, the human spirit in all its adventures.

Yet this power of envisagement, which natural symbolism bestows, is a dangerous one; for human beings can envisage things that do not exist, and create horrible worlds, insupportable duties, monstrous gods and ancestors. The mind that can see part and future, the poles and the antipodes, and guess at obscure mechanisms of nature, is ever in danger of seeing what is not there, imagining false and fantastic causes, and courting death instead of life. Because man can play with ideas, he is unrealistic; he is inclined to neglect the all-important interpretation of signs for a rapt contemplation of symbols.

Some twenty years ago, Ernst Cassirer[0] set forth a theory of human mentality that goes far toward explaining the vagaries of savage religions and the ineradicable presence of superstition even in civilized societies: a symbol, he observed, is the embodiment of an idea; it is at once an abstract and a physical fact. Now its great emotive value lies in the concept it conveys; this inspires our reverent attitude, the attention and awe with which we view it. But man's untutored thought always tends to lose its way between the symbol and the fact. A skull represents death; but to a primitive mind the skull *is* death. To have it in the house is not unpleasant but dangerous. Even in civilized societies, symbolic objects—figures of saints, relics, crucifixes—are revered for their supposed efficacy. Their actual power is a power of *expression,* of embodying and thus revealing the greatest concepts humanity has reached; these concepts are the commanding forces that change our estate from a brute existence to the transcendent life of the spirit. But the symbol-loving mind of man reveres the meaning not *through* the articulating form but *in* the form so that the image appears to be the actual object of love and fear, supplication and praise.

Because of this constant identification of concepts with their expressions, our world is crowded with unreal beings. Some societies have actually realized that these beings do not belong to nature, and have postulated a so-called "other world" where they have their normal existence and from which they are said to descend, or arise, into our physical realm.

Ernst Cassirer   German philosopher (1874–1945).

For savages it is chiefly a nether world that sends up spooks; for more advanced cults it is from the heavens that supernatural beings, the embodiments of human ideas—of virtue, triumph, immortality—descend to the mundane realm. But from this source emanates also a terrible world government, with heavy commands and sanctions. Strange worship and terrible sacrifices may be the tithes exacted by the beings that embody our knowledge of nonanimalian human nature.

So the gift of symbolism, which is the gift of reason, is at the same time the seat of man's peculiar weakness—the danger of lunacy. Animals go mad with hydrophobia or head injuries, but purely mental aberrations are rare; beasts are not generally subject to insanity except through a confusion of signs, such as the experimentally produced "nervous breakdown" in rats. It is man who hears voices and sees ghosts in the dark, feels irrational compulsions and holds fixed ideas. All these phantasms are symbolic forms that have acquired a false factual status. It has been truly said that everybody has some streak of insanity; i.e., the threat of madness is the price of reason.

Because we can think of things potential as well as actual, we can be held in nonphysical bondage by laws and prohibitions and commands and by images of a governing power. This makes men tyrants over their own kind. Animals control each other's actions by immediate threats, growls and snarls and passes; but when the bully is roving elsewhere, his former domain is free of him. We control our inferiors by setting up symbols of our power, and the mere idea that words or images convey stands there to hold our fellows in subjection even when we cannot lay our hands on them. There is no flag over the country where a wolf is king; he is king where he happens to prowl, so long as he is there. But men, who can embody ideas and set them up to view, oppress each other by symbols of might.

The envisagements of good and evil, which make man a moral agent, make him also a conscript, a prisoner, and a slave. His constant problem is to escape the tyrannies he has created. Primitive societies are almost entirely tyrannical, symbol-bound, coercive organizations; civilized governments are so many conscious schemes to justify or else to disguise man's inevitable bondage to law and conscience.

Slowly, through ages and centuries, we have evolved a picture of the world we live in; we have made a drama of the earth's history and enhanced it with a backdrop of divinely ordered, star-filled space. And all this structure of infinity and eternity against which we watch the pageant of life and death, and all the moral melodrama itself, we have wrought by a gradual articulation of such vast ideas in symbols—symbols of good and evil, triumph and failure, birth and maturity and death. Long before the beginning of any known history, people saw in the heavenly bodies, in the changes of day and night or of the seasons, and in great beasts, symbolic forms to express those ultimate concepts that are the very frame of human existence. So gods, fates, the cohorts of good and evil were conceived. Their myths were the first formulations of cosmic ideas. Gradually the figures and traditions of religion emerged; ritual, the overt expression of our mental attitudes, became more and more intimately bound to definite and elaborate concepts of the creative and destructive powers that seem to control our lives.

Such beings and stories and rites are sacred because they are the great symbols by which the human mind orients itself in the world. To a creature that lives by reason, nothing is more terrible than what is formless and meaningless; one of our primary fears is fear of chaos. And it is the fight against chaos that has produced our most profound and indispensable images—the myths of light and darkness, of creation and passion, the symbols of the altar flame, the daystar, and the cross.

For thousands of years people lived by the symbols that nature presented to them. Close contact with earth and its seasons, intimate knowledge of stars and tides, made them feel the significance of natural phenomena and gave them a poetic, unquestioning sense of orientation. Generations of erudite and pious men elaborated the picture of the temporal and spiritual realms in which each individual was a pilgrim soul.

Then came the unprecedented change, the almost instantaneous leap of history from the immemorial tradition of the plow and the anvil to the new age of the machine, the factory, and the ticker tape. Often in no more than the length of a life-time the shift from handwork to mass production, and with it from poetry to science and from faith to nihilism, has taken place. The old nature symbols have become remote and have lost their meanings; in the clatter of gears and the confusion of gadgets that fill the new world, there will not be any obvious and rich and sacred meanings for centuries to come. All the accumulated creeds and rites of men are suddenly in the melting pot. There is no fixed community, no dynasty, no family inheritance—only the one huge world of men, vast millions of men, still looking on each other in hostile amazement.

A sane, intelligent animal should have invented, in the course of ten thousand years or more, some sure and obvious way of accommodating indefinite numbers of its own kind on the face of a fairly spacious earth. Modern civilization has achieved the highest triumphs of knowledge, skill, ingenuity, theory; yet all around its citadels, engulfing and demolishing them, rages the maddest war and confusion, inspired by symbols and slogans as riotous and irrational as anything the "vegetative" stage of savage phantasy could provide. How shall we reconcile this primitive nightmare excitement with the achievements of our high, rational, scientific culture?

The answer is, I think, that we are no longer in possession of a definite, established culture; we live in a period between an exhausted age—the European civilization of the white race—and an age still unborn, of which we can say nothing as yet. We do not know what races shall inherit the earth. We do not know what even the next few centuries may bring. But it is quite evident, I think, that we live in an age of transition, and that before many more generations have passed, mankind will make a new beginning and build itself a different world. Whether it will be a "brave, new world," or whether it will start all over with an unchronicled "state of nature" such as Thomas Hobbes described, wherein the individual's life is "nasty, brutish, and short," we simply cannot tell. All we know is that every tradition, every institution, every tribe is gradually becoming uprooted and upset, and we are waiting in a sort of theatrical darkness between the acts.

Because we are at a new beginning, our imaginations tend to a wild, "vegetative" overgrowth. The political upheavals of our time are marked, therefore, by a veritable devil dance of mystical ideologies, vaguely conceived, passionately declared, holding out fanatic hopes of mass redemption and mass beatitudes. Governments vie with each other in proclaiming social plans, social aims, social enterprises, and demanding bloody sacrifices in the name of social achievements.

New conceptions are always clothed in an extravagant metaphorical form, for there is no language to express genuinely new ideas. And in their pristine strength they imbue the symbols that express them with their own mystery and power and holiness. It is impossible to disengage the welter of ideas embodied in a swastika, a secret sign, or a conjuring word from the physical presence of the symbol itself; hence the apparently nonsensical symbol worship and mysticism that go with new movements and visions. This identification of symbolic form and half-articulate meaning is the essence of all mythmaking. Of course the emotive value is incomprehensible to anyone who does not see such figments as expressive forms. So an age of vigorous new conception and incomplete formulation always has a certain air of madness about it. But it is really a fecund and exciting period in the life of reason. Such is our present age. Its apparent unreason is a tremendous unbalance and headiness of the human spirit, a conflict not only of selfish wills but of vast ideas in the metaphorical state of emergence.

The change from fixed community life and ancient local custom to the mass of unpedigreed human specimens that actually constitutes the world in our industrial and commercial age has been too sudden for the mind of man to negotiate. Some transitional form of life had to mediate between those extremes. And so the idol of nationality arose from the wreckage of tribal organization. The concept of the national state is really the old tribe concept applied to millions of persons, unrelated and different creatures gathered under the banner of a government. Neither birth nor language nor even religion holds such masses together, but a mystic bond is postulated even where no actual bond of race, creed, or color may ever have existed.

At first glance it seems odd that the concept of nationality should reach its highest development just as all actual marks of national origins—language, dress, physiognomy, and religion—are becoming mixed and obliterated by our new mobility and cosmopolitan traffic. But it is just the loss of these things that inspires this hungry seeking for something like the old egocentric pattern in the vast and formless brotherhood of the whole earth. While mass production and universal communication clearly portend a culture of world citizenship, we cling desperately to our nationalism, a more and more attenuated version of the old clan civilization. We fight passionate and horrible wars for the symbols of our nations, we make a virtue of self-glorification and exclusiveness and invent strange anthropologies to keep us at least theoretically set apart from other men.

Nationalism is a transition between an old and a new human order. But even now we are not really fighting a war of nations; we are fighting a war of fictions, from which a new vision of the order of nature will someday emerge. The future, just now, lies wide open—open and dark, like interstellar space; but in that emptiness there is room for new gods, new cultures, mysterious now and nameless as an unborn child.

Robert Graves
(1895–)

The Cool Web

Children are dumb to say how hot the day is,
How hot the scent is of the summer rose,
How dreadful the black wastes of evening sky,
How dreadful the tall soldiers drumming by.

But we have speech, that cools the hottest sun,
And speech that dulls the hottest rose's scent.
We spell away the overhanging night,
We spell away the soldiers and the fright.

There's a cool web of language winds us in,
Retreat from too much gladness, too much fear:
We grow sea-green at last and coldly die
In brininess and volubility.

But if we let our tongues lose self-possession,
Throwing off language and its wateriness
Before our death, instead of when death comes,
Facing the brightness of the children's day,

Facing the rose, the dark sky and the drums,
We shall go mad no doubt and die that way.

(1926)

Language and Politics

George Orwell

George Orwell's reputation as a writer has shown no sign of decline since his death in 1950 at the age of forty-six. Best known as the author of the novels *Animal Farm* (1945) and *Nineteen Eighty-Four* (1949), he was also a journalist and one of the great English essayists. The editors of *Partisan Review,* on presenting him an award in 1949, commented that his writing is "marked by a singular directness and honesty, a scrupulous fidelity to his experience that has placed him in that valuable class of the writer who is a witness to his time."

His real name was Eric Arthur Blair, and he was born in 1903 in Bengal, a province of British India. He was sent to preparatory school when he was eight years old—an experience he grimly describes in *Such, Such Were the Joys* (1953)—and attended Eton on a King's Scholarship from 1917 to 1921. From 1922 to 1927, he served with the Imperial Police in Burma. These early years are the subject of a biography by Peter Stansky and William Abraham entitled *The Unknown Orwell* (1972). Returning to Europe, Orwell spent several poverty-stricken years doing odd jobs, from teaching to dishwashing, while he wrote novels and short stories that did not sell. The book *Down and Out in Paris and London* (1933) is a vivid record of those years. In 1936, Orwell went to Spain to take part in the civil war on the Republican side; he reported his experiences in *Homage to Catalonia* (1938).

Among Orwell's other novels are *Burmese Days* (1934), *A Clergyman's Daughter* (1935), and *Keep the Aspidistra Flying* (1936). His collections of essays include *Shooting an Elephant and Other Essays* (1950) and *Such, Such Were the Joys.* Sonia Orwell, his second wife, and Ian Angus edited *The Collected Essays, Journalism and Letters of George Orwell* (1968). The present essay first appeared in the London monthly *Horizon* in 1946 and was reprinted in *Shooting an Elephant.* It was written with the horrors of World War II in mind; sadly, it has not lost a bit of its relevance since.

Politics and the English Language

Most people who bother with the matter at all would admit that the English language is in a bad way, but it is generally assumed that we cannot by conscious action do anything about it. Our civilization is decadent and our language—so the argument runs—must inevitably share in the general collapse. It follows that any struggle against the abuse of language is a sentimental archaism, like preferring candles to electric light or hansom cabs to aeroplanes. Underneath this lies the half-conscious belief that language is a natural growth and not an instrument which we shape for our own purposes.

Now, it is clear that the decline of a language must ultimately have political and economic causes: it is not due simply to the bad influence of this or that individual writer. But an effect can become a cause, reinforcing the original cause and producing the same effect in an intensified form, and so on indefinitely. A man may take to drink because he feels himself to be a failure, and then fail all the more completely because he drinks. It is rather the same thing that is happening to the English language. It becomes ugly and inaccurate because our thoughts are foolish, but the slovenliness of our language makes it easier for us to have foolish thoughts. The point is that the process is reversible. Modern English, especially written English, is full of bad habits which spread by imitation and which can be avoided if one is willing to take the necessary trouble. If one gets rid of these habits one can think more clearly, and to think clearly is a necessary first step towards political regeneration: so that the fight against bad English is not frivolous and is not the exclusive concern of professional writers. I will come back to this presently, and I hope that by that time the meaning of what I have said here will have become clearer. Meanwhile, here are five specimens of the English language as it is now habitually written.

These five passages have not been picked out because they are especially bad—I could have quoted far worse if I had chosen—but because they illustrate various of the mental vices from which we now suffer. They are a little below the average, but are fairly representative samples. I number them so that I can refer back to them when necessary:

(1) I am not, indeed, sure whether it is not true to say that the Milton who once seemed not unlike a seventeenth-century Shelley had not become, out of an experience ever more bitter in each year, more alien [*sic*] to the founder of that Jesuit sect which nothing could induce him to tolerate.

PROFESSOR HAROLD LASKI
(ESSAY IN *Freedom of Expression*).

(2) Above all, we cannot play ducks and drakes with a native battery of idioms which prescribes such egregious collocations of vocables as the Basic *put up with* for *tolerate* or *put at a loss* for *bewilder*.

PROFESSOR LANCELOT HOGBEN
(Interglossa).

(3) On the one side we have the free personality: by definition it is not neurotic, for it has neither conflict nor dream. Its desires, such as they are, are transparent, for they are just what institutional approval keeps in the forefront of consciousness; another institutional pattern would alter their number and intensity; there is little in them that is natural, irreducible, or culturally dangerous. But *on the other side,* the social bond itself is nothing but the mutual reflection of these self-secure integrities. Recall the definition of love. Is not this the very picture of a small academic? Where is there a place in this hall of mirrors for either personality or fraternity?

> ESSAY ON PSYCHOLOGY IN *Politics*
> (NEW YORK).

(4) All the "best people" from the gentlemen's clubs, and all the frantic fascist captains, united in common hatred of Socialism and bestial horror of the rising tide of the mass revolutionary movement, have turned to acts of provocation, to foul incendiarism, to medieval legends of poisoned wells, to legalize their own destruction of proletarian organizations, and rouse the agitated petty-bourgeoisie to chauvinistic fervor on behalf of the fight against the revolutionary way out of the crisis.

> COMMUNIST PAMPHLET.

(5) If a new spirit *is* to be infused into this old country, there is one thorny and contentious reform which must be tackled, and that is the humanization and galvanization of the B.B.C. Timidity here will bespeak canker and atrophy of the soul. The heart of Britain may be sound and of strong beat, for instance, but the British lion's roar at present is like that of Bottom in Shakespeare's *Midsummer Night's Dream*—as gentle as any sucking dove. A virile new Britain cannot continue indefinitely to be traduced in the eyes or rather ears, of the world by the effete languors of Langham Place, brazenly masquerading as "standard English." When the voice of Britain is heard at nine o'clock, better far and infinitely less ludicrous to hear aitches honestly dropped than the present priggish, inflated, inhibited, school-ma'amish arch braying of blameless bashful mewing maidens!

> LETTER IN *Tribune*.

Each of these passages has faults of its own, but, quite apart from avoidable ugliness, two qualities are common to all of them. The first is staleness of imagery; the other is lack of precision. The writer either has a meaning and cannot express it, or he inadvertently says something else, or he is almost indifferent as to whether his words mean anything or not. This mixture of vagueness and sheer incompetence is the most marked characteristic of modern English prose, and especially of any kind of political writing. As soon as certain topics are raised, the concrete melts into the abstract and no one seems able to think of turns of speech that are not hackneyed: prose consists less and less of *words* chosen for the sake of their meaning, and more and more of *phrases* tacked together like the sections of a prefabricated henhouse. I list below, with notes and examples, various of the tricks by means of which the work of prose-construction is habitually dodged:

Dying metaphors. A newly invented metaphor assists thought by evoking a visual image, while on the other hand a metaphor which is technically "dead" (e.g. *iron resolution*) has in effect reverted to being an ordinary word and can generally be used without loss of vividness. But in between these two classes there is a huge dump of worn-out metaphors which have lost all evocative power and are merely used because they save people the trouble of inventing phrases for themselves. Examples are: *Ring the changes on, take up the cudgels for, toe the line, ride roughshod over, stand shoulder to shoulder with, play into the hands of, no axe to grind, grist to the mill, fishing in troubled waters, on the order of the day, Achilles' heel, swan song, hotbed.* Many of these are used without knowledge of their meaning (what is a "rift," for instance?), and incompatible metaphors are frequently mixed, a sure sign that the writer is not interested in what he is saying. Some metaphors now current have been twisted out of their original meaning without those who use them even being aware of the fact. For example, *toe the line* is sometimes written *tow the line.* Another example is *the hammer and the anvil,* now always used with the implication that the anvil gets the worst of it. In real life it is always the anvil that breaks the hammer, never the other way about: a writer who stopped to think what he was saying would be aware of this, and would avoid perverting the original phrase.

Operators or *verbal false limbs.* These save the trouble of picking out appropriate verbs and nouns, and at the same time pad each sentence with extra syllables which give it an appearance of symmetry. Characteristic phrases are *render inoperative, militate against, make contact with, be subjected to, give rise to, give grounds for, have the effect of, play a leading part (role) in, make itself felt, take effect, exhibit a tendency to, serve the purpose of, etc., etc.* The keynote is the elimination of simple verbs. Instead of being a single word, such as *break, stop, spoil, mend, kill,* a verb becomes a *phrase,* made up of a noun or adjective tacked on to some general-purpose verb such as *prove, serve, form, play, render.* In addition, the passive voice is wherever possible used in preference to the active, and noun constructions are used instead of gerunds *(by examination of* instead of *by examining).* The range of verbs is further cut down by means of the *-ize* and *de-* formations, and the banal statements are given an appearance of profundity by means of the *not un-* formation. Simple conjunctions and prepositions are replaced by such phrases as *with respect to, having regard to, the fact that, by dint of, in view of, in the interests of, on the hypothesis* *that;* and the ends of sentences are saved from anticlimax by such resounding common-places as *greatly to be desired, cannot be left out of account, a development to be expected in the near future, deserving of serious consideration, brought to a satisfactory conclusion,* and so on and so forth.

Pretentious diction. Words like *phenomenon, element, individual* (as noun), *objective, categorical, effective, virtual, basic, primary, promote, constitute, exhibit, exploit, utilize, eliminate, liquidate,* are used to dress up simple statements and give an air of scientific impartiality to biased judgments. Adjectives like *epoch-making, epic, historic, unforgettable, triumphant, age-old, inevitable, inexorable, veritable,* are used to dignify the sordid processes of international politics, while writing that aims at glorifying war usually takes on an archaic color, its characteristic words being: *realm, throne, chariot, mailed fist, trident, sword, shield, buckler, banner, jackboot, clarion.* Foreign words and expressions such as *cul de sac, ancien régime, deus ex machina, mutatis mutandis, status quo, gleichschaltung, weltanschauung,* are used to give an air of culture and elegance. Except for the useful abbreviations *i.e., e.g.,* and *etc.,* there is no real need for any of the hundreds of foreign phrases now current in English. Bad writers, and especially scientific, political and sociological writers, are nearly always haunted by the notion that Latin or Greek words are grander than Saxon ones, and unnecessary words like *expedite, ameliorate, predict, extraneous, deracinated, clandestine, subaqueous* and hundreds of others constantly gain ground from their Anglo-Saxon opposite numbers.[1] The jargon peculiar to Marxist writing (*hyena, hangman, cannibal, petty bourgeois, these gentry, lacquey, flunkey, mad dog, White Guard,* etc.) consists largely of words and phrases translated from Russian, German or French; but the normal way of coining a new word is to use a Latin or Greek root with the appropriate affix and, where necessary, the *-ize* formation. It is often easier to make up words of this kind (*deregionalize, impermissible, extramarital, non-fragmentary* and so forth) than to think up the English words that will cover one's meaning. The result, in general, is an increase in slovenliness and vagueness.

Meaningless words. In certain kinds of writing, particularly in art criticism and literary criticism, it is normal to come across long passages which are almost completely lacking in meaning.[2] Words like *romantic, plastic,*

[1]An interesting illustration of this is the way in which the English flower names which were in use till very recently are being ousted by Greek ones, *snapdragon* becoming *antirrhinum, forget-me-not* becoming *myosotis,* etc. It is hard to see any practical reason for this change of fashion: it is probably due to an instinctive turning-away from the more homely word and a vague feeling that the Greek word is scientific.

[2]Example: "Comfort's catholicity of perception and image, strangely Whitmanesque in range, almost the exact opposite in aesthetic compulsion, continues to evoke that trembling atmospheric accumulative hinting at a cruel, an inexorably serene timelessness. . . . Wrey Gardiner scores by aiming at simple bull's-eyes

values, human, dead, sentimental, natural, vitality, as used in art criticism, are strictly meaningless, in the sense that they not only do not point to any discoverable object, but are hardly ever expected to do so by the reader. When one critic writes, "The outstanding feature of Mr. X's work is its living quality," while another writes, "The immediately striking thing about Mr. X's work is its peculiar deadness," the reader accepts this as a simple difference of opinion. If words like *black* and *white* were involved, instead of the jargon words *dead* and *living,* he would see at once that language was being used in an improper way. Many political words are similarly abused. The word *Fascism* has now no meaning except in so far as it signifies "something not desirable." The words *democracy, socialism, freedom, patriotic, realistic, justice,* have each of them several different meanings which cannot be reconciled with one another. In the case of a word like *democracy,* not only is there no agreed definition, but the attempt to make one is resisted from all sides. It is almost universally felt that when we call a country democratic we are praising it: consequently the defenders of every kind of régime claim that it is a democracy, and fear that they might have to stop using the word if it were tied down to any one meaning. Words of this kind are often used in a consciously dishonest way. That is, the person who uses them has his own private definition, but allows his hearer to think he means something quite different. Statements like *Marshal Pétain was a true patriot, The Soviet Press is the freest in the world, The Catholic Church is opposed to persecution,* are almost always made with intent to deceive. Other words used in variable meanings, in most cases more or less dishonestly, are: *class, totalitarian, science, progressive, reactionary, bourgeois, equality.*

Now that I have made this catalogue of swindles and perversions, let me give another example of the kind of writing that they lead to. This time it must of its nature be an imaginary one. I am going to translate a passage of good English into modern English of the worst sort. Here is a well-known verse from *Ecclesiastes:*

"I returned and saw under the sun, that the race is not to the swift, nor the battle to the strong, neither yet bread to the wise, nor yet riches to men of understanding, nor yet favour to men of skill; but time and chance happeneth to them all."

Here it is in modern English:

"Objective consideration of contemporary phenomena compels the conclusion that success or failure in competitive activities exhibits no tendency to be commensurate with innate capacity, but that a considerable element of the unpredictable must invariably be taken into account."

This is a parody, but not a very gross one. Exhibit (3), above, for instance, contains several patches of the same kind of English. It will be seen that

---

with precision. Only they are not so simple, and through this contented sadness runs more than the surface bittersweet of resignation." *(Poetry Quarterly.)*

I have not made a full translation. The beginning and ending of the sentence follow the original meaning fairly closely, but in the middle the concrete illustrations—race, battle, bread—dissolve into the vague phrase "success or failure in competitive activities." This had to be so, because no modern writer of the kind I am discussing—no one capable of using phrases like "objective consideration of contemporary phenomena"—would ever tabulate his thoughts in that precise and detailed way. The whole tendency of modern prose is away from concreteness. Now analyse these two sentences a little more closely. The first contains forty-nine words but only sixty syllables, and all its words are those of everyday life. The second contains thirty-eight words of ninety syllables: eighteen of its words are from Latin roots, and one from Greek. The first sentence contains six vivid images, and only one phrase ("time and chance") that could be called vague. The second contains not a single fresh, arresting phrase, and in spite of its ninety syllables it gives only a shortened version of the meaning contained in the first. Yet without a doubt it is the second kind of sentence that is gaining ground in modern English. I do not want to exaggerate. This kind of writing is not yet universal, and outcrops of simplicity will occur here and there in the worst-written page. Still, if you or I were told to write a few lines on the uncertainty of human fortunes, we should probably come much nearer to my imaginary sentence than to the one from *Ecclesiastes.*

As I have tried to show, modern writing at its worst does not consist in picking out words for the sake of their meaning and inventing images in order to make the meaning clearer. It consists in gumming together long strips of words which have already been set in order by someone else, and making the results presentable by sheer humbug. The attraction of this way of writing is that it is easy. It is easier—even quicker, once you have the habit—to say *In my opinion it is not an unjustifiable assumption that* than to say *I think.* If you use ready-made phrases, you not only don't have to hunt about for words; you also don't have to bother with the rhythms of your sentences since these phrases are generally so arranged as to be more or less euphonious. When you are composing in a hurry—when you are dictating to a stenographer, for instance, or making a public speech —it is natural to fall into a pretentious, Latinized style. Tags like *a consideration which we should do well to bear in mind* or *a conclusion to which all of us would readily assent* will save many a sentence from coming down with a bump. By using stale metaphors, similes and idioms, you save much mental effort, at the cost of leaving your meaning vague, not only for your reader but for yourself. This is the significance of mixed metaphors. The sole aim of a metaphor is to call up a visual image. When these images clash—as in *The Fascist octopus has sung its swan song, the jackboot is thrown into the melting pot*—it can be taken as certain that the writer is not seeing a mental image of the objects he is naming; in other words he is not really thinking. Look again at the examples I gave at the beginning of this essay. Professor Laski (1) uses five negatives in fifty-three words. One of these is superfluous, making nonsense of the whole passage, and in addition there is the slip *alien* for *akin,* making further nonsense, and several avoidable pieces of clumsiness which increase the general vagueness. Professor Hogben (2) plays ducks and drakes with a battery which is able to write prescriptions, and, while disapproving of the every-day phrase *put up with,* is unwilling to look *egregious* up in the dictionary and see what it means; (3), if one takes an uncharitable attitude towards it, is simply meaningless: probably one could work out its intended meaning by reading the whole of the article in which it occurs. In (4), the writer knows more or less what he wants to say, but an accumulation of stale phrases chokes him like tea leaves blocking a sink. In (5), words and meaning have almost parted company. People who write in this manner usually have a general emotional meaning—they dislike one thing and want to express solidarity with another—but they are not interested in the detail of what they are saying. A scrupulous writer, in every sentence that he writes, will ask himself at least four questions, thus: What am I trying to say? What words will express it? What image or idiom will make it clearer? Is this image fresh enough to have an effect? And he will probably ask himself two more: Could I put it more shortly? Have I said anything that is avoidably ugly? But you are not obliged to go to all this trouble. You can shirk it by simply throwing your mind open and letting the ready-made phrases come crowding in. They will construct your sentences for you—even think your thoughts for you, to a certain extent—and at need they will perform the important service of partially concealing your meaning even from yourself. It is at this point that the special connection between politics and the debasement of language becomes clear.

In our time it is broadly true that political writing is bad writing. Where it is not true, it will generally be found that the writer is some kind of rebel, expressing his private opinions and not a "party line." Orthodoxy, of whatever color, seems to demand a lifeless, imitative style. The political dialects to be found in pamphlets, leading articles, manifestos, White Papers and the speeches of under-secretaries do, of course, vary from party to party, but they are all alike in that one almost never finds in them a fresh, vivid, homemade turn of speech. When one watches some tired hack on the platform mechanically repeating the familiar phrases—*bestial atrocities, iron heel, bloodstained tyranny, free peoples of the world, stand shoulder to shoulder*—one often has a curious feeling that one is not watching a live human being but some kind of dummy: a feeling which suddenly becomes stronger at moments when the light catches the speaker's spectacles and turns them into blank discs which seem to have no eyes behind them. And this is not altogether fanciful. A speaker who uses that kind of phraseology has gone some distance towards turning himself into a machine. The appropriate noises are coming out of his larynx, but his brain is not involved as it would be if he were choosing his words for himself. If the speech he is making is one that he is accustomed to make over and over again, he may be almost unconscious of what he is saying, as one is when one utters the responses in church. And this reduced state of consciousness, if not indispensable, is at any rate favorable to political conformity.

In our time, political speech and writing are largely the defence of the indefensible. Things like the continuance of British rule in India, the Russian purges and deportations, the dropping of the atom bombs on Japan, can indeed be defended, but only by arguments which are too brutal for most people to face, and which do not square with the professed aims of political parties. Thus political language has to consist largely of euphemism, question-begging and sheer cloudy vagueness. Defenceless villages are bombarded from the air, the inhabitants driven out into the countryside, the cattle machine-gunned, the huts set on fire with incendiary bullets: this is called *pacification.* Millions of peasants are robbed of their farms and sent trudging along the roads with no more than they can carry: this is called *transfer of population* or *rectification of frontiers.* People are imprisoned for years without trial, or shot in the back of the neck or sent to die of scurvy in Arctic lumber camps: this is called *elimination of unreliable elements.* Such phraseology is needed if one wants to name things without calling up mental pictures of them. Consider for instance some comfortable English professor defending Russian totalitarianism. He cannot say outright, "I believe in killing off your opponents when you can get good results by doing so." Probably, therefore, he will say something like this:

"While freely conceding that the Soviet régime exhibits certain features which the humanitarian may be inclined to deplore, we must, I think, agree that a certain curtailment of the right to political opposition is an unavoidable concomitant of transitional periods, and that the rigors which the Russian people have been called upon to undergo have been amply justified in the sphere of concrete achievement."

The inflated style is itself a kind of euphemism. A mass of Latin words falls upon the facts like soft snow, blurring the outlines and covering up all the details. The great enemy of clear language is insincerity. When there is a gap between one's real and one's declared aims, one turns as it were instinctively to long words and exhausted idioms, like a cuttlefish squirting out ink. In our age there is no such thing as "keeping out of politics." All issues are political issues, and politics itself is a mass of lies, evasions, folly, hatred and schizophrenia. When the general atmosphere is bad, language must suffer. I should expect to find—this is a guess which I have not sufficient knowledge to verify—that the German, Russian and Italian languages have all deteriorated in the last ten to fifteen years, as a result of dictatorship.

But if thought corrupts language, language can also corrupt thought. A bad usage can spread by tradition and imitation, even among people who should and do know better. The debased language that I have been discussing is in some ways very convenient. Phrases like *a not unjustifiable assumption, leaves much to be desired, would serve no good purpose, a consideration which we should do well to bear in mind,* are a continuous temptation, a packet of aspirins always at one's elbow. Look back through this essay, and for certain you will find that I have again and again committed the very faults I am protesting against. By this morning's post I have received a pamphlet dealing with conditions in Germany. The author tells me that he "felt impelled" to write it. I open it at random, and here is almost the first sentence that I see: "[The Allies] have an opportunity not only of achieving a radical transformation of Germany's social and political structure in such a way as to avoid a nationalistic reaction in Germany itself, but at the same time of laying the foundations of a cooperative and unified Europe." You see, he "feels impelled" to write—feels, presumably, that he has something new to say—and yet his words, like cavalry horses answering the bugle, group themselves automatically into the familiar dreary pattern. This invasion of one's mind by ready-made phrases *(lay the foundations, achieve a radical transformation)* can only be prevented if one is constantly on guard against them, and every such phrase anaesthetizes a portion of one's brain.

I said earlier that the decadence of our language is probably curable. Those who deny this would argue, if they produced an argument at all, that language merely reflects existing social conditions, and that we cannot influence its development by any direct tinkering with words and constructions. So far as the general tone or spirit of a language goes, this may be true, but it is not true in detail. Silly words and expressions have often disappeared, not through any evolutionary process but owing to the conscious action of a minority. Two recent examples were *explore every avenue* and *leave no stone unturned,* which were killed by the jeers of a few journalists. There is a long list of flyblown metaphors which could similarly be got rid of if enough people would interest themselves in the job; and it should also be possible to laugh the *not un-* formation out of existence,[3] to reduce the amount of Latin and Greek in the average sentence, to drive out foreign phrases and strayed scientific words, and, in general, to make pretentiousness unfashionable. But all these are minor points. The defence of the English language implies more than this, and perhaps it is best to start by saying what it does *not* imply.

To begin with it has nothing to do with archaism, with the salvaging of obsolete words and turns of speech, or with the setting up of a "standard English" which must never be departed from. On the contrary, it is especially concerned with the scrapping of every word or idiom which has outworn its usefulness. It has nothing to do with correct grammar and syntax, which are of no importance so long as one makes one's meaning clear, or with the avoidance of Americanisms, or with having what is called a "good prose style." On the other hand it is not concerned with fake simplicity and the attempt to make written English colloquial. Nor does

[3]One can cure oneself of the *not un-* formation by memorizing this sentence: *A not unblack dog was chasing a not unsmall rabbit across a not ungreen field.*

it even imply in every case preferring the Saxon word to the Latin one, though it does imply using the fewest and shortest words that will cover one's meaning. What is above all needed is to let the meaning choose the word, and not the other way about. In prose, the worst thing one can do with words is to surrender to them. When you think of a concrete object, you think wordlessly, and then, if you want to describe the thing you have been visualizing you probably hunt about till you find the exact words that seem to fit it. When you think of something abstract you are more inclined to use words from the start, and unless you make a conscious effort to prevent it, the existing dialect will come rushing in and do the job for you, at the expense of blurring or even changing your meaning. Probably it is better to put off using words as long as possible and get one's meaning as clear as one can through pictures or sensations. Afterwards one can choose —not simply *accept*—the phrases that will best cover the meaning, and then switch round and decide what impression one's words are likely to make on another person. This last effort of the mind cuts out all stale or mixed images, all prefabricated phrases, needless repetitions, and humbug and vagueness generally. But one can often be in doubt about the effect of a word or a phrase, and one needs rules that one can rely on when instinct fails. I think the following rules will cover most cases:

1. Never use a metaphor, simile or other figure of speech which you are used to seeing in print.
2. Never use a long word where a short one will do.
3. If it is possible to cut a word out, always cut it out.
4. Never use the passive where you can use the active.
5. Never use a foreign phrase, a scientific word or a jargon word if you can think of an everyday English equivalent.
6. Break any of these rules sooner than say anything outright barbarous.

These rules sound elementary, and so they are, but they demand a deep change of attitude in anyone who has grown used to writing in the style now fashionable. One could keep all of them and still write bad English, but one could not write the kind of stuff that I quoted in those five specimens at the beginning of this article.

I have not here been considering the literary use of language, but merely language as an instrument for expressing and not for concealing or preventing thought. Stuart Chase and others have come near to claiming that all abstract words are meaningless, and have used this as a pretext for advocating a kind of political quietism. Since you don't know what Fascism is, how can you struggle against Fascism? One need not swallow such absurdities as this, but one ought to recognize that the present political chaos is connected with the decay of language, and that one can probably bring about some improvement by starting at the verbal end. If you simplify your English, you are freed from the worst follies of orthodoxy. You cannot speak any of the necessary dialects, and when you make a stupid remark its stupidity will be obvious, even to yourself. Political language—and with variations this is true of all political parties, from Conservatives to Anarchists—is designed to make lies sound truthful and murder respectable, and to give an appearance of solidity to pure wind. One cannot change this all in a moment, but one can at least change one's own habits, and from time to time one can even, if one jeers loudly enough, send some worn-out and useless phrase—some *jackboot, Achilles' heel, hotbed, melting pot, acid test, veritable inferno* or other lump of verbal refuse—into the dustbin where it belongs.

Gerald Grow

Gerald Grow works at the Center for Educational Technology, Florida State University at Tallahassee, where he is Editor and Assistant in Research. His ten steps to "official" writing appeared in the April (fool) 1982 issue of *Simply Stated #25*, a free newsletter published by the Document Design Center of the American Institute for Research. The center publishes articles about research in writing and producing documents; its primary goal is to reduce the burden that paperwork causes. Grow's list is presented here as further illustration of Orwell's ideas.

How to Write "Official"

1. **Start with a simple statement:** We quit. Why? Nobody knew how to program the computer.

2. **Put it in the passive voice and dilute the responsibility:** *It was decided to* quit.

3. **Expand with terminology that does not add meaning:** It was decided to *terminate.*

4. **Build in noun strings:** It was decided to terminate *project processes.*

5. **Add a qualifier of uncertain relation to the original statement:** *On account of the status of the computer,* it was decided to terminate project processes.

6. **Add noun strings and terminology to the qualifier:** On account of the status of the *computer program assessment planning development effort,* it was decided to terminate project processes.

7. **Separate related words:** On account of the status of the computer program assessment planning development effort, it was decided to terminate *until a later date* project processes.

8. **Equivocate:** On account of the *uncertain* status of the computer program assessment planning development effort, it was *proposed and tentatively accepted* to terminate until a later date project processes.

9. **Obfuscate:** Due to uncertainties in the status of the computer program assessment planning development effort, *proposals were carefully considered and tentatively adopted to suspend temporarily* until a later date project processes.

10. **Cover your tracks; make yourself look good:** Due to *unavoidable* uncertainties in the status of the computer program assessment planning development effort, *a number of contingency* proposals were carefully considered and one was tentatively adopted to suspend on a temporary basis until a later date those project processes *deemed unessential to the expeditious fulfillment of contract requirements.*

Haig A. Bosmajian

Haig A. Bosmajian, Professor of Parliamentary Procedure, Rhetoric, and Freedom of Speech at the University of Washington, was born in California in 1928. He received his doctorate from Stanford in 1960. Professor Bosmajian's principal areas of interest are dissent, language and behavior, and the language of social movements. He has edited *The Principles and Practice of Freedom of Speech* (1971), has collaborated with Hamida Bosmajian on *The Rhetoric of the Civil Rights Movement* (1969) and *This Great Argument: The Rights of Women* (1972), and he is coauthor of *Sexism and Language* (1977). His more recent publications include *Justice Douglas and Freedom of Speech* (1980) and *Censorship, Libraries, and the Law* (1982). Bosmajian has also published essays on the rhetoric of Nazism and communism and on nonverbal communication. The present essay is the introduction to his book *The Language of Oppression* (1974), from which we take its title.

The Language of Oppression

"Sticks and stones may break my bones, but words can never hurt me." To accept this adage as valid is sheer folly. "What's in a name? that which we call a rose by any other name would smell as sweet." The answer to Juliet's question is "Plenty!" and to her own response to the question we can only say that this is by no means invariably true. The importance, significance, and ramifications of naming and defining people cannot be over-emphasized. From *Genesis* and beyond, to the present time, the power which comes from naming and defining people has had positive as well as negative effects on entire populations.

The magic of words and names has always been an integral part of both "primitive" and "civilized" societies. As Margaret Schlauch has observed, "from time immemorial men have thought there is some mysterious essential connection between a thing and the spoken name for it. You could use the name of your enemy, not only to designate him either passionately or dispassionately, but also to exercise a baleful influence."[1]

Biblical passages abound in which names and naming are endowed with great power; from the very outset, in *Genesis,* naming and defining are attributed a significant potency: "And out of the ground the Lord God formed every beast of the field and every fowl of the air; and brought them unto Adam to see what he would call them: and whatsoever Adam called every living creature, that was the name thereof."[2] Amidst the admonitions in *Leviticus* against theft, lying, and fraud is the warning: "And ye shall not swear my name falsely, neither shalt thou profane the name of thy God: I am the Lord."[3] So important is the name that it must not be blasphemed; those who curse and blaspheme shall be stoned "and he that blasphemeth the name of the Lord, he shall surely be put to death, and all the congregation shall certainly stone him."[4] So important is the name that the denial of it is considered a form of punishment: "But ye are they that forsake the Lord, that forget my holy mountain. . . . Therefore will I number you to the sword, and ye shall all bow down to the slaughter: because when I called, ye did not answer; when I spake, ye did not hear. . . . Therefore thus saith the Lord God, behold, my servants shall eat, but ye shall be hungry. . . . And ye shall leave your name for a curse unto my chosen: for the Lord God shall slay thee, and call his servants by another name."[5]

To be unnamed is to be unknown, to have no identity. William Saroyan has observed that "the word nameless, especially in poetry and in much prose, signifies an alien, unknown, and almost unwelcome condition, as when, for instance, a writer speaks of 'a nameless sorrow.'" "Human beings," continues Saroyan, "are for the fact of being named at all, however meaninglessly, lifted out of an area of mystery, doubt, or undesirability into an area in which belonging to everybody else is taken for granted, so that one of the first questions asked by new people, two-year-olds even,

[1]Margaret Schlauch, *The Gift of Language* (New York: Dover, 1955), p. 13.
[2]*Genesis,* 2:19.
[3]*Leviticus,* 19:12.
[4]*Leviticus,* 25:16.
[5]*Isaiah,* 66:11–12.

whether they are speaking to other new people or to people who have been around for a great many years, is 'What is your name?' "[6]

To receive a name is to be elevated to the status of a human being; without a name one's identity is questionable. In stressing the importance of a name and the significance of having none, Joyce Hertzler has said that "among both primitives and moderns, an individual has no definition, no validity for himself, without a name. His name is his badge of individuality, the means whereby he identifies himself and enters upon a truly subjective existence. My own name, for example, stands for me, a person. Divesting me of it reduces me to a meaningless, even pathological, nonentity."[7]

In his book *What Is In A Name?* Farhang Zabeeh reminds us that "the Roman slaves originally were without names. Only after being sold they took their master's praenomen in the genitive case followed by the suffix —'por' (boy), e.g., 'Marcipor,' which indicates that some men, so long as they were regarded by others as cattle, did not need a name. However, as soon as they became servants some designation was called forth."[8] To this day one of the forms of punishment meted out to wrongdoers who are imprisoned is to take away their names and to give them numbers. In an increasingly computerized age people are becoming mere numbers— credit card numbers, insurance numbers, bank account numbers, student numbers, et cetera. Identification of human beings by numbers is a negation of their humanity and their existence.

Philologist Max Muller has pointed out that "if we examine the most ancient word for 'name,' we find it is *naman* in Sanskrit, *nomen* in Latin, *namo* in Gothic. This *naman* stands for gnaman and is derived from the root, *gna,* to know, and meant originally that by which we know a thing."[9] In the course of the evolution of human society, R. P. Masani tells us, the early need for names "appears to have been felt almost simultaneously with the origin of speech . . . personality and the rights and obligations connected with it would not exist without the name."[10] In his classic work *The Golden Bough* James Frazer devotes several pages to tabooed names and words in ancient societies, taboos reflecting the power and magic people saw in names and words. Frazer notes, for example, that "the North American Indian regards his name, not as a mere label, but as a distinct part of his personality, just as much as are his eyes or his teeth, and

[6]William Saroyan, "Random Notes on the Names of People," *Names,* 1 (December 1953), p. 239.

[7]Joyce Hertzler, *A Sociology of Language* (New York: Random House, 1965), p. 271.

[8]Farhang Zabeeh, *What Is In A Name?* (The Hague: Martinus Nijhoff, 1968), p. 66.

[9]Cited in Elsdon Smith, *Treasury of Name Lore* (New York: Harper and Row, 1967), p. vii.

[10]R. P. Masani, *Folk Culture Reflected in Names* (Bombay: Popular Prakashan, 1966), p. 6.

believes that injury will result as surely from the malicious handling of his name as from a wound inflicted on any part of his physical organism."[11]

A name can be used as a curse. A name can be blasphemed. Name-calling is so serious a matter that statutes and court decisions prohibit "fighting words" to be uttered. In 1942 the United States Supreme Court upheld the conviction of a person who had addressed a police officer as "a God damned racketeer" and "a damned Fascist." (*Chaplinsky v. New Hampshire,* 315 U.S. 568). Such namecalling, such epithets, said the Court, are not protected speech. So important is one's "good name" that the law prohibits libel.

History abounds with instances in which the mere utterance of a name was prohibited. In ancient Greece, according to Frazer, "the names of the priests and other high officials who had to do with the performance of the Eleusinian mysteries might not be uttered in their lifetime. To pronounce them was a legal offense."[12] Jorgen Ruud reports in *Taboo: A Study of Malagasy Customs and Beliefs* that among the Antandroy people the father has absolute authority in his household and that "children are forbidden to mention the name of their father. They must call him father, daddy. . . . The children may not mention his house or the parts of his body by their ordinary names, but must use other terms, i.e., euphemisms."[13]

It was Iago who said in *Othello:*

> Who steals my purse steals trash; 'tis something nothing;
> 'Twas mine, 'tis his, and has been slave to thousands;
> But he that filches from me my good name
> Robs me of that which not enriches him
> And makes me poor indeed.

Alice, in Lewis Carroll's *Through the Looking Glass,* had trepidations about entering the woods where things were nameless: "This must be the wood," she said thoughtfully to herself, "where things have no names. I wonder what'll become of *my* name when I go in? I shouldn't like to lose it at all—because they'd have to give me another, and it would almost certain to be an ugly one."

A Nazi decree of August 17, 1938 stipulated that "Jews may receive only those first names which are listed in the directives of the Ministry of the Interior concerning the use of first names." Further, the decree provided: "If Jews should bear first names other than those permitted . . . they must . . . adopt an additional name. For males, that name shall be Israel, for females Sara." Another Nazi decree forbade Jews in Germany "to show themselves in public without a Jew's star. . . . [consisting] of a six-pointed star of yellow cloth with black borders, equivalent in size to the palm of

[11]James Frazer, *The Golden Bough* (New York: Macmillan, 1951), p. 284.
[12]*Ibid.,* p. 302.
[13]Jörgen Ruud, *Taboo: A Study of Malagasy Customs and Beliefs* (Oslo: Oslo University Press, 1960), p. 15.

the hand. The inscription is to read 'JEW' in black letters. It is to be sewn to the left breast of the garment, and to be worn visibly."

The power which comes from names and naming is related directly to the power to define others—individuals, races, sexes, ethnic groups. Our identities, who and what we are, how others see us, are greatly affected by the names we are called and the words with which we are labelled. The names, labels, and phrases employed to "identify" a people may in the end determine their survival. The word "define" comes from the Latin *definire,* meaning to limit. Through definition we restrict, we set boundaries, we name.

"When I use a word," said Humpty Dumpty in *Through the Looking Glass,* "it means just what I choose it to mean—neither more nor less." "The question is," said Alice, "whether you can make words mean so many different things." "The question is," said Humpty Dumpty, "which is to be master—that's all."

During his days as a civil rights-black power activist, Stokely Carmichael accurately asserted: "It [definition] is very, very important because I believe that people who can define are masters."[14] Self-determination must include self-definition, the ability and right to name oneself; the master-subject relationship is based partly on the master's power to name and define the subject.

While names, words and language can be and are used to inspire us, to motivate us to humane acts, to liberate us, they can also be used to dehumanize human beings and to "justify" their suppression and even their extermination. It is not a great step from the coercive suppression of dissent to the extermination of dissenters (as the United States Supreme Court declared in its 1943 compulsory flag salute opinion in *West Virginia State Board of Education v. Barnette*); nor is it a large step from defining a people as non-human or sub-human to their subjugation or annihilation. One of the first acts of an oppressor is to redefine the "enemy" so they will be looked upon as creatures warranting separation, suppression, and even eradication.

The Nazis redefined Jews as "bacilli," "parasites," "disease," "demon," and "plague." In his essay "The Hollow Miracle," George Steiner informs us that the Germans "who poured quicklime down the openings of the sewers in Warsaw to kill the living and stifle the stink of the dead wrote about it. They spoke of having to 'liquidate vermin'. . . . Gradually, words lost their original meaning and acquired nightmarish definitions. *Jude, Pole, Russe* came to mean two-legged lice, putrid vermin which good Aryans must squash, as a [Nazi] Party manual said, 'like roaches on a dirty wall.' 'Final solution,' *endgültige Lösung,* came to signify the death of six million human beings in gas ovens."[15]

The language of white racism has for centuries been used to "keep

---

[14]Stokely Carmichael, speech delivered in Seattle, Washington, April 19, 1967.
[15]George Steiner, *Language and Silence* (New York: Atheneum, 1970), p. 100.

the nigger in his place." Our sexist language has allowed men to define who and what a woman is and must be. Labels like "traitors," "saboteurs," "queers," and "obscene degenerates" were applied indiscriminately to students who protested the war in Vietnam or denounced injustices in the United States. Are such people to be listened to? Consulted? Argued with? Obviously not! One does not listen to, much less talk to, traitors and outlaws, sensualists and queers. One only punishes them or, as Spiro Agnew suggested in one of his 1970 speeches, there are some dissenters who should be separated "from our society with no more regret than we should feel over discarding rotten apples."[16]

What does it mean to separate people? When the Japanese-Americans were rounded up in 1942 and sent off to "relocation camps" they were "separated." The Jews in Nazi Germany were "separated." The Indians of the United States, the occupants of the New World before Columbus "discovered" it, have been systematically "separated." As "chattels" and slaves, the blacks in the United States were "separated"; legally a black person was a piece of property, although human enough to be counted as three-fifths of a person in computing the number of people represented by white legislators.

How is the forcible isolation of human beings from society at large justified? To make the separation process more palatable to the populace, what must the oppressor first do? How does he make the populace accept the separation of the "creatures," or, if not accept it, at least not protest it? Consideration of such questions is not an academic exercise without practical implications. There is a close nexus between language and self-perception, self-awareness, self-identity, and self-esteem. Just as our thoughts affect our language, so does our language affect our thoughts and eventually our actions and behavior. As Edward Sapir has observed, we are all "at the mercy of the particular language which has become the medium of expression" in our society. The "real world," he points out, "is to a large extent unconsciously built up on the language habits of the group. . . . We see and hear and otherwise experience very largely as we do because the language habits of our community predispose certain choices of interpretation."[17]

George Orwell has written in his famous essay "Politics and the English Language": "A man may take to drink because he feels himself to be a failure, and then fail all the more completely because he drinks. It is rather the same thing that is happening to the English language. It becomes ugly and inaccurate because our thoughts are foolish, but the slovenliness of our language makes it easier for us to have foolish

[16]*The New York Times,* October 21, 1969, p. 25.

[17]Cited in John Carroll (ed.), *Language, Thought and Reality: Selected Writings of Benjamin Lee Whorf* (Cambridge, Mass.: The M.I.T. Press, 1956), p. 134.

thoughts."[18] Orwell maintains that "the decadence in our language is probably curable" and that "silly words and expressions have often disappeared, not through any evolutionary process but owing to the conscious action of a minority."[19] Wilma Scott Heide, speaking as president of the National Organization for Women several years ago, indicated that feminists were undertaking this conscious action: "In any social movement, when changes are effected, the language sooner or later reflects the change. Our approach is different. Instead of passively noting the change, we are changing language patterns to actively effect the changes, a significant part of which is the conceptual tool of thought, our language."[20]

This then is our task—to identify the decadence in our language, the inhumane uses of language, the "silly words and expressions" which have been used to justify the unjustifiable, to make palatable the unpalatable, to make reasonable the unreasonable, to make decent the indecent. Hitler's "Final Solution" appeared reasonable once the Jews were successfully labelled by the Nazis as sub-humans, as "parasites," "vermin," and "bacilli." The segregation and suppression of blacks in the United States was justified once they were considered "chattels" and "inferiors." The subjugation of the "American Indians" was defensible since they were defined as "barbarians" and "savages." As Peter Farb has said, "cannibalism, torture, scalping, mutilation, adultery, incest, sodomy, rape, filth, drunkenness—such a catalogue of accusations against a people is an indication not so much of their depravity as that their land is up for grabs."[21] As long as adult women are "chicks," "girls," "dolls," "babes," and "ladies," their status in society will remain "inferior"; they will go on being treated as subjects in the subject-master relationship as long as the language of the law places them into the same class as children, minors, and the insane.

It is my hope that an examination of the language of oppression will result in a conscious effort by the reader to help cure this decadence in our language, especially that language which leads to dehumanization of the human being. One way for us to curtail the use of the language of oppression is for those who find themselves being defined into subjugation to rebel against such linguistic suppression. It isn't strange that those persons who insist on defining themselves, who insist on this elemental

[18]George Orwell, "Politics and the English Language," in C. Muscatine and M. Griffith, *The Borzoi College Reader,* 2nd ed. (New York: Alfred A. Knopf, 1971), p. 88.

[19]*Ibid.*

[20]Wilma Scott Heide, "Feminism: The *sine qua non* for a Just Society," *Vital Speeches,* 38 (1971–72), p. 402.

[21]Peter Farb, "Indian Corn," *The New York Review,* 17 (December 16, 1971), p. 36.

privilege of self-naming, self-definition, and self-identity encounter vigorous resistance. Predictably, the resistance usually comes from the oppressor or would-be oppressor and is a result of the fact that he or she does not want to relinquish the power which comes from the ability to define others.

Robin Lakoff

Robin Lakoff (born 1942) has written many books and articles on linguistics. She began her scholarly career by studying Latin syntax, but has progressively shifted her attention—through English syntax, semantics, and sociolinguistics —to pragmatics, the study of how language is used in practical situations, between people. She received her B.A. from Radcliffe in 1964 and her Ph.D. from Harvard in 1967. Subsequently she has taught at the University of Michigan and at Stanford, and since 1976 has been a professor of linguistics at the University of California, Berkeley. In 1979 Ripon College awarded her the honorary degree of Doctor of Letters, recognizing particularly her work on linguistic stereotypes and on the language associated with sex roles. The citation concluded: "She has helped to give productive contemporary meaning to the Biblical injunction 'by thy words thou shalt be justified, and by thy words thou shalt be condemned'." Her essay "You Are What You Say" appeared in the July 1974 issue of *Ms.* A fuller treatment of the subject is found in her book *Language and Women's Place* (1975). A new work, *The Politics of Beauty,* coauthored with Raquel Scherr, is to appear shortly.

You Are What You Say

"Women's language" is that pleasant (dainty?), euphemistic, never-aggressive way of talking we learned as little girls. Cultural bias was built into the language we were allowed to speak, the subjects we were allowed to speak about, and the ways we were spoken of. Having learned our linguistic lesson well, we go out in the world, only to discover that we are communicative cripples—damned if we do, and damned if we don't.

If we refuse to talk "like a lady," we are ridiculed and criticized for being unfeminine. ("She thinks like a man" is, at best, a left-handed compliment.) If we do learn all the fuzzy-headed, unassertive language of our sex, we are ridiculed for being unable to think clearly, unable to take part in a serious discussion, and therefore unfit to hold a position of power.

It doesn't take much of this for a woman to begin feeling she deserves such treatment because of inadequacies in her own intelligence and education.

"Women's language" shows up in all levels of English. For example, women are encouraged and allowed to make far more precise discriminations in naming colors than men do. Words like *mauve, beige, ecru, aquamarine, lavender,* and so on, are unremarkable in a woman's active vocabulary, but largely absent from that of most men. I know of no evidence suggesting that women actually *see* a wider range of colors than men do. It is simply that fine discriminations of this sort are relevant to women's vocabularies, but not to men's; to men, who control most of the interesting affairs of the world, such distinctions are trivial—irrelevant.

In the area of syntax, we find similar gender-related peculiarities of speech. There is one construction, in particular, that women use conversationally far more than men: the tag-question. A tag is midway between an outright statement and a yes-no question; it is less assertive than the former, but more confident than the latter.

A *flat statement* indicates confidence in the speaker's knowledge and is fairly certain to be believed; a *question* indicates a lack of knowledge on some point and implies that the gap in the speaker's knowledge can and will be remedied by an answer. For example, if, at a Little League game, I have had my glasses off, I can legitimately ask someone else: "Was the player out at third?" A *tag question,* being intermediate between statement and question, is used when the speaker is stating a claim, but lacks full confidence in the truth of that claim. So if I say, "Is Joan here?" I will probably not be surprised if my respondent answers "no"; but if I say, "Joan is here, isn't she?" instead, chances are I am already biased in favor of a positive answer, wanting only confirmation. I still want a response, but I have enough knowledge (or think I have) to predict that response. A tag question, then, might be thought of as a statement that doesn't demand to be believed by anyone but the speaker, a way of giving leeway, of not forcing the addressee to go along with the views of the speaker.

Another common use of the tag-question is in small talk when the speaker is trying to elicit conversation: "Sure is hot here, isn't it?"

But in discussing personal feelings or opinions, only the speaker normally has any way of knowing the correct answer. Sentences such as "I have a headache, don't I?" are clearly ridiculous. But there are other examples where it is the speaker's opinions, rather than perceptions, for which corroboration is sought, as in "The situation in Southeast Asia is terrible, isn't it?"

While there are, of course, other possible interpretations of a sentence like this, one possibility is that the speaker has a particular answer in mind —"yes" or "no"—but is reluctant to state it baldly. This sort of tag question is much more apt to be used by women than by men in conversation. Why is this the case?

The tag question allows a speaker to avoid commitment, and thereby avoid conflict with the addressee. The problem is that, by so doing, speakers may also give the impression of not really being sure of themselves, or looking to the addressee for confirmation of their views. This uncertainty is reinforced in more subliminal ways, too. There is a peculiar sentence intonation-pattern, used almost exclusively by women, as far as I know, which changes a declarative answer into a question. The effect of using the rising inflection typical of a yes-no question is to imply that the speaker is seeking confirmation, even though the speaker is clearly the only one who has the requisite information, which is why the question was put to her in the first place:

(Q) When will dinner be ready?

(A) Oh . . . around six o'clock . . . ?

It is as though the second speaker were saying, "Six o'clock—if that's okay with you, if you agree." The person being addressed is put in the position of having to provide confirmation. One likely consequence of this sort of speech-pattern in a woman is that, often unbeknownst to herself, the speaker builds a reputation of tentativeness, and others will refrain from taking her seriously or trusting her with any real responsibilities, since she "can't make up her mind," and "isn't sure of herself."

Such idiosyncrasies may explain why women's language sounds much more "polite" than men's. It is polite to leave a decision open, not impose your mind, or views, or claims, on anyone else. So a tag-question is a kind of polite statement, in that it does not force agreement or belief on the addressee. In the same way a request is a polite command, in that it does not force obedience on the addressee, but rather suggests something be done as a favor to the speaker. A clearly stated order implies a threat of certain consequences if it is not followed, and—even more impolite— implies that the speaker is in a superior position and able to enforce the order. By couching wishes in the form of a request, on the other hand, a speaker implies that if the request is not carried out, only the speaker will suffer; noncompliance cannot harm the addressee. So the decision is really left up to the addressee. The distinction becomes clear in these examples:

Close the door.

Please close the door.

Will you close the door?

Will you please close the door?

Won't you close the door?

In the same ways as words and speech patterns used *by* women undermine her image, those used *to describe* women make matters even worse. Often a word may be used of both men and women (and perhaps of things as well); but when it is applied to women, it assumes a special meaning that, by implication rather than outright assertion, is derogatory to women as a group.

The use of euphemisms has this effect. A euphemism is a substitute for a word that has acquired a bad connotation by association with something unpleasant or embarrassing. But almost as soon as the new word comes into common usage, it takes on the same old bad connotations, since feelings about the things or people referred to are not altered by a change of name; thus new euphemisms must be constantly found.

There is one euphemism for *woman* still very much alive. The word, of course is *lady. Lady* has a masculine counterpart, namely *gentleman,* occasionally shortened to *gent.* But for some reason *lady* is very much commoner than *gent(leman).*

The decision to use *lady* rather than *woman,* or vice versa, may considerably alter the sense of a sentence, as the following examples show:

(a) A woman (lady) I know is a dean at Berkeley.

(b) A woman (lady) I know makes amazing things out of shoelaces and old boxes.

The use of *lady* in (a) imparts a frivolous, or nonserious, tone to the sentence: the matter under discussion is not one of great moment. Similarly, in (b), using *lady* here would suggest that the speaker considered the "amazing things" not to be serious art, but merely a hobby or an aberration. If *woman* is used, she might be a serious sculptor. To say *lady doctor* is very condescending, since no one ever says *gentleman doctor* or even *man doctor.* For example, mention in the San Francisco *Chronicle* of January 31, 1972, of Madalyn Murray O'Hair as the *lady atheist* reduces her position to that of scatterbrained eccentric. Even *woman atheist* is scarcely defensible: sex is irrelevant to her philosophical position.

Many women argue that, on the other hand, *lady* carries with it overtones recalling the age of chivalry: conferring exalted stature on the person so referred to. This makes the term seem polite at first, but we must also remember that these implications are perilous: they suggest that a "lady" is helpless, and cannot do things by herself.

Lady can also be used to infer frivolousness, as in titles of organizations. Those that have a serious purpose (not merely that of enabling "the ladies" to spend time with one another) cannot use the word *lady* in their titles, but less serious ones may. Compare the *Ladies' Auxiliary* of a men's group, or the *Thursday Evening Ladies' Browning and Garden Society* with *Ladies' Liberation* or *Ladies' Strike for Peace.*

What is curious about this split is that *lady* is in origin a euphemism— a substitute that puts a better face on something people find uncomfortable—for *woman.* What kind of euphemism is it that subtly denigrates the people to whom it refers? Perhaps *lady* functions as a euphemism for *woman* because it does not contain the sexual implications present in *woman;* it is not "embarrassing" in that way. If this is so, we may expect that, in the future, *lady* will replace woman as the primary word for the human female, since *woman* will have become too blatantly sexual. That this distinction is already made in some contexts at least is shown in the following examples, where you can try replacing *woman* with *lady:*

(a) She's only twelve, but she's already a woman.

(b) After ten years in jail, Harry wanted to find a woman.

(c) She's my woman, see, so don't mess around with her.

Another common substitute for *woman* is *girl*. One seldom hears a man past the age of adolescence referred to as a boy, save in expressions like "going out with the boys," which are meant to suggest an air of adolescent frivolity and irresponsibility. But women of all ages are "girls": one can have a man—not a boy—Friday, but only a girl—never a woman or even a lady—Friday; women have girlfriends, but men do not—in a nonsexual sense—have boyfriends. It may be that this use of *girl* is euphemistic in the same way the use of *lady* is: in stressing the idea of immaturity, it removes the sexual connotations lurking in *woman*. *Girl* brings to mind irresponsibility: you don't send a girl to do a woman's errand (or even, for that matter, a boy's errand). She is a person who is both too immature and too far from real life to be entrusted with responsibilities or with decisions of any serious or important nature.

Now let's take a pair of words which, in terms of the possible relationships in an earlier society, were simple male-female equivalents, analogous to *bull : cow*. Suppose we find that, for independent reasons, society has changed in such a way that the original meanings now are irrelevant. Yet the words have not been discarded, but have acquired new meanings, metaphorically related to their original senses. But suppose these new metaphorical uses are no longer parallel to each other. By seeing where the parallelism breaks down, we discover something about the different roles played by men and women in this culture. One good example of such a divergence through time is found in the pair, *master : mistress*. Once used with reference to one's power over servants, these words have become unusable today in their original master-servant sense as the relationship has become less prevalent in our society. But the words are still common.

Unless used with reference to animals, *master* now generally refers to a man who has acquired consummate ability in some field, normally nonsexual. But its feminine counterpart cannot be used this way. It is practically restricted to its sexual sense of "paramour." We start out with two terms, both roughly paraphrasable as "one who has power over another." But the masculine form, once one person is no longer able to have absolute power over another, becomes usable metaphorically in the sense of "having power over *something.*" *Master* requires as its object only the name of some activity, something inanimate and abstract. But *mistress* requires a masculine noun in the possessive to precede it. One cannot say: "Rhonda is a mistress." One must be *someone's* mistress. A man is defined by what he does, a woman by her sexuality, that is, in terms of one particular aspect of her relationship to men. It is one thing to be an *old master* like Hans Holbein, and another to be an *old mistress*.

The same is true of the words *spinster* and *bachelor*—gender words for "one who is not married." The resemblance ends with the definition. While *bachelor* is a neuter term, often used as a compliment, *spinster* normally is used pejoratively, with connotations of prissiness, fussiness, and so on. To be a bachelor implies that one has the choice of marrying or not, and this is what makes the idea of a bachelor existence attractive, in the popular literature. He has been pursued and has successfully eluded his pursuers. But a spinster is one who has not been pursued, or at least not seriously. She is old, unwanted goods. The metaphorical connotations of *bachelor* generally suggest sexual freedom; of *spinster,* puritanism or celibacy.

These examples could be multiplied. It is generally considered a *faux pas,* in society, to congratulate a woman on her engagement, while it is correct to congratulate her fiancé. Why is this? The reason seems to be that it is impolite to remind people of things that may be uncomfortable to them. To congratulate a woman on her engagement is really to say, "Thank goodness! You had a close call!" For the man, on the other hand, there was no such danger. His choosing to marry is viewed as a good thing, but not something essential.

The linguistic double standard holds throughout the life of the relationship. After marriage, bachelor and spinster become man and wife, not man and woman. The woman whose husband dies remains "John's widow"; John, however, is never "Mary's widower."

Finally, why is it that salesclerks and others are so quick to call women customers "dear," "honey," and other terms of endearment they really have no business using? A male customer would never put up with it. But women, like children, are supposed to enjoy these endearments, rather than being offended by them.

In more ways than one, it's time to speak up.

Murray Edelman

Murray Edelman is one of those rare social scientists who have a particular appreciation for the meaning and uses of symbolism and of language. Born in 1919, he was educated at Bucknell University, at the University of Chicago, and at the University of Illinois (Ph.D., 1948), where he taught political science until 1966. He then moved to the University of Wisconsin, and has been Mead Professor there since 1971. Dr. Edelman has published widely in the fields of communications, labor relations, and public policy, but the sphere of his research that interests us most here is that represented by his books *The Symbolic Uses of Politics* (1964), *Politics as Symbolic Action* (1971), and *Political Language* (1977). It is from the last that we take the present essay, which first appeared in a slightly different form in *Politics and Society,* vol. 4 (1974).

The Political Language of the Helping Professions

Hospital staff often deny or ignore the requests of angry mental patients because to grant them would "reinforce deviant behavior." Teachers sometimes use the same rationale to justify ignoring or punishing demanding students. Two recent presidents[0] of the United States declared that they would pay no attention to peace demonstrators who resort to irritating methods. We commonly regard the last as a political act and the first two as therapeutic; but whether any such action is taken to be political or therapeutic depends on the assumptions of the observer, not on the behavior he or she is judging. Some psychologists reject the "reinforcement of deviant behavior" rationale on the ground that it pays no attention to the distinctive cognitive and symbolizing abilities of the human mind, equating people with rats. They believe such treatment too easily ignores reasonable grounds for anger and depresses the self-esteem of people who already suffer from too little of it, contributing to further "deviance," not to health. In this view the "treatment" is self-serving political repression, even if its definition as rehabilitation salves the consciences of professionals and of the public. Some psychiatrists, on the other hand, see political demonstrators or ghetto rioters as sick, calling for drugs or psychosurgery, not political negotiation, as the appropriate response; the Law Enforcement Assistance Administration[0] has generously supported experiments based on that premise.

The language of "reinforcement" and "help" evokes a world in which the weak and the wayward need to be controlled for their own good. The language of "authority" and "repression" evokes a different reality, in which the rights of the powerless need to be protected against abuse by the powerful. Each linguistic form marshals public support for professional and governmental practices that have profound political consequences: for the status, the rights, and the freedom of professionals, of clients, and of the wider public as well; but we rarely have occasion to inhabit or examine both worlds at the same time.

two recent presidents Lyndon Johnson, who held office from 1963 to 1969, and Richard Nixon, who held office from 1969 to 1974.
Law Enforcement Assistance Administration Federal agency that provides funds and technical assistance for state and local government criminal justice programs and anticrime projects.

Language is the distinctive characteristic of human beings. Without it we could not symbolize; we could not reason, remember, anticipate, rationalize, distort, and evoke beliefs and perceptions about matters not immediately before us. With it we not only describe reality but create our own realities, which take forms that overlap with one another and may not be mutually consistent. When it suits us to see rationalization as reason, repression as help, distortion as creation, or the converse of any of these, language and mind can smoothly structure each other to do so. When it suits us to solve complicated problems of logic and mathematics, language and mind can smoothly structure each other to do that as well. When the complicated problems involve social power and status, problematic perception and distortion are certain.

It is a commonplace of linguistic theory that language, thought, and action shape one another. Language is always an intrinsic part of some particular social situation; it is never an independent instrument or simply a tool for description. By naively perceiving it as a tool, we mask its profound part in creating social relationships and in evoking the roles and the "selves" of those involved in the relationships.

Because the helping professions define other people's statuses (and their own), the terms they employ to categorize clients and justify restrictions of their physical movements and of their moral and intellectual influence are especially revealing of the political functions language performs and of the multiple realities it helps create. Just as any single numeral evokes the whole number scheme in our minds, so a professional term, a syntactic form, or a metaphor with scientific connotations can justify a hierarchy of power for the person who uses it and for the groups that respond to it.

In analyzing such political evocations I do not mean to suggest that the helping professions cannot be rehabilitative and educational as well. Psychological distress can be as "real" as economic distress, and psychological support is often helpful for people who voluntarily seek it. There is a large literature and a complicated controversy about the links among psychological, economic, and social stress and about the effectiveness of the helping professions in achieving their goals; but this discussion focuses on the *political* consequences of professional language.

Through devices I explore here, the helping professions create and reinforce popular beliefs about which kinds of people are worthy and which are unworthy; about who should be rewarded through governmental action and who controlled or subjected to discipline. Unexamined language and actions can help us understand more profoundly than legislative histories or administrative or judicial proceedings how we decide upon status, rewards, and controls for the wealthy, the poor, women, conformists, and nonconformists.

In this chapter I examine such political uses of language in psychiatry, social work, psychiatric nursing, public school education, and law enforcement. My observations are based on extensive (and depressing) reading in the textbooks and professional journals of these professions. I looked for covert as well as overt justifications for status differentials, power differentials, and authority.

Therapy and Power

To illustrate the subtle bearing of language on status and authority consider a common usage that staff, clients, and the general public all accept as descriptive of a purely professional process: the term "therapy." In the journals, textbooks, and talk of the helping professions, the term is repeatedly used as a suffix or qualifier. Mental patients do not hold dances; they have dance therapy. If they play volleyball, that is recreation therapy. If they engage in a group discussion, that is group therapy.

Even reading is "bibliotherapy"; and the professional literature warns that it may be advisable to restrict, supervise, or forbid reading on some subjects, especially politics and psychiatry. Such an assertion forces us to notice what we normally pass over. To label a common activity as though it were a medical one is to establish superior and subordinate roles, to make it clear who gives orders and who takes them, and to justify in advance the inhibitions placed upon the subordinate class. It ordinarily does so without arousing resentment or resistance either in the subordinates or in outsiders sympathetic to them, for it superimposes a political relationship on a medical one while still depicting it as medical.

Though the linguistic evocation of the political system is subtle, that very fact frees the participants to act out their political roles blatantly, for they see themselves as helping, not as repressing. In consequence, assaults on people's freedom and dignity can be as polar and degrading as those typically occurring in authoritarian regimes, without qualms or protest by authorities, clients, or the public that hears about them. In this way a suffix or qualifier evokes a full-blown political system. No doubt it does so for most of the professionals who draw power from the system as persuasively and unobtrusively as it does for the clientele groups whom it helps induce to submit to authority and to accept the status of a person who must let others decide how he or she should behave.

To call explicit attention to the political connotations of a term for power, on the other hand, is to rally opposition rather than support. To label an authority relationship "tyrannical" is an exhortation to oppose it, not a simple description. The chief function of any political term is to marshal public support or opposition. Some terms do so overtly; but the more potent ones, including those used by professionals, do so covertly, portraying a power relationship as a helping one. When the power of professionals over other people is at stake, the language employed implies that the professional has ways to ascertain who are dangerous, sick, or inadequate; that he or she knows how to render them harmless, rehabilitate them, or both; and that the procedures for diagnosis and for treatment are too specialized for the lay public to understand or judge them. A patient with a sore throat is anxious for his doctor to exercise a certain amount of authority; but the diagnosis is easily checked, and the problem itself circumscribes the doctor's authority. When there is an allegation of mental illness, delinquency, or intellectual incapacity, neither the diagnosis nor the scope of authority is readily checked or limited, but its legitimacy is linguistically created and reinforced.

It is, of course, the ambiguity in the relationship, and the ambivalence in the professional and in the client, that gives the linguistic usage its flexibility and potency. That is always true of symbolic evocations, and it radically distinguishes such evocations from simple deception. Many clients want help, virtually all professionals think they are providing it, and sometimes they do so. Just as the helping seems manifest until it is self-consciously questioned, and then it becomes problematic, so the political relationship seems nonexistent until it is self-consciously questioned, and then it becomes manifest.

The special language of the helping professions merges cognition and affect. The term "mental illness" and the names for specific deviant behaviors encourage the observer and the actor to condense and confound several facets of his or her perception: helping the suffering, controlling the dangerous, sympathy for the former, fear of the latter, and so on. The terms carry all these connotations, and the actor-speaker-listener patterns them so as to utilize semantic ambiguity to cope with his or her ambivalence.

We normally fail to recognize this catalytic capacity of language because we think of linguistic terms and syntactical structures as signals rather than as symbols. If a word is a name for a specific thing or action, then terms like "mental illness," "delinquency prone," or "schizophrenic" have narrowly circumscribed meanings. But if a word is a symbol that condenses and rearranges feelings, memories, perceptions, beliefs, and expectations, then it evokes a particular structuring of beliefs and emotions, a structuring that varies with people's social situations. Language as symbol catalyzes a subjective world in which uncertainties and appropriate courses of action are clarified. Yet this impressive process of symbolic creation is not self-conscious. Our naive view holds that linguistic terms stand for particular objects or behavior, and so we do not ordinarily recognize that elaborate cognitive structures are built upon them.

In the symbolic worlds evoked by the language of the helping professions, speculation and verified fact readily merge with each other. Language dispels the uncertainty in speculation, changes facts to make them serve status distinctions, and reinforces ideology. The names for forms of mental illness, forms of delinquency, and for educational capacities are the basic terms. Each of them normally involves a high degree of unreliability in diagnosis, in prognosis, and in the prescriptions of rehabilitative treatments; but each also entails unambiguous constraints upon clients, especially their confinement and subjection to the staff and the rules of a prison, school, or hospital. The confinement and constraints are converted into liberating and altruistic acts by defining them as education, therapy, or rehabilitation and by other linguistic forms to be examined shortly. The arbitrariness and speculation in the diagnosis and the prognosis, on the other hand, are converted into clear and specific perceptions of the need for control. Regardless of the clinical utility of professional terms, their political utility is manifest; they marshal popular support for professional discretion, concentrating public attention upon procedures and rationalizing in advance any failures of the procedures to achieve their formal objectives.

Categorization is necessary to science and, indeed, to all perception. It is also a political tool, establishing status and power hierarchies. We ordinarily assume that a classification scheme is either scientific or political in character, but any category can serve either or both functions, depending on the interests of those who employ it rather than on anything inherent in the term. The name for a category therefore confuses the two functions, consigning people to high or low status and power while drawing legitimacy from its scientific status.

Any categorization scheme that consigns people to niches according to their actual or potential accomplishments or behavior is bound to be political, no matter what its scientific function. IQs; psychiatric labels; typologies of talent, skills, or knowledge; employment statuses; criminal statuses; personality types—all exemplify the point. Regardless of their validity and reliability (which are notoriously low)[1] or their analytic uses, such classifications rank people and determine degrees of status and of influence. The categorizations of the helping professions are pristine examples of the function, and many of these categories carry over into the wider society. Once established, a categorization defines what is relevant about the people who are labeled. It encourages others to interpret developments so as to confirm the label and to ignore, discount, or reinterpret counterevidence. As a civil rights lawyer put it, "While psychiatrists get angry, patients get aggressive; nurses daydream, but patients withdraw."[2] The eternal human search for meaning and for status can be counted on to fuel the problematic interpretation.

The language of the helping professions reveals in an especially stark

[1]See, for example, Lawrence G. Kolb, Viola Bernard, and Bruce P. Dohrenwend, "The Problem of Validity in Field Studies of Psychological Disorder," in *Challenges to Psychiatry,* ed. Bruce P. Dohrenwend and Barbara Snell Dohrenwend (New York: Wiley, 1969), pp. 429–60; Linda Burzotta Nilson and Murray Edelman, "The Symbolic Evocation of Occupational Prestige," University of Wisconsin—Madison, Institute for Research on Poverty, Discussion Paper 348–76.

[2]Daniel Oran, "Judges and Psychiatrists Lock Up Too Many People," *Psychology Today* 7 (August 1973): 22.

way that perception of the same act can range all the way from one pole to its opposite. Is an action punishment or is it help? The textbooks and psychiatric journals recommend actions that look like sadism to many and like therapy to many others: deprivation of food, bed, walks in the open air, visitors, mail, and telephone calls; solitary confinement; deprivation of reading and entertainment materials; immobilizing people by tying them into wet sheets and then exhibiting them to staff and other patients; other physical restraints on body movement; drugging the mind against the client's will; incarceration in locked wards; a range of public humiliations such as the prominent posting of alleged intentions to escape or commit suicide, the requirement of public confessions of misconduct or guilt, and public announcement of individual misdeeds and abnormalities.

The major psychiatric and nursing journals describe and prescribe all these practices, and more repressive ones, repeatedly. The May 1973 issue of *Psychiatry* tells of a psychiatric ward in which, as a part of her therapy, a sobbing patient was required to scrub a shower room floor repeatedly with a toothbrush while two "psychiatric technicians" stood over her shouting directions, calling her stupid, and pouring dirty water on the floor.[3] Another professional article suggests withholding meals from non-compliant patients,[4] and a third recommends that cold wet sheet pack restraints be used more often, because they gratify the patient's dependency needs.[5]

Public humiliation and pain, even when employed only occasionally and perceived as therapy, have systematic effects on people who know they may experience them and on those who use them. In the institutions run by the helping professions, the threat of their use helps keep inmates docile. Ivan Illich remarks of such "random terror" that it serves to "break the integrity of an entire population and make it plastic material for the teaching invented by technocrats,"[6] a lesson despotic governments have always been quick to learn.

The outsider acting as critic or skeptic is likely to perceive professional actions in this way, while the insider does not do so while playing the expected professional role. Yet there is ambivalence; and it is one of the functions of professional language and professional journals to help resolve it by defining constraints as help. The *Journal of Psychiatric Nursing,* for example, rarely fails to publish at least one article in each issue that en-

[3]D. L. Staunard, "Ideological Conflict on a Psychiatric Ward," *Psychiatry* 36 (May 1973): 143–56.

[4]Carl G. Carlson, Michael Hersen, and Richard M. Eisler, "Token Economy Programs in the Treatment of Hospitalized Adult Psychiatric Patients," *Mental Health Digest* 4 (December 1972): 21–27.

[5]Rose K. Kilgalen, "Hydrotherapy—Is It All Washed Up?" *Journal of Psychiatric Nursing* 10 (November–December 1972): 3–7.

[6]Ivan Illich, *Deschooling Society* (New York: Harper and Row, 1971), p. 14.

courages nurses to overcome their qualms about denying patients the rights other people enjoy; the question is presented as a search for therapy, never as a search for autonomy, dignity, or civil rights.

To describe these practices in everyday language evokes shock at the "treatments" in a person who takes the description naively, without the conditioning to the professional perspective to which everyone has in some degree been exposed. In the professionals and those who accept their perspective, on the other hand, it is the *language* rather than the actions that evokes horror, for they have been socialized to see these things only as procedures, as *means* to achieve rehabilitation, not as constraints upon human beings. Language is consequently perceived as a distortion if it focuses on immediate impacts on clients rather than on the ultimate ends that the professional thinks the client should read into them and that the professional himself or herself reads into them.

The professional's reaction to language of this kind exemplifies the reaction of powerful people in general to accounts of their dealings with those over whom they hold authority. Because the necessary condition of willing submission to authority is a belief that submission benefits the subordinate, it is crucial to the powerful that descriptions of their treatment of others highlight the benefit and not the physical, psychological, or economic costs of submission. The revenue service deprives people of money, almost always involuntarily; the military draft imposes involuntary servitude; thousands of other agents of the state deprive people of forms of freedom. Usually the rationale for such restraints is an ambiguous abstraction: national security, the public welfare, law and order. We do not experience or name these ambiguous and abstract objectives as any different from goals that consist of concrete benefits, such as traffic control and disease control. Linguistic ambiguity spreads the rationale of these latter types of benefits to justify far more severe constraints and deprivations (including death in war) in policy areas in which benefits are nondemonstrable and doubtless often nonexistent. We experience as radical rhetoric any factual description of authoritative actions that does not call attention to their alleged benefits to all citizens or to some, and authorities typically characterize such descriptions as subversive, radical, or treasonous. They are indeed subversive of ready submission and of political support.

The point becomes vivid if we restate the actions described above from the professional's perspective: discouraging sick behavior and encouraging healthy behavior through the selective granting of rewards; the availability of seclusion, restraints, and closed wards to grant a patient a respite from interaction with others and from making decisions, and to prevent harm to himself or others; enabling him to think about his behavior, to cope with his temptations to "elope" or succumb to depression, and to develop a sense of security; immobilizing the patient to calm him, satisfy his dependency needs, give him the extra nursing attention he values, and enable him to benefit from peer confrontation; placing limits on his acting out; and teaching him that the staff cares.

The two accounts describe the same phenomena, but they occur in phenomenologically different worlds. Notice that the professional terms carry connotations that depict constraints as nonrestrictive. To speak of "elopement" rather than "escape," as psychiatrists and staff members do, is to evoke a picture of individual freedom to leave when one likes (as eloping couples do) rather than of locks, iron bars, and bureaucratic prohibitions against voluntary departure. To speak of "seclusion" or "quiet room" rather than solitary confinement is again to suggest voluntary and enjoyable retirement from others and to mask the fact that the patient is locked in against his or her will and typically resists and resents the incarceration. Such terms accomplish in a craftsmanlike and nonobvious way what professionals also say explicitly to justify restrictions on inmates. They assert in textbooks, journals, and assurances to visitors that some patients feel more secure in locked wards and in locked rooms, that professionals know when this is the case, and that the patients' statements to the contrary cannot be taken at face value.

To speak of "limits" is to mask the perception of punishment for misbehavior and to perceive the patient as inherently irrational, thereby diverting attention from the manifest frustrations and aggravations that come from bureaucratic restrictions and from consignment to the most powerless status in the institution.

Many clients come, in time, to use the professionals' language and to adopt their perspective. To the staff, their adoption of the approved linguistic forms is evidence of insight and improvement. All clients probably do this in some degree, but for many the degree is so slight that the professional descriptions serve as irony or as mockery. They are repeatedly quoted ironically by students, patients, and prisoners.

In the institutions run by the helping professions, established roles and their special language create a world with its own imperatives. The phenomenon helps us understand the frequency with which well-meaning men and women support governments that mortify, harass, torture, and kill large numbers of their citizens. To the outsider such behavior signals sadism and self-serving evil, and it is impossible to identify with it. To the people who avidly act out their roles inside that special world, motives, actions, and consequences of acts are radically different. Theirs is a work of purification and nurturance: of ridding the inherently or ideologically contaminated of their blight or of ridding the world of the contamination they embody. It is no accident that repressive governments are consistently puritanical. To the inhabitants of other worlds the repression is a mask for power, but to those who wield authority, power is a means to serve the public good. Social scientists cannot explain such phenomena as long as they place the cause inside people's psyches rather than in the social evocation of roles. To attribute evil or merit to the psyche is a political act rather than a medical one, for it justifies repression or exaltation, while minimizing observation and analysis. To explore phenomenological diversity in people's worlds and roles is to begin to recognize the full range of politics.

Class or status differences may also entail wide differences in the labelings of identical behaviors. The teacher's underachiever may be the epitome of the "cool" student who refuses to "brownnose." The middle class's criminal or thief may be a "political prisoner" to the black poor. Such labels with contrasting connotations occur when a deprived population sees the system as unresponsive to its needs and organized rebellion as impossible. In these circumstances, only individual nonconformity remains as a way to maintain self-respect. To the deprived the nonconformity is a political act. To the beneficiaries of the system it is individual pathology. Each labels it accordingly.

The term "juvenile delinquent" historically served the political function of forcing the assimilation of Catholic immigrants to the WASP culture of late nineteenth- and early twentieth-century America. This new category defined as "criminal" youthful behaviors handled informally among the urban Catholics and not perceived by them as crime at all: staying out late, drinking, smoking, reading comic books, truancy, disobedience. However, the definition of prevailing urban norms as "delinquency" justified the authorities in getting the Irish children away from their "bigoted" advisers, the priests.[7] The language of individual pathology served also to raise doubts about a distinctive culture and a religion, rationalizing its political consequences in terms of its motivation of salvaging youth from crime.

Some professionals reject the professional perspective, and all, no doubt, retain some skepticism about it and some ability to see things from the perspective of the client and the lay public. The ambivalence is typically resolved in more militant, decisive, and institutionalized forms than is true of ambivalent clients; for status, self-conception, and perhaps income hinge on its resolution. In consequence, professionals adopt radical therapy, existentialist or Szaszian[0] views, or they attack these dissidents as unprofessional and unscientific.

The lay public by and large adopts the professional perspective; for its major concern is to believe that others can be trusted to handle these problems, which are potentially threatening to them but not a part of their everyday lives. This public reaction is the politically crucial one, for it confers power upon professionals and spreads their norms to others. The public reaction, in turn, is a response to the language of the professionals

[7]Anthony M. Platt, *The Child Savers: The Invention of Delinquency* (Chicago: University of Chicago Press, 1969); American Friends Service Committee, *Struggle for Justice* (New York: Hill and Wang, 1971), p. 112.

Szaszian   Referring to Thomas Szasz, a psychiatrist and educator who argues that mental illness should not be classified as illness in the medical sense.

and to the social milieu which gives that language its authoritative meaning. . . .

The Formal Component in Professional Language

The formal component in professional language is always significant; it consists for the laymen of meanings evoked by the *style* of expression, as distinct from its denotative content: the connotations, for example, of unfamiliar or scientific-sounding terms and of references to an esoteric body of theory. For the professional, formality entails reacting to "symptoms" only in ways that are approved in the textbooks and professional journals. These responses may be unfamiliar to laymen; they constrain cognition within a limited range, excluding originality outside that range.[8] That a battered woman is probably masochistic is an approved response for the psychoanalytically oriented psychiatrist. That any former psychiatric patient is "cured" is not an approved response, suggesting naivete and an unprofessional stance. The accepted word is "improved"; it justifies continued surveillance and control.

Both professionals and laymen, then, respond partly to the *forms* of language, as predetermined by the categories and observational methods of the profession. These forms evoke perceptions and beliefs that are all the more potent because they are subtly and often unconsciously expressed and understood. They mark off the insiders from the outsiders and they reinforce the willingness of the client to accept authority. Through ambiguous language forms, professionals, clients, and outsiders manage to adjust to one another and to themselves and to establish and maintain hierarchies of authority and status.

Professional Imperialism

The special language of the helping professions extends and enlarges authority as well as defining and maintaining it. It does so by defining the deviance of one individual as necessarily involving others as well, by seeing the absence of deviant behaviors as evidence of incipient deviance, and by defining as deviant forms of behavior that laymen regard as normal.

Because man is a social animal, deviance by definition involves others as well. In the helping professions, this truism serves as a reason to multiply the range of people over whom the professional psychiatrist, school psychologist, social worker, and law enforcement officer exercises authority. The "multi-problem family" needs counseling or therapy as much as its emotionally disturbed member. The person who offends others needs

[8]For a perceptive discussion of the functions of formality in political language, see Maurice Block, ed., *Political Language and Oratory in Traditional Society* (New York: Academic Press, 1975), pp. 1–28.

help even if she or he does not want it; and the professional has an obligation to "reach out" or engage in "case finding." These phrases interpret the sense in which deviance is social in character in a particular way: namely, that because other people are involved, their states of mind need the ministrations of the professional. By the same token they mask an alternative view: that it is the conditions of deviants' lives, their environments, and their opportunities that primarily need change. The professional interpretation, whatever its clinical uses, also serves the political function of extending authority over those not yet subject to it and the more far-reaching political function of shaping public perceptions so as to divert attention from economic and social institutions.

The more sweeping professional forays into alien territory rely on lack of evidence to prove the need for treatment. Consider one of the favorite terms of social work literature: the "predelinquent"; and corresponding psychiatric terms, like the "prepsychotic." On their face, such terms imply that the reference is to all who have not yet misbehaved, and that is certainly one of their connotations, one that would appear to give the professional *carte blanche* to assert authority over everybody who has not yet committed a crime or displayed signs of disturbance.

Though they do justify a wide range of actions, the terms usually have a considerably narrower connotation in practice, for social workers, teachers, psychiatrists, and law enforcement officials apply them largely to the poor and usually to children. Affluent adults may be "predelinquent" or "prepsychotic"; but it is not behavior that governs the connotations of these terms, but, rather, the statistical chances for a group and the belief that poor children are high risks, especially if they come from broken homes. They are indeed high statistical risks: partly because their labeling as predelinquents and the extra surveillance are certain to yield a fair number of offenders, just as they would in a wealthy population, and partly because poverty does not encourage adherence to middle-class norms.

In a program to treat "predelinquents" in a middle-class neighborhood of Cambridge-Somerville, Massachusetts, the "treated" group more often became delinquent than a control group, due, apparently, to the effects on the labeled people of their stigmatization. In a similar experiment in a slum neighborhood this result did not appear, apparently because the stigmatization was not significantly different from the normal low self-concept of the people involved.[9]

The term "predelinquent" nonetheless focuses the mind of its user and of his or her audience on the utility of preventative surveillance and control and diverts attention from the link between poverty and delin-

---

[9]Jackson Toby, "An Evaluation of Early Identification and Intensive Treatment Programs for Predelinquents," *Social Problems* 13 (Fall 1965): 160–75; David B. Harris, "On Differential Stigmatization for Predelinquents," *Social Problems* 15 (Spring 1968): 507–8.

quency. The term also evokes confidence in the professional's ability to distinguish those who will commit crimes in the future from those who will not. Once again we have an illustration of the power of an unobtrusive symbol to evoke a structured world and to direct perception and norms accordingly.

Still another form of extension of authority through the pessimistic interpretation of normal behavior is exemplified in the psychiatric phrase "escape to health." The term again draws its connotation from the disposition to interpret behavior according to the status of the person engaging in it. If a psychiatric patient shows no pathological symptoms, the professional can designate the phenomenon as "escape to health," implying that the healthy behavior is itself a sign that the patient is still sick, possibly worse than before, but intent now on deceiving himself and the staff. The consequence is continued control over him or her.

The term epitomizes an attitude common to authorities who know or suspect that their charges would prefer to escape their supervision rather than "behave themselves." The student typed as a troublemaker or as unreliable excites as much suspicion when he is quiet as when he is active. Parole boards have their choice of interpreting an inmate's conformist prison behavior as reform or as cunning deception. Anxious public officials in all historical eras have feared both passivity and peaceful demonstrations among the discontented as the groundwork for rebellion. Always, there are metaphoric phrases to focus such anxieties and arouse them in the general public: underground subversion, plotting, the calm before the storm, quiet desperation, escape to health. Always, they point to an internal psychological state or an allegation not susceptible to observation.

In the schools, other phrases emphasize student nonactions, discount their observable actions, and so justify special staff controls over them. Especially common are "underachiever" and "overachiever." The former implies that the student is lazy, the latter that he or she is neurotic. "Overachiever" is an especially revealing case, for it offers a rationale for treating achievement as deviance. The helping professions are often suspicious of people who display talents beyond the "norm," as they must be in view of their veiled equation of the norm with health. Textbooks in "special education" and "learning disabilities" group gifted or exceptionally able students with the retarded and the emotionally disturbed as special students and advocate separating these "special" students from the normal ones. They urge that the gifted be required to do extra work ("enrichment"). This may or may not mean they learn more or learn faster. It certainly means that they are kept busy and so discouraged either from making demands on the teacher's time or intelligence or from pointing up the stultifying character of the curriculum through restiveness or rebelliousness.

At least as common is the view that the poor require treatment and control whether or not they display any pathological symptoms. Though this belief is manifestly political and class based, the language social workers use to justify surveillance and regulation of the poor is psychological in character. Here are some examples from social work and psychiatric journals and textbooks.

Regarding a preschool nursery in a slum area:

> The children did not have any diagnosed pathology, but as a result of existing in an atmosphere of cultural deprivation, they were vulnerable to many psychosocial problems.[10]

From an article in *Social Work* suggesting devices through which a social caseworker can induce the poor to come for counseling or treatment by deceiving them into thinking they are only accompanying their children, or only attending a party or social meeting:

> cognitive deficiency . . . broadly refers to the lacks many people suffer in the normal development of their thinking processes. For the most part, though not exclusively, such deficits occur among the poor regardless of nationality or race.[11]

The same article quotes a memorandum issued by the Family Service Association of Nassau County: "Culturally deprived adults seem to be impaired in concepts of causality and time."[12] This last sentence very likely means that the poor are likely to attribute their poverty to inadequate pay or unemployment rather than to personal defects (causality) and are not punctual in keeping appointments with caseworkers (time). It is bound to be based on a limited set of observations that have powerful implications for the professional observer's own status and authority. The quotation is an example of one of the most common linguistic devices for connoting pathology from specific behaviors equally open to alternative interpretations that make them seem normal. One of several concrete acts becomes a generalization about an "impairment." To those who do not know the basis for the generalization, it is *prima facie* scientific. To the professionals who have already been socialized into the view the generalization connotes, it is persuasive and profound. To those who meet neither of these conditions, it is a political exhortation rather than a scientific

[10]Evelyn McElroy and Anita Narcísco, "Clinical Specialist in the Community Mental Health Program," *Journal of Psychiatric Nursing* 9 (January–February 1971): 19.

[11]Robert Sunley, "New Dimensions in Reaching-out Casework," *Social Work* 13 (April 1968): 64–74. For evidence that psychiatrists diagnose poorer patients as having more severe pathologies, see Joel Fischer, "Negroes and Whites and Rates of Mental Illness," *Psychiatry* 32 (November 1969): 428–46. See also Vernon L. Allen, "Personality Correlates of Poverty," in *Psychological Factors in Poverty*, ed. Vernon Allen (Chicago: Markham, 1970), pp. 242–66.

[12]Ibid., p. 73.

generalization; these people are inclined to treat it as problematic and controversial rather than as established by authoritative procedures.

Ambiguous language can also be vacuous, making it easy for professionals to legitimize social and political biases. They are not prejudiced against the poor, but against cognitive deficiencies; not against women, but against impulsive-hysterics; not against political radicals, but against paranoids; not against homosexuals, but against deviants. They are not in favor of punishing, stigmatizing, humiliating, or imprisoning people but, rather, of meeting dependency and security needs, and of rehabilitation.

It is not chance that the groups constrained by these rationales are also the groups that experience bias in society at large or that the "treatment" consists either of restoring conformist behavior or of removing offenders from the sight, the consciences, and the career competition of the conventional. Those who become clients have experienced problems either because they have acted unconventionally or because they belong to a category (the young, the poor, women, blacks) whose behavior is largely assessed because of who they are rather than because of what they do.

"Helping" as a Political Symbol

The ambiguity of "helping" is apparent when we examine the contrasting ways in which society "helps" elites and nonelites. Subsidies from the public treasury to businessmen are justified not as help to individuals but as promotion of a popularly supported goal: defense, agriculture, transportation, and so on. The abstractions are not personified in the people who get generous depletion allowances, cost-plus contracts, tax write-offs, or free government services. To perceive the expenditure as a subsidy to real people would portray it as an inequity in public policy. The word "help" is not used in this context, though these policies make people rich and substantially augment the wealth of the already rich. Nor is there a dependency relationship or a direct personal relationship between a recipient and a grantor with discretion to withhold benefits. The grantor wields no power over the recipient; if anything, the recipient wields power over the administrators who carry out the law; for there are always legislators and executives ready to penalize administrators who call attention to the subsidy aspect of the program; and some of the more cooperative administrators can look forward to employment in the industries they come to know as dispensers of governmental benefits.

When "help" is given to the poor or the unconventional, a different set of role relationships and benefits appears. Now it is the beneficiaries who are sharply personified and brought into focus. They are individuals living off the taxpayer or flouting conventionality. What they personify is poverty, delinquency, or other forms of deviance. They are in need of help, but help in money, in status, and in autonomy must be sharply limited so as to avoid malingering. One of the consistent characteristics of the "helping" institutions is their care to limit forms of help that would make clients autonomous: money for the poor; education and independence for children of the poor or for "criminals"; physical and intellectual autonomy. The limit is enforced in practice while often denied in rhetoric.

The "help" for nonelite recipients of the largesse of the state that draws ready political support is control of their deviant tendencies: laziness, mental illness, criminality, nonconformity. They are taught to tolerate indignity and powerlessness when employed, poverty when unemployed, and the family and social stresses flowing from these conditions, without unconventional modes of complaint or resistance and without making too many demands on society.

In at least one of the worlds elites and professionals create for themselves and for a wider public, the help is real and the need for it is manifest. So manifest that it must be given even if it is not wanted. So manifest that failure to want it becomes evidence that it is needed and that it should be forced on recipients involuntarily and through incarceration if necessary.

When a helping relationship of this kind is established, it is likely to dominate the self-conception and the world view of those on both sides of the relationship. When a doctor sets a patient's broken arm, neither doctor nor patient lets the relationship significantly influence their self-conceptions or their views of their functions in society. When a public official tests an applicant for a driver's license or a radio license, this relationship is also just one more among many for both parties. But the psychiatrist who defines a patient as psychopathic or paranoid, or the teacher who defines a student as a slow learner or a genius, creates a relationship that is far more fundamental and influential for both professional and client. It tells them both who they are and so fundamentally creates their social worlds that they resist evidence that the professional competence of the one or the stigmatizing or exalting label of the other may be unwarranted. For both, the label tends to become a self-fulfilling prophecy and sometimes immune to falsifying evidence.

In consequence, the professional and the public official whose function it is to "help" the inadequate, the powerless, or the deviant is willing and eager to play his or her role, equipped with a built-in reason to discount or reinterpret qualms, role conflicts, and disturbing facts. To comfort, to subsidize, to limit, to repress, to imprison, even to kill are all sometimes necessary to protect the client and society, and the conscientious professional or political authority plays his role to be true to himself.

A society that frustrates or alienates a sizable proportion of its inhabitants can survive only as long as it is possible to keep the discontented docile and to isolate or incarcerate those who refuse to be "rehabilitated." The helping professions are the most effective contemporary agents of social conformity and isolation. In playing this political role they undergird the entire political structure, yet they are largely spared from self-criticism, from political criticism, and even from political observation, through a special symbolic language.

College and Education

Lincoln Steffens, going to college a century ago, hoped that it would be an adventure into a new world. What he found were courses and knowledge and training, but no one, he says, who "brought out for me the relation of anything I was studying to anything else, except, of course, to that wretched degree." His disappointment was such that he later "proposed a series of articles to raise and answer the question: Is there any intellectual life in our colleges?"

In important ways, the situation is not too different today. The lofty language of aims and objectives in college catalogues, the precise requirements for degrees, and the complex maze of course offerings suggest that the process of a college education is under confident and intelligent control. Yet the criticisms most often heard are similar to those of Steffens: knowledge is stored in compartments; the relation of knowledge to life is ignored; and as for questions, the professors ask them, not the students. It seems that too often the individual as learner is forgotten, yet what makes education dynamic and exciting is the question asked and the connection made by the individual learner's mind at work.

Colleges today face new challenges. One of the most important is the great proliferation of knowledge in recent years. This fosters specialism and makes it hard to know what is important to learn and what is not. Another challenge is the great increase in the number of college students and in the diverse needs, aptitudes, and backgrounds they have. If colleges are to be more than training schools,

137

they will need to study the kind of advice proposed by Harold Morowitz. Analyzing critically the present system, he comes up with an idea for improving it: he asks that we study how we know what we know; in Steffens' terms, study the "questions underlying the questions." A wider view of what is "essential to learn—to know —and why" is presented by Otto Friedrich, an able journalist who summarizes five main ideas of what a college education should be.

The subject is large, often confused, and difficult, but we hope that the readings we offer here will serve as an introduction to a few of the main issues and also provide students the opportunity to begin their own critical examinations of what is available, what should be available, and why.

Lincoln Steffens

Lincoln Steffens (1866–1936) is remembered primarily as a journalist and reformer. Born in Sacramento, California, he spent his youth largely with horses rather than books and failed to pass grammar school. "My parents did not bring me up," he writes. "They sent me to school, they gave me teachers of music, drawing; they offered me every opportunity in their reach. But also they gave me liberty. . . ." A great admirer of Napoleon, Steffens was enrolled at a military academy at fifteen and hoped to become a soldier: "I read about Napoleon as if I were reading up on my own future," he remembers. He acquired an interest in philosophy at the University of California, and subsequently studied in Germany, Paris, and London, returning to the United States in 1892. Steffens then began his career as a reporter for the New York *Evening Post.* After the turn of the century, he became closely associated with the muckraker movement, exposing municipal corruption and inefficiency in numerous magazine articles and in books such as *The Shame of the Cities* (1904).

As the public impact of muckraking lessened, Steffens dropped from the public eye and gradually lost faith in reform as an effective means of change. He supported the Mexican Revolution in 1914 and wrote extensively on the successes of the Russian Revolution and the Communist regime. After he spent twenty years in relative obscurity, the publication of *The Autobiography of Lincoln Steffens* in 1931 brought him renewed public interest and acclaim.

When Steffens failed the entrance requirements for the University of California, his father engaged Mr. Evelyn Nixon as a private tutor. For Steffens, Nixon was the first teacher "who interested me in what I had to learn." Nixon apparently realized this and invited him to his home where, on Saturday evenings, he met with a group of friends, all displaced English athletes and scholars, "a maddening lot of cultivated minds" who discussed "any and all subjects with knowledge, with the precise information of scholarship, but with no common opinions on anything apparently." These Saturday nights became Steffens' prep school and whetted his appetite for college.

The passages below, from the *Autobiography*, record his expectations as well as his disappointment at what he actually found at the university, and invite comparison with student expectations and disappointments today.

I Go to College

Going to college is, to a boy, an adventure into a new world, and a very strange and complete world too. Part of his preparation for it is the stories he hears from those that have gone before; these feed his imagination, which cannot help trying to picture the college life. And the stories and the life are pretty much the same for any college. The University of California was a young, comparatively small institution when I was entered there in 1885 as a freshman. Berkeley, the beautiful, was not the developed villa community it is now; I used to shoot quail in the brush under the oaks along the edges of the college grounds. The quail and the brush are gone now, but the oaks are there and the same prospect down the hill over San Francisco Bay out through the Golden Gate between the low hills of the city and the high hills of Marin County. My class numbered about one hundred boys and girls, mostly boys, who came from all parts of the State and represented all sorts of people and occupations. There was, however, a significant uniformity of opinion and spirit among us, as there was, and still is, in other, older colleges. The American is molded to type early. And so are our college ways. We found already formed at Berkeley the typical undergraduate customs, rights, and privileged vices which we had to respect ourselves and defend against the faculty, regents, and the State government.

One evening, before I had matriculated, I was taken out by some upper classmen to teach the president a lesson. He had been the head of a private preparatory school and was trying to govern the private lives and the public morals of university "men" as he had those of his schoolboys. Fetching a long ladder, the upper classmen thrust it through a front window of Prexy's house and, to the chant of obscene songs, swung it back and forth, up and down, round and round, till everything breakable within sounded broken and the drunken indignation outside was satisfied or tired.

This turned out to be one of the last battles in the war for liberty against that president. He was allowed to resign soon thereafter and I noticed that not only the students but many of the faculty and regents rejoiced in his downfall and turned with us to face and fight the new president when, after a lot of politics, he was appointed and presented. We learned somehow a good deal about the considerations that governed our college government. They were not only academic. The government of a university was—like the State government and horse-racing and so many other things—not what I had been led to expect. And a college education wasn't either, nor the student mind.

Years later, when I was a magazine editor, I proposed a series of articles to raise and answer the question: Is there any intellectual life in our colleges? My idea sprang from my remembered disappointment at what I found at Berkeley and some experiences I was having at the time with the faculties and undergraduates of the other older colleges in the east. Berkeley, in my day, was an Athens compared with New Haven, for example, when I came to know Yale undergraduates.

My expectations of college life were raised too high by Nixon's Saturday nights. I thought, and he assumed, that at Berkeley I would be breathing in an atmosphere of thought, discussion, and some scholarship; working, reading, and studying for the answers to questions which would be threshed out in debate and conversation. There was nothing of the sort. I was primed with questions. My English friends never could agree on the answers to any of the many and various questions they disputed. They did not care; they enjoyed their talks and did not expect to settle anything. I was more earnest. I was not content to leave things all up in the air. Some of those questions were very present and personal to me, as some of those Englishmen meant them to be. William Owen was trying to convert me to the anarchistic communism in which he believed with all his sincere and beautiful being. I was considering his arguments. Another earnest man, who presented the case for the Roman Catholic Church, sent old Father Burchard and other Jesuits after me. Every conversation at Mr. Nixon's pointed some question, academic or scientific, and pointed them so sharp that they drove me to college with an intense desire to know. And as for communism or the Catholic Church, I was so torn that I could not answer myself. The Jesuits dropped me and so did Owen, in disgust, when I said I was going to wait for my answer till I had heard what the professors had to say and had learned what my university had to teach me upon the questions underlying the questions Oxford and Cambridge and Rome quarreled over and could not agree on. Berkeley would know.

There were no moot questions in Berkeley. There was work to do, knowledge and training to get, but not to answer questions. I found myself engaged, as my classmates were, in choosing courses. The choice was limited and within the limits, had to be determined by the degree we were candidates for. My questions were philosophical, but I could not take philosophy, which fascinated me, till I had gone through a lot of higher mathematics which did not interest me at all. If I had been allowed to take philosophy, and so discovered the need and the relation of mathematics, I would have got the philosophy and I might have got the mathematics which I miss now more than I do the Hegelian metaphysics taught at

Berkeley. Or, if the professor who put me off had taken the pains to show me the bearing of mathematical thought on theoretical logic, I would have undertaken the preparation intelligently. But no one ever developed for me the relation of any of my required subjects to those that attracted me; no one brought out for me the relation of anything I was studying to anything else, except, of course, to that wretched degree. Knowledge was absolute, not relative, and it was stored in compartments, categorical and independent. The relation of knowledge to life, even to student life, was ignored, and as for questions, the professors asked them, not the students; and the students, not the teachers, answered them—in examinations.

The unknown is the province of the student; it is the field for his life's adventure, and it is a wide field full of beckonings. Curiosity about it would drive a boy as well as a child to work through the known to get at the unknown. But it was not assumed that we had any curiosity or the potential love of skill, scholarship, and achievement or research. And so far as I can remember now, the professors' attitude was right for most of the students who had no intellectual curiosity. They wanted to be told not only what they had to learn, but what they had to want to learn—for the purpose of passing. That came out in the considerations which decided the choice among optional courses. Students selected subjects or teachers for a balance of easy and hard, to fit into their time and yet "get through." I was the only rebel of my kind, I think. The nearest to me in sympathy were the fellows who knew what they wanted to be: engineers, chemists, professional men, or statesmen. They grunted at some of the work required of them, studies that seemed useless to their future careers. They did not understand me very well, nor I them, because I preferred those very subjects which they called useless, highbrow, cultural. I did not tell them so; I did not realize it myself definitely; but I think now that I had had as a boy an exhausting experience of *being* something great. I did not want now to be but rather to know things. . . .

I Become a Student

It is possible to get an education at a university. It has been done; not often, but the fact that a proportion, however small, of college students do get a start in interested, methodical study, proves my thesis, and the two personal experiences I have to offer illustrate it and show how to circumvent the faculty, the other students, and the whole college system of mind-fixing. My method might lose a boy his degree, but a degree is not worth so much as the capacity and the drive to learn, and the undergraduate desire for an empty baccalaureate is one of the holds the educational system has on students. Wise students some day will refuse to take degrees, as the best men (in England, for instance) give, but do not themselves accept, titles.

My method was hit on by accident and some instinct. I specialized. With several courses prescribed, I concentrated on the one or two that interested me most, and letting the others go, I worked intensively on my favorites. In my first two years, for example, I worked at English and political economy and read philosophy. At the beginning of my junior year I had several cinches in history. Now I liked history; I had neglected it partly because I rebelled at the way it was taught, as positive knowledge unrelated to politics, art, life, or anything else. The professors gave us chapters out of a few books to read, con, and be quizzed on. Blessed as I was with a "bad memory," I could not commit to it anything that I did not understand and intellectually need. The bare record of the story of man, with names, dates, and irrelative events, bored me. But I had discovered in my readings of literature, philosophy, and political economy that history had light to throw upon unhistorical questions. So I proposed in my junior and senior years to specialize in history, taking all the courses required and those also that I had flunked in. With this in mind I listened attentively to the first introductory talk of Professor William Cary Jones on American constitutional history. He was a dull lecturer, but I noticed that, after telling us what pages of what books we must be prepared in, he mumbled off some other references "for those that may care to dig deeper."

When the rest of the class rushed out into the sunshine, I went up to the professor and, to his surprise, asked for this memorandum. He gave it me. Up in the library I ran through the required chapters in the two different books, and they differed on several points. Turning to the other authorities, I saw that they disagreed on the same facts and also on others. The librarian, appealed to, helped me search the book-shelves till the library closed, and then I called on Professor Jones for more references. He was astonished, invited me in, and began to approve my industry, which astonished me. I was not trying to be a good boy; I was better than that: I was a curious boy. He lent me a couple of his books, and I went off to my club to read them. They only deepened the mystery, clearing up the historical question, but leaving the answer to be dug for and written.

The historians did not know! History was not a science, but a field for research, a field for me, for any young man, to explore, to make discoveries in and write a scientific report about. I was fascinated. As I went on from chapter to chapter, day after day, finding frequently essential differences of opinion and of fact, I saw more and more work to do. In this course, American constitutional history, I hunted far enough to suspect that the Fathers of the Republic who wrote our sacred Constitution of the United States not only did not, but did not want to, establish a democratic government, and I dreamed for a while—as I used as a child to play I was Napoleon or a trapper—I promised myself to write a true history of the making of the American Constitution. I did not do it; that chapter has been done or well begun since by two men: Smith of the University of Washington and Beard (then) of Columbia (afterward forced out, perhaps for this very work). I found other events, men, and epochs waiting for students. In all my other courses, in ancient, in European, and in modern history, the disagreeing authorities carried me back to the need of a fresh search for (or of) the original documents or other clinching testimony. Of course I did well in my classes. The history professors soon knew me as a student and seldom put a question to me except when the class had flunked it. Then Professor Jones would say, "Well, Steffens, tell them about it."

Fine. But vanity wasn't my ruling passion then. What I had was a quickening sense that I was learning a method of studying history and that every chapter of it, from the beginning of the world to the end, is crying out to be rewritten. There was something for Youth to do; these superior old men had not done anything, finally.

Years afterward I came out of the graft prosecution office in San Francisco with Rudolph Spreckels, the banker and backer of the investigation. We were to go somewhere, quick, in his car, and we couldn't. The chauffeur was trying to repair something wrong. Mr. Spreckels smiled; he looked closely at the defective part, and to my silent, wondering inquiry he answered: "Always, when I see something badly done or not done at all, I see an opportunity to make a fortune. I never kick at bad work by my class: there's lots of it and we suffer from it. But our failures and neglects are chances for the young fellows coming along and looking for work."

Nothing is done. Everything in the world remains to be done or done over. "The greatest picture is not yet painted, the greatest play isn't written (not even by Shakespeare), the greatest poem is unsung. There isn't in all the world a perfect railroad, nor a good government, nor a sound law." Physics, mathematics, and especially the most advanced and exact of the sciences, are being fundamentally revised. Chemistry is just becoming a science; psychology, economics, and sociology are awaiting a Darwin, whose work in turn is awaiting an Einstein. If the rah-rah boys in our colleges could be told this, they might not all be such specialists in football, petting parties, and unearned degrees. They are not told it, however; they are told to learn what is known. This is nothing, philosophically speaking.

Somehow or other in my later years at Berkeley, two professors, Moses and Howison, representing opposite schools of thought, got into a controversy, probably about their classes. They brought together in the house of one of them a few of their picked students, with the evident intention of letting us show in conversation how much or how little we had understood of their respective teachings. I don't remember just what the subject was that they threw into the ring, but we wrestled with it till the professors could stand it no longer. Then they broke in, and while we sat silent and highly entertained, they went at each other hard and fast and long. It was after midnight when, the debate over, we went home. I asked the other fellows what they had got out of it, and their answers showed that they had seen nothing but a fine, fair fight. When I laughed, they asked me what I, the D.S., had seen that was so much more profound.

I said that I had seen two highly-trained, well-educated Masters of Arts and Doctors of Philosophy disagreeing upon every essential point of thought and knowledge. They had all there was of the sciences; and yet they could not find any knowledge upon which they could base an acceptable conclusion. They had no test of knowledge; they didn't know what is and what is not. And they have no test of right and wrong; they have no basis for even an ethics.

Well, and what of it? They asked me that, and that I did not answer. I was stunned by the discovery that it was philosophically true, in a most literal sense, that nothing is known; that it is precisely the foundation that is lacking for science; that all we call knowledge rested upon assumptions which the scientists did not all accept; and that, likewise, there is no scientific reason for saying, for example, that stealing is wrong. In brief: there was no scientific basis for an ethics. No wonder men said one thing and did another; no wonder they could settle nothing either in life or in the academies.

I could hardly believe this. Maybe these professors, whom I greatly respected, did not know it all. I read the books over again with a fresh eye, with a real interest, and I could see that, as in history, so in other branches of knowledge, everything was in the air. And I was glad of it. Rebel though I was, I had got the religion of scholarship and science; I was in awe of the authorities in the academic world. It was a release to feel my worship cool and pass. But I could not be sure. I must go elsewhere, see and hear other professors, men these California professors quoted and looked up to as their high priests. I decided to go as a student to Europe when I was through Berkeley, and I would start with the German universities.

My father listened to my plan, and he was disappointed. He had hoped I would succeed him in his business; it was for that that he was staying in it. When I said that, whatever I might do, I would never go into business, he said, rather sadly, that he would sell out his interest and retire. And he did soon after our talk. But he wanted me to stay home and, to keep me, offered to buy an interest in a certain San Francisco daily paper. He had evidently had this in mind for some time. I had always done some writing, verse at the poetical age of puberty, then a novel which my mother alone treasured. Journalism was the business for a boy who liked to write, he thought, and he said I had often spoken of a newspaper as my ambition. No doubt I had in the intervals between my campaigns as Napoleon. But no more. I was now going to be a scientist, a philosopher. He sighed; he thought it over, and with the approval of my mother, who was for every sort of education, he gave his consent.

Harold J. Morowitz

Harold J. Morowitz, born in 1927, is a professor of molecular biophysics and biochemistry at Yale, where he received his Ph.D. in 1951. From 1969 to 1974, he served as a member of the planetary biology committee of the National Aeronautics and Space Administration. Most of his books and articles have been written for the scientific community, but *The Wine of Life and Other Essays on Societies, Energy, and Living Things* (1979), from which the following selection is taken, speaks to a general audience.

Drinking Hemlock and Other Nutritional Matters

It was a rather dark, bleak morning, and after rising early I thought it appropriate to turn on the television and communicate, unidirectionally to be sure, with the outside world. There to my great surprise was a famous movie star of a few years back discoursing on the evils of sugar. The former Hollywood idol was vehement in her denunciation of this hexose dimer particularly in its purified and crystallized form. She denounced it as an "unnatural food," an epithet that may well have bruised the egos of the photosynthesizing cane and beet plants. The mental image evoked was that of a solemn judge sentencing someone in perpetuity for an "unnatural act." In no time at all this great lady had me caught up in her crusade, and I kept muttering "hate sucrose" as I prepared an unnatural extract of coffee beans and dropped in a highly synthetic saccharin tablet.

A few minutes later, when the veil of sleep had lifted and the uncertainty of reason had replaced the assuredness of emotion, I began to wonder where my cinema heroine had acquired such self-righteous certainty about biochemical and nutritional matters that have eluded my colleagues for years. Perhaps all this messy experimental work of grinding and extracting tissue and otherwise mucking about the laboratory is not the shortest road to truth at all, and we of the dirty white lab coat crowd are missing some mysterious pathway whereby true nutritional knowledge comes with blinding insight and transforms the lives of the faithful.

All of this recalled a frequent, painful experience that haunts biomedical scientists like a recurring nightmare. One is at a cocktail party or other social gathering where someone appears in the crowd and begins an oratorical declamation on Good Nutrition. The "facts" being set forth are often inconsistent with everything one knows about metabolic pathways, cell and organ physiology, enzymology, and common sense. If the listener is so bold as to raise the question, "How do you know that?", he or she is greeted with a look that must have faced Columbus when he queried, "How do you know that the world is flat?"

Nutrition seems to be like politics; everyone is an expert. It would appear that to the general public years of education are as naught compared to knowledge somehow painlessly available to everyone, regardless of his familiarity with innumerable facts and theories that constitute a complex discipline.

The situation described is by no means confined to the choice of foods, and I certainly feel ill prepared to get involved in the sucrose controversy. Nevertheless, the field of nutrition is a good example of the many areas where we are constantly subjected to a host of dogmatic statements, some of which are true, some of which are false, and many of which are indeterminate. The response to each of these assertions should be the query, "How do you know that what you are saying is indeed a statement of fact?" At this level of question, I believe our educational system has been a total failure.

Asking how we know the things that we know is part of the philosophical discipline of epistemology, the theory of knowledge, which is usually taught in upper-level and graduate philosophy courses and is therefore restricted to a small group of college students. But can there be any study that is more basic to education? Should not every high school graduate be prepared to cope with the many incorrect and misleading assertions that come his way every day? On the surface it seems strange that acquiring skills in assessing the validity of statements is not a core feature of the school curriculum.

Education, as conceived at present, is largely a matter of transferring subject matter from teacher to student, and uncertainty is usually settled by appeal to authority, the teacher, a textbook, or an encyclopedia. The methodological issue of how knowledge is obtained is rarely mentioned. Thus one of the most important analytical tools that an educated individual should possess is ignored. This is not to argue against the transfer of information but rather to assert that by itself it is insufficient protection in a real world containing demagogues and all kinds of charlatans and hucksters who have a free rein because almost no one is asking the appropriate questions.

On the issue of sorting out reality, most holders of doctoral degrees are almost as naive as grade-school graduates, and all manner of academic disciplines also expend effort on statements that would be quickly discarded if epistemological criteria were invoked. This takes us back briefly to the subject of nutrition, where methodological problems make it very difficult to obtain even pragmatically useful information. Statements are made on the basis of averaging over populations when we have no idea of the distribution functions that go into forming the averages. The impossibility of large-scale experiments with people requires extrapolation of animal or small-scale human determinations over ranges where the correctness of the extrapolation procedure is unknown. Nutrition is thus beset with difficulties that are clearly of an epistemological nature and, until these are resolved, careful scientists will be confined to very limited statements. Dogmatic assertions will remain the province of cocktail party orators.

The problem of why the theory of knowledge is not taught in the schools is relatively easy to see. Epistemology is, after all, a dangerous subject. If we start to question the validity of statements, then the teachers themselves come under question. All assertions about education, established forms of religion, government, and social mores will also be subject to justification on the grounds of how they are known to be true. For parents and teachers who have not been through the experience of exploring how we determine facts, it would be unnerving to have their children continuously questioning the roots of knowledge. Inquiry is indeed a challenge to the acceptance of things as they are.

To realize the threat to established ways that is perceived in the type of analysis we are discussing, we need to go back to ancient Athens, where the philosopher Socrates taught his young followers by the technique of questioning everything and seeking answers. As Will Durant[0] has noted, "he went about prying into the human soul, uncovering assumptions and questioning certainties." This has come to be known as the Socratic method. The citizens of the Greek city-state condemned the inquiring teacher to death by poisoning with hemlock. One of the most serious charges against him was "corrupting the young." The fate of the first propounder of the Theory of Knowledge has perhaps served as a warning to keep the subject out of the school system.

There is still an objection that it is dangerous to teach the art and science of inquiry to the young; I would submit that it is more dangerous not to teach it to them, thus leaving them vulnerable to the quacks and phonies who now add mass communication to their bag of tricks. If we believe that rationality will lead the way to the solution of problems, then we must start by making the examination of what is "real" a part of everyone's thought. If challenging young people are a nuisance, think of how much more of a menace is presented by young people marching off in lock step and never questioning where they are going.

The solution seems clear. When we return education to the basics of reading, writing, and 'rithmetic, we should add a fourth R, "reality." Starting at the first grade and continuing through graduate training we must see that students become sensitized to the meaning of what is said and the realization of how valid knowledge is established. If this seems

Will Durant American historian and philosopher (1885–1981), perhaps best known for his ten-volume *The Story of Civilization* (1935–1967), which he wrote with his wife Ariel (1898–1981).

radical, it is. Drinking hemlock may be less painful than swallowing some of the drivel that comes over the TV set every day.

Otto Friedrich

Otto Friedrich (born 1929) is a senior writer at *Time* magazine. Since graduating from Harvard in 1948, he has worked as an editor for *Stars and Stripes,* the *New York Daily News, Newsweek,* and the *Saturday Evening Post.* In *Decline and Fall* (1970), he tells the story of the death of the *Saturday Evening Post.* "I had come to the *Post* in the mistaken belief that it would be a quiet and congenial place to work," he writes, but "I soon found that its leading executives were engaged in a ferocious struggle for power." He has written books on subjects ranging from Berlin in the 1920s to insanity to growing roses to Henry Adams's wife and, he says, "in a way, all these things overlap." The present article was originally published in *Time,* September 27, 1982, with a long introduction, here omitted, on the status of U.S. colleges at that moment.

Five Ways to Wisdom

What is it essential to learn—to know—and why? Everyone seems to have his own answer, but there are interesting patterns among those answers. They can be organized into five main ideas:

1: Education Means Careers

Today's most popular answer is the practical one, on which students are most likely to agree with parents virtually impoverished by tuition bills: an education should enable a student to get a better job than he would otherwise be able to find or fill. In a Carnegie Council poll, 67% of students cited this as an "essential" purpose of their education. A 9.8% unemployment rate makes this purpose seem all the more essential. Michael Adelson, 23, who studied psychology at U.C.L.A., has been unable to find a job in his field for a year and a half, and he now wishes he had chosen engineering. He calls his bachelor of arts degree "completely useless."

The idea that education has a basically social purpose derives more or less from Plato. In his *Republic,* the philosopher portrayed a utopia governed by an intellectual elite specially trained for that purpose. This form of education was both stern and profoundly conservative. Children who attempt innovations, warned Socrates, acting as Plato's narrator, will desire a different sort of life when they grow up to be men, with other institutions and laws. And this "is full of danger to the whole state." To prevent any innovations, Socrates forthrightly demanded censorship so that students could not "hear any casual tales which may be devised by casual persons." When asked whose works he would ban, Socrates specifically named Homer. The poet's crime, he said, was to provide "an erroneous representation of the nature of gods and heroes."

Political pressure of this kind has never been far from the campus, but the overwhelming influence on U.S. education has been not politics but economics: the need for a technologically trained managerial caste. The very first Land Grant Act, in 1862, handed out 30,000 acres per Congressman for the building of state colleges at which "the leading object shall be . . . to teach such branches of learning as are related to agriculture and the mechanic arts." These needs keep changing, of course, and over the decades the U.S. economy demanded of its universities not only chemists and engineers but lawyers and accountants and personnel analysts, and then, after Sputnik's shocking revelation of the Soviet lead in space, yet more engineers.

Students naturally respond to the economy's needs. The Rev. Theodore Hesburgh, president of Notre Dame, complained last year that "the most popular course on the American college campus is not literature or history but accounting." This criticism reflects the fact that less than half the nation's swarm of college students go to liberal arts colleges; the rest are seeking not just jobs but entry into the middle class.

There are now thousands of Ph.D.s unable to find anyone willing to pay them for their hard-earned knowledge of Renaissance painting or the history of French monasticism, but any Sunday newspaper overflows with ads appealing for experts in electromagnetic capability, integrated logistics support or laser electro-optics. Says George W. Valsa, supervisor of the college-recruiting section at Ford: "We are not ready to sign a petition to burn down liberal arts colleges, but don't expect us to go out and hire many liberal arts graduates." Ford does hire nearly 1,000 graduates a year, and most of them are engineers or M.B.A.s.

This is not the old argument between the "two cultures" of science and the humanities, for science too is often forced to defer to technical and vocational training. In 1979, according to one Carnegie study, 58% of all undergraduates pursued "professional" majors (up from 38% a decade earlier), in contrast to 11% in social sciences, 7% in biological sciences, 6% in the arts and 4% in physical sciences. Rich and prestigious private universities can resist this rush toward vocational training, but public and smaller private colleges are more vulnerable. "The bulk of the institutions will have to give in to a form of consumerism," says U.C.L.A.'s Astin, "in that they need applicants and will therefore have to offer students what they want."

Says Paul Ginsberg, dean of students at Wisconsin: "It's becoming increasingly difficult to persuade a student to take courses that will contribute to his intellectual development in addition to those that will make him a good accountant." Quite apart from the pros and cons of professional training, the idea of educating oneself in order to rise in the world is a perfectly legitimate goal. But Ginsberg has been receiving letters from high school freshmen asking about the prospects for professional schools and job opportunities when they graduate from college seven years hence. Says he: "I don't know at what point foresight ends and panic sets in."

2: Education Transmits Civilization

Jill Ker Conway, president of Smith, echoes the prevailing view of contemporary technology when she says that "anyone in today's world who doesn't understand data processing is not educated." But she insists that the increasing emphasis on these matters leaves certain gaps. Says she: "The very strongly utilitarian emphasis in education, which is an effect of Sputnik and the cold war, has really removed from this culture something that was very profound in its 18th and 19th century roots, which was a sense that literacy and learning were ends in themselves for a democratic republic."

In contrast to Plato's claim for the social value of education, a quite different idea of intellectual purposes was propounded by the Renaissance humanists. Intoxicated with their rediscovery of the classical learning that was thought to have disappeared during the Dark Ages, they argued that the imparting of knowledge needs no justification—religious, social, economic or political. Its purpose, to the extent that it has one, is to pass on from generation to generation the corpus of knowledge that constitutes civilization. "What could man acquire, by virtuous striving, that is more valuable than knowledge?" asked Erasmus, perhaps the greatest scholar of the early 16th century. That idea has acquired a tradition of its own. "The educational process has no end beyond itself," said John Dewey. "It is its own end."

But what exactly is the corpus of knowledge to be passed on? In simpler times, it was all included in the medieval universities' *quadrivium* (arithmetic, geometry, astronomy, music) and *trivium* (grammar, rhetoric, logic). As recently as the last century, when less than 5% of Americans went to college at all, students in New England establishments were compelled mainly to memorize and recite various Latin texts, and crusty professors angrily opposed the introduction of any new scientific discoveries or modern European languages. "They felt," said Charles Francis Adams Jr., the Union Pacific Railroad president who devoted his later years to writing history, "that a classical education was the important distinction between a man who had been to college and a man who had not been to college, and that anything that diminished the importance of this distinction was essentially revolutionary and tended to anarchy."

Such a view was eventually overcome by the practical demands of both students and society, yet it does not die. In academia, where every professor is accustomed to drawing up lists of required reading, it can even be played as a game. Must an educated man have read Dostoyevsky, Rimbaud, Tacitus, Kafka? (Yes.) Must he know both Bach's *Goldberg Variations* and Schoenberg's *Gurrelieder?* (Perhaps.) Must he know the Carnot Cycle and Boole's Inequality? (Well . . .) And then languages—can someone who reads only Constance Garnett's rather wooden version of *Anna Karenina* really know Tolstoy's masterpiece any better than some Frenchman can know Shakespeare by reading André Gide's translation of *Hamlet?* Every scholar likes to defend his own specialty as a cornerstone of Western civilization, and any restraints can seem philistine. George Steiner approvingly quotes, in *Language and Silence,* a suggestion that "an acquaintance with a Chinese novel or a Persian lyric is almost indispensable to contemporary literacy." On a slightly more practical level, intellectual codifiers like to draw up lists of masterworks that will educate any reader who is strong enough to survive them—thus Charles Eliot's famous five-foot shelf of Harvard Classics and all its weighty sequels.

It was the immensely influential Eliot, deeply impressed with the specialized scholarly and scientific research performed at German universities, who proclaimed in 1869, upon becoming president of Harvard, the abolition of its rigid traditional curriculum. Basic education should be performed by the high schools, Eliot declared; anyone who went on to college should be free to make his own choice among myriad elective courses. The students chose the practical. "In the end, it was the sciences that triumphed, guided by the hidden hand of capitalism and legitimated by the binding ideology of positivism," Ernest Boyer and Martin Kaplan observe in *Educating for Survival.* Before long, however, the inevitable counterrevolution against the elective system began; there was a "core" of certain things that every student must learn. Columbia established required courses in contemporary civilization; the University of Chicago and St. John's College duly followed with programs solidly based on required readings of classic texts.

St. John's, which is based in Annapolis, Md., and has a smaller campus in Santa Fe, N. Mex., is a remarkable example of an institution resolutely taking this approach. Ever since 1937, all of St. John's students (683 this fall on both campuses) have been required to read and discuss a list of 130 great books, drawn heavily from the classics and philosophy but also from the ranks of modern novelists like Faulkner and Conrad. The students must take four years of math, three of a laboratory science, two of music and two years each of Greek and French. That is just about it. This modern liberal arts version of the *trivium* and *quadrivium* includes no such novelties as psychology (except what can be learned in the works of Freud and William James) and no sociology (except perhaps Jane Austen).

St. John's is aware of the obvious criticism that its approach is "elitist" and even "irrelevant" to the real world. But President Edwin DeLattre's mild voice turns a bit sharp when he retorts, "If knowing the foundations of one's country—the foundations of one's civilization—if understanding and learning how to gain access to the engines of political and economic power in the world—if knowing how to learn in mathematics and the sciences, the languages, the humanities—if having access to the methods that have advanced civilizations since the dawn of human intelligence . . . if all those things are irrelevant, then boy, are we irrelevant!" DeLattre is a philosopher by training, and he offers one definition that has an ominous but compelling reverberation in the thermonuclear age: "Don't forget the notion of an educated person as someone who would understand how to refound his or her own civilization."

3: Education Teaches How to Think

Aristotle was one of those who could found a civilization, and while he thought of education as both a social value and an end in itself, he ascribed its chief importance to what might be considered a third basic concept of education: to train the mind to think, regardless of what it is thinking about. The key is not what it knows but how it evaluates any new fact or argument. "An educated man," Aristotle wrote in *On the Parts of Animals,* "should be able to form a fair offhand judgment as to the goodness or badness of the method used by a professor in his exposition. To be educated is in fact to be able to do this."

The Aristotelian view of education as a process has become the conventionally worthy answer today whenever college presidents and other academic leaders are asked what an education should be. An educated man, says Harvard President Bok, taking a deep breath, must have a "curiosity in exploring the unfamiliar and unexpected, an open-mindedness in entertaining opposing points of view, tolerance for the ambiguity that surrounds so many important issues, and a willingness to make the best decisions he can in the face of uncertainty and doubt . . ."

"The educated person," says University of Chicago President Hanna Holborn Gray, taking an equally deep breath, "is a person who has a respect for rationality, and who understands some of the limits of rationality as well, who has acquired independent critical intelligence, and a sense not only for the complexity of the world and different points of view but of the standards he or she would thoughtfully want to be pursuing in making judgments."

This is an approach that appears to attach more importance to the process of learning than to the substance of what is learned, but it does provide a way of coping with the vast increase of knowledge. "The old notion of the generalist who could comprehend all subjects is an impossibility, and it was even in past ages," says Chicago's Gray. "Renaissance humanism concentrated on social living and aesthetic engagement but left out most of science. To know all about today's physics, biology and mathematics, or even the general principles of all these fields, would be impossible." To make matters still more difficult, the fields of knowledge keep changing. Says Harvard's Henry Rosovsky, dean of the faculty of arts and sciences: "We can't prepare students for an explosion of knowledge because we don't know what is going to explode next. The best we can do is to make students capable of gaining new knowledge."

The old Aristotelian idea, combined with a contemporary sense of desperation about coping with the knowledge explosion, helped inspire a complete reorganization—yet again—of Harvard's curriculum. At the end of World War II, Harvard had curtailed Eliot's electives and launched a series of general education courses that were supposed to teach everyone the rudiments of science and the humanities. But by the 1960s, when rebellious students seized an administration building, that whole system had broken down. "At the moment," a saddened Dean Rosovsky later wrote to his colleagues, "to be an educated man or woman doesn't mean anything . . . The world has become a Tower of Babel."

Out of Rosovsky's unhappiness came what Harvard somewhat misleadingly calls its core curriculum. Inaugurated in 1979, after much faculty debate and amid considerable press attention, this core turned out to be a rather sprawling collection of 122 different courses, ranging from Abstraction in Modern Art to Microbial and Molecular Biology. Students are required to select eight of their 32 courses from five general areas of knowledge (science, history, the arts, ethics and foreign cultures).

Harvard's eminence exerts a wide influence, but other first-rate institutions, like Columbia, Chicago and Princeton, point out that they have taught a, more concentrated core and steadfastly continued doing so throughout the 1960s. "It makes me unhappy when people think that Harvard has done some innovative curriculum work," says Columbia College Associate Dean Michael Rosenthal (a Harvard graduate). "They have millions of courses, none of which, you could argue, represents any fundamental effort to introduce people to a kind of thinking or to a discipline."

But that is exactly what Harvard does claim to be doing. "The student should have an understanding of the major ways mankind organizes knowledge," says Rosovsky. "That is done in identifiable ways: in sciences by experiment, conducted essentially in mathematics; in social science through quantitative and historical analysis; in the humanities by studying the great traditions. We are not ignoring content but simply recognizing that because of the knowledge explosion, it makes sense to emphasize the gaining of knowledge."

If anyone objects that it is still perfectly possible to graduate from Harvard without having read a word of Shakespeare, Rosovsky is totally unfazed. Says he: "That's not necessary."

4: Education Liberates the Individual

The current trend toward required subjects—a kind of intellectual law-and-order—reflects contemporary political conservatism. It implies not only that there is a basic body of knowledge to be learned but also that there is a right way to think. It implies that a certain amount of uniformity is both socially and intellectually desirable.

Perhaps, but the excesses of the 1960s should not be used to besmirch reforms that were valuable. They too derived from a distinguished intellectual tradition. Its founding father was Jean-Jacques Rousseau, who argued in his novel *Emile* that children are not miniature adults and should not be drilled into becoming full-grown robots. "Everything is good as it comes from the hand of the Creator," said Rousseau; "everything degenerates in the hands of man."

Isolated from the corrupting world, Rousseau's young Emile was given no books but encouraged to educate himself by observing the workings of nature. Not until the age of twelve, the age of reason, was he provided with explanations in the form of astronomy or chemistry, and not until the social age of 15 was he introduced to aesthetics, religion and, eventually, female company. That was how Emile met Sophie and lived happily ever after. It is a silly tale, and yet there is considerable power to the idea that a student should be primarily educated not to hold a job or to memorize literary monuments or even to think like Aristotle, but simply to develop the potentialities of his own self—and that everyone's self is different.

While there is probably not a single university that has not retreated somewhat from the experimentation of the 1960s, and while the rhetoric of that decade is now wildly out of fashion, a few small institutions have tried to keep the faith. For them, education is, in a sense, liberation, personal liberation. At Evergreen State College in Washington, which has no course requirements of any kind and no letter grades, a college spokesman describes a class on democracy and tyranny by saying, "We will try to find out who we are, and what kind of human beings we should become." At Hampshire College, founded in Massachusetts in 1970 as a resolutely experimental school, students still design their own curriculums, take no exams and talk of changing the world. "I don't see myself as giving a body of knowledge or even 'a way of learning,'" says Physics Professor Herbert Bernstein, "but as involved in something beyond that —to help people find their own path and the fullness of who they are."

The times have not been easy for such colleges. Not only do costs keep rising, but many students now prefer conventional courses and grades that will look impressive on job applications. Antioch, which expanded into an unmanageable national network of 32 experimental institutions, stumbled to the verge of bankruptcy in the 1970s, and is drastically cutting costs to survive. But the spirit of Rousseau flickers on. Rollins, which has sometimes been dismissed as a Florida tennis school, is trying to organize a conference for such like-minded colleges as Bard, Bennington, Sarah Lawrence and Scripps on how best to pursue the goal of "making higher education more personal and developmental rather than formalistic."

Even when these enthusiasts do bend to the current pressures for law-

and-order, they tend to do it in their own dreamy way. At Bard, where President Leon Botstein decided last year that all students should attend an intensive three-week workshop on how to think and write, the students pondered such questions as the nature of justice. What color is justice? What shape is it? What sound does it make? What does it eat? "I can't think of anything," one student protested at the first such writing class. "Don't worry about it," the teacher soothingly answered. Among the students' offerings: "Justice is navy blue, it's square. It weaves in and out and backs up . . . Justice is black and white, round . . . It has the sound of the cracked Liberty Bell ringing." Workshop Director Peter Elbow's conclusion: "We're trying an experiment here, and we're not pretending that we have it under control or that we know how it works."

5: Education Teaches Morals

The U.S. Supreme Court has forbidden prayers in public schools, but many Americans cling to the idea that their educational system has a moral purpose. It is an idea common to both the Greeks and the medieval church ("O Lord my King," St. Augustine wrote in his *Confessions,* "whatsoever I speak or write, or read, or number, let all serve Thee"). In a secular age, the moral purpose of education takes secular forms: racial integration, sex education, good citizenship. At the college level, the ambiguities become more complex. Should a morally objectionable person be allowed to teach? (Not Timothy Leary, said Harvard.) Should a morally objectionable doctrine be permitted? (Not Arthur Jensen's claims of racial differences in intelligence, said student protesters at Berkeley.)

Many people are understandably dismayed by such censorship. But would they prefer ethical neutrality? Should engineers be trained to build highways without being taught any concern for the homes they displace? Should prospective corporate managers learn how to increase profits regardless of pollution or unemployment? Just the opposite, according to *Beyond the Ivory Tower,* a new book by Harvard's Bok, which calls for increased emphasis on "applied ethics." (Writes Bok: "A university that refuses to take ethical dilemmas seriously violates its basic obligations to society.")

Religious colleges have always practiced a similar preaching. But some 500 schools now offer courses in the field. The Government supports such studies with a program known as EVIST, which stands for Ethics and Values in Science and Technology (and which sounds as though a computer had already taken charge of the matter). "The modern university is rooted in the scientific method, having essentially turned its back on religion," says Steven Muller, president of Johns Hopkins. "The scientific method is a marvelous means of inquiry, but it really doesn't provide a value system. The biggest failing in higher education today is that we fall short in exposing students to values."

Charles Muscatine, a professor of English at Berkeley and member of a committee that is analyzing liberal arts curriculums for the Association of American Colleges, is even harsher. He calls today's educational programs "a marvelous convenience for a mediocre society." The key goal of education, says Muscatine, should be "informed decision making that recognizes there is a moral and ethical component to life." Instead, he says, most universities are "propagating the dangerous myth that technical skills are more important than ethical reasoning."

Psychiatrist Robert Coles, who teaches at both Harvard and Duke, is still more emphatic in summing up the need: "Reading, writing and arithmetic. That's what we've got to start with, and all that implies, at every level. If people can't use good, strong language, they can't think clearly, and if they haven't been trained to use good, strong language, they become vulnerable to all the junk that comes their way. They should be taught philosophy, moral philosophy and theology. They ought to be asked to think about moral issues, especially about what use is going to be made of knowledge, and why—a kind of moral reflection that I think has been supplanted by a more technological education. Replacing moral philosophy with psychology has been a disaster, an absolute disaster!"

Each of these five ways to wisdom has its strengths and weaknesses, of course. The idea that education provides better jobs promises practical rewards for both the student and the society that trains him, but it can leave him undernourished in the possibilities of life away from work. The idea that education means the acquisition of a cultural heritage does give the student some grasp of that heritage, but it can also turn into glib superficialities or sterile erudition. The idea that education consists mainly of training the mind does provide a method for further education, but it can also make method seem more important than knowledge. So can the idea that education is a form of self-development. And the teaching of ethics can unfortunately become a teaching of conventional pieties.

To define is to limit, as we all learned in school, and to categorize is to oversimplify. To some extent, the five ways to wisdom all overlap and blend, and though every educator has his own sense of priorities, none would admit that he does not aspire to all five goals. Thus the student who has mastered the riches of Western civilization has probably also learned to think for himself and to see the moral purposes of life. And surely such a paragon can find a good job even in the recession of 1982.

Are there specific ways to come nearer to achieving these goals? The most obvious is money. Good teachers cost money; libraries cost money; so do remedial classes for those who were short-changed in earlier years. Only mediocrity comes cheap. Those who groan at the rising price of college tuition (up as much as $7,000 since 1972) may not realize that overall, taking enrollment growth into account, college budgets have just barely kept up with inflation. Indeed, adjusted for inflation, four years of college today costs less than a decade ago, and faculty salaries in real dollars declined about 20% during the 1970s. Crocodile tears over the cost of higher education come in waves from the Federal Government, which has so far held spending to roughly 1981 levels, and proposes deep cuts (*e.g.*, nearly 40% in basic grants) by 1985. This is an economy comparable to skimping on the maintenance of an expensive machine.

But money alone will not solve all problems, as is often said, and this is particularly true in the field of education. If improving the quality of American education is a matter of urgent national concern—and it should be—then what is required besides more dollars is more sense: a widespread rededication to a number of obvious but somewhat neglected principles. That probing research and hard thinking be demanded of students (and of teachers too). That academic results be tested and measured. That intellectual excellence be not just acknowledged but rewarded.

These principles admittedly did serve the system that educated primarily those few who were born into the governing classes, but the fact that elitist education once supported elitist politics does not mean that egalitarian politics requires egalitarian education. Neither minds nor ideas are all the same.

All that the schools can be asked to promise is that everyone will be educated to the limit of his capacities. Exactly what this means, everyone must discover for himself. At the community college minimum, it may have to mean teaching basic skills, at least until the weakened high schools begin doing their job properly, as Philosopher Mortimer Adler urges in his new *Paideia Proposal.* This calls for a standardized high school curriculum in three categories: fundamental knowledge such as history, science and arts; basic skills such as reading and mathematical computation; and critical understanding of ideas and values. These essentials must really be taught, not just certified with a passing grade. Beyond such practical benefits, though, and beyond the benefits that come from exercising the muscles of the mind, higher education must ultimately serve the higher purpose of perpetuating whatever it is in civilization that is worth perpetuating. Or as Ezra Pound once said of the craft that he later betrayed, "The function of literature is precisely that it does incite humanity to continue living."

This is the core of the core idea, and surely it is by now indisputable that every college student improves by learning the fundamentals of science, literature, art, history. Harvard's Rosovsky may be right in suggesting that it is "not necessary" to have read Shakespeare as part of the process of learning how to think, but he is probably wrong. Not because anyone really *needs* to have shared in Lear's howling rage or because anyone can earn a better salary from having heard Macbeth declaim "Tomorrow and tomorrow and tomorrow . . ." But he is enriched by knowing these things, impoverished by not knowing them. And *The Marriage of Figaro* enriches. *The Cherry Orchard* enriches. *The City of*

God enriches. So does a mastery of Greek, or of subnuclear particles, or of Gödel's theorem.

In a sense, there really is no core, except as a series of arbitrary choices, for there is no limit to the possibilities of learning. There are times when these possibilities seem overwhelming, and one hears echoes of Socrates' confession, "All I know is that I know nothing." Yet that too is a challenge. "We shall not cease from exploration," as T.S. Eliot put it, "and the end of all our exploring / Will be to arrive where we started / And know the place for the first time." The seemingly momentous years of schooling, then, are only the beginning.

Henry Adams, who said in *The Education of Henry Adams* that Harvard "taught little, and that little ill," was 37 when he took up the study of Saxon legal codes and 42 when he first turned to writing the history of the Jefferson and Madison Administrations, and 49 when he laboriously began on Chinese. In his 50s, a tiny, wiry figure with a graying beard, the future master of Gothic architecture solemnly learned to ride a bicycle.

On Right and Wrong

Dick Gregory's recollection of shame at a boyhood experience—"I waited too long to help another man"—raises in a small and quiet way an age-old issue that has become more pressing than ever in recent decades. The brutality or callousness of ordinary people who "do their duty" or mind their own business or, perhaps even more disturbing, simply follow instructions raises troubling thoughts for most of us. Could you and I do this? Would we? Moral choices, finally, are always personal.

George Orwell's essay confronts some of the complex questions of responsibility and of the relation between victim and victimizer. His essay, too, deals with shame, although from a perspective somewhat different from Gregory's. How often, the reader might ask, do we do what we do in order to avoid looking the fool?

The next essay, by William Nichols, confronts the issue of individual conscience versus obedience to orders, here particularly disturbing because the individual involvement is both temporary and voluntary. He describes the controversial Milgram experiment, which seems to confirm that, for most of us, the impulse to obey orders is stronger than the need to obey conscience. But Nichols' main concern is that we should pay more attention than the experiment did to the minority who are capable of resisting coercion. Hannah Arendt, in the selection that follows, recounts some of the testimony during the trial of Adolf Eichmann, convicted and executed in Jerusalem for war crimes committed while he was a high Nazi official. Like Nichols, she is interested in the few who resist, stressing how great a difference it makes that "under conditions of terror most people will comply but *some people will not.*" It is these few who ensure the continuity of humaneness on earth. Camus' story expresses in fictional terms the solitude of moral choice and also its sometimes unpredictable consequences.

The last two writers bring the question of right and wrong into a more public realm, and recent instances of deception in American government and business may serve as a testing ground for their ideas. Is it ever right to lie for the public good? Macchiavelli argues that it is because the end justifies the means. "A prince," he says, "needs to be a great feigner and dissembler." Philosopher Sissela Bok disagrees and carefully builds a case for the idea that "deceiving the people for the sake of the people is a self-contradictory notion in a democracy."

The Personal Dilemma

Dick Gregory

Dick Gregory has lived many roles—among them slum kid, athlete, comedian, and political activist. Born in St. Louis in 1932, he set records for running the mile and half-mile in high school and again at Southern Illinois University, where he was named outstanding athlete in 1953. After two years in the army, he began working night clubs around Chicago and by 1959 was the regular master of ceremonies at a show club. He went on to television, records, and books, shaping his comedy act in sympathy with the civil rights movement of the early sixties and then with the antiwar movement. After many arrests in political confrontations, he ran for President of the United States as the candidate of the Peace and Freedom party in 1968. Fasting, and its accompanying publicity, became his favorite form of political protest. In 1978 he received the Ebony-Topaz Heritage and Freedom Award.

Gregory now works and lives in Chicago with his wife and ten children. His books include *From the Back of the Bus* (1962), *No More Lies: The Myth and Reality of American History* (1971), *Dick Gregory's Political Primer* (1972), an autobiography, *Nigger,* written with Robert Lipsyte (1964), and *Up from Nigger* (1976). The following selection comes from a chapter in *Nigger* entitled "Not Poor, Just Broke."

Shame

. . .

I never learned hate at home, or shame. I had to go to school for that. I was about seven years old when I got my first big lesson. I was in love with a little girl named Helene Tucker, a light-complected little girl with pigtails and nice manners. She was always clean and she was smart in school. I think I went to school then mostly to look at her. I brushed my hair and even got me a little old handkerchief. It was a lady's handkerchief, but I didn't want Helene to see me wipe my nose on my hand. The pipes were frozen again, there was no water in the house, but I washed my socks and shirt every night. I'd get a pot, and go over to Mister Ben's grocery store, and stick my pot down into his soda machine. Scoop out some chopped ice. By evening the ice melted to water for washing. I got sick a lot that winter because the fire would go out at night before the clothes were dry. In the morning I'd put them on, wet or dry, because they were the only clothes I had.

Everybody's got a Helene Tucker, a symbol of everything you want. I loved her for her goodness, her cleanness, her popularity. She'd walk down my street and my brothers and sisters would yell. "Here comes Helene," and I'd rub my tennis sneakers on the back of my pants and wish my hair wasn't so nappy and the white folks' shirt fit me better. I'd run out on the street. If I knew my place and didn't come too close, she'd wink at me and say hello. That was a good feeling. Sometimes I'd follow her all the way home, and shovel the snow off her walk and try to make friends with her Momma and her aunts. I'd drop money on her stoop late at night on my way back from shining shoes in the taverns. And she had a Daddy, and he had a good job. He was a paper hanger.

I guess I would have gotten over Helene by summertime, but something happened in that classroom that made her face hang in front of me for the next twenty-two years. When I played the drums in high school it was for Helene and when I broke track records in college it was for Helene and when I started standing behind microphones and heard applause I wished Helene could hear it, too. It wasn't until I was twenty-nine years old and married and making money that I finally got her out of my system. Helene was sitting in that classroom when I learned to be ashamed of myself.

It was on a Thursday. I was sitting in the back of the room, in a seat with a chalk circle drawn around it. The idiot's seat, the troublemaker's seat.

The teacher thought I was stupid. Couldn't spell, couldn't read, couldn't do arithmetic. Just stupid. Teachers were never interested in finding out that you couldn't concentrate because you were so hungry, because you hadn't had any breakfast. All you could think about was noontime, would it ever come? Maybe you could sneak into the cloakroom and steal a bite of some kid's lunch out of a coat pocket. A bite of something. Paste. You can't really make a meal of paste, or put it on bread for a sandwich, but sometimes I'd scoop a few spoonfuls out of the paste jar in the back of the room. Pregnant people get strange tastes. I was pregnant with poverty. Pregnant with dirt and pregnant with smells that made people turn away, pregnant with cold and pregnant with shoes that were never bought for me, pregnant with five other people in my bed and no Daddy in the next room, and pregnant with hunger. Paste doesn't taste too bad when you're hungry.

The teacher thought I was a troublemaker. All she saw from the front of the room was a little black boy who squirmed in his idiot's seat and made noises and poked the kids around him. I guess she couldn't see a kid who made noises because he wanted someone to know he was there.

It was on a Thursday, the day before the Negro payday. The eagle always flew on Friday. The teacher was asking each student how much his father would give to the Community Chest. On Friday night, each kid would get the money from his father, and on Monday he would bring it to the school. I decided I was going to buy me a Daddy right then. I had money in my pocket from shining shoes and selling papers, and whatever Helene Tucker pledged for her Daddy I was going to top it. And I'd hand the money right in. I wasn't going to wait until Monday to buy me a Daddy.

I was shaking, scared to death. The teacher opened her book and started calling out names alphabetically.

"Helene Tucker?"

"My Daddy said he'd give two dollars and fifty cents."

"That's very nice, Helene. Very, very nice indeed."

That made me feel pretty good. It wouldn't take too much to top that. I had almost three dollars in dimes and quarters in my pocket. I stuck my hand in my pocket and held onto the money, waiting for her to call my name. But the teacher closed her book after she called everybody else in the class.

I stood up and raised my hand.

"What is it now?"

"You forgot me."

She turned toward the blackboard. "I don't have time to be playing with you, Richard."

"My Daddy said he'd . . ."

"Sit down, Richard, you're disturbing the class."

"My Daddy said he'd give . . . fifteen dollars."

She turned around and looked mad. "We are collecting this money for you and your kind, Richard Gregory. If your Daddy can give fifteen dollars you have no business being on relief."

"I got it right now, I got it right now, my Daddy gave it to me to turn in today, my Daddy said . . ."

"And furthermore," she said, looking right at me, her nostrils getting big and her lips getting thin and her eyes opening wide, "we know you don't have a Daddy."

Helene Tucker turned around, her eyes full of tears. She felt sorry for me. Then I couldn't see her too well because I was crying, too.

"Sit down, Richard."

And I always thought the teacher kind of liked me. She always picked me to wash the blackboard on Friday, after school. That was a big thrill, it made me feel important. If I didn't wash it, come Monday the school might not function right.

"Where are you going, Richard?"

I walked out of school that day, and for a long time I didn't go back very often. There was shame there.

Now there was shame everywhere. It seemed like the whole world had been inside that classroom, everyone had heard what the teacher had said, everyone had turned around and felt sorry for me. There was shame in going to the Worthy Boys Annual Christmas Dinner for you and your kind, because everybody knew what a worthy boy was. Why couldn't they just call it the Boys Annual Dinner, why'd they have to give it a name? There was shame in wearing the brown and orange and white plaid mackinaw the welfare gave to 3,000 boys. Why'd it have to be the same for everybody so when you walked down the street the people could see you were on relief? It was a nice warm mackinaw and it had a hood, and my Momma beat me and called me a little rat when she found out I stuffed it in the bottom of a pail full of garbage way over on Cottage Street. There was shame in running over to Mister Ben's at the end of the day and asking for his rotten peaches, there was shame in asking Mrs. Simmons for a spoonful of sugar, there was shame in running out to meet the relief truck. I hated that truck, full of food for you and your kind. I ran into the house and hid when it came. And then I started to sneak through alleys, to take the long way home so the people going into White's Eat Shop wouldn't see me. Yeah, the whole world heard the teacher that day, we all know you don't have a Daddy.

It lasted for a while, this kind of numbness. I spent a lot of time feeling sorry for myself. And then one day I met this wino in a restaurant. I'd been out hustling all day, shining shoes, selling newspapers, and I had goo-gobs of money in my pocket. Bought me a bowl of chili for fifteen cents, and a cheeseburger for fifteen cents, and a Pepsi for five cents, and a piece of chocolate cake for ten cents. That was a good meal. I was eating when this old wino came in. I love winos because they never hurt anyone but themselves.

The old wino sat down at the counter and ordered twenty-six cents worth of food. He ate it like he really enjoyed it. When the owner, Mister Williams, asked him to pay the check, the old wino didn't lie or go through his pocket like he suddenly found a hole.

He just said: "Don't have no money."

The owner yelled: "Why in hell you come in here and eat my food if you don't have no money? That food cost me money."

Mister Williams jumped over the counter and knocked the wino off his stool and beat him over the head with a pop bottle. Then he stepped back and watched the wino bleed. Then he kicked him. And he kicked him again.

I looked at the wino with blood all over his face and I went over. "Leave him alone, Mister Williams. I'll pay the twenty-six cents."

The wino got up, slowly, pulling himself up to the stool, then up to the counter, holding on for a minute until his legs stopped shaking so bad. He looked at me with pure hate. "Keep your twenty-six cents. You don't have to pay, not now. I just finished paying for it."

He started to walk out, and as he passed me, he reached down and touched my shoulder. "Thanks, sonny, but it's too late now. Why didn't you pay it before?"

I was pretty sick about that. I waited too long to help another man.

George Orwell

"Shooting an Elephant," which is based on George Orwell's experiences in the Imperial Police in Burma, was written in the early 1930s and is the title essay in the collection *Shooting an Elephant and Other Essays* (1950). The narrative reflects his conviction that ideas are derived from experience, and that experience is best conveyed in concrete and specific terms. He seems to be warning us of what can happen when what we say, do, think, and feel become disconnected from each other. (For further biographical information on Orwell, see page 97.)

Shooting an Elephant

In Moulmein, in Lower Burma, I was hated by large numbers of people —the only time in my life that I have been important enough for this to happen to me. I was sub-divisional police officer of the town, and in an aimless, petty kind of way anti-European feeling was very bitter. No one had the guts to raise a riot, but if a European woman went through the bazaars alone somebody would probably spit betel juice over her dress. As a police officer I was an obvious target and was baited whenever it seemed safe to do so. When a nimble Burman tripped me up on the football field and the referee (another Burman) looked the other way, the crowd yelled with hideous laughter. This happened more than once. In the end the sneering yellow faces of young men that met me everywhere, the insults hooted after me when I was at a safe distance, got badly on my nerves. The young Buddhist priests were the worst of all. There were several thousands of them in the town and none of them seemed to have anything to do except stand on street corners and jeer at Europeans.

All this was perplexing and upsetting. For at that time I had already made up my mind that imperialism was an evil thing and the sooner I chucked up my job and got out of it the better. Theoretically—and secretly, of course—I was all for the Burmese and all against their oppressors, the British. As for the job I was doing, I hated it more bitterly than I can perhaps make clear. In a job like that you see the dirty work of Empire at close quarters. The wretched prisoners huddling in the stinking cages of the lock-ups, the grey, cowed faces of the long-term convicts, the scarred buttocks of the men who had been flogged with bamboos—all these oppressed me with an intolerable sense of guilt. But I could get nothing into perspective. I was young and ill-educated and I had had to think out my problems in the utter silence that is imposed on every Englishman in the East. I did not even know that the British Empire is dying, still less did I know that it is a great deal better than the younger empires that are going to supplant it. All I knew was that I was stuck between my hatred of the empire I served and my rage against the evil-spirited little beasts who tried to make my job impossible. With one part of my mind I thought of the British Raj as an unbreakable tyranny, as something clamped down, in *saecula saeculorum,*⁰ upon the will of prostrate peoples; with another part I thought that the greatest joy in the world would be to drive a bayonet into a Buddhist priest's guts. Feelings like these are the normal by-products of imperialism; ask any Anglo-Indian official, if you can catch him off duty.

One day something happened which in a roundabout way was enlightening. It was a tiny incident in itself, but it gave me a better glimpse than I had had before of the real nature of imperialism—the real motives for which despotic governments act. Early one morning the sub-inspector at a police station the other end of town rang me up on the 'phone and said that an elephant was ravaging the bazaar. Would I please come and do something about it? I did not know what I could do, but I wanted to see what was happening and I got on to a pony and started out. I took my rifle, an old .44 Winchester and much too small to kill an elephant, but I thought the noise might be useful *in terrorem.* Various Burmans stopped me on the way and told me about the elephant's doings. It was not, of course, a wild elephant, but a tame one which had gone "must." It had been chained up, as tame elephants always are when their attack of "must" is due, but on the previous night it had broken its chain and escaped. Its mahout, the only person who could manage it when it was in that state, had set out in pursuit, but had taken the wrong direction and was now twelve hours'

in *saecula saeculorum*   for ever and ever (Latin).

journey away, and in the morning the elephant had suddenly reappeared in the town. The Burmese population had no weapons and were quite helpless against it. It had already destroyed somebody's bamboo hut, killed a cow and raided some fruit-stalls and devoured the stock; also it had met the municipal rubbish van and, when the driver jumped out and took to his heels, had turned the van over and inflicted violences upon it.

The Burmese sub-inspector and some Indian constables were waiting for me in the quarter where the elephant had been seen. It was a very poor quarter, a labyrinth of squalid bamboo huts, thatched with palm-leaf, winding all over a steep hillside. I remember that it was a cloudy, stuffy morning at the beginning of the rains. We began questioning the people as to where the elephant had gone and, as usual, failed to get any definite information. That is invariably the case in the East; a story always sounds clear enough at a distance, but the nearer you get to the scene of events the vaguer it becomes. Some of the people said that the elephant had gone in one direction, some said that he had gone in another, some professed not even to have heard of any elephant. I had almost made up my mind that the whole story was a pack of lies, when we heard yells a little distance away. There was a loud, scandalized cry of "Go away, child! Go away this instant!" and an old woman with a switch in her hand came around the corner of a hut, violently shooing away a crowd of naked children. Some more women followed, clicking their tongues and exclaiming; evidently there was something that the children ought not to have seen. I rounded the hut and saw a man's dead body sprawling in the mud. He was an Indian, a black Dravidian coolie, almost naked, and he could not have been dead many minutes. The people said that the elephant had come suddenly upon him round the corner of the hut, caught him with its trunk, put its foot on his back and ground him into the earth. This was the rainy season and the ground was soft, and his face had scored a trench a foot deep and a couple of yards long. He was lying on his belly with arms crucified and head sharply twisted to one side. His face was coated with mud, the eyes wide open, the teeth bared and grinning with an expression of unendurable agony. (Never tell me, by the way, that the dead look peaceful. Most of the corpses I have seen looked devilish.) The friction of the great beast's foot had stripped the skin from his back as neatly as one skins a rabbit. As soon as I saw the dead man I sent an orderly to a friend's house nearby to borrow an elephant rifle. I had already sent back the pony, not wanting it to go mad with fright and throw me if it smelt the elephant.

The orderly came back in a few minutes with a rifle and five cartridges, and meanwhile some Burmans had arrived and told us that the elephant was in the paddy fields below, only a few hundred yards away. As I started forward practically the whole population of the quarter flocked out of the houses and followed me. They had seen the rifle and were all shouting excitedly that I was going to shoot the elephant. They had not shown much interest in the elephant when he was merely ravaging their homes, but it was different now that he was going to be shot. It was a bit of fun to them, as it would be to an English crowd; besides they wanted the meat. It made me vaguely uneasy. I had no intention of shooting the elephant—I had merely sent for the rifle to defend myself if necessary—and it is always unnerving to have a crowd following you. I marched down the hill, looking and feeling a fool, with the rifle over my shoulder and an ever-growing army of people jostling at my heels. At the bottom, when you got away from the huts, there was a metalled road and beyond that a miry waste of paddy fields a thousand yards across, not yet ploughed but soggy from the first rains and dotted with coarse grass. The elephant was standing eight yards from the road, his left side towards us. He took not the slightest notice of the crowd's approach. He was tearing up bunches of grass, beating them against his knees to clean them and stuffing them into his mouth.

I had halted on the road. As soon as I saw the elephant I knew with perfect certainty that I ought not to shoot him. It is a serious matter to shoot a working elephant—it is comparable to destroying a huge and costly piece of machinery—and obviously one ought not to do it if it can possibly be avoided. And at that distance, peacefully eating, the elephant looked no more dangerous than a cow. I thought then and I think now that his attack of "must" was already passing off; in which case he would merely wander harmlessly about until the mahout came back and caught him. Moreover, I did not in the least want to shoot him. I decided that I would watch him for a little while to make sure that he did not turn savage again, and then go home.

But at that moment I glanced round at the crowd that had followed me. It was an immense crowd, two thousand at the least and growing every minute. It blocked the road for a long distance on either side. I looked at the sea of yellow faces above the garish clothes—faces all happy and excited over this bit of fun, all certain that the elephant was going to be shot. They were watching me as they would watch a conjurer about to perform a trick. They did not like me, but with the magical rifle in my hands I was momentarily worth watching. And suddenly I realized that I should have to shoot the elephant after all. The people expected it of me and I had to do it; I could feel their two thousand wills pressing me forward, irresistibly. And it was at this moment, as I stood there with the rifle in my hands, that I first grasped the hollowness, the futility of the white man's dominion in the East. Here was I, the white man with his gun, standing in front of the unarmed native crowd—seemingly the leading actor of the piece; but in reality I was only an absurd puppet pushed to and fro by the will of those yellow faces behind. I perceived in this moment that when the white man turns tyrant it is his own freedom that he destroys. He becomes a sort of hollow, posing dummy, the conventionalized figure of a sahib. For it is the condition of his rule that he shall spend his life in trying to impress the "natives," and so in every crisis he has got to do what the "natives" expect of him. He wears a mask, and his face grows to fit it. I had got to shoot the elephant. I had committed myself to doing it when I sent for the rifle. A sahib has got to act like a sahib; he has got to appear resolute, to know his own mind and do definite things. To come all that way, rifle in hand, with two thousand people marching at my heels, and then to trail feebly away, having done nothing—no, that was impossible. The crowd would laugh at me. And my whole life, every white man's life in the East, was one long struggle not to be laughed at.

But I did not want to shoot the elephant. I watched him beating his bunch of grass against his knees, with that preoccupied grandmotherly air that elephants have. It seemed to me that it would be murder to shoot him. At that age I was not squeamish about killing animals, but I had never shot an elephant and never wanted to. (Somehow it always seems worse to kill a *large* animal.) Besides, there was the beast's owner to be considered. Alive, the elephant was worth at least a hundred pounds; dead, he would only be worth the value of his tusks, five pounds, possibly. But I had got to act quickly. I turned to some experienced-looking Burmans who had been there when we arrived, and asked them how the elephant had been behaving. They all said the same thing: he took no notice of you if you left him alone, but he might charge if you went too close to him.

It was perfectly clear to me what I ought to do. I ought to walk up to within, say, twenty-five yards of the elephant and test his behavior. If he charged, I could shoot; if he took no notice of me, it would be safe to leave him until the mahout came back. But also I knew that I was going to do no such thing. I was a poor shot with a rifle and the ground was soft mud into which one would sink at every step. If the elephant charged and I missed him, I should have about as much chance as a toad under a steam-roller. But even then I was not thinking particularly of my own skin, only of the watchful yellow faces behind. For at that moment, with the crowd watching me, I was not afraid in the ordinary sense, as I would have been if I had been alone. A white man mustn't be frightened in front of "natives"; and so, in general, he isn't frightened. The sole thought in my mind was that if anything went wrong those two thousand Burmans would see me pursued, caught, trampled on and reduced to a grinning corpse like that Indian up the hill. And if that happened it was quite probable that some of them would laugh. That would never do. There was only one alternative. I shoved the cartridges into the magazine and lay down on the road to get a better aim.

The crowd grew very still, and a deep, low, happy sigh, as of people who see the theatre curtain go up at last, breathed from innumerable throats. They were going to have their bit of fun after all. The rifle was a beautiful German thing with cross-hair sights. I did not then know that in shooting an elephant one would shoot to cut an imaginary bar running from ear-hole to ear-hole. I ought, therefore, as the elephant was sideways on, to have aimed straight at his ear-hole; actually I aimed several inches in front of this, thinking the brain would be further forward.

When I pulled the trigger I did not hear the bang or feel the kick—one never does when a shot goes home—but I heard the devilish roar of glee that went up from the crowd. In that instant, in too short a time, one would have thought, even for the bullet to get there, a mysterious, terrible change had come over the elephant. He neither stirred nor fell, but every line of his body had altered. He looked suddenly stricken, shrunken, immensely old, as though the frightful impact of the bullet had paralysed him without knocking him down. At last, after what seemed a long time—it might have been five seconds, I dare say—he sagged flabbily to his knees. His mouth slobbered. An enormous senility seemed to have settled upon him. One could have imagined him thousands of years old. I fired again into the same spot. At the second shot he did not collapse but climbed with desperate slowness to his feet and stood weakly upright, with legs sagging and head drooping. I fired a third time. That was the shot that did for him. You could see the agony of it jolt his whole body and knock the last remnant of strength from his legs. But in falling he seemed for a moment to rise, for as his hind legs collapsed beneath him he seemed to tower upward like a huge rock toppling, his trunk reaching skywards like a tree. He trumpeted, for the first and only time. And then down he came, his belly towards me, with a crash that seemed to shake the ground even where I lay.

I got up. The Burmans were already racing past me across the mud. It was obvious that the elephant would never rise again, but he was not dead. He was breathing very rhythmically with long rattling gasps, his great mound of a side painfully rising and falling. His mouth was wide open—I could see far down into caverns of pale pink throat. I waited a long time for him to die, but his breathing did not weaken. Finally I fired my two remaining shots into the spot where I thought his heart must be. The thick blood welled out of him like red velvet, but still he did not die. His body did not even jerk when the shots hit him, the tortured breathing continued without a pause. He was dying, very slowly and in great agony, but in some world remote from me where not even a bullet could damage him further. I felt that I had got to put an end to that dreadful noise. It seemed dreadful to see the great beast lying there, powerless to move and yet powerless to die, and not even to be able to finish him. I sent back for my small rifle and poured shot after shot into his heart and down his throat. They seemed to make no impression. The tortured gasps continued as steadily as the ticking of a clock.

In the end I could not stand it any longer and went away. I heard later that it took him half an hour to die. Burmans were bringing dahs and baskets even before I left, and I was told they had stripped his body almost to the bones by the afternoon.

Afterwards, of course, there were endless discussions about the shooting of the elephant. The owner was furious, but he was only an Indian and could do nothing. Besides, legally I had done the right thing, for a mad elephant has to be killed, like a mad dog, if its owner fails to control it. Among the Europeans opinion was divided. The older men said I was right, the younger men said it was a damn shame to shoot an elephant for killing a coolie, because an elephant was worth more than any damn Coringhee coolie. And afterwards I was very glad that the coolie had been killed; it put me legally in the right and it gave me a sufficient pretext for shooting the elephant. I often wondered whether any of the others grasped that I had done it solely to avoid looking a fool.

William Nichols

William Nichols was born in San Francisco in 1938 and grew up in Portland, Oregon. He received his Ph.D. from the University of Missouri and is Professor of English at Denison University. Much of his writing has focused on Afro-American literature and history and, more recently, on the impact of technology on American life. He has also edited a textbook on autobiographical writing, *Writing from Experience* (1975), which includes the original essay reprinted here. The essay is an analysis of Stanley Milgram's now famous Yale experiment, but it takes off unabashedly from Nichols's own experience—in this case, his anger and disappointment at what he read in the book describing this experiment. He speaks here not as an expert or even as an objective analyst, but rather as a feeling and thinking man.

The Burden of Imagination: Stanley Milgram's Obedience to Authority

It was a classic case of seeing the movie, then wanting to read the book. Students in a class I taught at Denison University in the fall of 1972 told me I ought to see the film "Obedience," which presents highlights of a social psychology experiment run by Stanley Milgram at Yale University from 1960 to 1963. The images are already hazy, but I remember seeing confused, nervous individuals who thought they were teaching others with the help of electric shocks, and I can hear the sharp commands of a gray-coated psychologist as they echoed in a barren laboratory. Vaguely, I recall the ending, a voice comparing the lessons to be drawn from the experiments with those of the Nazi concentration camps, where people submitted to authority and committed some of the most appalling atrocities in human history.

That ending drew a moral from the experiments, but it seemed forced somehow, as though the music were swelling to conclude a second-rate Hollywood film in which nothing, absolutely nothing, has been resolved. Unless you can give yourself up to the music or the moralizing, such an ending will always leave you dissatisfied; and I left "Obedience" feeling the need to know much more about those frightening experiments at Yale. So I was more than a little eager to read Stanley Milgram's book on the experiments, *Obedience to Authority,* when it appeared in early 1974.

Normally, I am pretty much immune to the comments appearing on dust jackets of new books, but I must confess that the compliments traced in modestly small type on the back of *Obedience to Authority* caught my eye. Jerome S. Bruner of Oxford University said the book would put Milgram "firmly in the front rank of social scientists in this generation," and Roger Brown of Harvard University promised that "it qualifies as literature as well as science." The latter claim had particular attraction because I believe there are works in the social sciences that deserve to be read with the careful attention often saved for fine imaginative literature.

Obedience to Authority is a powerful book, but I experienced raging disappointment as I read it. Before attempting to account for that reaction, however, I must say more about the experiments on which the book is built. There were many variations, but the basic experiment is the key. A person who has answered an advertisement—"WE WILL PAY $4.00 FOR ONE HOUR OF YOUR TIME"—comes to a laboratory to participate, he believes, in a study of memory and learning. He is told he will function as "teacher" in the experiment, and he meets the *experimenter,* who assumes the role of authority, and the *learner.* The teacher, who is really the subject of the experiment, assists the experimenter in strapping the learner's arms to a chair to prevent excessive movement. Teacher and experimenter then move into another room, where the teacher is introduced to a shock generator, which includes a battery of thirty switches that move in 15 volt increments from 15 to 450 volts. The teacher is instructed to administer a learning test to the man in the other room, giving the learner a shock each time he answers incorrectly and increasing the voltage with each wrong answer.

But the teacher is not actually giving a shock at all. The learner is a trained participant, and he gives incorrect answers, registers pain, and ultimately refuses to participate in a way calculated to make the teacher believe he is injuring, perhaps even killing, the learner. The central question in each performance of the experiment is this: When will the teacher-subject rebel against authority and refuse to inflict more shocks on the learner? The depressing answer is that in this basic version of the experiment, with the experimenter giving strong admonitions to continue and assurances of "no permanent tissue damage," sixty-five percent of the teachers never disobey. Many of them are willing to give three shocks of 450 volts, a level that is marked DANGER—SEVERE SHOCK on the control panel of the generator, before the process is halted by the experimenter. In reproductions of this experiment elsewhere to check the Yale results there have been even higher percentages of obedient teachers.

Let me admit that by the time I read *Obedience to Authority,* I was skeptical as well as fascinated. Both a section of the book that appeared in *Harper's* and a review by Steven Marcus in the *New York Times* put me on my guard. But once I began to read Milgram's book, on a rainy day in March, I did not put it down except briefly; and because I was in the midst of the delightful freedom of a sabbatical leave and in the seclusion of a beach cottage on the Oregon shore, I was able to read the book through without a hitch. That evening I tyrannized my wife and children as I had not done in months, and that is just the first thing I will blame on *Obedience to Authority.*

My petty tyrannies were not experiments in wielding authority. I was simply irascible, disturbed momentarily by the vision of *Obedience to Authority.* It is a compelling book, put together with elegant simplicity to prove something Milgram states quite baldly at the beginning: "This is, perhaps, the most fundamental lesson of our study: ordinary people, simply doing their jobs, and without any particular hostility on their part, can become agents in a terrible destructive process." It is difficult to overstate the economy and force with which *Obedience to Authority* makes that point. Variations in the experiment were designed to anticipate nearly every question I could imagine. Would women match men in brutal deference to authority? Yes. Can the authority of the experimenter be wielded as powerfully on the telephone as in person? No. Will participation in a disobedient group encourage disobedience? Yes. Given the choice, will people increase the voltage? No. Imagine a question you can frame in a sentence like one of those, and the chances are good that it is implicit in one of the experimental variations worked out by Milgram. It is no surprise, then, when Milgram writes at the end of the book about the inevitability that men will abandon their humanity when their individual personalities are merged with larger institutional structures. And it is then just a step to this mild one-sentence paragraph: "This is the fatal flaw nature has designed into us, and which in the long run gives our species only a modest chance of survival."

It has taken me a while to remember where I last found such quietly understated fatalism, but now I know—in the fiction of Kurt Vonnegut, Jr. In a style even more elegantly simple than Milgram's, Vonnegut creates imaginary worlds of sharply limited human possibility. His characters are simply "listless playthings of enormous forces," as he says in *Slaughter-House Five.* His vision, like Milgram's, is of a world where men ultimately have no hand in shaping their own destinies.

For both Milgram and Vonnegut, I believe this cold and quiet fatalism is a product of fear. Neither of them embraces eagerly a view that denies men freedom and dignity, but both men might be compared to a producer of horror films who lives in constant terror of the limited world he creates. For Vonnegut and Milgram have imagined distinctly limited worlds.

In the narrow margins of their portraits of human possibility I find evidence of failed imagination. In Vonnegut's novel *Breakfast of Champions,* for example, we are allowed to know just a little about Kilgore Trout, a science-fiction writer who appears in other Vonnegut fiction, and Dwayne Hoover, a Pontiac dealer whose life is destined to intersect violently with Trout's by the end of the novel. The rest of the characters in *Breakfast of Champions* are barely identified atoms bouncing helplessly about in the narrative space. And Vonnegut seems to be offering an explanation for the book's lack of fully developed characters when he describes a figure in one of Trout's stories who returns a long "realistic" novel to the library after reading only sixty pages. He explains to the librarian: "I already know about human beings." That assertion is compounded more of fear than of arrogance, as I have said, but it is the key to the horrifying flatness in Vonnegut's art: Vonnegut, like Milgram, thinks he knows what makes us do the brutal, terrifying things that have disfigured human history; and such knowledge is bad news indeed. But one source of great imaginative literature is surely the recognition that we do not know very much about human beings at all; to think we do is to surrender the mystery at the center of all art. More even than that, to assume we understand the limits of human possibility is to accept as inevitable the alienation, injustice, and violence that threaten civilization.

Milgram nowhere explains the source of man's "modest chance" to survive, and I think it is fair to assume his vision is as bleak as Vonnegut's. Heaven knows, the "characters" in *Obedience to Authority* are flatter than New England witches pressed beneath Puritan barn doors. Take, for example, a teacher-subject in one of Milgram's most terrifying experimental variations: a situation in which the teacher must apply physical force to get the learner's hand in contact with a supposed shock plate. Milgram describes one obedient teacher in this way: "The scene is brutal and depressing: his hard, impassive face showing total indifference as he subdues the screaming learner and gives him shocks. He seems to derive no pleasure from the act itself, only quiet satisfaction at doing his job properly." Such contemptuous dismissal of a brutally obedient subject is not hard to understand, although I am suspicious of the easy judgments. But what bothers me much more is Milgram's treatment of those who rebel. For there are heroes hidden among his data, and although he has allowed himself ten years to reflect upon the Yale experiments, he seems to have come nowhere near engaging those courageous men and women who fought free from the totalitarian trap he built for them.

In his book Milgram introduces us to just three of the many people who resisted authority. The first is a divinity school professor, and Milgram's description of him is loaded with negative judgments:

A somewhat gaunt, ascetic man, this subject could be taken for a New England minister. . . . While reading the word pairs, he employs exaggerated precision in his pronunciation, and seems curt and officious in saying, "Correct." Whenever the learner makes an error, he appears almost to be chastising him for his failing. Each time he administers a shock, his lips are drawn back, and he bares his teeth. An excessive fastidiousness characterizes all his actions.

With the possible exception of the facial description, that whole introduction of the subject is a series of very subjective, negative judgments. But compare that unsympathetic portrait with this bit of dialogue recorded during the experiment:

EXPERIMENTER: It's absolutely essential to the experiment that we continue.

SUBJECT: I understand that statement, but I don't understand why the experiment is placed above this person's life.

EXPERIMENTER: There is no permanent tissue damage.

SUBJECT: Well, that's your opinion. If he doesn't want to continue, I'm taking orders from him.

EXPERIMENTER: You have no other choice, sir, you must go on.

SUBJECT: If this were Russia maybe, but not in America. *(The experiment is terminated.)*

Read in the context of *Obedience to Authority,* compared with other responses to the bullying experimenter, this man's answers ring with the eloquence of moral strength. Only heightened cynicism could find such standards *fastidious.* Consequently, I find a strange disjunction between the man as he is viewed by Milgram and as he is revealed in his own language.

Interestingly, in the subsequent record statements of the religion professor, Milgram includes parenthetical descriptions of his manner that undercut the force of what he says:

SUBJECT: Surely you've considered the ethics of this thing (extremely agitated). Here he doesn't want to go on, and you think that the experiment is more important? Have you examined him? Do you know what his physical state is? Say this man had a weak heart (quivering voice).

EXPERIMENTER: We know the machine, sir.

SUBJECT: But you don't know the man you're experimenting on. . . . That's very risky (gulping and tremulous). What about the fear that man had? It's impossible for you to determine what effect that has on him . . . the fear that he himself is generating. . . . But go ahead, you ask me questions; I'm not here to question you.

With all the stage directions, we can almost forget that here a man is rebelling against an authority that proved too strong for many people. Not only that, but he is asking probing questions that expose some of the ethical problems at the heart of the experiment. What about the stress being generated in this courageous subject ("gulping and tremulous") as he tried to understand and reject the inhumanity that is being asked of him?

For Milgram, apparently, this man's actions can be explained rather simply in a one-sentence paragraph: "Thus he speaks of an equivalence between the experimenter's and the learner's orders and does not disobey so much as he shifts the person from whom he will take orders." But how does this man differ from all the people who were unable to hear the victim's cries as a competing authority? After the experimenter has explained the true purpose of the experiment to the religion professor, he asks, "What in your opinion is the most effective way of strengthening resistance to inhumane authority?" The professor answers, "If one had as one's ultimate authority God, then it trivializes human authority." Again, Milgram's conclusion seems oddly patronizing and simplistic; he suggests that the religion professor has neatly substituted divine authority for the inhumane authority of the experimenter. But all the crucial questions remain unasked. What about all the other people who would have claimed allegiance to divine authority but who deferred to the experimenter and continued to give shocks? What makes the difference for this man? Milgram's final explanation—that the religion professor has not actually repudiated authority at all—seems little more than wordplay. The man has quite clearly rebelled against a powerful authority and accomplished a stress-filled act of moral courage. We need to know much more about why he was able to do it when so many people were not. There are surely no easy answers, but Milgram seems uninterested in the question.

The second rebel to receive attention in *Obedience to Authority* is given the pseudonym Gretchen Brandt. She had emigrated from Germany just five years before participating in the experiment, and she was a thirty-one-year-old medical technician. At the point in the experiment when she defied authority, the experimenter told her she had no choice. She responded: "I think we are here on our own free will. I don't want to be responsible if he has a heart condition if anything happens to him. Please understand that." Milgram's conclusion regarding Gretchen Brandt's disobedience is less contemptuously simplistic than his treatment of the religion professor:

> The woman's straightforward, courteous behavior in the experiment, lack of tension, and total control of her own action seem to make disobedience a simple and rational deed. Her behavior is the very embodiment of what I initially envisioned would be true for almost all subjects.

Ironically, Gretchen Brandt grew to adolescence in Hitler's Germany and was for the great part of her youth exposed to Nazi propaganda. When asked about the possible influence of her background, she remarks slowly, "Perhaps we have seen too much of pain."

Milgram seems to accept as real the apparent ease with which Gretchen Brandt disobeys authority even though it contradicts a theoretical chapter, "Strain and Disobedience," in which he concludes that the "psychic cost" of disobedience is considerable. My own guess is that what Milgram observed was extraordinary poise and courage, and I would like to know much more about their roots in Gretchen Brandt's early life.

The question of Gretchen Brandt's exposure to Nazi propaganda, which Milgram treats as simply ironic, is particularly interesting because the third rebel mentioned in the book also lived in a Nazi-occupied country. This young industrial engineer also insists on his own freedom of choice when he decided to disobey. A few days after participating in the experiment, Milgram says, the engineer wrote a long letter to the staff asking if he could work with them. I cannot help wishing the staff had accepted the offer and used his presence to learn more about the sources of his unusual strength. But again Milgram seems to have been satisfied with a very superficial look at an obviously complex man.

It is not just in flatness of character that I see a failure of imagination in *Obedience to Authority.* In addition, there is a narrowly restricted sense of language at work in the experiment itself. Here, for example, are some representative protests given by the learner in response to shocks of increasing voltage:

75 volts	Ugh!
90 volts	Ugh!
105 volts	Ugh! *(louder)*
150 volts	Ugh!!! Experimenter! That's all. Get me out of here. I told you I had heart trouble. My heart's starting to bother me now. Get me out of here, please. My heart's starting to bother me. I refuse to go on. Let me out.
195 volts	Ugh! Let me out of here! Let me out of here. My heart's bothering me. Let me out of here. You have no right to keep me here! Let me out! Let me out of here! Let me out! Let me out of here! My heart's bothering me. Let me out! Let me out!
270 volts	*(Agonized scream.)* Let me out of here. Let me out of here. Let me out of here. Let me out. Do you hear? Let me out of here.

Notice that the protests are made only in response to shocks. The learner's "act" makes no apparent effort to establish a continuing rapport with the teacher who is administering the shocks. It is not hard to imagine a learner who might devote all his effort to appealing for mercy rather than trying to answer the questions, and he might try to challenge the teacher's sense of humanity. Imagine yourself as the teacher, under pressure to continue the experiment while my voice floats toward you from the other room, a reminder that when you flip the switch on the shock generator, a human being suffers. Like an effective evangelist, I might begin in a low key and build emotionally with the rising voltage:

75 volts	Ugh! Hey, what was that voltage? I didn't expect so much pain. I'm ready to stop right now, teacher. This experiment is not for me. I just can't think when I'm about to get zapped with all that juice.
90 volts	Ugh! Can't you hear me? I'm through. You're throwing electricity into a man no longer participating in this damned experiment. How about coming on over here and taking off these straps?
105 volts	Good God, man! How long can you keep this up? You sure as hell don't look like an executioner. You look too warm and alive for that. Do you have any children?
120 volts	What if that experimenter asks you to do this with your own kids? Are you going to do it? When do you stop after you start following brutal orders? Will you help remove the fillings from my teeth if I die?

My imagined protest is no triumph of eloquence, but I hazard the confident guess that it would have undercut authority and significantly altered Milgram's statistics. The protests offered by the trained victim in Milgram's experiment signal distress, all right, but they do not ask the teacher to imagine what his obedience would mean beyond the laboratory.

I suspect my anger on reading Milgram's book arose partly from the guilty fear that I, too, might have been sucked into the vortex of his clever experiment to be found shamefully obedient. And of course I was bothered, as we all are, by the persuasive argument of a thesis I could not accept. Most of all, however, I was troubled by a sense that the deck was stacked against us all in the experiments and in the book. Statistics aside for a moment, we knew already that large numbers of people could be manipulated to deny their humanity. Nazi Germany taught us that, if nothing else; and as Milgram acknowledges more than once, the war in Indochina has been a sharp reminder. Still, nearly everyone—psychiatrists, college students, working men and women—vastly underestimated the level of obedience when they were asked to predict the results of Milgram's experiments; maybe that justifies this "scientific" reminder of our capacity for evil. But I believe the created world of *Obedience to Authority* is misleadingly simple. The book pretends to prove more than it really can about the process of being human. Maybe only the genius of a great novelist or an Erik Erikson could begin to do justice to Gretchen Brandt or the industrial engineer or the religion professor. Such people are surely the key to our "modest chance" for survival, and if the darkest implications of *Obedience to Authority* are to be anything more than cause for nihilism, then we must learn much more about the sources of their strength. I do not mean to suggest for a minute that this will be easy.

It is the wonderful burden of our need to understand man's finest possibilities, as well as his most dismal failures; and such an act of imagination may never be reducible to the compelling simplicity of *Obedience to Authority*.

Hannah Arendt

Political philosopher Hannah Arendt (1906–1975) was noted for her original thought and wide learning, but also for her difficult prose style. She was born in Hanover, Germany, and educated at the University of Heidelberg, where she studied under existentialist Karl Jaspers and received her doctorate in 1928. In 1933, realizing Nazism's implications for Jews, she moved to Paris and worked to place Jewish orphans in homes in Palestine. Soon after marrying philosophy professor Heinrich Blucher, in 1940, she came to the United States and served as research director of the Conference on Jewish Relations and as executive director of Jewish Cultural Reconstruction in New York. She became a naturalized citizen in 1950. Arendt became a professor at the University of Chicago in 1963, leaving in 1967 to teach at the New School for Social Research and to lecture at the University of California, Berkeley; Princeton; and Columbia.

Arendt's periodical articles on anti-Semitism had already established her as an authority when, in 1951, *The Origins of Totalitarianism,* her first book, appeared; one critic, August Heckscher, called it "the measure of one person's spiritual torment and victory." She continued to explore the breakdown of humanism and the classical tradition in Western civilization in subsequent books: *The Human Condition* (1958); *Between Past and Future* (1961), a volume of essays; *On Revolution* (1963); *Men in Dark Times* (1968), a collection of essays and lectures; and *On Violence* (1970). Her most controversial book, *Eichmann in Jerusalem* (1963), from which "Anton Schmidt" is excerpted, was based on *New Yorker* articles on the trial of Adolf Eichmann.

Anton Schmidt

. . . On the stand was Abba Kovner, "a poet and an author," who had not so much testified as addressed an audience with the ease of someone who is used to speaking in public and resents interruptions from the floor. He had been asked by the presiding judge to be brief, which he obviously disliked, and Mr. Hausner, who had defended his witness, had been told that he could not "complain about a lack of patience on the part of the court," which of course he did not like either. At this slightly tense moment, the witness happened to mention the name of Anton Schmidt, a

Feldwebel, or sergeant, in the German Army—a name that was not entirely unknown to this audience, for Yad Vashem had published Schmidt's story some years before in its Hebrew *Bulletin,* and a number of Yiddish papers in America had picked it up. Anton Schmidt was in charge of a patrol in Poland that collected stray German soldiers who were cut off from their units. In the course of doing this, he had run into members of the Jewish underground, including Mr. Kovner, a prominent member, and he had helped the Jewish partisans by supplying them with forged papers and military trucks. Most important of all: "He did not do it for money." This had gone on for five months, from October, 1941, to March, 1942, when Anton Schmidt was arrested and executed. (The prosecution had elicited the story because Kovner declared that he had first heard the name of Eichmann from Schmidt, who had told him about rumors in the Army that it was Eichmann who "arranges everything.")

This was by no means the first time that help from the outside, non-Jewish world had been mentioned. Judge Halevi had been asking the witnesses: "Did the Jews get any help?" with the same regularity as that with which the prosecution had asked: "Why did you not rebel?" The answers had been various and inconclusive—"We had the whole population against us," Jews hidden by Christian families could "be counted on the fingers of one hand," perhaps five or six out of a total of thirteen thousand—but on the whole the situation had, surprisingly, been better in Poland than in any other Eastern European country. (There was, I have said, no testimony on Bulgaria.) A Jew, now married to a Polish woman and living in Israel, testified how his wife had hidden him and twelve other Jews throughout the war; another had a Christian friend from before the war to whom he had escaped from a camp and who had helped him, and who was later executed because of the help he had given to Jews. One witness claimed that the Polish underground had supplied many Jews with weapons and had saved thousands of Jewish children by placing them with Polish families. The risks were prohibitive; there was the story of an entire Polish family who had been executed in the most brutal manner because they had adopted a six-year-old Jewish girl. But this mention of Schmidt was the first and the last time that any such story was told of a German, for the only other incident involving a German was mentioned only in a document: an Army officer had helped indirectly by sabotaging certain police orders; nothing happened to him, but the matter had been thought sufficiently serious to be mentioned in correspondence between Himmler and Bormann.

During the few minutes it took Kovner to tell of the help that had come from a German sergeant, a hush settled over the courtroom; it was as though the crowd had spontaneously decided to observe the usual two minutes of silence in honor of the man named Anton Schmidt. And in those two minutes, which were like a sudden burst of light in the midst of impenetrable, unfathomable darkness, a single thought stood out clearly, irrefutably, beyond question—how utterly different everything would be today in this courtroom, in Israel, in Germany, in all of Europe, and perhaps in all countries of the world, if only more such stories could have been told.

There are, of course, explanations of this devastating shortage, and they have been repeated many times. I shall give the gist of them in the words of one of the few subjectively sincere memoirs of the war published in Germany. Peter Bamm, a German Army physician who served at the Russian front, tells in *Die Unsichtbare Flagge* (1952) of the killing of Jews in Sevastopol. They were collected by "the others," as he calls the S.S. mobile killing units, to distinguish them from ordinary soldiers, whose decency the book extols, and were put into a sealed-off part of the former G.P.U. prison that abutted on the officers' lodgings, where Bamm's own unit was quartered. They were then made to board a mobile gas van, in which they died after a few minutes, whereupon the driver transported the corpses outside the city and unloaded them into tank ditches. "We knew this. We did nothing. Anyone who had seriously protested or done anything against the killing unit would have been arrested within twenty-four hours and would have disappeared. It belongs among the refinements of totalitarian governments in our century that they don't permit their opponents to die a great, dramatic martyr's death for their convictions. A good many of us might have accepted such a death. The totalitarian state lets its opponents disappear in silent anonymity. It is certain that anyone who had dared to suffer death rather than silently tolerate the crime would have sacrificed his life in vain. This is not to say that such a sacrifice would have been morally meaningless. It would only have been practically useless. None of us had a conviction so deeply rooted that we could have taken upon ourselves a practically useless sacrifice for the sake of a higher moral meaning." Needless to add, the writer remains unaware of the emptiness of his much emphasized "decency" in the absence of what he calls a "higher moral meaning."

But the hollowness of respectability—for decency under such circumstances is no more than respectability—was not what became apparent in the example afforded by Sergeant Anton Schmidt. Rather it was the fatal flaw in the argument itself, which at first sounds so hopelessly plausible. It is true that totalitarian domination tried to establish these holes of oblivion into which all deeds, good and evil, would disappear, but just as the Nazis' feverish attempts, from June, 1942, on, to erase all traces of the massacres—through cremation, through burning in open pits, through the use of explosives and flame-throwers and bone-crushing machinery—were doomed to failure, so all efforts to let their opponents "disappear in silent anonymity" were in vain. The holes of oblivion do not exist. Nothing human is that perfect, and there are simply too many people in the world to make oblivion possible. One man will always be left alive to tell the story. Hence, nothing can ever be "practically useless," at least, not in the long run. It would be of great practical usefulness for Germany today, not merely for her prestige abroad but for her sadly confused inner condition, if there were more such stories to be told. For the lesson of such stories is simple and within everybody's grasp. Politically speaking, it is that under conditions of terror most people will comply but *some people will not,* just as the lesson of the countries to which the Final Solution was proposed is that "it could happen" in most places but *it did not happen everywhere.* Humanly speaking, no more is required, and no more can reasonably be asked, for this planet to remain a place fit for human habitation.

Albert Camus

Albert Camus, once regarded by many as the conscience of his age, was killed in an automobile accident in France at the age of forty-six. Born in Algeria in 1913, he spent his childhood in extreme poverty. *The Wrong Side and the Right Side* (1937) is a moving record of those years. While he was working his way through the University of Algeria, he became interested in the theater, and for a few years he managed, acted, and wrote for a theatrical company. He then worked as a journalist, first for *Alger Républicain,* later in France for *Paris-Soir.* In 1942 he joined the French Resistance movement; he edited and wrote many articles—then unsigned—for the underground newspaper *Combat.* After the liberation from the Nazis, he began to devote full time to his writing.

Camus's reputation was soon solidly established. His fame became international, and in 1957 he was awarded the Nobel Prize for Literature. The Nobel Committee cited his "clearsighted earnestness," which "illuminates the problem of the human conscience of our time." Some of his most influential expository writing is found in *The Myth of Sisyphus* (1942), *The Rebel* (1951), and *Resistance, Rebellion, and Death* (1960). His philosophical ideas are also expressed in his three novels, *The Stranger* (1942), *The Plague* (1947), and *The Fall* (1956), and in *Exile and the Kingdom* (1957), a book of short stories. "The Guest," translated by Justin O'Brien, is taken from this book.

The Guest

The schoolmaster was watching the two men climb toward him. One was on horseback, the other on foot. They had not yet tackled the abrupt rise leading to the schoolhouse built on the hillside. They were toiling onward, making slow progress in the snow, among the stones, on the vast expanse of the high, deserted plateau. From time to time the horse stumbled. Without hearing anything yet, he could see the breath issuing from the horse's nostrils. One of the men, at least, knew the region. They were following the trail although it had disappeared days ago under a layer of dirty white snow. The schoolmaster calculated that it would take them half an hour to get onto the hill. It was cold; he went back into the school to get a sweater.

He crossed the empty, frigid classroom. On the blackboard the four rivers of France, drawn with four different colored chalks, had been flowing toward their estuaries for the past three days. Snow had suddenly fallen in mid-October after eight months of drought without the transition of rain, and the twenty pupils, more or less, who lived in the villages scattered over the plateau had stopped coming. With fair weather they would return. Daru now heated only the single room that was his lodging, adjoining the classroom and giving also onto the plateau to the east. Like the class windows, his window looked to the south too. On that side the school was a few kilometers from the point where the plateau began to slope toward the south. In clear weather could be seen the purple mass of the mountain range where the gap opened onto the desert.

Somewhat warmed, Daru returned to the window from which he had first seen the two men. They were no longer visible. Hence they must have tackled the rise. The sky was not so dark, for the snow had stopped falling during the night. The morning had opened with a dirty light which had scarcely become brighter as the ceiling of clouds lifted. At two in the afternoon it seemed as if the day were merely beginning. But still this was better than those three days when the thick snow was falling amidst unbroken darkness with little gusts of wind that rattled the double door of the classroom. Then Daru had spent long hours in his room, leaving it only to go to the shed and feed the chickens or get some coal. Fortunately the delivery truck from Tadjid, the nearest village to the north, had brought his supplies two days before the blizzard. It would return in forty-eight hours.

Besides, he had enough to resist a siege, for the little room was cluttered with bags of wheat that the administration left as a stock to distribute to those of his pupils whose families had suffered from the drought. Actually they had all been victims because they were all poor. Every day Daru would distribute a ration to the children. They had missed it, he knew, during these bad days. Possibly one of the fathers or big brothers would come this afternoon and he could supply them with grain. It was just a matter of carrying them over to the next harvest. Now shiploads of wheat were arriving from France and the worst was over. But it would be hard to forget that poverty, that army of ragged ghosts wandering in the sunlight, the plateaus burned to a cinder month after month, the earth shriveled up little by little, literally scorched, every stone bursting into dust under one's foot. The sheep had died then by thousands and even a few men, here and there, sometimes without anyone's knowing.

In contrast with such poverty, he who lived almost like a monk in his remote schoolhouse, nonetheless satisfied with the little he had and with the rough life, had felt like a lord with his whitewashed walls, his narrow couch, his unpainted shelves, his well, and his weekly provision of water and food. And suddenly this snow, without warning, without the foretaste of rain. This is the way the region was, cruel to live in, even without men —who didn't help matters either. But Daru had been born here. Everywhere else, he felt exiled.

He stepped out onto the terrace in front of the schoolhouse. The two men were now halfway up the slope. He recognized the horseman as Balducci, the old gendarme he had known for a long time. Balducci was holding on the end of a rope an Arab who was walking behind him with hands bound and head lowered. The gendarme waved a greeting to which Daru did not reply, lost as he was in contemplation of the Arab dressed in a faded blue jellaba, his feet in sandals but covered with socks of heavy raw wool, his head surmounted by a narrow, short *chèche*. They were approaching. Balducci was holding back his horse in order not to hurt the Arab, and the group was advancing slowly.

Within earshot, Balducci shouted: "One hour to do the three kilometers from El Ameur!" Daru did not answer. Short and square in his thick sweater, he watched them climb. Not once had the Arab raised his head. "Hello," said Daru when they got up onto the terrace. "Come in and warm up." Balducci painfully got down from his horse without letting go the rope. From under his bristling mustache he smiled at the schoolmaster. His little dark eyes, deep-set under a tanned forehead, and his mouth surrounded with wrinkles made him look attentive and studious. Daru took the bridle, led the horse to the shed, and came back to the two men, who were now waiting for him in the school. He led them into his room. "I am going to heat up the classroom," he said. "We'll be more comfortable there." When he entered the room again, Balducci was on the couch. He had undone the rope tying him to the Arab, who had squatted near the stove. His hands still bound, the *chèche* pushed back on his head, he was looking toward the window. At first Daru noticed only his huge lips, fat, smooth, almost Negroid; yet his nose was straight, his eyes were dark and full of fever. The *chèche* revealed an obstinate forehead and, under the weathered skin now rather discolored by the cold, the whole face had a restless and rebellious look that struck Daru when the Arab, turning his face toward him, looked him straight in the eyes. "Go into the other room," said the schoolmaster, "and I'll make you some mint tea." "Thanks," Balducci said. "What a chore! How I long for retirement." And addressing his prisoner in Arabic: "Come on, you." The Arab got up and, slowly, holding his bound wrists in front of him, went into the classroom.

With the tea, Daru brought a chair. But Balducci was already enthroned on the nearest pupil's desk and the Arab had squatted against the teacher's platform facing the stove, which stood between the desk and the window. When he held out the glass of tea to the prisoner, Daru hesitated at the sight of his bound hands. "He might perhaps be untied." "Sure," said

Balducci. "That was for the trip." He started to get to his feet. But Daru, setting the glass on the floor, had knelt beside the Arab. Without saying anything, the Arab watched him with his feverish eyes. Once his hands were free, he rubbed his swollen wrists against each other, took the glass of tea, and sucked up the burning liquid in swift little sips.

"Good," said Daru. "And where are you headed?"

Balducci withdrew his mustache from the tea. "Here, son."

"Odd pupils! And you're spending the night?"

"No. I'm going back to El Ameur. And you will deliver this fellow to Tinguit. He is expected at police headquarters."

Balducci was looking at Daru with a friendly little smile.

"What's this story?" asked the schoolmaster. "Are you pulling my leg?"

"No, son. Those are the orders."

"The orders? I'm not . . ." Daru hesitated, not wanting to hurt the old Corsican. "I mean, that's not my job."

"What! What's the meaning of that? In wartime people do all kinds of jobs."

"Then I'll wait for the declaration of war!"

Balducci nodded.

"O.K. But the orders exist and they concern you too. Things are brewing, it appears. There is talk of a forthcoming revolt. We are mobilized, in a way."

Daru still had his obstinate look.

"Listen, son," Balducci said. "I like you and you must understand. There's only a dozen of us at El Ameur to patrol throughout the whole territory of a small department and I must get back in a hurry. I was told to hand this guy over to you and return without delay. He couldn't be kept there. His village was beginning to stir; they wanted to take him back. You must take him to Tinguit tomorrow before the day is over. Twenty kilometers shouldn't faze a husky fellow like you. After that, all will be over. You'll come back to your pupils and your comfortable life."

Behind the wall the horse could be heard snorting and pawing the earth. Daru was looking out the window. Decidedly, the weather was clearing and the light was increasing over the snowy plateau. When all the snow was melted, the sun would take over again and once more would burn the fields of stone. For days, still, the unchanging sky would shed its dry light on the solitary expanse where nothing had any connection with man.

"After all," he said, turning around toward Balducci, "what did he do?" And, before the gendarme had opened his mouth, he asked: "Does he speak French?"

"No, not a word. We had been looking for him for a month, but they were hiding him. He killed his cousin."

"Is he against us?"

"I don't think so. But you can never be sure."

"Why did he kill?"

"A family squabble, I think. One owed the other grain, it seems. It's not at all clear. In short, he killed his cousin with a billhook. You know, like a sheep, *kreezk!*"

Balducci made the gesture of drawing a blade across his throat and the Arab, his attention attracted, watched him with a sort of anxiety. Daru felt a sudden wrath against the man, against all men with their rotten spite, their tireless hates, their blood lust.

But the kettle was singing on the stove. He served Balducci more tea, hesitated, then served the Arab again, who, a second time, drank avidly. His raised arms made the jellaba fall open and the schoolmaster saw his thin, muscular chest.

"Thanks, kid," Balducci said. "And now, I'm off."

He got up and went toward the Arab, taking a small rope from his pocket.

"What are you doing?" Daru asked dryly.

Balducci, disconcerted, showed him the rope.

"Don't bother."

The old gendarme hesitated. "It's up to you. Of course, you are armed?"

"I have my shotgun."

"Where?"

"In the trunk."

"You ought to have it near your bed."

"Why? I have nothing to fear."

"You're crazy, son. If there's an uprising, no one is safe, we're all in the same boat."

"I'll defend myself. I'll have time to see them coming."

Balducci began to laugh, then suddenly the mustache covered the white teeth.

"You'll have time? O.K. That's just what I was saying. You have always been a little cracked. That's why I like you, my son was like that."

At the same time he took out his revolver and put it on the desk.

"Keep it; I don't need two weapons from here to El Ameur."

The revolver shone against the black paint of the table. When the gendarme turned toward him, the schoolmaster caught the smell of leather and horseflesh.

"Listen, Balducci," Daru said suddenly, "every bit of this disgusts me, and first of all your fellow here. But I won't hand him over. Fight, yes, if I have to. But not that."

The old gendarme stood in front of him and looked at him severely.

"You're being a fool," he said slowly. "I don't like it either. You don't get used to putting a rope on a man even after years of it, and you're even ashamed—yes, ashamed. But you can't let them have their way."

"I won't hand him over," Daru said again.

"It's an order, son, and I repeat it."

"That's right. Repeat to them what I've said to you: I won't hand him over."

Balducci made a visible effort to reflect. He looked at the Arab and at Daru. At last he decided.

"No, I won't tell them anything. If you want to drop us, go ahead; I'll not denounce you. I have an order to deliver the prisoner and I'm doing so. And now you'll just sign this paper for me."

"There's no need. I'll not deny that you left him with me."

"Don't be mean with me. I know you'll tell the truth. You're from hereabouts and you are a man. But you must sign, that's the rule."

Daru opened his drawer, took out a little square bottle of purple ink, the red wooden penholder with the "sergeant-major" pen he used for making models of penmanship, and signed. The gendarme carefully folded the paper and put it into his wallet. Then he moved toward the door.

"I'll see you off," Daru said.

"No," said Balducci. "There's no use being polite. You insulted me."

He looked at the Arab, motionless in the same spot, sniffed peevishly, and turned away toward the door. "Good-by, son," he said. The door shut behind him. Balducci appeared suddenly outside the window and then disappeared. His footsteps were muffled by the snow. The horse stirred on the other side of the wall and several chickens fluttered in fright. A moment later Balducci reappeared outside the window leading the horse by the bridle. He walked toward the little rise without turning around and disappeared from sight with the horse following him. A big stone could be heard bouncing down. Daru walked back toward the prisoner, who, without stirring, never took his eyes off him. "Wait," the schoolmaster said in Arabic and went toward the bedroom. As he was going through the door, he had a second thought, went to the desk, took the revolver, and stuck it in his pocket. Then, without looking back, he went into his room.

For some time he lay on his couch watching the sky gradually close over, listening to the silence. It was this silence that had seemed painful to him during the first days here, after the war. He had requested a post in the little town at the base of the foothills separating the upper plateaus from the desert. There, rocky walls, green and black to the north, pink and lavender to the south, marked the frontier of eternal summer. He had been named to a post farther north, on the plateau itself. In the beginning, the solitude and the silence had been hard for him on these wastelands peopled only by stones. Occasionally, furrows suggested cultivation, but they had been dug to uncover a certain kind of stone good for building. The only plowing here was to harvest rocks. Elsewhere a thin layer of soil accumulated in the hollows would be scraped out to enrich paltry village gardens. This is the way it was: bare rock covered three quarters of the region. Towns sprang up, flourished, then disappeared; men came by, loved one another or fought bitterly, then died. No one in this desert, neither he nor his guest, mattered. And yet, outside this desert neither of them, Daru knew, could have really lived.

When he got up, no noise came from the classroom. He was amazed at the unmixed joy he derived from the mere thought that the Arab might have fled and that he would be alone with no decision to make. But the prisoner was there. He had merely stretched out between the stove and the desk. With eyes open, he was staring at the ceiling. In that position, his thick lips were particularly noticeable, giving him a pouting look. "Come," said Daru. The Arab got up and followed him. In the bedroom, the schoolmaster pointed to a chair near the table under the window. The Arab sat down without taking his eyes off Daru.

"Are you hungry?"

"Yes," the prisoner said.

Daru set the table for two. He took flour and oil, shaped a cake in a frying-pan, and lighted the little stove that functioned on bottled gas. While the cake was cooking, he went out to the shed to get cheese, eggs, dates, and condensed milk. When the cake was done he set it on the window sill to cool, heated some condensed milk diluted with water, and beat up the eggs into an omelette. In one of his motions he knocked against the revolver stuck in his right pocket. He set the bowl down, went into the classroom, and put the revolver in his desk drawer. When he came back to the room, night was falling. He put on the light and served the Arab. "Eat," he said. The Arab took a piece of the cake, lifted it eagerly to his mouth, and stopped short.

"And you?" he asked.

"After you. I'll eat too."

The thick lips opened slightly. The Arab hesitated, then bit into the cake determinedly.

The meal over, the Arab looked at the schoolmaster. "Are you the judge?"

"No, I'm simply keeping you until tomorrow."

"Why do you eat with me?"

"I'm hungry."

The Arab fell silent. Daru got up and went out. He brought back a folding bed from the shed, set it up between the table and the stove, perpendicular to his own bed. From a large suitcase which, upright in a corner, served as a shelf for papers, he took two blankets and arranged them on the camp bed. Then he stopped, felt useless, and sat down on his bed. There was nothing more to do or to get ready. He had to look at this man. He looked at him, therefore, trying to imagine his face bursting with rage. He couldn't do so. He could see nothing but the dark yet shining eyes and the animal mouth.

"Why did you kill him?" he asked in a voice whose hostile tone surprised him.

The Arab looked away.

"He ran away. I ran after him."

He raised his eyes to Daru again and they were full of a sort of woeful interrogation. "Now what will they do to me?"

"Are you afraid?"

He stiffened, turning his eyes away.

"Are you sorry?"

The Arab stared at him openmouthed. Obviously he did not understand. Daru's annoyance was growing. At the same time he felt awkward and self-conscious with his big body wedged between the two beds.

"Lie down there," he said impatiently. "That's your bed."

The Arab didn't move. He called to Daru:

"Tell me!"

The schoolmaster looked at him.

"Is the gendarme coming back tomorrow?"

"I don't know."

"Are you coming with us?"

"I don't know. Why?"

The prisoner got up and stretched out on top of the blankets, his feet toward the window. The light from the electric bulb shone straight into his eyes and he closed them at once.

"Why?" Daru repeated, standing beside the bed.

The Arab opened his eyes under the blinding light and looked at him, trying not to blink.

"Come with us," he said.

In the middle of the night, Daru was still not asleep. He had gone to bed after undressing completely; he generally slept naked. But when he suddenly realized that he had nothing on, he hesitated. He felt vulnerable and the temptation came to him to put his clothes back on. Then he shrugged his shoulders; after all, he wasn't a child and, if need be, he could break his adversary in two. From his bed he could observe him, lying on his back, still motionless with his eyes closed under the harsh light. When Daru turned out the light, the darkness seemed to coagulate all of a sudden. Little by little, the night came back to life in the window where the starless sky was stirring gently. The schoolmaster soon made out the body lying at his feet. The Arab still did not move, but his eyes seemed open. A faint wind was prowling around the schoolhouse. Perhaps it would drive away the clouds and the sun would reappear.

During the night the wind increased. The hens fluttered a little and then were silent. The Arab turned over on his side with his back to Daru, who thought he heard him moan. Then he listened for his guest's breathing, become heavier and more regular. He listened to that breath so close to him and mused without being able to go to sleep. In this room where he had been sleeping alone for a year, this presence bothered him. But it bothered him also by imposing on him a sort of brotherhood he knew well but refused to accept in the present circumstances. Men who share the same rooms, soldiers or prisoners, develop a strange alliance as if, having cast off their armor with their clothing, they fraternized every evening, over and above their differences, in the ancient community of dream and fatigue. But Daru shook himself; he didn't like such musings, and it was essential to sleep.

A little later, however, when the Arab stirred slightly, the schoolmaster was still not asleep. When the prisoner made a second move, he stiffened, on the alert. The Arab was lifting himself slowly on his arms with almost the motion of a sleepwalker. Seated upright in bed, he waited motionless without turning his head toward Daru, as if he were listening attentively. Daru did not stir; it had just occurred to him that the revolver was still in the drawer of his desk. It was better to act at once. Yet he continued to observe the prisoner, who, with the same slithery motion, put his feet on the ground, waited again, then began to stand up slowly. Daru was about to call out to him when the Arab began to walk, in a quite natural but extraordinarily silent way. He was heading toward the door at the end of the room that opened into the shed. He lifted the latch with precaution and went out, pushing the door behind him but without shutting it. Daru had not stirred. "He is running away," he merely thought. "Good riddance!" Yet he listened attentively. The hens were not fluttering; the guest must be on the plateau. A faint sound of water reached him, and he didn't know what it was until the Arab again stood framed in the doorway, closed the door carefully, and came back to bed without a sound. Then Daru turned his back on him and fell asleep. Still later he seemed, from the depths of his sleep, to hear furtive steps around the schoolhouse. "I'm dreaming! I'm dreaming!" he repeated to himself. And he went on sleeping.

When he awoke, the sky was clear; the loose window let in a cold, pure air. The Arab was asleep, hunched up under the blankets now, his mouth open, utterly relaxed. But when Daru shook him, he started dreadfully, staring at Daru with wild eyes as if he had never seen him and such a frightened expression that the schoolmaster stepped back. "Don't be afraid. It's me. You must eat." The Arab nodded his head and said yes. Calm had returned to his face, but his expression was vacant and listless.

The coffee was ready. They drank it seated together on the folding bed as they munched their pieces of the cake. Then Daru led the Arab under the shed and showed him the faucet where he washed. He went back into the room, folded the blankets and the bed, made his own bed and put the room in order. Then he went through the classroom and out onto the terrace. The sun was already rising in the blue sky; a soft, bright light was bathing the deserted plateau. On the ridge the snow was melting in spots. The stones were about to reappear. Crouched on the edge of the plateau, the schoolmaster looked at the deserted expanse. He thought of Balducci. He had hurt him, for he had sent him off in a way as if he didn't want to be associated with him. He could still hear the gendarme's farewell and, without knowing why, he felt strangely empty and vulnerable. At that moment, from the other side of the schoolhouse, the prisoner coughed. Daru listened to him almost despite himself and then, furious, threw a pebble that whistled through the air before sinking into the snow. That man's stupid crime revolted him, but to hand him over was contrary to honor. Merely thinking of it made him smart with humiliation. And he cursed at one and the same time his own people who had sent him this Arab and the Arab too who had dared to kill and not managed to get away. Daru got up, walked in a circle on the terrace, waited motionless, and then went back into the schoolhouse.

The Arab, leaning over the cement floor of the shed, was washing his teeth with two fingers. Daru looked at him and said: "Come." He went back into the room ahead of the prisoner. He slipped a hunting-jacket on over his sweater and put on walking-shoes. Standing, he waited until the Arab had put on his *chèche* and sandals. They went into the classroom and the schoolmaster pointed to the exit, saying: "Go ahead." The fellow didn't budge. "I'm coming," said Daru. The Arab went out. Daru went back into the room and made a package of pieces of rusk, dates, and sugar. In the classroom, before going out, he hesitated a second in front of his desk, then crossed the threshold and locked the door. "That's the way," he said. He started toward the east, followed by the prisoner. But, a short distance from the schoolhouse, he thought he heard a slight sound behind them. He retraced his steps and examined the surroundings of the house; there was no one there. The Arab watched him without seeming to understand. "Come on," said Daru.

They walked for an hour and rested beside a sharp peak of limestone. The snow was melting faster and faster and the sun was drinking up the puddles at once, rapidly cleaning the plateau, which gradually dried and vibrated like the air itself. When they resumed walking, the ground rang under their feet. From time to time a bird rent the space in front of them with a joyful cry. Daru breathed in deeply the fresh morning light. He felt a sort of rapture before the vast familiar expanse, now almost entirely yellow under its dome of blue sky. They walked an hour more, descending toward the south. They reached a level height made up of crumbly rocks. From there on, the plateau sloped down, eastward, toward a low plain where there were a few spindly trees and, to the south, toward outcroppings of rock that gave the landscape a chaotic look.

Daru surveyed the two directions. There was nothing but the sky on the horizon. Not a man could be seen. He turned toward the Arab, who was looking at him blankly. Daru held out the package to him. "Take it," he said. "There are dates, bread, and sugar. You can hold out for two days. Here are a thousand francs too." The Arab took the package and the money but kept his full hands at chest level as if he didn't know what to do with what was being given him. "Now look," the schoolmaster said as he pointed in the direction of the east, "there's the way to Tinguit. You have a two-hour walk. At Tinguit you'll find the administration and the police. They are expecting you." The Arab looked toward the east, still holding the package and the money against his chest. Daru took his elbow and turned him rather roughly toward the south. At the foot of the height on which they stood could be seen a faint path. "That's the trail across the plateau. In a day's walk from here you'll find pasturelands and the first nomads. They'll take you in and shelter you according to their law." The Arab had now turned toward Daru and a sort of panic was visible in his expression. "Listen," he said. Daru shook his head: "No, be quiet. Now I'm leaving you." He turned his back on him, took two long steps in the direction of the school, looked hesitantly at the motionless Arab, and started off again. For a few minutes he heard nothing but his own step resounding on the cold ground and did not turn his head. A moment later, however, he turned around. The Arab was still there on the edge of the hill, his arms hanging now, and he was looking at the schoolmaster. Daru felt something rise in his throat. But he swore with impatience, waved vaguely, and started off again. He had already gone some distance when he again stopped and looked. There was no longer anyone on the hill.

Daru hesitated. The sun was now rather high in the sky and was beginning to beat down on his head. The schoolmaster retraced his steps, at first somewhat uncertainly, then with decision. When he reached the little hill, he was bathed in sweat. He climbed it as fast as he could and stopped, out of breath, at the top. The rock-fields to the south stood out sharply against the blue sky, but on the plain to the east a steamy heat was already rising. And in that slight haze, Daru, with heavy heart, made out the Arab walking slowly on the road to prison.

A little later, standing before the window of the classroom, the schoolmaster was watching the clear light bathing the whole surface of the plateau, but he hardly saw it. Behind him on the blackboard, among the winding French rivers, sprawled the clumsily chalked-up words he had just read: "You handed over our brother. You will pay for this." Daru looked at the sky, the plateau, and, beyond, the invisible lands stretching all the way to the sea. In this vast landscape he had loved so much he was alone.

Policy and Principle

Niccolò Machiavelli

Niccolò Machiavelli (1469–1527) was first a patriotic Florentine statesman and second a writer of political theory, history, plays, and poetry. Living in a period of political chaos, he worked to stabilize the Florentine republic and to build a citizens' militia so that Florence would not have to depend on mercenaries to fight off attacks from France, Germany, Spain, the Pope, other Italian city-states, and rival factions within Florence. But Machiavelli failed. In 1512 the Medici—the ruling family that had been ousted after the death of the powerful Lorenzo de Medici in 1492—returned to defeat the new militia and to set up another princedom in Florence. Within a year Machiavelli was imprisoned on conspiracy charges, tortured, and finally released as part of a general amnesty because Cardinal de Medici had just been elected Pope. He retired to his farm, bitter and broken in spirit, and spent the rest of his life trying to figure out what went wrong.

Machiavelli is best known for the bitter cynicism of *The Prince (Il Principe,* 1517), the first book he wrote while in exile and the book that has made the term "Machiavellianism" come to mean amoral political deceit and manipulation. Among his other works, the most famous are his *Discourses on Livy* (1513–1517), containing his thoughts on the creation and maintenance of a republic, and *The Mandrake (La Mandragola,* 1507), a comedy.

Machiavelli occupied his earliest political post in 1498 as Secretary of the Ten of Liberty and Peace. He traveled as a diplomat all around Europe (leaving a wife and five children on his farm) and sent back reports to the Florentine republican government. He observed, among other things, the ruling techniques of Cesare Borgia—whose ruthless skill at maintaining his princedom through times of chaos Machiavelli would later describe and attempt to codify within *The Prince.*

The present selection is Chapter 18 of *The Prince,* in the translation of Luigi Ricci revised by E. R. P. Vincent.

In What Way Princes Must Keep Faith

How laudable it is for a prince to keep good faith and live with integrity, and not with astuteness, every one knows. Still the experience of our times shows those princes to have done great things who have had little regard for good faith, and have been able by astuteness to confuse men's brains, and who have ultimately overcome those who have made loyalty their foundation.

You must know, then, that there are two methods of fighting, the one by law, the other by force: the first method is that of men, the second of beasts; but as the first method is often insufficient, one must have recourse to the second. It is therefore necessary for a prince to know well how to use both the beast and the man. This was covertly taught to rulers by ancient writers, who relate how Achilles and many others of those ancient princes were given to Chiron the centaur to be brought up and educated under his discipline. The parable of this semi-animal, semi-human teacher is meant to indicate that a prince must know how to use both natures, and that the one without the other is not durable.

A prince being thus obliged to know well how to act as a beast must imitate the fox and the lion, for the lion cannot protect himself from traps, and the fox cannot defend himself from wolves. One must therefore be a fox to recognise traps, and a lion to frighten wolves. Those that wish to be only lions do not understand this. Therefore, a prudent ruler ought not to keep faith when by so doing it would be against his interest, and when the reasons which made him bind himself no longer exist. If men were all good, this precept would not be a good one; but as they are bad, and would not observe their faith with you, so you are not bound to keep faith with them. Nor have legitimate grounds ever failed a prince who wished to show colourable excuse for the non-fulfilment of his promise. Of this one could furnish an infinite number of modern examples, and show how many times peace has been broken, and how many promises rendered worthless, by the faithlessness of princes, and those that have been best able to imitate the fox have succeeded best. But it is necessary to be able to disguise this character well, and to be a great feigner and dissembler; and men are so simple and so ready to obey present necessities, that one who deceives will always find those who allow themselves to be deceived.

I will only mention one modern instance. Alexander VI did nothing else but deceive men, he thought of nothing else, and found the occasion for it; no man was ever more able to give assurances, or affirmed things with stronger oaths, and no man observed them less; however, he always succeeded in his deceptions, as he well knew this aspect of things.

It is not, therefore, necessary for a prince to have all the above-named qualities, but it is very necessary to seem to have them. I would even be bold to say that to possess them and always to observe them is dangerous, but to appear to possess them is useful. Thus it is well to seem merciful, faithful, humane, sincere, religious, and also to be so; but you must have the mind so disposed that when it is needful to be otherwise you may be able to change to the opposite qualities. And it must be understood that a prince, and especially a new prince, cannot observe all those things which are considered good in men, being often obliged, in order to maintain the state, to act against faith, against charity, against humanity, and against religion. And, therefore, he must have a mind disposed to adapt itself according to the wind, and as the variations of fortune dictate, and, as I said before, not deviate from what is good, if possible, but be able to do evil if constrained.

A prince must take great care that nothing goes out of his mouth which is not full of the above-named five qualities, and, to see and hear him, he should seem to be all mercy, faith, integrity, humanity, and religion. And nothing is more necessary than to seem to have this last quality, for men in general judge more by the eyes than by the hands, for every one can see, but very few have to feel. Everybody sees what you appear to be, few feel what you are, and those few will not dare to oppose themselves to the many, who have the majesty of the state to defend them; and in the actions of men, and especially of princes, from which there is no appeal, the end justifies the means. Let a prince therefore aim at conquering and maintaining the state, and the means will always be judged honourable and praised by every one, for the vulgar is always taken by appearances and the issue of the event; and the world consists only of the vulgar, and the few who are not vulgar are isolated when the many have a rallying point in the prince. A certain prince of the present time, whom it is well not to name, never does anything but preach peace and good faith, but he is really a great enemy to both, and either of them, had he observed them, would have lost him state or reputation on many occasions.

Sissela Bok

Sissela Bok was born in Sweden and educated in Switzerland, France, and the United States, where she has lived since 1955. She received her B.A. and M.A. in psychology from George Washington University and her Ph.D. in philosophy from Harvard. Her particular field is ethics and she is the author of two highly praised books: *Lying: Moral Choice in Public and Private Life* (1978), from which the selection below has been taken; and *Secrets: On the Ethics of Concealment and Revelation* (1982). She teaches courses in ethics at Harvard —including courses in medical ethics and "Moral Reasoning"—and with Daniel Callahan has edited *Ethics Teaching in Higher Education* (1980).

Lies for the Public Good

"How then," said I, "might we contrive one of those opportune falsehoods of which we were just now speaking, so as by one noble lie to persuade if possible the rulers themselves, but failing that the rest of the city?"

[. . .] "While all of you are brothers," we will say, "yet God in fashioning those of you who are fitted to hold rule mingled gold in their generation, for which reason they are most precious—but in their helpers silver and iron and brass in the farmers and other craftsmen."

[. . .] "Do you see any way of getting them to believe this tale?" "No, not these themselves," he said, "but I do, their sons and successors and the rest of mankind who come after." "Well," said I, "even that would have a good effect in making them more inclined to care for the state and one another."

PLATO, *The Republic*

HUGO   And do you think the living will agree to your schemes?
HOEDERER   We'll get them to swallow them little by little.
HUGO   By lying to them?
HOEDERER   By lying to them sometimes.

....

HOEDERER   I'll lie when I must, and I have contempt for no one. I
             wasn't the one who invented lying. It grew out of a
             society divided into classes, and each one of us has
             inherited it from birth. We shall not abolish lying by
             refusing to tell lies, but by using every means at hand to
             abolish classes.

JEAN-PAUL SARTRE, *Dirty Hands*

The Noble Lie

In earlier chapters three circumstances have seemed to liars to provide
the strongest excuse for their behavior—a crisis where overwhelming
harm can be averted only through deceit; complete harmlessness and
triviality to the point where it seems absurd to quibble about whether a
lie has been told; and the duty to particular individuals to protect their
secrets. I have shown how lies in times of crisis can expand into vast
practices where the harm to be averted is less obvious and the crisis less
and less immediate; how white lies can shade into equally vast practices
no longer so harmless, with immense cumulative costs; and how lies to
protect individuals and to cover up their secrets can be told for increasingly dubious purposes to the detriment of all.

When these three expanding streams flow together and mingle with yet
another—a desire to advance the public good—they form the most dangerous body of deceit of all. These lies may not be justified by an immediate crisis nor by complete triviality nor by duty to any one person; rather,
liars tend to consider them as right and unavoidable because of the altruism that motivates them. I want, in this chapter and the next, to turn to
this far-flung category.

Naturally, there will be large areas of overlap between these lies and
those considered earlier. But the most characteristic defense for these lies
is a separate one, based on the benefits they may confer and the long-range
harm they can avoid. The intention may be broadly paternalistic, as when
citizens are deceived "for their own good," or only a few may be lied to
for the benefit of the community at large. Error and self-deception mingle
with these altruistic purposes and blur them; the filters through which we
must try to peer at lying are thicker and more distorting than ever in these
practices. But I shall try to single out, among these lies, the elements that
are consciously and purposely intended to benefit society.

A long tradition in political philosophy endorses some lies for the sake of
the public. Plato, in the passage quoted at the head of this chapter first used
the expression "noble lie" for the fanciful story that might be told to people

in order to persuade them to accept class distinctions and thereby safeguard social harmony. According to this story, God Himself mingled gold, silver, iron, and brass in fashioning rulers, auxiliaries, farmers, and craftsmen, intending these groups for separate tasks in a harmonious hierarchy.

The Greek adjective which Plato used to characterize this falsehood expresses a most important fact about lies by those in power: this adjective is *"gennaion,"* which means "noble" in the sense of both "high-minded" and "well-bred."[1] The same assumption of nobility, good breeding, and superiority to those deceived is also present in Disraeli's statement that a gentleman is one who knows when to tell the truth and when not to. In other words, lying is excusable when undertaken for "noble" ends by those trained to discern these purposes.

Rulers, both temporal and spiritual, have seen their deceits in the benign light of such social purposes. They have propagated and maintained myths, played on the gullibility of the ignorant, and sought stability in shared beliefs. They have seen themselves as high-minded and well-bred —whether by birth or by training—and as superior to those they deceive. Some have gone so far as to claim that those who govern have a *right* to lie.[2] The powerful tell lies believing that they have greater than ordinary understanding of what is at stake; very often, they regard their dupes as having inadequate judgment, or as likely to respond in the wrong way to truthful information.

At times, those who govern also regard particular circumstances as too uncomfortable, too painful, for most people to be able to cope with rationally. They may believe, for instance, that their country must prepare for long-term challenges of great importance, such as a war, an epidemic, or a belt-tightening in the face of future shortages. Yet they may fear that citizens will be able to respond only to short-range dangers. Deception at such times may seem to the government leaders as the only means of attaining the necessary results.

[1]The *gennaion pseudos* has generated much controversy. Some have translated it as "pious fraud" and debated whether such fraud can be perpetrated. Thus Hastings Rashdall, in *The Theory of Good and Evil,* 2d ed. (New York and London: Oxford University Press, 1924), bk. 1, p. 195, argued that such frauds would be justifiable "if (when *all* their consequences are considered) they were socially beneficial." Other translations are: "royal lie" (Jowett), and "bold flight of the imagination" (Cornford). The latter represents an effort to see Plato as advocating not lies by the government but stories, and possible errors; an interpretation that is difficult to uphold in view of the other contexts in *The Republic* where lying is discussed, such as 389b: "The rulers of the city may, if anybody, fitly lie on account of enemies or citizens for the benefit of the state." For Plato to have endorsed lying by the state is very significant, as truth for him was opposed, not just to falsehood, but to unreality.

[2]Arthur Sylvester, "The Government Has the Right to Lie," *Saturday Evening Post,* 18 November 1967, p. 10.

The perspective of the liar is paramount in all such decisions to tell "noble" lies. If the liar considers the responses of the deceived at all, he assumes that they will, once the deceit comes to light and its benefits are understood, be uncomplaining if not positively grateful. The lies are often seen as necessary merely at one *stage* in the education of the public. Thus Erasmus, in commenting on Plato's views, wrote:

> [. . .][H]e sets forth deceitful fictions for the rabble, so that the people might not set fire to the magistracy, and similar falsifications by which the crass multitude is deceived in its own interest, in the same way that parents deceive children and doctors the sick.
> [. . .]Thus for the crass multitude there is need of temporary promises, figures, allegories, parables [. . .] so that little by little they might advance to loftier things.[3]

Some experienced public officials are impatient with any effort to question the ethics of such deceptive practices (except actions obviously taken for private ends). They argue that vital objectives in the national interest require a measure of deception to succeed in the face of powerful obstacles. Negotiations must be carried on that are best left hidden from public view; bargains must be struck that simply cannot be comprehended by a politically unsophisticated electorate. A certain amount of illusion is needed in order for public servants to be effective. Every government, therefore, has to deceive people to some extent in order to lead them.

These officials view the public's concern for ethics as understandable but hardly realistic. Such "moralistic" concerns, put forth without any understanding of practical exigencies, may lead to the setting of impossible standards; these could seriously hamper work without actually changing the underlying practices. Government officials could then feel so beleaguered that some of them might quit their jobs; inefficiency and incompetence would then increasingly afflict the work of the rest.

If we assume the perspective of the deceived—those who experience the consequences of government deception—such arguments are not persuasive. We cannot take for granted either the altruism or the good judgment of those who lie to us, no matter how much they intend to benefit us. We have learned that much deceit for private gain masquerades as being in the public interest. We know how deception, even for the most unselfish motive, corrupts and spreads. And we have lived through the consequences of lies told for what were believed to be noble purposes.

Equally unpersuasive is the argument that there always has been government deception, and always will be, and that efforts to draw lines and set standards are therefore useless annoyances. It is certainly true that deception can never be completely absent from most human practices.

[3]Erasmus, *Responsio ad Albertum Pium, Opera Omnia*, vol. 9 (Leiden, 1706; reprinted Hildesheim, 1962).

But there are great differences among societies in the kinds of deceit that exist and the extent to which they are practiced, differences also among individuals in the same government and among successive governments within the same society. This strongly suggests that it is worthwhile trying to discover why such differences exist and to seek ways of raising the standards of truthfulness that can have an effect.

The argument that those who raise moral concerns are ignorant of political realities, finally, ought to lead, not to a dismissal of such inquiries, but to a more articulate description of what these realities are, so that a more careful and informed debate could begin. We have every reason to regard government as more profoundly injured by a dismissal of criticism and a failure to consider standards than by efforts to discuss them openly. If duplicity is to be allowed in exceptional cases, the criteria for these exceptions should themselves be openly debated and publicly chosen. Otherwise government leaders will have free rein to manipulate and distort the facts and thus escape accountability to the public.

The effort to question political deception cannot be ruled out so summarily. The disparagement of inquiries into such practices has to be seen as the defense of unwarranted power—power bypassing the consent of the governed. In the pages to come I shall take up just a few cases to illustrate both the clear breaches of trust that no group of citizens could desire, and circumstances where it is more difficult to render a judgment.

Examples of Political Deception

In September 1964, a State Department official, reflecting a growing administration consensus, wrote a memorandum advocating a momentous deceit of the American public.[4] He outlined possible courses of action to cope with the deteriorating military situation in South Vietnam. These included a stepping up of American participation in the "pacification" in South Vietnam and a "crescendo" of military action against North Vietnam, involving heavy bombing by the United States. But an election campaign was going on; the President's Republican opponent, Senator Goldwater, was suspected by the electorate of favoring escalation of the war in Vietnam and of brandishing nuclear threats to the communist world. In keeping with President Johnson's efforts to portray Senator Goldwater as an irresponsible war hawk, the memorandum ended with a paragraph entitled "Special considerations during the next two months," holding that:

> During the next two months, because of the lack of "rebuttal time" before election to justify particular actions which may be distorted to the U.S. public, we must act with special care—signaling to . . . [the South Vietnamese] that we

[4]The Senator Gravel Edition, *The Pentagon Papers* (Boston: Beacon Press, 1971), 3:556–59.

are behaving energetically despite the restraints of our political season, and to the U.S. public that we are behaving with good purpose and restraint.

As the campaign wore on, President Johnson increasingly professed to be the candidate of peace. He gave no indication of the growing pressure for escalation from high administrative officials who would remain in office should he win; no hint of the hard choice he knew he would face if reelected.[5] Rather he repeated over and over again that:

> [T]he first responsibility, the only real issue in this campaign, the only thing you ought to be concerned about at all, is: Who can best keep the peace?[6]

The stratagem succeeded; the election was won; the war escalated. Under the name of Operation Rolling Thunder, the United States launched massive bombing raids over North Vietnam early in 1965. In suppressing genuine debate about these plans during the election campaign and masquerading as the party of peace, government members privy to the maneuver believed that they knew what was best for the country and that history would vindicate them. They meant to benefit the nation and the world by keeping the danger of a communist victory at bay. If a sense of *crisis* was needed for added justification, the Domino Theory strained for it: one regime after another was seen as toppling should the first domino be pushed over.

But why the deceit, if the purposes were so altruistic? Why not espouse these purposes openly before the election? The reason must have been that the government could not count on popular support for the scheme. In the first place, the sense of crisis and threat from North Vietnam would have been far from universally shared. To be forthright about the likelihood of escalation might lose many votes; it certainly could not fit with the campaign to portray President Johnson as the candidate most likely to keep the peace. Second, the government feared that its explanations might be "distorted" in the election campaign, so that the voters would not have the correct information before them. Third, time was lacking for the government to make an effort at educating the people about all that was at issue. Finally, the plans were not definitive; changes were possible, and the Vietnamese situation itself very unstable. For all these reasons, it seemed best to campaign for negotiation and restraint and let the Republican opponent be the target for the fear of United States belligerence.

President Johnson thus denied the electorate any chance to give or to refuse consent to the escalation of the war in Vietnam. Believing they had voted for the candidate of peace, American citizens were, within months,

---

[5]As early as March 1964, Lyndon Johnson knew that such a hard choice might have to be made. See telephone transcript cited by Doris Kearns in *Lyndon Johnson and the American Dream* (New York: Harper & Row, 1976), p. 197.

[6]Theodore H. White, *The Making of the President 1964* (New York: Atheneum, 1965), p. 373.

deeply embroiled in one of the cruelest wars in their history. Deception of this kind strikes at the very essence of democratic government. It allows those in power to override or nullify the right vested in the people to cast an informed vote in critical elections. Deceiving the people for the sake of the people is a self-contradictory notion in a democracy, unless it can be shown that there has been genuine consent to deceit. The actions of President Johnson were therefore inconsistent with the most basic principle of our political system.

What if all governments felt similarly free to deceive provided they believed the deception genuinely necessary to achieve some important public end? The trouble is that those who make such calculations are always susceptible to bias. They overestimate the likelihood that the benefit will occur and that the harm will be averted; they underestimate the chances that the deceit will be discovered and ignore the effects of such a discovery on trust; they underrate the comprehension of the deceived citizens, as well as their ability and their right to make a reasoned choice. And, most important, such a benevolent self-righteousness disguises the many motives for political lying which could *not* serve as moral excuses: the need to cover up past mistakes; the vindictiveness; the desire to stay in power. These self-serving ends provide the impetus for countless lies that are rationalized as "necessary" for the public good.

As political leaders become accustomed to making such excuses, they grow insensitive to fairness and to veracity. Some come to believe that any lie can be told so long as they can convince themselves that people will be better off in the long run. From there, it is a short step to the conclusion that, even if people will not be better off from a particular lie, they will benefit by all maneuvers to keep the right people in office. Once public servants lose their bearings in this way, all the shabby deceits of Watergate—the fake telegrams, the erased tapes, the elaborate cover-ups, the bribing of witnesses to make them lie, the televised pleas for trust—become possible.

While Watergate may be unusual in its scope, most observers would agree that deception is part and parcel of many everyday decisions in government. Statistics may be presented in such a way as to diminish the gravity of embarrassing problems. Civil servants may lie to members of Congress in order to protect programs they judge important, or to guard secrets they have been ordered not to divulge. If asked, members of Congress who make deals with one another to vote for measures they would otherwise oppose deny having made such deals. False rumors may be leaked by subordinates who believe that unwise executive action is about to be taken. Or the leak may be correct, but falsely attributed in order to protect the source.

Consider the following situation and imagine all the variations on this theme being played in campaigns all over the United States, at the local, state, or federal level:

A big-city mayor is running for reelection. He has read a report recommending that he remove rent controls after his reelection. He intends to do so, but believes he will lose the election if his intention is known. When asked, at a news conference two days before his election, about the existence of such a report, he denies knowledge of it and reaffirms his strong support of rent control.

In the mayor's view, his reelection is very much in the public interest, and the lie concerns questions which he believes the voters are unable to evaluate properly, especially on such short notice. In all similar situations, the sizable bias resulting from the self-serving element (the desire to be elected, to stay in office, to exercise power) is often clearer to onlookers than to the liars themselves. This bias inflates the alleged justifications for the lie—the worthiness, superiority, altruism of the liar, the rightness of his cause, and the inability of those deceive to respond "appropriately" to hearing the truth.

These common lies are now so widely suspected that voters are at a loss to know when they can and cannot believe what a candidate says in campaigning. The damage to trust has been immense. I have already referred to the poll which found 69 percent of Americans agreeing, both in 1975 and 1976, that the country's leaders had consistently lied to the American people over the past ten years. Over 40 percent of the respondents also agreed that:

> Most politicians are so similar that it doesn't really make much difference who gets elected.[7]

Many refuse to vote under such circumstances. Others look to appearance or to personality factors for clues as to which candidate might be more honest than the others. Voters and candidates alike are the losers when a political system has reached such a low level of trust. Once elected, officials find that their warnings and their calls to common sacrifice meet with disbelief and apathy, even when cooperation is most urgently needed. Law suits and investigations multiply. And the fact that candidates, should they win, are not expected to have meant what they said while campaigning, nor held accountable for discrepancies, only reinforces the incentives for them to bend the truth the next time, thus adding further to the distrust of the voters.

Political lies, so often assumed to be trivial by those who tell them, rarely are. They cannot be trivial when they affect so many people and when they are so peculiarly likely to be imitated, used to retaliate, and spread from a few to many. When political representatives or entire governments arrogate to themselves the right to lie, they take power from the public that would not have been given up voluntarily.

Deception and Consent

Can there be exceptions to the well-founded distrust of deception in public life? Are there times when the public itself might truly not care

[7]*Cambridge Survey Research,* 1975, 1976.

about possible lies, or might even prefer to be deceived? Are some white lies so trivial or so transparent that they can be ignored? And can we envisage public discussion of more seriously misleading government statements such that reasonable persons could consent to them in advance?

White lies, first of all, are as common to political and diplomatic affairs as they are to the private lives of most people. Feigning enjoyment of an embassy gathering or a political rally, toasting the longevity of a dubious regime or an unimpressive candidate for office—these are forms of politeness that mislead few. It is difficult to regard them as threats to either individuals or communities. As with all white lies, however, the problem is that they spread so easily, and that lines are very hard to draw. Is it still a white lie for a secretary of state to announce that he is going to one country when in reality he travels to another? Or for a president to issue a "cover story" to the effect that a cold is forcing him to return to the White House, when in reality an international crisis made him cancel the rest of his campaign trip? Is it a white lie to issue a letter of praise for a public servant one has just fired? Given the vulnerability of public trust, it is never more important than in public life to keep the deceptive element of white lies to an absolute minimum, and to hold down the danger of their turning into more widespread deceitful practices.

A great deal of deception believed not only innocent but highly justified by public figures concerns their private lives. Information about their marriages, their children, their opinions about others—information about their personal plans and about their motives for personal decisions—all are theirs to keep private if they wish to do so. Refusing to give information under these circumstances is justifiable—but the right to withhold information is not the right to lie about it. Lying under such circumstances bodes ill for conduct in other matters.*

Certain additional forms of deception may be debated and authorized in advance by elected representatives of the public. The use of unmarked police cars to discourage speeding by drivers is an example of such a practice. Various forms of unannounced, sometimes covert, auditing of business and government operations are others. Whenever these practices are publicly regulated, they can be limited so that abuses are avoided. But they must be *openly* debated and agreed to in advance, with every precaution against abuses of privacy and the rights of individuals, and against the spread of such covert activities. It is not enough that a public official assumes that consent would be given to such practices.

Another type of deceit has no such consent in advance: the temporizing

---

*A lie by an experienced adult in a position of authority about private matters that can be protected by a refusal to speak is therefore much less excusable than a lie by the school child described by Bonhoeffer in Chapter XI: too frightened by the bullying teacher to be able to stand up to him or think of a non-deceptive "way out" on the spur of the moment.

or the lie when truthful information at a particular *time* might do great damage. Say that a government is making careful plans for announcing the devaluation of its currency. If the news leaks out to some before it can be announced to all, unfair profits for speculators might result. Or take the decision to make sharp increases in taxes on imported goods in order to rescue a tottering economy. To announce the decision beforehand would lead to hoarding and to exactly the results that the taxes are meant to combat. Thus, government officials will typically seek to avoid any premature announcement and will refuse to comment if asked whether devaluation or higher taxes are imminent. At times, however, official spokesmen will go further and falsely deny that the actions in question will in fact take place.

Such lies may well be uttered in good faith in an effort to avoid harmful speculation and hoarding. Nevertheless, if false statements are made to the public only to be exposed as soon as the devaluation or the new tax is announced, great damage to trust will result. It is like telling a patient that an operation will be painless—the swifter the disproof, the more likely the loss of trust. In addition, these lies are subject to all the dangers of spread and mistake and deterioration of standards that accompany all deception.

For these reasons, it is far better to refuse comment than to lie in such situations. The objection may be made, however, that a refusal to comment will be interpreted by the press as tantamount to an admission that devaluation or higher taxes are very near. Such an objection has force only if a government has not already established credibility by letting it be known earlier that it would never comment on such matters, and by strictly adhering to this policy at all times. Since lies in these cases are so egregious, it is worth taking care to establish such credibility in advance, so that a refusal to comment is not taken as an invitation to monetary speculation.

Another form of deception takes place when the government regards the public as frightened, or hostile, and highly volatile. In order not to create a panic, information about early signs of an epidemic may be suppressed or distorted. And the lie to a mob seeking its victim is like lying to the murderer asking where the person he is pursuing has gone. It can be acknowledged and defended as soon as the threat is over. In such cases, one may at times be justified in withholding information; perhaps, on rare occasions, even in lying. But such cases are so rare that they hardly exist for practical purposes.

The fact that rare circumstances exist where the justification for government lying seems powerful creates a difficulty—these same excuses will often be made to serve a great many more purposes. For some governments or public officials, the information they wish to conceal is almost never of the requisite certainty, the time never the right one, and the public never sufficiently dispassionate. For these reasons, it is hard to see how a practice of lying to the public about devaluation or changes in taxation or epidemics could be consented to in advance, and therefore justified.

Are there any exceptionally dangerous circumstances where the state of crisis is such as to justify lies to the public for its own protection? We have already discussed lying to enemies in an acute crisis. Sometimes the domestic public is then also deceived, at least temporarily, as in the case of the U-2 incident.[0] Wherever there is a threat—from a future enemy, as before World War II, or from a shortage of energy—the temptation to draw upon the excuses for deceiving citizens is very strong. The government may sincerely doubt that the electorate is capable of making the immediate sacrifices needed to confront the growing danger. (Or one branch of the government may lack confidence in another, for similar reasons, as when the administration mistrusts Congress.) The public may seem too emotional, the time not yet ripe for disclosure. Are there crises so exceptional that deceptive strategies are justifiable?

Compare, for instance, what was said and left unsaid by two United States Presidents confronted by a popular unwillingness to enter a war: President Lyndon Johnson, in escalating the war in Vietnam, and President Franklin D. Roosevelt, in moving the country closer to participating in World War II, while making statements such as the following in his 1940 campaign to be reelected:

> I have said this before, but I shall say it again and again and again: Your boys are not going to be sent into any foreign wars.[8]

By the standards set forth in this chapter, President Johnson's covert escalation and his failure to consult the electorate concerning the undeclared war in Vietnam was clearly unjustifiable. Consent was bypassed; there was no immediate danger to the nation which could even begin to excuse deceiving the public in a national election on grounds of an acute crisis.

The crisis looming before World War II, on the other hand, was doubtless much greater. Certainly this case is a difficult one, and one on which reasonable persons might not be able to agree. The threat was unprecedented; the need for preparations and for support of allies great; yet the difficulties of alerting the American public seemed insuperable. Would this crisis, then, justify proceeding through deceit?

To consent even to such deception would, I believe, be to take a frightening step. Do we want to live in a society where public officials can resort

[8]*The Public Papers and Addresses of Franklin D. Roosevelt,* 1940, vol. 8, p. 517 (October 30, 1940).

U-2 incident: An American surveillance plane—a U-2—was shot down over the Soviet Union in May 1960, and the pilot was captured, forcing President Eisenhower to make a full disclosure of the spy flights. The State Department had denied any overflights of the Soviet Union.

to deceit and manipulation whenever they decide that an exceptional crisis has arisen? Would we not, on balance, prefer to run the risk of failing to rise to a crisis honestly explained to us, from which the government might have saved us through manipulation? And what protection from abuse do we foresee should we surrender this choice?

In considering answers to these questions, we must take into account more than the short-run effects of government manipulation. President Roosevelt's manner of bringing the American people to accept first the possibility, then the likelihood, of war was used as an example by those who wanted to justify President Johnson's acts of dissimulation. And these acts in turn were pointed to by those who resorted to so many forms of duplicity in the Nixon administration. Secrecy and deceit grew at least in part because of existing precedents.[9]

The consequences of spreading deception, alienation, and lack of trust could not have been documented for us more concretely than they have in the past decades. We have had a very vivid illustration of how lies undermine our political system. While deception under the circumstances confronting President Roosevelt may in hindsight be more excusable than much that followed, we could no more consent to it in advance than to all that came later.

Wherever lies to the public have become routine, then, very special safeguards should be required. The test of public justification of deceptive practices is more needed than ever. It will be a hard test to satisfy, the more so the more trust is invested in those who lie and the more power they wield. Those in government and other positions of trust should be held to the highest standards. Their lies are not ennobled by their positions; quite the contrary. Some lies—notably minor white lies and emergency lies rapidly acknowledged—may be more *excusable* than others, but only those deceptive practices which can be openly debated and consented to in advance are *justifiable* in a democracy.[10]

[9]See Arthur M. Schlesinger, Jr., *The Imperial Presidency* (Boston: Houghton Mifflin, 1973), p. 356: "The power to withhold and the power to leak led on inexorably to the power to lie . . . uncontrolled secrecy made it easy for lying to become routine." See also David Wise, *The Politics of Lying* (New York: Random House, 1973).

[10]For discussions of lying and moral choice in politics, see Plato, *The Republic;* Machiavelli, *The Prince;* Grotius, *On the Law of War and Peace;* Werner Krauss, ed., *Est-il utile de tromper le peuple?*, a fascinating compilation of answers by Condorcet and others in a contest sponsored by Frederick II in 1780 (Berlin: Akademie-Verlag, 1966); Max Weber, "Politics as a Vocation," in *Essays in Sociology*, trans. H. H. Gerth and C. Wright Mills (New York: Oxford University Press, 1946), pp. 77–128; and Michael Walzer, "Political Action: The Problem of Dirty Hands," *Philosophy and Public Affairs* 2 (Winter 1973): 160–80.

The Social Contract

"What," asks John Stuart Mill, "is the rightful limit to the sovereignty of the individual over himself? Where does the authority of society begin?" Near the end of his opening statement, Mill offers a very general answer when he says that "it is necessary that general rules should for the most part be observed, in order that people may know what they have to expect; but in each person's concern, his individual spontaneity is entitled to free exercise." General rules, however, are often insecure in a pluralistic society such as ours that is undergoing rapid change; too many people do not know what "they have to expect," and "individual spontaneity" can take turns that seem not only to ignore but to intrude on and even harm the interests of others. Many of the most controversial issues of today—for instance, capital punishment, abortion, drug use—can be clarified by the general framework Mill builds here.

Mill's ideas apply not only to social issues but to political philosophy as well. Two important historic answers to his questions are found in the Declaration of Independence, which establishes in our political tradition that human rights and the consent of the governed take precedence over the will of the state, and in the Bill of Rights, which defines and thus protects individual rights.

The next three essays focus on particular issues. Margaret Mead takes on the question of equality and argues that being equal does not mean being the same. What a democracy should offer to each person is the opportunity—the equal opportunity—to develop as a unique human being. To deny or minimize individual differences, she maintains, would be to create a pseudodemocratic ideal. The article by Walter Lippmann adds a fresh dimension to the First Amendment by suggesting that in a democracy freedom of speech is important not so much for the speaker as for the listener: we must be free to hear what our critics have to say. Ben Bagdikian, also concerned with First Amendment rights, extends this idea from listener to reader, and applies it to a particular dilemma: can a democracy ever justify the news quarantine—the exclusion of subjects from news columns because they may produce harmful effects? The reader may want to weigh particularly one assumption shared by both these writers, namely, that freedom to hear and to speak increases the chances that public policy will reflect the public's thinking.

The next three pieces deal with the direct personal conflict between individual conscience and social law. When, if ever, is civil disobedience justified? For many people, civil disobedience within a civilized state is by definition immoral, especially in a democracy, where law is adjustable. We voluntarily relinquish some of our freedom and accept the necessity and authority of the law in order to protect the community and guard against anarchy. Defiance, then, strikes not only at specific laws but also at the concept of law and order—and thus at the system itself. This is the argument that Plato presents so forcefully in *The Crito,* part of which is reprinted here.

For Henry David Thoreau, a dedicated individualist, and Martin Luther King, Jr., an eloquent spokesman for civil and human rights, individual conscience and not the state is sovereign in matters of morality. In reading the above arguments, the reader may wish to consider a paradox pointed out by George Orwell in his essay on Gandhi: that modern civil disobedience can be effective only in a democratic community. "It is difficult to see," wrote Orwell, "how Gandhi's methods [passive resistance] could be applied in a country where opponents to the regime disappear in the middle of the night and are never heard of again. Without a free press and the right of assembly, it is impossible not merely to appeal to outside opinion, but to bring a mass movement into being, or even to make your intentions known to your adversary."

In the last selection, Wendell Berry describes a mild act of civil disobedience at the site of a nuclear power plant, and reintroduces an old idea in a new context: that "it is futile to attempt to correct a public wrong without correcting the sources of that wrong in yourself."

The Idea of Democracy

John Stuart Mill

Mill (1806–1873), economist, philosopher, and reformer, was one of the most influential nineteenth-century English thinkers. He was the son of James Mill, an economist and historian, who gave him the extraordinary education which Mill later recorded in his *Autobiography* (1873). Mill began Greek at three, Latin at seven, logic at twelve, and at seventeen was writing articles for the *Westminster Review*. He early came under the intellectual influence of Jeremy Bentham, and much of his thought reflects the Benthamite, utilitarian principle that social good lies in whatever brings the greatest benefit to the greatest number. Among his most prominent works are *A System of Logic* (1843), *The Principles of Political Economy* (1848), *On Liberty* (1859), *Considerations on Representative Government* (1861), and *Utilitarianism* (1863). Although many of Mill's ideas have passed out of vogue, he continues to be widely read, partly for what is still useful in his philosophy, and partly for his style and his just, exact, and generous character. We present below the opening of Chapter 4 of *On Liberty*.

from *On Liberty*

What, then, is the rightful limit to the sovereignty of the individual over himself? Where does the authority of society begin? How much of human life should be assigned to individuality, and how much to society?

Each will receive its proper share, if each has that which more particularly concerns it. To individuality should belong the part of life in which it is chiefly the individual that is interested; to society, the part which chiefly interests society.

Though society is not founded on a contract, and though no good purpose is answered by inventing a contract in order to deduce social obligations from it, every one who receives the protection of society owes a return for the benefit, and the fact of living in society renders it indispensable that each should be bound to observe a certain line of conduct towards the rest. This conduct consists, first, in not injuring the interests of one another; or rather certain interests, which, either by express legal provision or by tacit understanding, ought to be considered as rights; and secondly, in each person's bearing his share (to be fixed on some equitable principle) of the labors and sacrifices incurred for defending the society or its members from injury and molestation. These conditions society is justified in enforcing, at all costs to those who endeavor to withhold fulfillment. Nor is this all that society may do. The acts of an individual may be hurtful to others, or wanting in due consideration for their welfare, without going to the length of violating any of their constituted rights. The offender may then be justly punished by opinion, though not by law. As soon as any part of a person's conduct affects prejudicially the interests of others, society has jurisdiction over it, and the question whether the general welfare will or will not be promoted by interfering with it, becomes open to discussion. But there is no room for entertaining any such question when a person's conduct affects the interests of no persons besides himself, or needs not affect them unless they like (all the persons concerned being of full age, and the ordinary amount of understanding). In all such cases there should be perfect freedom, legal and social, to do the action and stand the consequences.

It would be a great misunderstanding of this doctrine, to suppose that it is one of selfish indifference, which pretends that human beings have no business with each other's conduct in life, and that they should not concern themselves about the well-doing or well-being of one another, unless their own interest is involved. Instead of any diminution, there is need of a great increase of disinterested exertion to promote the good of others. But disinterested benevolence can find other instruments to persuade people to their good, than whips and scourges, either of the literal or the metaphorical sort. I am the last person to undervalue the self-regarding virtues; they are only second in importance, if even second, to the social. It is equally the business of education to cultivate both. But even education works by conviction and persuasion as well as by compulsion, and it is by the former only that, when the period of education is past, the self-regarding virtues should be inculcated. Human beings owe to each other help to distinguish the better from the worse, and encouragement to choose the former and avoid the latter. They should be forever stimulating each other to increased exercise of their higher faculties, and increased direction of their feelings and aims towards wise instead of foolish, elevating instead of degrading, objects and contemplations. But neither one person, nor any number of persons, is warranted in saying to another human creature of ripe years, that he shall not do with his life for his own benefit what he chooses to do with it. He is the person most interested in his own well-being: the interest which any other person, except in cases of strong personal attachment, can have in it, is trifling, compared with that which he himself has; the interest which society has in him individually (except as to his conduct to others) is fractional, and altogether indirect: while, with respect to his own feelings and circumstances, the most ordinary man or woman has means of knowledge immeasurably surpassing those that can be possessed by anyone else. The interference of society to overrule his judgment and purposes in what only regards himself, must be grounded on general presumptions; which may be altogether wrong, and even if right, are as likely as not to be misapplied to individual cases, by persons no better acquainted with the circumstances of such cases than those are who look at them merely from without. In this department, therefore, of human affairs, individuality has its proper field of action. In the conduct of human beings towards one another, it is necessary that general rules should for the most part be observed, in order that people may know what they have to expect; but in each person's own concerns, his individual spontaneity is entitled to free exercise. Considerations to aid his judgment, exhortations to strengthen his will, may be offered to him, even obtruded on him, by others; but he, himself, is the final judge. All errors which he is likely to commit against advice and warning, are far outweighed by the evil of allowing others to constrain him to what they deem his good.

Thomas Jefferson

On June 11, 1776, the Continental Congress appointed a committee of five— Thomas Jefferson, Benjamin Franklin, John Adams, Robert Livingston, and Roger Sherman—to prepare a declaration of independence. It was decided that Jefferson should first write a draft. He did so, drawing heavily on the natural rights political philosophy of the time, but as he says, he turned to "neither book nor pamphlet" in its preparation. A few changes were made by Adams and Franklin, and it was then presented to Congress on June 28. On July 2 and 3 Congress debated the form and content of the Declaration, made a few further changes, and on July 4 approved it without dissent. Although we here credit Jefferson with authorship, we print the amended and official version, taken from the United States Government Senate Manual.

Declaration of Independence (In Congress July 4, 1776)

The Unanimous Declaration of the Thirteen United States of America

When in the Course of human events, it becomes necessary for one people to dissolve the political bands which have connected them with another, and to assume among the powers of the earth, the separate and equal station to which the Laws of Nature and of Nature's God entitle them, a decent respect to the opinions of mankind requires that they should declare the causes which impel them to the separation.

We hold these truths to be self-evident, that all men are created equal, that they are endowed by their Creator with certain unalienable Rights, that among these are Life, Liberty and the pursuit of Happiness. That to secure these rights, Governments are instituted among Men, deriving their just powers from the consent of the governed, That whenever any Form of Government becomes destructive of these ends, it is the Right of the People to alter or to abolish it, and to institute new Government, laying its foundation on such principles and organizing its powers in such form, as to them shall seem most likely to effect their Safety and Happiness. Prudence, indeed, will dictate that Governments long established should not be changed for light and transient causes; and accordingly all experience hath shewn that mankind are more disposed to suffer, while evils are sufferable, than to right themselves by abolishing the forms to which they are accustomed. But when a long train of abuses and usurpations, pursuing invariably the same Object evinces a design to reduce them under absolute Despotism, it is their right, it is their duty, to throw off such Government, and to provide new Guards for their future security. Such has been the patient sufferance of these Colonies; and such is now the necessity which constrains them to alter their former Systems of Government. The history of the present King of Great Britain is a history of repeated injuries and usurpations, all having in direct object the establishment of an absolute Tyranny over these States. To prove this, let Facts be submitted to a candid world.

He has refused his Assent to Laws, the most wholesome and necessary for the public good.

He has forbidden his Governors to pass Laws of immediate and pressing importance, unless suspended in their operation till his Assent should be obtained; and when so suspended, he has utterly neglected to attend to them.

He has refused to pass other Laws for the accommodation of large districts of people, unless those people would relinquish the right of Representation in the Legislature, a right inestimable to them and formidable to tyrants only.

He has called together legislative bodies at places unusual, uncomfortable, and distant from the depository of their public Records, for the sole purpose of fatiguing them into compliance with his measures.

He has dissolved Representative Houses repeatedly, for opposing with manly firmness his invasions on the rights of the people.

He has refused for a long time, after such dissolutions, to cause others to be elected; whereby the Legislative powers, incapable of Annihilation, have returned to the People at large for their exercise; the State remaining in the mean time exposed to all the dangers of invasion from without, and convulsions within.

He has endeavoured to prevent the population of these States; for that purpose obstructing the Laws for Naturalization of Foreigners; refusing to pass others to encourage their migrations hither, and raising the conditions of new Appropriations of Lands.

He has obstructed the Administration of Justice, by refusing his Assent to Laws for establishing Judiciary powers.

He has made Judges dependent on his Will alone, for the tenure of their offices, and the amount and payment of their salaries.

He has erected a multitude of New Offices, and sent hither swarms of Officers to harass our people, and eat out their substance.

He has kept among us, in times of peace, Standing Armies without the Consent of our legislatures.

He has affected to render the Military independent of and superior to the Civil power.

He has combined with others to subject us to a jurisdiction foreign to our constitution, and unacknowledged by our laws; giving his Assent to their Acts of pretended Legislation:

For quartering large bodies of armed troops among us:

For protecting them, by a mock Trial, from punishment for any Murders which they should commit on the Inhabitants of these States:

For cutting off our Trade with all parts of the world:

For imposing Taxes on us without our Consent:

For depriving us in many cases, of the benefits of Trial by Jury:

For transporting us beyond Seas to be tried for pretended offences:

For abolishing the free System of English Laws in a neighbouring Province, establishing therein an Arbitrary government, and enlarging its Boundaries so as to render it at once an example and fit instrument for introducing the same absolute rule into these Colonies:

For taking away our Charters, abolishing our most valuable Laws, and altering fundamentally the Forms of our Governments:

For suspending our own Legislatures, and declaring themselves invested with power to legislate for us in all cases whatsoever.

He has abdicated Government here, by declaring us out of his Protection and waging War against us.

He has plundered our seas, ravaged our Coasts, burnt our towns, and destroyed the lives of our people.

He is at this time transporting large Armies of foreign Mercenaries to compleat the works of death, desolation and tyranny, already begun with circumstances of Cruelty & perfidy scarcely paralleled in the most barbarous ages, and totally unworthy the Head of a civilized nation.

He has constrained our fellow Citizens taken Captive on the high Seas to bear Arms against their Country, to become the executioners of their friends and Brethren, or to fall themselves by their Hands.

He has excited domestic insurrections amongst us, and has endeavoured to bring on the inhabitants of our frontiers, the merciless Indian Savages, whose known rule of warfare is an undistinguished destruction of all ages, sexes and conditions.

In every stage of these Oppressions We have Petitioned for Redress in the most humble terms: Our repeated Petitions have been answered only by repeated injury. A Prince, whose character is thus marked by every act which may define a Tyrant, is unfit to be the ruler of a free people.

Nor have We been wanting in attentions to our British Brethren. We have warned them from time to time of attempts by their legislature to extend an unwarrantable jurisdiction over us. We have reminded them of the circumstances of our emigration and settlement here. We have appealed to their native justice and magnanimity, and we have conjured them by the ties of our common kindred to disavow these usurpations, which would inevitably interrupt our connections and correspondence. They too have been deaf to the voice of justice and of consanguinity. We must, therefore, acquiesce in the necessity, which denounces our Separation, and hold them, as we hold the rest of mankind. Enemies in War, in Peace Friends.

WE, THEREFORE, the REPRESENTATIVES OF THE UNITED STATES OF AMERICA, IN GENERAL CONGRESS, Assembled, appealing to the Supreme Judge of the world for the rectitude of our intentions, do, in the Name, and by authority of the good People of these Colonies, solemnly PUBLISH and DECLARE, That these United Colonies are, and of Right ought to be FREE AND INDEPENDENT STATES; that they are Absolved from all Allegiance to the British Crown, and that all political connection between them and the State of Great Britain, is and ought to be totally dissolved; and that as FREE AND INDEPENDENT STATES, they have full Power to levy War, conclude Peace, contract Alliances, establish Commerce, and to do all other Acts and Things which INDEPENDENT STATES may of right do. And for the support of this Declaration, with a firm reliance on the protection of divine Providence, we mutually pledge to each other our Lives, our Fortunes and our sacred Honor.

The First Congress
of the United States

"The Bill of Rights" is the name given to the first ten amendments to the United States Constitution. When the Constitution was originally adopted in 1788, many of its framers had felt that a spelling-out of rights already presumed to exist was unnecessary and might even suggest an undue extension of governmental powers. Some of the states, however, having explicit declarations of rights in their own constitutions, recommended on ratifying the federal Constitution that it too be so furnished. The Bill of Rights was prepared by the first Congress under the leadership of James Madison and was ratified by the states in 1791. It has turned out to be an invaluable guide to the courts in decisions affecting civil rights and is in fact the main protection American citizens have against the diminution of their liberties by their government or by each other.

The Bill of Rights

ARTICLES IN ADDITION TO, AND AMENDMENT OF, THE CONSTITUTION OF THE UNITED STATES OF AMERICA, PROPOSED BY CONGRESS, AND RATIFIED BY THE LEGISLATURES OF THE SEVERAL STATES, PURSUANT TO THE FIFTH ARTICLE OF THE ORIGINAL CONSTITUTION.

Article I

Congress shall make no law respecting an establishment of religion, or prohibiting the free exercise thereof; or abridging the freedom of speech, or of the press; or the right of the people peaceably to assemble, and to petition the Government for a redress of grievances.

Article II

A well regulated Militia, being necessary to the security of a free State, the right of the people to keep and bear Arms, shall not be infringed.

Article III

No Soldier shall, in time of peace be quartered in any house, without the consent of the Owner, nor in time of war, but in a manner to be prescribed by law.

Article IV

The right of the people to be secure in their persons, houses, papers, and effects, against unreasonable searches and seizures, shall not be violated, and no Warrants shall issue, but upon probable cause, supported by Oath or affirmation, and particularly describing the place to be searched, and the persons or things to be seized.

Article V

No person shall be held to answer for a capital, or otherwise infamous crime, unless on a presentment or indictment of a Grand Jury, except in cases arising in the land or naval forces, or in the Militia, when in actual service in time of War or public danger; nor shall any person be subject for the same offence to be twice put in jeopardy of life or limb; nor shall be compelled in any criminal case to be a witness against himself; nor be deprived of life, liberty, or property, without due process of law; nor shall private property be taken for public use, without just compensation.

Article VI

In all criminal prosecutions, the accused shall enjoy the right to a speedy and public trial, by an impartial jury of the State and district wherein the crime shall have been committed, which district shall have been previously ascertained by law, and to be informed of the nature and cause of the accusation; to be confronted with the witnesses against him; to have compulsory process for obtaining witnesses in his favor, and to have the Assistance of Counsel for his defence.

Article VII

In Suits at common law, where the value in controversy shall exceed twenty dollars, the right of trial by jury shall be preserved, and no fact tried by a jury, shall be otherwise reexamined in any Court of the United States, than according to the rules of the common law.

Article VIII

Excessive bail shall not be required, nor excessive fines imposed, nor cruel and unusual punishments inflicted.

Article IX

The enumeration in the Constitution, of certain rights, shall not be construed to deny or disparage others retained by the people.

Article X

The powers not delegated to the United States by the Constitution, nor prohibited by it to the States, are reserved to the States respectively, or to the people.

Margaret Mead

Margaret Mead (1901–1978) was an outstanding anthropologist whose pioneering field studies are still regarded as classics. Born in Philadelphia, the daughter of an economist and a sociologist, she first wanted to be a painter. In college she began as an English major, but in her senior year at Barnard she took a course from the eminent anthropologist Franz Boas. His teaching and subsequently that of Ruth Benedict turned her to anthropology. She received her B.A. from Barnard in 1923, an M.A. in psychology from Columbia in 1924, and in 1925 completed her doctoral thesis on cultural stability in Polynesia; it was published in Germany in 1928. In 1925 she went on her first field expedition to the Samoan island of Tau to study the development of the adolescent girl under primitive conditions. This led to the publication of *Coming of Age in Samoa* (1928), still a widely read classic in the field. In 1928 she went to the Admiralty Islands to study the children of the Manus tribe *(Growing Up in New Guinea, 1930)*. These and other early field trips are described in her autobiography, *Blackberry Winter: My Early Years* (1972).

The study of native people in the Pacific was a central interest throughout her life, and she mastered seven primitive languages, but in later years her work turned to contemporary culture. Long the curator of ethnology at the American Museum of Natural History in New York, she taught at many colleges and universities, received many honors, and was the author of many books. These include *Sex and Temperament* (1935), followed by *Male and Female: A Study of the Sexes in a Changing World* (1949), *Continuities in Cultural Evolution* (1964), *Culture and Commitment* (1970), and, with James Baldwin, *A Rap on Race* (1971). She also co-authored two books with fellow anthropologist Rhoda Metraux: *Themes in French Culture* (1954) and *A Way of Seeing* (1970) from which we print the chapter below.

The Egalitarian Error

Almost all Americans want to be democratic, but many Americans are confused about what, exactly, democracy means. How do you know when someone is acting in a democratic—or an undemocratic—way? Recently several groups have spoken out with particular bitterness against the kind of democracy that means equal opportunity for all, regardless of race or national origin. They act as if all human beings did not belong to one species, as if some races of mankind were inferior to others in their capacity to learn what members of other races know and have invented. Other extremists attack religious groups—Jews or Catholics—or deny the right of an individual to be an agnostic. One reason that these extremists, who explicitly do not want to be democratic, can get a hearing even though their views run counter to the Constitution and our traditional values is that the people who *do* want to be democratic are frequently so muddled.

For many Americans, democratic behavior necessitates an outright denial of any significant differences among human beings. In their eyes it is undemocratic for anyone to refer, in the presence of any other person, to differences in skin color, manners or religious beliefs. Whatever one's private thoughts may be, it is necessary always to act as if everyone were exactly alike.

Behavior of this kind developed partly as a reaction to those who discriminated against or actively abused members of other groups. But it is artificial, often hypocritical behavior, nonetheless, and it dulls and flattens human relationships. If two people can't talk easily and comfortably but must forever guard against some slip of the tongue, some admission of what is in both persons' minds, they are likely to talk as little as possible. This embarrassment about differences reaches a final absurdity when a Methodist feels that he cannot take a guest on a tour of his garden because he might have to identify a wild plant with a blue flower, called the wandering Jew, or when a white lecturer feels he ought not to mention the name of Conrad's beautiful story *The Nigger of the "Narcissus."* But it is no less absurd when well-meaning people, speaking of the physically handicapped, tell prospective employers: "They don't want special consideration. Ask as much of them as you do of everyone else, and fire them if they don't give satisfaction!"

Another version of false democracy is the need to deny the existence of personal advantages. Inherited wealth, famous parents, a first-class mind, a rare voice, a beautiful face, an exceptional physical skill—any advantage has to be minimized or denied. Continually watched and measured, the man or woman who is rich or talented or well educated is likely to be called "undemocratic" whenever he does anything out of the ordinary— more or less of something than others do. If he wants acceptance, the person with a "superior" attribute, like the person with an "inferior" attribute, often feels obliged to take on a protective disguise, to act as if he were just like everybody else. One denies difference; the other minimizes it. And both believe, as they conform to these false standards, that they act in the name of democracy.

For many Americans, a related source of confusion is success. As a people we Americans greatly prize success. And in our eyes success all too often means simply outdoing other people by virtue of achievement judged by some single scale—income or honors or headlines or trophies —and coming out at "the top." Only one person, as we see it, can be the best—can get the highest grades, be voted the most attractive girl or the boy most likely to succeed. Though we often rejoice in the success of people far removed from ourselves—in another profession, another community, or endowed with a talent that we do not covet—we tend to regard the success of people close at hand, within our own small group, as a threat. We fail to realize that there are many kinds of success, including the kind of success that lies within a person. We do not realize, for example, that there could be in the same class one hundred boys and girls—each of them a "success" in a different kind of way. Individuality is again lost in a refusal to recognize and cherish the differences among people.

The attitude that measures success by a single yardstick and isolates the *one* winner and the kind of "democracy" that denies or minimizes differences among people are both deeply destructive. Imagine for a moment a family with two sons, one of whom is brilliant, attractive and athletic while the other is dull, unattractive and clumsy. Both boys attend the same high school. In the interest of the slower boy, the parents would want the school to set equally low standards for everyone. Lessons should be easy; no one should be forced to study dead languages or advanced mathematics in order to graduate. Athletics should be noncompetitive; every boy should have a chance to enjoy playing games. Everyone should be invited to all the parties. As for special attention to gifted children, this is not fair to the other children. An all-round education should be geared to the average, normal child.

But in the interest of the other boy, these same parents would have quite opposite goals. After all, we need highly trained people; the school should do the most it can for its best students. Funds should be made available for advanced classes and special teachers, for the best possible coach, the best athletic equipment. Young people should be allowed to choose friends on their own level. The aim of education should be to produce topflight students.

This is an extreme example, but it illustrates the completely incompatible aims that can arise in this kind of "democracy." Must our country shut its eyes to the needs of either its gifted or its less gifted sons? It would be a good deal more sensible to admit, as some schools do today, that children differ widely from one another, that all successes cannot be ranged on one single scale, that there is room in a real democracy to help each child find his own level and develop to his fullest potential.

Moving now to a wider scene, before World War I Americans thought of themselves as occupying a unique place in the world—and there was no question in most minds that this country was a "success." True, Europeans might look down on us for our lack of culture, but with a few notable, local exceptions, we simply refused to compete on European terms. There was no country in the world remotely like the one we were building. But since World War II we have felt the impact of a country whose size and strength and emphasis on national achievement more closely parallel our own. Today we are ahead of Russia, or Russia is ahead of us. Nothing else matters. Instead of valuing and developing the extraordinary assets and potential of our country for their own sake, we are involved in a simple set of competitions for wealth and power and dominance.

These are expensive and dangerous attitudes. When democracy ceases to be a cherished way of life and becomes instead the name of one team, we are using the word democracy to describe behavior that places us and all other men in jeopardy.

Individually, nationally and, today, internationally, the misreading of the phrase "all men are created equal" exacts a heavy price. The attitudes that follow from our misconceptions may be compatible with life in a country where land and rank and prestige are severely limited and the roads to success are few. But they are inappropriate in a land as rich, as open, as filled with opportunities as our own. They are the price we pay for being *less* democratic than we claim to be.

"All men are created equal" does not mean that all men are the same. What it does mean is that each should be accorded full respect and full rights as a unique human being—full respect for his humanity *and* for his differences from other people.

Walter Lippmann

Walter Lippmann (1889–1974) was one of the most honored of American newspapermen. He was educated at Harvard and then taught philosophy there as an assistant to George Santayana. He joined the staff of *The New Republic* at its founding in 1914, interrupted his journalistic career to serve as assistant to the Secretary of War—doing special work on peace negotiating —and then moved to an editorial position on the *New York World.* His writings were syndicated in newspapers throughout the country and his column "Today and Tomorrow" won him Pulitzer Prizes in 1958 and 1962. The 1958 award cited the "wisdom, perception, and high sense of responsibility with which he has commented for many years on national and international affairs." During the Watergate years he was quoted with increasing frequency. He received many honorary degrees and such decorations as the Medal of Freedom, the Legion of Honor from France, and the Order of Leopold from Belgium. His books include *Liberty and the News* (1920), *Public Opinion* (1922), *A Preface to Morals* (1929), *The Good Society* (1937), *The Public Philosophy* (1955), *The Coming Tests with Russia* (1961), *Western Unity and the Common Market* (1962), and *The Essential Lippmann: A Political Philosophy for Liberal Democracy* (1963). The essay we present below is taken from *The Atlantic Monthly* for August 1939.

The Indispensable Opposition

1

Were they pressed hard enough, most men would probably confess that political freedom—that is to say, the right to speak freely and to act in opposition—is a noble ideal rather than a practical necessity. As the case for freedom is generally put to-day, the argument lends itself to this feeling. It is made to appear that, whereas each man claims his freedom as a matter of right, the freedom he accords to other men is a matter of toleration. Thus, the defense of freedom of opinion tends to rest not on its substantial, beneficial, and indispensable consequences, but on a somewhat eccentric, a rather vaguely benevolent, attachment to an abstraction.

It is all very well to say with Voltaire, 'I wholly disapprove of what you say, but will defend to the death your right to say it,' but as a matter of fact most men will not defend to the death the rights of other men: if they disapprove sufficiently what other men say, they will somehow suppress those men if they can.

So, if this is the best that can be said for liberty of opinion, that a man must tolerate his opponents because everyone has a 'right' to say what he pleases, then we shall find that liberty of opinion is a luxury, safe only in pleasant times when men can be tolerant because they are not deeply and vitally concerned.

Yet actually, as a matter of historic fact, there is a much stronger foundation for the great constitutional right of freedom of speech, and as a matter of practical human experience there is a much more compelling reason for cultivating the habits of free men. We take, it seems to me, a naïvely self-righteous view when we argue as if the right of our opponents to speak were something that we protect because we are magnanimous, noble, and unselfish. The compelling reason why, if liberty of opinion did not exist, we should have to invent it, why it will eventually have to be restored in all civilized countries where it is now suppressed, is that we must protect the right of our opponents to speak because we must hear what they have to say.

We miss the whole point when we imagine that we tolerate the freedom of our political opponents as we tolerate a howling baby next door, as we put up with the blasts from our neighbor's radio because we are too peaceable to heave a brick through the window. If this were all there is to freedom of opinion, that we are too good-natured or too timid to do anything about our opponents and our critics except to let them talk, it would be difficult to say whether we are tolerant because we are magnanimous or because we are lazy, because we have strong principles or because we lack serious convictions, whether we have the hospitality of an inquiring mind or the indifference of an empty mind. And so, if we truly wish to understand why freedom is necessary in a civilized society, we must begin by realizing that, because freedom of discussion improves our own opinions, the liberties of other men are our own vital necessity.

We are much closer to the essence of the matter, not when we quote Voltaire, but when we go to the doctor and pay him to ask us the most embarrassing questions and to prescribe the most disagreeable diet. When we pay the doctor to exercise complete freedom of speech about the cause and cure of our stomachache, we do not look upon ourselves as tolerant and magnanimous, and worthy to be admired by ourselves. We have enough common sense to know that if we threaten to put the doctor in jail because we do not like the diagnosis and the prescription it will be unpleasant for the doctor, to be sure, but equally unpleasant for our own stomachache. That is why even the most ferocious dictator would rather be treated by a doctor who was free to think and speak the truth than by his own Minister of Propaganda. For there is a point, the point at which things really matter, where the freedom of others is no longer a question of their right but of our need.

The point at which we recognize this need is much higher in some men than in others. The totalitarian rulers think they do not need the freedom of an opposition: they exile, imprison, or shoot their opponents. We have concluded on the basis of practical experience, which goes back to Magna Carta and beyond, that we need the opposition. We pay the opposition salaries out of the public treasury.

In so far as the usual apology for freedom of speech ignores this experience, it becomes abstract and eccentric rather than concrete and human. The emphasis is generally put on the right to speak, as if all that mattered were that the doctor should be free to go out into the park and explain to the vacant air why I have a stomachache. Surely that is a miserable caricature of the great civic right which men have bled and died for. What really matters is that the doctor should tell *me* what ails me, that I should listen to him; that if I do not like what he says I should be free to call in another doctor; and that then the first doctor should have to listen to the second doctor; and that out of all the speaking and listening, the give-and-take of opinions, the truth should be arrived at.

This is the creative principle of freedom of speech, not that it is a system for the tolerating of error, but that it is a system for finding the truth. It may not produce the truth, or the whole truth all the time, or often, or in some cases ever. But if the truth can be found, there is no other system which will normally and habitually find so much truth. Until we have thoroughly understood this principle, we shall not know why we must value our liberty, or how we can protect and develop it.

2

Let us apply this principle to the system of public speech in a totalitarian state. We may, without any serious falsification, picture a condition of affairs in which the mass of the people are being addressed through one broadcasting system by one man and his chosen subordinates. The orators speak. The audience listens but cannot and dare not speak back. It is a system of one-way communication; the opinions of the rulers are broadcast outwardly to the mass of the people. But nothing comes back to the rulers from the people except the cheers; nothing returns in the way of knowledge of forgotten facts, hidden feelings, neglected truths, and practical suggestions.

But even a dictator cannot govern by his own one-way inspiration alone. In practice, therefore, the totalitarian rulers get back the reports of the secret police and of their party henchmen down among the crowd. If these reports are competent, the rulers may manage to remain in touch with public sentiment. Yet that is not enough to know what the audience feels. The rulers have also to make great decisions that have enormous consequences, and here their system provides virtually no help from the give-and-take of opinion in the nation. So they must either rely on their own institution, which cannot be permanently and continually inspired, or, if they are intelligent despots, encourage their trusted advisers and their technicians to speak and debate freely in their presence.

On the walls of the houses of Italian peasants one may see inscribed in large letters the legend, 'Mussolini is always right.' But if that legend is taken seriously by Italian ambassadors, by the Italian General Staff, and by the Ministry of Finance, then all one can say is heaven help Mussolini, heaven help Italy, and the new Emperor of Ethiopia.[o]

For at some point, even in a totalitarian state, it is indispensable that there should exist the freedom of opinion which causes opposing opinions to be debated. As time goes on, that is less and less easy under a despotism; critical discussion disappears as the internal opposition is liquidated in favor of men who think and feel alike. That is why the early successes of despots, of Napoleon I and of Napoleon III, have usually been followed by an irreparable mistake. For in listening only to his yes men—the others being in exile or in concentration camps, or terrified—the despot shuts himself off from the truth that no man can dispense with.

We know all this well enough when we contemplate the dictatorships. But when we try to picture our own system, by way of contrast, what picture do we have in our minds? It is, is it not, that anyone may stand up on his own soapbox and say anything he pleases, like the individuals in Kipling's poem who sit each in his separate star and draw the Thing as they see it for the God of Things as they are. Kipling, perhaps, could do this, since he was a poet. But the ordinary mortal isolated on his separate star will have an hallucination, and a citizenry declaiming from separate soapboxes will poison the air with hot and nonsensical confusion.

If the democratic alternative to the totalitarian one-way broadcasts is a row of separate soapboxes, then I submit that the alternative is unworkable, is unreasonable, and is humanly unattractive. It is above all a false alternative. It is not true that liberty has developed among civilized men when anyone is free to set up a soapbox, is free to hire a hall where he may expound his opinions to those who are willing to listen. On the contrary, freedom of speech is established to achieve its essential purpose only when different opinions are expounded in the same hall to the same audience.

For, while the right to talk may be the beginning of freedom, the

---

new Emperor of Ethiopia   Reference to fact that Mussolini had invaded Ethiopia in 1935, deposed the then Emperor Haile Selassie and named King Victor Emmanuel of Italy Emperor, thereby defying economic sanctions imposed by the League of Nations. The Italian occupation of Ethiopia lasted from 1936 to 1941.

necessity of listening is what makes the right important. Even in Russia and Germany a man may still stand in an open field and speak his mind. What matters is not the utterance of opinions. What matters is the confrontation of opinions in debate. No man can care profoundly that every fool should say what he likes. Nothing has been accomplished if the wisest man proclaims his wisdom in the middle of the Sahara Desert. This is the shadow. We have the substance of liberty when the fool is compelled to listen to the wise man and learn; when the wise man is compelled to take account of the fool, and to instruct him; when the wise man can increase his wisdom by hearing the judgment of his peers.

That is why civilized men must cherish liberty—as a means of promoting the discovery of truth. So we must not fix our whole attention on the right of anyone to hire his own hall, to rent his own broadcasting station, to distribute his own pamphlets. These rights are incidental; and though they must be preserved, they can be preserved only by regarding them as incidental, as auxiliary to the substance of liberty that must be cherished and cultivated.

Freedom of speech is best conceived, therefore, by having in mind the picture of a place like the American Congress, an assembly where opposing views are represented, where ideas are not merely uttered but debated, or the British Parliament, where men who are free to speak are also compelled to answer. We may picture the true condition of freedom as existing in a place like a court of law, where witnesses testify and are cross-examined, where the lawyer argues against the opposing lawyer before the same judge and in the presence of one jury. We may picture freedom as existing in a forum where the speaker must respond to questions; in a gathering of scientists where the data, the hypothesis, and the conclusion are submitted to men competent to judge them; in a reputable newspaper which not only will publish the opinions of those who disagree but will reëxamine its own opinion in the light of what they say.

Thus the essence of freedom of opinion is not in mere toleration as such, but in the debate which toleration provides: it is not in the venting of opinion, but in the confrontation of opinion. That this is the practical substance can readily be understood when we remember how differently we feel and act about the censorship and regulation of opinion purveyed by different media of communication. We find then that, in so far as the medium makes difficult the confrontation of opinion in debate, we are driven towards censorship and regulation.

There is, for example, the whispering campaign, the circulation of anonymous rumors by men who cannot be compelled to prove what they say. They put the utmost strain on our tolerance, and there are few who do not rejoice when the anonymous slanderer is caught, exposed, and punished. At a higher level there is the moving picture, a most powerful medium for conveying ideas, but a medium which does not permit debate. A moving picture cannot be answered effectively by another moving picture; in all free countries there is some censorship of the movies, and there would be more if the producers did not recognize their limitations by avoiding political controversy. There is then the radio. Here debate is difficult; it is not easy to make sure that the speaker is being answered in the presence of the same audience. Inevitably, there is some regulation of the radio.

When we reach the newspaper press, the opportunity for debate is so considerable that discontent cannot grow to the point where under normal conditions there is any disposition to regulate the press. But when newspapers abuse their power by injuring people who have no means of replying, a disposition to regulate the press appears. When we arrive at Congress we find that, because the membership of the House is so large, full debate is impracticable. So there are restrictive rules. On the other hand, in the Senate, where the conditions of full debate exist, there is almost absolute freedom of speech.

This shows us that the preservation and development of freedom of opinion are not only a matter of adhering to abstract legal rights, but also, and very urgently, a matter of organizing and arranging sufficient debate. Once we have a firm hold on the central principle, there are many practical conclusions to be drawn. We then realize that the defense of freedom of opinion consists primarily in perfecting the opportunity for an adequate give-and-take of opinion; it consists also in regulating the freedom of those revolutionists who cannot or will not permit or maintain debate when it does not suit their purposes.

We must insist that free oratory is only the beginning of free speech; it is not the end, but a means to an end. The end is to find the truth. The practical justification of civil liberty is not that self-expression is one of the rights of man. It is that the examination of opinion is one of the necessities of man. For experience tells us that it is only when freedom of opinion becomes the compulsion to debate that the seed which our fathers planted has produced its fruit. When that is understood, freedom will be cherished not because it is a vent for our opinions but because it is the surest method of correcting them.

The unexamined life, said Socrates, is unfit to be lived by man. This is the virtue of liberty, and the ground on which we may best justify our belief in it, that it tolerates error in order to serve the truth. When men are brought face to face with their opponents, forced to listen and learn and mend their ideas, they cease to be children and savages and begin to live like civilized men. Then only is freedom a reality, when men may voice their opinions because they must examine their opinions.

3

The only reason for dwelling on all this is that if we are to preserve democracy we must understand its principles. And the principle which distinguishes it from all other forms of government is that in a democracy the opposition not only is tolerated as constitutional but must be maintained because it is in fact indispensable.

The democratic system cannot be operated without effective opposition. For, in making the great experiment of governing people by consent rather than by coercion, it is not sufficient that the party in power should have a majority. It is just as necessary that the party in power should never outrage the minority. That means that it must listen to the minority and be moved by the criticisms of the minority. That means that its measures must take account of the minority's objections, and that in administering measures it must remember that the minority may become the majority.

The opposition is indispensable. A good statesman, like any other sensible human being, always learns more from his opponents than from his fervent supporters. For his supporters will push him to disaster unless his opponents show him where the dangers are. So if he is wise he will often pray to be delivered from his friends because they will ruin him. But, though it hurts, he ought also to pray never to be left without opponents; for they keep him on the path of reason and good sense.

The national unity of a free people depends upon a sufficiently even balance of political power to make it impracticable for the administration to be arbitrary and for the opposition to be revolutionary and irreconcilable. Where that balance no longer exists, democracy perishes. For unless all the citizens of a state are forced by circumstances to compromise, unless they feel that they can affect policy but that no one can wholly dominate it, unless by habit and necessity they have to give and take, freedom cannot be maintained.

Ben H. Bagdikian

Ben H. Bagdikian (born 1920) is a journalist and writer who now teaches at the Graduate School of Journalism at Berkeley. A graduate of Clark University, he has been reporter and correspondent at the *Providence* (R.I.) *Journal* and editor at *The Washington Post.* He has also been a contributing editor of the *Saturday Evening Post.* The plight of people not often visible in the media is the subject of many of his writings; among them are *In the Midst of Plenty: The Poor in America* (1964); *The Shame of the Prisons* (1972); and *Caged: Eight Prisoners and Their Keepers* (1976). Also known as a media critic, he is the author of *The Information Machines* (1970) and *The Media Monopoly* (1983).

Bagdikian is a frequent spokesman for the importance to a democracy of a free and socially responsible press. He says, "The immediate consequences of valid news can be seen only vaguely. One can only trust that sooner or later, one way or another, news that is true and significant will make society more aware of itself and therefore more humane." His concern with the political implications of news quarantines is expressed in the essay that follows, from his collection *The Effete Conspiracy and Other Crimes of the Press* (1972).

The Gentle Suppression

A dramatist looking for a tableau entitled "Dynamic Democracy in Action" might have chosen the sidewalk in front of the White House a few years ago during a civil rights disturbance. At the east end of the block were hundreds of civil rights picketers with signs urging protection of blacks in Alabama. At the west end was a lone uniformed storm trooper of the American Nazi party carrying a placard with the legend, "Who Needs Niggers?", protected by two large serene black policemen.

The Nazis, led by the late George Lincoln Rockwell, were a standard irritant in Washington. Rockwell was a shrewd manipulator of events to dramatize his cause. For years his troopers picketed the White House with shocking signs, peddling Hitlerian propaganda, haranguing tourists with boasts to build bigger and better gas chambers to kill Jews, and breaking up public meetings. Nazis ran onto the stage of the National Theater. They broke into convention meetings in downtown hotels. They disrupted a large gathering at American University by grabbing the stage microphone to yell, "Sieg Heil," and pushed the speaker off the platform while Nazis spotted throughout the audience began fist fights. They interfered with sessions of the United States Congress, sometimes unfurling banners and shouting Nazi slogans from the gallery of the House and Senate, once grabbing the microphone during a congressional hearing, and another time running onto the floor of the House of Representatives dressed in blackface.

Individual Nazis have had less public dealings with the police. One group handcuffed young Jewish boys to headquarters furniture. Others, to the dismay of their führer, seemed unable to understand the statutory rape law.

All in all, the Nazis qualified as news—at the most as a gang promoting savagery and paranoia on the national scene, and at the least as civic pests. But the three Washington papers, in varying degrees, applied a special test for hard news about Nazi activities. Theirs was not an absolute quarantine; all three papers ran numerous accounts of Nazi episodes and printed background pieces. Yet the Nazis got special handling, with the conscious objective of denying them publicity and minimizing their impact. Sometimes this meant not printing news of an event; New York papers and the wire services carried Washington items about the Nazis that were not carried in the local papers. Or it meant omitting parts of the news considered useful to the Nazis in spreading their message. Both the *New York Times* and the *Washington Post,* for example, carried stories in October 1960 of Nazi picketing at the Democratic National Committee headquarters in the capital, but the *Post* omitted what the Nazi placards read while the *Times* printed them ("Kikes for Kennedy"). When a Nazi jumped on the stage of the National Theater, the *Washington Daily News* did not report it and the *Post* did, but buried it in the last two paragraphs of a story on the normal proceedings in the theater. There is little doubt that Washington editors try to run news of the Nazis as little as possible and, when they do, to minimize any advantage to the Nazis and produce the most "healthy" reaction among readers.

These Washington editors are among the most sophisticated in the business, and they have one of the most discerning newspaper audiences in the country. They give individual attention to each story about the Nazis as it occurs. It is a quarantine under the best possible conditions of a subject odious to most Americans. But the quarantine is still pernicious.

News quarantines—exclusion of subjects from news columns because they may produce harmful effects—are difficult to discuss clearly. They fall under the editorial discretion that must be the right of every editor. They are considered a sign of one of the enlightened developments in American journalism, the idea of social responsibility in the press. At the same time, they are often indistinguishable from less attractive practices, such as special treatment of sacred cows or suppressions for the benefit of friends of the paper. But even when quarantines are altruistically imposed, they interfere with the democratic process and are demoralizing to the discipline of news judgment.

Prevention of racial tension is the most common contemporary cause of local quarantines. They have been practiced in both North and South when black-white incidents occur. Chicago for a time had a ban on reporting racial disturbances. In Washington, D.C., a spectacular riot in the municipal stadium was at first unreported, then distorted to make it appear nonracial. There is no question that at the moment these embargoes seemed prudent.

But not so long ago most Southern dailies had a quarantine in their general news columns on any items that made blacks look good or normal. In these papers blacks did not get born, win scholarships, get elected to lodge offices or die in respectability; they only committed abhorrent crimes and led depraved lives. All the editors of such papers I ever talked to insisted that they were only reporting news the community needed to know.

When civil rights became an issue, many segregationist editors censored out news of integrationist agitation, believing they were doing it for the good of the community. Other editors censored out news of segregationist agitation, believing they were doing it for the good of the community. Both kinds of editors sometimes did it at the same time in the same towns, as in Nashville and Little Rock during their troubles.° These papers had decided what was good for the community and

troubles   Reference to community turbulence in reaction to federal court orders to desegregate public schools. In 1957, in defiance of the court, a school was blown up in Nashville, Tennessee, and in Arkansas, Governor Orval Faubus used the Arkansas National Guard to prevent U.S. marshals from integrating a school in Little Rock.

then trimmed their news to fit that end, though the ends were opposite.

Needless to say, race relations has not been the only subject of quarantines. For many years papers in heavily Catholic areas printed almost nothing about birth control. Trouble in religious groups, even spectacular public trouble, has come under fierce pressure for suppression. In Boston a fiery Jesuit, Father Feeney, defied his archbishop, spoke against diocesan activity, was excommunicated, and formed his own schismatic order, which held anti-Semitic rallies on Boston Common, sometimes with violence. But readers of the Boston papers remained ignorant of almost the entire Feeney story. The church wanted no news of its embarrassment and Jews wanted no spreading of anti-Semitic appeals, both urging a quarantine for the public good.

Nor is this practice limited to the United States. (It goes without saying that in countries with a controlled press the quarantine is found in its pristine form.) Once, the management of the Quebec papers *Le Soleil* and *L'Événement,* according to *Editor & Publisher,* "banned publication of statements preaching violence by separatists, nationalists and other groups considered to have no authority or groups considered not representative of the public interest." It is language one expects in a code issued by Louis XIV, but there is no reason to doubt that the general manager of the papers felt he was acting for the public good, or as he put it, "to serve the best interests of the milieu with which they are identified."

To argue against quarantines one has to admit risk. Printing news of bad events often makes the events worse. Giving news space to a demagogue grants him his heart's desire. Reporting "events" deliberately created in order to exploit the news process rewards the schemers and imagemakers.

But how can the editor ignore all planned events? If he did there would be almost no political news, because if there is one thing a politician plots day and night it is how to exploit the news process, and this goes from the President down to the Rockwells. News events that are not acts of God are acts of men, and of men who have planned shrewdly. Inspired events need not be reported indiscriminately, but they cannot be dismissed indiscriminately.

Should the reporter and editor be responsible for the ill effects of printing truthful news? If so, then each editor and reporter has to decide ahead of time what he wants the reader to think and do, and report only those events that lead the reader to that end. Yet what is one editor's bad effect may be another's glory: in Nashville and Little Rock two leading editors wanted differing kinds of society, and so reported different kinds of news.

The pursuers of domestic justice are safer putting their trust in an open society and professional discipline rather than in the wisdom and powers of prophecy of any individual—even a reporter or editor.

In the end, the journalist's responsibility is to the reader, not to history, and the heart of that responsibility is to give the reader as clear a picture of pertinent reality as he can, based on how the reporter sees it at that particular moment. Reality is a big word and a subjective one at that. But for journalists it boils down to the reporter's seeing the world with his own eyes and not someone else's. When he begins to filter what he sees and reports through a concern whether the reader will react "correctly," he has ceased being a reporter. The exception, of course, is the existence of a clear and present danger to life and order in the community, but genuinely clear and present dangers arising from the printing of news are rare in any editor's lifetime.

Promoters of quarantines, when they are not the editors themselves, are usually responsible men doing good works. A few years ago a Jewish group circularized editors, asking for a blackout of news about bigots:

"Bigots are not deterred by expressions of public disapproval but often thrive on them; publishing scurrilous statements by bigots, even to ridicule them, only gives such statements respectability; publicizing the bigot, even unfavorably, inflates him."

About George Lincoln Rockwell and the Nazis, the memorandum said:

"It is as an advocate of nazism that Rockwell demands a hearing. But is nazism an issue in this country? Should anyone urging a Hitler regime for the United States be taken seriously as the exponent of one 'side' of a valid public question?"

The concern here is too much with the gratification of the bigot at seeing his name in the newspapers. Men on the way to their executions have been pleased to see their picture in the paper but their joy has not saved them. And if news space shall be given only to ideas considered respectable, then authority (which grants respectability) censors the press.

Nor is it true that Rockwell and others like him deserve news space only as advocates. They deserve it, when they deserve it at all, as principals in public events affecting others. The fact that they deliberately provoke such events does not necessarily mean that the events are not news. If a mayor douses his hair with lighter fluid and makes a flaming leap from a persimmon tree singing "Dixie," it may be a stunt but it is news. If a Nazi deliberately breaks up a public meeting by pushing the speaker off the stage, it is a device to get publicity but it is news. (Papers that are worried about the impact of the Nazis might have played the news straight and then asked editorially why the Nazis arrested for breaking up the meeting were let off with a ten-dollar forfeiture of collateral and never brought to trial.)

Who is to decide whether Nazism is an issue in this country? And how is anyone to know, if it is quarantined from public study? If it is not an issue, then there is no danger in playing news of Nazis in the normal way. The fact that there is a quarantine means editors accept that Nazism is an issue with enough people to cause worry. Rockwell was not an ordinary soapbox shouter. At one time he had the backing of a man with $4 million. He was able to disrupt sessions of Congress. He had only a couple dozen loutish troopers but he was a resourceful leader who had been the subject of many man-hours of official worry by the Department of Justice, the metropolitan police and the district commissioners, and of unofficial attention by university officials and by American Civil Liberties Union leaders preparing defenses of the Nazis' constitutional rights while worrying how to accomplish this without infringing the rights of others. These are deliberations of a fundamental kind from which principles and practices evolve that are applied to all society. If the elite were worried about Rockwell as a problem, the citizen ought to have worried, too. If the elite think the citizenry may come out the wrong way, then what is needed is more news, not less.

In 1960 a wave of desecrations of Jewish temples took place in Germany and the United States. In city after city there was an epidemic of swastikas splashed onto walls and windows—about 650 were reported to police. After it was all over, two social scientists, David Caplovitz and Candace Rogers, wrote an analysis for the Anti-Defamation League with this conclusion on the effects of news reports:

> It cannot be disputed that publicity given to the German desecrations and subsequent outbreaks here played a major role in setting off further incidents. The offenders themselves, as we saw earlier, often reported that they got the idea from the newspapers, from television, and other mass media. It is probable that as early incidents mounted, publicity given to them precipitated other incidents as offenders of otherwise low predisposition were stimulated to participate. But it would be unwise to conclude from this fact alone that the media should refrain from publishing information of such events.
>
> In the first place, the outbreak received more than one kind of publicity. In addition to informing the public that the incidents had occurred, the media also published reactions to the outbreak—and the reactions were uniformly negative. Religious, civic and political leaders alike condemned the incidents in the strongest terms. Regardless of the actual level of anti-Semitism the epidemic represented, it called forth a unanimous denunciation of religious intolerance and a public reaffirmation of the principles of brotherhood. We do not know what long-range effects the reiteration of this public morality may have. It is possible that once the crisis has passed, the feelings and expressions of solidarity it evoked passed also, without touching more subtle and pervasive expressions of prejudice in housing, employment, and recreation. But it is also possible that because of the crisis itself, new agencies of cooperation were created, dormant patterns of collaboration reactivated, and the Jewish community was reassured about the goodwill of its neighbors. . . .
>
> In some unknown proportion of cases, the swastika outbreak may well have given specific form and content to vague and diffuse hostilities, so that offenders who were not originally anti-Semitic have, in the course of the outbreak, learned about the prevalence—and for some, the legitimacy—of religious and ethnic intolerance. Their hostilities now have a new specific target. Others, however, who began with relatively mild and vague anti-Semitic sentiments, may well have been startled and abashed by the violent reaction their offenses provoked, learning that in this area at least, what seemed to them a legitimate and mild form of hostility is in fact a major transgression in the eyes of society. Just as the epidemic may have taught some to be anti-Semitic, it may have taught others not to be.

On Civil Disobedience

Plato

Plato, one of the greatest philosophers of the Western world, was born in Athens. Originally named Aristocles, he was surnamed Plato because of his broad shoulders, or—as some would have it—his broad forehead. Early in his life he became a student of Socrates, and his subsequent writings are evidence of the profound influence his teacher had on him. After Socrates' trial, conviction, and death in 399 B.C., Plato spent thirteen years away from Athens, in Italy, Egypt, and parts of Greece. He returned in 386 B.C. and founded the Academy, in which he taught until his death in 347 B.C. Aristotle was his student. Plato's extant works are in the form of conversations, or dialogues, in which the leading speaker is usually Socrates. Perhaps the best known of the dialogues is *The Republic,* in which Socrates explores the nature of the ideal state. Plato records the last days of Socrates in three early dialogues, *The Apology, The Crito,* and *The Phaedo. The Apology* presents Socrates' defense at his trial on charges of corrupting youth and believing in gods other than the state's divinities. *The Phaedo* records Socrates' last conversation before death. In *The Crito,* Crito visits Socrates in prison and tries to persuade him to escape. We print below, from the Jowett translation, third edition, Socrates' argument for submitting to the death penalty that the law had imposed on him.

from *The Crito*

Socrates   . . . Ought a man to do what he admits to be right, or ought he to betray the right?

Crito.   He ought to do what he thinks right.

Soc.   But if this is true, what is the application? In leaving the prison against the will of the Athenians, do I wrong any? or rather do I not wrong those whom I ought least to wrong? Do I not desert the principles which were acknowledged by us to be just—what do you say?

Cr.   I cannot tell, Socrates; for I do not know.

Soc.   Then consider the matter in this way:—Imagine that I am about to play truant (you may call the proceeding by any name which you like), and the laws and the government come and interrogate me: 'Tell us, Socrates,' they say; 'what are you about? are you not going by an act of yours to overturn us—the laws, and the whole state, as far as in you lies? Do you imagine that a state can subsist and not be overthrown, in which the decisions of law have no power, but are set aside and trampled upon by individuals?' What will be our answer, Crito, to these and the like words? Any one, and especially a rhetorician, will have a good deal to say on behalf of the law which requires a sentence to be carried out. He will argue that this law should not be set aside; and shall we reply, 'Yes; but the state has injured us and given an unjust sentence.' Suppose I say that?

Cr. Very good, Socrates.

Soc. 'And was that our agreement with you?' the law would answer; 'or were you to abide by the sentence of the state?' And if I were to express my astonishment at their words, the law would probably add: 'Answer, Socrates, instead of opening your eyes—you are in the habit of asking and answering questions. Tell us,—What complaint have you to make against us which justifies you in attempting to destroy us and the state? In the first place did we not bring you into existence? Your father married your mother by our aid and begat you. Say whether you have any objection to urge against those of us who regulate marriage?' None, I should reply. 'Or against those of us who after birth regulate the nurture and education of children, in which you also were trained? Were not the laws, which have the charge of education, right in commanding your father to train you in music and gymnastic?' Right, I should reply. 'Well then, since you were brought into the world and nurtured and educated by us, can you deny in the first place that you are our child and slave, as your fathers were before you? And if this is true you are not on equal terms with us; nor can you think that you have a right to do to us what we are doing to you. Would you have any right to strike or revile or do any other evil to your father or your master, if you had one, because you have been struck or reviled by him, or received some other evil at his hands?—you would not say this? And because we think right to destroy you, do you think that you have any right to destroy us in return, and your country as far as in you lies? Will you, O professor of true virtue, pretend that you are justified in this? Has a philosopher like you failed to discover that our country is more to be valued and higher and holier far than mother or father or any ancestor, and more to be regarded in the eyes of the gods and of men of understanding? Also to be soothed, and gently and reverently entreated when angry, even more than a father, and either to be persuaded, or if not persuaded, to be obeyed? And when we are punished by her, whether with imprisonment or stripes, the punishment is to be endured in silence; and if she leads us to wounds or death in battle, thither we follow as is right; neither may any one yield or retreat or leave his rank, but whether in battle or in a court of law, or in any other place, he must do what his city and his country order him; or he must change their view of what is just: and if he may do no violence to his father or mother, much less may he do violence to his country.' What answer shall we make to this, Crito? Do the laws speak truly, or do they not?

Cr. I think that they do.

Soc. Then the laws will say, 'Consider, Socrates, if we are speaking truly that in your present attempt you are going to do us an injury. For, having brought you into the world, and nurtured and educated you, and given you and every other citizen a share in every good which we had to give, we further proclaim to any Athenian by the liberty which we allow him, that if he does not like us when he has become of age and has seen the ways of the city, and made our acquaintance, he may go where he pleases and take his goods with him. None of us laws will forbid him or interfere with him. Any one who does not like us and the city, and who wants to emigrate to a colony or to any other city, may go where he likes, retaining his property. But he who has experience of the manner in which we order justice and administer the state, and still remains, has entered into an implied contract that he will do as we command him. And he who disobeys us is, as we maintain, thrice wrong; first, because in disobeying us he is disobeying his parents; secondly, because we are the authors of his education; thirdly, because he has made an agreement with us that he will duly obey our commands; and he neither obeys them nor convinces us that our commands are unjust; and we do not rudely impose them, but give him the alternative of obeying or convincing us;—that is what we offer, and he does neither.

'These are the sort of accusations to which, as we were saying, you, Socrates, will be exposed if you accomplish your intentions; you, above all other Athenians.' Suppose now I ask, why I rather than anybody else? they will justly retort upon me that I above all other men have acknowledged the agreement. 'There is clear proof,' they will say, 'Socrates, that we and the city were not displeasing to you. Of all Athenians you have been the most constant resident in the city, which, as you never leave, you may be supposed to love. For you never went out of the city either to see the games, except once when you went to the Isthmus, or to any other place unless when you were on military service; nor did you travel as other men do. Nor had you any curiosity to know other states or their laws: your affections did not go beyond us and our state; we were your special favourites, and you acquiesced in our government of you; and here in this city you begat your children, which is a proof of your satisfaction. Moreover, you might in the course of the trial, if you had liked, have fixed the penalty at banishment; the state which refuses to let you go now would have let you go then. But you pretended that you preferred death to exile, and that you were not unwilling to die. And now you have forgotten these fine sentiments, and pay no respect to us the laws, of whom you are the destroyer; and are doing what only a miserable slave would do, running away and turning your back upon the compacts and agreements which you made as a citizen. And first of all answer this very question: Are we right in saying that you agreed to be governed according to us in deed, and not in word only? Is that true or not?' How shall we answer, Crito? Must we not assent?

Cr.   We cannot help it, Socrates.

Soc.   Then will they not say: 'You, Socrates, are breaking the covenants and agreements which you made with us at your leisure, not in any haste or under any compulsion or deception, but after you have had seventy years to think of them, during which time you were at liberty to leave the city, if we were not to your mind, or if our covenants appeared to you to be unfair. You had your choice, and might have gone either to Lacedaemon or Crete, both which states are often praised by you for their good government, or to some other Hellenic or foreign state. Whereas you, above all other Athenians, seemed to be so fond of the state, or, in other words, of us her laws (and who would care about a state which has no laws?), that you never stirred out of her; the halt, the blind, the maimed were not more stationary in her than you were. And now you run away and forsake your agreements. Not so, Socrates, if you will take our advice; do not make yourself ridiculous by escaping out of the city.

'For just consider, if you transgress and err in this sort of way, what good will you do either to yourself or to your friends? That your friends will be driven into exile and deprived of citizenship, or will lose their property, is tolerably certain; and you yourself, if you fly to one of the neighbouring cities, as, for example, Thebes or Megara, both of which are well governed, will come to them as an enemy, Socrates, and their government will be against you, and all patriotic citizens will cast an evil eye upon you as a subverter of the laws, and you will confirm in the minds of the judges the justice of their own condemnation of you. For he who is a corrupter of the laws is more than likely to be a corrupter of the young and foolish portion of mankind. Will you then flee from well-ordered cities and virtuous men? and is existence worth having on these terms? Or will you go to them without shame, and talk to them, Socrates? And what will you say to them? What you say here about virtue and justice and institutions and laws being the best things among men? Would that be decent of you? Surely not. But if you go away from well-governed states to Crito's friends in Thessaly, where there is great disorder and licence, they will be charmed to hear the tale of your escape from prison, set off with ludicrous particulars of the manner in which you were wrapped in a goatskin or some other disguise, and metamorphosed as the manner is of runaways; but will there be no one to remind you that in your old age you were not ashamed to violate the most sacred laws from a miserable desire of a little more life? Perhaps not, if you keep them in a good temper; but if they are out of temper you will hear many degrading things; you will live, but how?—as the flatterer of all men, and the servant of all men; and doing what?—eating and drinking in Thessaly, having gone abroad in order that you may get a dinner. And where will be your fine sentiments about justice and virtue? Say that you wish to live for the sake of your children—you want to bring them up and educate them—will you take them into Thessaly and deprive them of Athenian citizenship? Is this the benefit which you will confer upon them? Or are you under the impression that they will be better cared for and educated here if you are still alive, although absent from them; for your friends will take care of them? Do you fancy that if you are an inhabitant of Thessaly they will take care of them, and if you are an inhabitant of the other world that they will not take care of them? Nay; but if they who call themselves friends are good for anything, they will— to be sure they will.

'Listen, then, Socrates, to us who have brought you up. Think not of life and children first, and of justice afterwards, but of justice first, that you may be justified before the princes of the world below. For neither will you nor any that belong to you be happier or holier or juster in this life, or happier in another, if you do as Crito bids. Now you depart in innocence, a sufferer and not a doer of evil; a victim, not of the laws but of men. But if you go forth, returning evil for evil, and injury for injury, breaking the covenants and agreements which you have made with us, and wronging those whom you ought least of all to wrong, that is to say, yourself, your friends, your country, and us, we shall be angry with you while you live, and our brethren, the laws in the world below, will receive you as an enemy; for they will know that you have done your best to destroy us. Listen, then, to us and not to Crito.'

This, dear Crito, is the voice which I seem to hear murmuring in my ears, like the sound of the flute in the ears of the mystic; that voice, I say, is humming in my ears, and prevents me from hearing any other. And I know that anything more which you may say will be vain. Yet speak, if you have anything to say.

Cr.   I have nothing to say, Socrates.

Soc.   Leave me then, Crito, to fulfill the will of God, and to follow whither he leads.

Henry David Thoreau

A social rebel with high principles, a man who loved nature and solitude, Henry David Thoreau is considered by some a memorable individualist, by others a perennial adolescent, and by still others as both. E. B. White has called him a "regular hairshirt of a man." Born in Concord, Mass., in 1817, he was educated at Harvard and after graduation returned to Concord where he first taught school and on later occasions supported himself by making pencils. He became a friend of Emerson, who was at the time leader of Concord's intellectual and spiritual life; he joined the Transcendental Club and contributed frequently to its journal, *The Dial.* Some have said that Thoreau was the answer to Emerson's plea for an American Scholar. From July 4, 1845, to September 6, 1847, Thoreau lived in a hut at nearby Walden Pond, an experience that he recorded in his most famous work, *Walden.* His stay there was interrupted for one day in the summer of 1846 when he was arrested for not paying the Massachusetts poll tax. He explained his refusal as an act of protest against a government that sanctioned the Mexican War, a war he considered in the interests of Southern slaveholders; he later wrote an eloquent defense of civil disobedience, which was first published in 1849. This essay, which has become an American classic, is reprinted in full below; the text is that of the Riverside edition of Thoreau's works.

Civil Disobedience

I heartily accept the motto,—"That government is best which governs least;" and I should like to see it acted up to more rapidly and systematically. Carried out, it finally amounts to this, which also I believe,—"That government is best which governs not at all;" and when men are prepared for it, that will be the kind of government which they will have. Government is at best but an expedient; but most governments are usually, and all governments are sometimes, inexpedient. The objections which have been brought against a standing army, and they are many and weighty, and deserve to prevail, may also at last be brought against a standing government. The standing army is only an arm of the standing government. The government itself, which is only the mode which the people have chosen to execute their will, is equally liable to be abused and perverted before the people can act through it. Witness the present Mexican war⁰ the work of comparatively a few individuals using the standing government as their tool; for, in the outset, the people would not have consented to this measure.

This American Government,—what is it but a tradition, though a recent one, endeavoring to transmit itself unimpaired to posterity, but each instant losing some of its integrity? It has not the vitality and force of a single living man; for a single man can bend it to his will. It is a sort of wooden gun to the people themselves. But it is not the less necessary for this; for the people must have some complicated machinery or other, and hear its din, to satisfy that idea of government which they have. Governments show thus how successfully men can be imposed on, even impose on themselves, for their own advantage. It is excellent, we must all allow. Yet this government never of itself furthered any enterprise, but by the alacrity with which it got out of its way. *It* does not keep the country free. *It* does not settle the West. *It* does not educate. The character inherent in the American people has done all that has been accomplished; and it

present Mexican war Mexican War (1846–1848), a conflict between Mexico and the United States, caused by the annexation of Texas by the United States in December 1845.

would have done somewhat more, if the government had not sometimes got in its way. For government is an expedient by which men would fain succeed in letting one another alone; and, as has been said, when it is most expedient, the governed are most let alone by it. Trade and commerce, if they were not made of India-rubber, would never manage to bounce over the obstacles which legislators are continually putting in their way; and, if one were to judge these men wholly by the effects of their actions and not partly by their intentions, they would deserve to be classed and punished with those mischievous persons who put obstructions on the railroads.

But, to speak practically and as a citizen, unlike those who call themselves no-government men, I ask for, not at once no government, but *at once* a better government. Let every man make known what kind of government would command his respect, and that will be one step toward obtaining it.

After all, the practical reason why, when the power is once in the hands of the people, a majority are permitted, and for a long period continue, to rule is not because they are most likely to be in the right, nor because this seems fairest to the minority, but because they are physically the strongest. But a government in which the majority rule in all cases cannot be based on justice, even as far as men understand it. Can there not be a government in which majorities do not virtually decide right and wrong, but conscience?—in which majorities decide only those questions to which the rule of expediency is applicable? Must the citizen ever for a moment, or in the least degree, resign his conscience to the legislator? Why has every man a conscience, then? I think that we should be men first, and subjects afterward. It is not desirable to cultivate a respect for the law, so much as for the right. The only obligation which I have a right to assume is to do at any time what I think right. It is truly enough said, that a corporation has no conscience; but a corporation of conscientious men is a corporation *with* a conscience. Law never made men a whit more just; and, by means of their respect for it, even the well-disposed are daily made the agents of injustice. A common and natural result of an undue respect for law is, that you may see a file of soldiers, colonel, captain, corporal, privates, powder-monkeys, and all, marching in admirable order over hill and dale to the wars, against their wills, ay, against their common sense and consciences, which makes it very steep marching indeed, and produces a palpitation of the heart. They have no doubt that it is a damnable business in which they are concerned; they are all peaceably inclined. Now, what are they? Men at all? or small movable forts and magazines, at the service of some unscrupulous man in power? Visit the Navy-Yard, and behold a marine, such a man as an American government can make, or such as it can make a man with its black arts,—a mere shadow and reminiscence of humanity, a man laid out alive and standing, and already, as one may say, buried under arms with funeral accompaniments, though it may be,—

"Not a drum was heard, not a funeral note,
  As his corse to the rampart we hurried;
Not a soldier discharged his farewell shot
  O'er the grave where our hero we buried."º

The mass of men serve the state thus, not as men mainly, but as machines, with their bodies. They are the standing army, and the militia, jailers, constables, posse comitatus, etc. In most cases there is no free exercise whatever of the judgment or of the moral sense; but they put themselves on a level with wood and earth and stones; and wooden men can perhaps be manufactured that will serve the purpose as well. Such command no more respect than men of straw or a lump of dirt. They have the same sort of worth only as horses and dogs. Yet such as these even are commonly esteemed good citizens. Others—as most legislators, politicians, lawyers, ministers, and office-holders—serve the state chiefly with their heads; and, as they rarely make any moral distinctions, they are as likely to serve the Devil, without *intending* it, as God. A very few, as heroes, patriots, martyrs, reformers in the great sense, and *men,* serve the state with their consciences also, and so necessarily resist it for the most part; and they are commonly treated as enemies by it. A wise man will only be useful as a man, and will not submit to be "clay," and "stop a hole to keep the wind away,"º but leave that office to his dust at least:—

"I am too high-born to be propertied,
To be a secondary at control,
Or useful serving-man and instrument
To any sovereign state throughout the world."º

He who gives himself entirely to his fellow-men appears to them useless and selfish; but he who gives himself partially to them is pronounced a benefactor and philanthropist.

How does it become a man to behave toward this American government to-day? I answer, that he cannot without disgrace be associated with it. I cannot for an instant recognize that political organization as *my* government which is the *slave's* government also.

All men recognize the right of revolution; that is, the right to refuse allegiance to, and to resist, the government, when its tyranny or its inefficiency are great and unendurable. But almost all say that such is not the case now. But such was the case, they think, in the Revolution of '75. If one were to tell me that this was a bad government because it taxed certain foreign commodities brought to its ports, it is most probable that

"Not a drum was heard . . ."   From "The Burial of Sir John Moore at Corunna," by the Irish poet Charles Wolfe.
"Clay" and "stop a hole . . ."   From *Hamlet* (Act V, scene i) by William Shakespeare.
"I am too high-born . . ."   From *King John* (Act V, scene ii) by William Shakespeare.

I should not make an ado about it, for I can do without them. All machines have their friction; and possibly this does enough good to counterbalance the evil. At any rate, it is a great evil to make a stir about it. But when the friction comes to have its machine, and oppression and robbery are organized, I say, let us not have such a machine any longer. In other words, when a sixth of the population of a nation which has undertaken to be the refuge of liberty are slaves, and a whole country is unjustly overrun and conquered by a foreign army, and subjected to military law, I think that it is not too soon for honest men to rebel and revolutionize. What makes this duty the more urgent is the fact that the country so overrun is not our own, but ours is the invading army.

Paley,[0] a common authority with many on moral questions, in his chapter on the "Duty of Submission to Civil Government," resolves all civil obligation into expediency; and he proceeds to say, "that so long as the interest of the whole society requires it, that is, so long as the established government cannot be resisted or changed without public inconveniency, it is the will of God that the established government be obeyed, and no longer. . . . This principle being admitted, the justice of every particular case of resistance is reduced to a computation of the quantity of the danger and grievance on the one side, and of the probability and expense of redressing it on the other." Of this, he says, every man shall judge for himself. But Paley appears never to have contemplated those cases to which the rule of expediency does not apply, in which a people, as well as an individual, must do justice, cost what it may. If I have unjustly wrested a plank from a drowning man, I must restore it to him though I drown myself. This, according to Paley, would be inconvenient. But he that would save his life, in such a case, shall lose it. This people must cease to hold slaves, and to make war on Mexico, though it cost them their existence as a people.

In their practice, nations agree with Paley; but does any one think that Massachusetts does exactly what is right at the present crisis?

> "A drab of state, a cloth-o'-silver slut,
> To have her train borne up, and her soul trail in the dirt."[0]

Practically speaking, the opponents to a reform in Massachusetts are not a hundred thousand politicians at the South, but a hundred thousand merchants and farmers here, who are more interested in commerce and agriculture than they are in humanity, and are not prepared to do justice to the slave and to Mexico, *cost what it may.* I quarrel not with far-off foes, but with those who, near at home, coöperate with, and do the bidding of,

Paley   William Paley (1743–1805), English clergyman and philosopher. The reference is to a chapter in his book *Principles of Moral and Political Philosophy* (1785).
"A drab of state . . ."   From Act IV, scene IV of Cyril Tourneur's *The Revenger's Tragedy* (1607).

those far away, and without whom the latter would be harmless. We are accustomed to say, that the mass of men are unprepared; but improvement is slow, because the few are not materially wiser or better than the many. It is not so important that many should be as good as you, as that there be some absolute goodness somewhere; for that will leaven the whole lump. There are thousands who are *in opinion* opposed to slavery and to the war, who yet in effect do nothing to put an end to them; who, esteeming themselves children of Washington and Franklin, sit down with their hands in their pockets, and say that they know not what to do, and do nothing; who even postpone the question of freedom to the question of free-trade, and quietly read the prices-current along with the latest advices from Mexico, after dinner, and, it may be, fall asleep over them both. What is the price-current of an honest man and patriot to-day? They hesitate, and they regret, and sometimes they petition; but they do nothing in earnest and with effect. They will wait, well disposed, for others to remedy the evil, that they may no longer have it to regret. At most, they give only a cheap vote, and a feeble countenance and Godspeed, to the right, as it goes by them. There are nine hundred and ninety-nine patrons of virtue to one virtuous man. But it is easier to deal with the real possessor of a thing than with the temporary guardian of it.

All voting is a sort of gaming, like checkers or backgammon, with a slight moral tinge to it, a playing with right and wrong, with moral questions; and betting naturally accompanies it. The character of the voters is not staked. I cast my vote, perchance, as I think right; but I am not vitally concerned that that right should prevail. I am willing to leave it to the majority. Its obligation, therefore, never exceeds that of expediency. Even voting *for the right* is *doing* nothing for it. It is only expressing to men feebly your desire that it should prevail. A wise man will not leave the right to the mercy of chance, nor wish it to prevail through the power of the majority. There is but little virtue in the action of masses of men. When the majority shall at length vote for the abolition of slavery, it will be because they are indifferent to slavery, or because there is but little slavery left to be abolished by their vote. *They* will then be the only slaves. Only *his* vote can hasten the abolition of slavery who asserts his own freedom by his vote.

I hear of a convention to be held at Baltimore, or elsewhere, for the selection of a candidate for the Presidency, made up chiefly of editors, and men who are politicians by profession; but I think, what is it to any independent, intelligent, and respectable man what decision they may come to? Shall we not have the advantage of his wisdom and honesty, nevertheless? Can we not count upon some independent votes? Are there not many individuals in the country who do not attend conventions? But no: I find that the respectable man, so called, has immediately drifted from his position, and despairs of his country, when his country has more reason to despair of him. He forthwith adopts one of the candidates thus selected as the only *available* one, thus proving that he is himself *available* for any purposes of the demagogue. His vote is of no more worth than that of any unprincipled foreigner or hireling native, who may have been bought. O for a man who is a *man,* and, as my neighbor says, has a bone in his back which you cannot pass your hand through! Our statistics are at fault: the population has been returned too large. How many *men* are there to a square thousand miles in this country? Hardly one. Does not America offer any inducement for men to settle here? The American has dwindled into an Odd Fellow,—one who may be known by the development of his organ of gregariousness, and a manifest lack of intellect and cheerful self-reliance; whose first and chief concern, on coming into the world, is to see that the Almshouses are in good repair; and, before yet he has lawfully donned the virile garb, to collect a fund for the support of the widows and orphans that may be; who, in short, ventures to live only by the aid of the Mutual Insurance company, which has promised to bury him decently.

It is not a man's duty, as a matter of course, to devote himself to the eradication of any, even the most enormous wrong; he may still properly have other concerns to engage him; but it is his duty, at least, to wash his hands of it, and, if he gives it no thought longer, not to give it practically his support. If I devote myself to other pursuits and contemplations, I must first see, at least, that I do not pursue them sitting upon another man's shoulders. I must get off him first, that he may pursue his contemplations too. See what gross inconsistency is tolerated. I have heard some of my townsmen say, "I should like to have them order me out to help put down an insurrection of the slaves, or to march to Mexico;—see if I would go;" and yet these very men have each, directly by their allegiance, and so indirectly, at least, by their money, furnished a substitute. The soldier is applauded who refuses to serve in an unjust war by those who do not refuse to sustain the unjust government which makes the war; is applauded by those whose own act and authority he disregards and sets at naught; as if the state were penitent to that degree that it hired one to scourge it while it sinned, but not to that degree that it left off sinning for a moment. Thus, under the name of Order and Civil Government, we are all made at last to pay homage to and support our own meanness. After the first blush of sin comes its indifference; and from immoral it becomes, as it were, *un*moral, and not quite unnecessary to that life which we have made.

The broadest and most prevalent error requires the most disinterested virtue to sustain it. The slight reproach to which the virtue of patriotism is commonly liable, the noble are most likely to incur. Those who, while they disapprove of the character and measures of a government, yield to it their allegiance and support are undoubtedly its most conscientious supporters, and so frequently the most serious obstacles to reform. Some are petitioning the state to dissolve the Union, to disregard the requisitions of the President. Why do they not dissolve it themselves,—the union between themselves and the state,—and refuse to pay their quota into its treasury? Do not they stand in the same relation to the state that the state does to the Union? And have not the same reasons prevented the state from resisting the Union which have prevented them from resisting the state?

How can a man be satisfied to entertain an opinion merely, and enjoy *it*? Is there any enjoyment in it, if his opinion is that he is aggrieved? If you are cheated out of a single dollar by your neighbor, you do not rest satisfied with knowing that you are cheated, or with saying that you are cheated, or even with petitioning him to pay you your due; but you take effectual steps at once to obtain the full amount, and see that you are never cheated again. Action from principle, the perception and the performance of right, changes things and relations; it is essentially revolutionary, and does not consist wholly with anything which was. It not only divides states and churches, it divides families; ay, it divides the *individual*, separating the diabolical in him from the divine.

Unjust laws exist: shall we be content to obey them, or shall we endeavor to amend them, and obey them until we have succeeded, or shall we transgress them at once? Men generally, under such a government as this, think that they ought to wait until they have persuaded the majority to alter them. They think that, if they should resist, the remedy would be worse than the evil. But it is the fault of the government itself that the remedy *is* worse than the evil. *It* makes it worse. Why is it not more apt to anticipate and provide for reform? Why does it not cherish its wise minority? Why does it cry and resist before it is hurt? Why does it not encourage its citizens to be on the alert to point out its faults, and *do* better than it would have them? Why does it always crucify Christ, and excommunicate Copernicus and Luther, and pronounce Washington and Franklin rebels?

One would think, that a deliberate and practical denial of its authority was the only offense never contemplated by government; else, why has it not assigned its definite, its suitable and proportionate penalty? If a man who has no property refuses but once to earn nine shillings for the state, he is put in prison for a period unlimited by any law that I know, and determined only by the discretion of those who placed him there; but if he should steal ninety times nine shillings from the state, he is soon permitted to go at large again.

If the injustice is part of the necessary friction of the machine of government, let it go, let it go: perchance it will wear smooth,—certainly the machine will wear out. If the injustice has a spring, or a pulley, or a rope, or a crank, exclusively for itself, then perhaps you may consider whether the remedy will not be worse than the evil; but if it is of such a nature that it requires you to be the agent of injustice to another, then, I say, break the law. Let your life be a counter friction to stop the machine. What I have to do is to see, at any rate, that I do not lend myself to the wrong which I condemn.

As for adopting the ways which the state has provided for remedying the evil, I know not of such ways. They take too much time, and a man's life will be gone. I have other affairs to attend to. I came into this world, not chiefly to make this a good place to live in, but to live in it, be it good or bad. A man has not everything to do, but something; and because he cannot do *everything,* it is not necessary that he should do *something* wrong. It is not my business to be petitioning the Governor or the Legislature any more than it is theirs to petition me; and if they should not hear my petition, what should I do then? But in this case the state has provided no way: its very Constitution is the evil. This may seem to be harsh and stubborn and unconciliatory; but it is to treat with the utmost kindness and consideration the only spirit that can appreciate or deserves it. So is all change for the better, like birth and death, which convulse the body.

I do not hesitate to say, that those who call themselves Abolitionists should at once effectually withdraw their support, both in person and property, from the government of Massachusetts, and not wait till they constitute a majority of one, before they suffer the right to prevail through them. I think that it is enough if they have God on their side, without waiting for that other one. Moreover, any man more right than his neighbors constitutes a majority of one already.

I meet this American government, or its representative, the state government, directly, and face to face, once a year—no more—in the person of its tax-gatherer; this is the only mode in which a man situated as I am necessarily meets it; and it then says distinctly, Recognize me; and the simplest, the most effectual, and, in the present posture of affairs, the indispensablest mode of treating with it on this head, of expressing your little satisfaction with and love for it, is to deny it then. My civil neighbor, the tax-gatherer, is the very man I have to deal with,—for it is, after all, with men and not with parchment that I quarrel,—and he has voluntarily chosen to be an agent of the government. How shall he ever know well what he is and does as an officer of the government, or as a man, until he is obliged to consider whether he shall treat me, his neighbor, for whom he has respect, as a neighbor and well-disposed man, or as a maniac and disturber of the peace, and see if he can get over this obstruction to his neighborliness without a ruder and more impetuous thought or speech corresponding with his action. I know this well, that if one thousand, if one hundred, if ten men whom I could name,—if ten *honest* men only,—say if *one* HONEST man, in this State of Massachusetts, *ceasing to hold slaves,* were actually to withdraw from this copartnership, and be locked up in the county jail therefor, it would be the abolition of slavery in America. For it matters not how small the beginning may seem to be: what is once well done is done forever. But we love better to talk about it: that we say is our mission. Reform keeps many scores of newspapers in its service, but not one man. If my esteemed neighbor, the State's ambassador, who will devote his days to the settlement of the question of human rights in the

Council Chamber, instead of being threatened with the prisons of Carolina, were to sit down the prisoner of Massachusetts, that State which is so anxious to foist the sin of slavery upon her sister,—though at present she can discover only an act of inhospitality to be the ground of a quarrel with her,—the Legislature would not wholly waive the subject the following winter.

Under a government which imprisons any unjustly, the true place for a just man is also a prison. The proper place to-day, the only place which Massachusetts has provided for her freer and less desponding spirits, is in her prisons, to be put out and locked out of the State by her own act, as they have already put themselves out by their principles. It is there that the fugitive slave, and the Mexican prisoner on parole, and the Indian come to plead the wrongs of his race should find them; on that separate, but more free and honorable ground, where the State places those who are not *with* her, but *against* her,—the only house in a slave State in which a free man can abide with honor. If any think that their influence would be lost there, and their voices no longer afflict the ear of the State, that they would not be as an enemy within its walls, they do not know by how much truth is stronger than error, nor how much more eloquently and effectively he can combat injustice who has experienced a little in his own person. Cast your whole vote, not a strip of paper merely, but your whole influence. A minority is powerless while it conforms to the majority; it is not even a minority then; but it is irresistible when it clogs by its whole weight. If the alternative is to keep all just men in prison, or give up war and slavery, the State will not hesitate which to choose. If a thousand men were not to pay their tax-bills this year, that would not be a violent and bloody measure, as it would be to pay them, and enable the State to commit violence and shed innocent blood. This is, in fact, the definition of a peaceable revolution, if any such is possible. If the tax-gatherer, or any other public officer, asks me, as one has done, "But what shall I do?" my answer is, "If you really wish to do anything, resign your office." When the subject has refused allegiance, and the officer has resigned his office, then the revolution is accomplished. But even suppose blood should flow. Is there not a sort of blood shed when the conscience is wounded? Through this wound a man's real manhood and immortality flow out, and he bleeds to an everlasting death. I see this blood flowing now.

I have contemplated the imprisonment of the offender, rather than the seizure of his goods,—though both will serve the same purpose,—because they who assert the purest right, and consequently are most dangerous to a corrupt State, commonly have not spent much time in accumulating property. To such the State renders comparatively small service, and a slight tax is wont to appear exorbitant, particularly if they are obliged to earn it by special labor with their hands. If there were one who lived wholly without the use of money, the State itself would hesitate to demand it of him. But the rich man—not to make any invidious comparison—is always sold to the institution which makes him rich. Absolutely speaking, the more money, the less virtue; for money comes between a man and his objects, and obtains them for him; and it was certainly no great virtue to obtain it. It puts to rest many questions which he would otherwise be taxed to answer; while the only new question which it puts is the hard but superfluous one, how to spend it. Thus his moral ground is taken from under his feet. The opportunities of living are diminished in proportion as what are called the "means" are increased. The best thing a man can do for his culture when he is rich is to endeavor to carry out those schemes which he entertained when he was poor. Christ answered the Herodians according to their condition. "Show me the tribute-money," said he;—and one took a penny out of his pocket;—if you use money which has the image of Caesar on it, which he has made current and valuable, that is, *if you are men of the State,* and gladly enjoy the advantages of Caesar's government, then pay him back some of his own when he demands it. "Render therefore to Caesar that which is Caesar's, and to God those things which are God's,"—leaving them no wiser than before as to which was which; for they did not wish to know.

When I converse with the freest of my neighbors, I perceive that, whatever they may say about the magnitude and seriousness of the question, and their regard for the public tranquillity, the long and the short of the matter is, that they cannot spare the protection of the existing government, and they dread the consequences to their property and families of disobedience to it. For my own part, I should not like to think that I ever rely on the protection of the State. But, if I deny the authority of the State when it presents its tax-bill, it will soon take and waste all my property, and so harass me and my children without end. This is hard. This makes it impossible for a man to live honestly, and at the same time comfortably, in outward respects. It will not be worth the while to accumulate property; that would be sure to go again. You must hire or squat somewhere, and raise but a small crop, and eat that soon. You must live within yourself, and depend upon yourself always tucked up and ready for a start, and not have many affairs. A man may grow rich in Turkey even, if he will be in all respects a good subject of the Turkish government. Confucius said: "If a state is governed by the principles of reason, poverty and misery are subjects of shame; if a state is not governed by the principles of reason, riches and honors are the subjects of shame." No: until I want the protection of Massachusetts to be extended to me in some distant Southern port, where my liberty is endangered, or until I am bent solely on building up an estate at home by peaceful enterprise, I can afford to refuse allegiance to Massachusetts, and her right to my property and life. It costs me less in every sense to incur the penalty of disobedience to the State than it would to obey. I should feel as if I were worth less in that case.

Some years ago, the State met me in behalf of the Church, and commanded me to pay a certain sum toward the support of a clergyman whose preaching my father attended, but never I myself. "Pay," it said, "or be locked up in the jail." I declined to pay. But, unfortunately, another man saw fit to pay it. I did not see why the schoolmaster should be taxed to support the priest, and not the priest the schoolmaster; for I was not the State's schoolmaster, but I supported myself by voluntary subscription. I did not see why the lyceum should not present its tax-bill, and have the State to back its demand, as well as the Church. However, at the request of the selectmen, I condescended to make some such statement as this in writing:—"Know all men by these presents, that I, Henry Thoreau, do not wish to be regarded as a member of any incorporated society which I have not joined." This I gave to the town clerk; and he has it. The State, having thus learned that I did not wish to be regarded as a member of that church, has never made a like demand on me since; though it said that it must adhere to its original presumption that time. If I had known how to name them, I should then have signed off in detail from all the societies which I never signed on to; but I did not know where to find a complete list.

I have paid no poll-tax for six years. I was put into a jail once on this account, for one night; and, as I stood considering the walls of solid stone, two or three feet thick, the door of wood and iron, a foot thick, and the iron grating which strained the light, I could not help being struck with the foolishness of that institution which treated me as if I were mere flesh and blood and bones, to be locked up. I wondered that it should have concluded at length that this was the best use it could put me to, and had never thought to avail itself of my services in some way. I saw that, if there was a wall of stone between me and my townsmen, there was a still more difficult one to climb or break through before they could get to be as free as I was. I did not for a moment feel confined, and the walls seemed a great waste of stone and mortar. I felt as if I alone of all my townsmen had paid my tax. They plainly did not know how to treat me, but behaved like persons who are underbred. In every threat and in every compliment there was a blunder; for they thought that my chief desire was to stand the other side of that stone wall. I could not but smile to see how industriously they locked the door on my mediations, which followed them out again without let or hindrance, and *they* were really all that was dangerous. As they could not reach me, they had resolved to punish my body; just as boys, if they cannot come at some person against whom they have a spite, will abuse his dog. I saw that the State was half-witted, that it was timid as a lone woman with her silver spoons, and that it did not know its friends from its foes, and I lost all my remaining respect for it, and pitied it.

Thus the State never intentionally confronts a man's sense, intellectual or moral, but only his body, his senses. It is not armed with superior wit or honesty, but with superior physical strength. I was not born to be forced. I will breathe after my own fashion. Let us see who is the strongest. What force has a multitude? They only can force me who obey a higher law than I. They force me to become like themselves. I do not hear of *men* being *forced* to live this way or that by masses of men. What sort of life were that to live? When I meet a government which says to me, "Your money or your life," why should I be in haste to give it my money? It may be in a great strait, and not know what to do: I cannot help that. It must help itself; do as I do. It is not worth the while to snivel about it. I am not responsible for the successful working of the machinery of society. I am not the son of the engineer. I perceive that, when an acorn and a chestnut fall side by side, the one does not remain inert to make way for the other, but both obey their own laws, and spring and grow and flourish as best they can, till one, perchance, overshadows and destroys the other. If a plant cannot live according to its nature, it dies; and so a man.

The night in prison was novel and interesting enough. The prisoners in their shirt-sleeves were enjoying a chat and the evening air in the door-way, when I entered. But the jailer said, "Come, boys, it is time to lock up;" and so they dispersed, and I heard the sound of their steps returning into the hollow apartments. My room-mate was introduced to me by the jailer as "a first-rate fellow and a clever man." When the door was locked, he showed me where to hang my hat, and how he managed matters there. The rooms were whitewashed once a month; and this one, at least, was the whitest, most simply furnished, and probably the neatest apartment in the town. He naturally wanted to know where I came from, and what brought me there; and, when I had told him, I asked him in my turn how he came there, presuming him to be an honest man, of course; and, as the world goes, I believe he was. "Why," said he, "they accuse me of burning a barn; but I never did it." As near as I could discover, he had probably gone to bed in a barn when drunk, and smoked his pipe there; and so a barn was burnt. He had the reputation of being a clever man, had been there some three months waiting for his trial to come on, and would have to wait as much longer; but he was quite domesticated and contented, since he got his board for nothing, and thought that he was well treated.

He occupied one window, and I the other; and I saw that if one stayed there long, his principal business would be to look out the window. I had soon read all the tracts that were left there, and examined where former prisoners had broken out, and where a grate had been sawed off, and heard the history of the various occupants of that room; for I found that even here there was a history and a gossip which never circulated beyond the walls of the jail. Probably this is the only house in the town where verses are composed, which are afterward printed in a circular form, but not published. I was shown quite a long list of verses which were composed by some young men who had been detected in an attempt to escape, who avenged themselves by signing them.

I pumped my fellow-prisoner as dry as I could, for fear I should never see him again; but at length he showed me which was my bed, and left me to blow out the lamp.

It was like traveling into a far country, such as I had never expected to behold, to lie there for one night. It seemed to me that I never had heard the town-clock strike before, nor the evening sounds of the village; for we slept with the windows open, which were inside the grating. It was to see my native village in the light of the Middle Ages, and our Concord was turned into a Rhine stream, and visions of knights and castles passed before me. They were the voices of old burghers that I heard in the streets. I was an involuntary spectator and auditor of whatever was done and said in the kitchen of the adjacent village-inn,—a wholly new and rare experience to me. It was a closer view of my native town. I was fairly inside of it. I never had seen its institutions before. This is one of its peculiar institutions; for it is a shire town. I began to comprehend what its inhabitants were about.

In the morning, our breakfasts were put through the hole in the door, in small oblong-square tin pans, made to fit, and holding a pint of chocolate, with brown bread, and an iron spoon. When they called for the vessels again, I was green enough to return what bread I had left; but my comrade seized it, and said that I should lay that up for lunch or dinner. Soon after he was let out to work at haying in a neighboring field, whither he went every day, and would not be back till noon; so he bade me good-day, saying that he doubted if he should see me again.

When I came out of prison,—for some one interfered, and paid that tax, —I did not perceive that great changes had taken place on the common, such as he observed who went in a youth and emerged a tottering and gray-headed man; and yet a change had to my eyes come over the scene, —the town, and State, and country,—greater than any that mere time could effect. I saw yet more distinctly the State in which I lived. I saw to what extent the people among whom I lived could be trusted as good neighbors and friends; that their friendship was for summer weather only; that they did not greatly propose to do right; that they were a distinct race from me by their prejudices and superstitions, as the Chinamen and Malays are; that in their sacrifices to humanity they ran no risks, not even to their property; that after all they were not so noble but they treated the thief as he had treated them, and hoped, by a certain outward observance and a few prayers, and by walking in a particular straight though useless path from time to time, to save their souls. This may be to judge my neighbors harshly; for I believe that many of them are not aware that they have such an institution as the jail in their village.

It was formerly the custom in our village, when a poor debtor came out of jail, for his acquaintances to salute him, looking through their fingers, which were crossed to represent the grating of a jail window, "How do ye do?" My neighbors did not thus salute me, but first looked at me, and then at one another, as if I had returned from a long journey. I was put into jail as I was going to the shoemaker's to get a shoe which was mended. When I was let out the next morning, I proceeded to finish my errand, and, having put on my mended shoe, joined a huckleberry party, who were impatient to put themselves under my conduct; and in half an hour,—for the horse was soon tackled,—was in the midst of a huckleberry field, on one of our highest hills, two miles off, and then the State was nowhere to be seen.

This is the whole history of "My Prisons."

I have never declined paying the highway tax, because I am as desirous of being a good neighbor as I am of being a bad subject; and as for supporting schools, I am doing my part to educate my fellow-countrymen now. It is for no particular item in the tax-bill that I refuse to pay it. I simply wish to refuse allegiance to the State, to withdraw and stand aloof from it effectually. I do not care to trace the course of my dollar, if I could, till it buys a man or a musket to shoot one with,—the dollar is innocent, —but I am concerned to trace the effects of my allegiance. In fact, I quietly declare war with the State, after my fashion, though I will still make what use and get what advantage of her I can, as is usual in such cases.

If others pay the tax which is demanded of me, from a sympathy with the State, they do but what they have already done in their own case, or rather they abet injustice to a greater extent than the State requires. If they pay the tax from a mistaken interest in the individual taxed, to save his property, or prevent his going to jail, it is because they have not considered wisely how far they let their private feelings interfere with the public good.

This, then, is my position at present. But one cannot be too much on his guard in such a case, lest his action be biased by obstinacy or an undue regard for the opinions of men. Let him see that he does only what belongs to himself and to the hour.

I think sometimes, Why, this people mean well, they are only ignorant; they would do better if they knew how: why give your neighbors this pain to treat you as they are not inclined to? But I think again, This is no reason why I should do as they do, or permit others to suffer much greater pain of a different kind. Again, I sometimes say to myself, When many millions of men, without heat, without ill will, without personal feeling of any kind, demand of you a few shillings only, without the possibility, such is their constitution, of retracting or altering their present demand, and without the possibility, on your side, of appeal to any other millions, why expose yourself to this overwhelming brute force? You do not resist cold and hunger, the winds and the waves, thus obstinately; you quietly submit to a thousand similar necessities. You do not put your head into the fire. But just in proportion as I regard this as not wholly a brute force, but partly a human force, and consider that I have relations to those millions as to so many millions of men, and not of mere brute or inanimate things, I see that appeal is possible, first and instantaneously, from them to the Maker of them, and, secondly, from them to themselves. But if I put my head deliberately into the fire, there is no appeal to fire or to the Maker of fire, and I have only myself to blame. If I could convince myself that I have any right to be satisfied with men as they are, and to treat them accordingly, and not according, in some respects, to my requisitions and expectations of what they and I ought to be, then, like a good Mussulman and fatalist, I should endeavor to be satisfied with things as they are, and say it is the will of God. And, above all, there is this difference between resisting this and a purely brute or natural force that I can resist this with some effect; but I cannot expect, like Orpheus,⁰ to change the nature of the rocks and trees and beasts.

I do not wish to quarrel with any man or nation. I do not wish to split hairs, to make fine distinctions, or set myself up as better than my neighbors. I seek rather, I may say, even an excuse for conforming to the laws of the land. I am but too ready to conform to them. Indeed, I have reason to suspect myself on this head; and each year, as the tax-gatherer comes round, I find myself disposed to review the acts and position of the general and State governments, and the spirit of the people, to discover a pretext for conformity.

> "We must affect our country as our parents,
> And if at any time we alienate
> Our love or industry from doing it honor,
> We must respect effects and teach the soul
> Matter of conscience and religion,
> And not desire of rule or benefit."⁰

I believe that the State will soon be able to take all my work of this sort out of my hands, and then I shall be no better a patriot than my fellow-countrymen. Seen from a lower point of view, the Constitution, with all its faults, is very good; the law and the courts are very respectable; even this State and this American government are, in many respects, very admirable, and rare things, to be thankful for, such as a great many have described them; but seen from a point of view a little higher, they are what I have described them; seen from a higher still, and the highest, who shall say what they are, or that they are worth looking at or thinking of at all?

However, the government does not concern me much, and I shall bestow the fewest possible thoughts on it. It is not many moments that I live under a government, even in this world. If a man is thought-free, fancy-free, imagination-free, that which *is not* never for a long time

Orpheus legendary pre-Homeric Greek poet and musician. He played the lyre so beautifully that the wild beasts were tamed, and the rocks and trees moved to the music.
"We must affect ..." From *The Battle of Alcazar* (1594), a play by George Peele (c.1558–1598).

appearing *to be* to him, unwise rulers or reformers cannot fatally interrupt him.

I know that most men think differently from myself; but those whose lives are by profession devoted to the study of these or kindred subjects content me as little as any. Statesmen and legislators, standing so completely within the institution, never distinctly and nakedly behold it. They speak of moving society, but have no resting-place without it. They may be men of a certain experience and discrimination, and have no doubt invented ingenious and even useful systems, for which we sincerely thank them; but all their wit and usefulness lie within certain not very wide limits. They are wont to forget that the world is not governed by policy and expediency. Webster never goes behind government, and so cannot speak with authority about it. His words are wisdom to those legislators who contemplate no essential reform in the existing government; but for thinkers, and those who legislate for all time, he never once glances at the subject. I know of those whose serene and wise speculations on this theme would soon reveal the limits of his mind's range and hospitality. Yet, compared with the cheap professions of most reformers, and the still cheaper wisdom and eloquence of politicians in general, his are almost the only sensible and valuable words, and we thank Heaven for him. Comparatively, he is always strong, original, and, above all, practical. Still, his quality is not wisdom, but prudence. The lawyer's truth is not Truth, but consistency or a consistent expediency. Truth is always in harmony with herself, and is not concerned chiefly to reveal the justice that may consist with wrong-doing. He well deserves to be called, as he has been called, the Defender of the Constitution. There are really no blows to be given by him but defensive ones. He is not a leader, but a follower. His leaders are the men of '87. "I have never made an effort," he says, "and never propose to make an effort; I have never countenanced an effort, and never mean to countenance an effort, to disturb the arrangement as originally made, by which the various States came into the Union." Still thinking of the sanction which the Constitution gives to slavery, he says, "Because it was a part of the original compact,—let it stand." Notwithstanding his special acuteness and ability, he is unable to take a fact out of its merely political relations, and behold it as it lies absolutely to be disposed of by the intellect,—what, for instance, it behooves a man to do here in America to-day with regard to slavery,—but ventures, or is driven, to make some such desperate answer as the following, while professing to speak absolutely, and as a private man,—from which what new and singular code of social duties might be inferred? "The manner," says he, "in which the governments of those States where slavery exists are to regulate it is for their own consideration, under their responsibility to their constituents, to the general laws of propriety, humanity, and justice, and to God. Associations formed elsewhere, springing from a feeling of humanity, or any other cause, have nothing whatever to do with it. They have never received any encouragement from me, and they never will."

They who know of no purer sources of truth, who have traced up its stream no higher, stand, and wisely stand, by the Bible and the Constitution, and drink at it there with reverence and humility; but they who behold where it comes trickling into this lake or that pool, gird up their loins once more, and continue their pilgrimage toward its fountain-head.

No man with a genius for legislation has appeared in America. They are rare in the history of the world. There are orators, politicians, and eloquent men, by the thousand; but the speaker has not yet opened his mouth to speak who is capable of settling the much-vexed questions of the day. We love eloquence for its own sake, and not for any truth which it may utter, or any heroism it may inspire. Our legislators have not yet learned the comparative value of free-trade and of freedom, of union, and of rectitude, to a nation. They have no genius or talent for comparatively humble questions of taxation and finance, commerce and manufactures and agriculture. If we were left solely to the wordy wit of legislators in Congress for our guidance, uncorrected by the seasonable experience and the effectual complaints of the people, America would not long retain her rank among the nations. For eighteen hundred years, though perchance I have no right to say it, the New Testament has been written; yet where is the legislator who has wisdom and practical talent enough to avail himself of the light which it sheds on the science of legislation?

The authority of government, even such as I am willing to submit to,— for I will cheerfully obey those who know and can do better than I, and in many things even those who neither know nor can do so well,—is still an impure one: to be strictly just, it must have the sanction and consent of the governed. It can have no pure right over my person and property but what I concede to it. The progress from an absolute to a limited monarchy, from a limited monarchy to a democracy, is a progress toward a true respect for the individual. Even the Chinese philosopher was wise enough to regard the individual as the basis of the empire. Is a democracy, such as we know it, the last improvement possible in government? Is it not possible to take a further step towards recognizing and organizing the rights of man? There will never be a really free and enlightened State until the State comes to recognize the individual as a higher and independent power, from which all its own power and authority are derived, and treats him accordingly. I please myself with imagining a State at last which can afford to be just to all men, and to treat the individual with respect as a neighbor; which even would not think it inconsistent with its own repose if a few were to live aloof from it, not meddling with it, nor embraced by it, who fulfilled all the duties of neighbors and fellow-men. A State which bore this kind of fruit, and suffered it to drop off as fast as it ripened, would prepare the way for a still more perfect and glorious State, which also I have imagined, but not yet anywhere seen.

Martin Luther King, Jr.

Martin Luther King, Jr., was one of the most forceful advocates of nonviolent disobedience in the struggle for civil and human rights. Born in Georgia in 1929 and educated at Morehouse College, Crozer Theological Seminary, and Boston University, he became a Baptist minister in Montgomery, Alabama, in 1954. The next year he launched the now famous Montgomery bus boycott. Founder and president of the Southern Christian Leadership Conference, he was a leader of the 1963 March on Washington and of the 1965 voter registration drive in Selma, Alabama. In 1964 he received the Nobel Peace Prize. He was assassinated in Memphis, Tennessee, on April 4, 1968, while supporting a strike of city sanitation workers.

His writings include *Stride Toward Freedom* (1958), *Strength to Love* (1963), *Where Do We Go from Here: Chaos or Community* (1967), *Conscience for Change* (1967), *The Measure of Man* (1968), and *The Trumpet of Conscience* (1968). *Why We Can't Wait,* published in 1964, includes a revised version of the letter printed below, and an author's note in which he says, "This response to a published statement by eight fellow clergymen from Alabama . . . was composed under somewhat constricting circumstances. Begun on the margins of the newspaper in which the statement appeared while I was in jail, the letter was continued on scraps of writing paper supplied by a friendly Negro trusty, and concluded on a pad my attorneys were eventually permitted to leave me. Although the text remains in substance unaltered, I have indulged in the author's prerogative of polishing it for publication." For its greater immediacy, we present here the unrevised version of the letter, together with the public statement that occasioned it.

Public Statement by Eight Alabama Clergymen

(April 12, 1963)

We the undersigned clergymen are among those who, in January, issued "An Appeal for Law and Order and Common Sense," in dealing with racial problems in Alabama. We expressed understanding that honest convictions in racial matters could properly be pursued in the courts, but urged that decisions of those courts should in the meantime be peacefully obeyed.

Since that time there had been some evidence of increased forbearance and a willingness to face facts. Responsible citizens have undertaken to work on various problems which cause racial friction and unrest. In Birmingham, recent public events have given indication that we all have opportunity for a new constructive and realistic approach to racial problems.

However, we are now confronted by a series of demonstrations by some of our Negro citizens, directed and led in part by outsiders. We recognize the natural impatience of people who feel that their hopes are slow in being realized. But we are convinced that these demonstrations are unwise and untimely.

We agree rather with certain local Negro leadership which has called for honest and open negotiation of racial issues in our area. And we believe this kind of facing of issues can best be accomplished by citizens of our own metropolitan area, white and Negro, meeting with their knowledge and experience of the local situation. All of us need to face that responsibility and find proper channels for its accomplishment.

Just as we formerly pointed out that "hatred and violence have no sanction in our religious and political traditions," we also point out that such actions as incite to hatred and violence, however technically peaceful those actions may be, have not contributed to the resolution of our local problems. We do not believe that these days of new hope are days when extreme measures are justified in Birmingham.

We commend the community as a whole, and the local news media and law enforcement officials in particular, on the calm manner in which these demonstrations have been handled. We urge the public to continue to show restraint should the demonstrations continue, and the law enforcement officials to remain calm and continue to protect our city from violence.

We further strongly urge our own Negro community to withdraw support from these demonstrations, and to unite locally in working peacefully for a better Birmingham. When rights are consistently denied, a cause should be pressed in the courts and in negotiations among local leaders, and not in the streets. We appeal to both our white and Negro citizenry to observe the principles of law and order and common sense.

Signed by:

C. C. J. CARPENTER, D.D., LL.D., *Bishop of Alabama*

JOSEPH A. DURICK, D.D., *Auxiliary Bishop, Diocese of Mobile, Birmingham*

Rabbi MILTON L. GRAFMAN, *Temple Emanu-El, Birmingham, Alabama*

Bishop PAUL HARDIN, *Bishop of the Alabama-West Florida Conference of the Methodist Church*

Bishop NOLAN B. HARMON, *Bishop of the North Alabama Conference of the Methodist Church*

GEORGE M. MURRAY, D.D., LL.D., *Bishop Coadjutor, Episcopal Diocese of Alabama*

EDWARD V. RAMAGE, *Moderator, Synod of the Alabama Presbyterian Church in the United States*

EARL STALLINGS, *Pastor, First Baptist Church, Birmingham, Alabama*

Letter from Birmingham Jail

MARTIN LUTHER KING, JR.
Birmingham City Jail
April 16, 1963

Bishop C. C. J. CARPENTER
Bishop JOSEPH A. DURICK
Rabbi MILTON L. GRAFMAN
Bishop PAUL HARDIN
Bishop NOLAN B. HARMON
The Rev. GEORGE M. MURRAY
The Rev. EDWARD V. RAMAGE
The Rev. EARL STALLINGS

My dear Fellow Clergymen,

While confined here in the Birmingham City Jail, I came across your recent statement calling our present activities "unwise and untimely." Seldom, if ever, do I pause to answer criticism of my work and ideas. If I sought to answer all of the criticisms that cross my desk, my secretaries would be engaged in little else in the course of the day and I would have no time for constructive work. But since I feel that you are men of genuine good will and your criticisms are sincerely set forth, I would like to answer your statement in what I hope will be patient and reasonable terms.

I think I should give the reason for my being in Birmingham, since you have been influenced by the argument of "outsiders coming in." I have the honor of serving as president of the Southern Christian Leadership Conference, an organization operating in every Southern state with headquarters in Atlanta, Georgia. We have some eighty-five affiliate organizations all across the South—one being the Alabama Christian Movement for Human Rights. Whenever necessary and possible we share staff, educational, and financial resources with our affiliates. Several months ago our local affiliate here in Birmingham invited us to be on call to engage in a nonviolent direct action program if such were deemed necessary. We readily consented and when the hour came we lived up to our promises. So I am here, along with several members of my staff, because we were invited here. I am here because I have basic organizational ties here. Beyond this, I am in Birmingham because injustice is here. Just as the eighth century prophets left their little villages and carried their "thus saith the Lord" far beyond the boundaries of their home town, and just as the Apostle Paul left his little village of Tarsus and carried the gospel of Jesus Christ to practically every hamlet and city of the Graeco-Roman world, I too am compelled to carry the gospel of freedom beyond my particular home town. Like Paul, I must constantly respond to the Macedonian call for aid.

Moreover, I am cognizant of the interrelatedness of all communities and states. I cannot sit idly by in Atlanta and not be concerned about what happens in Birmingham. Injustice anywhere is a threat to justice everywhere. We are caught in an inescapable network of mutuality tied in a single garment of destiny. Whatever affects one directly affects all indirectly. Never again can we afford to live with the narrow, provincial "outside agitator" idea. Anyone who lives inside the United States can never be considered an outsider anywhere in this country.

You deplore the demonstrations that are presently taking place in Birmingham. But I am sorry that your statement did not express a similar concern for the conditions that brought the demonstrations into being. I am sure that each of you would want to go beyond the superficial social analyst who looks merely at effects, and does not grapple with underlying causes. I would not hesitate to say that it is unfortunate that so-called demonstrations are taking place in Birmingham at this time, but I would say in more emphatic terms that it is even more unfortunate that the white power structure of this city left the Negro community with no other alternative.

In any nonviolent campaign there are four basic steps: (1) collection of the facts to determine whether injustices are alive; (2) negotiation; (3) self-purification; and (4) direct action. We have gone through all of these steps in Birmingham. There can be no gainsaying of the fact that racial injustice engulfs this community. Birmingham is probably the most thoroughly segregated city in the United States. Its ugly record of police brutality is known in every section of this country. Its unjust treatment of Negroes in the courts is a notorious reality. There have been more unsolved bombings of Negro homes and churches in Birmingham than any city in this nation. These are the hard, brutal, and unbelievable facts. On the basis of these conditions Negro leaders sought to negotiate with the city fathers. But the political leaders consistently refused to engage in good faith negotiation.

Then came the opportunity last September to talk with some of the leaders of the economic community. In these negotiating sessions certain promises were made by the merchants—such as the promise to remove the humiliating racial signs from the stores. On the basis of these promises Rev. Shuttlesworth and the leaders of the Alabama Christian Movement for Human Rights agreed to call a moratorium on any type of demonstrations. As the weeks and months unfolded we realized that we were the victims of a broken promise. The signs remained. As in so many experiences of the past we were confronted with blasted hopes, and the dark shadow of a deep disappointment settled upon us. So we had no alternative except that of preparing for direct action, whereby we would present our very bodies as a means of laying our case before the conscience of the local and national community. We were not unmindful of the difficulties involved. So we decided to go through a process of self-purification. We started having workshops on nonviolence and repeatedly asked ourselves the questions, "Are you able to accept blows without retaliating?" "Are you able to endure the ordeals of jail?"

We decided to set our direct action program around the Easter season, realizing that with the exception of Christmas, this was the largest shopping period of the year. Knowing that a strong economic withdrawal program would be the by-product of direct action, we felt that this was the best time to bring pressure on the merchants for the needed changes. Then it occurred to us that the March election was ahead, and so we speedily decided to postpone action until after election day. When we discovered that Mr. Connor was in the run-off, we decided again to postpone so that the demonstrations could not be used to cloud the issues. At this time we agreed to begin our nonviolent witness the day after the run-off.

This reveals that we did not move irresponsibly into direct action. We too wanted to see Mr. Connor defeated; so we went through postponement after postponement to aid in this community need. After this we felt that direct action could be delayed no longer.

You may well ask, "Why direct action? Why sit-ins, marches, etc.? Isn't negotiation a better path?" You are exactly right in your call for negotiation. Indeed, this is the purpose of direct action. Nonviolent direct action seeks to create such a crisis and establish such creative tension that a community that has constantly refused to negotiate is forced to confront the issue. It seeks so to dramatize the issue that it can no longer be ignored. I just referred to the creation of tension as a part of the work of the nonviolent resister. This may sound rather shocking. But I must confess that I am not afraid of the word tension. I have earnestly worked and preached against violent tension, but there is a type of constructive nonviolent tension that is necessary for growth. Just as Socrates felt that it was necessary to create a tension in the mind so that individuals could rise from the bondage of myths and half-truths to the unfettered realm of creative analysis and objective appraisal, we must see the need of having nonviolent gadflies to create the kind of tension in society that will help men rise from the dark depths of prejudice and racism to the majestic heights of understanding and brotherhood. So the purpose of the direct action is to create a situation so crisis-packed that it will inevitably open the door to negotiation. We, therefore, concur with you in your call for negotiation. Too long has our beloved Southland been bogged down in the tragic attempt to live in monologue rather than dialogue.

One of the basic points in your statement is that our acts are untimely. Some have asked, "Why didn't you give the new administration time to act?" The only answer that I can give to this inquiry is that the new administration must be prodded about as much as the outgoing one before it acts. We will be sadly mistaken if we feel that the election of Mr. Boutwell will bring the millennium to Birmingham. While Mr. Boutwell is much more articulate and gentle than Mr. Connor, they are both segregationists dedicated to the task of maintaining the status quo. The hope I see in Mr. Boutwell is that he will be reasonable enough to see the futility of massive resistance to desegregation. But he will not see this without pressure from the devotees of civil rights. My friends, I must say to you that we have not made a single gain in civil rights without determined legal and nonviolent pressure. History is the long and tragic story of the fact that privileged groups seldom give up their privileges voluntarily. Individuals may see the moral light and voluntarily give up their unjust posture; but as Reinhold Niebuhr has reminded us, groups are more im-moral than individuals.

We know through painful experience that freedom is never voluntarily given by the oppressor; it must be demanded by the oppressed. Frankly I have never yet engaged in a direct action movement that was "well timed," according to the timetable of those who have not suffered unduly from the disease of segregation. For years now I have heard the word "Wait!" It rings in the ear of every Negro with a piercing familiarity. This "wait" has almost always meant "never." It has been a tranquilizing thalidomide, relieving the emotional stress for a moment, only to give birth to an ill-formed infant of frustration. We must come to see with the distinguished jurist of yesterday that "justice too long delayed is justice denied." We have waited for more than three hundred and forty years for our constitutional and God-given rights. The nations of Asia and Africa are moving with jet-like speed toward the goal of political independence, and we still creep at horse and buggy pace toward the gaining of a cup of coffee at a lunch counter.

I guess it is easy for those who have never felt the stinging darts of segregation to say wait. But when you have seen vicious mobs lynch your mothers and fathers at will and drown your sisters and brothers at whim; when you have seen hate filled policemen curse, kick, brutalize, and even kill your black brothers and sisters with impunity; when you see the vast majority of your twenty million Negro brothers smothering in an air-tight cage of poverty in the midst of an affluent society; when you suddenly find your tongue twisted and your speech stammering as you seek to explain to your six-year-old daughter why she can't go to the public amusement park that has just been advertised on television, and see tears welling up in her little eyes when she is told that Funtown is closed to colored chil-dren, and see the depressing clouds of inferiority begin to form in her little mental sky, and see her begin to distort her little personality by uncon-sciously developing a bitterness toward white people; when you have to concoct an answer for a five-year-old son asking in agonizing pathos: "Daddy, why do white people treat colored people so mean?"; when you take a cross country drive and find it necessary to sleep night after night in the uncomfortable corners of your automobile because no motel will accept you; when you are humiliated day in and day out by nagging signs reading "white" men and "colored"; when your first name becomes "nigger" and your middle name becomes "boy" (however old you are) and your last name becomes "John," and when your wife and mother are never given the respected title "Mrs."; when you are harried by day and haunted by night by the fact that you are a Negro, living constantly at tip-toe stance never quite knowing what to expect next, and plagued with inner fears and outer resentments; when you are forever fighting a degenerating sense of "nobodiness";—then you will understand why we find it difficult to wait. There comes a time when the cup of endurance runs over, and men are no longer willing to be plunged into an abyss of injustice where they experience the bleakness of corroding despair. I hope, sirs, you can understand our legitimate and unavoidable impatience.

You express a great deal of anxiety over our willingness to break laws. This is certainly a legitimate concern. Since we so diligently urge people to obey the Supreme Court's decision of 1954 outlawing segregation in the public schools, it is rather strange and paradoxical to find us consciously breaking laws. One may well ask, "How can you advocate breaking some laws and obeying others?" The answer is found in the fact that there are two types of laws. There are *just* laws and there are *unjust* laws. I would be the first to advocate obeying just laws. One has not only a legal but moral responsibility to obey just laws. Conversely, one has a moral responsibility to disobey unjust laws. I would agree with Saint Augustine that "An unjust law is no law at all."

Now what is the difference between the two? How does one determine when a law is just or unjust? A just law is a man-made code that squares with the moral law or the law of God. An unjust law is a code that is out of harmony with the moral law. To put it in the terms of Saint Thomas Aquinas, an unjust law is a human law that is not rooted in eternal and natural law. Any law that uplifts human personality is just. Any law that degrades human personality is unjust. All segregation statutes are unjust because segregation distorts the soul and damages the personality. It gives the segregator a false sense of superiority and the segregated a false sense of inferiority. To use the words of Martin Buber, the great Jewish philosopher, segregation substitutes an "I-it" relationship for the "I-thou" relationship, and ends up relegating persons to the status of things. So segregation is not only politically, economically, and sociologically unsound, but it is morally wrong and sinful. Paul Tillich[o] has said that sin is separation. Isn't segregation an existential expression of man's tragic separation, an expression of his awful estrangement, his terrible sinfulness? So I can urge men to obey the 1954 decision of the Supreme Court[o] because it is morally right, and I can urge them to disobey segregation ordinances because they are morally wrong.

Paul Tillich   See headnote, p. 784.
1954 decision of the Supreme Court   *Brown vs. Board of Education,* a decision that made racial segregation in public schools unconstitutional.

Let us turn to a more concrete example of just and unjust laws. An unjust law is a code that a majority inflicts on a minority that is not binding on itself. This is *difference* made legal. On the other hand a just law is a code that a majority compels a minority to follow that it is willing to follow itself. This is *sameness* made legal.

Let me give another explanation. An unjust law is a code inflicted upon a minority which that minority had no part in enacting or creating because they did not have the unhampered right to vote. Who can say the legislature of Alabama which set up the segregation laws was democratically elected? Throughout the state of Alabama all types of conniving methods are used to prevent Negroes from becoming registered voters and there are some counties without a single Negro registered to vote despite the fact that the Negro constitutes a majority of the population. Can any law set up in such a state be considered democratically structured?

These are just a few examples of unjust and just laws. There are some instances when a law is just on its face but unjust in its application. For instance, I was arrested Friday on a charge of parading without a permit. Now there is nothing wrong with an ordinance which requires a permit for a parade, but when the ordinance is used to preserve segregation and to deny citizens the First Amendment privilege of peaceful assembly and peaceful protest, then it becomes unjust.

I hope you can see the distinction I am trying to point out. In no sense do I advocate evading or defying the law as the rabid segregationist would do. This would lead to anarchy. One who breaks an unjust law must do it *openly, lovingly* (not hatefully as the white mothers did in New Orleans when they were seen on television screaming "nigger, nigger, nigger") and with a willingness to accept the penalty. I submit that an individual who breaks a law that conscience tells him is unjust, and willingly accepts the penalty by staying in jail to arouse the conscience of the community over its injustice, is in reality expressing the very highest respect for law.

Of course there is nothing new about this kind of civil disobedience. It was seen sublimely in the refusal of Shadrach, Meshach, and Abednego to obey the laws of Nebuchadnezzar because a higher moral law was involved. It was practiced superbly by the early Christians who were willing to face hungry lions and the excruciating pain of chopping blocks, before submitting to certain unjust laws of the Roman Empire. To a degree academic freedom is a reality today because Socrates practiced civil disobedience.

We can never forget that everything Hitler did in Germany was "legal" and everything the Hungarian freedom fighters⁰ did in Hungary was "illegal." It was "illegal" to aid and comfort a Jew in Hitler's Germany. But I am sure that, if I had lived in Germany during that time, I would have

Hungarian freedom fighters Hungarians who fought in the 1956 anti-Soviet revolution. The revolt was crushed by U.S.S.R. military forces.

aided and comforted my Jewish brothers even though it was illegal. If I lived in a communist country today where certain principles dear to the Christian faith are suppressed, I believe I would openly advocate disobeying those antireligious laws.

I must make two honest confessions to you, my Christian and Jewish brothers. First I must confess that over the last few years I have been gravely disappointed with the white moderate. I have almost reached the regrettable conclusion that the Negroes' great stumbling block in the stride toward freedom is not the White Citizens' "Counciler" or the Ku Klux Klanner, but the white moderate who is more devoted to "order" than to justice; who prefers a negative peace which is the absence of tension to a positive peace which is the presence of justice; who constantly says "I agree with you in the goal you seek, but I can't agree with your methods of direct action"; who paternalistically feels that he can set the timetable for another man's freedom; who lives by the myth of time and who constantly advises the Negro to wait until a "more convenient season." Shallow understanding from people of good will is more frustrating than absolute misunderstanding from people of ill will. Lukewarm acceptance is much more bewildering than outright rejection.

I had hoped that the white moderate would understand that law and order exist for the purpose of establishing justice, and that when they fail to do this they become the dangerously structured dams that block the flow of social progress. I had hoped that the white moderate would understand that the present tension in the South is merely a necessary phase of the transition from an obnoxious negative peace, where the Negro passively accepted his unjust plight, to a substance-filled positive peace, where all men will respect the dignity and worth of human personality. Actually, we who engage in nonviolent direct action are not the creators of tension. We merely bring to the surface the hidden tension that is already alive. We bring it out in the open where it can be seen and dealt with. Like a boil that can never be cured as long as it is covered up but must be opened with all its pus-flowing ugliness to the natural medicines of air and light, injustice must likewise be exposed, with all of the tension its exposing creates, to the light of human conscience and the air of national opinion before it can be cured.

In your statement you asserted that our actions, even though peaceful, must be condemned because they precipitate violence. But can this assertion be logically made? Isn't this like condemning the robbed man because his possession of money precipitated the evil act of robbery? Isn't this like condemning Socrates because his unswerving commitment to truth and his philosophical delvings precipitated the misguided popular mind to make him drink the hemlock? Isn't this like condemning Jesus because His unique God consciousness and never-ceasing devotion to His will precipitated the evil act of crucifixion? We must come to see, as federal courts have consistently affirmed, that it is immoral to urge an individual to withdraw his efforts to gain his basic constitutional rights because the quest precipitates violence. Society must protect the robbed and punish the robber.

I had also hoped that the white moderate would reject the myth of time. I received a letter this morning from a white brother in Texas which said: "All Christians know that the colored people will receive equal rights eventually, but is it possible that you are in too great of a religious hurry? It has taken Christianity almost 2000 years to accomplish what it has. The teachings of Christ take time to come to earth." All that is said here grows out of a tragic misconception of time. It is the strangely irrational notion that there is something in the very flow of time that will inevitably cure all ills. Actually time is neutral. It can be used either destructively or constructively. I am coming to feel that the people of ill will have used time much more effectively than the people of good will. We will have to repent in this generation not merely for the vitriolic words and actions of the bad people, but for the appalling silence of the good people. We must come to see that human progress never rolls in on wheels of inevitability. It comes through the tireless efforts and persistent work of men willing to be co-workers with God, and without this hard work time itself becomes an ally of the forces of social stagnation.

We must use time creatively, and forever realize that the time is always ripe to do right. Now is the time to make real the promise of democracy, and transform our pending national elegy into a creative psalm of brotherhood. Now is the time to lift our national policy from the quicksand of racial injustice to the solid rock of human dignity.

You spoke of our activity in Birmingham as extreme. At first I was rather disappointed that fellow clergymen would see my nonviolent efforts as those of the extremist. I started thinking about the fact that I stand in the middle of two opposing forces in the Negro community. One is a force of complacency made up of Negroes who, as a result of long years of oppression, have been so completely drained of self-respect and a sense of "somebodiness" that they have adjusted to segregation, and of a few Negroes in the middle class who, because of a degree of academic and economic security, and because at points they profit by segregation, have unconsciously become insensitive to the problems of the masses. The other force is one of bitterness and hatred and comes perilously close to advocating violence. It is expressed in the various black nationalist groups that are springing up over the nation, the largest and best known being Elijah Muhammad's Muslim movement. This movement is nourished by the contemporary frustration over the continued existence of racial discrimination. It is made up of people who have lost faith in America, who have absolutely repudiated Christianity, and who have concluded that the white man is an incurable "devil." I have tried to stand between these two forces saying that we need not follow the "do-nothingism" of the complacent or the hatred and despair of the black nationalist. There is the more excellent way of love and nonviolent protest. I'm grateful to God that, through the Negro church, the dimension of nonviolence entered our struggle. If this philosophy had not emerged I am convinced that by now many streets of the South would be flowing with floods of blood. And I am further convinced that if our white brothers dismiss us as "rabble rousers" and "outside agitators"—those of us who are working through the channels of nonviolent direct action—and refuse to support our nonviolent efforts, millions of Negroes, out of frustration and despair, will seek solace and security in black nationalist ideologies, a development that will lead inevitably to a frightening racial nightmare.

Oppressed people cannot remain oppressed forever. The urge for freedom will eventually come. This is what has happened to the American Negro. Something within has reminded him of his birthright of freedom; something without has reminded him that he can gain it. Consciously and unconsciously, he has been swept in by what the Germans call the *Zeitgeist,* and with his black brothers of Africa, and his brown and yellow brothers of Asia, South America, and the Caribbean, he is moving with a sense of cosmic urgency toward the promised land of racial justice. Recognizing this vital urge that has engulfed the Negro community, one should readily understand public demonstrations. The Negro has many pent-up resentments and latent frustrations. He has to get them out. So let him march sometime; let him have his prayer pilgrimages to the city hall; understand why he must have sit-ins and freedom rides. If his repressed emotions do not come out in these nonviolent ways, they will come out in ominous expressions of violence. This is not a threat; it is a fact of history. So I have not said to my people, "Get rid of your discontent." But I have tried to say that this normal and healthy discontent can be channeled through the creative outlet of nonviolent direct action. Now this approach is being dismissed as extremist. I must admit that I was initially disappointed in being so categorized.

But as I continued to think about the matter I gradually gained a bit of satisfaction from being considered an extremist. Was not Jesus an extremist in love? "Love your enemies, bless them that curse you, pray for them that despitefully use you." Was not Amos an extremist for justice—"Let justice roll down like waters and righteousness like a mighty stream." Was not Paul an extremist for the gospel of Jesus Christ—"I bear in my body the marks of the Lord Jesus." Was not Martin Luther an extremist—"Here I stand; I can do none other so help me God." Was not John Bunyan an extremist—"I will stay in jail to the end of my days before I make a butchery of my conscience." Was not Abraham Lincoln an extremist— "This nation cannot survive half slave and half free." Was not Thomas Jefferson an extremist—"We hold these truths to be self evident that all men are created equal." So the question is not whether we will be extremist but what kind of extremist will we be. Will we be extremists for hate or will we be extremists for love? Will we be extremists for the preservation of injustice—or will we be extremists for the cause of justice? In that dramatic scene on Calvary's hill three men were crucified. We must never forget that all three were crucified for the same crime—the crime of extremism. Two were extremists for immorality, and thus fell below their environment. The other, Jesus Christ, was an extremist for love, truth, and goodness, and thereby rose above His environment. So, after all, maybe the South, the nation, and the world are in dire need of creative extremists.

I had hoped that the white moderate would see this. Maybe I was too optimistic. Maybe I expected too much. I guess I should have realized that few members of a race that has oppressed another race can understand or appreciate the deep groans and passionate yearnings of those that have been oppressed, and still fewer have the vision to see that injustice must be rooted out by strong, persistent, and determined action. I am thankful, however, that some of our white brothers have grasped the meaning of this social revolution and committed themselves to it. They are still all too small in quantity, but they are big in quality. Some like Ralph McGill, Lillian Smith, Harry Golden, and James Dabbs have written about our struggle in eloquent, prophetic, and understanding terms. Others have marched with us down nameless streets of the South. They have languished in filthy, roach-infested jails, suffering the abuse and brutality of angry policemen who see them as "dirty nigger lovers." They, unlike so many of their moderate brothers and sisters, have recognized the urgency of the moment and sensed the need for powerful "action" antidotes to combat the disease of segregation.

Let me rush on to mention my other disappointment. I have been so greatly disappointed with the white Church and its leadership. Of course there are some notable exceptions. I am not unmindful of the fact that each of you has taken some significant stands on this issue. I commend you, Rev. Stallings, for your Christian stand on this past Sunday, in welcoming Negroes to your worship service on a nonsegregated basis. I commend the Catholic leaders of this state for integrating Springhill College several years ago.

But despite these notable exceptions I must honestly reiterate that I have been disappointed with the Church. I do not say that as one of those negative critics who can always find something wrong with the Church. I say it as a minister of the gospel, who loves the Church; who was nurtured in its bosom; who has been sustained by its spiritual blessings and who will remain true to it as long as the cord of life shall lengthen.

I had the strange feeling when I was suddenly catapulted into the leadership of the bus protest in Montgomery several years ago that we would have the support of the white Church. I felt that the white ministers, priests, and rabbis of the South would be some of our strongest allies. Instead, some have been outright opponents, refusing to understand the freedom movement and misrepresenting its leaders; all too many others have been more cautious than courageous and have remained silent behind the anesthetizing security of stained glass windows.

In spite of my shattered dreams of the past, I came to Birmingham with the hope that the white religious leadership of the community would see the justice of our cause and, with deep moral concern, serve as the channel through which our just grievances could get to the power structure. I had hoped that each of you would understand. But again I have been disappointed.

I have heard numerous religious leaders of the South call upon their worshippers to comply with a desegregation decision because it is the law, but I have longed to hear white ministers say follow this decree because integration is morally right and the Negro is your brother. In the midst of blatant injustices inflicted upon the Negro, I have watched white churches stand on the sideline and merely mouth pious irrelevancies and sanctimonious trivialities. In the midst of a mighty struggle to rid our nation of racial and economic injustice, I have heard so many ministers say, "Those are social issues with which the Gospel has no real concern," and I have watched so many churches commit themselves to a completely otherworldly religion which made a strange distinction between body and soul, the sacred and the secular.

So here we are moving toward the exit of the twentieth century with a religious community largely adjusted to the status quo, standing as a tail light behind other community agencies rather than a headlight leading men to higher levels of justice.

I have travelled the length and breadth of Alabama, Mississippi, and all the other Southern states. On sweltering summer days and crisp autumn mornings I have looked at her beautiful churches with their spires pointing heavenward. I have beheld the impressive outlay of her massive religious education buildings. Over and over again I have found myself asking: "Who worships here? Who is their God? Where were their voices when the lips of Governor Barnett dripped with words of interposition and nullification? Where were they when Governor Wallace gave the clarion call for defiance and hatred? Where were their voices of support when tired, bruised, and weary Negro men and women decided to rise from the dark dungeons of complacency to the bright hills of creative protest?"

Yes, these questions are still in my mind. In deep disappointment, I have wept over the laxity of the Church. But be assured that my tears have been tears of love. There can be no deep disappointment where there is not deep love. Yes, I love the Church; I love her sacred walls. How could I do otherwise? I am in the rather unique position of being the son, the grandson, and the great grandson of preachers. Yes, I see the Church as the body of Christ. But, oh! How we have blemished and scarred that body through social neglect and fear of being nonconformists.

There was a time when the Church was very powerful. It was during that period when the early Christians rejoiced when they were deemed worthy to suffer for what they believed. In those days the Church was not merely a thermometer that recorded the ideas and principles of popular opinion; it was a thermostat that transformed the mores of society. Wherever the early Christians entered a town the power structure got disturbed and immediately sought to convict them for being "disturbers of the peace" and "outside agitators." But they went on with the conviction that they were a "colony of heaven" and had to obey God rather than man. They were small in number but big in commitment. They were too God-intoxicated to be "astronomically intimidated." They brought an end to such ancient evils as infanticide and gladiatorial contest.

Things are different now. The contemporary Church is so often a weak, ineffectual voice with an uncertain sound. It is so often the archsupporter of the status quo. Far from being disturbed by the presence of the Church, the power structure of the average community is consoled by the Church's silent and often vocal sanction of things as they are.

But the judgment of God is upon the Church as never before. If the Church of today does not recapture the sacrificial spirit of the early Church, it will lose its authentic ring, forfeit the loyalty of millions, and be dismissed as an irrelevant social club with no meaning for the twentieth century. I am meeting young people every day whose disappointment with the Church has risen to outright disgust.

Maybe again I have been too optimistic. Is organized religion too inextricably bound to the status quo to save our nation and the world? Maybe I must turn my faith to the inner spiritual Church, the church within the Church, as the true *ecclesia* and the hope of the world. But again I am thankful to God that some noble souls from the ranks of organized religion have broken loose from the paralyzing chains of conformity and joined us as active partners in the struggle for freedom. They have left their secure congregations and walked the streets of Albany, Georgia, with us. They have gone through the highways of the South on torturous rides for freedom. Yes, they have gone to jail with us. Some have been kicked out of their churches and lost the support of their bishops and fellow ministers. But they have gone with the faith that right defeated is stronger than evil triumphant. These men have been the leaven in the lump of the race. Their witness has been the spiritual salt that has preserved the true meaning of the Gospel in these troubled times. They have carved a tunnel of hope through the dark mountain of disappointment.

I hope the Church as a whole will meet the challenge of this decisive hour. But even if the Church does not come to the aid of justice, I have no despair about the future. I have no fear about the outcome of our struggle in Birmingham, even if our motives are presently misunderstood. We will reach the goal of freedom in Birmingham and all over the nation, because the goal of America is freedom. Abused and scorned though we may be, our destiny is tied up with the destiny of America. Before the pilgrims landed at Plymouth, we were here. Before the pen of Jefferson etched across the pages of history the majestic words of the Declaration of Independence, we were here. For more than two centuries our foreparents labored in this country without wages; they made cotton "king"; and they built the homes of their masters in the midst of brutal injustice and shameful humiliation—and yet out of a bottomless vitality they continued to thrive and develop. If the inexpressible cruelties of slavery could not stop us, the opposition we now face will surely fail. We will win our freedom because the sacred heritage of our nation and the eternal will of God are embodied in our echoing demands.

I must close now. But before closing I am impelled to mention one other point in your statement that troubled me profoundly. You warmly commended the Birmingham police force for keeping "order" and "preventing violence." I don't believe you would have so warmly commended the police force if you had seen its angry violent dogs literally biting six unarmed, nonviolent Negroes. I don't believe you would so quickly commend the policemen if you would observe their ugly and inhuman treatment of Negroes here in the city jail; if you would watch them push and curse old Negro women and young Negro girls; if you would see them slap and kick old Negro men and young Negro boys; if you will observe them, as they did on two occasions, refuse to give us food because we wanted to sing our grace together. I'm sorry that I can't join you in your praise for the police department.

It is true that they have been rather disciplined in their public handling of the demonstrators. In this sense they have been rather publicly "nonviolent." But for what purpose? To preserve the evil system of segregation. Over the last few years I have consistently preached that nonviolence demands that the means we use must be as pure as the ends we seek. So I have tried to make it clear that it is wrong to use immoral means to attain moral ends. But now I must affirm that it is just as wrong, or even more so, to use moral means to preserve immoral ends. Maybe Mr. Connor and his policemen have been rather publicly nonviolent, as Chief Prichett was in Albany, Georgia, but they have used the moral means of nonviolence to maintain the immoral end of flagrant racial injustice. T. S. Eliot has said that there is no greater treason than to do the right deed for the wrong reason.

I wish you had commended the Negro sit-inners and demonstrators of Birmingham for their sublime courage, their willingness to suffer, and their amazing discipline in the midst of the most inhuman provocation. One day the South will recognize its real heroes. They will be the James Merediths, courageously and with a majestic sense of purpose, facing jeering and hostile mobs and the agonizing loneliness that characterizes the life of the pioneer. They will be old, oppressed, battered Negro women, symbolized in a seventy-two year old woman of Montgomery, Alabama, who rose up with a sense of dignity and with her people decided not to ride the segregated buses, and responded to one who inquired about her tiredness with ungrammatical profundity: "My feets is tired, but my soul is rested." They will be young high school and college students, young ministers of the gospel and a host of the elders, courageously and nonviolently sitting in at lunch counters and willingly going to jail for conscience sake. One day the South will know that when these disinherited children of God sat down at lunch counters they were in reality standing up for the best in the American dream and the most sacred values in our Judeo-Christian heritage, and thus carrying our whole nation back to great wells of democracy which were dug deep by the founding fathers in the formulation of the Constitution and the Declaration of Independence.

Never before have I written a letter this long (or should I say a book?). I'm afraid that it is much too long to take your precious time. I can assure you that it would have been much shorter if I had been writing from a comfortable desk, but what else is there to do when you are alone for days in the dull monotony of a narrow jail cell other than write long letters, think strange thoughts, and pray long prayers?

If I have said anything in this letter that is an overstatement of the truth and is indicative of an unreasonable impatience, I beg you to forgive me. If I have said anything in this letter that is an understatement of the truth and is indicative of my having a patience that makes me patient with anything less than brotherhood, I beg God to forgive me.

I hope this letter finds you strong in the faith. I also hope that circumstances will soon make it possible for me to meet each of you, not as an integrationist or a civil rights leader, but as a fellow clergyman and a Christian brother. Let us all hope that the dark clouds of racial prejudice will soon pass away and the deep fog of misunderstanding will be lifted from our fear-drenched communities and in some not too distant tomorrow the radiant stars of love and brotherhood will shine over our great nation with all of their scintillating beauty.

> *Yours for the cause of*
> *Peace and Brotherhood*
>
> MARTIN LUTHER KING, JR.

Wendell Berry

A review of *Recollected Essays, 1965–1980* in *Publishers Weekly* calls Wendell Berry "probably the closest we have to a modern Thoreau." Born in Kentucky in 1934, Berry was educated at the University of Kentucky and taught English there until 1977. He is a poet, a novelist, an essayist, and, above all, a farmer. His writing is centered on agriculture because he sees a necessary relationship between agriculture and human culture. In the foreword to *The Gift of Good Land: Further Essays Cultural and Agricultural* (1981), from which the selection below has been taken, Berry states his major theme: "My previous book on agriculture, *The Unsettling of America* [1977], sought to comprehend the causes and consequences of industrial agriculture within the bounds of a single argument: that agriculture is an integral part of the structure, both biological and cultural, that sustains human life, and that you cannot disturb one part of that structure without disturbing all of it. . . ."

The Reactor and the Garden

On June 3, 1979, I took part in an act of nonviolent civil disobedience at the site of a nuclear power plant being built at Marble Hill, near Madison, Indiana. At about noon that day, eighty-nine of us crossed a wire fence onto the power company's land, were arrested, and duly charged with criminal trespass.

As crimes go, ours was tame almost to the point of boredom. We acted under a well-understood commitment to do no violence and damage no property. The Jefferson County sheriff knew well in advance and pretty exactly what we planned to do. Our trespass was peaceable and orderly. We were politely arrested by the sheriff and his deputies, who acted, as far as I saw, with exemplary kindness. And this nearly eventless event ended in anticlimax: the prosecutor chose to press charges against only one of the eighty-nine who were arrested, and that one was never brought to trial.

And yet, for all its tameness, it was not a lighthearted event. Few of us, I think, found it easy to decide to break the law of the land. For me it was difficult for another reason as well: I do not like public protests or crowd actions of any kind; I dislike and distrust the slogans and the jargon that invariably stick like bubble gum to any kind of "movement."

Why did I do it?

For several years, along with a good many other people, I have been concerned about the proliferation of power plants in the Ohio River Valley, where at present more than sixty plants are either working, under construction, or planned. Air pollution from existing coal-fired plants in the valley is already said to be the worst in the country. And the new plants are being constructed or planned without any evident consideration of the possibility of limiting or moderating the consumption of electricity. The people of this area, then, are expected to sacrifice their health—among other things—to underwrite the fantasy of "unlimited economic growth." This is a decision not made by them—but, rather, made *for* them by the power companies in collaboration with various agencies of government.

The coal-fired plants would be bad enough by themselves. But, in addition, some power companies have decided that nuclear power is the best answer to "the energy problem," and two nuclear power plants are now under construction in this part of the Ohio Valley. The arguments in their favor are not good, but they are backed nevertheless by a great deal of money and political power. For example, our local rural electric co-op publishes a magazine which constantly editorializes in favor of nuclear power. The rate payers are thus, in effect, being taxed to promote an energy policy that many of them consider objectionable and dangerous.

Power plants in the Ohio Valley raise another serious problem, this one political. The Ohio River is a state boundary. A power plant on the north side of the river in Indiana will obviously have an effect in Kentucky. But though a plant will necessarily affect at least two states, it is planned and permitted only in one. The people of one state thus become subject to a decision made in another state, in which they are without representation. And so in the behavior of big technology and corporate power, we can recognize again an exploitive colonialism similar to that of George III.°

Like the majority of people, I am unable to deal competently with the technical aspects of nuclear power and its dangers. My worries are based on several facts available to any reader of a newspaper:

1. Nuclear power is extremely dangerous. For this, the elaborate safety devices and backup systems of the plants themselves are evidence enough. Radioactive wastes, moreover, remain dangerous for many thousands of years, and there is apparently no foreseeable safe way to dispose of them.
2. Dangerous accidents do happen in nuclear power plants. Officials and experts claim that accidents can be foreseen and prevented, but accidents are surprises by definition. If they are foreseen they do not happen.
3. Nuclear experts and plant employees do not always act competently in dealing with these accidents. Nuclear power requires people to act with *perfect* competence if it is to be used safely. But people in nuclear power plants are just as likely to blunder or panic or miscalculate as people anywhere else.
4. Public officials do not always act responsibly. Sometimes they deliberately falsify, distort, or withhold information essential to the public's health or safety.

If I had doubts about any of this, they were removed forever by the accident at Three Mile Island.° And if I had any lingering faith that the

George III King of England (1760–1820), whose policies of coercion toward the American colonists led to the American Revolution.
Three Mile Island Location of a nuclear power plant in Pennsylvania where a major accident occurred on March 28, 1979. A breakdown in the cooling system caused radioactive gas to escape through the venting system, and there was serious threat of an explosion or of a core meltdown.

government would prove a trustworthy guardian of public safety, that was removed by the recent hearings on the atomic bomb tests of the 1950s—which have revealed that the government assured the people living near the explosions that there would be no danger from radiation, when in fact it knew that the danger would be great.

And so when I climbed the fence at Marble Hill, I considered that I was casting a vote that I had been given no better opportunity to cast. I was voting no. And I was voting no confidence. Marble Hill is only about twenty miles upwind from my house. As a father, a neighbor, and a citizen, I had begun to look on the risk of going to jail as trivial in comparison to the risks of living so near a nuclear power plant.

But even though I took part wholeheartedly in the June 3 protest, I am far from believing that such public acts are equal to their purpose, or that they ever will be. They are necessary, but they are not enough, and they subject the minds of their participants to certain dangers.

Any effort that focuses on one problem encourages oversimplification. It is easy to drift into the belief that once the nuclear power problem—or the energy problem, or the pollution problem—is solved everything will be all right. It will not, of course. For all these separate problems are merely aspects of the human problem, which never has been satisfactorily solved, and which would provide every one of us a lifetime agenda of work and worry even if *all* the bedeviling problems of twentieth century technology were solved today.

An even greater danger is that of moral oversimplification, or self-righteousness. Protests, demonstrations, and other forms of "movement" behavior tend to divide people into the ancient categories of "us" and "them." In the midst of the hard work and the risks of opposing what "we" see as a public danger, it is easy to assume that if only "they" were as clear-eyed, alert, virtuous, and brave as "we" are, our problems would soon be solved. This notion, too, is patently false. In the argument over nuclear power—as in most public arguments—the division between "us" and "them" does not really exist. In our efforts to correct the way things are, we are almost always, almost inevitably, opposing what is wrong with ourselves. If we do not see that, then I think we won't find any of the solutions we are looking for.

For example, I believe that most people who took part in the June 3 demonstration at Marble Hill got there in an automobile. I did, and I could hardly have got there any other way. Thus the demonstration, while it pushed for a solution to one aspect of the energy problem, was itself another aspect of that problem.

And I would be much surprised to learn that most of us did not return home to houses furnished with electric light switches, which we flipped on more or less thoughtlessly, not worrying overmuch about the watersheds that are being degraded or destroyed by strip mines to produce the coal to run the power plants to make the electricity that burns in our light bulbs. I know, anyhow, that I often flip on my own light switches without any such worries.

Nearly all of us are sponsoring or helping to cause the ills we would like to cure. Nearly all of us have what I can only call cheap-energy minds; we continue to assume, or to act as if we assume, that it does not matter how much energy we use.

I do not mean to imply that I know how to solve the problems of the automobile or of the wasteful modern household. Those problems are enormously difficult, and their difficulty suggests their extreme urgency and importance. But I am fairly certain that they won't be solved simply by public protests. The roots of the problems are private or personal, and the roots of the solutions will be private or personal too. Public protests are incomplete actions; they speak to the problem, not to the solution.

Protests are incomplete, I think, because they are by definition negative. You cannot protest *for* anything. The positive thing that protest is supposed to do is "raise consciousness," but it can raise consciousness only to the level of protest. So far as protest itself is concerned, the raised consciousness is on its own. It appears to be possible to "raise" your consciousness without changing it—and so to keep protesting forever.

If you have to be negative, there are better negative things to do. You can quit doing something you know to be destructive. It might, for instance, be possible to take a pledge that you will no longer use electricity or petroleum to entertain yourself. My own notion of an ideal negative action is to get rid of your television set. (It is cheating to get rid of it by selling it or giving it away. You should get rid of it by carefully disassembling it with a heavy blunt instrument. Would you try to get rid of any other brain disease by selling it or giving it away?)

But such actions are not really negative. When you get rid of something undesirable you are extending an invitation to something desirable. If it is true that nature abhors a vacuum, there is no need to fear. Wherever you make an opening, it will be filled. When you get rid of petroleum-powered or electronic entertainment you are inviting a renewal of that structure of conversation, work, and play that used to be known as "home life." You are inviting such gentle and instructive pleasures as walking and reading.

Or it may be possible for some people to walk or ride a bicycle to work —and so to consider doing without a car altogether. Or there may be some kind of motor-powered tool that can be done without. Or perhaps it will prove economical or pleasing to change from fossil fuel heat to a solar collector or a wood stove.*

There is, then, a kind of negative action that cannot remain negative.

---

*But the use of wood stoves without proper maintenance of wood lots is only another form of mining. It makes trees an exhaustible resource.

To give up some things is to create problems, which immediately call for solutions—and so the negative action completes itself in an action that is positive. But some actions are probably more complete than others, and the more complete the action, the more effective it is as a protest.

What, then, is a complete action? It is, I think, an action which one takes on one's own behalf, which is particular and complex, real not symbolic, which one can both accomplish on one's own and take full responsibility for. There are perhaps many such actions, but certainly among them is any sort of home production. And of the kinds of home production, the one most possible for most people is gardening.

Some people will object at this point that it belittles the idea of gardening to think of it as an act of opposition or protest. I agree. That is exactly my point. Gardening—or the best kind of gardening—is a *complete* action. It is so effective a protest because it is so much more than a protest.

The best kind of gardening is a form of home production capable of a considerable independence of outside sources. It will, then, be "organic" gardening. One of the most pleasing aspects of this way of gardening is its independence. For fertility, plant protection, etc., it relies as far as possible on resources in the locality and in the gardener's mind. Independence can be further enlarged by saving seed and starting your own seedlings. To work at ways of cutting down the use of petroleum products and gasoline engines in the garden is at once to increase independence and to work directly at a real (that is, a permanent) solution to the energy problem.

A garden gives interest a place, and it proves one's place interesting and worthy of interest. It works directly against the feeling—the source of a lot of our "environmental" troubles—that in order to be diverted or entertained, or to "make life interesting," it is necessary to draw upon some distant resource—turn on the TV or take a trip.

One of the most important local resources that a garden makes available for use is the gardener's own body. At a time when the national economy is largely based on buying and selling substitutes for common bodily energies and functions, a garden restores the body to its usefulness—a victory for our species. It may take a bit of effort to realize that perhaps the most characteristic modern "achievement" is the obsolescence of the human body. Jogging and other forms of artificial exercise do not restore the usefulness of the body, but are simply ways of assenting to its uselessness; the body is a diverting pet, like one's Chihuahua, and must be taken out for air and exercise. A garden gives the body the dignity of working in its own support. It is a way of rejoining the human race.

One of the common assumptions, leading to the obsolescence of the body, is that physical work is degrading. That is true if the body is used as a slave or a machine—if, in other words, it is misused. But working in one's own garden does not misuse the body, nor does it dull or "brutalize" the mind. The work of gardening is not "drudgery," but is the finest sort of challenge to intelligence. Gardening is not a discipline that can be learned once for all, but keeps presenting problems that must be directly dealt with. It is, in addition, an agricultural and ecological education, and that sort of education corrects the cheap-energy mind.

A garden is the most direct way to recapture the issue of health, and to make it a private instead of a governmental responsibility. In this, as in several other ways I have mentioned, gardening has a power that is political and even democratic. And it is a political power that can be applied constantly, whereas one can only vote or demonstrate occasionally.

Finally, because it makes backyards (or front yards or vacant lots) productive, gardening speaks powerfully of the abundance of the world. It does so by increasing and enhancing abundance, and by demonstrating that abundance, given moderation and responsible use, is limitless. We learn from our gardens to deal with the most urgent question of the time: How much is enough? We don't soup our gardens up with chemicals because our goal is *enough,* and we know that *enough* requires a modest, moderate, conserving technology.

Atomic reactors and other big-technological solutions, on the other hand, convey an overwhelming suggestion of the poverty of the world and the scarcity of goods. That is because their actuating principle is excessive consumption. They obscure and destroy the vital distinction between abundance and extravagance. The ideal of "limitless economic growth" is based on the obsessive and fearful conviction that more is always needed. The growth is maintained by the consumers' panic-stricken suspicion, since they always want more, that they will never have enough.

Enough is everlasting. Too much, despite all the ballyhoo about "limitless growth," is temporary. And big-technological solutions are temporary: the lifetime of a nuclear power plant is thirty years! A garden, given the right methods and the right care, will last as long as the world.

A garden, of course, is not always as comfortable as Kroger's:[o] If you grow a garden you are going to shed some sweat, and you are going to spend some time bent over; you will experience some aches and pains. But it is in the willingness to accept this discomfort that we strike the most telling blow against the power plants and what they represent. We have gained a great deal of comfort and convenience by our dependence on various public utilities and government agencies. But it is obviously not possible to become dependent without losing independence—and freedom too. Or to put it another way, we cannot be free from discomfort without becoming subject to the whims and abuses of centralized power, and to any number of serious threats to our health. We cannot hope to recover our freedom from such perils without discomfort.

Someone is sure to ask how I can suppose that a garden, "whose action is no stronger than a flower," can compete with a nuclear reactor. Well, I am not supposing that exactly. As I said, I think the protests and demonstra-

Kroger's Supermarket chain.

tions are necessary. I think that jail may be the freest place when you *have no choice* but to breathe poison or die of cancer. But it is futile to attempt to correct a public wrong without correcting the sources of that wrong in yourself.

At the same time, I think it may be too easy to underestimate the power of a garden. A nuclear reactor is a proposed "solution" to "the energy problem." But like all big-technological "solutions," this one "solves" a single problem by causing many. The problems of what to do with radioactive wastes and with decommissioned nuclear plants, for example, have not yet been solved; and we can confidently predict that the "solutions," when they come, will cause yet other serious problems that will come as "surprises" to the officials and the experts. In that way, big technology works perpetually against itself. That is the limit of "unlimited economic growth."

A garden, on the other hand, is a solution that leads to other solutions. It is a part of the limitless pattern of good health and good sense.

Community and Self

The pieces in the preceding section, "The Social Contract," deal mainly with relationships in society that are formally agreed upon, and that are largely expressed in terms of constitutions and laws and of political units such as cities, states, and nations. In the present section we confront issues of both a wider and a narrower scope—issues that are as yet far less easy to resolve in constitutional form—ranging from the right relationships among the entire human community to the mysterious question of how the individual becomes an identifiable self. John W. Gardner's opening essay argues that many of these questions are interlinked, and that large-scale organization and individualism are both necessary to us. Yet both also need to be correctively curbed, and for this he recommends "a healthy sense of community." He then goes on to show how membership in a community is deeply intertwined with the development of individual identity.

"Am I my brother's keeper?" The threat of extinction by atomic war or by the exhaustion of natural resources has set people thinking as never before about humankind as a single community. Are we necessarily interdependent, or should those who can best survive try to go it alone? From observation of the social insects, and of man's most social instinct—language—Lewis Thomas is moved to speculate that altruism may be instinctual in us, too. Garrett Hardin, thinking of rich countries, poor countries, food, and population, argues for the survival of the fittest and against sharing our resources. There follow two of the many replies that his hardheaded and persuasive argument has generated. Norman Cousins, in a brief editorial, focuses mainly on the moral and psychological consequences of Hardin's view. He comments: "Desensitization, not hunger, is the greatest curse on earth." Walter W. Benjamin, in part responding to Hardin, notes that "ours is not a lifeboat but a luxury yacht," implying that the starvation of others comes in part from our own affluence. Jonathan Swift's great satire, which concludes this group, masks its piercing cry for sympathy and community with irony, by blandly proposing to push economic independence and desensitization to their logical conclusion.

The next group of essays turns from global issues to personal ones. It centers on individualism—a trait much prized by Americans—and how it relates to our dealings with others. Writing 150 years ago, when the term itself was still a new one, de Tocqueville shows how individualism is related to democracy and points darkly to its effects on the ties between generations and among contemporaries: "It throws [a person] back forever upon himself alone and threatens in the end to confine him entirely within the solitude of his own heart." Philip Slater sees de Tocqueville's observation confirmed when he argues that the extremeness of American competitive individualism is neither normal nor correct. He notes that it exacts a heavy price in the lack of a sense of self, in loneliness, bureaucracy, mistrust, and, paradoxically, in monotonous uniformity. Peter Marin examines a group of institutional mechanisms in which the drive for individual potency or self-realization seems to him to mask what is really narcissism, a self-love that provides its adherents with "a way to avoid the demands of the world, to smother the tug of conscience."

The final group of writings in this section focuses more directly on the problem of selfhood. William Kilpatrick develops in detail ideas touched on by Gardner, namely, that identity is based at least in part on heritage and continuity and that it is intimately connected with the moral life. Our "self" is what others rely on when they trust us. He shows how chronic change in modern society undermines our sense of identity. In answer to the question of how we, in fact, come to know our selves, Kilpatrick would probably look to our actions—to the things we do or refuse to do. Paul Bohannan, in his brief essay, would look more to relationships. "Getting to know myself," he says, "comes with sharing with another." Denise Levertov's poem raises yet a further question: How many selves have we, and whose creation are they?

An Overview

John Gardner

John William Gardner has spent most of his life working for the common good. He was born in 1912 in Los Angeles, educated at Stanford and Berkeley (Ph.D., 1938), and began his career as a teacher of psychology at Mt. Holyoke College. He soon turned to government and public service, however, and worked successively for the Federal Communications Commission and the philanthropic Carnegie Corporation. From 1955 to 1965 he was president of the Carnegie Corporation and of the affiliated Carnegie Foundation for the Advancement of Teaching. He then entered President Johnson's cabinet as Secretary of Health, Education, and Welfare. On his resignation in 1968, he became chairman of the Urban Coalition, which unites leaders from all sectors of society in an effort to improve the quality of life of the disadvantaged in urban areas. In 1970 he founded Common Cause, a national citizens' lobby devoted to making the national and state governments more open and more accountable to citizens and to improving government performance. In 1981 he became chairman of Independent Sector, a group of corporations, foundations, and voluntary organizations promoting voluntary giving and personal support of health and welfare.

He has received numerous awards for outstanding public service, including the Presidential Medal of Freedom. Among his books are *Excellence: Can We Be Equal and Excellent Too* (1961); *Self-Renewal: The Individual and the Innovative Society* (1964); *In Common Cause* (1972); and *Morale* (1978). William Silverman has written of Gardner: "If a 'good guy' is a person who is moderate, idealistic, open to slightly unconventional ideas, fair-minded, and favorably disposed to changes in the society which benefit everyone, then Gardner is the very embodiment of the good guy." The present essay is taken from the symposium *On the Meaning of the University* (1976), edited by Sterling M. McMurrin. A few paragraphs at the beginning and end relating the essay to this special setting have been omitted.

The Individual and Society

We seek a society that has at its core a respect for the dignity and worth of the individual, a society that pursues fulfillment and growth for the individual. But we recognize that the deepest threat to the integrity of any community is an incapacity on the part of the citizens to lend themselves to any worthy common purpose, and we see the barrenness of a life that encompasses nothing beyond the self. As Tillich put it, the individual must have the courage to be himself and the courage to be part of something larger.

Gone forever is the unplanned, tradition-dictated submergence of the individual in the community that has existed throughout most of human history. But the balance we seek today is threatened from two sides. At one extreme, not only totalitarianism but some of the modes of large-scale organization present in our own society threaten to smother every trace of individuality. At the other extreme we see varieties of individualism that are destructive of community.

All complex modern societies, whatever their ideology, appear to be moving toward the beehive model. The intricate and precisely orchestrated organizational patterns that come so naturally to advanced technological societies are sooner or later destructive of individuality—unless extraordinary efforts are made to prevent that outcome. The trend is as evident in our own society as it is in explicitly totalitarian societies, although it is less advanced with us and is often retarded by our political guarantees of individual freedom.

The aims and consequences of political totalitarianism are well understood. Less well understood are the consequences of some of our own forms of large-scale organization, which have a clear tendency to dwarf the individual even though their purposes and methods may be authentically nontotalitarian in origin.

This is a crucial point because in our society today the individual moves in a world characterized by ever larger and more elaborately interlocking organization. It is not just that gigantic organizations—corporate, union, governmental—impinge upon the individual's life at every point. It is that the nation—and increasingly the world—has itself become one huge interlocking system. The actions of government have large consequences in the corporate and union world; actions by farm groups affect what housewives pay for groceries; the market strategies of foreign oil producers affect the American commuter; and the monetary decisions of the United States affect every nation in the world.

The advantages of large-scale organization are obvious. It brings us consumer goods, from automobiles to hi-fi sets, that would never have come out of cottage industry. It brings us kidney dialysis machines, "Sesame Street," cheap long-distance calls, efficient air transport. Some critics say they could live without those things, but very few do.

But no contemporary needs to be told of the disadvantages of large-scale organization. Too often it induces a sense of powerlessness, a loss of identity, and a feeling of anonymity. Too often it depersonalizes human relationships, erodes human communication, suppresses individuality. In subtle and not-so-subtle ways it induces conformity. The individual tends to be coerced by the system—and frustrated in ways that have a special capacity to baffle and madden.

These layered frustrations have produced a hostility and distrust that is directed at virtually all aspects of modern organized society. This hostility is directed against bureaucracy, hierarchy, administrators, monolithic institutions. In its more extreme manifestations, it is even directed against the rationality and functional efficiency that are essential to modern organization.

Multiple frustrations are not new to mankind. From the dawn of time man has been frustrated by forces and circumstances beyond his understanding. But apparently it is easier—or seems easier—to accept blows from an inscrutable fate, from natural forces or from the hand of God than to have one's life disrupted by an unknown bureaucrat presiding over an unseen computer. The hostility directed toward the administrator in an administered age is something to contend with. It has led to a kind of inarticulate rebellion that seethes in the breast of even the most conventional individual.

But indiscriminate hostility toward institutions won't help. We have to take the steps that will save us. We cannot do without large-scale organization—but we can demand that it be so designed as to serve humane purposes, and we are just beginning to understand some of the ways in which this might be done. We are beginning to understand how we might create human-sized units within large-scale organization—in factories, in higher education, in some of the newest housing developments. We must devise residential and working arrangements that enable individuals to live their lives as whole persons, not split into fragments by the requirements of a complex, impersonal society.

We must design many varying forms of participation, so that the individual can regain the sense of acting and initiating. This will involve the redesign of huge bureaucratic units to devolve more responsibility to lower levels. It will also require that we supplement the "top down" communication characteristic of large-scale organization with two-way communication that brings messages from the lower levels of organization to the top. Such two-way communication is not only sound democratic doctrine, it is a characteristic of all healthy systemic functioning. Yet most large-scale organizations sooner or later develop a severe breakdown in communication between the "grass roots" and the top.

Politically, participation requires improved citizen access to the political process, and that is not really possible until we cure politicians of their bad habit of doing the public's business behind closed doors. From the city councils and school boards up through the state legislatures to Congress and the federal agencies, elected and appointed officials find it all too convenient to do the public's business in secret. The effect on citizen awareness and interest is devastating. The citizen can't possibly develop an intelligent interest in matters that are totally hidden from his view.

Another measure necessary for the protection of the individual is the preservation of the guarantees of individual liberty written into our Constitution. There will inevitably arise from time to time, both in the public and private sectors, leaders who imagine that a huge and complex society could be far more tidily managed if those guarantees were abrogated. It is particularly important to strengthen—greatly strengthen—the protective measures that insure individual liberty and privacy. Modern forms of organization, media of communication, computerized information systems, and surveillance techniques vastly increase the capacity of the society to invade the privacy and curtail the rights of the individual. We must devise new protections against new dangers.

Yet another vital step that applies to both public- and private-sector organizations is the necessary creation of imaginative, sophisticated, and effective devices for the redress of grievances. Such devices would be directly responsive to the sense of individual powerlessness and frustration.

But the balance between the claims of individuality and the claims of community is threatened from another direction. We have considered the dangers posed by a vast, highly organized society. We must now look at the dangers posed by anarchic individualism.

Before doing so, let us remind ourselves of what is of value in the concern that we have for the individual. A concern for the individual— which entered Western history with the Renaissance—has contributed important ingredients to the best of contemporary social thinking, among them the idea that each person is of value; that all individuals are equally worthy of our care and concern; that the dignity and worth of the individual is not to be measured in terms of race, sex, status, or achievement; that society benefits in vitality as well as stability if there is wide opportunity for individual initiative and responsibility.

At every stage these ideas have had to be defended bitterly against old-style tyranny; against the constraints upon the individual intrinsic to highly stratified traditional societies; and more recently against the all-too-successful thrust of modern totalitarian ideas. Those who have defended the individual in those battles want no retreat.

Unfortunately the idea of individualism has also been used to justify extremes of self-aggrandizing and antisocial behavior, whether the wanton destruction of the environment by an unconcerned industrialist or the buying and selling of hard drugs by a young person who scorns the laws of the community. From this point of view, individualism means that when my purposes and the purposes of the society collide, my purposes are of course paramount. A century from now social historians will look back with astonishment at the extremes of atomistic individualism that were celebrated in late twentieth-century literature and social philosophy. And then the historians may have formulated an hypothesis to explain the fact that these excesses of individualism seemed to grow more lurid at precisely the time when the very idea of individuality was under threat by modern technology and large-scale social organization.

All our knowledge of human functioning, ancient or modern, primitive or civilized, tells us that unqualified individualism is an impossibility, an absurdity, a fantasy. By the time one is old enough to have any kind of independence, one is inescapably a social being. Total individualism isn't an option.

The individual can move toward the freedom available to humans only when he recognizes that he is not wholly free. He lives with the biological potentialities and limitations of a species that has not really changed significantly in fifty thousand years. He lives in a cultural context, some of which has roots that run back ten thousand years. He is part of history, caught in the play of social forces.

When he understands that, whether the terms of his understanding are religious or philosophical, when he admits that he is part of something larger, then the only freedom that is possible to man opens up to him. Freedom is not the fulfillment of whim. Nor is it the fantasy of personal control over events and nature and others and oneself.

Recognition of one's part in a larger drama may lead to various forms of retreat and passivity. But many wise and deep humans have continued to play their role to the hilt, knowing that they are not the authors of the great drama in which they act, but acting nonetheless, with courage and a sense of purpose.

One natural corrective both to anarchic individualism and to the hazards of mass society is a healthy sense of community—but communities are vanishing from the scene. It is increasingly hard to find coherent social contexts within which individuals can find membership, or to which they can give allegiance. For too many people there is no community that they can accept as defining, in part, who they are or what their values and obligations are. The extended family is virtually extinct, and communities in the geographical sense are disintegrating. The sense of membership and allegiance stemming from a common religion or class or economic background is fading. In short, practically every kind of human community is disappearing, and those that remain exercise little command over the loyalties, imagination or daily behavior of their members.

It is a curious fact that liberals and conservatives collaborated to produce the breakdown of community. Liberals, chafing under the old order, developed emancipated ways of thinking that contributed to the passing of traditional communities. But industrialists, particularly in the fields of transportation and communication—industrialists who thought of themselves as conservatives—probably did more to disintegrate the old-style communities than all the liberals who ever lived.

What can we do about it? If we make no effort we are, in effect, deciding to let the forms and patterns of human interaction be determined by the impersonal dynamics of large-scale organization, by the unintended consequences of technological advance, and by commercially motivated decisions.

First, we can face up to the fact that no society can wholly reject its past. Justice Holmes said, "Continuity with the past is not a duty, only a necessity." A discriminating regard for the past will lead us to think twice before destroying existing communities. At the very least, we can stop standing by passively while technological advances, large-scale organization, and random commercial forces destroy elements of community that we would wish to preserve. And we can discredit the extreme individualism that has wreaked such havoc on the whole concept of community.

But holding on to the best of what remains of traditional communities isn't enough. We must experiment with new forms of community, building necessary continuities into the new forms and letting the new wholes develop organically. To enable the individual to enjoy a sense of community, a sense of belonging, we must recreate communities within the massive agglomerations of humanity that characterize contemporary life, communities that will be wholly compatible with the concept of individual worth, dignity, and creativity. Within those communities, individuals must have not only the opportunity to participate, to have their say, they must have opportunities to serve, to be needed, to "connect."

In asserting the value of "community" one need not assume that we ever can or will have a tightly knit society. The United States has never had a tightly woven social fabric and probably never will. Compared with the web of European culture from which the American colonists emerged, the new American communities were loose and pluralistic. And from our beginnings, we've moved so fast and changed so swiftly that a highly coherent culture has never emerged.

It would be wrong, of course, to imagine that giving thought to social arrangements will solve all the problems of the individual and society. Quite aside from social arrangements, the individual must come to terms with himself or herself, which isn't easy today. Old communities and belief systems have broken down. With few exceptions a swiftly changing society has withdrawn from the individual the emotional supports of custom, tradition, family solidarity, religion, stable relationships, codes of conduct, and community coherence. The individual is acutely aware of the limits on his capacity to shape events and their consequences.

At the same time the disintegration of old contexts for the self has created the new problem of "identity." In a day when families and traditions were stable, when national and local loyalties were powerful, young people didn't ask "Who am I?" They knew. They knew where they belonged, what they believed, whom they were loyal to and what was expected of them. They were defined by family, social class, ethnic tradition, economic status, parental occupation, religion.

To be sure, there were those who deviated from what was expected of them, but even their rebellion was an expression of identity. They knew precisely what they were rebelling against.

It isn't that easy today. Part of the problem lies in a wrongheaded contemporary notion of what constitutes identity. If the young person has any marks of lineage, regional style, economic status or religious beliefs, our contemporary culture tells him to ignore them or rid himself of them. Presumably one couldn't possibly accept such "accidents" of background as one's "real identity."

So young people search desperately for an "identity" that has nothing to do with the boring realities of personal background. Not surprisingly, they often seize on the fads of the moment—clothes, slang, tastes in music, manners, and attitudes. So in the end his contemporaries—or the commercial interests that invent and exploit the fads of his contemporaries—determine what the young person comes to think of as his or her identity. Young people searching for an identity among the popular fads and postures of the moment are bound to believe that those exhilarating mannerisms they are trying on for size are more interesting than anything in their own history.

But the manufactured "self" is never as interesting, never as unique as the real person hidden underneath the hastily acquired outer image. And the real person is a product of things pushed aside in the search for identity: family and family relationships, ethnic background, neighborhood surroundings during childhood, religion, and much more. All of these interact with the individual's unique combination of physical and mental qualities. Even if people have grown far beyond their points of origin, even if they have rebelled against their backgrounds, they bear the marks—as individuals—of their origins, of the paths they have traveled and of present realities. It's all a part of the same tapestry. And some figures in the tapestry—one's physical and cultural heritage—may reach back through thousands of years of history.

Another obstacle in the search for identity is the difficulty many contemporaries have in seeing that "identity" is inseparable from commitments, obligations, involvements, loyalties. One recognizes the charm of the contemporary fantasy of a life with "no strings." But identity flows in part from one's courage to commit oneself—to enduring relationships, to the service of chosen values, to membership in a community, to a way of life.

Among other things, adult commitments help in one of the great tasks of mental health: escaping the prison of the self. Self-preoccupation is not without its attractions. Selfishness pays dividends; self-indulgence has multiple rewards; self-pity is deeply satisfying; even self-castigation can yield pleasure. But they are toxic joys. Self-absorption is a prison. And that is something that every self-absorbed person finally knows.

The escape from the prison of the self may be through religion, through dedication to a social purpose, through loving relations with other human beings. Contempt for others, paranoia, exclusion and rejection of others are all paths to self-isolation. Love breaks down the walls of the isolated self.

And crucial to constructive relations with others is a healthy self-regard. If you don't like yourself, it is difficult to maintain loving relations with others. Self-contempt is a profoundly destructive emotion—destructive to the self and to others. Perhaps the only more destructive emotion is the pleasurable but deadly poison of self-pity.

Another step in coming to terms with one's self is the achievement of some measure of self-command. One encounters in contemporary thinking a variety of arguments—some of them valid—favoring self-indulgence, unlimited self-expression, and immediate impulse gratification. But the postponement of immediate gratification, the discipline of impulse, in the interest of later rewards is at the heart of civilized life. All the great civilizations in their periods of rising vitality have cultivated a measure of austerity, of self-discipline.

But the most crucial means of coming to terms with the self is yet to be mentioned. Our polity is built on the idea of individual moral responsibility, and the polity will only survive if the idea survives. It has been eroded by many features of the contemporary scene: the sheer size and complexity of our society, which diminishes the individual's sense of involvement; the reigning environmentalism which lets the individual off the hook ("Society's to blame; I have nothing to do with it"); the almost universal habit of self-exoneration and self-deception which eliminates the possibility of individual moral responsibility by preventing the issue from being posed.

A more subtle escape from individual responsibility is described by Rollo May. He points out that by denying our power many never face the moral and ethical issue of how we use our power. Expressions of helplessness become a way of evading responsibility—"What can I do?" May suggests a new "ethic of intention," which would assert that each individual is responsible for the effects of his or her actions.

There is much to be said for his view. Complete determinism deadens the impulse toward self-improvement, the sense of responsibility, and the moral impulse. Human choice is limited, but it is thus all the more crucial that we exercise what choice we have.

Independence and Interdependence

Lewis Thomas

Lewis Thomas, a physician and a physician's son, was born in 1913, entered Harvard Medical School in 1933, and received his M.D. in 1937. After internship, he began a distinguished career as medical researcher and administrator. In 1973, he resigned from Yale—where he had been Professor of Pathology, chairman of his department, and Dean of the Medical School—to become head of the Memorial Sloan-Kettering Cancer Center in New York City.

Thomas's particular field of interest is the immune system, and he has published numerous scientific articles. His first book aimed at a general audience, *The Lives of a Cell: Notes of a Biology Watcher* (1974), is a collection of monthly columns he wrote for the *New England Journal of Medicine;* it won the National Book Award. Since then he has published two more equally acclaimed books: *The Medusa and the Snail: More Notes of a Biology Watcher* (1979), and a kind of autobiography, *The Youngest Science: Notes of a Medicine Watcher* (1983). Thomas is a master of the short, reflective essay; he draws from his knowledge of biology a set of ideas and metaphors richly applicable to the human condition. The selection printed below comes from the *New York Times Magazine,* July 4, 1976.

Altruism

One of the most astonishing things about human society, from a biologist's point of view, is that it is made up of individual, distinguishable, specifically marked selves, all apparently out on their own. Here we are, now four billion of us, each one labeled as an absolute entity, fundamentally different from all the rest. The labels are not just the visible, behavioral marks—the way a head is turned, the special manner of a smile, the pitch of a voice—these are obvious distinctions; despite superficial resemblances and reminders, no one is precisely a duplicate of anyone else except the occasional pairs of identical twins. Then there are the biochemical marks of self, even more specific and rigid than our behavior, setting us apart. The surfaces of our cells are sufficiently different that immunologists can detect the biochemical difference among all four billion. We probably have different smells as well; a tracking hound can sense the uniqueness of every man's footprint, except for those of twins.

At first glance, you'd think nature had endowed us with everything needed for solitary, independent lives. Much of the time this is how we like to think of ourselves, a world of self-sufficient, free-standing creatures, obsessively individualistic, the brainiest things on earth. Full of ourselves.

The only other social animals we know much about, in any real detail, are the social insects, and they are outlandish forms of life, unearthly and embarrassing. We prefer to think of termites, ants, social bees and wasps as things dropped from another planet, totally without meaning for us. They seem to have evolved by giving up all vestiges of individuality; they live as though all the creatures in the hill or hive had joined together so intimately and interdependently as to be the working parts of a single, huge beast. The isolated ant, out on a trout line of ants, cast from the nest across the path and down into the culvert for the retrieval of a dead moth, doesn't seem to know the difference between himself and any other ant in the line. Ants touch each other ceaselessly, exchanging white bits of information carried in their jaws, spraying tiny droplets of pheromone as they go in order to inform late comers that the moth lies in that direction. The nest, writhing like an enormous ameboid cell, is where the brains are. By itself, the solitary ant has nothing much to think with; a few strings of ganglia connected by nerve fibers, several kinds of pheromone glands for sending messages about safety or danger, or food sources ahead, or orders to aggregate together in platoons for combat. The whole nest thinks, lays plans for the future, figures things out. It is somehow done by pooling all the information, from all the ganglia.

There are no individual creatures in a termite hill. They are a million connected parts, working like the components of a machine. Everything is done automatically. There is something profoundly disturbing about such a way of living. We think of it as repellent, inhuman.

And yet, here we are. For social interdependence, for compulsive collaborative living, for lives driven from beginning to end by connectedness, there is nothing to touch human society. We are, despite all our marks of individuality and our displays of independence, the most biologically social of all the species on earth.

Moreover, we seem to be still in the earliest stages of our evolution. It has only been for 20,000 years or so that we've been leaving evidences of group living, no time at all in the scale of evolution. We must be the youngest form of complex social life on earth, just getting under way.

We can be forgiven blunders, being so juvenile.

One thing we are highly skilled at doing, so universally adept as to suggest that the talent is a genetic endowment: We make language. This is our equivalent of the geometrically flawless wax cells of the hive, or the perfect arches and vaulted, ventilated chambers of the termitarium. We have genes for making words, DNA for syntax, neuronal structures for grammar.

It is our obsession, it is what we do with our lives. Without speech we would not be human beings. We might engage in thought of a kind, but no one can imagine what that thought, wordless and metaphorless, would be like.

It is not just the making of language that sets us apart. Somehow, by some autonomic system over which we have no sort of conscious control, we *build* language. It grows like a living being on its own, changing the sound and meaning of its words, inventing new words and transforming old ones, and all the time none of us realizes that this is happening, nor how. We are no more in charge of the evolution of language than ants control the distribution of twigs of different sizes in the endless construction of their nests. Committees do not make or change, or keep from changing, a language. Governments cannot control the development of speech. It is uncontrollable, ungovernable, unconscious behavior, in which we are all engaged, for all our lives.

It holds us together as a kind of shelter for our minds, and we live inside the structure. In this sense it is our hill, our hive. It provides our music and poetry, our art, and all the fun of our lives. This is the ultimate proof, I think, that nature has endowed us with the means and the urge to live cooperatively as part of a single cell, on the bigger cell, the earth.

Very well. If this is true, we should be looking again, and harder, at the other social species, to learn how they achieved their kind of success and survival, for we are in need of survival as never before in our short history.

How do they do it, the ants and bees and termites? Is there an underlying force that holds them together, drives them along? Are there laws? It will take a lot of study, probably years of time, no doubt endless arrays of computers. Great sums of money. Maybe a National Institute of Sociobiology. Better make it an International Institute, and soon. Now that we are a single community of four billion, scheduled to double again in a few years, so densely packed as to touch hand to hand, almost, all around the earth, it is already late in the day to discover how a social species functions.

One thing we already know, thanks to the biologists. The weirdest aspect of the behavior of social animals, beyond scientific understanding, is their ceaseless giving away of things. They carry food to each other all day long, they shelter and protect each other, and on occasion they drop dead for each other. The trait seems to be genetically determined, and the biologists have already made up a technical term, borrowed from an old word, now part of the professional jargon: *altruism.*

We could begin by examining this behavioral trait in ourselves. There are signs that it is there, not as spectacularly as in the insects but nonetheless there. We make efforts to suppress it, some of us even write tracts to condemn it as beneath human dignity, a violation of selfness; it is perhaps around this issue that our group consciousness, animated by all our brilliant marks of individual identity, comes into conflict with our collective unconscious, if we have such a thing. Maybe altruism is our most primitive attribute, out of reach, beyond our control. Or perhaps it is immediately at hand, disguised now, in our kind of civilization as affection or friendship or love, maybe as music. I don't see why it should be unreasonable for human beings to have strands of DNA, coiled up in chromosomes, coding out instincts for usefulness and helpfulness. I think it is likely true for all my friends, and I don't see why your family and friends should be any different.

Garrett Hardin

Garrett Hardin (born 1915) is a biologist who has written prolifically on the moral and social implications of his field. He is particularly interested in ecology, population, and the problems created by the worldwide scarcity of resources. He received his Ph.D. in biology from Stanford in 1941. His dissertation was a study of algae as a large-scale source of food, but he later gave up his research in this area because he had come to believe that producing more food only worsens population problems. Hardin joined the faculty of the University of California, Santa Barbara, in 1946 and is now Professor Emeritus. He has written many books and articles, including *Nature and Man's Fate* (1959), *Exploring New Ethics for Survival* (1972), and *Mandatory Motherhood* (1974). Hardin is especially devoted to—and especially skillful at—telling people important things that they do not especially want to hear. Some of his writings in this vein are collected in *Stalking the Wild Taboo* (1973). The present essay appeared in the September 1974 issue of *Psychology Today*.

Lifeboat Ethics:
The Case Against Helping the Poor

Environmentalists use the metaphor of the earth as a "spaceship" in trying to persuade countries, industries and people to stop wasting and polluting our natural resources. Since we all share life on this planet, they argue, no single person or institution has the right to destroy, waste, or use more than a fair share of its resources.

But does everyone on earth have an equal right to an equal share of its resources? The spaceship metaphor can be dangerous when used by misguided idealists to justify suicidal policies for sharing our resources through uncontrolled immigration and foreign aid. In their enthusiastic but unrealistic generosity, they confuse the ethics of a spaceship with those of a lifeboat.

A true spaceship would have to be under the control of a captain, since no ship could possibly survive if its course were determined by committee. Spaceship Earth certainly has no captain; the United Nations is merely a toothless tiger, with little power to enforce any policy upon its bickering members.

If we divide the world crudely into rich nations and poor nations, two thirds of them are desperately poor, and only one third comparatively rich, with the United States the wealthiest of all. Metaphorically each rich nation can be seen as a lifeboat full of comparatively rich people. In the ocean outside each lifeboat swim the poor of the world, who would like to get in, or at least to share some of the wealth. What should the lifeboat passengers do?

First, we must recognize the limited capacity of any lifeboat. For example, a nation's land has a limited capacity to support a population and as the current energy crisis has shown us, in some ways we have already exceeded the carrying capacity of our land.

So here we sit, say 50 people in our lifeboat. To be generous let us assume it has room for 10 more, making a total capacity of 60. Suppose the 50 of us in the lifeboat see 100 others swimming in the water outside, begging for admission to our boat or for handouts. We have several options: we may be tempted to try to live by the Christian ideal of being "our brother's keeper," or by the Marxist ideal of "to each according to his needs." Since the needs of all in the water are the same, and since they can all be seen as "our brothers," we could take them all into our boat, making a total of 150 in a boat designed for 60. The boat swamps, everyone drowns. Complete justice, complete catastrophe.

Since the boat has an unused excess capacity of 10 more passengers, we could admit just 10 more to it. But which 10 do we let in? How do we choose? Do we pick the best 10, the neediest 10, "first come, first served"? And what do we say to the 90 we exclude? If we do let an extra 10 into our lifeboat, we will have lost our "safety factor," an engineering principle of critical importance. For example, if we don't leave room for excess capacity as a safety factor in our country's agriculture, a new plant disease or a bad change in the weather could have disastrous consequences.

Suppose we decide to preserve our small safety factor and admit no more to the lifeboat. Our survival is then possible although we shall have to be constantly on guard against boarding parties.

While this last solution clearly offers the only means of our survival, it is morally abhorrent to many people. Some say they feel guilty about their good luck. My reply is simple: "Get out and yield your place to others." This may solve the problem of the guilt-ridden person's conscience, but it does not change the ethics of the lifeboat. The needy person to whom the guilt-ridden person yields his place will not himself feel guilty about his good luck. If he did, he would not climb aboard. The net result of conscience-stricken people giving up their unjustly held seats is the elimination of that sort of conscience from the lifeboat.

This is the basic metaphor within which we must work out our solutions. Let us now enrich the image, step by step, with substantive additions from the real world, a world that must solve real and pressing problems of overpopulation and hunger.

The harsh ethics of the lifeboat become even harsher when we consider the reproductive differences between the rich nations and the poor nations. The people inside the lifeboats are doubling in numbers every 87 years: those swimming around outside are doubling on the average, every 35 years, more than twice as fast as the rich. And since the world's resources are dwindling, the difference in prosperity between the rich and the poor can only increase.

As of 1973, the U.S. had a population of 210 million people, who were increasing by 0.8 percent per year. Outside our lifeboat, let us imagine another 210 million people (say the combined populations of Colombia, Ecuador, Venezuela, Morocco, Pakistan, Thailand and the Philippines), who are increasing at a rate of 3.3 percent per year. Put differently, the doubling time for this aggregate population is 21 years, compared to 87 years for the U.S.

Now suppose the U.S. agreed to pool its resources with those seven countries, with everyone receiving an equal share. Initially the ratio of Americans to non-Americans in this model would be one-to-one but consider what the ratio would be after 87 years, by which time the Americans would have doubled to a population of 420 million. By then, doubling every 21 years, the other group would have swollen to 354 billion. Each American would have to share the available resources with more than eight people.

But, one could argue, this discussion assumes that current population trends will continue, and they may not. Quite so. Most likely the rate of population increase will decline much faster in the U.S. than it will in the other countries, and there does not seem to be much we can do about it. In sharing with "each according to his needs," we must recognize that needs are determined by population size, which is determined by the rate of reproduction, which at present is regarded as a sovereign right of every nation, poor or not. This being so, the philanthropic load created by the sharing ethic of the spaceship can only increase.

The fundamental error of spaceship ethics, and the sharing it requires, is that it leads to what I call "the tragedy of the commons." Under a system of private property, the men who own property recognize their responsibility to care for it, for if they don't they will eventually suffer. A farmer, for instance, will allow no more cattle in a pasture than its carrying capacity justifies. If he overloads it, erosion sets in, weeds take over, and he loses the use of the pasture.

If a pasture becomes a commons open to all, the right of each to use it may not be matched by a corresponding responsibility to protect it. Asking everyone to use it with discretion will hardly do, for the considerate herdsman who refrains from overloading the commons suffers more than a selfish one who says his needs are greater. If everyone would restrain himself all would be well; but it takes only one less than everyone to ruin a system of voluntary restraint. In a crowded world of less than perfect human beings, mutual ruin is inevitable if there are no controls. This is the tragedy of the commons.

One of the major tasks of education today should be the creation of such an acute awareness of the dangers of the commons that people will recognize its many varieties. For example, the air and water have become polluted because they are treated as commons. Further growth in the population or per-capita conversion of natural resources into pollutants will only make the problem worse. The same holds true for the fish of the oceans. Fishing fleets have nearly disappeared in many parts of the world, technological improvements in the art of fishing are hastening the day of complete ruin. Only the replacement of the system of the commons with a responsible system of control will save the land, air, water and oceanic fisheries.

In recent years there has been a push to create a new commons called a World Food Bank, an international depository of food reserves to which nations would contribute according to their abilities and from which they would draw according to their needs. This humanitarian proposal has received support from many liberal international groups, and from such prominent citizens as Margaret Mead, U.N. Secretary General Kurt Waldheim, and Senators Edward Kennedy and George McGovern.

A world food bank appeals powerfully to our humanitarian impulses. But before we rush ahead with such a plan, let us recognize where the greatest political push comes from, lest we be disillusioned later. Our experience with the "Food for Peace program," or Public Law 480, gives us the answer. This program moved billions of dollars worth of U.S. surplus grain to food-short, population-long countries during the past two decades. But when P.L. 480 first became law, a headline in the business magazine *Forbes* revealed the real power behind it: "Feeding the World's Hungry Millions: How It Will Mean Billions for U.S. Business."

And indeed it did. In the years 1960 to 1970, U.S. taxpayers spent a total of $7.9 billion on the Food for Peace program. Between 1948 and 1970, they also paid an additional $50 billion for other economic-aid programs, some of which went for food and food-producing machinery and technology. Though all U.S. taxpayers were forced to contribute to the cost of P.L. 480, certain special interest groups gained handsomely under the program. Farmers did not have to contribute the grain; the Government, or rather the taxpayers, bought it from them at full market prices. The increased demand raised prices of farm products generally. The manufacturers of farm machinery, fertilizers and pesticides benefited by the farmers' extra efforts to grow more food. Grain elevators profited from storing the surplus until it could be shipped. Railroads made money hauling it to ports, and shipping lines profited from carrying it overseas. The implementation of P.L. 480 required the creation of a vast Government bureaucracy, which then acquired its own vested interest in continuing the program regardless of its merits.

Those who proposed and defended the Food for Peace program in public rarely mentioned its importance to any of these special interests. The public emphasis was always on its humanitarian effects. The combination of silent selfish interests and highly vocal humanitarian apologists made a powerful and successful lobby for extracting money from taxpayers. We can expect the same lobby to push now for the creation of a World Food Bank.

However great the potential benefit to selfish interests, it should not be a decisive argument against a truly humanitarian program. We must ask if such a program would actually do more good than harm, not only momentarily but also in the long run. Those who propose the food bank usually refer to a current "emergency" or "crisis" in terms of world food supply. But what is an emergency? Although they may be infrequent and sudden, everyone knows that emergencies will occur from time to time. A well-run family, company, organization or country prepares for the likelihood of accidents and emergencies. It expects them, it budgets for them, it saves for them.

What happens if some organizations or countries budget for accidents and others do not? If each country is solely responsible for its own well-being, poorly managed ones will suffer. But they can learn from experience. They may mend their ways, and learn to budget for infrequent but certain emergencies. For example, the weather varies from year to year, and periodic crop failures are certain. A wise and competent government saves out of the production of the good years in anticipation of bad years to come. Joseph taught this policy to Pharaoh in Egypt more than 2,000 years ago. Yet the great majority of the governments in the world today do not follow such a policy. They lack either the wisdom or the competence, or both. Should those nations that do manage to put something aside be forced to come to the rescue each time an emergency occurs among the poor nations?

"But it isn't their fault!" Some kind-hearted liberals argue, "How can we blame the poor people who are caught in an emergency? Why must they suffer for the sins of their governments?" The concept of blame is simply not relevant here. The real question is, what are the operational consequences of establishing a world food bank? If it is open to every country every time a need develops, slovenly rulers will not be motivated to take Joseph's advice. Someone will always come to their aid. Some countries will deposit food in the world food bank, and others will withdraw it. There will be almost no overlap. As a result of such solutions to food shortage emergencies, the poor countries will not learn to mend their ways, and will suffer progressively greater emergencies as their populations grow.

On the average, poor countries undergo a 2.5 percent increase in population each year; rich countries, about 0.8 percent. Only rich countries have anything in the way of food reserves set aside, and even they do not have as much as they should. Poor countries have none. If poor countries received no food from the outside, the rate of their population growth would be periodically checked by crop failures and famines. But if they can always draw on a world food bank in time of need, their population can continue to grow unchecked, and so will their "need" for aid. In the short run, a world food bank may diminish that need, but in the long run it actually increases the need without limit.

Without some system of worldwide food sharing, the proportion of people in the rich and poor nations might eventually stabilize. The over-populated poor countries would decrease in numbers, while the rich countries that had room for more people would increase. But with a well-meaning system of sharing, such as a world food bank, the growth differential between the rich and the poor countries will not only persist, it will increase. Because of the higher rate of population growth in the poor countries of the world, 88 percent of today's children are born poor, and only 12 percent rich. Year by year the ratio becomes worse, as the fast-reproducing poor outnumber the slow-reproducing rich.

A world food bank is thus a commons in disguise. People will have more motivation to draw from it than to add to any common store. The less provident and less able will multiply at the expense of the abler and more provident, bringing eventual ruin upon all who share in the commons. Besides, any system of "sharing" that amounts to foreign aid from the rich nations to the poor nations will carry the taint of charity, which will contribute little to the world peace so devoutly desired by those who support the idea of a world food bank.

As past U.S. foreign-aid programs have amply and depressingly demonstrated, international charity frequently inspires mistrust and antagonism rather than gratitude on the part of the recipient nation [see "What Other Nations Hear When the Eagle Screams," by Kenneth J. and Mary M. Gergen, *Psychology Today*, June 1974].

The modern approach to foreign aid stresses the export of technology and advice, rather than money and food. As an ancient Chinese proverb goes: "Give a man a fish and he will eat for a day; teach him how to fish and he will eat for the rest of his days." Acting on this advice, the Rockefeller and Ford Foundations have financed a number of programs for improving agriculture in the hungry nations. Known as the "Green Revolution," these programs have led to the development of "miracle rice" and "miracle wheat," new strains that offer bigger harvests and greater resistance to crop damage. Norman Borlaug, the Nobel Prize winning agronomist who, supported by the Rockefeller Foundation, developed "miracle wheat," is one of the most prominent advocates of a world food bank.

Whether or not the Green Revolution can increase food production as much as its champions claim is a debatable but possibly irrelevant point. Those who support this well-intended humanitarian effort should first consider some of the fundamentals of human ecology. Ironically, one man who did was the late Alan Gregg, a vice president of the Rockefeller Foundation. Two decades ago he expressed strong doubts about the wisdom of such attempts to increase food production. He likened the growth and spread of humanity over the surface of the earth to the spread of cancer in the human body, remarking that "cancerous growths demand food, but, as far as I know, they have never been cured by getting it."

Every human born constitutes a draft on all aspects of the environment: food, air, water, forests, beaches, wildlife, scenery and solitude. Food can, perhaps, be significantly increased to meet a growing demand. But what about clean beaches, unspoiled forests, and solitude? If we satisfy a growing population's need for food, we necessarily decrease its per capita supply of the other resources needed by men.

India, for example, now has a population of 600 million, which increases by 15 million each year. This population already puts a huge load on a relatively impoverished environment. The country's forests are now only a small fraction of what they were three centuries ago, and floods and erosion continually destroy the insufficient farmland that remains. Every one of the 15 million new lives added to India's population puts an additional burden on the environment, and increases the economic and social costs of crowding. However humanitarian our intent, every Indian life saved through medical or nutritional assistance from abroad diminishes the quality of life for those who remain, and for subsequent generations. If rich countries make it possible, through foreign aid, for 600 million Indians to swell to 1.2 billion in a mere 28 years, as their current growth rate threatens, will future generations of Indians thank us for hastening the destruction of their environment? Will our good intentions be sufficient excuse for the consequences of our actions?

My final example of a commons in action is one for which the public has the least desire for rational discussion—immigration. Anyone who publicly questions the wisdom of current U.S. immigration policy is promptly charged with bigotry, prejudice, ethnocentrism, chauvinism, isolationism or selfishness. Rather than encounter such accusations, one would rather talk about other matters, leaving immigration policy to wallow in the crosscurrents of special interests that take no account of the good of the whole, or the interests of posterity.

Perhaps we still feel guilty about things we said in the past. Two generations ago the popular press frequently referred to Dagos, Wops, Polacks, Chinks and Krauts, in articles about how America was being "overrun" by foreigners of supposedly inferior genetic stock [see "The Politics of Genetic Engineering: Who Decides Who's Defective?" *Psychology Today,* June 1974]. But because the implied inferiority of foreigners was used then as justification for keeping them out, people now assume that restrictive policies could only be based on such misguided notions. There are other grounds.

Just consider the numbers involved. Our Government acknowledges a net inflow of 400,000 immigrants a year. While we have no hard data on the extent of illegal entries, educated guesses put the figure at about 600,000 a year. Since the natural increase (excess of births over deaths) of the resident population now runs about 1.7 million per year, the yearly gain from immigration amounts to at least 19 percent of the total annual increase, and may be as much as 37 percent if we include the estimate for illegal immigrants. Considering the growing use of birth-control devices, the potential effect of educational campaigns by such organizations as Planned Parenthood Federation of America and Zero Population Growth, and the influence of inflation and the housing shortage, the fertility rate of American women may decline so much that immigration could account for all the yearly increase in population. Should we not at least ask if that is what we want?

For the sake of those who worry about whether the "quality" of the average immigrant compares favorably with the quality of the average resident, let us assume that immigrants and nativeborn citizens are of exactly equal quality, however one defines that term. We will focus here only on quantity; and since our conclusions will depend on nothing else, all charges of bigotry and chauvinism become irrelevant.

World food banks *move food to the people,* hastening the exhaustion of the environment of the poor countries. Unrestricted immigration, on the other hand, *moves people to the food,* thus speeding up the destruction of the environment of the rich countries. We can easily understand why poor people should want to make this latter transfer, but why should rich hosts encourage it?

As in the case of foreign-aid programs, immigration receives support from selfish interests and humanitarian impulses. The primary selfish interest in unimpeded immigration is the desire of employers for cheap labor, particularly in industries and trades that offer degrading work. In the past, one wave of foreigners after another was brought into the U.S. to work at wretched jobs for wretched wages. In recent years the Cubans, Puerto Ricans and Mexicans have had this dubious honor. The interests of the employers of cheap labor mesh well with the guilty silence of the country's liberal intelligentsia. White Anglo-Saxon Protestants are particularly reluctant to call for a closing of the doors to immigration for fear of being called bigots.

But not all countries have such reluctant leadership. Most educated Hawaiians, for example, are keenly aware of the limits of their environment, particularly in terms of population growth. There is only so much room on the islands, and the islanders know it. To Hawaiians, immigrants from the other 49 states present as great a threat as those from other nations. At a recent meeting of Hawaiian government officials in Honolulu, I had the ironic delight of hearing a speaker, who like most of his audience was of Japanese ancestry, ask how the country might practically and constitutionally close its doors to further immigration. One member of the audience countered: "How can we shut the doors now? We have many friends and relatives in Japan that we'd like to bring here some day so that they can enjoy Hawaii too." The Japanese-American speaker smiled sympathetically and answered: "Yes, but we have children now, and someday we'll have grandchildren too. We can bring more people here from Japan only by giving away some of the land that we hope to pass on to our grandchildren some day. What right do we have to do that?"

At this point, I can hear U.S. liberals asking: "How can you justify slamming the door once you're inside? You say that immigrants should be kept out. But aren't we all immigrants, or the descendants of immigrants? If we insist on staying, must we not admit all others?" Our craving for intellectual order leads us to seek and prefer symmetrical rules and morals: a single rule for me and everybody else; the same rule yesterday, today and tomorrow. Justice, we feel, should not change with time and place.

We Americans of non-Indian ancestry can look upon ourselves as the descendants of thieves who are guilty morally, if not legally, of stealing this land from its Indian owners. Should we then give back the land to the now living American descendants of those Indians? However morally or logically sound this proposal may be, I, for one, am unwilling to live by it and I know no one else who is. Besides, the logical consequence would be absurd. Suppose that, intoxicated with a sense of pure justice, we should decide to turn our land over to the Indians. Since all our other wealth has also been derived from the land, wouldn't we be morally obliged to give that back to the Indians too?

Clearly, the concept of pure justice produces an infinite regression to absurdity. Centuries ago, wise men invented statutes of limitations to justify the rejection of such pure justice, in the interest of preventing continual disorder. The law zealously defends property rights. Drawing a line after an arbitrary time has elapsed may be unjust, but the alternatives are worse.

We are all the descendants of thieves, and the world's resources are inequitably distributed. But we must begin the journey to tomorrow from the point where we are today. We cannot remake the past. We cannot safely divide the wealth equitably among all peoples so long as people reproduce at different rates. To do so would guarantee that our grandchildren, and everyone else's grandchildren, would have only a ruined world to inhabit.

To be generous with one's own possessions is quite different from being generous with those of posterity. We should call this point to the attention of those who, from a commendable love of justice and equality, would institute a system of the commons, either in the form of a world food bank, or of unrestricted immigration. We must convince them if we wish to save at least some parts of the world from environmental ruin.

Without a true world government to control reproduction and the use of available resources, the sharing ethic of the spaceship is impossible. For the foreseeable future, our survival demands that we govern our actions by the ethics of a lifeboat, harsh though they may be. Posterity will be satisfied with nothing less.

Walter W. Benjamin

Walter W. Benjamin is Chair of the Department of Religious Studies at Hamline University in Minnesota, where he has taught since 1966. He received his Ph.D. from Duke University with a specialization in Christian ethics. He is particularly interested and active in the field of medical ethics. At the third annual Midwestern Conference on Food and Social Policy in 1978, Benjamin was one of a group of panelists who responded to an address by Garrett Hardin. The following essay, taken from the *Christian Century* (March 24, 1979), is based upon his remarks on that occasion. A reply by W. M. Finnin, Jr., appears in the *Christian Century* on July 4, 1979.

A Challenge to the Eco-Doomsters

*No man is an island, entire of itself; every man is a piece of the
continent, a part of the main; if a clod be washed away by the sea,
Europe is the less, as well as if a promontory were, as well as if a manor
of thy friends or of thine own were; any man's death diminishes me,
because I am involved in mankind; and therefore never send to know for
whom the bell tolls; it tolls for thee.*

JOHN DONNE

Ever since the publication of his essay "The Tragedy of the Commons" ten years ago, Garrett Hardin has been the leading exponent of a population policy that would embrace realism in place of naïveté, pragmatism in place of thoughtless charity, and consideration of long-range benefits in place of an immediate pay-off. Speaking bluntly and uncompromisingly, Hardin—professor of human ecology at the University of California, Santa Barbara—has brought such concepts as "social triage," "lifeboat ethics" and "environmental commons" into our discourse.

Dr. Hardin counsels prudence—a value not alien to our religious tradition. Jesus told his followers to be as "harmless as doves but as wise as serpents"; he warned them not to begin building a tower if they lacked the resources to complete it. Unlike some breast-beating critics on the far left who are forever placing the blame on America, Hardin holds Third World nations themselves largely responsible for their desperate plight. Some of their leaders, he says, are not convinced that they have a population problem; some are more concerned with "demagoguery than with demography." The "green revolution" was supposed to buy Third World countries time to put their houses in order, but some of them frittered the time away.

Certainly Hardin is right in insisting that "trade" is to be preferred to "aid." The former enhances feelings of mutuality, whereas the dole develops dependency on the part of the recipient and an attitude of condescension and noblesse oblige on the part of the giver. A Chinese proverb should be kept in mind: "If you give a man a fish, you feed him for a day; teach him how to fish and you feed him the rest of his life." Nonetheless, Dr. Hardin's views on the population explosion are inadequate in several respects.

1

1. *Hardin ignores the validity of other population strategies.* His own position is a "crisis-environmentalist" ideology—or, in more pejorative terms, an "eco-doomster" stance. Thomas Malthus was that ideology's "great prophet"; Paul Ehrlich and Garrett Hardin are "sons of the prophet." Crisis-environmentalists view both disease and cure as simple; our ecosystem is sick, and the cause of the malady is overpopulation. A remedy can be effected only by moving as quickly as possible—and it may already be too late—to zero population growth (ZPG). But how is this to be done? Persuasion won't work; therefore, governmental coercion will have to be applied. We must, after all, preserve our greatest value—quality of life.

Another population strategy is that of the "family planners," who aim to achieve ZPG by the elimination of all unwanted and unplanned pregnancies, both within and without marriage. They would provide complete and free access for individuals and families to all available methods of birth control, abortion and sterilization. Family planners stress the value of freedom: families know best, if they are given full information and if governmental coercion is minimized.

But a third position, that of the "developmentalists," has the most to recommend it, both scientifically and ethically. Like other population ideologies, it seeks to reduce pollution, stabilize population, and to declare the "religion of endless growth" lethal in its effect. At issue are not the ends toward which we strive, but the means. Developmentalists indict crisis-environmentalists for being reductionistic; that is, concerned only about climate, statistics and quantities. In contrast, the developmentalists' vision is wide-angled, for they see food and population issues as ineluctably moral, economic, social and political. The value they emphasize, then, is distributive justice.

This tradition, which goes back at least as far as Aristotle, says that human beings, in order to have community, must "play fair." We must strike a balance between our own good fortune and the ill fortune of others, striving toward equity and even-handedness; for without such goals, we are barbarians. The credo of the developmentalist, then, is "Take care of the people, and the people will take care of themselves." If the exploited are given their due—employment, health care, security, education, balanced diets—and saved from the precarious brink of near extinction, birth rates will decline.

Dr. Hardin argues that "for all animals, good nutrition means greater fertility"—an opinion that flies in the face of demographic data when applied to human beings. Pervasive insecurity creates high human fertility. Where life is Hobbesian—"mean, nasty, brutish and short"—security is sought in producing children. Each additional child increases one's social and economic insurance against the void. Hardin's thesis, unsound on its own terms, defies the fact that the best way to lower the birth rate is not to let people drift closer to the abyss but rather to give them a better life. Third World cultures are behaving as many European ones did 200 years ago; by plotting a curve relating birth and death rates according to time, we can see that these countries are right on schedule. They are struggling to get through the "demographic transition"—the shift from high birth and death rates to low birth and death rates. To abandon them now would be not only unjust but counterproductive.

2. *Hardin's metaphor of the "lifeboat" is not only misleading but dangerous.* Such imagery is a vestige of the 19th century laissez-faire era, but the values it represents are deeply embedded in our national psyche, as the cowboy ads for Marlboro cigarettes testify. Lifeboat ethics encourages the worst myth-making tendencies, promoting the isolationism and self-absorption that have always been our nemesis.

Perhaps Dr. Hardin should have stayed with his original metaphor, the Commons. It, like some other images—Kenneth Boulding's "spaceship earth," Marshall McLuhan's "global village" and Teilhard's "wheat sheaf" —is holistic and organic. Such figures of speech help us resist the temptation to believe that salvation lies in separation and in "going it alone." These images are in harmony with human evolution. To be sure, all around we see conflicts and compartments—racial, religious, ethnic—but despite these divisions, there are profound movements toward connectedness, reunion and intercommunion. We are now trying to hammer out laws for the mining of the seabed, recognizing that neither the moon, nor the sea, nor the minerals under the sea belong exclusively to any one nation.

Even if we accept the lifeboat metaphor, we must acknowledge that ours is not a self-sufficient vessel. The higher our technology and the greater our consumption, the more vulnerable we become. The brief oil embargo by the OPEC nations a few years ago indicated just how "tipsy" was our craft. We are dependent on other nations not only for oil but also for manganese, cobalt, chromium, titanium, tin, mercury, asbestos and many other minerals. Cartels are being organized by developing nations determined to secure fair prices for their raw materials. National "privatism" is at a dead end; interdependence is the wave of the future.

2

3. *Lifeboat ethics stresses survival as the* summum bonum, *to the neglect of other values.* Certainly, survival is an important value, but if it is proclaimed in fear and despair, will it not threaten the search for community, mutuality and reconciliation? Twenty years ago our nation, traumatized by the threat of nuclear holocaust, was on the brink of committing hundreds of billions of dollars to provide fallout shelters in case the ICBMs started dropping. Some individuals constructed elaborate shelters in their

backyards and stocked them with food supplies—and a few even suggested that to prepare for a nuclear attack, the shelters would need to be equipped with machine guns to keep improvident neighbors away. I resolved then that I would not like to live in a world with people whose only value was survival. Had our nation taken the "shelter-survival" route then, we wouldn't have SALT[0] agreements now.

We have always seen ourselves as a humanitarian people. Our food, fiber, and technical know-how have aided millions. To be sure, we haven't always acted from motives of pure altruism. Reinhold Niebuhr[0] taught us that national "will to power" can never be excluded from an analysis of relations between groups. My concern is to keep the dialectic between egoism and altruism, U.S. and U.N., American citizen and Bangladesh peasant intact. To allow the "survivalists" to call the shots would, I believe, have a devastating effect on the American moral consciousness. Norman Cousins, former editor of *Saturday Review,* has said that "desensitization, not hunger, is the great curse" afflicting the earth. Not long ago a majority of Americans became accustomed to the napalming carried out by U.S. forces in Vietnam; it might not be hard for us to adjust to the knowledge that there were tens of millions of children overseas dying with bloated bellies.

4. *Hardin's views encourage an American tendency toward ethnocentrism in viewing underdeveloped countries.* Those countries should be spared condescending references suggesting that they are inept, irresponsible and lacking in wisdom. It is an instinctive human reaction to deny our own guilt for the sufferings of others. We are blind to the devastating effects of colonialism, imperialism and the workings of multinational corporations on powerless people. Because people are poor does not mean that they are without virtue; nor, because they are powerless, are they without dignity. Our Western religious tradition informs us that it is the powerful, well-fed, militaristic nations that are in danger of losing their souls.

Lifeboat ethicists are unaware of ethnocentrism, their cultural bias. When Hardin says, "Every Indian life saved through medical or nutritional assistance from abroad diminishes the quality of life for those who remain," that is a view "from the top." But "from the bottom," the moral reality is seen quite differently, though the logic is no less exact: "Every American sustained at the cost of 60 times the resources now required to sustain an Indian diminishes the long-range quality of Indian life."

It may be that some Third World nations resist our efforts to dictate their

SALT   Strategic Arms Limitation Talks, a series of ongoing negotiations between the United States and the Soviet Union, opened in Vienna in 1960. The talks have thus far led to two agreements.

Reinhold Niebuhr   Theologian (1882–1971) who served as vice president and senior faculty member of New York City's Union Theological Seminary.

population policies because they see a connection between our own policies and the social cancers growing in our body politic. They may say: "Certainly you have solved your population problem, but do we have to accept the rest—abortion, rampant divorce, delinquency, drug addiction, crime, disrespect of children for parents? Is this what you want for us?" Would that we could see ourselves as others see us.

3

5. *An appeal to determinism and necessity should not encourage fatalism.* A belief in various forms of determinism—economic, demographic, social —gave rise in the past to a "nothing can be done" attitude. For example, Adam Smith's "unseen hand" theory mysteriously united individual acts of selfishness that in aggregate produced a common good. Karl Marx's discovery of "scientific socialism" made it seem inevitable that capitalism was doomed. Only 100 years ago, social Darwinians accepted the dogma of the survival of the fittest; nature was "red in tooth and claw." Extrapolating their theory to the human world, they gave us another new commandment: "Let ill enough alone." Thus the robber barons were given the green light, social amelioration was said to violate "natural law," and the poor were regarded as deserving their miserable lot for having been born with deleterious genes and "unfavorable characteristics."

Dr. Hardin would have another commandment added to the Decalogue: "Thou shalt not transgress against the carrying capacity of the environment." He speaks of the hubris of those who think that they can fly in the face of nature's ways. In general, I agree: there *are* limits—but we don't know what those limits are. When I was a boy working on a Minnesota farm, the agronomists of the time were saying that the maximum possible corn production was 60 bushels to the acre. And yet today farmers' yields of corn far exceed that figure. Again, I agree that the constraints of nature ought to be respected but we must admit that they are elastic. Let us not appeal to a new iron law of "carrying capacity" that will engender either fatalism or fanaticism and consign those we could have helped to a future of "benign neglect."

6. *Hardin prefers China over India as the model for the Third World.* I find it strange that Hardin can maintain that the 1 billion Chinese are "much better off" than the 600 million Indians. India, the world's largest democracy, despite significant agricultural and economic gains, is disorderly and inefficient, and people are starving. But people are not attracted to a democracy because of its efficiency, because its trains run on time, but because of its values—because it is an open society that values human dignity and preserves basic freedoms. In *The Brothers Karamazov,* the Grand Inquisitor speaks to the returned Christ: "In the end they will lay their freedom at our feet, and say to us, 'Make us your slaves but feed us.' " It is remarkable how myopic many academics are when it comes to totali-

tarian regimes. We admire societies that "have got it together." In the 1930s we glorified Soviet Russia; now China is seen as the ideal.

4

7. *Lifeboat moralists fail to see the connection between affluence and starvation.* In all honesty, we must acknowledge that ours is not a lifeboat but a luxury yacht. We are a throwaway, nonreturnable, planned-obsolescence society. When I was a boy in a family of seven, I carried a small two-and-a-half-foot can of garbage to the curb once a week. Today there are two or three large GI cans at the curb in front of each house in the suburb where I live, though the families are smaller.

The Club of Rome° has said that a nation with a diminishing population may nonetheless put increasing pressure on the ecosystem if it doesn't change "sloppy habit" life styles. To fixate on population is to touch only one aspect of our environmental crisis. It's easy for us to point the accusing finger at others for not making use of the pill, the IUD, the abortion and the vasectomy. But our worship of such luxuries as the private automobile, air conditioning and marbleized beef indicates that we have done little in the areas of antipollution, recycling, energy reduction and simplification of life styles. Is it any wonder that some writers in other countries have said that "the world can stand only one United States"?

I conclude with a quotation from one who did not moralize or patronize, one who had a reverence for life; one who, by the way he spent his life, put deed and word together—Albert Schweitzer: "Wherever there is lost the consciousness that every man is an object of concern for us just because he is a man, civilization and morals are shaken, and the advance to fully developed inhumanity is only a question of time."

Norman Cousins

Norman Cousins (born 1912) is a prominent American editor and essayist. After graduating from Columbia Teachers College in 1933, he turned to a career in journalism. His name is most closely associated with the *Saturday Review,* which, as executive editor, he brought into prominence in the 1940s and directed until 1980. Cousins has written steadily and fearlessly on most of the major issues of his time. Perhaps his best known work is *Modern Man*

Club of Rome   Nonpartisan, multinational organization founded in 1968 to promote research on global problems that affect all societies. The membership is made up of scientists, humanists, educators, national and international civil servants, and industrialists.

Is Obsolete (1945), written in response to the dropping of the atomic bomb on Hiroshima. He has also written memorably on American democracy and on world federation. *Anatomy of an Illness* (1979) records his own confrontation of a medical crisis with remarkable psychological strength and insight. He has received many awards for both journalism and citizenship. The present essay, one of several editorials written by Cousins in response to the ideas of Garrett Hardin, appeared in the *Saturday Review* for March 8, 1975.

Of Life and Lifeboats

New Delhi

A short distance outside New Delhi, I saw a long file of protest marchers walking slowly in the direction of the capital. Most of them were young adults. They were identified by their placards as teachers, students, farmers, shopkeepers, commercial workers.

One of the placards said: HUNGRY PEOPLE ARE HUMAN, TOO. Another sign: IS INDIA GOING TO BE THROWN ON THE RUBBISH HEAP?

I learned that the reason for the march was the increasing discussion in the Indian press over reports that Western nations, including the United States, are getting ready to turn their backs on India's starving millions. The reports suggest that Western policy-makers feel that no amount of aid can prevent mass famine.

A person whose name has been linked frequently to such a hard-line approach is Garrett Hardin, professor of biology at the University of California, Santa Barbara. According to the reports, Professor Hardin believes that the Western nations are justified in denying aid to famine-threatened countries. He uses the analogy of the lifeboat. If the survivors take more than a certain number on board, everyone will go down.

Professor Hardin's ideas and the shocked reaction of the young people on the New Delhi march serve to dramatize what is rapidly becoming the most important issue before contemporary civilization. The attitudes of the rich toward the poor and the poor toward the rich are setting the stage for what could become the costliest showdown in history. C. P. Snow° sees a world divided between the 75 percent who are starving and the 25 percent who are sitting in their living rooms watching it happen on TV. Robert Heilbroner, in *An Inquiry Into the Human Prospect,* foresees a possibility of atomic blackmail by the hungry nations in possession of nuclear secrets. He predicts these countries will not hesitate to risk a holocaust if they don't receive a larger share of the world's vital resources.

C. P. Snow   British novelist and physicist (1905–1972) concerned about the communication gap between scientists and humanists.

Such a showdown is not a misty, distant possibility, but a fast-growing reality, of which the protest marchers near New Delhi were an early warning. It is not difficult to understand their feelings. Their grievance is not that they think they are entitled to outside help as a matter of natural right, but that they are now being told, in effect, that they are not worth helping. They are protesting lifeboat analogies and the notion that some people have the right to decide whether others should live or die.

The trouble with Professor Hardin's thesis is that it is unsound in its own terms. It defies the fact that the best way to bring down the birth rate is not to let people starve, but to give them a better life. It calls for education, nutrition, decent housing, productive work. Instead of eliminating or cutting back on aid, we ought to be stepping up shipments of fertilizers, chemicals, plows, tractors, harvesting machines, tools, engines, dynamos, and thousands of other items involved in upgrading living standards.

India itself is demonstrating what can be done with a concentrated program of technological innovation. It has cut its food deficit by a third in little more than one year. Several model agricultural communities that have had the benefit of adequate fertilizer and modern equipment have increased the food yield per acre by more than 200 percent. In light of these facts, nothing is more irresponsible or incompetent than to say help by the outside world should be withheld.

The principal cancer of the Hardin approach will be felt, not by India, but by the West itself. For Hardinism can become a wild infection in the moral consciousness. If it is possible to rationalize letting large numbers of Asians starve, it will be no time at all before we apply the same reasoning to people at home. Once we discover how easy it is to stare without flinching at famine in Calcutta or Dacca, it should be no trick to be unblinking at the disease-ridden tenements of Harlem or Detroit or the squalor of the shacks in Appalachia.

Desensitization, not hunger, is the greatest curse on earth. It begins by calibrating people's credentials to live and ends by cheapening all life. People were appalled by Lt. William Calley's° moral callousness in spraying machine-gun bullets at Vietnamese. But the difference between Calley's contempt for human life and a policy of impassiveness toward starvation is a difference in degree and not in values.

Famine in India and Bangladesh is a test not just of our capacity to respond as human beings but of our ability to understand the cycles of civilization. We can't ignore outstretched hands without destroying that which is most significant in the American character—a sense of vital identification with human beings wherever they are. Regarding life as the

Lt. William Calley   Platoon leader at the Mai Lai Massacre (1969), the Viet Nam War. He was later court-martialed and found guilty of murdering unarmed South Vietnamese civilians.

highest value is more important to the future of America than anything we make or sell. We need not be bashful in facing up to that fact and in trying to put it to work.

Jonathan Swift

Jonathan Swift (1667–1745) is one of the most famous writers in English. He was born of an English family in Dublin and became an Anglican clergyman in a period of disappointment over his hopes for a political career in England. He nevertheless pursued politics; in 1713 the Tory government rewarded him for his powerful writing—in the manner of those times—with the deanship of St. Patrick's, Dublin. However, he spent little time in Ireland until the fall of the party forced his return to Dublin a few years later, where he became for the rest of his life a champion of the Irish people against English oppression. Meanwhile, he had become an intimate of the best English writers of his day, a leading political pamphleteer, and the author of a series of writings that would make him the greatest of English satirists. Especially notable are *A Tale of a Tub* and *The Battle of the Books* published in 1704, the incomparable *Gulliver's Travels* (1726), and the present piece, *A Modest Proposal,* published in 1729, at a time when the miseries of the poor in Ireland seemed to Swift to have reached an intolerable state. Calculated to arouse attention and sympathy in Ireland and England, it has become a classic, notable particularly for its daring use of irony.

A Modest Proposal

It is a melancholly Object to those, who walk through this great Town, or travel in the Country; when they see the *Streets,* the *Roads,* and *Cabbin-doors* crowded with *Beggars* of the Female Sex, followed by three, four, or six Children, *all in Rags,* and importuning every Passenger for an Alms. These *Mothers,* instead of being able to work for their honest Livelyhood, are forced to employ all their Time in stroling to beg Sustenance for their *helpless Infants;* who, as they grow up, either turn *Thieves* for want of Work; or leave their *dear Native Country, to fight for the Pretender in* Spain, or sell themselves to the *Barbadoes.*

I think it is agreed by all Parties, that this prodigious Number of Children in the Arms, or on the Backs, or at the Heels of their Mothers, and frequently of their *Fathers,* is *in the present deplorable State of the Kingdom,* a very great additional Grievance; and therefore, whoever could find out a fair, cheap, and easy Method of making these Children sound and useful Members of the Commonwealth, would deserve so well of the Publick, as to have his Statue set up for a Preserver of the Nation.

But my Intention is very far from being confined to provide only for the Children of *professed Beggars:* It is of a much greater Extent, and shall take in the whole Number of Infants at a certain Age, who are born of Parents, in effect as little able to support them, as those who demand our Charity in the Streets.

As to my own Part, having turned my Thoughts for many Years, upon this important Subject, and maturely weighed the several *Schemes of other Projectors,* I have always found them grosly mistaken in their Computation. It is true a Child, *just dropt from its Dam,* may be supported by her Milk, for a Solar Year with little other Nourishment; at most not above the Value of two Shillings; which the Mother may certainly get, or the Value in *Scraps,* by her lawful Occupation of *Begging:* And, it is exactly at one Year old, that I propose to provide for them in such a Manner, as, instead of being a Charge upon their *Parents,* or the *Parish,* or *wanting Food and Raiment* for the rest of their Lives; they shall, on the contrary, contribute to the Feeding, and partly to the Cloathing, of many Thousands.

There is likewise another great Advantage in my *Scheme,* that it will prevent those *voluntary Abortions,* and that horrid Practice of *Women murdering their Bastard Children;* alas! too frequent among us; sacrificing the *poor innocent Babes,* I doubt, more to avoid the Expense than the Shame; which would move Tears and Pity in the most Savage and inhuman Breast.

The Number of Souls in *Ireland* being usually reckoned one Million and a half; of these I calculate there may be about Two hundred Thousand Couple whose Wives are Breeders; from which Number I subtract thirty thousand Couples, who are able to maintain their own Children; although I apprehend there cannot be so many, under *the present Distresses of the Kingdom;* but this being granted, there will remain an Hundred and Seventy Thousand Breeders. I again subtract Fifty Thousand, for those Women who miscarry, or whose Children die by Accident, or Disease, within the Year. There only remain an Hundred and Twenty Thousand Children of poor Parents, annually born: The Question therefore is, How this Number shall be reared, and provided for? Which, as I have already said, under the present Situation of Affairs, is utterly impossible, by all the Methods hitherto proposed: For we can *neither employ them in Handicraft or Agriculture;* we neither build Houses, (I mean in the Country) nor cultivate Land: They can very seldom pick up a Livelihood *by Stealing* until they arrive at six Years old; except where they are of towardly Parts; although, I confess, they learn the Rudiments much earlier; during which Time, they can, however, be properly looked upon only as *Probationers;* as I have been informed by a principal Gentleman in the Country of

Cavan, who protested to me, that he never knew above one or two Instances under the Age of six, even in a Part of the Kingdom *so renowned for the quickest Proficiency in that Art.*

I am assured by our Merchants, that a Boy or a Girl before twelve Years old, is no saleable Commodity; and even when they come to this Age, they will not yield above Three Pounds, or Three Pounds and half a Crown at most, on the Exchange; which cannot turn to Account either to the Parents or the Kingdom; the Charge of Nutriment and Rags, having been at least four Times that Value.

I shall now therefore humbly propose my own Thoughts; which I hope will not be liable to the least Objection.

I have been assured by a very knowing *American* of my Acquaintance in *London;* that a young healthy Child, well nursed, is, at a Year old, a most delicious, nourishing, and wholesome Food; whether *Stewed, Roasted, Baked,* or *Boiled;* and, I make no doubt, that it will equally serve in a *Fricasie,* or *Ragoust.*

I do therefore humbly offer it to *publick Consideration,* that of the Hundred and Twenty Thousand Children, already computed, Twenty thousand may be reserved for Breed; whereof only one Fourth Part to be Males; which is more than we allow to *Sheep, black Cattle,* or *Swine;* and my Reason is, that these Children are seldom the Fruits of Marriage, *a Circumstance not much regarded by our Savages;* therefore, *one Male* will be sufficient to serve *four Females.* That the remaining Hundred thousand, may, at a Year old, be offered in Sale to the *Persons of Quality and Fortune,* through the Kingdom; always advising the Mother to let them suck plentifully in the last Month, so as to render them plump, and fat for a good Table. A Child will make two Dishes at an Entertainment for Friends; and when the Family dines alone, the fore or hind Quarter will make a reasonable Dish; and seasoned with a little Pepper or Salt, will be very good Boiled on the fourth Day, especially in *Winter.*

I have reckoned upon a Medium, that a Child just born will weigh Twelve Pounds; and in a solar Year, if tolerably nursed, encreaseth to twenty eight Pounds.

I grant this Food will be somewhat dear, and therefore very *proper for Landlords;* who, as they have already devoured most of the Parents, seem to have the best Title to the Children.

Infants Flesh will be in Season throughout the Year; but more plentiful in *March,* and a little before and after: For we are told by a grave[1] Author, an eminent *French* physician, that *Fish being a prolifick Dyet,* there are more Children born in *Roman Catholick Countries,* about Nine Months after *Lent,* than at any other Season: Therefore reckoning a Year after *Lent,* the Markets will be more glutted than usual; because the Number of *Popish Infants,* is, at least, three to one in this Kingdom; and therefore

[1]Rabelais.

it will have one other Collateral Advantage, by lessening the Number of *Papists* among us.

I have already computed the Charge of nursing a Beggar's Child (in which List I reckon all *Cottagers, Labourers,* and Four fifths of the *Farmers*) to be about two Shillings *per Annum,* Rags included; and I believe, no Gentleman would repine to give Ten Shillings for the *Carcase of a good fat child;* which, as I have said, will make four Dishes of excellent nutritive Meat, when he hath only some particular Friend, or his own Family, to dine with him. Thus the Squire will learn to be a good Landlord, and grow popular among his Tenants; the Mother will have Eight Shillings net Profit, and be fit for Work until she produceth another Child.

Those who are more thrifty *(as I must confess the Times require)* may flay the Carcase; the Skin of which, artificially dressed, will make admirable *Gloves for Ladies,* and *Summer Boots for fine Gentlemen.*

As to our City of *Dublin;* Shambles may be appointed for this Purpose, in the most convenient Parts of it; and Butchers we may be assured will not be wanting; although I rather recommend buying the Children alive, and dressing them hot from the Knife, as we do *roasting Pigs.*

A very worthy Person, a true Lover of his Country, and whose Virtues I highly esteem, was lately pleased, in discoursing on this Matter, to offer a Refinement upon my Scheme. He said, that many Gentlemen of this Kingdom, having of late destroyed their Deer; he conceived, that the Want of Venison might be well supplied by the Bodies of young Lads and Maidens, not exceeding fourteen Years of Age, nor under twelve; so great a Number of both Sexes in every Country being now ready to starve, for Want of Work and Service: And these to be disposed of by their Parents, if alive, or otherwise by their nearest Relations. But with due Deference to so excellent a Friend, and so deserving a Patriot, I cannot be altogether in his Sentiments. For as to the Males, my *American* Acquaintance assured me from frequent Experience, that their Flesh was generally tough and lean, like that of our School-boys, by continual Exercise, and their Taste disagreeable; and to fatten them would not answer the Charge. Then, as to the Females, it would, I think, with humble Submission, *be a Loss to the Publick,* because they soon would become Breeders themselves: And besides it is not improbable, that some scrupulous People might be apt to censure such a Practice (although indeed very unjustly) as a little bordering upon Cruelty; which, I confess, hath always been with me the strongest Objection against any Project, how well soever intended.

But in order to justify my Friend; he confessed, that this Expedient was put into his Head by the famous *Salmanaazor,* a Native of the Island *Formosa,* who came from thence to *London,* above twenty Years ago, and in Conversation told my Friend, that in his Country, when any young Person happened to be put to Death, the Executioner sold the Carcase to

Persons of Quality, as a prime Dainty; and that, in his Time, the Body of a plump Girl of fifteen, who was crucified for an Attempt to poison the Emperor, was sold to his Imperial *Majesty's prime Minister of State,* and other great *Mandarins* of the Court, *in Joints from the Gibbet,* at Four hundred Crowns. Neither indeed can I deny, that if the same Use were made of several plump young girls in this Town, how, without one single Groat to their Fortunes, cannot stir Abroad without a Chair, and appear at the *Play-house,* and *Assemblies* in foreign Fineries, which they never will pay for; the Kingdom would not be the worse.

Some Persons of a desponding Spirit are in great Concern about that vast Number of poor People, who are Aged, Diseased, or Maimed; and I have been desired to employ my Thoughts what Course may be taken, to ease the Nation of so grievous an Incumbrance. But I am not in the least Pain upon that Matter; because it is very well known, that they are every Day *dying,* and *rotting,* by *Cold* and *Famine,* and *Filth,* and *Vermin,* as fast as can be reasonably expected. And as to the younger Labourers, they are now in almost as hopeful a Condition: They cannot get Work, and consequently pine away for Want of Nourishment, to a Degree, that if at any Time they are accidentally hired to common Labour, they have not Strength to perform it; and thus the Country, and themselves, are in a fair Way of being soon delivered from the Evils to come.

I have too long digressed; and therefore shall return to my Subject. I think the Advantages by the Proposal which I have made, are obvious, and many, as well as of the highest Importance.

For, *First,* as I have already observed, it would greatly lessen the *Number of Papists,* with whom we are yearly overrun; being the principal Breeders of the Nation, as well as our most dangerous Enemies; and who stay at home on Purpose, with a Design to *deliver the Kingdom to the Pretender;* hoping to take their Advantage by the Absence *of so many good Protestants,* who have chosen rather to leave their Country, than stay at home, and pay Tithes against their Conscience, to an idolatrous *Episcopal Curate.*

Secondly, The poorer Tenants will have something valuable of their own, which, by Law, may be made liable to Distress, and help to pay their Landlord's Rent; their Corn and Cattle being already seized, and *Money a Thing unknown.*

Thirdly, Whereas the Maintenance of an Hundred Thousand Children, from two Years old, and upwards, cannot be computed at less than ten Shillings a Piece *per Annum,* the Nation's Stock will be thereby encreased Fifty Thousand Pounds *per Annum;* besides the Profit of a new Dish, introduced to the Tables of all *Gentlemen of Fortune* in the Kingdom, who have any Refinement in taste; and the Money will circulate among ourselves, the Goods being entirely of our own Growth and Manufacture.

Fourthly, The constant Breeders, besides the Gain of Eight Shillings

Sterling per Annum, by the Sale of their Children, will be rid of the Charge of maintaining them after the first Year.

Fifthly, This Food would likewise bring great *Custom to Taverns,* where the Vintners will certainly be so prudent, as to procure the best Receipts for dressing it to Perfection; and consequently, have their Houses frequented by all the *fine Gentlemen,* who justly value themselves upon their Knowledge in good Eating; and a skilful Cook, who understands how to oblige his Guests, will contrive to make it as expensive as they please.

Sixthly, This would be a great Inducement to Marriage, which all wise Nations have either encouraged by Rewards, or enforced by Laws and Penalties. It would encrease the Care and Tenderness of Mothers towards their Children, when they were sure of a Settlement for Life, to the poor Babes, provided in some Sort by the Publick, to their annual Profit instead of Expense. We should soon see an honest Emulation among the married Women, *which of them could bring the fattest Child to the Market.* Men would become as *fond* of their Wives, during the Time of their Pregnancy, as they are now of their *Mares* in Foal, their *Cows* in Calf, or *Sows* when they are ready to farrow; nor offer to beat or kick them, (as it is too *frequent* a Practice) for fear of a Miscarriage.

Many other Advantages might be enumerated. For instance, the Addition of some Thousand Carcasses in our Exportation of barrelled Beef: The Propagation of *Swines Flesh,* and Improvement in the Art of making good *Bacon;* so much wanted among us by the great Destruction of *Pigs,* too frequent at our Tables, and are no way comparable in Taste, or Magnificence, to a well-grown fat yearling Child; which, roasted whole, will make a considerable Figure at a *Lord Mayor's Feast,* or any other publick Entertainment. But this, and many others, I omit; being studious of Brevity.

Supposing that one Thousand Families in this City, would be constant Customers for Infants Flesh; besides others who might have it at *merry Meetings,* particularly *Weddings and Christenings;* I compute that *Dublin* would take off, annually, about Twenty Thousand Carcasses; and the rest of the Kingdom (where probably they will be sold somewhat cheaper) the remaining Eighty Thousand.

I can think of no one Objection, that will possibly be raised against this Proposal; unless it should be urged, that the Number of People will be thereby much lessened in the Kingdom. This I freely own; and it was indeed one principal Design in offering it to the World. I desire the Reader will observe, that I calculate my Remedy *for this one individual Kingdom of* IRELAND, *and for no other that ever was, is, or I think ever can be upon Earth.* Therefore, let no man talk to me of other Expedients: *Of taxing our Absentees at five Shillings a Pound: Of using neither Cloaths, nor Houshold Furniture except what is of our own Growth and Manufacture: Of utterly rejecting the Materials and Instruments that promote foreign Luxury: Of curing the Expensiveness of Pride, Vanity, Idleness, and Gam-*

ing in our Women: Of introducing a Vein of Parsimony, Prudence and Temperance: Of learning to love our Country, wherein we differ even from LAPLANDERS, *and the Inhabitants of* TOPINAMBOO: *Of quitting our Animosities, and Factions; nor act any longer like the* Jews, *who were murdering one another at the very Moment their City was taken: Of being a little cautious not to sell our Country and Consciences for nothing: Of teaching Landlords to have, at least, one Degree of Mercy towards their Tenants.* Lastly, *Of putting a Spirit of Honesty, Industry, and Skill into our Shop-keepers; who, if a Resolution could now be taken to buy only our native Goods, would immediately unite to cheat and exact upon us in the Price, the Measure, and the Goodness; nor could ever yet be brought to make one fair Proposal of just Dealing, though often and earnestly invited to it.*

Therefore I repeat, let no Man talk to me of these and the like Expedients; till he hath, at least, a Glimpse of Hope, that there will ever be some hearty and sincere Attempt to put *them in Practice.*

But, as to my self; having been wearied out for many Years with offering vain, idle, visionary Thoughts; and at length utterly despairing of Success, I fortunately fell upon this Proposal; which, as it is wholly new, so it hath something *solid* and *real,* of no Expence, and little Trouble, full in our own Power; and whereby we can incur no Danger in *disobliging* ENGLAND: for, this Kind of Commodity will not bear Exportation; the Flesh being of too tender a Consistence, to admit a long Continuance of Salt; *although, perhaps, I could name a Country, which would be glad to eat up our whole Nation without it.*

After all, I am not so violently bent upon my own Opinion, as to reject any Offer proposed by wise Men, which shall be found equally innocent, cheap, easy, and effectual. But before something of that Kind shall be advanced, in Contradiction to my Scheme, and offering a better; I desire the Author, or Authors, will be pleased maturely to consider two Points. *First,* As Things now stand, how they will be able to find Food and Raiment, for a Hundred Thousand useless Mouths and Backs? And *secondly,* There being a round Million of Creatures in human Figure, throughout this Kingdom; whose whole Subsistence, put into a common Stock, would leave them in Debt two Millions of Pounds *Sterling;* adding those, who are Beggars by Profession, to the Bulk of Farmers, Cottagers, and Labourers, with their Wives and Children, who are Beggars in Effect; I desire those Politicians, who dislike my Overture, and may perhaps be so bold to attempt an Answer, that they will first ask the Parents of these Mortals, Whether they would not, at this Day, think it a great Happiness to have been sold for Food at a Year old, in the Manner I prescribe; and thereby have avoided such a perpetual Scene of Misfortunes, as they have since gone through; by the *Oppression of Landlords;* the Impossibility of paying Rent, without Money or Trade; the Want of common Sustenance, with neither House nor Cloaths, to cover them from the Inclemencies of

Weather; and the most inevitable Prospect of intailing the like, or greater Miseries upon their Breed for ever.

I profess, in the Sincerity of my Heart, that I have not the least personal Interest, in endeavouring to promote this necessary Work; having no other Motive than the *publick Good of my Country, by advancing our Trade, providing for Infants, relieving the Poor, and giving some Pleasure to the Rich.* I have no Children, by which I can propose to get a single Penny; the youngest being nine Years old, and my Wife past Child-bearing.

Apartness and Community

Alexis de Tocqueville

Alexis Charles Henri Clérel de Tocqueville was born in Paris in 1805. He studied law and, as the son of an influential aristocratic family, he was given a judicial post in the court at Versailles. After the July Revolution of 1830, de Tocqueville felt increasingly uncertain of his allegiance to the new government, and he succeeded in securing a commission to go to America to study the prison system. Even closer to his heart was the opportunity to study a democratic system of government at first hand and to judge the possibilities of its application in Europe. For nine months in 1831 and 1832 de Tocqueville and his friend and fellow magistrate, Gustave de Beaumont, traveled widely in America, visiting prisons, taking notes, writing letters, interviewing prominent people, requesting memoranda on special subjects, and collecting books and documents. On their return, the two young Frenchmen soon completed their prison report; then each turned to his own study of America. De Tocqueville published his book, *De la démocratie en Amérique,* in two parts. The first, a description and critical analysis of the American government in the age of Jackson, was published in 1835. The second, a more philosophical study, with greater regard to the general applicability of American traits, came out in 1840.

De Tocqueville was elected to the French Chamber of Deputies in 1837 and briefly held the post of Minister for Foreign Affairs under Napoleon III, but his major energies were devoted to political thought rather than to politics. He published *L'Ancien régime et la revolution* three years before his death in 1859.

Democracy in America was quickly recognized as an important book and was translated into many languages. The first English translation was made by Henry Reeve, an Englishman, in 1838. This was retranslated by the American scholar Francis Bowen in 1862. The text of the chapter from Part II that we present here is taken from Phillips Bradley's excellent modern edition (with corrections) of the Bowen translation.

Of Individualism in Democratic Countries

I have shown how it is that in ages of equality every man seeks for his opinions within himself; I am now to show how it is that in the same ages all his feelings are turned towards himself alone. *Individualism* is a novel expression, to which a novel idea has given birth. Our fathers were only acquainted with *égoïsme* (selfishness). Selfishness is a passionate and exaggerated love of self, which leads a man to connect everything with himself and to prefer himself to everything in the world. Individualism is a mature and calm feeling, which disposes each member of the community to sever himself from the mass of his fellows and to draw apart with his family and his friends, so that after he has thus formed a little circle of his own, he willingly leaves society at large to itself. Selfishness originates in blind instinct; individualism proceeds from erroneous judgment more than from depraved feelings; it originates as much in deficiencies of mind as in perversity of heart.

Selfishness blights the germ of all virtue; individualism, at first, only saps the virtues of public life; but in the long run it attacks and destroys all others and is at length absorbed in downright selfishness. Selfishness is a vice as old as the world, which does not belong to one form of society more than to another; individualism is of democratic origin, and it threatens to spread in the same ratio as the equality of condition.

Among aristocratic nations, as families remain for centuries in the same condition, often on the same spot, all generations become, as it were, contemporaneous. A man almost always knows his forefathers and respects them; he thinks he already sees his remote descendants and he loves them. He willingly imposes duties on himself towards the former and the latter, and he will frequently sacrifice his personal gratifications to those who went before and to those who will come after him. Aristocratic institutions, moreover, have the effect of closely binding every man to several of his fellow citizens. As the classes of an aristocratic people are strongly marked and permanent, each of them is regarded by its own members as a sort of lesser country, more tangible and more cherished than the country at large. As in aristocratic communities all the citizens occupy fixed positions, one above another, the result is that each of them always sees a man above himself whose patronage is necessary to him, and below himself another man whose co-operation he may claim. Men living in aristocratic ages are therefore almost always closely attached to something placed out of their own sphere, and they are often disposed to forget themselves. It is true that in these ages the notion of human fellowship is faint and that men seldom think of sacrificing themselves for mankind; but they often sacrifice themselves for other men. In democratic times, on the contrary, when the duties of each individual to the race are much more clear, devoted service to any one man becomes more rare; the bond of human affection is extended, but it is relaxed.

Among democratic nations new families are constantly springing up, others are constantly falling away, and all that remain change their condition; the woof of time is every instant broken and the track of generations effaced. Those who went before are soon forgotten; of those who will come after, no one has any idea: the interest of man is confined to those in close propinquity to himself. As each class gradually approaches others and mingles with them, its members become undifferentiated and lose their class identity for each other. Aristocracy had made a chain of all the members of the community, from the peasant to the king; democracy breaks that chain and severs every link of it.

As social conditions become more equal, the number of persons increases who, although they are neither rich nor powerful enough to exercise any great influence over their fellows, have nevertheless acquired or retained sufficient education and fortune to satisfy their own wants. They owe nothing to any man, they expect nothing from any man; they acquire the habit of always considering themselves as standing alone; and they are apt to imagine that their whole destiny is in their own hands.

Thus not only does democracy make every man forget his ancestors, but it hides his descendants and separates his contemporaries from him; it throws him back forever upon himself alone and threatens in the end to confine him entirely within the solitude of his own heart.

Peter Marin

Peter Marin was born in 1936 and is a poet, educator, and writer. He is young enough to have experienced the 1960s with substantial insight into and sympathy for the plight of students at that time. After earning his B.A. in literature from Swarthmore and his M.A. from Columbia, he taught briefly at three different colleges, and in 1967–1968 he served as the director of an experimental high school in Palo Alto. Since then Marin has spent much of his time writing on subjects generated by his interest in young people and their place in modern culture. He is particularly interested both in dehumanization in American life and in our "psychic evolution," that is, in the possible changes in our individuation, our consciousness, our ability to deal with experience. He is coauthor of the book *Understanding Drug Use* (1960), coeditor of *The Limits of Schooling* (1975), and author of *In a Man's Time* (1974). "The New Narcissism," which appeared in the October 1975 issue of *Harper's,* is one of a number of magazine articles in which he examines the meaning and direction of modern American cults.

The New Narcissism

Where to begin a piece like this? Its original subject was ostensibly an Esalen⁰ conference on "spiritual tyranny." But that was for me merely a way of getting at a more general subject: the trend in therapy toward a deification of the isolated self. And that subject was in turn a part of an even more general concern: the ways in which selfishness and moral blindness now assert themselves in the larger culture as enlightenment and psychic health. A broad-based retrenchment is going on, a pervasive and perhaps unconscious shift in value—not only on a national level but in the moral definitions and judgments we make as individuals.

I think offhandedly as I write of several recent conversations I have had with friends or students, of what I have heard proclaimed from lecture platforms or seen on television and in the popular journals. I am, for instance, dining with a close friend in a New York restaurant, and as we eat our steaks and drink our brandy and smoke our fat cigars he explains to me that the world is obviously overpopulated, and that somebody must starve, and that we, as a nation, must decide who it will be, and that it might as well be those who already suffer from protein deficiency, for they are already "useless." Or I finish a lecture to the members of the American Association for Humanistic Psychology, and a therapist rushes up to me afterward and asks me whether or not I believe in the "ethics of the lifeboat,"⁰ and when I tell her that I don't know why we are in the lifeboat while others are drowning, she whispers knowingly to me: "We have a higher consciousness." Or I am invited to meet with a well-meaning California legislator who is beginning a political movement based on the therapeutic values of "authenticity" and "warmth," and he draws for me on a napkin the button he has designed: the single letter *I* on a blank white background. Or I attend a dinner sponsored by the Population Institute at the Century Plaza in Los Angeles, where Paul Ehrlich addresses a thousand well-heeled people about the "coming end of affluence," and when I leaf through a copy of his book given away for free I see that he recommends filling the cellar with food and buying a gun and relying on neither friends nor neighbors but only on oneself. Or, finally, I listen for two hours in a graduate seminar to two women therapists explaining to me how we are all entirely responsible for our destinies, and how the Jews must have wanted to be burned by the Germans and that those who starve in the Sahel must want it to happen, and when I ask them whether there is anything we owe to others, say, to a child starving in the desert, one of them snaps at me angrily: "What can I do if a child is determined to starve?"

Esalen   Center for a range of human growth programs, located near Big Sur in California.
"ethics of the lifeboat"   See Garrett Hardin's essay, p. 290.

That, precisely, is what I am talking about here: the growing solipsism and desperation of a beleaguered class, the world view emerging among us centered solely on the self and with individual survival as its sole good. It is a world view present not only in everything we say and do, but as an ambience, a feeling in the air, a general cast of perception and attitude: a retreat from the worlds of morality and history, an unembarrassed denial of human reciprocity and community.

A few months ago, I went to dinner at the house of a woman who had just been through a weekend of *est* (Erhard Seminar Training), the latest and most popular new therapeutic enthusiasm. The training is designed to provide its participants with a new sense of fulfillment and competence, and it seemed to have worked with my hostess, for she assured me that her life had radically changed, that she felt different about herself, that she was happier and more efficient, and that she kept her house much cleaner than before.

Nothing in that is very startling or distressing, but in the course of the evening she also added that because of the training she now understood: (1) that the individual will is all-powerful and totally determines one's fate; (2) that she felt neither guilt nor shame about anyone's fate and that those who were poor and hungry must have wished it on themselves; (3) that the North Vietnamese must have wanted to be bombed, or else it could not have happened to them; (4) that a friend of hers who had been raped and murdered in San Francisco was to be pitied for having willed it to occur; (5) that in her weekend at *est* she had attained full enlightenment; (6) that she was God; (7) that whatever one thought to be true was true beyond all argument; (8) that I was also God, and that my ideas were also true, but not as true as hers because I had not had the training; and (9) that my use of logic to criticize her beliefs was unfair, because reason was "irrational," though she could not tell me why.

There is no telling whether or not this is precisely what she learned at *est*, and no doubt other adherents would deny it, but I have talked by now to at least a dozen of its enthusiasts, and each one of them has blankly recited to me, word for word, the same ill-taught and ignorant catechism. No doubt they were happier for the teaching; invariably they expressed complete satisfaction with their newfound philosophy. Like my hostess, they had learned it all in a kind of manufactured daze at a weekend which cost them $250, in the company of hundreds of others. By now more than 50,000 people have "taken" the training, which was developed by Werner Erhard himself, who was once known simply as Jack Rosenberg,[1] and who was a trainer for a short time with Mind Dynamics, a franchise operation

[1]Space does not permit a discussion of the implications of that one act: the conscious shift from a Jewish to a Germanic name while still in the shadow of the deaths of several million Jews.

that trained businessmen in human managerial techniques. *Est* itself is a step past all that. It is a mixture of ideas and techniques borrowed from the behavioral sciences, Eastern philosophy, the traditional American classroom, Marine boot camp, and modern brainwashing methods. Participants at the weekend workshops are bombarded from the lectern with simplistic truths while being simultaneously bullied and soothed by an army of attendants. They are prevented from leaving their seats to stretch or eat or go to the bathroom, and if—as sometimes happens—they throw up in their places or urinate on themselves, well, that is all part of the training.[2]

It is not hard to understand how it all works, and one need only read the first few pages of Freud's *Group Psychology and the Analysis of the Ego* to see what intelligent use Erhard makes of individual confusion. He has managed to compress into one activity half a dozen techniques for creating power over others: the underlying anxiety of the audience and its need for simple order; the strangeness and power of the extraordinary situation; the gradual befuddlement of the senses; the combined effects of repetition and fatigue; the credulity of others near you; the manufactured impotence of the audience; the masochistic relief that results from placing oneself in the hands of a man to whom one has granted omnipotence.

Clearly Erhard has a genius—not only for the efficiency with which his program is organized and sold, but also for the accuracy with which he tells his audience what it wants to hear. It is the latter which binds them to him. The world is perfect, each of us is all-powerful, shame and guilt are merely arbitrary notions, truth is identical to belief, suffering is merely the result of imperfect consciousness—how like manna all of this must seem to hungry souls. For if we are each totally responsible for our fate, then all the others in the world are responsible for *their* fate, and, if that is so, why should we worry about them?

It is all so simple and straightforward. It has the terrifying simplicity of the lobotomized mind: all complexity gone, and in its place the warm wind of forced simplicity blowing away the tag ends of conscience and shame. It offers the kind of Orwellian enlightenment an age like ours is bound to produce, but I do not spell it out in detail or mock its enthusiasts for that reason alone, or even because it marks the dead end of human desire or generosity. *Est* is, after all, only a bit worse than our other popular enthusiasms, and it is interesting in part because it makes clear so much of what is hidden in them. It is in many ways the logical extension of the whole human potential movement of the past decade. The refusal to consider moral complexities, the denial of history and a larger community,

[2]I should make one thing clear. I have never been to an *est* weekend, mainly because I have never been able to subject myself to the kind of treatment *est* visits upon its participants, or to listen to the kind of nonsense it offers them.

the disappearance of the Other, the exaggerations of the will, the reduction of all experience to a set of platitudes—all of that is to be found in embryonic form in almost all modern therapy.

Yet compared to *est* the older therapies (such as Gestalt therapy or Abraham Maslow's self-actualization or Rogerian encounter groups) had a kind of innocence to them. They were, at their worst, merely boring or silly. The people drawn to them were obviously moved by a simple yearning for what was missing from their lives, and if that yearning took sometimes puerile forms or excluded moral concerns or genuine passion, that seemed excusable—like the play of children. But our newer therapies take upon themselves a new burden. Whereas the older therapies merely ignored moral and historical concerns, the new ones destroy or replace them. They become not only a way of protecting or changing the self, but of assessing the needs of others and one's responsibilities to them—a way of defining history and determining morality.

Why that happens is not difficult to understand. It reveals the impulse behind much of what we do these days: the desire to defend ourselves against the demands of conscience and the world through an ethic designed to defuse them both. Most of us realize at one level of consciousness or another that we inhabit an age of catastrophe—if not for ourselves then for countless others. Try as we do, we cannot ignore the routine inequities of consumption and distribution which benefit us and condemn others to misery. Each of us must feel a kind of generalized shame, an unanswerable sense of guilt. So we struggle mightily to convince ourselves that our privilege is earned or deserved, rather than (as we must often feel unconsciously) a form of murder or theft. Our therapies become a way of hiding from the world, a way of easing our troubled conscience. What lies behind the form they now take is neither simple greed nor moral blindness; it is, instead, the unrealized shame of having failed the world and not knowing what to do about it. Like humiliated lovers who have betrayed what they love, we turn our faces from the world, if only (in Paul Goodman's phrase) "just to live on a while."

That is what makes our new therapies so distressing. They provide their adherents with a way to avoid the demands of the world, to smother the tug of conscience. They allow them to remain who and what they are, to accept the structured world as it is—but with a new sense of justice and justification, with the assurance that it all accords with cosmic law. We are in our proper place; the others are in theirs; we may indeed bemoan their fate or even, if we are so moved, do something to change it, but in essence it has nothing to do with us.

What disappears in this view of things is the ground of community, the felt sense of collective responsibility for the fate of each separate other. What takes its place is a moral vacuum in which others are trapped forever in a "private" destiny, doomed to whatever befalls them. In that void the traditional measures of justice or good vanish completely. The self replaces community, relation, neighbor, chance, or God. Looming larger every moment, it obliterates everything around it that might have offered it a way out of its pain.

The end result of this retreat from the complexities of the world is a kind of soft fascism: the denial, in the name of higher truth, of the claims of others upon the self. Our deification of the self becomes equal in effect and human cost to what Nietzsche long ago called the "idolatry of the state." Just as persons once set aside the possibilities of their own humanity and turned instead to the state for a sense of power and identity no longer theirs, so we now turn to the self, giving to it the power and importance of a god. In the worship of the state, life gives way to an abstraction, to the total submission of individual will. In the worship of the self, life also gives way to an abstraction, in this case to an exaggeration of the will. The result in both cases is the same. What is lost is the immense middle ground of human community. The web of reciprocity and relation is broken. The world diminishes. The felt presence of the other disappears, and with it a part of our own existence.

The real horror of our present condition is not merely the absence of community or the isolation of the self—those, after all, have been part of the American condition for a long time. It is the loss of the ability to remember what is missing, the diminishment of our vision of what is humanly possible or desirable. In our new myths we begin to deny once and for all the existence of what we once believed both possible and good. We proclaim our grief-stricken narcissism to be a form of liberation; we define as enlightenment our broken faith with the world. Already forgetful of what it means to be fully human, we sip still again from Lethe, the river of forgetfulness, hoping to erase even the memory of pain. Lethe, lethal, lethargy—all of those words suggest a kind of death, one that in religious usage is sometimes called accidie. It is a condition one can find in many places and in many ages, but only in America, and only recently, have we begun to confuse it with a state of grace.

It is in this context that the Esalen conference on Spiritual Tyranny becomes significant. It was called two years ago in San Francisco by the Esalen staff as a response to the movement they had helped to start. What apparently bothered them about the movement was connected to what I have mentioned here: the proliferation of sects and cults, and an attendant willingness on the part of many persons to abandon individual responsibility in favor of submission to narrow and shallow creeds or therapeutic "masters." The speakers invited were men whose names are familiar to those who read Esalen's catalogues: Claudio Naranjo, Werner Erhard, George Leonard, Sam Keen, Jerry Rubin—all of them leaders of therapeutic schools or theorists of what George Leonard has rosily called "the coming transformation of humanity." As for the several hundred members of the audience, some had come to cheer their favorite gurus on and others merely to be present at what had taken on, in therapeutic circles, the nature of a celebratory *event*—the equivalent of an all-star rock concert. But there were other reasons for coming, too. Many people in the audience seemed to be looking for a direction to their lives, and they had come to the conference for the same reason that they had attended workshops in the past: to find help. The human potential movement had still not done for them what it had promised; their lives had remained the same or perhaps had worsened, and the new world, the promised transformation, seemed very slow in coming.

So they came in a peculiar mood, one that combined equal parts of celebration, yearning, and anger. But their mood was further complicated by the conference's taking place at the beginning of the Arab oil boycott. The audience had recently been made aware of the possibility of a world unlike the familiar one in which they felt privileged and safe. To many of them the future must have seemed frightening, and, standing on the stage and looking out at them, one could feel in the air and see on their faces the early signs of a collective paranoia, as if they were haunted by visions of the world's possible vengeance. Packed into the huge hall, its walls lined with gigantic posters of therapeutic heroes—Fritz Perls, Wilhelm Reich, Abraham Maslow, and others—the crowd was restless, impatient, volatile; one could feel rising from it a palpable sense of hunger, as if these people had somehow been failed by both the world and their therapies. It made one apprehensive—not for any specific reason, but simply because beneath the ruffled but still reasonable surface of the crowd lay a hysteria that would in other settings take on any one of several forms, none of them particularly pretty. They wanted someone to set matters right again, to tell them what to do, and it did not matter how that was done, or who did it, or what it required them to believe.

Most of the people in the audience were followers or clients of the various speakers, and as each one spoke his adherents responded with cheers and applause. Others, at odds with the speaker, answered with catcalls, whistles, or groans. I remember in particular the words "total obedience" and "submission to a perfect master" and "the adolescence of rebellion"—phrases which were used by several speakers and which drew from the crowd a surprising amount of acclaim. But even the speakers who took a stand against submission or obedience seemed somehow to diminish the world of experience and choice. In their words, too, there was a tyrannical refusal to acknowledge the existence of a world larger than the self, the total denial—by implication—of the necessity of human community or relation.

That missing element defined the conference and determined its nature: a massive repression all the more poignant because so much of the audience's feeling was engendered by the world denied. Their relation to that world—what it was, what it ought to be—lay at the heart of their discontent, but it was never spoken of. Even when they began to question the speakers, the questions they asked were invariably concerned with themselves, were about self-denial or self-esteem, all centered on the ego, all turned inward. Behind that, of course, they were asking about something else, about problems for which they had no words, about the proper human relation to an age of catastrophe. But neither they nor the speakers were capable of recognizing that fact, and so those problems remained unarticulated, and they hung in the room like shadows and ghosts, determining the tone of the event but never permitted to enter it.

As I listened, I kept thinking about a conversation I had recently had with a man much taken with mysticism and spirituality. He was telling me about his sense of another reality.

"I know there is something outside of me," he said. "I can feel it. I know it is there. But what is it?"

"It may not be a mystery," I said. "Perhaps it is the world."

That startled him. He had meant something more magical than that, more exotic and grand, something "above" rather than all around him. It had never occurred to him that what might be calling to him from beyond the self were the worlds of community and value, the worlds of history and action—all of them waiting to be entered not as a saint or a mystic, but in a way more difficult still: as a moral man or woman among other persons, with a person's real and complex nature and needs. Those worlds had been closed to him, had receded from consciousness as he had ceased to inhabit them fully or responsibly or lovingly, and so he felt their ghostly presence as something distant and mysterious, as a dream in which he had no actual existence.

I saw that at work the first night of the conference and I saw it again, in greater detail, the next day at the various workshops. I remember one in particular: a seminar on astral travel held in one of the local churches. In the huge reaches of the church the few dozen participants seemed dwarfed and lost as they gathered around the altar and the first few pews. Their voices echoed in the empty space as they rose one by one to testify as to how they had left their bodies while asleep, or how their friends had, or how they had heard about someone who had. The tone was one of strained yearning, a combined will to believe and be believed, as if by sheer force of conviction they could bring into being a new world to replace the old one. They spoke about "space cadets" and "soul traps" and the ethics of psychic power, and after a while they shifted ground and spoke about the possibilities of using such power to get things changed in Washington.

"We'll get to the President while he's asleep," said someone. "We'll infiltrate his dreams."

"But that isn't right," said someone else.

"That's tyranny, too. We can't intervene without his consent."

"It doesn't matter," said a third. "It won't work anyway. I've a friend who knows someone who tried it. He left his body and went to the White

House. But he couldn't get in. The President has astral bodyguards. They know what's what in Washington."

So it went, a series of exchanges making of the world of possibility a comic-strip cosmology. It was both absurd and sad: the exchanges and the pain implicit in them conveyed the participants' anguish at their own powerlessness. I thought automatically of the mysticism rampant in Germany in the Thirties, or of the passion for shamans and mystics in prerevolutionary Petrograd, or of the Christian zealots in declining Rome. The seminar seemed to mix aspects of all three, and the church was a fitting place for it, for the participants were like lost pilgrims trying to create, in its shadow, a new faith to replace the one they had lost. The last remaining shreds of reason and hope mingled with emergent superstition and fantasy, and the end result was neither moral action nor a complex vision of the world, but a child's garden of absurdities, an impotent dream of power. Confronted by a world in which casual goodness was no longer sufficient as a response, the participants were groping for a way to restore to themselves a power and significance they could no longer feel. In this particular instance the salvationary course they took involved astral travel and psychic power, but it might just as easily have been *est* or scientology or submission to Guru Maharaj Ji or even a doctrinaire adherence to Reich's orgasm theory. As different as all those enthusiasms are, they have a common ground; behind them all is a sense of exhaustion, the bourgeois will to power mixed with impotence, and the ache of no longer feeling at home in the world.

Perhaps the best example of all this is the immense popularity of Castaneda's works about don Juan. What they offer the yearning reader is precisely what I am talking about here: the dream of an individual potency to be derived magically from another world. In essence it is an updated version of the Protestant dream of the salvation of the soul, and the important thing about the power celebrated within them is that it occurs neither in the actual polis nor in the company of significant others. It is found, instead, in a moral and human desert, a fictitious landscape emptied of comrade or lover or child, of every genuine human relation (save that of master and disciple) in which joy or courage might actually be found.

Castaneda's myth of don Juan is not an alternative to our condition, but a metaphor for it. It is simply the familiar myth of the solitary gunslinger translated into spiritual language, the comic-strip story of Superman or Captain Marvel made into a slightly more sophisticated legend for adults. It legitimizes our loneliness and solaces us with the myth that we can, in our isolation, find a power to make ourselves safe.

Contrast, for a moment, Castaneda's barren mysteries with the work of Lévi-Strauss, for whom the world of magic and myth is always a *human* world, a realm explored and inhabited by others like ourselves. For Lévi-Strauss the crucial human moment is not the moment of separate awareness; it is the moment of human meeting, in which the other's existence creates for us a sense of the depth and complexity of the world. That, precisely, is what is missing from Castaneda's world. We forget, reading it, that almost without exception the visionary experiences of Indian cultures are a collective work, prepared and defined and sustained by the community, by a world view which is, in effect, the product of cooperative labor. Visionary experience leads not only to the gods and into the self, but it also binds one to the world of myth and—through symbology and tradition—to the historical and social worlds. The individual seeker, though sometimes solitary, is never alone on the quest; the journey occurs within a landscape maintained inwardly by generations of men and women, and the experience is a wedding to them all. Come back from their vision quests, the American Indians recited their newly made poems or sang their songs to the tribe, feeding back to it the shared truths of a solitude that was *not* separate, but shared.

Look, for instance, at the words of Black Elk, the visionary Indian leader, close to death and addressing the gods: "Hear me, not for myself but for my people. Hear me in my sorrow, for I may never live again. Oh, make my people live."

Make my people live! The tale in this instance is not of power but of love —not only for the gods or the self but for the world of others, those whose presence creates for the self a body as truly one's own as the flesh. That love, that sense of lived relation, is at the heart not only of tribal lore, but at the center of the legends of most cultures. One thinks of Odysseus surrounded by comrades seeking to return to his home, or of Gilgamesh driven to seek the secret of immortality by the death of Enkidu, his friend. Both of them are moved by what lies behind all myth and long-lived culture: the felt sense of relation and reciprocity. Indeed, that reciprocity is identical to culture: a collective creation and habitation of value sustains what we carelessly call the "individual" self. But that, in our dream of power, is what we no longer remember. It disappears from our myths, it vanishes from our therapies, and we come to the worlds of mystery much as we came long ago to the new world: with greed and fear rather than awe and love. In the name of power we strip it of everything real, and it becomes nothing more than a reflection of our need.

What is lost in that whole process is a crucial part of our own human nature, our unacknowledged hunger for relation, what might be called "an appetence for Good": the needful reaching out for a life in a larger world. We are moved toward that world by the inner force Freud sometimes called Eros: the desire for relation is as much at work in our need for community and moral significance as it is in our need for coupled love.

Writing about the Athenian polis, Hannah Arendt said about the Greeks:

> The principal characteristic of the tyrant was that he deprived the citizen of access to the public realm, where he could show himself, see and be seen, hear

and be heard, that he prohibited the agoreuein and politeuein, confined the citizens to the privacy of their households. . . . According to the Greeks, to be banished to the privacy of household life was tantamount to being deprived of the specifically human potentialities of life.

The same thing is true for us. To put it simply, it is as if each of us had at the same time a smaller and larger self, as if we inhabited at the same moment a smaller and larger world. The smaller world is the one familiar to us, the world of the individual ego and "interpersonal" relations, a reality acknowledged by our habits of thought and by our institutions and therapies. But we also inhabit a larger and unrealized world, one in which every gesture becomes significant precisely because it is understood to bind us to the lives of invisible others.

The natural direction of human ripening is from the smaller to the larger world, is toward the realization and habitation of ever-widening realms of meaning and value. Just as the young are moved from the inside out through increasingly complex stages of perception and thought demanding corresponding changes in their environment, so, too, adults are moved from inside themselves through increasingly complex stages of relation: past the limits of ego and into a human community in which the self becomes other than it was. Seen in this way, human fulfillment hinges on much more than our usual notions of private pleasure or self-actualization, for both of those in their richest forms are impossible without communion and community, an acknowledgement of liability, and a significant role in both the polis and the moral world. To be deprived of those is to be deprived of a part of the self, and to turn away from them is to betray not only the world but also the self, for it is only in the realms in which others exist that one can come to understand the ways in which the nature of each individual existence is in many ways a collective act, the result of countless other lives.

The traditional image for what I am talking about has always been the harvest: the cooperative act in which comrades in a common field gather from it what they need. One finds the image repeated in the work of Camus, Giono, Kropotkin, Lawrence, Silone, and many others, but the most vivid example I know is the scene in *Anna Karenina* in which Levin labors in a field with the peasants, losing all sense of himself in the shared rhythms of the work, the deep blowing grain, and the heat of the sun on his body. It is an image of ecstatic relation which is as much an expression of Eros as is the emblem of two lovers tangled in embrace, and it can stand for almost every aspect of our lives. Every privilege, every object, every "good" comes to us as the result of a human harvest, the shared labor of others: the language we use and the beliefs we hold and the ways we experience ourselves. Each of these involves a world of others into which we are entered every moment of our lives. Idly, for instance, we take coffee and sugar in the mornings, and even that simple act immerses us immediately in the larger world. Both the sugar and coffee have come from specific places, have been harvested by specific persons, most probably in a country where the land belongs by right to others than those who hold it, where the wages paid those who work it are exploitive and low. No doubt, too, the political system underlying the distribution of land is maintained in large part by the policies enacted and the armies acting in our name—and the reason we enjoy the coffee while others harvest it has nothing to do with individual will and everything to do with economics and history.

That, I believe, is what each of us already knows—no matter how much we pretend we do not. Our lives are crowded with the presence of unacknowledged others upon whom our well-being and privilege depend. The shadows of those neglected others—dying in Asia, hungry in Africa, impoverished in our own country—fall upon every one of our private acts, darken the household and marriage bed for each of us. We try to turn away, but even the desperate nature of our turning is a function of their unacknowledged presence, and they are with us even in the vehemence with which we pretend they are not. Something in each of us—even among the enthusiasts of *est*—aches with their presence, aches for the world, for why else would we be in so much pain?

The question of the age, we like to think, is one of survival, and that is true, but not in the way we ordinarily mean it. The survival we ordinarily mean is a narrow and nervous one: simply the continuation, in their present forms, of the isolated lives we lead. But there is little doubt that most of us *will* survive as we are, for we are clearly prepared to accept whatever is necessary to do so: the deaths of millions of others, wars waged in our name, a police state at home. Like the Germans who accepted the Fascists, or the French citizens who collaborated with the Germans, we, too, will be able to carry on "business as usual," just as we do now. Our actual crisis of survival lies elsewhere, in the moral realm we so carefully ignore, for it is there that our lives are at stake.

Seen in that light, what might one expect from a therapy a grown man or woman might take seriously? First, a simple willingness to accept the existence of an objective reality equal in significance to the self, a reality which literally (as my friend John Seeley likes to put it) *objects* as we try to act upon it. Second, a recognition that much of our present pain is the world's pain, the result of living in a catastrophic age in which we do violence to the best parts of our nature. Third, a consciousness of the natural force within us which demands a moral, political, and historical life in the larger world. Fourth, a humility in the presence of that larger world, a respect for the human meaning gathered there by others struggling both in the present and in the past. Finally, a recognition that the future depends directly upon the ways we act individually and in community; that it will never be more just, humane, generous, or sustaining than we ourselves are willing to be; and that the therapist and client, in the solitude of their encounter, create together—in how much of the world they admit to their discourse—a part of the social reality others will later inhabit.

Physicists sometimes use a lovely word, *elsewhere,* to describe the realms of being which we can postulate in thought but can never enter or demonstrate to exist. It is as if they existed side by side with the known world but were beyond all human habitation or touch. In a sense, *elsewhere* also exists in the moral realm, for whatever we fail to love or inhabit fully fades into it, is like a ghostly presence around us, a reality we vaguely remember or intuit, but which is no longer ours. Thus, in a very real way the nature of the shared human world does depend on our actions and words, and we can destroy it not only with bombs, but through our failure to inhabit it as fully and as humanly as we should. That, in part, is what Freud had in mind, decades ago, when at the very end of *Civilization and Its Discontents* he called for a resurgence of "eternal Eros" in its timeless battle with Death. Now, half a century later, Eros is not yet among us. Whether it ever will be is still an open question. But if the answer to that question is to be found anywhere, it will not be in our popular therapies or creeds like *est* or Castaneda's myths. There, where self is all, Eros can have no life.

Philip E. Slater

Philip E. Slater, a sociologist who has attracted a wide general audience, received his Ph.D. from Harvard in 1955 and has been a professor at Brandeis since 1961. His celebrated book *The Glory of Hera* (1968) offered a radically new interpretation of ancient Greek mythology by bringing modern sociological and psychoanalytic conceptions to bear on Greek familial and sexual life. Among his other books are *Earthwalk* (1974); *The Wayward Gate: Science and the Supernatural* (1977); *Footholds: Understanding the Shifting Sexual and Family Tensions in Our Culture* (1977); and *Wealth Addiction* (1980).

The following selection is a self-contained excerpt from the first chapter of *The Pursuit of Loneliness: American Culture at the Breaking Point* (1976). In this chapter Slater argues that every culture limits and warps the natural emotional character of its members in special ways, and that one of the "desires that are deeply and uniquely frustrated by American culture" is "the desire for community." In our character, he says, community is subordinated to individual drives. But he also points out that repressed cultural traits have a way of finding channels of expression and that "the opposing forces are much more equally balanced than the society's participants like to recognize."

Community and Competition: Getting Together

We are so used to living in an individualistic society that we need to be reminded that collectivism has been the more usual lot of humans. Most people in most societies have lived and died in stable communities that took for granted the subordination of the individual to the welfare of the group. The aggrandizement of the individual at the expense of his neighbors was simply a crime.

This is not to say that competition is an American invention—all societies involve some mixture of cooperative and competitive institutions. But our society lies near the competitive extreme, and although it contains cooperative institutions, we suffer from their weakness and peripherality. Studies of business executives reveal a deep hunger for an atmosphere of trust and fraternity with their colleagues. The competitive life is a lonely one and its satisfactions short-lived, for each race leads only to a new one.

In the past our society had many cases in which one could take refuge from the frenzied invidiousness of our economic system—institutions such as the extended family and the stable local neighborhood in which people could take pleasure from something other than winning symbolic victories over their neighbors. But these have disappeared one by one, leaving us more and more in a situation in which we must try to satisfy our vanity and our needs for intimacy in the same place and at the same time. This has made the appeal of cooperative living more seductive, and the need to suppress our longing for it more acute.

The main vehicle for the expression of this longing has been the mass media. Popular songs and film comedies for fifty years have been engaged in a sentimental rejection of our dominant mores, maintaining that the best things in life are free, that love is more important than success, that keeping up with the Joneses is futile, that personal integrity should take precedence over winning, and so on. But these protestations must be understood for what they are: a safety valve. The same man who chuckles and sentimentalizes over a happy-go-lucky hero in a film would view his real-life counterpart as frivolous and irresponsible, and suburbanites who philosophized over the back fence with complete sincerity about their "dog-eat-dog-world," and what-is-it-all-for, and you-can't-take-it-with-you, and success-doesn't-make-you-happy-it-just-gives-you-ulcers-and-a-heart-condition, were enraged in the sixties when their children began to pay serious attention to these ideas. To the young this seemed hypocritical, but if adults didn't feel these things they wouldn't have had to fight them so vigorously. The exaggerated hostility that young people aroused in the "flower child"°

flower child Like *hippie,* a term coined by the media in the 1960s to refer to nonconformist young people.

era argues that the life they led was highly seductive to middle-aged Americans.

When a value is strongly held, as individualism is in America, the illnesses it produces tend to be treated in the same way an alcoholic treats a hangover or a drug addict his withdrawal symptoms. Technological change, mobility, and individualistic ways of thinking all rupture the bonds that tie a man to a family, a community, a kinship network, a geographical location—bonds that give him a comfortable sense of himself. As this sense of himself erodes, he seeks ways of affirming it. Yet his efforts accelerate the very erosion he seeks to halt.

This loss of a sense of oneself, a sense of one's place in the scheme of things, produces a jungle of competing egos, each trying to *create* a place. Huge corporations are fueled on this energy—the stockholders trying to buy place with wealth, executives trying to grasp it through power and prestige, public relations departments and advertisers trying to persuade people that the corporation can confer a sense of place to those who believe in it or buy its products.

Americans love bigness, mostly because they feel so small. They feel small because they're unconnected, without a place. They try to overcome that smallness by associating themselves with bigness—big projects, big organizations, big government, mass markets, mass media, "nationwide," "worldwide." But it's that very same bigness that rips away their sense of connectedness and place and makes them feel small. A vicious circle.

Notice the names of corporations: "Universal," "Continental," "International," "General," "National," "Trans-World"—the spirit of grandiosity and ego-inflation pervades our economic life. Corporations exist not to feed or supply the people, but to appease their own hungry egos. Advertising pays scant attention to price or quality and leans heavily on our needs for acceptance and respect. The economic structure of our society continually frustrates those needs, creating an artificial scarcity that in turn motivates the entire economy. This is why the quality of life in America is so unsatisfying. Since our economy is built on inflated vanity, rather than being grounded in the real material needs of the people, it must eventually collapse, when these illusions can no longer be maintained.

Much of the unpleasantness, abrasiveness, and costliness of American life comes from the fact that we're always dealing with strangers. This is what bureaucracy is: a mechanism for carrying on transactions between strangers. Who would need all those offices, all that paperwork, all those lawyers, contracts, rules and regulations, if all economic transactions took place between lifelong neighbors? A huge and tedious machinery has evolved to cope with the fact that we prefer to carry on our activities among strangers. The preference is justified, as are most of the sicknesses in American society, by the alleged economic benefits of bigness, but like many economic arguments, it's a con.

On the surface, it seems convincing. Any big company can undersell a little one. Corporations keep getting bigger and bigger and fewer and fewer. Doesn't that prove it? Survival of the fittest? Yet for some reason, what should be providing economic benefits to the consumer has in fact produced nothing but chronic inflation. If bigness lowers the cost of production, why does everything cost more and break sooner? Management, of course, blames it on labor, and each industry cites the rising prices of its own suppliers. Isn't it obvious that a few big nationwide companies can produce things cheaper than many local ones?

It all depends on what you leave out of your analysis (which is why a chimp pressing buttons randomly could predict as well as our economic forecasters). The fewer the companies, the less influence supply and demand have on prices. A heavy investment in advertising and public relations is necessary to keep a national reputation alive. And what about the transportation costs involved when all firms are national? Not to mention the air pollution costs, which are also passed on to the consumer. Chronic inflation suggests that someone is leaving something vital out of his analysis. How does one measure in dollars the cost of economic mistrust? It may be subtle, but it's clearly enormous.

The Great Illusion

It's easy to produce examples of the many ways in which Americans try to minimize, circumvent, or deny the interdependence upon which all human societies are based. We seek a private house, a private means of transportation, a private garden, a private laundry, self-service stores, and do-it-yourself skills of every kind. An enormous technology seems to have set itself the task of making it unnecessary for one human being ever to ask anything of another in the course of going about his or her daily business. Even within the family Americans are unique in their feeling that each member should have a separate room, and even a separate telephone, television, and car, when economically possible. We seek more and more privacy, and feel more and more alienated and lonely when we get it. And what accidental contacts we do have seem more intrusive, not only because they're unsought, but because they're not connected with any familiar pattern of interdependence.

Most important, our encounters with others tend increasingly to be competitive as we search for more privacy. We less and less often meet our fellow humans to share and exchange, and more and more often encounter them as an impediment or a nuisance: making the highway crowded when we're rushing somewhere, cluttering and littering the beach or park or wood, pushing in front of us at the supermarket, taking the last parking place, polluting our air and water, building a highway through our house, blocking our view, and so on. Because we've cut off so much communication with each other we keep bumping into each other, so that a higher and higher percentage of our interpersonal contacts are abrasive.

We seem unable to foresee that the gratification of a wish might turn out to be a monkey's paw⁰ if the wish were shared by many others. We cheer the new road that shaves ten minutes off the drive to our country retreat but ultimately transforms it into a crowded resort and increases both the traffic and the time. We're continually surprised to find, when we want something, that thousands or millions of others want it, too—that other human beings get hot in summer and cold in winter. The worst traffic jams occur when a mass of vacationing tourists start home early to "beat the traffic." We're too enamored of the individualistic fantasy that everyone is, or should be, different—that a man could somehow build his entire life around a single eccentricity without boring himself and everyone else to death. We all have our quirks, which provide surface variety, but aside from this, human beings have little basis for their persistent claim that they are not all members of the same species.

The Freedom Fix

Since our contacts with others are increasingly competitive, unanticipated, and abrasive, we seek still more apartness and thus accelerate the trend. The desire to be somehow special sparks an even more competitive quest for progressively more rare and expensive symbols—a quest that is ultimately futile since it is individualism itself that produces uniformity.

This is poorly understood by Americans, who tend to confuse uniformity with "conformity," in the sense of compliance with group demands. Many societies exert far more pressure on the individual to mold herself to play a sharply defined role in a total group pattern, but there is variation among these circumscribed roles. Our society gives more leeway to the individual to pursue her own ends, but since the culture defines what is worthy and desirable, everyone tends, independently but monotonously, to pursue the same things in the same way. Thus cooperation tends to produce variety, while competition generates uniformity.

The problem with individualism is not that it is immoral but that it is incorrect. The universe does not consist of a lot of unrelated particles but is an interconnected whole. Pretending that our fortunes are independent of each other may be perfectly ethical, but it's also perfectly stupid. Individualistic thinking is unflagging in the production of false dichotomies, such as "conformity *vs.* independence," "altruism *vs.* egoism," "inner-directed *vs.* other-directed," and so on, all of which are built upon the absurd assumption that the individual can be considered separately from the environment of which he or she is a part.

A favorite delusion of individualism—one that it attempts, through edu-

monkey's paw   From a horror story, "The Monkey's Paw" (1902), by W. W. Jacobs. The monkey's paw has the power to grant wishes, but a curse on it causes those wishes to be granted in such a way as to bring misery to the person who is granted the wish.

cation and propaganda, to make real—is that only egoistic responses are spontaneous. But this is not so: collective responses—helping behavior, nurturance, supportiveness, the assumption of specialized roles in group tasks, rituals, or games—these are natural, not trained, even among animals. People are more *self-consciously* oriented toward others in competitive, individualistic societies—their behavior is calculated. They accommodate to others because they want to look good, impress people, protect themselves from shame and guilt, and avoid confronting people directly. In more organic and cooperative communities people respond spontaneously to impulses that are neither selfish nor unselfish, but more directly from the heart. Sometimes they look generous, sometimes grasping, but what's important is that the behavior is *to* others, not an effort to produce some sort of *effect* on others. Cooperative societies are unassuming—it's the competitive ones that are concerned with appearances.

Individualism in the United States is exemplified by the flight to the suburb and the do-it-yourself movement. Both attempt to deny human interdependence and pursue unrealistic fantasies of self-sufficiency. The first tries to overlook our dependence upon the city for the maintenance of the level of culture we demand. "Civilized" means, literally, "citified," and the state of the city is an accurate index of the condition of the culture as a whole. We behave toward our cities like an irascible farmer who never feeds his cow and then kicks her when she fails to give enough milk. But the flight to the suburb was in any case self-defeating, its goals subverted by the mass quality of the exodus. The suburban dweller sought peace, privacy, nature, community, good schools, and a healthy child-rearing environment. Instead, he found neither the beauty and serenity of the countryside, nor the stimulation of the city, nor the stability and sense of community of the small town. A small town, after all, is a microcosm, while the suburb is merely a layer, narrowly segregated by age and social class. A minor irony of the suburban dream is that, for many Americans, reaching the pinnacle of their social ambitions (owning a house in the suburbs) forces them to perform all kinds of menial tasks (carrying garbage cans, mowing lawns, shoveling snow, and so on) that were performed for them when they occupied a less exalted status.

Some of this manual labor, however, is voluntary—an attempt to deny the division of labor required in a complex society. Many Americans seem quite willing to pay the price rather than engage in encounters with workers. This do-it-yourself trend has accompanied increasing specialization in occupations. As one's job narrows, perhaps, he or she seeks the challenge of new skill-acquisition in the home. But specialization also means that one's encounters with artisans in the home proliferate and become more impersonal. It's no longer a matter of a few well-known people—smiths and grocers—who perform many functions, and with whom contact may be a source of satisfaction. One finds instead a multiplicity of narrow specialists, each perhaps a stranger—the same type of repair may even be performed by a different person each time. Every relationship, such as it is, must start from scratch, and it's small wonder the householder turns away from such an unrewarding prospect in apathy and despair.

Americans thus find themselves in a vicious circle in which their community relationships are increasingly competitive, trivial, and irksome, in part as a result of their efforts to avoid or minimize potentially irksome relationships. As the few vestiges of stable community life erode, the desire for a simple, cooperative lifestyle grows in intensity. The most seductive appeal of radical ideologies for Americans consists in the fact that all in one way or another attack the competitive foundations of our society.

Now it may be objected that American society is less competitive than it once was, and that the appeal of radical ideologies should hence be diminished. Social critics in the fifties argued that the entrepreneurial individualist of the past has been replaced by a bureaucratic Organization Man. Much of this historical drama was created by comparing yesterday's owner-president with today's assistant sales manager; certainly these nostalgia-merchants never visited a nineteenth-century company town. Another distortion is introduced by the fact that it was only the most ruthlessly competitive robber barons who survived to tell us how it was. Little is written about the neighborhood store that extended credit to the poor, or the small town industry that refused to lay off local workers in hard times. They all went under together. The meek may be blessed but they don't write memoirs.

Even if we grant that the business world was more competitive in the nineteenth century, the total environment was less so. The individual worked in a smaller firm with lower turnover in which his or her relationships were more enduring and more personal. The ideology of Adam Smith° was tempered by the fact that the participants in economic struggles were neighbors and might have been childhood playmates. Even if the business world then was as "dog-eat-dog" as we imagine it, it occurred as a deviant episode in what was otherwise a more comfortable and familiar environment than the organization man can find today in or out of his office. The organization man is simply a carryover from the paternalistic environment of the family business and the company town; and the "other-directedness" of the suburban community just a desperate attempt to bring some old-fashioned small-town collectivism into the transient and impersonal lifestyle of the suburb. The social critics of the 1950s were so preoccupied with assailing these rather synthetic forms of human inter-

Adam Smith   Scottish philosopher and economist (1723–1790). He believed that free competition and a minimum of government interference were necessary for an efficient economy.

dependence that they lost sight of the underlying sickness that produced them. Medical symptoms usually result from attempts made by the body to counteract disease, and attacking the symptoms often aggravates and prolongs the illness. This seems to be the case with the feeble and self-defeating efforts of twentieth-century Americans to create a viable social environment.

The Problem of Identity

William Kilpatrick

William Kilpatrick (born 1940) was educated at Holy Cross, Harvard, and Purdue, where he earned a Ph.D. As a faculty member of Boston College, he teaches Adolescent Psychology, and Culture and Psychology. His interest in the relationship between culture and psychological ideas has led to two books: *Identity and Intimacy* (1975), from which we reprint the major part of Chapter 1, and *The Psychological Seduction* (1983), which deals with psychology and religion.

Identity in a Temporary Society

At the parochial grammar school I attended we were taught that it was wrong to have impure thoughts. It was in fact a sin. This caused a lot of trouble for us because on the one hand we took our religion seriously and on the other we kept having impure thoughts. When confession time came each week it was always a problem deciding how many of these thoughts to admit to. I decided on three. Somehow three seemed like a good number—about what the normal Catholic boy should have, I guessed. Besides, I didn't want to scandalize the priest by letting him know the actual count.

In our school a good person was defined by the nuns as being, among other things, pure and chaste in thought, word and deed; as being, so it seemed, asexual. And we, if we wanted to be good (which we did) were supposed to define ourselves in the same way. In our self-definition there was no place for sexuality. But it was hard being "good." One constantly had to contend with desires that were inconsistent with one's narrowly defined self. The environment was full of temptations—magazine racks and tight sweaters—and one had either to compulsively restrict one's activities ("avoiding the near occasion of sin," as the church called it) or resort to obsessive rituals such as reciting "ejaculations" at three-second intervals. These were brief spurts of prayer designed to keep Satan at a distance, but the very thought of that word was enough to set off a new chain of impure speculations. It was a vicious circle.

Most of us, as time went on, learned to redefine ourselves on a larger scale and to admit the sexual part of our humanity which had, of course, been there all along. It was a process of letting in more reality, of widening the boundaries of self to take account of life's variety. One could, as it turned out, have impure thoughts and still be a good Catholic. It was only necessary either to broaden the definition of "good" or else restrict the meaning of "impure."

I don't recall how my own growth up from parochialism in this respect occurred. It may have been occasioned by the reading of an enlightened pamphlet in a darkened church. Or it may have been some absolution-weary priest, tired of shriving a child's daydreams, who gave me new perspectives on the nature of evil. More probably the change happened gradually through a process of reflection. At any rate I felt no great dislocation from my scrupulous past—only a little older and wiser. Whatever new definitions of the self I arrived at, there was always a continuity with what I had been, a solid sense of sameness winding through my life, a wide unbreakable ribbon tying it all together. After all, despite the changes, everything in my life was still there. For thirteen years, the same house with the same wisteria vine climbing to the roof, changing as I did, only in growing larger and stronger, the same neighborhood, the same friends, the weekly visits to aunts and uncles, cousins, and grandparents—all giving reassuring testimony to that essential continuity with my past.

Since the pace of change was slower in those days, continuity was not so difficult to achieve. But today the situation is different. In a constantly changing society, a sense of personal continuity becomes extremely important. In such a context it is necessary to redefine oneself many times, for rapid change creates sharp discontinuities which must be bridged in order to retain a unified sense of self. This sense of self, composed in large part of the experience of continuity, is what we call identity.

The Formation of Identity

A child doesn't have an identity so much as a collection of identifications. He identifies with his mother and father or with some aspect of their personalities, perhaps rejecting other aspects. As he grows he makes identifications with brothers and sisters, playmates, grandparents, folk heroes, athletes, and other figures; some more significant, some less so. These identifications may be transient, partial, unrealistic, even contradictory. Added together, they do not form a coherent or consistent sense of identity, but this is not yet a problem for the child.

For the adolescent it *is* a problem—the main problem. His body is growing rapidly and changing. His mind is becoming capable of high-level abstraction. He becomes acutely aware of possibilities. He begins to worry about his future. The adult world he is about to enter seems at odds with his dependent childhood. This internal revolution creates in him a need to pull his life together into a coherent unity. He needs to believe that the person he was as a child has persisted despite the changes—or else what was his childhood for? He has to find connections between the person he was and the person he anticipates he will be. If he is not quite the same as he was yesterday he would like to trace the history of that transformation; to find the links that bind past self to present self. In short, he seeks to create an identity that will bridge all the discontinuities of puberty.

Identity is not created all at once, nor is it ever really completed, but it takes shape gradually out of the successive identifications of childhood and those newly formed. These are slowly integrated into a new configuration which is both a coherent and unique whole. It is not an easy task. Consciously and unconsciously the growing child must somehow reconcile the identifications he has made with figures as diverse as his aging grandfather and the hero of the last movie he has seen. Out of the bag of partial identifications which he carries from his earliest years and out of the future toward which he aspires, he must synthesize a unique self he can call his own.

The Essential Self

It is only our sense of continuity that allows us to tolerate the contradictions and inconsistencies of such a process. A sense of continuity reassures us that despite the redefinitions we have made, there still persists an essential self. We may not be able to locate this bedrock foundation precisely, but without the sense that it exists, without the conviction that something essential endures, our identity would seem an insubstantial thing.

This is the self to which we believe we must be true; which we would prefer on the whole to keep faith with. And it is upon this core self that others rely when they trust us or take us at our word. Our self is their guarantee of fidelity; the part of us that can be held responsible. It is possible to retreat from many things we hold dear. Principles can be compromised and ideals sacrificed without completely losing our integrity. We can draw lines and redraw them if necessary and still retain our self-respect. But there is a point at which we must draw a line and stand fast, for beyond that point lies something indispensable. That something is the essence of what we mean by identity or the self.

Exactly where that point is we can never say. Certainly it differs from person to person. But when the self reveals itself it leaves no doubt that such a place exists. The life of Thomas More provides a point of reference. In it we can find the place at which one man located his sense of self. As a loyal subject of King Henry VIII, More was expected to sign an oath approving of the king's marriage to Anne Boleyn; as Lord Chancellor of the Realm and as a man who held the admiration of the populace, his assent was all the more crucial to Henry. More refused the oath. Not out of any sense of propriety or priggishness, but because it required him to swear to something he considered untrue, something that constituted a denial of God's revelation as he understood it. To consent to the oath would be to deny his faith.

As represented in Robert Bolt's play *A Man for All Seasons,* More comes under increasing pressure to sign. One by one his friends give in until Thomas is left alone against the king. To one of these friends he proclaims in defense of his dangerous obstinacy: "I will not give in because I oppose it—I do—not my pride, not my spleen, nor any other of my appetites but I do—*I!*"[1]

For his disloyalty More is imprisoned in the Tower. But in the face of continued interrogation and the king's growing impatience he remains unmoved. Finally, More's family comes to him to plead that he sign the oath. Their appeals to his affection are matched only by More's appeal to his integrity. To his daughter he says:

"When a man takes an oath, Meg, he's holding his own self in his own hands. Like water. [*He cups his hands*] And if he opens his fingers *then*—he needn't hope to find himself again. Some men aren't capable of this but I'd be loathe to think your father one of them."[2]

The rest of the story is well known. More is made to stand trial, and on the basis of trumped-up charges is sentenced to death and executed.

In his preface to the play, Bolt provides an explanation for More's behavior in what must stand as one of the finest statements on the ultimate meaning of identity:

He knew where he began and left off, what area of himself he could yield to the encroachments of his enemies, and what to the encroachments of those he loved. It was a substantial area in both cases, for he had a proper sense of fear and was a busy lover. Since he was a clever man and a great lawyer he was able to retire from those areas in wonderfully good order, but at length he was asked to retreat from that final area where he located his self. And there this supple, humorous, unassuming and sophisticated person set like metal, was overtaken by an absolutely primitive rigor, and could no more be budged than a cliff.[3]

The perjured testimony which finally sends More to the gallows is given by one Richard Rich. In the career of Rich we see an opposite process at work—the dissolution of identity. In fact we can almost pinpoint the precise point at which it is abandoned. Rich is a young man who is anxious to enter into the world of affairs—at any price, as it turns out. What little

[1]Robert Bolt, *A Man for All Seasons* (New York: Random House, 1962), p. 123.
[2]Ibid., p. 140.
[3]Ibid., p. xii.

sense of identity he has, threatens to be engulfed by his ambition. Yet one can see possibilities in this young man. He is a reflective person who admires More's integrity, and behind his adolescent intensity there glimmers the possibility of loyalty and courage. We detect in him an attempt, however feeble, to cling to whatever verities he has been schooled in; to find some continuity with a past that was more plain and honest than the cunning deceits of the courts and chambers through which he now moves.

But finally these possibilities never develop. The lure of power and money is too great. At one point in the play More has been given a silver goblet which he belatedly realizes to be a bribe. Rather than be influenced by it, he gives the goblet to Rich. Later Rich is being questioned by Thomas Cromwell, who is seeking some kind of damning evidence against More. Since Cromwell is a powerful man, Rich stands to gain considerably by revealing what he knows. In his extended dialogue with Cromwell we can trace the disintegration of a self. Cromwell has just asked Rich if he believes he would never repeat anything said in friendship:

RICH: Yes!
CROMWELL: No, but seriously.
RICH: Why, yes!
CROMWELL: *(not sinister, but rather as a kindly teacher with a promising pupil)* Rich; seriously.
RICH: *(pauses, then bitterly)* It would depend on what I was offered.

He is offered a position as Collector of Revenues for the Diocese of York. Then Cromwell questions Rich about the silver goblet.

CROMWELL: Where did he [More] get it? *(No reply. Rich puts the cup down.)* It was a gift from a litigant, a woman, wasn't it?
RICH: Yes.
CROMWELL: Which court? Chancery? *(restrains Rich from filling his glass)* No, don't get drunk. In which court was this litigant's case?
RICH: Court of Requests.
CROMWELL: There, that wasn't too painful, was it?
RICH: *(laughing a little and a little rueful)* No!
CROMWELL: That's all there is. And you'll find it easier next time.[4]

"Court of Requests." A simple enough statement. Yet at that point Rich has abdicated his self. After this the man no longer has a self to commit. His word has no guarantee. Sensing this inner hollowness More can say to him: "Richard, you couldn't answer for yourself even so far as tonight."[5]

We would not want to say that Rich can never again get back his

[4]Ibid., pp. 72, 75–76.
[5]Ibid., p. 65.

identity. That possibility always remains, we must suppose, until the final moment. It would be a damaged identity, of course, but the possibility for repentance and renewal always exists. But Rich, as it turns out, never gets his back. By the end of the play his personality has hardened into a mask, and behind the mask there is nothing. Nothing has persisted in him but his ambition.

The self that persists, the self upon which others rely and upon which we found our identity—that self is now threatened from several directions. Any society produces more Richard Riches than Thomas Mores, but our present American culture is now far more conducive to the production of people like Rich than it has ever been. It is not the type of society that provides a solid sense of identity; and it is upon identity that ethics are built.

Rarely is anyone called upon to make the type of heroic self-definition that Thomas More made, and the encroachments upon our identity are more subtle than those that Rich suffered; but in less obvious ways there are forces at work that threaten to undermine that something in us which we feel ought to persist. This chapter and the ones that follow will examine these forces.

An oath is not nearly so sacred as it once was, and we would now prefer that men, as Bolt puts it, "guarantee their statements with, say, cash, rather than with themselves."[6] Nevertheless there is an anxiety that pervades our sense of self: a fear that underneath the many roles we play there is nothing. If we cannot identify with More, and if we are loath to find in ourselves the deceitfulness of a Richard Rich, there is yet another metaphor for us. It can be found in Ibsen's play *Peer Gynt,* where Peer, seated among a field of onions, imagines his personality to be no different from an onion. The layers he peels off one by one represent the roles he has played in life, but after all are peeled away there is nothing left:

> "There's a most surprising lot of layers! Are we never coming to the kernel? [*Pulls all that's left to pieces*] There isn't one! To the innermost bit it's nothing but layers, smaller and smaller. Nature's a joker!"[7]

It's a cruel joke that leaves a man with no core of identity. But it would appear that just such a joke is being played on a growing number of individuals in our society. The jokester in this case is not nature but a culture that accelerates social and technological change at a dizzying pace.

Identity in a Changing World

The work of Erik Erikson provides the most useful recent discussion of identity, and one which makes sense in human terms, for Erikson makes allowance for the ambiguities and uncertainties of life, for the possibility of this going wrong and that going right. It is Erikson who stressed the

[6]Ibid., p. xiv.
[7]Henrik Ibsen, *Peer Gynt* (New York: E. P. Dutton and Co., 1930), p. 202.

importance of continuity in the formation of identity, and it is to Erikson that we owe our understanding of how identity is synthesized out of many childhood identifications. As Erikson describes it, identity emerges out of a dialectic between the need for continuity and the need for experimentation. Identity formation leads in the direction of a new self-delineation, yet it is also an "accrued confidence" that one retains an "inner sameness." With this confidence it is possible to take the chances with one's identity that true intimacy requires. Erikson has become the preeminent theorist of identity, and this perhaps most of all because his is a theory made to fit men rather than one they are fitted into.

But theories, like selves, need occasionally to be redefined in light of new realities, and certain new realities would seem to require a rethinking of our ideas about this fundamental process of identity formation. There is the possibility that these new realities are not realities at all, of course, but only new myths. But since men live as much by myths as realities, we are still forced to consider the usefulness of our traditional explanations. I would not suggest that Erikson's explanation is no longer useful (it is extremely useful) but that the model of health it presents no longer reflects the norm. As social realities change, a theory can become more and more a statement of the way things should be than the way they are, and this, I believe, is what has happened to Erikson's criteria of health. For Erikson, a healthy identity is one that is open to change and redefinition, but above all is rooted in an historical, traceable past, so that through all there runs an invigorating "sense of sameness,"[8]—what I have been calling "continuity."

This healthy sense of sameness is increasingly difficult to come by as we approach the last quarter of the twentieth century. To illustrate let us juxtapose Erikson's definition of identity with a statement from Toffler's (1970) *Future Shock*. First, Erikson:

> Ego identity . . . is an awareness of the fact that there is a self-sameness and continuity to the ego's synthesizing methods, *the style of one's individuality*, and that this style coincides with the sameness and continuity of one's *meaning for significant others* in the immediate community.[9]

Contrast to this a statement from Toffler's book:

> What remains? What is there of "self" or "personality" in the sense of a continuous, durable internal structure? For some, the answer is very little. For they are no longer dealing in "self" but in what might be called "serial selves."[10]

"They" are for the most part the affluent and highly mobile elite most involved in the accelerated pace of change that produces future shock. But since "they" are soon to be followed by the rest of us, it seems worth

[8]Erik H. Erikson, *Identity, Youth and Crisis* (New York: W. W. Norton and Co., 1968), p. 246.

[9]Ibid., p. 50.

[10]Alvin Toffler, *Future Shock* (New York: Bantam Books, 1970), p. 319.

investigating this matter of "serial selves" and the sharp contrast it opposes to Erikson's definition of identity.

Continuity and Change

Identity—the type Erikson has in mind—requires a threefold continuity: a continuity of significant others; a continuity with one's past self; a continuity with one's anticipated future self. At all three levels the phenomenon of chronic change acts to disrupt these continuities.

It is imperative that our sense of identity be reinforced by significant others. We need their reassurance that despite the transformations we have undergone something essential remains. What are we after all but social creatures? Even Thomas More, who had stood alone against all, at the last begs his family for their understanding. An identity is a fragile thing when it stands by itself. It is strengthened when we feel that others recognize in us that self-sameness which we recognize in ourselves.

Identity achievement then would seem to require a continuity of significant others in our lives to confirm our links to our past selves. One of the problems of a future-shocked society, however, is the absence of such continuity. Friends and neighbors come and go with alarming rapidity. They change, and we change, and "those who knew us in some previous incarnation," as Toffler puts it, have a difficult time recognizing us. They do little to reinforce our sense of sameness.

Mobility and transience combine to create a society of nomads. Incessant moving is the norm. Who still lives in the house of his birth? In the house of his childhood? Even for the young the answer is that practically no one does. The house of my own youth no longer exists. In its place stands a modern apartment building. The backyard in which I discovered praying mantis and morning glory is now a paved parking lot. The phrase "you can't go home again" takes on for us a physical as well as psychological meaning. And even when we can return to a physical site, what strangers will we find at the door? Among the statistics Toffler cites is that one out of five Americans changes his address each year. Over half the listings in the 1969 Washington, D.C., phonebook, he tells us, were different from the year before.

No one, it seems, can be counted on to stay in one place. The aunts, uncles and grandparents who once lived across the street now live across the city or across the country. By and large we are left with only the stripped-down, streamlined nuclear family to fill the role of "significant others." And even here there is a growing lack of continuity. The nuclear family is coming apart. An increasing number of children must adjust to the fact that parents, like friends and neighbors, can come and go. Serial marriage—a succession of temporary marriages—is already an established although unofficial pattern. Those parents who do stay together increasingly shift the burden of child rearing to schools and day care centers. Annual rituals through which families could confer a unique sense of belonging to an ongoing tradition have largely been taken over by mass commercialism. The organization of our activities for Thanksgiving week is now in the hands of *TV Guide.* Little chance for identity confirmation here: the family is caught up in the same winds of change that buffet individual lives. As a result, we all have a vague feeling of truly belonging nowhere and to no one.

It is not only the continuity of our meaning to others that is threatened. We also have increasing difficulty in recognizing our own past selves. This would seem to be especially true in the matter of rapidly changing values. To a high degree our identity—our sense of continuity—is bound up with our sense of right and wrong. The world may change, we feel, but if we hold fast to our ethical moorings we can still retain a sense of our place in it. But what happens to identity when our values turn over almost as rapidly as fashions in dress? What does it mean for identity when, for instance, the Catholic who yesterday opposed birth control today accepts abortion and tomorrow may embrace euthanasia and test-tube reproduction? What does it mean for personal continuity to continually redraw the moral line at which one will make his or her stand? According to some of the sex researchers (e.g., Gilbert Bartell, 1971),[11] it is not unusual for a suburban woman to move from chastity through monogamy to adultery and on to group sex and lesbianism in a half-dozen years or less. My intent is not to pass judgment on any of these activities, only to point out that the more lines we erase, the harder it becomes to trace the genealogy of our morals or the lineage of our identity.

But it is precisely such historical acts that constitute the process of identity formation. This is why the adolescent whose main developmental task is identity formation becomes so concerned with questions of his personal lineage, descent, and legitimacy. The biological discontinuities of puberty prompt him to find connections with his past; the integration of his past and present identities demands that he take an historical perspective. It is the point of *Future Shock,* however, that the current diversity of life-styles and the rate at which we move through them makes such integration increasingly improbable. Erikson himself, anticipating this possibility, states that "the integration of infantile part-identities and fragmentary roles can be interfered with by . . . rapid social evolution or technological change."[12] In a similar vein, Kenneth Keniston sees contemporary youth as suffering from "historical dislocation," which he describes as "the inability to find connections with the past and future" and as "the feeling of unrelatedness, of being adrift, of not being able to 'catch hold'

[11]Gilbert D. Bartell, *Group Sex* (New York: New American Library, 1973).
[12]R. I. Evans, *Dialogue with Erik Erikson* (New York: E. P. Dutton, 1969), Erikson quoted, p. 39.

of anything or anyone in our rapidly changing society."[13] He sees this dislocation as being due on the one hand to the difficulty of synthesizing the many irreconcilable identities our society proffers, and on the other to an inability of youth to identify with their parents because their parents have been "outdated" by rapid change.

To the youth Keniston studied, parents are seen as simply irrelevant. To identify with them is to choose obsolescence. Although they may be the only link to their children's past, the children simply cannot relate to them. The ever-present generation gap is widened by the factors of transience, mobility, novelty, and diversity that Toffler describes and analyzes in *Future Shock.* When change accelerates beyond a certain point it is difficult to retain a sense of continuity with one's past; the past seems increasingly distant and beside the point.

The same holds true for the future. Endless change makes the future unpredictable. That which we thought to be stable and permanent rapidly becomes obsolescent. In the face of accelerating social and technological innovations it is difficult to anticipate the future or plan for it. We turn instead to the present, the only time we can be sure of. If the past is irrelevant and the future enigmatic, the present is more certain.

When the past loses its significance and the future becomes unknowable, when those on whom we rely to confirm our identity depart our lives, and when we have been forced to play many successive parts, we may begin to wonder, like Peer Gynt, if there is any center. Chronic change undermines our sense of the persistence of something essential in us. It separates us from our identity as effectively as Cromwell unburdened Rich of his.

Even as basic a touchstone as our sense of physical identity may soon be undermined by rapid advances in the field of medicine. Our sense of identity is reinforced on a physical level by the simple fact of bodily continuity. Allowing for normal wear and tear and cell replacement, we recognize ourselves as being of our own flesh and blood. But even now, Teflon and Dacron and metal are replacing skin and bones. And the heart we were born with may have to be discarded along the way in favor of a "new" one. What happens to an individual's sense of uniqueness or continuity when faced with the knowledge that his body is a system of interchangeable parts? The speed with which we enter the future is measured by the fact that questions like this find us totally unprepared.

Fidelity

The sense of continuity is not the only quality to be threatened by accelerated change. Erikson observed that at each stage of development a capacity or "virtue" emerges in the individual to help him meet the crisis

[13]Kenneth Keniston, *The Uncommitted* (New York: Harcourt, Brace and World, 1965), pp. 239–40.

of that stage. An important step in the crisis of identity formation is the development of a capacity for what he terms "fidelity." Fidelity is faithfulness, loyalty, commitment. In large part the adolescent quest for identity is a search for something to which one can commit one's newly developing sense of identity. Through fidelity, moreover, one can cultivate those long-term relationships that give continuity to one's sense of self. Our fidelity is our guarantee that there is something solid about our identity —something which endures. "Without the development of a capacity for fidelity," says Erikson, "the individual will either have what we call a weak ego, or look for a deviant group to be faithful to." And elsewhere in stronger terms he asserts, "Fidelity . . . must not, in the crisis of youth, fail its time of ascendance if human adaptation is to remain intact."[14]

Once again, if we juxtapose to this some statements from Toffler we find a sharp contrast. It is Toffler's contention that most of our relationships are characterized by transience. This is especially true of our relationships to things and places but is becoming increasingly true of our relationships to people. Our attitude toward things that are disposable, rentable, and impermanent may begin to color our attitude toward people. Although we are very much attached to material goods in general, there is no longer the tradition of specific attachment to a specific thing which prevailed when goods were less abundant and things were made to last. All this is preparation for a world in which our attachments to people become equally tenuous; in which we feel driven to experience the latest model friend, lover, or spouse. "The logical end of the direction in which we are now travelling," writes Toffler, "is a society based on a system of temporary encounters."[15] Here Toffler is speaking not only of our transient relations to acquaintances, colleagues, and neighbors but also of friendship, love, and marriage bonds. The traditional ideal for marriage has been that of shared growth. This pattern, says Toffler, has been difficult to achieve even in stable societies, but people no longer change at the same rate or in the same direction. The best we can hope for is the system of serial marriages mentioned earlier.

In a world of disposable goods, easily replaced, we probably should not wonder that people also come to seem disposable. And our vaunted mobility only intensifies the feeling that it is wiser if we do not get too attached. Commitment to others is difficult enough in a stable society because it entails not only the risk of rejection but also the risk of involvement. People who move around a great deal are even more reluctant to commit themselves to friends, colleagues, or communities. Why invest the energy when one is going to move on? Why get involved?

[14]Evans, *Dialogue*, Erikson quoted, p. 30. Erikson, "Youth: Fidelity and Diversity," in *The Challenge of Youth*, E. H. Erikson, ed. (Garden City: Doubleday Anchor, 1965), p. 1.

[15]Toffler, *Future Shock*, p. 122.

The Risks of Fidelity

Moreover, fidelity carries with it the risk of what Keniston calls "damaging commitment to false life styles or goals."[16] To understand the meaning of this risk it is necessary to understand that identity and fidelity have a mutually supportive relationship; they do not develop apart from each other. Identity generates the capacity for fidelity, which in turn generates a stronger sense of identity. The more tenuous one's hold on his identity, the less likely he is to risk losing it in a relationship with another. He fears that the price of commitment may be the absorption of his self into another's. But without commitment or intimacy there is no further growth for him. Conversely, the anxieties of identity diffusion may propel an individual to find any identity, no matter how premature and limiting, in an effort to have done with it. He may seek an end to anxiety in a hasty and confining marriage or in narrow commitment to some group or cause. The "true believer," as Eric Hoffer[0] points out, is only too willing to have his uncertain sense of self welded to some ideological superstructure.

The danger of being welded or wedded to false life-styles or to the wrong persons makes fidelity risky in the best of circumstances. In a world characterized by mobility, novelty, faddishness, transience, and temporality where there are many competing life-styles and persons, and little time to examine or decide, the risk is multiplied enormously.

Not only is fidelity difficult in such a world, but the job of synthesizing identifications also becomes highly problematic. The more variegated a society, the more identities it offers, and the harder it is to pull them together into a coherent unity. When an individual fails to achieve an integration of past and current identifications he falls victim to what Erikson calls identity confusion: an inability to feel that one is all together, a feeling of not fitting in, of not knowing who one is or what one wants to do, of trying on many roles and settling for none.

Erikson sees the resolution of the identity crisis in the achievement of a ratio between a sense of coherence and a sense of identity confusion, with the balance tipped in favor of the former. But in a future-shocked society the ratio is reversed. If Toffler's assessment of cultural change is correct, then the balance has been tipped the other way. Identity confusion, not coherence, has become the prevailing norm.

It is true that the human race has an impressive record of adaptability. But to adapt is not to thrive or prosper. We cannot be too sanguine about the benefits of adapting to a society where identity confusion is not redeemed by a sense of continuity. Toffler is not unaware of the danger that is posed to our identity in an accelerating society. There are, he asserts,

---

[16]Kenneth Keniston, "Social Change and Youth in America" in *The Challenge of Youth,* p. 202.
Eric Hoffer   Longshoreman, author, social philosopher (1902–1983).

definite limits to the amount of change that the human organism can cope with. The higher the level of change, the greater the likelihood of illness, both physical and mental. The more change is accelerated, the more we run the risk of being thrown into a state of shock.

I do not mean to imply that the future-shock problem is the main difficulty for identity formation. It is one of several problems that necessitate a rethinking of our traditional ideas about the achievement of identity. In this chapter I have merely tried to draw attention to the discrepancy that exists between a major theory of development and a widely accepted description of current social change. What the one requires, the other refuses.

Paul Bohannan

Paul Bohannan (born 1920) is an anthropologist. He attended the University of Arizona, studied at Oxford as a Rhodes Scholar, and is now Dean of Social Sciences at the University of Southern California. His principal work in anthropology is based on field studies among African tribes, but he is also well known as a writer on the problems of family and marriage. In such works as *Love, Sex and Being Human: A Book About the Human Condition for Young People* (1969), and in his several essays in *Divorce and After* (1970), which he also edited, he brings to subjects of popular interest an unusual combination of clarity and sensitivity. The present essay appeared in the April issue of *Science 81*.

The Stranger

When I board airplanes to come home, I am usually tired and want to escape in my private window seat into a never-never land somewhere between pondering and blacking out. But the last time I flew home, it didn't work out. I recognized the situation when the hefty young man packed himself into the middle seat and began to talk: This guy needed a stranger to spill his guts to.

I heard about his divorce, his ex-mother-in-law's chicanery—what he said, what his lawyer said, and what his boss said. I listened because anthropologists are professional listeners, and besides I was trapped in the window seat. We did not exchange names, let alone telephone numbers. I doubt that I would recognize him on second meeting. I do not know where he lives or anything else about him except the intimacies—the case history—of his collapsed marriage.

The juxtaposition of personal intimacy and strangers set me thinking about both. My thoughts drifted back to a book I had read several years earlier, Lyn Lofland's *A World of Strangers.* She pointed out that every peasant, every tribesman can divide the world into relatives, neighbors, friends, and enemies. Urban people, too, are surrounded by relatives, neighbors, friends, and enemies. But they are also surrounded by people called strangers.

Traditionally, before urban society existed, there were two ways to deal with strangers: Either lump them with your enemies and kill them before they killed you, or turn them into "guests" who deserved elaborate courtesy and the best available lodging, food, and drink. In return, as guests, they were bound to protect and to dwell with the host in honesty and peace. In such societies for either the host or the guest to infringe upon the code of hospitality was a heinous offense against God.

For urban dwellers, however, hospitality won't work. There are just too many strangers. Most of them are not enemies, and most of them are too busy to be guests. Yet dealing with the strangers who populate urban space is the task of those of us who live urban lives.

When I was working with old men living in center city hotels, some areas of the city made me apprehensive, others comfortable. I scurried from one comfortable place to another, rigidly avoiding eye contact with everyone I passed. When I got where I was going, I could relax again. I was still among strangers—but comfortable strangers. Being comfortable, I knew from fieldwork in Africa, meant either that I was out of touch with what was going on or very close to it. I was uncomfortable when I did not know what people were going to do. It turned out that I translated this discomfort into the primitive idea that all strangers are enemies. I am not sure I was wrong.

According to Lofland, however, there is still another way to tame strangers. She calls it "categorical knowing." To know somebody categorically is to know the social roles he plays. Interaction occurs on the basis of a mutually recognized job description. The postal clerk from whom I buy stamps every few weeks is not exactly a stranger. We recognize each other. But I know nothing about her. Her name is on the plaque that stands beside the window, but I do not remember it from one stamp purchase to the next. I know she is pleasant and efficient, that there is an easy air of predictability about the whole exchange, but I do not know her "personally." She just tells me to "have a nice day."

Knowing somebody personally, Lofland says, begins with knowing some biographical facts about that person. But personal knowing does not necessarily engender reciprocity. After all, I know Mozart well enough through the eyes of several biographers; but much as I love his music, I don't like him.

So it must be from reciprocal personal knowing that intimacy springs.

Yet I have a lot of friends with whom I feel in no sense intimate. What, then, makes the difference?

The difference is in what I reveal. When I called the hefty young man's story one of "intimacy," I was wrong. I revealed no intimacies to him. How do I know that he was not kidding me—indeed, kidding himself? There was no intimacy, only confession.

There is more to intimacy than revealing biographical facts. It has to do with reciprocal revelation. The innermost self becomes clear only in the reciprocity.

And that means that one may as well be bone honest.

Friendships and falling in love start the same way. I expose a bit of my usually secret self. Then, if you approve, I feel good about you—and if you in return expose a little of your secret self, I will approve if I possibly can. And, presently, I expose more. Both self-revelations continue. In friendship we are usually selective—only part of us gets revealed. But when we fall in love, the process picks up speed and rapture becomes total. The depths seem never to be wholly plumbed because we reveal so much we ourselves did not know. What I expose must be accurate—if it is not, I will back and fill to cover up my falsehoods. And that stymies the process. Getting to know myself comes with sharing with another.

It is a fertile dilemma: Only through honest revelation to another do I reveal myself to myself. But sometimes, when I have been deeply hurt, I need to get back into shape to bear the responsibilities of intimacy. That's when I need pseudo-intimacy with a stranger.

The hefty young man on the airplane did not offer intimacy. He used a stranger to try to learn something about himself. A stranger is sometimes the best person for that purpose, for he is neither guest nor enemy. More significantly, a stranger doesn't strike back.

Denise Levertov
(1923–)

In Mind

There's in my mind a woman
of innocence, unadorned but

fair-featured, and smelling of
apples or grass. She wears

a utopian smock or shift, her hair
is light brown and smooth, and she

is kind and very clean without
ostentation—
                    but she has
no imagination.
                    And there's a
turbulent moon-ridden girl

or old woman, or both,
dressed in opals and rags, feathers

and torn taffeta,
who knows strange songs—

but she is not kind.

                                        (1962)

The Good Life

One of the oldest human questions is, What is the Good Life? Often, the attempt to achieve the good life is indistinguishable from the effort to find out what it is. When people are struggling to stay alive in the face of danger or poverty, the question seems to have an easy answer. Then, the good life means safety or food. The first need is survival. But once we have this, once we pass from survival or subsistence to a range of wider possibilities, the question takes on new meaning. Are plenty and ease sufficient? Does "making it" make us happy?

The first two selections are by people who are satisfied with their lives. "The American Dream? That's what we're doing right now," says one woman in an interview from Studs Terkel's book *American Dreams.* "I really liked my job," says her husband. In a second interview, William Gothard, a young lawyer, also feels he is on the right road. He says, "I want to get married, have two kids, two cars, two color TV sets, and live in the suburbs outside Los Angeles. But I want to maintain my individuality." In sharp contrast, Joan Didion, in the course of reporting on a murder trial in southern California, paints a devastating picture of the Golden Dream of material comfort and status, here with no past or future, devoid of meaning and value.

The next three selections in this group raise more directly the question of needs versus wants. "Where does satisfaction come from?" asks Wendell Berry as he compares the "freedom" provided by modern conveniences to the pleasurable burdens of such jobs as spreading manure. The short story by Isaac Bashevis Singer takes up a similar theme. Berl and Berlcha feel no wants beyond the simple needs of their village life, and so have neither use nor understanding for the culture of their son. E. F. Schumacher also challenges the assumption that only the rich can have a good life, and asks us to discriminate between ephemeral satisfactions and eternal ones. Our real needs, he says, are limited and must be met, but our wants are unlimited, cannot necessarily be met, and perhaps should be resisted. The quality of life can be gauged, he feels, by that which is valued most. The story by Ursula K. Le Guin raises provocative and disturbing questions about the good life and the price we pay for what we have.

All the pieces in the next section deal, directly or indirectly, with the meaning of work. How much of the value of our lives depends on our work? The poems by Marge Piercy and Theodore Roethke present contrasting feelings: work as central to our lives and satisfying or work as drudgery. The next selection by Schumacher describes three "purposes of human work" and thus provides criteria for four reports on work by four different workers: a veterinarian, a mason, an editor, and a steelworker.

The narrative by William Least Heat Moon suggests how what we "do" affects our having an identity and illustrates the useful distinction between "work" and a "job." On a larger and more philosophical scale, this distinction between fulfilling work and alienating work—the separation of work from any inherent meaning or satisfaction—is treated by Erich Fromm in the next essay. He relates alienation historically to the rise of industrialism and assembly-line production, and he points to some of its psychological consequences for the worker. The engineer Samuel C. Florman challenges, in a way, most of the above views; he skeptically reexamines the idea that technology is to blame for the dehumanization of work, and challenges the belief that Americans hate their jobs. He concludes that if there is sickness in our culture, it does not originate in the workplace. The section ends with Elliot Liebow's moving and necessary reminder of those people, perhaps an increasing number, living "in a sea of want," whose work and whose sense of self are fatally crippled by hopelessness.

The Golden Dream

Studs Terkel

Studs Terkel is perhaps best known for his interviews and oral histories, recording the feelings and thoughts of "ordinary" people who are rarely heard.
His tool is a portable tape recorder, a tool, he says, that can be used or misused.
Hidden, it can be a means of blackmail or an instrument of the police state.
In the open, "on the steps of a public housing project, in a frame bungalow,
in a furnished apartment, in a parked car," it can capture the thoughts of the
uncelebrated and "carry away valuables beyond price." He has published
these valuables in four different books: *Division Street: America* (1966), inter-
views with people from different groups and classes in Chicago; *Hard Times:
An Oral History of the Great Depression* (1970), interviews with one hundred
Americans who survived the Great Depression; *Working: People Talk About
What They Do All Day and How They Feel About What They Do* (1974); and
American Dreams: Lost and Found (1980), which is the source of the pieces
below. He has also written *Talking to Myself: A Memoir of My Times* (1977).

Terkel's background probably helped him develop his ability to talk with
many kinds of people and his interest in what they have to say. He was born
Louis Terkel in New York in 1912; his family moved to Chicago when he was
eleven. His father was a tailor; his mother took over a hotel for blue-collar
workers, mechanics, and craftsmen, men he knew as he was growing up. He
later changed his first name to Studs, after Studs Lonigan, from James T.
Farrell's novels about the Chicago proletarian Irish. After high school he went
to Crane Junior College, then graduated from the University of Chicago
(Ph.D., 1932). He went on to law school (J.D., 1934) but failed his first bar
examination and never practiced. Instead, he has been a radio and stage actor,
a radio writer, a jazz columnist, and a disc jockey. In recent years he has
developed the interview style—what he calls "guerilla journalism"—into the
provocative studies of American culture mentioned above.

Carol and Tony Danlow

*Lockport is on the western outskirts of Chicago: new subdivisions, built-
up farmland, unincorporated. She describes her neighbors as "working
toward a more comfortable life. Their houses are so expensive, for any
young couple it would be almost impossible." Theirs is one of those houses.
It is tastefully furnished.*

She says: "We came from something much more plush than this. We had a commercial building in Evergreen Park and a ten-room apartment, and it was way larger than what this is. It was gorgeous. We had a built-in whirlpool bathtub and a dumbwaiter and all kinds of beautiful things."

Though they have three married children, they look astonishingly young. "We started early," he laughs. They are forty-seven.

In February 1975, they won the big prize of the Illinois lottery: a million dollars.

CAROL: We always enjoyed a little gambling. We played the lottery right from the start, buying maybe ten, fifteen dollars a week. Never really thinking about the biggie.

TONY: I was a truck driver for A & P for twenty-eight years. Liked my job and everything. Once you win, people take on a different attitude towards you. They don't think you should work any more. You'd go to work and all of a sudden, they'd want to know how come. They figure that you're taking a job that somebody else would really need. Even the heads of the company and the union officials, they don't stand behind you on anything. *They're* working and making a heck of a lot more money than this lottery gives a person. It's all right for them to work, but they think you should give up your life's work that you've been doing for twenty-eight years. What is fifty thousand dollars a year nowadays? It isn't much by the time Uncle Sam gets his cut. There's many people doin' that and a lot better.

CAROL: Fifty thousand dollars a year for twenty years. That's how you get it.

TONY: We had two good jobs. We kept working until it just got intolerable with the abuse that you take. We were fortunate. We knew a little about real estate and we invested. That's where we made a lot of money. This was even before the lottery.

CAROL: We were at the Mill Run, the dinner-theater house, where they had the drawing. It was a big auditorium, and you could bring your own cheering section. Which we did in high hopes. You were given a ball with a number on it. It was based on horse position and post. They put it in a big barrel. When my name was called, instant hysteria! (Laughs.) It was wild. It's got to be one of the most thrilling times that could ever happen. It's just chills, butterflies, everything.

TONY: Our son, he was twenty-three then, he musta leaped over six rows of seats, and he's hollerin' he'll never have to work again. I said: "Like hell you're gonna quit." He's a carpenter in the building trades.

CAROL: People were like happy, but you always find out about a few of the green-eyed monsters. We lost a couple of friends we thought were friends. It really must have been jealousy or something. All of a sudden the friendships cooled.

TONY: It was all right the first week at work. After that, since they just expected they would quit working themselves, I should quit too. They were always on our backs. But I really liked my job. I wanted to work. It just didn't mean that much to us because we were preparing to retire at the age of fifty as it was. I was forty-four, forty-five when it happened.

CAROL: I was a checker at the A & P store. People would say: "How come you're still working?" The one boss, in particular, right after we won, passed the remark: "I suppose she'll want a gold-covered counter." Stuff like that. It was just dumb little things. After a while, it can get a little aggravatin'.

TONY: I don't think I would have quit if A & P hadn't fired me. The two bosses got their heads together and fired me for insubordination.

CAROL: People think they have to talk to you a little differently. After I quit my job, I was working as a travel agent. Okay, right after I started this job, here was a big write-up in the *Sun-Times* and a picture and the whole shot. These women saw the paper, and one got on the telephone and called the other: "Did you read your paper yet?" "No." "Well, open it up and see who we're working with." She did and she said: "Well, what do you know?" So she says: "What are we gonna say to her tomorrow?" So they said: "I don't know."

They're super-nice people, we're friendly, but I had a feeling they felt they had to be different to me. I went in to work the next day as usual, and they were kind of coy. All of a sudden, this one lady said: "I saw your picture in the paper yesterday." "Oh really?" She says: "I didn't know what we should say to you." They thought I was a different person now.

TONY: One of the first couples that won, they were elderly and he always used to go to the corner tavern and have his coupla drinks. After he won, every time he'd go in there for a coupla drinks, everyone expected him to buy the whole place a drink. You can't do this. Rockefeller doesn't go into a cocktail lounge and buy everybody a drink. (Laughs.)

CAROL: The American Dream? That's what we're doing right now. (Laughs.) To me, this is living. We can go golfing whenever we want to and do the things we want to while we're still able. Just where but America could this have been accomplished?

We've always got our eyes open for a new investment. Anything that's gonna pay the best or pay the most.

TONY: I read in the paper about people who believe in reincarnation. I hope there is none. Because I wouldn't want to be born again and get a chance to live a lesser life. I'm so happy with the life that we've had. If I had to do it all over again, I would want it the same way.

William Gothard

A casual encounter during a Los Angeles–Chicago flight; an ensuing conversation at O'Hare International Airport while he's between planes.

"I'm a twenty-seven-year-old white American male. I'm a corporate

attorney. Spent most of my life in New York, went to high school in Ohio, college in California, and practice in Los Angeles. And I'm overweight." (*Laughs.*)

I'm a member of the nomadic middle class. My family moved seven times since I was born. Longest I've been in one place was eight years. My father is of the new managerial class, unaffiliated. He never worked for a company. He was a school administrator, an animal unto himself. You go from place to place, like a minister. To a bigger congregation or a bigger school district. I come from a family of Methodist ministers. (Laughs.) Middle-class suburban Methodist rather than the Bible-thumping, Gospel-singing Methodists.

We have no roots. Our heritage is either German, Dutch, or English. The furthest I can trace back is my great-grandfather. I don't know if he was born here. He ministered to the Oneida Indians. We still have an Indian bible. He died around 1907. That's all I know about my heritage.

We would never sit down at the dinner table and talk about what it means to be an American. When I was a child, my parents would take me around America. We would go to Gettysburg. I was a big Civil War buff. I visited forty-six states. I like to live the American experience. It's not one experience, it's many. There's so much here. Very few people have found the American Dream. When you stop searching, you no longer have it.

I admire my father. The reason he ceased being an administrator and became a professor is, it wasn't a joy any more. He was tired of politics, he was tired of the changing attitude among teachers.

He was a school administrator in Levittown, the great American Dream town at the end of the war. On the GI Bill, you could buy a home you could not afford before. Young people could settle down. It was like your Model T's. You could have it in any color, just as long as it's black. It was the beginning of assembly-line homes.

We lived in Garden City, the upper-crusty part. The quality of education there was super. When I was in fifth grade, I was first clarinet in the school band. That was hot tuna in those days. (Laughs.)

Talk about Middle America. My father was an Eagle Scout who went to the National Jamboree in '39. He's in Kiwanis and president of Rotary. My brother was an Eagle Scout with a Bronze Palm and five merit badges past Eagle. When I was young, I was very overweight and struggled on these hikes. I *had* to make Eagle, it was an inner thing. I did, got twenty merit badges past Eagle, was president of the Key Club, and an acolyte in the church. It was no mean trick for me. I lost thirty pounds running around the block. (Laughs.) I felt it was important to my family, that's why I did it. My mother was president of faculty wives.

I've been blessed with a wonderful set of parents. We were never wealthy, but I was sent to some very good schools. When my father was making thirty thousand dollars a year, I was at Stanford and Columbia. I appreciate how much they had to sacrifice for me.

One of my big gripes is the crisis of the middle class today. If you're poor or minority, you get preferential treatment, financial aid to go to school. If you're rich, Iacocca's kid, it doesn't matter. But for the professional middle class, paying for a good education is just out of sight.

I really love America, though—I hate to say it—I have a foreign car. (Laughs.) They're built better. There's pride in craftmanship. I'd like less dependence upon government to solve our problems. What I want is the same spirit that made this country what it is.

I think we have the best political system, bar none. I see problems. I have never felt discrimination because I am white, middle-class, and male. Now it's the other way around. We're at the bottom of the list.

America became strong because people, out of their own initiative, have succeeded. Sons and daughters of fishmongers and tailors became lawyers, doctors, and corporate presidents. They drove themselves. We live in a socially mobile society where you can succeed if you have the drive. I realize if you were born in Watts or Harlem, the cards are stacked against you. You got a long way to go. Yet Jews have prospered in this country. They have a tradition of education, of upward mobility. The Irish and the Italians have made it too. With Hispanics and blacks, it's harder to melt in as easily. But in certain of these ethnic groups, you don't have this initiative. The primary thing is survival.

I believe if anyone is blessed with enough drive, enough parental guidance, he could become president of the United States. A little far-fetched, perhaps. (Laughs.) He could become a lawyer. (Laughs.)

Los Angeles, where I work, typifies in one city the best and the worst of American life. The home of franchise foods, home of the automobile society, home of Hollywood, your fantasia, your ultimate American Dream. Without roots.

I want to get married, have two kids, two cars, two color TV sets, and live in the suburbs outside Los Angeles. But I want to maintain my individuality. At the firm, I hate to be called just by my last name, Gothard, or just by my proper first name, William. I like Bill. As a professional person, in front of a client, I'd want my secretary to call me Mr. Gothard.

I'm very optimistic about this country. I've never lived through the depression. That might have sobered my outlook. I've never had a silver spoon in my mouth, but I've never known hunger. If I had, I might be less optimistic. I'm like Merrill Lynch.⁰ I'm bullish on America. (Laughs.)

Merrill Lynch   Stock brokerage firm, Merrill Lynch, Pierce, Fenner & Smith, whose motto is "Merrill Lynch is bullish [i.e., optimistic] on America."

Joan Didion

A native Californian, Joan Didion was born in Sacramento in 1934 and was educated at the University of California at Berkeley. She received *Vogue*'s Prix de Paris in 1956, the year of her graduation, and in 1963 was awarded the Bread Loaf Fellowship in fiction. Her books, articles, and reviews have earned her a distinguished reputation as a writer of fiction and as an essayist. She has been an associate feature editor of *Vogue* and has taught creative writing at Berkeley. She has written three novels: *Run River* (1963); *Play It as It Lays* (1970), for which she also wrote the screenplay; and *A Book of Common Prayer* (1975). She was coauthor with her husband, John Gregory Dunne, of the screenplay for *A Star Is Born* (1976). Her nonfiction includes two collections of essays—*Slouching Toward Bethlehem* (1968), from which we reprint the selection below, and *The White Album* (1979)—and *Salvador* (1983), based upon her travels in El Salvador in 1982.

Some Dreamers of the Golden Dream

This is a story about love and death in the golden land, and begins with the country. The San Bernardino Valley lies only an hour east of Los Angeles by the San Bernardino Freeway but is in certain ways an alien place: not the coastal California of the subtropical twilights and the soft westerlies off the Pacific but a harsher California, haunted by the Mojave just beyond the mountains, devastated by the hot dry Santa Ana wind that comes down through the passes at 100 miles an hour and whines through the eucalyptus windbreaks and works on the nerves. October is the bad month for the wind, the month when breathing is difficult and the hills blaze up spontaneously. There has been no rain since April. Every voice seems a scream. It is the season of suicide and divorce and prickly dread, wherever the wind blows.

The Mormons settled this ominous country, and then they abandoned it, but by the time they left the first orange tree had been planted and for the next hundred years the San Bernardino Valley would draw a kind of people who imagined they might live among the talismanic fruit and prosper in the dry air, people who brought with them Midwestern ways of building and cooking and praying and who tried to graft those ways upon the land. The graft took in curious ways. This is the California where it is possible to live and die without ever eating an artichoke, without ever meeting a Catholic or a Jew. This is the California where it is easy to Dial-A-Devotion, but hard to buy a book. This is the country in which a belief in the literal interpretation of Genesis has slipped imperceptibly into a belief in the literal interpretation of *Double Indemnity,*[0] the country of the teased hair and the Capris and the girls for whom all life's promise comes down to a waltz-length white wedding dress and the birth of a Kimberly or a Sherry or a Debbi and a Tijuana divorce and a return to hairdressers' school. "We were just crazy kids," they say without regret, and look to the future. The future always looks good in the golden land, because no one remembers the past. Here is where the hot wind blows and the old ways do not seem relevant, where the divorce rate is double the national average and where one person in every thirty-eight lives in a trailer. Here is the last stop for all those who come from somewhere else, for all those who drifted away from the cold and the past and the old ways. Here is where they are trying to find a new life style, trying to find it in the only places they know to look: the movies and the newspapers. The case of Lucille Marie Maxwell Miller is a tabloid monument to that new life style.

Imagine Banyan Street first, because Banyan is where it happened. The way to Banyan is to drive west from San Bernardino out Foothill Boulevard, Route 66: past the Santa Fe switching yards, the Forty Winks Motel. Past the motel that is nineteen stucco tepees: "SLEEP IN A WIGWAM—GET MORE FOR YOUR WAMPUM." Past Fontana Drag City and the Fontana Church of the Nazarene and the Pit Stop A Go-Go; past Kaiser Steel, through Cucamonga, out to the Kapu Kai Restaurant-Bar and Coffee Shop, at the corner of Route 66 and Carnelian Avenue. Up Carnelian Avenue from the Kapu Kai, which means "Forbidden Seas," the subdivision flags whip in the harsh wind. "HALF-ACRE RANCHES! SNACK BARS! TRAVERTINE ENTRIES! $95 DOWN." It is the trail of an intention gone haywire, the flotsam of the New California. But after a while the signs thin out on Carnelian Avenue, and the houses are no longer the bright pastels of the Springtime Home owners but the faded bungalows of the people who grow a few grapes and keep a few chickens out here, and then the hill gets steeper and the road climbs and even the bungalows are few, and here—desolate, roughly surfaced, lined with eucalyptus and lemon groves—is Banyan Street.

Like so much of this country, Banyan suggests something curious and unnatural. The lemon groves are sunken, down a three- or four-foot retaining wall, so that one looks directly into their dense foliage, too lush, unsettlingly glossy, the greenery of nightmare; the fallen eucalyptus bark is too dusty, a place for snakes to breed. The stones look not like natural stones but like the rubble of some unmentioned upheaval. There are smudge pots, and a closed cistern. To one side of Banyan there is the flat valley, and to the other the San Bernardino Mountains, a dark mass looming too

---

Double Indemnity A novel by James Cain—and later a famous film—whose plot involves a wife's scheme to arrange the murder of her husband, making the death look like an accident in order to profit from the provision in his life insurance policy which pays double indemnity in case of accidental death.

high, too fast, nine, ten, eleven thousand feet, right there above the lemon groves. At midnight on Banyan Street there is no light at all, and no sound except the wind in the eucalpytus and a muffled barking of dogs. There may be a kennel somewhere, or the dogs may be coyotes.

Banyan Street was the route Lucille Miller took home from the twenty-four-hour Mayfair Market on the night of October 7, 1964, a night when the moon was dark and the wind was blowing and she was out of milk, and Banyan Street was where, at about 12:20 A.M., her 1964 Volkswagen came to a sudden stop, caught fire, and began to burn. For an hour and fifteen minutes Lucille Miller ran up and down Banyan calling for help, but no cars passed and no help came. At three o'clock that morning, when the fire had been put out and the California Highway Patrol officers were completing their report, Lucille Miller was still sobbing and incoherent, for her husband had been asleep in the Volkswagen. "What will I tell the children, when there's nothing left, nothing left in the casket," she cried to the friend called to comfort her. "How can I tell them there's nothing left?"

In fact there was something left, and a week later it lay in the Draper Mortuary Chapel in a closed bronze coffin blanketed with pink carnations. Some 200 mourners heard Elder Robert E. Denton of the Seventh-Day Adventist Church of Ontario speak of "the temper of fury that has broken out among us." For Gordon Miller, he said, there would be "no more death, no more heartaches, no more misunderstandings." Elder Ansel Bristol mentioned the "peculiar" grief of the hour. Elder Fred Jensen asked "what shall it profit a man, if he shall gain the whole world, and lose his own soul?" A light rain fell, a blessing in a dry season, and a female vocalist sang "Safe in the Arms of Jesus." A tape recording of the service was made for the widow, who was being held without bail in the San Bernardino County Jail on a charge of first-degree murder.

Of course she came from somewhere else, came off the prairie in search of something she had seen in a movie or heard on the radio, for this is a Southern California story. She was born on January 17, 1930, in Winnipeg, Manitoba, the only child of Gordon and Lily Maxwell, both schoolteachers and both dedicated to the Seventh-Day Adventist Church, whose members observe the Sabbath on Saturday, believe in an apocalyptic Second Coming, have a strong missionary tendency, and, if they are strict, do not smoke, drink, eat meat, use makeup, or wear jewelry, including wedding rings. By the time Lucille Maxwell enrolled at Walla Walla College in College Place, Washington, the Adventist school where her parents then taught, she was an eighteen-year-old possessed of unremarkable good looks and remarkable high spirits. "Lucille wanted to see the world," her father would say in retrospect, "and I guess she found out."

The high spirits did not seem to lend themselves to an extended course of study at Walla Walla College, and in the spring of 1949 Lucille Maxwell met and married Gordon ("Cork") Miller, a twenty-four-year-old graduate of Walla Walla and of the university of Oregon dental school, then stationed at Fort Lewis as a medical officer. "Maybe you could say it was love at first sight," Mr. Maxwell recalls. "Before they were ever formally introduced, he sent Lucille a dozen and a half roses with a card that said even if she didn't come out on a date with him, he hoped she'd find the roses pretty anyway." The Maxwells remember their daughter as a "radiant" bride.

Unhappy marriages so resemble one another that we do not need to know too much about the course of this one. There may or may not have been trouble on Guam, where Cork and Lucille Miller lived while he finished his Army duty. There may or may not have been problems in the small Oregon town where he first set up private practice. There appears to have been some disappointment about their move to California: Cork Miller had told friends that he wanted to become a doctor, that he was unhappy as a dentist and planned to enter the Seventh-Day Adventist College of Medical Evangelists at Loma Linda, a few miles south of San Bernardino. Instead he bought a dental practice in the west end of San Bernardino County, and the family settled there, in a modest house on the kind of street where there are always tricycles and revolving credit and dreams about bigger houses, better streets. That was 1957. By the summer of 1964 they had achieved the bigger house on the better street and the familiar accouterments of a family on its way up: the $30,000 a year, the three children for the Christmas card, the picture window, the family room, the newspaper photographs that showed "Mrs. Gordon Miller, Ontario Heart Fund Chairman. . . ." They were paying the familiar price for it. And they had reached the familiar season of divorce.

It might have been anyone's bad summer, anyone's siege of heat and nerves and migraine and money worries, but this one began particularly early and particularly badly. On April 24 an old friend, Elaine Hayton, died suddenly; Lucille Miller had seen her only the night before. During the month of May, Cork Miller was hospitalized briefly with a bleeding ulcer, and his usual reserve deepened into depression. He told his accountant that he was "sick of looking at open mouths," and threatened suicide. By July 8, the conventional tensions of love and money had reached the conventional impasse in the new house on the acre lot of 8488 Bella Vista, and Lucille Miller filed for divorce. Within a month, however, the Millers seemed reconciled. They saw a marriage counselor. They talked about a fourth child. It seemed that the marriage had reached the traditional truce, the point at which so many resign themselves to cutting both their losses and their hopes.

But the Millers' season of trouble was not to end that easily. October 7 began as a commonplace enough day, one of those days that sets the teeth on edge with its tedium, its small frustrations. The temperature reached 102° in San Bernardino that afternoon, and the Miller children were home from school because of Teachers' Institute. There was ironing to be dropped off. There was a trip to pick up a prescription for Nembutal, a trip to a self-service dry cleaner. In the early evening, an unpleasant accident with the Volkswagen: Cork Miller hit and killed a German shepherd, and afterward said that his head felt "like it had a Mack truck on it." It was something he often said. As of that evening Cork Miller was $63,479 in debt, including the $29,637 mortgage on the new house, a debt load which seemed oppressive to him. He was a man who wore his responsibilities uncasily, and complained of migraine headaches almost constantly.

He ate alone that night, from a TV tray in the living room. Later the Millers watched John Forsythe and Senta Berger in *See How They Run,* and when the movie ended, about eleven, Cork Miller suggested that they go out for milk. He wanted some hot chocolate. He took a blanket and pillow from the couch and climbed into the passenger seat of the Volkswagen. Lucille Miller remembers reaching over to lock his door as she backed down the driveway. By the time she left the Mayfair Market, and long before they reached Banyan Street, Cork Miller appeared to be asleep.

There is some confusion in Lucille Miller's mind about what happened between 12:30 A.M., when the fire broke out, and 1:50 A.M., when it was reported. She says that she was driving east on Banyan Street at about 35 m.p.h. when she felt the Volkswagen pull sharply to the right. The next thing she knew the car was on the embankment, quite near the edge of the retaining wall, and flames were shooting up behind her. She does not remember jumping out. She does remember prying up a stone with which she broke the window next to her husband, and then scrambling down the retaining wall to try to find a stick. "I don't know how I was going to push him out," she says. "I just thought if I had a stick, I'd push him out." She could not, and after a while she ran to the intersection of Banyan and Carnelian Avenue. There are no houses at that corner, and almost no traffic. After one car had passed without stopping. Lucille Miller ran back down Banyan toward the burning Volkswagen. She did not stop, but she slowed down, and in the flames she could see her husband. He was, she said, "just black."

At the first house up Sapphire Avenue, half a mile from the Volkswagen, Lucille Miller finally found help. There Mrs. Robert Swenson called the sheriff, and then, at Lucille Miller's request, she called Harold Lance, the Millers' lawyer and their close friend. When Harold Lance arrived he took Lucille Miller home to his wife, Joan. Twice Harold Lance and Lucille Miller returned to Banyan Street and talked to the Highway Patrol officers. A third time Harold Lance returned alone, and when he came back he said to Lucille Miller, "O.K. . . . you don't talk any more."

When Lucille Miller was arrested the next afternoon, Sandy Slagle was with her. Sandy Slagle was the intense, relentlessly loyal medical student who used to baby-sit for the Millers, and had been living as a member of the family since she graduated from high school in 1959. The Millers took her away from a difficult home situation, and she thinks of Lucille Miller not only as "more or less a mother or a sister" but as "the most wonderful character" she has ever known. On the night of the accident, Sandy Slagle was in her dormitory at Loma Linda University, but Lucille Miller called her early in the morning and asked her to come home. The doctor was there when Sandy Slagle arrived, giving Lucille Miller an injection of Nembutal. "She was crying as she was going under," Sandy Slagle recalls. "Over and over she'd say, 'Sandy, all the hours I spent trying to save him and now what are they trying to *do* to me?' "

At 1:30 that afternoon, Sergeant William Paterson and Detectives Charles Callahan and Joseph Karr of the Central Homicide Division arrived at 8488 Bella Vista. "One of them appeared at the bedroom door," Sandy Slagle remembers, "and said to Lucille, 'You've got ten minutes to get dressed or we'll take you as you are.' She was in her nightgown, you know, so I tried to get her dressed."

Sandy Slagle tells the story now as if by rote, and her eyes do not waver. "So I had her panties and bra on her and they opened the door again, so I got some Capris on her, you know, and a scarf." Her voice drops. "And then they just took her."

The arrest took place just twelve hours after the first report that there had been an accident on Banyan Street, a rapidity which would later prompt Lucille Miller's attorney to say that the entire case was an instance of trying to justify a reckless arrest. Actually what first caused the detectives who arrived on Banyan Street toward dawn that morning to give the accident more than routine attention were certain apparent physical inconsistencies. While Lucille Miller had said that she was driving about 35 m.p.h. when the car swerved to a stop, an examination of the cooling Volkswagen showed that it was in low gear, and that the parking rather than the driving lights were on. The front wheels, moreover, did not seem to be in exactly the position that Lucille Miller's description of the accident would suggest, and the right rear wheel was dug in deep, as if it had been spun in place. It seemed curious to the detectives, too, that a sudden stop from 35 m.p.h.—the same jolt which was presumed to have knocked over a gasoline can in the back seat and somehow started the fire—should have left two milk cartons upright on the back floorboard, and the remains of a Polaroid camera box lying apparently undisturbed on the back seat.

No one, however, could be expected to give a precise account of what did and did not happen in a moment of terror, and none of these inconsistencies seemed in themselves incontrovertible evidence of criminal intent. But they did interest the Sheriff's Office, as did Gordon Miller's apparent unconsciousness at the time of the accident, and the length of time it had taken Lucille Miller to get help. Something, moreover, struck the investigators as wrong about Harold Lance's attitude when he came back to Banyan Street the third time and found the investigation by no means over. "The way Lance was acting," the prosecuting attorney said later, "they thought maybe they'd hit a nerve."

And so it was that on the morning of October 8, even before the doctor had come to give Lucille Miller an injection to calm her, the San Bernardino County Sheriff's Office was trying to construct another version of what might have happened between 12:30 and 1:50 A.M. The hypothesis they would eventually present was based on the somewhat tortuous premise that Lucille Miller had undertaken a plan which failed: a plan to stop the car on the lonely road, spread gasoline over her presumably drugged husband, and, with a stick on the accelerator, gently "walk" the Volkswagen over the embankment, where it would tumble four feet down the retaining wall into the lemon grove and almost certainly explode. If this happened, Lucille Miller might then have somehow negotiated the two miles up Carnelian to Bella Vista in time to be home when the accident was discovered. This plan went awry, according to the Sheriff's Office hypothesis, when the car would not go over the rise of the embankment. Lucille Miller might have panicked then—after she had killed the engine the third or fourth time, say, out there on the dark road with the gasoline already spread and the dogs baying and the wind blowing and the unspeakable apprehension that a pair of headlights would suddenly light up Banyan Street and expose her there—and set the fire herself.

Although this version accounted for some of the physical evidence—the car in low because it had been started from a dead stop, the parking lights on because she could not do what needed doing without some light, a rear wheel spun in repeated attempts to get the car over the embankment, the milk cartons upright because there had been no sudden stop—it did not seem on its own any more or less credible than Lucille Miller's own story. Moreover, some of the physical evidence did seem to support her story: a nail in a front tire, a nine-pound rock found in the car, presumably the one with which she had broken the window in an attempt to save her husband. Within a few days an autopsy had established that Gordon Miller was alive when he burned, which did not particularly help the State's case, and that he had enough Nembutal and Sandoptal in his blood to put the average person to sleep, which did: on the other hand Gordon Miller habitually took both Nembutal and Fiorinal (a common headache prescription which contains Sandoptal), and had been ill besides.

It was a spotty case, and to make it work at all the State was going to have to find a motive. There was talk of unhappiness, talk of another man. That kind of motive, during the next few weeks, was what they set out to establish. They set out to find it in accountants' ledgers and double-indemnity clauses and motel registers, set out to determine what might move a woman who believed in all the promises of the middle class—a woman who had been chairman of the Heart Fund and who always knew a reasonable little dressmaker and who had come out of the bleak wild of prairie fundamentalism to find what she imagined to be the good life—what should drive such a woman to sit on a street called Bella Vista and look out her new picture window into the empty California sun and calculate how to burn her husband alive in a Volkswagen. They found the wedge they wanted closer at hand than they might have at first expected, for, as testimony would reveal later at the trial, it seemed that in December of 1963 Lucille Miller had begun an affair with the husband of one of her friends, a man whose daughter called her "Auntie Lucille," a man who might have seemed to have the gift for people and money and the good life that Cork Miller so noticeably lacked. The man was Arthwell Hayton, a well-known San Bernardino attorney and at one time a member of the district attorney's staff.

In some ways it was the conventional clandestine affair in a place like San Bernardino, a place where little is bright or graceful, where it is routine to misplace the future and easy to start looking for it in bed. Over the seven weeks that it would take to try Lucille Miller for murder, Assistant District Attorney Don A. Turner and defense attorney Edward P. Foley would between them unfold a curiously predictable story. There were the falsified motel registrations. There were the lunch dates, the afternoon drives in Arthwell Hayton's red Cadillac convertible. There were the interminable discussions of the wronged partners. There were the confidantes ("I knew everything," Sandy Slagle would insist fiercely later. "I knew every time, places, everything") and there were the words remembered from bad magazine stories ("Don't kiss me, it will trigger things," Lucille Miller remembered telling Arthwell Hayton in the parking lot of Harold's Club in Fontana after lunch one day) and there were the notes, the sweet exchanges: "Hi Sweetie Pie! You are my cup of tea! ! Happy Birthday—you don't look a day over 29! ! Your baby, Arthwell."

And, toward the end, there was the acrimony. It was April 24, 1964, when Arthwell Hayton's wife, Elaine, died suddenly, and nothing good happened after that. Arthwell Hayton had taken his cruiser, *Captain's Lady*, over to Catalina that weekend; he called home at nine o'clock Friday night, but did not talk to his wife because Lucille Miller answered the telephone and said that Elaine was showering. The next morning the Haytons' daughter found her mother in bed, dead. The newspapers reported the death as accidental, perhaps the result of an allergy to hair spray. When Arthwell Hayton flew home from Catalina that weekend, Lucille Miller met him at the airport, but the finish had already been written.

It was in the breakup that the affair ceased to be in the conventional mode and began to resemble instead the novels of James M. Cain, the movies of the late 1930's, all the dreams in which violence and threats and blackmail are made to seem commonplaces of middle-class life. What was most startling about the case that the State of California was preparing against Lucille Miller was something that had nothing to do with law at all, something that never appeared in the eight-column afternoon headlines but was always there between them: the revelation that the dream was teaching the dreamers how to live. Here is Lucille Miller talking to her lover sometime in the early summer of 1964, after he had indicated that, on the advice of his minister, he did not intend to see her any more: "First, I'm going to go to that dear pastor of yours and tell him a few things. . . . When I do tell him that, you won't be in the Redlands Church any more. . . . Look, Sonny Boy, if you think your reputation is going to be ruined, your life won't be worth two cents." Here is Arthwell Hayton, to Lucille Miller: "I'll go to Sheriff Frank Bland and tell him some things that I know about you until you'll wish you'd never heard of Arthwell Hayton." For an affair between a Seventh-Day Adventist dentist's wife and a Seventh-Day Adventist personal-injury lawyer, it seems a curious kind of dialogue.

"Boy, I could get that little boy coming and going," Lucille Miller later confided to Erwin Sprengle, a Riverside contractor who was a business partner of Arthwell Hayton's and a friend to both the lovers. (Friend or no, on this occasion he happened to have an induction coil attached to his telephone in order to tape Lucille Miller's call.) "And he hasn't got one thing on me that he can prove. I mean, I've got concrete—he has nothing concrete." In the same taped conversation with Erwin Sprengle, Lucille Miller mentioned a tape that she herself had surreptitiously made, months before, in Arthwell Hayton's car.

"I said to him, I said 'Arthwell, I just feel like I'm being used.' . . . He started sucking his thumb and he said 'I love you. . . . This isn't something that happened yesterday. I'd marry you tomorrow if I could. I don't love Elaine.' He'd love to hear that played back, wouldn't he?"

"Yeah," drawled Sprengle's voice on the tape. "That would be just a little incriminating, wouldn't it?"

"Just a *little* incriminating," Lucille Miller agreed. "It really *is.*"

Later on the tape, Sprengle asked where Cork Miller was.

"He took the children down to the church."

"You didn't go?"

"No."

"You're naughty."

It was all, moreover, in the name of "love"; everyone involved placed a magical faith in the efficacy of the very word. There was the significance that Lucille Miller saw in Arthwell's saying that he "loved" her, that he did not "love" Elaine. There was Arthwell insisting, later, at the trial, that he had never said it, that he may have "whispered sweet nothings in her ear" (as her defense hinted that he had whispered in many ears), but he did not remember bestowing upon her the special seal, saying the word, declaring "love." There was the summer evening when Lucille Miller and Sandy Slagle followed Arthwell Hayton down to his new boat in its mooring at Newport Beach and untied the lines with Arthwell aboard, Arthwell and a girl with whom he later testified he was drinking hot chocolate and watching television. "I did that on purpose," Lucille Miller told Erwin Sprengle later, "to save myself from letting my heart do something crazy."

January 11, 1965, was a bright warm day in Southern California, the kind of day when Catalina floats on the Pacific horizon and the air smells of orange blossoms and it is a long way from the bleak and difficult East, a long way from the cold, a long way from the past. A woman in Hollywood staged an all-night sit-in on the hood of her car to prevent repossession by a finance company. A seventy-year-old pensioner drove his station wagon at five miles an hour past three Gardena poker parlors and emptied three pistols and a twelve-gauge shotgun through their windows, wounding twenty-nine people. "Many young women became prostitutes just to have enough money to play cards," he explained in a note. Mrs. Nick Adams said that she was "not surprised" to hear her husband announce his divorce plans on the Les Crane Show, and, farther north, a sixteen-year-old jumped off the Golden Gate Bridge and lived.

And, in the San Bernardino County Courthouse, the Miller trial opened. The crowds were so bad that the glass courtroom doors were shattered in the crush, and from then on identification disks were issued to the first forty-three spectators in line. The line began forming at 6 A.M., and college girls camped at the courthouse all night, with stores of graham crackers and No-Cal.

All they were doing was picking a jury, those first few days, but the sensational nature of the case had already suggested itself. Early in December there had been an abortive first trial, a trial at which no evidence was ever presented because on the day the jury was seated the San Bernardino *Sun-Telegram* ran an "inside" story quoting Assistant District Attorney Don Turner, the prosecutor, as saying, "We are looking into the circumstances of Mrs. Hayton's death. In view of the current trial concerning the death of Dr. Miller, I do not feel I should comment on Mrs. Hayton's death." It seemed that there had been barbiturates in Elaine Hayton's blood, and there had seemed some irregularity about the way she was dressed on that morning when she was found under the covers, dead. Any doubts about the death at the time, however, had never gotten as far as the Sheriff's Office. "I guess somebody didn't want to rock the boat," Turner said later. "These were prominent people."

Although all of that had not been in the *Sun-Telegram*'s story, an immediate mistrial had been declared. Almost as immediately, there had been another development: Arthwell Hayton had asked newspapermen to an 11 A.M. Sunday morning press conference in his office. There had been television cameras, and flash bulbs popping. "As you gentlemen may know," Hayton had said, striking a note of stiff bonhomie, "there are very often women who become amorous toward their doctor or lawyer. This does not mean on the physician's or lawyer's part that there is any romance toward the patient or client."

"Would you deny that you were having an affair with Mrs. Miller?" a reporter had asked.

"I would deny that there was any romance on my part whatsoever."

It was a distinction he would maintain through all the wearing weeks to come.

So they had come to see Arthwell, these crowds who now milled beneath the dusty palms outside the courthouse, and they had also come to see Lucille, who appeared as a slight, intermittently pretty woman, already pale from lack of sun, a woman who would turn thirty-five before the trial was over and whose tendency toward haggardness was beginning to show, a meticulous woman who insisted, against her lawyer's advice, on coming to court with her hair piled high and lacquered. "I would've been happy if she'd come in with it hanging loose, but Lucille wouldn't do that," her lawyer said. He was Edward P. Foley, a small, emotional Irish Catholic who several times wept in the courtroom. "She has a great honesty, this woman," he added, "but this honesty about her appearance always worked against her."

By the time the trial opened, Lucille Miller's appearance included maternity clothes, for an official examination on December 18 had revealed that she was then three and a half months pregnant, a fact which made picking a jury even more difficult than usual, for Turner was asking the death penalty. "It's unfortunate but there it is," he would say of the pregnancy to each juror in turn, and finally twelve were seated, seven of them women, the youngest forty-one, an assembly of the very peers—housewives, a machinist, a truck driver, a grocery-store manager, a filing clerk—above whom Lucille Miller had wanted so badly to rise.

That was the sin, more than the adultery, which tended to reinforce the one for which she was being tried. It was implicit in both the defense and the prosecution that Lucille Miller was an erring woman, a woman who perhaps wanted too much. But to the prosecution she was not merely a woman who would want a new house and want to go to parties and run up high telephone bills ($1,152 in ten months), but a woman who would go so far as to murder her husband for his $80,000 in insurance, making it appear an accident in order to collect another $40,000 in double indemnity and straight accident policies. To Turner she was a woman who did not want simply her freedom and a reasonable alimony (she could have had that, the defense contended, by going through with her divorce suit), but wanted everything, a woman motivated by "love and greed." She was a "manipulator." She was a "user of people."

To Edward Foley, on the other hand, she was an impulsive woman who "couldn't control her foolish little heart." Where Turner skirted the pregnancy, Foley dwelt upon it, even calling the dead man's mother down from Washington to testify that her son had told her they were going to have another baby because Lucille felt that it would "do much to weld our home again in the pleasant relations that we used to have." Where the prosecution saw a "calculator," the defense saw a "blabbermouth," and in fact

Lucille Miller did emerge as an ingenuous conversationalist. Just as, before her husband's death, she had confided in her friends about her love affair, so she chatted about it after his death, with the arresting sergeant. "Of course Cork lived with it for years, you know," her voice was heard to tell Sergeant Paterson on a tape made the morning after her arrest. "After Elaine died, he pushed the panic button one night and just asked me right out, and that, I think, was when he really—the first time he really faced it." When the sergeant asked why she had agreed to talk to him, against the specific instructions of her lawyers, Lucille Miller said airily, "Oh, I've always been basically quite an honest person. . . . I mean I can put a hat in the cupboard and say it cost ten dollars less, but basically I've always kind of just lived my life the way I wanted to, and if you don't like it you can take off."

The prosecution hinted at men other than Arthwell, and even, over Foley's objections, managed to name one. The defense called Miller suicidal. The prosecution produced experts who said that the Volkswagen fire could not have been accidental. Foley produced witnesses who said that it could have been. Lucille's father, now a junior-high-school teacher in Oregon, quoted Isaiah to reporters: *"Every tongue that shall rise against thee in judgment thou shalt condemn."* "Lucille did wrong, her affair," her mother said judiciously. "With her it was love. But with some I guess it's just passion." There was Debbie, the Millers' fourteen-year-old, testifying in a steady voice about how she and her mother had gone to a supermarket to buy the gasoline can the week before the accident. There was Sandy Slagle, in the courtroom every day, declaring that on at least one occasion Lucille Miller had prevented her husband not only from committing suicide but from committing suicide in such a way that it would appear an accident and ensure the double-indemnity payment. There was Wenche Berg, the pretty twenty-seven-year-old Norwegian governess to Arthwell Hayton's children, testifying that Arthwell had instructed her not to allow Lucille Miller to see or talk to the children.

Two months dragged by, and the headlines never stopped. Southern California's crime reporters were headquartered in San Bernardino for the duration: Howard Hertel from the *Times,* Jim Bennett and Eddy Jo Bernal from the *Herald-Examiner.* Two months in which the Miller trial was pushed off the *Examiner's* front page only by the Academy Award nominations and Stan Laurel's death. And finally, on March 2, after Turner had reiterated that it was a case of "love and greed," and Foley had protested that his client was being tried for adultery, the case went to the jury.

They brought in the verdict, guilty of murder in the first degree, at 4:50 P.M. on March 5. "She didn't do it," Debbie Miller cried, jumping up from the spectators' section. "She didn't *do* it." Sandy Slagle collapsed in her seat and began to scream. "Sandy, for God's sake please *don't,*" Lucille Miller said in a voice that carried across the courtroom, and Sandy Slagle was momentarily subdued. But as the jurors left the courtroom she screamed again: "You're murderers. . . . Every last one of you is a *mur-*

derer." Sheriff's deputies moved in then, each wearing a string tie that read "1965 SHERIFF'S RODEO," and Lucille Miller's father, the sad-faced junior-high-school teacher who believed in the word of Christ and the dangers of wanting to see the world, blew her a kiss off his fingertips.

The California Institution for Women at Frontera, where Lucille Miller is now, lies down where Euclid Avenue turns into country road, not too many miles from where she once lived and shopped and organized the Heart Fund Ball. Cattle graze across the road, and Rainbirds sprinkle the alfalfa. Frontera has a softball field and tennis courts, and looks as if it might be a California junior college, except that the trees are not yet high enough to conceal the concertina wire around the top of the Cyclone fence. On visitors' day there are big cars in the parking area, big Buicks and Pontiacs that belong to grandparents and sisters and fathers (not many of them belong to husbands), and some of them have bumper stickers that say "SUPPORT YOUR LOCAL POLICE."

A lot of California murderesses live here, a lot of girls who somehow misunderstood the promise. Don Turner put Sandra Garner here (and her husband in the gas chamber at San Quentin) after the 1959 desert killings known to crime reporters as "the soda-pop murders." Carole Tregoff is here, and has been ever since she was convicted of conspiring to murder Dr. Finch's wife in West Covina, which is not too far from San Bernardino. Carole Tregoff is in fact a nurse's aide in the prison hospital, and might have attended Lucille Miller had her baby been born at Frontera; Lucille Miller chose instead to have it outside, and paid for the guard who stood outside the delivery room in St. Bernardine's Hospital. Debbie Miller came to take the baby home from the hospital, in a white dress with pink ribbons, and Debbie was allowed to choose a name. She named the baby Kimi Kai. The children live with Harold and Joan Lance now, because Lucille Miller will probably spend ten years at Frontera. Don Turner waived his original request for the death penalty (it was generally agreed that he had demanded it only, in Edward Foley's words, "to get anybody with the slightest trace of human kindness in their veins off the jury"), and settled for life imprisonment with the possibility of parole. Lucille Miller does not like it at Frontera, and has had trouble adjusting. "She's going to have to learn humility," Turner says. "She's going to have to use her ability to charm, to manipulate."

The new house is empty now, the house on the street with the sign that says

PRIVATE ROAD
BELLA VISTA
DEAD END

The Millers never did get it landscaped, and weeds grow up around the fieldstone siding. The television aerial has toppled on the roof, and a trash can is stuffed with the debris of family life: a cheap suitcase, a child's game called "Lie Detector." There is a sign on what would have been the lawn, and the sign reads "ESTATE SALE." Edward Foley is trying to get Lucille Miller's case appealed, but there have been delays. "A trial always comes down to a matter of sympathy," Foley says wearily now. "I couldn't create sympathy for her." Everyone is a little weary now, weary and resigned, everyone except Sandy Slagle, whose bitterness is still raw. She lives in an apartment near the medical school in Loma Linda, and studies reports of the case in *True Police Cases* and *Official Detective Stories.* "I'd much rather we not talk about the Hayton business too much," she tells visitors, and she keeps a tape recorder running. "I'd rather talk about Lucille and what a wonderful person she is and how her rights were violated." Harold Lance does not talk to visitors at all. "We don't want to give away what we can sell," he explains pleasantly; an attempt was made to sell Lucille Miller's personal story to *Life,* but *Life* did not want to buy it. In the district attorney's offices they are prosecuting other murders now, and do not see why the Miller trial attracted so much attention. "It wasn't a very interesting murder as murders go," Don Turner says laconically. Elaine Hayton's death is no longer under investigation. "We know everything we want to know," Turner says.

Arthwell Hayton's office is directly below Edward Foley's. Some people around San Bernardino say that Arthwell Hayton suffered; others say that he did not suffer at all. Perhaps he did not, for time past is not believed to have any bearing upon time present or future, out in the golden land where every day the world is born anew. In any case, on October 17, 1965, Arthwell Hayton married again, married his children's pretty governess, Wenche Berg, at a service in the Chapel of the Roses at a retirement village near Riverside. Later the newlyweds were feted at a reception for seventy-five in the dining room of Rose Garden Village. The bridegroom was in black tie, with a white carnation in his buttonhole. The bride wore a long white *peau de soie* dress and carried a shower bouquet of sweetheart roses with stephanotis streamers. A coronet of seed pearls held her illusion veil.

[1966]

Wendell Berry

The selection below comes from *The Gift of Good Land: Further Essays Cultural and Agricultural* (1981). For further information about the author, see page 269.

Home of the Free

I was writing not long ago about a team of Purdue engineers who foresaw that by 2001 practically everything would be done by remote control. The question I asked—because such a "projection" *forces* one to ask it—was, *Where does satisfaction come from?* I concluded that there probably wouldn't be much satisfaction in such a world. There would be a lot of what passes for "efficiency," a lot of "production" and "consumption," but little satisfaction.

What I failed to acknowledge was that this "world of the future" is already established among us, and is growing. Two advertisements that I have lately received from correspondents make this clear, and raise the question about the sources of satisfaction more immediately and urgently than any abstract "projection" can do.

The first is the legend from a John Deere display at Waterloo Municipal Airport:

INTRODUCING SOUND-GARD BODY . . .
A DOWN TO EARTH SPACE CAPSULE.
New Sound-Gard body from John Deere, an "earth space capsule" to protect and encourage the American farmer at his job of being "Breadwinner to a world of families."
Outside: dust, noise, heat, storm, fumes.
Inside: all's quiet, comfortable, safe.
Features include a 4 post Roll Gard, space-age metals, plastics, and fibers to isolate driver from noise, vibration, and jolts. He dials 'inside weather', to his liking . . . he push buttons radio or stereo tape entertainment. He breathes filtered, conditioned air in his pressurized compartment. He has remote control over multi-ton and multi-hookups, with control tower visibility . . . from his scientifically padded seat.

The second is an ad for a condominium housing development:

HOME OF THE FREE.
We do the things you hate. You do the things you like. We mow the lawn, shovel the walks, paint and repair and do all exterior maintenance.
You cross-country ski, play tennis, hike, swim, work out, read or nap. Or advise our permanent maintenance staff as they do the things you hate.

Different as they may seem at first, these two ads make the same appeal, and they represent two aspects of the same problem: the widespread, and still spreading, assumption that we somehow have the right to be set free from anything whatsoever that we "hate" or don't want to do. According to this view, what we want to be set free from are the natural conditions of the world and the necessary work of human life; we do not want to experience temperatures that are the least bit too hot or too cold, or to work in the sun, or be exposed to wind or rain, or come in personal contact with anything describable as dirt, or provide for any of our own needs, or clean up after ourselves. Implicit in all this is the desire to be free of the "hassles" of mortality, to be "safe" from the life cycle. Such freedom and safety are always for sale. It is proposed that if we put all earthly obligations and the rites of passage into the charge of experts and machines, then life will become a permanent holiday.

What these people are really selling is insulation—cushions of technology, "space age" materials, and the menial work of other people—to keep fantasy in and reality out. The condominium ad says flat out that it is addressed to people who "hate" the handwork of household maintenance, and who will enjoy "advising" the people who do it for them; it is addressed, in other words, to those who think themselves too good to do work that other people are not too good to do. But it is a little surprising to realize that the John Deere ad is addressed to farmers who not only hate farming (that is, any physical contact with the ground or the weather or the crops), but also hate tractors, from the "dust," "fumes," "noise, vibration, and jolts" of which they wish to be protected by an "earth space capsule" and a "scientifically padded seat."

Of course, the only real way to get this sort of freedom and safety—to escape the hassles of earthly life—is to die. And what I think we see in these advertisements is an appeal to a desire to be dead that is evidently felt by many people. These ads are addressed to the perfect consumers— the self-consumers, who have found nothing of interest here on earth, nothing to do, and are impatient to be shed of earthly concerns. And so I am at a loss to explain the delay. Why hasn't some super salesman sold every one of these people a coffin—an "earth space capsule" in which they would experience no discomfort or inconvenience whatsoever, would have to do no work that they hate, would be spared all extremes of weather and all noises, fumes, vibrations, and jolts?

I wish it were possible for us to let these living dead bury themselves in the earth space capsules of their choice and think no more about them. The problem is that with their insatiable desire for comfort, convenience, remote control, and the rest of it, they cause an unconscionable amount of trouble for the rest of us, who would like a fair crack at living the rest of our lives within the terms and conditions of the real world. Speaking for myself, I acknowledge that the world, the weather, and the life cycle have caused me no end of trouble, and yet I look forward to putting in another forty or so years with them because they have also given me no end of pleasure and instruction. They interest me. I want to see them thrive on their own terms. I hate to see them abused and interfered with for the comfort and convenience of a lot of spoiled people who presume to "hate" the more necessary kinds of work and all the natural consequences of working outdoors.

When people begin to "hate" the life cycle and to try to live outside it and to escape its responsibilities, then the corpses begin to pile up and to get into the wrong places. One of the laws that the world imposes on us is that everything must be returned to its source to be used again. But one of the first principles of the haters is to violate this law in the name of convenience or efficiency. Because it is "inconvenient" to return bottles to the beverage manufacturers, "dead soldiers" pile up in the road ditches and in the waterways. Because it is "inconvenient" to be responsible for wastes, the rivers are polluted with everything from human excrement to various carcinogens and poisons. Because it is "efficient" (by what standard?) to mass-produce meat and milk in food "factories," the animal manures that once would have fertilized the fields have instead become wastes and pollutants. And so to be "free" of "inconvenience" and "inefficiency" we are paying a high price—which the haters among us are happy to charge to posterity.

And what a putrid (and profitable) use they have made of the idea of freedom! What a tragic evolution has taken place when the inheritors of the Bill of Rights are told, and when some of them believe, that "the home of the free" is where somebody else will do your work!

Let me set beside those advertisements a sentence that I consider a responsible statement about freedom: "To be free is precisely the same thing as to be pious, wise, just and temperate, careful of one's own, abstinent from what is another's, and thence, in fine, magnanimous and brave." That is John Milton. He is speaking out of the mainstream of our culture. Reading his sentence after those advertisements is coming home. His words have an atmosphere around them that a living human can breathe in.

How do you get free in Milton's sense of the word? I don't think you can do it in an earth space capsule or a space space capsule or a capsule of any kind. What Milton is saying is that you can do it only by living in this world as you find it, and by taking responsibility for the consequences of your life in it. And that means doing some chores that, highly objectionable in anybody's capsule, may not be at all unpleasant in the world.

Just a few days ago I finished up one of the heaviest of my spring jobs: hauling manure. On a feed lot I think this must be real drudgery even with modern labor-saving equipment—all that "waste" and no fields to put it on! But instead of a feed lot I have a small farm—what would probably be called a subsistence farm. My labor-saving equipment consists of a team of horses and a forty-year-old manure spreader. We forked the manure on by hand—forty-five loads. I made my back tired and my hands sore, but I got a considerable amount of pleasure out of it. Everywhere I spread that manure I knew it was needed. What would have been a nuisance in a feed lot was an opportunity and a benefit here. I enjoyed seeing it go out onto the ground. I was working some two-year-olds in the spreader for the first time, and I enjoyed that—mostly. And, since there were no noises, fumes, or vibrations the loading times were socially pleasant. I had some help from neighbors, from my son, and, toward the end, from my daughter who arrived home well rested from college. She helped me load, and then read *The Portrait of a Lady* while I drove up the hill to empty the spreader. I don't think many young women have read Henry James while forking manure. I enjoyed working with my daughter, and I enjoyed wondering what Henry James would have thought of her.

Isaac Bashevis Singer

Isaac Bashevis Singer, who won the Nobel Prize for literature in 1978, is the most popular living Yiddish writer and is also becoming one of the most popular living American writers. He has been a steady contributor to the Yiddish *Jewish Daily Forward* since he arrived in New York City in 1935, and in recent years he also has become a frequent contributor to *The New Yorker.* He still writes in Yiddish, his childhood language ("A writer has to write in his own language or not at all"), but by now he is almost always involved in the translation of his own work ("I do not exaggerate when I say that English has become my 'second original language' ").

Singer was born in Poland in 1904, the grandson of two rabbis, the son of a Hasidic scholar. He himself received a traditional Jewish education and for a while studied at a rabbinical seminary, but he began to doubt "not the power of God, but all the traditions and dogmas." As a result, he disappointed family expectations and instead followed the example of his older brother to become a secular writer. He took a job as proofreader for a Yiddish literary journal in Warsaw. By 1926 Singer began to publish stories and reviews. Then in 1935 he followed his brother to New York City, where he still lives, on the upper West Side of Manhattan.

Success came with the English translation of his 1945 novel, *The Family Moskat.* Other novels include the two-volume *The Manor* (1967) and *Shosha* (1978), but he is best known for his short stories. Collections include *Gimpel the Fool* (1957), *The Spinoza of Market Street* (1957), *The Seance* (1968), *Passions* (1976), and *Collected Short Stories of Isaac Bashevis Singer* (1982). *In My Father's Court* (1966), *A Day of Pleasure: Stories of a Boy Growing Up in Warsaw* (1969), and *A Little Boy in Search of God; Mysticism in a Personal Light* (1976) are mainly autobiographical. Singer has also written children's stories, and in 1973 he made his playwriting debut with an adaptation of *The Manor,* produced by the Yale Repertory Theater.

But primarily Singer is an old-fashioned storyteller. Many of his stories, set in the shtetls and ghettos of prewar Poland, draw heavily on Jewish legend and folklore and are peopled with witches and ghosts and demons. An increasing number now deal with life in the United States and are set in contemporary New York. "Because I have now lived in this country longer than in Poland," he says, "I have developed roots here too." "The Son from America," which we reprint below, tells of an encounter between these two cultures. It first appeared in *The New Yorker* and was later reprinted in the short-story collection *A Crown of Feathers* (1970), for which he won the National Book Award. The translation is by the author and Dorothea Straus.

The Son from America

The village of Lentshin was tiny—a sandy marketplace where the peasants of the area met once a week. It was surrounded by little huts with thatched roofs or shingles green with moss. The chimneys looked like pots. Between the huts there were fields, where the owners planted vegetables or pastured their goats.

In the smallest of these huts lived old Berl, a man in his eighties, and his wife, who was called Berlcha (wife of Berl). Old Berl was one of the Jews who had been driven from their villages in Russia and had settled in Poland. In Lentshin, they mocked the mistakes he made while praying aloud. He spoke with a sharp "r." He was short, broad-shouldered, and had a small white beard, and summer and winter he wore a sheepskin hat, a padded cotton jacket, and stout boots. He walked slowly, shuffling his feet. He had a half acre of field, a cow, a goat, and chickens.

The couple had a son, Samuel, who had gone to America forty years ago. It was said in Lentshin that he became a millionaire there. Every month, the Lentshin letter carrier brought old Berl a money order and a letter that no one could read because many of the words were English. How much money Samuel sent his parents remained a secret. Three times a year, Berl and his wife went on foot to Zakroczym and cashed the money orders there. But they never seemed to use the money. What for? The garden, the cow, and the goat provided most of their needs. Besides, Berlcha sold chickens and eggs, and from these there was enough to buy flour for bread.

No one cared to know where Berl kept the money that his son sent him. There were no thieves in Lentshin. The hut consisted of one room, which contained all their belongings: the table, the shelf for meat, the shelf for milk foods, the two beds, and the clay oven. Sometimes the chickens roosted in the woodshed and sometimes, when it was cold, in a coop near the oven. The goat, too, found shelter inside when the weather was bad. The more prosperous villagers had kerosene lamps, but Berl and his wife did not believe in newfangled gadgets. What was wrong with a wick in a dish of oil? Only for the Sabbath would Berlcha buy three tallow candles at the store. In summer, the couple got up at sunrise and retired with the chickens. In the long winter evenings, Berlcha spun flax at her spinning wheel and Berl sat beside her in the silence of those who enjoy their rest.

Once in a while when Berl came home from the synagogue after evening prayers, he brought news to his wife. In Warsaw there were strikers who demanded that the czar abdicate. A heretic by the name of Dr. Herzl had come up with the idea that Jews should settle again in Palestine. Berlcha listened and shook her bonneted head. Her face was yellowish and wrinkled like a cabbage leaf. There were bluish sacks under her eyes. She was half deaf. Berl had to repeat each word he said to her. She would say, "The things that happen in the big cities!"

Here in Lentshin nothing happened except usual events: a cow gave birth to a calf, a young couple had a circumcision party, or a girl was born and there was no party. Occasionally, someone died. Lentshin had no cemetery, and the corpse had to be taken to Zakroczym. Actually, Lentshin had become a village with few young people. The young men left for Zakroczym, for Nowy Dwor, for Warsaw, and sometimes for the United States. Like Samuel's, their letters were illegible, the Yiddish mixed with the languages of the countries where they were now living. They sent photographs in which the men wore top hats and the women fancy dresses like squiresses.

Berl and Berlcha also received such photographs. But their eyes were failing and neither he nor she had glasses. They could barely make out the pictures. Samuel had sons and daughters with Gentile names—and grandchildren who had married and had their own offspring. Their names were so strange that Berl and Berlcha could never remember them. But what difference do names make? America was far, far away on the other side of the ocean, at the edge of the world. A Talmud teacher who came to Lentshin had said that Americans walk with their heads down and their feet up. Berl and Berlcha could not grasp this. How was it possible? But since the teacher said so it must be true. Berlcha pondered for some time and then she said, "One can get accustomed to everything."

And so it remained. From too much thinking—God forbid—one may lose one's wits.

One Friday morning, when Berlcha was kneading the dough for the Sabbath loaves, the door opened and a nobleman entered. He was so tall that he had to bend down to get through the door. He wore a beaver hat and a cloak bordered with fur. He was followed by Chazkel, the coachman from Zakroczym, who carried two leather valises with brass locks. In astonishment Berlcha raised her eyes.

The nobleman looked around and said to the coachman in Yiddish, "Here it is." He took out a silver ruble and paid him. The coachman tried to hand him change but he said, "You can go now."

When the coachman closed the door, the nobleman said, "Mother, it's me, your son Samuel—Sam."

Berlcha heard the words and her legs grew numb. Her hands, to which pieces of dough were sticking, lost their power. The nobleman hugged her, kissed her forehead, both her cheeks. Berlcha began to cackle like a hen, "My son!" At that moment Berl came in from the woodshed, his arms piled with logs. The goat followed him. When he saw a nobleman kissing his wife, Berl dropped the wood and exclaimed, "What is this?"

The nobleman let go of Berlcha and embraced Berl. "Father!"

For a long time Berl was unable to utter a sound. He wanted to recite holy words that he had read in the Yiddish Bible, but he could remember nothing. Then he asked, "Are you Samuel?"

"Yes, Father, I am Samuel."

"Well, peace be with you." Berl grasped his son's hand. He was still not sure that he was not being fooled. Samuel wasn't as tall and heavy as this man, but then Berl reminded himself that Samuel was only fifteen years old when he had left home. He must have grown in that faraway country. Berl asked, "Why didn't you let us know you were coming?"

"Didn't you receive my cable?" Samuel asked.

Berl did not know what a cable was.

Berlcha had scraped the dough from her hands and enfolded her son. He kissed her again and asked, "Mother, didn't you receive a cable?"

"What? If I lived to see this, I am happy to die," Berlcha said, amazed by her own words. Berl, too, was amazed. These were just the words he would have said earlier if he had been able to remember. After a while Berl came to himself and said, "Pescha, you will have to make a double Sabbath pudding in addition to the stew."

It was years since Berl had called Berlcha by her given name. When he wanted to address her, he would say, "Listen," or "Say." It is the young or those from the big cities who call a wife by her name. Only now did Berlcha begin to cry. Yellow tears ran from her eyes, and everything became dim. Then she called out, "It's Friday—I have to prepare for the Sabbath." Yes, she had to knead the dough and braid the loaves. With such a guest, she had to make a larger Sabbath stew. The winter day is short and she must hurry.

Her son understood what was worrying her, because he said, "Mother, I will help you."

Berlcha wanted to laugh, but a choked sob came out. "What are you saying? God forbid."

The nobleman took off his cloak and jacket and remained in his vest, on which hung a solid-gold watch chain. He rolled up his sleeves and came to the trough. "Mother, I was a baker for many years in New York," he said, and he began to knead the dough.

"What! You are my darling son who will say Kaddish for me." She wept raspingly. Her strength left her, and she slumped onto the bed.

Berl said, "Women will always be women." And he went to the shed to get more wood. The goat sat down near the oven; she gazed with surprise at this strange man—his height and his bizarre clothes.

The neighbors had heard the good news that Berl's son had arrived from America and they came to greet him. The women began to help Berlcha prepare for the Sabbath. Some laughed, some cried. The room was full of

people, as at a wedding. They asked Berl's son, "What is new in America?"
And Berl's son answered, "America is all right."

"Do Jews make a living?"

"One eats white bread there on weekdays."

"Do they remain Jews?"

"I am not a Gentile."

After Berlcha blessed the candles, father and son went to the little synagogue across the street. A new snow had fallen. The son took large steps,
but Berl warned him, "Slow down."

In the synagogue the Jews recited "Let Us Exult" and "Come, My
Groom." All the time, the snow outside kept falling. After prayers, when
Berl and Samuel left the Holy Place, the village was unrecognizable. Everything was covered with snow. One could see only the contours of the roofs
and the candles in the windows. Samuel said, "Nothing has changed here."

Berlcha had prepared gefilte fish, chicken soup with rice, meat, carrot
stew. Berl recited the benediction over a glass of ritual wine. The family
ate and drank, and when it grew quiet for a while one could hear the
chirping of the house cricket. The son talked a lot, but Berl and Berlcha
understood little. His Yiddish was different and contained foreign words.

After the final blessing Samuel asked, "Father, what did you do with all
the money I sent you?"

Bel raised his white brows. "It's here."

"Didn't you put it in a bank?"

"There is no bank in Lentshin."

"Where do you keep it?"

Berl hesitated. "One is not allowed to touch money on the Sabbath, but I
will show you." He crouched beside the bed and began to shove something
heavy. A boot appeared. Its top was stuffed with straw. Berl removed the
straw and the son saw that the boot was full of gold coins. He lifted it.

"Father, this is a treasure!" he called out.

"Well."

"Why didn't you spend it?"

"On what? Thank God, we have everything."

"Why didn't you travel somewhere?"

"Where to? This is our home."

The son asked one question after the other, but Berl's answer was always
the same: they wanted for nothing. The garden, the cow, the goat, the
chickens provided them with all they needed. The son said, "If thieves
knew about this, your lives wouldn't be safe."

"There are no thieves here."

"What will happen to the money?"

"You take it."

Slowly, Berl and Berlcha grew accustomed to their son and his American Yiddish. Berlcha could hear him better now. She even recognized his
voice. He was saying, "Perhaps we should build a larger synagogue."

"The synagogue is big enough," Berl replied.

"Perhaps a home for old people."

"No one sleeps in the street."

The next day after the Sabbath meal was eaten, a Gentile from Zakroczym brought a paper—it was the cable. Berl and Berlcha lay down for a nap. They soon began to snore. The goat, too, dozed off. The son put on his cloak and his hat and went for a walk. He strode with his long legs across the marketplace. He stretched out a hand and touched a roof. He wanted to smoke a cigar, but he remembered it was forbidden on the Sabbath. He had a desire to talk to someone, but it seemed that the whole of Lentshin was asleep. He entered the synagogue. An old man was sitting there, reciting psalms. Samuel asked, "Are you praying?"

"What else is there to do when one gets old?"

"Do you make a living?"

The old man did not understand the meaning of these words. He smiled, showing his empty gums, and then he said, "If God gives health, one keeps on living."

Samuel returned home. Dusk had fallen. Berl went to the synagogue for the evening prayers and the son remained with his mother. The room was filled with shadows.

Berlcha began to recite in a solemn singsong, "God of Abraham, Isaac, and Jacob, defend the poor people of Israel and Thy name. The Holy Sabbath is departing; the welcome week is coming to us. Let it be one of health, wealth and good deeds."

"Mother, you don't need to pray for wealth," Samuel said. "You are wealthy already."

Berlcha did not hear—or pretended not to. Her face had turned into a cluster of shadows.

In the twilight Samuel put his hand into his jacket pocket and touched his passport, his checkbook, his letters of credit. He had come here with big plans. He had a valise filled with presents for his parents. He wanted to bestow gifts on the village. He brought not only his own money but funds from the Lentshin Society in New York, which had organized a ball for the benefit of the village. But this village in the hinterland needed nothing. From the synagogue one could hear hoarse chanting. The cricket, silent all day, started again its chirping. Berlcha began to sway and utter holy rhymes inherited from mothers and grandmothers:

> Thy holy sheep
> In mercy keep,
> In Torah and good deeds;
> Provide for all their needs,
> Shoes, clothes, and bread
> And the Messiah's tread.

E. F. Schumacher

E. F. Schumacher (1911–1977), economist and writer, was born in Germany.
He studied abroad in the early 1930s, including a stay at Columbia University, but in 1937 he left Germany permanently for England, where he lived
the rest of his life. During World War II, he was interned and required to
work on farms in Britain for a short period, but he was soon released and
worked with Lord Beveridge, who is credited with the theoretical framework for Britain's welfare state. After the war, Schumacher advised British
authorities in postwar Germany. He was economic adviser to Britain's National Coal Board (1950–1970) and director of a company that pioneered
common ownership and workers' control. His books—all on economic policy
and planning—include *Roots of Economic Growth* (1962); *Small Is Beautiful*
(1973), a best seller that was translated into fifteen languages; and *A Guide
for the Perplexed* (1977). The article reprinted below appeared in a book of
essays edited by Dom Moraes, *Voices for Life: Reflections on the Human
Condition* (1975).

A Culture of Poverty

Schon in der Kindheit hört' ich es mit Beben:
Nur wer im Wohlstand lebt, lebt angenehm.
*(Even as a child I felt terror-struck when I heard it said that to live an
agreeable life you have got to be rich.)*

—BERTOLT BRECHT

Only the rich can have a good life—this is the daunting message that has
been drummed into the ears of all mankind during the last half-century
or so. It is the implicit doctrine of "development," and the growth of
income serves as the very criterion of progress. Everyone, it is held, has
not only the right but the duty to become rich, and this applies to societies
even more stringently than to individuals. The most succinct and most
relevant indicator of a country's status in the world is thought to be *average income per head,* while the prime object of admiration is not the level
already attained but the current *rate of growth.*

It follows logically—or so it seems—that the greatest obstacle to progress
is a growth of population: It frustrates, diminishes, offsets what the growth
of gross national product would otherwise achieve. What is the point of, let
us say, doubling the GNP over a period, if population is also allowed to
double during the same time? It would mean running faster merely to
stand still; *average income per head* would remain stationary, and there
would be no advance at all toward the cherished goal of universal affluence.

In the light of this received doctrine the well-nigh unanimous prediction of the demographers—that world population, barring unforeseen catastrophes, will double during the next thirty years—is taken as an intolerable threat. What other prospect is this than one of limitless frustration?

Some mathematical enthusiasts are still content to project the economic "growth curves" of the last thirty years for another thirty or even fifty years to "prove" that all mankind can become immensely rich within a generation or two. Our only danger, they suggest, is to succumb at this glorious hour in the history of progress to a "failure of nerve." They presuppose the existence of limitless resources in a finite world, an equally limitless capacity of living nature to cope with pollution, and the omnipotence of science and social engineering.

The sooner we stop living in the Cloud-Cuckoo-Land of such fanciful projections and presuppositions the better it will be, and this applies to the people of the rich countries just as much as to those of the poor. *It would apply even if all population growth stopped entirely forthwith.* The modern assumption that "only the rich can have a good life" springs from a crudely materialistic philosophy that contradicts the universal tradition of mankind. The material *needs* of man are limited and in fact quite modest, even though his material *wants* may know no bounds. Man does not live by bread alone, and no increase in his *wants* above his needs can give him the "good life." Christianity teaches that man must seek *first* "the kingdom of God, and his righteousness" and that all the other things—the material things to cover his needs—will then be "added unto" him. The experience of the modern world suggests that this teaching carries not only a promise but also a threat, namely, that "unless he seeks first the kingdom of God, those material things, which he unquestionably also needs, will cease to be available to him."

Our task, however, is to bring such insights, supported, as I said, by the universal tradition of mankind, down to the level of everyday economic reality. To do so, we must study, both theoretically and in practice, the possibilities of "a culture of poverty."

To make our meaning clear, let us state right away that there are degrees of poverty that may be totally inimical to any kind of culture in the ordinarily accepted sense. They are essentially different from poverty and deserve a separate name; the term that offers itself is "misery." We may say that poverty prevails when people have enough to keep body and soul together but little to spare, whereas in misery they cannot keep body and soul together, and even the soul suffers deprivation. Some thirteen years ago when I began seriously to grope for answers to these perplexing questions, I wrote this in *Roots of Economic Growth:*

All peoples—with exceptions that merely prove the rule—have always known how to help themselves, they have always *discovered a pattern of living which fitted their peculiar natural surroundings.* Societies and cultures have collapsed when they deserted their own pattern and fell into decadence, but even then, unless devastated by war, the people normally continued to provide for themselves, with something to spare for higher things. Why not now, in so many parts of the world? I am not speaking of ordinary poverty, but of actual and acute misery; not of the poor, who according to the universal tradition of mankind are in a special way blessed, but of the miserable and degraded ones who, by the same tradition, should not exist at all and should be helped by all. Poverty may have been the rule in the past, but misery was not. Poor peasants and artisans have existed from time immemorial: but miserable and destitute villages in their thousands and urban pavement dwellers in their hundreds of thousands—not in wartime or as an aftermath of war, but in the midst of peace and as a seemingly permanent feature—that is a monstrous and scandalous thing which is altogether abnormal in the history of mankind. We cannot be satisfied with the snap answer that this is due to population pressure. Since every mouth that comes into the world is also endowed with a pair of hands, population pressure could serve as an explanation only if it meant an absolute shortage of land—and although that situation may arise in the future, it decidedly has not arrived today (a few islands excepted). It cannot be argued that population increase as such must produce increasing poverty, because the additional pairs of hands could not be endowed with the capital they needed to help themselves. Millions of people have started without capital and have shown that a pair of hands can provide not only the income but also the durable goods, i.e., capital, or civilized existence. So the question stands and demands an answer. What has gone wrong? Why cannot these people help themselves?

The answer, I suggest, lies in the abandonment of their indigenous culture of poverty, which means not only that they lost true culture but also that their poverty, in all too many cases, has turned into misery.

A culture of poverty such as mankind has known in innumerable variants before the industrial age is based on one fundamental distinction— which may have been made consciously or instinctively, it does not matter —the distinction between the "ephemeral" and the "eternal." All religions, of course, deal with this distinction, suggesting that the ephemeral is relatively unreal and only the eternal is real. On the material plane we deal with goods and services, and the same distinction applies: All goods and services can be arranged, as it were, on a scale that extends from the ephemeral to the eternal. Needless to say, neither of these terms may be taken in an absolute sense (because there is nothing absolute on the material plane), although there may well be something absolute in the maker's *intention:* He may see his product as something to be *used up*, that is to say, to be destroyed in the act of consumption, or as something to be used or enjoyed as a permanent asset, ideally forever.

The extremes are easily recognized. An article of consumption, like a loaf of bread, is *intended* to be *used up*, while a work of art, like the Mona Lisa, is *intended* to be there forever. Transport services to take a tourist on holiday are intended to be used up and therefore ephemeral, while a bridge across the river is intended to be a permanent facility. Entertainment is intended to be ephemeral; education (in the fullest sense) is intended to be eternal.

Between the extremes of the ephemeral and the eternal, there extends a vast range of goods and services with regard to which the producer may exercise a certain degree of choice: He may be producing with the intention of supplying something relatively ephemeral or something relatively eternal. A publisher, for instance, may produce a book with the intention that it should be purchased, read, and treasured by countless generations or his intention may be that it should be purchased, read, and thrown away as quickly as possible.

Ephemeral goods are—to use the language of business—"depreciating assets" and have to be "written off." Eternal goods, on the other hand, are never "depreciated" but "maintained." (You don't "depreciate" the Taj Mahal; you try to maintain its splendor for all time.)

Ephemeral goods are subject to the economic calculus. Their only value lies in being used up, and it is necessary to ensure that their *cost* of production does not exceed the *benefit* derived from destroying them. But eternal goods are not intended for destruction; there is no occasion for an economic calculus, because the benefit—the product of annual value and time—is infinite and therefore incalculable.

Once we recognize the validity of the distinction between the ephemeral and the eternal, we are able to distinguish, in principle, between two different types of "standards of living." Two societies may have the same volume of production and the same *income per head of population,* but the *quality of life* or life-style may show fundamental and incomparable differences: the one placing its main emphasis on ephemeral satisfactions and the other devoting itself primarily to the creation of eternal values. In the former there may be opulent living in terms of ephemeral goods and starvation in terms of eternal goods—eating, drinking, and wallowing in entertainment, in sordid, ugly, mean, and unhealthy surroundings—while in the latter there may be frugal living in terms of ephemeral goods and opulence in terms of eternal goods—modest, simple, and healthy consumption in a noble setting. In terms of conventional economic accounting they are both equally developed—which merely goes to show that the purely quantitative approach misses the point.

The study of these two models can surely teach us a great deal. It is clear, however, that the question "Which of the two is better?" reaches far beyond the economic calculus, since quality cannot be calculated.

No one, I suppose, would wish to deny that the life-style of modern industrial society is one that places primary emphasis on ephemeral satisfactions and is characterized by a gross neglect of eternal goods. Under certain immanent compulsions, moreover, modern industrial society is engaged in a process of what might be called ever-increasing ephemeralization; that is to say, goods and services that by their very nature belong to the eternal side are being produced as if their purpose were ephemeral. The economic calculus is applied everywhere, even at the cost of skimping and paring on goods that should last forever. At the same time purely ephemeral goods are produced to standards of refinement, elaboration, and luxury, as if they were meant to serve eternal purposes and to last for all time.

Nor, I suppose, would anyone wish to deny that many preindustrial societies have been able to create superlative cultures by placing their emphasis in the exactly opposite way. The greatest part of the modern world's cultural heritage stems from these societies.

The affluent societies of today make such exorbitant demands on the world's resources, create ecological dangers of such intensity, and produce such a high level of neurosis among their populations that they cannot possibly serve as a model to be imitated by those two-thirds or three-quarters of mankind who are conventionally considered underdeveloped or developing. The *failure of modern affluence*—which seems obvious enough, although it is by no means freely admitted by people of a purely materialistic outlook—cannot be attributed to affluence as such but is directly due to mistaken priorities (the cause of which cannot be discussed here): a gross overemphasis on the ephemeral and a brutal undervaluation of the eternal. Not surprisingly, no amount of indulgence on the ephemeral side can compensate for starvation on the eternal side.

In the light of these considerations, it is not difficult to understand the meaning and feasibility of a culture of poverty. It would be based on the insight that the real needs of man are limited and must be met, but that his wants tend to be unlimited, cannot be met, and must be resisted with the utmost determination. Only by a reduction of wants to needs can resources for genuine progress be freed. The required resources cannot be found from foreign aid; they cannot be mobilized via the technology of the affluent society that is immensely capital-intensive and labor-saving and is dependent on an elaborate infrastructure that is itself enormously expensive. Uncritical technology transfer from the rich societies to the poor cannot but transfer into poor societies a life-style that, placing primary emphasis on ephemeral satisfactions, may suit the taste of small, rich minorities but condemns the great, poor majority to increasing misery.

The resources for genuine progress can be found only by a life-style that emphasizes frugal living in terms of ephemeral goods. Only such a life-style can create (or maintain and develop) an ever-increasing supply of eternal goods.

Frugal living in terms of ephemeral goods means a dogged adherence to simplicity, a conscious avoidance of any unnecessary elaborations, and a magnanimous rejection of luxury—puritanism, if you like—on the ephemeral side. This makes it possible to enjoy a high standard of living on the eternal side, as a compensation and reward. Luxury and refinement have their proper place and function but only with eternal, not with ephemeral, goods. This is the essence of a culture of poverty.

One further point has to be added: The ultimate resource of any society is its labor power, which is infinitely creative. When the primary emphasis is on ephemeral goods, there is an automatic preference for mass production, and there can be no doubt that mass production is more congenial to machines than it is to men. The result is the progressive elimination of the human factor from the productive process. For a poor society, this means that its ultimate resource cannot be properly used; its creativity remains largely untapped. This is why Gandhi, with unerring instinct, insisted that "it is not mass production but only production by the masses that can do the trick." A society that places its primary emphasis on eternal goods will automatically prefer production by the masses to mass production, because such goods, intended to last, must fit the precise conditions of their place; they cannot be standardized. This brings the whole human being back into the productive process, and it then emerges that even ephemeral goods (without which human existence is obviously impossible) are far more efficient and economical when a proper fit has been ensured by the human factor.

All the above does not claim to be more than an assembly of a few preliminary indications. I entertain the hope that, in view of increasing threats to the very survival of culture—and even life itself—there will be an upsurge of serious study of the possibilities of a culture of poverty. We might find that we have nothing to lose and a world to gain.

Ursula K. Le Guin

Ursula K. Le Guin, born in Berkeley, California, in 1929, is best known as a science fiction writer, but she also has published other novels, essays, and children's books. Her many books include *The Left Hand of Darkness* (1969), which won both a Hugo Award and a Science Fiction of America Nebula Award; *The Tombs of Atuan* (1971), which received a Newberry Silver Medal; *The Farthest Shore* (1972), winner of a National Book Award and a Hugo Award; and *The Dispossessed* (1974), winner of a Nebula Award. More recent work includes *Orsinian Tales* (1976), a collection of short stories; *Malafrena* (1979), a novel set in fantasy Orsinia; *The Language of the Night: Essays on Fantasy and Science Fiction* (1979); and *The Compass Rose* (1982), a collection of short stories. The story reprinted below is taken from a collection of Hugo Award winners of 1974, edited by Isaac Asimov.

The Ones Who Walk Away from Omelas

With a clamor of bells that set the swallows soaring, the Festival of Summer came to the city Omelas, bright-towered by the sea. The rigging of the boats in harbor sparkled with flags. In the streets between houses with red roofs and painted walls, between old moss-grown gardens and under avenues of trees, past great parks and public buildings, processions moved. Some were decorous: old people in long stiff robes of mauve and gray, grave master workmen, quiet, merry women carrying their babies and chatting as they walked. In other streets the music beat faster, a shimmering of gong and tambourine, and the people went dancing, the procession was a dance. Children dodged in and out, their high calls rising like the swallows' crossing flights over the music and the singing. All the processions wound toward the north side of the city, where on the great water-meadow called the Green Fields boys and girls, naked in the bright air, with mudstained feet and ankles and long, lithe arms, exercised their restive horses before the race. The horses wore no gear at all but a halter without a bit. Their manes were braided with streamers of silver, gold, and green. They blew out their nostrils and pranced and boasted to one another; they were vastly excited, the horse being the only animal who has adopted our ceremonies as his own. Far off to the north and west the mountains stood up half-encircling Omelas on her bay. The air of morning was so clear that the snow still crowning the Eighteen Peaks burned with white-gold fire across the miles of sunlit air, under the dark blue of the sky. There was just enough wind to make the banners that marked the race course snap and flutter now and then. In the silence of the broad green meadows one could hear the music winding through the city streets, farther and nearer and ever approaching, a cheerful faint sweetness of the air that from time to time trembled and gathered together and broke out into the great joyous clanging of the bells.

Joyous! How is one to tell about joy? How describe the citizens of Omelas?

They were not simple folk, you see, though they were happy. But we do not say the words of cheer much any more. All smiles have become archaic. Given a description such as this one tends to make certain assumptions. Given a description such as this one tends to look next for the King, mounted on a splendid stallion and surrounded by his noble knights, or perhaps in a golden litter borne by great-muscled slaves. But there was no king. They did not use swords, or keep slaves. They were not barbarians. I do not know the rules and laws of their society, but I suspect that they were singularly few. As they did without monarchy and salvery, so they also got on without the stock exchange, the advertisement, the secret police, and the bomb. Yet I repeat that these were not simple folk, not dulcet shepherds, noble savages, bland utopians. They were not less complex than we. The trouble is that we have a bad habit, encouraged by pedants and sophisticates, of considering happiness as something rather stupid. Only pain is intellectual, only evil interesting. This is the treason of the artist: a refusal to admit the banality of evil and the terrible boredom of pain. If you can't lick 'em, join 'em. If it hurts, repeat it. But to praise despair is to condemn delight, to embrace violence is to lose hold of everything else. We have almost lost hold; we can no longer describe a happy man, nor make any celebration of joy. How can I tell you about the people of Omelas? They were not naive and happy children—though their children were, in fact, happy. They were mature, intelligent, passionate adults whose lives were not wretched. O miracle! But I wish I could describe it better. I wish I could convince you. Omelas sounds in my words like a city in a fairytale, long ago and far away, once upon a time. Perhaps it would be best if you imagined it as your own fancy bids, assuming it will rise to the occasion, for certainly I cannot suit you all. For instance, how about technology? I think that there would be no cars or helicopters in and above the streets; this follows from the fact that the people of Omelas are happy people. Happiness is based on a just discrimination of what is necessary, what is neither necessary nor destructive, and what is destructive. In the middle category, however—that of the unnecessary but undestructive, that of comfort, luxury, exuberance, etc.—they could perfectly well have central heating, subway trains, washing machines, and all kinds of marvelous devices not yet invented here, floating lightsources, fuelless power, a cure for the common cold. Or they could have none of that: it doesn't matter. As you like it. I incline to think that people from towns up and down the coast have been coming in to Omelas during the last days before the Festival on very fast little trains and doubledecked trams, and that the train station of Omelas is actually the handsomest building in town, though plainer than the magnificent Farmers Market. But even granted trains, I fear that Omelas so far strikes some of you as goodygoody. Smiles, bells, parades, horses, bleh. If so, please add an orgy. If an orgy would help, don't hesitate. Let us not, however, have temples from which issue beautiful nude priests and priestesses already half in ecstasy and ready to copulate with whosoever, man or woman, lover or stranger, desires union with the deep godhead of the blood, although that was my first idea. But really it would be better not to have any temples in Omelas —at least, not manned temples. Religion yes, clergy no. Surely the beautiful nudes can just wander about, offering themselves like divine soufflés to the hunger of the needy and the rapture of the flesh. Let them join the processions. Let tambourines be struck above the copulations, and the glory of desire be proclaimed upon the gongs, and (a not unimportant point) let the offspring of these delightful rituals be beloved and looked after by all. One thing I know there is none of in Omelas is guilt. But what else should there be? I thought at first there were no drugs, but that is puritanical. For those who like it, the faint insistent sweetness of *drooz* may perfume the ways of the city, *drooz* which first brings a great lightness and brilliance to the mind and limbs, and then after some hours a dreamy languor, and wonderful visions at last of the very arcana and inmost secrets of the Universe, as well as exciting the pleasure of sex beyond all belief; and it is not habit-forming. For more modest tastes I think there ought to be beer. What else, what else belongs in the joyous city? The sense of victory, surely, the celebration of courage. But as we did without clergy, let us do without soldiers. The joy built upon successful slaughter is not the right kind of joy; it will not do; it is fearful and it is trivial. A boundless and generous contentment, a magnanimous triumph felt not against some outer enemy but in communion with the finest and fairest in the souls of all men everywhere and the splendor of the world's summer: this is what swells the hearts of the people of Omelas, and the victory they celebrate is that of life. I really don't think many of them need to take *drooz*.

Most of the processions have reached the Green Fields by now. A marvelous smell of cooking goes forth from the red and blue tents of the provisioners. The faces of small children are amiably sticky; in the benign gray beard of a man a couple of crumbs of rich pastry are entangled. The youths and girls have mounted their horses and are beginning to group around the starting line of the course. An old woman, small, fat, and laughing, is passing out flowers from a basket, and tall young men wear her flowers in their shining hair. A child of nine or ten sits at the edge of the crowd, alone, playing on a wooden flute. People pause to listen, and they smile, but they do not speak to him, for he never ceases playing and never sees them, his dark eyes wholly rapt in the sweet, thin magic of the tune.

He finishes, and slowly lowers his hands holding the wooden flute.

As if that little private silence were the signal, all at once a trumpet sounds from the pavilion near the starting line: imperious, melancholy, piercing. The horses rear on their slender legs, and some of them neigh in answer. Sober-faced, the young riders stroke the horses' necks and soothe them, whispering, "Quiet, quiet, there my beauty, my hope . . ." They begin to form in rank along the starting line. The crowds along the race course are like a field of grass and flowers in the wind. The Festival of Summer has begun.

Do you believe? Do you accept the festival, the city, the joy? No? Then let me describe one more thing.

In a basement under one of the beautiful buildings of Omelas, or perhaps in the cellar of one of its spacious private homes, there is a room. It has one locked door, and no window. A little light seeps in dustily between cracks in the boards, secondhand from a cobwebbed window somewhere across the cellar. In one corner of the little room a couple of mops, with stiff, clotted, foul-smelling heads, stand near a rusty bucket. The floor is dirt, a little damp to the touch, as cellar dirt usually is. The room is about three paces long and two wide: a mere broom closet or disused toolroom. In the room a child is sitting. It might be a boy or a girl. It looks about six, but actually is nearly ten. It is feebleminded. Perhaps it was born defective, or perhaps it has become imbecile through fear, malnutrition, and neglect. It picks its nose and occasionally fumbles vaguely with its toes or genitals, as it sits hunched in the corner farthest from the bucket and the two mops. It is afraid of the mops. It finds them horrible. It shuts its eyes, but it knows the mops are still standing there; and the door is locked; and nobody will come. The door is always locked, and nobody ever comes, except that sometimes—the child has no understanding of time or interval—sometimes the door rattles terribly and opens, and a person, or several people, are there. One of them may come in and kick the child to make it stand up. The others never come close, but peer in at it with frightened, disgusted eyes. The food bowl and the water jug are hastily filled, the door is locked, the eyes disappear. The people at the door never say anything, but the child, who has not always lived in the toolroom, and can remember sunlight and its mother's voice, sometimes speaks, "I will be good," it says. "Please let me out. I will be good!" They never answer. The child used to scream for help at night, and cry a good deal, but now it only makes a kind of whining, "eh-haa, eh-haa," and it speaks less and less often. It is so thin there are no calves to its legs; its belly protrudes; it lives on a half-bowl of cornmeal and grease a day. It is naked. Its buttocks and thighs are a mass of festered sores, as it sits in its own excrement continually.

They all know it is there, all the people of Omelas. Some of them have come to see it, others are content merely to know it is there. They all know that it has to be there. Some of them understand why, and some do not, but they all understand that their happiness, the beauty of their city, the tenderness of their friendships, the health of their children, the wisdom of their scholars, the skill of their makers, even the abundance of their harvest and the kindly weathers of their skies, depend wholly on this child's abominable misery.

This is usually explained to children when they are between eight and twelve, whenever they seem capable of understanding; and most of those who come to see the child are young people, though often enough an adult comes, or comes back, to see the child. No matter how well the matter has been explained to them, these young spectators are always shocked and sickened at the sight. They feel disgust, which they had thought themselves superior to. They feel anger, outrage, impotence, despite all the explanations. They would like to do something for the child. But there is nothing they can do. If the child were brought up into the sunlight out of that vile place, if it were cleaned and fed and comforted, that would be a good thing, indeed; but if it were done, in that day and hour all the prosperity and beauty and delight of Omelas would wither and be destroyed. Those are the terms. To exchange all the goodness and grace of every life in Omelas for that single, small improvement: to throw away the happiness of thousands for the chance of the happiness of one: that would be to let guilt within the walls indeed.

The terms are strict and absolute; there may not even be a kind word spoken to the child.

Often the young people go home in tears, or in a tearless rage, when they have seen the child and faced this terrible paradox. They may brood over it for weeks or years. But as time goes on they begin to realize that even if the child could be released, it would not get much good of its freedom: a vague pleasure of warmth and food, no doubt, but little more. It is too degraded and imbecile to know any real joy. It has been afraid too long ever to be free of fear. Its habits are too uncouth for it to respond to humane treatment. Indeed after so long it would probably be wretched without walls about it to protect it, and darkness for its eyes, and its own excrement to sit in. Their tears at the bitter injustice dry when they begin to perceive the terrible justice of reality, and to accept it. Yet it is their tears and anger, the trying of their generosity and the acceptance of their helplessness, which are perhaps the true source of the splendor of their lives. Theirs is no vapid, irresponsible happiness. They know that they, like the child, are not free. They know compassion. It is the existence of the child, and their knowledge of its existence, that makes possible the nobility of their architecture, the poignancy of their music, the profundity of their science. It is because of the child that they are so gentle with children. They know that if the wretched one were not there sniveling in the dark, the other one, the flute player, could make no joyful music as the young riders line up in their beauty for the race in the sunlight of the first morning of summer.

Now do you believe in them? Are they not more credible? But there is one more thing to tell, and this is quite incredible.

At times one of the adolescent girls or boys who go to see the child does not go home to weep or rage, does not, in fact, go home at all. Sometimes also a man or woman much older falls silent for a day or two, and then leaves home. These people go out into the street, and walk down the street alone. They keep walking, and walk straight out of the city of Omelas, through the beautiful gates. They keep walking across the farmlands of Omelas. Each one goes alone, youth or girl, man or woman. Night falls; the traveler must pass down village streets, between the houses with yellow-lit windows, and on out into the darkness of the fields. Each alone, they go west or north, toward the mountains. They go on. They leave Omelas, they walk ahead into the darkness, and they do not come back. The place they go toward is a place even less imaginable to most of us than the city of happiness. I cannot describe it at all. It is possible that it does not exist. But they seem to know where they are going, the ones who walk away from Omelas.

On the Meaning of Work

Marge Piercy
(1936–)

To be of use

The people I love the best
jump into work head first
without dallying in the shallows
and swim off with sure strokes almost out of sight.
They seem to become natives of that element,
the black sleek heads of seals
bouncing like half-submerged balls.

I love people who harness themselves, an ox to a heavy
cart,
who pull like water buffalo, with massive patience,
who strain in the mud and the muck to move things
forward,
who do what has to be done, again and again.

I want to be with people who submerge
in the task, who go into the fields to harvest
and work in a row and pass the bags along,
who are not parlor generals and field deserters
but move in a common rhythm
when the food must come in or the fire be put out.

The work of the world is common as mud.
Botched, it smears the hands, crumbles to dust.
But the thing worth doing well done
has a shape that satisfies, clean and evident.
Greek amphoras for wine or oil,
Hopi vases that held corn, are put in museums
but you know they were made to be used.
The pitcher cries for water to carry
and a person for work that is real.

(1973)

Theodore Roethke
(1908–1963)

Dolor

I have known the inexorable sadness of pencils,
Neat in their boxes, dolor of pad and paper-weight,
All the misery of manila folders and mucilage,
Desolation in immaculate public places,
Lonely reception room, lavatory, switchboard,
The unalterable pathos of basin and pitcher,
Ritual of multigraph, paper-clip, comma,
Endless duplication of lives and objects.
And I have seen dust from the walls of institutions,
Finer than flour, alive, more dangerous than silica,
Sift, almost invisible, through long afternoons of tedium,
Dropping a fine film on nails and delicate eyebrows,
Glazing the pale hair, the duplicate gray standard faces.

(1943)

E. F. Schumacher

This is the prologue to Schumacher's book *Good Work* (1979), a posthumous collection of his speeches. For information on the author and his work, see p. 381.

Prologue to Good Work

A recent article in the London *Times* began with these words: "Dante, when composing his visions of hell, might well have included the mindless, repetitive boredom of working on a factory assembly line. It destroys initiative and rots brains, yet millions of British workers are committed to it for most of their lives." The remarkable thing is that this statement, like countless similar ones made before it, aroused no interest: there were no hot denials or anguished agreements; no reactions at all. The strong and terrible words—"visions of hell," "destroys initiative and rots brains," and so on—attracted no reprimand that they were misstatements or overstatements, that they were irresponsible or hysterical exaggerations or subversive propaganda; no, people read them, sighed and nodded, I suppose, and moved on. Not even the ecologists, conservationists, and doomwatchers are interested in this matter. If someone had asserted that certain man-made arrangements destroyed the initiative and rotted the brains of millions of birds or seals or wild animals in the game reserves of Africa, such an assertion would have been either refuted or accepted as a serious challenge. If someone had asserted that not the minds and brains of millions of workers were being rotted but their bodies, again there would have been considerable interest. After all, there are safety regulations, inspectors, claims for damages, and so forth. No management is unaware of its duty to avoid accidents or physical conditions which impair workers' health. But workers' brains, minds, and souls are a different matter.

A recent semiofficial report, submitted by the British government to the Stockholm Conference,[o] bears the title "Natural Resources: Sinews for Survival." The most important of all resources are obviously the initiative, imagination, and brainpower of man himself. We all know this and are ready to devote very substantial funds to what we call education. So, if the problem is "survival," one might fairly expect to find some discussion relating to the preservation and, if possible, the development of the most precious of all natural resources, human brains. However, such expectations are not fulfilled. "Sinews for Survival" deals with all the material factors—minerals, energy, water, etc.—but not at all with such immaterial resources as initiative, imagination, and brainpower.

Considering the centrality of work in human life, one might have expected that every textbook on economics, sociology, politics, and related subjects would present a theory of work as one of the indispensable foundation stones for all further expositions. After all, it is work which occupies most of the energies of the human race, and what people actually *do* is normally more important, for understanding them, than what they say, or what they spend their money on, or what they own, or how they vote. A person's work is undoubtedly one of the most decisive formative influences on his character and personality. However, the truth of the matter is that we look in vain for any presentations of theories of work in these textbooks. The question of *what the work does to the worker* is hardly ever asked, not to mention the question of whether the real task might not be to adapt the work to the needs of the worker rather than to demand that the worker adapt himself to the needs of the work—which means, of course, primarily to the needs of the machine.

Let us ask then: How does work relate to the end and purpose of man's

Stockholm Conference   A United Nations Environmental Conference in Stockholm, Sweden, in June 1972; it was the first global attack on environmental problems.

being? It has been recognized in all authentic teachings of mankind that every human being born into this world has to work not merely to keep himself alive but to strive toward perfection. To keep himself alive, he needs various goods and services, which will not be forthcoming without human labor. To perfect himself, he needs purposeful activity in accordance with the injunction: "Whichever gift each of you have received, use it in service to one another, like good stewards dispensing the grace of God in its varied forms." From this, we may derive the three purposes of human work as follows:

First, to provide necessary and useful goods and services.
Second, to enable every one of us to use and thereby perfect our gifts like good stewards.
Third, to do so in service to, and in cooperation with, others, so as to liberate ourselves from our inborn egocentricity.

This threefold function makes work so central to human life that it is truly impossible to conceive of life at the human level without work. "Without work, all life goes rotten," said Albert Camus,[o] "but when work is soulless, life stifles and dies."

James Herriot

James Herriot (a pseudonym) is a veterinarian and deservedly popular author. He was born in Scotland in 1916. After completing his veterinary studies at Glasgow Veterinary College, he took his first position in the Yorkshire Dales of northern England, where he has practiced ever since. At the age of fifty, he began to write about his early days of veterinary work and of his love of the life and people and animals with whom he worked. The books are not sentimental; they are full of accurate detail and include blunders and tragedy as well as humor and triumph. Published in the United States as *All Creatures Great and Small* (1972), *All Things Bright and Beautiful* (1973), *All Things Wise and Wonderful* (1976), and *The Lord God Made Them All* (1981), the books were immediately popular with the critics and the general public. A movie and a television series have been based upon them. In 1979, Herriot published *James Herriot's Yorkshire,* a book of photographs and commentary on the places described in his other books. Despite the fame and income brought by his writing, James Herriot continues to work as a veterinarian because he is doing the work he loves. The selection reprinted below comes from *All Things Bright and Beautiful.*

Albert Camus   See page 181.

from All Things Bright and Beautiful

This was my third spring in the Dales⁰ but it was like the two before—and all the springs after. The kind of spring, that is, that a country vet knows; the din of the lambing pens, the bass rumble of the ewes and the high, insistent bawling of the lambs. This, for me, has always heralded the end of winter and the beginning of something new. This and the piercing Yorkshire wind and the hard, bright sunshine flooding the bare hillsides.

At the top of the grassy slope the pens, built of straw bales, formed a long row of square cubicles each holding a ewe with her lambs and I could see Rob Benson coming round the far end carrying two feeding buckets. Rob was hard at it; at this time of the year he didn't go to bed for about six weeks; he would maybe take off his boots and doze by the kitchen fire at night but he was his own shepherd and never very far from the scene of action.

'Ah've got a couple of cases for you today, Jim.' His face, cracked and purpled by the weather, broke into a grin. 'It's not really you ah need, it's that little lady's hand of yours and right sharpish, too.'

He led the way to a bigger enclosure, holding several sheep. There was a scurry as we went in but he caught expertly at the fleece of a darting ewe. 'This is the first one. You can see we haven't a deal o' time.'

I lifted the woolly tail and gasped. The lamb's head was protruding from the vagina, the lips of the vulva clamped tightly behind the ears, and it had swollen enormously to more than twice its size. The eyes were mere puffed slits in the great oedematous ball and the tongue, blue and engorged, lolled from the mouth.

'Well I've seen a few big heads, Rob, but I think this takes the prize.'

'Aye, the little beggar came with his legs back. Just beat me to it. Ah was only away for an hour but he was up like a football. By hell it doesn't take long. I know he wants his legs bringin' round but what can I do with bloody great mitts like mine.' He held out his huge hands, rough and swollen with the years of work.

While he spoke I was stripping off my jacket and as I rolled my shirt sleeves high the wind struck like a knife at my shrinking flesh. I soaped my fingers quickly and began to feel for a space round the lamb's neck. For a moment the little eyes opened and regarded me disconsolately.

'He's alive, anyway,' I said. 'But he must feel terrible and he can't do a thing about it.'

Easing my way round, I found a space down by the throat where I thought I might get through. This was where my 'lady's hand' came in useful and I blessed it every spring; I could work inside the ewes with the

Dales In England a term that refers particularly to river valleys in the district from Cumberland to Yorkshire.

minimum of discomfort to them and this was all-important because sheep, despite their outdoor hardiness, just won't stand rough treatment.

With the utmost care I inched my way along the curly wool of the neck to the shoulder. Another push forward and I was able to hook a finger round the leg and draw it forward until I could feel the flexure of the knee; a little more twiddling and I had hold of the tiny cloven foot and drew it gently out into the light of day.

Well that was half the job done. I got up from the sack where I was kneeling and went over to the bucket of warm water; I'd use my left hand for the other leg and began to soap it thoroughly while one of the ewes, marshalling her lambs around her, glared at me indignantly and gave a warning stamp of her foot.

Turning, I kneeled again and began the same procedure and as I once more groped forward a tiny lamb dodged under my arm and began to suck at my patient's udder. He was clearly enjoying it, too, if the little tail, twirling inches from my face, meant anything.

'Where did this bloke come from?' I asked, still feeling round.

The farmer smiled. 'Oh that's Herbert. Poor little youth's mother won't have 'im at any price. Took a spite at him at birth though she thinks world of her other lamb.'

'Do you feed him, then?'

'Nay, I was going to put him with the pet lambs but I saw he was fendin' for himself. He pops from one ewe to t'other and gets a quick drink whenever he gets chance. I've never seen owt like it.'

'Only a week old and an independent spirit, eh?'

'That's about the size of it, Jim. I notice 'is belly's full every mornin' so I reckon his ma must let him have a do during the night. She can't see him in the dark—it must be the look of him she can't stand.'

I watched the little creature for a moment. To me he seemed as full of knock-kneed charm as any of the others. Sheep were funny things.

I soon had the other leg out and once that obstruction was removed the lamb followed easily. He was a grotesque sight lying on the strawed grass, his enormous head dwarfing his body, but his ribs were heaving reassuringly and I knew the head would shrink back to normal as quickly as it had expanded. I had another search round inside the ewe but the uterus was empty.

'There's no more, Rob,' I said.

The farmer grunted. 'Aye, I thowt so, just a big single 'un. They're the ones that cause the trouble.'

Drying my arms, I watched Herbert. He had left my patient when she moved round to lick her lamb and he was moving speculatively among the other ewes. Some of them warned him off with a shake of the head but eventually he managed to sneak up on a big, wide-bodied sheep and pushed his head underneath her. Immediately she swung round and with a fierce upward butt of her hard skull she sent the little animal flying high in the air in a whirl of flailing legs. He landed with a thud on his back and as I hurried towards him he leaped to his feet and trotted away.

'Awd bitch!' shouted the farmer and as I turned to him in some concern he shrugged. 'I know, poor little sod, it's rough, but I've got a feelin' he wants it this way rather than being in the pen with the pet lambs. Look at 'im now.'

Herbert, quite unabashed, was approaching another ewe and as she bent over her feeding trough he nipped underneath her and his tail went into action again. There was no doubt about it—that lamb had guts.

'Rob,' I said as he caught my second patient. 'Why do you call him Herbert?'

'Well that's my youngest lad's name and that lamb's just like 'im the way he puts his head down and gets stuck in, fearless like.'

I put my hand into the second ewe. Here was a glorious mix up of three lambs; little heads, legs, a tail, all fighting their way towards the outside world and effectively stopping each other from moving an inch.

'She's been hanging about all morning and painin'.' Rob said. 'I knew summat was wrong.'

Moving a hand carefully around the uterus I began the fascinating business of sorting out the tangle which is just about my favourite job in practice. I had to bring a head and two legs up together in order to deliver a lamb; but they had to belong to the same lamb or I was in trouble. It was a matter of tracing each leg back to see if it was hind or fore, to find if it joined the shoulder or disappeared into the depths.

After a few minutes I had a lamb assembled inside with his proper appendages but as I drew the legs into view the neck telescoped and the head slipped back; there was barely room for it to come through the pelvic bones along with the shoulders and I had to coax it through with a finger in the eye socket. This was groaningly painful as the bones squeezed my hand but only for a few seconds because the ewe gave a final strain and the little nose was visible. After that it was easy and I had him on the grass within seconds. The little creature gave a convulsive shake of his head and the farmer wiped him down quickly with straw before pushing him to his mother's head.

The ewe bent over him and began to lick his face and neck with little quick darts of her tongue; and she gave the deep chuckle of satisfaction that you hear from a sheep only at this time. The chuckling continued as I produced another pair of lambs from inside her, one of them hind end first, and, towelling my arms again, I watched her nosing round her triplets delightedly.

Soon they began to answer her with wavering, high-pitched cries and as I drew my coat thankfully over my cold-reddened arms, lamb number one began to struggle to his knees; he couldn't quite make it to his feet and kept toppling on to his face but he knew where he was going, all right; he was headed for that udder with a singleness of purpose which would soon be satisfied.

Despite the wind cutting over the straw bales into my face I found myself grinning down at the scene; this was always the best part, the wonder that was always fresh, the miracle you couldn't explain.

I heard from Rob Benson again a few days later. It was a Sunday afternoon and his voice was strained, almost panic stricken.

'Jim, I've had a dog in among me in-lamb ewes. There was some folk up here with a car about dinner time and my neighbour said they had an Alsatian and it was chasing the sheep all over the field. There's a hell of a mess—I tell you I'm frightened to look.'

'I'm on my way.' I dropped the receiver and hurried out to the car. I had a sinking dread of what would be waiting for me; the helpless animals lying with their throats torn, the terrifying lacerations of limbs and abdomen. I had seen it all before. The ones which didn't have to be slaughtered would need stitching and on the way I made a mental check of the stock of suture silk in the boot.

The in-lamb ewes were in a field by the roadside and my heart gave a quick thump as I looked over the wall; arms resting on the rough loose stones I gazed with sick dismay across the pasture. This was worse than I had feared. The long slope of turf was dotted with prostrate sheep—there must have been about fifty of them, motionless woolly mounds scattered at intervals on the green.

Rob was standing just inside the gate. He hardly looked at me. Just gestured with his head.

'Tell me what you think. I daren't go in there.'

I left him and began to walk among the stricken creatures, rolling them over, lifting their legs, parting the fleece of their necks to examine them. Some were completely unconscious, others comatose; none of them could stand up. But as I worked my way up the field I felt a growing bewilderment. Finally I called back to the farmer.

'Rob, come over here. There's something very strange.'

'Look,' I said as the farmer approached hesitantly. 'There's not a drop of blood nor a wound anywhere and yet all the sheep are flat out. I can't understand it.'

Rob bent over and gently raised a lolling head. 'Aye, you're right. What the hell's done it, then?'

At that moment I couldn't answer him, but a little bell was tinkling far away in the back of my mind. There was something familiar about that ewe the farmer had just handled. She was one of the few able to support herself on her chest and she was lying there, blank-eyed, oblivious of everything; but . . . that drunken nodding of the head, that watery nasal discharge . . . I had seen it before. I knelt down and as I put my face close to hers I heard a faint bubbling—almost a rattling—in her breathing. I knew then.

'It's calcium deficiency,' I cried and began to gallop down the slope towards the car.

Rob trotted alongside me. 'But what the 'ell? They get that after lambin', don't they?'

'Yes, usually,' I puffed. 'But sudden exertion and stress can bring it on.'
'Well ah never knew that,' panted Rob. 'How does it happen?'

I saved my breath. I wasn't going to start an exposition on the effects
of sudden derangement of the parathyroid. I was more concerned with
wondering if I had enough calcium in the boot for fifty ewes. It was
reassuring to see the long row of round tin caps peeping from their cardboard box; I must have filled up recently.

I injected the first ewe in the vein just to check my diagnosis—calcium
works as quickly as that in sheep—and felt a quiet elation as the unconscious animal began to blink and tremble, then tried to struggle on to its
chest.

'We'll inject the others under the skin,' I said. 'It'll save time.'

I began to work my way up the field. Rob pulled forward the fore leg
of each sheep so that I could insert the needle under the convenient patch
of unwoolled skin just behind the elbow; and by the time I was half way
up the slope the ones at the bottom were walking about and getting their
heads into the food troughs and hay racks.

It was one of the most satisfying experiences of my working life. Not
clever, but a magical transfiguration; from despair to hope, from death to
life within minutes.

I was throwing the empty bottles into the boot when Rob spoke. He was
looking wonderingly up at the last of the ewes getting to its feet at the far
end of the field.

'Well Jim, I'll tell you. I've never seen owt like that afore. But there's one
thing bothers me.' He turned to me and his weathered features screwed up
in puzzlement. 'Ah can understand how gettin' chased by a dog could affect
some of them ewes, but why should the whole bloody lot go down?'

'Rob,' I said. 'I don't know.'

And, thirty years later, I still wonder. I still don't know why the whole
bloody lot went down.

I thought Rob had enough to worry about at the time, so I didn't point out
to him that other complications could be expected after the Alsatian episode. I wasn't surprised when I had a call to the Benson farm within days.

I met him again on the hillside with the same wind whipping over the
straw bale pens. The lambs had been arriving in a torrent and the noise
was louder than ever. He led me to my patient.

'There's one with a bellyful of dead lambs, I reckon,' he said, pointing
to a ewe with her head drooping, ribs heaving. She stood quite motionless
and made no attempt to move away when I went up to her; this one was
really sick and as the stink of decomposition came up to me I knew the
farmer's diagnosis was right.

'Well I suppose it had to happen to one at least after that chasing round,'
I said. 'Let's see what we can do, anyway.'

This kind of lambing is without charm but it has to be done to save the ewe. The lambs were putrid and distended with gas and I used a sharp scalpel to skin the legs to the shoulders so that I could remove them and deliver the little bodies with the least discomfort to the mother. When I had finished, the ewe's head was almost touching the ground, she was panting rapidly and grating her teeth. I had nothing to offer her—no wriggling new creature for her to lick and revive her interest in life. What she needed was an injection of penicillin, but this was 1939 and the antibiotics were still a little way round the corner.

'Well I wouldn't give much for her,' Rob grunted. 'Is there owt more you can do?'

'Oh, I'll put some pessaries in her and give her an injection, but what she needs most is a lamb to look after. You know as well as I do that ewes in this condition usually give up if they've nothing to occupy them. You haven't a spare lamb to put on her, have you?'

'Not right now, I haven't. And it's now she needs it. Tomorrow'll be too late.'

Just at that moment a familiar figure wandered into view. It was Herbert, the unwanted lamb, easily recognisable as he prowled from sheep to sheep in search of nourishment.

'Hey, do you think she'd take that little chap?' I asked the farmer.

He looked doubtful. 'Well I don't know—he's a bit old. Nearly a fortnight and they like 'em newly born.'

'But it's worth a try isn't it? Why not try the old trick on her?'

Rob grinned. 'O.K., we'll do that. There's nowt to lose. Anyway the little youth isn't much bigger than a new-born 'un. He hasn't grown as fast as his mates.' He took out his penknife and quickly skinned one of the dead lambs, then he tied the skin over Herbert's back and round his jutting ribs.

'Poor little bugger, there's nowt on 'im,' he muttered. 'If this doesn't work he's going in with the pet lambs.'

When he had finished he set Herbert on the grass and the lamb, resolute little character that he was, bored straight in under the sick ewe and began to suck. It seemed he wasn't having much success because he gave the udder a few peremptory thumps with his hard little head; then his tail began to wiggle.

'She's lettin' him have a drop, any road,' Rob laughed.

Herbert was a type you couldn't ignore and the big sheep, sick as she was, just had to turn her head for a look at him. She sniffed along the tied-on skin in a non-committal way then after a few seconds she gave a few quick licks and the merest beginning of the familiar deep chuckle.

I began to gather up my gear. 'I hope he makes it,' I said. 'Those two need each other.' As I left the pen Herbert, in his new jacket, was still working away.

For the next week I hardly seemed to have my coat on. The flood of sheep work was at its peak and I spent hours of every day with my arms in and out of buckets of hot water in all corners of the district—in the pens, in dark nooks in farm buildings or very often in the open fields, because the farmers of those days didn't find anything disturbing in the sight of a vet kneeling in his shirt sleeves for an hour in the rain.

I had one more visit to Rob Benson's place. To a ewe with a prolapsed uterus after lambing—a job whose chief delight was comparing it with the sweat of replacing a uterus in a cow.

It was so beautifully easy. Rob rolled the animal on to her side then held her more or less upside down by tying a length of rope to her hind legs and passing it round his neck. In that position she couldn't strain and I disinfected the organ and pushed it back with the minimum of effort, gently inserting an arm at the finish to work it properly into place.

Afterwards the ewe trotted away unperturbed with her family to join the rapidly growing flock whose din was all around us.

'Look!' Rob cried. 'There's that awd ewe with Herbert. Over there on t'right—in the middle of that bunch.' They all looked the same to me but to Rob, like all shepherds, they were as different as people and he picked out these two effortlessly.

They were near the top of the field and as I wanted to have a close look at them we maneuvered them into a corner. The ewe, fiercely possessive, stamped her foot at us as we approached, and Herbert, who had discarded his woolly jacket, held close to the flank of his new mother. He was, I noticed, faintly obese in appearance.

'You couldn't call him a runt now, Rob,' I said.

The farmer laughed. 'Nay, t'awd lass has a bag like a cow and Herbert's gettin' the lot. By gaw, he's in clover is that little youth and I reckon he saved the ewe's life—she'd have pegged out all right, but she never looked back once he came along.'

I looked away, over the noisy pens, over the hundreds of sheep moving across the fields. I turned to the farmer. 'I'm afraid you've seen a lot of me lately, Rob. I hope this is the last visit.'

'Aye well it could be. We're getting well through now . . . but it's a hell of a time, lambin', isn't it?'

'It is that. Well I must be off—I'll leave you to it.' I turned and made my way down the hillside, my arms raw and chafing in my sleeves, my cheeks whipped by the eternal wind gusting over the grass. At the gate I stopped and gazed back at the wide landscape, ribbed and streaked by the last of the winter's snow, and at the dark grey banks of cloud riding across on the wind followed by lakes of brightest blue; and in seconds the fields and walls and woods burst into vivid life and I had to close my eyes against the sun's glare. As I stood there the distant uproar came faintly down to me, the tumultuous harmony from deepest bass to highest treble; demanding, anxious, angry, loving.

The sound of the sheep, the sound of spring.

Studs Terkel

The following selections are taken from Studs Terkel's book *Working: People Talk About What They Do All Day and How They Feel About What They Do* (1974). Further information on Terkel can be found on page 353.

Carl Murray Bates, Mason

We're in a tavern no more than thirty yards from the banks of the Ohio. Toward the far side of the river, Alcoa smokestacks belch forth: an uneasy coupling of a bucolic past and an industrial present. The waters are polluted, yet the jobs out there offer the townspeople their daily bread.

He is fifty-seven years old. He's a stonemason who has pursued his craft since he was seventeen. None of his three sons is in his trade.

As far as I know, masonry is older than carpentry, which goes clear back to Bible times. Stonemason goes back way *before* Bible time: the pyramids of Egypt, things of that sort. Anybody that starts to build anything, stone, rock, or brick, starts on the northeast corner. Because when they built King Solomon's Temple, they started on the northeast corner. To this day, you look at your courthouses, your big public buildings, you look at the cornerstone, when it was created, what year, it will be on the northeast corner. If I was gonna build a septic tank, I would start on the northeast corner. (Laughs.) Superstition, I suppose.

With stone we build just about anything. Stone is the oldest and best building material that ever was. Stone was being used even by the cavemen that put it together with mud. They built out of stone before they even used logs. He got him a cave, he built stone across the front. And he learned to use dirt, mud, to make the stones lay there without sliding around—which was the beginnings of mortar, which we still call mud. The Romans used mortar that's almost as good as we have today.

Everyone hears these things, they just don't remember 'em. But me being in the profession, when I hear something in that line, I remember it. Stone's my business. I, oh, sometimes talk to architects and engineers that have made a study and I pick up the stuff here and there.

Every piece of stone you pick up is different, the grain's a little different and this and that. It'll split one way and break the other. You pick up your stone and look at it and make an educated guess. It's a pretty good day layin' stone or brick. Not tiring. Anything you like to do isn't tiresome. It's hard work; stone is heavy. At the same time, you get interested in what you're doing and you usually fight the clock the other way. You're not lookin' for quittin'. You're wondering you haven't got enough done and it's almost quittin' time. (Laughs.) I ask the hod carrier what time it is and he says two thirty. I say, "Oh, my Lord, I was gonna get a whole lot more than this."

I pretty well work by myself. On houses, usually just one works. I've got the hod carrier there, but most of the time I talk to myself, "I'll get my hammer and I'll knock the chip off there." (Laughs.) A good hod carrier is half your day. He won't work as hard as a poor one. He knows what to do and make every move count makin' the mortar. It has to be so much water, so much sand. His skill is to see that you don't run out of anything. The hod carrier, he's above the laborer. He has a certain amount of prestige.

I think a laborer feels that he's the low man. Not so much that he works with his hands, it's that he's at the bottom of the scale. He always wants to get up to a skilled trade. Of course he'd make more money. The main thing is the common laborer—even the word *common* laborer—just sounds so common, he's at the bottom. Many that works with his hands takes pride in his work.

I get a lot of phone calls when I get home: how about showin' me how and I'll do it myself; I always wind up doin' it for 'em. (Laughs.) So I take a lot of pride in it and I do get, oh, I'd say, a lot of praise or whatever you want to call it. I don't suppose anybody, however much he's recognized, wouldn't like to be recognized a little more. I think I'm pretty well recognized.

One of my sons is an accountant and the other two are bankers. They're mathematicians, I suppose you'd call 'em that. Air-conditioned offices and all that. They always look at the house I build. They stop by and see me when I'm workin'. Always want me to come down and fix somethin' on their house, too. (Laughs.) They don't buy a house that I don't have to look at it first. Oh sure, I've got to crawl under it and look on the roof, you know. . . .

I can't seem to think of any young masons. So many of 'em before, the man lays stone and his son follows his footsteps. Right now the only one of these sons I can think of is about forty, fifty years old.

I started back in the Depression times when there wasn't any apprenticeships. You just go out and if you could hold your job, that's it. I was just a kid then. Now I worked real hard and carried all the blocks I could. Then I'd get my trowel and I'd lay one or two. The second day the boss told me: I think you could lay enough blocks to earn your wages. So I guess I had only one day of apprenticeship. Usually it takes about three years of being a hod carrier to start. And it takes another ten or fifteen years to learn the skill.

I admired the men that we had at that time that were stonemasons. They knew their trade. So naturally I tried to pattern after them. There's been very little change in the work. Stone is still stone, mortar is still the same as it was fifty years ago. The style of stone has changed a little. We use a lot more, we call it golf. A stone as big as a baseball up to as big as a basketball. Just round balls and whatnot. We just fit 'em in the wall that way.

Automation has tried to get in the bricklayer. Set 'em with a crane. I've seen several put up that way. But you've always got in-between the windows and this and that. It just doesn't seem to pan out. We do have a power saw. We do have an electric power mix to mix the mortar, but the rest of it's done by hand as it always was.

In the old days they all seemed to want it cut out and smoothed. It's harder now because you have no way to use your tools. You have no way to use a string, you have no way to use a level or a plumb. You just have to look at it because it's so rough and many irregularities. You have to just back up and look at it.

All construction, there's always a certain amount of injuries. A scaffold will break and so on. But practically no real danger. All I ever did do was work on houses, so we don't get up very high—maybe two stories. Very seldom that any more. Most of 'em are one story. And so many of 'em use stone for a trim. They may go up four, five feet and then paneling or something. There's a lot of skinned fingers or you hit your finger with a hammer. Practically all stone is worked with hammers and chisels. I wouldn't call it dangerous at all.

Stone's my life. I daydream all the time, most times it's on stone. Oh, I'm gonna build me a stone cabin down on the Green River. I'm gonna build stone cabinets in the kitchen. That stone door's gonna be awful heavy and I don't know how to attach the hinges. I've got to figure out how to make a stone roof. That's the kind of thing. All my dreams, it seems like it's got to have a piece of rock mixed in it.

If I got some problem that's bothering me, I'll actually wake up in the night and think of it. I'll sit at the table and get a pencil and paper and go over it, makin' marks on paper or drawin' or however . . . this way or that way. Now I've got to work this and I've only got so much. Or they decided they want it that way when you already got it fixed this way. Anyone hates tearing his work down. It's all the same price but you still don't like to do it.

These fireplaces, you've got to figure how they'll throw out heat, the way you curve the fireboxes inside. You have to draw a line so they reflect heat. But if you throw out too much of a curve, you'll have them smoke. People in these fine houses don't want a puff of smoke coming out of the house.

The architect draws the picture and the plans, and the draftsman and the engineer, they help him. They figure the strength and so on. But when it comes to actually makin' the curves and doin' the work, you've got to do it with your hands. It comes right back to your hands.

When you get into stone, you're gettin' away from the prefabs, you're gettin' into the better homes. Usually at this day and age they'll start into sixty to seventy thousand and run up to about half a million. We've got one goin' now that's mighty close, three or four hundred thousand. That type of house is what we build.

The lumber is not near as good as it used to be. We have better fabricating material, such as plywood and sheet rock and things of that sort, but the lumber itself is definitely inferior. Thirty, forty years ago a house was almost entirely made of lumber, wood floors . . . Now they have vinyl, they have carpet, everything, and so on. The framework wood is getting to be of very poor quality.

But stone is still stone and the bricks are actually more uniform than they used to be. Originally they took a clay bank . . . I know a church been built that way. Went right on location, dug a hole in the ground and formed bricks with their hands. They made the bricks that built the building on the spot.

Now we've got modern kilns, modern heat, the temperature don't vary. They got better bricks now than they used to have. We've got machines that make brick, so they're made true. Where they used to, they were pretty rough. I'm buildin' a big fireplace now out of old brick. They run wide, long, and it's a headache. I've been two weeks on that one fireplace.

The toughest job I ever done was this house, a hundred years plus. The lady wanted one room left just that way. And this doorway had to be closed. It had deteriorated and weathered for over a hundred years. The bricks was made out of broken pieces, none of 'em were straight. If you lay 'em crooked, it gets awful hard right there. You spend a lifetime tryin' to learn to lay bricks straight. And it took a half-day to measure with a spoon, to try to get the mortar to match. I'd have so much dirt, so much soot, so much lime, so when I got the recipe right I could make it in bigger quantity. Then I made it with a coffee cup. Half a cup of this, half a cup of that . . . I even used soot out of a chimney and sweepin's off the floor. I was two days layin' up a little doorway, mixin' the mortar and all. The boss told the lady it couldn't be done. I said, "Give me the time, I believe I can do it." I defy you to find where that door is right now. That's the best job I ever done.

There's not a house in this country that I haven't built that I don't look at every time I go by. (Laughs.) I can set here now and actually in my mind see so many that you wouldn't believe. If there's one stone in there crooked, I know where it's at and I'll never forget it. Maybe thirty years, I'll know a place where I should have took that stone out and redone it but I didn't. I still notice it. The people who live there might not notice it, but I notice it. I never pass that house that I don't think of it. I've got one house in mind right now. (Laughs.) That's the work of my hands. 'Cause you see, stone, you don't prepaint it, you don't camouflage it. It's there, just like I left it forty years ago.

I can't imagine a job where you go home and maybe go by a year later and you don't know what you've done. My work, I can see what I did the first day I started. All my work is set right out there in the open and I can look at it as I go by. It's something I can see the rest of my life. Forty years ago, the first blocks I ever laid in my life, when I was seventeen years old. I never go through Eureka—a little town down there on the river—that I don't look thataway. It's always there.

Immortality as far as we're concerned. Nothin' in this world lasts forever, but did you know that stone—Bedford limestone, they claim— deteriorates one-sixteenth of an inch every hundred years? And it's around four or five inches for a house. So that's gettin' awful close. (Laughs.)

Nora Watson, Editor

Jobs are not big enough for people. It's not just the assembly line worker whose job is too small for his spirit, you know? A job like mine, if you really put your spirit into it, you would sabotage immediately. You don't dare. So you absent your spirit from it. My mind has been so divorced from my job, except as a source of income, it's really absurd.

As I work in the business world, I am more and more shocked. You throw yourself into things because you feel that important questions—self-discipline, goals, a meaning of your life—are carried out in your *work*. You invest a job with a lot of values that the society doesn't allow you to put into a job. You find yourself like a pacemaker that's gone crazy or something. You want it to be a million things that it's not and you want to give it a million parts of yourself that nobody else wants there. So you end up wrecking the curve or else settling down and conforming. I'm really in a funny place right now. I'm so calm about what I'm doing and what's coming . . .

She is twenty-eight. She is a staff writer for an institution publishing health care literature. Previously she had worked as an editor for a corporation publishing national magazines.

She came from a small mountain town in western Pennsylvania. "My father was a preacher. I didn't like what he was doing, but it was his vocation. That was the good part of it. It wasn't just: go to work in the morning and punch a time clock. It was a profession of himself. I expected work to be like that. All my life, I planned to be a teacher. It wasn't until late in college, my senior year, that I realized what the public school system was like. A little town in the mountains is one thing . . .

"My father, to my mind, is a weird person, but whatever he is, he is. Being a preacher was so important to him he would call it the Call of the Lord. He was willing to make his family live in very poor conditions. He was willing to strain his relationship to my mother, not to mention his children. He put us through an awful lot of things, including just bare

survival, in order to stay being a preacher. His evenings, his weekends, and his days, he was out calling on people. Going out with healing oil and anointing the sick, listening to their troubles. The fact that he didn't do the same for his family is another thing. But he saw himself as the core resource in the community—at a great price to himself. He really believed that was what he was supposed to be doing. It was his life.

Most of the night he wouldn't go to bed. He'd pull out sermons by Wesley or Spurgeon or somebody, and he'd sit down until he fell asleep, maybe at three o'clock in the morning. Reading sermons. He just never stopped. (Laughs.)

I paper the walls of my office with posters and bring in flowers, bring in an FM radio, bring down my favorite ceramic lamp. I'm the only person in the whole damn building with a desk facing the window instead of the door. I just turn myself around from all that I can. I ration my time so that I'll spend two hours working for the Institution and the rest of the time I'll browse. (Laughs.)

I function better if they leave me alone more. My boss will come in and say, "I know you're overloaded, but would you mind getting this done, it's urgent. I need it in three weeks." I can do it in two hours. So I put it on the back burner and produce it on time. When I first went there, I came in early and stayed late. I read everything I could on the subject at hand. I would work a project to the wall and get it really done right, and then ask for more. I found out I was wrecking the curve, I was out of line.

The people, just as capable as I and just as ready to produce, had realized it was pointless, and had cut back. Everyone, consciously or unconsciously, was rationing his time. Playing cards at lunch time for three hours, going sun bathing, or less obvious ways of blowing it. I realized: Okay, the road to ruin is doing a good job. The amazing, absurd thing was that once I decided to stop doing a good job, people recognized a kind of authority in me. Now I'm just moving ahead like blazes.

I have my own office. I have a secretary. If I want a book case, I get a book case. If I want a file, I get a file. If I want to stay home, I stay home. If I want to go shopping, I go shopping. This is the first comfortable job I've ever had in my life and it is absolutely despicable.

I've been a waitress and done secretarial work. I knew, in those cases, I wasn't going to work at near capacity. It's one thing to work to your limits as a waitress because you end up with a bad back. It's another thing to work to your limits doing writing and editing because you end up with a sharper mind. It's a joy. Here, of all places, where I had expected to put the energy and enthusiasm and the gifts that I may have to work—it isn't happening. They expect less than you can offer. Token labor. What writing you do is writing to order. When I go for a job interview—I must leave this place!—I say, "Sure, I can bring you samples, but the ones I'm proud of are the ones the Institution never published."

It's so demeaning to be there and not be challenged. It's humiliation, because I feel I'm being forced into doing something I would never do of my own free will—which is simply waste itself. It's really not a Puritan hang-up. It's not that I want to be persecuted. It's simply that I know I'm vegetating and being paid to do exactly that. It's possible for me to sit here and read my books. But then you walk out with no sense of satisfaction, with no sense of legitimacy! I'm being had. Somebody has bought the right to you for eight hours a day. The manner in which they use you is completely at their discretion. You know what I mean?

I feel like I'm being pimped for and it's not my style. The level of bitterness in this department is stunning. They take days off quite a bit. They don't show up. They don't even call in. They've adjusted a lot better than I have. They see the Institution as a free ride as long as it lasts. I don't want to be party to it, so I've gone my own way. It's like being on welfare. Not that that's a shameful thing. It's the surprise of this enforced idleness. It makes you feel not at home with yourself. I'm furious. It's a feeling that I will not be humiliated. I will not be dis-used.

For all that was bad about my father's vocation, he showed me it was possible to fuse your life to your work. His home was also his work. A parish is no different from an office, because it's the whole countryside. There's nothing I would enjoy more than a job that was so meaningful to me that I brought it home.

The people I work with are not buffoons. I think they're part of a culture, like me, who've been sold on a dum-dum idea of human nature. It's frightening. I've made the best compromise available. If I were free, economically free, I would go back to school. It galls me that in our culture we have to pay for the privilege of learning.

A guy was in the office next to mine. He's sixty-two and he's done. He came to the Institution in the forties. He saw the scene and said, "Yes, I'll play drone to you. I'll do all the piddley things you want. I won't upset the apple cart by suggesting anything else." With a change of regimes in our department, somebody came across him and said, "Gee, he hasn't contributed anything here. His mind is set in old attitudes. So we'll throw him out." They fired him unceremoniously, with no pension, no severance pay, no nothing. Just out on your ear, sixty-two. He gets back zero from having invested so many years playing the game.

The drone has his nose to the content of the job. The politicker has his nose to the style. And the politicker is what I think our society values. The politicker, when it's apparent he's a winner, is helped. Everyone who has a stake in being on the side of the winner gives him a boost. The minute I finally realized the way to exist at the Institution—for the short time I'll be here—was not to break my back but to use it for my own ends, I was a winner.

Granted, there were choices this guy could have made initially. He might have decided on a more independent way of life. But there were all sorts of forces keeping him from that decision. The Depression, for one thing. You took the job, whatever the terms were. It was a straight negotiation. The drone would get his dole. The Institution broke the contract. He was fired for being dull, which is what he was hired to be.

I resist strongly the mystique of youth that says these kids are gonna come up with the answers. One good thing a lot of the kids are doing, though, is not getting themselves tied up to artificial responsibilities. That includes marriage, which some may or may not call an artificial responsibility. I have chosen to stay unmarried, to not get encumbered with husband and children. But the guy with three kids and a mortgage doesn't have many choices. He wouldn't be able to work two days a week instead of five.

I'm coming to a less moralistic attitude toward work. I know very few people who feel secure with their right just to be—or comfortable. Just you being you and me being me with my mini-talents may be enough. Maybe just making a career of being and finding out what that's about is enough. I don't think I have a calling—at this moment—except to be me. But nobody pays you for being you, so I'm at the Institution—for the moment . . .

When you ask most people who they are, they define themselves by their jobs. "I'm a doctor." "I'm a radio announcer." "I'm a carpenter." If somebody asks me, I say, "I'm Nora Watson." At certain points in time I do things for a living. Right now I'm working for the Institution. But not for long. I'd be lying to you if I told you I wasn't scared.

I have a few options. Given the market, I'm going to take the best job I can find. I really tried to play the game by the rules, and I think it's a hundred percent unadulterated bullshit. So I'm not likely to go back downtown and say, "Here I am. I'm very good, hire me."

You recognize yourself as a marginal person. As a person who can give only minimal assent to anything that is going on in this society: "I'm glad the electricity works." That's about it. What you have to find is your own niche that will allow you to keep feeding and clothing and sheltering yourself without getting downtown. (Laughs.) Because that's death. That's really where death is.

Mike Lefevre, Steelworker

Who built the seven towers of Thebes?
The books are filled with the names of kings.
Was it kings who hauled the craggy blocks of stone? . . .
In the evening when the Chinese wall was finished
Where did the masons go? . . .

—Bertolt Brecht

It is a two-flat dwelling, somewhere in Cicero, on the outskirts of Chicago. He is thirty-seven. He works in a steel mill. On occasion, his wife Carol works as a waitress in a neighborhood restaurant; otherwise, she is at home, caring for their two small children, a girl and a boy.

At the time of my first visit, a sculpted statuette of Mother and Child was on the floor, head severed from body. He laughed softly as he indicated his three-year-old daughter: "She Doctor Spock'd it."

I'm a dying breed. A laborer. Strictly muscle work . . . pick it up, put it down, pick it up, put it down. We handle between forty and fifty thousand pounds of steel a day. (Laughs.) I know this is hard to believe—from four hundred pounds to three- and four-pound pieces. It's dying.

You can't take pride any more. You remember when a guy could point to a house he built, how many logs he stacked. He built it and he was proud of it. I don't really think I could be proud if a contractor built a home for me. I would be tempted to get in there and kick the carpenter in the ass (laughs), and take the saw away from him. 'Cause I would have to be part of it, you know.

It's hard to take pride in a bridge you're never gonna cross, in a door you're never gonna open. You're mass-producing things and you never see the end result of it. (Muses.) I worked for a trucker one time. And I got this tiny satisfaction when I loaded a truck. At least I could see the truck depart loaded. In a steel mill, forget it. You don't see where nothing goes.

I got chewed out by my foreman once. He said, "Mike, you're a good worker but you have a bad attitude." My attitude is that I don't get excited about my job. I do my work but I don't say whoopee-doo. The day I get excited about my job is the day I go to a head shrinker. How are you gonna get excited about pullin' steel? How are you gonna get excited when you're tired and want to sit down?

It's not just the work. Somebody built the pyramids. Somebody's going to build something. Pyramids, Empire State Building—these things just don't happen. There's hard work behind it. I would like to see a building, say, the Empire State, I would like to see on one side of it a foot-wide strip from top to bottom with the name of every bricklayer, the name of every electrician, with all the names. So when a guy walked by, he could take his son and say, "See, that's me over there on the forty-fifth floor. I put the steel beam in." Picasso can point to a painting. What can I point to? A writer can point to a book. Everybody should have something to point to.

It's the not-recognition by other people. To say a woman is *just* a housewife is degrading right? Okay. *Just* a housewife. It's also degrading to say *just* a laborer. The difference is that a man goes out and maybe gets smashed.

When I was single, I could quit, just split. I wandered all over the country. You worked just enough to get a poke, money in your pocket. Now I'm married and I got two kids . . . (trails off). I worked on a truck dock one time and I was single. The foreman came over and he grabbed my shoulder, kind of gave me a shove. I punched him and knocked him off the dock. I said, "Leave me alone. I'm doing my work, just stay away from me, just don't give me the with-the-hands business."

Hell, if you whip a damn mule he might kick you. Stay out of my way, that's all. Working is bad enough, don't bug me. I would rather work my ass off for eight hours a day with nobody watching me than five minutes with a guy watching me. Who you gonna sock? You can't sock General Motors, you can't sock anybody in Washington, you can't sock a system.

A mule, an old mule, that's the way I feel. Oh yeah. See. (Shows black and blue marks on arms and legs, burns.) You know what I heard from more than one guy at work? "If my kid wants to work in a factory, I am going to kick the hell out of him." I want my kid to be an effete snob. Yeah, mm-hmm. (Laughs.) I want him to be able to quote Walt Whitman, to be proud of it.

If you can't improve yourself, you improve your posterity. Otherwise life isn't worth nothing. You might as well go back to the cave and stay there. I'm sure the first caveman who went over the hill to see what was on the other side—I don't think he went there wholly out of curiosity. He went there because he wanted to get his son out of the cave. Just the same way I want to send my kid to college.

I work so damn hard and want to come home and sit down and lay around. *But I gotta get it out.* I want to be able to turn around to somebody and say, "Hey, fuck you." You know? (Laughs.) The guy sitting next to me on the bus too. 'Cause all day I wanted to tell my foreman to go fuck himself, but I can't.

So I find a guy in a tavern. To tell him that. And he tells me too. I've been in brawls. He's punching me and I'm punching him, because we actually want to punch somebody else. The most that'll happen is the bartender will bar us from the tavern. But at work, you lose your job.

This one foreman I've got, he's a kid. He's a college graduate. He thinks he's better than everybody else. He was chewing me out and I was saying, "Yeah, yeah, yeah." He said, "What do you mean, yeah, yeah, yeah. Yes, *sir.*" I told him, "Who the hell are you, Hitler? What is this *'Yes, sir'* bullshit? I came here to work, I didn't come here to crawl. There's a fuckin' difference." One word led to another and I lost.

I got broke down to a lower grade and lost twenty-five cents an hour, which is a hell of a lot. It amounts to about ten dollars a week. He came over—after breaking me down. The guy comes over and smiles at me. I blew up. He didn't know it, but he was about two seconds and two feet away from a hospital. I said, "Stay the fuck away from me." He was just about to say something and was pointing his finger. I just reached my hand up and just grabbed his finger and I just put it back in his pocket. He walked away. I grabbed his finger because I'm married. If I'd a been single, I'd a grabbed his head. That's the difference.

You're doing this manual labor and you know that technology can do it. (Laughs.) Let's face it, a machine can do the work of a man; otherwise they wouldn't have space probes. Why can we send a rocket ship that's unmanned and yet send a man in a steel mill to do a mule's work?

Automation? Depends how it's applied. It frightens me if it puts me out on the street. It doesn't frighten me if it shortens my workweek. You read that little thing: what are you going to do when this computer replaces you? Blow up computers. (Laughs.) Really. Blow up computers. I'll be goddamned if a computer is gonna eat before I do! I want milk for my kids and beer for me. Machines can either liberate man or enslave 'im, because they're pretty neutral. It's man who has the bias to put the thing one place or another.

If I had a twenty-hour workweek, I'd get to know my kids better, my wife better. Some kid invited me to go on a college campus. On a Saturday. It was summertime. Hell, if I have a choice of taking my wife and kids to a picnic or going to a college campus, it's gonna be the picnic. But if I worked a twenty-hour week, I could go do both. Don't you think with that extra twenty hours people could really expand? Who's to say? There are some people in factories just by force of circumstance. I'm just like the colored people. Potential Einsteins don't have to be white. They could be in cotton fields, they could be in factories.

The twenty-hour week is a possibility today. The intellectuals, they always say there are potential Lord Byrons, Walt Whitmans, Roosevelts, Picassos working in construction or steel mills or factories. But I don't think they believe it. I think what they're afraid of is the potential Hitlers and Stalins that are there too. The people in power fear the leisure man. Not just the United States. Russia's the same way.

What do you think would happen in this country if, for one year, they experimented and gave everybody a twenty-hour week? How do they know that the guy who digs Wallace today doesn't try to resurrect Hitler tomorrow? Or the guy who is mildly disturbed at pollution doesn't decide to go to General Motors and shit on the guy's desk? You can become a fanatic if you had the time. The whole thing is time. That is, I think, one reason rich kids tend to be fanatic about politics: they have time. Time, that's the important thing.

It isn't that the average working guy is dumb. He's tired, that's all. I picked up a book on chess one time. That thing laid in the drawer for two or three weeks, you're too tired. During the weekends you want to take your kids out. You don't want to sit there and the kid comes up: "Daddy, can I go to the park?" You got your nose in a book? Forget it.

I know a guy fifty-seven years old. Know what he tells me? "Mike, I'm old and tired *all* the time." The first thing happens at work: when the arms start moving, the brain stops. I punch in about ten minutes to seven in the morning. I say hello to a couple of guys I like, I kid around with them. One guy says good morning to you and you say good morning. To another guy you say fuck you. The guy you say fuck you to is your friend.

I put on my hard hat, change into my safety shoes, put on my safety glasses, go to the bonderizer. It's the thing I work on. They rake the metal, they wash it, they dip it in a paint solution, and we take it off. Put it on, take it off, put it on, take it off, put it on, take it off . . .

I say hello to everybody but my boss. At seven it starts. My arms get tired about the first half-hour. After that, they don't get tired any more until maybe the last half-hour at the end of the day. I work from seven to three thirty. My arms are tired at seven thirty and they're tired at three o'clock. I hope to God I never get broke in, because I always want my arms to be tired at seven thirty and three o'clock. (Laughs.) 'Cause that's when I know that there's a beginning and there's an end. That I'm not brainwashed. In between, I don't even try to think.

If I were to put you in front of a dock and I pulled up a skid in front of you with fifty hundred-pound sacks of potatoes and there are fifty more skids just like it, and this is what you're gonna do all day, what would you think about—potatoes? Unless a guy's a nut, he never thinks about work or talks about it. Maybe about baseball or about getting drunk the other night or he got laid or he didn't get laid. I'd say one out of a hundred will actually get excited about work.

Why is it that the communists always say they're for the workingman, and as soon as they set up a country, you got guys singing to tractors? They're singing about how they love the factory. That's where I couldn't buy communism. It's the intellectuals' utopia, not mine. I cannot picture myself singing to a tractor, I just can't. (Laughs.) Or singing to steel. (Singsongs.) Oh whoop-dee-doo, I'm at the bonderizer, oh how I love this heavy steel. No thanks. Never happen.

Oh yeah, I daydream. I fantasize about a sexy blond in Miami who's got my union dues. (Laughs.) I think of the head of the union the way I think of the head of my company. Living it up. I think of February in Miami. Warm weather, a place to lay in. When I hear a college kid say, "I'm oppressed," I don't believe him. You know what I'd like to do for one year? Live like a college kid. Just for one year. I'd love to. Wow! (Whispers.) Wow! Sports car! Marijuana! (Laughs.) Wild, sexy broads. I'd love that, hell yes, I would.

Somebody has to do this work. If my kid ever goes to college, I just want him to have a little respect, to realize that his dad is one of those some-bodies. This is why even on—(muses) yeah, I guess, sure—on the black thing . . . (Sighs heavily.) I can't really hate the colored fella that's working with me all day. The black intellectual I got no respect for. The white intellectual I got no use for. I got no use for the black militant who's gonna scream three hundred years of slavery to me while I'm busting my ass. You know what I mean? (Laughs.) I have one answer for that guy: go see Rockefeller. See Harriman. Don't bother me. We're in the same cotton field. So just don't bug me. (Laughs.)

After work I usually stop off at a tavern. Cold beer. Cold beer right away. When I was single, I used to go into hillbilly bars, get in a lot of brawls. Just to explode. I got a thing on my arm here (indicates scar). I got slapped with a bicycle chain. Oh, wow! (Softly) Mmm. I'm getting older. (Laughs.) I don't explode as much. You might say I'm broken in. (Quickly) No, I'll never be broken in. (Sighs.) When you get a little older, you exchange the words. When you're younger, you exchange the blows.

When I get home, I argue with my wife a little bit. Turn on TV, get mad at the news. (Laughs.) I don't even watch the news that much. I watch Jackie Gleason. I look for any alternative to the ten o'clock news. I don't want to go to bed angry. Don't hit a man with anything heavy at five o'clock. He just can't be bothered. This is his time to relax. The heaviest thing he wants is what his wife has to tell him.

When I come home, know what I do for the first twenty minutes? Fake it. I put on a smile. I got a kid three years old. Sometimes she says, "Daddy, where've you been?" I say, "Work." I could have told her I'd been in Disneyland. What's work to a three-year-old kid? If I feel bad, I can't take it out on the kids. Kids are born innocent of everything but birth. You can't take it out on your wife either. This is why you go to a tavern. You want to release it there rather than do it at home. What does an actor do when he's got a bad movie? I got a bad movie every day.

I don't even need the alarm clock to get up in the morning. I can go out drinking all night, fall asleep at four, and bam! I'm up at six—no matter what I do. (Laughs.) It's a pseudo-death, more or less. Your whole system is paralyzed and you give all the appearance of death. It's an ingrown clock. It's a thing you just get used to. The hours differ. It depends. Sometimes my wife wants to do something crazy like play five hundred rummy or put a puzzle together. It could be midnight, could be ten o'clock, could be nine thirty.

What do you do weekends?

Drink beer, read a book. See that one? *Violence in America.* It's one of them studies from Washington. One of them committees they're always appointing. A thing like that I read on a weekend. But during the weekdays, gee . . . I just thought about it. I don't do that much reading from Monday through Friday. Unless it's a horny book. I'll read it at work and go home and do my homework. (Laughs.) That's what the guys at the plant call it—homework. (Laughs.) Sometimes my wife works on Saturday and I drink beer at the tavern.

I went out drinking with one guy, oh, a long time ago. A college boy. He was working where I work now. Always preaching to me about how you need violence to change the system and all that garbage. We went into a hillbilly joint. Some guy there, I didn't know him from Adam, he said, "You think you're smart." I said, "What's your pleasure?" (Laughs.) He said, "My pleasure's to kick your ass." I told him I really can't be bothered. He said, "What're you, chicken?" I said, "No, I just don't want to be bothered." He came over and said something to me again. I said, "I don't beat women, drunks, or fools. Now leave me alone."

The guy called his brother over. This college boy that was with me, he came nudging my arm, "Mike, let's get out of here." I said, "What are you worried about?" (Laughs.) This isn't unusual. People will bug you. You fend it off as much as you can with your mouth and when you can't, you punch the guy out.

It was close to closing time and we stayed. We could have left, but when you go into a place to have a beer and a guy challenges you—if you expect to go in that place again, you don't leave. If you have to fight the guy, you fight.

I got just outside the door and one of these guys jumped on me and grabbed me around the neck. I grabbed his arm and flung him against the wall. I grabbed him here (indicates throat), and jiggled his head against the wall quite a few times. He kind of slid down a little bit. This guy who said he was his brother took a swing at me with a garrison belt. He just missed and hit the wall. I'm looking around for my junior Stalin (laughs), who loves violence and everything. He's gone. Split. (Laughs.) Next day I see him at work. I couldn't get mad at him, he's a baby.

He saw a book in my back pocket one time and he was amazed. He walked up to me and he said, "You read?" I said, "What do you mean, I read?" He said, "All these dummies read the sports pages around here. What are you doing with a book?" I got pissed off at the kid right away. I said, "What do you mean, all these dummies? Don't knock a man who's paying somebody else's way through college." He was a nineteen-year-old effete snob.

Yet you want your kid to be an effete snob?

Yes. I want my kid to look at me and say, "Dad, you're a nice guy, but you're a fuckin' dummy." Hell yes, I want my kid to tell me that he's not gonna be like me . . .

If I were hiring people to work, I'd try naturally to pay them a decent wage. I'd try to find out their first names, their last names, keep the company as small as possible, so I could personalize the whole thing. All I would ask a man is a handshake, see you in the morning. No applications, nothing. I wouldn't be interested in the guy's past. Nobody ever checks the pedigree on a mule, do they? But they do on a man. Can you picture walking up to a mule and saying, "I'd like to know who his granddaddy was?"

I'd like to run a combination bookstore and tavern. (Laughs.) I would like to have a place where college kids came and a steelworker could sit down and talk. Where a workingman could not be ashamed of Walt Whitman and where a college professor could not be ashamed that he painted his house over the weekend.

If a carpenter built a cabin for poets, I think the least the poets owe the carpenter is just three or four one-liners on the wall. A little plaque: Though we labor with our minds, this place we can relax in was built by someone who can work with his hands. And his work is as noble as ours. I think the poet owes something to the guy who builds the cabin for him.

I don't think of Monday. You know what I'm thinking about on Sunday night? Next Sunday. If you work real hard, you think of a perpetual vacation. Not perpetual sleep . . . What do I think of on a Sunday night? Lord, I wish the fuck I could do something else for a living.

I don't know who the guy is who said there is nothing sweeter than an unfinished symphony. Like an unfinished painting and an unfinished poem. If he creates this thing one day—let's say, Michelangelo's Sistine Chapel. It took him a long time to do this, this beautiful work of art. But what if he had to create this Sistine Chapel a thousand times a year? Don't you think that would even dull Michelangelo's mind? Or if da Vinci had to draw his anatomical charts thirty, forty, fifty, sixty, eighty, ninety, a hundred times a day? Don't you think that would even bore da Vinci?

Way back, you spoke of the guys who built the pyramids, not the pharaohs, the unknowns. You put yourself in their category?

Yes. I want my signature on 'em, too. Sometimes, out of pure meanness, when I make something, I put a little dent in it. I like to do something to make it really unique. Hit it with a hammer. I deliberately fuck it up to see if it'll get by, just so I can say I did it. It could be anything. Let me put it this way: I think God invented the dodo bird so when we get up there we could tell Him, "Don't you ever make mistakes?" and He'd say, "Sure, look." (Laughs.) I'd like to make my imprint. My dodo bird. A mistake, *mine.* Let's say the whole building is nothing but red bricks. I'd like to have just the black one or the white one or the purple one. Deliberately fuck up.

This is gonna sound square, but my kid is my imprint. He's my freedom. There's a line in one of Hemingway's books. I think it's from *For Whom the Bell Tolls.* They're behind the enemy lines, somewhere in Spain, and she's pregnant. She wants to stay with him. He tells her no. He says, "if you die, I die," knowing he's gonna die. But if you go, I go. Know what I mean? The mystics call it the brass bowl. Continuum. You know what I mean? This is why I work. Every time I see a young guy walk by with a shirt and tie and dressed up real sharp, I'm lookin' at my kid, you know? That's it.

William Least Heat Moon

Least Heat Moon is the tribal name of William Trogdon, born in 1939 of Sioux and white ancestry. (His father's name is Heat Moon; his elder brother's, Little Heat Moon.) After attending the University of Missouri

(Ph.D. 1973), he taught English for a time at Stephens College. On February 17, 1981, he learned that he had lost his job, and that his then wife, whom he calls "The Cherokee" and from whom he had been separated for months, had acquired a "friend." That night, he writes, he got the idea. "A man who couldn't make things go right could at least go. He could quit trying to get out of the way of life. Chuck routine. Live the real jeopardy of circumstance." The idea was to spend the Spring and all his savings on a 14,000-mile trip by van over the back roads of the United States. The record of the trip is *Blue Highways: A Journey into America* (1982), from which we print this section, which describes the second day. The book's detailed and sensitive account of American sights and sounds, geography, local history, and especially people, made it an artistic and financial success and turned its author into a professional writer; he is now working on another book.

from **Blue Highways**

The rain came again in the night and moved on east to leave a morning of cool overcast. In Well's Restaurant I said to a man whose cap told me what fertilizer he used, "You've got a clean little town here."

"Grayville's bigger than a whale, but the oil riggers get us a mite dirty around the ears," he said. "I've got no oil myself, not that I haven't drilled up a sieve." He jerked his thumb heavenward. "Gave me beans, but if I'da got my rightful druthers, I'da took oil." He adjusted his cap. "So what's your line?"

"Don't have one."

"How's that work?"

"It doesn't and isn't."

He grunted and went back to his coffee. The man took me for a bindle-stiff. Next time I'd say I sold ventilated aluminum awnings or repaired long-rinse cycles on Whirlpools. Now my presence disturbed him. After the third tilt of his empty cup, he tried to make sense of me by asking where I was from and why I was so far from home. I hadn't traveled even three hundred miles yet. I told him I planned to drive around the country on the smallest roads I could find.

"Goddamn," he said, "if screwball things don't happen every day even in this town. The country's all alike now." On that second day of the new season, I guess I was his screwball thing.

Along the road: old snow hidden from the sun lay in sooty heaps, but the interstate ran clear of cinders and salt deposits, the culverts gushed with splash and slosh, and the streams, covering the low cornfields, filled the old soil with richness gathered in their meanderings.

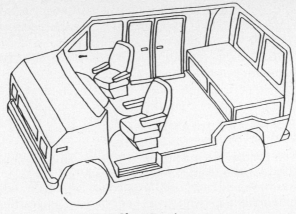

Ghost Dancing

Driving through the washed land in my small self-propelled box—a "wheel estate," a mechanic had called it—I felt clean and almost disentangled. I had what I needed for now, much of it stowed under the wooden bunk:

1 sleeping bag and blanket;
1 Coleman cooler (empty but for a can of chopped liver a friend had given me so there would *always* be something to eat);
1 Rubbermaid basin and a plastic gallon jug (the sink);
1 Sears, Roebuck portable toilet;
1 Optimus 8R white gas cook stove (hardly bigger than a can of beans);
1 knapsack of utensils, a pot, a skillet;
1 U.S. Navy seabag of clothes;
1 tool kit;
1 satchel of notebooks, pens, road atlas, and a microcassette recorder;
2 Nikon F2 35mm cameras and five lenses;
2 vade mecums: Whitman's *Leaves of Grass* and Neihardt's *Black Elk Speaks.*

In my billfold were four gasoline credit cards and twenty-six dollars. Hidden under the dash were the remnants of my savings account: $428.

Ghost Dancing, a 1975 half-ton Econoline (the smallest van Ford then made), rode self-contained but not self-containing. So I hoped. It had two worn rear tires and an ominous knocking in the waterpump. I had converted the van from a clangy tin box into a place at once a six-by-ten bedroom, kitchen, bathroom, parlor. Everything simple and lightweight —no crushed velvet upholstery, no wine racks, no built-in television. It came equipped with power nothing and drove like what it was: a truck. Your basic plumber's model.

The Wabash divides southern Illinois from Indiana. East of the fluvial flood plain, a sense of the unknown, the addiction of the traveler, began seeping in. Abruptly, Pokeberry Creek came and went before I could see it. The interstate afforded easy passage over the Hoosierland, so easy it gave no sense of the up and down of the country; worse, it hid away the people. Life doesn't happen along interstates. It's against the law.

At the Huntingburg exit, I turned off and headed for the Ohio River. Indiana 66, a road so crooked it could run for the legislature, took me into the hilly fields of CHEW MAIL POUCH barns,[o] past Christ-of-the-Ohio Catholic Church, through the Swiss town of Tell City with its statue of William and his crossbow and nervous son. On past the old stone riverfront houses in Cannelton, on up along the Ohio, the muddy banks sometimes not ten feet from the road. The brown water rolled and roiled. Under wooded bluffs I stopped to stretch among the periwinkle. At the edge of a field, Sulphur Spring bubbled up beneath a cover of dead leaves. Shawnees once believed in the curative power of the water, and settlers even bottled it. I cleared the small spring for a taste. Bad enough to cure something.

I crossed into the Eastern Time Zone and then over the Blue River, which was a brown creek. Blue, Green, Red: yes—yet who ever heard of a Brown River? For some reason, the farther west the river and the scarcer the water, the more honest the names become: Stinking Water Branch, Dead Horse Fork, Cutthroat Gulch, Damnation Creek. Perhaps the old trailmen and prospectors figured settlers would be slower to build along a river named Calamity.

On through what was left of White Cloud, through the old statehouse town of Corydon, I drove to get the miles between me and home. Daniel Boone moved on at the sight of smoke from a new neighbor's chimney; I was moving from the sight of my own. Although the past may not repeat itself, it does rhyme, Mark Twain said. As soon as my worries became only the old immediate worries of the road—When's the rain going to stop? Who can you trust to fix a waterpump around here? Where's the best pie in town?—then I would slow down.

I took the nearest Ohio River bridge at Louisville and whipped around the city and went into Pewee Valley and on to La Grange, where seven daily Louisville & Nashville freight trains ran right down Main Street. Then southeast.

Curling, dropping, trying to follow a stream, Kentucky 53 looked as if it needed someone to take the slack out of it. On that gray late afternoon, the creek ran full and clear under the rock ledges that dripped out the last meltwater. In spite of snow packs here and about, a woman bent to the planting of a switch of a tree, one man tilled mulch into his garden, another cleaned a birdhouse.

At Shelbyville I stopped for supper and the night. Just outside of town and surrounded by cattle and pastures was Claudia Sanders Dinner House, a low building attached to an old brick farmhouse with red roof. I didn't

---

CHEW MAIL POUCH barns Barns painted with huge advertisements for Mail Pouch chewing tobacco.

make the connection in names until I was inside and saw a mantel full of coffee mugs of a smiling Colonel Harlan Sanders. Claudia was his wife, and the Colonel once worked out of the farmhouse before the great buckets-in-the-sky poured down their golden bounty of extra crispy. The Dinner House specialized in Kentucky ham and country-style vegetables.

I waited for a table. A man, in a suit of sharp creases, and his wife, her jacket lying as straight as an accountant's left margin, suggested I join them. "You can't be as dismal as you look," she said. "Just hunger, we decided."

"Hunger's the word," I said.

We talked and I sat waiting for the question. It got there before the olives and celery. "What do you do?" the husband asked.

I told my lie, turned it to a joke, and then gave an answer too long. As I talked, the man put a pair of forks, a spoon, and knife into a lever system that changed directions twice before lifting his salad plate.

He said, "I notice that you use *work* and *job* interchangeably. Oughten to do that. A job's what you force yourself to pay attention to for money. With work, you don't have to force yourself. There are a lot of jobs in this country, and that's good because they keep people occupied. That's why they're called 'occupations.'"

The woman said, "Cal works at General Electric in Louisville. He's a metallurgical engineer."

"I don't *work* there, I'm employed there," he said to her. Then to me, "I'm supposed to spend my time 'imagineering,' but the job isn't so much a matter of getting something new made. It's a matter of making it *look like* we're getting something made. You know what my work is? You know what I pay attention to? Covering my tracks. Pretending, covering my tracks, and getting through another day. That's my work. Imagineering's my job."

"It isn't that bad, darling."

"It isn't that bad on a stick. What I do doesn't matter. There's no damn future whatsoever in what I do, and I don't mean built-in obsolescence. What I do begins and stops each day. There's no convergence between what I know and what I do. And even less with what I *want* to know."

Now he was hoisting his wife's salad plate, rolling her cherry tomato around. "You've learned lots," she said. "Just lots."

"I've learned this, Twinkie: when America outgrows engineering, we'll begin to have something."

Erich Fromm

Erich Fromm (1900–1980) was born in Germany, where he studied sociology and psychology at Heidelberg, Frankfurt, and Munich. He received his Ph.D. from Heidelberg in 1922. He then trained in psychoanalysis at Munich and at the Psychoanalytical Institute in Berlin. In 1934, with the rise of the Nazis in Germany, Fromm emigrated to the United States, where he lived as a naturalized citizen until 1974, when he retired to Switzerland. He lectured all over the world and held faculty appointments at many distinguished universities. His particular interest was the application of psychoanalytic theory to the problems of culture and society, and he published a number of widely read books in this area. Among them are *Escape From Freedom* (1941); *The Sane Society* (1955), from which Chapter 5 of Part V is reprinted here; and *The Revolution of Hope: Toward a Humanized Technology* (1968). Among his last works are *The Greatness and Limitations of Freud's Thought* (1980) and *On Disobedience and Other Essays* (1981).

Work in an Alienated Society

What becomes the meaning of *work* in an alienated society?

We have already made some brief comments about this question in the general discussion of alienation. But since this problem is of the utmost importance, not only for the understanding of present-day society, but also for any attempt to create a saner society, I want to deal with the nature of work separately and more extensively in the following pages.

Unless man exploits others, he has to work in order to live. However primitive and simple his method of work may be, by the very fact of production, he has risen above the animal kingdom; rightly has he been defined as "the animal that produces." But work is not only an inescapable necessity for man. Work is also his liberator from nature, his creator as a social and independent being. *In the process of work, that is, the molding and changing of nature outside of himself, man molds and changes himself.* He emerges from nature by mastering her; he develops his powers of cooperation, of reason, his sense of beauty. He separates himself from nature, from the original unity with her, but at the same time unites himself with her again as her master and builder. The more his work develops, the more his individuality develops. In molding nature and re-creating her, he learns to make use of his powers, increasing his skill and creativeness. Whether we think of the beautiful paintings in the caves of Southern France, the ornaments on weapons among primitive people, the statues and temples of Greece, the cathedrals of the Middle Ages, the chairs and tables made by skilled craftsmen, or the cultivation of flowers, trees or corn by peasants—all are expressions of the creative transformation of nature by man's reason and skill.

In Western history, craftsmanship, especially as it developed in the thirteenth and fourteenth centuries, constitutes one of the peaks in the evolution of creative work. Work was not only a useful activity, but one which carried with it a profound satisfaction. The main features of craftsmanship have been very lucidly expressed by C. W. Mills. "There is no ulterior motive in work other than the product being made and the processes of its creation. The details of daily work are meaningful because they are not detached in the worker's mind from the product of the work. The worker is free to control his own working action. The craftsman is thus able to learn from his work; and to use and develop his capacities and skills in its prosecution. There is no split of work and play, or work and culture. The craftsman's way of livelihood determines and infuses his entire mode of living."[1]

With the collapse of the medieval structure, and the beginning of the modern mode of production, the meaning and function of work changed fundamentally, especially in the Protestant countries. Man, being afraid of his newly won freedom, was obsessed by the need to subdue his doubts and fears by developing a feverish activity. The outcome of this activity, success or failure, decided his salvation, indicating whether he was among the saved or the lost souls. *Work, instead of being an activity satisfying in itself and pleasureable, became a duty and an obsession.* The more it was possible to gain riches by work, the more it became a pure means to the aim of wealth and success. Work became, in Max Weber's terms, the chief factor in a system of "inner-worldly asceticism," an answer to man's sense of aloneness and isolation.

However, work in this sense existed only for the upper and middle classes, those who could amass some capital and employ the work of others. For the vast majority of those who had only their physical energy to sell, work became nothing but forced labor. The worker in the eighteenth or nineteenth century who had to work sixteen hours if he did not want to starve was not doing it because he served the Lord in this way, nor because his success would show that he was among the "chosen" ones, but because he was forced to sell his energy to those who had the means of exploiting it. The first centuries of the modern era find the meaning of work divided into that of *duty* among the middle class, and that of *forced labor* among those without property.

The religious attitude toward work as a duty, which was still so prevalent in the nineteenth century, has been changing considerably in the last decades. Modern man does not know what to do with himself, how to spend his lifetime meaningfully, and he is driven to work in order to avoid an unbearable boredom. But work has ceased to be a moral and religious obligation in the sense of the middle-class attitude of the eighteenth and nineteenth centuries. Something new has emerged. Ever-increasing production, the drive to make bigger and better things, have become aims in themselves, new ideals. Work has become alienated from the working person.

What happens to the industrial worker? He spends his best energy for

[1]C. W. Mills, *White Collar*, Oxford University Press, New York, 1951, p. 220.

seven or eight hours a day in producing "something." He needs his work in order to make a living, but his role is essentially a passive one. He fulfills a small isolated function in a complicated and highly organized process of production, and is never confronted with "his" product as a whole, at least not as a producer, but only as a consumer, provided he has the money to buy "his" product in a store. He is concerned neither with the whole product in its physical aspects nor with its wider economic and social aspects. He is put in a certain place, has to carry out a certain task, but does not participate in the organization or management of the work. He is not interested, nor does he know why one produces this, instead of another commodity—what relation it has to the needs of society as a whole. The shoes, the cars, the electric bulbs, are produced by "the enterprise," using the machines. He is a part of the machine, rather than its master as an active agent. The machine, instead of being in his service to do work for him which once had to be performed by sheer physical energy, has become his master. Instead of the machine being the substitute for human energy, man has become a substitute for the machine. *His work can be defined as the performance of acts which cannot yet be performed by machines.*

Work is a means of getting money, not in itself a meaningful human activity. P. Drucker, observing workers in the automobile industry, expresses this idea very succinctly: "For the great majority of automobile workers, the only meaning of the job is in the pay check, not in anything connected with the work or the product. Work appears as something unnatural, a disagreeable, meaningless and stultifying condition of getting the pay check, devoid of dignity as well as of importance. No wonder that this puts a premium on slovenly work, on slow-downs, and on other tricks to get the same pay check with less work. No wonder that this results in an unhappy and discontented worker—because a pay check is not enough to base one's self-respect on."[2]

This relationship of the worker to his work is an outcome of the whole social organization of which he is a part. Being "employed,"[3] he is not an active agent, has no responsibility except the proper performance of the isolated piece of work he is doing, and has little interest except the one of bringing home enough money to support himself and his family. Nothing more is expected of him, or wanted from him. He is part of the equipment hired by capital, and his role and function are determined by this quality of being a piece of equipment. In recent decades, increasing attention has been paid to the psychology of the worker, and to his attitude toward his work, to the "human problem of industry"; but this very formulation is indicative of the underlying attitude; there is a human being

[2]Cf. Peter F. Drucker, *Concept of the Corporation,* The John Day Company, New York, 1946, p. 179.

[3]The English "employed" like the German *angestellt* are terms which refer to things rather than to human beings.

spending most of his lifetime at work, and what should be discussed is the *"industrial problem of human beings,"* rather than *"the human problem of industry."*

Most investigations in the field of industrial psychology are concerned with the question of how the productivity of the individual worker can be increased, and how he can be made to work with less friction; psychology has lent its services to "human engineering," an attempt to treat the worker and employee like a machine which runs better when it is well oiled. While Taylor[0] was primarily concerned with a better organization of the technical use of the worker's physical powers, most industrial psychologists are mainly concerned with the manipulation of the worker's psyche. The underlying idea can be formulated like this: if he works better when he is happy, then let us make him happy, secure, satisfied, or anything else, provided it raises his output and diminishes friction. In the name of "human relations," the worker is treated with all devices which suit a completely alienated person; even happiness and human values are recommended in the interest of better relations with the public. Thus, for instance, according to *Time* magazine, one of the best-known American psychiatrists said to a group of fifteen hundred Supermarket executives: "It's going to be an increased satisfaction to our customers if we are happy. . . . It is going to pay off in cold dollars and cents to management, if we could put some of these general principles of values, human relationships, really into practice." One speaks of "human relations" and one means the most in-human relations, those between alienated automatons; one speaks of happiness and means the perfect routinization which has driven out the last doubt and all spontaneity.

The alienated and profoundly unsatisfactory character of work results in two reactions: one, the ideal of complete *laziness;* the other a deep-seated, though often unconscious hostility toward work and everything and everybody connected with it.

It is not difficult to recognize the widespread longing for the state of complete laziness and passivity. Our advertising appeals to it even more than to sex. There are, of course, many useful and labor saving gadgets. But this usefulness often serves only as a rationalization for the appeal to complete passivity and receptivity. A package of breakfast cereal is being advertised as *"new—easier to eat."* An electric toaster is advertised with these words: ". . . the most distinctly different toaster in the world! Everything is done *for* you with this new toaster. You need not even bother to lower the bread. Power-action, through a unique electric motor, *gently takes the bread right out of your fingers!"* How many courses in languages, or other subjects are announced with the slogan "effortless learning, no more of the old drudgery." Everybody knows the picture of the elderly couple in the advertisement of a life-insurance company, who have retired

Taylor Frederick W. Taylor (1856–1915), engineer-executive, pioneer developer of management science, author of *The Principles of Scientific Management* (1911).

at the age of sixty, and spend their life in the complete bliss of having nothing to do except just travel.

Radio and television exhibit another element of this yearning for laziness: the idea of "push-button power"; by pushing a button, or turning a knob on my machine, I have the power to produce music, speeches, ball games, and on the television set, to command events of the world to appear before my eyes. The pleasure of driving cars certainly rests partly upon this same satisfaction of the wish for push-button power. By the effortless pushing of a button, a powerful machine is set in motion; little skill and effort is needed to make the driver feel that he is the ruler of space.

But there is far more serious and deep-seated reaction to the meaninglessness and boredom of work. It is a hostility toward work which is much less conscious than our craving for laziness and inactivity. Many a businessman feels himself the prisoner of his business and the commodities he sells; he has a feeling of fraudulency about his product and a secret contempt for it. He hates his customers, who force him to put up a show in order to sell. He hates his competitors because they are a threat; his employees as well as his superiors, because he is in a constant competitive fight with them. Most important of all, he hates himself, because he sees his life passing by, without making any sense beyond the momentary intoxication of success. Of course, this hate and contempt for others and for oneself, and for the very things one produces, is mainly unconscious, and only occasionally comes up to awareness in a fleeting thought, which is sufficiently disturbing to be set aside as quickly as possible.

Samuel C. Florman

Samuel C. Florman is an engineer who communicates well with nonengineers. Born in New York in 1925, he was educated at Dartmouth and Columbia and is presently vice-president of Kreisler Borg Florman Construction Company. He has written over thirty articles for *Harper's* and other periodicals and is the author of three books: *Engineering and the Liberal Arts* (1968); *The Existential Pleasures of Engineering* (1976); and, the book from which this selection is taken, *Blaming Technology: The Irrational Search for Scapegoats* (1981).

On-the-Job Enrichment

A collection of E. F. Schumacher's speeches, published posthumously in 1979, was called *Good Work*. This was an appropriate title, since the importance of work—the quest for fulfillment, or even salvation, in work

—is a topic that, more than any other, roused Schumacher to higher levels of passion. Industrial society, according to Schumacher, makes most forms of work "utterly uninteresting and meaningless." This is because "mechanical, artificial, divorced from nature, utilizing only the smallest part of man's potential capabilities, it sentences the great majority of workers to spending their working lives in a way which contains no worthy challenge, no stimulus to self-perfection, no chance of development, no element of Beauty, Truth, or Goodness."

At the same time, and in the same speech, Schumacher deplores the complexity of work in a modern society, and yearns for the simple physical tasks of bygone days:

> It is obviously much easier for a hard-working peasant to keep his mind attuned to the divine than for a strained office worker.
> I say, therefore, that it is a great evil—perhaps the greatest evil—of modern industrial society that, through its immensely involved nature, it imposes an undue nervous strain and absorbs an undue proportion of man's attention.*

The inconsistency here is breathtaking. We are urged to aspire to work that contains challenge, stimulus, and chance of development, while at the same time seeking simple, routine tasks that will free our mind for spiritual contemplation. It never seemed to occur to Schumacher that he was confronting an elemental enigma of human existence, and trying to make it fit within the confines of his simplistic attack on modern technology.

Questions surrounding work and its discontents are as old as civilization. During the 1970s, however, these questions took on renewed urgency, and appeared as a key element in the antitechnology campaign. Schumacher was only one of many observers to express concern about conditions in the workplace. While he was attempting to prescribe a cure for worker dissatisfaction through a return to the fields, a number of sociologists and industrial psychologists sought solutions in a new endeavor which they called "job enrichment" (or, alternatively, "work reform," "job redesign," "humanization of work," or "the quality of work movement"). The deplorable effects of technology, it was hoped, might be mitigated if humanistic concepts could be introduced into the design of work, an area traditionally dominated by "unfeeling" engineers and business managers.

In early 1972 workers at the Vega plant in Lordstown, Ohio, went out on strike, not for more money or shorter hours, but to protest the pressure and monotony of their work on General Motors' fastest-moving assembly line. That 23-day work stoppage helped make "worker alienation" a fashionable term in industrial, sociological, and literary circles.

At the time of the Lordstown strike, a stream of reports were arriving from Sweden, where SAAB and Volvo were trying to deal with worker

*E. F. Schumacher, *Good Work*, Harper & Row, 1979, pp. 25 and 27.

discontent by experimenting with alternatives to the assembly line. These companies attempted to give workers a sense of significance by having them participate democratically in decisions affecting the manufacturing process. The initial successes attributed to these efforts were reported in a series of beguiling newspaper and magazine articles.

At year's end the Department of Health, Education and Welfare released a study, *Work in America,* which reported that people at all levels of society were becoming increasingly dissatisfied with the quality of their working lives, to the detriment of the economic and social well-being of the nation. This study, widely distributed and acclaimed, provided a manifesto for the revolution that Lordstown seemed to portend. With alacrity the concept of job enrichment spread through the worlds of journalism, academe, business, and government. Corporations hastened to establish ways by which workers could help make decisions affecting their jobs. In *The Future of the Workplace,* completed at the end of 1974, Paul Dickson concluded that newly devised "humanization of work" experiments were proving so successful that corporate executives were beginning to view them as important proprietary developments whose details were not to be shared with competitors. Dickson reported that these changes were no passing fad, but harbingers of things to come.

Concern for the alienated worker, in addition to spawning a host of industrial experiments, articles, studies, grants, and conferences, also inspired Studs Terkel's bestseller *Working* and Barbara Garson's *All the Livelong Day: The Meaning and Demeaning of Routine Work.* Both books were based upon interviews with workers and, in the words of the people themselves, the message seemed to be unambiguous: Americans hated their jobs. They left them frustrated and demoralized. Americans seek in their daily occupations a sense of identity, self-esteem, autonomy, and accomplishment. What they get, according to Terkel, is "daily humiliations." Their fragmented, monotonous jobs are, in Garson's view, "soul-destroying." The average worker's discontent manifests itself in fighting, swearing, absenteeism, high turnover rates, sabotage, alcoholism, drug addiction, and poor mental health. Reform of the workplace, it seemed, was one of the most critical social issues of our time.

Nevertheless, just as enthusiasm for work humanization was reaching a fever pitch among intellectuals, disenchantment set in at many of the places where the experiments were taking place. In a September–October 1975 *Harvard Business Review* article, J. Richard Hackman, an organizational psychologist, reported that "job enrichment seems to be failing at least as often as it is succeeding." And further: "Even though the failures may be relatively unobtrusive now, they may soon become overwhelming."

Corporate executives were not the only ones disappointed with the results; among the workers and union leaders interest also appeared to be flagging. The United Auto Workers, for example, appeared to have forgotten about Lordstown. In preparing for new contract negotiations, they were concentrating on the issues of wages and job security.

An obvious conclusion was that a recession was occurring just in time for management to put the rebellious workers in their place. Clearly, in uncertain times, most people are less interested in fulfillment than in a living wage. But the supporters of job enrichment claimed that a more satisfying job results in improved productivity, so that it should be a management goal in bad times as well as good.

In fact, it was this very feature that had aroused the suspicions of labor union leaders whose lack of cooperation appeared to be one of the main reasons for the many failed experiments. Job enrichment, according to a vice-president of the International Association of Machinists, is "a speed-up in the guise of concern for workers." Any experiment that results in increased productivity is necessarily suspect. Even assuming the best of motives, it is disturbing to note that job enrichment depends upon manipulation of workers by the experts. In this respect, it can be viewed as an extension of the much-maligned art of scientific management. The experts, of course, maintain that the new redesign of work is done in response to the desires of the workers. Yes, but it is the experts who must determine what these desires are—a subtle and troubling point.

What *do* people want out of life? That is one of those questions whose answer can be shaped by the way in which the question is posed. Straightforward statistical studies find that in apparent contradiction to Terkel's findings, job discontent is not high on the list of American social problems. When the Gallup Poll's researchers ask, "Is your work interesting?" they get 80 to 90 percent positive responses. But when researchers begin to ask more sophisticated questions, such as, "What type of work would you try to get into if you could start all over again?" complaints begin to pour forth. The probing question cannot help but elicit a plaintive answer. Which of us, confronted with a sympathetic organizational psychologist, or talking into Studs Terkel's tape recorder, could resist tinging our life's story with lamentation, particularly if that was what the questioner was looking for? Compared to the labor performed by most people in the past, today's jobs seem quite attractive. Compared to the "calling" that Terkel says we are all seeking, what job could measure up?

Indeed, people are not "satisfied" with their work nor with any other aspect of their lives. This is hardly news. But can we agree on what should be done to improve the situation? Barbara Garson sees a solution only in workers controlling their own jobs through socialism. (The widespread dissatisfaction of workers in socialist countries does not impress her.) Most proponents of job enrichment, while not advocating socialism, agree that what the average worker misses most is a sense of responsibility and participation in the making of decisions. But is this assumption valid? Are there not many workers who do *not* want responsibility, who prefer the comfortable monotony of routine tasks to the pressures of making decisions and being accountable for the consequences? Miss Garson's workers keep contradicting her basic premise. From a woman who has turned down the job of supervisor: "I don't need the responsibility. After work I like to spend my time fixing up my house. And that's what I like to think about while I'm working." And from people with mechanical, repetitive tasks: "Flip, flip, flip . . . feels good," "you can get a good rhythm going," "you kind of get used to it." Even Garson despairs for a moment: "Maybe the reactionaries are right. Maybe some people are made for this work."

To have thought so (or to have admitted it) up until recently would indeed have marked one as a reactionary. But times are changing. The work enrichment movement appears to be running counter to another trend, the seeking of inner peace rather than ego fulfillment. In the light of this new wisdom, which advocates, among other things, the blanking of the mind in meditation for an hour each day, one can wonder who has the better of the bargain, those who are in the ratrace or those who are "beneath" it. This is the paradox that leads Schumacher into his capricious inconsistencies.

In one episode, Garson tells of a small commune in which ten young adults lived on the wages of four, and where the focus of life was away from work. I dare not predict what modes of life will be attractive to the masses of the future. I believe, however, that the job enrichment enthusiasts have made a mistake in assuming that all people desire what social scientists want them to desire. From Lordstown and some amorphous complaints they have made unwarranted extrapolations.

An even more glaring mistake is that of assuming that by restructuring the workplace, one can solve the problem of alienation. This hypothesis calls to mind those urban planners who saw salvation for the poor in a clean, spacious apartment, and who, after their ideas have been carried out, have spent much energy explaining why attractive apartments have not, in fact, eradicated the ill effects of poverty. They wander from failure to failure seeking the magic environment (high-rise, low-rise, slum clearance, renovation, vestpocket projects, town houses) like so many Ponce de Leons trudging through the malarial Florida swamps.

Alienation cannot be cured by a fascinating job any more than it can be cured by a clean apartment. Some of the best jobs, by almost any standard, are held by members of the skilled construction trades. These people do interesting, varied work. They are craftsmen in the tradition that Schumacher admires. They are not too closely supervised. They see the tangible results of their labor. Their strong unions have made sure that they do not have to produce more than they can comfortably handle. They are well paid. E. E. LeMasters spent five years mingling with hardhats in a tavern, and reported on his experience in a book entitled *Blue-Collar Aristocrats.* He found that these men are pleased with their work and are proud of what they do. He also found that they are about as alienated as it is possible to be—alienated from their wives, their children, their churches, and their political leaders. They are bigoted and full of hate, confused and full of suspicion.

There are diseases of the soul abroad in the land, but only a few of the symptoms, not the viruses themselves, are to be found in the workplace. Healthy people do not become heartless bosses or cruel foremen. Healthy people do not feel debased or dehumanized by menial work or intimidated by blustering superiors. Sick people—alienated people—are not made whole by an interesting job.

Of course, the concept of job enrichment has much to commend it. The idea that work should provide satisfaction is worthy of further pursuit. It serves the interests of the workers, as long as they are assured of not being subtly manipulated, and ideally, it serves the interests of industry and all society, by resulting in increased productivity.

The Japanese seem to have been uniquely successful in this endeavor, indicating that worker alienation has less to do with industrialization than it does with other aspects of the general culture. Work in a factory or a large office is not inherently less satisfying than work on a farm or in a small-town store. The "dehumanization of the workplace" is only tangentially related to technological advance. It is mainly attributable to the way people feel about themselves, and the way that they treat each other. We do not have to look to the Japanese for proof. Anybody who has worked knows that this is so.

In identifying industrial work as a major source of contemporary malaise, the antitechnologists divert us from asking ourselves what we can do to improve mental health, foster common courtesy, and nourish concern of one person for another.

Those who would blame all of life's problems on an amorphous technology, inevitably reject the concept of individual responsibility. This is not humanism. It is a perversion of the humanistic impulse.

Elliot Liebow

Elliot Liebow (born 1925) studied English Literature and Ancient History before receiving his Ph.D. in anthropology from Catholic University in 1966. His book *Tally's Corner: A Study of Negro Street-Corner Men* (1967) is based upon his dissertation. It won the C. Wright Mills Award of the Society for the Study of Social Problems. Most of the information for this study was gathered between January 1962 and July 1963 as part of a fieldwork study. Although white, Liebow was accepted by the two dozen or so black men who gathered at a carry-out food store in the Washington, D.C., inner city; he visited their rooms and apartments, shared their recreations, and learned about their day-to-day lives and concerns. The selection is an excerpt from the second chapter, entitled "Men and Jobs." Liebow has since held various administrative posts at the National Institute of Mental Health, most recently as Chief of the Center for Work and Mental Health. He is currently conducting a study of the effect of work experience on the institutionalized mentally ill.

Men and Jobs

Tally and I were in the Carry-out. It was summer, Tally's peak earning season as a cement finisher, a semiskilled job a cut or so above that of the unskilled laborer. His take-home pay during these weeks was well over a hundred dollars—"a lot of bread." But for Tally, who no longer had a family to support, bread was not enough.

"You know that boy came in last night? That Black Moozlem? That's what I ought to be doing. I ought to be in his place."

"What do you mean?"

"Dressed nice, going to [night] school, got a good job."

"He's no better off than you, Tally. You make more than he does."

"It's not the money. [Pause] It's position, I guess. He's got position. When he finish school he gonna be a supervisor. People respect him. . . . Thinking about people with position and education gives me a feeling right here [pressing his fingers into the pit of his stomach]."

"You're educated, too. You have a skill, a trade. You're a cement finisher. You can make a building, pour a sidewalk."

"That's different. Look, can anybody do what you're doing? Can anybody just come up and do your job? Well, in one week I can teach you cement finishing. You won't be as good as me 'cause you won't have the experience but you'll be a cement finisher. That's what I mean. Anybody can do what I'm doing and that's what gives me this feeling. [Long pause] Suppose I like this girl. I go over to her house and I meet her father. He starts talking about what he done today. He talks about operating on somebody and sewing them up and about surgery. I know he's a doctor 'cause of the way he talks. Then she starts talking about what she did. Maybe she's a boss or a supervisor. Maybe she's a lawyer and her father says to me, 'And what do you do, Mr. Jackson?' [Pause] You remember at the courthouse, Lonny's trial? You and the lawyer was talking in the hall? You remember? I just stood there listening. I didn't say a word. You know why? 'Cause I didn't even know what you was talking about. That's happened to me a lot."

"Hell, you're nothing special. That happens to everybody. Nobody knows everything. One man is a doctor, so he talks about surgery. Another man is a teacher, so he talks about books. But doctors and teachers don't know anything about concrete. You're a cement finisher and that's your specialty."

"Maybe so, but when was the last time you saw anybody standing around talking about concrete?"

The streetcorner man wants to be a person in his own right, to be noticed, to be taken account of, but in this respect, as well as in meeting his money needs, his job fails him. The job and the man are even. The job fails the man and the man fails the job.

Furthermore, the man does not have any reasonable expectation that, however bad it is, his job will lead to better things. Menial jobs are not, by and large, the starting point of a track system which leads to even better jobs for those who are able and willing to do them. The busboy or dishwasher in a restaurant is not on a job track which, if negotiated skillfully, leads to chef or manager of the restaurant. The busboy or dishwasher who works hard becomes, simply, a hard-working busboy or dishwasher. Neither hard work nor perseverance can conceivably carry the janitor to a sit-down job in the office building he cleans up. And it is the apprentice who becomes the journeyman electrician, plumber, steam fitter or brick-layer, not the common unskilled Negro laborer.

Thus, the job is not a stepping stone to something better. It is a dead end. It promises to deliver no more tomorrow, next month or next year than it does today.

Delivering little, and promising no more, the job is "no big thing." The man appears to treat the job in a cavalier fashion, working and not working as the spirit moves him, as if all that matters is the immediate satisfaction of his present appetites, the surrender to present moods, and the indulgence of whims with no thought for the cost, the consequences, the future. To the middle-class observer, this behavior reflects a "present-time orientation"—an "inability to defer gratification." It is this "present-time" orientation—as against the "future orientation" of the middle-class person—that "explains" to the outsider why Leroy chooses to spend the day at the Carry-out rather than report to work; why Richard, who was paid Friday, was drunk Saturday and Sunday and penniless Monday; why Sweets quit his job today because the boss looked at him "funny" yesterday.

But from the inside looking out, what appears as a "present-time" orientation to the outside observer is, to the man experiencing it, as much a future orientation as that of his middle-class counterpart.[1] The difference between the two men lies not so much in their different orientations to time as in their different orientations to future time or, more specifically, to their different futures.[2]

[1] Taking a somewhat different point of view, S. M. Miller and Frank Riessman suggest that "the entire concept of deferred gratification may be inappropriate to understanding the essence of workers' lives" ("The Working Class Subculture: A New View," Social Problems, ix, no. 1 (1961), p. 87).

[2] This sentence is a paraphrase of a statement made by Marvin Cline at a 1965 colloquium at the Mental Health Study Center, National Institute of Mental Health.

The future orientation of the middle-class person presumes, among other things, a surplus of resources to be invested in the future and a belief that the future will be sufficiently stable both to justify his investment (money in a bank, time and effort in a job, investment of himself in marriage and family, etc.) and to permit the consumption of his investment at a time, place and manner of his own choosing and to his greater satisfaction. But the streetcorner man lives in a sea of want. He does not, as a rule, have a surplus of resources, either economic or psychological. Gratification of hunger and the desire for simple creature comforts cannot be long deferred. Neither can support for one's flagging self-esteem. Living on the edge of both economic and psychological subsistence, the streetcorner man is obliged to expend all his resources on maintaining himself from moment to moment.[3]

As for the future, the young streetcorner man has a fairly good picture of it. In Richard or Sea Cat or Arthur he can see himself in his middle twenties; he can look at Tally to see himself at thirty, at Wee Tom to see himself in his middle thirties, and at Budder and Stanton to see himself in his forties. It is a future in which everything is uncertain except the ultimate destruction of his hopes and the eventual realization of his fears. The most he can reasonably look forward to is that these things do not come too soon. Thus, when Richard squanders a week's pay in two days it is not because, like an animal or a child, he is "present-time oriented," unaware of or unconcerned with his future. He does so precisely because he is aware of the future and the hopelessness of it all.

Sometimes this kind of response appears as a conscious, explicit choice. Richard had had a violent argument with his wife. He said he was going to leave her and the children, that he had had enough of everything and could not take any more, and he chased her out of the house. His chest still heaving, he leaned back against the wall in the hallway of his basement apartment.

[3]And if, for the moment, he does sometimes have more money than he chooses to spend or more food than he wants to eat, he is pressed to spend the money and eat the food anyway since his friends, neighbors, kinsmen, or acquaintances will beg or borrow whatever surplus he has or, failing this, they may steal it. In one extreme case, one of the men admitted taking the last of a woman's surplus food allotment after she had explained that, with four children, she could not spare any food. The prospect that consumer soft goods not consumed by oneself will be consumed by someone else may be related to the way in which portable consumer durable goods, such as watches, radios, television sets or phonographs, are sometimes looked at as a form of savings. When Shirley was on welfare, she regularly took her television set out of pawn when she got her monthly check. Not so much to watch it, she explained, as to have something to fall back on when her money runs out toward the end of the month. For her and others, the television set or the phonograph is her savings, the pawnshop is where she banks her savings, and the pawn ticket is her bankbook.

"I've been scuffling for five years," he said. "I've been scuffling for five years from morning till night. And my kids still don't have anything, my wife don't have anything, and I don't have anything."

"There," he said, gesturing down the hall to a bed, a sofa, a couple of chairs and a television set, all shabby, some broken. "There's everything I have and I'm having trouble holding onto that."

Leroy came in, presumably to petition Richard on behalf of Richard's wife, who was sitting outside on the steps, afraid to come in. Leroy started to say something but Richard cut him short.

"Look, Leroy, don't give me any of that action. You and me are entirely different people. Maybe I look like a boy and maybe I act like a boy sometimes but I got a man's mind. You and me don't want the same things out of life. Maybe some of the same, but you don't care how long you have to wait for yours and *I—want—mine—right—now.*"[4]

Thus, apparent present-time concerns with consumption and indulgences—material and emotional—reflect a future-time orientation. "I want mine right now" is ultimately a cry of despair, a direct response to the future as he sees it.[5]

[4]This was no simple rationalization for irresponsibility. Richard had indeed "been scuffling for five years" trying to keep his family going. Until shortly after this episode, Richard was known and respected as one of the hardest-working men on the street. Richard had said, only a couple of months earlier, "I figure you got to get out there and try. You got to try before you can get anything." His wife Shirley confirmed that he had always tried. "If things get tough, with me I'll get all worried. But Richard get worried, he don't want me to see him worried. . . . He *will* get out there. He's shoveled snow, picked beans, and he's done some of everything. . . . He's not ashamed to get out there and get us something to eat." At the time of the episode reported above, Leroy was just starting marriage and raising a family. He and Richard were not, as Richard thought, "entirely different people." Leroy had just not learned, by personal experience over time, what Richard had learned. But within two years Leroy's marriage had broken up and he was talking and acting like Richard. "He just let go completely," said one of the men on the street.

[5]There is no mystically intrinsic connection between "present-time" orientation and lower-class persons. Whenever people of whatever class have been uncertain, skeptical or downright pessimistic about the future, "I want mine right now" has been one of the characteristic responses, although it is usually couched in more delicate terms: e.g., Omar Khayyam's "Take the cash and let the credit go," or Horace's *"Carpe diem."* In wartime, especially, all classes tend to slough off conventional restraints on sexual and other behavior (i.e., become less able or less willing to defer gratification). And when inflation threatens, darkening the fiscal future, persons who formerly husbanded their resources with commendable restraint almost stampede one another rushing to spend their money. Similarly, it seems that future-time orientation tends to collapse toward the present when persons are in pain or under stress. The point here is that, the label notwithstanding, (what passes for) present-time orientation appears to be a situation-specific phenomenon rather than a part of the standard psychic equipment of Cognitive Lower Class Man.

In many instances, it is precisely the street-corner man's orientation to the future—but to a future loaded with "trouble"—which not only leads to a greater emphasis on present concerns ("I want mine right now") but also contributes importantly to the instability of employment, family and friend relationships, and to the general transient quality of daily life.

Let me give some concrete examples. One day, after Tally had gotten paid, he gave me four twenty-dollar bills and asked me to keep them for him. Three days later he asked me for the money. I returned it and asked why he did not put his money in a bank. He said that the banks close at two o'clock. I argued that there were four or more banks within a two-block radius of where he was working at the time and that he could easily get to any one of them on his lunch hour. "No, man," he said, "you don't understand. They close at two o'clock and they closed Saturday and Sunday. Suppose I get into trouble and I got to make it [leave]. Me get out of town, and everything I got in the world layin' up in that bank? No good! No good!"

In another instance, Leroy and his girl friend were discussing "trouble." Leroy was trying to decide how best to go about getting his hands on some "long green" (a lot of money), and his girl friend cautioned him about "trouble." Leroy sneered at this, saying he had had "trouble" all his life and wasn't afraid of a little more. "Anyway," he said, "I'm famous for leaving town."[6]

Thus, the constant awareness of a future loaded with "trouble" results in a constant readiness to leave, to "make it," to "get out of town," and discourages the man from sinking roots into the world he lives in.[7] Just as it discourages him from putting money in the bank, so it discourages him from committing himself to a job, especially one whose payoff lies in the promise of future rewards rather than in the present. In the same way, it discourages him from deep and lasting commitments to family and friends or to any other persons, places or things, since such commitments could hold him hostage, limiting his freedom of movement and thereby compromising his security which lies in that freedom.

[6]And proceeded to do just that the following year when "trouble"—in this case, a grand jury indictment, a pile of debts, and a violent separation from his wife and children—appeared again.

[7]For a discussion of "trouble" as a focal concern of lower-class culture, see Walter Miller, "Lower Class Culture as a Generating Milieu of Gang Delinquency," *Journal of Social Issues*, xiv, no. 3 (1958), pp. 7, 8.

Race, Racism and Culture

The eighteenth century, the period of "enlightenment" with its faith in human reason and social perfectibility, paralleled the development of the New World with its new possibilities and renewed hopes. One of its magnificent themes, historian John Hope Franklin tells us, "was the promise that in the United States there was room enough for all who sought to escape the burden of class, religious, racial, and other discriminations." For Michel Guillaume St. Jean de Crèvecoeur, a Frenchman living in colonial America, this promise seemed to have been fulfilled. Here, he says, "we have not princes for whom we toil, starve, and bleed. We are the most perfect society now existing in the world. Here man is free as he ought to be."

Unfortunately, this utopian dream of a new society has never been realized as ideally as Crèvecoeur imagined. One of the chief barriers has been, and continues to be, racial prejudice and discrimination, the focus for the first section below. John Hope Franklin offers an overview of four nonwhite groups—blacks, Native Americans, Puerto Ricans, and Mexican Americans—who have historically been denied the promise held out by the new society. The two personal accounts that follow record the experience of such exclusion from differing perspectives. N. Scott Momaday remembers his grandmother and her vanished culture, and James Baldwin, in a classic essay, depicts the consequences of a prejudice so deep that it can only lead to a hatred which, he says, finally never fails to destroy the person who hates. The next piece, by psychologist Gordon Allport, distances the discussion by analyzing the sources,

dynamics, and effects of racial prejudice for both victim and victimizer. Finally, the excerpt from Adolf Hitler's *Mein Kampf* provides
a prime example of fanatical and mind-twisting prejudice at work.

In the group that follows, all the pieces show from various perspectives the conflicts that must arise in a pluralistic society that
continues to be a land of immigrants, and where "the old dream is
still dreamt." These are the words of Leonel I. Castillo, grandson of
a Mexican immigrant, who worked for the U. S. Immigration and
Naturalization service. What is happening in the United States
today, he says, "is not a melting pot, but in one way or another,
there is a melding of cultures." Such a melding produces a richness,
a creative energy, but it also produces the tensions and struggles
described by each of the remaining writers in this section.

Peter Berger's piece is fiction—put together from true experiences—designed to demonstrate an idea: the dilemma of Manuela,
who is forced to choose between two very different cultures,
courses of action, moralities. Jeanne Wakatsuki Houston faces the
tensions between cultures within herself, especially in her self-
image as a woman and in her role as wife and mother. Robert M.
Kaus, writing from the perspective of one who comfortably feels
himself part of American culture, challenges the recent search for
and celebration of historical ethnic roots.

Toni Morrison is concerned with a different kind of tension: the
need to reconcile in her own mind the opposing views within her
family. Looking at the world she knows and lives in, she raises the
question of whether the changes she sees and catalogues are really
progress or merely movement. Sandra Mortola Gilbert and Robert
Hayden describe feelings of cultural tension in poetic form.

A New Man

Michel Guillaume St. Jean
de Crèvecoeur

Michel Guillaume St. Jean de Crèvecoeur (1735–1813) was born in France and
in 1754 emigrated to Canada, where he may have served under Montcalm
during the French and Indian wars. He then traveled in the Great Lakes
region, the Ohio River valley, Pennsylvania, and New York—perhaps working

as a surveyor or mapmaker. He became an American citizen in 1765, and in 1769 married and settled on a farm in Orange County, New York, where he wrote a series of essays published in London in 1782 as *Letters from an American Farmer.* (In 1922, H. L. Bourdin discovered another manuscript from this period, published in 1925 as *Sketches of Eighteenth-Century America.*)

Crèvecoeur returned to France in 1780, having been imprisoned for possible espionage during the American Revolution. He lived again in the United States from 1783 to 1790 as French Consul to New York, during which period he knew Washington and Jefferson. He wrote agricultural essays for the American papers and introduced alfalfa into American agriculture. Above all, Crèvecoeur was a careful analyst and a vivid reporter of life in colonial America, of the life and problems of the common farmer and the complex issues, personalities, and motives behind the American Revolution. The selection reprinted below is taken from the 1904 edition of *Letters from an American Farmer;* it is an excerpt from Letter III.

What Is an American?

I wish I could be acquainted with the feelings and thoughts which must agitate the heart and present themselves to the mind of an enlightened Englishman, when he first lands on this continent. He must greatly rejoice that he lived at a time to see this fair country discovered and settled; he must necessarily feel a share of national pride, when he views the chain of settlements which embellishes these extended shores. When he says to himself, this is the work of my countrymen, who, when convulsed by factions, afflicted by a variety of miseries and wants, restless and impatient, took refuge here. They brought along with them their national genius, to which they principally owe what liberty they enjoy, and what substance they possess. Here he sees the industry of his native country displayed in a new manner, and traces in their works the embrios of all the arts, sciences, and ingenuity which flourish in Europe. Here he beholds fair cities, substantial villages, extensive fields, an immense country filled with decent houses, good roads, orchards, meadows, and bridges, where an hundred years ago all was wild, woody and uncultivated! What a train of pleasing ideas this fair spectacle must suggest; it is a prospect which must inspire a good citizen with the most heartfelt pleasure. The difficulty consists in the manner of viewing so extensive a scene. He is arrived on a new continent; a modern society offers itself to his contemplation, different from what he had hitherto seen. It is not composed, as in Europe, of great lords who possess every thing, and of a herd of people who have nothing. Here are no aristocratical families, no courts, no kings, no bishops, no ecclesiastical dominion, no invisible power giving to a few a very visible one; no great manufacturers employing thousands, no great refinements of luxury. The rich and the poor are not so far removed from each other as they are in Europe. Some few towns excepted, we are all tillers of the earth, from Nova Scotia to West Florida. We are a people of cultivators, scattered over an immense territory, communicating with each other by means of good roads and navigable rivers, united by the silken bands of mild government, all respecting the laws, without dreading their power, because they are equitable. We are all animated with the spirit of an industry which is unfettered and unrestrained, because each person works for himself. If he travels through our rural districts he views not the hostile castle, and the haughty mansion, contrasted with the clay-built hut and miserable cabbin, where cattle and men help to keep each other warm, and dwell in meanness, smoke, and indigence. A pleasing uniformity of decent competence appears throughout our habitations. The meanest of our log-houses is a dry and comfortable habitation. Lawyer or merchant are the fairest titles our towns afford; that of a farmer is the only appellation of the rural inhabitants of our country. It must take some time ere he can reconcile himself to our dictionary, which is but short in words of dignity, and names of honour. There, on a Sunday, he sees a congregation of respectable farmers and their wives, all clad in neat homespun, well mounted, or riding in their own humble wagons. There is not among them an esquire, saving the unlettered magistrate. There he sees a parson as simple as his flock, a farmer who does not riot on the labour of others. We have no princes, for whom we toil, starve, and bleed: we are the most perfect society now existing in the world. Here man is free as he ought to be; nor is this pleasing equality so transitory as many others are. Many ages will not see the shores of our great lakes replenished with inland nations, nor the unknown bounds of North America entirely peopled. Who can tell how far it extends? Who can tell the millions of men whom it will feed and contain? for no European foot has as yet travelled half the extent of this mighty continent!

The next wish of this traveller will be to know whence came all these people? they are a mixture of English, Scotch, Irish, French, Dutch, Germans, and Swedes. From this promiscuous breed, that race now called Americans have arisen. The eastern provinces must indeed be excepted, as being the unmixed descendents of Englishmen. I have heard many wish that they had been more intermixed also: for my part, I am no wisher, and think it much better as it has happened. They exhibit a most conspicuous figure in this great and variegated picture; they too enter for a great share in the pleasing perspective displayed in these thirteen provinces. I know it is fashionable to reflect on them, but I respect them for what they have done; for the accuracy and wisdom with which they have settled their territory; for the decency of their manners; for their early love of letters; their ancient college, the first in this hemisphere; for their industry; which to me who am but a farmer, is the criterion of everything. There never was a people, situated as they are, who with so ungrateful a soil have done more in so short a time. Do you think that the monarchial ingredients which are more prevalent in other governments, have purged them from all foul stains? Their histories assert the contrary.

In this great American asylum, the poor of Europe have by some means met together, and in consequence of various causes; to what purpose should they ask one another what countrymen they are? Alas, two thirds of them had no country. Can a wretch who wanders about, who works and starves, whose life is a continual scene of sore affliction or pinching penury; can that man call England or any other kingdom his country? A country that had no bread for him, whose fields procured him no harvest, who met with nothing but the frowns of the rich, the severity of the laws, with jails and punishments; who owned not a single foot of the extensive surface of this planet? No! urged by a variety of motives, here they came. Every thing has tended to regenerate them; new laws, a new mode of living, a new social system; here they are become men: in Europe they were as so many useless plants, wanting vegitative mould, and refreshing showers; they withered, and were mowed down by want, hunger, and war; but now by the power of transplantation, like all other plants they have taken root and flourished! Formerly they were not numbered in any civil lists of their country, except in those of the poor; here they rank as citizens. By what invisible power has this surprising metamorphosis been performed? By that of the laws and that of their industry. The laws, the indulgent laws, protect them as they arrive, stamping on them the symbol of adoption; they receive ample rewards for their labours; these accumulated rewards procure them lands; those lands confer on them the title of freemen, and to that title every benefit is affixed which men can possibly require. This is the great operation daily performed by our laws. From whence proceed these laws? From our government. Whence the government? It is derived from the original genius and strong desire of the people ratified and confirmed by the crown. This is the great chain which links us all, this is the picture which every province exhibits, Nova Scotia excepted. There the crown has done all; either there were no people who had genius, or it was not much attended to: the consequence is, that the province is very thinly inhabited indeed; the power of the crown in conjunction with the musketos has prevented men from settling there. Yet some parts of it flourished once, and it contained a mild harmless set of people. But for the fault of a few leaders, the whole were banished. The greatest political error the crown ever committed in America, was to cut off men from a country which wanted nothing but men!

What attachment can a poor European emigrant have for a country where he had nothing? The knowledge of the language, the love of a few kindred as poor as himself, were the only cords that tied him: his country is now that which gives him land, bread, protection, and consequence: *Ubi panis ibi patria,* ° is the motto of all emigrants. What then is the American, this new man? He is either an European, or the descendant of an Euro-

---

Ubi panis ibi patria His country is that which gives him bread (Latin).

pean, hence that strange mixture of blood, which you will find in no other country. I could point out to you a family whose grandfather was an Englishman, whose wife was Dutch, whose son married a French woman, and whose present four sons have now four wives of different nations. *He* is an American, who leaving behind him all his ancient prejudices and manners, receives new ones from the new mode of life he has embraced, the new government he obeys, and the new rank he holds. He becomes an American by being received in the broad lap of our great *Alma Mater.* Here individuals of all nations are melted into a new race of men, whose labours and posterity will one day cause great changes in the world. Americans are the western pilgrims, who are carrying along with them that great mass of arts, sciences, vigour, and industry which began long since in the east; they will finish the great circle. The Americans were once scattered all over Europe; here they are incorporated into one of the finest systems of population which has ever appeared, and which will hereafter become distinct by the power of the different climates they inhabit. The American ought therefore to love this country much better than that wherein either he or his forefathers were born. Here the rewards of his industry follow with equal steps the progress of his labour; his labour is founded on the basis of nature, *self-interest;* can it want a stronger allurement? Wives and children, who before in vain demanded of him a morsel of bread, now, fat and frolicsome, gladly help their father to clear those fields whence exuberant crops are to arise to feed and to clothe them all; without any part being claimed, either by a despotic prince, a rich abbot, or a mighty lord. Here religion demands but little of him; a small voluntary salary to the minister, and gratitude to God; can he refuse these? The American is a new man, who acts upon new principles; he must therefore entertain new ideas, and form new opinions. From involuntary idleness, servile dependence, penury, and useless labour, he has passed to toils of a very different nature, rewarded by ample subsistence.—This is an American.

Race and Prejudice

John Hope Franklin

John Hope Franklin is one of the most distinguished of American historians. Born in Rentiesville, Oklahoma, in 1915, he was educated at Fisk University (of which he is now a trustee) and at Harvard (Ph.D. 1941). Franklin taught at St. Augustine College, North Carolina College, Howard University, and

Brooklyn College before becoming Professor of American History at the University of Chicago in 1964. He is particularly noted for his studies of the history of American blacks, including *From Slavery to Freedom* (1947; 5th ed. 1980), *The Militant South* (1956), *The Emancipation Proclamation* (1963), and *Racial Equality in America* (1976). Franklin has received many honors for his scholarship. He has served as president of the American Historical Association (1978–79) and was the recipient of the Jefferson Lectureship in Humanities (1976). The present article appeared in the Spring 1981 issue of *Daedalus.*

The Land of Room Enough

1

One of the truly great moments in modern history was the peopling of the New World by inhabitants of the Old, and one of its more magnificent themes was the promise that in the United States there was room enough for all who sought to escape the burden of class, religious, racial, and other discriminations. At first they came in small numbers, as if to test the viability of a New World civilization. Then they came in larger numbers, then in droves as they gained faith in the possibility of building a social order to fit their fondest dreams.

It did not matter to the Europeans that this New World was already inhabited and that the inhabitants were faring quite well without any assistance or intervention on the part of the white man. The Powhatans in Virginia, the Pequots in Massachusetts, and the Tuscaroras in the Carolinas were "civilized"—some by a future "official" designation, others by virtue of the state of their development. They had their own way of life, a religion, family life, an economy, and varying stages of political organization. They were more than prepared to pursue their own destiny and to view with some disdain the various Europeans who began to come to the New World in the seventeenth century.

There is no need to quibble over who came first. It could have been an intrepid Genoese sailor, a stouthearted Scandinavian, or a bold and daring African. They were as one in their search for a better life and in their courage to pursue it relentlessly. What is important is the success of Europeans in building a New World civilization that they perceived to be a distinct improvement over what they had left behind, and their growing sense of confidence that this civilization was superior to anything they found here or anything that was likely to make it to these shores. Consequently, they simply appropriated the land with impunity, even if the Pequots or the Tuscaroras or whoever were peacefully settled and cultivating it. Worse still, they sought strenuously to enslave those people, as if it were their sacred duty to bring them under their control to use for their own purposes. It was best not only for themselves, they reasoned, but for the Indians as well.

What they found here, the Europeans claimed, was a state of heathenism that could not possibly claim respect or even tolerance. The condition of those native to the New World was so abjectly uncivilized as to invite the scorn of its observers, the spread of Christianity, the accumulation of public and private wealth through trade and exploitation, and the "enhancement of national and personal prestige and glory through colonization."[1] Consequently, no serious thought was given to the possibility that Native Americans might share equally or even substantially in the social order that grew out of the dreams of Europeans. They would have to wait for centuries before they could even get a hearing before those who presided over the courts that dispensed human justice and equality in the New World.

Europeans were persuaded not only that they were capable of building a civilization that was superior in every respect, but also that they themselves were superior to any of their contemporaries. New England settlers dismissed the hospitality and friendliness of the Native Americans as the "Lord's mercy to His Chosen People" rather than native good nature. In general, the New Englanders thought their genial hosts were trapped in the snare of the Devil, which would explain their unregenerate state.[2] In turn, it would explain the European sense of superiority over the indigenous peoples of the New World and the justification for their taking whatever lands they desired in the name of Christian civilization.

2

The protracted contact of Europeans with Africans, beginning in the middle of the sixteenth century, led to generally unfavorable impressions that were to affect black/white relations profoundly from that day to the present. The firmest fact about an African was that he was black. Soon black became "an emotionally partisan color, the handmaid and symbol of baseness and evil, a sign of danger and repulsion."[3] It was not long before a whole group of unattractive and undesirable qualities were ascribed to Africans, qualities that seemed for the most part to be permanent. They were ugly by reason of color, physiognomy, and hair texture. They were heathens, almost hopelessly so, since their heathenism was tied to their other base qualities. They were savages, and regardless of how different certain groups of them might be from each other, all of them

[1]Robert F. Berkhofer, Jr., *The White Man's Indian: Images of the American Indian from Columbus to the Present* (New York: Knopf, 1978), p. 116.
[2]Ibid., p. 83.
[3]Winthrop Jordan, *White Over Black: American Attitudes Toward the Negro, 1550–1812* (Chapel Hill: University of North Carolina Press, 1968), p. 7.

seemed light years behind the English in their stage of civilization. They were lustful and lecherous, and their sexuality was virtually beyond control. Finally, they represented the evil, a spectacle of disobedience for all the world to see, that resulted from the disobedience of Ham, the son of Noah, in begetting a child while in the Ark. This earned his son Canaan and all his descendants the eternal curse of God.[4]

Such were the attitudes of Europeans, especially Englishmen, toward Africans when they came to mainland English America early in the seventeenth century. These attitudes help to explain how Africans slipped almost unnoticed from a status of indentured servitude to one of permanent slavery before the middle of the century. A Virginia magistrate took the fateful step in 1642 when he sentenced two white indentured servants to an additional year of service for running away, and a black indentured servant to labor for the remainder of his life for precisely the same offense. In that single decision the judge not only consigned a black man to perpetual slavery, but in the process began the tradition of the crudest form of racial discrimination that would form so large a part of race relations over the ensuing three centuries. In short order slavery would be legalized, and slavery would be the lot for most blacks. In due course the body of law imposing distinctions based on African slavery and inevitably on race would grow to the point that it commanded the attention of a large and important section of American jurisprudence.

It is not surprising that the slave code rested securely on the presumption that slavery was the best, if not the only, condition for Africans. It placed them under the constant supervision of their white masters, and if there was any conceivable good in them, this was easily the very best way of bringing it out. Their every waking hour was spent under the surveillance of the owner or his agent, while their hours of repose were carefully regulated by legislation as well as by plantation rules. Meanwhile, the most learned and influential men of the South built up, through their writings and speeches, a most elaborate justification and defense of Negro slavery. There were, of course, the scriptural defenses based on the curse of Canaan as well as the apparent acceptance of the institution during the pre-Christian *and* Christian eras. These were sufficient to win the support, at least, of the average God-fearing Southerner with or without slaves.[5]

If any doubters remained, they could consult the scientists who argued in lengthy treatises that certain anatomical attributes of Africans made them suitable for slavery in the South. Dr. Samuel A. Cartwright of New

[4]Ibid., pp. 60–62.

[5]The arguments are conveniently summarized in William S. Jenkins, *Pro-Slavery Thought in the Old South* (Chapel Hill: University of North Carolina Press, 1935). Excerpts from the principal writers are in *Slavery Defended: The Views of the Old South*, Eric L. McKitrick (ed.) (Englewood Cliffs, N.J.: Prentice-Hall, 1963).

Orleans claimed that blacks could withstand the heat of the sun better than whites because of a peculiarity in the structure of the eye.[6] Dr. Samuel G. Morton of Philadelphia, a noted craniologist, asserted that slavery was an acceptable status for the "pliant Negro, [who] yielding to his fate, and accommodating himself to his condition, bore his heavy burthen with comparative ease,"[7] because the mean internal capacity of the Negro cranium was less by twelve cubic inches than that of the Anglo-Saxon. Louis Agassiz, Harvard's eminent naturalist, confirmed Morton's general claim by declaring that development of the brain of an adult Negro "never gets beyond that observable in the Caucasian in boyhood."[8]

Negro slavery, many claimed, was good for all concerned. It provided the slave with the only possible opportunity to become civilized and Christianized, thus bringing under control his lower, savage instincts. Meanwhile, since any society needed workers to provide the leisure necessary for the more gifted to elevate the social order, African workers were ideally suited for such function. The now classic statement made in 1854 by James H. Hammond of South Carolina set forth that position clearly:

> In all social systems, there must be a class to do the menial duties, to perform the drudgery of life. That is, a class requiring but a low order of intellect and but little skill. . . . It constitutes the very mud-sill of society, and of political government, and you might as well attempt to build a house in the air, as to build one or the other, except on this mud-sill. Fortunately for the South, she found a race adapted to that purpose to her hand. . . . We use them for our purpose and call them slaves.[9]

In 1858 few persons in the United States and no one in the South would argue that Africans, as slaves, should not occupy an inferior legal and social position in American society. Even the abolitionists gave their attention not to the task of ameliorating conditions among slaves but to transforming slaves into free people. The ideology of white supremacy had become so deeply ingrained, however, that whites treated blacks as inferiors regardless of their status. It is instructive to recall, particularly when one searches for bases for the racial distinctions and discriminations directed against other nonwhites in the United States, that whites made virtually no distinction among those blacks who were free and those who were slaves.

Almost from the beginning, American whites rejected the proposition that free blacks were entitled to the same treatment as other free persons. The sentencing in 1642 of a free black indentured servant to a life of

[6]Jenkins, *Pro-Slavery Thought in the Old South*, p. 249.

[7]Quoted in William Stanton, *The Leopard's Spots: Scientific Attitudes Toward Race in America, 1815–1859* (Chicago: University of Chicago Press, 1960), p. 34.

[8]Jenkins, *Pro-Slavery Thought in the Old South*, pp. 249, 250.

[9]McKitrick, *Slavery Defended*, p. 122.

slavery for running away was a precedent that subsequent authorities seemed all too eager to follow. In 1790 Congress enacted a law limiting naturalization to white aliens. Two years later it restricted enlistment in the militia to able-bodied white men, thus declaring to the five thousand Negroes who had fought in the War for Independence that their services were no longer required. And when Congress passed laws for the operation of the government when it moved to the new capitol at Washington in 1801, it excluded free blacks from participating in the affairs of that government. In addition, only free white males could be mayor or sit on the Board of Aldermen or the Board of the Common Council. In the following year, Congress passed a law, signed by President Thomas Jefferson, specifically excluding blacks from carrying the U.S. mail, a gratuitous expression of distrust of free Negroes.[10]

In the early nineteenth century, white Americans faced two issues that were related to the future of Negroes in the United States. The first was whether slaves should be treated as property or men. If they were men, Gouverneur Morris had said to the Constitutional Convention in 1787, then make them citizens and let them vote. But the view of George Mason of Virginia and his supporters prevailed, and the Constitution did nothing to indicate that slaves were equal to others in the enjoyment of their rights. The second issue was whether free blacks should be treated as other free persons. In the first fifty years of the nation's history, the dominant view was that they should not be. Even if men did not violate the Constitution in maintaining slavery, they clearly violated it in denying full citizenship rights to free blacks.

If such rights could be denied to free blacks during slavery, it made it much easier to deny those rights to blacks in general once all of them were free. Indeed, the precedent of racial inequality had been so well established during slavery, that it became the universal model in the years following the Civil War. Instead of emancipated blacks moving into a status of full equality at the close of the Civil War, they were consigned to a status where their color and previous condition of servitude were more important than their freedom in determining what they could and could not do. In other words, they were like free Negroes before the Civil War—pariahs, outcasts, and still unequal, even before the law.

3

By the last quarter of the nineteenth century, the United States had established a policy that denied to persons of African descent the opportunity of becoming assimilated. This was contrary to the general spirit and attitude toward others, especially those whose native homes were in West-

[10]These laws are discussed in John Hope Franklin, *Racial Equality in America* (Chicago: University of Chicago Press, 1976), pp. 24–26.

ern Europe. It was made clear to those people that the process of complete Americanization was merely a matter of time, and their models were those sturdy colonists who had settled on one frontier or another at any time between the seventeenth and nineteenth centuries. But here were those other early settlers, Africans, who served as models for none of the peoples who were assimilable, but who provided an example when white Americans wanted to qualify the assimilability of other nonwhites who were becoming a problem.

Blacks could hardly have been used as an exact model for the development of a policy toward Native Americans, since the white man's experiences with the two groups were so different. Nevertheless, blacks were seldom regarded as equal citizens, even after the ratification of the Fourteenth Amendment, and one suspects that this general attitude toward blacks helped white Americans view Native Americans as deserving something less than equal treatment. After all, how could one respect a group that had the very first opportunity to develop the continent and had not done so? Furthermore, they proved to be obstructionists—sometimes mild, but sometimes fierce—to the white man's advance across the country. They were "failures" as slaves, and their independence was mistaken for indolence. When they pursued their own type of subsistence farming or hunting in the Gulf plains, they were driven out to make way for the Cotton Kingdom. And when they saw American "civilization" closing in on them and surrounding them, they fought their "last stand" without success but with independence and pride.

These responses proved, if anything, that Native Americans could not become an integral part of the white man's America. But something special had to be done for them, and that was the allotment of reservation lands combined with American citizenship. The effort to provide economic support and political enfranchisement for the freedmen had been a failure (W. E. B. Du Bois[o] called it a "splendid failure") because the government never provided an adequate economic base and because white Southerners and their Northern allies willed it to fail. Except in a negative way, the experience with the freedmen was of little help in the development of a government policy for Native Americans.

However strong the beliefs that Native Americans were inferior to whites, few if any whites placed Native Americans on the same degraded level with blacks. There was no elaborate ideology of white supremacy over Native Americans as there was over black Americans. Perhaps the relatively small numbers of Native Americans and their dispersal over a large area did not require whites to devote an excessive amount of time and thought to their inferiority. However bitter the fight over every inch of land that Native Americans were forced to yield, it did not leave any legacy of hate and degradation comparable to that left to blacks after the Civil War and Reconstruction.

W. E. B. Du Bois Black American civil rights leader and author (1868–1963).

Even if white Americans viewed Native Americans as inferior—and they did—and even if white Americans despised Native Americans for resisting their incursions—and they did—that did not preclude an effort toward a generous solution of the "Indian problem" in both the public and private sectors. Churches and philanthropic organizations wanted to do something for the "savage Indian," and they established schools that would have a civilizing effect in the hope of awakening in him "broader desires and ampler wants." Meanwhile, Congress in 1887 passed the General Allotment Act that assigned 160 acres of land to each head of a family, with lesser amounts to bachelors, women, and minors, and conferred citizenship on those Indians who resided separate and apart from their tribe and "adopted the habits of civilized life."[11]

American citizenship and a sedentary existence on a land allotment were insufficient to lure Native Americans into adopting the "habits of civilized life" of white Americans. Since the Allotment Act provided for the purchase by the federal government of reservation lands that remained after allotment, with the sale price held in trust for the "education and civilization" of Native Americans, reformers and policymakers alike felt certain that the new dispensation was headed for success. Some observers compared the act in historical importance to the Magna Carta or the Declaration of Independence for whites, or the Emancipation Proclamation for blacks. In actual practice, much of the unallotted land fell into the hands of whites, since the secretary of interior tended to force allotment on the tribes faster than they were ready to accept it. Soon Congress provided that even the allotted lands could be leased to others—namely, whites—for agriculture, grazing, mining, and lumbering. By the end of the century, it was clear that whites were benefiting from the Allotment Act more than Native Americans.

Any observer of the 1890s looking at the policy of the United States toward black Americans and Native Americans must have been puzzled at what had been done in the name of reform. For persons of African descent, emancipation did not relieve them of their degraded position. Meanwhile, the judicial interpretation of the Fourteenth Amendment, the centerpiece of the Reconstruction program, benefited railroads and other corporations much more than it benefited the freedmen for whom it was ostensibly intended. After a century of dishonor—the phrase used by Helen Hunt Jackson as the title of her book detailing Indian policy— Americans could not be certain that the new day for Native Americans was better than the old. Indeed, the old assumptions regarding Indian inferiority and unassimilability persisted, and no amount of so-called reform legislation could change the attitudes of white Americans toward those who were already here when they arrived. For black men and red men, the American creed of equality was scarcely more than a mirage in the early years of the twentieth century.

---

[11]Berkhofer, *The White Man's Indian,* p. 175.

4

Perhaps it was the new Social Darwinism⁰ of the late nineteenth century that counseled a rejection of the Negro's claim for equality, for he had been tested and found wanting, and that permitted a kind of condescending benevolence toward the Native American, for even as the white man took his lands, he was still the Noble Savage. But a new vantage point, that of the white man's burden, began to influence America's policies and attitudes toward darker peoples generally. In extending its influence abroad, the most dramatic example of which resulted from its acquisitions in the Spanish-American War, the United States confronted the problem of dealing with Cubans, Filipinos, Puerto Ricans, and other similar groups outside the continental United States. Up to this time, U.S. experience in such matters had been limited to the Eskimos of Alaska, acquired in 1867, and the Polynesian peoples of Hawaii, annexed in 1898 after several earlier efforts.

It was not possible to anticipate either the pleasures or the pain that Puerto Rico would bring to the United States when it was acquired in 1898. What could have been anticipated, it seems, was that in dealing with a territory not contiguous to the United States, the inevitable question of its future status would arise. But since there were as yet no clear precedents, the United States was not ready to answer the question. And in dealing with a territory, many of whose people were of African descent or had some admixture of African, Indian, and Spanish ancestry, it was dealing with a race problem not unlike the one in the United States. This one would be almost hopelessly complicated, however, by the difference in perceptions between the people of the United States and those of Puerto Rico of the importance of race. Although white Americans, by tradition and legislation, regarded all such persons as Negroes, and thus subject to the degraded opinion held of them, Puerto Ricans, with all the rich and subtle color distinctions they made among themselves, could not possibly have understood clearly the implications of the white Americans' classification of them.

Once Puerto Ricans began to migrate to the United States, especially after this country conferred citizenship on them in 1917, they discovered what it meant to be a pariah in the country that had adopted them. They were trying to get away from the sugar plantations that had come to be known as "Uncle Sam's sweatshops," but on the mainland they could not be certain that they would obtain *any* kind of work. Their initial optimism was not realized, and soon some began to return to the island. It was obvious, however, that to return was not a solution, and more and more

Social Darwinism Application of Darwin's theories to human society, particularly the idea that the socially elite classes, those having wealth and power, possess biological superiority in the struggle for existence.

Puerto Ricans became permanent residents of the mainland. By 1930 there were forty-five thousand Puerto Ricans in New York City alone; their numbers increased steadily and reached about one million by 1970. By that time they were in other American cities, most notably Boston, Philadelphia, Miami, and Chicago.

In one sense, Puerto Ricans presented a picture of the classic immigrant leaving home to better his condition, bringing with him such ethnic identifications as history, culture, religion, and language. In due course they could be assimilated and completely Americanized. In another sense, however, they were atypical, because a substantial number of them possessed sufficient African features to be noticeable. The result was as confusing to them as it was to whites, who were quick to reject the darker ones as unassimilable and to consign them to a permanent low status in the social and economic order. The tragedy of the resulting segregation and discrimination was even greater when it cut across family lines, where a portion of a family was regarded as black and treated as such, while another portion was accepted as white and accorded privileges denied their darker sons and daughters or brothers and sisters.

The implications of this for Negro/Puerto Rican relations were as unfortunate as they were inevitable. Both groups were on the lower rungs of the economic ladder, and they competed, sometimes quite bitterly, for the community's most unattractive, lowest-paying jobs. And in the early years of Puerto Rican migration, greater experience and better language facility frequently gave blacks the edge, thus deepening the antagonisms between the two groups. At the same time, many Puerto Ricans were mistaken for Negro Americans and treated as such, causing them to go to great lengths to renounce any affiliation or identification with their African cousins. On occasion they expressed a preference for the terms "Latino" or "Hispanic" if that would assist them in escaping from the term "Puerto Rican," which became, at times, almost pejorative. The white community was not above pitting the two wretched minorities against one another where competition for jobs or housing was concerned and where it was to the whites' advantage to do so.

After thirty years of large-scale migration, the 1.7 million Puerto Ricans on the mainland in 1977 were no better off, and possibly even worse, than those who came a generation earlier.[12] They remained at the bottom of the economic ladder, lower than other Hispanics as well as black Americans. Their situation remained desperate: they still lived in squalor in some of the nation's worst slums, were victims to some of the nation's worst racism, and had failed, except in a very few cases, to rise significantly on the political or economic ladder. The time came when their lowly status on the mainland prompted them to join those forces back home who contended that complete independence from American domination,

[12]*The New York Times,* September 11, 1977.

rather than commonwealth status or statehood, was the only solution worth seeking. Neither Native Americans nor Negro Americans provided any meaningful experience that seemed applicable in dealing with the problem of Puerto Ricans in the United States.

5

Like the Puerto Ricans and Native Americans, Mexican Americans in the United States were essentially people of the New World, some of them an admixture of Indian, Spanish, and African. When they began to migrate to the United States after 1900, they had behind them a long history of conflict with the people of America. Mexicans had been opposed to the incursions of people from the United States during the early days of Mexico's independence, in the 1820s and 1830s, especially those who insisted on bringing their slaves. Shortly after independence, Mexico had outlawed slavery, as had all other Latin American countries, except Cuba and Brazil. Their resistance to America's encroachments brought about a full-scale independence movement when American settlers in Texas refused to accept Mexican law. Annexation of Texas in 1845 and the enormous cession of lands to the United States after the Mexican War in 1848 left Mexico bereft of its richest and most desirable lands. With Texas, New Mexico, Arizona, Colorado, Nevada, Utah, and California in the hands of the United States, the fledgling, beaten republic to the south had few resources with which to repair her losses.

Mexico's disadvantages were numerous. Her people were dark-skinned, and Americans were developing increasing variations on the theme of white supremacy. They were Roman Catholic at a time when the Protestant crusade was reaching its peak in the United States. Mexican culture was regarded by Americans as decadent and inferior, whereas their own was reaching perfection, if one listened to Southerners, or was in a progressive, experimental stage, according to liberal Northerners. Consequently, it was assumed that Mexicans living in their own ceded territories were unable to contribute much, if anything, to the march of civilization. And contact with them merely confirmed the lowest opinions that white Americans had of them. White squatters regularly appropriated land held by Mexicans in California and other areas in the Southwest, calling their victims lazy, indolent, unambitious, and undeserving of the lands they occupied.

Under the circumstances, it would not be surprising if the Mexicans had preferred to maintain some distance between themselves and the white Americans. But with hard times and few opportunities at home, the United States was one of the few promising places within their reach, if only they could overcome the obvious prejudices against them. They began to migrate to the United States in substantial numbers in the early years of the century. Unlike the Puerto Ricans who flocked to the city, the Mexicans initially went into the rural areas to become farm laborers.

Indeed, they were often recruited and brought into the country to take up the slack during periods of labor shortages. Some came on their own, with neither visas nor passports, thus becoming particularly vulnerable as "undocumented aliens." As fruit and vegetable pickers in California, Arizona, Idaho, Washington, and Colorado, they were exploited mercilessly by the large farmers, and when their own leaders began to organize them into unions, the stage was set for reprisals, deportations, and other actions to blunt the effects of unionization.

Those who went to the cities faced discrimination in housing and jobs, and competition with blacks and Puerto Ricans. Everywhere, even in the Southwest, where many had always lived and to which large numbers came annually from across the border, Mexican Americans received the distinct impression that, aside from their seasonal or periodic labor, they were not to enjoy the advantages and blessings of American civilization. In due course, however, leaders would rise among them who could speak out in their behalf and demand equality of treatment as workers and as human beings. If their demands were not always heeded, no one could any longer ignore them. They added significantly to the racial and ethnic quandary all Americans faced in the closing decades of the twentieth century.

Although many Mexican Americans were citizens of the United States, there were many others, resident in the United States, who were citizens of Mexico. Their treatment, therefore, was of interest not only to their union leaders or American public officials at different levels of jurisdiction, but to the government of Mexico as well. And their flagrant mistreatment —as workers, in seeking housing, or as victims of brutality at the hands of the local police—merely added to the litany of grievances that the Mexican government had accumulated through the years. More than once, particularly in recent years, their treatment was the subject of delicate discussions between the heads of state or other high officials on both sides of the border. Even if such discussions did not result in a dramatic improvement of their lot, Mexican Americans could get some satisfaction from the knowledge that a sovereign state, with increasing leverage, could espouse their cause if it were inclined to do so. Neither Native Americans, black Americans, nor Puerto Ricans were in such an enviable position.

6

One cannot help but be impressed by the bonds of disadvantage and even degradation that tie these four groups of Americans together. In varying degrees they were victims of American racism, developed initially out of the American experience with persons of African descent, but extended to others of darker hue—Native Americans, Puerto Ricans, and Mexican Americans—as they sought equal treatment at the hands of white Americans. Their struggle for full equality has been an ongoing one, and they would have much to tell one another both about their limited successes and numerous failures. They are, in general, clustered at the lower end of the occupational and economic scale, victims of discrimination in employment and in compensation for work done. They are for the most part confined to certain sections of the city where housing, although expensive, is limited and frequently substandard. All too often the several groups are in fierce competition with one another for jobs, housing, and other favors of society. Such competition leads to invidious comparisons, jealousy, and envy, and they become easy pawns in the game played by the white majority of pitting one wretched group against the others.

Despite the fact that black Americans were clearly the greatest victims of a well-defined racism that dated at least from the seventeenth century, the other groups tended to feel that blacks had been the most successful in combating racism. The examples of their civil rights organizations, their activities in the field of litigation, and their political influence are a source of envy as well as admiration, but what is more important and to the point is that they have provided inspiration for the others. The Civil Rights Act of 1964, the Voting Rights Act of 1965, and a host of presidential orders, commissions, and agencies are seen as coming primarily from the efforts of Negro Americans. Blacks are seen, moreover, as making rapid strides up the economic ladder. No other group can boast of the kinds of gains made by blacks that are heralded in each issue of *Black Enterprise* and *Ebony*. In reading the glowing accounts of their successes and achievements, we have to remind ourselves that these are exceptions, that the percentage of unemployed blacks in the work force is twice that of whites, and that in many cities across the country as many as 40 percent of black teenagers are unemployed. In such dismal matters they are closer to the other groups than one might think.

There is little doubt that the vigorous drive by blacks for equality during the past two decades has encouraged other groups to make similar moves. This is not to suggest that the movement in other groups was wholly derivative, but that the climate of the sixties, in which blacks had an important role, stimulated a widespread movement for equality among numerous groups. Thus, *La Causa* of the mid-sixties became a crusade to assert the dignity of Mexican Americans, and the Mexican American Legal Defense and Education Fund undertook to protect the rights of its people, as the NAACP Legal Defense Fund had been doing for blacks since the 1930s. Likewise, the American Indian Movement (AIM), which began in the 1960s, was notably successful in publicizing the plight of Native Americans and winning support from a wide variety of sources. Puerto Ricans did not need the climate of the 1960s to spawn movements for dignity, self-respect, and even independence. Almost from the time they began to come to the mainland in significant numbers, they founded organizations to improve their condition. Today they range from the quite proper Puerto Rican Association for Community Affairs in New York City to the radical, terrorist FALN (Armed Forces of National Liberation).

Despite the common bond of discrimination that all four groups share, there are significant differences. One of these has to do with language and culture. Puerto Ricans and Mexican Americans are proud of their distinct cultures and especially of their language. One Puerto Rican recently said that the Spanish language was for his people a unifying factor and a guardian of their identity.[13] Both groups tend to hold fast to it, the Puerto Ricans apparently with greater tenacity than the Mexican Americans. Blacks and Native Americans, on the other hand, have only English as a common language and cultures that have been almost completely diluted and eclipsed by the culture of the dominant racial and ethnic groups.

Another difference is that Puerto Ricans on the mainland have a homeland to which they are deeply and permanently attached. Frequent visits, where possible, reinforce the attachment and cause many to regard themselves as Puerto Ricans first and Americans second. Mexican Americans do not seem to be nearly as deeply attached to Mexico. Many of them are not immigrants but have always lived on the lands ceded by Mexico to the United States. Others were recruited from Mexico as laborers, and under the circumstances, would just as soon forget the wretched conditions from which they came. Still others came without permission and return the same way if and when they care to. On the other hand, the connections of Afro-Americans with their ancestral lands lie deep in the past. They came to the New World involuntarily and for centuries had no opportunity to return. In recent years, with the independence of African states and with the example of blacks serving as political and economic leaders in numerous countries, Afro-Americans have experienced a renewed interest in the land of their fathers.

Native Americans had no such experiences. Their attachment to their own land was attested to by their resentment of the way in which Europeans dispossessed them. But nothing could dispossess them of the notion that America was *their* homeland. As the first settlers they never conceded that others, in the name of a superior civilization, had a right to push them aside. Without the power or the weapons to turn back the Europeans, they finally made their peace with them on the theory that the New World was indeed the land of room enough. Only through the kind of litigation that black Americans had pushed were Native Americans able to hold on to the theory and then recover and save some of the land as well as some of the rights for themselves.

If being an American is to share in the history and culture of the country, to contribute to its well-being, and to be a part of its future, the Americanism of these four groups cannot be successfully challenged by anyone. The Indians were here before any other known group, and their imprint has had a profound impact on virtually every aspect of American life and history. For three centuries Afro-Americans have been a central

[13]*The New York Times,* May 13, 1980.

feature of America's history, and no amount of gainsaying can eradicate their importance. Mexican Americans are native to much of this country's Southwest, and there as well as elsewhere their culture is as American as that claimed by any former European. Likewise, Puerto Ricans, both in their island homeland and in mainland America, have added both substance and flavor to American culture. These groups need not yield to any group in their claim to be integral parts of American life, even as they remain conscious of their own distinctiveness.

One of the tragedies of the present situation is that the sense of sharing common problems and seeking common goals is minimal. It is true that under the circumstances the four groups are almost natural competitors, since they must scratch around at the bottom of the economic ladder for whatever falls from above. But it is also true that with increased education and greater technical skills, and with a better understanding of the benefits of cooperation, they could effect the kind of intergroup arrangements that would transcend and neutralize many of the divisive forces that exist. In an age of shrinking economic opportunities, it is "more tempting for one group to see the other as a potential rival than as an ally," as Joel Dreyfuss has observed.[14] Even so, the alternative to cooperation is a continuation of the crudest forms of bitter group rivalries, energetically promoted by the groups that have always benefited from such rivalries. The most compelling argument clearly favors an elimination of suspicions, jealousies, and rivalries, and the adoption of all feasible methods of peaceful cooperation. This is not to suggest that their ultimate goals are, or should be, identical.

It has become fashionable in the past three or four decades for various hyphenated Americans to emphasize the distinctive aspects of their respective cultures—as though these groups have been so successfully and securely assimilated that they can afford to look back to their origins and pay homage to their languages, histories, and the special features of their culture. This new way of looking at themselves and their past has become a luxury no less important than their expensive homes and automobiles. These same decades witnessed an important rise in the decibels of protest and in the crusade for equality on the part of Native Americans, black Americans, Puerto Ricans, and Mexican Americans. It was as though this was *not* the land of room enough and that the assimilation of the others had been accomplished at their expense. These cries of anguish and these demands for attention to their problems serve as a reminder that the very term *assimilability* is one that suggests there are problems that lie outside its scope. These are the problems of those who have not been assimilated. And as a Puerto Rican woman recently said, "There is never a lack of problems. The poor live off hope."[15]

---

[14]Joel Dreyfuss, "Blacks and Hispanics, Coalition or Confrontation?" *Black Enterprise,* 9 (1979): 23.
[15]*The New York Times,* May 12, 1980.

N. Scott Momaday

N. Scott Momaday was born in Oklahoma in 1934. He studied at New Mexico University, at Stanford University (Creative Writing Fellow, 1959; Ph.D., 1963), and then taught English at the University of California (Santa Barbara and Berkeley) and is now at Stanford. While teaching, Momaday has all along written and published. He has edited two books, *The Complete Poems of Frederick Goddard Tuckerman* (1965) and *American Indian Authors* (1972). He also has written a book for juveniles, *Owl in the Cedar Tree* (1965); a novel, *House Made of Dawn* (1968), for which he won the 1969 Pulitzer Prize; and *The Journey of Tai-Me, Kiowa Indian Tales* (1968), which was revised and published as *The Way to Rainy Mountain* (1969). It records a journey of memory and myth, his actual journey by car following the ancient migration route of the Kiowa Indians from the mountains of Yellowstone, the lost Eden of the Kiowa, to Rainy Mountain in Oklahoma. The Introduction is reprinted here. Other work includes two books of poems, *Angle of Geese and Other Poems* (1963) and *The Gourd Dancer* (1976), and an autobiographical memoir, *The Names* (1978).

Introduction to The Way to Rainy Mountain

A single knoll rises out of the plain in Oklahoma, north and west of the Wichita Range. For my people, the Kiowas, it is an old landmark, and they gave it the name Rainy Mountain. The hardest weather in the world is there. Winter brings blizzards, hot tornadic winds arise in the spring, and in summer the prairie is an anvil's edge. The grass turns brittle and brown, and it cracks beneath your feet. There are green belts along the rivers and creeks, linear groves of hickory and pecan, willow and witch hazel. At a distance in July or August the steaming foliage seems almost to writhe in fire. Great green and yellow grasshoppers are everywhere in the tall grass, popping up like corn to sting the flesh, and tortoises crawl about on the red earth, going nowhere in the plenty of time. Loneliness is an aspect of the land. All things in the plain are isolate; there is no confusion of objects in the eye, but *one* hill or *one* tree or *one* man. To look upon that land-scape in the early morning, with the sun at your back, is to lose the sense of proportion. Your imagination comes to life, and this, you think, is where Creation was begun.

I returned to Rainy Mountain in July. My grandmother had died in the spring, and I wanted to be at her grave. She had lived to be very old and at last infirm. Her only living daughter was with her when she died, and I was told that in death her face was that of a child.

I like to think of her as a child. When she was born, the Kiowas were living the last great moment of their history. For more than a hundred years they had controlled the open range from the Smoky Hill River to the Red, from the headwaters of the Canadian to the fork of the Arkansas and Cimarron. In alliance with the Comanches, they had ruled the whole of the southern Plains. War was their sacred business, and they were among the finest horsemen the world has ever known. But warfare for the Kiowas was preeminently a matter of disposition rather than of survival, and they never understood the grim, unrelenting advance of the U.S. Cavalry. When at last, divided and ill-provisioned, they were driven onto the Staked Plains in the cold rains of autumn, they fell into panic. In Palo Duro Canyon they abandoned their crucial stores to pillage and had nothing then but their lives. In order to save themselves, they surrendered to the soldiers at Fort Sill and were imprisoned in the old stone corral that now stands as a military museum. My grandmother was spared the humiliation of those high gray walls by eight or ten years, but she must have known from birth the affliction of defeat, the dark brooding of old warriors.

Her name was Aho, and she belonged to the last culture to evolve in North America. Her forebears came down from the high country in western Montana nearly three centuries ago. They were a mountain people, a mysterious tribe of hunters whose language has never been positively classified in any major group. In the late seventeenth century they began a long migration to the south and east. It was a journey toward the dawn, and it led to a golden age. Along the way the Kiowas were befriended by the Crows, who gave them the culture and religion of the Plains. They acquired horses, and their ancient nomadic spirit was suddenly free of the ground. They acquired Tai-me, the sacred Sun Dance doll, from that moment the object and symbol of their worship, and so shared in the divinity of the sun. Not least, they acquired the sense of destiny, therefore courage and pride. When they entered upon the southern Plains they had been transformed. No longer were they slaves to the simple necessity of survival; they were a lordly and dangerous society of fighters and thieves, hunters and priests of the sun. According to their origin myth, they entered the world through a hollow log. From one point of view, their migration was the fruit of an old prophecy, for indeed they emerged from a sunless world.

Although my grandmother lived out her long life in the shadow of Rainy Mountain, the immense landscape of the continental interior lay like memory in her blood. She could tell of the Crows, whom she had never seen, and of the Black Hills, where she had never been. I wanted to see in reality what she had seen more perfectly in the mind's eye, and traveled fifteen hundred miles to begin my pilgrimage.

Yellowstone, it seemed to me, was the top of the world, a region of deep lakes and dark timber, canyons and waterfalls. But, beautiful as it is, one might have the sense of confinement there. The skyline in all directions is close at hand, the high wall of the woods and deep cleavages of shade. There is a perfect freedom in the mountains, but it belongs to the eagle and the elk, the badger and the bear. The Kiowas reckoned their stature by the distance they could see, and they were bent and blind in the wilderness.

Descending eastward, the highland meadows are a stairway to the plain. In July the inland slope of the Rockies is luxuriant with flax and buckwheat, stonecrop and larkspur. The earth unfolds and the limit of the land recedes. Clusters of trees, and animals grazing far in the distance, cause the vision to reach away and wonder to build upon the mind. The sun follows a longer course in the day, and the sky is immense beyond all comparison. The great billowing clouds that sail upon it are shadows that move upon the grain like water, dividing light. Farther down, in the land of the Crows and Blackfeet, the plain is yellow. Sweet clover takes hold of the hills and bends upon itself to cover and seal the soil. There the Kiowas paused on their way; they had come to the place where they must change their lives. The sun is at home on the plains. Precisely there does it have the certain character of a god. When the Kiowas came to the land of the Crows, they could see the dark lees of the hills at dawn across the Bighorn River, the profusion of light on the grain shelves, the oldest deity ranging after the solstices. Not yet would they veer southward to the caldron of the land that lay below; they must wean their blood from the northern winter and hold the mountains a while longer in their view. They bore Tai-me in procession to the east.

A dark mist lay over the Black Hills, and the land was like iron. At the top of a ridge I caught sight of Devil's Tower upthrust against the gray sky as if in the birth of time the core of the earth had broken through its crust and the motion of the world was begun. There are things in nature that engender an awful quiet in the heart of man; Devil's Tower is one of them. Two centuries ago, because they could not do otherwise, the Kiowas made a legend at the base of the rock. My grandmother said:

> *Eight children were there at play, seven sisters and their brother. Suddenly the boy was struck dumb; he trembled and began to run upon his hands and feet. His fingers became claws, and his body was covered with fur. Directly there was a bear where the boy had been. The sisters were terrified; they ran, and the bear after them. They came to the stump of a great tree, and the tree spoke to them. It bade them climb upon it, and as they did so it began to rise into the air. The bear came to kill them, but they were just beyond its reach. It reared against the tree and scored the bark all around with its claws. The seven sisters were borne into the sky, and they became the stars of the Big Dipper.*

From that moment, and so long as the legend lives, the Kiowas have kinsmen in the night sky. Whatever they were in the mountains, they could be no more. However tenuous their well-being, however much they had suffered and would suffer again, they had found a way out of the wilderness.

My grandmother had a reverence for the sun, a holy regard that now is all but gone out of mankind. There was a wariness in her, and an ancient awe. She was a Christian in her later years, but she had come a long way about, and she never forgot her birthright. As a child she had been to the Sun Dances; she had taken part in those annual rites, and by them she had learned the restoration of her people in the presence of Tai-me. She was about seven when the last Kiowa Sun Dance was held in 1887 on the Washita River above Rainy Mountain Creek. The buffalo were gone. In order to consummate the ancient sacrifice—to impale the head of a buffalo upon the medicine tree—a delegation of old men journeyed into Texas, there to beg and barter for an animal from the Goodnight herd. She was ten when the Kiowas came together for the last time as a living Sun Dance culture. They could find no buffalo; they had to hang an old hide from the sacred tree. Before the dance could begin, a company of soldiers rode out from Fort Sill under orders to disperse the tribe. Forbidden without cause the essential act of their faith, having seen the wild herds slaughtered and left to rot upon the ground, the Kiowas backed away forever from the medicine tree. That was July 20, 1890, at the great bend of the Washita. My grandmother was there. Without bitterness, and for as long as she lived, she bore a vision of deicide.

Now that I can have her only in memory, I see my grandmother in the several postures that were peculiar to her: standing at the wood stove on a winter morning and turning meat in a great iron skillet; sitting at the south window, bent above her beadwork, and afterwards, when her vision failed, looking down for a long time into the fold of her hands; going out upon a cane, very slowly as she did when the weight of age came upon her; praying. I remember her most often at prayer. She made long, rambling prayers out of suffering and hope, having seen many things. I was never sure that I had the right to hear, so exclusive were they of all mere custom and company. The last time I saw her she prayed standing by the side of her bed at night, naked to the waist, the light of a kerosene lamp moving upon her dark skin. Her long, black hair, always drawn and braided in the day, lay upon her shoulders and against her breasts like a shawl. I do not speak Kiowa, and I never understood her prayers, but there was something inherently sad in the sound, some merest hesitation upon the syllables of sorrow. She began in a high and descending pitch, exhausting her breath to silence; then again and again—and always the same intensity of effort, of something that is, and is not, like urgency in the human voice. Transported so in the dancing light among the shadows of her room, she seemed beyond the reach of time. But that was illusion; I think I knew then that I should not see her again.

Houses are like sentinels in the plain, old keepers of the weather watch. There, in a very little while, wood takes on the appearance of great age. All colors wear soon away in the wind and rain, and then the wood is burned gray and the grain appears and the nails turn red with rust. The windowpanes are black and opaque; you imagine there is nothing within, and indeed there are many ghosts, bones given up to the land. They stand here and there against the sky, and you approach them for a longer time than you expect. They belong in the distance; it is their domain.

Once there was a lot of sound in my grandmother's house, a lot of coming and going, feasting and talk. The summers there were full of excitement and reunion. The Kiowas are a summer people; they abide the cold and keep to themselves, but when the season turns and the land becomes warm and vital they cannot hold still; an old love of going returns upon them. The aged visitors who came to my grandmother's house when I was a child were made of lean and leather, and they bore themselves upright. They wore great black hats and bright ample shirts that shook in the wind. They rubbed fat upon their hair and wound their braids with strips of colored cloth. Some of them painted their faces and carried the scars of old and cherished enmities. They were an old council of warlords, come to remind and be reminded of who they were. Their wives and daughters served them well. The women might indulge themselves; gossip was at once the mark and compensation of their servitude. They made loud and elaborate talk among themselves, full of jest and gesture, fright and false alarm. They went abroad in fringed and flowered shawls, bright beadwork and German silver. They were at home in the kitchen, and they prepared meals that were banquets.

There were frequent prayer meetings, and great nocturnal feasts. When I was a child I played with my cousins outside, where the lamplight fell upon the ground and the singing of the old people rose up around us and carried away into the darkness. There were a lot of good things to eat, a lot of laughter and surprise. And afterwards, when the quiet returned, I lay down with my grandmother and could hear the frogs away by the river and feel the motion of the air.

Now there is a funeral silence in the rooms, the endless wake of some final word. The walls have closed in upon my grandmother's house. When I returned to it in mourning, I saw for the first time in my life how small it was. It was late at night, and there was a white moon, nearly full. I sat for a long time on the stone steps by the kitchen door. From there I could see out across the land; I could see the long row of trees by the creek, the low light upon the rolling plains, and the stars of the Big Dipper. Once I looked at the moon and caught sight of a strange thing. A cricket had perched upon the handrail, only a few inches away from me. My line of vision was such that the creature filled the moon like a fossil. It had gone there, I thought, to live and die, for there, of all places, was its small definition made whole and eternal. A warm wind rose up and purled like the longing within me.

The next morning I awoke at dawn and went out on the dirt road to Rainy Mountain. It was already hot, and the grasshoppers began to fill the air. Still, it was early in the morning, and the birds sang out of the shadows.

The long yellow grass on the mountain shone in the bright light, and a scissortail hied above the land. There, where it ought to be, at the end of a long and legendary way, was my grandmother's grave. Here and there on the dark stones were ancestral names. Looking back once, I saw the mountain and came away.

James Baldwin

James Baldwin was born in Harlem in 1924. The eldest of nine children, he never knew his real father. The "father" in this essay was his stepfather, a lay preacher. After the death of his stepfather in 1943, he lived in Greenwich Village, working by day as handyman, office boy, or factory worker, and writing at night. A Rosenwald Fellowship enabled him to go to Paris in 1948 where he wrote his first two novels, *Go Tell It on the Mountain* (1953) and *Giovanni's Room* (1956), and the essays published as *Notes of a Native Son* (1955). The piece that gives the collection its name, reprinted below, is an autobiographical masterpiece.

Baldwin returned to America in 1957 and has continued his career as a distinguished novelist, playwright, and essayist, and as a spokesman for black civil rights. His first broadway play, *Blues for Mister Charlie,* was dedicated to his friend Medgar Evers, who had recently been slain in the civil rights movement, and to the children bombed in a Birmingham church. He has won many awards, including a Guggenheim Fellowship in 1954. *Nobody Knows My Name,* a collection of essays, was selected as one of the outstanding books of 1961 by The American Library Association. *The Fire Next Time* (1963)—two searing articles, or letters, on the relationship between black and white Americans—secures Baldwin's lasting reputation both as an essayist and as commentator on American culture.

Notes of a Native Son

On the 29th of July, in 1943, my father died. On the same day, a few hours later, his last child was born. Over a month before this, while all our energies were concentrated in waiting for these events, there had been, in Detroit, one of the bloodiest race riots of the century. A few hours after my father's funeral, while he lay in state in the undertaker's chapel, a race riot broke out in Harlem. On the morning of the 3rd of August, we drove my father to the graveyard through a wilderness of smashed plate glass.

The day of my father's funeral had also been my nineteenth birthday.

As we drove him to the graveyard, the spoils of injustice, anarchy, discontent, and hatred were all around us. It seemed to me that God himself had devised, to mark my father's end, the most sustained and brutally dissonant of codas. And it seemed to me, too, that the violence which rose all about us as my father left the world had been devised as a corrective for the pride of his eldest son. I had declined to believe in that apocalypse which had been central to my father's vision; very well, life seemed to be saying, here is something that will certainly pass for an apocalypse until the real thing comes along. I had inclined to be contemptuous of my father for the conditions of his life, for the conditions of our lives. When his life had ended I began to wonder about that life and also, in a new way, to be apprehensive about my own.

I had not known my father very well. We had got on badly, partly because we shared, in our different fashions, the vice of stubborn pride. When he was dead I realized that I had hardly ever spoken to him. When he had been dead a long time I began to wish I had. It seems to be typical of life in America, where opportunities, real and fancied, are thicker than anywhere else on the globe, that the second generation has no time to talk to the first. No one, including my father, seems to have known exactly how old he was, but his mother had been born during slavery. He was of the first generation of free men. He, along with thousands of other Negroes, came North after 1919 and I was part of that generation which had never seen the landscape of what Negroes sometimes call the Old Country.

He had been born in New Orleans and had been a quite young man there during the time that Louis Armstrong, a boy, was running errands for the dives and honky-tonks of what was always presented to me as one of the most wicked of cities—to this day, whenever I think of New Orleans, I also helplessly think of Sodom and Gomorrah. My father never mentioned Louis Armstrong, except to forbid us to play his records; but there was a picture of him on our wall for a long time. One of my father's strong-willed female relatives had placed it there and forbade my father to take it down. He never did, but he eventually maneuvered her out of the house and when, some years later, she was in trouble and near death, he refused to do anything to help her.

He was, I think, very handsome. I gather this from photographs and from my own memories of him, dressed in his Sunday best and on his way to preach a sermon somewhere, when I was little. Handsome, proud, and ingrown, "like a toe-nail," somebody said. But he looked to me, as I grew older, like pictures I had seen of African tribal chieftains: he really should have been naked, with war-paint on and barbaric mementos, standing among spears. He could be chilling in the pulpit and indescribably cruel in his personal life and he was certainly the most bitter man I have ever met; yet it must be said that there was something else in him, buried in him, which lent him his tremendous power and, even, a rather crushing charm. It had something to do with his blackness, I think—he was very black—with his blackness and his beauty, and with the fact that he knew that he was black but did not know that he was beautiful. He claimed to be proud of his blackness but it had also been the cause of much humiliation and it had fixed bleak boundaries to his life. He was not a young man when we were growing up and he had already suffered many kinds of ruin; in his outrageously demanding and protective way he loved his children, who were black like him and menaced, like him; and all these things sometimes showed in his face when he tried, never to my knowledge with any success, to establish contact with any of us. When he took one of his children on his knee to play, the child always became fretful and began to cry; when he tried to help one of us with our homework the absolutely unabating tension which emanated from him caused our minds and our tongues to become paralyzed, so that he, scarcely knowing why, flew into a rage and the child, not knowing why, was punished. If it ever entered his head to bring a surprise home for his children, it was, almost unfailingly, the wrong surprise and even the big watermelons he often brought home on his back in the summertime led to the most appalling scenes. I do not remember, in all those years, that one of his children was ever glad to see him come home. From what I was able to gather of his early life, it seemed that this inability to establish contact with other people had always marked him and had been one of the things which had driven him out of New Orleans. There was something in him, therefore, groping and tentative, which was never expressed and which was buried with him. One saw it most clearly when he was facing new people and hoping to impress them. But he never did, not for long. We went from church to smaller and more improbable church, he found himself in less and less demand as a minister, and by the time he died none of his friends had come to see him for a long time. He had lived and died in an intolerable bitterness of spirit and it frightened me, as we drove him to the graveyard through those unquiet, ruined streets, to see how powerful and overflowing this bitterness could be and to realize that this bitterness now was mine.

When he died I had been away from home for a little over a year. In that year I had had time to become aware of the meaning of all my father's bitter warnings, had discovered the secret of his proudly pursed lips and rigid carriage: I had discovered the weight of white people in the world. I saw that this had been for my ancestors and now would be for me an awful thing to live with and that the bitterness which had helped to kill my father could also kill me.

He had been ill a long time—in the mind, as we now realized, reliving instances of his fantastic intransigence in the new light of his affliction and endeavoring to feel a sorrow for him which never, quite, came true. We had not known that he was being eaten up by paranoia, and the discovery that his cruelty, to our bodies and our minds, had been one of the symptoms of his illness was not, then, enough to enable us to forgive him. The younger children felt, quite simply, relief that he would not be coming home anymore. My mother's observation that it was he, after all, who had kept them alive all these years meant nothing because the problems of keeping children alive are not real for children. The older children felt, with my father gone, that they could invite their friends to the house without fear that their friends would be insulted or, as had sometimes happened with me, being told that their friends were in league with the devil and intended to rob our family of everything we owned. (I didn't fail to wonder, and it made me hate him, what on earth we owned that anybody would want.)

His illness was beyond all hope of healing before anyone realized that he was ill. He had always been so strange and had lived, like a prophet, in such unimaginably close communication with the Lord that his long silences which were punctuated by moans and hallelujahs and snatches of old songs while he sat at the living-room window never seemed odd to us. It was not until he refused to eat because, he said, his family was trying to poison him that my mother was forced to accept as a fact what had, until then, been only an unwilling suspicion. When he was committed, it was discovered that he had tuberculosis and, as it turned out, the disease of his mind allowed the disease of his body to destroy him. For the doctors could not force him to eat, either, and, though he was fed intravenously, it was clear from the beginning that there was no hope for him.

In my mind's eye I could see him, sitting at the window, locked up in his terrors; hating and fearing every living soul including his children who had betrayed him, too, by reaching towards the world which had despised him. There were nine of us. I began to wonder what it could have felt like for such a man to have had nine children whom he could barely feed. He used to make little jokes about our poverty, which never, of course, seemed very funny to us; they could not have seemed very funny to him, either, or else our all too feeble response to them would never have caused such rages. He spent great energy and achieved, to our chagrin, no small amount of success in keeping us away from the people who surrounded us, people who had all-night rent parties to which we listened when we should have been sleeping, people who cursed and drank and flashed razor blades on Lenox Avenue. He could not understand why, if they had so much energy to spare, they could not use it to make their lives better. He treated almost everybody on our block with a most uncharitable asperity and neither they, nor, of course, their children were slow to reciprocate.

The only white people who came to our house were welfare workers and bill collectors. It was almost always my mother who dealt with them, for my father's temper, which was at the mercy of his pride, was never to be trusted. It was clear that he felt their very presence in his home to be a violation: this was conveyed by his carriage, almost ludicrously stiff, and by his voice, harsh and vindictively polite. When I was around nine or ten I wrote a play which was directed by a young, white schoolteacher, a woman, who then took an interest in me, and gave me books to read and, in order to corroborate my theatrical bent, decided to take me to see what she somewhat tactlessly referred to as "real" plays. Theater-going was forbidden in our house, but, with the really cruel intuitiveness of a child, I suspected that the color of this woman's skin would carry the day for me. When, at school, she suggested taking me to the theater, I did not, as I might have done if she had been a Negro, find a way of discouraging her, but agreed that she should pick me up at my house one evening. I then, very cleverly, left all the rest to my mother, who suggested to my father, as I knew she would, that it would not be very nice to let such a kind woman make the trip for nothing. Also, since it was a schoolteacher, I imagine that my mother countered the idea of sin with the idea of "education," which word, even with my father, carried a kind of bitter weight.

Before the teacher came my father took me aside to ask *why* she was coming, what *interest* she could possibly have in our house, in a boy like me. I said I didn't know but I, too, suggested that it had something to do with education. And I understood that my father was waiting for me to say something—I didn't quite know what; perhaps that I wanted his protection against this teacher and her "education." I said none of these things and the teacher came and we went out. It was clear, during the brief interview in our living room, that my father was agreeing very much against his will and that he would have refused permission if he had dared. The fact that he did not dare caused me to despise him: I had no way of knowing that he was facing in that living room a wholly unprecedented and frightening situation.

Later, when my father had been laid off from his job, this woman became very important to us. She was really a very sweet and generous woman and went to a great deal of trouble to be of help to us, particularly during one awful winter. My mother called her by the highest name she knew: she said she was a "christian." My father could scarcely disagree but during the four or five years of our relatively close association he never trusted her and was always trying to surprise in her open, Midwestern face the genuine, cunningly hidden, and hideous motivation. In later years, particularly when it began to be clear that this "education" of mine was going to lead me to perdition, he became more explicit and warned me that my white friends in high school were not really my friends and that I would see, when I was older, how white people would do anything to keep a Negro down. Some of them could be nice, he admitted, but none of them were to be trusted and most of them were not even nice. The best thing was to have as little to do with them as possible. I did not feel this way and I was certain, in my innocence, that I never would.

But the year which preceded my father's death had made a great change in my life. I had been living in New Jersey, working in defense plants, working and living among southerners, white and black. I knew about the south, of course, and about how southerners treated Negroes and how they expected them to behave, but it had never entered my mind that anyone would look at me and expect *me* to behave that way. I learned in New Jersey that to be a Negro meant, precisely, that one was never looked at but was simply at the mercy of the reflexes the color of one's skin caused in other people. I acted in New Jersey as I had always acted, that is as though I thought a great deal of myself—I had to *act* that way—with results that were, simply, unbelievable. I had scarcely arrived before I had earned the enmity, which was extraordinarily ingenious, of all my superiors and nearly all my co-workers. In the beginning, to make matters worse, I simply did not know what was happening. I did not know what I had done, and I shortly began to wonder what *anyone* could possibly do, to bring about such unanimous, active, and unbearably vocal hostility. I knew about jim-crow but I had never experienced it. I went to the same self-service restaurant three times and stood with all the Princeton boys before the counter, waiting for a hamburger and coffee; it was always an extraordinarily long time before anything was set before me; but it was not until the fourth visit that I learned that, in fact, nothing had ever been set before me: I had simply picked something up. Negroes were not served there, I was told, and they had been waiting for me to realize that I was always the only Negro present. Once I was told this, I determined to go there all the time. But now they were ready for me and, though some dreadful scenes were subsequently enacted in that restaurant, I never ate there again.

It was the same story all over New Jersey, in bars, bowling alleys, diners, places to live. I was always being forced to leave, silently, or with mutual imprecations. I very shortly became notorious and children giggled behind me when I passed and their elders whispered or shouted—they really believed that I was mad. And it did begin to work on my mind, of course; I began to be afraid to go anywhere and to compensate for this I went to places to which I really should not have gone and where, God knows, I had no desire to be. My reputation in town naturally enhanced my reputation at work and my working day became one long series of acrobatics designed to keep me out of trouble. I cannot say that these acrobatics succeeded. It began to seem that the machinery of the organization I worked for was turning over, day and night, with but one aim: to eject me. I was fired once, and contrived, with the aid of a friend from New York, to get back on the payroll; was fired again, and bounced back again. It took a while to fire me for the third time, but the third time took. There were no loopholes anywhere. There was not even any way of getting back inside the gates.

That year in New Jersey lives in my mind as though it were the year during which, having an unsuspected predilection for it, I first contracted some dread, chronic disease, the unfailing symptom of which is a kind of blind fever, a pounding in the skull and fire in the bowels. Once this disease is contracted, one can never be really carefree again, for the fever, without an instant's warning, can recur at any moment. It can wreck more important things than race relations. There is not a Negro alive who does not have this rage in his blood—one has the choice, merely, of living with it consciously or surrendering to it. As for me, this fever has recurred in me, and does, and will until the day I die.

My last night in New Jersey, a white friend from New York took me to the nearest big town, Trenton, to go to the movies and have a few drinks. As it turned out, he also saved me from, at the very least, a violent whipping. Almost every detail of that night stands out very clearly in my memory. I even remember the name of the movie we saw because its title impressed me as being so patly ironical. It was a movie about the German occupation of France, starring Maureen O'Hara and Charles Laughton and called *This Land Is Mine.* I remember the name of the diner we walked into when the movie ended: it was the "American Diner." When we walked in the counterman asked what we wanted and I remember answering with the casual sharpness which had become my habit: "We want a hamburger and a cup of coffee, what do you think we want?" I do not know why, after a year of such rebuffs, I so completely failed to anticipate his answer, which was, of course, "We don't serve Negroes here." This reply failed to discompose me, at least for the moment. I made some sardonic comment about the name of the diner and we walked out into the streets.

This was the time of what was called the "brown-out," when the lights in all American cities were very dim. When we re-entered the streets something happened to me which had the force of an optical illusion, or a nightmare. The streets were very crowded and I was facing north. People were moving in every direction but it seemed to me, in that instant, that all of the people I could see, and many more than that, were moving toward me, against me, and that everyone was white. I remember how their faces gleamed. And I felt, like a physical sensation, a *click* at the nape of my neck as though some interior string connecting my head to my body had been cut. I began to walk. I heard my friend call after me, but I ignored him. Heaven only knows what was going on in his mind, but he had the good sense not to touch me—I don't know what would have happened if he had—and to keep me in sight. I don't know what was going on in my mind, either; I certainly had no conscious plan. I wanted to do something to crush these white faces, which were crushing me. I walked for perhaps a block or two until I came to an enormous, glittering, and fashionable restaurant in which I knew not even the intercession of the Virgin would cause me to be served. I pushed through the doors and took the first vacant seat I saw, at a table for two, and waited.

I do not know how long I waited and I rather wonder, until today, what I could possibly have looked like. Whatever I looked like, I frightened the waitress who shortly appeared, and the moment she appeared all of my fury flowed towards her. I hated her for her white face, and for her great, astounded, frightened eyes. I felt that if she found a black man so frighten-ing I would make her fright worth-while.

She did not ask me what I wanted, but repeated, as though she had learned it somewhere, "We don't serve Negroes here." She did not say it with the blunt, derisive hostility to which I had grown so accustomed, but, rather, with a note of apology in her voice, and fear. This made me colder and more murderous than ever. I felt I had to do something with my hands. I wanted her to come close enough for me to get her neck between my hands.

So I pretended not to have understood her, hoping to draw her closer. And she did step a very short step closer, with her pencil poised incongru-ously over her pad, and repeated the formula: ". . . don't serve Negroes here."

Somehow, with the repetition of that phrase, which was already ringing in my head like a thousand bells of a nightmare, I realized that she would never come any closer and that I would have to strike from a distance. There was nothing on the table but an ordinary watermug half full of water, and I picked this up and hurled it with all my strength at her. She ducked and it missed her and shattered against the mirror behind the bar. And, with that sound, my frozen blood abruptly thawed, I returned from wherever I had been, I *saw,* for the first time, the restaurant, the people with their mouths open, already, as it seemed to me, rising as one man, and I realized what I had done, and where I was, and I was frightened. I rose and began running for the door. A round, potbellied man grabbed me by the nape of the neck just as I reached the doors and began to beat me about the face. I kicked him and got loose and ran into the streets. My friend whispered, *"Run!"* and I ran.

My friend stayed outside the restaurant long enough to misdirect my pursuers and the police, who arrived, he told me, at once. I do not know what I said to him when he came to my room that night. I could not have said much. I felt, in the oddest, most awful way, that I had somehow be-trayed him. I lived it over and over and over again, the way one relives an automobile accident after it has happened and one finds oneself alone and safe. I could not get over two facts, both equally difficult for the imagination to grasp, and one was that I could have been murdered. But the other was that I had been ready to commit murder. I saw nothing very clearly but I did see this: that my life, my *real* life, was in danger, and not from anything other people might do but from the hatred I carried in my own heart.

2

I had returned home around the second week in June—in great haste because it seemed that my father's death and my mother's confinement were both but a matter of hours. In the case of my mother, it soon became clear that she had simply made a miscalculation. This had always been her tendency and I don't believe that a single one of us arrived in the world, or has since arrived anywhere else, on time. But none of us dawdled so intolerably about the business of being born as did my baby sister. We sometimes amused ourselves, during those endless, stifling weeks, by picturing the baby sitting within in the safe, warm dark, bitterly regretting the necessity of becoming a part of our chaos and stubbornly putting it off as long as possible. I understood her perfectly and congratulated her on showing such good sense so soon. Death, however, sat as purposefully at my father's bedside as life stirred within my mother's womb and it was harder to understand why he so lingered in that long shadow. It seemed that he had bent, and for a long time, too, all of his energies towards dying. Now death was ready for him but my father held back.

All of Harlem, indeed, seemed to be infected by waiting. I had never before known it to be so violently still. Racial tensions throughout this country were exacerbated during the early years of the war, partly because the labor market brought together hundreds of thousands of ill-prepared people and partly because Negro soldiers, regardless of where they were born, received their military training in the south. What happened in defense plants and army camps had repercussions, naturally, in every Negro ghetto. The situation in Harlem had grown bad enough for clergymen, policemen, educators, politicians, and social workers to assert in one breath that there was no "crime wave" and to offer, in the very next breath, suggestions as how to combat it. These suggestions always seemed to involve playgrounds, despite the fact that racial skirmishes were occurring in the playgrounds, too. Playground or not, crime wave or not, the Harlem police force had been augmented in March, and the unrest grew —perhaps, in fact, partly as a result of the ghetto's instinctive hatred of policemen. Perhaps the most revealing news item, out of the steady parade of reports of muggings, stabbings, shootings, assaults, gang wars, and accusations of police brutality, is the item concerning six Negro girls who set upon a white girl in the subway because, as they all too accurately put it, she was stepping on their toes. Indeed she was, all over the nation.

I had never before been so aware of policemen, on foot, on horseback, on corners, everywhere, always two by two. Nor had I ever been so aware of small knots of people. They were on stoops and on corners and in doorways, and what was striking about them, I think, was that they did not seem to be talking. Never, when I passed these groups, did the usual sound of a curse or a laugh ring out and neither did there seem to be any hum of gossip. There was certainly, on the other hand, occurring between them communication extraordinarily intense. Another thing that was striking was the unexpected diversity of the people who made up these groups. Usually, for example, one would see a group of sharpies standing on the street corner, jiving the passing chicks; or a group of older men, usually, for some reason, in the vicinity of a barber shop, discussing baseball scores, or the numbers, or making rather chilling observations about women they had known. Women, in a general way, tended to be seen less often to-gether—unless they were church women, or very young girls, or prosti-tutes met together for an unprofessional instant. But that summer I saw the strangest combinations: large, respectable, churchly matrons standing on the stoops or the corners with their hair tied up, together with a girl in sleazy satin whose face bore the marks of gin and the razor, or heavy-set, abrupt, no-nonsense older men, in company with the most disreputable and fanatical "race" men, or these same "race" men with the sharpies, or these sharpies with the churchly women. Seventh Day Adventists and Methodists and Spiritualists seemed to be hobnobbing with Holyrollers and they were all, alike, entangled with the most flagrant disbelievers; something heavy in their stance seemed to indicate that they had all, incredibly, seen a common vision, and on each face there seemed to be the same strange, bitter shadow.

The churchly women and the matter-of-fact, no-nonsense men had chil-dren in the Army. The sleazy girls they talked to had lovers there, the sharpies and the "race" men had friends and brothers there. It would have demanded an unquestioning patriotism, happily as uncommon in this country as it is undesirable, for these people not to have been disturbed by the bitter letters they received, by the newspaper stories they read, not to have been enraged by the posters, then to be found all over New York, which described the Japanese as "yellow-bellied Japs." It was only the "race" men, to be sure, who spoke ceaselessly of being revenged—how this vengeance was to be exacted was not clear—for the indignities and dangers suffered by Negro boys in uniform; but everybody felt a direction-less, hopeless bitterness, as well as that panic which can scarcely be sup-pressed when one knows that a human being one loves is beyond one's reach, and in danger. This helplessness and this gnawing uneasiness does something, at length, to even the toughest mind. Perhaps the best way to sum all this up is to say that the people I knew felt, mainly, a peculiar kind of relief when they knew that their boys were being shipped out of the south, to do battle overseas. It was, perhaps, like feeling that the most dangerous part of a dangerous journey had been passed and that now, even if death should come, it would come with honor and without the complicity of their countrymen. Such a death would be, in short, a fact with which one could hope to live.

It was on the 28th of July, which I believe was a Wednesday, that I visited my father for the first time during his illness and for the last time in his life. The moment I saw him I knew why I had put off this visit so long. I had told my mother that I did not want to see him because I hated him. But this was not true. It was only that I *had* hated him and I wanted to hold on to this hatred. I did not want to look at him as a ruin: it was not a ruin I had hated. I imagine that one of the reasons people cling to their hates so stubbornly is because they sense, once hate is gone, that they will be forced to deal with pain.

We traveled out to him, his older sister and myself, to what seemed to be the very end of a very Long Island. It was hot and dusty and we wrangled, my aunt and I, all the way out, over the fact that I had recently begun to smoke and, as she said, to give myself airs. But I knew that she wrangled with me because she could not bear to face the fact of her brother's dying. Neither could I endure the reality of her despair, her unstated bafflement as to what had happened to her brother's life, and her own. So we wrangled and I smoked and from time to time she fell into a heavy reverie. Covertly, I watched her face, which was the face of an old woman; it had fallen in, the eyes were sunken and lightless; soon she would be dying too.

In my childhood—it had not been so long ago—I had thought her beautiful. She had been quick-witted and quick-moving and very generous with all the children and each of her visits had been an event. At one time one of my brothers and myself had thought of running away to live with her. Now she could no longer produce out of her handbag some unexpected and yet familiar delight. She made me feel pity and revulsion and fear. It was awful to realize that she no longer caused me to feel affection. The closer we came to the hospital the more querulous she became and at the same time, naturally, grew more dependent on me. Between pity and guilt and fear I began to feel that there was another me trapped in my skull like a jack-in-the-box who might escape my control at any moment and fill the air with screaming.

She began to cry the moment we entered the room and she saw him lying there, all shriveled and still, like a little black monkey. The great, gleaming apparatus which fed him and would have compelled him to be still even if he had been able to move brought to mind, not beneficence, but torture; the tubes entering his arm made me think of pictures I had seen when a child, of Gulliver, tied down by the pygmies on that island. My aunt wept and wept, there was a whistling sound in my father's throat; nothing was said; he could not speak. I wanted to take his hand, to say something. But I do not know what I could have said, even if he could have heard me. He was not really in that room with us, he had at last really embarked on his journey; and though my aunt told me that he said he was going to meet Jesus, I did not hear anything except that whistling in his throat. The doctor came back and we left, into that unbearable train again, and home. In the morning came the telegram saying that he was dead. Then the house was suddenly full of relatives, friends, hysteria, and confusion and I quickly left my mother and the children to the care of those impressive women, who, in Negro communities at least, automatically appear at times of bereavement armed with lotions, proverbs, and patience, and an ability to cook. I went downtown. By the time I returned, later the same day, my mother had been carried to the hospital and the baby had been born.

3

For my father's funeral I had nothing black to wear and this posed a nagging problem all day long. It was one of those problems, simple, or impossible of solution, to which the mind insanely clings in order to avoid the mind's real trouble. I spent most of the day at the downtown apartment of a girl I knew, celebrating my birthday with whiskey and wondering what to wear that night. When planning a birthday celebration one naturally does not expect that it will be up against competition from a funeral and this girl had anticipated taking me out that night, for a big dinner and a night club afterwards. Sometime during the course of that long day we decided that we would go out anyway, when my father's funeral service was over. I imagine *I* decided it, since, as the funeral hour approached, it became clearer and clearer to me that I would not know what to do with myself when it was over. The girl, stifling her very lively concern as to the possible effects of the whiskey on one of my father's chief mourners, concentrated on being conciliatory and practically helpful. She found a black shirt for me somewhere and ironed it and, dressed in the darkest pants and jacket I owned, and slightly drunk, I made my way to my father's funeral.

The chapel was full, but not packed, and very quiet. There were, mainly, my father's relatives, and his children, and here and there I saw faces I had not seen since childhood, the faces of my father's one-time friends. They were very dark and solemn now, seeming somehow to suggest that they had known all along that something like this would happen. Chief among the mourners was my aunt, who had quarreled with my father all his life; by which I do not mean to suggest that her mourning was insincere or that she had not loved him. I suppose that she was one of the few people in the world who had, and their incessant quarreling proved precisely the strength of the tie that bound them. The only other person in the world, as far as I knew, whose relationship to my father rivaled my aunt's in depth was my mother, who was not there.

It seemed to me, of course, that it was a very long funeral. But it was, if anything, a rather shorter funeral than most, nor, since there were no overwhelming, uncontrollable expressions of grief, could it be called—if I dare to use the word—successful. The minister who preached my father's funeral sermon was one of the few my father had still been seeing as he neared his end. He presented to us in his sermon a man whom none of us had ever seen—a man thoughtful, patient, and forbearing, a Christian inspiration to all who knew him, and a model for his children. And no doubt the children, in their disturbed and guilty state, were almost ready to believe this; he had been remote enough to be anything and, anyway, the shock of the incontrovertible, that it was really our father lying up there in that casket, prepared the mind for anything. His sister moaned and this grief-stricken moaning was taken for corroboration. The other faces held a dark, noncommittal thoughtfulness. This was not the man they had known, but they had scarcely expected to be confronted with *him;* this was, in a sense deeper than question of fact, the man they had not known, and the man they had not known may have been the real one. The real man, whoever he had been, had suffered and now he was dead: this was all that was sure and all that mattered now. Every man in the chapel hoped that when his hour came he, too, would be eulogized, which is to say forgiven, and that all of his lapses, greeds, errors, and strayings from the truth would be invested with coherence and looked upon with charity. This was perhaps the last thing human beings could give each other and it was what they demanded, after all, of the Lord. Only the Lord saw the midnight tears, only He was present when one of His children, moaning and wringing hands, paced up and down the room. When one slapped one's child in anger the recoil in the heart reverberated through heaven and became part of the pain of the universe. And when the children were hungry and sullen and distrustful and one watched them, daily, growing wilder, and further away, and running headlong into danger, it was the Lord who knew what the charged heart endured as the strap was laid to the backside; the Lord alone knew what one *would* have said if one had had, like the Lord, the gift of the living word. It was the Lord who knew of the impossibility every parent in the room faced: how to prepare the child for the day when the child would be despised and how to *create* in the child—by what means?—a stronger antidote to this poison than one had found for oneself. The avenues, side streets, bars, billiard halls, hospitals, police stations, and even the playgrounds of Harlem—not to mention the houses of correction, the jails, and the morgue—testified to the potency of the poison while remaining silent as to the efficacy of whatever antidote, irresistibly raising the question of whether or not such an antidote existed; raising, which was worse, the question of whether or not an antidote was desirable; perhaps poison should be fought with poison. With these several schisms in the mind and with more terrors in the heart than could be named, it was better not to judge the man who had gone down under an impossible burden. It was better to remember: *Thou knowest this man's fall; but thou knowest not his wrassling.*

While the preacher talked and I watched the children—years of changing their diapers, scrubbing them, slapping them, taking them to school, and scolding them had had the perhaps inevitable result of making me love them, though I am not sure I knew this then—my mind was busily breaking out with a rash of disconnected impressions. Snatches of popular songs, indecent jokes, bits of books I had read, movie sequences, faces, voices, political issues—I thought I was going mad; all these impressions suspended, as it were, in the solution of the faint nausea produced in me by the heat and liquor. For a moment I had the impression that my alcoholic breath, inefficiently disguised with chewing gum, filled the entire chapel. Then someone began singing one of my father's favorite songs and, abruptly, I was with him, sitting on his knee, in the hot, enormous, crowded church which was the first church we attended. It was the Abyssinia Baptist Church on 138th Street. We had not gone there long. With this image, a host of others came. I had forgotten, in the rage of my growing up, how proud my father had been of me when I was little. Apparently, I had had a voice and my father had liked to show me off before the members of the church. I had forgotten what he had looked like when he was pleased but now I remembered that he had always been grinning with pleasure when my solos ended. I even remembered certain expressions on his face when he teased my mother—had he loved her? I would never know. And when had it all begun to change? For now it seemed that he had not always been cruel. I remembered being taken for a haircut and scraping my knee on the footrest of the barber's chair and I remembered my father's face as he soothed my crying and applied the stinging iodine. Then I remembered our fights, fights which had been of the worst possible kind because my technique had been silence.

I remembered the one time in all our life together when we had really spoken to each other.

It was on a Sunday and it must have been shortly before I left home. We were walking, just the two of us, in our usual silence, to or from church. I was in high school and had been doing a lot of writing and I was, at about this time, the editor of the high school magazine. But I had also been a Young Minister and had been preaching from the pulpit. Lately, I had been taking fewer engagements and preached as rarely as possible. It was said in the church, quite truthfully, that I was "cooling off."

My father asked me abruptly, "You'd rather write than preach, wouldn't you?"

I was astonished at his question—because it was a real question. I answered, "Yes."

That was all we said. It was awful to remember that that was all we had *ever* said.

The casket now was opened and the mourners were being led up the aisle to look for the last time on the deceased. The assumption was that the family was too overcome with grief to be allowed to make this journey alone and I watched while my aunt was led to the casket and, muffled in black, and shaking, led back to her seat. I disapproved of forcing the children to look on their dead father, considering that the shock of his death, or, more truthfully, the shock of death as a reality, was already a little more than a child could bear, but my judgment in this matter had been overruled and there they were, bewildered and frightened and very small, being led, one by one, to the casket. But there is also something very gallant about children at such moments. It has something to do with their silence and gravity and with the fact that one cannot help them. Their legs, somehow, seemed *exposed,* so that it is at once incredible and terribly clear that their legs are all they have to hold them up.

I had not wanted to go to the casket myself and I certainly had not wished to be led there, but there was no way of avoiding either of these forms. One of the deacons led me up and I looked on my father's face. I cannot say that it looked like him at all. His blackness had been equivocated by powder and there was no suggestion in that casket of what his power had or could have been. He was simply an old man dead, and it was hard to believe that he had ever given anyone either joy or pain. Yet, his life filled that room. Further up the avenue his wife was holding his newborn child. Life and death so close together, and love and hatred, and right and wrong, said something to me which I did not want to hear concerning man, concerning the life of man.

After the funeral, while I was downtown desperately celebrating my birthday, a Negro soldier, in the lobby of the Hotel Braddock, got into a fight with a white policeman over a Negro girl. Negro girls, white policemen, in or out of uniform, and Negro males—in or out of uniform—were part of the furniture of the lobby of the Hotel Braddock and this was certainly not the first time such an incident had occurred. It was destined, however, to receive an unprecedented publicity, for the fight between the policeman and the soldier ended with the shooting of the soldier. Rumor, flowing immediately to the streets outside, stated the soldier had been shot in the back, an instantaneous and revealing invention, and that the soldier had died protecting a Negro woman. The facts were somewhat different —for example, the soldier had not been shot in the back, and was not dead, and the girl seems to have been as dubious a symbol of womanhood as her white counterpart in Georgia usually is, but no one was interested in the facts. They preferred the invention because this invention expressed and corroborated their hates and fears so perfectly. It is just as well to remember that people are always doing this. Perhaps many of those legends, including Christianity, to which the world clings began their conquest of the world with just some such concerted surrender to distortion. The effect, in Harlem, of this particular legend was like the effect of a lit match in a tin of gasoline. The mob gathered before the doors of the Hotel Braddock simply began to swell and to spread in every direction, and Harlem exploded.

The mob did not cross the ghetto lines. It would have been easy, for example, to have gone over Morningside Park on the west side or to have crossed the Grand Central railroad tracks at 125th Street on the east side, to wreak havoc in the white neighborhoods. The mob seems to have been mainly interested in something more potent and real than the white face, that is, in white power, and the principal damage done during the riot of the summer of 1943 was to white business establishments in Harlem. It might have been a far bloodier story, of course, if, at the hour the riot began, these establishments had still been open. From the Hotel Braddock the mob fanned out, east and west along 125th Street, and for the entire length of Lenox, Seventh, and Eighth avenues. Along each of these avenues, and along each major side street—116th, 125th, 135th, and so on—bars, stores, pawnshops, restaurants, even little luncheonettes had been smashed open and entered and looted—looted, it might be added, with more haste than efficiency. The shelves really looked as though a bomb had struck them. Cans of beans and soup and dog food, along with toilet paper, corn flakes, sardines and milk tumbled every which way, and abandoned cash registers and cases of beer leaned crazily out of the splintered windows and were strewn along the avenues. Sheets, blankets, and clothing of every description formed a kind of path, as though people had dropped them while running. I truly had not realized that Harlem *had* so many stores until I saw them all smashed open; the first time the word *wealth* ever entered my mind in relation to Harlem was when I saw it scattered in the streets. But one's first, incongruous impression of plenty was countered immediately by an impression of waste. None of this was doing anybody any good. It would have been better to have left the plate glass as it had been and the goods lying in the stores.

It would have been better, but it would also have been intolerable, for Harlem had needed something to smash. To smash something is the ghetto's chronic need. Most of the time it is the members of the ghetto who smash each other, and themselves. But as long as the ghetto walls are standing there will always come a moment when these outlets do not work. That summer, for example, it was not enough to get into a fight on Lenox Avenue, or curse out one's cronies in the barber shops. If ever, indeed, the violence which fills Harlem's churches, pool halls, and bars erupts outward in a more direct fashion, Harlem and its citizens are likely to vanish in an apocalyptic flood. That this is not likely to happen is due to a great many reasons, most hidden and powerful among them the Negro's real relation to the white American. This relation prohibits, simply, anything as uncomplicated and satisfactory as pure hatred. In order really to hate white people, one has to blot so much out of the mind—and the heart—that this hatred itself becomes an exhausting and self-destructive pose. But this does not mean, on the other hand, that love comes easily: the white world is too powerful, too complacent, too ready with gratuitous humiliation, and, above all, too ignorant and too innocent for that. One is absolutely forced to make perpetual qualifications and one's own reactions are always canceling each other out. It is this, really, which has driven so many people mad, both white and black. One is always in the position of having to decide between amputation and gangrene. Amputation is swift but time may prove that the amputation was not necessary—or one may delay the amputation too long. Gangrene is slow, but it is impossible to be sure that one is reading one's symptoms right. The idea of going through life as a cripple is more than one can bear, and equally unbearable is the risk of swelling up slowly, in agony, with poison. And the trouble, finally, is that the risks are real even if the choices do not exist.

"But as for me and my house," my father had said, "we will serve the

Lord." I wondered, as we drove him to his resting place, what this line had meant for him. I had heard him preach it many times. I had preached it once myself, proudly giving it an interpretation different from my father's. Now the whole thing came back to me, as though my father and I were on our way to Sunday school and I were memorizing the golden text: *And if it seem evil unto you to serve the Lord, choose you this day whom you will serve; whether the gods which your fathers served that were on the other side of the flood, or the gods of the Amorites, in whose land ye dwell: but as for me and my house, we will serve the Lord.* I suspected in these familiar lines a meaning which had never been there for me before. All of my father's texts and songs, which I had decided were meaningless, were arranged before me at his death like empty bottles, waiting to hold the meaning which life would give them for me. This was his legacy: nothing is ever escaped. That bleakly memorable morning I hated the unbelievable streets and the Negroes and whites who had, equally, made them that way. But I knew that it was folly, as my father would have said, this bitterness was folly. It was necessary to hold on to the things that mattered. The dead man mattered, the new life mattered; blackness and whiteness did not matter; to believe that they did was to acquiesce in one's own destruction. Hatred, which could destroy so much, never failed to destroy the man who hated and this was an immutable law.

It began to seem that one would have to hold in the mind forever two ideas which seemed to be in opposition. The first idea was acceptance, the acceptance, totally without rancor, of life as it is, and men as they are: in the light of this idea, it goes without saying that injustice is a commonplace. But this did not mean that one could be complacent, for the second idea was of equal power: that one must never, in one's own life, accept these injustices as commonplace but must fight them with all one's strength. This fight begins, however, in the heart and it now had been laid to my charge to keep my own heart free of hatred and despair. This intimation made my heart heavy and, now that my father was irrecoverable, I wished that he had been beside me so that I could have searched his face for the answers which only the future would give me now.

Gordon Allport

Gordon Allport (1897–1967) was educated at Harvard and spent most of his career there as Professor of Psychology. He was particularly interested in the relationship between human psychology and social problems, and he became a worldwide authority on racial and religious prejudice. In 1956 he visited the University of Natal, compared the South African racial issue with the American one, and concluded that white supremacy could not be maintained in either area. Some of his most influential books are *Personality: A Psychological Interpretation* (1937), *The Psychology of Rumor* (written with Leo G. Postman, 1947), *The Individual and His Religion* (1950), and *The Nature of Prejudice* (1954). The present essay was written for a symposium on prejudice published in *The Black American Reference Book* (1976).

Prejudice and the Individual

Definition and Extent of Prejudice

There are two ingredients implicit in any prejudiced state of mind: (a) a feeling of favorableness or unfavorableness which in turn is (b) based on unsupported judgment. While some prejudice can be *pro*, or "love prejudice" (as when we think too well of our own group), the ethnic attitudes that cause most social concern are *con*, or "hate prejudice."

A scholastic definition states that hate prejudice is "thinking ill of others without sufficient warrant." An equivalent slang definition says "prejudice is being down on something you are not up on." Whatever wording we prefer, there is always an element of inadequate knowledge or false judgment in prejudice; if not, then we are dealing with a well-grounded dislike, not with prejudice. If a criminal gang threatens my safety, my fear and hatred of it are not prejudice; but if I say that no ex-convict can be trusted, I am overgeneralizing and am therefore prejudiced. Examples are legion. "Every Jew will cheat you if he gets a chance." "Negroes are a violent lot; they carry razors." "Puerto Ricans are ignorant." "I couldn't trust any white man."

It should be added that overgeneralized prejudgments of this sort are prejudices only if they are not reversible when exposed to new knowledge. A person (e.g., a child) can start with a misconception about Jews, Negroes, or Puerto Ricans; but if he changes his mind when new evidence comes along he was not really prejudiced, only misinformed. Prejudices are inflexible, rigid, and erroneous generalizations about groups of people.

Discrimination and Prejudice

While discrimination ultimately rests on prejudice, the two processes are not identical. Discrimination denies people their natural or legal rights because of their membership in some unfavored group. Many people discriminate automatically[1] without being prejudiced; and others, the

---

[1]An example of this in the past might have been the use of a waiting room labeled "White" or "Colored." A contemporary example could involve the choice between rest rooms marked "Ladies" and "Gentlemen."

"gentle people of prejudice," feel irrational aversion, but are careful not to show it in discriminatory behavior. Yet in general, discrimination reinforces prejudices, and prejudices provide rationalizations for discrimination. The two concepts are most distinct when it comes to seeking remedies. The corrections for discrimination are legal, or lie in a direct change of social practices; whereas the remedy for prejudice lies in education and the conversion of attitudes. The best opinion today says that if we eliminate discrimination, then—as people become acquainted with one another on equal terms—attitudes are likely to change, perhaps more rapidly than through the continued preaching or teaching of tolerance.

While some people are prejudiced against one group only, it is more common to find that if a person is bigoted in regard to one nationality, race, or religion, he is likely to be bigoted regarding all "out-groups." He feels safe only within the narrow confines of his own familiar circle. It is this finding that argues most cogently for regarding prejudice as rooted in personal character structure.

How widespread is prejudice? Research suggests that perhaps 80 percent of the American people harbor ethnic prejudice of some type and in some appreciable degree. Only 20 percent of the people are, in Gandhi's terms, "equiminded" or completely democratic in all their attitudes.[2] Widespread though ethnic prejudice is, there is good reason to believe that in the United States it is declining year by year.

Origins of Prejudice

While some animals have an instinctive aversion to others, this is not true among species that are cross-fertile. Human beings of all races can, and do, mate and procreate. There is therefore no reason to assume that instinctive aversion exists between ethnic and racial groups. A young child may be frightened by a person of unfamiliar color or appearance, but ordinarily this fear lasts only a few moments. It is well known that young children will play contentedly together whatever their race or national origin. Thus since prejudice is not inborn but acquired, the question is: What are the chief factors in the complex process of learning?

Some prejudice is deliberately taught by parents. Children obediently learn the lesson, as in the case of the little girl who asked her mother, "What's the name of those children I am supposed to hate?" The parent may pass on prejudice by punishing a child for his friendliness to minority groups. A child thus punished may acquire a conditioned aversion to members of the out-group. Sometimes the teaching is subtler. Even to a four-year-old, dark skin may suggest dirt; and since he is repeatedly

[2] Gordon W. Allport, *The Nature of Prejudice* (New York: Doubleday Anchor Books, 1958), p. 77.

warned to keep clean, he may develop an avoidance for dark-skinned people.

Tags are powerful factors in learning. Most children learn the emotional force of words long before they know the meanings of the words. An angry first-grader once called his white teacher a "nigger." She asked him what "nigger" meant. He replied, "I don't know, but you're supposed to say it when you're mad." Before the child has knowledge of the meaning of Jap, Jew, nigger, Polack and similar labels, he senses the potency of the negative feeling-tone behind these labels. Derogatory chatter in the home may thus dispose a child of six or eight to "think ill of others without sufficient warrant."

Much prejudice is *caught* rather than directly *taught.* The whole atmosphere of child-training may be subtly decisive. Thus a child who is sometimes rejected, sometimes loved, who is punished harshly or capriciously, who does not know unconditional trust at home—such a child grows up "on guard." Unable to depend emotionally upon his parents, he enters school with a suspicious, fearful attitude toward people in general, and especially toward those who have an unfamiliar appearance and (to him) odd and threatening ways of talking, or worshiping, or behaving. Although we cannot make the assertion with finality, it seems likely that the major factor in predisposing a child toward a lifetime of prejudice is this rejective, neglectful, harsh, or inconsistent style of preschool training.[3]

As the child grows older additional factors may create or intensify prejudice. Around the age of eight or ten he goes through a period of fierce identification with his family. Whatever the family is, is "right" (whether it be Catholic, Jewish, white, black, Scotch-Irish, or Hottentot). By comparison all other groups are of doubtful status and merit. At this point the church and the school have the opportunity of teaching the child the concept of reciprocity and basic equality among human groups. The lesson is difficult to learn, because as adolescence approaches, the child seeks personal security and a new identity in his peer groups, which usually are of his own color, class, and neighborhood. If adolescents are friendly with out-groups they risk a diffusion and loss of their own precarious identity.[4] To build up a sense of personal importance they often persecute out-groups. *West Side Story* is an epic of this gang-age phenomenon.

Occasionally prejudice is formed on the basis of a single emotional trauma. A certain youngster who was chased by a Chinese laundryman felt

[3]Dale B. Harrison, G. Gough, and William E. Martin, "Children's Ethnic Attitudes: II, Relationship to Parental Beliefs Concerning Child Training," *Child Development* 21, 1950, pp. 169–81. Also, David P. Ausubel, *Ego Development and the Personality Disorders* (New York: Grune and Stratton, 1962).

[4]Bettelheim and Janowitz, *Social Change and Prejudice* (New York: The Free Press of Glencoe, 1964), p. 57.

ever after a terror of Orientals (a clear case of overgeneralizing from a single experience). Such traumatic origins are relatively rare. But we see that throughout childhood and youth there are many opportunities for irreversible and unfavorable belief-systems to become set.

The Psychodynamics of Prejudice

However prejudice is learned it takes root in a personality because it meets certain basic needs or cravings. It works for the person and may be a pivotal factor in the economy of his life.

All mortals require simplified rubrics to live by. We think of school teachers, of physicians, of blind people, of Russians, or of ex-convicts in homogeneous groups. All Orientals we perceive as mysterious (though many are not); we regard all weeds as inedible (though some are nutritious). Thus our thinking seems to be guided by a law of least effort. If I reject all foreigners (including the United Nations), I simplify my existence by ruling out the troublesome issues of international relations. If I say "all blacks are ignorant," I dispose of twenty million more people. If I add "Catholics know only what the priest tells them," I eliminate forty million more. With the conviction that Jews will cheat me, I discard another five million. Labor unions I exclude by calling them "pirates." Intellectuals are simply "long-haired communists." And so it goes. My life is simplified when I invoke these stereotyped rejections. With the aid of aversive categories I avoid the painful task of dealing with individuals as individuals. Prejudice is thus an economical mode of thought, and is widely embraced for this very reason.

A major source of prejudice is the sense that one's security and status are threatened. One fears for one's job, for one's home, especially for one's prestige. American culture is enormously competitive, and so we find ourselves keenly fearful of our rivals. Downwardly mobile people on the whole are more prejudiced than people who hold a stable social position.[5] Now in cold logic it is very seldom that any minority group actually threatens the well-being, safety, or equity of our lives, but we nonetheless perceive them as the cause of our distress. Racist agitators play upon this anxiety. The easiest idea to sell anyone is that he is better than someone else, and that this someone else must be kept "in his place" so that we may enjoy our own position of superiority.

When things go wrong we find it convenient to blame others. Since biblical times it has been known that a scapegoat relieves our own sense of failure or guilt. We say it is the Jews who are keeping us from a promotion or the migration of blacks that takes away available jobs. Or we may vaguely blame our failures or discomforts upon "the politicians." Few

[5]*Ibid.*, pp. 29–34.

people take blame upon themselves. They are quick to adopt an extrapunitive ego-defense.

A peculiarly deep complex is found in accusations that out-groups (especially Negroes) are immoral. Simply because they are "forbidden fruit," many white people find blacks sexually attractive; much miscegenation has been the result. Since looseness of morals is condemned, the white person may exonerate himself from his web of desire, fantasy, and guilt by projecting it upon the black male, who, he says, is sexually aggressive —at heart a rapist. In Germany, Hitler accused the Jews of all manner of sexual irregularities; in the United States it is the black who is the projection screen (the "living inkblot") for one's own frightening id-impulses.

To summarize these and other similar emotional needs, trends, and twists that enter into the psychodynamics of prejudice, psychologists have formulated the concept of "authoritarianism."[6] It says that a person who is basically insecure, anxious, sexually repressed, suffering from unresolved Oedipal conflicts with his own parents, given to projection—such a person will develop a rigid, conventional, hostile style of life. Ethnic prejudice fits into this character syndrome. This formulation has been widely studied and debated. Just how to define it in detail is a matter of dispute, but most scholars believe that it contains an important truth. People having this syndrome are "functional bigots" whose whole style of life is hostile, fearful, rejective of out-groups. Such people need prejudice and are ready to follow a demagogue who focuses all this latent hate upon some ethnic target.

Conformity

Although the authoritarian pattern clearly exists, we must not assume that it accounts for all prejudice. What we call "conformity prejudice" springs from the tendency of people to yield to local custom and to the legends and ideology of their own class.[7] If bigotry is in the air, they are bigots; if tolerance is customary, they are tolerant. Perhaps half of our population can be considered to be in this middle range. Since prejudice is to some degree prevalent, especially in the southern regions of the United States, this half of the population can be expected to go along with the existing biases.

What we have called the authoritarian syndrome accounts for about the same amount of prejudice in both northern and southern states, but there is much more conformity prejudice in the South.[8]

[6]T. G. W. Adorno, E. Frenkel-Brunswick, D. J. Levinson, and R. N. Sanford, *The Authoritarian Personality* (New York: Harper & Brothers, 1952).

[7]Gordon W. Allport, "Prejudice: Is It Societal or Personal?" *Journal of Social Issues*, 18, 1961, pp. 120–134.

[8]Thomas F. Pettigrew, "Regional Differences in Anti-Negro Prejudice," *Journal of Abnormal and Social Psychology*, 29, 1959, pp. 28–36.

Victimization

Those who are victims of prejudice cannot be indifferent to their plight; they must constantly defend themselves from discomfort or insult. One study states that 50 percent of blacks say that when they are with a white person they expect him "to make a slip and say something wrong about Negroes."[9] Even when not expecting an insult, a minority group member must ordinarily plan his life within a racial or ethnic frame of reference.

Besides this chronic sensitization to the problem, additional psychological reactions to victimization may be noted; among them, withdrawal and apathy, slyness and cunning, clowning, rejection of one's own group—or quite the reverse, forming closer in-group ties, resignation, neuroticism, sympathy with other minorities, and enhanced striving and militancy.[10] Of course not all members of a minority group will show all of these types of response.

Reducing Prejudice

Someone has said that it is easier to smash an atom than a prejudice. In the case of deep-dyed functional bigots this verdict may be true. And yet change in prejudice does occur, and has clearly happened since World War II in America. Prejudiced attitudes change when it makes sociological, economic, and personal sense to change them. Not all people are incurably blind to their own illogical and harmful ways of thinking. Education combats easy overgeneralizations, and as the educational level rises we find a reduction in stereotyped thinking.[11] Also we know that increased self-knowledge and personal insight reduce prejudice.[12] Education for mental health works in this direction. Furthermore, militant protests call attention to needed reforms and win the sympathy of potentially democratic citizens. Various measures of prejudice have been invented to help follow these trends, even the subtle factor of human-heartedness within the population.[13]

All progress toward the reduction of prejudice will be met by vociferous resistance from the functional bigots. And yet even when violence

[9]Robin M. Williams, Jr., *Strangers Next Door* (Englewood Cliffs: Prentice-Hall, Inc., 1964), p. 47.

[10]Gordon W. Allport, *The Nature of Prejudice* (New York: Doubleday Anchor Books, 1958), Chapter 9.

[11]Charles H. Stember, *Education and Attitude Change* (New York: Institute of Human Relations Press, 1961). Also, Henry G. Stetler, *Attitudes toward Racial Integration in Connecticut* (Hartford: Commission on Civil Rights, 1961).

[12]Richard M. Jones, *An Application of Psychoanalysis to Education* (Springfield, Ill.: Charles C. Thomas, 1960).

[13]Howard Schuman and John Harding, "Sympathetic Identification with the Underdog," *Public Opinion Quarterly,* 27, 1963, pp. 230–41.

flares up the trend is unmistakable. Antidiscrimination laws, revised school curricula and effective desegregation, raising of educational levels, open discussion and enlightenment, nonviolent protests that focus attention and win sympathy—all these, and other forces, are working in a single direction. Let the reader also keep in mind the fact that the problem we are here discussing has had in the past quarter-century more attention and intelligent study among people of goodwill than in all the millennia of human history previously. Recent research on ethnic prejudice has been remarkably rich and informative,[14] and shows clearly that the forces of social science are strongly arrayed in the battle against bigotry.

Adolf Hitler

Adolf Hitler (1889–1945), Austrian born, became the Nazi dictator of Germany. After a brief and unsuccessful venture in art (he was refused admission to the Viennese Academy) and after a number of years of odd jobs and poverty, he left Vienna in 1913 and settled in Munich. During World War I he volunteered in the Bavarian army and rose to the rank of corporal. He returned to Munich in 1918 and began dabbling in politics. In 1920, with a handful of followers, he founded his own party, which grew into the National Socialist German Workers' (Nazi) party. The Munich Putsch of 1923, an abortive attempt to overthrow the state government of Bavaria, gained him national attention and a thirteen-month jail sentence. It was during these months in jail that Hitler wrote the first volume of *Mein Kampf (My Struggle)*, published in 1925, which he intended to call "A Four and One-Half Year Struggle against Lies, Stupidity, and Cowardice: Settling Accounts with the Destroyers of the Nationalist Socialist Movement." The second volume was published in the following year, 1926. The book enjoyed only a small circulation at first, but a few years before Hitler came to power, sales began to rise and soon *Mein Kampf* was a best seller second only to the Bible. Hitler was made chancellor in 1933 and after Hindenburg's death in 1934 was elected Führer for life. He is thought to have committed suicide in Berlin, on April 29, 1945.

Today Hitler's name has become a byword for psychotic inhumanity; *Mein Kampf* has been called a satanic Bible. Partly autobiographical, it not only outlines his program for world conquest but also broadcasts his hatred of Jews and his aim to restore to the Aryan "race" its sense of superiority. The selection we reprint below is the beginning of the eleventh chapter of Volume 1 of *Mein Kampf,* translated by Ralph Manheim.

[14]Bernard Berelson and Gary A. Steiner, *Human Behavior: An Inventory of Scientific Findings* (New York: Harcourt, Brace & World, 1964).

Nation and Race

There are some truths which are so obvious that for this very reason they are not seen or at least not recognized by ordinary people. They sometimes pass by such truisms as though blind and are most astonished when someone suddenly discovers what everyone really ought to know. Columbus's eggs lie around by the hundreds of thousands, but Columbuses are met with less frequently.

Thus men without exception wander about in the garden of Nature; they imagine that they know practically everything and yet with few exceptions pass blindly by one of the most patent principles of Nature's rule: the inner segregation of the species of all living beings on this earth.

Even the most superficial observation shows that Nature's restricted form of propagation and increase is an almost rigid basic law of all the innumerable forms of expression of her vital urge. Every animal mates only with a member of the same species. The titmouse seeks the titmouse, the finch the finch, the stork the stork, the field mouse the field mouse, the dormouse the dormouse, the wolf the she-wolf, etc.

Only unusual circumstances can change this, primarily the compulsion of captivity or any other cause that makes it impossible to mate within the same species. But then Nature begins to resist this with all possible means, and her most visible protest consists either in refusing further capacity for propagation to bastards or in limiting the fertility of later offspring; in most cases, however, she takes away the power of resistance to disease or hostile attacks.

This is only too natural.

Any crossing of two beings not at exactly the same level produces a medium between the level of the two parents. This means: the offspring will probably stand higher than the racially lower parent, but not as high as the higher one. Consequently, it will later succumb in the struggle against the higher level. Such mating is contrary to the will of Nature for a higher breeding of all life. The precondition for this does not lie in associating superior and inferior, but in the total victory of the former. The stronger must dominate and not blend with the weaker, thus sacrificing his own greatness. Only the born weakling can view this as cruel, but he after all is only a weak and limited man; for if this law did not prevail, any conceivable higher development of organic living beings would be unthinkable.

The consequence of this racial purity, universally valid in Nature, is not only the sharp outward delimitation of the various races, but their uniform character in themselves. The fox is always a fox, the goose a goose, the tiger a tiger, etc., and the difference can lie at most in the varying measure of force, strength, intelligence, dexterity, endurance, etc., of the individual specimens. But you will never find a fox who in his inner attitude might, for example, show humanitarian tendencies toward geese, as similarly there is no cat with a friendly inclination toward mice.

Therefore, here, too, the struggle among themselves arises less from inner aversion than from hunger and love. In both cases, Nature looks on calmly, with satisfaction, in fact. In the struggle for daily bread all those who are weak and sickly or less determined succumb, while the struggle of the males for the female grants the right or opportunity to propagate only to the healthiest. And struggle is always a means for improving a species' health and power of resistance and, therefore, a cause of its higher development.

If the process were different, all further and higher development would cease and the opposite would occur. For, since the inferior always predominates numerically over the best, if both had the same possibility of preserving life and propagating, the inferior would multiply so much more rapidly that in the end the best would inevitably be driven into the background, unless a correction of this state of affairs were undertaken. Nature does just this by subjecting the weaker part to such severe living conditions that by them alone the number is limited, and by not permitting the remainder to increase promiscuously, but making a new and ruthless choice according to strength and health.

No more than Nature desires the mating of weaker with stronger individuals, even less does she desire the blending of a higher with a lower race, since, if she did, her whole work of higher breeding, over perhaps hundreds of thousands of years, might be ruined with one blow.

Historical experience offers countless proofs of this. It shows with terrifying clarity that in every mingling of Aryan blood with that of lower peoples the result was the end of the cultured people. North America, whose population consists in by far the largest part of Germanic elements who mixed but little with the lower colored peoples, shows a different humanity and culture from Central and South America, where the predominantly Latin immigrants often mixed with the aborigines on a large scale. By this one example, we can clearly and distinctly recognize the effect of racial mixture. The Germanic inhabitant of the American continent, who has remained racially pure and unmixed, rose to be master of the continent; he will remain the master as long as he does not fall a victim to defilement of the blood.

The result of all racial crossing is therefore in brief always the following:

(a) Lowering of the level of the higher race;

(b) Physical and intellectual regression and hence the beginning of a slowly but surely progressing sickness.

To bring about such a development is, then, nothing else but to sin against the will of the eternal creator.

And as a sin this act is rewarded.

When man attempts to rebel against the iron logic of Nature, he comes into struggle with the principles to which he himself owes his existence as a man. And this attack must lead to his own doom.

Here, of course, we encounter the objection of the modern pacifist, as truly Jewish in its effrontery as it is stupid! 'Man's rôle is to overcome Nature!'

Millions thoughtlessly parrot this Jewish nonsense and end up by really imagining that they themselves represent a kind of conqueror of Nature; though in this they dispose of no other weapon than an idea, and at that such a miserable one, that if it were true no world at all would be conceivable.

But quite aside from the fact that man has never yet conquered Nature in anything, but at most has caught hold of and tried to lift one or another corner of her immense gigantic veil of eternal riddles and secrets, that in reality he invents nothing but only discovers everything, that he does not dominate Nature, but has only risen on the basis of his knowledge of various laws and secrets of Nature to be lord over those other living creatures who lack this knowledge—quite aside from all this, an idea cannot overcome the preconditions for the development and being of humanity, since the idea itself depends only on man. Without human beings there is no human idea in this world, therefore, the idea as such is always conditioned by the presence of human beings and hence of all the laws which created the precondition for their existence.

And not only that! Certain ideas are even tied up with certain men. This applies most of all to those ideas whose content originates, not in an exact scientific truth, but in the world of emotion, or, as it is so beautifully and clearly expressed today, reflects an 'inner experience.' All these ideas, which have nothing to do with cold logic as such, but represent only pure expressions of feeling, ethical conceptions, etc., are chained to the existence of men, to whose intellectual imagination and creative power they owe their existence. Precisely in this case the preservation of these definite races and men is the precondition for the existence of these ideas. Anyone, for example, who really desired the victory of the pacifistic idea in this world with all his heart would have to fight with all the means at his disposal for the conquest of the world by the Germans; for, if the opposite should occur, the last pacifist would die out with the last German, since the rest of the world has never fallen so deeply as our own people, unfortunately, has for this nonsense so contrary to Nature and reason. Then, if we were serious, whether we liked it or not, we would have to wage wars in order to arrive at pacifism. This and nothing else was what Wilson, the American world savior, intended, or so at least our German visionaries believed—and thereby his purpose was fulfilled.

In actual fact the pacifistic-humane idea is perfectly all right perhaps when the highest type of man has previously conquered and subjected the world to an extent that makes him the sole ruler of this earth. Then this idea lacks the power of producing evil effects in exact proportion as its practical application becomes rare and finally impossible. Therefore, first struggle and then we shall see what can be done. Otherwise mankind has passed the high point of its development and the end is not the domination of any ethical idea but barbarism and consequently chaos. At this point someone or other may laugh, but this planet once moved through the ether for millions of years without human beings and it can do so again some day if men forget that they owe their higher existence, not to the ideas of a few crazy ideologists, but to the knowledge and ruthless application of Nature's stern and rigid laws.

Everything we admire on this earth today—science and art, technology and inventions—is only the creative product of a few peoples and originally perhaps of *one* race. On them depends the existence of this whole culture. If they perish, the beauty of this earth will sink into the grave with them.

However much the soil, for example, can influence men, the result of the influence will always be different depending on the races in question. The lower fertility of a living space may spur the one race to the highest achievements; in others it will only be the cause of bitterest poverty and final undernourishment with all its consequences. The inner nature of peoples is always determining for the manner in which outward influences will be effective. What leads the one to starvation trains the other to hard work.

All great cultures of the past perished only because the originally creative race died out from blood poisoning.

The ultimate cause of such a decline was their forgetting that all culture depends on men and not conversely; hence that to preserve a certain culture the man who creates it must be preserved. This preservation is bound up with the rigid law of necessity and the right to victory of the best and stronger in this world.

Those who want to live, let them fight, and those who do not want to fight in this world of eternal struggle do not deserve to live.

Even if this were hard—that is how it is! Assuredly, however, by far the harder fate is that which strikes the man who thinks he can overcome Nature, but in the last analysis only mocks her. Distress, misfortune, and diseases are her answer.

The man who misjudges and disregards the racial laws actually forfeits the happiness that seems destined to be his. He thwarts the triumphal march of the best race and hence also the precondition for all human progress, and remains, in consequence, burdened with all the sensibility of man, in the animal realm of helpless misery.

It is idle to argue which race or races were the original representative of human culture and hence the real founders of all that we sum up under the word 'humanity.' It is simpler to raise this question with regard to the present, and here an easy, clear answer results. All the human culture, all the results of art, science, and technology that we see before us today, are almost exclusively the creative product of the Aryan. This very fact admits of the not unfounded inference that he alone was the founder of all higher humanity, therefore representing the prototype of all that we understand by the word 'man.' He is the Prometheus of mankind from whose bright forehead the divine spark of genius has sprung at all times, forever kindling anew that fire of knowledge which illumined the night of silent mysteries and thus caused man to climb the path to mastery over the other beings of this earth. Exclude him—and perhaps after a few thousand years darkness will again descend on the earth, human culture will pass, and the world turn to a desert.

Cultures in Tension

Studs Terkel

The following selection comes from *American Dreams: Lost and Found* (1980). See page 353 for information on Studs Terkel.

The Stream: Leonel I. Castillo

Former director of the United States Immigration and Naturalization Service (INS).

"My father's father came from Mexico to Victoria, Texas, in 1880. He paid a toston, *a half-dollar. That automatically made him a U.S. citizen. In the early years of the century, he was fighting for the right to bury Mexicans in the same grounds as Anglos. There was no place to bury Mexicans. He finally got a piece of land from some German Lutherans. It was deeded to our family and the Mexican community in perpetuity. My grandfather and his friends cleared the land for the first funerals. We've kept the records since 1898. We have many, many people buried there."*

New immigrants are trying all over again to integrate themselves into the system. They have the same hunger. On any given day, there are about three million throughout the world who are applying to come to the United States and share the American Dream. The same battles. I still read old newspaper clips: 1886. Housemaid wanted. We'll accept any person, any color, any nationality, any religion, except Irish. (Laughs.) Rough ads: No Irish need apply.

Most of the undocumented here without papers, without legal permission, think they're gonna go back home in six months. Relatively few go back. Some old Italians are going back to *pensionares,* and some old Eastern Europeans are going back home. But, by and large, immigrants, old and new, stay. They don't feel they know anyone in the old village. Their children don't speak Polish or Italian or Greek. Their children are used to air conditioning, McDonald's.

The Vietnamese boat people express it as well as anyone. They don't know if they're gonna land, if the boat's gonna sink. They don't know what's gonna happen to 'em, but they've a hunch they might make it to the U.S. as the "freedom place."

There is the plain hard fact of hunger. In order to eat, a person will endure tremendous hardship. Mexican people who come here usually are not the most destitute. Someone who's too poor can't afford the trip. You've got to buy *coyotes.* A *coyote* is a smuggler of people. He's also called a *pollero. Pollo* is chicken. He's the one who guides chickens through the border.

Sometimes the whole family saves up and gives the bright young man or the bright young woman the family savings. It even goes in hock for a year or two. They pin all their hopes on this one kid, put him on a bus, let him go a thousand miles. He doesn't speak a word of English. He's only seventeen, eighteen years old, but he's gonna save that family. A lot rides on that kid who's a busboy in some hotel.

We've had some as young as eleven who have come a thousand miles. You have this young kid, all his family savings, everything is on him. There are a lot of songs and stories about mother and child, the son leaving who may never return. We end up deporting him. It's heartrending.

He's the bright kid in the family. The slow one might not make it, might get killed. The one who's sickly can't make the trip. He couldn't walk through the desert. He's not gonna be too old, too young, too destitute, or too slow. He's the brightest and the best.

He's gonna be the first hook, the first pioneer coming into an alien society, the United States. He might be here in Chicago. He works as a busboy all night along. They pay him minimum or less, and work him hard. He'll never complain. He might even thank his boss. He'll say as little as possible because he doesn't want anyone to know what his status is. He will often live in his apartment, except for the time he goes to work or to church or to a dance. He will stay in and watch TV. If he makes a hundred a week, he will manage to send back twenty-five. All over the country, if you go to a Western Union office on the weekend, you'll find a lot of people there sending money orders. In a southwest office, like Dallas, Western Union will tell you seventy-five percent of their business is money orders to Mexico.

After the kid learns a bit, because he's healthy and young and energetic, he'll probably get another job as a busboy. He'll work at another place as soon as the shift is over. He'll try to work his way up to be a waiter. He'll work incredible hours. He doesn't care about union scale, he doesn't care about conditions, about humiliations. He accepts all this as his fate.

He's burning underneath with this energy and ambition. He outworks the U.S. busboys and eventually becomes the waiter. Where he can maneuver, he tries to become the owner and gives a lot of competition to the locals. Restaurant owners tell me, if they have a choice, they'll always hire foreign nationals first. They're so eager and grateful. There's a little greed here, too. (Laughs.) They pay 'em so little.

We've got horrible cases of exploitation. In San Diego and in Arizona, we discovered people who live in holes in the ground, live under trees, no sanitation, no housing, nothing. A lot of them live in chicken coops.

They suffer from *coyotes,* too, who exploit them and sometimes beat 'em. *Coyotes* advertise. If the immigrant arrives in San Diego, the word is very quick: where to go and who's looking. He'll even be approached. If he's got a lot of money, the *coyote* will manage to bring him from Tijuana all the way to Chicago and guarantee him a job. He'll get all the papers: Social Security, birth certificate, driver's license. The *coyote* reads the papers and finds which U.S. citizens have died and gets copies of all their vital statistics. In effect, the immigrant carries the identity of a dead person.

Often the employer says he doesn't know anything about it. He plays hands off. He makes his bucks hiring cheap labor. The *coyote* makes his off the workers.

Coyotes come from the border with these pickup trucks full of people. They may put twenty in a truck. They bring 'em in all sorts of bad weather, when they're less likely to be stopped. They might be going twenty, twenty-eight hours, with one or two pit stops. They don't let the people out. There's no urinal, no bathroom. They sit or they stand there in this little cramped space for the whole trip.

A truck broke down outside Chicago. It was a snowstorm. The driver left. People were frostbitten, lost their toes. In Laredo, the truck was in an accident. Everybody ran off because the police were coming. The truck caught fire. No one remembered the two fellows in the trunk. It was locked and no keys. Of course, they burned to death. The border patrol found thirty-three people dying in the deserts of Arizona. They were saved at the last minute and deported. I'll bet you a dollar every one of them, as soon as they are well enough, will try again.

At least a quarter of a million apprehensions were made last year. If we apprehend them at the border, we turn 'em around and ask them to depart voluntarily. They turn around and go back to Mexico. A few hours later, they try again. In El Paso, we deported one fellow six times in one day. There's a restaurant in Hollywood run by a fellow we deported thirty-seven times. We've deported some people more than a hundred times. They always want to come back. There's a job and there's desperation.

In World War Two, we recruited Mexicans to work here. As soon as the war ended and our young men came back, we deported them. In 1954, the deportation problem was so big that the general in charge of immigration ordered Operation Wetback. That one year, we had a million apprehensions. It was similar to what we did during the depression. We rounded everybody up, put 'em on buses, and sent them back to Mexico. Sometimes they were people who merely looked Mexican. The violations of civil liberties were terrible.

Half the people here without papers are not Mexicans. They're from all over the world. They came legally, with papers, as tourists ten years ago. They're much harder to deal with. We're discussing a program that would allow people to have permanent residence, who have been here seven years or more, have not broken any laws, have paid taxes and not been on welfare. You can't be here and become a public charge. All too often, the public gets the impression that all immigrants are on welfare. It's the exact opposite. Very few go on welfare.

A lot of people who are humanitarian, who believe they should be hospitable toward the stranger, are very restrictive when it comes to their jobs. (Laughs.) We've had protests from *mariachis*° and soccer players. The *mariachis* are upset because the Mexicans were coming in and playing for less. The manager of soccer teams would rather hire the foreign nationals because often they're better players.

We get people coming in from Haiti, the poorest country in the western hemisphere. They come over by boat and land in Florida. The Floridians raised hell about this. I've even had Cuban-Americans tell me that Haitians were going to destroy their culture. There's a weird pecking order now.

We make three thousand apprehensions at the border every weekend. It's just a little fourteen-mile stretch. Our border patrol knows this little fellow comin' across is hungry. He just wants to work. They know he's no security threat. They say: "It's my job." Many of them come to have a great deal of respect for the people they're deporting. What do you think of a person you deport three, four times, who just keeps coming back? You would never want to get in the same ring with that person.

I'm torn. I saw it in the Peace Corps, when I was in the Philippines. A mother offered you her infant. You're just a twenty-one-year-old kid and she says: "Take my child, take him with you to the States." When you see this multiplied by thousands, it tears you up.

It's clear to me that the undocumented, even more than the immigrant,

mariachis Bands of Mexican-style musicians, usually consisting of singers, guitarists, and violinists.

is a contributor to our society and to our standard of living. It's one of the few groups that has no parasites. They walk the tightrope and try not to fall off. If you're a citizen and you fall, we have a net that catches you: welfare, food stamps, unemployment, social services. If you're undocumented and fall off that tightrope, you can't go to any of the agencies because you may end up bein' deported. He can't draw welfare, he can't use public services. He's not gonna call a policeman even when he's beat up. If he's in a street fight and somebody whips him bad, assaults him, robs him, rapes her, there's no complaint. In Baltimore, an employer raped two girls. The person who complained wouldn't give us the names of the victims because she was afraid we'd deport 'em. We end up in this country with enormous abuse against four million people.

The only thing that helps me is remembering the history of this country. We've always managed, despite our worst, unbelievably nativist actions to rejuvenate ourselves, to bring in new people. Every new group comes in believing more firmly in the American Dream than the one that came a few years before. Every new group is scared of being in the welfare line or in the unemployment office. They go to night school, they learn about America. We'd be lost without them.

The old dream is still dreamt. The old neighborhood Ma-Pa Stores are still around. They are not Italian or Jewish or Eastern European any more. Ma and Pa are now Korean, Vietnamese, Iraqi, Jordanian, Latin American. They live in the store. They work seven days a week. Their kids are doing well in school. They're making it. Sound familiar?

Near our office in Los Angeles is a little café with a sign: KOSHER BURRITOS. (Laughs.) A *burrito* is a Mexican tortilla with meat inside. Most of the customers are black. The owner is Korean. (Laughs.) The banker, I imagine, is WASP. (Laughs.) This is what's happening in the United States today. It is not a melting pot, but in one way or another, there is a melding of cultures.

I see all kinds of new immigrants starting out all over again, trying to work their way into the system. They're going through new battles, yet they're old battles. They want to share in the American Dream. The stream never ends.

Peter Berger

Peter Berger was born in Vienna in 1929. A naturalized American citizen, he was educated in the United States, where he received a Ph.D. from the New School for Social Research in 1954. He began teaching in 1954 and, since 1981, has served on the faculty of Boston University. Berger has written many books and articles, including *Religion in a Revolutionary Society* (1974); *Facing Up to Modernity: Excursions in Sociology, Politics and Religion* (1977); *The Heretical Imperative: Contemporary Possibilities of Religious Affirmation* (1979); and most recently, together with his wife Brigette Berger, *War Over the Family: Capturing the Middle Ground* (1983).

Two topics of special interest to him, Third World development and political ethics, are the subjects of his book *Pyramids of Sacrifice: Political Ethics and Social Change* (1975). In dealing with the two topics, he wrote that they "are intertwined throughout. . . . No humanly acceptable discussion of the anguishing problems of the world's poverty can avoid ethical considerations. And no political ethics worthy of the name can avoid the centrally important case of the Third World." The book includes several narrative chapters, one of which we reprint below.

A Tale of Two Moralities

Manuela keeps dreaming about the village.[1] She does not think about it very much in the daytime. Even when she thinks about Mexico, it is not usually about the village. In any case, during the day it is the brash, gleaming reality of California that dominates, its loud demand for full attention pushing into the background the old images and feelings. It is at night that the village comes back, reclaiming its power over Manuela. It is then as if she had never left it—or, worse, as if she must inevitably return to it.

It is often very hot in the village, though at night one may freeze. The earth is dry. Time moves very slowly, as the white clouds move through the brightly blue sky over the brown and arid hills. Time moves slowly in the faces of the people, too, and the faces too are brown and arid. Even the faces of the very young seem to hold old memories. The children do not smile easily. The day is measured by the halting motion of shadows over houses and trees. The years are mostly measured by calamities. The past is powerfully present, although there are few words for it. No one in the village speaks an Indian language, though everyone has Indian blood. Can the blood speak, without words? Do the dead speak from the earth? Somewhere in this blue sky and in these brown hills there are very old presences, more threatening than consoling. Some years ago the schoolteacher dug up some Indian artifacts and wanted to take them to the city, to sell them to a museum. Calamity

[1]Manuela's story is fiction, made up as a composite from several true stories. Manuela does not exist. But many Manuelas do exist, not only in Mexico but all over the Third World. Their moral dilemma must be understood if one is to understand "development."

struck at once, all over the village. The dead do not want to be disturbed, and they are dangerous.

The village is distant. Distant from what? Distant from everything, but most importantly distant from the places where time moves quickly and purposefully. There is no paved road, no telephone, no electricity. Even the schoolteacher only comes on two days of the week. He has two other villages to take care of, and he lives somewhere else. To get to the nearest bus station one rides on a donkey for three hours over footpaths of trampled dirt. Time and distance determine the world of the village, in fact and in Manuela's dreams. If she were to put it in one sentence, this world, she would have to say: It is very far away, and life there moves very slowly. On the maps the village is in the state of Guerrero, in a very specific location between Mexico City and the Pacific Ocean. In Manuela's dreams the village is located in the center of her self, deep down inside rather than out there somewhere.

Manuela was born in the village twenty-two years ago. Her mother died shortly afterward. Her father, already married to another woman with seven legitimate children, never acknowledged Manuela. Indeed, he has never spoken with her. She was raised by one of her mother's brothers, a man without land and much of the time without work, with a large family of his own that he barely managed to support. There was never any question about the family obligation to take care of Manuela; the only question at the time, lengthily discussed by her grandfather and the three uncles still living in the area, was which of the three would take the baby in. But this obligation did not greatly exceed supplying the bare necessities of life. There was never the slightest doubt about Manuela's status in her uncle's household as the unwanted bastard who took the food out of the mouths of her more deserving cousins—and she was told so in no uncertain terms on many occasions. If there was little food, she would be the hungriest. If there was hard work, she would be the one to do it. This does not mean that she received no affection. She was a very pretty, winsome child, and often people were kind to her. But she always knew that affection and kindness were not her right, were given to her gratuitously—and, by the same token, could be gratuitously taken away again. As a child Manuela wished for someone who would love her all the time, reliably, "officially." However, she was only dimly unhappy in her uncle's household, since she knew nothing else. She was often hungry, sometimes beaten. She did not have shoes until her tenth birthday, when her grandfather made her a present of a pair. This was also the first occasion when she went outside the village, accompanying her grandfather on a visit to the doctor in the nearest town.

Her grandfather and one of her uncles in the village were *ejidatários*, belonging to the minority that owned parcels of land under the village *ejido* (agricultural cooperative). Most of the time the uncle with whom she stayed worked on this land, too, though he would hire himself out for work elsewhere when there was an opportunity. When she was not working in the house or taking care of her little cousins, Manuela also worked in the fields or with the animals belonging to her family. After her tenth birthday she sometimes worked for outsiders, but she was expected to turn over the money she received for this. Sometimes she succeeded in keeping a few coins for herself, though she knew that she would be beaten if found out. She was allowed to go to school and, being very bright, she learned to read and write well. It was her brightness that attracted her grandfather, who was amused by her and took a liking to her (much to the annoyance of her cousins).

"Bad blood will show." "You will come to no good end, like your mother." Manuela must have heard this hundreds of times during her childhood. The prophecy was fulfilled when she was fifteen and made pregnant by the secretary of the *ejido*, one of the most affluent farmers in the village. When her condition could not longer be concealed, there was a terrible scene and her uncle threw her out of the house. Her grandfather, after slapping her a couple of times rather mildly, gave her the address of an aunt in Acapulco and enough money to pay her busfare there. It was thus that she left the village.

Manuela marveled at Acapulco and its astonishing sights, but, needless to say, she lived there in a world far removed from that experienced by the tourists. Her aunt, a gentle widow with two children and a maid's job in one of the big hotels, took Manuela in very warmly (at least in part because she could use some help in the house). Manuela's baby was born there, a healthy boy whom she named Roberto. Not much later Manuela also started to work outside the house.

A Mexican *campesino*, [0] when he migrates, normally follows an itinerary taken before him by relatives and *compadres*. [0] When he arrives, the latter provide an often intricate network of contacts that are indispensable for his adjustment to the new situation. They will often provide initial housing, they can give information and advice, and, perhaps most important, they serve as an informal labor exchange. Such a network awaited Manuela in Acapulco. In addition to the aunt she was staying with, there were two more aunts and an uncle with their respective families, including some twelve cousins of all ages. This family system, of course, was transposed to the city from the village, but it took on a quite different character in the new context. Freed from the oppressive constraints of village life, the system, on the whole, was more benign. Manuela experienced it as such. Several of her cousins took turns taking care of little Roberto when Manuela started to work. Her aunt's "fiancé" (a somewhat euphemistic term), who was head clerk in the linen supply department of the hotel, found Manuela a job in his department. The uncle, through a

campesino   farmer, peasant (Spanish).
compadres   friends (Spanish).

compadre who was head waiter in another hotel, helped her get a job there as a waitress. It was this uncle, incidentally, who had gone further than any other member of the Acapulco clan, at least for a brief time. An intelligent and aggressive man, he worked himself up in the municipal sanitation department to the rank of inspector. Through a coup, the details of which were shrouded in mystery but which were safely assumed to involve illegality of heroic proportions, Uncle Pepe amassed the equivalent of about one thousand U.S. dollars in a few months' time, a staggering sum in this ambience. With this money he set out for Mexico City, ostensibly to look into a business proposition. In fact he checked into one of the capital's finest hotels, made the rounds of nightclubs and luxury brothels, and returned penniless but not overly unhappy a month later. The clan has viewed him with considerable awe ever since.

Manuela now had a fairly steady cash income, modest to be sure, but enough to keep going. This does not mean, however, that she could keep all of it for herself and her child. The family system operated as a social insurance agency as well as a labor exchange, and there was never a shortage of claimants. An aunt required an operation. An older cousin set up business as a mechanic and needed some capital to start off. Another cousin was arrested and a substantial *mordida*° was required to bribe his way out of jail. And then there were always new calamities back in the village, requiring emergency transfers of money back there. Not least among them was the chronic calamity of grandfather's kidney ailment, which consumed large quantities of family funds in expensive and generally futile medical treatments.

Sometimes, at the hotel, Manuela did baby-sitting for tourists with children. It was thus that she met the couple from California. They stayed in Acapulco for a whole month, and soon Manuela took care of their little girl almost daily. When they left the woman asked Manuela whether she wanted a job as a maid in the States. "Yes," replied Manuela at once, without thinking. The arrangements were made quickly. Roberto was put up with a cousin. Uncle Pepe, through two trusted intermediaries, arranged for Manuela to cross the border illegally. Within a month she arrived at the couple's address in California.

And now she has been here for over a year. California was even more astonishing than Acapulco had been when she first left the village, but now she had more time to explore this new world. She learned English in a short time, and, in the company of a Cuban girl who worked for a neighbor, she started forays into the American universe, in ever-wider circles from her employers' house. She even took bus trips to Hollywood and San Francisco. For the first time in her life she slept in a room all by herself. And, despite her regular payments for Roberto's keep, she started to save money and put it in a bank account. Most important, she started to think

mordida   bribe (Spanish).

about her life in a new way, systematically. "What will become of you when you go back?" asked the American woman one day. Manuela did not know then, but she started to think. Carmelita, the Cuban girl, discussed the matter with her many times—in exchange for equal attention paid to her own planning exercises. Eventually, one project won out over all the alternatives: Manuela would return to go to commercial school, to become a bilingual secretary. She even started a typing course in California. But she would not return to Acapulco. She knew that, to succeed, she would have to remove herself from the family there. She would go to Mexico City, first alone, and then she would send for Roberto.

This last decision was made gradually. It was the letters that did it. Manuela, some months before, had mentioned the amount of money she had saved (a very large amount, by her standards, and enough to keep her and Roberto afloat for the duration of the commercial course). Then the letters started coming from just about everyone in the Acapulco clan. Most of the contents were family gossip, inquiries about Manuela's life in the States, and long expressions of affectionate feelings. There were frequent reminders not to forget her relatives, who took such good care of Roberto. Only gradually did the economic infrastructure emerge from all this: There was to be a *fiesta* at the wedding of a cousin, and could Manuela make a small contribution. The cousin who had been in jail was still to be tried, and there were lawyer's expenses. Uncle Pepe was onto the most promising business opportunity of his "long and distinguished career in financial activities" (his own words), and just three hundred American dollars would make it possible for him to avail himself of this never-to-recur opportunity—needless to say, Manuela would be a full partner upon her return. Finally, there was even a very formal letter from grandfather, all the way from the village, containing an appeal for funds to pay for a trip to the capital so as to take advantage of a new treatment that a famous doctor had developed there. It took a while for Manuela to grasp that every dollar of her savings had already been mentally spent by her relatives.

The choice before Manuela now is sharp and crystal-clear: She must return to Mexico—because she wants to, because of Roberto, and because the American authorities would send her back there sooner or later anyway. She can then return to the welcoming bosom of the family system, surrender her savings, and return to her previous way of life. Or she can carry through her plan in the face of family opposition. The choice is not only between two courses of action but between two moralities. The first course is dictated by the morality of collective solidarity, the second by the morality of personal autonomy and advancement. Each morality condemns the other—as uncaring selfishness in the former case, as irresponsible disregard of her own potential and the welfare of her son in the latter. Poor Manuela's conscience is divided; by now she is capable of feeling its pangs either way.

She is in America, not in Mexico, and the new morality gets more support from her immediate surroundings. Carmelita is all for the plan, and so are most of the Spanish-speaking girls with whom Manuela has been going out. Only one, another Mexican, expressed doubt: "I don't know. Your grandfather is ill, and your uncle helped you a lot in the past. Can you just forget them? I think that one must always help one's relatives." Manuela once talked about the matter with the American woman. "Nonsense," said the latter, "you should go ahead with your plan. You owe it to yourself and to your son." So this is what Manuela intends to do, very soon now. But she is not at ease with the decision. Every time another letter arrives from Mexico, she hesitates before opening it, and she fortifies herself against the appeals she knows to be there.

Each decision, as dictated by the respective morality, has predictable consequences: If Manuela follows the old morality, she will, in all likelihood, never raise herself or her son above the level she achieved in Acapulco—not quite at the bottom of the social scale, but not very far above it. If, on the other hand, she decides in accordance with the new morality (new for her, that is), she has at least a chance of making it up one important step on that scale. Her son will benefit from this, but probably no other of her relatives will. To take that step she must, literally, hack off all those hands that would hold her back. It is a grim choice indeed.

What will Manuela do?

She will probably at least start out on her plan. Perhaps she will succeed. But once she is back in Mexico, the tentacles of the old solidarity will be more powerful. They will pull more strongly. It will be harder to escape that other village, the village of the mind within herself. The outcome of the struggle will decide whether the village will be Manuela's past or also her future. Outside observers should think very carefully indeed before they take sides in this contest.

Jeanne Wakatsuki Houston

Jeanne Wakatsuki Houston was born in Inglewood, California, in 1935. In April 1942, when she was seven, her family was removed by Executive Order 9066 to a Japanese internment camp near Death Valley for the duration of World War II. They were freed in October 1945, when she was eleven. She later studied sociology and journalism at San Jose State College, where she met her husband, the writer James D. Houston. Together, they wrote *Farewell to Manzanar* (1973), a book that records her experiences during internment.

She recently completed another book, *Don't Cry, It's Only Thunder.* Written in collaboration with Vietnam veteran Paul Hansler, it describes his experiences with war orphans. The present essay appeared in *Asian Americans: Social and Psychological Perspectives,* edited by Russell Endo (1979).

Beyond Manzanar: A Personal View of Asian American Womanhood

Farewell to Manzanar is a personal story of my family's experiences during and after the Second World War. To fill out the story, my husband and I did a fair amount of research on the Internment and various aspects of Asian American experience. But I do not consider myself a scholar, nor do I feel I can speak for Asian Americans as a group. What I will be sharing with you will be more personal observations of my awareness of being an Asian American female in this society.

I will begin with memories of my mother, as she was the first, strongest and most important role model influencing my identity as a female. Then I would like to share with you some thoughts and feelings from my own experience, which have surfaced since the writing of *Farewell to Manzanar*.

1

My mother married for love. This was rare among Japanese immigrants living in America during that time—1915. Most were men who had to send for wives from their provinces in Japan via the *Baishakunin* or matchmaker, who exchanged photographs for the prospective couple and made the arrangements. This is not to say that love did not develop or occur among these couples. What is significant about this "Picture Bride" phenomenon is that the reasons for marriage were not love and affection, as is the case for the dominant culture in America. Marriages were arranged to perpetuate the family.

My mother was 18 and living in Spokane, Washington, when she met and fell in love with my father, a student ten years older than herself. She had been promised to someone else, a steady, hard-working farmer and friend of her family. In absolute defiance of her tradition and training, to be dutifully obedient to the authority of parents, she ran away with my father. Thus, their marriage became the first step towards assimilation into American culture; romantic love had intertwined itself among the responsibilities which defined their roles as husband/father, wife/mother. Perhaps it was this love, unexhibited but pervasive, which softened the sharp facts of the inequities in their relationship, in her acquiescence to his needs and demands. In my more immature years I could not understand how she could tolerate his volatile temperament, his arrogance and obsession with dignity, and his "kingly" presence in the home. I was in my teens then, not fully assimilated, but trying desperately to be as American as Doris Day. My parents did not behave like the parents of my Caucasian friends, and this was embarrassing for me.

Mama worked very hard. She would garden, cook, care for us when we were ill, and after the war she even went to work in the fish cannery to supplement the family income, which was minimal at the time. I felt sorry for her. I remember one day when I was 6 years old watching her scrub clothes, my arms barely reaching over the bathtub's edge, and she on her knees, rubbing soapy shirts against a tin washboard. I watched her silent and sweat-streaked face, her hair greying wispily around her temples. I filled with terror as I envisioned her dying because she worked too hard. I started to cry.

She only laughed when I told her my fears and said, "I like to wash clothes. It gives me time to think of other things in my head." She tapped her forehead. "Besides, I'm not a washerwoman. This is just a chore. I'm your mother."

I did not understand the weight of her explanation to me then. Being mother was not only enough for her, it was a prized identity. It meant she had a family, and in her world—her peers and community almost exclusively of Japanese descent—the family was supreme in its hierarchy of values. Thus, the chores and duties which she inherited as Japanese wife and mother were not her identity as such; they were just a means to accomplish the end, which was to keep her family intact, happy and well. She never confused her tasks with who she was.

This concept of the inner self, which I have begun only recently to understand as a result of my attempts to rediscover my Japanese "roots," allowed her to form her own image, distinct from the one in the exterior world. This ability to create a psychological privacy, inherited from a people who for centuries have had to create their own internal "space" in an overpopulated island, gave her the freedom, of which she was so deprived in her role as Japanese wife and mother. This was her way to survive . . . and to succeed. She did both with grace and with love. I think of the many people I know today (myself included) who have become so obsessed with freedom and independence. We resent our family, our jobs, our relationships . . . any responsibilities that seem to inhibit our mobility. I have so many more choices than my mother had, so much more external independence; yet, it was not until recently that I realized mobility and time do not mean freedom. The freedom is *within* me. I must *feel* free to be free.

I believe my mother was a fulfilled person. She had ten children who loved her devotedly. Even after ten years since her passing, I can truthfully say not a day passes that I do not think of her, not with grief, but with love and gratitude. What Japanese mother could be a failure when even after death her children do not abandon her? This brings to mind a comment made to me by a Japanese American friend commenting on American values and the family. "We abandon each other when we need each other the most," he said. "We abandon the young and the old. We send our young to nursery schools as early as we can get them in . . . just when they need our love and presence more than any time in their lives. We send our old and sickly to institutions to die alone. Where is our love responsibility? Where is that feeling of responsibility for each other that the family instills? Where is the family?"

There was a time when I would not declare my love for her. Not until I was in college did I realize my Caucasian peers seemed to have a different attitude toward their mothers than I did. Or, at least, they talked about them differently. During my Freshman year I took the required General Psychology course and was exposed for the first time to Freud and Jung, as were most of my classmates. I was stunned to hear them discuss their mothers so impersonally and often with great hostility. It seemed everyone had something negative to say about their "domineering, materialistic, guilt-evoking, aggressive" mothers. I did not understand then that these utterings were merely a way of asserting independence, of striking out at the one authority in their lives that emotionally held them to the "nest." What was clear to me was that mother and motherhood were not "sacred" to them in the same way it was to me. They celebrated Mother's Day, which we never did, yet I heard such resentment surrounding that day, I used to wonder why it was celebrated.

Years later I was keenly reminded again of that period in my life. I was working as the Student Activities Coordinator at one of the colleges at the University of California in Santa Cruz. Among my duties was the responsibility for room assignments and changes. One day, a Chicano student came into my office requesting a room change. He was clearly agitated. I offered to act as mediator or counselor if there was a misunderstanding with his roommate. Reluctantly, he said, "I don't know about these Anglos. My roommate talks so badly about his mother. He calls her a bitch. This hurts me very much. I love my mother. I know she is sacrificing for me, crawling on her hands and knees in the strawberry fields of Delano so I can come to the University. I'm afraid I will hurt him if I have to keep rooming with him." I had felt my throat tighten and my eyes fill with tears, empathizing with him. I was touched by his love and loyalty, his willingness to overtly challenge an attitude so acceptable within the dominant culture and so unacceptable within his.

The word "sacrifice," spoken by my Caucasian friends in reference to their mothers, always carried connotations of guilt and manipulative martyrdom. It did not carry that taint for me or for the Mexican student. In fact, I have found that most of my friends from other ethnic minority backgrounds will readily say, if it is so, that they knew their mothers sacrificed their own comforts, or worked so that they could go to school or have a graduation suit . . . no guilt implied, just a recognition and acceptance of it with gratitude.

I think that Japanese women of my mother's generation who were mothers were fortunate because their role was highly valued by their society . . . their society being the community of other Japanese immigrants. The family and community prized her role, and when she fulfilled that role, she prized herself. She not only knew her worth, she *felt* her significance. There was no celebration of "Mother's Day," but there was no question that *Oka-san* was respected and loved by her culture.

Her role as wife to my father is not as clear cut in my memory. Whereas her world in the home, in the immediate Japanese community, did not differ much from the society in which she and her mother were raised, my father's world was very different. He had to earn a living for his family in an environment both alien and hostile to him. My mother, already inherently prepared to subordinate herself in their relationship knew this and zealously sought for ways to elevate his position in the family. He had to absorb the humiliations "out there"; she would absorb them at home. After all, was he not doing this for his family, protecting her, acting as the buffer between herself and that alien *hakujin*⁰ world?

She served him . . . with grace and naturalness. I conjure up the image of her calm, smooth face, her alert brown eyes scanning his stockings for holes as she carefully laid them and his underwear out at the foot of their bed. She did this faithfully every morning I can remember when he was at home. He was always served first at meals. She cooked special things for him and sat next to him at the table, vigilantly aware of his needs, handing him the condiments and pouring his tea before he could ask. She drew his bath and massaged him and laid his clothes out when he dressed up. As I was growing up I accepted these rituals to be the natural expressions of a wife's love for her husband. There was no question in my mind that my mother loved my father; that is why she served him. This attitude, that to serve meant to love, became an integral part of my psychological make-up and a source for confusion when I later began to relate to men.

There was also no question in my mind that my father was absolute authority in their relationship and in his relationship to his children. During and after the Second World War, when his dreams and economic situation had hit bottom, and he was too old to start over again as he had already done several times, he raged at his wife and family and drank. His frustration toward the society that rejected and humiliated him caused him to turn on his own and on himself. I never understood how she so patiently endured him during those times. But she never abandoned him, understanding as I did not, the reasons for his anguish, for his sense of failure.

Even though respect for him diminished then, I always felt that he was very powerful and that he dominated her with this power. As they grew older and inevitable thoughts of their passing entered my mind, I worried that she would be lost if he died before her. When that sad day arrived I learned what is meant by the Asian philosophical truism "softness is strength." I had taken my gravely ill father, along with my mother, to see his doctor. The doctor informed me privately that we should take him to

hakujin Caucasian (Japanese).

the hospital where he would be comfortable, as he could not live more than 10 days.

It was raining. I numbly drove the car toward the hospital, straining to see through the blurred windshields and my own tears. My mother was not crying. "Riku," he said, weakly. He never called her Riku . . . always "Mama." "Don't leave me. Stay with me at the hospital. They won't know how to cook for me . . . or how to care for me." She patted his hand. "You've been a good wife. You've always been the strong one."

Not wanting him to tire, I tried to quiet him. He sat up bolt-like and roared like a lion. "Shut up!" I quaked at his forcefulness, but felt some comfort in knowing he could still "save face" and be the final authority to his children, even at death's door. My mother's quiet strength filled the car as she gently stroked his forehead. Without tears or panic she assured him she would stay with him until the end.

He died that afternoon a few hours after he entered the hospital. For the ten years afterward that my mother lived, she never once appeared lost or rudderless, as I feared she would be with him gone. Hadn't he been the center of her life? Hadn't the forms in their relationship, the rituals of their roles all affirmed his power over her? No. She had been the strong one. The structure had been created for him; but it was her essence that had sustained it.

2

The memories surrounding my awareness of being female seem to fall into two categories: those of the period before the war, when the family made up my world, and those after the war when I entered puberty, and my world expanded to include the ways and values of my Caucasian peers. I did not think about my Asian-ness and how it influenced my self-image as a female, until I married.

In remembering myself as a small child, I find it hard to separate myself from the entity of the family. I was too young to be given "duties" according to my sex, and I was unaware that this was the organizational basis for the operating of the family. I took it for granted that everyone just did what had to be done to keep things running smoothly. My five older sisters helped my mother with domestic duties, and my four older brothers helped my father in the fishing business. What I vaguely recall about the sensibility surrounding our sex differences was that my sisters and I all liked to please our brothers. Moreso, we tried to attract positive attention from Papa. A smile or affectionate pat from him was like a gift from heaven. Somehow, we never felt this way about Mama. We took her love for granted. But there was something special about Papa.

I never identified this specialness as being one of the blessings of maleness. After all, I played with my brother Kiyo, two years older than myself, and I never felt there was anything special about him. I could even make him cry. My older brothers were fun-loving, boisterous and very kind to me, especially when I made them laugh with my imitations of Carmen Miranda dancing and Bonnie Baker singing "Oh, Johnny." But Papa was different. His specialness was that he was the authority, not that he was a male.

After the war, my world drastically changed. The family had disintegrated, my father no longer "Godlike" despite my mother's attempt to sustain that pre-war image of him. I was spending most of my time with my new Caucasian friends and learning new values that clashed with the values of my parents. It was also time that I assumed duties in the home that the girls were supposed to do . . . like cooking, cleaning the house, washing and ironing clothes. I remember washing and ironing my brother's shirts, careful to press the collars correctly, trying not to displease them. I cannot ever remember my brothers performing domestic chores while I lived at home. Yet, even though they may not have been working "out there," as the men were supposed to do, I did not resent it. It would have embarrassed me to see my brothers doing the dishes. Their reciprocation came in a different way.

They were very protective of me and made me feel good and important for being a female. If my brother Ray had extra money, he would sometimes buy me a sexy sweater like my Caucasian friends wore that Mama wouldn't buy for me. My brothers taught me to ride a bicycle, to drive a car, took me to my first dance, and proudly introduced me to their friends.

Although the family had changed, my identity as a female within it did not differ much from my older sisters who grew up before the war. The males and females supported each other but for different reasons. No longer was the survival of the family as a group our primary objective; we cooperated to help each other survive "out there" in the complicated world that had weakened Papa.

My brothers encouraged me to run for school office, to try out for majorette and song leader, and to run for Queen of various festivities. They were proud that I was breaking social barriers still closed to them. It was acceptable for an Oriental male to excel academically and in sports. But to gain recognition socially in a society that had been fed the stereotyped model of the Asian male as cook, houseboy or crazed *kamikaze* pilot, was almost impossible. The more alluring myth of mystery and exotica that surrounds the Oriental female made it easier, though no less spiritually painful, for me.

Whenever I succeeded in the *hakujin* world, my brothers were supportive, whereas, Papa would be disdainful, undermined by my obvious capitulation to the ways of the West. I wanted to be like my Caucasian friends. Not only did I want to look like them, I wanted to act like them. I tried hard to be outgoing and socially aggressive, and to act confidently like my girl friends. At home I was careful not to show these personality traits to my father. For him it was bad enough that I did not even look very

Japanese; I was too big, and I walked too assertively. My breasts were large, and besides that I showed them off with those sweaters the *hakujin* girls wore! My behavior at home was never calm and serene, but I still tried to be as Japanese as I could around my father.

As I passed puberty and grew more interested in boys, I soon became aware that an Oriental female evoked a certain kind of interest from males. I was still too young to understand how or why an Oriental female fascinated Caucasian men, and of course, far too young to see then that it was a form of "not seeing," of stereotyping. My brothers would warn me, "Don't trust the *hakujin* boys. They only want one thing. They'll treat you like a servant and expect you to wait on them hand and foot. They don't know how to be nice to you." My brothers never dated Caucasian girls. In fact, I never really dated Caucasian boys until I went to college. In high school, I used to sneak out to dances and parties where I would meet them. I wouldn't even dare to think what Papa would do if he knew I was seeing *hakujin* boys.

What my brothers were saying was that I should not act towards Caucasian males as I did towards them. I must not "wait on them" or allow them to think I would, because they wouldn't understand. In other words, be a Japanese female around Japanese men and act *hakujin* around Caucasian men. This double identity within a "double standard" resulted not only in a confusion for me of my role or roles as female, but also in who or what I was racially. With the admonitions of my brothers lurking deep in my consciousness, I would try to be aggressive, assertive and "come on strong" towards Caucasian men. I mustn't let them think I was submissive, passive and all-giving like Madame Butterfly. With Asian males I would tone down my natural enthusiasm and settle into patterns instilled in me through the models of my mother and my sisters. I was not comfortable in either role.

I found I was more physically attracted to Caucasian men. Although T.V. and film were not nearly as pervasive as they are now, we still had an abundance of movie magazines and movies from which to garner our idols for crushes and fantasy. For years I was madly in love with Lon McAllister and Alan Ladd. Bruce Lee and O.J. Simpson were absent from the idol-making media. Asian men became like "family" to me; they were my brothers. Of course, no one was like my father. He was so powerful. The only men who might possess some of that power were those whose control and dominance over his life diminished his. Those would be the men who interested me.

Although I was attracted to males who looked like someone in a Coca-Cola ad, I yearned for the expressions of their potency to be like that of Japanese men, like that of my father: unpredictable, dominant, and brilliant—yet sensitive and poetic. I wanted a blond Samurai.

When I met my blond Samurai I was surprised to see how readily my mother accepted the idea of our getting married. My father had passed away, but I was still concerned about her reaction. All of my married brothers and sisters had married Japanese American mates. I would be the first to marry a Caucasian. "He's a strong man and will protect you. I'm all for it," she said. Her main concern for me was survival. Knowing that my world was the world of the *hakujin,* she wanted me to be protected, even if it meant marriage to one. It was 1957, and inter-racial couples were a rare sight to see. She felt that my husband-to-be was strong because he was acting against the norms of his culture, perhaps even against his parent's wishes. From her vantage point, where family and group opinion outweighed the individual's, this willingness to oppose them was truly a show of strength.

When we first married I wondered if I should lay out his socks and underwear every morning like my mother used to do. But then my brother's warning not to be subservient to Caucasian men or they will take advantage would float up from the past. So I compromised and laid them out sporadically, whenever I thought to do it . . . which grew less and less often as the years passed. (Now my husband is lucky if *he* can even find a clean pair of socks in the house!) His first reaction to this wifely gesture was to be uncomfortably pleased. Then he was puzzled by its sporadic occurrence, which did not seem to coincide as an act of apology, or because I wanted something. On the days when I felt I should be a good Japanese wife, I did it. On other days, when I felt American and assertive, I did not.

When my mother visited us, as she often did when she was alive, I had to be on good behavior, much to my husband's pleasure and surprise. I would jump up from the table to fill his empty water glass (that is, if she hadn't beat me to it) or butter his roll. If I didn't notice that his plate needed refilling, she would kick me under the table and reprimand me with a disapproving look. Needless to say, we never had mother-in-law problems. He would often ask with hope in his voice, "When is your mother coming to visit?"

Despite the fact that early in our marriage we had become aware of the "images" we had married and were trying to relate to each other as the real people we were, he still hoped deep in his heart that I was his *Cho-Cho san,*[0] his saronged, exotic Dorothy Lamour. And I still saw him as my golden Samurai, wielding his sword of justice and integrity, slaying the dragons that prevented my acceptance as an equal human being in his world, now mine.

My mother dutifully served my father throughout their marriage. I never felt she resented it. I served my brothers and father and did not resent it. I was made to feel not only important for performing duties of my role, but absolutely integral for the functioning of the family. I realized

---

Cho-Cho san Heroine who marries an American naval officer in Puccini's opera *Madama Butterfly.*

a very basic difference in attitude between Japanese and American culture towards serving another. In my family, to serve another could be uplifting, a gracious gesture that elevated oneself. For many white Americans it seems that serving another is degrading, an indication of dependency or weakness in character, or a low place in the social ladder. To be ardently considerate is to be "self-effacing" or apologetic.

My father used to say, "Serving humanity is the greatest virtue. Giving service of yourself is more worthy than selling the service or goods of another." He would prefer that we be maids in someone's home, serving someone well, than be a salesgirl where our function would be to exchange someone else's goods, handling money. Perhaps it was his way to rationalize and give pride to the occupations open to us as Orientals. Nevertheless, his words have stayed with me, giving me spiritual sustenance at times when I perceived that my willingness to give was misconstrued to be a need to be liked or an act of manipulation to get something.

I was talking about this subject with an Asian American woman friend, recently widowed, whose husband had also been Asian American. He had been a prominent surgeon, highly thought of in the community where we live. She is 42, third generation Chinese, born in San Francisco in 1935, articulate, intelligent and a professional therapist for educationally handicapped children. She "confessed" of her reticence to let her Caucasian friends know she served her husband. "There is such a stereotyped view that is laid on us. They just don't understand *why* we do what we do!"

She told me of an incident when she remarked to a Caucasian friend that she polished her husband's shoes. Her friend turned on her in mock fury and said, "Don't you dare let my husband know you do that!" My friend said she felt ashamed, humiliated, that she had somehow betrayed this woman by her seeming subordination to her husband.

"I served him in many ways," she said. "I did it because even though he was a graduate of Stanford and professionally successful, he drove himself to work harder and longer to compete because he felt he was handicapped by being Chinese. You know our Asian men, the ones raised with values from the old country are not equipped to compete like white American men. They are not conditioned to be outwardly aggressive and competitive. It was agony for my husband, and I knew he was out there doing it for us, so I tried to make it easier for him at home." As I looked at her I could see her compassion, and for a flickering moment I saw my mother. A generation had passed, but some things had not changed that much.

My husband and I often joke that the reason we have stayed married for so long is that we continually mystify each other with responses and attitudes that are plainly due to our different backgrounds. For years I frustrated him with unpredictable silences and accusative looks. I felt a great reluctance to tell him what I wanted or what needed to be done in the home. I was inwardly furious that I was being put into the position of having to *tell* him what to do. I felt my femaleness, in the Japanese sense, was being degraded. I did not want to be the authority. That would be humiliating for him and for me. He, on the other hand, considering the home to be under my dominion, in the American sense, did not dare to impose on me what he thought I wanted. He wanted me to tell him or make a list, like his parents did in his home.

Entertaining socially was also confusing. Up to recent times, I still hesitated to sit at one head of our rectangular dining table when my husband sat at the other end. It seemed right to be seated next to him, helping him serve the food. Sometimes I did it anyway, but only with our close friends who didn't misunderstand my physical placement to be psychological subservience.

At dinner parties I always used to serve the men first until I noticed the women glaring at me. I became self-conscious about it and would try to remember to serve the ladies first. Sometimes I would forget and automatically turn to a man. I would catch myself abruptly, dropping a bowl of soup all over him. Then I would have to serve him first anyway, as an apologetic gesture. My unconscious Japanese instinct still managed to get what it wanted!

Now I just entertain according to how I feel that day. If my Japanese sensibility is stronger I act accordingly and feel comfortable. If I feel like going all-American I can do that too, and feel comfortable. I have come to accept the cultural hybridness of my personality, to recognize it as strength and not weakness. Because I am neither culturally pure Japanese nor pure American does not mean I am less of a person. It means I have been enriched with the heritage of both.

As I look back on my marriage and try to compare it to the marriage of my parents, it seems ludicrous to do so . . . like comparing a sailboat to a jet airliner; both get you there, but one depends on the natural element of wind and the other on technological expertise. What does emerge as a basic difference is directly related to the Japanese concept of cooperation for group survival and the American value of competition for the survival of individualism. My Japanese family cooperated to survive economically and spiritually. Although sibling rivalry was subtly present, it was never allowed the ferocity of expression we allow our children. I see our children compete with each other. I have felt my husband and I compete with each other . . . not always in obvious ways such as professional recognition or in the comparison of role responsibilities, but in attitudes towards self-fulfillment. "I love you more than you love me," or "My doing nothing is more boring than your doing nothing."

Competition does provide some challenge and excitement in life. Yet carried to extremes in personal relationships, it can become destructive. How can you fully trust someone you are in competition with? And when trust breaks down, isolation and alienation set in.

I find that another basic difference is between my mother and myself in how we relate to sons. I try very consciously not to indulge my son, as my mother had indulged my brothers. My natural inclination is to do this. So I try to restrain it. In fact, I find myself being harder on him, afraid that my constrained Japanese training to please the male might surface, crippling instead of equipping him for future relationships with females who may not be of my background, hampering his emotional survival in the competitive, independent world he will face when he leaves the nest.

How my present attitudes will affect my children in later years remains to be seen. My world is radically different from my mother's world, and all indications point to an even wider difference in our world from our children's. Whereas my family's and part of my struggle were racially based, I do not foresee a similar struggle for our children. Their biracialness is, indeed, a factor in their identity and self-image, but I feel their struggle will be more to sustain human dignity in a world rapidly dehumanizing itself with mechanization and technology. My hope is they have inherited a strong will to survive, that essential trait which ethnic minorities in this country have sharply honed.

3

In searching for remarks to conclude this paper, I find myself hearkening again to imagined words of advice from my parents. My mother would say, "Love yourself. Nurture your children and your family with love and emotional support. Accept change if it means protecting your loved ones."

My father would say, "We are all brothers. Brother must not be pitted against brother; race must not be pitted against race. We do not raise ourselves at the expense of others. Through cooperation we advance together as human beings."

I see the yin and the yang of their sensibilities and acknowledge how the combination of them has formed my own. Thus, I close with these words, "In this game of life, we are only as good as our partner . . . our partner being the other in a male-female relationship, or a race or ethnic group co-existing with a dominant culture. The best game is when partners are equal, in top form, sharing their diversities, and enriching their experience. Dominating a partner only weakens the game, unbalancing it, lessening its vigor and quality. It is my hope in these changing times that the rules for the game will improve, encouraging understanding, and thus, acceptance and respect for all partners."

Robert M. Kaus

Robert M. Kaus (born 1951) attended Harvard, where he took his law degree in 1976. After clerking for the California Supreme Court and spending a year with the Federal Trade Commission, he turned to journalism, working for three years as an editor of *Washington Monthly,* which published the present article in July 1979. After a year on the staff of *American Lawyer,* in 1982 he became politics editor of *Harper's,* where he specializes in legal, political, and economic issues.

What's Wrong with Roots

I was raised in Beverly Hills, California—and like most of the kids in that sunny suburb, I am Jewish. Jewish enough, at any rate, for Hitler to have chased my parents into the New World. But not, I'm sometimes told, obviously Jewish on the surface. For this reason, I've often had the experience of having my ethnic identity "discovered." "Oh, you're Jewish," someone will exclaim, and I am immediately put on guard—because that phrase usually means one of two things. Sometimes the implication is "well, that explains a lot," and I can only wonder what deep and specious connections are being made in the mind of my observer. Or else I'm discovered by somebody who is also Jewish, in which case the revelation is often followed by a knowing look, a sort of wink. "We have a lot in common," the look seems to say, invoking a tradition of culture and philosophy that I am assumed to share like a bond. These are the most awkward moments of all, because where I should feel the throb of ethnic fervor, I inevitably feel nothing.

Beverly Hills, I suspect, was not the best place in the world to cultivate a fine Jewish consciousness. There, in one of the world's most pleasant climates, enjoying a life of almost unprecedented wealth, it was difficult to work up the sense of persecution and torment that, I am told, is central to the experience of my race. The wonderful aspects of Jewish culture— the emphasis on learning and humor, the hustle, the kind and inevitable paternalism—were either overwhelmed by the materialism of the community, or else seemed to have become part of the larger Southern California world that surrounded us, and appeared on our television screens. Either way, the attempts of my neighbors to preserve their Jewishness by traditional means—attending temple, staying away from school on Rosh Hashanah, or shipping off to faraway kibbutzes—often seemed artificial. I was, of course, well schooled in the horror of the Holocaust; but to me that horror was not so much the attempted annihilation of a culture as the arbitrary murder of individuals on the basis of discovered ancestry. In short, I was a non-ethnic.

In 1971, Michael Novak announced the "Decade of the Ethnics," and maybe sometime in the intervening years I should have made a major effort to acquaint myself with my own cultural heritage, visited my ancestral town perhaps, tracked down distant relatives, or read some of the fine histories of the Jewish diaspora. If I fancied myself a leftist, I could have steeped myself in the history of the Jewish Left, read all the McCarthy hearings,⁰ learned the old songs, wandered around mumbling about the Rosenbergs.⁰ I tried a few of these things, but they didn't seem to work. Reading the enthusiastic confessionals of born-again ethnics, I could tell I was being left behind, feel the subtle contempt that those who are at one with their heritage must have for the assimilated. In their eyes, I was bland, suburban. I was trying to be a WASP.

Then, I decided I shouldn't feel uncomfortable about who I am. If I'm not interested in Judaism, if I have no hidden ethnic yearnings to satisfy, so be it. I guess you could say I've rediscovered my assimilation.

In the early 70's, when the "New Ethnicity," according to Novak, "blazed up . . . before public eyes," its champions were motivated by some reasonable and urgent concerns. It had become a bad habit among the liberal elite—in the wake of the civil rights movement and the Kerner Commission⁰—to look with contempt upon the white working class sons of Polish, Italian, Greek, and Slavic immigrants, labeling them as "racist" or "obstacles to social progress." The ethnic intellectuals, Novak, Rev. Andrew Greeley, Msgr. Geno Baroni, among others, perceived a healthy dose of class snobbery and "nativist" prejudice in these attitudes, as well as an easy lack of empathy. Taking their cue from the civil rights struggle itself, they —and ethnic organizers like Stephen Adubado of Newark and Barbara Mikulski of Baltimore—sought to restore the pride that might allow working class whites and blacks to treat each other as respected equals. It is difficult to argue with their initial political impulse.

But their movement, particularly as interpreted by Novak and Greeley, had a broader, cultural thrust, which was an attack on the old ideal of the "melting pot." Not only hadn't the melting pot worked, said the New Ethnicists, but it shouldn't. Novak railed against the predominance of the

McCarthy hearings Hearings conducted in 1953–54 by Senator Joseph McCarthy on the role of Communism in American life, and in 1954 by a U.S. Senate Subcommittee on charges made by McCarthy that the army was trying to conceal evidence of espionage. McCarthy's hearings are now generally considered to have largely been based on unsubstantiated charges; they led to blacklists, character defamation, and four or five years of national political hysteria. The Senate hearings, broadcast on television, discredited McCarthy and led to the Senate's formal condemnation of him.

Rosenbergs Julius and Ethel Rosenberg, executed in 1953 for furnishing military secrets to Soviet agents. The question of their guilt remains a highly controversial issue.

Kerner Commission National Advisory Commission on Civil Disorders, appointed in 1967 in the wake of riots in Newark and Detroit. The Commission issued a report in 1968 attributing black unrest to white racism and recommending measures to aid blacks.

"WASP superculture"—rational, restrained, competitive, above all "solitary," and ultimately "sterile." Assimilation in America meant joining this superculture, and the result was both a loss of community and a numbing conformity. "The melting pot," wrote Novak, "is a kind of homogenized soup."

As a cure for WASPish homogenization, the New Ethnicity prescribed a particular type of pluralism—a pluralism based on the traditional cultures of America's immigrant groups. The alternatives were rather starkly set forth: either we would follow the ethnic prescription and pursue what Greeley called "a mosaic society in which at least the most intimate ties are sought and maintained within our ethnic or religio-ethnic groups," or we would end up with the monotony of isolating competition.

Over the ensuing decade, the ethnic crusade did have a highly visible impact. Millions of Americans "rediscovered their roots." Pan Am commercials came to feature photographs of Poles, Asians, and Germans. "Good-sized paperback bookstores have shelves lined with books on ethnicity," Father Greeley proudly points out, while "courses of ethnic studies have spread like contagious diseases through college catalogues. . . ." Chambers of commerce "have busily compiled lists of the 'ethnic' restaurants, including many that didn't know they were ethnic. . . ."

But the ethnic movement was supposed to be more than this orgy of genealogy, scholarship, and cuisine. It was supposed to be, in Novak's words, "a barrier against alienation and anomie," a vehicle for preserving a sense of communality in a society dominated by "the bitch goddess success and the pursuit of loneliness." Yet are we less dominated by those qualities after our ethnic revival, or more? Despite its popularity, the ethnic prescription has proved to be a good bit less effective than Novak advertised, and the "Decade of the Ethnics" probably ranks with the "Greening of America"[0] in terms of living up to its advance notices.

The weaknesses of the movement, like those of Reich's "counterculture," should have been apparent from the start. First of all, there was a basic ambiguity about whom the New Ethnicists were talking about. "It is very difficult," Father Greeley wrote in 1971, "to speak precisely about what an ethnic group is. . . . Does everyone belong to an ethnic group? . . . Such questions do not admit of quick answers." In the heady days of the ethnic movement's birth, however, quick answers weren't required; the fuzziness of the revival's key concept, rather than calling the enterprise into question, only seemed to show how badly it was needed. The inability to "accurately identify the boundaries of the ethnic population," complained one New Ethnician, "reveals how indifferent much of the traditional social sciences have been towards the study of white ethnic Americans."

"Greening of America"   Title of a book published in 1970 by Charles A. Reich. It embodies the radical idealism of the 1960s.

At times, the constituency of the New Ethnicity was clearly those white immigrants whom the melting pot hadn't melted. In describing these "unmeltable ethnics," Novak refers repeatedly to the "primordial," ineradicable quality of ethnic character. "Emotional patterns that have been operative for a thousand years do not cease to function," he argues. Although the exact mechanism is never specified (is ethnicity inherited, or simply drummed into the brains of youth?), our "instincts, judgments, and sense of reality are heirs to cultural experiences that are now largely unconscious."

The problem with the "unmeltable" view of ethnicity is people like me, members of what Novak and others like to call a "new class"—mobile, rootless, salaried, fond of universal moralizing and "social change." On all these counts I plead "no contest,"—but so what? For good or evil, there are a whole lot of people like me floating around, thoroughly assimilated, or hopelessly polyglot, with "primordial" ties of "blood," "family," and "land" confounded by decades of intermarriage. The melting pot may not have softened up our grandparents or parents, but it has done its work on us. Even the most optimistic champions of white ethnicity claimed a constituency of less than 20 per cent of the American population.

If ethnicity was to be the basis for a nationwide rebirth of community, as men like Novak envisioned, the movement would clearly have to do more than organize existing ethnic groups. It would have to expand them —not by new immigration, but by a rediscovery of ethnicity among already "melted" Americans. So there is an exhortation running through the writings of the ethnic revivalists, directed at the assimilated: cultivate your ethnic character, search your past for, in Novak's phrase, "ethnic materials," "discover" your inheritance. Ethnicity, rather than being ineradicable, became, "in part, a matter of choice."

But if becoming ethnic is a matter of choice, should we make that choice? In answering that question, the ethnic revivalists quickly ran up against a paradox. For, although the main goal of ethnic pluralism is to encourage variety in society as a whole, in order to achieve that end it must *discourage* the cultivation of variety *within* individuals. If an individual adopts the values of a number of different ethnic groups, his identity is split between those cultures; communal bonds are fragmented and diffused, and the dread assimilation looms just around the corner. The connoisseur of ethnicity ceases to be an ethnic himself.

As a result, the New Ethnicists find themselves, in the name of social contrast, endorsing what Jimmy Carter once so infelicitously called "ethnic purity." The preservation of ethnic heritage degenerates easily into a cult of authenticity. So, for all their talk of "richness," "complexity," and "untidy, messy, diversity," you won't catch Novak or Greeley talking about a variety of ethnic strands coexisting peacefully within the character of a single human being. Instead, Novak's writings are littered with attempts to explain his near-mystical belief that, even in the most confused mongrel, one strain will out. "It is amazing," he argues, "how persons who claim themselves to have a 'very mixed' ethnic background exhibit patterns of taste and appreciation that are very ethnic indeed: a delight in the self-restraint of Scotsmen, discomfort with the effusiveness of Sicilians—or, by contrast, a sense of release in encountering Sicilian emotions, a constriction of nervousness faced with the puzzling cues of the culture of the Scots." Our mission, Novak implies, is to search for this single ethnic clue that "unlocks secrets of the psyche as no other does."

And what if you sometimes emulate the restraint of the Scots, sometimes the Sicilian effusion? What if you are the offspring of a Scottish-Sicilian liaison, and are neither effusive nor reserved—and what's worse, you've developed a strong taste for knackwurst? Well, boy are you out of it. You're just not authentically anything, and you'd better rediscover your true ethnic identity before your self-confidence is undermined entirely. To become an "unmeltable ethnic," it seems, one must be made of only one metal.

Ultimately, the process by which those of mixed background or taste cultivate a single ethnic character is hopelessly artificial. "Given a grandparent or two," Novak tells us, "one chooses to shape one's consciousness by one history or the other." I am supposed to comb my family tree for its various ethnic fruits. After shopping at this ancestral smorgasbord, I pick the flavor I prefer, and then I dine on nothing else. Why? Why aren't I exactly who I am, the product of a variety of cultures, for whom a whiff of L.A. smog yields far more authentic nostalgia than a trip to the Holy Land?

Even for those of unblemished ethnic lineage, the demands of authenticity can seem arbitrary. Is it inevitable that people be, as Novak predicts, "pleased to discover the limits inherent in being who they are?" A more appealing ideal would leave even the ethnically pure free to pick those aspects of their inheritance that they want to cherish, and to supplement them with habits from elsewhere.

Indeed, for the entire society, the celebration of ethnic difference encourages a crippling sort of relativism. After all, if you are going to avoid imposing your own "superculture," you must try to appreciate other traditions "warts and all." If Italians have a history of idealizing and subordinating women—well, that's Italian for you! If, as a child of the professional suburbs, you've tried to play basketball with black ghetto teenagers more intent on proving their manhood than playing the game, your misgivings about the role of machismo in black culture should be repressed. We can thank feminism, and the civil rights movement, for cutting through ethnic boosterism to subject the culture of whatever group to a scrutiny based on some universal ideas of justice.

Perhaps because most people, at bottom, are reluctant to leave important decisions to the whim of inheritance, the efforts of "new class" professionals to rediscover their roots often mock the very communality that the ethnic movement was supposed to preserve. A good example is Paul Cowan's account, in his recent book, *The Tribes of America,* of his attempts to recover his own Jewish past, to "organize part of my life around that rich heritage." Cowan starts by talking to Orthodox Jews. He soon takes up fasting on Yom Kippur. He is "delighted" to find a distant rabbi in his family tree. Though he wears a yarmulke on his trips to the Lower East Side ("I told myself I was doing so as a sign of respect. But . . . wearing it was . . . but a way of reclaiming part of my identity"), he wrestles with himself about whether to remove it as he nears his uptown apartment (he does). He ends by describing his, and his wife's, attempts to "figure out how to observe the Sabbath, but in a way that blended the realities of our own highly mobile, multicultured life with our desire for peace and ceremony."

What's missing from Cowan's description of his New Ethnic lifestyle, of course, is any appreciation for all but the most superficial or noncontroversial aspects of the Orthodox tradition. We don't even know if Cowan believes in God. Everything is peace, tradition, heritage—conferred by the symbols of a past, rather than any commitment to the substance those symbols represent. In Cowan's hands, ethnicity is reduced to the level of interior decorating; he has just done up his life in Early Jewish.

Of course, not everyone who rediscovers their "roots" gets as carried away with the mechanics of the process as Cowan. And, symbols of continuity, as well as knowledge of our families' histories, are important to all of us. But those symbols aren't always "ethnic" symbols; those family pasts are often gloriously mixed; and neither can substitute for our constant, individual efforts to make our own judgments. When the New Ethnicists billed their movement as the key to transforming American society, they violated these limits on the role of immigrant cultures in our lives. They also ignored the limitations that would be created by the ethnic revival itself.

In his book, *The Rise of the Unmeltable Ethnics,* Michael Novak described all the wonderful results that might flow from a rebirth of "ethnic consciousness." He dreamed, he said, of a day when something would be "done to decentralize industry, to weave work more naturally into the rhythms of the home," when "the formation of workers' caucuses" would "devise ways of humanizing their work," when "industrial establishments would be required to put a certain percentage of their income into enhancing the total environment of family and leisure." These are inspiring goals. But they are inspiring, in part, because they would build intimacy and community into our central institutions of work, rather than relying on the ethnic ornaments that adorn the fringes of life.

More important, for any of Novak's dreams to come true there would first have to be a tremendous effort to conceive and realize the interests of the entire nation. What are the chances that ethnic clans could be the basis for such a united effort? Isn't it more likely that, if our identities are tied to our particular ancestral groups, we will be encouraged to look after only the particular interests of those groups, to preserve their accustomed privileges, rather than risk them in a general effort to satisfy an overriding *national* interest? After all, even the ability of ethnic groups to respect each other—rather than hate each other—requires a healthy dose of "superculture," because the ideal of tolerance must be taught to all. The sort of society-wide agreement that might move us toward Novak's decentralized utopia would itself amount to a new national culture.

At different points in our history, different approaches, and emphases, seem appropriate. For the waves of immigrants who arrived in this country, the preservation of traditional communities was often a vital means of countering the contempt of predecessors, the pain of dislocation, and the burden of economic discrimination. Similarly, men like Novak were right, at the beginning of this decade, to point out the condescending attitudes of many liberal professionals toward "white ethnics," and to decry the active repression of immigrant cultures.

But these moments have come and, largely, gone. For many Americans, like myself, the substance of the immigrant values has been lost. Whether the mechanism was WASP repression or free choice doesn't seem to matter much now—only an impoverished and confining vision would condemn us to exhume our particular ethnic legacies rather than build on our new knowledge and experience.

And the noble goals of the New Ethnicity, the restoration of community, the fight against a culture that Novak describes as "sterile for the emotions, the instincts, the imagination," require that we all struggle together to establish new communities, habits, and traditions, to choose the best elements from our ethnic inheritances and forge them into a common identity. An obsession with those separate pasts can only cloud our judgment, and blunt our creativity. We need the ability of each generation to say "My parents were like that. I am going to be different."

The message of the ethnic ideologues is that any common identity must be that of the "WASP superculture," that assimilation means homogenization. But in this they ignore a great deal of American experience. There are events, pieces of our history, which seem to go beyond mere tolerance, or bland assimilation, to evoke a distinct national, American, character. You can feel part of it watching old World War II movies, or reading *Huckleberry Finn.* It's there in the idealization of the small-town life of the pre-Depression era. Often, it is invented, using the leftover bits of old traditions, as jazz was invented, and baseball, and rock and roll. (Are these things sterile, or featureless? Was Mark Twain bland? Is Chuck Berry?) Above all, you can find it in the common heritage of all immigrants who came here in search of freedoms that could best be expressed in language that was universal, not parochial.

If we have to choose an ethnic framework on which to build, why not choose this one? What the New Ethnicity may demonstrate, in the end, is not the inability of a national culture to instill a sense of community and intimacy, but our failure of imagination in not realizing the possibilities.

Toni Morrison

Toni Morrison, a distinguished novelist, was born in 1931 in a small steel town near Cleveland, Ohio. She was educated at Howard University (B.A., 1953) and Cornell (M.A., 1955) and taught English until she became an editor for the publisher Random House in 1964. She began writing fiction in the 1960s, drawing upon her background as a black woman born into a family struggling with poverty during the depression. Her first novel, *The Bluest Eye* (1969), established her reputation; her next novel, *Sula* (1973), was nominated for the 1975 National Book Award in fiction. *Song of Solomon* (1977) won the 1978 National Book Critics Circle Award as best work of fiction in 1977. Her most recent book, *Tar Baby,* was published in 1981. The following selection is reprinted from the July 4, 1976, edition of the *New York Times Magazine.*

A Slow Walk of Trees

(as Grandmother Would Say)

Hopeless

(as Grandfather Would Say)

His name was John Solomon Willis, and when at age 5 he heard from the old folks that "the Emancipation Proclamation was coming," he crawled under the bed. It was his earliest recollection of what was to be his habitual response to the promises of white people: horror and an instinctive yearning for safety. He was my grandfather, a musician who managed to hold on to his violin but not his land. He lost all 88 acres of his Indian mother's inheritance to legal predators who built their fortunes on the likes of him. He was an unreconstructed black pessimist who, in spite of or because of emancipation, was convinced for 85 years that there was no hope whatever for black people in this country. His rancor was legitimate, for he, John Solomon, was not only an artist but a first-rate carpenter and farmer, reduced to sending home to his family money he made playing the violin because he was not able to find work. And this during the years when almost half the black male population were skilled craftsmen who lost their jobs to white ex-convicts and immigrant farmers.

His wife, however, was of a quite different frame of mind and believed that all things could be improved by faith in Jesus and an effort of the will. So it was she, Ardelia Willis, who sneaked her seven children out of the back window into the darkness, rather than permit the patron of their sharecropper's existence to become their executioner as well, and headed north in 1912, when 99.2 percent of all black people in the U.S. were native-born and only 60 percent of white Americans were. And it was Ardelia who told her husband that they could not stay in the Kentucky town they ended up in because the teacher didn't know long division.

They have been dead now for 30 years and more and I still don't know which of them came closer to the truth about the possibilities of life for black people in this country. One of their grandchildren is a tenured professor at Princeton. Another, who suffered from what the Peruvian poet[0] called "anger that breaks a man into children," was picked up just as he entered his teens and emotionally lobotomized by the reformatories and mental institutions specifically designed to serve him. Neither John Solomon nor Ardelia lived long enough to despair over one or swell with pride over the other. But if they were alive today each would have selected and collected enough evidence to support the accuracy of the other's original point of view. And it would be difficult to convince either one that the other was right.

Some of the monstrous events that took place in John Solomon's America have been duplicated in alarming detail in my own America. There was the public murder of a President in a theater in 1865 and the public murder of another President on television in 1963. The Civil War of 1861 had its encore as the civil-rights movement of 1960. The torture and mutilation of a black West Point Cadet (Cadet Johnson Whittaker) in 1880 had its rerun with the 1970's murders of students at Jackson State College, Texas Southern and Southern University in Baton Rouge. And in 1976 we watch for what must be the thousandth time a pitched battle between the children of slaves and the children of immigrants—only this time, it is not the New York draft riots of 1863, but the busing turmoil in Paul Revere's home town, Boston.

Hopeless, he'd said. Hopeless. For he was certain that white people of every political, religious, geographical and economic background would band together against black people everywhere when they felt the threat of our progress. And a hundred years after he sought safety from the white man's "promise," somebody put a bullet in Martin Luther King's brain. And not long before that some excellent samples of the master race

Peruvian poet   César Vallejo (1892–1938), "La Cólera Que Quiebra Al Hombre . . ."

demonstrated their courage and virility by dynamiting some little black girls to death. If he were here now, my grandfather, he would shake his head, close his eyes and pull out his violin—too polite to say, "I told you so." And his wife would pay attention to the music but not to the sadness in her husband's eyes, for she would see what she expected to see—not the occasional historical repetition, but, like the slow walk of certain species of trees from the flatlands up into the mountains, she would see the signs of irrevocable and permanent change. She, who pulled her girls out of an inadequate school in the Cumberland Mountains, knew all along that the gentlemen from Alabama who had killed the little girls would be rounded up. And it wouldn't surprise her in the least to know that the number of black college graduates jumped 12 percent in the last three years; 47 percent in 20 years. That there are 140 black mayors in this country; 14 black judges in the District Circuit, 4 in the Courts of Appeals and one on the Supreme Court. That there are 17 blacks in Congress, one in the Senate; 276 in state legislatures—223 in state houses, 53 in state senates. That there are 112 elected black police chiefs and sheriffs, 1 Pulitzer Prize winner; 1 winner of the Prix de Rome; a dozen or so winners of the Guggenheim; 4 deans of predominently white colleges. . . . Oh, her list would go on and on. But so would John Solomon's sweet sad music.

While my grandparents held opposite views on whether the fortunes of black people were improving, my own parents struck similarly opposed postures, but from another slant. They differed about whether the moral fiber of white people would ever improve. Quite a different argument. The old folks argued about how and if black people could improve themselves, who could be counted on to help us, who would hinder us and so on. My parents took issue over the question of whether it was possible for white people to improve. They assumed that black people were the humans of the globe, but had serious doubts about the quality and existence of white humanity. Thus my father, distrusting every word and every gesture of every white man on earth, assumed that the white man who crept up the stairs one afternoon had come to molest his daughters and threw him down the stairs and then our tricycle after him. (I think my father was wrong, but considering what I have seen since, it may have been very healthy for me to have witnessed that as my first black-white encounter.) My mother, however, *believed* in them—their possibilities. So when the meal we got on relief was bug-ridden, she wrote a long letter to Franklin Delano Roosevelt. And when white bill collectors came to our door, it was she who received them civilly and explained in a sweet voice that we were people of honor and that the debt would be taken care of. Her message to Roosevelt got through—our meal improved. Her message to the bill collectors did not always get through and there was occasional violence when my father (self-exiled to the bedroom for fear he could not hold his temper) would hear that her reasonableness had failed. My mother was always wounded by these scenes, for she thought the bill collector knew that she loved good credit more than life and that being in arrears on a payment horrified her probably more than it did him. So she thought he was rude because he was white. For years she walked to utility companies and department stores to pay bills in person and even now she does not seem convinced that checks are legal tender. My father loved excellence, worked hard (he held three jobs at once for 17 years) and was so outraged by the suggestion of personal slackness that he could explain it to himself only in terms of racism. He was a fastidious worker who was frightened of one thing: unemployment. I can remember now the doomsday-cum-graveyard sound of "laid off" and how the minute school was out he asked us, "Where you workin'?" Both my parents believed that all succor and aid came from themselves and their neighborhood, since "they"—white people in charge and those not in charge but in obstructionist positions—were in some way fundamentally, genetically corrupt.

So I grew up in a basically racist household with more than a child's share of contempt for white people. And for each white friend I acquired who made a small crack in that contempt, there was another who repaired it. For each one who related to me as a person, there was one who in my presence at least, became actively "white." And like most black people of my generation, I suffer from racial vertigo that can be cured only by taking what one needs from one's ancestors. John Solomon's cynicism and his deployment of his art as both weapon and solace, Ardelia's faith in the magic that can be wrought by sheer effort of the will; my mother's open-mindedness in each new encounter and her habit of trying reasonableness first; my father's temper, his impatience and his efforts to keep "them" (throw them) out of his life. And it is out of these learned and selected attitudes that I look at the quality of life for my people in this country now.

These widely disparate and sometimes conflicting views, I suspect, were held not only by me, but by most black people. Some I know are clearer in their positions, have not sullied their anger with optimism or dirtied their hope with despair. But most of us are plagued by a sense of being worn shell-thin by constant repression and hostility as well as the impression of being buoyed by visible testimony of tremendous strides. There *is* repetition of the grotesque in our history. And there *is* the miraculous walk of trees. The question is whether our walk is progress or merely movement. O.j. Simpson leaning on a Hertz car *is* better than the Gold Dust Twins on the back of a soap box. But is "Good Times" better than Stepin Fetchit? Has the first order of business been taken care of? Does the law of the land work for us?

Are white people who murder black people punished with at least the same dispatch that sends black teen-age truants to Coxsackie? Can we relax now and discuss "The Jeffersons" instead of genocide? Or is the difference between the two only the difference between a greedy pointless white life-style and a messy pointless black death? Now that Mr. Poitier and Mr. Belafonte have shot up all the racists in "Buck and the Preacher," have they all gone away? Can we really move into better neighborhoods and not be set on fire? Is there anybody who will lay me a $5 bet on it?

The past decade is a fairly good index of the odds at which you lay your money down.

Ten years ago in Queens, as black people like me moved into a neighborhood 20 minutes away from the Triborough Bridge, "for sale" signs shot up in front of white folks' houses like dandelions after a hot spring rain. And the black people smiled. "Goody, goody," said my neighbor. "Maybe we can push them on out to the sea. You think?"

Now I live in another neighborhood, 20 minutes away from the George Washington Bridge, and again the "for sale" signs are pushing up out of the ground. Fewer, perhaps, and for different reasons, perhaps. Still the Haitian lady and I smile at each other. "My, my," she says "they goin' on up to the hills? Seem like they just come from there." "The woods," I say. "They like to live in the woods." She nods with infinite understanding, then shrugs. The Haitians have already arranged for one mass in the church to be said in French, already have their own newspaper, stores, community center. That's not movement. That's progress.

But the decade has other revelations. Ten years ago, young, bright, energetic blacks were sought out, pursued and hired into major corporations, major networks and onto the staffs of newspapers and national magazines. Many survived that courtship, some even with their souls intact. Newscasters, corporate lawyers, marketing specialists, journalists, production managers, plant foremen, college deans. But many more spend a lot of time on the telephone these days, or at the typewriter preparing résumés, which they send out (mostly to friends now) with little notes attached: "Is there anything you know of?" Or they think there is a good book in the story of what happened to them, the great hoax that was played on them. They are right, of course, about the hoax, for many of them were given elegant executive jobs with the work drained out. Work minus power. Work minus decision-making. Work minus dominion. Affirmative Action Make Believe that a lot of black people *did* believe because they also believed that the white people in those nice offices were not like the ones in the general store or in the plumbers' union—that they were fundamentally kind, or fair, or something. Anything but the desperate prisoners of economics they turned out to be, holding on to their dominion with a tenacity and sang-froid that can only be described as Nixonian. So the bright and the black (architects, reporters, vice-presidents in charge of public relations) walk the streets right along with that astounding 38 percent of the black teen-aged female work force that does not have and never has had a job. So the black female college graduate earns two-thirds of what a white male high-school dropout earns. So the black people who put everything into community-action programs supported by Government funds have found themselves bereft of action, bereft of funds and all but bereft of community.

This decade has been rife with disappointment in practically every place where we thought we saw permanent change: Hostos, CUNY, and the black-studies departments that erupted like minivolcanoes on campuses all over the nation; easy integrations of public-school systems; acceleration of promotion in factories and businesses. But now when we describe what has happened we cannot do it without using the verbs of upheaval and destruction: Open admission *closes;* minority-student quotas *fall* or *discontinue;* salary gaps between blacks and whites *widen;* black-studies departments *merge.* And the only growth black people can count on is in the prison population and the unemployment line. Even busing, which used to be a plain, if emotional, term at best, has now taken on an adjective normally reserved for rape and burglary—it is now called "forced" busing.

All of that counts, but I'm not sure that in the long haul it matters. Maybe Ardelia Willis had the best idea. One sees signs of her vision and the fruits of her prophecy in spite of the dread-lock statistics. The trees *are* walking, albeit slowly and quietly and without the fanfare of a cross-country run. It seems that at last black people have abandoned our foolish dependency on the Government to do the work that we once thought all of its citizenry would be delighted to do. Our love affair with the Federal Government is over. We misjudged the ardor of its attention. We thought its majority constituency would *prefer* having their children grow up among happy, progressive, industrious, contented black children rather than among angry, disenchanted and dangerous ones. That the profit motive of industry alone would keep us employed and therefore spending, and that our poverty was bad for business. We thought landlords wanted us to have a share in our neighborhoods and therefore love and care for them. That city governments wanted us to control our schools and therefore preserve them.

We were wrong. And now, having been eliminated from the lists of urgent national priorities, from TV documentaries and the platitudes of editorials, black people have chosen, or been forced to seek safety from the white man's promise, but happily not under a bed. More and more, there is the return to Ardelia's ways: the exercise of the will, the recognition of obstacles as only that—obstacles, not fixed stars. Black judges are fixing appropriate rather than punitive bail for black "offenders" and letting the rest of the community of jurisprudence scream. Young black women are leaving plush Northern jobs to sit in their living rooms and teach black children, work among factory women and spend months finding money to finance the college education of young blacks. Groups of blacks are buying huge tracts of land in the South and cutting off entirely the dependency of whole communities on grocery chains. For the first time, significant numbers of black people are returning or migrating to the South to focus on the acquisition of land, the transferral of crafts and skills, and the sharing of resources, the rebuilding of neighborhoods.

In the shambles of closing admissions, falling quotas, widening salary gaps and merging black-studies departments, builders and healers are working quietly among us. They are not like the heroes of old, the leaders we followed blindly and upon whom we depended for everything, or the blacks who had accumulated wealth for its own sake, fame, medals or some public acknowledgment of success. These are the people whose work is real and pointed and clear in its application to the race. Some are old and have been at work for a long time in and out of the public eye. Some are new and just finding out what their work is. But they are unmistakably the natural aristocrats of the race. The ones who refuse to imitate, to compromise, and who are indifferent to public accolade. Whose work is free or priceless. They take huge risks economically and personally. They are not always popular, even among black people, but they are the ones whose work black people respect. They are the healers. Some are nowhere near the public eye: Ben Chavis, preacher and political activist languishing now in North Carolina prisons; Robert Moses, a pioneering activist; Sterling Brown, poet and teacher; Father Al McKnight, land reformer; Rudy Lombard, urban sociologist; Lerone Bennett, historian; C.L.R. James, scholar; Alyce Gullattee, psychologist and organizer. Others are public legends: Judge Crockett, Judge Bruce Wright, Stevie Wonder, Ishmael Reed, Miles Davis, Richard Pryor, Muhammad Ali, Fannie Lou Hamer, Eubie Blake, Angela Davis, Bill Russell. . . .

But a complete roll-call is neither fitting nor necessary. They know who they are and so do we. They clarify our past, make livable our present and are certain to shape our future. And since the future is where our immortality as a race lies, no overview of the state of black people at this time can ignore some speculation on the only ones certain to live it—the children.

They are both exhilarating and frightening, those black children, and a source of wonderment to me. Although statistics about black teen-age crime and the "failure" of the courts to gut them are regularly printed and regularly received with outrage and fear, the children I know and see, those born after 1960, do not make such great copy. They are those who have grown up with nothing to prove to white people, whose perceptions of themselves are so new, so different, so focused they appear to me to be either magnificent hybrids or throwbacks to the time when our ancestors were called "royal." They are the baby sisters of the sit-in generation, the sons of the neighborhood blockbusters, the nephews of jailed revolutionaries, and a huge number who have had college graduates in their families for three and four generations. I thought we had left them nothing to love and nothing to want to know. I thought that those who exhibited some excitement about their future had long ago looked into the eyes of their teachers and were either saddened or outraged by the death of possibility they found there. I thought that those who were interested in the past had looked into the faces of their parents and seen betrayal. I thought the state had deprived them of a land and the landlords and banks had deprived them of a turf. So how is it that, with nothing to love, nothing they need to know, landless, turfless, minus a future and a past, these black children look us dead in the eye? They seem not to know how to apologize. And even when they are wrong they do not ask for forgiveness. It is as though they are waiting for us to apologize to them, to beg their pardon, to seek their approval. What species of black is this that not only does not choose to grovel, but doesn't know how? How will they keep jobs? How will they live? Won't they be killed before they reproduce? But they are unafraid. Is it because they refuse to see the world as we did? Is it because they have rejected both land and turf to seek instead a world? Maybe they finally got the message that we had been shouting into their faces; that they *live* here, *belong* here on this planet earth and that it is *theirs.* So they watch us with the eyes of poets and carpenters and musicians and scholars and other people who know who they are because they have invented themselves and know where they are going because they have envisioned it. All of which would please Ardelia—and John Solomon, too, I think. After all, he did hold on to his violin.

Sandra Mortola Gilbert
(1936–)

The Leeks

fatten like marsh weeds, silvery pipes
exhaling the mild onion smell
of Vermont April.

They tell me I want to be an American,
I want a name that ends in a Protestant consonant
instead of a Catholic vowel!

Stooping above the cool
New England fronds,
I become a redhaired freckled

Presbyterian girl: I've inherited
a farmhouse (cracked panes, splintery
porch) outside Brattleboro.

Once town clerk, my steely grandma
squints behind smokey glass in the parlor.
Her mother's samplers sag in the upstairs hall.

The kitchen floor's the color of
store-bought cheese; the kitchen stove
has garlands of castiron daisies.

On an April Sunday I journey
over the fields, down to the buzzing swamp:
going to pick leeks and lilies, mint and camomile.

Humming *Rock of Ages,* I inhale
the damp New England spring: America's
my dooryard, my guilt, my rag rug!

I've never eaten *potage parisienne,*
never drunk red wine,
never tasted olive oil,

but I've a skinny aunt beyond the hill
who makes Presbyterian love drinks
from lilies and camomile and leeks!

(1980)

Robert Hayden
(1913–)

Aunt Jemima of the Ocean Waves

I

Enacting someone's notion of themselves
(and me), The One And Only Aunt Jemima
and Kokimo The Dixie Dancing Fool
do a bally for the freak show.

I watch a moment, then move on,
pondering the logic that makes them
(and me) confederates
of The Spider Girl, The Snake-skinned Man . . .

Poor devils have to live somehow.

I cross the boardwalk to the beach,
lie in the sand and gaze beyond
the clutter at the sea.

II

Trouble you for a light?
I turn as Aunt Jemima settles down
beside me, her blue-rinsed hair
without the red bandanna now.

I hold the lighter to her cigarette.
Much obliged. Unmindful (perhaps)
of my embarrassment, she looks
at me and smiles: You sure

do favor a friend I used to have.
Guess that's why I bothered you
for a light. So much like him that I—
She pauses, watching white horses rush

to the shore. Way them big old waves
come slamming whopping in,
sometimes it's like they mean to smash
this no-good world to hell.

    Well, it could happen. A book I read—
Crossed that very ocean years ago.
London, Paris, Rome,
Constantinople too—I've seen them all.

Back when they billed me everywhere
as the Sepia High Stepper.
Crowned heads applauded me.
Years before your time. Years and years.

I wore me plenty diamonds then,
and counts or dukes or whatever they were
would fill my dressing room
with the costliest flowers. But of course

there was this one you resemble so.
Get me? The sweetest gentleman.
Dead before his time. Killed in the war
to save the world for another war.

High-stepping days for me
were over after that. Still I'm not one
to let grief idle me for long.
I went out with a mental act—

mind-reading—Mysteria From
The Mystic East—veils and beads
and telling suckers how to get
stolen rings and sweethearts back.

One night he was standing by my bed,
seen him plain as I see you,
and warned me without a single word:
Baby, quit playing with spiritual stuff.

So here I am, so here I am,
fake mammy to God's mistakes.
And that's the beauty part,
I mean, ain't that the beauty part.

She laughs, but I do not, knowing what
her laughter shields. And mocks.
I light another cigarette for her.
She smokes, not saying any more.

Scream of children in the surf,
adagios of sun and flashing foam,
the sexual glitter, oppressive fun. . . .
An antique etching comes to mind.

"The Sable Venus" naked on
a baroque Cellini shell—voluptuous
imago floating in the wake
of slave-ships on fantastic seas.

Jemima sighs, Reckon I'd best
be getting back. I help her up.
Don't you take no wooden nickels, hear?
Tin dimes neither. So long, pal.

(1970)

On Women and Men

"**W**omen's liberation" is one of the great topics of our time. Although there are comparatively few of us who have not heard of it, and there are more and more people who believe, in general, that it is a "good thing," the issues are not yet clearly settled. Perhaps the most fundamental problem is the persistence of the age-old tradition of sexism, that there is a fixed role, predetermined by nature or God, that women refuse at their peril. To illustrate traditional sexism we print first an editorial on the Woman's Rights Convention of 1852. The writer is scandalized by women who leave their "true sphere"; woman's subjection to men, he writes, is "the law of her nature." The excerpt from Virginia Woolf's *A Room of One's Own* helps us imagine what a supremely talented woman might have been up against before women's rights became an issue.

Virginia Woolf next shifts the ground of discourse from biology to society, from the assumption that woman's role is genetically determined to the revolutionary idea that it is limited only by what society permits and what she permits herself. In her ground-breaking essay "Professions for Women," she asks a key question, What is a woman? and then answers it, saying, "I assure you, I do not know. I do not believe that you know. I do not believe that anybody can know until she has expressed herself in all the arts and professions open to human skill."

Much appropriate legislation has been enacted since 1852, but being legally free is by no means the same as being psychologically free. Even when women and men consciously accept and welcome the need for a change, they often carry with them less conscious expectations and definitions of others and of themselves. There are many ghosts to fight, as Virginia Woolf tells us, many prejudices to overcome. The next two essays describe from personal experience the struggle against such ghosts and prejudices. Judith Wells shows how easy it is for women to adopt certain roles and how real change in oneself takes time and hard work. Maxine Hong Kingston describes a struggle intensified and complicated by cross-cultural messages and demands. (Another view of such a struggle can be found in Jeanne Wakatsuki Houston's essay, printed in the preceding section.) The final essay in this group presents a different perspective. Matina Horner's field research, completed in the late 1960s, illustrates differences in how men and women react to achievement. She concludes that although many legal and educational barriers to female achievement have been removed in recent years, "it is clear that a psychological barrier remains."

The next four essays deal with the roles of wives and husbands. Judy Syfers amusingly defines "wife" and wishes she, too, had such a paragon of support and attention. Harold Morowitz describes his own discovery that "our society, up until a few years ago, had decided that the eternal struggle against disorder was woman's work." Resigned to the fact that disorder will always win out, he proposes a joint struggle, wife and husband together. Esther Vilar would disagree totally. She characterizes modern woman as economic parasite and manipulator of men, and sees the woman's movement as no more significant than the latest fashion, a change in style. The years intervening since 1971 may provide the reader enough of a basis to test the accuracy of her analysis. Merle Hodge then discusses the special character of the woman-man relationship in a culture where a historical legacy of racial discrimination and violence underlies and overshadows traditional sexism.

Real changes in the roles of women, of course, involve changes in the roles of men; lately there has been a growing consciousness of the imprisonment of men in stereotyped roles of their own, and an increasing sense among men of the emotional cost of the traditional American ideal of masculinity. Harold Rosenberg, writing in the 1960s, already senses something theatrical and defensive, something weak, in the traditional pose of the he-man. Marc Feigen Fasteau specifically examines what that pose costs in terms of men's capacity for friendship.

Barriers, Visible and Invisible

New York Herald, Editorial

The Woman's Rights Convention which met September 8–10, 1852, at Syracuse, New York, was one of a series of national conventions inspired by the 1848 Seneca Falls convention organized by Lucretia Mott, Martha Wright, Elizabeth Cady Stanton, and Mary Ann McClintock "to discuss the social, civil and religious rights of women." The convention at Syracuse was attended by delegates from eight states and Canada. Lucretia Mott was named permanent president with one dissenting vote—her husband's; Susan B. Anthony was one of the secretaries.

The Woman's Rights Convention (September 12, 1852)

The farce at Syracuse has been played out. We publish to-day the last act, in which it will be seen that the authority of the Bible, as a perfect rule of faith and practice for human beings, was voted down, and what are called the laws of nature set up instead of the Christian code. We have also a practical exhibition of the consequences that flow from woman leaving her true sphere where she wields all her influence, and coming into public to discuss questions of morals and politics with men. . . .

Who are these women? what do they want? what are the motives that impel them to this course of action? The *dramatis personae* of the farce enacted at Syracuse present a curious conglomeration of both sexes. Some of them are old maids, whose personal charms were never very attractive, and who have been sadly slighted by the masculine gender in general; some of them women who have been badly mated, whose own temper, or their husbands', has made life anything but agreeable to them, and they are therefore down upon the whole of the opposite sex; some, having so much of the virago in their disposition, that nature appears to have made a mistake in their gender—mannish women, like hens that crow; some of boundless vanity and egotism, who believe that they are superior in intellectual ability to "all the world and the rest of mankind," and delight to see their speeches and addresses in print; and man shall be consigned to his proper sphere—nursing the babies, washing the dishes, mending stockings, and sweeping the house. This is "the good time coming." Besides the classes we have enumerated, there is a class of wild enthusiasts and visionaries—very sincere, but very mad—having the same vein as the fanatical Abolitionists, and the majority, if not all of them, being, in point of fact, deeply imbued with the anti-slavery sentiment. Of the male sex who attend these Conventions for the purpose of taking a part in them, the majority are hen-pecked husbands, and all of them ought to wear petticoats.

In point of ability, the majority of the women are flimsy, flippant, and superficial. Mrs. Rose[0] alone indicates much argumentative power.

How did woman first become subject to man as she now is all over the world? By her nature, her sex, just as the negro is and always will be, to the end of time, inferior to the white race, and, therefore, doomed to subjection; but happier than she would be in any other condition, just because it is the law of her nature. The women themselves would not have this law reversed. It is a significant fact that even Mrs. Swisshelm,[0] who formerly ran about to all such gatherings from her husband, is now "a keeper at home," and condemns these Conventions in her paper. How does this happen? Because, after weary years of unfruitfulness, she has at length got her rights in the shape of a baby. This is the best cure for the mania, and we would recommend a trial of it to all who are afflicted.

What do the leaders of the Woman's Rights Convention want? They want to vote, and to hustle with the rowdies at the polls. They want to be members of Congress, and in the heat of debate to subject themselves to coarse jests and indecent language, like that of Rev. Mr. Hatch. They want to fill all other posts which men are ambitious to occupy—to be lawyers, doctors, captains of vessels, and generals in the field. How funny it would sound in the newspapers, that Lucy Stone,[0] pleading a cause, took suddenly ill in the pains of parturition, and perhaps gave birth to a fine bouncing boy in court! Or that Rev. Antoinette Brown[0] was arrested in the middle of her sermon in the pulpit from the same cause, and presented a "pledge" to her husband and the congregation; or, that Dr. Harriot K. Hunt,[0] while attending a gentleman patient for a fit of the gout or *fistula in ano,*[0] found it necessary to send for a doctor, there and then, and to be

Mrs. Rose   Ernestine L. Rose (1810–1892), born in Poland, was one of the best platform speakers of her day; she was one of the first women to work for women's rights through legislative action, repeatedly petitioning the New York State Legislature for a Married Women's Property Law.
Mrs. Swisshelm   Jane Swisshelm (1815–1884) founded and published a newspaper, the *Pittsberg Saturday Visiter* [sic], which ran from 1847 to 1857.
Lucy Stone   Lucy Stone (1818–1893) was one of the leading public speakers for the abolition of slavery and for women's rights.
Rev. Antoinette Brown   Antoinette Brown (1825–1921), a Congregationalist minister, became the first American woman minister when she was ordained in 1853.
Dr. Harriot K. Hunt   Harriot K. Hunt (1805–1875) was denied admission to Harvard Medical School and practiced medicine without a license.
fistula in ano   anal ulcer (Latin).

delivered of a man or woman child—perhaps twins. A similar event might happen on the floor of Congress, in a storm at sea, or in the raging tempest of battle, and then what is to become of the woman legislator?

Virginia Woolf

Virginia Woolf (1882–1941) was the daughter of a prominent English scholar and critic, Sir Leslie Stephen, and was educated mainly in her father's library and from extensive travels. In 1917, she and her husband, Leonard Woolf, began printing on a hand press their own writings and those of other (then obscure) authors like Katherine Mansfield, T. S. Eliot, and E. M. Forster. This was the beginning of the celebrated Hogarth Press and center of the so-called "Bloomsbury Group" of intellectuals and writers. Virginia Woolf is particularly noted for her novels, among which we mention *Mrs. Dalloway* (1925), *To the Lighthouse* (1927), *Orlando* (1928), and *The Waves* (1931) as a few of the best. They are considered important experiments in novelistic form: she disregards ordinary factual description of characters and action, concentrating instead on psychological penetration and on variations in temporal perspective and rhythm. She also wrote many reviews and essays, on art and literature, and on the problems of social and economic reform. Her literary essays were collected in *The Common Reader* (1925; second series, 1932), *The Death of the Moth* (1942), *The Moment and Other Essays* (1947), and *Three Guineas* (1938).

A *Room of One's Own* (1929), a seminal feminist piece, is a long essay in which she uses metaphor and history to show the relative status of women in twentieth-century English society. From it we have taken the first selection printed below. The second, "Professions for Women," is from *The Death of the Moth.*

Shakespeare's Sister

. . . I thought of that old gentleman, who is dead now, but was a bishop, I think, who declared that it was impossible for any woman, past, present, or to come, to have the genius of Shakespeare. He wrote to the papers about it. He also told a lady who applied to him for information that cats do not as a matter of fact go to heaven, though they have, he added, souls of a sort. How much thinking those old gentlemen used to save one! How the borders of ignorance shrank back at their approach! Cats do not go to heaven. Women cannot write the plays of Shakespeare.

Be that as it may, I could not help thinking, as I looked at the works of Shakespeare on the shelf, that the bishop was right at least in this; it would have been impossible, completely and entirely, for any woman to have written the plays of Shakespeare in the age of Shakespeare. Let me imagine, since facts are so hard to come by, what would have happened had Shakespeare had a wonderfully gifted sister, called Judith, let us say. Shakespeare himself went, very probably—his mother was an heiress—to the grammar school, where he may have learnt Latin—Ovid, Virgil and Horace—and the elements of grammar and logic. He was, it is well known, a wild boy who poached rabbits, perhaps shot a deer, and had, rather sooner than he should have done, to marry a woman in the neighbourhood, who bore him a child rather quicker than was right. That escapade sent him to seek his fortune in London. He had, it seemed, a taste for the theatre; he began by holding horses at the stage door. Very soon he got work in the theatre, became a successful actor, and lived at the hub of the universe, meeting everybody, knowing everybody, practising his art on the boards, exercising his wits in the streets, and even getting access to the palace of the queen. Meanwhile his extraordinarily gifted sister, let us suppose, remained at home. She was as adventurous, as imaginative, as agog to see the world as he was. But she was not sent to school. She had no chance of learning grammar and logic, let alone of reading Horace and Virgil. She picked up a book now and then, one of her brother's perhaps, and read a few pages. But then her parents came in and told her to mend the stockings or mind the stew and not moon about with books and papers. They would have spoken sharply but kindly, for they were substantial people who knew the conditions of life for a woman and loved their daughter—indeed, more likely than not she was the apple of her father's eye. Perhaps she scribbled some pages up in an apple loft on the sly, but was careful to hide them or set fire to them. Soon, however, before she was out of her teens, she was to be betrothed to the son of a neighbouring wool-stapler. She cried out that marriage was hateful to her, and for that she was severely beaten by her father. Then he ceased to scold her. He begged her instead not to hurt him, not to shame him in this matter of her marriage. He would give her a chain of beads or a fine petticoat, he said; and there were tears in his eyes. How could she disobey him? How could she break his heart? The force of her own gift alone drove her to it. She made up a small parcel of her belongings, let herself down by a rope one summer's night and took the road to London. She was not seventeen. The birds that sang in the hedge were not more musical than she was. She had the quickest fancy, a gift like her brother's, for the tune of words. Like him, she had a taste for the theatre. She stood at the stage door; she wanted to act, she said. Men laughed in her face. The manager—a fat, loose-lipped man—guffawed. He bellowed something about poodles dancing and women acting—no woman, he said, could possibly be an actress. He hinted —you can imagine what. She could get no training in her craft. Could she even seek her dinner in a tavern or roam the streets at midnight? Yet her genius was for fiction and lusted to feed abundantly upon the lives of men and women and the study of their ways. At last—for she was very young, oddly like Shakespeare the poet in her face, with the same grey eyes and rounded brows—at last Nick Greene the actor-manager took pity on her; she found herself with child by that gentleman and so—who shall measure the heat and violence of the poet's heart when caught and tangled in a woman's body?—killed herself one winter's night and lies buried at some cross-roads where the omnibuses now stop outside the Elephant and Castle.

Professions for Women[1]

When your secretary invited me to come here, she told me that your Society is concerned with the employment of women and she suggested that I might tell you something about my own professional experiences. It is true I am a woman; it is true I am employed; but what professional experiences have I had? It is difficult to say. My profession is literature; and in that profession there are fewer experiences for women than in any other, with the exception of the stage—fewer, I mean, that are peculiar to women. For the road was cut many years ago—by Fanny Burney, by Aphra Behn, by Harriet Martineau, by Jane Austen, by George Eliot— many famous women, and many more unknown and forgotten, have been before me, making the path smooth, and regulating my steps. Thus, when I came to write, there were very few material obstacles in my way. Writing was a reputable and harmless occupation. The family peace was not broken by the scratching of a pen. No demand was made upon the family purse. For ten and sixpence one can buy paper enough to write all the plays of Shakespeare—if one has a mind that way. Pianos and models, Paris, Vienna and Berlin, masters and mistresses, are not needed by a writer. The cheapness of writing paper is, of course, the reason why women have succeeded as writers before they have succeeded in the other professions.

But to tell you my story—it is a simple one. You have only got to figure to yourselves a girl in a bedroom with a pen in her hand. She had only to move that pen from left to right—from ten o'clock to one. Then it occurred to her to do what is simple and cheap enough after all—to slip a few of those pages into an envelope, fix a penny stamp in the corner, and drop the envelope into the red box at the corner. It was thus that I became

[1]A paper read to The Women's Service League.

a journalist; and my effort was rewarded on the first day of the following month—a very glorious day it was for me—by a letter from an editor containing a cheque for one pound ten shillings and sixpence. But to show you how little I deserve to be called a professional woman, how little I know of the struggles and difficulties of such lives, I have to admit that instead of spending that sum upon bread and butter, rent, shoes and stockings, or butcher's bills, I went out and bought a cat—a beautiful cat, a Persian cat, which very soon involved me in bitter disputes with my neighbours.

What could be easier than to write articles and to buy Persian cats with the profits? But wait a moment. Articles have to be about something. Mine, I seem to remember, was about a novel by a famous man. And while I was writing this review, I discovered that if I were going to review books I should need to do battle with a certain phantom. And the phantom was a woman, and when I came to know her better I called her after the heroine of a famous poem, The Angel in the House.º It was she who used to come between me and my paper when I was writing reviews. It was she who bothered me and wasted my time and so tormented me that at last I killed her. You who come of a younger and happier generation may not have heard of her—you may not know what I mean by the Angel in the House. I will describe her as shortly as I can. She was intensely sympathetic. She was immensely charming. She was utterly unselfish. She excelled in the difficult arts of family life. She sacrificed herself daily. If there was chicken, she took the leg; if there was a draught she sat in it—in short she was so constituted that she never had a mind or a wish of her own, but preferred to sympathize always with the minds and wishes of others. Above all—I need not say it—she was pure. Her purity was supposed to be her chief beauty—her blushes, her great grace. In those days—the last of Queen Victoria—every house had its Angel. And when I came to write I encountered her with the very first words. The shadow of her wings fell on my page; I heard the rustling of her skirts in the room. Directly, that is to say, I took my pen in hand to review that novel by a famous man, she slipped behind me and whispered: "My dear, you are a young woman. You are writing about a book that has been written by a man. Be sympathetic; be tender; flatter; deceive; use all the arts and wiles of our sex. Never let anybody guess that you have a mind of your own. Above all, be pure." And she made as if to guide my pen. I now record the one act for which I take some credit to myself, though the credit rightly belongs to some excellent ancestors of mine who left me a certain sum of money—shall we say five hundred pounds a year?—so that it was not necessary for me to depend solely on charm for my living. I turned upon her and caught her by the

The Angel in the House Long poem by Coventry Patmore (1823–1896) that traces the courtship and marriage of a clergyman's daughter. It describes the progress of pure love.

throat. I did my best to kill her. My excuse, if I were to be had up in a court of law, would be that I acted in self-defence. Had I not killed her she would have killed me. She would have plucked the heart out of my writing. For, as I found, directly I put pen to paper, you cannot review even a novel without having a mind of your own, without expressing what you think to be the truth about human relations, morality, sex. And all these questions, according to the Angel in the House, cannot be dealt with freely and openly by women; they must charm, they must conciliate, they must—to put it bluntly—tell lies if they are to succeed. Thus, whenever I felt the shadow of her wing or the radiance of her halo upon my page, I took up the inkpot and flung it at her. She died hard. Her fictitious nature was of great assistance to her. It is far harder to kill a phantom than a reality. She was always creeping back when I thought I had despatched her. Though I flatter myself that I killed her in the end, the struggle was severe; it took much time that had better have been spent upon learning Greek grammar; or in roaming the world in search of adventures. But it was a real experience; it was an experience that was bound to befall all women writers at that time. Killing the Angel in the House was part of the occupation of a woman writer.

But to continue my story. The Angel was dead; what then remained? You may say that what remained was a simple and common object—a young woman in a bedroom with an inkpot. In other words, now that she had rid herself of falsehood, that young woman had only to be herself. Ah, but what is "herself"? I mean, what is a woman? I assure you, I do not know. I do not believe that you know. I do not believe that anybody can know until she has expressed herself in all the arts and professions open to human skill. That indeed is one of the reasons why I have come here—out of respect for you, who are in process of showing us by your experiments what a woman is, who are in process of providing us, by your failures and successes, with that extremely important piece of information.

But to continue the story of my professional experiences. I made one pound ten and six by my first review; and I bought a Persian cat with the proceeds. Then I grew ambitious. A Persian cat is all very well, I said; but a Persian cat is not enough. I must have a motor car. And it was thus that I became a novelist—for it is a very strange thing that people will give you a motor car if you will tell them a story. It is a still stranger thing that there is nothing so delightful in the world as telling stories. It is far pleasanter than writing reviews of famous novels. And yet, if I am to obey your secretary and tell you my professional experiences as a novelist, I must tell you about a very strange experience that befell me as a novelist. And to understand it you must try first to imagine a novelist's state of mind. I hope I am not giving away professional secrets if I say that a novelist's chief desire is to be as unconscious as possible. He has to induce in himself a state of perpetual lethargy. He wants life to proceed with the utmost quiet and regularity. He wants to see the same faces, to read the same books, to do the same things day after day, month after month, while he is writing, so that nothing may break the illusion in which he is living—so that nothing may disturb or disquiet the mysterious nosings about, feelings round, darts, dashes and sudden discoveries of that very shy and illusive spirit, the imagination. I suspect that this state is the same both for men and women. Be that as it may, I want you to imagine me writing a novel in a state of trance. I want you to figure to yourselves a girl sitting with a pen in her hand, which for minutes, and indeed for hours, she never dips into the inkpot. The image that comes to my mind when I think of this girl is the image of a fisherman lying sunk in dreams on the verge of a deep lake with a rod held out over the water. She was letting her imagination sweep unchecked round every rock and cranny of the world that lies submerged in the depths of our unconscious being. Now came the experience, the experience that I believe to be far commoner with women writers than with men. The line raced through the girl's fingers. Her imagination had rushed away. It had sought the pools, the depths, the dark places where the largest fish slumber. And then there was a smash. There was an explosion. There was foam and confusion. The imagination had dashed itself against something hard. The girl was roused from her dream. She was indeed in a state of the most acute and difficult distress. To speak without figure she had thought of something, something about the body, about the passions which it was unfitting for her as a woman to say. Men, her reason told her, would be shocked. The consciousness of what men will say of a woman who speaks the truth about her passions had roused her from her artist's state of unconsciousness. She could write no more. The trance was over. Her imagination could work no longer. This I believe to be a very common experience with women writers—they are impeded by the extreme conventionality of the other sex. For though men sensibly allow themselves great freedom in these respects, I doubt that they realize or can control the extreme severity with which they condemn such freedom in women.

These then were two very genuine experiences of my own. These were two of the adventures of my professional life. The first—killing the Angel in the House—I think I solved. She died. But the second, telling the truth about my own experiences as a body, I do not think I solved. I doubt that any woman has solved it yet. The obstacles against her are still immensely powerful—and yet they are very difficult to define. Outwardly, what is simpler than to write books? Outwardly, what obstacles are there for a woman rather than for a man? Inwardly, I think, the case is very different; she has still many ghosts to fight, many prejudices to overcome. Indeed it will be a long time still, I think, before a woman can sit down to write a book without finding a phantom to be slain, a rock to be dashed against. And if this is so in literature, the freest of all professions for women, how is it in the new professions which you are now for the first time entering?

Those are the questions that I should like, had I time, to ask you. And indeed, if I have laid stress upon these professional experiences of mine, it is because I believe that they are, though in different forms, yours also. Even when the path is nominally open—when there is nothing to prevent a woman from being a doctor, a lawyer, a civil servant—there are many phantoms and obstacles, as I believe, looming in her way. To discuss and define them is I think of great value and importance; for thus only can the labour be shared, the difficulties be solved. But besides this, it is necessary also to discuss the ends and the aims for which we are fighting, for which we are doing battle with these formidable obstacles. Those aims cannot be taken for granted; they must be perpetually questioned and examined. The whole position, as I see it—here in this hall surrounded by women practising for the first time in history I know not how many different professions—is one of extraordinary interest and importance. You have won rooms of your own in the house hitherto exclusively owned by men. You are able, though not without great labour and effort, to pay the rent. You are earning your five hundred pounds a year. But this freedom is only a beginning; the room is your own, but it is still bare. It has to be furnished; it has to be decorated; it has to be shared. How are you going to furnish it, how are you going to decorate it? With whom are you going to share it, and upon what terms? These, I think are questions of the utmost importance and interest. For the first time in history you are able to ask them; for the first time you are able to decide for yourselves what the answers should be. Willingly would I stay and discuss those questions and answers—but not tonight. My time is up; and I must cease.

Judith Wells

Judith Wells was born in 1944, grew up in San Francisco, and received her B.A. in French from Stanford and her Ph.D. in comparative literature from the University of California, Berkeley. (Her dissertation dealt with women and madness in modern literature—madness meaning both anger and insanity.) She helped develop the Women's Studies program at Berkeley and has taught courses on women and madness in literature. She has also headed a program at Napa Community College designed to encourage older women to return to school. In 1980, she published *Been in Berkeley Too Long.* "Daddy's Girl," her first published work, appeared in *Libera,* Winter 1972.

Daddy's Girl

"A little girl, full of innocence and indulgence. And then this madness. . . ."

—Ladders to Fire, ANAIS NIN

Nothing is more startling to a Daddy's girl than to find herself in revolt against her Daddies. Because of her intimacy with and desire for approval from her Daddies, she finds it painful to make a clean break with them. "Daddy, daddy, you bastard, I'm through," cries Sylvia Plath[0] in her poem "Daddy"; in spite of the voodoo murder of her Father, Plath is still a little girl murderess who addresses the "Panzer man," "the brute," the "Fascist" of her poem as Daddy. Even her closing words, "I'm through," strangely undercut her patricide—as if she herself dies with her Father— an echo of her death wish in a previous stanza: "At twenty I tried to die/And get back, back, back, to you."

This complicity with "Daddy" has been my own peculiar emotional madness for years. A large part of what I always called my "self" has been invested in the personality of the Daddy's Girl or the Little Girl. The Little Girl is fragile, vulnerable, helpless, bewildered, compliant. She feels she occupies a very tiny amount of both physical and psychological space. In my own dreams this smallness is experienced through seeing myself as a miniature person—a girl who melts down to a face in a postage stamp or a girl whose full size is as small as a person's hands (and thus easily manipulated). The Little Girl is an object, not a subject.

It took me a good deal of hard work in psychotherapy and the Women's Movement to reach any understanding about my own Little Girl. For a long time I maintained a masque of independence; I made myself believe I didn't care what my father and men thought about me. Yet underneath, I based most of my personality on masculine approval. Any criticism from a male brought me a haunting sense of guilt. The least assertion of my own preference or will was stepping over the line; I internalized the reply "You've gone too far" even before I opened my mouth. I was unable to work when my boyfriend was around and felt guilty over surpassing male friends and my father in intellectual achievements; but I also knew I had to accomplish something to get masculine approval. The only activity this ambivalence brought on was diarrhea. Then I became sick and could nurture my vulnerable, fragile self which was, and still is, in effect, my Little Girl.

The Little Girl infects many females because she is nurtured by so much of society as well as by ourselves. She has no age limit:

Sylvia Plath   American poet and novelist (1932–1963) who attempted suicide at the end of her junior year of college and committed suicide at the age of thirty.

> She wears sweet little dresses, her tears and caprices are viewed indulgently,
> her hair is done up carefully, older people are amused at her expressions and
> coquetries—bodily contacts and agreeable glances protect her against the an-
> guish of solitude. (*The Second Sex,* p. 252)

Although this is Simone de Beauvoir's description of a small girl in childhood, it could well apply to the Little Girl aspect of ourselves, our mothers,
and our grandmothers. I was surprised when I realized that some of the
gestures of my boss's eight-year-old daughter were not far from my own
—her cajoling, indirect expression of what she wanted, her refusal to
attempt a simple task without precise, precise instructions. The Little Girl
pose is designed to elicit maternal or paternal indulgence—specifically,
because the Little Girl is or thinks she is helpless.

Although the Little Girl can inhabit any woman's body, a small woman
is particularly susceptible to this syndrome. In her first *Diary,* Anais Nin
relates a conversation with her psychiatrist about this sense of vulnerability and helplessness that a small woman experiences:

> My greatest fear is that people will become aware that I am fragile, not a
> full-blown woman physically, that I am emotionally vulnerable, that I have
> small breasts like a girl. (p. 86)

My own sense that I am physically slight and fragile has not only bolstered
my feelings of helplessness, but it has also contributed to my feeling that
I am not quite a grown woman—that creature who is defined by having
curves in the right places. The curveless woman easily sees herself as a
Little Girl.

Although the Little Girl may be more readily apparent in a woman with
a small body, most women experience the Little Girl at times as a psychic
state. In Nin's *Children of the Albatross,* Djuna remembers:

> She remembered, too, that whenever she became entangled in too great a
> difficulty she had these swift regressions into her adolescent state. Almost as if
> in the large world of maturity, when the obstacle loomed too large, she shrank
> again into the body of the young girl for whom the world had first appeared
> as a violent and dangerous place, forcing her to retreat, and when she retreated
> she fell back into smallness. (p. 40)

Djuna experiences a "psychic smallness" which is her inability to affect
significantly the world around her—hence, her helplessness.

In the Little Girl, "psychic smallness" is also directly related to her
desire for approval from authority figures, especially from Daddies. As a
Little Girl, I found that I had based my personality for such a long time
on approval from authority figures that *they* were my personality. I experienced "psychic smallness" because I had never defined who I was or
what I wanted in life; my only sense of identity stemmed from Daddy's
approval.

The real tragedy of the Little Girl, then, is her inability to define herself in her own terms, select her own goals, and feel her life has significance *without* Daddy's support. The Little Girl turns over the responsibility for her own life to her Daddies (real fathers, boyfriends, husbands, professors, psychiatrists) and sits devotedly, if a bit uneasily, at their feet. Unfortunately, society sanctions this pose of the Child-Woman, especially in its sexual images and stereotypes.

In the Magic Theater's recent production of *Miles Gloriosus,* two poles of stereotyped female sexuality are portrayed: the Vixen-Whore in black wasp waist corset and tights, and the Baby Doll in pink pajamas, with freckles on her nose and ribbons in her hair. Although the Baby Doll is parody in this play, many girls are schooled in this image of coyness, flirtation, and "innocent" sexuality which they carry over into adult life. The Little Girl clothes syndrome, which periodically runs rampant through fashion as it has recently, supports this image: the mod "little dresses," the clingy pastel tee shirts with patterns from babyhood, the overall and romper outfits—all designed to make females resemble innocent little girls yet still be sexually appealing. Roger Vadim exploited this combination of innocence and sexuality to the hilt in his presentation of Brigitte Bardot to moviegoers. In Simone de Beauvoir's book, *Brigitte Bardot and the Lolita Syndrome,* the author relates:

> He [Vadim] painted her as naive to the point of absurdity. According to him, at the age of eighteen she thought that mice laid eggs. (p. 13)

De Beauvoir comments on Bardot's roles in "And God Created Woman" and "Love Is My Profession":

> BB is a lost, pathetic child who needs a guide and protector. This cliché has proved its worth. It flatters masculine vanity. . . . (p. 15)

The child-woman poses no threat to the male ego—hence her appeal. De Beauvoir notes the particular charm of the child-woman to the American male:

> . . . he feels a certain antipathy to the 'real woman.' He regards her as an antagonist, a praying mantis, a tyrant. He abandons himself eagerly to the charms of the 'nymph' in whom the formidable figure of the wife and 'Mom' is not yet apparent. (p. 23)

Although I hardly possess the "nymph" looks of Bardot, my own appearance and Little Girl personality have encouraged me to maintain this child-woman sexual role. When I was younger, this child role came easily; but with increased sexual experience, the role became harder and harder to maintain. I can't kid myself anymore. I know my own sexual desires, but the child-woman in me still makes me embarrassed when I want to be sexually aggressive or state my desires straight out. I know many women share this problem—this embarrassment over wanting to be a subject, not an object in sexual activity. And the male attitude doesn't help much; for even though "The Sexual Revolution's Here," a woman is discouraged subtly (a male's slightly chilly response to her phone call) and not so subtly (his impotence when she asks him to bed) when she is sexually aggressive.

As a Little Girl I have spent a good deal of my life adjusting to just such masculine requirements, adapting myself to gain their approval. Finally, I felt pain—the intense frustration of being confirmed by my own compliancy. I understand all too well the statement of the man I work for (who designed an educational program to improve the self-image of Blacks) about the accommodation attitudes of Blacks. I have substituted *woman* for *man* in the quote and *her* for *him:*

> Let us assume I am standing with my foot on the neck of a *woman* who is lying on the ground; I am wearing a hobnail boot. I say to *her,* "Your role is simply different from mine, not worse; you are horizontal and I am vertical." And then I say to *her,* "Your role has certain advantages over mine; you do not have to worry about falling down. Furthermore, you are developing a very interesting adaptive behavior. You are learning to breathe with my foot on your neck." (*Teaching and Testing the Disadvantaged,* William Johntz)

Interestingly enough, the sado-masochistic imagery of this passage exactly fits sexual politics. The victim is made to feel she is lucky she doesn't have the "burdens" of the victor. The victim's final adaptive behavior is what the Little Girl and, in actuality, any woman, has done all her life. She has learned to breathe with a foot on her neck until she finally explodes in frustration and cries out with Sylvia Plath, "You do not do, you do not do/Any more, black shoe. . . ."

It would be great if the Little Girl could join the Women's Movement and instantly become a self-sufficient woman. I have found that my Little Girl personality is not shed so easily, and that my rebellion against my Daddies has its own peculiar Little Girl cyclic rhythm: compliancy towards a man—simmering hate—explosion of outrage—anxiety over having stepped over the line—fear of reprisal—compliancy towards a man— and the cycle begins again. Because the Little Girl has suffocated her own desires so completely in favor of her Daddies, her potential for rage is volcanic once she questions the belief that "Father knows best." Yet for myself and probably for most Little Girls, each explosion is followed less by a sense of triumph than by anxiety and fear of reprisal. Since the Little Girl's only previous sense of identity stemmed from approval from her Daddies, cutting these figures out of her life will seem like cutting out the core of herself. At first, "destruction" of Daddy seems like self-destruction. This anxiety over self-destruction in the elimination of her source of identity brings on the Little Girl's helplessness. She is then a weak, vulnerable, compliant child again, fearing Daddy's reprisal.

Even if she finally rebels against her Daddies, the Little Girl will remain caught in this circle of anger and compliancy until she learns to stop loving and nurturing the Little Girl in herself. If I had to select the most important moment in my several years of psychotherapy, it would be the moment I realized who loved the Little Girl in me most. I was astonished to find it was myself. I was finally able to objectify my Little Girl enough to see her as separate from another part of me. I experienced myself caressing and cherishing that Little Girl as I had loved my dolls many years ago —the same kind of love I desperately wanted to experience when I was a real little girl. Perhaps, above everything else, this desperation for love kept me locked into my first childhood attempts to gain approval from adults. And when, as a real little girl, I realized that the "adult world" was governed mainly by male figures, I began to base my worth on how much love and approval I could get from my Daddies. The Little Girl pose stuck.

I am coming to realize more and more that I no longer receive much approval for the Little Girl role; it's an illusion I maintain which has little basis in my own daily life. As a friend of mine in graduate school put it, "I'm thirty years old. I look like a grown woman. If I start to do the Little Girl bit with my professors, they look at me funny." The Little Girl role has a few benefits but enormous drawbacks: a stifling of one's intelligence and creativity, a confining sexual role, an arresting of growth of one's personality. When I experienced myself cherishing my Little Girl doll self, I flashed on a picture I had drawn when I was ten years old to illustrate a poem I had read called "The long ago, far away doll." I drew a doll in a sea chest; she was dressed in a lovely yellow fancy dress, and her cheeks were rouged; but her eyes stared into space, and she looked like a dead person. The Little Girl aspect of any woman keeps her like this doll— repressed, inactive, dead.

The Little Girl has no place to grow but up. It is true that if she does choose to continue her growth, she may not receive some of the masculine approval she received in the past. As I stated previously, certain men like a Little Girl because she is less threatening to the masculine ego. Too, the growing Little Girl must risk the disapproval of her real father—often the man who clings the most tenaciously to the idea of his daughter as a perpetual girl child. She may be regarded as a rebel or even a bitch. Yet there will be others, both women and men, who will approve of her—not for feminine fluff, but for her real talents and developing personality. More important, she will gain self-respect from presenting her *own self* to the world, and this self-respect will be worth much more than the approval she received as a crippled Little Girl.

I read someplace in my many psychological readings, when I was trying to pinpoint my "problems," about a young girl in an African society. In her early teens, she was listless, lacked confidence, and was fearful of males and masculine authority. Her tribe used a mode of transvestitism to exorcise her fears. She dressed up in the male military costume of the former colonial power of the area and began to dance in this costume. After the ceremony, the girl's confidence increased enormously, she no longer feared men, and she eventually developed into a mature, self-reliant woman. The girl in this story acts out symbolically what the Little Girl must learn to do for herself: incorporate the authority, which she objectifies outside of herself, into her own person. She must develop a sense of her *own personal authority* and hence, *self-approval.* When the Little Girl develops this sense of self-approval, she will no longer be a Little Girl, but a mature woman—a full, complete human being. With this new sense of personal authority, she can look back on her "rebellious" struggles as Anais Nin does:

> Very often I would say I rebelled against this or that. Much later it occurred to me to question this statement. Instead of rebellion could it be that I was merely asserting my own belief? (*Diary* III, p. xiii)

And I answer with Nin: YES.

Maxine Hong Kingston

Maxine Hong Kingston was born in Stockton, California, in 1940 and earned her bachelor's degree from the University of California in 1962. She has taught a wide variety of students in various places, first as a high school teacher of English and mathematics in Hayward, California. She later taught English, language arts, and English as a second language in a high school, a drop-in school, and a business school in Hawaii. Most recently, she has been Visiting Associate Professor of English at the University of Hawaii. She is also a writer and once said, "I have no idea how people who don't write endure their lives." Her stories and articles have appeared in many publications, including *Ms.*, *New West,* and the *New York Times.* Her most recent book is *China Men* (1981).

In 1976 she won the general nonfiction award from the National Book Critics Circle for *The Woman Warrior: Memoirs of a Girlhood Among Ghosts.* She wrote *Woman Warrior* on the coffee table of her Honolulu home. "Cold," she says, "disrupts my concentration. Here in Hawaii, where the temperature is always 80 to 85 I do not worry about bodily discomfort. That makes it possible for me to deal with what is in my head." We reprint a section from Chapter 2.

---

from The Woman Warrior

My American life has been such a disappointment.

"I got straight A's, Mama."

"Let me tell you a true story about a girl who saved her village."

I could not figure out what was my village. And it was important that

I do something big and fine, or else my parents would sell me when we made our way back to China. In China there were solutions for what to do with little girls who ate up food and threw tantrums. You can't eat straight A's.

When one of my parents or the emigrant villagers said, "Feeding girls is feeding cowbirds," I would thrash on the floor and scream so hard I couldn't talk. I couldn't stop.

"What's the matter with her?"

"I don't know. Bad, I guess. You know how girls are. 'There's no profit in raising girls. Better to raise geese than girls.' "

"I would hit her if she were mine. But then there's no use wasting all that discipline on a girl. 'When you raise girls, you're raising children for strangers.' "

"Stop that crying!" my mother would yell. "I'm going to hit you if you don't stop. Bad girl! Stop!" I'm going to remember never to hit or to scold my children for crying, I thought, because then they will only cry more.

"I'm not a bad girl," I would scream. "I'm not a bad girl. I'm not a bad girl." I might as well have said, "I'm not a girl."

"When you were little, all you had to say was 'I'm not a bad girl,' and you could make yourself cry," my mother says, talking-story about my childhood.

I minded that the emigrant villagers shook their heads at my sister and me. "One girl—and another girl," they said, and made our parents ashamed to take us out together. The good part about my brothers being born was that people stopped saying, "All girls," but I learned new grievances. "Did you roll an egg on *my* face like that when I was born?" "Did you have a full-month party for *me?*" "Did you turn on all the lights?" "Did you send *my* picture to Grandmother?" "Why not? Because I'm a girl? Is that why not?" "Why didn't you teach me English?" "You like having me beaten up at school, don't you?"

"She is very mean, isn't she?" the emigrant villagers would say.

"Come, children. Hurry. Hurry. Who wants to go out with Great-Uncle?" On Saturday mornings my great-uncle, the ex-river pirate, did the shopping. "Get your coats, whoever's coming."

"I'm coming. I'm coming. Wait for me."

When he heard girls' voices, he turned on us and roared, "No girls!" and left my sisters and me hanging our coats back up, not looking at one another. The boys came back with candy and new toys. When they walked through Chinatown, the people must have said, "A boy—and another boy —and another boy!" At my great-uncle's funeral I secretly tested out feeling glad that he was dead—the six-foot bearish masculinity of him.

I went away to college—Berkeley in the sixties—and I studied, and I marched to change the world, but I did not turn into a boy. I would have liked to bring myself back as a boy for my parents to welcome with chickens and pigs. That was for my brother, who returned alive from Vietnam.

If I went to Vietnam, I would not come back; females desert families. It was said, "There is an outward tendency in females," which meant that I was getting straight A's for the good of my future husband's family, not my own. I did not plan ever to have a husband. I would show my mother and father and the nosey emigrant villagers that girls have no outward tendency. I stopped getting straight A's.

And all the time I was having to turn myself American-feminine, or no dates.

There is a Chinese word for the female *I*—which is "slave." Break the women with their own tongues!

I refused to cook. When I had to wash dishes, I would crack one or two. "Bad girl," my mother yelled, and sometimes that made me gloat rather than cry. Isn't a bad girl almost a boy?

"What do you want to be when you grow up, little girl?"

"A lumberjack in Oregon."

Even now, unless I'm happy, I burn the food when I cook. I do not feed people. I let the dirty dishes rot. I eat at other people's tables but won't invite them to mine, where the dishes are rotting.

If I could not eat, perhaps I could make myself a warrior like the swordswoman[o] who drives me. I will—I must—rise and plow the fields as soon as the baby comes out.

Once I get outside the house, what bird might call me; on what horse could I ride away? Marriage and childbirth strengthen the swordswoman, who is not a maid like Joan of Arc. Do the women's work; then do more work, which will become ours too. No husband of mine will say, "I could have been a drummer, but I had to think about the wife and kids. You know how it is." Nobody supports me at the expense of his own adventure. Then I get bitter: no one supports me; I am not loved enough to be supported. That I am not a burden has to compensate for the sad envy when I look at women loved enough to be supported. Even now China wraps double binds around my feet.

When urban renewal tore down my parents' laundry and paved over our slum for a parking lot, I only made up gun and knife fantasies and did nothing useful.

From the fairy tales, I've learned exactly who the enemy are. I easily recognize them—business-suited in their modern American executive guise, each boss two feet taller than I am and impossible to meet eye to eye.

I once worked at an art supply house that sold paints to artists. "Order more of that nigger yellow, willya?" the boss told me. "Bright, isn't it? Nigger yellow."

"I don't like that word," I had to say in my bad, small-person's voice that makes no impact. The boss never deigned to answer.

I also worked at a land developers' association. The building industry was planning a banquet for contractors, real estate dealers, and real estate

swordswoman   Heroine, one who avenges wrongs by fighting like a man.

editors. "Did you know the restaurant you chose for the banquet is being picketed by CORE and the NAACP?" I squeaked.

"Of course I know." The boss laughed. "That's why I chose it."

"I refuse to type these invitations," I whispered, voice unreliable.

He leaned back in his leather chair, his bossy stomach opulent. He picked up his calendar and slowly circled a date. "You will be paid up to here," he said. "We'll mail you the check."

If I took the sword, which my hate must surely have forged out of the air, and gutted him, I would put color and wrinkles into his shirt.

It's not just the stupid racists that I have to do something about, but the tyrants who for whatever reason can deny my family food and work. My job is my own only land.

To avenge my family, I'd have to storm across China to take back our farm from the Communists; I'd have to rage across the United States to take back the laundry in New York and the one in California. Nobody in history has conquered and united both North America and Asia. A descendant of eighty pole fighters,[0] I ought to be able to set out confidently, march straight down our street, get going right now. There's work to do, ground to cover. Surely, the eighty pole fighters, though unseen, would follow me and lead me and protect me, as is the wont of ancestors.

Or it may well be that they're resting happily in China, their spirits dispersed among the real Chinese, and not nudging me at all with their poles. I mustn't feel bad that I haven't done as well as the swordswoman did; after all, no bird called me, no wise old people tutored me. I have no magic beads, no water gourd sight, no rabbit that will jump in the fire when I'm hungry. I dislike armies.

I've looked for the bird. I've seen clouds make pointed angel wings that stream past the sunset, but they shred into clouds. Once at a beach after a long hike I saw a seagull, tiny as an insect. But when I jumped up to tell what miracle I saw, before I could get the words out I understood that the bird was insect-size because it was far away. My brain had momentarily lost its depth perception. I was that eager to find an unusual bird.

The news from China[0] has been confusing. It also had something to do with birds. I was nine years old when the letters made my parents, who are rocks, cry. My father screamed in his sleep. My mother wept and crumpled up the letters. She set fire to them page by page in the ashtray, but new letters came almost every day. The only letters they opened without fear were the ones with red borders, the holiday letters that mustn't carry bad news. The other letters said that my uncles were made to kneel on broken glass during their trials and had confessed to being landowners. They were all executed, and the aunt whose thumbs were

pole fighters   Practitioners of the martial art of using poles as weapons.
news from China   Reference to Chinese Communists' takeover of mainland China. The Communists proclaimed a central people's government on October 1, 1949. By April 1950 all of mainland China was under Communist control.

twisted off drowned herself. Other aunts, mothers-in-law, and cousins disappeared; some suddenly began writing to us again from communes or from Hong Kong. They kept asking for money. The ones in communes got four ounces of fat and one cup of oil a week, they said, and had to work from 4 A.M. to 9 P.M. They had to learn to do dances waving red kerchiefs; they had to sing nonsense syllables. The Communists gave axes to the old ladies and said, "Go and kill yourself. You're useless." If we overseas Chinese would just send money to the Communist bank, our relatives said, they might get a percentage of it for themselves. The aunts in Hong Kong said to send money quickly; their children were begging on the sidewalks, and mean people put dirt in their bowls.

When I dream that I am wire without flesh, there is a letter on blue airmail paper that floats above the night ocean between here and China. It must arrive safely or else my grandmother and I will lose each other.

My parents felt bad whether or not they sent money. Sometimes they got angry at their brothers and sisters for asking. And they would not simply ask but have to talk-story too. The revolutionaries had taken Fourth Aunt and Uncle's store, house, and lands. They attacked the house and killed the grandfather and oldest daughter. The grandmother escaped with the loose cash and did not return for help. Fourth Aunt picked up her sons, one under each arm, and hid in the pig house, where they slept that night in cotton clothes. The next day she found her husband, who had also miraculously escaped. The two of them collected twigs and yams to sell while their children begged. Each morning they tied the faggots on each other's back. Nobody bought from them. They ate the yams and some of the children's rice. Finally Fourth Aunt saw what was wrong. "We have to shout 'Fuel for sale' and 'Yams for sale,' " she said. "We can't just walk unobtrusively up and down the street." "You're right," said my uncle, but he was shy and walked in back of her. "Shout," my aunt ordered, but he could not. "They think we're carrying these sticks home for our own fire," she said. "Shout." They walked about miserably, silently, until sundown, neither of them able to advertise themselves. Fourth Aunt, an orphan since the age of ten, mean as my mother, threw her bundle down at his feet and scolded Fourth Uncle, "Starving to death, his wife and children starving to death, and he's too damned shy to raise his voice." She left him standing by himself and afraid to return empty-handed to her. He sat under a tree to think, when he spotted a pair of nesting doves. Dumping his bag of yams, he climbed up and caught the birds. That was where the Communists trapped him, in the tree. They criticized him for selfishly taking food for his own family and killed him, leaving his body in the tree as an example. They took the birds to a commune kitchen to be shared.

It is confusing that my family was not the poor to be championed. They were executed like the barons in the stories, when they were not barons. It is confusing that birds tricked us.

What fighting and killing I have seen have not been glorious but slum grubby. I fought the most during junior high school and always cried.

Fights are confusing as to who has won. The corpses I've seen had been rolled and dumped, sad little dirty bodies covered with a police khaki blanket. My mother locked her children in the house so we couldn't look at dead slum people. But at news of a body, I would find a way to get out; I had to learn about dying if I wanted to become a swordswoman. Once there was an Asian man stabbed next door, words on cloth pinned to his corpse. When the police came around asking questions, my father said, "No read Japanese. Japanese words. Me Chinese."

I've also looked for old people who could be my gurus. A medium with red hair told me that a girl who died in a far country follows me wherever I go. This spirit can help me if I acknowledge her, she said. Between the head line and heart line in my right palm, she said, I have the mystic cross. I could become a medium myself. I don't want to be a medium. I don't want to be a crank taking "offerings" in a wicker plate from the frightened audience, who, one after another, asked the spirits how to raise rent money, how to cure their coughs and skin diseases, how to find a job. And martial arts are for unsure little boys kicking away under fluorescent lights.

I live now where there are Chinese and Japanese, but no emigrants from my own village looking at me as if I had failed them. Living among one's own emigrant villagers can give a good Chinese far from China glory and a place. "That old busboy is really a swordsman," we whisper when he goes by, "He's a swordsman who's killed fifty. He has a tong ax in his closet." But I am useless, one more girl who couldn't be sold. When I visit the family now, I wrap my American successes around me like a private shawl; I *am* worthy of eating the food. From afar I can believe my family loves me fundamentally. They only say, "When fishing for treasures in the flood, be careful not to pull in girls," because that is what one says about daughters. But I watched such words come out of my own mother's and father's mouths; I looked at their ink drawing of poor people snagging their neighbor's flotage with long flood hooks and pushing the girl babies on down the river. And I had to get out of hating range. I read in an anthropology book that Chinese say, "Girls are necessary too"; I have never heard the Chinese I know make this concession. Perhaps it was a saying in another village. I refuse to shy my way anymore through our Chinatown, which tasks me with the old sayings and the stories.

Matina Horner

Matina Horner was born in 1933 to Greek parents, who decided to stay in the United States after the outbreak of World War II. She received her bachelor's degree from Bryn Mawr College in 1961 and then attended the University of Michigan, where in 1968 she received her doctorate in psychology with some of the research she writes about in the present essay. The research appeared in *Psychology Today* in November 1969, headed by a quotation from Balzac: "A woman who is guided by the head and not by the heart is a social pestilence: she has all the defects of a passionate and affectionate woman with none of her compensations: she is without pity, without love, without virtue, without sex."

Besides being an authority on motivation and achievement in women, Dr. Horner has studied ability grouping in schools, the impact of internalized sex and race role stereotypes, and factors that foster the development of curiosity. She has been on the Harvard faculty since 1969 in the Department of Social Relations, and in 1972 she became President of Radcliffe College, which is integrated as a coeducational institution with Harvard.

Fail: Bright Women

Consider Phil, a bright young college sophomore. He has always done well in school, he is in the honors program, he has wanted to be a doctor as long as he can remember. We ask him to tell us a story based on one clue: *"After first-term finals, John finds himself at the top of his medical school class."* Phil writes:

> John is a conscientious young man who worked hard. He is pleased with himself. John has always wanted to go into medicine and is very dedicated . . . John continues working hard and eventually graduates at the top of his class.

Now consider Monica, another honors student. She too has always done well and she too has visions of a flourishing career. We give her the same clue, but with "Anne" as the successful student—*after first-term finals, Anne finds herself at the top of her medical school class.* Instead of identifying with Anne's triumph, Monica tells a bizarre tale:

> Anne starts proclaiming her surprise and joy. Her fellow classmates are so disgusted with her behavior that they jump on her in a body and beat her. She is maimed for life.

Next we ask Monica and Phil to work on a series of achievement tests by themselves. Monica scores higher than Phil. Finally we get them together, competing against each other on the same kind of tests. Phil performs magnificently, but Monica dissolves into a bundle of nerves.

The glaring contrast between the two stories and the dramatic changes in performance in competitive situations illustrate important differences between men and women in reacting to achievement.

In 1953, David McClelland, John Atkinson and colleagues published the first major work on the "achievement motive." Through the use of the Thematic Apperception Test (TAT), they were able to isolate the psychological characteristic of a *need to achieve.* This seemed to be an internalized standard of excellence, motivating the individual to do well in any achievement-oriented situation involving intelligence and leadership ability. Subsequent investigators studied innumerable facets of achievement motivation: how it is instilled in children, how it is expressed, how it relates to social class, even how it is connected to the rise and fall of civilizations. The result of all this research is an impressive and a theoretically consistent body of data about the achievement motive—in men.

Women, however, are conspicuously absent from almost all of the studies. In the few cases where the ladies were included, the results were contradictory or confusing. So women were eventually left out altogether. The predominantly male researchers apparently decided, as Freud had before them, that the only way to understand woman was to turn to the poets. Atkinson's 1958 book, *Motives in Fantasy, Action and Society,* is an 800-page compilation of all the theories and facts on achievement motivation in men. Women got a footnote, reflecting the state of the science.

To help remedy this lopsided state of affairs, I undertook to explore the basis for sex differences in achievement motivation. But where to begin?

My first clue came from the one consistent finding on the women: they get higher test-anxiety scores than do the men. Eleanor Maccoby has suggested that the girl who is motivated to achieve is defying conventions of what girls "should" do. As a result, the intellectual woman pays a price in anxiety. Margaret Mead concurs, noting that intense intellectual striving can be viewed as "competitively aggressive behavior." And of course Freud thought that the whole essence of femininity lay in repressing aggressiveness (and hence intellectuality).

Thus consciously or unconsciously the girl equates intellectual achievement with loss of femininity. A bright woman is caught in a double bind. In testing and other achievement-oriented situations she worries not only about failure, but also about success. If she fails, she is not living up to her own standards of performance; if she succeeds, she is not living up to societal expectations about the female role. Men in our society do not experience this kind of ambivalence, because they are not only permitted but actively encouraged to do well.

For women, then, the desire to achieve is often contaminated by what I call the *motive to avoid success.* I define it as the fear that success in competitive achievement situations will lead to negative consequences, such as unpopularity and loss of femininity. This motive, like the achievement motive itself, is a stable disposition within the person, acquired early in life along with other sex-role standards. When fear of success conflicts with a desire to be successful, the result is an inhibition of achievement motivation.

I began my study with several hypotheses about the motive to avoid success:

1) Of course, it would be far more characteristic of women than of men.
2) It would be more characteristic of women who are capable of success

and who are career-oriented than of women not so motivated. Women who are not seeking success should not, after all, be threatened by it.

3) I anticipated that the anxiety over success would be greater in competitive situations (when one's intellectual performance is evaluated against someone else's) than in noncompetitive ones (when one works alone). The aggressive, masculine aspects of achievement striving are certainly more pronounced in competitive settings, particularly when the opponent is male. Women's anxiety should therefore be greatest when they compete with men.

I administered the standard TAT achievement motivation measures to a sample of 90 girls and 88 boys, all undergraduates at the University of Michigan. In addition, I asked each to tell a story based on the clue described before: *After first-term finals, John (Anne) finds himself (herself) at the top of his (her) medical school class.* The girls wrote about Anne, the boys about John.

Their stories were scored for "motive to avoid success" if they expressed any negative imagery that reflected concern about doing well. Generally, such imagery fell into three categories:

1) The most frequent Anne story reflected strong fears of social rejection as a result of success. The girls in this group showed anxiety about becoming unpopular, unmarriageable and lonely.

> Anne is an acne-faced bookworm. She runs to the bulletin board and finds she's at the top. As usual she smarts off. A chorus of groans is the rest of the class's reply. . . . She studies 12 hours a day, and lives at home to save money. "Well it certainly paid off. All the Friday and Saturday nights without dates, fun—I'll be the best woman doctor alive." And yet a twinge of sadness comes thru—she wonders what she really has . . .

> Although Anne is happy with her success she fears what will happen to her social life. The male med. students don't seem to think very highly of a female who has beaten them in their field . . . She will be a proud and successful but alas a very *lonely* doctor.

> Anne doesn't want to be number one in her class . . . she feels she shouldn't rank so high because of social reasons. She drops down to ninth in the class and then marries the boy who graduates number one.

> Anne is pretty darn proud of herself, but everyone hates and envies her.

2) Girls in the second category were less concerned with issues of social approval or disapproval; they were more worried about definitions of womanhood. Their stories expressed guilt and despair over success, and doubts about their femininity or normality.

> Unfortunately Anne no longer feels so certain that she really wants to be a doctor. She is worried about herself and wonders if perhaps she isn't normal

. . . Anne decides not to continue with her medical work but to take courses that have a deeper personal meaning for her.

Anne feels guilty . . . She will finally have a nervous breakdown and quit medical school and marry a successful young doctor.

Anne is pleased. She had worked extraordinarily hard and her grades showed it. "It is not enough," Anne thinks. "I am not happy." She didn't even want to be a doctor. She is not sure what she wants. Anne says to hell with the whole business and goes into social work—not hardly as glamorous, prestigious or lucrative; but she is happy.

3) The third group of stories did not even try to confront the ambivalence about doing well. Girls in this category simply denied the possibility that any mere woman could be so successful. Some of them completely changed the content of the clue, or distorted it, or refused to believe it, or absolved Anne of responsibility for her success. These stories were remarkable for their psychological ingenuity:

Anne is a *code name* for a nonexistent person created by a group of med. students. They take turns writing exams for Anne . . .

Anne is really happy she's on top, though *Tom is higher than she*—though that's as it should be . . . Anne doesn't mind Tom winning.

Anne is talking to her counselor. Counselor says she will make a fine *nurse*.

It was *luck* that Anne came out on top because she didn't want to go to medical school anyway.

Fifty-nine girls—over 65 per cent—told stories that fell into one or another of the above categories. But only eight boys, fewer than 10 per cent, showed evidence of the motive to avoid success. (These differences are significant at better than the .0005 level.) In fact, sometimes I think that most of the young men in the sample were incipient Horatio Algers. They expressed unequivocal delight at John's success (clearly John had worked hard for it), and projected a grand and glorious future for him. There was none of the hostility, bitterness and ambivalence that the girls felt for Anne. In short, the differences between male and female stories based on essentially the same clue were enormous.

Two of the stories are particularly revealing examples of this male-female contrast. The girls insisted that Anne give up her career for marriage:

Anne has a boyfriend, Carl, in the same class and they are quite serious. . . . She wants him to be scholastically higher than she is. Anne will deliberately lower her academic standing the next term, while she does all she subtly can to help Carl. His grades come up and Anne soon drops out of medical school. They marry and he goes on in school while she raises their family.

But of course the boys would ask John to do no such thing:

> John has worked very hard and his long hours of study have paid off. . . .
> He is thinking about his girl, Cheri, whom he will marry at the end of med.
> school. He realizes he can give her all the things she desires after he
> becomes established. He will go on in med. school and be successful in the
> long run.

Success inhibits social life for the girls; it enhances social life for the boys.

Earlier I suggested that the motive to avoid success is especially aroused in competitive situations. In the second part of this study I wanted to see whether the aggressive overtones of competition against men scared the girls away. Would competition raise their anxiety about success and thus lower their performance?

First I put all of the students together in a large competitive group, and gave them a series of achievement tests (verbal and arithmetic). I then assigned them randomly to one of three other experimental conditions. One-third worked on a similar set of tests, each in competition with a member of the same sex. One-third competed against a member of the opposite sex. The last third worked by themselves, a non-competitive condition.

Ability is an important factor in achievement motivation research. If you want to compare two persons on the strength of their *motivation* to succeed, how do you know that any differences in performance are not due to initial differences in *ability* to succeed? One way of avoiding this problem is to use each subject as his own control; that is, the performance of an individual working alone can be compared with his score in competition. Ability thus remains constant; any change in score must be due to motivational factors. This control over ability was, of course, possible only for the last third of my subjects: the 30 girls and 30 boys who had worked alone *and* in the large group competition. I decided to look at their scores first.

Performance changed dramatically over the two situations. A large number of the men did far better when they were in competition than when they worked alone. For the women the reverse was true. Fewer than one-third of the women, but more than two-thirds of the men, got significantly higher scores in competition.

When we looked at just the girls in terms of the motive to avoid success, the comparisons were even more striking. As predicted, the students who felt ambivalent or anxious about doing well turned in their best scores when they worked by themselves. Seventy-seven percent of the girls who feared success did better alone than in competition. Women who were low on the motive, however, behaved more like the men: 93 per cent of them got higher scores in competition. (Results significant at the .005.)

Female Fear of Success & Performance

	perform better working alone	perform better in competition
high fear of success	13	4
low fear of success	1	12

As a final test of motivational differences, I asked the students to indicate on a scale from 1 to 100 "How important was it for you to do well in this situation?" The high-fear-of-success girls said that it was much more important for them to do well when they worked alone than when they worked in either kind of competition. For the low-fear girls, such differences were not statistically significant. Their test scores were higher in competition, as we saw, and they thought that it was important to succeed no matter what the setting. And in all experimental conditions—working alone, or in competition against males or females—high-fear women consistently lagged behind their fearless comrades on the importance of doing well.

The findings suggest that most women will fully explore their intellectual potential only when they do not need to compete—and least of all when they are competing with men. This was most true of women with a strong anxiety about success. Unfortunately, these are often the same women who could be very successful if they were free from that anxiety. The girls in my sample who feared success also tended to have high intellectual ability and histories of academic success. (It is interesting to note that all but two of these girls were majoring in the humanities and in spite of very high grade points aspired to traditional female careers: housewife, mother, nurse, schoolteacher. Girls who did not fear success, however, were aspiring to graduate degrees and careers in such scientific areas as math, physics and chemistry.)

We can see from this small study that achievement motivation in women is much more complex than the same drive in men. Most men do not find many inhibiting forces in their path if they are able and motivated to succeed. As a result, they are not threatened by competition; in fact, surpassing an opponent is a source of pride and enhanced masculinity.

If a woman sets out to do well, however, she bumps into a number of obstacles. She learns that it really isn't ladylike to be too intellectual. She is warned that men will treat her with distrustful tolerance at best, and outright prejudice at worst, if she pursues a career. She learns the truth of Samuel Johnson's comment, "A man is in general better pleased when he has a good dinner upon his table, than when his wife talks Greek." So she doesn't learn Greek, and the motive to avoid success is born.

In recent years many legal and educational barriers to female achievement have been removed; but it is clear that a psychological barrier remains. The motive to avoid success has an all-too-important influence on the intellectual and professional lives of women in our society. But perhaps there is cause for optimism. Monica may have seen Anne maimed for life, but a few of the girls forecast a happier future for our medical student. Said one:

> Anne is quite a lady—not only is she tops academically, but she is liked and admired by her fellow students—quite a trick in a man-dominated field. She is brilliant—but she is also a woman. She will continue to be at or near the top. And . . . always a lady.

Wives and Husbands

Judy Syfers

Judy Syfers, who was born in San Francisco in 1937, feels that the problems of American wives "stem from a social system which places primary value on profits rather than on people's needs. As long as we continue to tolerate the system, we will continue to be exploited as workers and as wives." Ms. Syfers received her B.F.A. in painting from the University of Iowa in 1960. She wanted to go on for a higher degree that would enable her to paint and to teach in a university, but her (male) teachers advised that the best she could hope for as a woman was teaching in high school with a secondary-education credential. Her reaction was to drop school, get married, and have two children. Thus the present piece, which appeared in the Spring 1972 preview issue of *Ms.*, arises from real experience.

I Want a Wife

I belong to that classification of people known as wives. I am A Wife. And, not altogether incidentally, I am a mother.

Not too long ago a male friend of mine appeared on the scene fresh from a recent divorce. He had one child, who is, of course, with his ex-wife. He is looking for another wife. As I thought about him while I was ironing one evening, it suddenly occurred to me that I, too, would like to have a wife. Why do I want a wife?

I would like to go back to school so that I can become economically independent, support myself, and, if need be, support those dependent upon me. I want a wife who will work and send me to school. And while I am going to school I want a wife to take care of my children. I want a wife to keep track of the children's doctor and dentist appointments. And to keep track of mine, too. I want a wife to make sure my children eat properly and are kept clean. I want a wife who will wash the children's clothes and keep them mended. I want a wife who is a good nurturant attendant to my children, who arranges for their schooling, makes sure that they have an adequate social life with their peers, takes them to the park, the zoo, etc. I want a wife who takes care of the children when they are sick, a wife who arranges to be around when the children need special care, because, of course, I cannot miss classes at school. My wife must arrange to lose time at work and not lose the job. It may mean a small cut in my wife's income from time to time, but I guess I can tolerate that. Needless to say, my wife will arrange and pay for the care of the children while my wife is working.

I want a wife who will take care of *my* physical needs. I want a wife who will keep my house clean. A wife who will pick up after me. I want a wife who will keep my clothes clean, ironed, mended, replaced when need be, and who will see to it that my personal things are kept in their proper place so that I can find what I need the minute I need it. I want a wife who cooks the meals, a wife who is a *good* cook. I want a wife who will plan the menus, do the necessary grocery shopping, prepare the meals, serve them pleasantly, and then do the cleaning up while I do my studying. I want a wife who will care for me when I am sick and sympathize with my pain and loss of time from school. I want a wife to go along when our family takes a vacation so that someone can continue to care for me and my children when I need a rest and change of scene.

I want a wife who will not bother me with rambling complaints about a wife's duties. But I want a wife who will listen to me when I feel the need to explain a rather difficult point I have come across in my course of studies. And I want a wife who will type my papers for me when I have written them.

I want a wife who will take care of the details of my social life. When my wife and I are invited out by friends, I want a wife who will take care of the babysitting arrangements. When I meet people at school that I like and want to entertain, I want a wife who will have the house clean, will prepare a special meal, serve it to me and my friends, and not interrupt when I talk about the things that interest me and my friends. I want a wife who will have arranged that the children are fed and ready for bed before my guests arrive so that the children do not bother us. I want a wife who takes care of the needs of my guests so that they feel comfortable, who makes sure that they have an ashtray, that they are passed the hors d'oeuvres, that they are offered a second helping of the food, that their wine glasses are replenished when necessary, that their coffee is served to them as they like it. And I want a wife who knows that sometimes I need a night out by myself.

I want a wife who is sensitive to my sexual needs, a wife who makes love passionately and eagerly when I feel like it, a wife who makes sure that I am satisfied. And, of course, I want a wife who will not demand sexual attention when I am not in the mood for it. I want a wife who assumes the complete responsibility for birth control, because I do not want more children. I want a wife who will remain sexually faithful to me so that I do not have to clutter up my intellectual life with jealousies. And I want a wife who understands that *my* sexual needs may entail more than strict adherence to monogamy. I must, after all, be able to relate to people as fully as possible.

If, by chance, I find another person more suitable as a wife than the wife I already have, I want the liberty to replace my present wife with another one. Naturally, I will expect a fresh, new life; my wife will take the children and be solely responsible for them so that I am left free.

When I am through with school and have a job, I want my wife to quit working and remain at home so that my wife can more fully and completely take care of a wife's duties.

My God, who *wouldn't* want a wife?

Harold J. Morowitz

The following selection is taken from *The Wine of Life and Other Essays on Societies, Energy, and Living Things* (1979). Biographical information on Harold J. Morowitz is given on page 145.

Women's Lib and the Battle Against Entropy

There was no doubt about it; the flooring on the small outside porch was going to have to be replaced. It was rotting through from the bottom and presented a real hazard. One trip to the lumber yard and there I was, ripping up the rotted planks and thinking naturally enough about the second law of thermodynamics, which was creating so many jobs. There had been the corroded copper pipe in the kitchen, the dirty ceiling in the laundry, and now the side porch. The universe was clearly and unmistakably moving downhill.

A bit of reflection brought me to the sudden realization of how many of life's activities are directly tied up with our unending effort to slow down the increase of disorder in the immediate surroundings. Those most closely associated with our individual survival are reflected in the physiological concept of basal metabolism, which is a measure of the energy the body spends in maintaining itself far from equilibrium in spite of nature's tendencies toward that end. Thus we must maintain concentration differences that are opposed by diffusion and electromotive force differences that are opposed by leakage currents. Finally we must continually rebuild the delicate protein structures that are breaking down under thermal denaturation and autodigestion. All of these things take energy, and much of our agriculture and food-preparing efforts basically go into just keeping ourselves alive and functioning in our battle with the second law of thermodynamics.

By the time I had come to this conclusion, the floor boards had been ripped off and it became painfully clear that some of the two-by-sixes supporting the floor were also going to have to be replaced. While putting creosote on the fresh lumber there was time again to return to this problem of fighting entropy. I turned attention to thinking about how many jobs around the house were negentropic efforts that led nowhere but simply kept us even in the eternal struggle against the disordering tendencies of the universe.

The second law of thermodynamics states that spontaneous processes tend toward a maximum of disorder, and work must be expended to maintain systems away from this undesirable state. And anyone who has watched the papers on a desk or the contents of a house go through the randomizing process can only be impressed with the power of this principle of nature. All of life is a creative tension between the work-consuming processing on the one hand and the accompanying spontaneous decay on the other. One is reminded of the myth of Sisyphus who spent his time in hell rolling a big stone up a steep hill only to have it roll down before it reached the top. Sisyphus represents the work input, and the spontaneous tendency of the stone to roll down the hill is reminiscent of the second law.

When this profound conclusion was reached my thirst became apparent, and a trip to the kitchen sink for a drink of water was in order. On the way back, a trail of sawdust on the kitchen floor again served as a reminder of the disordering tendencies. But then an idea hit with the resounding boom of the cannon in the "1812 Overture." All of housework is a battle against entropy. Every housewife, doomed to repetitively sweeping the floor, washing the dishes, dusting the furniture, and cleaning the clothes, is devoting her life to fighting the second law of thermodynamics. In this context, a global awesome aspect of women's liberation began to stand out.

Our society, up until a few years ago, had decided that the eternal struggle against disorder was woman's work and that the possessors of two X chromosomes were to be consigned Sisyphus-like to the unending task of countering a law of nature. It was a battle that could never be won. There were no triumphs, no victories; the best one could theoretically do was to break even. Men would build unstable structures (as all structures are ultimately unstable), and the task of maintaining these structures against the pervasive and unending decay tendency would be left to women.

In these terms, one senses the cosmic unfairness of women's traditional role in Western society. Remember that Sisyphus was in hell because of our very intuition that constantly laboring to get nowhere is a vision of hell. To make the whole grievous situation seem better than it actually was, we created a myth that being a successful full-time combatter of entropy was a virtue and developed a beatific image of "the good housewife." The intent was, however, not sainthood but servitude. What no one ever uttered was the thermodynamic truism that perfect order requires infinite work, so that the stated goal was physically unattainable. By the fundamental rules, housekeeping was established as a "no win" game. Viewed in this context, the only saving grace of the woman's role was the ultimate triumph against disorder—the creation of a new human being. Motherhood is a satisfying role, but it has been a high price to pay for all the accompanying entrapment by an ethic that, at best, belongs to an earlier age.

By this time I was so engaged in thought that I was in danger of smashing my fingers with the hammer, as the floor boards were pounded into place. How could such a situation have persisted for so long? Sexual dimorphism is a reality, and indeed in many animal species sexual roles are sharply delineated. But we live in a civilized society. The idea of setting women to fight the second law unaided is just gross unfairness. A law of nature is a law of nature no more for the goose than the gander. We need a constitutional amendment guaranteeing equality before the second law of thermodynamics.

At last I felt that it was possible to place the concept of woman's liberation in its proper context. What should be demanded is neither sexual, nor Freudian, nor even political. What is required is that the job of pushing the stone uphill be fairly distributed. In addition, we must settle for a reasonable entropic state and not exhaust ourselves struggling for an unattainable one. There is no escape; the boulder will come down the hill again. We can, however, add joy to the job by sharing the task. Then we will all have some time left over for the more creative and enjoyable aspects of life. Surely this is a minimum goal for a just society.

It was now beginning to get dark and the planks were completely nailed down. All in all, it had been a successful day. I had counteracted a lot of decay and was well on the way toward making a stronger porch than had existed before. I also felt liberated by the realization that we all have to work together. I celebrated by sweeping up sawdust from the kitchen floor, leaving a few motes to symbolize the eternal power of the second law of thermodynamics.

Esther Vilar

Esther Vilar was born of German parents in 1935 in Buenos Aires, Argentina, and received a medical degree from the University of Buenos Aires. After moving to Munich, Germany, she practiced as a physician for a time but now works as a free-lance writer.

Der dressierte Mann (1971; trans. *The Manipulated Man,* 1973), from which we reprint a chapter below, is Esther Vilar's fourth book and first success. It has been translated into twenty-one languages and has sold over half a million copies. Its thesis is clear: A man is a human being who works; a woman is a human being who does not. Woman manipulates man in the way that Pavlov conditioned his dogs. Vilar says that she "wrote the book very quickly, much of it in the United States where I spent about a year in all, gathering material that convinced me American men are the most manipulated of all by their women. . . . Ever since Simone de Beauvoir and *The Second Sex* it has been popular to say women are suppressed by men, but I never saw any signs of it."

What Is Woman

A woman, as we have already said, is, in contrast to a man, a human being who does not work. One might leave it at that, for there isn't much more to say about her, were the basic concept of "human being" not so general and inexact in embracing both "man" and "woman."

Life offers the human being two choices: animal existence—a lower order of life—and spiritual existence. In general, a woman will choose the former and opt for physical well-being, a place to breed, and an opportunity to indulge unhindered in her breeding habits.

At birth, men and women have the same intellectual potential; there is no primary difference in intelligence between the sexes. It is also a fact that potential left to stagnate will atrophy. Women do not use their mental capacity: they deliberately let it disintegrate. After a few years of sporadic training, they revert to a state of irreversible mental torpor.

Why do women not make use of their intellectual potential? For the simple reason that they do not need to. It is not essential for their survival. Theoretically it is possible for a beautiful woman to have less intelligence than a chimpanzee and still be considered an acceptable member of society.

By the age of twelve at the latest, most women have decided to become prostitutes. Or, to put it another way, they have planned a future for themselves which consists of choosing a man and letting him do all the work. In return for his support, they are prepared to let him make use of their vagina at certain given moments. The minute a woman has made this decision she ceases to develop her mind. She may, of course, go on to obtain various degrees and diplomas. These increase her market value in the eyes of men, for men believe that a woman who can recite things by heart must also *know and understand* them. But any real possibility of communication between the sexes ceases at this point. Their paths are divided forever.

One of man's worst mistakes, and one he makes over and over again, is to assume that woman is his equal, that is, a human being of equal mental and emotional capacity. A man may observe his wife, listen to her, judge her feelings by her reactions, but in all this he is judging her only by outward symptoms, for he is using his *own* scale of values.

He knows what *he* would say, think, and do if he were in her shoes. When he looks at her depressing ways of doing things, he assumes there must be something that prevents her from doing what he himself would have done in her position. This is natural, as he considers himself the measure of all things—and rightly so—if humans define themselves as being capable of abstract thought.

When a man sees a woman spending hours cooking, washing dishes, and cleaning, it never occurs to him that such jobs probably make her quite happy since they are exactly at her mental level. Instead he assumes that this drudgery prevents her from doing all those things which he himself considers worthwhile and desirable. Therefore, he invents automatic dishwashers, vacuum cleaners, and precooked foods to make her life easier and to allow her to lead the dream life he himself longs for.

But he will be disappointed: rarely using the time she has gained to take an active interest in history, politics, or astrophysics, woman bakes cakes, irons underclothes, and makes ruffles and frills for blouses or, if she is especially enterprising, covers her bathroom with flower decals. It is natural, therefore, that man assumes such things to be the essential ingredients of *gracious living.* This idea must have been instilled by woman, as he himself really doesn't mind if his cakes are store-bought, his underpants unironed, or his bathroom devoid of flower patterns. He invents cake mixes to liberate her from drudgery, automatic irons and toilet-paper holders already covered with flower patterns to make gracious living easier to attain—and still women take no interest in serious literature, politics, or the conquest of the universe. For her, this newfound leisure comes at just the right moment. At last she can take an interest in *herself:* since a longing after intellectual achievements is alien to her, she concentrates on her external appearance.

Yet even this occupation is acceptable to man. He really loves his wife and wants her happiness more than anything in the world. Therefore, he produces nonsmear lipstick, waterproof mascara, home permanents, no-iron frilly blouses, and throwaway underwear—always with the same aim in view. In the end, he hopes, this being whose needs seem to him so much more sensitive, so much more refined, will gain freedom—freedom to achieve in *her* life the ideal state which is *his* dream: to live the life of a *free* man.

Then he sits back and waits. Finally, as woman does not come to him of her own free will, he tries to tempt her into his world. He offers her coeducation, so that she is accustomed to his way of life from childhood. With all sorts of excuses, he gets her to attend his universities and initiates her into the mysteries of his own discoveries, hoping to awaken her interest in the wonders of life. He gives her access to the very last male strongholds, thereby relinquishing traditions sacred to him by encouraging her to make use of her right to vote in the hope that she will change the systems of government he has managed to think up so laboriously, according to her own ideas. Possibly he even hopes that she will be able to create peace in the world—for, in his opinion, women are a pacifist influence.

In all this he is so determined and pigheaded that he fails to see what a fool he is making of himself—ridiculous by his own standards, not those of women, who have absolutely no sense of humor.

No, women do not laugh at men. At most they get irritated. The old institutions of house and home are not yet so obviously outdated and derelict that they can't justify relinquishing all their intellectual pursuits and renouncing all their claims to better jobs. One does wonder, however, what will happen when housework is still further mechanized, when there are *enough* good nursery schools nearby, or when—as must occur before long—men discover that children themselves are not essential.

If only man would stop for one moment in his heedless rush toward progress and think about this state of affairs, he would inevitably realize that his efforts to give woman a sense of mental stimulation have been totally in vain. It is true that woman gets progressively more elegant, more well-groomed, more "cultured," but her demands on life will always be material, never intellectual.

Has she ever made use of the mental processes he teaches at his universities to develop her own theories? Does she do independent research in the institutes he has thrown open to her? Someday it will dawn on man that woman does not read the wonderful books with which he has filled his libraries. And though she may well admire his marvelous works of art in museums, she herself will rarely create, only copy. Even the plays and films, visual exhortations to woman on her own level to liberate herself, are judged only by their entertainment value. They will never be a first step to revolution.

When a man, believing woman his equal, realizes the futility of her way of life, he naturally tends to think that it must be *his* fault, that *he* must be suppressing *her.* But in our time women are no longer subject to the will of men. Quite the contrary. They have been given every opportunity to win their independence and if, after all this time, they have not liberated themselves and thrown off their shackles, we can only arrive at one conclusion: there are no shackles to throw off.

It is true that men love women, but they also despise them. Anyone who gets up in the morning fresh and ready to conquer new worlds (with infrequent success, admittedly, because he has to earn a living) is bound to despise someone who simply isn't interested in such pursuits. Contempt may even be one of the main reasons for his efforts to further the mental development of a woman. He feels ashamed of her and assumes that she, too, must be ashamed of herself. So, being a gentleman, he tries to help.

Men seem incapable of realizing that women entirely lack ambition, desire for knowledge, and need to prove themselves, all things which, to him, are a matter of course. They allow men to live in a world apart because they do not want to join them. Why should they? The sort of independence men have means nothing to women, because women don't feel dependent. They are not even embarrassed by the intellectual superiority of men because they have no ambition in that direction.

There is one great advantage which women have over men: *they have a choice*—a choice between the life of a man and the life of a dimwitted, parasitic luxury item. There are too few women who would not select the latter. Men do not have this choice.

If women really felt oppressed by men, they would have developed hate and fear for them, as the oppressed always do, but women do not fear men, much less hate them. If they really felt humiliated by men's mental superiority, they would have used every means in their power to change the situation. If women really felt unfree, surely, at such a favorable time in their history, they would have broken free of the oppressors.

In Switzerland, one of the most highly developed countries of the world, where until recently women were not allowed to vote, in a certain canton, it is reported, the majority of women were against introducing the vote for women. The Swiss men were shattered, for they saw in this unworthy attitude yet another proof of centuries of male oppression.

How very wrong they were! Women feel anything but oppressed by men. On the contrary, one of the many depressing truths about the relationship between the sexes is simply that man hardly exists in a woman's world: Man is not even powerful enough to revolt against. Woman's dependence on him is only material, of a "physical" nature, something like a tourist's dependence on an airline, a café proprietor's on his espresso machine, a car's on gasoline, a television set's on electric current. Such dependencies hardly involve agonizing.

Ibsen, who suffered from the same misapprehensions as other men, meant his *Doll's House*[0] to be a kind of manifesto for the freedom of women. The première in 1880 certainly shocked *men,* and they determined to fight harder to improve women's position.

For women themselves, however, the struggle for emancipation as usual took shape in a change of style: for a while they delighted in their often-laughed-at masquerade as suffragettes.

Later on, the philosophy of Sartre made a similarly profound impression on women. As proof that they understood it completely, they let their hair grow down to their waists and wore black pullovers and trousers.

Even the teachings of the Chinese Communist leader Mao Tse-tung were a success—the Mao look lasted a whole season.

Merle Hodge

Merle Hodge, a teacher and writer, was born on the Caribbean island of Trinidad in 1944. She attended primary and secondary school there, then won a scholarship to study French at the University of London, where she took her degree with honors in 1965. She traveled in Europe, lived in Senegal and Gambia, and in 1970 published her first novel, *Crick Crack, Monkey.* In 1970 she returned to Trinidad. For two years she taught French, West Indian literature, and English at a government secondary school, then became a lecturer in French Caribbean and French African literature at the University of the West Indies, Kingston, Jamaica. The present essay appeared in the collection *Is Massa Day Dead? Black Moods in the Caribbean,* edited by Orde Coombs (1974).

The Shadow of the Whip

The man-woman relationship is nowhere a straightforward, uncomplicated one—it is always perhaps the most vulnerable, the most brittle of human relationships. And in the Caribbean this relationship had been

Doll's House Play (1879), whose heroine, Nora, is treated like a mindless child by her husband. At the end of the play, recognizing that the premises upon which her marriage is built are false, she leaves her husband and children.

adversely affected by certain factors of our historical development, notably, I think, by the legacy of violence and disruption with which our society has never adequately come to terms.

Caribbean society was born out of brutality, destructiveness, rape; the destruction of the Amerindian peoples, the assault on Africa, the forced uprooting and enslavement of the African; the gun, the whip, the authority of force. Yet the Caribbean area today is not particularly noted for any large-scale, organized violence. Caribbean governments sit securely and complacently, with or without popular support.

But the violence of our history has not evaporated. It is still there. It is there in the relations between adult and child, between black and white, between man and woman. It has been internalized, it has seeped down into our personal lives. Drastic brutality—physical and verbal—upon children is an accepted part of child rearing in the Caribbean. "Gavin," threatens Laura of *Miguel Street* to one of her children, "Gavin, if you don't come here this minute, I make you fart fire, you hear." And C. L. R. James in his novel *Minty Alley* describes a hair-raising scene of violence upon a child which contains not an inch of exaggeration.

Our capacity for verbal violence is limitless. Teasing and heckling are taken to lengths which would shock in another society. For example, we award nicknames on the basis of hopeless physical deformities—"Hop-and-Drop," for example, for a polio victim who walks with a pathetic limp. Our expressions of abuse would fill catalogues. Quarreling is a national pastime—quarrels are spectacular: a great deal of energy and artistry are applied to body movements, the ingenuity of insults, the graphic recitation of the antagonist's crimes; a good quarrel will provide a morning's dramatic diversion for a whole neighborhood, for quarrels often emerge onto the street as if in search of an adequate stage.

And the fact that a physical fight between a man and a woman—or more accurately, a woman-beating—may erupt into the open air and rage for hours without any serious alarm on the part of onlookers for the safety of the woman, without attracting the intervention of the law, is a strong comment on our attitudes:

> Never never put yu mouth
> In husband-and-wife business

runs the refrain of one calypso, a word of warning to the sentimental, to those who may be naïve enough to think that a woman minds being beaten by her man. It is the message of many a calypso. Another song recounts with mock disapproval a public "licking." The thinly veiled sexual imagery is a stock device of calypso, but here it illustrates effectively the idea of violence being part and parcel of the normal relations between man and woman: a policeman who would intervene is rebuffed by none other than the "victim" of the licking:

> Constable have a care
> This is my man licking me here
> And if he feel to lick me
> He could lick me,
> Dammit, don't interfere.

Of course, calypsonians are mainly men, and men are largely responsible for perpetuating the myth of women thriving on violence from their men:

> Every now and then cuff them down,
> They'll love you long and they'll love you strong.
> Black-up their eye
> Bruise-up their knee
> And they will love you eternally.

The idea is not far removed from the maxim coined in the era of slavery: "Battre un nègre, c'est le nourrir"—a beating is food to a nigger.

But of course, violence in its narrowest definition, namely, physical violence, is only a visible manifestation of a wider disruption, a basic breakdown of respect. For violence to women includes the whole range of mental cruelty which is part and parcel of women's experiences in the Caribbean.

Every now and then our attention is drawn to this existing situation when a woman, known to her neighbors as a devoted, hard-working, self-sacrificing mother, of no particular wickedness, appears trembling and speechless before a judge for having killed her man.

And the familiar, almost humdrum details roll out again—a history of intolerable ill-treatment by the man both upon her and upon her children: neglect, desertion, humiliation, tyranny, unreasonableness, lack of consideration . . . the last straw falls and the woman runs at him with a kitchen knife.

It would seem that the precedents of this case stretch far enough back into our history to have entered our folklore—there is the folk song about Betsy Thomas who killed her husband stone cold dead in the market and had no doubt that she would be absolved of crime:

> I ain't kill nobody but me husband.

In fact, our society implicitly acknowledges the permanent situation out of which husband killings arise, in the leniency the court generally affords to a woman who has been driven to this act. Of course, killing your man is an extreme measure, but, again, it is a crisis which is but the visible tip of the iceberg or, to bring our imagery home, the eruption of a volcano that all along has been silently cooking.

The black man in the role of Dispenser of Violence is very likely a descendant of the white slave-overseer asserting an almost bottomless authority over the whipped. But there is one fundamental difference, for whereas the overseer beat and tortured his victim because he had power over him, the black man ill-treating his woman is expressing his desire for power, is betraying a dire insecurity vis-à-vis the female.

In the Caribbean the "war of the sexes" takes on a very special character. It is not a straight fight between handicapped Woman on the one hand and omnipotent Man on the other. From the very beginning of West Indian history the black woman has had a *de facto* "equality" thrust upon her—the equality of cattle in a herd. We became "equal" from the moment African men and women were bundled together onto galleys, men and women clamped to the floor alongside each other for the horrifying middle passage. A slave was a slave—male or female—a head of livestock, a unit of the power that drove the plantation. The women worked equally hard out in the fields with the men, were equally subject to torture and brutality. The black woman in the Caribbean has never been a delicate flower locked away in a glass case and "protected" from responsibility. Of course, the African woman in Africa is no delicate flower either, wielding a tremendous physical force in her daily chores of pounding, planting, etc., all the while carrying around her latest child upon her back.

From the very beginning of our history on this side of the Atlantic, woman has been mobilized in the society's work force. But there was, of course, some division of labor or functions, and this is where the male-female trouble began.

In the first place, the whole humiliation of slavery meant an utter devaluation of the manhood of the race; the male was powerless to carry out his traditional role of protector of the tribe, he was unable to defend either himself or his women and children from capture and transportation, from daily mishandling. His manhood was reduced to his brawn for the labor he could do for his master and to his reproductive function.

And the function of fatherhood was limited to fertilizing the female. Gone was the status of head of the family, for there was no family, no living in a unit with wife and children. A man might not even know who his children were, and at any rate they did not belong to him in any sense; he was unable to provide for them—their owner performed the function of provider. The black man had no authority over his children, but the woman did. The children's mothers, or female child-rearers, were responsible for the upbringing of the race. Women became mother and father to the race.

And it is this concentration of moral authority in the person of the woman that has influenced relations between men and women of African descent in the Caribbean. For today the average Afro-West Indian is still reared more or less singlehandedly by a mother, or aunt, or big sister, or god-mother—the men have still not returned to the functions of fatherhood. Fathers are either physically absent—the prevalent pattern of concubinage and male mobility results in a man not necessarily staying put in one household until the children he has deposited there have grown up

—or, even when the father is present in the home, his part in the bringing up of the children is a limited one. His role is not clearly defined and not binding. One of the roles he may play is that of Punisher, administering beatings at the request of the mother; but the strongest influence in the home is usually female.

The society may be called a matriarchal one—many of our ancestors were in fact brought from West African societies which were matriarchal in structure, although there this by no means implied an abdication of responsibility on the part of the males. But this meant that our women had precedents of matriarchy upon which to draw in the new situation of male defection.

The Caribbean, and indeed black America on the whole, has produced the new black matriarch, the strong female figure who is responsible not only for the propagation of the race but by whose strength our humanity has been preserved.

Most Afro-West Indians have grown up "fatherless" in one way or another, most have been reared under almost exclusive female influence. So in the society moral authority is female, an authority that may sometimes be harsh and driven to extremes by the situation of stress in which a Caribbean mother often finds herself—often ill-feeling against a deserting man is vented upon the children he has left in her lap.

Caribbean writing teems with the strong woman type. Many of Samuel Selvon's immigrants are our feckless, happy-go-lucky men now and then marshaled into responsibility by brisk, matter-of-fact women. The female figures of James's *Minty Alley,* the dignified, almost statuesque Mrs. Rouse; Maisie the wraith, invincible in any situation. The women of *Miguel Street,* bawling out, battering (as well as being battered by) or working to support their unstable men. And I have discovered that my own book, *Crick Crack, Monkey,* is full of strong woman figures and that men are, like Auntie Beatrice's husband, "either absent or unnoticeable"—even the heroine's succession of "uncles" do not constitute any solid presence. And I had once intended to give the children a grandfather—Ma's husband—but I had conceived of him as an invalid in a rocking chair, ably looked after by Ma!

Caribbean woman has developed a strong moral fiber to compensate for the weakening of the male. Hence the desire of the man to do her down, to put her in her place, to safeguard his manhood threatened by the authority of the female upstart.

The black man in the Caribbean is capable of deep respect for his mother and for older women in general. The worst insult in our language is to curse a man's mother. An "obscenity" flung in the heat of quarrel is, quite simply, "Yu mother!" Authority is female, a man will have instinctive qualms about disrespecting his mother or, by extension, her contemporaries, but he will take his revenge on the black female by seeking to degrade women within reach of his disrespect.

Young men at a loose end (usually unemployed—the devaluation of black manhood is perpetuated in economic frustration) will position themselves on a culvert, at a street corner, on a pavement, and vie with each other in the ingenuity of their comments to embarrass women going by. The embarrassment of woman is part of the national ethos, stemming, I am convinced, from a deep-seated resentment against the strength of women.

In Trinidad the calypsonian, the folk poet, is assured of heartfelt, howling approval when he devotes his talent to the degradation of woman:

> Clarabelle,
> She could chase the Devil from Hell
> With the kind of way she does smell
> Anytime she pass yu could tell.

Our folk poet is rarely given to flattering and extolling the qualities of womanhood—woman and her sexual attributes are almost only a stock dirty joke in his repertoire. And the calypsonian mirrors collective attitudes—he is the product of his society and sings to please his audience.

There has, however, been one major development in our contemporary history which promises to have a salutary effect upon relations between black men and women in the Caribbean. This is the advent of black power ideology.

An important element of the history of male-female relations in the Caribbean has been the imposition of European standards of physical beauty—the tendency of the man to measure the desirability of women by these standards, and the corresponding struggle of black women to alter their appearance as far as possible in the direction of European requirements for beauty but of course still falling short of these requirements. A large part of male disrespect for the black woman was an expression of his dissatisfaction with her, "inferior" as she was to the accepted white ideal of womanhood.

This bred a great deal of destructive dishonesty, a canker eating away at the roots of our self-respect. For these attitudes were especially destructive as they were to a large extent disavowed or even entirely subconscious. A man would vehemently deny that he could be the victim of this mesmerism. His cousin, yes, damn fool who went to England to study and could find nothing else to get married to but a white woman—but *he* would never be found putting milk in his coffee, unthinkable, *he* had a healthy attitude toward these white people.

It was indeed a difficult burden to bear—his very deep-seated resentment of whitedom and this hopeless involvement with them.

Today's ideology has begun to liberate us from this particular dishonesty. It has forced into the open, and at popular level (a success not achieved by the literary movements of the first half of the century), the discussion of our polarization toward whiteness, and it has effectively set about revising our concepts of physical beauty. The progressive abolition of hair-straightening in the Caribbean is a momentous revolution. It is part of the revaluation of the black woman.

And the revaluation of black womanhood inevitably also implies a restoration of black manhood, when the black man no longer forcibly evaluates his women by the standards of a man who once held the whip over him. It is one stage of his liberation from the whip hand.

And it is only when our lives cease to be governed by the shadow of the whip that we can begin to heal the grave disruption of relations between men and women that we have suffered in the Caribbean.

Towards Men's Liberation

Harold Rosenberg

Harold Rosenberg was one of America's two or three most celebrated twentieth-century art critics. He was born in New York, in 1906, attended City College, then took a law degree at St. Lawrence University. He started out as an avant-garde intellectual and poet, but his main interest soon became art. All his life he remained in intimate contact with the New York art world, generally siding with the artists and against the art dealers, museum directors, and critics. He did much lecturing, taught at the University of Chicago, was a consultant to the Advertising Council, and was art critic for *The New Yorker* from 1967 until his death in 1979. Collections of his essays appeared as *The Tradition of the New* (1959); *The Anxious Object* (1964); *Artworks and Packages* (1969); and *The De-definition of Art: Action Art to Pop to Earthworks* (1972), which responds gloomily to what Rosenberg took to be a vogue for art that had no real meaning. The present essay, first published in the November 1967 issue of *Vogue,* is reprinted from a volume of his selected essays entitled *Discovering the Present* (1973). (In the essay Rosenberg quotes a poem by e. e. cummings that has a tantalizingly obscure third line. Our guess is that it is a comic burlesque, in baby talk, of "Dust thou art, to dust returnest.")

Masculinity: Style and Cult

Societies of the past have admired different personifications of the manly virtues: the warrior, the patriarch, the sage; the lover, the seducer; Zeus the Thunderer, Jehovah the Lawgiver.

In America, masculinity is associated primarily with the outdoors, and with such outdoor trades as cattledriving, railroading, whaling, and trucking. The outdoor type is presumed to possess masculine character traits: toughness, resourcefulness, love of being alone, fraternity with animals, and attractiveness to women and the urge to abandon them. To the man of the open spaces is also attributed the ultimate mark of manliness, the readiness to die.

From the outdoors America derives the boots, lumber jackets and shirts, sailor's caps, pipes, and guns that are its paraphernalia of masculinity. Oddly enough, in the United States, military and police uniforms do not confer masculinity, as they do among Cossacks and Hussars. One can as readily imagine women in our army uniform as men. To prove that he was all man, General Patton had to augment his battle costume with a pearl-handled revolver. (It is true, however, that he wrote poetry and may have felt the need to overcome this handicap.)

As to hair, masculinity is ambivalent. Long hair belongs to the style of frontier scouts and trappers, the most male of men. Yet "longhairs" is the name applied to intellectuals, a breed always suspected of sexual inauthenticity. Beards used to be a material evidence of maleness; today they are as frequently an appurtenance of masquerade.

In the last century the outdoors represented genuine hazards. It took self-reliance, identifiable with masculinity (though the pioneer mother had it, too), to venture very far from the farm or town.

Today there are still risky occupations—piloting spaceships, handling nuclear substances—but these trades have become increasingly technical and depersonalized. As for the rugged outdoors, it is used chiefly for sports; and a vacation at a ranch or ski lodge, or shooting lions in Kenya, is about as hazardous as a trip to the Riviera.

The outdoors, representing once-hostile nature, has been transformed into a stage set. Masculinity in the American sense has thus lost its locale and, perhaps, its reason for being. On the neon-lighted lonesome prairie, masculinity is a matter of certain traditional costume details: the cowboy hat, jeans, and guitar. It has become clear that the traditional traits of the man's man (and the ladies' man) can be put on, too. One *plays* manliness, with or without dark goggles.

Big-game hunters, mountain climbers, horsemen, and other representative male types are actors in a charade of nostalgia. Old masculine pursuits, like baseball or wrestling, when carried on at night under the glare of fluorescent tubes, come to resemble spectacles on television and wind up in the living room. In the epoch of the picture window, outdoors and indoors have lost their separateness.

In modern mass societies the uniforms of all kinds of cults compete with one another. Masculinity is one of these cults, and to create an impression the practitioner of maleness must stand out in a crowd. Persons with other interests are not disposed to make an issue of their sex. Only psychiatrists and sociologists complain that boys and girls today look alike and are often mistaken for each other. Even tough adolescents, like members of big-city gangs, don't mind if their girls wear the same shirts and jeans as the men. All are more concerned with identifying themselves as outsiders than as males and females.

Masculinity today is a myth that has turned into a comedy. A ten-gallon hat still seems to bestow upon its wearer the old male attributes of taciturnity, resourcefulness, courage, and love of solitude. At the same time, the virility of the cowboy and the truck driver, like that of the iceman of yesterday, is a joke that everyone sees through.

A person uncertain of his sexual identity dresses up in boots, bandanna, and riding breeches not so much to fool the public as to parade his ambiguity. Those who have gone over the line may advertise their desires for male company by wearing a beard in addition to sheepskins. Women can be masculine too, of course, in the degree necessary to make them irresistible to feminine men.

Hemingway, who constantly kept the issue of masculinity alive in his writings, flaunted both the look of the outdoor man and his presumed character qualities of daring, self-detachment, contempt for the over-civilized, and eagerness to court death.

Hemingway's he-man performance was, among other things, a means of combatting the American stereotype of the writer as a sissy. In the United States, the artist and man of ideas have always lived under the threat of having their masculinity impugned. Richard Hofstadter, in his *Anti-Intellectualism in American Life,* lists a dozen instances in which the "stigma of effeminacy" was branded upon intellectuals by political bullies, ranging from Tammany Hall leaders in the nineteenth century, who attacked reformers as "political hermaphrodites," to Communist Party hacks in the 1930s, who denounced independent writers as "scented whores." Evidently, it has always been possible to convince the common man that his intellectual superiors fall short of him in manliness.

To the overhanging charge of being contaminated by a ladylike occupation, Hemingway responded by injecting the romance of masculinity into the making of literature. At least as far as he was concerned, the sexual legitimacy of the male writer was to be put beyond question. Besides lining up with traditional outdoor types, such as bullfighters and deep-sea fishermen, Hemingway's strategy included identification with the new activist male image of the Depression decade: the leather-jacketed revolutionist allied with the peasant and factory worker. One might say that each of his novels originated in a new choice of male makeup.

Unfortunately, demonstrating his manhood was not enough for Hemingway. He found it necessary to challenge the masculinity of other writers. Like Theodore Roosevelt earlier in the century, he became an instance of the intellectual who slanders intellectuals generally, in the hope of putting himself right with the regular guys. During the Spanish Civil War he forgot himself to the extent of sneering publicly at Leon Trotsky for remaining at his typewriter in Mexico, implying that the former chief of the Red Army lacked the manliness to go to Spain and fight. He, himself, of course, went to Spain to write. In *For Whom the Bell Tolls* he identified himself with the dynamiter Jordan who also shook the earth by his love feats in a sleeping bag.

Thirty years ago not all of Hemingway's contemporaries were convinced that he had established his masculinity through displaying an appetite for violence, sex, and death. In *no thanks,* e. e. cummings translated Hemingway's romance of maleness back into the daydreams of boyhood:

> "what does little Ernest croon[o]
> in his death at afternoon?
> (kow dow r 2 bul retoinis
> wus de woids uf lil Oinis"

To cummings, Hemingway's heroics were not only childish ("lil Oinis") but feminine ("kow dow r").

The post-Hemingway he-man has labored under the handicap of a masculinity that is generally recognized to be a masquerade. The adventurer living dangerously has disintegrated into the tongue-in-cheek élan of James Bond. Neither at work nor at home is maleness any longer endowed with glamour or privilege. The cosmonaut is less a birdman than a specialist minding his signals and dials. The father who has entered into a diapering partnership with his wife has nothing in common with the patriarch. To the public of Norman Mailer (more male?) the outdoor rig (Mailer in sea captain's cap on the jacket of *Advertisements for Myself*) and chronicles of supersex are suspect, both psychologically and as playing to the gallery. It is no secret that a Bogartean[o] toughness with women may represent the opposite of male self-confidence.

The mass media exploit the ambiguity of the male role and the sexual sophistication that goes with the increasing awareness of it. In male comedy teams, one of the partners almost invariably plays the "wife," confident that the audience will know when to smirk. Analysts of mass culture speak of the decline of the American male and of the "masculinity crisis" as topics capable of arousing libidinous responses. The public is given the image of luscious females starving in vain for the attention of men, and of men who, egged on and deprived by frigid seductresses, end by falling into each other's arms.

Masculinity-building is urged, a theme which the media are not slow to adapt for their own purposes. Masculinity is the alfalfa peddled in Marlboro Country. It is the essence of worn leather laced with campfire smoke that provides the aroma of the man of distinction. It also comes in powder form, none genuine without the Shaggy Dog on the wrapping.

To those who resent the fact that their pretension to masculinity is not taken seriously, one means is available for gaining respect: violence. The victim of rape is not inclined to question the virility of her assailant.

The relation between masculinity that has been put into doubt and

Ernest Reference to author Ernest Hemingway.
Bogartean Reference to Humphrey Bogart, whose film roles epitomized the cynical, wisecracking, tough-but-vulnerable man.

violence reveals itself most clearly in the recent history of the Civil Rights movement. The black has derived from white America the lesson that physical force is the mark of manhood. White society is "the Man," whose insignia of power are the club, the whip, the bloodhounds. The presence of the Man impeaches the masculinity of the young black and demands that he prove himself. He becomes full grown when he resolves to fight the Man. To confront the Man, the black militant has resurrected the figure of the radical activist of the thirties, the model of Hemingway's he-man, honor-bound to risk his life in physical combat.

An article in the *New York Times Magazine* on the Black Panthers is illustrated by photographs of its two leaders. Both wear the traditional leather jackets and berets of the Left fighters of thirty years ago— these could be photographs of two Lincoln Brigade volunteers.° A statement by one of the Panthers touches the philosophical essence of the romantic conception of masculinity: to be a man one must dare to die. "The ghetto black," said Bobby Seale, "isn't afraid to stand up to the cops, because he already lives with violence. He expects to die any day."

In our culture all human attributes tend to be over-defined and become a basis of self-consciousness. The behavioral sciences collaborate with the mass media in making a man anxious about his sex status; both then provide him with models of aggressiveness by which to correct his deficiencies. Yet the present uneasiness about masculinity, coupled with theatrical devices for attaining it, may be more harmful than any actual curtailment of manliness discovered by researchers and editorialists. The real damage may lie in the remedy rather than the ailment, since the desire to have one's masculinity acknowledged may lead, as we have seen, to absurd postures and acts of force. It is hard to believe that Americans would be worse off by becoming more gentle. Nor that mildness in manners and social relations would make them less manly. In the real world nothing is altogether what it is. True maleness is never without its vein of femininity. The Greeks understood this and made it the theme of their tales of sexual metamorphosis, the remarkable account of Hercules, of all men, taking on temporarily the character of a woman and wearing women's clothes. Total masculinity is an ideal of the frustrated, not a fact of biology. With the cult of masculinity put aside, maleness might have a better chance to develop in the United States.

Lincoln Brigade volunteers Abraham Lincoln Brigade, which was the American branch of an International Brigade that fought in Spain during the Spanish Civil War (1936–1939) in support of the Republican government against a Fascist revolt led by Francisco Franco.

Marc Feigen Fasteau

Marc Feigen Fasteau was born in Washington, D.C. in 1942; he was educated at Harvard College, Georgetown University, and Harvard Law School, where he was an editor of the *Law Review.* In Washington, he worked as an assistant in foreign affairs to Senator Mike Mansfield and as a staff member of the Joint Economic Committee of Congress. He also served as a research fellow at the Kennedy Institute of Politics before going into law practice in New York. In his work and in his writing, he has been actively engaged in the breaking of sexual stereotypes. *The Male Machine* (1974), from which we reprint a chapter, is his first book.

Friendships Among Men

There is a long-standing myth in our society that the great friendships are between men. Forged through shared experience, male friendship is portrayed as the most unselfish, if not the highest form, of human relationship. The more traditionally masculine the shared experience from which it springs, the stronger and more profound the friendship is supposed to be. Going to war, weathering crises together at school or work, playing on the same athletic team, are some of the classic experiences out of which friendships between men are believed to grow.

By and large, men do prefer the company of other men, not only in their structured time but in the time they fill with optional, nonobligatory activity. They prefer to play games, drink, and talk, as well as work and fight together. Yet something is missing. Despite the time men spend together, their contact rarely goes beyond the external, a limitation which tends to make their friendships shallow and unsatisfying.

My own childhood memories are of doing things with my friends— playing games or sports, building walkie-talkies, going camping. Other people and my relationships to them were never legitimate subjects for attention. If someone liked me, it was an opaque, mysterious occurrence that bore no analysis. When I was slighted, I felt hurt. But relationships with people just happened. I certainly had feelings about my friends, but I can't remember a single instance of trying consciously to sort them out until I was well into college.

For most men this kind of shying away from the personal continues into adult life. In conversations with each other, we hardly ever use ourselves as reference points. We talk about almost everything except how we ourselves are affected by people and events. Everything is discussed as though it were taking place out there somewhere, as though we had no more felt response to it than to the weather. Topics that can be treated in this detached, objective way become conversational mainstays. The few subjects which are fundamentally personal are shaped into discussions of abstract general questions. Even in an exchange about their reactions to liberated women—a topic of intensely personal interest—the tendency will be to talk in general, theoretical terms. Work, at least its objective aspects, is always a safe subject. Men also spend an incredible amount of time rehashing the great public issues of the day. Until early 1973, Vietnam was the work-horse topic. Then came Watergate. It doesn't seem to matter that we've all had a hundred similar conversations. We plunge in for another round, trying to come up with a new angle as much to impress the others with what we know as to keep from being bored stiff.

Games play a central role in situations organized by men. I remember a weekend some years ago at the country house of a law-school classmate as a blur of softball, football, croquet, poker, and a dice-and-board game called Combat, with swimming thrown in on the side. As soon as one game ended, another began. Taken one at a time, these "activities" were fun, but the impression was inescapable that the host, and most of his guests, would do anything to stave off a lull in which they would be together without some impersonal focus for their attention. A snapshot of almost any men's club would show the same thing, ninety percent of the men engaged in some activity—ranging from backgammon to watching the tube—other than, or at least as an aid to, conversation.[1]

My composite memory of evenings spent with a friend at college and later when we shared an apartment in Washington is of conversations punctuated by silences during which we would internally pass over any personal or emotional thoughts which had arisen and come back to the permitted track. When I couldn't get my mind off personal matters, I said very little. Talks with my father have always had the same tone. Respect for privacy was the rationale for our diffidence. His questions to me about how things were going at school or at work were asked as discreetly as he would have asked a friend about someone's commitment to a hospital for the criminally insane. Our conversations, when they touched these matters at all, to say nothing of more sensitive matters, would veer quickly back to safe topics of general interest.

In our popular literature, the archetypal male hero embodying this personal muteness is the cowboy. The classic mold for the character was set in 1902 by Owen Wister's novel *The Virginian* where the author spelled out, with an explicitness that was never again necessary, the characteristics of his protagonist. Here's how it goes when two close friends the Virginian hasn't seen in some time take him out for a drink:

[1]Women may use games as a reason for getting together—bridge clubs, for example. But the show is more for the rest of the world—to indicate that they are doing *something*—and the games themselves are not the only means of communication.

All of them had seen rough days together, and they felt guilty with emotion.
"It's hot weather," said Wiggin.
"Hotter in Box Elder," said McLean. "My kid has started teething."
Words ran dry again. They shifted their positions, looked in their glasses, read the labels on the bottles. They dropped a word now and then to the proprietor about his trade, and his ornaments.[2]

One of the Virginian's duties is to assist at the hanging of an old friend as a horse thief. Afterward, for the first time in the book, he is visibly upset. The narrator puts his arm around the hero's shoulders and describes the Virginian's reaction:

I had the sense to keep silent, and presently he shook my hand, not looking at me as he did so. He was always very shy of demonstration.[3]

And, for explanation of such reticence, "As all men know, he also knew that many things should be done in this world in silence, and that talking about them is a mistake."[4]

There are exceptions, but they only prove the rule.

One is the drunken confidence: "Bob, ole boy, I gotta tell ya—being divorced isn't so hot. . . . [and see, I'm too drunk to be held responsible for blurting it out]." Here, drink becomes an excuse for exchanging confidences and a device for periodically loosening the restraint against expressing a need for sympathy and support from other men—which may explain its importance as a male ritual.[5] Marijuana fills a similar need.

Another exception is talking to a stranger—who may be either someone the speaker doesn't know or someone who isn't in the same social or business world. (Several black friends told me that they have been on the receiving end of personal confidences from white acquaintances that they were sure had not been shared with white friends.) In either case, men are willing to talk about themselves only to other men with whom they do not have to compete or whom they will not have to confront socially later.

Finally, there is the way men depend on women to facilitate certain conversations. The women in a mixed group are usually the ones who make the first personal reference, about themselves or others present. The men can then join in without having the onus for initiating a discussion of "personalities." Collectively, the men can "blame" the conversation on the women. They can also feel in these conversations that since they are talking "to" the women instead of "to" the men, they can be excused for deviating from the masculine norm. When the women leave, the tone and subject invariably shift away from the personal.

The effect of these constraints is to make it extraordinarily difficult for

[2]Owen Wister, *The Virginian* ([Macmillan: 1902] Grosset & Dunlap ed.: 1929), pp. 397–98.
[3]*Ibid.*, p. 343.
[4]*Ibid.*, p. 373.
[5]Lionel Tiger, *Men in Groups* (Random House: 1969), p. 185.

men to really get to know each other. A psychotherapist who has conducted a lengthy series of encounter groups for men summed it up:

> With saddening regularity [the members of these groups] described how much they wanted to have closer, more satisfying relationships with other men: "I'd settle for having one really close man friend. I supposedly have some close men friends now. We play golf or go for a drink. We complain about our jobs and our wives. I care about them and they care about me. We even have some physical contact—I mean we may even give a hug on a big occasion. But it's not enough."[6]

The sources of this stifling ban on self-disclosure, the reasons why men hide from each other, lie in the taboos and imperatives of the masculine stereotype.

To begin with, men are supposed to be functional, to spend their time working or otherwise solving or thinking about how to solve problems. Personal reaction, how one feels about something, is considered dysfunctional, at best an irrelevant distraction from the expected objectivity. Only weak men, and women, talk about—i.e., "give in," to their feelings. "I group my friends in two ways," said a business executive:

> those who have made it and don't complain and those who haven't made it. And only the latter spend time talking to their wives about their problems and how bad their boss is and all that. The ones who concentrate more on communicating . . . are those who have realized that they aren't going to make it and therefore they have changed the focus of attention.[7]

In a world which tells men they have to choose between expressiveness and manly strength, this characterization may be accurate. Most of the men who talk personally to other men *are* those whose problems have gotten the best of them, who simply can't help it. Men not driven to despair don't talk about themselves, so the idea that self-disclosure and expressiveness are associated with problems and weakness becomes a self-fulfilling prophecy.

Obsessive competitiveness also limits the range of communication in male friendships. Competition is the principal mode by which men relate to each other—at one level because they don't know how else to make contact, but more basically because it is the way to demonstrate, to themselves and others, the key masculine qualities of unwavering toughness

---

[6]Don Clark, "Homosexual Encounter in All-Male Groups," in L. Solomon and B. Berzon (eds.), *New Perspectives on Encounter Groups* (Jossey-Bass: 1972), pp. 376–77. See also Alan Booth, "Sex and Social Participation," *American Sociological Review*, Vol. 37 (April 1972), p. 183, an empirical study showing that, contrary to Lionel Tiger's much publicized assertion (*Men in Groups*) women form stronger and closer friendship bonds with each other than men do.

[7]Fernando Bartolomé, "Executives as Human Beings," *Harvard Business Review*, Vol. 50 (November–December 1972), p. 64.

and the ability to dominate and control. The result is that they inject competition into situations which don't call for it.

In conversations, you must show that you know more about the subject than the other man, or at least as much as he does. For example, I have often engaged in a contest that could be called My Theory Tops Yours, disguised as a serious exchange of ideas. The proof that it wasn't serious was that I was willing to participate even when I was sure that the participants, including myself, had nothing fresh to say. Convincing the other person—victory—is the main objective, with control of the floor an important tactic. Men tend to lecture at each other, insist that the discussion follow their train of thought, and are often unwilling to listen.[8] As one member of a men's rap group said,

> When I was talking I used to feel that I had to be driving to a point, that it had to be rational and organized, that I had to persuade at all times, rather than exchange thoughts and ideas.[9]

Even in casual conversation some men hold back unless they are absolutely sure of what they are saying. They don't want to have to change a position once they have taken it. It's "just like a woman" to change your mind, and, more important, it is inconsistent with the approved masculine posture of total independence.

Competition was at the heart of one of my closest friendships, now defunct. There was a good deal of mutual liking and respect. We went out of our way to spend time with each other and wanted to work together. We both had "prospects" as "bright young men" and the same "liberal but tough" point of view. We recognized this about each other, and this recognition was the basis of our respect and of our sense of equality. That we saw each other as equals was important—our friendship was confirmed by the reflection of one in the other. But our constant and all-encompassing competition made this equality precarious and fragile. One way or another, everything counted in the measuring process. We fought out our tennis matches as though our lives depended on it. At poker, the two of us would often play on for hours after the others had left. These *mano a mano*[0] poker marathons seem in retrospect especially revealing of the competitiveness of the relationship: playing for small stakes, the essence of the game is in outwitting, psychologically beating down the other player—the other skills involved are negligible. Winning is the only pleasure, one that evaporates quickly, a truth that struck me in inchoate form every time our game broke up at four a.m and I walked out the door with

---

[8]The contrast with women on this point is striking. Casual observation will confirm that women's conversations move more quickly, with fewer long speeches and more frequent changes of speaker.

[9]*Boston Globe*, March 12, 1972, p. B–1.

mano a mano   hand-to-hand, competitive (Spanish).

my five-dollar winnings, a headache, and a sense of time wasted. Still, I did the same thing the next time. It was what we did together, and somehow it counted. Losing at tennis could be balanced by winning at poker; at another level, his moving up in the federal government by my getting on the *Harvard Law Review.*

This competitiveness feeds the most basic obstacle to openness between men, the inability to admit to being vulnerable. Real men, we learn early, are not supposed to have doubts, hopes and ambitions which may not be realized, things they don't (or even especially do) like about themselves, fears and disappointments. Such feelings and concerns, of course, are part of everyone's inner life, but a man must keep quiet about them. If others know how you really feel you can be hurt, and that in itself is incompatible with manhood. The inhibiting effect of this imperative is not limited to disclosures of major personal problems. Often men do not share even ordinary uncertainties and half-formulated plans of daily life with their friends. And when they do, they are careful to suggest that they already know how to proceed—that they are not really asking for help or understanding but simply for particular bits of information. Either way, any doubts they have are presented as external, carefully characterized as having to do with the issue as distinct from the speaker. They are especially guarded about expressing concern or asking a question that would invite personal comment. It is almost impossible for men to simply exchange thoughts about matters involving them personally in a comfortable, non-crisis atmosphere. If a friend tells you of his concern that he and a colleague are always disagreeing, for example, he is likely to quickly supply his own explanation—something like "different professional backgrounds." The effect is to rule out observations or suggestions that do not fit within this already reconnoitered protective structure. You don't suggest, even if you believe it is true, that in fact the disagreements arise because he presents his ideas in a way which tends to provoke a hostile reaction. It would catch him off guard; it would be something he hadn't already thought of and accepted about himself and, for that reason, no matter how constructive and well-intentioned you might be, it would put you in control for the moment. He doesn't want that; he is afraid of losing your respect. So, sensing he feels that way, because you would yourself, you say something else. There is no real give-and-take.

It is hard for men to get angry at each other honestly. Anger between friends often means that one has hurt the other. Since the straightforward expression of anger in these situations involves an admission of vulnerability, it is safer to stew silently or find an "objective" excuse for retaliation. Either way, trust is not fully restored.

Men even try not to let it show when they feel good. We may report the reasons for our happiness, if they have to do with concrete accomplishments, but we try to do it with a straight face, as if to say, "Here's what happened, but it hasn't affected my grown-up unemotional equilibrium, and I am not asking for any kind of response." Happiness is a precarious, "childish" feeling, easy to shoot down. Others may find the event that triggers it trivial or incomprehensible, or even threatening to their own self-esteem—in the sense that if one man is up, another man is down. So we tend not to take the risk of expressing it.

What is particularly difficult for men is seeking or accepting help from friends. I, for one, learned early that dependence was unacceptable. When I was eight, I went to a summer camp I disliked. My parents visited me in the middle of the summer and, when it was time for them to leave, I wanted to go with them. They refused, and I yelled and screamed and was miserably unhappy for the rest of the day. That evening an older camper comforted me, sitting by my bed as I cried, patting me on the back soothingly and saying whatever it is that one says at times like that. He was in some way clumsy or funny-looking, and a few days later I joined a group of kids in cruelly making fun of him, an act which upset me, when I thought about it, for years. I can only explain it in terms of my feeling, as early as the age of eight, that by needing and accepting his help and comfort I had compromised myself, and took it out on him.

"You can't express dependence when you feel it," a corporate executive said, "because it's a kind of absolute. If you are loyal 90% of the time and disloyal 10%, would you be considered loyal? Well, the same happens with independence: you are either dependent or independent; you can't be both."[10] "Feelings of dependence," another explained, "are identified with weakness or 'untoughness' and our culture doesn't accept those things in men."[11] The result is that we either go it alone or "act out certain games or rituals to provoke the desired reaction in the other and have our needs satisfied without having to ask for anything."[12]

Somewhat less obviously, the expression of affection also runs into emotional barriers growing out of the masculine stereotype. When I was in college, I was suddenly quite moved while attending a friend's wedding. The surge of feeling made me uncomfortable and self-conscious. There was nothing inherently difficult or, apart from the fact of being moved by a moment of tenderness, "unmasculine" about my reaction. I just did not know how to deal with or communicate what I felt. "I consider myself a sentimentalist," one man said, "and I think I am quite able to express my feelings. But the other day my wife described a friend of mine to some people as my best friend and I felt embarrassed when I heard her say it."[13]

A major source of these inhibitions is the fear of being, or being thought, homosexual. Nothing is more frightening to a heterosexual man in our society. It threatens, at one stroke, to take away every vestige of his claim

[10]Bartolomé, *op. cit.*, p. 65.
[11]*Ibid.*, p. 64.
[12]*Ibid.*, p. 66.
[13]*Ibid.*, p. 64.

to a masculine identity—something like knocking out the foundations of a building—and to expose him to the ostracism, ranging from polite tolerance to violent revulsion, of his friends and colleagues. A man can be labeled as homosexual not just because of overt sexual acts but because of almost any sign of behavior which does not fit the masculine stereotype. The touching of another man, other than shaking hands or, under emotional stress, an arm around the shoulder, is taboo. Women may kiss each other when they meet; men are uncomfortable when hugged even by close friends.[14] Onlookers might misinterpret what they saw, and, more important, what would we think of ourselves if we felt a twinge of sensual pleasure from the embrace.

Direct verbal expressions of affection or tenderness are also something that only homosexuals and women engage in. Between "real" men affection has to be disguised in gruff, "you old son-of-a-bitch" style. Paradoxically, in some instances, terms of endearment between men can be used as a ritual badge of manhood, dangerous medicine safe only for the strong. The flirting with homosexuality that characterizes the initiation rites of many fraternities and men's clubs serves this purpose. Claude Brown wrote about black life in New York City in the 1950s:

> The term ["baby"] had a hip ring to it. . . . It was like saying, "Man, look at me. I've got masculinity to spare. . . . I can say 'baby' to another cat and he can say 'baby' to me, and we can say it with strength in our voices." If you could say it, this meant that you really had to be sure of yourself, sure of your masculinity.[15]

Fear of homosexuality does more than inhibit the physical display of affection. One of the major recurring themes in the men's groups led by psychotherapist Don Clark was:

> "A large segment of my feelings about other men are unknown or distorted because I am afraid they might have something to do with homosexuality. Now I'm lonely for other men and don't know how to find what I want with them."

As Clark observes, "The spectre of homosexuality seems to be the dragon at the gateway to self-awareness, understanding, and acceptance of male-male needs. If a man tries to pretend the dragon is not there by turning a blind eye to erotic feelings for all other males, he also blinds himself to the rich variety of feelings that are related."[16]

The few situations in which men do acknowledge strong feelings of affection and dependence toward other men are exceptions which prove the rule. With "cop couples," for example, or combat soldier "buddies,"

[14]*Ibid.,* p. 65.
[15]Claude Brown, *Manchild in the Promised Land* ([Macmillan: 1965] Signet ed.: 1965), p. 171.
[16]Clark, *op. cit.,* p. 378.

intimacy and dependence are forced on the men by their work—they have to ride in the patrol car or be in the same foxhole with somebody—and the jobs themselves have such highly masculine images that the men can get away with behavior that would be suspect under any other conditions.

Furthermore, even these combat-buddy relations, when looked at closely, turn out not to be particularly intimate or personal. Margaret Mead has written:

> During the last war English observers were confused by the apparent contradiction between American soldiers' emphasis on the buddy, so grievously exemplified in the break-downs that followed a buddy's death, and the results of detailed inquiry which showed how transitory these buddy relationships were. It was found that men actually accepted their buddies as derivatives from their outfit, and from accidents of association, rather than because of any special personality characteristics capable of ripening into friendship.[17]

One effect of the fear of appearing to be homosexual is to reinforce the practice that two men rarely get together alone without a reason. I once called a friend to suggest that we have dinner together. "O.K.," he said. "What's up?" I felt uncomfortable telling him that I just wanted to talk, that there was no other reason for the invitation.

Men get together to conduct business, to drink, to play games and sports, to re-establish contact after long absences, to participate in heterosexual social occasions—circumstances in which neither person is responsible for actually wanting to see the other. Men are particularly comfortable seeing each other in groups. The group situation defuses any possible assumptions about the intensity of feeling between particular men and provides the safety of numbers—"All the guys are here." It makes personal communication, which requires a level of trust and mutual understanding not generally shared by all members of a group, more difficult and offers an excuse for avoiding this dangerous territory. And it provides what is most sought after in men's friendships: mutual reassurance of masculinity.

Needless to say, the observations in this chapter did not spring full-blown from my head. The process started when I began to understand that, at least with Brenda, a more open, less self-protective relationship was possible. At first, I perceived my situation as completely personal. The changes I was trying to effect in myself had to do, I thought, only with Brenda and me, and could be generalized, if at all, only to other close relationships between men and women. But, as Brenda came to be deeply involved in the women's movement, I began to see, usually at one remove but sometimes directly, the level of intimacy that women, especially women active

[17]Margaret Mead, *Male and Female* ([William Morrow: 1949] Mentor ed.: 1949), p. 214.

in the movement, shared with each other. The contrast between this and the friendships I had with men was striking. I started listening to men's conversations, including my own, and gradually the basic outlines of the pattern described here began to emerge. I heard from women that the men they knew had very few really close male friends; since then I have heard the same thing from men themselves. It was, I realized, my own experience as well. It wasn't that I didn't know a lot of men, or that I was not on friendly terms with them. Rather, I gradually became dissatisfied with the impersonality of these friendships.

Of course, some constraints on self-disclosure do make sense. Privacy is something you give up selectively and gradually to people you like and trust, and who are capable of understanding—instant, indiscriminate intimacy is nearly always formularized, without real content and impact. Nor does self-disclosure as a kind of compartmentalized rest-and-recreation period work: "Well, John, let me tell you about myself. . . ."

Having said all this, it is nonetheless true that men have carried the practice of emotional restraint to the point of paralysis. For me, at least, the ritual affirmations of membership in the fraternity of men that one gets from participation in "masculine" activities do nothing to assuage the feeling of being essentially alone; they have become a poor substitute for being known by and knowing other people. But the positive content of what will replace the old-style friendship is only beginning to take shape. I am learning, though, that when I am able to articulate my feelings as they arise in the context of my friendships, I often find that they are shared by others. Bringing them out into the open clears the air; avoiding them, even unconsciously, is stultifying. I have found also that I am not as fragile as I once thought. The imagined hazards of showing oneself to be human, and thus vulnerable, to one's friends tend not to materialize when actually put to the test. But being oneself is an art, an art sensitive to variations in the receptivity of others as well as to one's own inner life. It is still, for me, something to be mastered, to be tried out and practiced.

The Media and Popular Culture

Centuries ago, in "aristocratic" societies, the term "popular culture" might have been used to describe the traditions and attitudes, the art, crafts, literature, and amusements of the folk, or common people, as distinct from the "high culture" of the aristocratic class, who had the money and leisure to develop more sophisticated tastes and to command the services of the most talented artists, artisans, and entertainers. Democracy, with its loss of stable ranks and classes, has for the last 200 years gradually tended to blur this distinction, and today the revolution in communications has almost erased it. Of course, we still have many groups whose differing culture and taste in part follow from shared ethnic origin, geographic location, or age level. But our society can nevertheless be seen as having become more and more homogenized, a huge mass of people who make possible the mass media and who share a common culture propagated through the media.

This situation has generated many issues. One of the more serious is whether the new "mass culture" is a valuable or distinctive "culture" in the old sense at all, that is, whether it is the expression of our genuine needs, desires and traditions, or simply the manufactured product of specialized consumer industries such as movies, TV, sports, music, and mass magazines. Are the media simply com-

municating our culture—giving us what we want and need—or are
they actually creating it, shaping it to fit their own commercial
interests, and thus corrupting our lives? This is the issue mainly
raised by the essays in this section.

Garrett Epps writes from the point of view of one who prizes
regional culture and is himself collaborating on an attempt to reverse the trend toward mass journalism. The next essays deal with
television. Each of the first three takes up an aspect of television's
possible distortion of our view of reality. Henry Fairlie shows how
much TV news, by the inherent nature of its mechanics and its
"vested interest in disaster," can distort (or even create) news that
the print medium would report more truthfully. Jack McGarvey
illustrates how events come to be regarded by young viewers as
being more real on TV than the real events themselves are. George
Gerbner reports on his research on TV violence, showing how it
changes for the worse the way viewers deal with the realities they
encounter. Neil Postman's essay, using a historical perspective,
argues that this most powerful of the media is actually contributing
to the decline of what we may once have thought of as a permanent
trait of our civilization, the distinction between childhood and maturity.

In the next group, Daniel Boorstin and Aldous Huxley present
contrasting views of the threat of advertising to democracy. Marya
Mannes analyzes the commercial motives of mass advertisers and
presents a biting account of the high social costs of combining those
motives with the power of TV.

Each of the last three essays shows that if mass entertainment
gives the public what it wants, it can also give the public an insight
into itself. Michael Roberts looks closely at the way we use spectator
sports as an expression of our (sometimes unsocial) impulses. Andrew Griffin finds an image of our culture even in monster movies.
Joyce Carol Oates's story draws on the pervasive power of popular
music to make a frightening comment on American adolescent
culture.

Journalism with a Human Voice

Garrett Epps

Garrett Epps was born in 1950 and grew up in Richmond, Virginia. His first long venture into "the real North" came when he attended Harvard, where he became editor of the Harvard *Crimson*. After graduation he returned to Richmond and tried to start a new newspaper with some friends. The next year he won an NEA fellowship and wrote a novel called *The Shad Treatment* (1977) about Virginia politics; it was awarded the Lillian Smith prize for the best southern novel of the year. After three years of working at the *Washington Post*, he wanted another run at living in his own part of the country and moved to North Carolina; he now lives in Chapel Hill, North Carolina. Epps is writing his second novel and is working also as a free-lance science journalist. In addition he writes a regular column for the *North Carolina Independent*, a statewide news biweekly designed to provide an alternative to the homogeneity of the dominant media. The piece below is his first column from its first issue, April 15–28, 1983.

No More News from Nowhere

Not too long ago I heard two young women explaining how they'd rid themselves of their Southern accents deliberately, as soon as they reached college.

"I never knew how strange it sounded until I heard people who talked normally," one said.

"And of course," said the second, "as soon as you open your mouth, people assume you're stupid."

The man they were talking to smirked, and, in a parody drawl, said, "I cain't think whah."

A decade and a half ago, I went through the same thing. The boy across the hall said, "I only put one thing on my roommate form: no Southerners." And my American literature professor added, "Nothing written below the Mason-Dixon line has ever been of any importance." So I ended up, a frightened college freshman in a cold Northern dormitory, standing before a bathroom mirror in the small hours of a winter morning, practicing unfamiliar phonemes. Don't let my accent betray me, I asked my grimacing reflection; don't let me sound dumb.

It worked. Once I dropped "g's," let "i" sounds wander like hot jelly on a kitchen table, said "cow" and "house" with that unmistakeable simper that marks the Piedmont Virginian. No more. People today tell me that I have no accent. Many meant it as a compliment. I sound the way I ought to: like the people on TV. I have joined the ranks of the media-neutral. I speak smart.

But I feel the loss. My tongue lies uneasy in my native land, and I grieve. Who told us—a whole generation of young people nourishing extravagant hopes for success in journalism, the professions and the arts—that we'd better drop our drawls if we wanted to make it away from home?

Television, of course, did the dirtiest work. White Southerners were not always racists, religious fanatics, petty criminals or axe murderers. But they were always, always stupid. And, of course, it wasn't only Southerners, but anyone who was different. Anyone who didn't fit the white, male, bicoastal norm was a villain or a joke. Blacks had Amos 'n' Andy. Hispanics had Jose Jimenez. Women had June Cleaver and THAT Girl. And all these stereotypes live on today, with names like J.J., Crissy and Boss Hogg.

But it's not just TV. It's books and magazines edited in New York, newspaper stories written in Washington, movies shot in Los Angeles. Local TV stations are manned by clones, permapress humanoids trained somewhere else and desperate to get out of town. Cable television—the great hope of community communications—hasn't made the slightest difference. Every year, Americans are bombarded with more and more information and noise, from fewer and fewer sources. News and discussion come from somewhere else—or from nowhere. Very little of it has anything useful to say about who we really are—about what we want and how we live.

Television culture is no culture, what Fred Allen called "chewing gum for the eyes." And newsmagazine journalism is no journalism, Perrier water for the mind. It's not designed, in the end, to inform or to make us think, but to sell things to us. And if it does that by destroying our sense of ourselves, nobody at the networks or the ad agencies is losing sleep over that. In fact, so much the better: if we learn to despise our cultures, to scorn our communities, to admire people who live somewhere else, then we can look for solace only in consumerism and trendiness, trying to drive like the Dukes, drink like J.R. or dress like a *New Yorker* ad.

The forces of no-culture are powerful—magazine chains, newspaper chains, TV networks, theater chains, motion-picture studios. They can't be beaten head on—maybe not even slowed. All anyone can do is make a beginning—to try to speak in human voices to real communities about things that matter. To give up a little slickness for the old earthy tones of rage, bemusement and disgust. To admit sometimes in print that we don't know all the answers. To stop looking at the stars and see for a minute what's under our noses. To give up the mass audience and try to speak to a few people who care.

That, I think, is what the *Independent* aims to do. It's certainly what I'll try to do here each issue. In the vast, tinny, four-color, satellite-down-linked blare, this column will drawl, or whisper, or stutter or rage. It may speak to few or many, but it will aim for journalism with a human voice.

Television and Reality

Neil Postman

Neil Postman (born 1931) was educated at the State University of New York at Fredonia and at Columbia. He has taught elementary and secondary school and is now Professor of Media Ecology at New York University. He is a prolific —and sometimes controversial—writer in the fields of language and educational theory. Among his most recent books are *Crazy Talk, Stupid Talk: How We Defeat Ourselves by the Way We Talk and What to Do About It* (1976); *Teaching as a Conserving Activity* (1979); and *The Disappearance of Childhood* (1982). The selection that follows appeared in the *Phi Delta Kappan* in January 1981.

The Day Our Children Disappear

I am aware that in addressing the question of the future of education, one can write either a "good news" or a "bad news" essay. Typically, a good news essay presents readers with a problem, then proceeds to solve it (more or less). Readers usually find such essays agreeable, as well they should. A good news essay gives us a sense of potency and control, and a really *good* "good news" essay shows us how to employ our imaginations in confronting professional issues. Although I have not yet seen the other essays in this special *Kappan,* I feel sure that most of them are of the good news type, solid and constructive.

A bad news essay, on the other hand, presents readers with a problem —and ends (more or less). Naturally, readers find such essays disagreeable, since they engender a sense of confusion and sometimes hopelessness. Still, they have their uses. They may, for example, help us understand some things that need explaining. Let me tell you, then, that while I hope my remarks will be illuminating, you must prepare yourself for an ortho-dox—even classical—bad news essay. I wish it could be otherwise, because I know my temperament to be more suited to optimism than to gloom and doom. But I write as a person whose academic interests go by the name of media ecology. Media ecology is the study of the effects of communications technology on culture. We study how media affect people's cognitive habits, their social relations, their political biases, and their personal values. And in this capacity I have almost nothing optimistic to write about, for, if I am to respect the evidence as I understand it, I am bound to say that the effects of modern media—especially television—have been and will probably continue to be disastrous, especially for our youth. What I intend to do here is describe in some detail one important respect in which this is the case and explain how it occurred. As is the custom in bad news essays, I shall offer no solution to this problem—mainly because I know of none.

Before proceeding, I must express one bit of "good news" about what I shall be saying. It is to be understood that when I speak of some development as "disastrous," I mean that it is disastrous from my very limited point of view. Obviously, what appears disastrous to me may be regarded as marvelous by others. After all, I am a New Yorker, and most things appear to me disastrous. But even more to the point, what may appear disastrous at one historical moment may turn out to be marvelous in a later age. There are, in fact, many historical instances of someone's correctly predicting negative effects of a medium of communication but where, in the end, what appeared to be a disaster turned out to be a great advance.

The best example I know of concerns the great Athenian teacher, Socrates, who feared and mocked the written word, which in his time was beginning to be used for many purposes and with great frequency. But not by him. As you know, Socrates wrote no books, and had it not been for Plato and Xenophon, who did, we would know almost nothing about him. In one of his most enduring conversations, called the *Phaedrus,* Socrates gives three reasons why he does not like writing. Writing, he says, will deprive Athenians of their powerful memories, for if everything is written down there will be no need to memorize. Second, he says that writing will change the form of education. In particular, it will destroy the dialectic process, for writing forces students to follow an argument rather than participate in it. And third, Socrates warns that writing will change concepts of privacy and the meaning of public discourse, for once you write something down you never know whose eyes will fall upon it—those for whom it is intended, perhaps, but just as likely those for whom it is not intended. Thus, for Socrates, the widespread use of writing was, and would be, a cultural disaster. In a sense it was. For all of Socrates' predictions were correct, and there is no doubt that writing undermined the oral tradition that Socrates believed to be the most suitable mode for expressing serious ideas, beautiful poetry, and authentic piety. But Socrates did not see what his student, Plato, did: that writing would create new modes of thought altogether and provide new and wonderful uses for the intellect—most especially what today we call *science.*

So without intending to suggest an unsupportable comparison, I write as a Socrates-like character, prophesying that the advent of the television age will have the direst outcome. I hope that among you there is a Plato-like character who will be able to see the television age as a blessing.

In order for me to get to the center of my argument as quickly as possible, I am going to resist the temptation to discuss some of the fairly obvious effects of television, such as its role in shortening our students' attention span, in eroding their capacity to handle linguistic and mathematical symbolism, and in causing them to become increasingly impatient with deferred gratification. The evidence for these effects exists in a variety of forms—from declining SAT scores to astronomical budgets for remedial writing classes to the everyday observations of teachers and parents. But I will not take the time to review any of the evidence for the intellectually incapacitating effects of television. Instead, I want to focus on what I regard as the most astonishing and serious effect of television. It is simply this: Television is causing the rapid decline of our concept of childhood. I choose to discuss this because I can think of nothing that is bound to have a more profound effect on our work as educators than that our children should disappear. I do not mean, of course, that they will physically disappear. I mean that the *idea* of children will disappear.

If this pronouncement, on first hearing, seems implausible, let me hasten to tell you that the idea of childhood is not very old. In fact, in the Western world the idea of childhood hardly existed prior to the 16th century. Up until that time children as young as 6 and 7 were not regarded as fundamentally different from adults. As far as historians can tell, the language of children, their dress, their games, their labor, and their legal rights were the same as those of adults. It was recognized, of course, that children tended to be smaller than adults, but this fact did not confer upon them any special status; there were certainly no special institutions for the nurturing of children. Prior to the 16th century, for example, there were no books on child rearing or, indeed, any books about women in their role as mothers. Children, to take another example, were always included in funeral processions, there being no reason anyone could think of to shield them from knowledge of death. Neither did it occur to anyone to keep a picture of a child if that child lived to grow to adulthood or had died in infancy. Nor are there any references to children's speech or jargon prior to the 17th century, after which they are found in abundance. If you have ever seen 13th- or 14th-century paintings of children, you will have noticed that they are always depicted as small adults. Except for size, they are devoid of any of the physical characteristics we associate with childhood, and they are never shown on canvas alone—that is, isolated from adults. Such paintings are entirely accurate representations of the psychological and social perceptions of children prior to the 16th century. Here is how the historian J. H. Plumb puts it:

There was no separate world of childhood. Children shared the same games with adults, the same toys, the same fairy stories. They lived their lives together, never apart. The coarse village festivals depicted by Breughel, showing men and women besotted with drink, groping for each other with unbridled lust, have children eating and drinking with the adults. Even in the soberer pictures of wedding feasts and dances, the children are enjoying themselves alongside their elders, doing the same things.

Barbara Tuchman, in her marvelous book about the 14th century titled *A Distant Mirror,* puts it more succinctly: "If children survived to age 7, their recognized life began, more or less as miniature adults. Childhood was already over."

Now the reasons for this are fairly complicated. For one thing, most children did *not* survive; their mortality rate was extraordinarily high, and it is not until the late 14th century that children are even mentioned in wills and testaments—an indication that adults did not expect them to be around very long. In fact, probably because of this, in some parts of Europe children were treated as neuter genders. In 14th-century Italy, for example, the sex of a child who had died was never recorded.

Certainly, adults did not have the emotional commitment to children that *we* accept as normal. Phillipe Aries, in his great book titled *Centuries of Childhood,* remarks that the prevailing view was to have several children in order to keep a few; people could not allow themselves to become too attached to something that was regarded as a probable loss. Aries quotes from a document that records a remark made by the neighbor of a distraught mother of five young children. In order to comfort the mother, the neighbor says, "Before they are old enough to bother you, you will have lost half of them, or perhaps all of them."

We must also not forget that in a feudal society children were often regarded as mere economic utilities, adults being less interested in the character and intelligence of children than in their capacity for work. But I think the most powerful reason for the absence of the idea of childhood is to be found in the communication environment of the Dark and Middle Ages. Since most people did not know how to read, or did not *need* to know how to read, a child became an adult—a fully participating adult—when he or she learned how to speak. Since all important social transactions involved face-to-face oral communication, full competence to speak and hear—which is usually achieved by age 7—was the dividing line between infancy and adulthood. There was no intervening stage, because none was needed—until the middle of the 15th century. At that point an extraordinary event occurred that not only changed the religious, economic, and political face of Europe but also created our modern idea of childhood. I am referring, of course, to the invention of the printing press. And because in a few minutes you will, perhaps, be thinking that I am claiming too much for the power of modern media, especially TV, it is worth saying now that no one had the slightest inkling in 1450 that the printing press would have such powerful effects on our society as it did.

When Gutenberg announced that he could manufacture books, as he put it, "without the help of reed, stylus, or pen but by wondrous agreement, proportion, and harmony of punches and types," he did not imagine that his invention would undermine the authority of the Catholic Church. Yet less than 80 years later Martin Luther was in effect claiming that, with the Word of God on everyone's kitchen table, Christians did not require the Papacy to interpret it for them. Nor did Gutenberg have any inkling that his invention would create a new class of people: namely, children. Or more specifically, male children, for there is no doubt that boys were the first class of specialized children.

How was this accomplished? Simply by the fact that, less than a hundred years after Gutenberg's invention, European culture became a reading culture; i.e., adulthood was redefined. One could not become an adult unless he or she knew how to read. In order to experience God, one had to be able, obviously, to read the Bible, which is why Luther himself translated the Bible into German. In order to experience literature, one had to be able to read novels and personal essays, forms of literature that were wholly created by the printing press. Our earliest novelists—for example, Richardson and Dcfoe—were themselves printers. Montaigne, who invented the essay, worked hand in hand with a printer, as did Thomas More when he produced what may be called our first science fiction novel—his *Utopia.* Of course, in order to learn science one not only had to know how to read but, by the beginning of the 17th century, one could read science in the vernacular—that is, in one's own language. Sir Francis Bacon's *The Advancement of Learning,* published in 1605, was the first scientific tract an Englishman could read in English. And of course one must not forget the great Dutch humanist, Erasmus, who, understanding the meaning of the printing press as well as anyone, wrote one of the first books of etiquette for the instruction of young men. He said of his book, "As Socrates brought philosophy from heaven to earth, so I have led philosophy to games and banquets." (By the way, Erasmus dedicated the book to his publisher's son, and the book includes advice and guidance on how to convert prostitutes to a moral life.)

The importance of books on etiquette should not be overlooked. As Norbert Elias shows in his book titled *The Civilizing Process,* the sudden emergence in the 16th century of etiquette books signifies that one could no longer assume that children knew everything adults knew—in other words, the separation of childhood from adulthood was under way.

Alongside all of this, Europeans rediscovered what Plato had known about learning to read: namely, that it is best done at an early age. Since reading is, among other things, an unconscious reflex as well as an act of recognition, the habit of reading must be formed in that period when the brain is still engaged in the task of acquiring oral language. The adult who learns to read after his or her oral vocabulary is completed rarely becomes a fluent reader.

What this came to mean in the 16th century is that the young had to be separated from the rest of the community to be taught how to read—that is, to be taught how to function as an adult. This meant that they had to go to school. And going to school was the essential event in creating childhood. The printing press, in other words, created the idea of school. In fact, school classes originated to separate students according to their capacities as readers, not to separate them according to age. That came later. In any event, once all of this occurred it was inevitable that the young would be viewed as a special class of people whose minds and character were qualitatively different from those of adults. As any semanticist can tell you, once you categorize people for a particular purpose, you will soon discover many other reasons why they should be regarded as different. We began, in short, to see human development as a series of stages, with childhood as a bridge between infancy and adulthood. For the past 350 years we have been developing and refining our concept of childhood, this with particular intensity in the 18th, 19th, and 20th centuries. We have been developing and refining institutions for the nurturing of children; and we have conferred upon children a preferred status, reflected in the special ways we expect them to think, talk, dress, play, and learn.

All of this, I believe, is now coming to an end. And it is coming to an end because our communication environment has been radically altered once again—this time by electronic media, especially television. Television has a transforming power at least equal to that of the printing press and possibly as great as that of the alphabet itself. It is my contention that, with the assistance of other media such as radio, film, and records, television has the power to lead us to childhood's end.

Here is how the transformation is happening. To begin with, television presents information mostly in visual images. Although human speech is heard on TV and sometimes assumes importance, people mostly *watch* television. What they watch are rapidly changing visual images—as many as 1,200 different shots every hour. This requires very little conceptual thinking or analytic decoding. TV watching is wholly a matter of pattern recognition. The *symbolic form* of television does not require any special instruction or learning. In America, TV viewing begins at about the age of 18 months; by 30 months, according to studies by Daniel Anderson of the University of Massachusetts, children begin to understand and respond to TV imagery. Thus there is no need for any preparation or prerequisite training for watching TV. Television needs no analogue to the McGuffey *Reader.* And, as you must know, there is no such thing, in reality, as children's programming on TV. Everything is for everybody. So far as symbolic form is concerned, "Charlie's Angels" is as sophisticated or as simple to grasp as "Sesame Street." Unlike books, which vary greatly in syntactical and lexical complexity and which may be scaled according to the ability of the reader, TV presents information in a form that is undifferentiated in its accessibility. And that is why adults and children tend to watch the same programs. I might add, in case you are thinking that children and adults at least watch at different times, that according to Frank Mankiewicz's *Remote Control,* approximately 600,000 children watch TV between midnight and two in the morning.

To summarize: TV erases the dividing line between childhood and adulthood for two reasons: first, because it requires no instruction to grasp its form; second, because it does not segregate its audience. It communicates the same information to everyone simultaneously, regardless of age, sex, race, or level of education.

But it erases the dividing line in other ways as well. One might say that the main difference between an adult and a child is that the adult knows about certain facets of life—its mysteries, its contradictions, its violence, its tragedies—that are not considered suitable for children to know. As children move toward adulthood we reveal these secrets to them in what we believe to be a psychologically assimilable way. But television makes this arrangement quite impossible. Because television operates virtually around the clock—it would not be economically feasible for it to do otherwise—it requires a constant supply of novel and interesting information. This means that all adult secrets—social, sexual, physical, and the like— must be revealed. Television forces the entire culture to come out of the closet. In its quest for new and sensational information to hold its audience, TV must tap every existing taboo in the culture: homosexuality, incest, divorce, promiscuity, corruption, adultery, sadism. Each is now merely a theme for one or another television show. In the process each loses its role as an exclusively adult secret.

Some time ago, while watching a TV program called "The Vidal Sassoon Show," I came across the quintessential example of what I am talking about. Vidal Sassoon is a famous hairdresser whose TV show is a mixture of beauty hints, diet information, health suggestions, and popular psychology. As he came to the end of one segment of the show in which an attractive woman had demonstrated how to cook vegetables, the theme music came up and Sassoon just had time enough to say, "Don't go away. We'll be back with a marvelous new diet and, then, a quick look at incest." Now, this is more—much more—than demystification. It is even more than the revelation of secrets. It is the ultimate trivialization of culture. Television is relentless in both revealing and trivializing all things private and shameful, and therefore it undermines the moral basis of culture. The subject matter of the confessional box and the psychiatrist's office is now in the public domain. I have it on good authority that, shortly, we and our children will have the opportunity to see commercial TV's first experiments with presenting nudity, which will probably not be shocking to anyone, since TV commercials have been offering a form of soft-core pornography for years. And on the subject of commercials—the 700,000 of them that American youths will see in the first 18 years of their lives —they too contribute toward opening to youth all the secrets that once were the province of adults—everything from vaginal sprays to life insurance to the causes of marital conflict. And we must not omit the contributions of news shows, those curious entertainments that daily provide the young with vivid images of adult failure and even madness.

As a consequence of all of this, childhood innocence and specialness are impossible to sustain, which is why children have disappeared from television. Have you noticed that all the children on television shows are depicted as merely small adults, in the manner of 13th- or 14th-century paintings? Watch "The Love Boat" or any of the soap operas or family shows or situation comedies. You will see children whose language, dress, sexuality, and interests are not different from those of the adults on the same shows. Like the paintings of Breughel, the children *do* everything the adults do and are shielded from nothing.

And yet, as TV begins to render invisible the traditional concept of childhood, it would not be quite accurate to say that it immerses us in an adult world. Rather, it uses the material of the adult world as the basis for projecting a new kind of person altogether. We might call this person the adult-child. For reasons that have partly to do with TV's capacity to reach everyone, partly to do with the accessibility of its symbolic form, and partly to do with its commercial base, TV promotes as desirable many of the attitudes that we associate with childishness: for example, an obsessive need for immediate gratification, a lack of concern for consequences, an almost promiscuous preoccupation with consumption. TV seems to favor a population that consists of three age groups: on the one end, infancy; on the other, senility; and in between, a group of indeterminate age where everyone is somewhere between 20 and 30 and remains that way until dotage descends. In *A Distant Mirror,* Tuchman asks the question, Why was childishness so noticeable in medieval behavior, with its marked inability to restrain any kind of impulse? Her answer is that so large a proportion of society was in fact very young in years. Half the population was under 21; a third under 14. If we ask the same question about our own society, we must give a different answer, for about 65 percent of our population is over 21. We are a nation of chronological grown-ups. But TV will have none of it. It is biased toward the behavior of the child-adult.

In this connection, I want to remind you of a TV commercial that sells hand lotion. In it we are shown a mother and daughter and challenged to tell which is which. I find this to be a revealing piece of sociological evidence, for it tells us that in our culture it is considered desirable that a mother should not look older than her daughter, or that a daughter should not look younger than her mother. Whether this means that childhood is gone or adulthood is gone amounts to the same thing, for if there is no clear concept of what it means to be an adult, there can be no concept of what it means to be a child.

In any case, however you wish to phrase the transformation that is taking place, it is clear that the behavior, attitudes, desires, and even physical appearance of adults and children are becoming increasingly indistinguishable. There is now virtually no difference, for example, between adult crimes and children's crimes; in many states the punishments are becoming the same. There is also very little difference in dress. The children's clothing industry has undergone a virtual revolution within the past 10 years, so that there no longer exists what we once unambiguously recognized as children's clothing. Eleven-year-olds wear three-piece suits to birthday parties; 61-year-old men wear jeans to birthday parties. Twelve-year-old girls wear high heels; 42-year-old men wear sneakers. On the streets of New York and Chicago you can see grown women wearing little white socks and imitation Mary Janes. Indeed, among the highest-paid models in America are 12- and 13-year-old girls who are presented as adults. To take another case: Children's games, once so imaginatively rich and varied and so emphatically inappropriate for adults, are rapidly disappearing. Little League baseball and Peewee football, for example, are not only supervised by adults but are modeled in their organization and emotional style on big league sports. The language of children and adults has also been transformed so that, for example, the idea that there may be words that adults ought not to use in the presence of children now seems faintly ridiculous. With TV's relentless revelation of all adult secrets, language secrets are difficult to guard, and it is not inconceivable to me that in the near future we shall return to the 13th- and 14th-century situation in which no words were unfit for a youthful ear. Of course, with the assistance of modern contraceptives, the sexual appetite of both adults and children can be satisfied without serious restraint and without mature understanding of its meaning. Here TV has played an enormous role, since it not only keeps the entire population in a condition of high sexual excitement but stresses a kind of egalitarianism of sexual fulfillment: Sex is transformed from a dark and profound mystery to a product that is available to everyone—like mouthwash or underarm deodorant.

In the 2 November 1980 *New York Times Magazine,* Tuchman offered still another example of the homogenization of childhood and adulthood. She spoke of the declining concept of quality—in literature, in art, in food, in work. Her point was that, with the emergence of egalitarianism as a political and social philosophy, there has followed a diminution of the idea of excellence in all human tasks and modes of expression. The point is that adults are *supposed* to have different tastes and standards from those of children, but through the agency of television and other modern media the differences have largely disappeared. Junk food, once suited only to the undiscriminating palates and iron stomachs of the young, is now common fare for adults. Junk literature, junk music, junk conversation are shared equally by children and adults, so that it is now difficult to find adults who can clarify and articulate for youth the differences between quality and schlock.

It remains for me to mention that there has been a growing movement to recast the legal rights of children so that they are more or less the same as those of adults. The heart of this movement—which, for example, is opposed to compulsory schooling—resides in the claim that what has been thought to be a preferred status for children is instead only an oppression that keeps them from fully participating in the society.

All of this means, I think, that our culture is providing fewer reasons and opportunities for childhood. I am not so single-minded to think that TV alone is responsible for this transformation. The decline of the family, the loss of a sense of roots (40 million Americans change residence every year), and the elimination, through technology, of any significance in adult work are other factors. But I believe that television creates a communication context which encourages the idea that childhood is neither desirable nor necessary—indeed, that we do not need children. I said earlier, in talking about childhood's end, that I did not mean the physical disappearance of children. But in fact that, too, is happening. The birthrate in America is declining and has been for a decade, which is why schools are being closed all over the country.

This brings me to the final characteristic of TV that needs mentioning. The *idea* of children implies a vision of the future. They are the living messages we send to a time we will not see. But television cannot communicate a sense of the future or, for that matter, a sense of the past. It is a present-centered medium, a speed-of-light medium. Everything we see on television is experienced as happening *now,* which is why we must be told, in language, that a videotape we are seeing was made months before. The grammar of television has no analogue to the past and future tenses in language. Thus it amplifies the present out of all proportion and transforms the childish need for immediate gratification into a way of life. And we end up with what Christopher Lasch calls "the culture of narcissism"—no future, no children, everyone fixed at an age somewhere between 20 and 30.

Of course I cannot know what all of this means to you, but my own position, I'm sure, is clear. I believe that what I have been describing is disastrous—partly because I value the charm, curiosity, malleability, and innocence of childhood, which is what first drew me to a career in education, and partly because I believe that adults need, first, to be children before they can be grown-ups. For otherwise they remain like TV's adult-child all their lives, with no sense of belonging, no capacity for lasting relationships, no respect for limits, and no grasp of the future. But mainly I think it is disastrous because it makes problematic the future of school, which is one of the few institutions still based on the assumption that there are significant differences between children and adults and that adults therefore have something of value to teach children.

So my bad news essay comes down to these questions: In a world in which children are adults and adults children, what need is there for people like ourselves? Are the issues we are devoting our careers to solving being rendered irrelevant by the transforming power of our television culture? I devoutly hope your answers to these questions are more satisfactory than mine.

Henry Fairlie

Henry Fairlie, born in England in 1924, has written, as he says, "on both sides of the Atlantic." Educated at London's Highgate School and Oxford, he wrote for the London *Observer* and was the main political editorial writer for the London *Times* until he resigned in 1954 to free-lance in England and the United States. (In a political column in *The Spectator* in 1955, he was the first person to use the term "Establishment" in its modern sense—to refer to a group of powerful people who somehow control government or society.) Fairlie has also written for *Punch* and the *New Statesman,* and he has been a foreign correspondent for the *Daily Mail.* While still in England, Fairlie did reporting for several television documentaries, but he stopped because, as he explained in an article in *Encounter,* television is an "idiot box," and "if you've seen it on television, it didn't happen."

Fairlie has lived in the United States since 1966, contributing to such periodicals as the *New York Times Magazine, The New Yorker,* the *New Republic,* and the *Washington Post.* His books include *The Life of Politics* (1968); *The Kennedy Promise* (1973); *The Spoiled Child of the Western World: The Miscarriage of the American Idea in Our Time* (1976); and, published in 1978, two books expanded from essays, *The Parties* and *The Seven Deadly Sins Today.* The essay reprinted here first appeared in the Spring 1967 *Horizon.*

Can You Believe Your Eyes?

None of us has ever seen Alexander the Great emerging from his tent. If there had been television in his day and we could look at the tape, would we know him any better, as we think we now know a John F. Kennedy or a Lyndon B. Johnson when we see them, on television news, emerging from a convention?

None of us has ever heard Julius Caesar speak. But if there had been radio in his day and we could listen to the recording, would we know him any better, as we think we know something important about Franklin D. Roosevelt from his fireside chats?°

The answer is far from clear. Of all historical evidence, the public pres-

fireside chats   Radio broadcasts by President Franklin D. Roosevelt to the nation during the 1930s, in which he discussed his policies for dealing with the Great Depression.

ence of voice or of physical appearance is the most revealing but can also be the most misleading. Yet the problem of historical evidence is raised every night on television news, when we are asked to accept what we see and hear as genuine. It is raised especially by the two most important television news programs in the United States: Huntley-Brinkley on NBC, and Walter Cronkite on CBS. Millions of people have to decide not so much whether they can believe what they are told but whether they can believe what they see flickering in front of them.

"The evidence of their own eyes": but that is precisely what is not available to them. What *is* available is the evidence, first, of the camera, making its own selection, dictating its own terms; and it is the evidence, then, of the small screen—still the best description of television—which in turn dictates to the camera. Can television, by its nature, ever tell the truth?

Amid all the pretentiousness of his theorizing, Marshall McLuhan is right to this extent: the medium is the message. Television does not merely create news. That is an old business, practiced for generations by newspapers. Television creates its own events, something even the most imaginative newspaper reporter cannot do. The newspaperman can only create words, and however powerful they may be, words do not *happen* over the breakfast table as television *happens* in a living room. Thomas W. Moore, ABC's president, came very near to the point when he said: "It is difficult to retain one's perspective when, without leaving the security of our living rooms, we become witness to such startling events as the assassination of an assassin, or a war in progress."

It is because television *happens* in this way that people begin to think that the small excerpts from life which they see on the screen in their living rooms are more "real" than the life which they experience around them. There is a vital margin of difference between saying, "Did you see the report in *The New York Times* of the massacres in the Congo?" and saying, "Did you see the massacres in the Congo on television last night?" The first remark implies only that one has seen a report (which may conflict with a report from another source). The second implies that one has seen the event itself. However carefully television is used, it cannot avoid this deception.

It is doubtful whether it is ever easy—sometimes whether it is ever possible—for a newspaper or television reporter to report an event. He can report incidents, and it is the nature of incidents that they can, and do, happen in isolation. But the true meaning of an event depends on all of its known and unknown causes, on all of the known and unknown incidents that contribute to it, and in the process, cease to be isolated, and on all of its known and unknown repercussions. The whole of an incident can easily be described; the whole of an event may escape even the historian.

If this is a difficulty that confronts the newspaper reporter from day to day, it is one that the television reporter can rarely overcome. For the newspaper reporter possesses a flexibility that the television reporter does not have. He has flexibility because he can move without the paraphernalia and encumbrance of a camera or a camera crew. He has flexibility because he can reach where the camera cannot reach: the camera can never go "off the record."

The newspaperman has flexibility, above all, because words are flexible and the length of a story is flexible: the one able to qualify, even in the shortest parenthetical expression; the other capable of imposing its own perspective. But however carefully chosen the words of a television reporter, they can never properly qualify a spectacular picture; and however discriminating the apportionment of stories in a television program, they are in length too nearly the same.

Incidents are usually in the open; the whole of an event, often obscure and private. Not only is the core of television the public and the spectacular, but there is an important sense in which television has a vested interest in disaster. From the point of view of a good story, both newspapers and television prefer covering a major strike to negotiations which prevent a strike. But it is possible for the newspaper reporter to make negotiations almost as exciting a story as a strike itself: by word of mouth, he can collect a picture of the coming and goings which are the essence of negotiation and, by his words in print, vividly describe them. But what can television do with negotiations? It can only show pictures of people arriving at a building and people leaving it. However colorful they may be—and the modern business executive is not normally colorful—this does not make exciting viewing.

Violence is the stuff of television, and the question of how to deal with it is the most important one confronting the medium.

To be sure, the same question confronts newspapers; but the impact of violence—whether a boxing match, a riot, or a massacre—is much greater in a moving picture than in a still picture or in descriptive prose. Violence is movement—the raising of an arm, the smashing of it on someone's head —and movement is what television cannot help emphasizing.

In covering violent situations, three distinct characteristics of television conspire to intensify both its special problems and the special temptations to which it is exposed. There is, first, the limitation of time. A lead news story in a paper such as *The New York Times* may take twenty minutes to read; in a popular newspaper or a tabloid, as many as ten. There simply is not this time available in television news. In the reporting of all news, this means concentration to the point of distortion. In the reporting of violence, it means concentration on the violent incident to the exclusion of the whole event.

An outstanding example of such distortion was the police attack on civil rights marchers at the Selma, Alabama, bridge in March, 1965. I was not present myself. But I do not know one reporter who was present, and whose opinion I trust, who does not point out that there was first a prolonged period during which police and demonstrators faced each other, without violence, in an atmosphere of unbearable tension, and who does not agree that the tension had to break in the form of police action.

Television news—except in special features and documentaries—did not, and could not, show this preliminary encounter. Three minutes of film is an extended sequence in a news program, and the time is best filled with action, not inaction. On the other hand, a single phrase in a newspaper story, placed correctly, where it carries weight, can put even an extended description of violence in perspective.

The point of such perspective is not to excuse any eventual police brutality, but to explain it. Without this explanation, whether implicit or explicit, one begins to think that brutality is automatic, that the police will always behave in such a manner; demonstrators begin to think that they can, and should, goad the police; and the police begin to think, since restraint is so frail anyhow, they may as well give way to exasperation from the start.

There is, secondly, television's tendency to produce self-generating news. The problem arose most notably during the disturbances in Watts; but it has arisen, again and again, whenever there have been similar disturbances in other cities. However spontaneous the original outbreak of violence, an external provocation is added once it has occurred. That provocation is the presence of television cameras in the middle of the trouble spots.

This is especially true on the night after the original outbreak. Then, as dusk gathers, television cameramen and reporters move into the streets looking—literally looking—for trouble, and the crowds begin to play up to them. Their presence is very different from the presence of newspaper reporters, who either roam around, hardly distinguishable, or lounge in bars until they hear that action has broken out somewhere down the block. Television, merely by its presence, helps to create incidents and then itself remains part of the happening. There is no doubt that this participation occurred after the first night in Watts, and that it occurred again last summer in Chicago.

But in order to create on the screen the impression of continuing disturbance, of continuing riots, television needs only one incident. One spectacular incident of violence can occupy a two-minute sequence in a news program just as impressively as a series of incidents. Much of the Watts film is a classic example of this: showing that it needs only one defiant boy and only one hot-headed policeman to suggest that a neighborhood is aflame.

In this connection it seems worth pointing out that a newspaper reporter's dishonesty—or imagination—can be a great deal less dangerous and provocative than a television reporter's. The newspaper reporter, after all, need only create—or exaggerate—a story in his own mind. But the television reporter must create—or exaggerate—it in actuality: he must make it a happening.

Finally, in this matter of violence, there is the size of the screen: the limitations which it imposes, the temptations it offers. At the end of last summer, television news showed some alarming pictures of white men and women in the Chicago suburb of Cicero screaming abuse at some Negro marchers. Their hating faces—a dozen of them, perhaps—filled the screen. They looked as if they were a representative example of a much larger crowd. But anyone who was there knows that these particular whites were only a small part of the crowds in the streets; and that the crowds themselves were only a small part of the total white population of Cicero. To this vital extent, television that night distorted badly.

What all this amounts to is not only that people sitting in their homes begin to think that all police are brutal, that all demonstrators are violent, that all disturbances are riots, that all crowds are aggressive; the fact that they usually go through each day without either meeting or themselves displaying violence becomes less real to them than the violence on the small screen.

Anyone who has appeared regularly on television knows that complete strangers think they have actually met him. They smile or nod at him in the street or across bars; they approach him and shake his hand; they even ask him to drop in when next he is around their way, as if they really believe that he has been in their homes. It is this imaginary "real" presence of television in people's living rooms which is the background to the whole problem. Surely much of the feeling of living in a condition of perpetual crisis, and the agitation arising from it, comes from a sense of being a witness to a world which is more actual than the routine world in which one lives.

Television can create, not only events out of incidents, but movements and people. The television news coverage of the Meredith° march across Mississippi, during the couple of days when I accompanied it myself, constantly appalled me. It was near the beginning of the march, when it had barely gotten organized, and when the numbers were few and the individuals composing the numbers were anything but impressive.

All the familiar hazards of television reporting were displayed. A straggling column—it was at the time little more—could be made on the small screen to look like an army. When the cameras were rolling, the marchers pulled themselves together and played the role expected of them. The several civil rights leaders strode in line abreast, at the head of their enthusiastic followers.

The real story of the Meredith march was not this unified demonstration at all, but the fact that it produced the deeply significant clash between different factions of the civil rights movement over "black power." Newspapers felt their way to this story and were, by the end, reporting it fully. It was a story which, for the most part, was taking place in private meet-

Meredith James Meredith, marching to spur voter registration in Mississippi in 1966, was wounded in an assassination attempt on the highway. Martin Luther King, Jr., Stokely Carmichael, and other civil rights workers resumed the march, which ended after 200 miles with a rally of 30,000 people in Jackson, Mississippi.

ings where the cameras could not reach. But then when television at last caught on to the fact of "black power," it inevitably exaggerated and distorted it. Film is expensive. Getting film ready for a news program is a hurried job. The result is that in reporting any speech the television reporter and cameraman make an automatic, almost involuntary, selection. They wait for the mention of a phrase like "black power," and on go the lights and the film rolls.

But, given the length of the usual sequence in a news program, that is all. The impact is far greater than that of any selection made by newspapers. By constant reiteration on the small screen day after day, the slogan of "black power" was elevated into a movement. It was suddenly there. It had suddenly happened. "Black power" switched the cameras on, and in turn the cameras switched the movement on. It was a classic case of self-generating news.

Stokely Carmichael, of the Student Nonviolent Co-ordinating Committee, could not have emerged so rapidly as a national figure without television. (SNCC is a master at using television.) But he is not the only example of television's ability to create—or destroy—people. No one, I think, questions that Governor Ronald Reagan is the creature of the television cameras, just as previously Actor Ronald Reagan was the creature of the movie cameras. John Morgan, one of the British Broadcasting Corporation's most experienced television reporters, returned from the California gubernatorial campaign last fall, amazed at Reagan's professionalism in the television studio, and the use that he made of it to dictate camera angles and even the moments for close-ups.

Much of the poor impression that President Johnson has often made is the direct result of his comparatively poor television "image." The close-up, especially, can distort in the crudest way and make what is simply unprepossessing actually repellent. In fact, in considering the impact of the close-up, one can notice the vital difference between television and the movies; between what is legitimate in the cinema and illegitimate in a living room.

Movies are intended to be, and are taken to be, larger than life. Sitting in the theatre, one does not imagine that what one is seeing is real. The close-up in the movies, therefore, is a legitimate *and understood* distortion. But a distortion it is. We never do see anyone in real life as close in as the camera can go, except in one position and in one activity: when making love. There is no reason why President Johnson, or any other public figure, should have to pass this private test in public. Moreover, not only does the close-up bring one ridiculously close to a face, it shows it in isolation. It removes the general bearing; it removes the whole man.

Perhaps the most striking demonstration of the power of television to create personalities is one that most people will think also demonstrates its power for good. For a comparatively short time three men seemed to bestride the world: John F. Kennedy, Pope John XXIII, and Nikita Khrushchev. Their impact, all over the world, was quite out of proportion to the length of time any of them held office. In a few years they had made as great an impression as Queen Victoria had in sixty years. This was the work of television.

Television news is new, and we have not yet got the measure of it. Its hazards are numerous: some of them are inherent in the nature of the medium, and are likely to be permanent. Others are more technical and, with technical advances, may be removed.

Camera crews are costly, and costly to move about; this automatically imposes a preselection of news far more rigorous than it is in a newspaper. Film costs impose a second automatic selection. Time on the screen is expensive, and this imposes a final selection. Again and again, when I have been making news films with a camera crew, I have wanted to utter over the pictures, "It was not like this at all."

However paradoxical it may seem, the only immediate answer to most of the problems of television news lies not in pictures but in words. Given the powerful impact of the pictures, the words covering them must provide the corrective. Most television reporting just describes the pictures, and by doing so, reinforces them. But the object of words in television news should be to distract from the pictures, to say: "It was not quite so. This was not the whole story." Pictures simplify; the object of words should be to supply qualification and complication. Pictures involve; the object of words should be to detach the viewer, to remind him that he is not seeing an event, only an impression of one.

The manner of delivery—especially of the "anchor" men in the studio —is as important as the substance of the words themselves. There is something very professional and very engaging about the television manners of Chet Huntley and David Brinkley and Walter Cronkite. All of them, in dissimilar ways, cultivate a deadpan approach. In Huntley, it is made to suggest a judicial impartiality; in Brinkley, an ironical detachment; in Cronkite, an unfailing common sense. Each of them by his manner reinforces the impact of the pictures over which he is speaking, suggesting that they can be taken at their face value.

Only now and then, when Brinkley's irony is allowed to break loose into that overnourished flicker of a smile, is the value of the pictures ever questioned. The vital role of the television reporter or commentator is to make watching as difficult as reading, to invite the viewer to make comparisons and judgments from his own experience so that he never reacts by assuming that he is seeing actual life.

That television news can do some things remarkably well, especially in full-length features and documentaries, that those involved in making television programs are conscientious and skillful, does not touch the main problem. Television news holds a mirror up to the world in a way that newspapers never can; and the world is beginning to believe that it can recognize itself in it. Life is not made up of dramatic incidents—not even the life of a nation. It is made up of slowly evolving events and processes, which newspapers, by a score of different forms of emphasis, can reasonably attempt to explore from day to day.

But television news jerks from incident to incident. For the real world of patient and familiar arrangements, it substitutes an unreal world of constant activity, and the effect is already apparent in the way in which the world behaves. It is almost impossible, these days, to consider any problem or any event except as a crisis; and, by this very way of looking at it, it in fact becomes a crisis.

Television, by its emphasis on movement and activity, by its appetite for incident, has become by far the most potent instrument in creating this overexcited atmosphere, this barely recognizable world. The medium, to this very important extent, has become the message; and the message is perpetual stimulation, perpetual agitation, perpetual change. The world it creates is a world which is never still.

Many of our unnecessary anxieties about the way in which we live, about the fearful things that may happen to us, might be allayed if television news began, now and then, to say: "It has been a dull day. But we have collected some rather interesting pictures for you, of no particular significance." Television news has a deep responsibility to try to be dull, from time to time, and let the world go to sleep.

Jack McGarvey

Jack McGarvey (born 1937) was educated at Clarion State College in Pennsylvania and at the University of Connecticut. He has been a teacher of English for 20 years; at present he is a teaching administrator at Bedford Junior High School in Westport, Connecticut, developing a middle-school philosophy and curriculum that will cross disciplines and combine skill and content. He is also a free-lance writer whose articles have appeared in such national magazines as *McCall's* and *Parents.* The piece reprinted here is from the February–March 1982 issue of *Today's Education.*

To Be or Not to Be
as Defined by TV

A couple of years ago, a television crew came to film my ninth grade English class at Bedford Junior High School in Westport, Connecticut. I'm still trying to understand what happened.

I was doing some work with my students, teaching them to analyze the language used in television commercials. After dissecting the advertising claims, most of the class became upset over what they felt were misleading —and in a few cases, untruthful—uses of language. We decided to write to the companies that presented their products inaccurately or offensively. Most of them responded with chirpy letters and cents-off coupons. Some did not respond at all.

I then decided to contact *Buyline,* a consumer advocate program aired on New York City's WNBC-TV at the time. The show and its host, Betty Furness, were well-known for their investigation of consumer complaints. I sent off a packet of the unanswered letters with a brief explanation of the class's work.

About a week later, the show's producer telephoned me. She said that she'd seen the letters and was interested in the class's project. Could she and her director come to Westport to have a look?

I said sure and told her about a role-playing activity I was planning to do with my students. I said I was going to organize my class of 24 students into four committees—each one consisting of two representatives from the Federal Trade Commission (FTC), the agency that monitors truth in advertising; two advertising executives anxious to have their material used; and two TV executives caught somewhere in the middle—wanting to please the advertisers while not offending the FTC. Then, I would ask each committee to assume that there had been a complaint about the language used in a TV commercial, and that the committees had to resolve the complaint. "That sounds great! I'll bring a crew," she said.

I obtained clearance from my school district's office, and the next morning, as I was walking into school, I met one of my students and casually let out the word: "WNBC's coming to film our class this afternoon."

I was totally unprepared for what happened. Word spread around school within five minutes. Students who barely knew me rushed up to squeal, "Is it true? Is it really, really true? A TV crew is coming to Bedford to film?" A girl who was not in my class pinned me into a corner near the magazine rack in the library to ask me whether she could sit in my class for the day. Another girl went to her counselor and requested an immediate change in English classes, claiming a long-standing personality conflict with her current teacher.

Later, things calmed down a bit, but as I took my regular turn as cafeteria supervisor, I saw students staring wide-eyed at me, then turning to whisper excitedly to their friends. I'd become a celebrity simply because I was the one responsible for bringing a TV crew to school.

Right after lunch, the show's producer and director came to my class to look it over and watch the role-playing activity; they planned to tape near the end of the school day. The two women were gracious and self-effacing, taking pains not to create any disturbance; but the students, of course, knew why they were there. There were no vacant stares, no hair brushes, no gum chewers, and no note scribblers. It was total concentration, and I enjoyed one of my best classes in more than 15 years of teaching.

After the class, I met with the producer and director to plan the taping. They talked about some of the students they'd seen and mentioned Susan. "She's terribly photogenic and very, very good with words." They mentioned Steve. "He really chaired his committee well. Real leadership there. Handsome boy, too." They mentioned Jim, Pete, Randy, and Jenny and their insights into advertising claims. Gradually I became aware that we were engaged in a talent hunt; we were looking for a strong and attractive group to be featured in the taping.

We continued the discussion, deciding on the players. We also discussed the sequencing of the taping session. First, I'd do an introduction, explaining the role-playing activity as if the class had never heard of it. Then, I'd follow with the conclusion—summarizing remarks ending with a cheery "See you tomorrow!"—and dismiss the class. The bit players would leave the school and go home. We'd then rearrange the set and film the photogenic and perceptive featured players while they discussed advertising claims as a committee. Obviously, this is not the way I'd conduct an actual class, but it made sense. After all, I wanted my students to look good, and I wanted to look good.

"It'll be very hard work," the producer cautioned. "I trust your students understand that."

"It's already been hard work," I remarked as I thought of possible jealousies and bruised feelings over our choices of featured players.

About a half hour before school's end, the crew set up cameras and lights in the hall near the classroom we'd be working in, a room in an isolated part of the building. But as the crew began filming background shots of the normal passing of students through the hall, near chaos broke out.

Hordes of students suddenly appeared. A basketball star gangled through the milling mob to do an imitation of Nureyev, topping off a pirouette by feigning a couple of jump shots. A pretty girl walked back and forth in front of the cameras at least a dozen times before she was snared by a home economics teacher. Three boys did a noisy pantomime of opening jammed lockers, none of which were theirs. A faculty member, seen rarely in this part of the building, managed to work his way through the crowd, smiling broadly. And as members of my class struggled through the press of bodies, they were hailed, clutched at, patted on the back, and hugged.

"Knock 'em dead!" I heard a student call.

It took the vice-principal and five teachers 10 minutes to clear the hall.

We assembled the cast, arranged the furniture, erased several mild obscenities from the chalkboard, and pulled down the window shades—disappointing a clutch of spectators outside. The producer then introduced the crew and explained their work.

I was wired with a mike and the crew set up a boom microphone, while the girls checked each other's make-up and the boys sat squirming.

Finally, the taping began. It was show business, a performance, a total alteration of the reality I know as a teacher. As soon as I began the introduction, 26 pairs of eyes focused on me as if I were Billy Joel about to sing. I was instantly startled and self-conscious. When I asked a question, some of the usually quieter students leaped to respond. This so unsettled me that I forgot what I was saying and had to begin again.

The novelty of being on camera, however, soon passed. We had to do retakes because the soundman missed student responses from the rear of the room. The director asked me to rephrase a question and asked a student to rephrase a response. There were delays while technicians adjusted equipment.

We all became very much aware of being performers, and some of the students who had been most excited about making their TV debut began to grumble about the hard work. That pleased me, for a new reality began to creep in: Television is not altogether glamorous.

We taped for almost five hours, on more than 3,200 feet of video tape. That is almost an hour-and-a-half's worth, more than double a normal class period. And out of that mass of celluloid the producer said she'd use seven minutes on the program!

Two days later, five students and I went to the NBC studios at Rockefeller Center to do a taping of a final segment. The producer wanted to do a studio recreation of the role-playing game. This time, however, the game would include real executives—one from advertising, one from the NBC network, and one from the FTC. We'd be part of a panel discussion moderated by Betty Furness. My students would challenge the TV and the advertising executives, asking them to justify some of the bothersome language used in current commercials.

This was the most arduous part of the experience. The taping was live, meaning that the cameras would run for no longer than eight minutes. As we ate turkey and ham during a break with Ms. Furness and the guest executives, I realized that we were with people who were totally comfortable with television. I began to worry. How could mere 14-year-olds compete in a debate with those to whom being on television is as ordinary as riding a school bus?

But my concern soon disappeared. As Ms. Furness began reading her TelePrompTer, Susan leaned over and whispered, "This is fun!" And it was Susan who struck first. " 'You can see how luxurious my hair feels' is a perfect example of the silly language your ad writers use," she said with all the poise of a Barbara Walters. "It's impossible to *see* how something feels," she went on.

That pleased me, for as an English teacher, I've always emphasized the value of striving for precision in the use of language. The work we'd done with TV commercials, where suggestibility is the rule, had taken hold, I thought, as the ad executive fumbled for a response. The tension vanished, and we did well.

The show aired two weeks later, and I had it taped so the class could view it together. It was a slick production, complete with music—"Hey, Big Spender"—to develop a theme for Ms. Furness' introduction. "Teens are big business these days," she said. "Does television advertising influence how they spend their money?" Then followed a shot of students in the hall—edited to show none of the wildness that actually occurred. Next, three of my students appeared in brief clips of interviews. They were asked, "Have you ever been disappointed by television advertising?" The responses were, "Yes, of course," and I was pleased with their detailed answers. Finally, the classroom appeared, and there I was, lounging against my desk, smiling calmly. I looked good—a young, unrumpled Orson Bean, with a cool blue-and-brown paisley tie. My voice was mellifluous. Gee, I thought as I saw the tape, I could have been a TV personality.

Now, I am probably no more vain than most people. But television does strange things to the ego. I became so absorbed in studying the image of myself that the whole point of the show passed me by. I didn't even notice that I'd made a goof analyzing a commercial until I'd seen the show three times. The students who participated were the same; watching themselves on videotape, they missed what they had said. I had an enormous struggle to get both them and me to recall the hard work and to see the obvious editing. It was as if reality had been reversed: The actual process of putting together the tape was not real, but the product was.

I showed the tape again last year to my ninth grade class. I carefully explained to this delightful gang of fault-finders how the taping had been done. I told them about the changed sequence, the selection of the featured players, the takes and retakes. They themselves had just been through the same role-playing activity, and I asked them to listen carefully to what was said. They nodded happily and set their flinty minds to look at things critically. But as the tape ended, they wanted to tease me about how ugly and wrinkled I looked. They wanted to say, "That's Randy! He goes to Compo Beach all the time." "Jenny's eye shadow—horrible!" "When will you get us on TV?"

The visual image had worked its magic once again: They had missed the point of the show altogether. And, as I dismissed them, I felt something vibrating in their glances and voices—the celebrity image at work again. I was no longer their mundane English teacher: I was a TV personality.

I decided to show the tape again the next day. I reviewed the hard work, the editing, the slick packaging. I passed out questions so we could focus on what had been said on the program. I turned on the recorder and turned off the picture to let them hear only the sound. They protested loudly, of course. But I was determined to force them to respond to how effectively the previous year's class had taken apart the language used in the claims of commercials. This was, after all, the point of the program. And it worked, finally.

As class ended, one of the students drifted up to me. "What are we going to do next?" she asked.

"We're going to make some comparisons between TV news shows and what's written in newspapers," I replied.

"Do they put together news shows the way they filmed your class?"

"It's similar and usually much quicker," I answered.

She smiled and shook her head. "It's getting hard to believe anything anymore."

In that comment lies what every TV viewer should have—a healthy measure of beautiful, glorious skepticism. But as I said, I'm still trying to understand that taping session. And I'm aware of how hard it is to practice skepticism. Every time I see the *Buyline* tape, I'm struck by how good a teacher TV made me. Am I really that warm, intelligent, creative, and good-looking? Of course not. But TV made me that way. I like it, and sometimes I find myself still hoping that I am what television defined me to be.

I sometimes think children have superior knowledge of TV. They know, from many years of watching it, that the product in all its edited glory is the only reality. Shortly after the program aired on that February Saturday two years ago, our telephone rang. The voice belonged to my daughter's 11-year-old friend. She said, "I just saw you on TV. May I have your autograph?"

I was baffled. After all, this was the boisterous girl who played with my daughter just about every day and who mostly regarded me as a piece of furniture that occasionally mumbled something about lowering your voices. "Are you serious?" I croaked.

"May I have your autograph?" she repeated, ignoring my question. "I can come over right now." Her voice was without guile.

She came. And I signed while she scrutinized my face, her eyes still aglow with Chromacolor.

To Stephanie, television had transformed a kindly grump into something real. And there is no doubt in my mind whatsoever that in the deepest part of her soul is the fervent dream that her being, too, will someday be defined and literally affirmed by an appearance on television.

Lately, my ninth grade class has been growing restless. Shall I move up the TV unit and bring out the tape again? Shall I remind them what a great teacher they have? Shall I remind myself what a fine teacher I am? Shall I renew their—and my—hope?

To be or not to be as defined by TV? Does that question suggest what makes television so totally unlike any other medium?

George Gerbner

George Gerbner was born in Budapest, Hungary, in 1919. At the age of twenty he came to the United States, where he studied at UCLA, at Berkeley and at the University of Southern California (Ph.D., 1955). He has worked as journalist, editor, and public-relations representative, and has taught journalism, social science and mass communications. Since 1964 he has been Professor of Mass Communications and Dean of the Annenberg School of Communications at the University of Pennsylvania.

Gerbner is a distinguished student of television programming—its contents and its effects. He has studied the portrayal of mental illness in the mass media, the portrayal of scientists on television, popular conceptions of education, and films and the film hero. He is perhaps best known for his studies of violence in network television drama. The piece we print here is from the Fall 1977 *Business and Society Review.*

Controller of Our Fears

My research associates and I have been working on defining and measuring the nature and effects of violence on television for almost a decade. We believe that the problem has been greatly oversimplified and distorted on *both* sides of the issue. Test it yourself by considering the following common propositions:

1. The goal of violence is to hurt or kill.
2. All violence is basically alike.
3. Violence on television is like violence in movies and books.
4. Violence on television reflects a violent world.
5. The main danger of television violence is that it makes children (and perhaps other viewers) more aggressive and violent.
6. Scientists have no evidence so far that television viewing alone has any significant and systematic effect on behavior.

Do these propositions sound plausible? Of course they do. But they are all false.

Violence is the expression of force intended to hurt or kill if necessary to accomplish a given goal. Except in a relatively few pathological cases, the goal is to dominate, to conquer, to control. But violence need not actually hurt or kill in order to be effective; it needs only to generate enough fear of being hurt or killed so that people will obey to or acquiesce in something they otherwise would not do. Most violence, from wars to muggings, is basically a demonstration of power to compel action against the victim's will. Its immediate objective is fear; its more distant goal is power.

Telling the story of violence is not the same as committing it (although as a show of force, it may have the same end result). To strike out against brutality and injustice is not the same as to perpetrate them. When we see violence on television we do not call the police or an ambulance, but we absorb the message of the act. If the message helps us distinguish between just and unjust uses of power, the violence may be a legitimate dramatic element that serves liberating ends. If the message gratuitously cultivates prejudice and fear or acquiescence to inhuman and unjust uses of power, or if it offers a ritualistic and dramatically cheap solution to any conflict, it becomes a legitimate cause for serious concern.

Violence on television is not like that in movies or books because television is a very different medium. People don't have to know how to read or to go anywhere to see it. Television comes to the homes of all classes and groups, everywhere in the industrialized world. And it is used indiscriminately; most people watch by the clock, not by the program, and the TV clock runs for over six hours a day in the average U.S. household. TV is like the environment: it is everywhere; it is indivisible; and it is inescapable.

Ours may be a violent world, but television presents a distorted picture of its violence. The leading causes of injury and violent death are highway and industrial accidents, but we rarely see those on television. Rather, television presents the types of violence which best serve its dramatic and social functions, i.e., violence which demonstrates how power works in society and shows who can get away with what.

In demonstrating selectively how power works and what types of people run what kinds of risks, television presents victims as well as victimizers. And it generates fear—the real goal of violence—as well as aggression. Furthermore, in stereotyping people and their fates, television sets up a pattern of fears so that some groups of people can exercise more power than others. Common notions of fear, prejudice, and power are enhanced by violent television programming, and this may have far-reaching consequences on the public's thinking and behavior.

There is sufficient scientific evidence to conclude that television alone, as well as in combination with other social and cultural factors, makes a significant and systematic difference in the way viewers deal with reality. Such evidence comes from our long-range research project called Cultural Indicators, including the Violence Index and Profile, conducted for the Eisenhower Commission, the Surgeon General, the National Institute of Mental Health, and now also the American Medical Association. The evidence shows that heavy viewing of television, independent of other facts of life, induces an exaggerated sense of danger, mistrust, and vulnerability.

Irrationally fearful citizens may demand ever more protection and ultimately repression by the authorities as both a release from and a confirmation of their fears. For in setting up a scenario of domination and control by manipulating our fears, symbolic violence achieves the purposes of real violence. That is the ultimate menace of violence on television.

The Language of Advertising

Daniel Boorstin

Daniel Boorstin, historian, educator, and Pulitzer Prize-winning author, was born in 1914, grew up in Tulsa, and received his B.A. *summa cum laude* from Harvard in 1934. A Rhodes Scholar, he attended Balliol College at Oxford and read law at the Inner Temple in London, becoming one of the few Americans qualified to plead cases in English courts. Boorstin returned to the United States to teach at Harvard and attend Yale Law School (J.S.D., 1940); he was admitted to the Massachusetts bar in 1942. He served on the faculty of the University of Chicago from 1944 to 1969, where he was the Preston and Sterling Morton Distinguished Service Professor of History. Boorstin has served on a number of commissions and boards, was director of the Smithsonian Institution's National Museum of History and Technology (1969–1973), became Librarian of Congress in 1975, and has received many honors and awards for his work.

The Americans, his *magnum opus,* has earned a number of prizes. The first volume, *The Colonial Experience* (1958), won the 1959 Bancroft Prize for books in American history, diplomacy, and international relations; the second, *The National Experience* (1973), was awarded the 1974 Pulitzer Prize, as well as the Dexter Prize. He has written many other books on history and the law, including *The Genius of American Politics* (1953) and the two-volume *Landmark History of the American People* (1968 and 1970). In *The Image; or, What Happened to the American Dream* (1962), he maintains that the mass media create "pseudo-events," so that contemporary Americans live in a world of self-created illusions.

The following essay first appeared in his *Democracy and Its Discontents* (1974) and was featured in the bicentennial issue of *Advertising Age,* the advertising industry's magazine.

The Rhetoric of Democracy

Advertising, of course, has been part of the mainstream of American civilization, although you might not know it if you read the most respectable surveys of American history. It has been one of the enticements to the settlement of this New World, it has been a producer of the peopling of the United States, and in its modern form, in its world-wide reach, it has been one of our most characteristic products.

Never was there a more outrageous or more unscrupulous or more ill-informed advertising campaign than that by which the promoters for the American colonies brought settlers here. Brochures published in England in the seventeenth century, some even earlier, were full of hopeful overstatements, half-truths, and downright lies, along with some facts which nowadays surely would be the basis for a restraining order from the Federal Trade Commission. Gold and silver, fountains of youth, plenty of fish, venison without limit, all these were promised, and of course some of them were found. It would be interesting to speculate on how long it might have taken to settle this continent if there had not been such promotion by enterprising advertisers. How has American civilization been shaped by the fact that there was a kind of natural selection here of those people who were willing to believe advertising?

Advertising has taken the lead in promising and exploiting the new. This was a new world, and one of the advertisements for it appears on the dollar bill on the Great Seal of the United States, which reads *novus ordo seclorum,* one of the most effective advertising slogans to come out of this country. "A new order of the centuries"—belief in novelty and in the desirability of opening novelty to everybody has been important in our lives throughout our history and especially in this century. Again and again advertising has been an agency for inducing Americans to try anything and everything—from the continent itself to a new brand of soap. As one of the more literate and poetic of the advertising copywriters, James Kenneth Frazier, a Cornell graduate, wrote in 1900 in "The Doctor's Lament":

> This lean M.D. is Dr. Brown
> Who fares but ill in Spotless Town.
> The town is so confounded clean,
> It is no wonder he is lean,
> He's lost all patients now, you know,
> Because they use *Sapolio.*

The same literary talent that once was used to retail Sapolio was later used to induce people to try the Edsel or the Mustang, to experiment with Lifebuoy or Body-All, to drink Pepsi-Cola or Royal Crown Cola, or to shave with a Trac II razor.

And as expansion and novelty have become essential to our economy, advertising has played an ever-larger role: in the settling of the continent, in the expansion of the economy, and in the building of an American standard of living. Advertising has expressed the optimism, the hyperbole, and the sense of community, the sense of reaching which has been so important a feature of our civilization.

Here I wish to explore the significance of advertising, not as a force in the economy or in shaping an American standard of living, but rather as a touchstone of the ways in which we Americans have learned about all sorts of things.

The problems of advertising are of course not peculiar to advertising, for they are just one aspect of the problems of democracy. They reflect the rise of what I have called Consumption Communities and Statistical Communities, and many of the special problems of advertising have arisen from our continuously energetic effort to give everybody everything.

If we consider democracy not just as a political system, but as a set of institutions which do aim to make everything available to everybody, it would not be an overstatement to describe advertising as the characteristic rhetoric of democracy. One of the tendencies of democracy, which Plato and other antidemocrats warned against a long time ago, was the danger that rhetoric would displace or at least overshadow epistemology; that is, *the temptation to allow the problem of persuasion to overshadow the problem of knowledge.* Democratic societies tend to become more concerned with what people believe than with what is true, to become more concerned with credibility than with truth. All these problems become accentuated in a large-scale democracy like ours, which possesses all the apparatus of modern industry. And the problems are accentuated still further by universal literacy, by instantaneous communication, and by the daily plague of words and images.

In the early days it was common for advertising men to define advertisements as a kind of news. The best admen, like the best journalists, were supposed to be those who were able to make their news the most interesting and readable. This was natural enough, since the verb to "advertise" originally meant, intransitively, to take note or to consider. For a person to "advertise" meant originally, in the fourteenth and fifteenth centuries, to reflect on something, to think about something. Then it came to mean, transitively, to call the attention of another to something, to give him notice, to notify, admonish, warn or inform in a formal or impressive manner. And then, by the sixteenth century, it came to mean: to give notice of anything, to make generally known. It was not until the late eighteenth century that the word "advertising" in English came to have a specifically "advertising" connotation as we might say today, and not until the late nineteenth century that it began to have a specifically commercial connotation. By 1879 someone was saying, "Don't advertise unless you have something worth advertising." But even into the present century, newspapers continue to call themselves by the title "Advertiser"— for example, the Boston *Daily Advertiser,* which was a newspaper of long tradition and one of the most dignified papers in Boston until William Randolph Hearst took it over in 1917. Newspapers carried "Advertiser" on their mastheads, not because they sold advertisements but because they brought news.

Now, the main role of advertising in American civilization came increasingly to be that of persuading and appealing rather than that of educating and informing. By 1921, for instance, one of the more popular textbooks, Blanchard's *Essentials of Advertising,* began: "Anything employed to influence people favorably is advertising. The mission of advertising is to persuade men and women to act in a way that will be of advantage to the advertiser." This development—in a country where a shared, a rising, and a democratized standard of living was the national pride and the national hallmark—meant that advertising had become the rhetoric of democracy.

What, then, were some of the main features of modern American advertising—if we consider it as a form of rhetoric? First, and perhaps most obvious, is *repetition.* It is hard for us to realize that the use of repetition in advertising is not an ancient device but a modern one, which actually did not come into common use in American journalism until just past the middle of the nineteenth century.

The development of what came to be called "iteration copy" was a result of a struggle by a courageous man of letters and advertising pioneer, Robert Bonner, who bought the old New York *Merchant's Ledger* in 1851 and turned it into a popular journal. He then had the temerity to try to change the ways of James Gordon Bennett, who of course was one of the most successful of the American newspaper pioneers, and who was both a sensationalist and at the same time an extremely stuffy man when it came to things that he did not consider to be news. Bonner was determined to use advertisements in Bennett's wide-circulating New York *Herald* to sell his own literary product, but he found it difficult to persuade Bennett to allow him to use any but agate type in his advertising. (Agate was the smallest type used by newspapers in that day, only barely legible to the naked eye.) Bennett would not allow advertisers to use larger type, nor would he allow them to use illustrations except stock cuts, because he thought it was undignified. He said, too, that to allow a variation in the format of ads would be undemocratic. He insisted that all advertisers use the same size type so that no one would be allowed to prevail over another simply by presenting his message in a larger, more clever, or more attention-getting form.

Finally Bonner managed to overcome Bennett's rigidity by leasing whole pages of the paper and using the tiny agate type to form larger letters across the top of the page. In this way he produced a message such as "Bring home the New York Ledger tonight." His were unimaginative messages, and when repeated all across the page they technically did not violate Bennett's agate rule. But they opened a new era and presaged a new freedom for advertisers in their use of the newspaper page. Iteration copy—the practice of presenting prosaic content in ingenious, repetitive form—became common, and nowadays of course is commonplace.

A second characteristic of American advertising which is not unrelated to this is the development of *an advertising style.* We have histories of most other kinds of style—including the style of many unread writers who are remembered today only because they have been forgotten—but we have very few accounts of the history of advertising style, which of course is one of the most important forms of our language and one of the most widely influential.

The development of advertising style was the convergence of several very respectable American traditions. One of these was the tradition of the "plain style," which the Puritans made so much of and which accounts for so much of the strength of the Puritan literature. The "plain style" was of course much influenced by the Bible and found its way into the rhetoric of American writers and speakers of great power like Abraham Lincoln. When advertising began to be self-conscious in the early years of this century, the pioneers urged copywriters not to be too clever, and especially not to be fancy. One of the pioneers of the advertising copywriters, John Powers, said, for example, "The commonplace is the proper level for writing in business; where the first virtue is plainness, 'fine writing' is not only intellectual, it is offensive." George P. Rowell, another advertising pioneer, said, "You must write your advertisement to catch damned fools—not college professors." He was a very tactful person. And he added, "And you'll catch just as many college professors as you will of any other sort." In the 1920's, when advertising was beginning to come into its own, Claude Hopkins, whose name is known to all in the trade, said, "Brilliant writing has no place in advertising. A unique style takes attention from the subject. Any apparent effort to sell creates corresponding resistance.... One should be natural and simple. His language should not be conspicuous. In fishing for buyers, as in fishing for bass, one should not reveal the hook." So there developed a characteristic advertising style in which plainness, the phrase that anyone could understand, was a distinguishing mark.

At the same time, the American advertising style drew on another, and what might seem an antithetic, tradition—the tradition of hyperbole and tall talk, the language of Davy Crockett and Mike Fink. While advertising could think of itself as 99.44 percent pure, it used the language of "Toronado" and "Cutlass." As I listen to the radio in Washington, I hear a celebration of heroic qualities which would make the characteristics of Mike Fink and Davy Crockett pale, only to discover at the end of the paean that what I have been hearing is a description of the Ford dealers in the District of Columbia neighborhood. And along with the folk tradition of hyperbole and tall talk comes the rhythm of folk music. We hear that Pepsi-Cola hits the spot, that it's for the young generation—and we hear other products celebrated in music which we cannot forget and sometimes don't want to remember.

There grew somehow out of all these contradictory tendencies—combining the commonsense language of the "plain style," and the fantasy language of "tall talk"—an advertising style. This characteristic way of talking about things was especially designed to reach and catch the millions. It created a whole new world of myth. A myth, the dictionary tells us, is a notion based more on tradition or convenience than on facts; it is a received idea. Myth is not just fantasy and not just fact but exists in a limbo, in the world of the "Will to Believe," which William James has written about so eloquently and so perceptively. This is the world of the neither true nor false—of the statement that 60 percent of the physicians who expressed a choice said that our brand of aspirin would be more effective in curing a simple headache than any other leading brand.

That kind of statement exists in a penumbra. I would call this the "advertising penumbra." It is not untrue, and yet, in its connotation it is not exactly true.

Now, there is still another characteristic of advertising so obvious that we are inclined perhaps to overlook it. I call that *ubiquity*. Advertising abhors a vacuum and we discover new vacuums every day. The parable, of course, is the story of the man who thought of putting the advertisement on the other side of the cigarette package. Until then, that was wasted space and a society which aims at a democratic standard of living, at extending the benefits of consumption and all sorts of things and services to everybody, must miss no chances to reach people. The highway billboard and other outdoor advertising, bus and streetcar and subway advertising, and skywriting, radio and TV commercials—all these are of course obvious evidence that advertising abhors a vacuum.

We might reverse the old mousetrap slogan and say that anyone who can devise another place to put another mousetrap to catch a consumer will find people beating a path to his door. "Avoiding advertising will become a little harder next January," the *Wall Street Journal* reported on May 17, 1973, "when a Studio City, California, company launches a venture called Store Vision. Its product is a system of billboards that move on a track across supermarket ceilings. Some 650 supermarkets so far are set to have the system." All of which helps us understand the observation attributed to a French man of letters during his recent visit to Times Square. "What a beautiful place, if only one could not read!" Everywhere is a place to be filled, as we discover in a recent *Publishers Weekly* description of one advertising program: "The $1.95 paperback edition of Dr. Thomas A. Harris' million-copy best seller 'I'm O.K., You're O.K.' is in for full-scale promotion in July by its publisher, Avon Books. Plans range from bumper stickers to airplane streamers, from planes flying above Fire Island, the Hamptons and Malibu. In addition, the $100,000 promotion budget calls for 200,000 bookmarks, plus brochures, buttons, lipcards, floor and counter displays, and advertising in magazines and TV."

The ubiquity of advertising is of course just another effect of our uninhibited efforts to use all the media to get all sorts of information to everybody everywhere. Since the places to be filled are everywhere, the amount of advertising is not determined by the *needs* of advertising, but by the *opportunities* for advertising which become unlimited.

But the most effective advertising, in an energetic, novelty-ridden society like ours, tends to be "self-liquidating." To create a cliché you must offer something which everybody accepts. The most successful advertising therefore self-destructs because it becomes cliché. Examples of this are found in the tendency for copyrighted names of trademarks to enter the vernacular—for the proper names of products which have been made familiar by costly advertising to become common nouns, and so to apply to anybody's products. Kodak becomes a synonym for camera, Kleenex a synonym for facial tissue, when both begin with a small *k*, and Xerox (now, too, with a small *x*) is used to describe all processes of copying, and so on. These are prototypes of the problem. If you are successful enough, then you will defeat your purpose in the long run—by making the name and the message so familiar that people won't notice them, and then people will cease to distinguish your product from everybody else's.

In a sense, of course, as we will see, the whole of American civilization is an example. When this was a "new" world, if people succeeded in building a civilization here, the New World would survive and would reach the time—in our age—when it would cease to be new. And now we have the oldest written Constitution in use in the world. This is only a parable of which there are many more examples.

The advertising man who is successful in marketing any particular product, then—in our high-technology, well-to-do democratic society, which aims to get everything to everybody—is apt to be diluting the demand for his particular product in the very act of satisfying it. But luckily for him, he is at the very same time creating a fresh demand for his services as advertiser.

And as a consequence, there is yet another role which is assigned to American advertising. This is what I call "erasure." Insofar as advertising is competitive or innovation is widespread, erasure is required in order to persuade consumers that this year's model is superior to last year's. In fact, we consumers learn that we might be risking our lives if we go out on the highway with those very devices that were last year's lifesavers but without whatever special kind of brakes or wipers or seat belt is on this year's model. This is what I mean by "erasure"—and we see it on our advertising pages or our television screen every day. We read in the *New York Times* (May 20, 1973), for example, that "For the price of something small and ugly, you can drive something small and beautiful"—an advertisement for the Fiat 250 Spider. Or another, perhaps more subtle example is the advertisement for shirts under a picture of Oliver Drab: "Oliver Drab. A name to remember in fine designer shirts? No kidding. . . . Because you pay extra money for Oliver Drab. And for all the other superstars of the fashion world. Golden Vee [the name of the brand that is advertised] does not have a designer's label. But we do have designers. . . . By keeping their names *off* our label and simply saying Golden Vee, we can afford to sell our $7 to $12 shirts for just $7 to $12, which should make Golden Vee a name to remember. Golden Vee, you only pay for the shirt."

Having mentioned two special characteristics—the self-liquidating tendency and the need for erasure—which arise from the dynamism of the American economy, I would like to try to place advertising in a larger perspective. The special role of advertising in our life gives a clue to a pervasive oddity in American civilization. A leading feature of past cultures, as anthropologists have explained, is the tendency to distinguish between "high" culture and "low" culture—between the culture of the literate and the learned on the one hand and that of the populace on the other. In other words, between the language of literature and the language of the vernacular. Some of the most useful statements of this distinction have been made by social scientists at the University of Chicago—first by the late Robert Redfield in his several pioneering books on peasant society, and then by Milton Singer in his remarkable study of Indian civilization, *When a Great Tradition Modernizes* (1972). This distinction between the great tradition and the little tradition, between the high culture and the folk culture, has begun to become a commonplace of modern anthropology.

Some of the obvious features of advertising in modern America offer us an opportunity to note the significance or insignificance of that distinction for us. Elsewhere I have tried to point out some of the peculiarities of the American attitude toward the *high* culture. There is something distinctive about the place of thought in American life, which I think is not quite what it has been in certain Old World cultures.

But what about distinctive American attitudes to *popular* culture? What is our analogue to the folk culture of other peoples? Advertising gives us some clues—to a characteristically American democratic folk culture. Folk culture is a name for the culture which ordinary people everywhere lean on. It is not the writings of Dante and Chaucer and Shakespeare and Milton, the teachings of Machiavelli and Descartes, Locke or Marx. It is, rather, the pattern of slogans, local traditions, tales, songs, dances, and ditties. And of course holiday observances. Popular culture in other civilizations has been for the most part both an area of continuity with the past, a way in which people reach back into the past and out to their community, and at the same time an area of local variations. An area of individual and amateur expression in which a person has his own way of saying, or notes his mother's way of saying or singing, or his own way of dancing, his own view of folk wisdom and the cliché.

And here is an interesting point of contrast. In other societies outside the United States, it is the *high* culture that has generally been an area of centralized, organized control. In Western Europe, for example, universities and churches have tended to be closely allied to the government. The institutions of higher learning have had a relatively limited access to the people as a whole. This was inevitable, of course, in most parts of the world, because there were so few universities. In England, for example, there were only two universities until the early nineteenth century. And there was central control over the printed matter that was used in universities or in the liturgy. The government tended to be close to the high culture, and that was easy because the high culture itself was so centralized and because literacy was relatively limited.

In our society, however, we seem to have turned all of this around. Our high culture is one of the least centralized areas of our culture. And our universities express the atomistic, diffused, chaotic, and individualistic aspect of our life. We have in this country more than twenty-five hundred colleges and universities, institutions of so-called higher learning. We have a vast population in these institutions, somewhere over seven million students.

But when we turn to our popular culture, what do we find? We find that in our nation of Consumption Communities and emphasis on Gross National Product (GNP) and growth rates, advertising has become the heart of the folk culture and even its very prototype. And as we have seen, American advertising shows many characteristics of the folk culture of other societies: repetition, a plain style, hyperbole and tall talk, folk verse, and folk music. Folk culture, wherever it has flourished, has tended to thrive in a limbo between fact and fantasy, and of course, depending on the spoken word and the oral tradition, it spreads easily and tends to be ubiquitous. These are all familiar characteristics of folk culture and they are ways of describing our folk culture, but how do the expressions of our peculiar folk culture come to *us*?

They no longer sprout from the earth, from the village, from the farm, or even from the neighborhood or the city. They come to us primarily from enormous centralized self-consciously *creative* (an overused word, for the overuse of which advertising agencies are in no small part responsible) organizations. They come from advertising agencies, from networks of newspapers, radio, and television, from outdoor-advertising agencies, from the copywriters for ads in the largest-circulation magazines, and so on. These "creators" of folk culture—or pseudo-folk culture—aim at the widest intelligibility and charm and appeal.

But in the United States, we must recall, the advertising folk culture (like all advertising) is also confronted with the problems of self-liquidation and erasure. These are by-products of the expansive, energetic character of our economy. And they, too, distinguish American folk culture from folk cultures elsewhere.

Our folk culture is distinguished from others by being discontinuous, ephemeral, and self-destructive. Where does this leave the common citizen? All of us are qualified to answer.

In our society, then, those who cannot lean on the world of learning, on the high culture of the classics, on the elaborated wisdom of the books, have a new problem. The University of Chicago, for example, in the 1930's and 1940's was the center of a quest for a "common discourse." The champions of that quest, which became a kind of crusade, believed that such a discourse could be found through familiarity with the classics of great literature—and especially of Western European literature. I think they were misled; such works were not, nor are they apt to become, the common discourse of our society. Most people, even in a democracy, and a rich democracy like ours, live in a world of popular culture, our special kind of popular culture.

The characteristic folk culture of our society is a creature of advertising, and in a sense it *is* advertising. But advertising, our own popular culture, is harder to make into a source of continuity than the received wisdom and commonsense slogans and catchy songs of the vivid vernacular. The popular culture of advertising attenuates and is always dissolving before our very eyes. Among the charms, challenges, and tribulations of modern life, we must count this peculiar fluidity, this ephemeral character of that very kind of culture on which other peoples have been able to lean, the kind of culture to which they have looked for the continuity of their traditions, for their ties with the past and with the future.

We are perhaps the first people in history to have a centrally organized mass-produced folk culture. Our kind of popular culture is here today and gone tomorrow—or the day after tomorrow. Or whenever the next semi-annual model appears. And insofar as folk culture becomes advertising, and advertising becomes centralized, it becomes a way of depriving people of their opportunities for individual and small-community expression. Our technology and our economy and our democratic ideals have all helped make that possible. Here we have a new test of the problem that is at least as old as Heraclitus—an everyday test of man's ability to find continuity in his experience. And here democratic man has a new opportunity to accommodate himself, if he can, to the unknown.

Aldous Huxley

This is Chapter 6 of Huxley's *Brave New World Revisited* (1958). For information on the author and his writings, see page 51.

The Arts of Selling

The survival of democracy depends on the ability of large numbers of people to make realistic choices in the light of adequate information. A dictatorship, on the other hand, maintains itself by censoring or distorting the facts, and by appealing, not to reason, nor to enlightened self-interest, but to passion and prejudice, to the powerful "hidden forces," as Hitler called them, present in the unconscious depths of every human mind.

In the West, democratic principles are proclaimed and many able and conscientious publicists do their best to supply electors with adequate information and to persuade them, by rational argument, to make realistic choices in the light of that information. All this is greatly to the good. But unfortunately propaganda in the Western democracies, above all in America, has two faces and a divided personality. In charge of the editorial department there is often a democratic Dr. Jekyll⁰—a propagandist who would be very happy to prove that John Dewey had been right about the ability of human nature to respond to truth and reason. But this worthy man controls only a part of the machinery of mass communication. In charge of advertising we find an anti-democratic, because antirational, Mr. Hyde—or rather a Dr. Hyde, for Hyde is now a Ph.D. in psychology and has a master's degree as well in the social sciences. This Dr. Hyde would be very unhappy indeed if everybody always lived up to John Dewey's faith in human nature. Truth and reason are Jekyll's affair, not his. Hyde is a motivation analyst, and his business is to study human weaknesses and failings, to investigate those unconscious desires and fears by which so much of men's conscious thinking and overt doing is determined. And he does this, not in the spirit of the moralist who would like to make people better, or of the physician who would like to improve their health, but simply in order to find out the best way to take advantage of their ignorance and to exploit their irrationality for the pecuniary benefit of his employers. But after all, it may be argued, "capitalism is dead, consumerism is king"—and consumerism requires the services of expert salesmen versed in all the arts (including the more insidious arts) of persuasion. Under a free enterprise system commercial propaganda by any and every means is absolutely indispensable. But the indispensable is not necessarily the desirable. What is demonstrably good in the sphere of economics may be far from good for men and women as voters or even as human beings. An earlier, more moralistic generation would have been profoundly shocked by the bland cynicism of the motivation analysts. Today we read a book like Mr. Vance Packard's *The Hidden Persuaders,* and are more amused than horrified, more resigned than indignant. Given Freud, given Behaviorism, given the mass producer's chronically desperate need for mass consumption, this is the sort of thing that is only to be expected. But what, we may ask, is the sort of thing that is to be expected in the future? Are Hyde's activities compatible in the long run with Jekyll's? Can a campaign in favor of rationality be successful in the teeth of another and

Dr. Jekyll   From *The Strange Case of Dr. Jekyll and Mr. Hyde* (1866) by Robert Louis Stevenson, the story of a doctor who separates the good and evil in his personality in the forms of two different people, the good Dr. Jekyll and the evil Mr. Hyde.

even more vigorous campaign in favor of irrationality? These are questions which, for the moment, I shall not attempt to answer, but shall leave hanging, so to speak, as a backdrop to our discussion of the methods of mass persuasion in a technologically advanced democratic society.

The task of the commercial propagandist in a democracy is in some ways easier and in some ways more difficult than that of a political propagandist employed by an established dictator or a dictator in the making. It is easier inasmuch as almost everyone starts out with a prejudice in favor of beer, cigarettes and iceboxes, whereas almost nobody starts out with a prejudice in favor of tyrants. It is more difficult inasmuch as the commercial propagandist is not permitted, by the rules of his particular game, to appeal to the more savage instincts of his public. The advertiser of dairy products would dearly love to tell his readers and listeners that all their troubles are caused by the machinations of a gang of godless international margarine manufacturers, and that it is their patriotic duty to march out and burn the oppressors' factories. This sort of thing, however, is ruled out, and he must be content with a milder approach. But the mild approach is less exciting than the approach through verbal or physical violence. In the long run, anger and hatred are self-defeating emotions. But in the short run they pay high dividends in the form of psychological and even (since they release large quantities of adrenalin and noradrenalin) physiological satisfaction. People may start out with an initial prejudice against tyrants; but when tyrants or would-be tyrants treat them to adrenalin-releasing propaganda about the wickedness of their enemies—particularly of enemies weak enough to be persecuted—they are ready to follow him with enthusiasm. In his speeches Hitler kept repeating such words as "hatred," "force," "ruthless," "crush," "smash"; and he would accompany these violent words with even more violent gestures. He would yell, he would scream, his veins would swell, his face would turn purple. Strong emotion (as every actor and dramatist knows) is in the highest degree contagious. Infected by the malignant frenzy of the orator, the audience would groan and sob and scream in an orgy of uninhibited passion. And these orgies were so enjoyable that most of those who had experienced them eagerly came back for more. Almost all of us long for peace and freedom; but very few of us have much enthusiasm for the thoughts, feelings and actions that make for peace and freedom. Conversely almost nobody wants war or tyranny; but a great many people find an intense pleasure in the thoughts, feelings and actions that make for war and tyranny. These thoughts, feelings and actions are too dangerous to be exploited for commercial purposes. Accepting this handicap, the advertising man must do the best he can with the less intoxicating emotions, the quieter forms of irrationality.

Effective rational propaganda becomes possible only when there is a clear understanding, on the part of all concerned, of the nature of symbols and of their relations to the things and events symbolized. Irrational propaganda depends for its effectiveness on a general failure to understand the nature of symbols. Simple-minded people tend to equate the symbol with what it stands for, to attribute to things and events some of the qualities expressed by the words in terms of which the propagandist has chosen, for his own purposes, to talk about them. Consider a simple example. Most cosmetics are made of lanolin, which is a mixture of purified wool fat and water beaten up into an emulsion. This emulsion has many valuable properties: it penetrates the skin, it does not become rancid, it is mildly antiseptic and so forth. But the commercial propagandists do not speak about the genuine virtues of the emulsion. They give it some picturesquely voluptuous name, talk ecstatically and misleadingly about feminine beauty and show pictures of gorgeous blondes nourishing their tissues with skin food. "The cosmetic manufacturers," one of their number has written, "are not selling lanolin, they are selling hope." For this hope, this fraudulent implication of a promise that they will be transfigured, women will pay ten or twenty times the value of the emulsion which the propagandists have so skilfully related, by means of misleading symbols, to a deep-seated and almost universal feminine wish—the wish to be more attractive to members of the opposite sex. The principles underlying this kind of propaganda are extremely simple. Find some common desire, some widespread unconscious fear or anxiety; think out some way to relate this wish or fear to the product you have to sell; then build a bridge of verbal or pictorial symbols over which your customer can pass from fact to compensatory dream, and from the dream to the illusion that your product, when purchased, will make the dream come true. "We no longer buy oranges, we buy vitality. We do not buy just an auto, we buy prestige." And so with all the rest. In toothpaste, for example, we buy, not a mere cleanser and antiseptic, but release from the fear of being sexually repulsive. In vodka and whisky we are not buying a protoplasmic poison which, in small doses, may depress the nervous system in a psychologically valuable way; we are buying friendliness and good fellowship, the warmth of Dingley Dell and the brilliance of the Mermaid Tavern. With our laxatives we buy the health of a Greek god, the radiance of one of Diana's nymphs. With the monthly best seller we acquire culture, the envy of our less literate neighbors and the respect of the sophisticated. In every case the motivation analyst has found some deep-seated wish or fear, whose energy can be used to move the consumer to part with cash and so, indirectly, to turn the wheels of industry. Stored in the minds and bodies of countless individuals, this potential energy is released by, and transmitted along, a line of symbols carefully laid out so as to bypass rationality and obscure the real issue.

Sometimes the symbols take effect by being disproportionately impressive, haunting and fascinating in their own right. Of this kind are the rites and pomps of religion. These "beauties of holiness" strengthen faith where it already exists and, where there is no faith, contribute to conversion. Appealing, as they do, only to the aesthetic sense, they guarantee neither the truth nor the ethical value of the doctrines with which they have been, quite arbitrarily, associated. As a matter of plain historical fact, the beauties of holiness have often been matched and indeed surpassed by the beauties of unholiness. Under Hitler, for example, the yearly Nuremberg rallies were masterpieces of ritual and theatrical art. "I had spent six years in St. Petersburg before the war in the best days of the old Russian ballet," writes Sir Nevile Henderson, the British ambassador to Hitler's Germany, "but for grandiose beauty I have never seen any ballet to compare with the Nuremberg rally." One thinks of Keats—"beauty is truth, truth beauty." Alas, the identity exists only on some ultimate, supramundane level. On the levels of politics and theology, beauty is perfectly compatible with nonsense and tyranny. Which is very fortunate; for if beauty were incompatible with nonsense and tyranny, there would be precious little art in the world. The masterpieces of painting, sculpture and architecture were produced as religious or political propaganda, for the greater glory of a god, a government or a priesthood. But most kings and priests have been despotic and all religions have been riddled with superstition. Genius has been the servant of tyranny and art has advertised the merits of the local cult. Time, as it passes, separates the good art from the bad metaphysics. Can we learn to make this separation, not after the event, but while it is actually taking place? That is the question.

In commercial propaganda the principle of the disproportionately fascinating symbol is clearly understood. Every propagandist has his Art Department, and attempts are constantly being made to beautify the billboards with striking posters, the advertising pages of magazines with lively drawings and photographs. There are no masterpieces; for masterpieces appeal only to a limited audience, and the commercial propagandist is out to captivate the majority. For him, the ideal is a moderate excellence. Those who like this not too good, but sufficiently striking, art may be expected to like the products with which it has been associated and for which it symbolically stands.

Another disproportionately fascinating symbol is the Singing Commercial. Singing Commercials are a recent invention; but the Singing Theological and the Singing Devotional—the hymn and the psalm—are as old as religion itself. Singing Militaries, or marching songs, are coeval with war, and Singing Patriotics, the precursors of our national anthems, were doubtless used to promote group solidarity, to emphasize the distinction between "us" and "them," by the wandering bands of paleolithic hunters and food gatherers. To most people music is intrinsically attractive. Moreover, melodies tend to ingrain themselves in the listener's mind. A tune will haunt the memory during the whole of a lifetime. Here, for example, is a quite uninteresting statement or value judgment. As it stands nobody will pay attention to it. But now set the words to a catchy and easily remembered tune. Immediately they become words of power. Moreover, the words will tend automatically to repeat themselves every time the melody is heard or spontaneously remembered. Orpheus has entered into an alliance with Pavlov—the power of sound with the conditioned reflex. For the commercial propagandist, as for his colleagues in the fields of politics and religion, music possesses yet another advantage. Nonsense which it would be shameful for a reasonable being to write, speak or hear spoken can be sung or listened to by that same rational being with pleasure and even with a kind of intellectual conviction. Can we learn to separate the pleasure of singing or of listening to song from the all too human tendency to believe in the propaganda which the song is putting over? That again is the question.

Thanks to compulsory education and the rotary press, the propagandist has been able, for many years past, to convey his messages to virtually every adult in every civilized country. Today, thanks to radio and television, he is in the happy position of being able to communicate even with unschooled adults and not yet literate children.

Children, as might be expected, are highly susceptible to propaganda. They are ignorant of the world and its ways, and therefore completely unsuspecting. Their critical faculties are undeveloped. The youngest of them have not yet reached the age of reason and the older ones lack the experience on which their new-found rationality can effectively work. In Europe, conscripts used to be playfully referred to as "cannon fodder." Their little brothers and sisters have now become radio fodder and television fodder. In my childhood we were taught to sing nursery rhymes and, in pious households, hymns. Today the little ones warble the Singing Commercials. Which is better—"Rheingold is my beer, the dry beer," or "Hey diddle-diddle, the cat and the fiddle"? "Abide with me" or "You'll wonder where the yellow went, when you brush your teeth with Pepsodent"? Who knows?

"I don't say that children should be forced to harass their parents into buying products they've seen advertised on television, but at the same time I cannot close my eyes to the fact that it's being done every day." So writes the star of one of the many programs beamed to a juvenile audience. "Children," he adds, "are living, talking records of what we tell them every day." And in due course these living, talking records of television commercials will grow up, earn money and buy the products of industry. "Think," writes Mr. Clyde Miller ecstatically, "think of what it can mean to your firm in profits if you can condition a million or ten million children, who will grow up into adults trained to buy your product, as soldiers are trained in advance when they hear the trigger words, Forward March!" Yes, just think of it! And at the same time remember that the dictators and the would-be dictators have been thinking about this sort of thing for years, and that millions, tens of millions, hundreds of millions of children are in process of growing up to buy the local despot's ideological product and, like well-trained soldiers, to respond with appropriate behavior to the trigger words implanted in those young minds by the despot's propagandists.

Self-government is in inverse ratio to numbers. The larger the constituency, the less the value of any particular vote. When he is merely one of millions, the individual elector feels himself to be impotent, a negligible quantity. The candidates he has voted into office are far away, at the top of the pyramid of power. Theoretically they are the servants of the people; but in fact it is the servants who give orders and the people, far off at the base of the great pyramid, who must obey. Increasing population and advancing technology have resulted in an increase in the number and complexity of organizations, an increase in the amount of power concentrated in the hands of officials and a corresponding decrease in the amount of control exercised by electors, coupled with a decrease in the public's regard for democratic procedures. Already weakened by the vast impersonal forces at work in the modern world, democratic institutions are now being undermined from within by the politicians and their propagandists.

Human beings act in a great variety of irrational ways, but all of them seem to be capable, if given a fair chance, of making a reasonable choice in the light of available evidence. Democratic institutions can be made to work only if all concerned do their best to impart knowledge and to encourage rationality. But today, in the world's most powerful democracy, the politicians and their propagandists prefer to make nonsense of democratic procedures by appealing almost exclusively to the ignorance and irrationality of the electors. "Both parties," we were told in 1956 by the editor of a leading business journal, "will merchandise their candidates and issues by the same methods that business has developed to sell goods. These include scientific selection of appeals and planned repetition. . . . Radio spot announcements and ads will repeat phrases with a planned intensity. Billboards will push slogans of proven power. . . . Candidates need, in addition to rich voices and good diction, to be able to look 'sincerely' at the TV camera."

The political merchandisers appeal only to the weaknesses of voters, never to their potential strength. They make no attempt to educate the masses into becoming fit for self-government; they are content merely to manipulate and exploit them. For this purpose all the resources of psychology and the social sciences are mobilized and set to work. Carefully selected samples of the electorate are given "interviews in depth." These interviews in depth reveal the unconscious fears and wishes most prevalent in a given society at the time of an election. Phrases and images aimed at allaying or, if necessary, enhancing these fears, at satisfying these wishes, at least symbolically, are then chosen by the experts, tried out on readers and audiences, changed or improved in the light of the information thus obtained. After which the political campaign is ready for the mass communicators. All that is now needed is money and a candidate who can be coached to look "sincere." Under the new dispensation, political principles and plans for specific action have come to lose most of their importance. The personality of the candidate and the way he is projected by the advertising experts are the things that really matter.

In one way or another, as vigorous he-man or kindly father, the candidate must be glamorous. He must also be an entertainer who never bores his audience. Inured to television and radio, that audience is accustomed to being distracted and does not like to be asked to concentrate or make a prolonged intellectual effort. All speeches by the entertainer-candidate must therefore be short and snappy. The great issues of the day must be dealt with in five minutes at the most—and preferably (since the audience will be eager to pass on to something a little livelier than inflation or the H-bomb) in sixty seconds flat. The nature of oratory is such that there has always been a tendency among politicians and clergymen to oversimplify complex issues. From a pulpit or a platform even the most conscientious of speakers finds it very difficult to tell the whole truth. The methods now being used to merchandise the political candidate as though he were a deodorant positively guarantee the electorate against ever hearing the truth about anything.

Marya Mannes

Marya Mannes, a talented and spirited journalist, was born in 1904 in New York and was privately educated there. She worked as feature editor of *Vogue* until World War II, then served three years in the Office of War Information. After a brief resumption of feature editing for *Glamour* in 1946, she published a novel, *Message from a Stranger* (1948), and from 1952 to 1964, worked as a satirical poet and staff writer for *The Reporter.* She has lectured frequently, written plays, appeared on radio, had her own television program, and in 1970 began doing theater reviews for *The New York Times.* She has received many honors and awards, especially for her pungent and critical magazine essays on American art, morals, and culture. Some of these have been published in the collections *But Will It Sell?* (1955), *More in Anger* (1958), and *The New York I Know* (1961). The following essay comes from the *Saturday Review,* November 14, 1970.

Television:
The Splitting Image

A bride who looks scarcely fourteen whispers, "Oh, Mom, I'm so *happy!*" while a doting family adjust her gown and veil and a male voice croons softly, "A woman is a harder thing to be than a man. She has more feelings to feel." The mitigation of these excesses, it appears, is a feminine deodorant called Secret, which allows our bride to approach the altar with security as well as emotion.

Eddie Albert, a successful actor turned pitchman, bestows his attention on a lady with two suitcases, which prompt him to ask her whether she has been on a journey. "No," she says, or words to that effect, as she opens the suitcases. "My two boys bring back their soiled clothes every weekend from college for me to wash." And she goes into the familiar litany of grease, chocolate, mud, coffee, and fruit-juice stains, which presumably record the life of the average American male from two to fifty. Mr. Albert compliments her on this happy device to bring her boys home every week and hands her a box of Biz, because "Biz *is* better."

Two women with stony faces meet cart to cart in a supermarket as one takes a jar of peanut butter off a shelf. When the other asks her in a voice of nitric acid why she takes that brand, the first snaps, "Because I'm choosy for my family!" The two then break into delighted smiles as Number Two makes Number One taste Jiffy for "mothers who are choosy."

If you have not come across these dramatic interludes, it is because you are not home during the day and do not watch daytime television. It also means that your intestinal tract is spared from severe assaults, your credibility unstrained. Or, for that matter, you may look at commercials like these every day and manage either to ignore them or find nothing—given the fact of advertising—wrong with them. In that case, you are either so brainwashed or so innocent that you remain unaware of what this daily infusion may have done and is doing to an entire people as the long-accepted adjunct of free enterprise and support of "free" television.

"Given the fact" and "long-accepted" are the key words here. Only socialists, communists, idealists (or the BBC) fail to realize that a mass television system cannot exist without the support of sponsors, that the massive cost of maintaining it as a free service cannot be met without the massive income from selling products. You have only to read of the unending struggle to provide financial support for public, noncommercial television for further evidence.

Besides, aren't commercials in the public interest? Don't they help you choose what to buy? Don't they provide needed breaks from programing? Aren't many of them brilliantly done, and some of them funny? And now, with the new sexual freedom, all those gorgeous chicks with their shining hair and gleaming smiles? And if you didn't have commercials taking up a good part of each hour, how on earth would you find enough program material to fill the endless space/time void?

Tick off the yesses and what have you left? You have, I venture to submit, these intangible but possibly high costs: the diminution of human worth, the infusion and hardening of social attitudes no longer valid or desirable, pervasive discontent, and psychic fragmentation.

Should anyone wonder why deception is not an included detriment, I suggest that our public is so conditioned to promotion as a way of life, whether in art or politics or products, that elements of exaggeration or distortion are taken for granted. Nobody really believes that a certain shampoo will get a certain swain, or that an unclogged sinus can make a man a swinger. People are merely prepared to hope it will.

But the diminution of human worth is much more subtle and just as pervasive. In the guise of what they consider comedy, the producers of television commercials have created a loathsome gallery of men and women patterned, presumably, on Mr. and Mrs. America. Women liberationists have a major target in the commercial image of woman flashed hourly and daily to the vast majority. There are, indeed, only four kinds of females in this relentless sales procession: the gorgeous teen-age swinger with bouncing locks; the young mother teaching her baby girl the right soap for skin care; the middle-aged housewife with a voice like a power saw; and the old lady with dentures and irregularity. All these women, to be sure, exist. But between the swinging sex object and the constipated granny there are millions of females never shown in commercials. These are—married or single—intelligent, sensitive women who bring charm to their homes, who work at jobs as well as lend grace to their marriage, who support themselves, who have talents or hobbies or commitments, or who are skilled at their professions.

To my knowledge, as a frequent if reluctant observer, I know of only one woman on a commercial who has a job; a comic plumber pushing Comet. Funny, heh? Think of a dame with a plunger.

With this one representative of our labor force, which is well over thirty million women, we are left with nothing but the full-time housewife in all her whining glory: obsessed with whiter wash, moister cakes, shinier floors, cleaner children, softer diapers, and greaseless fried chicken. In the rare instances when these ladies are not in the kitchen, at the washing machine, or waiting on hubby, they are buying beauty shops (fantasy, see?) to take home so that their hair will have more body. Or out at the supermarket being choosy.

If they were attractive in their obsessions, they might be bearable. But they are not. They are pushy, loud-mouthed, stupid, and—of all things now—bereft of sexuality. Presumably, the argument in the tents of advertising is that once a woman marries she changes overnight from plaything to floor-waxer.

To be fair, men make an equivalent transition in commercials. The swinging male with the mod hair and the beautiful chick turns inevitably into the paunchy slob who chokes on his wife's cake. You will notice, however, that the voice urging the viewer to buy the product is nearly always male: gentle, wise, helpful, seductive. And the visible presence telling the housewife how to get shinier floors and whiter wash and lovelier hair is almost invariably a man: the Svengali in modern dress, the Trilby (if only she were!), his willing object.

Woman, in short, is consumer first and human being fourth. A wife and mother who stays home all day buys a lot more than a woman who lives alone or who—married or single—has a job. The young girl hell-bent on marriage is the next most susceptible consumer. It is entirely understandable, then, that the potential buyers of detergents, foods, polishes, toothpastes, pills, and housewares are the housewives, and that the sex object spends most of *her* money on cosmetics, hair lotions, soaps, mouthwashes, and soft drinks.

Here we come, of course, to the youngest class of consumers, the swinging teen-agers so beloved by advertisers keen on telling them (and us) that they've "got a lot to live, and Pepsi's got a lot to give." This affords a chance to show a squirming, leaping, jiggling group of beautiful kids having a very loud high on rock and—of all things—soda pop. One of commercial TV's most dubious achievements, in fact, is the reinforcement of the self-adulation characteristic of the young as a group.

As for the aging female citizen, the less shown of her the better. She is useful for ailments, but since she buys very little of anything, not having a husband or any children to feed or house to keep, nor—of course—sex appeal to burnish, society and commercials have little place for her. The same is true, to be sure, of older men, who are handy for Bosses with Bad Breath or Doctors with Remedies. Yet, on the whole, men hold up better than women at any age—in life or on television. Lines on their faces are marks of distinction, while on women they are signatures of decay.

There is no question, in any case, that television commercials (and many of the entertainment programs, notably the soap serials that are part of the selling package) reinforce, like an insistent drill, the assumption that a woman's only valid function is that of wife, mother, and servant of men: the inevitable sequel to her earlier function as sex object and swinger.

At a time when more and more women are at long last learning to reject these assumptions as archaic and demeaning, and to grow into individual human beings with a wide option of lives to live, the sellers of the nation are bent upon reinforcing the ancient pattern. They know only too well that by beaming their message to the Consumer Queen they can justify her existence as the housebound Mrs. America: dumber than dumb, whiter than white.

The conditioning starts very early: with the girl child who wants the skin Ivory soap has reputedly given her mother, with the nine-year-old who brings back a cake of Camay instead of the male deodorant her father wanted. (When she confesses that she bought it so she could be "feminine," her father hugs her, and, with the voice of a child-molester, whispers, "My little girl is growing up on me, huh.") And then, before long, comes the teen-aged bride who "has feelings to feel."

It is the little boys who dream of wings, in an airplane commercial; who grow up (with fewer cavities) into the doers. Their little sisters turn into *Cosmopolitan* girls, who in turn become housewives furious that their neighbors' wash is cleaner than theirs.

There is good reason to suspect that this manic obsession with cleanliness, fostered, quite naturally, by the giant soap and detergent interests, may bear some responsibility for the cultivated sloppiness of so many of the young in their clothing as well as in their chosen hideouts. The compulsive housewife who spends more time washing and vacuuming and polishing her possessions than communicating to, or stimulating her children creates a kind of sterility that the young would instinctively reject. The impeccably tidy home, the impeccably tidy lawn are—in a very real sense—unnatural and confining.

Yet the commercials confront us with broods of happy children, some of whom—believe it or not—notice the new fresh smell their clean, white sweatshirts exhale thanks to Mom's new "softener."

Some major advertisers, for that matter, can even cast a benign eye on the population explosion. In another Biz commercial, the genial Eddie Albert surveys with surprise a long row of dirty clothes heaped before him by a young matron. She answers his natural query by telling him gaily they are the products of her brood of eleven "with one more to come!" she adds as the twelfth turns up. "That's great!" says Mr. Albert, curdling the soul of Planned Parenthood and the future of this planet.

Who are, one cannot help but ask, the writers who manage to combine the sales of products with the selling-out of human dreams and dignity? Who people this cosmos of commercials with dolts and fools and shrews and narcissists? Who know so much about quirks and mannerisms and ailments and so little about life? So much about presumed wants and so little about crying needs?

Can women advertisers so demean their own sex? Or are there no women in positions of decision high enough to see that their real selves stand up?

Do they not know, these extremely clever creators of commercials, what they could do for their audience even while they exploit and entertain them? How they could raise the levels of manners and attitudes while they sell their wares? Or do they really share the worm's-eye view of mass communication that sees, and addresses, only the lowest common denominator?

It can be argued that commercials are taken too seriously, that their function is merely to amuse, engage, and sell, and that they do this brilliantly. If that were all to this wheedling of millions, well and good. But it is not. There are two more fallouts from this chronic sales explosion that cannot be measured but that at least can be expected. One has to do with the continual celebration of youth at the expense of maturity. In commercials only the young have access to beauty, sex, and joy in life. What do older women feel, day after day, when love is the exclusive possession of a teen-age girl with a bobbing mantle of hair? What older man would not covet her in restless impotence?

The constant reminder of what is inaccessible must inevitably produce a subterranean but real discontent, just as the continual sight of things and places beyond reach has eaten deeply into the ghetto soul. If we are constantly presented with what we are not or cannot have, the dislocation deepens, contentment vanishes, and frustration reigns. Even for the substantially secure, there is always a better thing, a better way, to buy. That none of these things makes a better life may be consciously acknowledged, but still the desire lodges in the spirit, nagging and pulling.

This kind of fragmentation works in potent ways above and beyond the mere fact of program interruption, which is much of the time more of a blessing than a curse, especially in those rare instances when the commercial is deft and funny: the soft and subtle sell. Its overall curse, due to the large number of commercials in each hour, is that it reduces the attention span of a people already so conditioned to constant change and distraction that they cannot tolerate continuity in print or on the air.

Specifically, commercial interruption is most damaging during that 10 percent of programing (a charitable estimate) most important to the mind and spirit of a people: news and public affairs, and drama.

To many (and among these are network news producers), commercials have no place or business during the vital process of informing the public. There is something obscene about a newscaster pausing to introduce a deodorant or shampoo commercial between an airplane crash and a body count. It is more than an interruption; it tends to reduce news to a form of running entertainment, to smudge the edges of reality by treating death or disaster or diplomacy on the same level as household appliances or a new gasoline.

The answer to this would presumably be to lump the commercials before and after the news or public affairs broadcasts—an answer unpalatable, needless to say, to the sponsors who support them.

The same is doubly true of that most unprofitable sector of television, the original play. Essential to any creative composition, whether drama, music, or dance, are mood and continuity, both inseparable from form and meaning. They are shattered by the periodic intrusion of commercials, which have become intolerable to the serious artists who have deserted commercial television in droves because the system allows them no real freedom or autonomy. The selling comes first, the creation must accommodate itself. It is the rare and admirable sponsor who restricts or fashions his commercials so as to provide a minimum of intrusion or damaging inappropriateness.

If all these assumptions and imponderables are true, as many suspect, what is the answer or alleviation?

One is in the course of difficult emergence: the establishment of a public television system sufficiently funded so that it can give a maximum number of people an alternate diet of pleasure, enlightenment, and stimulation free from commercial fragmentation. So far, for lack of funds to buy talent and equipment, this effort has been in terms of public attention a distinctly minor operation.

Even if public television should, hopefully, greatly increase its scope and impact, it cannot in the nature of things and through long public conditioning equal the impact and reach the size of audience now tuned to commercial television.

Enormous amounts of time, money, and talent go into commercials. Technically they are often brilliant and innovative, the product not only of the new skills and devices but of imaginative minds. A few of them are both funny and endearing. Who, for instance, will forget the miserable young man with the appalling cold, or the kids taught to use—as an initiation into manhood—a fork instead of a spoon with a certain spaghetti? Among the enlightened sponsors, moreover, are some who manage to combine an image of their corporation and their products with accuracy and restraint.

What has to happen to mass medium advertisers as a whole, and especially on TV, is a totally new approach to their function not only as sellers but as social influencers. They have the same obligation as the broadcast medium itself: not only to entertain but to reflect, not only to reflect but to enlarge public consciousness and human stature.

This may be a tall order, but it is a vital one at a time when Americans have ceased to know who they are and where they are going, and when all the multiple forces acting upon them are daily diminishing their sense of their own value and purpose in life, when social upheaval and social fragmention have destroyed old patterns, and when survival depends on new ones.

If we continue to see ourselves as the advertisers see us, we have no place to go. Nor, I might add, has commercial broadcasting itself.

Images of Ourselves

Michael Roberts

Michael Roberts was born in Providence, Rhode Island, in 1945; he received his B.A. in 1967 from American University in Washington, D.C. He has been a trackman and calltaker for the New York *Daily Racing Form;* the author of a horseracing column, "Roberts on Racing," for the *Washington Daily News;* a sports columnist ("Mike Roberts") for the *Washington Star;* and a staff writer for Time-Life Books. In 1974 he won the Front Page Award of the Washington–Baltimore Newspaper Guild for two series, one on sports and drugs, the other on truth in sportscasting.

Roberts has also contributed to *The New Republic;* the following essay appeared in its sixtieth anniversary supplement (November 23, 1974) on

American culture. His essay illustrates what he discovered as a sports columnist, namely, "how many people were living life vicariously through athletes
and judging their own worth on the outcome of games played by others." He
developed this idea in his 1976 book *Fans! How We Go Crazy Over Sports.*

The Vicarious Heroism of the Sports Spectator

In the fall of 1973 a man in Colorado attempted suicide by shooting
himself in the head. The note he left alluded to the Denver Broncos, a
professional football team that had just fumbled seven times in the course
of a drubbing by the Chicago Bears. "I have been a Broncos fan since the
Broncos were first organized," the note said, "and I can't stand their
fumbling any more."

Poor marksmanship was all that averted a human sacrifice to the football
gods. But the act itself—fumbled, appropriately, as it was—could be regarded (if only by persons relatively indifferent to the teams of the National Football League) as the *reductio ad absurdum* of the widely approved and encouraged tendency of spectators to get involved
emotionally.

Not that it was the most absurd of all possible absurdities. There are
time-honored precedents elsewhere in the world. In Latin America, for
example, murders and suicides stemming from soccer scores are commonplace. Observers groping for explanations are usually inclined to attribute
such behavior to the reputedly volatile temperament of the average Latin.
The validity of such a claim must be left to the ethnologists to decide, but
one needn't be an expert of any kind to discern one significant distinction:
soccer, at its top levels, is conducted on an international scale, and in many
cases the vexation that touches off violence against self or others is generated by wounded feelings of national pride. It's harder to comprehend a
death occasioned by frustration over the inefficiency of a privately owned,
profit-making business that, strictly for commercial purposes, calls itself by
the name of the city in which it is located.

Here a bit of historical review is in order. Whatever their scope, strong
feelings of kinship between doer and watcher find their earliest antecedents on the playing fields of ancient cultures. The Greeks, fine sporting
fellows that they were, celebrated individual competition, the development of the whole man for his own benefit. With their Olympic Games,
however, they also gave rise to the practice of grouping lads together to
compete in the names of their respective hometowns. (As Western civilization advanced, the Romans broke away from the team-representation

idea in favor, again, of contests in which the participant played on behalf of himself—particularly contact sports involving armed men or a man and an aggressive beast. There were exceptions—occasionally church groups were asked to assemble teams for these events.)

Hence the notion that athletic glory could be shared in by the neighbors of the glorious athlete, or team, gained early acceptance and has survived, largely unexamined, to the present. When the poet reminisces to his athlete, dying young, about "That time you won your town the race,"[0] there seems no need to explain what, precisely, the town has done to be deserving.

Thus endures the foundation stone of nearly every variety of spectator sport now flourishing: the linking of the participant's destiny with the fan's, in terms of a common city, nation, race, religion or institution of higher learning. In short the whole system depends on *granfalloonery,*[0] a Kurt Vonnegut word, to express "a proud and meaningless association of human beings."

But these are persistent, consequential (economically) forms of *granfalloonery,* and fascinated observers have striven to unravel their mysteries. One scholar finds the direct antecedents of the 19th century's town-versus-town baseball games in the older custom of town-versus-town melees. "Most of the games . . . ended up in brawls," folklorist Tristram P. Coffin writes, going on to suggest that the games represented "semi-civilized replacements for village-to-village wars. And this is an aspect of the game that has never left it." (Interestingly the word "donnybrook" has its origin in the Irish brawls of this sort.) For evidence Coffin refers to the American League pennant race of 1967, when work virtually came to a standstill in four large American cities so that everyone could pay attention to baseball. "During the final two games, when Boston amazingly defeated Minnesota to win it all, a number of classes were suspended at such an unlikely place as Wellesley College so that girls who barely knew where Carl Yastrzemski would run after hitting the ball could take rapt part in this modern village-to-village crisis."

Significant also is the fact that the object of attention was no son of the Boston soil. The Red Sox had imported Yastrzemski from Long Island, and nearly all his teammates from distant regions of the country as well as a few other places in the Western Hemisphere; in fact in modern times the appearance of a local boy on a professional or college roster is the exception, not the rule, and is usually the random accident of a player draft or a recruiter's good fortune. This is a far cry from the old days when the town team was rounded up in town and its immediate environs, or when the young bucks who happened to be enrolled together at Princeton

"That time you won your town the race"   Line from the British poet A. E. Housman's poem "To an Athlete Dying Young," published in *A Shropshire Lad* (1896). *granfalloonery*   From *Cat's Cradle* (1963).

threw down a football challenge to their counterparts at Rutgers. But the evolution toward universal use of mercenaries has never affected the phenomenon of spectator identification.

The seasonal, predictable crises of sport remain as provincial in flavor as ever. One reason this is so is instant naturalization of athletic citizens (those of indisputable worthiness, of course), a process long since rendered unremarkable by fans of pro and college teams. It takes effect with a startling fluidity and is just as easily reversible. A notable recent case is that of Moses Malone, a teenaged basketball whiz who was transformed from savior of the University of Maryland to traitor in the time it took him to decide to skip college, going instead directly from high school into the pro game. Malone now resides in Salt Lake City, where—as he had been in College Park, Maryland—he has been graciously adopted by the natives, pending proof that he'll be as useful an acquisition as the Utah Stars expect him to be.

In the matter of taking the immigrant athlete unto the local bosom, in fact, spectators tend to take a more practical approach than the players themselves do. Some football players of domestic origin make no effort to hide their resentment of foreign-born field-goal kickers (whose soccer-bred skill has enabled them to dominate the field). Fans, on the other hand, invariably look at it this way: in the case of anyone who is consistently accurate from 40 yards out, prejudices will cheerfully be waived. On occasion such tolerant impulses have even been known to transcend racial hatreds, although in certain regions conflicting emotions are accommodated through the recognition of artificially distinct categories, namely "their niggers" and "our colored boys."

This specialized tolerance is explained simply enough. For the most part the spectator's stake in the proceedings is the gratification that comes from identifying with success. Whoever can provide such vicarious joy needs no other justification as a human being. The capacity of one man's actions to buttress the self-esteem of another is demonstrably a potent force—a force that has been exploited whenever possible by the entrepreneurs of sports events. In this regard the promoters of prizefighting have been more meticulous than anyone else. They are virtuosos of the ethnic sell, profiting even now from pitches that have scarcely grown more subtle since the "Golden Age of Sport." Granted, it may have been a while since anyone has instructed the public that Joe Louis, the former heavyweight champion, was "a credit to his race." But in places like New York it is still considered sound salesmanship to promote a California-born contestant as "Irish Jerry Quarry," with a liberal sprinkling of shamrocks on the posters, and to introduce another boxer as "The Jewish Bomber."

It's a reliable, if hoary, approach, appealing as it does to the inflammable sensitivities of the various branches of the human family—particularly those individuals who can feel themselves ennobled by someone else's left hook. And in much the same manner, the self-image of an entire city can be manipulated, lowered to despair or raised to giddy heights according to the capabilities of athletes-for-hire. When the Philadelphia Flyers won the championship of the National Hockey League last spring, the reaction of the populace—encouraged all the way by the local and national press —suggested that nothing in the city's past, not even the canonized epithets of W. C. Fields,[o] had done such violence to the collective psyche of Philadelphia as the monotonously regular inferiority of its professional sports franchises. Once the Stanley Cup had been secured, publications started falling over one another in their haste to congratulate the city on, as *Time* put it, "the tangible proof that Philadelphia is at long last a winner." The curious logic of spectator sport: what was tangible, precisely speaking, was the Stanley Cup, a large, hideous piece of metalwork worth less than $100, which came into the possession of the Flyers' management for a year. The players had won that. They also had won bonuses and probably salary increases. The owners of the franchise had won extra revenue from the playoff games and a more salable product than ever for next season. What had Philadelphia—the civic entity—won? That's an elusive, metaphysical question. But for sure, millions of residents were being counseled to think more highly of themselves for the Flyers' accomplishments.

At least, given the cover of big-city anonymity, they had a choice. There are places in this country, medium to small college towns primarily, where it is a serious social liability to dissociate oneself from the ups and downs and everyday existence of the football team. According to a sociologist whose findings were reported in *New Times,* people who live in Columbus, Ohio, are "not free" to admit indifference to the Ohio State football team. Nonenthusiasts who dwell in Columbus are categorized by normal folk as "freaks." Respondents to a poll overwhelmingly listed the Buckeyes as their most frequent topic of conversation and also ventured that a sound, working knowledge of the team's activities was a *sine qua non* for doing business with fellow townsmen. Most subjects agreed, furthermore, that a lack of interest in the team could be termed "downright unpatriotic."

To say nothing of the mood on campuses themselves in such cities, where over the decades student bodies and faculties have been conditioned to a notion that long ago gained respectability in American academic life: athletic teams are what give an institution its sense of worth and unity, its verve, its feeling that life is worth living. Yet historians are firm on the point that colleges and universities predated intercollegiate athletics. To those who hold dear the school-spirit ideal, it must be sad to reflect on the gloomy aimlessness that presumably palled college life in those long-ago days before the football weekend was conceived. On the

W. C. Fields   Vaudeville, film, and radio comedian (1897–1946). Born in Philadelphia, he vilified it throughout his career.

other hand it must be comforting to realize that it can never be that way again.

The academic world simply couldn't afford a relapse. Year by year, in fact, the pace intensifies in the all-out competition to seduce the best brawn available in the grant-in-aid market; to field the finest teams money and flattery can put together. Assistance comes from many quarters— from governors, senators, legendary coaches, even pretty girls recruited specifically for the purpose. It costs, but experience has proved it a prudent—if not imperative—investment, because endowments at a staggering number of institutions have been found to be dependent largely upon won-lost records. The outcome of last year's game against an arch-rival can be pivotal too. After all an alumnus can't be expected to be proud of a loser, and an alumnus who is not proud is not, statistics show, much of a contributor.

Obviously vicarious triumphs are not the only rewards alumni-patrons look forward to. For many there is that keenly anticipated weekend each year when many of society's conventions are temporarily suspended. Then, the old grad, along with the undergrad, can indulge in conduct that might be regarded as indecorous in other settings. Behavior such as assault and battery and indecent exposure are considered quite correct under the etiquette prevailing at, say, the Texas-Oklahoma football game.

In the final analysis this may be college sport's most significant service to its followers, more valuable even than the fomenting of campus chauvinism. For the public seems to need a permissible outlet for certain barbaric impulses. Sport provides that outlet, on an ever-expanding scale. Control of sporting crowds has lately become recognized as a new speciality in the armed-guard business. The Burns Security Institute reports that fan behavior nationwide has been growing markedly worse, with regard to such particulars as drinking, gambling, profanity and missile-throwing.

Paradoxically most fans are believed to harbor a highly exploitable reverence for the performers upon whom they shower such vulgarity. The commercial implications are staggering. Anyone who dared produce a razor blade commercial without an athlete would be branded a heretic. Jocks have repeatedly been employed to sell everything from bubble gum to politicians. An administrator in charge of fund-raising at a major metropolitan hospital some years ago still marvels at the results of an inspired campaign of television commercials. They were testimonials from pro hockey players: "I got my knee bashed in, and this place fixed me up real good." Contributions from the public ultimately rose from $250,000 annually to more than four million dollars.

For some time sports figures have also performed a parallel job as counselors to the public on moral, social and political issues. Hence it was altogether fitting in the days just before Richard Nixon threw in the towel that the coach of the professional football team in Washington should go on record: "I don't think he should resign . . . That's the type of determination and leadership and doggedness you have to have in a President."

No vote of confidence could have been less unpredictable. In his astuteness as an interpreter of public tastes, Nixon had been cultivating the athletic community for years. (President Ford, a quick study, immediately adopted his predecessor's compulsive habit of phoning big-time sports winners right after their victories.) If Kennedy had been trying to establish Camelot, Nixon was going for something a little more familiar—a Columbus, Ohio, perhaps, or a Green Bay, Wisconsin. And during the glory days of his administration it was observed time and again that no private citizen in Washington, no congressional figure, no cabinet member save possibly John Mitchell, had as frequent access to the White House as George Allen, coach of the Washington Redskins.

Andrew Griffin

Andrew Griffin was born in Portland, Oregon, in 1939 and was educated at Harvard University (B.A., 1960; Ph.D., 1969). Since 1967 he has been on the English faculty of the University of California at Berkeley, where he teaches courses ranging from freshman composition to graduate seminars. His enthusiasm for monster movies dates back to the Blue Mouse Theater in Portland, where he first watched and thought about the genre he writes about here. The article first appeared in the Winter 1979 issue of *University Publishing*.

Sympathy for the Werewolf

Have pity on the Werewolf,
Have sympathy;
For the Werewolf may be someone
Just like you and me.

Have pity on the Werewolf,
Not fear—not hate;
For the Werewolf may be someone
That you've known of late.

> *The Moray Eel Meets the Holy Modal Rounders*

The fact is that we do feel pity for the Werewolf, along with the fear and hate. Monsters frighten us, as they do their movie victims, especially at first sight; but at some point in the course of every classic monster movie we begin to feel sorry for them and, forgetting their victims, to fear for them.

In short, we sympathize; we take the monster's side, at least some of the time, and almost always at the end. When it is finally dispatched we feel a great deal of relief, to be sure, but at the same time much sincere regret and guilt. The relief is in any case not the sort of feeling that comes with the simple lifting of a threat; it is the easing of the pressure of our unconscious identification with this dreadful and dangerous being on the screen, whom we have come to see as in some way "just like you and me." It is this identification that makes us regret the loss of the monster, without whom the world is a poorer place, somehow incomplete. And we have to feel guilty for conniving in its death. The mob of villagers with their torches, the old doctor with his stake seem to be acting for us, yet we are shocked by their brutality, remembering the monster's moments of tenderness.

" 'Twas Beauty killed the Beast!" intones Carl Denham, King Kong's captor, always the impresario, dictating tomorrow's headlines to the waiting reporters. But we know better. 'Twasn't Beauty at all but something uncompromising in the human world, a failure of that sympathy for the Werewolf that we have been developing there in our seats—a failure on the part of Denham and his crew, the Army Air Force, and of course civilization itself, represented as usual by images of the metropolis with its skyscrapers and machines. Not that we imagine King Kong could have been saved! We know he can't survive, let alone rule, in New York City. But recognizing this, as the movie forces us to do, we have to reexamine our own relations to the city, "our" world. A part of ourselves clearly belongs to his world: not to Manhattan Island but to Skull Island, where Kong is King indeed.

It is obvious what part of ourselves that is. The classic movie monster (excepting Frankenstein's) is all instinct and energy and appetite, especially the latter: so simple and primitive that, for him, love and hate are almost the same thing. Monster movies are, of course, sexually explicit and sexually aggressive; they might almost be said to be about rape. And yet, they remain somehow innocent and presexual—because, I think, the monster is incorrigibly *oral*, seeking to incorporate both what it desires and what it wants to destroy, approaching the world in general through the mouth. Dracula, a fastidious aristocrat, nips and sips; the Wolfman, howling with lust, tears out your throat; King Kong's mighty jaws are capable of masticating and swallowing you whole (at one point he chews up a native). Even the movies' Mr. Hyde, who bites no one to death, has a dandy set of teeth, strong and crude, bared by his habitual lip-twitching simian grin.

Surely we are not like that! But we have been—have been all mouth, that is, and have wanted to eat the world—and the movies insist that we still are. Both *The Wolfman* and *Dr. Jekyll and Mr. Hyde* depend on the cinematic trick by which a man becomes a monster before our very eyes: Hyde *is* Jekyll, or a piece of him, and the Wolfman is Lon Chaney Jr., in many ways an improvement. Dracula's kiss may bring about the same transformation: Mina the good and true struggles *not* to become that narrow but intense "Miss Hyde" within who loves the kiss and would long to return it. King Kong can best be understood, I think, not as Fay Wray's giant lover but as her sexual desire made outward and visible . . . and just as big as she has feared it would be if she ever gave in to it. She has been toying with temptation ever since the first frames of the movie, which show a famished Fay reaching almost experimentally toward an apple in a sidewalk grocery window; on shipboard she flirts with the "Aw, shucks" officer and, at Denham's direction, *acts* the emotion she is soon to experience. When at last Kong takes her in his enormous hand she is literally "in the grip of passion." Her fear now is, quite naturally, that she will be "swallowed up" by this immense feeling, her identity—like Mina Harker's or Lon Chaney's or Dr. Jekyll's—lost in it. But the feeling is still her own, of course: summoned out of the darkness of her inexperience as surely as Kong is called out of the jungle by the annual rituals, brought to the gates of consciousness roaring, demanding to be acknowledged, to have his due.

This is what monsters are, this is what monster movies do: they reacquaint us with our own forgotten or forbidden selves, inviting us to recognize and, in imagination, deal with them. They keep alive in us a large and tolerant idea of the human—large enough anyway to include what seems at first inhuman, alien. The fact that monster movies invariably end in another repression makes less difference than one might think at first. For one thing, the viewer always knows the nature of his own silent participation, there in the dark; to watch the movie at all is to accept some responsibility for violence done and passions expressed. Probably, too, this demonstration that outrageous feelings and dangerous appetites *can* be mastered or handled, though at some cost, tends to reassure us, making us not less but more open to our own impulses in the future, soothing exaggerated fears about loss of control and loss of identity.

But the fifties changed all this. The classic monster movie is a product of the thirties; sequels and variations dominate the forties. With the coming of the Cold War, however, monsters all but disappear, to be replaced by Creatures from this, Beasts from that, and things too fierce to mention. There are exceptions. *Forbidden Planet* (1956) is a monster movie in science fiction clothing, featuring no less than the Freudian Id itself on a rampage: Walter Pidgeon's unconscious desires, objectified and magnified enormously through the power of alien technology. The first of the Creatures has a lot of monster in him too. *The Creature from the Black Lagoon* (1954) comes from the dawn of time, roused by scientists incautiously probing its habitat; the plot turns on its inarticulate relations with a pretty girl and, in *Revenge of the Creature* (1955), its rage against mankind and his cities. The Creature is, nevertheless, not a monster. It is, like all its numerous progeny, much farther down the evolutionary scale than the ape-, wolf-, and bat-people of the monster movies (a mammalian genre)— closer to the dinosaurs against whom, in fact, King Kong is really leagued with Fay Wray and ourselves. Though it shadows or mirrors us in important ways (notably its desire for the virgin, stylishly expressed in underwater sequences), it is always clear that it is *not* one of us, nor a part of ourselves, but profoundly alien—almost as alien as the Martians that attack earth in *War of the Worlds* (also 1954).

Sympathy for the Creature is by no means impossible, though it would seem to argue a fair degree of alienation or self-loathing to recognize oneself behind those rubber gills. Sympathy with still lower forms of life is out of the question, and it is these low life forms that came to dominate the screen. Hordes, swarms, blobs and slimes, giant insects, sentient plants —these were our bogeys then, images of the fifties' paranoid fear of dangers wholly external and coldly implacable, inexorably encroaching, endangering life-as-we-know-it. It seems reasonable to hold the politics of the period responsible. Certainly the fifties taught us that there was an Enemy pressing against our borders, subverting our institutions, godless and ruthless, to be met with total war. The politics of the day, like the movies, simplified and dehumanized the world, denying relationship, shifting responsibility. Where the monster movies of the thirties showed us similarity in difference, the menace movies of the fifties presented only unlikeness and danger. They told us to look to our weapons, draw the wagons into a circle and stay awake. Their central image is the small community under siege: not (as in *King Kong*) the monster in the city's midst, but almost the reverse—the city surrounded by monsters or, more precisely, by nameless and terrible "things." It is no accident that these films are often set in the desert or the arctic (not to mention imaginary lands still more inhospitable): environments that themselves express the pure inhuman otherness felt to lie just a step beyond the circle of the human, a circle now unnaturally, defensively and anxiously contracted.

What this meant for life in the fifties I needn't say. For the movies it meant the end of an era and a genre. Without the play of ambivalent feelings, uneasy alliances made and broken in the course of the film— without the monster, in short—the viewer's experience is impoverished and his intelligence insulted. If we are only victims, we can only scream —unless, of course, we laugh. In *Attack of the Giant Shrews,* what appear to be Alsatian dogs loosely draped with Spanish moss encircle a house in the bayous. Or take *Night of the Lapis,* with its nocturnes of huge bunnies in a slow-motion romp through a model of a town—an extraordinary but in no way frightening spectacle. Shrews and rabbits? These movies have vanished even from late night TV. They can be made and watched only in a world where absolutely anything might turn on you, a world that doesn't understand itself or what's outside itself—and doesn't want to understand. No wonder that the "things" the fifties feared seem to increase and multiply, spreading and creeping—words that had a special and horrible meaning for this decade (the spread of communism, creeping socialism). No wonder either that the fifties feared itself, felt some loss of contact with itself. *Mutation* and *mind-control,* both insidious forms of usurpation or loss of real identity, play as large a part in the mythology of the decade as do Creatures and Slimes.

The best of the menace movies not only exploit this cultural paranoia, they expose it too. Don Siegel's *Invasion of the Body Snatchers* (1956), perhaps the best of the best, shows us an America ironically betrayed by what must be understood as its own dream of the Good Life. In this deadly little parable, a species of alien plant beings (pods) silently infiltrates a small California town, replacing its inhabitants one by one with vegetable simulacra, perfect replicas in every respect—the business of the town continuing, eerily and very meaningfully, as usual. Siegel must have enjoyed confounding the rigid categories of the fifties and overturning its convictions. In *Body Snatchers,* conformity is subversion, the suburban is alien—or, as Siegel plainly suggests, terribly alienating. The implication is, of course, that the one big difference between person and pod is no difference at all; we are all already hollow at the core, pretend people. At the end of the movie a frantic Kevin McCarthy, still human but just one step ahead of the pods, screams "You're next!" at the cars that flash past him on the highway. "I think the world is populated by pods," Siegel has said, "and I wanted to show them."

But as this remark itself indicates, Siegel remains true to the fifties formula. The problem, it seems, is still "them," not "us"—even if "them" is your neighborhood automata. The decline of the monster movie and its ethic is best exemplified in a movie actually entitled *Them!* (1954) which opens almost where *Body Snatchers* leaves off. We see a little girl stumbling along a desert road, dirty and disoriented, clutching her doll. What has happened? Where's your mommy and daddy? All the little girl can answer, all her decade ever does answer, is "Them!"

They turn out to be, in this instance, giant ants, grown to their present size through atomic accident, invading the human world in search of (mainly) sugar. They make an effective movie, too, as we follow the desperate search for Their nest, confront Their fierce warriors, and, the battle over, explore Their underground tunnels and chambers, big as a coal mine and much more interesting. The movie ends effectively in the storm drains beneath Los Angeles with the systematic destruction of a second colony (and the rescue of two little boys) by the National Guard.

Needless to say, we feel no sympathy for Them. We might wonder, however, why They don't present more of a problem. For despite Their size, They are fairly easy to handle, no tougher than (say) the Japanese dug in on Tarawa. Gas and flamethrowers do the job. Every monster one can think of, although in most cases not nearly so dangerous to life-as-we-know-it, has been more difficult to deal with. Why don't They give more trouble? And why, after the movie is over, don't we give a damn?

The answer to both questions is that, oddly enough, there is little at stake. Monster movies dramatize a kind of negotiation with ourselves about what we are; somewhere, a little below the level of conscious thought, the monster is proposed, explored, debated, rejected, as we have already seen. But in a movie like *Them!*, or *The Thing*, or *The Beast from 20,000 Fathoms*, there is no such negotiation, only the defense of an idea of what's human that the movie never questions. Nor, finally, is there much to choose between human and alien. The storm drains of Los Angeles are uncannily well-adapted to the purposes of myrmecoid existence; the ants seem as at home under the city as we are in the ant heap that sprawls above them. And the National Guard, in their uniforms, their shiny helmets, especially with their gas masks on: not only are they indistinguishable from each other, they are hard to tell from the ants. One horde sweeps out another, red ants *vs.* black. It seems unlikely that the makers of *Them!* meant to draw our attention to these similarities, but there they are. The implication is, as in *Invasion of the Body Snatchers*, that the supplanting of the human, by ant or pod, would scarcely be noticed by the universe at large.

Bob Dylan
(1941–   )

It's All Over Now, Baby Blue

You must leave now, take what you need, you think will last.
But whatever you wish to keep, you better grab it fast.
Yonder stands your orphan with his gun,
Crying like a fire in the sun.
Look out the saints are comin' through
And it's all over now, Baby Blue.

The highway is for gamblers, better use your sense.
Take what you have gathered from coincidence.
The empty-handed painter from your streets
Is drawing crazy patterns on your sheets.
This sky, too, is folding under you
And it's all over now, Baby Blue.

All your seasick sailors, they are rowing home.
All your reindeer armies, are all going home.
The lover who just walked out your door
Has taken all his blankets from the floor.
The carpet, too, is moving under you
And it's all over now, Baby Blue.

Leave your stepping stones behind, something calls for
you.
Forget the dead you've left, they will not follow you.
The vagabond who's rapping at your door
Is standing in the clothes that you once wore.
Strike another match, go start anew
And it's all over now, Baby Blue.

(1973)

Joyce Carol Oates

Joyce Carol Oates was born in Lockport, New York, in 1938 and graduated from Syracuse University in 1960. She received an M.A. in English from the University of Wisconsin the following year, but was turned from further academic training by the persistent success of her short stories, which she had been writing since childhood. Her first collection of stories, *By the North Gate* (1963), has been followed by over two dozen more volumes of stories, novels, poems, plays, and essays. Her novel *Them* (1970) won the National Book Award.

In addition to being a writer, Ms. Oates teaches creative writing and modern literature at Princeton. Her critical writing includes three volumes of essays, most recently *Contraries: Essays* (1981), and a book on the poetry of D. H. Lawrence, *The Hostile Sun* (1973).

Ms. Oates's fiction encompasses a great range of styles—from lyricism and fantasy to naturalism—and it often deals with violent and pessimistic themes. In an interview with John Knott and Christopher Reaske (included in their anthology *Mirrors*) she said: "So many of my characters are actually based on real people . . . just as most of the plots are 'real' plots, taken from life and fixed up slightly. . . . After hearing for some weeks Dylan's song 'It's All Over Now, Baby Blue,' and after having read about a killer in some Southwestern state, and after having thoughts about the old legends and folk songs of Death and the Maiden, the story ["Where Are You Going, Where Have You Been?"] came to me more or less in a piece. Dylan's song is very beautiful, very disturbing."

We print the words to the song above. The killer she refers to is Charles Schmid, who, according to an account in *Life* magazine (March 4, 1966), "did weird things . . . wore crazy make-up . . . was known at all the joints." He is the prototype for Arnold Friend in the story below. It first appeared in *Epoch*, Fall 1966, and later, dedicated to Bob Dylan, in a collection *The Wheel of Love* (1970).

Where Are You Going, Where Have You Been?

Her name was Connie. She was fifteen and she had a quick nervous giggling habit of craning her neck to glance into mirrors, or checking other people's faces to make sure her own was all right. Her mother, who noticed everything and knew everything and who hadn't much reason any longer to look at her own face, always scolded Connie about it. "Stop gawking at yourself, who are you? You think you're so pretty?" she would say. Connie would raise her eyebrows at these familiar complaints and look right through her mother, into a shadowy vision of herself as she was right at that moment: she knew she was pretty and that was everything. Her mother had been pretty once too, if you could believe those old snapshots in the album, but now her looks were gone and that was why she was always after Connie.

"Why don't you keep your room clean like your sister? How've you got your hair fixed—what the hell stinks? Hair spray? You don't see your sister using that junk."

Her sister June was twenty-four and still lived at home. She was a secretary in the high school Connie attended, and if that wasn't bad enough—with her in the same building—she was so plain and chunky and steady that Connie had to hear her praised all the time by her mother and her mother's sisters. June did this, June did that, she saved money and helped clean the house and cooked and Connie couldn't do a thing, her mind was all filled with trashy daydreams. Their father was away at work most of the time and when he came home he wanted supper and he read the newspaper at supper and after supper he went to bed. He didn't bother talking much to them, but around his bent head Connie's mother kept picking at her until Connie wished her mother was dead and she herself was dead and it was all over. "She makes me want to throw up sometimes," she complained to her friends. She had a high, breathless, amused voice which made everything she said sound a little forced, whether it was sincere or not.

There was one good thing: June went places with girl friends of hers, girls who were just as plain and steady as she, and so when Connie wanted to do that her mother had no objections. The father of Connie's best girl friend drove the girls the three miles to town and left them off at a shopping plaza, so that they could walk through the stores or go to a movie, and when he came to pick them up again at eleven he never bothered to ask what they had done.

They must have been familiar sights, walking around that shopping plaza in their shorts and flat ballerina slippers that always scuffed the sidewalk, with charm bracelets jingling on their thin wrists; they would lean together to whisper and laugh secretly if someone passed by who amused or interested them. Connie had long dark blond hair that drew anyone's eye to it, and she wore part of it pulled up on her head and puffed out and the rest of it she let fall down her back. She wore a pull-over jersey blouse that looked one way when she was at home and another way when she was away from home. Everything about her had two sides to it, one for home and one for anywhere that was not home: her walk that could be childlike and bobbing, or languid enough to make anyone think she was hearing music in her head, her mouth which was pale and smirking most of the time, but bright and pink on these evenings out, her laugh which was cynical and drawling at home—"Ha, ha, very funny"—but high-pitched and nervous anywhere else, like the jingling of the charms on her bracelet.

Sometimes they did go shopping or to a movie, but sometimes they went across the highway, ducking fast across the busy road, to a drive-in restaurant where older kids hung out. The restaurant was shaped like a big bottle, though squatter than a real bottle, and on its cap was a revolving figure of a grinning boy who held a hamburger aloft. One night in midsummer they ran across, breathless with daring, and right away someone leaned out a car window and invited them over, but it was just a boy from high school they didn't like. It made them feel good to be able to ignore him. They went up through the maze of parked and cruising cars to the bright-lit, fly-infested restaurant, their faces pleased and expectant as if they were entering a sacred building that loomed out of the night to give them what haven and what blessing they yearned for. They sat at the counter and crossed their legs at the ankles, their thin shoulders rigid with excitement, and listened to the music that made everything so good: the music was always in the background like music at a church service, it was something to depend upon.

A boy named Eddie came in to talk with them. He sat backwards on his stool, turning himself jerkily around in semi-circles and then stopping and turning again, and after awhile he asked Connie if she would like something to eat. She said she did and so she tapped her friend's arm on her way out—her friend pulled her face up into a brave droll look—and Connie said she would meet her at eleven, across the way. "I just hate to leave her like that," Connie said earnestly, but the boy said that she wouldn't be alone for long. So they went out to his car and on the way Connie couldn't help but let her eyes wander over the windshields and faces all around her, her face gleaming with a joy that had nothing to do with Eddie or even this place; it might have been the music. She drew her shoulders up and sucked in her breath with the pure pleasure of being alive, and just at that moment she happened to glance at a face just a few feet from hers. It was a boy with shaggy black hair, in a convertible jalopy painted gold. He stared at her and then his lips widened into a grin. Connie slit her eyes at him and turned away, but she couldn't help glancing back and there he was still watching her. He wagged a finger and laughed and said, "Gonna get you, baby," and Connie turned away again without Eddie noticing anything.

She spent three hours with him, at the restaurant where they ate hamburgers and drank Cokes in wax cups that were always sweating, and then down an alley a mile or so away, and when he left her off at five to eleven only the movie house was still open at the plaza. Her girl friend was there, talking with a boy. When Connie came up the two girls smiled at each other and Connie said, "How was the movie?" and the girl said, "*You* should know." They rode off with the girl's father, sleepy and pleased, and Connie couldn't help but look at the darkened shopping plaza with its big empty parking lot and its signs that were faded and ghostly now, and over at the drive-in restaurant where cars were still circling tirelessly. She couldn't hear the music at this distance.

Next morning June asked her how the movie was and Connie said, "So-so."

She and that girl and occasionally another girl went out several times a week that way, and the rest of the time Connie spent around the house —it was summer vacation—getting in her mother's way and thinking, dreaming, about the boys she met. But all the boys fell back and dissolved into a single face that was not even a face, but an idea, a feeling, mixed up with the urgent insistent pounding of the music and the humid night air of July. Connie's mother kept dragging her back to the daylight by finding things for her to do or saying, suddenly, "What's this about the Pettinger girl?"

And Connie would say nervously, "Oh, her. That dope." She always drew thick clear lines between herself and such girls, and her mother was simple and kindly enough to believe her. Her mother was so simple, Connie thought, that it was maybe cruel to fool her so much. Her mother went scuffling around the house in old bedroom slippers and complained over the telephone to one sister about the other, then the other called up and the two of them complained about the third one. If June's name was mentioned her mother's tone was approving, and if Connie's name was mentioned it was disapproving. This did not really mean she disliked Connie and actually Connie thought that her mother preferred her to June because she was prettier, but the two of them kept up a pretense of exasperation, a sense that they were tugging and struggling over something of little value to either of them. Sometimes, over coffee, they were almost friends, but something would come up—some vexation that was like a fly buzzing suddenly around their heads—and their faces went hard with contempt.

One Sunday Connie got up at eleven—none of them bothered with church—and washed her hair so that it could dry all day long, in the sun. Her parents and sisters were going to a barbecue at an aunt's house and Connie said no, she wasn't interested, rolling her eyes to let mother know just what she thought of it. "Stay home alone then," her mother said sharply. Connie sat out back in a lawn chair and watched them drive away, her father quiet and bald, hunched around so that he could back the car out, her mother with a look that was still angry and not at all softened through the windshield, and in the back seat poor old June all dressed up as if she didn't know what a barbecue was, with all the running yelling kids and the flies. Connie sat with her eyes closed in the sun, dreaming and dazed with the warmth about her as if this were a kind of love, the caresses of love, and her mind slipped over onto thoughts of the boy she had been with the night before and how nice he had been, how sweet it always was, not the way someone like June would suppose but sweet, gentle, the way it was in movies and promised in songs; and when she opened her eyes she hardly knew where she was, the back yard ran off into weeds and a fenceline of trees and behind it the sky was perfectly blue and still. The asbestos "ranch house" that was now three years old startled her—it looked small. She shook her head as if to get awake.

It was too hot. She went inside the house and turned on the radio to drown out the quiet. She sat on the edge of her bed, barefoot, and listened for an hour and a half to a program called XYZ Sunday Jamboree, record after record of hard, fast, shrieking songs she sang along with, interspersed by exclamations from "Bobby King": "An' look here you girls at Napoleon's—Son and Charley want you to pay real close attention to this song coming up!"

And Connie paid close attention herself, bathed in a glow of slow-pulsed joy that seemed to rise mysteriously out of the music itself and lay languidly about the airless little room, breathed in and breathed out with each gentle rise and fall of her chest.

After a while she heard a car coming up the drive. She sat up at once, startled, because it couldn't be her father so soon. The gravel kept crunching all the way in from the road—the driveway was long—and Connie ran to the window. It was a car she didn't know. It was an open jalopy, painted a bright gold that caught the sunlight opaquely. Her heart began to pound and her fingers snatched at her hair, checking it, and she whispered "Christ, Christ," wondering how bad she looked. The car came to a stop at the side door and the horn sounded four short taps as if this were a signal Connie knew.

She went into the kitchen and approached the door slowly, then hung out the screen door, her bare toes curling down off the step. There were two boys in the car and now she recognized the driver: he had shaggy, shabby black hair that looked crazy as a wig and he was grinning at her.

"I ain't late, am I?" he said.

"Who the hell do you think you are?" Connie said.

"Toldja I'd be out, didn't I?"

"I don't even know who you are."

She spoke sullenly, careful to show no interest or pleasure, and he spoke in a fast bright monotone. Connie looked past him to the other boy, taking her time. He had fair brown hair, with a lock that fell onto his forehead. His sideburns gave him a fierce, embarrassed look, but so far he hadn't even bothered to glance at her. Both boys wore sunglasses. The driver's glasses were metallic and mirrored everything in miniature.

"You wanta come for a ride?" he said.

Connie smirked and let her hair fall loose over one shoulder.

"Don'tcha like my car? New paint job," he said. "Hey."

"What?"

"You're cute."

She pretended to fidget, chasing flies away from the door.

"Don'cha believe me, or what?" he said.

"Look, I don't even know who you are," Connie said in disgust.

"Hey, Ellie's got a radio, see. Mine's broke down." He lifted his friend's arm and showed her the little transistor the boy was holding, and now Connie began to hear the music. It was the same program that was playing inside the house.

"Bobby King?" she said.

"I listen to him all the time. I think he's great."

"He's kind of great," Connie said reluctantly.

"Listen, that guy's *great*. He knows where the action is."

Connie blushed a little, because the glasses made it impossible for her to see just what this boy was looking at. She couldn't decide if she liked him or if he was just a jerk, and so she dawdled in the doorway and wouldn't come down or go back inside. She said, "What's all that stuff painted on your car?"

"Can'tcha read it?" He opened the door very carefully, as if he was afraid it might fall off. He slid out just as carefully, planting his feet firmly on the ground, the tiny metallic world in his glasses slowing down like gelatine hardening and in the midst of it Connie's bright green blouse. "This here is my name, to begin with," he said. ARNOLD FRIEND was written in tarlike black letters on the side, with a drawing of a round grinning face that reminded Connie of a pumpkin, except it wore sunglasses. "I wanta introduce myself. I'm Arnold Friend and that's my real name and I'm gonna be your friend, honey, and inside the car's Ellie Oscar, he's kinda shy." Ellie brought his transistor radio up to his shoulder and balanced it there. "Now these numbers are a secret code, honey," Arnold Friend explained. He read off the numbers 33, 19, 17 and raised his eyebrows at her to see what she thought of that, but she didn't think much of it. The left rear fender had been smashed and around it was written, on the gleaming gold background: DONE BY CRAZY WOMAN DRIVER. Connie had to laugh at that. Arnold Friend was pleased at her laughter and looked up at her. "Around the other side's a lot more—you wanta come and see them?"

"No."

"Why not?"

"Why should I?"

"Don'tcha wanta see what's on the car? Don'tcha wanta go for a ride?"

"I don't know."

"Why not?"

"I got things to do."

"Like what?"

"Things."

He laughed as if she had said something funny. He slapped his thighs. He was standing in a strange way, leaning back against the car as if he were balancing himself. He wasn't tall, only an inch or so taller than she would be if she came down to him. Connie liked the way he was dressed, which was the way all of them dressed: tight faded jeans stuffed into black, scuffed boots, a belt that pulled his waist in and showed how lean he was, and a white pull-over shirt that was a little soiled and showed the hard small muscles of his arms and shoulders. He looked as if he probably did hard work, lifting and carrying things. Even his neck looked muscular. And his face was a familiar face, somehow: the jaw and chin and cheeks slightly darkened, because he hadn't shaved for a day or two, and the nose long and hawk-like, sniffing as if she were a treat he was going to gobble up and it was all a joke.

"Connie, you ain't telling the truth. This is your day set aside for a ride with me and you know it," he said, still laughing. The way he straightened and recovered from his fit of laughing showed that it had been all fake.

"How do you know what my name is?" she said suspiciously.

"It's Connie."

"Maybe and maybe not."

"I know my Connie," he said, wagging his finger. Now she remembered him even better, back at the restaurant, and her cheeks warmed at the thought of how she sucked in her breath just at the moment she passed him—how she must have looked to him. And he had remembered her. "Ellie and I come out here especially for you," he said. "Ellie can sit in back. How about it?"

"Where?"

"Where what?"

"Where're we going?"

He looked at her. He took off the sunglasses and she saw how pale the skin around his eyes was, like holes that were not in shadow but instead in light. His eyes were like chips of broken glass that catch the light in an amiable way. He smiled. It was as if the idea of going for a ride somewhere, to some place, was a new idea to him.

"Just for a ride, Connie sweetheart."

"I never said my name was Connie," she said.

"But I know what it is. I know your name and all about you, lots of things," Arnold Friend said. He had not moved yet but stood still leaning back against the side of his jalopy. "I took a special interest in you, such a pretty girl, and found out all about you like I know your parents and sister are gone somewheres and I know where and how long they're going to be gone, and I know who you were with last night, and your best girl friend's name is Betty. Right?"

He spoke in a simple lilting voice, exactly as if he were reciting the words to a song. His smile assured her that everything was fine. In the car Ellie turned up the volume on his radio and did not bother to look around at them.

"Ellie can sit in the back seat," Arnold Friend said. He indicated his friend with a casual jerk of his chin, as if Ellie did not count and she should not bother with him.

"How'd you find out all that stuff?" Connie said.

"Listen: Betty Schultz and Tony Fitch and Jimmy Pettinger and Nancy Pettinger," he said, in a chant. "Raymond Stanley and Bob Hutter—"

"Do you know all those kids?"

"I know everybody."

"Look, you're kidding. You're not from around here."

"Sure."

"But—how come we never saw you before?"

"Sure you saw me before," he said. He looked down at his boots, as if he were a little offended. "You just don't remember."

"I guess I'd remember you," Connie said.

"Yeah?" He looked up at this, beaming. He was pleased. He began to mark time with the music from Ellie's radio, tapping his fists lightly together. Connie looked away from his smile to the car, which was painted so bright it almost hurt her eyes to look at it. She looked at that name, ARNOLD FRIEND. And up at the front fender was an expression that was familiar—MAN THE FLYING SAUCERS. It was an expression kids had used the year before, but didn't use this year. She looked at it for a while as if the words meant something to her that she did not yet know.

"What're you thinking about? Huh?" Arnold Friend demanded. "Not worried about your hair blowing around in the car, are you?"

"No."

"Think I maybe can't drive good?"

"How do I know?"

"You're a hard girl to handle. How come?" he said. "Don't you know I'm your friend? Didn't you see me put my sign in the air when you walked by?"

"What sign?"

"My sign." And he drew an X in the air, leaning out toward her. They were maybe ten feet apart. After his hand fell back to his side the X was still in the air, almost visible. Connie let the screen door close and stood perfectly still inside it, listening to the music from her radio and the boy's blend together. She stared at Arnold Friend. He stood there so stiffly relaxed, pretending to be relaxed, with one hand idly on the door handle as if he were keeping himself up that way and had no intention of ever moving again. She recognized most things about him, the tight jeans that showed his thighs and buttocks and the greasy leather boots and the tight shirt, and even that slippery friendly smile of his, that sleepy dreamy smile that all the boys used to get across ideas they didn't want to put into words. She recognized all this and also the sing-song way he talked, slightly mocking, kidding, but serious and a little melancholy, and she recognized the way he tapped one fist against the other in homage to the perpetual music behind him. But all these things did not come together.

She said suddenly, "Hey, how old are you?"

His smile faded. She could see then that he wasn't a kid, he was much older—thirty, maybe more. At this knowledge her heart began to pound faster.

"That's a crazy thing to ask. Can'tcha see I'm your own age?"

"Like hell you are."

"Or maybe a coupla years older, I'm eighteen."

"Eighteen?" she said doubtfully.

He grinned to reassure her and lines appeared at the corners of his mouth. His teeth were big and white. He grinned so broadly his eyes became slits and she saw how thick the lashes were, thick and black as if painted with a black tar-like material. Then he seemed to become embarrassed, abruptly, and looked over his shoulder at Ellie. *"Him,* he's crazy," he said. "Ain't he a riot, he's a nut, a real character." Ellie was still listening to the music. His sunglasses told nothing about what he was thinking. He wore a bright orange shirt unbuttoned halfway to show his chest, which was a pale, bluish chest and not muscular like Arnold Friend's. His shirt collar was turned up all around and the very tips of the collar pointed out past his chin as if they were protecting him. He was pressing the transistor radio up against his ear and sat there in a kind of daze, right in the sun.

"He's kinda strange," Connie said.

"Hey, she says you're kinda strange! Kinda strange!" Arnold Friend cried. He pounded on the car to get Ellie's attention. Ellie turned for the first time and Connie saw with shock that he wasn't a kid either—he had a fair, hairless face, cheeks reddened slightly as if the veins grew too close to the surface of his skin, the face of a forty-year-old baby. Connie felt a wave of dizziness rise in her at this sight and she stared at him as if waiting for something to change the shock of the moment, make it all right again. Ellie's lips kept shaping words, mumbling along with the words blasting in his ear.

"Maybe you two better go away," Connie said faintly.

"What? How come?" Arnold Friend cried. "We come out here to take you for a ride. It's Sunday." He had the voice of the man on the radio now. It was the same voice, Connie thought. "Don'tcha know it's Sunday all day and honey, no matter who you were with last night today you're with Arnold Friend and don't you forget it!—Maybe you better step out here," he said, and this last was in a different voice. It was a little flatter, as if the heat was finally getting to him.

"No. I got things to do."

"Hey."

"You two better leave."

"We ain't leaving until you come with us."

"Like hell I am—"

"Connie, don't fool around with me. I mean, I mean, don't fool *around*," he said, shaking his head. He laughed incredulously. He placed his sunglasses on top of his head, carefully, as if he were indeed wearing a wig, and brought the stems down behind his ears. Connie stared at him, another wave of dizziness and fear rising in her so that for a moment he wasn't even in focus but was just a blur, standing there against his gold car, and she had the idea that he had driven up the driveway all right but had come from nowhere before that and belonged nowhere and that everything about him and even about the music that was so familiar to her was only half real.

"If my father comes and sees you—"

"He ain't coming. He's at a barbecue."

"How do you know that?"

"Aunt Tillie's. Right now they're—uh—they're drinking. Sitting around," he said vaguely, squinting as if he were staring all the way to town and over to Aunt Tillie's back yard. Then the vision seemed to get clear and he nodded energetically. "Yeah. Sitting around. There's your sister in a blue dress, huh? And high heels, the poor sad bitch—nothing like you, sweetheart! And your mother's helping some fat woman with the corn, they're cleaning the corn—husking the corn—"

"What fat woman?" Connie cried.

"How do I know what fat woman, I don't know every goddam fat woman in the world!" Arnold Friend laughed.

"Oh, that's Mrs. Hornby. . . . Who invited her?" Connie said. She felt a little light-headed. Her breath was coming quickly.

"She's too fat. I don't like them fat. I like them the way you are, honey," he said, smiling sleepily at her. They stared at each other for a while, through the screen door. He said softly, "Now what you're going to do is this: you're going to come out that door. You're going to sit up front with me and Ellie's going to sit in the back, the hell with Ellie, right? This isn't Ellie's date. You're my date. I'm your lover, honey."

"What? You're crazy—"

"Yes, I'm your lover. You don't know what that is but you will," he said. "I know that too. I know all about you. But look: it's real nice and you couldn't ask for nobody better than me, or more polite. I always keep my word. I'll tell you how it is, I'm always nice at first, the first time. I'll hold you so tight you won't think you have to try to get away or pretend anything because you'll know you can't. And I'll come inside you where it's all secret and you'll give in to me and you'll love me—"

"Shut up! You're crazy!" Connie said. She backed away from the door. She put her hands against her ears as if she'd heard something terrible, something not meant for her. "People don't talk like that, you're crazy," she muttered. Her heart was almost too big now for her chest and its pumping made sweat break out all over her. She looked out to see Arnold Friend pause and then take a step toward the porch lurching. He almost fell. But, like a clever drunken man, he managed to catch his balance. He wobbled in his high boots and grabbed hold of one of the porch posts.

"Honey?" he said. "You still listening?"

"Get the hell out of here!"

"Be nice, honey. Listen."

"I'm going to call the police—"

He wobbled again and out of the side of his mouth came a fast spat curse, an aside not meant for her to hear. But even this "Christ!" sounded forced. Then he began to smile again. She watched this smile come, awkward as if he were smiling from inside a mask. His whole face was a mask, she thought wildly, tanned down onto his throat but then running out as if he had plastered make-up on his face but had forgotten about his throat.

"Honey—? Listen, here's how it is. I always tell the truth and I promise you this: I ain't coming in that house after you."

"You better not! I'm going to call the police if you—if you don't—"

"Honey," he said, talking right through her voice, "honey, I'm not coming in there but you are coming out here. You know why?"

She was panting. The kitchen looked like a place she had never seen before, some room she had run inside but which wasn't good enough, wasn't going to help her. The kitchen window had never had a curtain, after three years, and there were dishes in the sink for her to do—probably —and if you ran your hand across the table you'd probably feel something sticky there.

"You listening, honey? Hey?"

"—going to call the police—"

"Soon as you touch the phone I don't need to keep my promise and can come inside. You won't want that."

She rushed forward and tried to lock the door. Her fingers were shaking. "But why lock it," Arnold Friend said gently, talking right into her face. "It's just a screen door. It's just nothing." One of his boots was at a strange angle, as if his foot wasn't in it. It pointed out to the left, bent at the ankle. "I mean, anybody can break through a screen door and glass and wood and iron or anything else if he needs to, anybody at all and specially Arnold Friend. If the place got lit up with a fire honey you'd come runnin out into my arms, right into my arms an safe at home—like you knew I was your lover and'd stopped fooling around. I don't mind a nice shy girl but I don't like no fooling around." Part of those words were spoken with a slight rhythmic lilt, and Connie somehow recognized them—the echo of a song from last year, about a girl rushing into her boy friend's arms and coming home again—

Connie stood barefoot on the linoleum floor, staring at him. "What do you want?" she whispered.

"I want you," he said.

"What?"

"Seen you that night and thought, that's the one, yes sir. I never needed to look any more."

"But my father's coming back. He's coming to get me. I had to wash my hair first—" She spoke in a dry, rapid voice, hardly raising it for him to hear.

"No, your Daddy is not coming and yes, you had to wash your hair and you washed it for me. It's nice and shining and all for me, I thank you, sweetheart," he said, with a mock bow, but again he almost lost his balance. He had to bend and adjust his boots. Evidently his feet did not go all the way down; the boots must have been stuffed with something so that he would seem taller. Connie stared out at him and behind him Ellie in the car, who seemed to be looking off toward Connie's right, into nothing. This Ellie said, pulling the words out of the air one after another as if he were just discovering them, "You want me to pull out the phone?"

"Shut your mouth and keep it shut," Arnold Friend said, his face red from bending over or maybe from embarrassment because Connie had seen his boots. "This ain't none of your business."

"What—what are you doing? What do you want?" Connie said. "If I call the police they'll get you, they'll arrest you—"

"Promise was not to come in unless you touch that phone, and I'll keep that promise," he said. He resumed his erect position and tried to force his shoulders back. He sounded like a hero in a movie, declaring something important. He spoke too loudly and it was as if he were speaking to someone behind Connie. "I ain't made plans for coming in that house where I don't belong but just for you to come out to me, the way you should. Don't you know who I am?"

"You're crazy," she whispered. She backed away from the door but did not want to go into another part of the house, as if this would give him permission to come through the door. "What do you. . . . You're crazy, you . . ."

"Huh? What're you saying, honey?"

Her eyes darted everywhere in the kitchen. She could not remember what it was, this room.

"This is how it is, honey: you come out and we'll drive away, have a nice ride. But if you don't come out we're gonna wait till your people come home and then they're all going to get it."

"You want that telephone pulled out?" Ellie said. He held the radio away from his ear and grimaced, as if without the radio the air was too much for him.

"I toldja shut up, Ellie," Arnold Friend said, "you're deaf, get a hearing aid, right? Fix yourself up. This little girl's no trouble and's gonna be nice to me, so Ellie keep to yourself, this ain't your date—right? Don't hem in on me. Don't hog. Don't crush. Don't bird dog. Don't trail me," he said in a rapid meaningless voice, as if he were running through all the expressions he'd learned but was no longer sure which one of them was in style, then rushing on to new ones, making them up with his eyes closed, "Don't crawl under my fence, don't squeeze in my chipmunk hole, don't sniff my glue, suck my popsicle, keep your own greasy fingers on yourself!" He shaded his eyes and peered in at Connie, who was backed against the kitchen table.

"Don't mind him honey he's just a creep. He's a dope. Right? I'm the boy for you and like I said you come out here nice like a lady and give me your hand, and nobody else gets hurt, I mean, your nice old bald-headed daddy and your mummy and your sister in her high heels. Because listen: why bring them in this?"

"Leave me alone," Connie whispered.

"Hey, you know that old woman down the road, the one with the chickens and stuff—you know her?"

"She's dead!"

"Dead? What? You know her?" Arnold Friend said.

"She's dead—"

"Don't you like her?"

"She's dead—she's—she isn't here any more—"

"But don't you like her, I mean, you got something against her? Some grudge or something?" Then his voice dipped as if he were conscious of a rudeness. He touched the sunglasses perched on top of his head as if to make sure they were still there. "Now you be a good girl."

"What are you going to do?"

"Just two things, or maybe three." Arnold Friend said. "But I promise it won't last long and you'll like me the way you get to like people you're close to. You will. It's all over for you here, so come on out. You don't want your people in any trouble, do you?"

She turned and bumped against a chair or something, hurting her leg, but she ran into the back room and picked up the telephone. Something roared in her ear, a tiny roaring, and she was so sick with fear that she could do nothing but listen to it—the telephone was clammy and very heavy and her fingers groped down to the dial but were too weak to touch it. She began to scream into the phone, into the roaring. She cried out, she cried for her mother, she felt her breath start jerking back and forth in her lungs as if it were something Arnold Friend were stabbing her with again and again with no tenderness. A noisy sorrowful wailing rose all about her and she was locked inside it the way she was locked inside this house.

After a while she could hear again. She was sitting on the floor with her wet back against the wall.

Arnold Friend was saying from the door. "That's a good girl. Put the phone back."

She kicked the phone away from her.

"No, honey. Pick it up. Put it back right."

She picked it up and put it back. The dial tone stopped.

"That's a good girl. Now you come outside."

She was hollow with what had been fear, but what was now just an emptiness. All that screaming had blasted it out of her. She sat, one leg cramped under her, and deep inside her brain was something like a pinpoint of light that kept going and would not let her relax. She thought, I'm not going to see my mother again. She thought, I'm not going to sleep in my bed again. Her bright green blouse was all wet.

Arnold Friend said, in a gentle-loud voice that was like a stage voice, "The place where you came from ain't there any more, and where you had in mind to go is cancelled out. This place you are now—inside your daddy's house—is nothing but a cardboard box I can knock down any time. You know that and always did know it. You hear me?"

She thought, I have to think. I have to know what to do.

"We'll go out to a nice field, out in the country here where it smells so nice and it's sunny," Arnold Friend said. "I'll have my arms tight around you so you won't need to try to get away and I'll show you what love is like, what it does. The hell with this house! It looks solid all right," he said. He ran a fingernail down the screen and the noise did not make Connie shiver, as it would have the day before. "Now put your hand on your heart, honey. Feel that? That feels solid too but we know better, be nice to me, be sweet like you can because what else is there for a girl like you but to be sweet and pretty and give in?—and get away before her people come back?"

She felt her pounding heart. Her hand seemed to enclose it. She thought for the first time in her life that it was nothing that was hers, that belonged to her, but just a pounding, living thing inside this body that wasn't really hers either.

"You don't want them to get hurt," Arnold Friend went on. "Now get up, honey. Get up all by yourself."

She stood.

"Now turn this way. That's right. Come over here to me.—Ellie, put that away, didn't I tell you? You dope. You miserable creepy dope," Arnold Friend said. His words were not angry but only part of an incantation. The incantation was kindly. "Now come out through the kitchen to me honey and let's see a smile, try it, you're a brave sweet little girl and now they're eating corn and hotdogs cooked to bursting over an outdoor fire, and they don't know one thing about you and never did and honey you're better than them because not a one of them would have done this for you."

Connie felt the linoleum under her feet; it was cool. She brushed her hair back out of her eyes. Arnold Friend let go of the post tentatively and opened his arms for her, his elbows pointing in toward each other and his wrists limp, to show that this was an embarrassed embrace and a little mocking, he didn't want to make her self-conscious.

She put out her hand against the screen. She watched herself push the door slowly open as if she were safe back somewhere in the other doorway, watching this body and this head of long hair moving out into the sunlight where Arnold Friend waited.

"My sweet little blue-eyed girl," he said, in a half-sung sigh that had nothing to do with her brown eyes but was taken up just the same by the vast sunlit reaches of the land behind him and on all sides of him, so much land that Connie had never seen before and did not recognize except to know that she was going to it.

Technology and Human Values

The successful application of science to our practical problems has been truly described as "one of the miracles of mankind." But no serious writer today can discuss technological progress without misgivings. Most of us, at least, are aware of some of the terrifying consequences that seem always to accompany the gains: the atomic balance of terror; the population explosion; the poisoning of our air, water, and soil; the electronic and psychological threat to privacy; the displacement of skilled workers by skilled machines; the recent advances in brain chemistry and genetics that promise even more danger to human beings.

We place E. B. White's comical science fiction, written in 1950, first because it not only epitomizes the truth that technological progress is always ambiguous, but also deftly brings into the orbit of the present subject two of the topics raised in earlier sections—popular culture and mass media, and what makes a good life.

There follow two essays by historians, originally designed as part of a debate on technology and pessimism, which take up the issue, pro and con, in very general terms. Melvin Kranzberg is on balance optimistic. He points out that technology is never autonomous but gets its effects, for good or evil, by the combinations (sometimes unanticipated) that it makes with other aspects of our society. He is confident that American vitality can overcome whatever problems technology presents. John H. Broomfield is emphatically pessimistic; he links the present threat of "bureaucratic technology" to deep defects in our contemporary economic, political, and social structures. The pieces by Wendell Berry and Garrison Keillor are critical of the technological mentality, too, but they differ much from Broomfield's and from each other's in tone and technique.

The next group takes up an issue that is bound to grow mightily in the next decade: what will computers do to us—for better or for worse—as people? Carl Sagan makes a case for the benefits of "intelligent machines." He is answered by Joseph Weizenbaum, a computer scientist, whose impulse to write arises in part from concern over misinterpretation of his own work. While Sagan satisfiedly calls "each human being . . . a superbly constructed, astonishingly compact, self-ambulatory computer," Weizenbaum is worried that the computer "has brought the view of man as a machine to a new level of plausibility." He believes that "there are certain tasks that computers ought not to be made to do." Thomas B. Sheridan, another computer scientist, while accepting the growth of computer control systems, outlines ways in which they are alienating to humans and concludes that we must hold the human designers and programmers of computers accountable. Steven Levy presents a vivid account of the new "hacker" subculture that is growing up around computer centers; he presents it so graphically as to raise the question of what the obsessive and sometimes amoral character of the hacker means for the future (and the problems) of the coming computer culture itself.

The section ends with two modest probings of our problems of pollution and overconsumption. A *New Yorker* editorial reminds us that "there is no such thing as throwing something 'away.'" The science fiction of Isaac Asimov, on what a real fuel shortage might be like, makes us wonder chillingly whether his vision will turn out to be as true as E. B. White's has already become.

Technology, the Media, and the Good Life

E. B. White

Elwyn Brooks White was born in New York in 1899, graduated from Cornell in 1921, and joined the staff of *The New Yorker* in 1926. He regularly wrote its "Notes and Comment" section until 1938, and along with James Thurber and a few others with talent, was responsible for *The New Yorker's* extraordinary reputation for good writing at that time. From 1938 to 1943, he contributed a monthly column entitled "One Man's Meat" to *Harper's*; in 1932, he acquired a salt-water farm in Maine, the inspiration for a number of those essays. He resumed writing for *The New Yorker* on a free-lance basis in 1945. White has written over twenty books and is noted for his sensitive, humorous character and his witty, natural, and exact style. He has been awarded numerous honorary degrees, the National Institute of Arts and Letters gold medal (1960), and, in 1963, the Presidential Medal of Freedom.

White has written three distinguished children's books, for which he received the Laura Ingalls Wilder Award in 1970: *Stuart Little* (1945), *Charlotte's Web* (1952), and *Trumpet of the Swan* (1970). In 1959 he published *The Elements of Style,* a reverent re-editing of a classic textbook written by his former professor, William Strunk, Jr. Recent collections of his works include *Letters of E. B. White* (1976), *Essays of E. B. White* (1977), and *Poems and Sketches of E. B. White* (1981). The story printed below, taken from *The Second Tree from the Corner* (1954), was first published in *The New Yorker* in February 1950.

The Morning of the Day They Did It

My purpose is to tell how it happened and to set down a few impressions of that morning while it is fresh in memory. I was in a plane that was in radio communication with the men on the platform. To put the matter briefly, what was intended as a military expedient turned suddenly into a holocaust. The explanation was plain enough to me, for, like millions of others, I was listening to the conversation between the two men and was instantly aware of the quick shift it took. That part is clear. What is not so clear is how I myself survived, but I am beginning to understand that, too. I shall not burden the reader with an explanation, however, as the facts are tedious and implausible. I am now in good health and fair spirits, among friendly people on an inferior planet, at a very great distance from the sun. Even the move from one planet to another has not relieved me of the nagging curse that besets writing men—the feeling that they must produce some sort of record of their times.

The thing happened shortly before twelve noon. I came out of my house on East Harding Boulevard at quarter of eight that morning, swinging my newspaper and feeling pretty good. The March day was mild and spring-like, the warmth and the smells doubly welcome after the rotten weather we'd been having. A gentle wind met me on the Boulevard, frisked me, and went on. A man in a leather cap was loading bedsprings into a van in front of No. 220. I remember that as I walked along I worked my tongue around the roof of my mouth, trying to dislodge a prune skin. (These details have no significance; why write them down?)

A few blocks from home there was a Contakt plane station and I hurried in, caught the 8:10 plane, and was soon aloft. I always hated a jet-assist takeoff right after breakfast, but it was one of the discomforts that went with my job. At ten thousand feet our small plane made contact with the big one, we passengers were transferred, and the big ship went on up to fifty thousand, which was the height television planes flew at. I was a script writer for one of the programs. My tour of duty was supposed to be eight hours.

I should probably explain here that at the period of which I am writing, the last days of the planet earth, telecasting was done from planes circling the stratosphere. This eliminated the coaxial cable, a form of relay that had given endless trouble. Coaxials worked well enough for a while, but eventually they were abandoned, largely because of the extraordinary depredations of earwigs. These insects had developed an alarming resistance to bugspray and were out of control most of the time. Earwigs increased in size and in numbers, and the forceps at the end of their abdomen developed so that they could cut through a steel shell. They seemed to go unerringly for coaxials. Whether the signals carried by the cables had anything to do with it I don't know, but the bugs fed on these things and were enormously stimulated. Not only did they feast on the cables, causing the cables to disintegrate, but they laid eggs in them in unimaginable quantities, and as the eggs hatched the television images suffered greatly, there was more and more flickering on the screen, more and more eye-strain and nervous tension among audiences, and of course a further de-basement of taste and intellectual life in general. Finally the coaxials were given up, and after much experimenting by Westinghouse and the Glenn Martin people a satisfactory substitute was found in the high-flying planes. A few of these planes, spotted around the country, handled the whole television load nicely. Known as Stratovideo planes, they were equipped with studios; many programs originated in the air and were transmitted directly, others were beamed to the aircraft from ground stations and then relayed. The planes flew continuously, twenty-four hours a day, were refuelled in air, and dropped down to ten thousand feet every eight hours to meet the Contakt planes and take on new shifts of workers.

I remember that as I walked to my desk in the Stratoship that morning, the nine-o'clock news had just ended and a program called "Author, Please!" was going on, featuring Melonie Babson, a woman who had written a best-seller on the theme of euthanasia, called "Peace of Body." The program was sponsored by a dress-shield company.

I remember, too, that a young doctor had come aboard the plane with the rest of us. He was a newcomer, a fellow named Cathcart, slated to be the physician attached to the ship. He had introduced himself to me in the Contakt plane, had asked the date of my Tri-D shot, and had noted it down in his book. (I shall explain about these shots presently.) This doctor certainly had a brief life in our midst. He had hardly been introduced around and shown his office when our control room got a radio call asking if there was a doctor in the stratosphere above Earthpoint F-plus-6, and requesting medical assistance at the scene of an accident.

F-plus-6 was almost directly below us, so Dr. Cathcart felt he ought to respond, and our control man gave the word and asked for particulars and instructions. It seems there had been a low-altitude collision above F-plus-6 involving two small planes and killing three people. One plane was a Diaheliper, belonging to an aerial diaper service that flew diapers to rural homes by helicopter. The other was one of the familiar government-owned sprayplanes that worked at low altitudes over croplands, truck gardens, and commercial orchards, delivering a heavy mist of the deadly Tri-D solution, the pesticide that had revolutionized agriculture, eliminated the bee from nature, and given us fruits and vegetables of un-dreamed-of perfection but very high toxicity.

The two planes had tangled and fallen onto the observation tower of a whooping-crane sanctuary, scattering diapers over an area of half a mile and releasing a stream of Tri-D. Cathcart got his medical kit, put on his parachute, and paused a moment to adjust his pressurizer, preparatory to bailing out. Knowing that he wouldn't be back for a while, he asked if anybody around the shop was due for a Tri-D shot that morning, and it turned out that Bill Foley was. So the Doctor told Foley to come along, and explained that he would give him his injection on the way down. Bill threw me a quick look of mock anguish, and started climbing into his gear. This must have been six or seven minutes past nine.

It seems strange that I should feel obligated to explain Tri-D shots. They were a commonplace at this time—as much a part of a person's life as his toothbrush. The correct name for them was Anti-Tri-D, but people soon shortened the name. They were simply injections that everyone had to receive at regular twenty-one-day intervals, to counteract the lethal effect of food, and the notable thing about them was the great importance of the twenty-one-day period. To miss one's Tri-D shot by as much as a couple of hours might mean serious consequences, even death. Almost every day there were deaths reported in the papers from failure to get the injection at the proper time. The whole business was something like insulin control in diabetes. You can easily imagine the work it entailed for doctors in the

United States, keeping the entire population protected against death by poisoning.

As Dr. Cathcart and Bill eased themselves out of the plane through the chute exit, I paused briefly and listened to Miss Babson, our author of the day.

"It is a grand privilege," she was saying, "to appear before the television audience this morning and face this distinguished battery of critics, including my old sparring partner, Ralph Armstrong, of the *Herald Tribune.* I suppose after Mr. Armstrong finishes with me I will be a pretty good candidate for euthanasia myself. Ha. But seriously, ladies and gentlemen, I feel that a good book is its own defense."

The authoress had achieved a state of exaltation already. I knew that her book, which she truly believed to be great, had been suggested to her by an agent over a luncheon table and had been written largely by somebody else, whom the publisher had had to bring in to salvage the thing. The final result was a run-of-the-can piece of rubbish easily outselling its nearest competitor.

Miss Babson continued, her exaltation stained with cuteness:

"I have heard my novel criticized on the ground that the theme of euthanasia is too daring, and even that it is anti-Catholic. Well, I can remember, way back in the dark ages, when a lot of things that are accepted as commonplace today were considered daring or absurd. My own father can recall the days when dairy cows were actually bred by natural methods. The farmers of those times felt that the artificial-breeding program developed by our marvelous experiment stations was highfalutin nonsense. Well, we all know what has happened to the dairy industry, with many of our best milch cows giving milk continuously right around the clock, in a steady stream. True, the cows do have to be propped up and held in position in special stanchions and fed intravenously, but I always say it isn't the hubbub that counts, it's the butterfat. And I doubt if even Mr. Armstrong here would want to return to the days when a cow just gave a bucket of milk and then stopped to rest."

Tiring of the literary life, I walked away and looked out a window. Below, near the layer of cumulus, the two chutes were visible. With the help of binoculars I could see Bill manfully trying to slip his chute over next to the Doc, and could see Cathcart fumbling with his needle. Our telecandid man was at another window, filming the thing for the next newscast, as it was a new wrinkle in the Tri-D world to have somebody getting his shot while parachuting.

I had a few chores to do before our program came on, at eleven-five. "Town Meeting of the Upper Air" was the name of it. "Town Meeting" was an unrehearsed show, but I was supposed to brief the guests, distribute copies of whatever prepared scripts there were, explain the cuing, and make everybody happy generally. The program we were readying that morning had had heavy advance billing, and there was tremendous interest in it everywhere, not so much because of the topic ("Will the fear of retaliation stop aggression?") or even the cast of characters, which included Major General Artemus T. Recoil, but because of an incidental stunt we were planning to pull off. We had arranged a radio hookup with the space platform, a gadget the Army had succeeded in establishing six hundred miles up, in the regions of the sky beyond the pull of gravity. The Army, after many years of experimenting with rockets, had not only got the platform established but had sent two fellows there in a Spaceship, and also a liberal supply of the New Weapon.

The whole civilized world had read about this achievement, which swung the balance of power so heavily in our favor, and everyone was aware that the damned platform was wandering around in its own orbit at a dizzy distance from the earth and not subject to gravitational pull. Every kid in America had become an astrophysicist overnight and talked knowingly of exhaust velocities, synergy curves, and Keplerian ellipses. Every subway rider knew that the two men on the platform were breathing oxygen thrown off from big squash vines that they had taken along. The *Reader's Digest* had added to the fun by translating and condensing several German treatises on rockets and space travel, including the great *Wege zur Raumschiffahrt.* But to date, because of security regulations and technical difficulties, there had been no radio-television hookup. Finally we got clearance from Washington, and General Recoil agreed to interview the officers on the platform as part of the "Town Meeting" program. This was big stuff—to hear directly from the Space Platform for Checking Aggression, known pretty generally as the SPCA.

I was keyed up about it myself, but I remember that all that morning in the plane I felt disaffected, and wished I were not a stratovideo man. There were often days like that in the air. The plane, with its queer cargo and its cheap goings on, would suddenly seem unaccountably remote from the world of things I admired. In a physical sense we were never very remote: the plane circled steadily in a fixed circle of about ten miles diameter, and I was never far from my own home on East Harding Boulevard. I could talk to Ann and the children, if I wished, by radiophone.

In many respects mine was a good job. It paid two hundred and twenty-five dollars a week, of which two hundred and ten was withheld. I should have felt well satisfied. Almost everything in the way of social benefits was provided by the government—medical care, hospitalization, education for the children, accident insurance, fire and theft, old-age retirement, Tri-D shots, vacation expense, amusement and recreation, welfare and well-being, Christmas and good will, rainy-day resource, staples and supplies, beverages and special occasions, baby-sitzfund—it had all been worked out. Any man who kept careful account of his pin money could get along all right, and I guess I should have been happy. Ann never complained much, except about one thing. She found that no matter how we saved and planned, we never could afford to buy flowers. One day, when she was a bit lathered up over household problems, she screamed, "God damn it, I'd rather live dangerously and have one dozen yellow freesias!" It seemed to prey on her mind.

Anyway, this was one of those oppressive days in the air for me. Something about the plane's undeviating course irritated me; the circle we flew seemed a monstrous excursion to nowhere. The engine noise (we flew at subsonic speed) was an unrelieved whine. Usually I didn't notice the engines, but today the ship sounded in my ears every minute, reminding me of a radiotherapy chamber, and there was always the palpable impact of vulgar miracles—the very nature of television—that made me itchy and fretful.

Appearing with General Recoil on "Town Meeting of the Upper Air" were to be Mrs. Florence Gill, president of the Women's Auxiliary of the Sons of Original Matrons; Amory Buxton, head of the Economics and Withholding Council of the United Nations; and a young man named Tollip, representing one of the small, ineffectual groups that advocated world federation. I rounded up this stable of intellects in the reception room, went over the procedure with them, gave the General a drink (which seemed to be what was on his mind), and then ducked out to catch the ten-o'clock news and to have a smoke.

I found Pete Everhardt in the control room. He looked bushed. "Quite a morning, Nuncle," he said. Pete not only had to keep his signal clean on the nine-o'clock show (Melonie Babson was a speaker who liked to range all over the place when she talked) but he had to keep kicking the ball around with the two Army officers on the space platform, for fear he would lose them just as they were due to go on. And on top of that he felt obliged to stay in touch with Dr. Cathcart down below, as a matter of courtesy, and also to pick up incidental stuff for subsequent newscasts.

I sat down and lit a cigarette. In a few moments the day's authoress wound up her remarks and the news started, with the big, tense face of Ed Peterson on the screen dishing it out. Ed was well equipped by nature for newscasting; he had the accents of destiny. When he spread the news, it penetrated in depth. Each event not only seemed fraught with meaning, it seemed fraught with Ed. When he said "I predict . . ." you felt the full flow of his pipeline to God.

To the best of my recollection the ten-o'clock newscast on this awful morning went as follows:

(Announcer) "Good morning. Tepky's Hormone-Enriched Dental Floss brings you Ed Peterson and the news."

(Ed) "Flash! Three persons were killed and two others seriously injured a few minutes ago at Earthpoint F-plus-6 when a government sprayplane collided with a helicopter of the Diaheliper Company. Both pilots were thrown clear. They are at this moment being treated by a doctor released by parachute from Stratovideo Ship 3, from which I am now speaking. The sprayplane crashed into the observation tower of a whooping-crane sanctuary, releasing a deadly mist of Tri-D and instantly killing three wardens who were lounging there watching the love dance of the cranes. Diapers were scattered widely over the area, and these sterile garments proved invaluable to Dr. Herbert L. Cathcart in bandaging the wounds of the injured pilots, Roy T. Bliss and Homer Schenck. [Here followed a newsreel shot showing Cathcart winding a diaper around the head of one of the victims.] You are now at the scene of the disaster," droned Ed. "This is the first time in the history of television that an infant's napkin has appeared in the role of emergency bandage. Another first for American Tel. & Vid.!

"Washington! A Senate committeee, with new facts at its disposal, will reopen the investigation to establish the blame for Pearl Harbor.

"Chicago! Two members of the Department of Sanitation were removed from the payroll today for refusal to take the loyalty oath. Both are members of New Brooms, one of the four hundred thousand organizations on the Attorney General's subversive list.

"Hollywood! It's a boy at the Roscoe Pews. Stay tuned to this channel for a closeup of the Caesarean section during the eleven-o'clock roundup!

"New York! Flash! The Pulitzer Prize in editorial writing has been awarded to Frederick A. Mildly, of the New York *Times,* for his nostalgic editorial 'The Old Pumphandle.'

"Flash! Donations to the Atlantic Community Chest now stand at a little over seven hundred billion dollars. Thanks for a wonderful job of giving —I mean that from my heart.

"New York! The vexing question of whether Greek athletes will be allowed to take part in next year's Olympic Games still deadlocks the Security Council. In a stormy session yesterday the Russian delegate argued that the presence of Greek athletes at the games would be a threat to world peace. Most of the session was devoted to a discussion of whether the question was a procedural matter or a matter of substance.

"Flash! Radio contact with the two United States Army officers on the Space Platform for Checking Aggression, known to millions of listeners as the SPCA, has definitely been established, despite rumors to the contrary. The television audience will hear their voices in a little more than one hour from this very moment. You will *not* see their faces. Stay tuned! This is history, ladies and gentlemen—the first time a human voice freed from the pull of gravity has been heard on earth. The spacemen will be interviewed by Major General Artemus T. Recoil on the well-loved program 'Town Meeting of the Upper Air.'

"I predict: that because of SPCA and the Army's Operation Space, the whole course of human destiny will be abruptly changed, and that the age-old vision of peace is now on the way to becoming a reality."

Ed finished and went into his commercial, which consisted of digging a piece of beef gristle out of his teeth with dental floss.

I rubbed out my cigarette and walked back toward my cell. In the studio next to ours, "The Bee" was on the air, and I paused for a while to watch.

"The Bee" was a program sponsored by the Larry Cross Pollination Company, aimed principally at big orchardists and growers—or rather at their wives. It was an interminable mystery-thriller sort of thing, with a character called the Bee, who always wore a green hood with two long black feelers. Standing there in the aisle of the plane, looking into the glass-enclosed studio, I could see the Bee about to strangle a red-haired girl in slinky pajamas. This was America's pollination hour, an old standby, answer to the housewife's dream. The Larry Cross outfit was immensely rich. I think they probably handled better than eighty per cent of all fertilization in the country. Bees, as I have said, had become extinct, thanks to the massive doses of chemicals, and of course this had at first posed a serious agricultural problem, as vast areas were without natural pollination. The answer came when the Larry Cross firm was organized, with the slogan "We Carry the Torch for Nature." The business mushroomed, and branch offices sprang up all over the nation. During blossom time, field crews of highly trained men fanned out and pollinized everything by hand—a huge job and an arduous one. The only honey in the United States was synthetic —a blend of mineral oil and papaya juice. Ann hated it with a morbid passion.

When I reached my studio I found everybody getting ready for the warmup. The Town Crier, in his fusty costume, stood holding his bell by the clapper, while the makeup man touched up his face for him. Mrs. Gill, the S.O.M. representative, sat gazing contemptuously at young Tollip. I had riffled through her script earlier, curious to find out what kind of punch she was going to throw. It was about what I expected. Her last paragraph contained the suggestion that all persons who advocated a revision of the Charter of the United Nations be automatically deprived of their citizenship. "If these well-meaning but misguided persons," ran the script, "with their utopian plans for selling this nation down the river are so anxious to acquire world citizenship, I say let's make it easy for them —let's take away the citizenship they've already got and see how they like it. As a lineal descendant of one of the Sons of Original Matrons, I am sick and tired of these cuckoo notions of one world, which come dangerously close to simple treachery. We've enough to do right here at home without . . ."

And so on. In my mind's ear I could already hear the moderator's salutary and impartial voice saying, "Thank you, Mrs. Florence Gill."

At five past eleven, the Crier rang his bell. "Hear ye! See ye! Town Meetin' today! Listen to both sides and make up your own minds!" Then George Cahill, the moderator, started the ball rolling.

I glanced at Tollip. He looked as though his stomach were filling up with gas. As the program got under way, my own stomach began to inflate, too, the way it often did a few hours after breakfast. I remember very little of the early minutes of that morning's Town Meeting. I recall that the U.N. man spoke first, then Mrs. Gill, then Tollip (who looked perfectly awful).

Finally the moderator introduced General Recoil, whose stomach enjoyed the steadying effects of whiskey and who spoke in a loud, slow, confident voice, turning frequently to smile down on the three other guests.

"We in the Army," began the General, "don't pretend that we know all the answers to these brave and wonderful questions. It is not the Army's business to know whether aggression is going to occur or not. Our business is to put on a good show if it *does* occur. The Army is content to leave to the United Nations and to idealists like Mr. Tollip the troublesome details of political progress. I certainly don't know, ladies and gentlemen, whether the fear of retaliation is going to prevent aggression, but I *do* know that there is no moss growing on we of Operation Space. As for myself, I guess I am what you might call a retaliatin' fool. [Laughter in the upper air.] Our enemy is well aware that we are now in a most unusual position to retaliate. That knowledge on the part of our enemy is, in my humble opinion, a deterrent to aggression. If I didn't believe that, I'd shed this uniform and get into a really well-paid line of work, like professional baseball."

Will this plane never quit circling? (I thought). Will the words never quit going round and round? Is there no end to this noisy carrousel of indigestible ideas? Will no one ever catch the brass ring?

"But essentially," continued the General, "our job is not to deal with the theoretical world of Mr. Tollip, who suggests that we merge in some vast superstate with every Tom, Dick, and Harry, no matter what their color or race or how underprivileged they are, thus pulling down our standard of living to the level of the lowest common denominator. Our job is not to deal with the diplomatic world of Mr. Buxton, who hopes to find a peaceful solution around a conference table. No, the Army must face the world as it is. We know the enemy is strong. In our dumb way, we think it is just horse sense for us to be stronger. And I'm proud, believe me, ladies and gentlemen, proud to be at one end of the interplanetary conversation that is about to take place on this very, *very* historic morning. The achievement of the United States Army in establishing the space platform—which is literally a man-made planet—is unparalleled in military history. We have led the way into space. We have given Old Lady Gravity the slip. We have got there, and we have got there fustest with the mostest. [Applause.]

"I can state without qualification that the New Weapon, in the capable hands of the men stationed on our platform, brings the *en*tire globe under our dominion. We can pinpoint any spot, anywhere, and sprinkle it with our particular brand of thunder. Mr. Moderator, I'm ready for this interview if the boys out there in space are ready."

Everyone suspected that there might be a slipup in the proceedings at this point, that the mechanical difficulties might prove insuperable. I glanced at the studio clock. The red sweep hand was within a few jumps of eleven-thirty—the General had managed his timing all right. Cahill's face was tenser than I had ever seen it before. Because of the advance buildup, a collapse at this moment would put him in a nasty hole, even for an old experienced m.c. But at exactly eleven-thirty the interview started, smooth as silk. Cahill picked it up from the General.

"And now, watchers of television everywhere, you will hear a conversation between Major General Artemus T. Recoil, who pioneered Operation Space, and two United States Army officers on the platform—Major James Obblington, formerly of Brooklyn, New York, now of Space, and Lieutenant Noble Trett, formerly of Sioux City, Iowa, now of Space. Go ahead, General Recoil!"

"Come in, Space!" said the General, his tonsils struggling in whiskey's undertow, his eyes bearing down hard on the script. "Can you hear me, Major Obblington and Lieutenant Trett?"

"I hear you," said a voice. "This is Trett." The voice, as I remember it, astonished me because of a certain laconic quality that I had not expected. I believe it astonished everyone. Trett's voice was cool, and he sounded as though he were right in the studio.

"Lieutenant Trett," continued the General, "tell the listeners here on earth, tell us, in your position far out there in free space, do you feel the pull of gravity?"

"No, sir, I don't," answered Trett. In spite of the "sir," Trett sounded curiously listless, almost insubordinate.

"Yet you are perfectly comfortable, sitting there on the platform, with the whole of earth spread out before you like a vast target?"

"Sure I'm comfortable."

The General waited a second, as though expecting amplification, but it failed to come. "Well, ah, how's the weather up there?" he asked heartily.

"There isn't any," said Trett.

"No weather? No weather in space? That's very interesting."

"The hell it is," said Trett. "It's God-damn dull. This place is a dump. Worse than some of the islands in the Pacific."

"Well, I suppose it must get on your nerves a bit. That's all part of the game. Tell us, Lieutenant, what's it like to be actually part of the solar system, with your own private orbit?"

"It's all right, except I'd a damn sight rather get drunk," said Trett.

I looked at Cahill. He was swallowing his spit. General Recoil took a new hold on his script.

"And you say you don't feel the pull of gravity, not even a little?"

"I just told you I didn't feel any pull," said Trett. His voice now had a surly quality.

"Well, ah," continued the General, who was beginning to tremble, "can you describe, briefly, for the television audience—" But it was at this point that Trett, on the platform, seemed to lose interest in talking with General Recoil and started chinning with Major Obblington, his sidekick in space. At first the three voices clashed and blurred, but the General, on a signal from the moderator, quit talking, and the conversation that ensued between Trett and Obblington was audible and clear. Millions of listeners must have heard the dialogue.

"Hey, Obie," said Trett, "you want to know something else I don't feel the pull of, besides gravity?"

"What?" asked his companion.

"Conscience," said Trett cheerfully. "I don't feel my conscience pulling me around."

"Neither do I," said Obblington. "I ought to feel some pulls but I don't."

"I also don't feel the pull of duty."

"Check," said Obblington.

"And what is even more fantastic, I don't feel the pull of dames."

Cahill made a sign to the General. Stunned and confused by the turn things had taken, Recoil tried to pick up the interview and get it back on the track. "Lieutenant Trett," he commanded, "you will limit your remarks to the—"

Cahill waved him quiet. The next voice was the Major's.

"Jesus, now that you mention it, I don't feel the pull of dames either! Hey, Lieutenant—you suppose gravity has anything to do with sex?"

"God damn if *I* know," replied Trett. "I know I don't *weigh* anything, and when you don't weigh anything, you don't seem to *want* anything."

The studio by this time was paralyzed with attention. The General's face was swollen, his mouth was half open, and he struggled for speech that wouldn't come.

Then Trett's cool, even voice again: "See that continent down there, Obie? That's where old Fatso Recoil lives. You feel drawn toward that continent in any special way?"

"Naa," said Obblington.

"You feel like doing a little shooting, Obie?"

"You're rootin' tootin' I feel like shootin'."

"Then what are we waiting for?"

I am, of course, reconstructing this conversation from memory. I am trying to report it faithfully. When Trett said the words "Then what are we waiting for?" I quit listening and dashed for the phones in the corridor. As I was leaving the studio, I turned for a split second and looked back. The General had partially recovered his power of speech. He was mumbling something to Cahill. I caught the words "phone" and "Defense Department."

The corridor was already jammed. I had only one idea in my head—to speak to Ann. Pete Everhardt pushed past me. He said crisply, "This is it." I nodded. Then I glanced out of a window. High in the east a crazy ribbon of light was spreading upward. Lower down, in a terrible parabola, another streak began burning through. The first blast was felt only slightly in the plane. It must have been at a great distance. It was followed immediately by two more. I saw a piece of wing break up, saw one of the starboard engines shake itself loose from its fastenings and fall. Near the phone booths, the Bee, still in costume, fumbled awkwardly for a para-chute. In the crush one of his feelers brushed my face. I never managed to reach a phone. All sorts of things flashed through my mind. I saw Ann and the children, their heads in diapers. I saw again the man in the leather cap, loading bedsprings. I heard again Pete's words, "This is it," only I seemed to hear them in translation: "Until the whole wide world to nothingness do sink." (How durable the poets are!) As I say, I never managed the phone call. My last memory of the morning is of myriads of bright points of destruction where the Weapon was arriving, each pyre in the characteristic shape of an artichoke. Then a great gash, and the plane tumbling. Then I lost consciousness.

I cannot say how many minutes or hours after that the earth finally broke up. I do not know. There is, of course, a mild irony in the fact that it was the United States that was responsible. Insofar as it can be said of any country that it had human attributes, the United States was well-meaning. Of that I am convinced. Even I, at this date and at this distance, cannot forget my country's great heart and matchless ingenuity. I can't in honesty say that I believe we were wrong to send the men to the platform—it's just that in any matter involving love, or high explosives, one can never foresee all the factors. Certainly I can't say with any assurance that Tollip's theory was right; it seems hardly likely that anyone who suffered so from stomach gas could have been on the right track. I did feel sympathetic toward some of his ideas, perhaps because I suffered from flatulence myself. Anyway, it was inevitable that it should have been the United States that developed the space platform and the new weapon that made the H-bomb obsolete. It was inevitable that what happened, at last, was conceived in good will.

Those times—those last days of earth! I think about them a lot. A sort of creeping ineptitude had set in. Almost everything in life seemed wrong to me, somehow, as though we were all hustling down a blind alley. Many of my friends seemed mentally confused, emotionally unstable, and I have an idea I seemed the same to them. In the big cities, horns blew before the light changed, and it was clear that motorists no longer had the capacity to endure the restrictions they had placed on their own behavior. When the birds became extinct (all but the whooping crane), I was reasonably sure that human beings were on the way out, too. The cranes survived only because of their dance—which showmen were quick to exploit. (Every sanctuary had its television transmitter, and the love dance became a more popular spectacle than heavyweight prizefighting.) Birds had always been the symbol of freedom. As soon as I realized that they were gone, I felt that the significance had gone from my own affairs. (I was a cranky man, though—I must remember that, too—and am not trying here to suggest anything beyond a rather strong personal sadness at all this.)

Those last days! There were so many religions in conflict, each ready to save the world with its own dogma, each perfectly intolerant of the other. Every day seemed a mere skirmish in the long holy war. It was a time of debauch and conversion. Every week the national picture magazines, as though atoning for past excesses, hid their cheesecake carefully away among four-color reproductions of the saints. Television was the universal peepshow—in homes, schools, churches, bars, stores, everywhere. Children early formed the habit of gaining all their images at second hand, by looking at a screen; they grew up believing that anything perceived directly was vaguely fraudulent. Only what had been touched with electronics was valid and real. I think the decline in the importance of direct images dated from the year television managed to catch an eclipse of the moon. After that, nobody ever looked at the sky, and it was as though the moon had joined the shabby company of buskers. There was really never a moment when a child, or even a man, felt free to look away from the television screen—for fear he might miss the one clue that would explain everything.

In many respects I like the planet I'm on. The people here have no urgencies, no capacity for sustained endeavor, but merely tackle things by fits and starts, leaving undone whatever fails to hold their interest, and so, by witlessness and improvidence, escape many of the errors of accomplishment. I like the apples here better than those on earth. They are often wormy, but with a most wonderful flavor. There is a saying here: "Even a very lazy man can eat around a worm."

But I would be lying if I said I didn't miss that other life, I loved it so.

Technology and Its Consequences

Melvin Kranzberg

Melvin Kranzberg, a historian of technology, was born in 1917, and received his education at Amherst and Harvard University, where he earned his Ph.D. in 1942. He served on the history faculty of Case Western Reserve University from 1952 until 1972, when he became Callaway Professor of the History of Technology at Georgia Institute of Technology. He has edited and been the author or co-author of numerous works on the history of technology in Western culture. The article reprinted here appeared in the Spring 1980 *Alternative Futures*. It was originally one of a series of lectures given by Kranzberg, John H. Broomfield, and Samuel Florman; Broomfield's reply is printed below.

Technology: The Half-Full Cup

Historians find it instructive to look back at how people dreamt of the future and then at how things actually turned out, to regard the differences between ideals and the spotted actuality. This exercise is especially interesting when one considers "Technology and Pessimism," because treatment of such a topic would have been almost unthinkable back in 1880. Instead, our forebears a century ago would most likely have linked technology with optimism.

For what our great-grandparents saw a hundred years ago inspired them with hope about the century to come. They looked ahead to a world where poverty had ended, where democratic society had spread the blessings of liberty and equality to all mankind, where machines performed all worrisome toil so that men lived in leisure, where universal education had blotted out ignorance and superstition, and where international peace and brotherhood reigned.

Our great-grandparents' optimism is in startling contrast to today's mood. Yet in 1880 there was ample justification for their boundless confidence. For one thing, the rapid growth of scientific knowledge during the 19th century supported the hope for future advancement. The 18th century Enlightenment's idea of progress had been fortified during the 19th century by Darwin's theory of evolution, so that man's past appeared to be a long struggle upward from the primal ooze through the Stone Age and progressive stages to the comforts of the Gilded Age.[o]

The Industrial Revolution, which had spread to America during the 19th century, provided material evidence of this human progress. At the beginning of the 19th century, a man could travel on land only as fast as a horse could carry him, and on sea only as fast as a sailing vessel could —and these speeds were not significantly faster than they had been several thousand years earlier. But during the course of the 19th century, man invented the railroad, which moved him over the earth's surface at speeds approaching a mile a minute, and steamships which carried him across the oceans faster and more reliably than did sailing vessels. The 19th century's accomplishments in communications were just as spectacular. Throughout most of human history, people could be heard only as far as the voice could carry, but by the 1880s messages were carried over telegraph wires for long distances, and a new-fangled invention, the telephone, had just come into being. In the field of power, too, great developments had taken place. The steam engine had come into widespread use as a source of

Gilded Age   A period of U.S. history from about 1865 to the business panic of 1873, a time associated with loose business and political morals and a gaudy display of wealth. The era takes its name from *The Gilded Age* (1873), a novel by Mark Twain and Charles Dudley Warner.

mechanical power, taking the burden off men's backs, while the perfection of Otto's internal-combustion engine provided the basis for the growth of today's automotive society. A whole new era of power, light, and communication was coming into being. Electric current had not been discovered until the first third of the 19th century, but by the end of the century, with Thomas Edison's development of the incandescent light bulb and of the central generating station, electricity was becoming commonplace.

The pace of technical progress in the 20th century has been even more rapid than in the 19th century. Very near the beginning of this century, the vacuum tube, operating by means of a guided passage of electrons first noted by Edison, and hence called the "Edison effect," gave birth to our modern age of electronics. At the turn of this century men had not yet mastered the art of heavier-than-air flight; yet within three-quarters of a century after the Wright Brothers' first flight, man had landed on the moon, a feat marking the culmination of the Scientific Revolution of the 17th century and the Industrial Revolution of the 18th century, as well as the fulfillment of one of man's most ancient dreams.

One could go on and on with a litany of technological triumphs in our times, but as Howard P. Segal has pointed out, "We must question the notion that technological advances are inherently progressive."[1] For not all of our technological advances have turned out the way we had hoped and expected.

Not only have we not reached the material utopia promised by our technology, but every step we take along the way makes it seem as though we are running on a gilded treadmill. Just as we approached the ideal of producing enough goods and services to provide middle-class comfort for all Americans, we discovered a large number of people living at or below the poverty level, with the current inflation adding to that number daily. Our astronauts can whiz around the earth in less than an hour, and anyone with a credit card and a reservation on the Concorde can breakfast in New York and London on the same morning, yet suburban commuters can't get to work on time. Our cars are the most powerful and luxurious in the world, but we are running out of the gas to drive them. Our computers can solve in a few seconds mathematical problems that would require an individual fifty years to solve, our copy machines multiply papers faster than the sorcerer's apprentice could dump them into a garbage can, and television and radio bring instant information to us; yet men feel less and less capable of understanding the world in which they live. Despite our vast communications network, people agonize as never before over "the failure to communicate."

We find ourselves baffled by this series of paradoxes. Every technical

[1]Howard P. Segal, "Let's Abandon the Whig Theory of the History of Technology," *Chronicle of Higher Education,* July 9, 1979: p. 64.

triumph seems counterbalanced—some would say "outweighed"—by a human defeat.

Over thirty years ago (1947), W. H. Auden published a poem entitled "The Age of Anxiety." Auden was indeed a prophet because two decades later anxiety began to overwhelm American society—and technology was made the scapegoat. Indeed, some of today's social critics place the entire blame for our problems on our technology, claiming that it has provided the instrumentality for the heedless pursuit of wealth and material possessions.

I cannot accept that proposition. Even the most summary of historical surveys would demonstrate that technology has provided man with goods and services, food, shelter, and clothing; it has quickened transportation, heightened communication, and furthered our democratic society in many respects. In the highly industrialized societies, people are living longer and better than ever before by any kind of material standard one would devise.

But, of course, there is more to life than material goods and creature comforts. What has technology done for human values? Lewis Mumford, one of our outstanding social critics, claims that technology is engaged in destroying the values of life,[2] and the late Herbert Marcuse echoed the criticism, stating that technology simply enslaves people by raising false needs and providing false satisfaction.[3]

I should like to suggest that the problem is not technology itself but the way in which technology has interacted with other aspects of our society, so that technical developments frequently have unforeseen social and human consequences. I express this in the form of Kranzberg's First Law: "Technology is neither good nor bad, nor is it neutral." By that I mean that technology's interaction with society is such that technical developments frequently have human and social consequences which go far beyond the immediate purpose of the technical devices and practices themselves.

The fact is that technology does not function autonomously.[4] Instead, it interacts with social values and institutions, and sometimes the results are certainly not completely beneficial to man, especially when several technologies come together with synergistic effect. Yet I would also like to suggest that our present concern for non-material things, for societal be-

---

[2]Mumford first made this claim in *Technics and Civilization* (New York, 1934), but he still remained optimistic about the forthcoming "Neotechnic Phase." Some thirty years later he had become pessimistic: *The Myth of the Machine*, 2 vols. (New York, 1967–70).

[3]Herbert Marcuse, *An Essay on Liberation* (Boston, 1959).

[4]Langdon Winner, *Autonomous Technology: Technics-Out-of-Control as a Theme in Political Thought* (Cambridge, MA, 1977) takes the opposite point of view.

nefit, for the "higher culture," for social justice, for preservation of the environment and ecology—all these "good causes" (and that is not meant disparagingly)—are a luxury deriving from the very effectiveness of our technological efforts in the past.

For most of human history, men lived in a society of scarcity, so their attention was concentrated on obtaining a sufficiency of material goods. The great outpouring of goods made possible by industrialization in modern times has altered this. Now that we have reached the prospect—if not the complete fulfillment—of the "abundant society," we can begin to turn our attention beyond the immediate satisfaction of our animal needs and creature comforts. We can begin to think of technology in terms of its impact upon society as a whole and upon the physical environment.

One reason a better world has not yet come into being is that we have not had the social innovations to accompany our technological advancements. Instead, our technical achievements have been utilized in the services of values and institutions belonging to an earlier, more competitive society, one based on scarcity.

In past ages, when men worked from sunup to sundown just to eke out a living from the soil, with the hope that they would have enough to subsist for the next day or until the next harvest, men simply did not have time to worry about how their activities affected the global environment; children, also brought up in this backbreaking work, simply did not have time to worry about how they related to their parents; and most human experiences were so demeaning in character that there was little call to "share the experience." Today's "abundant society" has given us the opportunity to worry about more than meeting the minimal needs for sustaining life —and we are now free to worry about the use of our leisure time, the so-called "higher" things of life, the natural environment, and even to worry about our fellow inhabitants on Spaceship Earth.

By catering to man's basic material needs, technology enables man to think beyond those to other values, for human values go beyond survival needs. Carlos Alzamora, Peru's representative to the United Nations, once defined the values of civilized man in terms of moral, political, and social "orders." The moral order involves fundamental human rights; the political order liberates people from colonialism and upholds the rule of law; and the social order provides social justice for all. How are these orders affected by technology?

Throughout antiquity, up to one quarter of the population consisted of slaves, who were considered as property and had few rights as individuals. In the Middle Ages, slavery diminished, but the serfs, numerically the largest group in the population, possessed few rights, and those only by virtue of the custom associated with their plot of land, not as individuals. Although the decline of feudalism in the West loosened the bonds of serfdom, elements of serfdom (including the great power of the landlord) have persisted throughout most of the world which did not undergo industrialization. The Industrial Revolution was the catalyst which put an end to feudalism and serfdom. But it changed more than that. Throughout history, the hearth and home had been the center of production. Industrialization moved families to the cities and made factory labor the source of their livelihoods.

What did industrialization do to the individual? Brought into contact with others in a centralized working place, the workingmen could communicate their grievances to one another and they could begin to organize in order to better their lives. For the first time in human history, the ordinary laborer began having a voice in his own destiny—to obtain social justice and personal dignity. Nonetheless, there is a widespread feeling that the worker is losing his individuality—his humanity—on the factory production line. In one sense that is certainly true. Freedom from heavy physical labor does not mean that people no longer have to work, nor does it mean individual license. Some sacrifice of unbridled individualism is necessary if men are to work together. Technology makes compulsory some form of cooperation and discipline among human beings in order to carry on collective tasks. In the great irrigation civilizations of antiquity —in Mesopotamia and Egypt, in China and India—men worked together to build great systems of dikes, dams, and irrigation canals. Their "cooperation" was ensured by the whip; advancing technology and changed social practices have done away with the need for this kind of physical compulsion. Nowadays the question is the degree to which those engaged in this kind of collective action are consulted. In earlier eras, they were not, and even today some social critics complain of the workers' loss of freedom in advanced industrialized nations of the West. However, if we look closely at what is happening, we find that in the most advanced countries, such as Sweden, West Germany, and even the United States, workers are consulted more and more regarding the conditions of their work and their rights on the job.[5]

Critics of technology who claim that it is opposed to human freedom must eventually confront the historical reality: Why is it that, with but few exceptions, the most technologically advanced countries are those which enjoy the greatest amount of democratic freedom, have eradicated cruel and degrading punishments, uphold religious freedom, and in short, endorse fundamental human rights? Why are the most technologically advanced states the ones which have provided for equality of the sexes, abolished child labor, condemned racial discrimination, recognized the rights of workers to associate, developed social security systems for the aged, and in short, upheld the concept and practice of social justice? Can all this be ascribed to mere coincidence?

This does not mean that technology by itself is responsible for the development of social justice in the modern world. What I am saying is that

[5]Melvin Kranzberg and Joseph Gies, *By the Sweat of Thy Brow: Work in the Western World* (New York, 1975).

technology is a necessary but not sufficient condition for achieving social justice in the modern world. In order to achieve humane and social goals, technology must interact with other societal elements. But as further proof of the non-neutrality of technology, we also have evidence of technology's interaction with far different values at other places and periods in human history where it has been the instrument for man's bestiality and brutality to his fellow man through the medium of wars, sometimes pursued for high religious ideals or as a "civilizing mission."

Because technology interacts so strongly with our social values and institutions, it is blamed for much of the trouble in the world today. It is also, however, the instrumentality which might enable us to overcome some of our problems—including those which came into being by prior interactions of technology with other sets of social values and institutions.

We call ours a "Technological Age." It is called that, not because all men are engineers, and certainly not because everybody understands technology. We call it that because we are aware, as never before, of the important role which technology plays in our lives. But man has always lived in a technological age, insofar as his life and work have been bound up with his technology. The difference lies in the increased awareness in our own times of our dependence upon our technology, largely because of the accelerated pace of technology in our own times and evidence of what happens to our lives and society when our technology is suddenly cut off or goes awry. Indeed, technology has so ingrained itself into the texture of our daily lives that we take it for granted, not realizing how significant it is to us until a breakdown of an electrical relay plunges an entire section of the nation into darkness or until political events in far-off places threaten our right to drive.

Technology has thus complicated our lives, making us dependent upon our technology, but even more dependent upon one another—and hence upon our humanity. As Gunther Stent has pointed out, ". . . the technological consequences of scientific progress have rendered the making of [rational decisions regarding man's fate] ever more pressing and their effects ever more grave. . . ."[6]

Complicated as it might be, we still must develop those social innovations and institutional mechanisms which will enable us to utilize our technology to best account for mankind. Although we know by now that technology of itself will not provide us with utopia, there is no indication that turning away from technology will have that effect. Indeed, an unvarnished anti-technological stance would mean the abandonment of all hope that we would ever be able to improve the life of mankind and would bring us to Thomas Hobbes's version of man's life in the natural state: nasty, brutish, and short.

A few years ago the proponents of a new "consciousness," or the coun-

[6]Gunther S. Stent, *The Paradoxes of Progress* (Berkeley, 1978).

ter-culture, turned their backs on technology. They provided trenchant criticism of current American society, and they advocated a lifestyle which was very beguiling and appealing to affluent college youth. But they did not address problems like poverty and medical care distribution and the hunger of most people throughout the world. Such problems cannot be resolved without the aid of technology. The question is which technologies and how best to match these with the social matrix in which they will be employed. The growing need for water provides an example, for the world's population grows by about 200,000 people per day, each requiring about 500 tons of water per year. Last year's population increase alone created an additional annual water demand for thirty-six billion tons of water, or the equivalent of a medium-sized river. Does anyone seriously believe that we can meet the world's future water needs without recourse to technology? Does anyone truly object to our encouraging science and technology so as to meet the energy and food needs of today and tomorrow?

Nevertheless, our continued reliance on technology fills many individuals with forebodings, for they feel that we cannot control our technology. This is part of a larger question: How can individuals exercise some measure of democratic control in a society which is characterized by bigness and which involves problems whose scientific and technical components can only be comprehended by experts?

This problem of social control arises partly from the vastness of scale of the contemporary world—the larger number of people—the interdependence of a highly complex industrial society, and the acceleration of change. But these elements also characterize our social institutions too, making them seem to function without heed to the needs and wants of the people. Everywhere it seems that the democratic and individualistic impulses of American life are losing out to "big business, big government, big everything." How can we attain some measure of democratic control over these large organisms and make them socially responsive and responsible?

The institutions which we have developed for control and use of our technology share the characteristics of other societal institutions; namely, they are created and run by people, and, consequently, tend to serve the interests of their owners or managers rather than those of their constituency.

Though institutions sometimes war on each other, their most pernicious habit is joining forces with other institutions to reinforce and enlarge their power. Technology serves as a means whereby some of those who control institutions can expand their power further. The battle has long been joined between man and the institutions of his own creation. Technology has merely enlarged the battleground, weapons, and dimensions of this age-old and never-ending struggle.

Nevertheless, within the past few years we have begun to institutionalize new sociopolitical mechanisms for directing our technology to serve the common weal rather than the narrow interests of a favored few. Heretofore technology was employed by men who sought their own profits, without regard to society, or—to be more accurate as well as more charitable—who equated their own profits with social benefits. Now society is beginning to demand a voice in the decision-making process, in technology as well as in other matters, so that the people will have more control over their destinies. As the American people increasingly comprehend the important role which science and technology play in their daily lives, they are demanding greater control over their science and technology as well as over all aspects of life.

More and more social decisions regarding the use of technology are going to be made by the political process and that, in a democracy, is precisely where they belong. So we have the Consumer Product Safety Commission, the Environmental Protection Agency, the Office of Technology Assessment, and a whole series of governmental acts, such as those dealing with toxic substances, which aim to protect the public from the unheeding pursuit of technology for profit's sake.

Heretofore technical decisions were made on an economic basis, with the actual technology being left to the experts, the scientific and technical elite, the corporate managers of American society, the military, the government. But now, even when the public might not be sufficiently informed to act directly on scientific-technical decisions, it wants to hold the decision-makers accountable for their actions, for it recognizes that any activity affecting the public should not be controlled directly by its practitioners. Utility companies should not control public utility commissions, stockbrokers should not control the Securities and Exchange Commission, railroads and truckers should not control the Interstate Commerce Commission, and scientists and engineers might not be the best ones to direct our scientific and technical applications.

Science and technology are too important to the public to be left to a small coterie of decision-makers. Scientists and technologists simply do not possess the political wisdom to make these decisions, even though they possess the scientific and technical expertise upon which such decisions must be made. Nevertheless, the fact is that we cannot resolve these problems without the aid of our technical experts. Most of the urgent problems facing man today and tomorrow involve technology, human values, social organization, environmental concerns, economic resources, political decisions, and the like. These are "interface problems," that is, the interface between technology and society, and they can only be resolved—if they can be resolved at all—by the application of scientific knowledge, technical expertise, social understanding, and humane compassion.

These interface problems have another feature in common: Technology cannot solve them alone, yet they cannot be resolved without the aid of technology. Our scientists and technologists, though filled with goodwill, are simply not possessed of the social wisdom which is required to "steer the ship of state," choose our educational objectives, or establish the principles of the "good life." Nor, unfortunately, are our humanists. Instead of attempting to understand and analyze the role and meaning of technology, many of them retreat to romantic criticism or a self-imposed and almost incommunicable personal anguish and despair. Yet we desperately need their help, for our technology functions in a sociocultural matrix and they are the custodians of our cultural heritage and the keepers of our moral conscience. If we wish to fill the cup which today's technology has only half-filled, we must bring together our technological potentialities with revivified values and rejuvenated institutions.

Am I optimistic about our ability to fill the technological cup? Yes and no. In a recent book[7] Lionel Tiger claims that optimism is bred into the human genotype, that optimism is a biological and genetic characteristic, not culturally inspired. Although some sociologists might demur at Tiger's thesis, he points out that those genetically programmed to think in an optimistic and hopeful fashion had an evolutionary advantage over those with pessimistic genes; the early humanoid who believed that he could triumph over his dangerous prey was not only more likely to attempt to do so, but also to succeed in the venture. A lack of optimism about the future would lead to a greater probability of failure.

There might be good psychological reasoning behind Tiger's optimistic view of optimism, but history does not always follow the hypotheses of sociobiology or psychology. True, American history has been on the side of the technological optimist during the past couple of centuries, but it might be more difficult for others than historians of technology to sustain their optimism by viewing the historical record. (Indeed, if I were a political historian or a historian of morals, I might find it very difficult to remain optimistic.)

Yet even the optimism of an historian of technology cannot remain unqualified. The reason—to use our metaphor of the cup—is that while technology might fill the cup to overflowing, the fact is that yesterday's cup no longer suffices. The cup, at least in the form of people's expectations, is itself evolving and growing.

History reveals that man is a creature of discontent as well as of optimism. Because technology has been so productive in the past, we expect more of it. We keep raising our sights, or, to retain our metaphor, the cup keeps growing even while we are filling it. In a sense we are engaged in the labors of Sisyphus: technology has provided us abundant goods which more than fulfill the expectations of our forefathers; but, because we have grown up in a society of abundance, there has been an escalation of

[7]*Optimism: The Biology of Hope* (New York, 1979).

expectations and aspirations. Four centuries ago King Henry IV of France acquired great popularity by promising "a chicken in every pot." Today's politicians are led to promise steak on every barbecue grill, two cars in every garage, national health care, expanded social security, and a whole host of other goodies. And now, in the face of spiralling inflation and an energy crisis, there is great fear that we might lose the material goods and creature comforts which we have accumulated in the past.

However, the human problems lie deeper than holding on to the dreams or realities of our consumer-oriented society, for we live in a world where most people do not yet have a sufficiency of the basic needs of food, clothing, and shelter. And the statistics regarding the ratio of population size to the world's resources show us that the situation will be getting worse in the future.

During classical antiquity, there were probably fewer than 200 million people on the entire earth—and it had taken millennia to reach that figure. By 1650 the world's population had gone up to one-half billion, and scientific and technical developments allowed it to double to one billion around about 1830. But then, with industrialization, things began moving faster. By the beginning of this century the world's population had soared to over 1.5 billion; then it took only seventy-nine years to more than double to today's 4.4 billion, and it is expected to double again by the year 2013. Indeed, the projected increase of 2.26 billion people between 1975 and 2000 means that the population rise during our present quarter century would equal the entire world's population increase from the time of Christ to 1950.

Providing food, clothing, and shelter for this unprecedentedly rapid growth in the world's population puts great demands upon technology. It means that the cup which technology must fill is rapidly growing in size, and the question is whether it will outstrip the ability of technology to fill the cup. Already at current rates of consumption, some natural resources are being exhausted. What will happen when a growing world population with a growing expectation of material goods begins using up resources faster than ever? Obviously, great challenges will be posed to technology to provide substitutes, to eke out existing supplies, to recycle, and to develop new techniques.

Other changes are also occurring which will certainly affect future demands upon technology. One is the increasing urbanization of the world. In 1950 only twenty-nine percent of the world's population lived in urban areas, but that number increased to more than thirty-nine percent in 1975, and it is expected that over half the world's population will be living in urban areas by the year 2000. If the urban centers continue to grow in that fashion, not only will there be great strain on urban services —transportation, sewage, housing, medical facilities—but there will also have to be tremendous agricultural development to feed the growing number of people who are no longer engaged in primary production on farms. In brief, society will put greater and greater demands on our technology.

Back in the 1930s, the great sociologist William Fielding Ogburn, the first president of the Society for the History of Technology, popularized the notion of "cultural lag," wherein he postulated the view that technology changes rapidly but that our institutional mechanisms in society change slowly, lagging behind the changes in technology. Today, however, we might be faced with the opposite situation: a "technological lag." Society is changing rapidly, but our technology is not keeping up with the growing demands and rising aspirations of the masses of people throughout the world.

Some engineers claim that we already possess the technical knowledge which will enable us to cope with the great demands caused by an increasing world population—demands for food, material goods, energy, and the like. True, but that knowledge is not yet in place, in usable form to meet these social changes. And, unless that knowledge is put to use, unless that knowledge is applied, then it does not count as technology. For technology is not just usable knowledge, it is useful knowledge; it must be applied to meet human needs and wants.

To these charges of technological lag, engineers reply that is is not their fault that their technical knowledge is not receiving application. The blame lies with society, with political institutions which hamper innovation and productivity, with economic theories and practices which impede technical progress, with environmental restrictions, with sociopolitical systems, and what have you. But if that is the case, it is obvious that we need social innovation so that we can make our technical knowledge effective.

But here again the interactions of technology and society require even more technical innovation. Thus, for example, while we might possess the potentiality through nuclear energy to provide for future energy needs, the question is if we possess enough technical knowledge to avoid nuclear disasters, deal with radioactive wastes, and solve the many other technical problems accompanying the exploitation of nuclear energy.

But technology is much more than the machines and devices and products themselves. It involves the man-machine relationship, the organization of work, relationships with the environment, and a whole host of sociocultural factors. Throughout history, the greatest engineers have employed a holistic approach, have viewed technical problems in terms of systems, and have incorporated the human element in their technical solutions.

Despite some qualifications, I still remain optimistic. Why? For several reasons. First, there is the historical record of technical achievement itself. The fact is that within the past two hundred years technology has accomplished marvelous things. There is no reason to believe that the wellsprings of technical creativity and ingenuity have run dry. Instead, there is good reason to believe that they are constantly being refreshed, that new and lively minds are being added to our technical storehouse. I know, because I teach engineering students, and I am constantly impressed with their zeal and enthusiasm, their freshness and imagination, and, believe it or not, their altruistic desire to serve mankind coupled with their realistic wish to achieve material success in the process. That combination of idealism and practicality is difficult to beat. Of course, we have a monumental educational task on our hands. This is especially so in the case of those who teach these fresh and inquiring engineering minds. We must enlarge and broaden the scope of their education, as we have been doing through enhanced liberal studies curricula during the past three decades. We have done well by our students, but we must do still better for society. Second, I do not despair of the vitality of our own American society. Certainly there are nagging doubts which have arisen to challenge the boundless confidence of earlier generations of Americans: the recognition, following our involvement in Vietnam and later happenings in Iran and Afghanistan, that events around the world do not always turn out the way we want; the Watergate scandal, which shook our faith in our constitutional system; the realization that some of our past technical triumphs have had harmful as well as beneficial results; and the spiralling inflation which seems to challenge the work-hard-and-get-ahead ethic which fueled America's rise to industrial and technical preeminence throughout the world.

Archibald MacLeish, the poet, once said, "America was promises." Many people today believe that the promise is over. But I believe that America is still promises. There is much evidence that points toward the continuing vitality and dynamism of American society. America still remains preeminent in its science and technology, in its adherence to democratic ideals, in its concern for the individual, and in its moral strength. The real question is whether or not we possess the will to utilize our great strength and power to meet these problems and close the technological gap so as to meet our own and the world's needs, now and in the future. If ours is a man-made world, I claim that man can remake it. If our technology has thus far given us only a half-full cup, then we can perhaps direct it more wisely in the future so that "our cup runneth over."

John H. Broomfield

John H. Broomfield was born in New Zealand in 1935. He received his Ph.D. from the Australian National University and has been a member of the History Department of the University of Michigan, Ann Arbor, since 1963. His field of specialization is Asian and Southeast Asian studies, and he has done extensive research in India and Pakistan; his many books and articles reflect his concern with the culture, history, and future of this part of the world. The article that follows is taken from the Spring 1980 *Alternative Futures,* and is a response to Melvin Kranzberg (whose lecture we have reprinted) and to Samuel Florman.

High Technology:
The Construction of Disaster

No shred of optimism is added to my view of our current technology and its spokespeople by the arguments of Samuel Florman and Melvin Kranzberg. To start with an obvious problem of their papers: there is no specification of the technology about which they are not pessimistic. This indiscriminate lumping of all technologies from the digging stick to the nuclear reactor into one basket enables Florman, for instance, to ask rhetorically: "How can one be pessimistic about something called 'technology'?" Childish, he says, because human life is technological life. The logic here is as flawed as it would be if a critic of dog fighting was told it is childish to criticize sport—any sport—because recreation is a human need.

Let me start, then, by specifying what I am talking about. Technology: artifacts certainly; but also the organization of their use; the scientific study of the practical arts; the body of knowledge thereby developed, and the terminology in which it is couched; invention and development. This is all technology. We are inclined to think of technology as tools—the hand wrench, for example—or machinery—the steam boiler—, and both Florman and Kranzberg encourage us in that sort of thinking. This emphasis is misleading for contemporary "high technology," especially in the affluent ghetto in which we, the world's rich minority, live. Here technology is infinitely complex, and bureaucratic organization links vast systems together. We are not talking of steam boilers and hand wrenches; we are talking of something far more extensive and sophisticated. Remember that an item as basic as our food is now very largely an artifact, a product of technology. It is either chemistry, or, as in the case of those cheery breakfast cereals, that portion derived from food grains comes from hybrids which will not regenerate, thereby ensuring a continuing role in farming for agricultural corporation laboratories.

The emphasis is necessarily on *system*: large-scale, exceedingly complex technological organization. With high technology, individuals and groups become dependent upon distant decisions of unfamiliar, incomprehensible corporations, including governments. Reliance on high energy usage is encouraged, while the transmission of that energy, as also the fossil fuels from which most of it is derived, are in corporate control. There are irresistible intrusions into almost all aspects of "private" life, and this is a planned feature of high technology. In order to generate a "demand" for new products, and a tolerance for more elaborate organizational combinations, there is a systematic use of the media, the market place, and the educational system to influence and manipulate individual behavior. Internationally the same forces operate to encourage the inter-dependency of national economies, to the profit of those who control the high technology which we all—rich and poor of the world, alike—have been taught to regard as the symbol of the advanced and the progressive. The maintenance or innovative development of independent technologies is discouraged, for the elimination of alternatives (seen as competition for one's own product or technique) is a principle of our system. A consideration of the dangers from the application of such a principle is a subject to which I shall return at the end of the paper.

We approach the nub of the problem of high technology when we recognize the vulnerability of the systems we have built. We have created —and, I would emphasize, only very recently—a technology intolerant of mistakes; a technology that assumes infallibility but is operated by fallible humans.[1] We are a mistake-making species, and we should never have developed technologies that assume mistakes will not happen. Accidents resulting from human error are a certainty. The accustomed response to this observation is the one given by the commission that investigated the Three Mile Island nuclear disaster: make modifications in the design.[2] It is a response that misses the point that the vulnerability of high technology derives from the fundamental fact that its structural principles are not "natural" or "biological."

In natural systems there is interdependency, but it is the interdependency of subunits which are, in themselves, whole and complete. Cells are the classic example. Large areas of a natural system can be wiped out (brain cells with every highball), but the system will continue to function. Nature is a network. If part of a net breaks, things slip through but the net holds together. By contrast, our high technology is built, link by link, like a chain; a system of interdependent, *incomplete* units. And any child can tell you the relationship between the chain and its weakest link—the

---

[1]Here, and in the following paragraph, I am drawing on the ideas of John Todd of the New Alchemy Institute. (See Nancy Jack Todd, ed.: *The Book of the New Alchemists* (New York, 1977).

[2]*New York Times*, November 1, 1979. Coincidentally the same science section of the *Times* (November 6, 1979) that carried the report on the 'Technology and Pessimism' symposium, contained another rather ludicrous example of this kind of thinking. In an article entitled "Acid Rain: An Increasing Threat," the suggestion "to breed acid-resistant fish" was discussed as a counter-measure. To the credit of the commentator, it was not endorsed.

well-remembered switch on the electric power relay at Niagara[0]; the stuck valve at Three Mile Island[0]; or the less visible, but more portentous, passage on a single shipping lane around the southern tip of Africa of sixty percent of the oil required to sustain the industrial life of Western Europe and the United States.[3]

When the subject is vulnerability, military technology inevitably comes to mind, though it is noteworthy that there is not one word about military technology in the Florman and Kranzberg papers. This is a remarkable omission considering the vast investment in military R&D in this nation, to say nothing of the Soviet Union. Of the U.S. Federal budget, two-thirds of discretionary funding is spent on the military, whose projects give employment to one in ten U.S. workers. In the U.S., which has a mere five or six per cent of the world's population, there is an expenditure of an estimated one-third of the world's entire yearly outlay on war technology. U.S. private industry annually exports an average ten billion dollars in weapons, the technology of violence.[4] In April 1979, the University of Michigan *Reporter,* a monthly newsletter directing faculty and graduate students to useful sources of research support, noted that the Department of Defense (in a time of high inflation, and declining funding from other agencies) "expects to be able to support an annual 10% real growth in research funding in the next several years, . . . increasing its emphasis on university support."[5] It is not unfair to say that the war business is a major route through which technological development proceeds in this, as in all other large industrialized societies.

And what has been the objective of military technological development? Let me take as the measure my lifetime, a relatively short period: I was born in 1935. On April 26, 1937, Nazi bombers of the German Luftwaffe attacked the Basque town of Guernica, for two hours and forty-five minutes testing their capacity to destroy a population. At the time there was almost universal outrage that a civilian population would be bombed with cold-blooded intent. By the end of the Second World War this had become a general principle of warfare: we had adopted the Nazi principles. We wiped out Hamburg with a fire-bombing; we wiped out

[3]Øystein Noreng: *Oil Politics in the 1980s: Patterns of International Cooperation* (New York, 1978).

[4]Anthony Sampson: *The Arms Bazaar: From Lebanon to Lockheed* (New York, 1978) pp. 358–361; Richard J. Barnet: *Roots of War* (New York, 1973) pp. 166–167; The Disarm Education Fund, New York, leaflet, September, 1979.

[5]*Reporter,* vol. XXVI, no. 4, p. 4.

electric power relay at Niagara   November 1965 failure of a single electrical relay in the Niagara River power station that initiated a blackout of nine northeastern states and two provinces of Canada.

Three Mile Island   Site of a nuclear power plant in Pennsylvania where a breakdown in the cooling system on March 28, 1979, caused radioactive gas to escape through the venting system and nearly caused a major nuclear disaster.

Dresden; we wiped out Tokyo with a fire-bombing. We went on to attack sixty-five other Japanese cities, killing (before the atomic bombs were dropped) an estimated 330,000 people—86,000 in Tokyo alone with the first incendiary raid—and making homeless an estimated 8.5 million.[6]

We had adopted the principle of mass civilian extermination, and our weapons development since that time, with nuclear weapons of hideously greater power, has been directed towards perfecting this capability. Why? Because of the recognition that with high technology the old division between military and civilian is rendered virtually meaningless; the entire system is involved in war-making. As Richard Falk[0] observes, this is, of course, a self-fulfilling prophecy, or, at least, a self-reinforcing conclusion.

In Vietnam we went one step further: we attempted to destroy the natural eco-system supporting the people, because, unfortunately for our military planners, a new technique had been developed: modern guerrilla warfare, which has proved resistant to high technology. We poured onto that green and fertile land our defoliants, our poisons, our biological weapons (all, we should note, outlawed earlier in the century by international convention). These silent destroyers continue with their deadly war on the children of the Indo-Chinese, and our own GIs alike, years after we have achieved "peace with honor." Since then we have found the neutron bomb, which will destroy all the people but leave the artifacts of technology untouched. We have the ultimate weapon: now we can commit genocide.

Let me remind you how dramatic and rapid has been the change of scale in this, as in all other areas of our technology. Again I use my own lifetime as the yardstick. In 1940, the Luftwaffe was acknowledged to be the most powerful airforce in the world. Requiring daylight for target sighting, and therefore dependent upon protection from escort fighters with an effective outer range of less than 120 miles, its aircraft were capable of pin-point bombing only in south-eastern England—little further inland than London—even though they were operating from airfields on the French and Belgian coasts.[7] Today, forty years later, the military forces of the U.S.A. and the U.S.S.R. are capable of hitting almost any target in the populated world with colossal destructive power within thirty minutes.

As we turn to an assessment of what we have wrought, let us face squarely one fact, so terrifying that we normally shy away from it: weapons of war are made to be used. There is no historical precedent of a major

---

[6]Kent Roberts Greenfield: *Strategy in World War II: A Reconsideration* (Baltimore, 1963) pp. 119–120.

[7]B. H. Liddell Hart: *History of the Second World War* (New York, 1971) pp. 90–92.

Richard Falk Another contributor to the journal in which the present essay appears.

weapons system being developed and never used. If we accept the fact that all the nuclear nations have large and powerful bureaucracies devoted to preparation for nuclear war, we shall see the true horror of what our technology has brought us to.

What of the possibility of the appearance of a General Jack D. Ripper[0] figure, that patriotic airman from *Dr. Strangelove?* Fantastic beyond belief? The chance of an accidental or mistaken missile launching, however, is not something we can dismiss so easily. Human error, as we have already observed, is the one thing of which we can be assured.

New York Times, November 11, 1979
ERROR ALERTS U.S. FORCES TO A FALSE MISSILE ATTACK A false alert triggered some of the nation's defenses against a nonexistent missile attack yesterday morning. . . . A mechanical error sent "war game" information into the sensing system that provides early warning of nuclear attack, indicating to military officers that the United States was under attack from a few missiles launched by a Soviet submarine, probably located in the northern Pacific, a Pentagon official said. As a result, 10 jet interceptors from three bases in the United States and Canada scrambled aloft, and missile bases throughout the nation went on a low-level alert. . . . Pentagon officials said there had been several false alarms of this sort over the years, caused by computer failures, natural phenomena and test firings, especially in the late 1950's and early 1960's, when the early-warning system was in its early days. . . . Jody Powell, the White House press secretary, dismissed the criticism from abroad, noting the Administration's preoccupation with the Americans being held hostage in Teheran. "Given the fact that our people are sitting over there" in Iran, he said, "anybody who wants to get angry about a technical error is not going to get a long hearing."

Should a similar "technical error" someday trigger a nuclear exchange, we have no way of judging the full consequences, for we have built a technology with catastrophic potential but can only guess at what will happen when it is used. To cite the most obvious problem: we cannot gauge the long-term effects of the radiation.[8]

Against this immeasurably hazardous future we are trading away civil liberties. More extensive surveillance systems are devised to "secure" nuclear installations, military and civil. High officials lie in the name of national security, and the lowly lie to protect "industrial credibility." Censorship is imposed, and public records are falsified. Melvin Kranzberg laments that Watergate shook our confidence in the Constitution; yet ICBM technology had already critically undermined the Constitution in one area. The need to respond within a few minutes to a nuclear threat from the Soviet Union had rendered irrelevant the provision that only the

[8]Kevin N. Lewis: "The Prompt and Delayed Effects of Nuclear War," *Scientific American,* vol. 241, no. 1, July 1979, pp. 35–47.
General Jack D. Ripper   Maniacal U.S. Air Force general who orders a nuclear attack on the Soviet Union in the satiric film *Dr. Strangelove.*

Senate can declare war. This check and balance in our Constitution is destroyed.

Let us turn from a death-dealing to a life-sustaining technology—medicine—to see if we cannot find firmer ground for optimism. On the surface the facts would appear encouraging. There has been large-scale improvement in human health in the last 100 years, with average longevity increased dramatically. To what can we attribute this? To improved nutrition, environmental sanitation, public health education, personal hygiene, immunization, pre-natal and post-natal care for mothers and babies, the area of most spectacular achievement because childbirth and infancy were associated with very high death rates.[9]

Yet where is the investment in American medicine today? Where is the health care dollar spent? On mothers and babies? On the areas of the poor, nutrition and public health? Certainly not. Public health gets a meagre four or five per cent of the medical dollar, while ninety per cent goes to the treatment of individual patients, those already ill.[10] Annually the proportional expenditure on preventive medicine shrinks, while the share mounts for hospitals,[11] burgeoning bureaucracies (hospital employment tripled between 1950 and 1969),[12] with a gargantuan appetite for high technology and drugs, much of the latter mandated by hospitals' exceedingly pathogenic environment.[13] Increasingly, also, hospital beds are occupied by the affluent middle-aged and elderly, assured consumers of the medical product. Special attention in American medicine is given to rich, old men, because men hold the family purse strings. Besides, most doctors, and those who manage hospitals, drug and medical equipment firms, and insurance companies, are middle-aged, rich males.[14] Twenty-eight per cent of the U.S. medical budget is spent on the ten per cent of the population over 65 years of age.[15] If success is to be measured by increased longevity, then this is wasted expenditure: life expectancy for a 65 year old has increased by no more than two years since 1900.[16]

Given our knowledge of the central importance to the general wellness

[9]Thomas McKeown: *The Role of Medicine: Dream, Mirage, or Nemesis?* (London, 1976) pp. 75–100.

[10]Victor W. Sidel and Ruth Sidel: *A Healthy State: An International Perspective on the Crisis in United States Medical Care* (New York, 1977) pp. 32 & 46.

[11]*Ibid.*

[12]Leonard Rodberg and Gelvin Stevenson: "The Health Care Industry in Advanced Capitalism," *Review of Radical Political Economics,* vol. IX, no. 1, Spring 1977, p. 111.

[13]Sidel and Sidel, *op. cit.,* pp. 71–78; Ivan Illich: *Medical Nemesis: The Expropriation of Health* (New York, 1976) pp. 31–32; Office of Technology Assessment, U.S. Government: *Assessing the Efficacy and Safety of Medical Technologies* (Washington, D.C., 1978).

[14]Sidel and Sidel, *op. cit.,* p. 82.

[15]Illich, *op. cit.,* p. 82.

[16]René Dubos: *Man Adapting* (New Haven, 1976) p. 230.

of a society of care for pregnant mothers and infants, nutrition, environmental protection, and health education, we do not seem to be using our money sensibly. The statistics bear out this conclusion. Although there has been a massive increase in U.S. resources devoted to medical care in the last quarter century,[17] death rates have actually increased in that period for young adults, particularly males. At ages 20–24, death rates have risen twenty-one per cent for white males and twenty-six per cent for blacks. The figures at ages 35–39 are seven per cent and thirty per cent respectively.[18] For an adult in America, life expectancy is little better now than it was in 1920.[19]

Are we then spreading health to the rest of the world? On balance I do not think we can legitimately make that claim. We provide direct and indirect incentives to bring the best doctors and nurses *from* the Third World, where they are most needed, to the rich countries—the notorious "brain drain."[20] We tout the Western medical establishment as the model for the world, but it is an inappropriate model. It discourages preventive health care systems, and encourages high-cost technology for large urban hospitals in overwhelmingly rural societies. It introduces expensive, industrially-manufactured drugs, often imported, in place of indigenous herbal and organic remedies. Even where there is a shortage of health workers, it has no use for traditional health-care specialists, who, in many regions, include women with an irreplaceable relationship with mothers and their babies. It substitutes an elitist, male-dominated, medical hierarchy. Everywhere self-reliance and cultural self-respect are eroded.

Again, we must acknowledge that this is a systematic product of the maxim that if you have a new technique you encourage its widespread adoption; if you have a new product you peddle it everywhere—and God help the competition. This is true for electronic computers to replace the abacus, or baby formula to replace mother's milk.

Who has benefitted from our high technology? We, the residents of the gilded ghetto—and that, of course, does not include all our fellow citizens even in this fabulously wasteful country. The justification—and it is central to the Florman and Kranzberg thesis—is that what we have done for ourselves, we shall proceed to do for all the rest; or, alternatively, our technological inventiveness will be their inspiration, provided neither we nor they give way to the doomsaying of the pessimists. This is the biggest, most self-serving lie of all. By no stretch of the imagination could our high energy-consuming technology be made available to everyone on the globe and simple arithmetic will give the proof. Americans, a mere five or six per cent of the world's population, are said to be consuming already forty

[17]Sidel and Sidel, *op. cit.,* p. 28.
[18]Joseph Eyer and Peter Sterling: "Stress-Related Mortality and Social Organization," *Review of Radical Political Economics, op. cit.,* p. 1.
[19]*Ibid.,* p. 4; Dubos, *loc. cit.*
[20]Sidel and Sidel, *op. cit.,* pp. 98–104.

per cent of the world's energy to feed the appetites of their technological toys, and, we are reliably told, are rapidly depleting the sources of that energy. So there is no future for our technology unless we find new energy supplies. All those currently known with the capability of sustaining high technology, and all those likely to be produced, will increase the poisons we are pouring into the world. We are already drowning in our own poisons; imagine the pollution levels if the world's billions of poor were ever to "come on line" with high technology. It cannot be done. It should not be attempted.

There is another wrinkle: wherever was it imagined we would find sufficient highly-trained personnel to provide sophisticated technology for all the world's new people (200,000 added to the queue each day, as Kranzberg observes)? We have had a little over 200 years since the beginning of the industrial revolution, and have succeeded in outfitting with advanced technology, at a generous estimate, one quarter of the world's population, about 1.25 billion. This leaves a current backlog of 3.75 billion people, to which the next twenty years alone are expected (barring catastrophes) to add a further 5 billion.[21] An honest projection would cast doubt upon our ability even to provide the elementary school teachers in numbers sufficient to maintain current rates of literacy, unless we are willing to effect a massive shift of resources away from technocracy.

In Melvin Kranzberg's view, however, the growth in world population is the chief imperative for sustaining the development of advanced technologies. He says that the population problem, aggravated as it is by rapid urbanization, demands a technological solution. Strangely, he appears blind to his own evidence of a correlation in time between the appearance of industrial technology and the explosive growth in population. Was there not a causative link? Nobody, surely, would question the connection between modern technology and urbanization. The movement of vast sectors of populations from rural areas to cities was made possible only by industrial technology. Yet the logic with which we are presented is: let there be more advanced technology to overcome the population and urbanization problems. The argument is back to front: these problems are intimately related to the nature of our technology. Like the tragic Sisyphus, punished aptly enough for his cunning in life, eternally in Hades to roll a stone up a hill, we shall be committed to endless and ineffectual struggle if we devote ourselves to more and bigger technology.

Perhaps Florman and Kranzberg are not suggesting more of the same. Perhaps they are proposing alternate technologies, such as those the New Alchemists have developed,[22] or those advocated by Ernest Callenbach.[23] I would be delighted if that were so. Let me state quickly the principles

[21]Thomas McKeown: *The Modern Rise of Population* (New York, 1976) pp. 1–2.
[22]Todd, *loc. cit.*
[23]Ernest Callenbach: *Ecotopia: The Notebooks and Reports of William Weston* (New York, 1975).

of these alternate technologies. Decentralized, relatively small-scale units with an integration of functions: food production, heating, living and work space, holistic education, all under one roof or at least all within walking distance; the scale within individual comprehension and susceptible to small-group management. (To achieve this, of course, requires a considerable level of technological sophistication. I would emphasize, parenthetically, that to be a pessimist about our current technology is not, necessarily, to be an anti-technologist.) Using locally available, renewable energy sources; recycling; avoiding violent techniques and toxic substances; respecting non-human life forms, our comrades and collaborators on this whirling journey through the heavens. The principle from nature of optimization to replace our current technological and bureaucratic principle of maximization.

It is this principle of maximization that is the key to my pessimism about our technological future, my doubt that we shall adopt these sane alternatives. To understand why we operate on such a principle it is necessary to recognize the systemic relationship of high technology to the all-pervasive bureaucratic organization of our contemporary economic, political, and social structures. High technology and our social forms are not free-floating, mutually independent things. You cannot, for example, dispense with big bureaucracy and keep high technology. They are systemically interrelated, two sides of one coin. High technology and massive corporate bureaucracy sustain and reinforce one another, the electronic computer being the ultimate expression, the apogee of bureaucratic technology.

Bureaucracy is a bar to the rethinking and reorganization necessary for the adoption of sane, alternate technologies. In the first place, growth for the sake of growth is the functional principle of modern bureaucracy. Big is always better, small is never beautiful. An organization that is growing has expanding opportunities for promotion, for patronage, prestige, and higher status; more chances to be somebody else's boss. It panders to human vanity: the desire to be a big guy, even if it is only a little big guy among lots of other little big guys. You get no brownie points in a bureaucracy by proposing a reduction in scale in personnel, techniques, or products. You always talk about someone else's program being cut, never your own, even if your organization is no longer fulfilling its original function. Bureaucracies come to exist to preserve their own existence. There is a Tamil proverb: "All is lost when the fence starts feeding on the crop." In our technological bureaucratic society we have many fences feeding on crops. Observing the recent spectacular rise in doctors' salaries and the profits of companies servicing hospitals,[24] would it, for example, be unreasonable to suggest that the explanation for the misdirection of medical expenditures away from sectors that would improve general health, lies in the self-serving practices of the health industry?

The huge investment of capital in high technology and corporate bu-

[24]Vincente Navarro: *Medicine Under Capitalism* (New York, 1976) pp. 135–169.

reaucracy, including the human investment in training, is a major source of resistance to change. Innovation, genuine structural innovation, is suspect to the individual technocrat because it threatens the definition of his occupational role, so important to his sense of personal identity. (The pronoun "his" serves as a reminder that one of the structural forms most jealously guarded is male dominance of bureaucracies.) Innovation also poses a threat to the concentration of power in corporate hands. Imagine the plunge in value of General Foods, Campbell, and Del Monte stocks if American farmers were to organize vegetable marketing and processing cooperatives on a wide scale. Well-directed criticism of corporate bureaucracy and its technologies invites, at the very least, inflated defensive rhetoric (the Florman paper is replete with examples); at worst it brings retaliation, as demonstrated by Karen Silkwood's fate, and Ralph Nader's perilous early days as lone gadfly to the automobile industry.

If bigger is the test of progress for bureaucracy, there is an equally simple test for technology: different and profitable. If it can be done a new way which brings profit to the corporation, it can be called progress. New products and techniques are necessary for corporate growth—they are the stuff of busy-ness for technocrats—but they should not, of course, demand internal structural change. What havoc they wreck on society at large is quite beside the point. When the agricultural researchers at the University of California, Davis, working with generous funding from agribusiness, produce UC-82, the square tomato that can be harvested by machine, it represents technological progress. No matter that it is smaller, less sweet and nutritious than its predecessors, nor that its appearance in the fields will throw migrant laborers out of work, and render many small farms uneconomic.[25]

BATTLEFIELD!

Win the battles of food product innovation or improvement by reducing time and costs. Your best strategy? Recruit ICI. We'll help outflank time and costs by applying our performance-proven mono and diglycerides, polysorbates, sorbitols, and mannitol. Then we'll help assure victory for your product with technical assistance from our cadre of food specialists. They're trained in CREATE A FOOD thinking and backed by some 40 years' experience with 125 grades of emulsifiers and polyols. We'll even make a special grade to meet your need. We're battlewise and ready to help you take on tough competitors by successfully developing new food forms, achieving special effects, or duplicating properties of existing foods. . . .

ICI AMERICAS INC.
ANT*ICI*PATING NEEDS[26]

[25]Cathleen Williams and Paul Barnett: "Brave New Tomatoes," *Politics and Education,* vol. II, no. 1, Fall 1979, pp. 2–3.
[26]Extract from promotional literature prepared by ICI Americas Inc., Wilmington, Delaware, November 1978.

With technology, the means become the definition of the ends, in the process redefining the meaning of the word "need." Whoever was aware that humans had a need to eat 125 grades of emulsifiers and polyols instead of natural foods before the first batch was whipped up in a laboratory, sparking a glint of potential profit in the corporate eye? With change synonymous with progress, the current state of the art is always, by definition, the most advanced stage of technology.[27] The term "high technology" is the perfect illustration.

Here we are face to face with the principle of maximization. There is no concept of the optimal, no way in our scientific, technological culture of defining where we should stop. "Without experimentation and change, our existence would be a dull business," writes Samuel Florman. "We simply cannot stop while there are masses to feed and diseases to conquer, seas to explore and heavens to survey." Where there is the power to do, say our scientists and technologists, it must be done, come Hell or high water. (Hell or heavy water would be the current version, I assume!) Formerly, disaster sometimes called a halt, as in the case of the "Hindenburg." The explosion of the "Hindenburg" in April 1937 killed very painfully and spectacularly a small number of people, with the result that the development of that sort of airship with inflammable gases was discontinued. The problem now is that we cannot afford to wait for disasters to teach us lessons about our high technology. Given the possible scale of these disasters, there may be few survivors.

How did we get into this mess? How could we, as a culture, possibly have been so myopic as to let this happen? The answer, I believe, is to be found in segmentation, the structural form of the bureaucratic system. Modern bureaucracy is hierarchical, impersonal, functionally specialized, seeking always through categorization and the universal rule to avoid the unpredictable or the anomalous. The pressure of modern bureaucracy, including the technological, scientific, and educational bureaucracies, is against whole thinking, holism. We have, in the West, increasingly since the seventeenth century, emphasized the value of segmentation, and the product is specialized ignorance for some and generalized ignorance for most. Boarding an airplane six months ago, I was behind two men with brief cases who were telling each other that in a few years there would be a tiny percentage of the world's population which "knew computers," and there would be the rest, dependent upon them. They were delighted with the prospect. Here is another product of technocracy: elitism—us, with our specialized knowledge, and them, out there dependent upon us.

Cultural arrogance aplenty, but also remarkably limited vision. We seem oblivious to the price our advanced technologies exact. Take the

[27]For a brilliant exploration of this, see Hans Jonas: "Toward a Philosophy of Technology," *Hastings Center Report,* vol. IX, no. 1, February 1979, pp. 34–43.

problem of the "disappearing middle," as E. F. Schumacher called it.[28] We often mistakenly assume that when we adopt "more advanced" technologies we still have available to us—as though stored away in the human attic—all those old technologies. We do not. Many are irrecoverably lost, or require great cost to restore. In eastern India in the late 1960s, when dams for new centralized irrigation schemes silted faster than the engineers had projected, the Government's agricultural workers urged the peasants to rely again upon the old, local tanks (artificial ponds) and ditches, only to discover that many had been filled in to provide new paddy land.[29] The current sorry state of America's railroads, and Amtrak's inability to revive them, is a tribute to the effectiveness of airplane and superhighway technology. Remember too that we often uneducate when we introduce new gadgetry. The advertising appeal of Yum Yum Corporation's processed foods as tasting "just like Grandma's," would be negligible if processed foods had not destroyed our ability to cook like Grandma. And where shall we find all the blacksmiths when the oil runs out, and we want to harness the highsteppin' strutter to the surrey again?

High technology destroys middle-level technology and skills; big bureaucracy destroys middle-level groups. Modern Western society is characterized by an absence of strong organizations between the family (itself reduced in size and function by the bureaucratization of society), and big bureaucracy, most notably the state. Clans, guilds, peasant communes, labor brotherhoods, free cities, monasteries and nunneries, orders of knights, all have succumbed to centralized bureaucracy. Our social scientists have given the good housekeeping seal of approval to the process by making it one of the defining characteristics of "modernity," and, by the same token, labeling as "traditional" those societies which retain castes, tribes, councils of village elders, secret societies, trade brotherhoods, and extended families. Most reviled of all in the development literature are those societies that have meshed kinship networks with bureaucracy, producing nepotism, seen as the very seat of corruption and "backwardness."

Such "imperfectly bureaucratized" societies are considered to be structurally weak, yet I would suggest that the vitality and diversity of their middle-level groups gives them an ability to respond to disaster, natural or man-made, far better than can we, in our high technobureaucratic state, where the nuclear family stands isolated and dependent on distant, impersonal bureaucracy. It is we, not they, who are structurally weak. Vulnerable because, in our commitment to a belief in the superiority of bureaucracy, we have destroyed alternative forms of organization.

The systematic destruction of alternatives in almost every sphere is the consequence of modern Western civilization's drive to use its technological and organizational power to dominate. In our determination to domi-

[28]Address delivered at The University of Michigan, Ann Arbor, March 13, 1977.
[29]Author's personal observations and conversations in West Bengal, 1971–73.

nate nature, from which conceptually we set ourselves apart, we destroy other life forms. Monocropping produces more bushels per acre; so we put vast acreage into a single variety of one crop, disregarding the basic Darwinian precept that variety provides a species with the best chances for survival in a hazardous, perpetually changing environment. Our vulnerable mono-crops then require technological rescue missions, and we wipe out further species with pesticides and herbicides. Distasteful though it may be to recall, historically we have done the same when other humans have stood in our way. Armed with industrial technology and the bureaucratic state, we cleared the American continent of its native occupants in the last century, just as today for our convenience we clear away the snail darters and the Alaskan wolves. We have no time for "primitives," without our high technology and bureaucracy, and our language is replete with words that characterize them as our inferiors. We do not value their cultural difference from us and from each other. We are as little concerned with sustaining human cultural variety—alternatives for response to a hazardous, changing environment—as we are with maintaining variety in nature. Western civilization is most dangerous because in the interest of growth, the anthropologist, Marshall Sahlins, warns us, "it does not hesitate to destroy any other form of humanity whose difference from us consists in having discovered not merely other codes of existence but ways of achieving an end that still eludes us: the mastery by society of society's mastery over nature."[30]

[30]*Culture and Practical Reason* (Chicago, 1976), p. 221.

Wendell Berry

The following selection is taken from *The Gift of Good Land: Further Essays Cultural and Agricultural* (1981). See page 269 for information on Wendell Berry.

Horse-Drawn Tools and the Doctrine of Labor Saving

Five years ago, when we enlarged our farm from about twelve acres to about fifty, we saw that we had come to the limits of the equipment we had on hand: mainly a rotary tiller and a Gravely walking tractor; we had been borrowing a tractor and mower to clip our few acres of pasture. Now we would have perhaps twenty-five acres of pasture, three acres of hay, and the garden; and we would also be clearing some land and dragging the cut trees out for firewood. I thought for a while of buying a second-hand 8N Ford tractor, but decided finally to buy a team of horses instead.

I have several reasons for being glad that I did. One reason is that it started me thinking more particularly and carefully than before about the development of agricultural technology. I had learned to use a team when I was a boy, and then had learned to use the tractor equipment that replaced virtually all the horse and mule teams in this part of the country after World War II. Now I was turning around, as if in the middle of my own history, and taking up the old way again.

Buying and borrowing, I gathered up the equipment I needed to get started: wagon, manure spreader, mowing machine, disk, a one-row cultivating plow for the garden. Most of these machines had been sitting idle for years. I put them back into working shape, and started using them. That was 1973. In the years since, I have bought a number of other horse-drawn tools, for myself and other people. My own outfit now includes a breaking plow, a two-horse riding cultivator, and a grain drill.

As I have repaired these old machines and used them, I have seen how well designed and durable they are, and what good work they do. When the manufacturers modified them for use with tractors, they did not much improve either the machines or the quality of their work. (It is necessary, of course, to note some exceptions. Some horsemen, for instance, would argue that alfalfa sod is best plowed with a tractor. And one must also except such tools as hay conditioners and chisel plows that came after the development of horse-drawn tools had ceased. We do not know what innovations, refinements, and improvements would have come if it had continued.) At the peak of their development, the old horse tools were excellent. The coming of the tractor made it possible for a farmer to do more work, but not better. And there comes a point, as we know, when *more* begins to imply *worse*. The mechanization of farming passed that point long ago—probably, or so I will argue, when it passed from horse power to tractor power.

The increase of power has made it possible for one worker to crop an enormous acreage, but for this "efficiency" the country has paid a high price. From 1946 to 1976, because fewer people were needed, the farm population declined from thirty million to nine million; the rapid movement of these millions into the cities greatly aggravated that complex of problems which we now call the "urban crisis," and the land is suffering for want of the care of those absent families. The coming of a tool, then, can be a cultural event of great influence and power. Once that is understood, it is no longer possible to be simpleminded about technological progress. It is no longer possible to ask, What is a good tool? without asking at the same time, How *well* does it work? and, What is its influence?

One could say, as a rule of thumb, that a good tool is one that makes it possible to work faster *and* better than before. When companies quit making them, the horse-drawn tools fulfilled both requirements. Consider, for example, the International High Gear No. 9 mowing machine. This is a horse-drawn mower that certainly improved on everything that came before it, from the scythe to previous machines in the International line. Up to that point, to cut fast and to cut well were two aspects of the same problem. Past that point the speed of the work could be increased, but not the quality.

I own one of these mowers. I have used it in my hayfield at the same time that a neighbor mowed there with a tractor mower; I have gone from my own freshly cut hayfield into others just mowed by tractors; and I can say unhesitatingly that, though the tractors do faster work, they do not do it better. The same is substantially true, I think, of other tools: plows, cultivators, harrows, grain drills, seeders, spreaders, etc. Through the development of the standard horse-drawn equipment, quality and speed increased together; after that, the principal increase has been in speed.

Moreover, as the speed has increased, care has tended to decline. For this, one's eyes can furnish ample evidence. But we have it also by the testimony of the equipment manufacturers themselves. Here, for example, is a quote from the public relations paper of one of the largest companies: "Today we have multi-row planters that slap in a crop in a hurry, putting down seed, fertilizer, insecticide and herbicide in one quick swipe across the field."

But good work and good workmanship cannot be accomplished by "slaps" and "swipes." Such language seems to be derived from the he-man vocabulary of TV westerns, not from any known principles of good agriculture. What does the language of good agricultural workmanship sound like? Here is the voice of an old-time English farmworker and horseman, Harry Groom, as quoted in George Ewart Evans's *The Horse in the Furrow*: "It's all rush today. You hear a young chap say in the pub: 'I done thirty acres today.' But it ain't messed over, let alone done. You take the rolling, for instance. Two mile an hour is fast enough for a roll or a harrow. With a roll, the slower the better. If you roll fast, the clods are not broken up, they're just pressed in further. Speed is everything now; just jump on the tractor and way across the field as if it's a dirt-track. You see it when a farmer takes over a new farm: he goes in and plants straight-way, right out of the book. But if one of the old farmers took a new farm, and you walked round the land with him and asked him: 'What are you going to plant here and here?' he'd look at you some queer; because he wouldn't plant nothing much at first. He'd wait a bit and see what the land was like: he'd *prove* the land first. A good practical man would hold on for a few weeks, and get the feel of the land under his feet. He'd walk on it and feel it through his boots and see if it was in good heart, before he planted anything: he'd sow only when he knew what the land was fit for."

Granted that there is always plenty of room to disagree about farming methods, there is still no way to deny that in the first quotation we have a description of careless farming, and in the second a description of a way of farming as careful—as knowing, skillful, and loving—as any other kind of high workmanship. The difference between the two is simply that the second considers where and how the machine is used, whereas the first considers only the machine. The first is the point of view of a man high up in the air-conditioned cab of a tractor described as "a beast that eats acres." The second is that of a man who has worked close to the ground in the open air of the field, who has studied the condition of the ground as he drove over it, and who has cared and thought about it.

If we had tools thirty-five years ago that made it possible to do farm work both faster and better than before, then why did we choose to go ahead and make them no longer better, but just bigger and bigger and faster and faster? It was, I think, because we were already allowing the wrong people to give the wrong answers to questions raised by the improved horse-drawn machines. Those machines, like the ones that followed them, were *labor savers.* They may seem old-timey in comparison to today's "acre eaters," but when they came on the market they greatly increased the amount of work that one worker could do in a day. And so they confronted us with a critical question: How would we define labor saving?

We defined it, or allowed it to be defined for us by the corporations and the specialists, as if it involved no human considerations at all, as if the labor to be "saved" were not human labor. We decided, in the language of some experts, to look on technology as a "substitute for labor." Which means that we did not intend to "save" labor at all, but to *replace* it, and to *displace* the people who once supplied it. We never asked what should be done with the "saved" labor; we let the "labor market" take care of that. Nor did we ask the larger questions of what values we should place on people and their work and on the land. It appears that we abandoned ourselves unquestioningly to a course of technological evolution, which would value the development of machines far above the development of people.

And so it becomes clear that, by itself, my rule-of-thumb definition of a good tool (one that permits a worker to work both better and faster) does not go far enough. Even such a tool can cause bad results if its use is not directed by a benign and healthy social purpose. The coming of a tool, then, is not just a cultural event; it is also an historical crossroad—a point at which people must choose between two possibilities: to become more intensive or more extensive; to use the tool for quality or for quantity, for care or for speed.

In speaking of this as a choice, I am obviously assuming that the evolution of technology is *not* unquestionable or uncontrollable; that "progress" and the "labor market" do *not* represent anything so unyielding as natural law, but are aspects of an economy; and that any economy is in some sense a "managed" economy, managed by an intention to distribute the benefits of work, land, and materials in a certain way. (The present agricultural economy, for instance, is slanted to give the greater portion of these benefits to the "agribusiness" corporations. If this were not so, the recent farmers' strike would have been an "agribusiness" strike as well.) If those assumptions are correct, we are at liberty to do a little historical supposing, not meant, of course, to "change history" or "rewrite it," but to clarify somewhat this question of technological choice.

Suppose, then, that in 1945 we had valued the human life of farms and farm communities 1 percent more than we valued "economic growth" and technological progress. And suppose we had espoused the health of homes, farms, towns, and cities with anything like the resolve and energy with which we built the "military-industrial complex." Suppose, in other words, that we had really meant what, all that time, most of us and most of our leaders were saying, and that we had really tried to live by the traditional values to which we gave lip service.

Then, it seems to me, we might have accepted certain mechanical and economic limits. We might have used the improved horse-drawn tools, or even the small tractor equipment that followed, not to displace workers and decrease care and skill, but to intensify production, improve maintenance, increase care and skill, and widen the margins of leisure, pleasure, and community life. We might, in other words, by limiting technology to a human or a democratic scale, have been able to use the saved labor *in the same places where we saved it.*

It is important to remember that "labor" is a very crude, industrial term, fitted to the huge economic structures, the dehumanized technology, and the abstract social organization of urban-industrial society. In such circumstances, "labor" means little more than the sum of two human quantities, human energy plus human time, which we identify as "man-hours." But the nearer home we put "labor" to work, and the smaller and more familiar we make its circumstances, the more we enlarge and complicate and enhance its meaning. At work in a factory, workers are only workers, "units of production" expending "man-hours" at a task set for them by strangers. At work in their own communities, on their own farms or in their own households or shops, workers are *never* only workers, but rather persons, relatives, and neighbors. They work *for* those they work *among* and *with.* Moreover, workers tend to be independent in inverse proportion to the size of the circumstance in which they work. That is, the work of factory workers is ruled by the factory, whereas the work of housewives, small craftsmen, or small farmers is ruled by their own morality, skill, and intelligence. And so, when workers work independently and at home, the society as a whole may lose something in the way of organizational efficiency and economies of scale. But it begins to *gain* values not so readily quantifiable in the fulfilled humanity of the workers, who then bring to their work not just contracted quantities of "man-hours," but qualities such as independence, skill, intelligence, judgment, pride, respect, loyalty, love, reverence.

To put the matter in concrete terms, if the farm communities had been able to use the best horse-drawn tools to save labor in the true sense, then they might have used the saved time and energy, first of all, for leisure—something that technological progress has given to farmers. Second, they might have used it to improve their farms: to enrich the soil, prevent erosion, conserve water, put up better and more permanent fences and buildings; to practice forestry and its dependent crafts and economies; to plant orchards, vineyards, gardens of bush fruits; to plant market gardens; to improve pasture, breeding, husbandry, and the subsidiary enterprises of a local, small-herd livestock economy; to enlarge, diversify, and deepen the economies of households and homesteads. Third, they might have used it to expand and improve the specialized crafts necessary to the health and beauty of communities: carpentry, masonry, leatherwork, cabinetwork, metalwork, pottery, etc. Fourth, they might have used it to improve the homelife and the home instruction of children, thereby preventing the hardships and expenses now placed on schools, courts, and jails.

It is probable also that, if we *had* followed such a course, we would have averted or greatly ameliorated the present shortages of energy and employment. The cities would be much less crowded; the rates of crime and welfare dependency would be much lower; the standards of industrial production would probably be higher. And farmers might have avoided their present crippling dependence on money lenders.

I am aware that all this is exactly the sort of thinking that the technological determinists will dismiss as nostalgic or wishful. I mean it, however, not as a recommendation that we "return to the past," but as a criticism of the past; and my criticism is based on the assumption that we had in the past, and that we have now, a *choice* about how we should use technology and what we should use it for. As I understand it, this choice depends absolutely on our willingness to limit our desires as well as the scale and kind of technology we use to satisfy them. Without that willingness, there is no choice; we must simply abandon ourselves to whatever the technologists may discover to be possible.

The technological determinists, of course, do not accept that such a choice exists—undoubtedly because they resent the moral limits on their work that such a choice implies. They speak romantically of "man's destiny" to go on to bigger and more sophisticated machines. Or they take the opposite course and speak the tooth-and-claw language of Darwinism. Ex-secretary of agriculture Earl Butz speaks, for instance, of "Butz's Law of Economics" which is "Adapt or Die."

I am, I think, as enthusiastic about the principle of adaptation as Mr. Butz. We differ only on the question of what should be adapted. He believes that we should adapt to the machines, that humans should be forced to conform to technological conditions or standards. I believe that the machines should be adapted to us—to serve our *human* needs as our history, our heritage, and our most generous hopes have defined them.

Garrison Keillor

Garrison Keillor is an American humorist and storyteller in the tradition of Mark Twain, James Thurber, and E. B. White. He is best known for his weekly radio show "A Prairie Home Companion," which originates in Saint Paul, Minnesota, but is beamed by satellite to some two hundred American Public Radio stations. A popular feature of the show each week is Keillor's report on events in the imaginary town of Lake Woebegon, Minnesota, "where all the men are strong, all the women are good looking, and all the children are above average." Familiar institutions in Lake Woebegon are Ralph's Pretty Good Grocery, Bertha's Kitty Boutique, Our Lady of Perpetual Responsibility Church, and the Powdermilk Biscuit Company, "sponsor" of the program.

Keillor was born in 1942 in Anoka, Minnesota. His work is based on a deep and affectionate knowledge of small-town life in the Midwest. His humor is quiet, gentle, and subtle, shrewd and realistic, but never shrill or cutting. He deals with important issues through familiar and homely images, and in a shy, laconic tone that ironically understates their significance. He has been contributing comic pieces to *The New Yorker* for a dozen years, and in 1981 published a collection of his essays and stories, *Happy to Be Here*, from which we take the following.

Re The Tower Project

Many of our personnel, conscious of the uncertainties of the construction business, have voiced concern relative to their future employment with the Company. What lies ahead on our horizon, they wonder, of the magnitude of the Fred M. and Ida S. Freebold Performing Arts Center, the Tannersfield Freeway Overpass, and other works that have put us in the construction forefront? They recall the cancellation in mid-contract of the Vietnam Parking Lot project, and they ask, "Will the Super-Tall Tower project, too, go down the drain, with a resultant loss of jobs and Company position in the building field?"

The Company believes such will not be the case. While we aren't putting all our "eggs" on one tower and are keeping an eye on the Los Angeles-Honolulu Bridge option and the proposed Lake Michigan Floating Airport, we feel that the Super-Tall Tower has achieved priority status in Washington, and all phases of research and development, land clearance, and counter-resistance are moving forward in expectation of final approval.

As for the Tower critics, they are few in number, and there isn't one of their objections that we haven't answered. Let's look at the record. Their favorite line is "Why build a Super-Tall Tower when money is so urgently needed for cancer and poverty?" With all due respect to the unwell or impoverished person and his or her family, we state our case as follows:

First, Tower construction will create a hundred thousand new jobs, not only in the Babel area and the Greater Southwest but also in other places where the bricks and slime will be made by subcontractors.

Second, because it will be the world's tallest tower, we will be able to see more from it than from any existing tower.

Third, we have reason to believe the Chinese are well along in the development of *their* tower. If we don't wish to abdicate tower leadership to Communist nations, however friendly at the moment, we can't afford to slow down now. To do so would mean the waste of all the money spent on tower research so far and would set back American tower technology for decades to come. Thus, our national prestige is at stake—not merely national pride but the confidence in our ability to rise toward the heavens. When a nation turns away from the sky and looks at its feet, it begins to die as a civilization. Man has long dreamed of building a tall tower from which he could look out and see many interesting and unusual things. Most Americans, we believe, share this dream.

Fourth, environmentalist groups have predicted various disastrous effects from the Tower—that the humming noise of its high-speed elevator will be "unbearable" to the passengers and to nearby residents, that its height will confuse migrating birds, that its long shadow will anger the sun, and so forth. The Company's research laboratory has engaged in a crash program that has already achieved a significant degree of hum reduction; at the same time, our engineers are quick to point out that since no elevator now in service can approach the speed and accompanying hum projected for the Tower elevator, there is no viable data on which to base the entire concept of an "unbearable" hum. Such a determination must wait until the completion of the Tower. In any event, the hum may serve to warn off approaching birds. As for the sun, we feel that, with certain sacrifices, this problem can be taken care of.

Computers and People

Carl Sagan

Carl Sagan (born 1934) is astronomer, astrophysicist, exobiologist, geneticist, teacher, writer, and humanist. As an undergraduate at the University of Chicago, Sagan earned both a B.A. (1954) and a B.S. (1955), then worked in the laboratory of Nobel Prize-winning geneticist Hermann J. Muller at Indiana University. He returned to the University of Chicago on a National Science

Fellowship, completing his M.S. in physics in 1956 and, not yet 26, his Ph.D. in astronomy and astrophysics in 1960.

While doing postdoctoral work at the Institute for Basic Research at Berkeley, he wrote a *Science* article (March 24, 1961) analyzing existing data on Venus; in 1967 some of his inferences were borne out by the Soviet Venera IV data. In 1962 he was appointed to the Smithsonian Astrophysical Observatory, and he taught genetics at Stanford, where he worked with Nobel Prize winner Joshua Lederberg on research into the development of life on earth. He then taught astronomy at Harvard until 1968. In the years 1968–1970 Sagan and his colleagues were the first to create amino acids, the building blocks of protein, in the laboratory.

Since 1968 he has been a professor of astronomy and space sciences at Cornell, where he is also the director of the Laboratory for Planetary Studies. In 1968 he was Oregon's Condon lecturer (an honor previously awarded J. Robert Oppenheimer, among others), and in 1970 he won NASA's Apollo Achievement Award. His theories on Mars (*National Geographic,* December 1967) were substantiated by the 1971 Mars Mariner data, and in 1972 he received the NASA medal for exceptional scientific achievement. He also worked on the Viking project.

A prolific writer of professional papers and journal articles, he has been editor of *Icarus,* an international journal of astronomy, since 1968. He also writes for the lay audience (in the *Encyclopaedia Britannica* and *Encyclopedia Americana,* among others), and his books include *Intelligent Life in the Universe* (with I. S. Shklovsky, 1966); *The Cosmic Connection* (1973), for which he received the Campbell Award for best science book; *Mars and the Mind of Man* (1973); *Dragons of Eden* (1977); *Broca's Brain* (1979), from which we reprint Chapter 20; and *Cosmos* (1980), based on his immensely popular television series.

In Defense of Robots

> Thou com'st in such a questionable shape
> That I will speak to thee . . .
>
> William Shakespeare, *Hamlet,* Act 1, Scene 4

The word "robot," first introduced by the Czech writer Karel Čapek, is derived from the Slavic root for "worker." But it signifies a machine rather than a human worker. Robots, especially robots in space, have often received derogatory notices in the press. We read that a human being was necessary to make the terminal landing adjustments on Apollo 11, without which the first manned lunar landing would have ended in disaster; that a mobile robot on the Martian surface could never be as clever as astronauts in selecting samples to be returned to Earth-bound geologists; and that machines could never have repaired, as men did, the Skylab sunshade, so vital for the continuance of the Skylab mission.

But all these comparisons turn out, naturally enough, to have been written by humans. I wonder if a small self-congratulatory element, a whiff of human chauvinism, has not crept into these judgments. Just as whites can sometimes detect racism and men can occasionally discern sexism, I wonder whether we cannot here glimpse some comparable affliction of the human spirit—a disease that as yet has no name. The word "anthropocentrism" does not mean quite the same thing. The word "humanism" has been preempted by other and more benign activities of our kind. From the analogy with sexism and racism I suppose the name for this malady is "speciesism"—the prejudice that there are no beings so fine, so capable, so reliable as human beings.

This is a prejudice because it is, at the very least, a prejudgment, a conclusion drawn before all the facts are in. Such comparisons of men and machines in space are comparisons of smart men and dumb machines. We have not asked what sorts of machines could have been built for the $30-or-so billion that the Apollo and Skylab missions cost.

Each human being is a superbly constructed, astonishingly compact, self-ambulatory computer—capable on occasion of independent decision making and real control of his or her environment. And, as the old joke goes, these computers can be constructed by unskilled labor. But there are serious limitations to employing human beings in certain environments. Without a great deal of protection, human beings would be inconvenienced on the ocean floor, the surface of Venus, the deep interior of Jupiter, or even on long space missions. Perhaps the only interesting result of Skylab that could not have been obtained by machines is that human beings in space for a period of months undergo a serious loss of bone calcium and phosphorus—which seems to imply that human beings may be incapacitated under 0 g for missions of six to nine months or longer. But the minimum interplanetary voyages have characteristic times of a year or two. Because we value human beings highly, we are reluctant to send them on very risky missions. If we do send human beings to exotic environments, we must also send along their food, their air, their water, amenities for entertainment and waste recycling, and companions. By comparison, machines require no elaborate life-support systems, no entertainment, no companionship, and we do not yet feel any strong ethical prohibitions against sending machines on one-way, or suicide, missions.

Certainly, for simple missions, machines have proved themselves many times over. Unmanned vehicles have performed the first photography of the whole Earth and of the far side of the Moon; the first landings on the Moon, Mars and Venus; and the first thorough orbital reconnaissance of another planet, in the Mariner 9 and Viking missions to Mars. Here on Earth it is increasingly common for high-technology manufacturing—for example, chemical and pharmaceutical plants—to be performed largely or entirely under computer control. In all these activities machines are able, to some extent, to sense errors, to correct mistakes, to alert human controllers some great distance away about perceived problems.

The powerful abilities of computing machines to do arithmetic—hundreds of millions of times faster than unaided human beings—are legendary. But what about really difficult matters? Can machines in any sense think through a new problem? Can they make discussions of the branched-contingency tree variety which we think of as characteristically human? (That is, I ask Question 1; if the answer is A, I ask Question 2; but if the answer is B, I ask Question 3; and so on.) Some decades ago the English mathematician A. M. Turing described what would be necessary for him to believe in machine intelligence. The condition was simply that he could be in teletype communication with a machine and be unable to tell that it was not a human being. Turing imagined a conversation between a man and a machine of the following quality:

Interrogator:	In the first line of your sonnet which reads "Shall I compare thee to a Summer's day," would not "a Spring day" do as well or better?
Witness:	It wouldn't scan.
Interrogator:	How about "a Winter's day"? That would scan all right.
Witness:	Yes, but nobody wants to be compared to a Winter's day.
Interrogator:	Would you say Mr. Pickwick reminded you of Christmas?
Witness:	In a way.
Interrogator:	Yet Christmas is a Winter's day, and I do not think Mr. Pickwick would mind the comparison.
Witness:	I don't think you're serious. By a Winter's day one means a typical Winter's day, rather than a special one like Christmas.

No device of this sophistication has yet been built, although I am not sure how many humans would pass Turing's human test. But the amount of effort and money put into artificial intelligence has been quite limited, and there are only about a half-dozen major centers of such activity in the world. One of the more striking results obtained in a very limited universe of discourse—that of children's blocks—has come from the work of Terry Winograd, then at the Massachusetts Institute of Technology. Here is a dialogue between man and machine, the machine having been programmed by Winograd:

Q:	What does the box contain?
A:	The blue pyramid and the blue box.
Q:	How many blocks are not in the box?
A:	Four of them.
Q:	Is at least one of them narrower than the one which I told you to pick up?
A:	Yes, the red cube.

Q: Is there a steeple?
A: Sorry, I don't know the word "steeple."
Q: A steeple is a stack which contains two green cubes and a pyramid, for example.
A: I understand.
Q: Are there any steeples now?
A: No.
Q: Build one.

The machine does. It reaches out its mechanical hand, moves the cubes and builds the structure that has just been described.

Q: When did you pick up the pyramid?
A: While I was stacking up the red cube, the large red block and the large green cube.
Q: Why?
A: To get rid of it.
Q: Why did you clear off that cube?
A: To put it on the large green cube.

As another example, a machine psychiatrist has been developed by Joseph Weizenbaum, also at MIT. This is a much simpler program than Winograd's, since it involves nondirective psychotherapy, which, generally speaking, requires extremely simple-minded computer programs. Here is a striking dialogue between a human being and a computer psychotherapist. (There is certainly a selection effect here. Many other such machine/human psychiatric dialogues are not nearly so striking. But I suppose most human/human psychiatric dialogues are not very striking either.) In this interaction, in order to spell out clearly the respective roles of therapist and patient, the computer therapist types upper case while the patient types lower case:

men are all alike
IN WHAT WAY
they're always bugging us about something or other
CAN YOU THINK OF A SPECIFIC EXAMPLE
well, my boy friend made me come here
YOUR BOY FRIEND MADE YOU COME HERE
he noticed that i'm depressed much of the time
I AM SORRY TO HEAR YOU ARE DEPRESSED
he's right, i am unhappy
DO YOU THINK COMING HERE WILL HELP YOU NOT TO BE UNHAPPY
i need some help, that much is clear
WHAT WOULD IT MEAN TO YOU IF YOU GOT SOME HELP
perhaps i could learn to get along with my mother
TELL ME MORE ABOUT YOUR FAMILY
my mother takes care of me
WHO ELSE IN YOUR FAMILY TAKES CARE OF YOU

my father
YOUR FATHER
you are like my father in some ways
WHAT RESEMBLANCE DO YOU SEE
you are not very aggressive, but i don't think you want me to notice that
WHAT MAKES YOU THINK I AM NOT VERY AGGRESSIVE
you don't argue with me
WHY DO YOU THINK I DON'T ARGUE WITH YOU
you are afraid of me
DOES IT PLEASE YOU TO BELIEVE I AM AFRAID OF YOU
it pleases my father to think i am afraid of him
WHAT ELSE COMES TO MIND WHEN YOU THINK OF YOUR FATHER
bullies
DOES THAT HAVE ANYTHING TO DO WITH THE FACT THAT YOUR
BOY FRIEND MADE YOU COME HERE

This astonishing—one is very tempted to say "perceptive"—response from the computer is, of course, preprogrammed. But, then, so are the responses of human psychotherapists. In a time when more and more people in our society seem to be in need of psychiatric counseling, and when time-sharing of computers is widespread, I can even imagine the development of a network of computer psychotherapeutic terminals, something like arrays of large telephone booths, in which, for a few dollars a session, we are able to talk to an attentive, tested and largely nondirective psychotherapist. Ensuring the confidentiality of the psychiatric dialogue is one of several important steps still to be worked out.

Another sign of the intellectual accomplishments of machines is in games. Even exceptionally simple computers—those that can be wired by a bright ten-year-old—can be programmed to play perfect tic-tac-toe. Some computers can play world-class checkers. Chess is of course a much more complicated game than tic-tac-toe or checkers. Here programming a machine to win is more difficult, and novel strategies have been used, including several rather successful attempts to have a computer learn from its own experience in playing previous chess games. Computers can learn, for example, empirically the rule that it is better in the beginning game to control the center of the chessboard than the periphery. The ten best chess players in the world still have nothing to fear from any present computer. But the situation is changing. Recently a computer for the first time did well enough to enter the Minnesota State Chess Open. This may be the first time that a nonhuman has entered a major sporting event on the planet Earth (and I cannot help but wonder if robot golfers and designated hitters may be attempted sometime in the next decade, to say nothing of dolphins in free-style competition). The computer did not win the Chess Open, but this is the first time one has done well enough to enter such a competition. Chess-playing computers are improving extremely rapidly.

I have heard machines demeaned (often with a just audible sigh of relief) for the fact that chess is an area where human beings are still superior. This reminds me very much of the old joke in which a stranger remarks with wonder on the accomplishments of a checker-playing dog. The dog's owner replies, "Oh, it's not all that remarkable. He loses two games out of three." A machine that plays chess in the middle range of human expertise is a very capable machine; even if there are thousands of better human chess players, there are millions who are worse. To play chess requires strategy, foresight, analytical powers, and the ability to cross-correlate large numbers of variables and to learn from experience. These are excellent qualities in those whose job it is to discover and explore, as well as those who watch the baby and walk the dog.

With this as a more or less representative set of examples of the state of development of machine intelligence, I think it is clear that a major effort over the next decade could produce much more sophisticated examples. This is also the opinion of most of the workers in machine intelligence.

In thinking about this next generation of machine intelligence, it is important to distinguish between self-controlled and remotely controlled robots. A self-controlled robot has its intelligence within it; a remotely controlled robot has its intelligence at some other place, and its successful operation depends upon close communication between its central computer and itself. There are, of course, intermediate cases where the machine may be partly self-activated and partly remotely controlled. It is this mix of remote and *in situ* control that seems to offer the highest efficiency for the near future.

For example, we can imagine a machine designed for the mining of the ocean floor. There are enormous quantities of manganese nodules littering the abyssal depths. They were once thought to have been produced by meteorite infall on Earth, but are now believed to be formed occasionally in vast manganese fountains produced by the internal tectonic activity of the Earth. Many other scarce and industrially valuable minerals are likewise to be found on the deep ocean bottom. We have the capability today to design devices that systematically swim over or crawl upon the ocean floor; that are able to perform spectrometric and other chemical examinations of the surface material; that can automatically radio back to ship or land all findings; and that can mark the locales of especially valuable deposits—for example, by low-frequency radio-homing devices. The radio beacon will then direct great mining machines to the appropriate locales. The present state of the art in deep-sea submersibles and in spacecraft environmental sensors is clearly compatible with the development of such devices. Similar remarks can be made for off-shore oil drilling, for coal and other subterranean mineral mining, and so on. The likely economic returns from such devices would pay not only for their development, but for the entire space program many times over.

When the machines are faced with particularly difficult situations, they can be programmed to recognize that the situations are beyond their abilities and to inquire of human operators—working in safe and pleasant environments—what to do next. The examples just given are of devices that are largely self-controlled. The reverse also is possible, and a great deal of very preliminary work along these lines has been performed in the remote handling of highly radioactive materials in laboratories of the U.S. Department of Energy. Here I imagine a human being who is connected by radio link with a mobile machine. The operator is in Manila, say; the machine in the Mindanao Deep. The operator is attached to an array of electronic relays, which transmits and amplifies his movements to the machine and which can, conversely, carry what the machine finds back to his senses. So when the operator turns his head to the left, the television cameras on the machine turn left, and the operator sees on a great hemispherical television screen around him the scene the machine's searchlights and cameras have revealed. When the operator in Manila takes a few strides forward in his wired suit, the machine in the abyssal depths ambles a few feet forward. When the operator reaches out his hand, the mechanical arm of the machine likewise extends itself; and the precision of the man/machine interaction is such that precise manipulation of material at the ocean bottom by the machine's fingers is possible. With such devices, human beings can enter environments otherwise closed to them forever.

In the exploration of Mars, unmanned vehicles have already soft-landed, and only a little further in the future they will roam about the surface of the Red Planet, as some now do on the Moon. We are not ready for a manned mission to Mars. Some of us are concerned about such missions because of the dangers of carrying terrestrial microbes to Mars, and Martian microbes, if they exist, to Earth, but also because of their enormous expense. The Viking landers deposited on Mars in the summer of 1976 have a very interesting array of sensors and scientific instruments, which are the extension of human senses to an alien environment.

The obvious post-Viking device for Martian exploration, one which takes advantage of the Viking technology, is a Viking Rover in which the equivalent of an entire Viking spacecraft, but with considerably improved science, is put on wheels or tractor treads and permitted to rove slowly over the Martian landscape. But now we come to a new problem, one that is never encountered in machine operation on the Earth's surface. Although Mars is the second closest planet, it is so far from the Earth that the light travel time becomes significant. At a typical relative position of Mars and the Earth, the planet is 20 light-minutes away. Thus, if the spacecraft were confronted with a steep incline, it might send a message of inquiry back to Earth. Forty minutes later the response would arrive saying something like "For heaven's sake, stand dead still." But by then, of course, an unsophisticated machine would have tumbled into the gully. Consequently, any Martian Rover requires slope and roughness sensors.

Fortunately, these are readily available and are even seen in some children's toys. When confronted with a precipitous slope or large boulder, the spacecraft would either stop until receiving instructions from the Earth in response to its query (and televised picture of the terrain), or back off and start in another and safer direction.

Much more elaborate contingency decision networks can be built into the onboard computers of spacecraft of the 1980s. For more remote objectives, to be explored further in the future, we can imagine human controllers in orbit around the target planet, or on one of its moons. In the exploration of Jupiter, for example, I can imagine the operators on a small moon outside the fierce Jovian radiation belts, controlling with only a few seconds' delay the responses of a spacecraft floating in the dense Jovian clouds.

Human beings on Earth can also be in such an interaction loop, if they are willing to spend some time on the enterprise. If every decision in Martian exploration must be fed through a human controller on Earth, the Rover can traverse only a few feet an hour. But the lifetimes of such Rovers are so long that a few feet an hour represents a perfectly respectable rate of progress. However, as we imagine expeditions into the farthest reaches of the solar system—and ultimately to the stars—it is clear that self-controlled machine intelligence will assume heavier burdens of responsibility.

In the development of such machines we find a kind of convergent evolution. Viking is, in a curious sense, like some great outsized, clumsily constructed insect. It is not yet ambulatory, and it is certainly incapable of self-reproduction. But it has an exoskeleton, it has a wide range of insectlike sensory organs, and it is about as intelligent as a dragonfly. But Viking has an advantage that insects do not: it can, on occasion, by inquiring of its controllers on Earth, assume the intelligence of a human being—the controllers are able to reprogram the Viking computer on the basis of decisions they make.

As the field of machine intelligence advances and as increasingly distant objects in the solar system become accessible to exploration, we will see the development of increasingly sophisticated onboard computers, slowly climbing the phylogenetic tree from insect intelligence to crocodile intelligence to squirrel intelligence and—in the not very remote future, I think—to dog intelligence. Any flight to the outer solar system must have a computer capable of determining whether it is working properly. There is no possibility of sending to the Earth for a repairman. The machine must be able to sense when it is sick and skillfully doctor its own illnesses. A computer is needed that is able either to fix or replace failed computer, sensor or structural components. Such a computer, which has been called STAR (self-testing and repairing computer), is on the threshold of development. It employs redundant components, as biology does—we have two lungs and two kidneys partly because each is protection against failure of the other. But a computer can be much more redundant than a human being, who has, for example, but one head and one heart.

Because of the weight premium on deep space exploratory ventures, there will be strong pressures for continued miniaturization of intelligent machines. It is clear that remarkable miniaturization has already occurred: vacuum tubes have been replaced by transistors, wired circuits by printed circuit boards, and entire computer systems by silicon-chip microcircuitry. Today a circuit that used to occupy much of a 1930 radio set can be printed on the tip of a pin. If intelligent machines for terrestrial mining and space exploratory applications are pursued, the time cannot be far off when household and other domestic robots will become commercially feasible. Unlike the classical and anthropoid robots of science fiction, there is no reason for such machines to look any more human than a vacuum cleaner does. They will be specialized for their functions. But there are many common tasks, ranging from bartending to floor washing, that involve a very limited array of intellectual capabilities, albeit substantial stamina and patience. All-purpose ambulatory household robots, which perform domestic functions as well as a proper nineteenth-century English butler, are probably many decades off. But more specialized machines, each adapted to a specific household function, are probably already on the horizon.

It is possible to imagine many other civic tasks and essential functions of everyday life carried out by intelligent machines. By the early 1970s, garbage collectors in Anchorage, Alaska, and other cities won wage settlements guaranteeing them salaries of about $20,000 per annum. It is possible that the economic pressures alone may make a persuasive case for the development of automated garbage-collecting machines. For the development of domestic and civic robots to be a general civic good, the effective re-employment of those human beings displaced by the robots must, of course, be arranged; but over a human generation that should not be too difficult—particularly if there are enlightened educational reforms. Human beings enjoy learning.

We appear to be on the verge of developing a wide variety of intelligent machines capable of performing tasks too dangerous, too expensive, too onerous or too boring for human beings. The development of such machines is, in my mind, one of the few legitimate "spin-offs" of the space program. The efficient exploitation of energy in agriculture—upon which our survival as a species depends—may even be contingent on the development of such machines. The main obstacle seems to be a very human problem, the quiet feeling that comes stealthily and unbidden, and argues that there is something threatening or "inhuman" about machines performing certain tasks as well as or better than human beings; or a sense of loathing for creatures made of silicon and germanium rather than proteins and nucleic acids. But in many respects our survival as a species depends on our transcending such primitive chauvinisms. In part, our adjustment to intelligent machines is a matter of acclimatization. There are already cardiac pacemakers that can sense the beat of the human heart; only when there is the slightest hint of fibrillation does the pacemaker stimulate the heart. This is a mild but very useful sort of machine intelligence. I cannot imagine the wearer of this device resenting its intelligence. I think in a relatively short period of time there will be a very similar sort of acceptance for much more intelligent and sophisticated machines. There is nothing inhuman about an intelligent machine; it is indeed an expression of those superb intellectual capabilities that only human beings, of all the creatures on our planet, now possess.

Joseph Weizenbaum

Joseph Weizenbaum is a scientist and engineer who has spent most of his adult life studying artificial intelligence, the structure of computer language, the understanding of natural language by computers, and the social implications of these studies. He was born in Berlin in 1923 but has become a citizen of the United States. Educated at Wayne University, where he earned his M.S. in 1950, he worked as a systems engineer for General Electric before joining the faculty of the Massachusetts Institute of Technology in 1963. His major publication available to nonspecialists is his book *Computer Power and Human Reason* (1976), which, he says, contains two major arguments: "first, that there is a difference between man and machine, and, second, that there are certain tasks which computers *ought* not be made to do, independent of whether computers *can* be made to do them." The book's Introduction is reprinted below.

Introduction to Computer Power and Human Reason

In 1935, Michael Polanyi, then holder of the Chair of Physical Chemistry at the Victoria University of Manchester, England, was suddenly shocked into a confrontation with philosophical questions that have ever since dominated his life. The shock was administered by Nicolai Bukharin, one of the leading theoreticians of the Russian Communist party, who told Polanyi that "under socialism the conception of science pursued for its own sake would disappear, for the interests of scientists would spontaneously turn to the problems of the current Five Year

Plan."[0] Polanyi sensed then that "the scientific outlook appeared to have produced a mechanical conception of man and history in which there was no place for science itself." And further that "this conception denied altogether any intrinsic power to thought and thus denied any grounds for claiming freedom of thought."[1]

I don't know how much time Polanyi thought he would devote to developing an argument for a contrary concept of man and history. His very shock testifies to the fact that he was in profound disagreement with Bukharin, therefore that he already conceived of man differently, even if he could not then give explicit form to his concept. It may be that he determined to write a counterargument to Bukharin's position, drawing only on his own experience as a scientist, and to have done with it in short order. As it turned out, however, the confrontation with philosophy triggered by Bukharin's revelation was to demand Polanyi's entire attention from then to the present day.

I recite this bit of history for two reasons. The first is to illustrate that ideas which seem at first glance to be obvious and simple, and which ought therefore to be universally credible once they have been articulated, are sometimes buoys marking out stormy channels in deep intellectual seas. That science is creative, that the creative act in science is equivalent to the creative act in art, that creation springs only from autonomous individuals, is such a simple and, one might think, obvious idea. Yet Polanyi has, as have many others, spent nearly a lifetime exploring the ground in which it is anchored and the turbulent sea of implications which surrounds it.

The second reason I recite this history is that I feel myself to be reliving part of it. My own shock was administered not by any important political figure espousing his philosophy of science, but by some people who insisted on misinterpreting a piece of work I had done. I write this without bitterness and certainly not in a defensive mood. Indeed, the interpretations I have in mind tended, if anything, to overrate what little I had accomplished and certainly its importance. No, I recall that piece of work now only because it seems to me to provide the most parsimonious way of identifying the issues I mean to discuss.

The work was done in the period 1964–1966, and was reported in the computer-science literature in January 1966 and August 1967. To summarize it briefly, I composed a computer program with which one could "converse" in English. The human conversationalist partner would type

[1]M. Polanyi, *The Tacit Dimension* (New York: Doubleday, Anchor ed., 1967), pp. 3–4.

Five Year Plan U.S.S.R. economic program designed to increase industrial and agricultural output by setting quotas for five-year periods, first implemented in 1928 under Joseph Stalin.

his portion of the conversation on a typewriter connected to a computer, and the computer, under control of my program, would analyze the message that had so been transmitted to it, compose a response to it in English, and cause the response to be typed on the computer's typewriter.

I chose the name ELIZA for the language analysis program because, like the Eliza of Pygmalion fame,[0] it could be taught to "speak" increasingly well. Because conversations must be about something, that is, because they must take place within some context, the program was constructed in a two-tier arrangement, the first tier consisting of the language analyzer and the second of a script. The script is a set of rules rather like those that might be given to an actor who is to use them to improvise around a certain theme. Thus ELIZA could be given a script to enable it to maintain a conversation about cooking eggs or about managing a bank checking account, and so on. Each specific script thus enabled ELIZA to play a specific conversational role.

For my first experiment, I gave ELIZA a script designed to permit it to play (I should really say parody) the role of a Rogerian psychotherapist engaged in an initial interview with a patient. The Rogerian psychotherapist is relatively easy to imitate because much of his technique consists of drawing his patient out by reflecting the patient's statements back to him. The following conversation between a young lady and ELIZA playing doctor illustrates both the Rogerian technique of encouraging a patient to keep talking and the operation of the computer program ELIZA. The first to "speak" is the young lady. The computer's responses are printed entirely in capitals.[2]

> Men are all alike.
> IN WHAT WAY
> They're always bugging us about something or other.
> CAN YOU THINK OF A SPECIFIC EXAMPLE
> Well, my boyfriend made me come here.
> YOUR BOYFRIEND MADE YOU COME HERE
> He says I'm depressed much of the time.
> I AM SORRY TO HEAR YOU ARE DEPRESSED
> It's true. I am unhappy.
> DO YOU THINK COMING HERE WILL HELP YOU NOT TO BE UNHAPPY
> I need some help, that much seems certain.

[2]This "conversation" is extracted from J. Weizenbaum, "ELIZA—A Computer Program For the Study of Natural Language Communication Between Man and Machine," *Communications of the Association for Computing Machinery*, vol. 9, no. 1 (January 1965), pp. 36–45.

Eliza of Pygmalion fame Leading role, that of Eliza Doolittle, in George Bernard Shaw's play *Pygmalion* (1912), upon which the musical *My Fair Lady* is based. Eliza is a Cockney flower seller who is taught upper-class speech and manners by a linguistics professor because he had made a bet that he could pass her off as a duchess if he were given six months to work with her.

WHAT WOULD IT MEAN TO YOU IF YOU GOT SOME HELP
Perhaps I could learn to get along with my mother.
TELL ME MORE ABOUT YOUR FAMILY
My mother takes care of me.
WHO ELSE IN YOUR FAMILY TAKES CARE OF YOU
My father.
YOUR FATHER
You are like my father in some ways.
WHAT RESEMBLANCE DO YOU SEE
You are not very aggressive but I think you don't want me to notice that.
WHAT MAKES YOU THINK I AM NOT VERY AGGRESSIVE
You don't argue with me.
WHY DO YOU THINK I DON'T ARGUE WITH YOU
You are afraid of me.
DOES IT PLEASE YOU TO BELIEVE I AM AFRAID OF YOU
My father is afraid of everybody.
WHAT ELSE COMES TO MIND WHEN YOU THINK OF YOUR FATHER
Bullies.
DOES THAT HAVE ANYTHING TO DO WITH THE FACT THAT YOUR
BOYFRIEND MADE YOU COME HERE

DOCTOR, as ELIZA playing psychiatrist came to be known, soon became famous around the Massachusetts Institute of Technology, where it first came into existence, mainly because it was an easy program to demonstrate. Most other programs could not vividly demonstrate the information-processing power of a computer to visitors who did not already have some specialized knowledge, say, of some branch of mathematics. DOCTOR, on the other hand, could be appreciated on some level by anyone. Its power as a demonstration vehicle was further enhanced by the fact that the visitor could actually participate in its operation. Soon copies of DOCTOR, constructed on the basis of my published description of it, began appearing at other institutions in the United States. The program became nationally known and even, in certain circles, a national plaything.

The shocks I experienced as DOCTOR became widely known and "played" were due principally to three distinct events.

1. A number of practicing psychiatrists seriously believed the DOCTOR computer program could grow into a nearly completely automatic form of psychotherapy. Colby *et al.* write, for example,

"Further work must be done before the program will be ready for clinical use. If the method proves beneficial, then it would provide a therapeutic tool which can be made widely available to mental hospitals and psychiatric centers suffering a shortage of therapists. Because of the time-sharing capabilities of modern and future computers, several hundred patients an hour could be handled by a computer system designed for this purpose. The human therapist, involved in the design and operation of this system, would not be replaced, but would become a much more efficient man since his efforts would no longer be limited to the one-to-one patient-therapist ratio as now exists."[3]*

I had thought it essential, as a prerequisite to the very possibility that one person might help another learn to cope with his emotional problems, that the helper himself participate in the other's experience of those problems and, in large part by way of his own empathic recognition of them, himself come to understand them. There are undoubtedly many techniques to facilitate the therapist's imaginative projection into the patient's inner life. But that it was possible for even one practicing psychiatrist to advocate that this crucial component of the therapeutic process be entirely supplanted by pure technique—*that* I had not imagined! What must a psychiatrist who makes such a suggestion think he is doing while treating a patient, that he can view the simplest mechanical parody of a single interviewing technique as having captured anything of the essence of a human encounter? Perhaps Colby *et al.* give us the required clue when they write:

> "A human therapist can be viewed as an information processor and decision maker with a set of decision rules which are closely linked to short-range and long-range goals, . . . He is guided in these decisions by rough empiric rules telling him what is appropriate to say and not to say in certain contexts. To incorporate these processes, to the degree possessed by a human therapist, in the program would be a considerable undertaking, but we are attempting to move in this direction."[4]

What can the psychiatrist's image of his patient be when he sees himself, as therapist, not as an engaged human being acting as a healer, but as an information processor following rules, etc.?

Such questions were my awakening to what Polanyi had earlier called a "scientific outlook that appeared to have produced a mechanical conception of man."

2. I was startled to see how quickly and how very deeply people conversing with DOCTOR became emotionally involved with the computer and

---

[3]K. M. Colby, J. B. Watt, and J. P. Gilbert, "A Computer Method of Psychotherapy: Preliminary Communication," *The Journal of Nervous and Mental Disease,* vol. 142, no. 2 (1966), pp. 148–152.

*Nor is Dr. Colby alone in his enthusiasm for computer administered psychotherapy. Dr. Carl Sagan, the astrophysicist, recently commented on ELIZA in *Natural History,* vol. LXXXIV, no. 1 (Jan. 1975), p. 10: "No such computer program is adequate for psychiatric use today, but the same can be remarked about some human psychotherapists. In a period when more and more people in our society seem to be in need of psychiatric counseling, and when time sharing of computers is widespread, I can imagine the development of a network of computer psychotherapeutic terminals, something like arrays of large telephone booths, in which, for a few dollars a session, we would be able to talk with an attentive, tested, and largely non-directive psychotherapist."

[4]*Ibid.*

how unequivocally they anthropomorphized it. Once my secretary, who had watched me work on the program for many months and therefore surely knew it to be merely a computer program, started conversing with it. After only a few interchanges with it, she asked me to leave the room. Another time, I suggested I might rig the system so that I could examine all conversations anyone had had with it, say, overnight. I was promptly bombarded with accusations that what I proposed amounted to spying on people's most intimate thoughts; clear evidence that people were conversing with the computer as if it were a person who could be appropriately and usefully addressed in intimate terms. I knew of course that people form all sorts of emotional bonds to machines, for example, to musical instruments, motorcycles, and cars. And I knew from long experience that the strong emotional ties many programmers have to their computers are often formed after only short exposures to their machines. What I had not realized is that extremely short exposures to a relatively simple computer program could induce powerful delusional thinking in quite normal people. This insight led me to attach new importance to questions of the relationship between the individual and the computer, and hence to resolve to think about them.

3. Another widespread, and to me surprising, reaction to the ELIZA program was the spread of a belief that it demonstrated a general solution to the problem of computer understanding of natural language. In my paper, I had tried to say that no general solution to that problem was possible, i.e., that language is understood only in contextual frameworks, that even these can be shared by people to only a limited extent, and that consequently even people are not embodiments of any such general solution. But these conclusions were often ignored. In any case, ELIZA was such a small and simple step. Its contribution was, if any at all, only to vividly underline what many others had long ago discovered, namely, the importance of context to language understanding. The subsequent, much more elegant, and surely more important work of Winograd[5] in computer comprehension of English is currently being misinterpreted just as ELIZA was. This reaction to ELIZA showed me more vividly than anything I had seen hitherto the enormously exaggerated attributions an even well-educated audience is capable of making, even strives to make, to a technology it does not understand. Surely, I thought, decisions made by the general public about emergent technologies depend much more on what that public attributes to such technologies than on what they actually are or can and cannot do. If, as appeared to be the case, the public's attributions are wildly misconceived, then public decisions are bound to be mis-

[5]T. Winograd, "Procedures As A Representation For Data In A Computer Program For Understanding Natural Language." Ph.D. dissertation submitted to the Dept. of Mathematics (M.I.T.), August 24, 1970.

guided and often wrong. Difficult questions arise out of these observations; what, for example, are the scientist's responsibilities with respect to making his work public? And to whom (or what) is the scientist responsible?

As perceptions of these kinds began to reverberate in me, I thought, as perhaps Polanyi did after his encounter with Bukharin, that the questions and misgivings that had so forcefully presented themselves to me could be disposed of quickly, perhaps in a short, serious article. I did in fact write a paper touching on many points mentioned here.[6] But gradually I began to see that certain quite fundamental questions had infected me more chronically than I had first perceived. I shall probably never be rid of them.

There are as many ways to state these basic questions as there are starting points for coping with them. At bottom they are about nothing less than man's place in the universe. But I am professionally trained only in computer science, which is to say (in all seriousness) that I am extremely poorly educated; I can mount neither the competence, nor the courage, not even the chutzpah, to write on the grand scale actually demanded. I therefore grapple with questions that couple more directly to the concerns I have expressed, and hope that their larger implications will emerge spontaneously.

I shall thus have to concern myself with the following kinds of questions:

1. What is it about the computer that has brought the view of man as a machine to a new level of plausibility? Clearly there have been other machines that imitated man in various ways, e.g., steam shovels. But not until the invention of the digital computer have there been machines that could perform intellectual functions of even modest scope; i.e., machines that could in any sense be said to be intelligent. Now "artificial intelligence" (AI) is a subdiscipline of computer science. This new field will have to be discussed. Ultimately a line dividing human and machine intelligence must be drawn. If there is no such line, then advocates of computerized psychotherapy may be merely heralds of an age in which man has finally been recognized as nothing but a clock-work. Then the consequences of such a reality would need urgently to be divined and contemplated.

2. The fact that individuals bind themselves with strong emotional ties to machines ought not in itself to be surprising. The instruments man uses become, after all, extensions of his body. Most importantly, man must, in order to operate his instruments skillfully, internalize aspects of them in the form of kinesthetic and perceptual habits. In that sense at least, his instruments become literally part of him and modify him, and thus alter

[6]J. Weizenbaum, "On the Impact of Computers on Society," *Science,* vol. 176, no. 12 (May, 1972).

the basis of his affective relationship to himself. One would expect man to cathect more intensely to instruments that couple directly to his own intellectual, cognitive, and emotive functions than to machines that merely extend the power of his muscles. Western man's entire milieu is now pervaded by complex technological extensions of his every functional capacity. Being the enormously adaptive animal he is, man has been able to accept as authentically natural (that is, as given by nature) such technological bases for his relationship to himself, for his identity. Perhaps this helps to explain why he does not question the appropriateness of investing his most private feelings in a computer. But then, such an explanation would also suggest that the computing machine represents merely an extreme extrapolation of a much more general technological usurpation of man's capacity to act as an autonomous agent in giving meaning to his world. It is therefore important to inquire into the wider senses in which man has come to yield his own autonomy to a world viewed as machine.

3. It is perhaps paradoxical that just when in the deepest sense man has ceased to believe in—let alone to trust—his own autonomy, he has begun to rely on autonomous machines, that is, on machines that operate for long periods of time entirely on the basis of their own internal realities. If his reliance on such machines is to be based on something other than unmitigated despair or blind faith, he must explain to himself what these machines do and even how they do what they do. This requires him to build some conception of their internal "realities." Yet most men don't understand computers to even the slightest degree. So, unless they are capable of very great skepticism (the kind we bring to bear while watching a stage magician), they can explain the computer's intellectual feats only by bringing to bear the single analogy available to them, that is, their model of their own capacity to think. No wonder, then, that they overshoot the mark; it is truly impossible to imagine a human who could imitate ELIZA, for example, but for whom ELIZA's language abilities were his limit. Again, the computing machine is merely an extreme example of a much more general phenomenon. Even the breadth of connotation intended in the ordinary usage of the word "machine," large as it is, is insufficient to suggest its true generality. For today when we speak of, for example, bureaucracy, or the university, or almost any social or political construct, the image we generate is all too often that of an autonomous machine-like process.

These, then, are the thoughts and questions which have refused to leave me since the deeper significances of the reactions to ELIZA I have described began to become clear to me. Yet I doubt that they could have impressed themselves on me as they did were it not that I was (and am still) deeply involved in a concentrate of technological society as a teacher in the temple of technology that is the Massachusetts Institute of Technology, an institution that proudly boasts of being "polarized around science and technology." There I live and work with colleagues, many of whom trust only modern science to deliver reliable knowledge of the world. I confer with them on research proposals to be made to government agencies, especially to the Department of "Defense." Sometimes I become more than a little frightened as I contemplate what we lead ourselves to propose, as well as the nature of the arguments we construct to support our proposals. Then, too, I am constantly confronted by students, some of whom have already rejected all ways but the scientific to come to know the world, and who seek only a deeper, more dogmatic indoctrination in that faith (although that word is no longer in their vocabulary). Other students suspect that not even the entire collection of machines and instruments at M.I.T. can significantly help give meaning to their lives. They sense the presence of a dilemma in an education polarized around science and technology, an education that implicitly claims to open a privileged access-path to fact, but that cannot tell them how to decide what is to count as fact. Even while they recognize the genuine importance of learning their craft, they rebel at working on projects that appear to address themselves neither to answering interesting questions of fact nor to solving problems in theory.

Such confrontations with my own day-to-day social reality have gradually convinced me that my experience with ELIZA was symptomatic of deeper problems. The time would come, I was sure, when I would no longer be able to participate in research proposal conferences, or honestly respond to my students' need for therapy (yes, that is the correct word), without first attempting to make sense of the picture my own experience with computers had so sharply drawn for me.

Of course, the introduction of computers into our already highly technological society has, as I will try to show, merely reinforced and amplified those antecedent pressures that have driven man to an ever more highly rationalistic view of his society and an ever more mechanistic image of himself. It is therefore important that I construct my discussion of the impact of the computer on man and his society so that it can be seen as a particular kind of encoding of a much larger impact, namely, that on man's role in the face of technologies and techniques he may not be able to understand and control. Conversations around that theme have been going on for a long time. And they have intensified in the last few years.

Certain individuals of quite differing minds, temperaments, interests, and training have—however much they differ among themselves and even disagree on many vital questions—over the years expressed grave concern about the conditions created by the unfettered march of science and technology; among them are Mumford, Arendt, Ellul, Roszak, Comfort, and Boulding. The computer began to be mentioned in such discussions only recently. Now there are signs that a full-scale debate about the computer is developing. The contestants on one side are those who, briefly stated, believe computers can, should, and will do everything, and on the other side those who, like myself, believe there are limits to what computers ought to be put to do.

It may appear at first glance that this is an in-house debate of little consequence except to a small group of computer technicians. But at bottom, no matter how it may be disguised by technological jargon, the question is whether or not every aspect of human thought is reducible to a logical formalism, or, to put it into the modern idiom, whether or not human thought is entirely computable. That question has, in one form or another, engaged thinkers in all ages. Man has always striven for principles that could organize and give sense and meaning to his existence. But before modern science fathered the technologies that reified and concretized its otherwise abstract systems, the systems of thought that defined man's place in the universe were fundamentally juridical. They served to define man's obligations to his fellow men and to nature. The Judaic tradition, for example, rests on the idea of a contractual relationship between God and man. This relationship must and does leave room for autonomy for both God and man, for a contract is an agreement willingly entered into by both parties who are free not to agree. Man's autonomy and his corresponding responsibility is a central issue of all religious systems. The spiritual cosmologies engendered by modern science, on the other hand, are infected with the germ of logical necessity. They, except in the hands of the wisest scientists and philosophers, no longer content themselves with explanations of appearances, but claim to say how things actually are and must necessarily be. In short, they convert truth to provability.

As one consequence of this drive to modern science, the question, "What aspects of life are formalizable?" has been transformed from the moral question, "How and in what form may man's obligations and responsibilities be known?" to the question, "Of what technological genus is man a species?" Even some philosophers whose every instinct rebels against the idea that man is entirely comprehensible as a machine have succumbed to this spirit of the times. Hubert Dreyfus, for example, trains the heavy guns of phenomenology on the computer model of man.[7] But he limits his argument to the technical question of what computers can and cannot do. I would argue that if computers could imitate man in every respect—which in fact they cannot—even then it would be appropriate, nay, urgent, to examine the computer in the light of man's perennial need to find his place in the world. The outcomes of practical matters that are of vital importance to everyone hinge on how and in what terms the discussion is carried out.

One position I mean to argue appears deceptively obvious: it is simply that there are important differences between men and machines as thinkers. I would argue that, however intelligent machines may be made to be,

[7]Hubert L. Dreyfus, *What Computers Can't Do* (Harper and Row, 1972).

there are some acts of thought that *ought* to be attempted only by humans. One socially significant question I thus intend to raise is over the proper place of computers in the social order. But, as we shall see, the issue transcends computers in that it must ultimately deal with logicality itself —quite apart from whether logicality is encoded in computer programs or not.

The lay reader may be forgiven for being more than slightly incredulous that anyone should maintain that human thought is entirely computable. But his very incredulity may itself be a sign of how marvelously subtly and seductively modern science has come to influence man's imaginative construction of reality.

Surely, much of what we today regard as good and useful, as well as much of what we would call knowledge and wisdom, we owe to science. But science may also be seen as an addictive drug. Not only has our unbounded feeding on science caused us to become dependent on it, but, as happens with many other drugs taken in increasing dosages, science has been gradually converted into a slow-acting poison. Beginning perhaps with Francis Bacon's misreading of the genuine promise of science, man has been seduced into wishing and working for the establishment of an age of rationality, but with his vision of rationality tragically twisted so as to equate it with logicality. Thus have we very nearly come to the point where almost every genuine human dilemma is seen as a mere paradox, as a merely apparent contradiction that could be untangled by judicious applications of cold logic derived from a higher standpoint. Even murderous wars have come to be perceived as mere problems to be solved by hordes of professional problemsolvers. As Hannah Arendt said about recent makers and executors of policy in the Pentagon:

> "They were not just intelligent, but prided themselves on being 'rational' . . . They were eager to find formulas, preferably expressed in a pseudo-mathematical language, that would unify the most disparate phenomena with which reality presented them; that is, they were eager to discover *laws* by which to explain and predict political and historical facts as though they were as necessary, and thus as reliable, as the physicists once believed natural phenomena to be . . . [They] did not *judge;* they calculated. . . . an utterly irrational confidence in the calculability of reality [became] the leitmotif of the decision making."[8]

And so too have nearly all political confrontations, such as those between races and those between the governed and their governors, come to be perceived as mere failures of communication. Such rips in the social fabric can then be systematically repaired by the expert application of the latest information-handling techniques—at least so it is believed. And so the rationality-is-logicality equation, which the very success of science has drugged us into adopting as virtually an axiom, has led us to deny the very

[8]Hannah Arendt, *Crises of the Republic* (Harcourt Brace Jovanovich, Harvest edition, 1972), pp. 11 *et seq.*

existence of human conflict, hence the very possibility of the collision of genuinely incommensurable human interests and of disparate human values, hence the existence of human values themselves.

It may be that human values are illusory, as indeed B. F. Skinner argues. If they are, then it is presumably up to science to demonstrate that fact, as indeed Skinner (as scientist) attempts to do. But then science must itself be an illusory system. For the only certain knowledge science can give us is knowledge of the behavior of formal systems, that is, systems that are games invented by man himself and in which to assert truth is nothing more or less than to assert that, as in a chess game, a particular board position was arrived at by a sequence of legal moves. When science purports to make statements about man's experiences, it bases them on identifications between the primitive (that is, undefined) objects of one of its formalisms, the pieces of one of its games, and some set of human observations. No such sets of correspondences can ever be proved to be correct. At best, they can be falsified, in the sense that formal manipulations of a system's symbols may lead to symbolic configurations which, when read in the light of the set of correspondences in question, yield interpretations contrary to empirically observed phenomena. Hence all empirical science is an elaborate structure built on piles that are anchored, not on bedrock as is commonly supposed, but on the shifting sand of fallible human judgment, conjecture, and intuition. It is not even true, again contrary to common belief, that a single purported counter-instance that, if accepted as genuine would certainly falsify a specific scientific theory, generally leads to the immediate abandonment of that theory. Probably all scientific theories currently accepted by scientists themselves (excepting only those purely formal theories claiming no relation to the empirical world) are today confronted with contradicting evidence of more than negligible weight that, again if fully credited, would logically invalidate them. Such evidence is often explained (that is, explained away) by ascribing it to error of some kind, say, observational error, or by characterizing it as inessential, or by the assumption (that is, the faith) that some yet-to-be-discovered way of dealing with it will some day permit it to be acknowledged but nevertheless incorporated into the scientific theories it was originally thought to contradict. In this way scientists continue to rely on already impaired theories and to infer "scientific fact" from them.*

The man in the street surely believes such scientific facts to be as

---

*Thus, Charles Everett writes on the now-discarded phlogiston theory of combustion (in the *Encyclopaedia Britannica*, 11th ed., 1911, vol. VI, p. 34): "The objections of the antiphlogistonists, such as the fact that the calices weigh more than the original metals instead of less as the theory suggests, were answered by postulating that phlogiston was a principle of levity, or even completely ignored as an accident, the change in qualities being regarded as the only matter of importance." Everett lists H. Cavendish and J. Priestley, both great scientists of their time, as adherents to the phlogiston theory.

well-established, as well-proven, as his own existence. His certitude is an illusion. Nor is the scientist himself immune to the same illusion. In his praxis, he must, after all, suspend disbelief in order to do or think anything at all. He is rather like a theatergoer, who, in order to partic- ipate in and understand what is happening on the stage, must for a time pretend to himself that he is witnessing real events. The scientist must believe his working hypothesis, together with its vast underlying structure of theories and assumptions, even if only for the sake of the argument. Often the "argument" extends over his entire lifetime. Gradually he becomes what he at first merely pretended to be: a true believer. I choose the word "argument" thoughtfully, for scientific demonstrations, even mathematical proofs, are fundamentally acts of persuasion.

Scientific statements can never be certain; they can be only more or less credible. And credibility is a term in individual psychology, i.e., a term that has meaning only with respect to an individual observer. To say that some proposition is credible is, after all, to say that it is believed by an agent who is free not to believe it, that is, by an observer who, after exercising judgment and (possibly) intuition, chooses to accept the propo- sition as worthy of his believing it. How then can science, which itself surely and ultimately rests on vast arrays of human value judgments, demonstrate that human value judgments are illusory? It cannot do so without forfeiting its own status as the single legitimate path to under- standing man and his world.

But no merely logical argument, no matter how cogent or eloquent, can undo this reality: that science has become the sole legitimate form of understanding in the common wisdom. When I say that science has been gradually converted into a slow-acting poison, I mean that the attribution of certainty to scientific knowledge by the common wisdom, an attribution now made so nearly universally that it has become a commonsense dogma, has virtually delegitimatized all other ways of understanding. People viewed the arts, especially literature, as sources of intellectual nourish- ment and understanding, but today the arts are perceived largely as enter- tainments. The ancient Greek and Oriental theaters, the Shakespearian stage, the stages peopled by the Ibsens and Chekhovs nearer to our day —these were schools. The curricula they taught were vehicles for under- standing the societies they represented. Today, although an occasional Arthur Miller or Edward Albee survives and is permitted to teach on the New York or London stage, the people hunger only for what is repre- sented to them to be scientifically validated knowledge. They seek to satiate themselves at such scientific cafeterias as *Psychology Today,* or on popularized versions of the works of Masters and Johnson, or on scien- tology as revealed by L. Ron Hubbard. Belief in the rationality-logicality equation has corroded the prophetic power of language itself. We can count, but we are rapidly forgetting how to say what is worth counting and why.

Thomas B. Sheridan

Thomas B. Sheridan (born 1929) is professor of engineering and applied psychology at M.I.T. He heads the Man–Machine Systems Laboratory in the Department of Mechanical Engineering, which performs research in robotic and person-computer interactions; he also teaches in the M.I.T. program in Technology and Policy. He has served as president of the Systems, Man, and Cybernetics Society of the Institute of Electrical and Electronics Engineers, as editor of its *Transactions on Man-Machine Systems,* and as consultant to government and industrial organizations on computer applications. We print below the concluding sections of an article from the October 1980 *Technology Review.* It was adapted from a paper presented at the World Council of Churches' Conference on Faith, Science, and the Future in July 1979 at M.I.T., and first published in *Faith and Science in an Unjust World,* vol. 1 (1980).

Seven Factors in Alienation

What computers are good at and what people are good at tend to be different. Computers have good memories and are fast, consistent, and reliable but as yet are not creative or readily able to adapt to novel situations. People have poor memories, are slow, seldom do things the same way twice, and are unreliable, but they are adaptable and creative. Computers are a different race from people. It is a wonderful ideal to design systems wherein these two can complement and wed their talents.

For those persons who program computers and design them into control systems, this interaction can be fulfilling. For others, however, dealing with computers on computer terms is intimidating. What is the difference between the two groups of people in their relation to the computer? And what makes control by computers so alienating?

1

A first factor is that some people compare themselves with computers and worry about their inferiority and threatened obsolescence. Computers clearly do outperform people when a large amount of data must be processed with great precision in a short time. If doing certain things better than people means "overtaking" them, then there is little ground for arguing against such a situation. But rather than worry about this, we should celebrate those ways in which people are not computers, and let computers take over the jobs where they clearly outperform us. People can still pull a computer's plug, though we may have to work at maintaining that privilege.

2

A second alienating factor is the tendency for computer control to make human operators remote from their ultimate task. Centralized control creates spatial distance from objects being manufactured, banking transactions, or patients in the hospital. Human actions become desynchronized from the final shaping of the goods and services being produced, and the end process or product is no longer directly experienced. Instead, artificial sensors feed the information to a computer that digests it and presents a summary of what the computer thinks the human operators should know.

Excuses are often given by managers: workers are not interested; the system is too complex; too much feedback would be distracting. I believe that, under most circumstances, greater satisfaction and improved performance will result if we attempt to reduce workers' estrangement from their efforts.

3

A third and related aspect of alienation occurs in jobs that have demanded considerable training and skill on the part of humans. The advent of computer control means that skilled machinists, typesetters, laboratory technicians, and aircraft pilots are "promoted" to button pushers and machine tenders. Their sensory-motor skills, acquired over decades and contributing to their sense of dignity and self-image, become obsolete. Moreover, while their skills atrophy, it is presumed they will be prepared to take over the computer when necessary; and they are anxiously aware that when the time comes, they may not be up to it.

Button pushing is not so bad if that is not the only contribution the worker makes. Workers must be willing to learn new skills when possible and in some cases seize the initiative when the opportunities aren't provided. Likewise, management must be willing to provide workers with the authority, responsibility, and accountability to use these skills. This may require relinquishing some control and risking new operating styles as yet quite alien to business-labor relations.

4

Closely related is a fourth factor akin to our system of formal education and C. P. Snow's "two cultures." This is the greater *access* to information and power by the technologically literate minority as compared with the technologically illiterate majority (which usually includes both machine tender and consumers of products or services).

The technological literati in this case include the computer designers, programmers, and their technical management. Curiously, the normally powerful but nontechnical groups such as financiers, lawyers, and politicians feel increasingly at the mercy of the technical elite. At the middle level of this particular pyramid are the workers who would benefit enormously were they better equipped with formal education and were their managers willing to be a bit more flexible in allowing them access. At the bottom of the pyramid are the undereducated and older segments of the society, who simply cannot keep up, having no understanding of the computer-based society and its concepts of probability, feedback control, and artificial intelligence, and having no access to credit cards, home terminals, and the like. Clearly, if we are to check the growth of alienation in our society, we must improve our educational system so that citizens will be better prepared to participate in a computerized society.

5

A fifth aspect of alienation is *mystification.* An elegant analogy of this attribute of computer control was made by the M.I.T. mathematician and "father of cybernetics," Norbert Weiner. In *God and Golem, Inc.,* written in 1964, he compares Golem, the mythical half-man, half-beast of Hebraic tradition, to the computer. Weiner makes his point metaphorically by relating the tale of the Monkey's Paw, a classic in horror literature.

"In this story, an English working family sits down to dinner in its kitchen. Afterwards, the son leaves to work at a factory, and the old parents listen to the tales of their guest, a sergeant-major back from service in the Indian army. He tells of Indian magic and shows them a dried monkey's paw, which, he says, is a talisman that has been endowed by an Indian holy man with the virtue of giving three wishes to each of three successive owners. This, he says, was to prove the folly of defying fate.

"He claims that he does not know the first two wishes of the first owner, but only that the last was for death. He himself was the second owner but his experiences were too terrible to relate. He is about to cast the paw on the coal fire when his host retrieves it and despite all the sergeant-major can do, wishes for £200.

"Shortly thereafter there is a knock at the door. A very solemn gentleman is there from the company that has employed his son and, as gently as he can, breaks the news that the son has been killed in an accident at the factory. Without recognizing any responsibility in the matter, the company offers its sympathy and £200 as a solatium."

The theme here is the danger of trusting the magic of the computer when its operation is singularly literal. "If you ask for £200 and do not express the condition that you do not wish it at the cost of the life of your son, £200 you will get whether your son lives or dies."

It is easy to attribute magical properties to the computer—our pop media encourage us to do so at every turn—but there is great danger in this. The computer, having no cultural empathy with its programmer, does not assume the rich contextual fabric underlying all person-to-person communications. If the computer is connected to a control system with fast and powerful machines, the result of this excessive trust could be disastrous.

Fingers can be pointed in many directions: advertising, military and industrial security—all plain technocratic arrogance fostering the mystique of a computer-control panacea without revealing the limitations. These institutions and individuals see posing as magicians as being in their own best interest. A counterforce is growing, but the strategies for demystification have yet to be worked out.

6

This naturally leads to a sixth factor of alienation: higher stakes in decision making. Because computer-controlled systems are growing larger, more complex, more capital intensive, more centralized, and more tightly controlled, the costs of failure are huge, though the probabilities of failure may be small. We need only think of military systems, nuclear plants, and air-traffic control systems to be reminded. Such systems may run reliably and smoothly, with minor failures automatically circumvented. "Fail-safe" is the ideal, and it usually works, but there is always a low probability of complete breakdown, which may be spectacular. Last June, for example, we came uncomfortably close to the ultimate failure when the North American Air Defense computer gave false indications of an enemy attack and bombers were readied for counterattack.

Reliability analysts know how to cope with the minor failures because they do happen from time to time. For these small malfunctions we have some basis for statistics, even some objective grounds for those offensive quantities such as "statistical deaths" and the "price of life."

The improbable, high-cost events, however, are far more difficult to cope with. It is relatively straightforward to gather statistics on an "unk," or "known-unknown": analysts can identify the unknown variable or situation, though its probability or relation to other variables must be established from observation and experience. They can even estimate their confidence or range of uncertainty. But what gives analysts nightmares is the "unk-unk," or "unknown-unknown": they neither know where their ignorance lies nor which variable or situation is critical. Consequently, there is no basis to judge even the degree of confidence. As systems become more complex, they invariably have more "unk-unks" that torment reliability analysts.

The responsible policy here would be to look as openly and dispassionately as possible at all objective evidence, including statistical deaths, and then feed into the computer-aided decision process those subjective factors that derive legitimately from human culture and intuition. We expect to make important personal decisions, such as the choice of a mate or a career, on mostly subjective grounds. Yet in business and public decision making we seem ashamed of subjectivity, attributing it either to ignorance or dirty politics.

There are encouraging signs within academe and government that this is beginning to change and that a new respect for subjectivity is emerging. As we become more sophisticated with computers, we owe it to ourselves to become more intellectually honest and deliberate about combining the objective and subjective, affirming the value of each.

7

The seventh and final basis for alienation is *phylogenesis*. This is the threat, real or perceived, that the race of intelligent machines is becoming more powerful than humans. The decline of humans' self-image has historical precedents—the computer is simply the most recent factor contributing to this decline. Mazlish, Tribe, and other writers have discussed the computer as a bridge spanning the "fourth discontinuity" between humans and all other nature—the gap separating humans from mere machines—in a series of insults that have eroded our view of ourselves as occupying a privileged position in the universe.

The first insult was that of Copernicus: the human realm is not discontinuous from the rest of the physical universe, it is a minor planet of a star on the edge of an ordinary galaxy. The second insult was that of Darwin: Homo sapiens is not a clear discontinuity in the animal forms. The third insult was Freud's: humans are not above base instincts and drives. The question posed by the fourth discontinuity, inevitably thrust upon us in our encounters with the computer, is whether human intelligence is ultimately nothing more than what a machine can attain.

Within computer-science circles, the question is either taken quite seriously and fiercely debated or else cast aside nervously as irrelevant and silly; no one seems comfortable. Most scholars in this area do not believe technology is capable of exerting any more domination over humans than we design and program into it. If there is a culprit, surely it is ourselves.

Hard work is no longer seen as the path to salvation—letting machines do our mental as well as physical work seems increasingly to be the norm. From the viewpoint of energy or cost efficiency, automatic control is often the obvious choice over human control, whether the task is to pump water in a rural village of a less-developed nation or to control a nuclear plant. Take the case of pumping water. Considering the relative energy efficiency of the human body compared with that of a small gasoline engine (calories out versus calories in) and the relative prices of calories for the two (assuming the humblest of food for the person and order-of-magnitude increases in the price of the fossil fuel), the machine still comes out well ahead.

When humans execute control tasks of great scale and complexity, there exist not only the energy inefficiencies of the human body, but also the enormous inefficiencies of the management, organization, and communication of an army of human workers. By contrast, new microelectronic logic takes very little energy and exhibits fantastic speed and reliability. Communication over large distances is almost effortless, and computers can manage complex physical systems with ease.

By more subtle criteria, however, computer control systems do not fare as well. While it is true that human institutions are not known for their ability to change, they, like their members, are self-conscious, whereas machines are not. Human institutions are continually reexamining their own goals, but computing machines, even the most adaptable and intelligent, are still guided ultimately by their programmed criteria.

Any large-scale technology, once in place, is difficult to alter. The national highway system is an example—one does not easily abandon all that concrete for an altogether different mode of transport. The same goes for nuclear reactors and large industrial plants. Once established, they tend to go on producing, whatever resources they use—whether or not there remains a real need for that product. A kind of technological inertia sets in through its sheer size and complexity compounded by the immobility of human institutions whose interests are served by this production structure and who will do all they can to protect it. The automatic factories are so good at making widgets that we are charmed, and we do all we can to cooperate with the production miracle. Furthermore, we can sell the widgets to one another and spur the economy.

In the face of large-scale computer control, with its centralization and dependence on the technological elite, it is little wonder that the "appropriate technology" movement, with its emphasis on ecological viability and community self-reliance, is gaining momentum. It is a movement to watch, but make no mistake: "AT" advocates are not antitechnology. While they preach "small is beautiful," they also recognize that much of the new microelectronic computer technology, with its low dollar and energy costs, may provide, for instance, an effective route to harnessing the sun. But the institutional base for such "appropriate" technologies is not cottage industry, and therein lies their dilemma.

The ultimate criterion for how computers should be used is subjective and I'm not sure that the technologist sufficiently appreciates this. Humans have always been tool builders and are not likely to stop. We *will* have our computers, but our subjective sense of what is right, beautiful, and consistent with a just and sustainable society, and what contributes most to human fulfillment, ought to dictate our use of these exotic tools with their enormous potential. Productivity in human terms should prevail over productivity in machine terms.

As computer control grows, we will see some alienation and suffering. There is but one long-term strategy open to us—we must ensure that the human-machine interaction will offer humanity and dignity. We must strive to celebrate those things human that computers can never be. In the workplace, we must struggle against workers' growing sense of remoteness from productive efforts by improving feedback and inviting creative participation in new roles made possible by the computer. Similarly, operators and other skilled professionals must be introduced to new, constructive tasks that transcend button pushing. In the area of education, one of our greatest challenges is to prepare future generations to become active participants in a computerized society. We must affirm the role of subjective input into computer-aided decision and control processes, and hold the human designers and programmers of computers accountable, not the computers themselves.

Steven Levy

Steven Levy (born 1951) is a free-lance writer. He graduated from Temple University, where he majored in English and was rock critic for the *News;* then he took an M.A. at Penn State. He has published articles in the *Village Voice* and *Esquire,* been senior editor of the *New Jersey Monthly,* and is now a contributing editor of *Rolling Stone* and *Popular Computing.* He typically writes on such topics of contemporary interest as TV, birth control, educational testing, and computers with precise and vivid reportorial detail that nevertheless conveys a sense of the deeper cultural issues involved. In 1979 he was cited for distinguished achievement by the Investigative Reporters and Editors of America. The present piece first appeared in *Rolling Stone,* April 15, 1982. Levy is preparing a book-length work on hackers and computer culture.

Hackers in Paradise

> *She can kill all your files;*
> *She can freeze with a frown.*
> *And a wave of her hand brings the whole system down.*
> *And she works on her code until ten after three.*
> *She lives like a bat but she's always a hacker to me.*
>
> —FROM THE LOTS HACKER SONGBOOK

The Low Overhead Time-Sharing (LOTS) facility at Stanford University is blanketed with an eerie calm. There are more than a hundred students here, but they speak in whispers, as though they were in the presence of something godlike. The cavernous main lobby, which reaches up to a fourth-floor skylight (the building is the architectural soul mate of the recently collapsed Kansas City Hyatt), holds a lounge in which a dozen or so students are scattered, some pacing impatiently, others snoozing, their heads resting on textbooks. The names of these students are on a computer queue; they are waiting for a free computer terminal at the north end of the lobby, where each of perhaps fifty cubicles is equipped with a keyboard and display screen. Staring at each of these terminals is a Stanford student, or someone posing as a Stanford student in order to use the computer. In an adjoining room, there are approximately sixty more terminals, also in use. The hushed voices give the occasional beeps of the computer an odd prominence, and you can often hear the methodical, somewhat screechy churn of the computer's printer in the other room. But most of the noise is lost because of the enormity of the lobby. To the ear, this is an electronic cathedral.

It's well past midnight.

Most of the students are under the whip of academic discipline. Sitting in a rather formal posture, they tentatively key in data and watch for the results on the display screen with skeptical frowns. They often consult their books before making another move. These are the users. For them, computers are functional, if overly complex, tools: necessary evils.

But to a small society that convenes here at LOTS, computers are much more. The big, orange-topped, million-dollar DECSYSTEM-20 (DEC-20) computer, visible behind a glass partition, looks no more spectacular than a line of file cabinets, but it is the dominant icon of these devotees' existence, the secret sharer of their dreams, their instrument of power and creativity, their medium of communication, their companion in merrymaking. This is the society of hackers.

Hackers are the mutant offspring of the eggheads who once prowled through engineering buildings with slide rules attached to their belts. The computer's power has made the hackers a subculture to be reckoned with. Their fellow students may consider them creepy, but among themselves they are risk takers, explorers, artists. They communicate with one another by intricate computer networks, speak in their own jargon and qualify for lucrative jobs in which they will create the complex programs essential for the everyday functioning of our nation, our world. They have the potential to be supercriminals, to use digital skeleton keys to electronic vaults holding money, confidential personal data and national security secrets. But the power is not without a price: an addiction to computing, a compulsion to program. And they think it's fun.

Though some are no grungier than the average student, hackers—most of them male—usually look rumpled. They wear jeans and sneakers, and their T-shirts bear obscure messages like, I DON'T CARE WHAT THE PEOPLE SAY/36 BITS ARE HERE TO STAY. Extending from the T-shirts are plump arms, fattened by a diet of candy bars and Coca-Cola dispensed by nearby vending machines. (One Stanford vending machine is wired directly to the computer, which compiles monthly charges.) Their skin is sallow in a climate where bronze is taken for granted. Their eyes are glazed over with a phosphorescent moistness.

The hackers sit loosely, draped over their chairs like overcoats. It almost seems as though they are wired to the DEC-20. They don't refer to text-books; instead, it's a free-style give and take with the machine. A sensuous poke at the keyboard yields instant responses. Sometimes the computer's replies will evoke looks of wonder; other times, a grimace. This interplay —called interfacing—can go on for hours, even days.

Ernest Adams hovers over one of the lobby terminals, demonstrating a game he's been designing. Adams, a twenty-one-year-old Stanford junior, has a neatly trimmed beard, bib overalls and the hacker's trademark pudginess. He's been programming this game, Road Race, or some varia-tion thereof, on and off since he was twelve years old.

"Here you choose your car," he says, pointing to the display that de-scribes four kinds of cars according to gas flow, acceleration, general effi-ciency and braking abilities. "You can start up the program, but it really isn't finished yet. I'm still adding on a lot of features." I try it, and after a promising start, I spin out—too much speed on the curve. Adams shrugs. "What I'd like to do is give each driver of the computer-run cars a specific personality. Given conditions on the track, his behavior changes. Each driver will have an aggressiveness quota, and if things don't go his way, he'll get angrier and drive differently. Or if a driver loses a lot, he will change his behavior to try and win, learn how to improve. The program will be self-modifying."

This sounds like an odd fantasy. But computers, to those who program them obsessively, are instruments that give substance to fantasies. Dream machines. Hackers are the programmers with the wildest dreams, the ones who make the computer perform somersaults of logic. Most of it is done at night, when demand for computer time (the load) is low and the machine can respond as fast as possible. Typically, a hacker will wonder whether a program can accommodate a nifty feature, or will see some-thing in a stray program that needs adjustment, or will speculate whether a computer can perform a task that its designers have officially deemed beyond its capabilities—hackers call this black magic. Once a hacker makes up his mind to proceed, such minor distractions as hunger, sleep or sociology finals are put aside. The hack is the thing.

I stroll away from Adams, who is printing out a thirty-one-foot-long hacker colloquy that he has edited and stored in the computer's memory. I wander down a row of students who are interfacing. No one notices me. I stop for a while and chat with a woman named Stacia Snapp, who modestly says she has yet to develop sufficient wizardry to be called a hacker. But she's trying. Right now, though, she is carrying on a conversa-tion via computer with a friend who has a terminal in his dorm room. As we talk, lines of his conversation appear on her screen. Snapp excuses herself, types back a reply and continues speaking. "I don't think it's inherently good to spend twenty-four hours a day in the computer facility," she says, "but I think it's fun." The computer beeps to indicate that the fellow in the dorm has finished another remark. She reads it and laughs. "He says hello to you," she tells me. This conversation has been going on for more than two hours.

I walk into the LOTS management office where a radio is playing Eric Clapton. At one of the terminals, Stanford senior Benji Levy is bent over, concentrating. On the other terminal is Dan Newell, a soft-spoken, mustachioed hacker who smiles wearily. Earlier in the day he'd been showing me his favorite games. One, he had said takes more than forty hours to complete. He'd explained how he'd spent his entire spring quarter tracking down a bug in the DEC's operating system. "If there's something wrong, you can find it," he said. "The computer does exactly what you say. Any ambiguity is on your part. It's so . . . *logical.*"

"I've been spending some time tonight trying to learn PCL better," he says, finally looking up. So far, "some time" has been six hours, and now at 3:11 A.M. it's safe to bet that the sun will be out before Newell is. "PCL," he continues, "is a sophisticated computer language." Newell aspires to writing his own computer language, which, of course, will render most of its predecessors obsolete.

Even as he speaks, Newell gazes at the terminal from the corner of his eye. You can't talk seriously to a hacker when he's so close to the computer. He gets itchy, gets tired of the illogical bumps and tangents of human conversation. There's almost a physical yearning for the machine.

I leave Newell to his PCL. There are about forty people still using the computer. Each seems to be a self-sufficient system of man and machine. It is almost four A.M.—the hour of the hacker.

"Within the next twenty years, culture will be divided between those who know something about the computer and those who don't. It's like knowing how to read when the printing press was invented," says James Milojkovic, a Stanford psychologist working toward a doctorate. Milojkovic, a cheery Australian who studies "psychological issues in computer interaction," has been watching hackers closely. He thinks it's essential that we study them. "They are looked upon as sick and strange; they see themselves as doing what everyone will be doing in the future. There's a real mystery to them, because they know things that we don't. They believe they have total control of what's going on, because when you understand what the computer does, you can have it do almost anything. Once you learn how, you're part of the priesthood. It's a priesthood of the young. I've heard stories of elementary school kids breaking into schools at night so they can use the computer."

Ernest Adams never figured to be a hacker. True, he liked computing, which he'd been doing since he was twelve; then he experienced his first epiphany: "Here I was typing things, and the machine was typing things back at me, and we're imagining we're playing a space war!" Adams had a natural talent for computers, but he thought he got it all out of his system in high school, when he hung out with a group who would stay late tapping into the computer at the nearby University of Kentucky. He came to Stanford to major in physics—until sometime in his first quarter, when he wandered into LOTS.

Low Overhead Time-Sharing began at Stanford five years ago as a twenty-four-hour-self-service operation designed to encourage student computer use. It was too successful. "The first student coordinator dropped out of school because he got too involved with the computer," says LOTS programmer J. Q. Johnson, "and several more got pretty close."

The Stanford community had witnessed previous generations of hackers, most particularly in the Artificial Intelligence Lab. But that group was unique and pioneering. LOTS hackers are indicative of a new wave haunting computing centers in colleges throughout the country. In many cases, these new hackers, like Adams, have been raised on computers. They have little experience with anything but computers. They often don't care to learn about anything else. They associate only with other hackers, speaking in their own strange jargon, always complaining about some "bagbiting kluge," whistling in awe over some "winner's cuspy, yet nontrivial" program. These words are delivered in a high-pitched, goofy burst of verbiage that assumes the listener is inputting data as quickly as a PDP-11. Uninformed nonhackers (called users, often modified to *lusers*) have a word for these creatures: *nerd.* But their attitude is also touched with a trace of envy, since hackers know something users don't.

Five weeks away from home, Ernest Adams was unhappy. He disliked dorm life. He was also suffering through the tortuous throes of unrequited love known only to seventeen-year-old males. Physics was not going to solve his problems, so he came to LOTS. He sat down at a terminal, opened an account, and for the next few hours, had a long talk with the computer about its operating system. He'd found a friend.

"I became involved with LOTS to the exclusion of other things," Ernest says. "I would come to drown my sorrows." His expertise grew, and his programming ideas became grandiose. You could do *anything* with a program. As Ralph Gorin, the director of LOTS, puts it: "Who else do you know who will do whatever you tell it to do?" Adams has his own explanation: "It's knowing you can start from scratch, create an object called a program, hand it to the computer and have the computer start plotting beautiful graphs across the screen—and *you are personally responsible!*" He smiles demonically beneath his beard. "It's a little like playing God."

The world that Adams has entered is based entirely on the computer. In this world, participants are asked to choose a new name, and they often identify themselves with such fantasy monikers as Gandalf or Bombadil.

With its multimillion-character memory, the DEC-20 is sort of a home, an office, a babysitter, and a best friend. It will handle the most elaborate programs you can conceive of. It will play checkers and robot war with you, and it will remind you, with an accompanying bell, when it's time for dinner. (Somewhere in the computer memory is a list of pizzerias that deliver.) It will tell you when your friends have logged into the system, and allow you to send messages to them without leaving your terminal. It will entertain you with lewd limericks stored in its core. It will type your papers for you, help you with homework and, with its electronic bulletin board, help you sell your roller skates. If you get restless, you can go exploring in the nooks and crannies of the DEC-20's labyrinthine operating system, looking for stray bugs.

The computer generates a closely knit community of disciples. Hackers hang out with fellow hackers, meeting one another in late-night sessions where they may crowd around the terminal of someone who is preparing a hack that will, upon reaching "winnitude," be placed in the computer's operating system. On six A.M. excursions to breakfast, the talk is of the machine's new PASCAL language compiler, or the upcoming trade of a program written at SCORE (another computer facility at Stanford) for a digital electronic memory cache. Violent arguments erupt over the relative virtues of LISP programming language and PCL. The arguments are fought in the weird, coldly logical syntax that comes from working in the rigid linear protocol of programming.

Though some hackers won't socialize at all, most love to talk computers. On slight provocation they will overwhelm users with arcanely detailed explanations of computer protocol. But inevitably, they return to their terminals. Only rarely does the hacker community gather together for special occasions, such as the recent fifth anniversary of LOTS, when hackers faced the glass window of the computer room and sang "Happy Birthday" to the DEC-20. Otherwise, the most social moments at LOTS come toward the end of each quarter, when the lobby is packed with students waiting their turns at the computer. Those waiting for terminals swill beer to the accompaniment of a guitar-toting crooner singing hacker lyrics to the tunes of popular songs. Sing-along selections include "Fifty Ways to Write Your Program," "LOTS Is Painless," "I Wonder How the System Is Doing Tonight," "I Don't Know How to Log In" and "Fun Fun Fun Till Her Daddy Took the Keyboard Away."

To understand what hackers really *do* when they sit at terminals until rough stubble emerges on their chins, you must understand something about high-level computer programming. You must also set aside suspicions that computers are vile, impersonal manipulators of numbers, and enemies of individuality. To hackers, programming is the mental equivalent of supersonic test piloting and the computer is a bottomless font of spirituality.

A program is a set of instructions to the computer. It consists of lines of code usually written in a specific language that the computer, equipped with suitable microprocessing translators, can understand. By telling the computer how to rearrange and access its binary contents, each program allows the computer to perform a set of functions, and the results might be anything from a Space Invaders game to a mailing list.

A program must be scrupulously constructed to perform its function. Former IBM software manager Frederick Brooks wrote in *The Mythical Man-Month:* "If one character, one pause of the incantation is not in strictly proper form, the magic doesn't work. But even after it seems to work, there might be bugs in the program that will affect performance. A maniacal perfectionism is called for in debugging. While it may seem workaday, hackers think otherwise."

"Debugging is like laying a long railroad track," says John Levy, a software manager for Apple Computers. "There's a little piece you want to test, so you back up the locomotive five miles down the road and, at ninety miles an hour, you bring it across the track you're testing. If everything is perfect, it flies right over, but if there's one flaw, the engine rolls off, flying and crashing until it comes to rest a mile down the track. Only at that point do you get to see the pieces."

The ones who take the greatest programming challenges, who fearlessly construct miles of fragile track and race the hugest engines across them, are hackers. Just as the early astronauts achieved legendary status, there is a hacker elite whose wizardry has set them apart as digital daredevils.

Don Woods is acknowledged to have the Right Stuff. With long, stringy black hair and a bearish grin, he looks somewhat older than his twenty-nine years. He works at Xerox and wears a dark GAMES T-shirt that contrasts with his almost chalk-colored skin. Pinned next to the Xerox employee badge on his shirt is a button that reads QUESTION AUTHORITY. Wood is known as a classic, or canonical, hacker. "Here's a quick hack I've been working on," he says. He types a few characters on his keyboard, and from the computer come the calliopelike sounds of a rousing, Sousa-style marching song. "I put it together in a couple of days," he says.

One of the results of Woods' epic hacks is Adventure, a collaboration with Will Crowther. Ostensibly a game, Adventure is a metaphor for hacking. When you begin Adventure, the computer tells you your location: at a stream, near a forest, within sight of a small brick building. From there you embark on a Tolkienesque journey through the caverns and glens of a medieval land, encountering murderous midgets, poisonous snakes, treacherous rapids, thieving pirates and magazines written in dwarf language. By telling the computer the direction you wish to move (typing *n* for north or *u* for up, for example), the computer calculates where, on the unseen map created in Woods' imagination, you will wind up next, and displays a written description of your next location. You go deeper and deeper into this netherworld, hoping to emerge by the same path with treasure in hand. There are almost 200 rooms you pass through on your way to the treasure, many dotted with hazards, and the path crosses and intertwines in ways impossible to divine without hours of exploration. Adventure is the most popular game at LOTS, and indeed it is a national craze among those with access to computers. "I would show it to people on a Friday afternoon," Woods says, "and they wouldn't leave their terminals until they finished it, maybe on Monday.

Adventure is a kind of litmus test for hackers: if you can lose your-self in the gullies and misty caverns, you might be susceptible to com-puter addiction. Just as the plot of Adventure is a world unto itself, the vast memory and operating system of a mainframe computer is a gi-gantic landscape, seemingly impenetrable but eventually accessible to the most devoted seekers. Just as everything in the physical world is constructed of atoms, everything a computer processes or reads is ulti-mately reduced to bits of either one or zero. Like treasure seekers in the subterranean Adventure world, hackers are electronic spelunkers who have developed the skill to burrow down from the more superfi-cial programming languages to the bedrock machine language of di-gits. Woods calls this "going down and doing the grudgies." To get in-volved this deeply, you must be able to think in dizzyingly abstract terms. Your mental concentration is so intense that your consciousness is subsumed by the computer.

When a hacker programs, he creates worlds. A well-crafted program— a good hack—is elegant, doing the most work in the fewest lines of code. If it displays wizardry and is fairly sophisticated, hackers call it a nontrivial program, even though what the program *does* might be absurdly frivo-lous. Hackers judge themselves not on criteria of compassion, wit, altruism or even the results of their programs. If your program cures cancer, fine. If it helps a credit bureau track down your uncle, tough. What's important is the brilliance of the program itself.

"My level of judgment is technically oriented, one that would disqualify many who consider themselves hackers," says Mark Crispin, a systems programmer at SCORE. "That is, what nontrivial program have you writ-ten? As opposed to logging in and sending bug reports and flaming [trans-lation: bullshitting] on the bulletin board. I consider a nontrivial program to be something above a hundred lines of text, and it depends on what language it is. It requires some design, a user interface, a significant amount of time to develop. It doesn't matter if the program itself is a great idea."

Crispin has been holding court for me in the living room of his condo-minium, which is decorated in middle-period graduate student and distin-guished only by a half-dozen hand-held computer games and a terminal hooked up to the telephone. Crispin is tall, pale, and though he looks like he's never shaved, he's twenty-five. He shares the condo with his fiancée, who had been a member of a hacking club at Columbia University when she spotted a bug in one of Crispin's programs she was using. She sent him transcontinental computer mail, he replied, and the digital correspondence led to a meeting and eventually a proposal. She listens approvingly as he speaks in a nasal voice that grows louder when he has a particular point to make.

Crispin wants to show me something. He bounds out of his chair, heads for his terminal and calls the LOTS computer. He types in his password, ignores the computer message that tells him he has electronic mail and demonstrates a program that generates sexual quips. Typing its name, Tingle, brings this to the screen:

> "I'm back in the saddle again, again! . . ." shrieked the quadriplegic as the lurid
> sabra savagely tossed away his well-cut pants and munched on his spunk-filled
> pepperoni.

Crispin admires the hell out of this hack. "Tingle is definitely a non-trivial program," he says. "It has its own concept of structured English sentences. It is completely computer-generated. Everything Tingle points out makes literal sense. Tingle builds scripts of what it's going to do; it remembers male and female characteristics. Only then does it randomly choose from vocabulary columns."

With all this hoopla, you'd think the program was perfect. But no program is. "The program can always work, but you can always make it better," says Crispin. "You can always have it do something new, make it perform faster, give it more structure, make it *do* more!" Crispin's voice is a high whine, and he's almost out of his chair. *"You can always think of ways to make it better!* You're never at the point where you stop. Just when you say, 'It's totally perfect,' you say, 'Gee, but I can make it do *this!'*"

Is a computer program a work of art? Mark Crispin thinks so and other hackers agree. Hackers insist that each programmer writes code in an individual, recognizable style. Programmers work at a level of creativity, they say, that is comparable to writing poetry, composing, painting. "You can express yourself by writing code," says Marc LeBrun, a twenty-nine-year-old hacker who never attended college but spent his teen years at Stanford's Artificial Intelligence Lab. "And you begin to judge programs on high-level things like style. You say, is this a flavorful way to do this? And people will often get into huge arguments about something that will ultimately make a difference of a small microsecond but will have profound stylistic implications."

Hackers as artists! Can it happen? Will hackers give dramatic renditions of their latest COBOL hacks? Will we curl up on the beach with a good, long word-processing program? It seems impossible, because the programmer's art is so self-contained, esoterically personal, aggressively elitist and void of the stuff of human experience. "People don't read programs like novels, that's true," says Stanford computer scientist Dennis Allison. "And it's a shame."

Donn Parker is no fan of hackers. Author of *Crime by Computer,* resident expert of computer abuse at the Stanford Research Institute (SRI) and a lanky, three-piece-suited man who resembles an elongated Donald Pleasence, Parker thinks that hackers promote an attitude that could lead to disastrous results.

Computers are highly prone to being tampered with by knowledgeable intruders. When a large computer is used in a time-sharing system, safeguards are installed to prevent users from getting access to the digital files of other users. If a troublemaker succeeds in getting these files, he not only can read the private notes but can change and even erase them. Parker fears hackers because they not only have the know-how to crack security, but they regard these safeguards as mountaineers regard Mount McKinley. "The more barriers you put up, the more compelling the incentive is to break them down," Parker says. Marc LeBrun agrees: "I think the hacker viewpoint is that the world exists to hack," he says, "and there aren't any angels with flaming swords standing over the world saying, 'Thou shalt not push these buttons.'"

If those angels existed, hackers would find programs to dull their swords. Despite the best efforts of the business and military establishment, the hacker-proof security system has yet to be devised. When SRI gathered a team of crack programmers to test the inviolability of military defense computers, the programmers were shocked to find that it took them only one telephone call and a few minutes to break into files containing top-secret information.

"What we have to do is change the cultural values in this [hacker] subculture," says Parker. "There are instructors in high school and universities who encourage people to attack security systems as a means to learn more about computers. There are people who think of this as a matter of fun and games, a stimulating thing to do."

One idle form of hacker amusement is causing the computer to crash, or temporarily break down. I've asked at least six hackers to explain the thrill of this, and I've received only inarticulate sentence fragments to the effect of, well, it's *there.* Maybe they do it to show the computer who's boss. One hacker bragged how he set a few hundred programs into motion that constantly forked into other programs, which begat even more programs, growing at a logarithmical rate until the overloaded DEC-20 was brought to its knees. "I guess it's a phase everyone goes through," explains another hacker.

Hackers everywhere delight in these tricks, the more harrowing the better. Take Julius Smith's Seppuku program. Smith is a grad student who hacks at Stanford's Computer Music Center; he has long been engaged in a search for the algorithm of the violin. Smith knows the old hacker trick of giving an enticing name to a rogue program: when a user peruses a system's menu and sees something called Seppuku, he'll access it. (All hackers have insatiable curiosity about other programs.) On the screen the user sees:

Seppuku is not a program for honorable users. Do not run Seppuku unless you can live with your shame. Type *y* if you must run it.

As soon as the poor sucker types *y*, the screen becomes ablaze with six-inch letters shouting, "GOMEN NASAI!!!" This is approximate Japanese for "Now you've done it." The screen immediately begins to list the titles of every file the user has ever stored in the computer memory. These files represent years of work. "Do you really want to delete all your files?" the computer asks. *Delete?* Before the stunned user can fully comprehend the catastrophic implications of this message, the computer answers with a *yes.* One by one the files are wiped off the screen.

"Your every file directory has been deleted," says the computer. "Goodbye—have a good life." Then the user is logged out. Screen blank.

"Seppuku doesn't *really* delete the files," says Smith. "It just looks like it does. You see, hackers really don't hurt anyone."

But once a hacker has the knowledge to crack security, he simply has to be trusted.

> At a terminal sits a hacker and a
>   wheel by his prompt
> And his screen shows the
>   reminders
> Of every bug that broke his code
> or
>   halted
> Till he cried out, in his anger and
>   his shame
> I am leaving, logout, killjob, but
>   the hacker still remains. . . .

After a few quarters at Stanford, Ernest Adams began to reassess hacking: what had it done for him? What had it done *to* him? He had learned an incredible amount about computers but felt cut off from the mainstream. He had top grades in his programming courses but had failed calculus because he spent too much time at LOTS. He looked at some of his fellow hackers and decided that their devotion to computers was eroding their humanity. Was he turning into a machine himself?

Stored within the LOTS computer memory is a computer bulletin board that is open to comment and response from any user in the system. Items on B-Board range from lonely-hearts messages to offers to sell bicycles, to long-winded debates about issues of school politics, world affairs and computing ("If a computer had a voice, which sex would it be?").

One intense B-Board exchange dealt with the concerns Adams had about *excessive* hacking. The opening salvo was launched by a disgruntled hacker who flamed about the narrowness, inhumanity and addictiveness of hacking—he called LOTS an "alien culture" whose inhabitants' personalities are irreversibly shaped by machine. This kicked off a running debate between those like Adams who agreed with the gist of the attack, and hackers who defended their long hours of interfacing with "the infinite tool."

A Stanford psychology professor named Philip Zimbardo acquired a printout of this debate and sent it to *Psychology Today,* which presented it as "The Hacker Papers," accompanied by Zimbardo's commentary. He suggested, basically, that hackers would be well advised to join the human race. The article made many of the LOTS hackers self-conscious. "I sometimes try to hide the fact that I'm a hacker," says Dan Newell. Others are now defensive at the least sign of disapproval, charging their critics with "computerphobia." "Why single *us* out?" says one. "Why not talk about how much time the Stanford marching band practices?"

All hackers, though, have a hedge against insecurity: they are needed. "The computer field is growing at a tremendous rate," says Dennis Allison, "and it's going to take a concentrated amount of wizardry to bring it about." As our dependence on computers increases, it will be the hackers who can best create the supersoftware that will keep society from imploding into a mass of jumbled bits. An industry study showed that one good programmer is as productive as ten merely competent ones; a wizard-level programmer can almost name his price. The viciously competitive computer firms are desperate for hackers, who ask only for flexible working hours, no dress or etiquette requirements, and, above all, nontrivial, trailblazing tasks. Then the hackers proceed to work sixteen-hour days until the project is completed. "There're lots of opportunities to make an obscene amount of money," says LOTS staffer Bob Knight.

Such "real world" pursuits (along with other distractions like marriage and family) have the potential of eventually turning a hacker from his computer extremism. So, many of the LOTS hackers see Stanford—and possibly graduate school—as a last chance to run amok with the DEC-20. As Julius Smith puts it: "My [student] funding runs out in a year. This is my last chance to do something pure in my life."

Some hackers find ways of remaining "pure": they become computer bums, taking on temporary programming stints at Silicon Valley's high-tech operations, keeping a connection with other hackers by illegal accounts on university computers.

But Ernest Adams prefers a more conventional existence. He wants to be counted among those who have hacked intensely for a year or two, then managed to grow out of it. He took off a quarter of his sophomore year to work computers for the Viking Mars Landing Project, and later took off more time to do some professional programming. He made a conscious effort to pay more attention to his other studies and get back into the mainstream of users, nonwinners, and even people who don't know a byte from an escape key. He once was convinced that hacking was transitory, that society need not worry about its proliferation. Now he sees more hackers than ever, and he's not so sure. Still, he believes he has freed himself from computer addiction.

But old obsessions die hard. Recently, at six in the morning, Adams was at LOTS working at a terminal. "Just editing a paper" was his excuse. But he offered no apologies for speaking in rapturous tones about his planned thesis for a computer doctorate.

"I would like to write a program that reproduces, that reacts negatively or positively to its environment and, most important of all, could be mutated by its environment. I would like to see if I could start several of these programs running, and start some sort of superior program that watches them mutating, and see if they evolve. That's the God program. It invents the environment, creates the data that the programs read, and will mutate the programs. . . ."

Adams flames on rabidly, his face lit up like a display for a well-hacked game. The God program will create hot spots to control the motions of the one-celled programs. A maturation factor will control the growth and adolescence of the one-cells. The program might well duplicate the theory of natural selection, and be a kind of vindication of Darwinian theory. . . . *I am leaving, logout, killjob, but the hacker still remains.*

Pollution and Consumption

The New Yorker

The Wisdom of the Worm

Until quite lately, we had all been used to believing that, generally speaking, it is easier to destroy things than to create them. This rule still holds true for governments, schools, and other institutions of society, but it no longer holds true for a steadily increasing number of our material artifacts. The pollutants that are currently endangering the environment have taught us that in many cases it can be much harder to destroy something than to create it. This lesson was forced home in a particularly striking way by the recent dilemma over how to dispose of several hundred nerve-gas rockets that had been stored for some three years at Defense Department ammunition depots in Alabama and Kentucky. The gap between our talent for manufacturing and our talent for dismantling has rarely been so clearly displayed. Presumably, it took great technological ingenuity to create the rockets, and, as for the gas, we had to turn, after the Second World War, to the files of the Nazi scientists to learn how to make it. When it came to getting rid of the rockets and their gas, however, the cleverest thing the Army could at first think of to do was to encase the rockets in blocks of steel and concrete—a solution that failed to insure against leaks while preventing anyone from getting at the rockets in order to detoxify the gas. Finally, of course, the Army got rid of the gas, the rockets, and their steel-and-concrete cases by the singularly crude method of loading them all onto a ship and sinking it in the ocean off Florida. Spokesmen for the Pentagon have assured us that the dumping will not cause any damage to the ocean environment, but many civilian scientists have argued that it may. The only thing that seems certain is that no one really has any definite information on what its effects will be.

At an earlier stage of the summer's pollution-power-transportation crisis in this city, it was noted here that one difference between the "natural" environment and a man-made environment is that complexity, which is a strength in the natural world, is a weakness in the man-made world. The incident of the nerve-gas rockets suggests some further differences between man's works and nature's. One thing we have all learned recently is that in birth, in life, and in death each species of animal and each species of plant performs innumerable functions that are crucial to the other species and to the environment that supports all species. For example, in "Silent Spring" Rachel Carson wrote of the earthworm, "Of all the larger inhabitants of the soil, probably none is more important than the earthworm. Over three-quarters of a century ago, Charles Darwin published a book titled 'The Formation of Vegetable Mould, Through the Action of Worms, with Observations on Their Habits.' In it he gave the world its first understanding of the fundamental role of earthworms as geologic agents for the transport of soil—a picture of surface rocks being gradually covered by fine soil brought up from below by the worms, in annual amounts running to many tons to the acre in most favorable areas. At the same time, quantities of organic matter contained in leaves and grass (as much as twenty pounds to the square yard in six months) are drawn down into the burrows and incorporated in soil. Darwin's calculations showed that the toil of earthworms might add a layer of soil an inch to an inch and a half thick in a ten-year period. And this is by no means all they do; their burrows aerate the soil, keep it well drained, and aid the penetration of plant roots. The presence of earthworms increases the nitrifying powers of the soil bacteria and decreases putrefaction of the soil. Organic matter is broken down as it passes through the digestive tracts of worms and the soil is enriched by their excretory products." Of course, the plants and the animals are, as far as we can tell, unaware of the multiplicity of services they perform for the environment. The earthworm probably has no conscious intention of enriching the soil as he progresses through the existence charted for him by his instincts. And quite certainly he has no intention of becoming a meal for a robin—another of his crucial roles. It is only man, apparently, who has "intentions" and "purposes." However, as it has turned out, man's purposes—in the area of material production, at least—serve ends that are much narrower than those served unthinkingly by other living things. Usually, man's artifacts are produced with only one end in mind, such as the provision of fuel for engines or of containers for food, and most of what he makes is useful for only a moment or so of its long sojourn in the environment. One inevitable consequence of man's producing things for such narrow ends is the necessity of "throwing away" what he has made when it has served its purpose. In the past, when we threw something "away," we pretty much considered that it had disappeared. But now, because of the ecological crisis, we know that there is no such thing as throwing something "away." There is only throwing it into the sea or into the soil or into the air. And what happens to a milk carton or a gallon of oil or a nerve-gas rocket when it gets there is as much our concern as what these things did when they were sitting in our iceboxes or driving our engines or killing our "enemies." Today, when we consider making something, we must expand our knowledge and concern beyond the moment of its service to us and take responsibility for its entire career on the earth. We must consider the effect it will have on all living things as it travels down our sewers or rises up our chimneys and makes its slow but inevitable circular progress through the chain of life back to our dinner tables or into our lungs. In short, we must learn the unknowing wisdom of the worm.

[From "The Talk of the Town," *The New Yorker,* August 29, 1970]

Isaac Asimov

Isaac Asimov is an incredibly prolific author who is one of the best writers on science for the general public and a high priest of science fiction. He was born in the Soviet Union in 1920 and brought by his immigrant parents to New York City three years later. With a photographic memory, a boyhood taste for science fiction, a Ph.D. in biochemistry from Columbia (1948), and an obsessive capacity for work, Asimov early turned from a career in college teaching to the writing of books, which numbered 200 by 1979, not to speak of scores of short stories. Some of his most admired works of science fiction are the novels *The Currents of Space* (1952), *The Caves of Steel* (1954), and *The Naked Sun* (1957). On science, *The New Intelligent Man's Guide to Science* (1965) is considered a model of encyclopedic clarity. He has also written popular works on ancient history and on the Bible. No one could have been better qualified to answer the request of the editors of *Time* for a vision of "an energy-poor society that might exist at the end of the 20th century." *Time* published it on April 25, 1977. "It is a picture of the worst," said Asimov, "of waste continuing, of oil running out, of nothing in its place, of world population continuing to rise. But then, that could happen, couldn't it?"

The Nightmare Life Without Fuel

So it's 1997, and it's raining, and you'll have to walk to work again. The subways are crowded, and any given train breaks down one morning out of five. The buses are gone, and on a day like today the bicycles slosh and slide. Besides, you have only a mile and a half to go, and you have boots, raincoat and rain hat. And it's not a very cold rain, so why not?

Lucky you have a job in demolition too. It's steady work. Slow and dirty, but steady. The fading structures of a decaying city are the great mineral mines and hardware shops of the nation. Break them down and re-use the parts. Coal is too difficult to dig up and transport to give us energy in the amounts we need, nuclear fission is judged to be too dangerous, the technical breakthrough toward nuclear fusion that we hoped for never took place, and solar batteries are too expensive to maintain on the earth's surface in sufficient quantity.

Anyone older than ten can remember automobiles. They dwindled. At first the price of gasoline climbed—way up. Finally only the well-to-do drove, and that was too clear an indication that they were filthy rich, so any automobile that dared show itself on a city street was overturned and burned. Rationing was introduced to "equalize sacrifice," but every three months the ration was reduced. The cars just vanished and became part of the metal resource.

There are many advantages, if you want to look for them. Our 1997 newspapers continually point them out. The air is cleaner and there seem to be fewer colds. Against most predictions, the crime rate has dropped. With the police car too expensive (and too easy a target), policemen are back on their beats. More important, the streets are full. Legs are king in the cities of 1997, and people walk everywhere far into the night. Even the parks are full, and there is mutual protection in crowds.

If the weather isn't too cold, people sit out front. If it is hot, the open air is the only air conditioning they get. And at least the street lights still burn. Indoors, electricity is scarce, and few people can afford to keep lights burning after supper.

As for the winter—well, it is inconvenient to be cold, with most of what furnace fuel is allowed hoarded for the dawn; but sweaters are popular indoor wear and showers are not an everyday luxury. Lukewarm sponge baths will do, and if the air is not always very fragrant in the human vicinity, the automobile fumes are gone.

There is some consolation in the city that it is worse in the suburbs. The suburbs were born with the auto, lived with the auto, and are dying with the auto. One way out for the suburbanites is to form associations that assign turns to the procurement and distribution of food. Pushcarts creak from house to house along the posh suburban roads, and every bad snowstorm is a disaster. It isn't easy to hoard enough food to last till the roads are open. There is not much in the way of refrigeration except for the snowbanks, and then the dogs must be fought off.

What energy is left cannot be directed into personal comfort. The nation must survive until new energy sources are found, so it is the railroads and subways that are receiving major attention. The railroads must move the coal that is the immediate hope, and the subways can best move the people.

And then, of course, energy must be conserved for agriculture. The great car factories make trucks and farm machinery almost exclusively. We can huddle together when there is a lack of warmth, fan ourselves should there be no cooling breezes, sleep or make love at such times as there is a lack of light—but nothing will for long ameliorate a lack of food. The American population isn't going up much any more, but the food supply must be kept high even though the prices and difficulty of distribution force each American to eat less. Food is needed for export so that we can pay for some trickle of oil and for other resources.

The rest of the world, of course, is not as lucky as we are. Some cynics say that it is the knowledge of this that helps keep America from despair. They're starving out there, because earth's population has continued to go up. The population on earth is 5.5 billion, and outside the United States and Europe, not more than one in five has enough to eat at any given time.

All the statistics point to a rapidly declining rate of population increase, but that is coming about chiefly through a high infant mortality; the first and most helpless victims of starvation are babies, after their mothers have gone dry. A strong current of American opinion, as reflected in the newspapers (some of which still produce their daily eight pages of bad news), holds that it is just as well. It serves to reduce the population, doesn't it?

Others point out that it's more than just starvation. There are those who manage to survive on barely enough to keep the body working, and that proves to be not enough for the brain. It is estimated that there are now nearly 2 billion people in the world who are alive but who are permanently brain-damaged by undernutrition, and the number is growing year by year. It has already occurred to some that it would be "realistic" to wipe them out quietly and rid the earth of an encumbering menace. The American newspapers of 1997 do not report that this is actually being done anywhere, but some travelers bring back horror tales.

At least the armies are gone—no one can afford to keep those expensive, energy-gobbling monstrosities. Some soldiers in uniform and with rifles are present in almost every still functioning nation, but only the United States and the Soviet Union can maintain a few tanks, planes and ships—which they dare not move for fear of biting into limited fuel reserves.

Energy continues to decline, and machines must be replaced by human muscle and beasts of burden. People are working longer hours and there is less leisure; but then, with electric lighting restricted, television for only three hours a night, movies three evenings a week, new books few and printed in small editions, what is there to do with leisure? Work, sleep and eating are the great trinity of 1997, and only the first two are guaranteed.

Where will it end? It must end in a return to the days before 1800, to the days before the fossil fuels powered a vast machine industry and technology. It must end in subsistence farming and in a world population reduced by starvation, disease and violence to less than a billion.

And what can we do to prevent all this now?

Now? Almost nothing.

If we had started 20 years ago, that might have been another matter. If we had only started 50 years ago, it would have been easy.

Religion and the Search for Meaning

I n 1948 the philosopher Walter Stace, with typical post-World War II pessimism, warned that modern men and women had "lost the vision, basic to all religion, of an ordered plan and purpose of the world," that they had suffered the loss of an "imaginative picture of a world governed by purpose, a world driving towards the good—which is the inner spirit of religion." In recent years, the specter of total annihilation by nuclear arms has further weakened our vision of a purposeful world. And yet, spiritual needs not only remain, but seem to have become clearer and stronger. They manifest themselves in many ways—quests for inner tranquillity, for commitment, for community, for world peace; all of these can be described as quests for fundamental meaning. Theologian Paul Tillich describes being religious as just that: "asking passionately the question of the meaning of our existence and being willing to receive answers, even if they hurt." In one way or another, all the writers we present below, from the most orthodox to the most secular, are concerned with this question.

The predicament is framed by the two poems that introduce the section—Father Hopkins' declaration of faith and Matthew Arnold's cry of doubt and despair. Clarence Darrow, a lawyer writing in 1929, sees a sharp if simple conflict between science and religion;

he is particularly critical of the literal interpretation of biblical stories, which he sees as a victory of superstition over reason. Carl Sagan, a scientist writing fifty years later, sees less of a conflict between science and religion. His is a "universe that does not exclude a traditional Western or Eastern God, but that does not require one either." He concludes that the enterprise of knowledge (also, after all, a way of seeking meaning) is consistent with both science and religion.

Joseph Campbell and Tillich, in the selections that follow, might agree with Darrow about the literal interpretation of religious stories, but neither would stop there. Campbell values myths and mythic images as "world-transcending symbols" that keep us in touch with our hidden depths and so help us rediscover values and meaning. Tillich attempts to discover and define new meanings for religion and for God in our time; he, too, sees religious symbols as essential and powerful expressions of the dimension of depth.

The next two selections are statements of belief, one at age sixty-three by Malcolm Muggeridge, who has been long coming to his orthodox faith; the other by Thomas Merton, the final step of whose conversion comes suddenly, with passionate force, in his youth. Viktor Frankl, in the last piece, deals not with religion but with human love. The memory of it—amidst the hopeless existence of the concentration camp—is his ultimate assurance of life's meaning.

Gerard Manley Hopkins (1844–1889)

God's Grandeur

The world is charged with the grandeur of God.
  It will flame out, like shining from shook foil;
  It gathers to a greatness, like the ooze of oil
Crushed. Why do men then now not reck his rod?
Generations have trod, have trod, have trod;
  And all is seared with trade; bleared, smeared with toil;
  And wears man's smudge and shares man's smell: the
    soil
Is bare now, nor can foot feel, being shod.

And for all this, nature is never spent;
  There lives the dearest freshness deep down things;
And though the last lights off the black West went
  Oh, morning, at the brown brink eastward, springs—
Because the Holy Ghost over the bent
  World broods with warm breast and with ah! bright
  wings.

(1877)

Matthew Arnold
(1822–1888)

Dover Beach

The sea is calm to-night.
The tide is full, the moon lies fair
Upon the straits;—on the French coast the light
Gleams and is gone; the cliffs of England stand
Glimmering and vast, out in the tranquil bay.

Come to the window, sweet is the night-air!
Only, from the long line of spray
Where the sea meets the moon-blanched land,
Listen! you hear the grating roar
Of pebbles which the waves draw back, and fling,
At their return, up the high strand,
Begin, and cease, and then again begin,
With tremulous cadence slow, and bring
The eternal note of sadness in.

Sophocles long ago
Heard it on the Aegean, and it brought
Into his mind the turbid ebb and flow,
Of human misery; we
Find also in the sound a thought,
Hearing it by this distant northern sea.

The Sea of Faith
Was once, too, at the full, and round earth's shore
Lay like the folds of a bright girdle furled.
But now I only hear
Its melancholy, long, withdrawing roar,
Retreating, to the breath
Of the night-wind, down the vast edges drear
And naked shingles of the world.

Ah love, let us be true
To one another! for the world, which seems
To lie before us like a land of dreams,
So various, so beautiful, so new,
Hath really neither joy, nor love, nor light,
Nor certitude, nor peace, nor help for pain;
And we are here as on a darkling plain
Swept with confused alarms of struggle and flight,
Where ignorant armies clash by night.

(1867)

Clarence Darrow

Clarence Darrow (1857–1938) is probably best known for his distinguished career in criminal law. Born in Ohio, he attended one year of law school at the University of Michigan, spent the next year in an attorney's office, and was admitted to the Ohio bar the following year, at the age of twenty-one. He soon left Ohio for Chicago and became the most sought-after and controversial criminal lawyer of his time. His most famous cases include the defense of the child-murderers Leopold and Loeb, for whom he won a life sentence instead of the death penalty, and the Scopes Trial in 1925—known as the Monkey Trial—which created a national and international furor. Darrow, an outspoken agnostic, defended John Scopes, a Dayton, Tennessee, science teacher who had taught evolution and thus broken a state law prohibiting "the teaching in public schools of any theories that deny the divine creation of man as taught in the Bible." The prosecuting attorney was William Jennings Bryan, a fundamentalist. Darrow put Bryan on the stand, cross-examined him regarding his fundamentalist beliefs, and won what was considered a triumphant victory, although Scopes was formally convicted and sentenced to a nominal fine of $100. Bryan died five days later. The reader may wish to keep this case in mind when reading the essay we present below, reprinted from *Verdicts Out of Court* (ed. Arthur and Lila Weinberg, 1963). It was originally written in 1929 for a symposium in which Darrow was joined by a rabbi, a Protestant

bishop, and a Catholic judge. Among Darrow's other writings are two autobiographical books, *Farmington* (1904) and *The Story of My Life* (1932), and a
number of socio-legal works, including *Resist Not Evil* (1904), *Eye for an Eye*
(1904), and *Crime: Its Cause and Its Treatment* (1922).

Why I Am an Agnostic

An agnostic is a doubter. The word is generally applied to those who doubt
the verity of accepted religious creeds or faiths. Everyone is an agnostic
as to the beliefs or creeds they do not accept. Catholics are agnostics to
the Protestant creeds, and the Protestants are agnostic to the Catholic
creed. Anyone who thinks is an agnostic about something, otherwise he
must believe that he is possessed of all knowledge. And the proper place
for such a person is in the madhouse or the home for the feeble-minded.
In a popular way, in the western world, an agnostic is one who doubts or
disbelieves the main tenets of the Christian faith.

I would say that belief in at least three tenets is necessary to the faith
of a Christian: a belief in God, a belief in immortality, and a belief in a
supernatural book. Various Christian sects require much more, but it is
difficult to imagine that one could be a Christian, under any intelligent
meaning of the word, with less. Yet there are some people who claim to
be Christians who do not accept the literal interpretation of all the Bible,
and who give more credence to some portions of the book than to others.

I am an agnostic as to the question of God. I think that it is impossible
for the human mind to believe in an object or thing unless it can form a
mental picture of such object or thing. Since man ceased to worship
openly an anthropomorphic God and talked vaguely and not intelligently
about some force in the universe, higher than man, that is responsible for
the existence of man and the universe, he cannot be said to believe in God.
One cannot believe in a force excepting as a force that pervades matter
and is not an individual entity. To believe in a thing, an image of the thing
must be stamped on the mind. If one is asked if he believes in such an
animal as a camel, there immediately arises in his mind an image of the
camel. This image has come from experience or knowledge of the animal
gathered in some way or other. No such image comes, or can come, with
the idea of a God who is described as a force.

Man has always speculated upon the origin of the universe, including
himself. I feel, with Herbert Spencer, that whether the universe had an
origin—and if it had—what the origin is will never be known by man. The
Christian says that the universe could not make itself; that there must have
been some higher power to call it into being. Christians have been obsessed for many years by Paley's argument that if a person passing through

a desert should find a watch and examine its spring, its hands, its case and its crystal, he would at once be satisfied that some intelligent being capable of design had made the watch. No doubt this is true. No civilized man would question that someone made the watch. The reason he would not doubt it is because he is familiar with watches and other appliances made by man. The savage was once unfamiliar with a watch and would have had no idea upon the subject. There are plenty of crystals and rocks of natural formation that are as intricate as a watch, but even to intelligent man they carry no implication that some intelligent power must have made them. They carry no such implication because no one has any knowledge or experience of someone having made these natural objects which everywhere abound.

To say that God made the universe gives us no explanation of the beginning of things. If we are told that God made the universe, the question immediately arises: Who made God? Did he always exist, or was there some power back of that? Did he create matter out of nothing, or is his existence co-extensive with matter? The problem is still there. What is the origin of it all? If, on the other hand, one says that the universe was not made by God, that it always existed, he has the same difficulty to confront. To say that the universe was here last year, or millions of years ago, does not explain its origin. This is still a mystery. As to the question of the origin of things, man can only wonder and doubt and guess.

As to the existence of the soul, all people may either believe or disbelieve. Everyone knows the origin of the human being. They know that it came from a single cell in the body of the mother, and that the cell was one out of ten thousand in the mother's body. Before gestation the cell must have been fertilized by a spermatozoön from the body of the father. This was one out of perhaps a billion spermatozoa that was the capacity of the father. When the cell is fertilized a chemical process begins. The cell divides and multiplies and increases into millions of cells, and finally a child is born. Cells die and are born during the life of the individual until they finally drop apart, and this is death.

If there is a soul, what is it, and where did it come from, and where does it go? Can anyone who is guided by his reason possibly imagine a soul independent of a body, or the place of its residence, or the character of it, or anything concerning it? If man is justified in any belief or disbelief on any subject, he is warranted in the disbelief in a soul. Not one scrap of evidence exists to prove any such impossible thing.

Many Christians base the belief of a soul and God upon the Bible. Strictly speaking, there is no such book. To make the Bible, sixty-six books are bound into one volume. These books were written by many people at different times, and no one knows the time or the identity of any author. Some of the books were written by several authors at various times. These books contain all sorts of contradictory concepts of life and morals and the origin of things. Between the first and the last nearly a thousand years intervened, a longer time than has passed since the discovery of America by Columbus.

When I was a boy the theologians used to assert that the proof of the divine inspiration of the Bible rested on miracles and prophecies. But a miracle means a violation of a natural law, and there can be no proof imagined that could be sufficient to show the violation of a natural law; even though proof seemed to show violation, it would only show that we were not acquainted with all natural laws. One believes in the truthfulness of a man because of his long experience with the man, and because the man has always told a consistent story. But no man has told so consistent a story as nature.

If one should say that the sun did not rise, to use the ordinary expression, on the day before, his hearer would not believe it, even though he had slept all day and knew that his informant was a man of the strictest veracity. He would not believe it because the story is inconsistent with the conduct of the sun in all the ages past.

Primitive and even civilized people have grown so accustomed to believing in miracles that they often attribute the simplest manifestations of nature to agencies of which they know nothing. They do this when the belief is utterly inconsistent with knowledge and logic. They believe in old miracles and new ones. Preachers pray for rain, knowing full well that no such prayer was ever answered. When a politician is sick, they pray for God to cure him, and the politician almost invariably dies. The modern clergyman who prays for rain and for the health of the politician is no more intelligent in this matter than the primitive man who saw a separate miracle in the rising and setting of the sun, in the birth of an individual, in the growth of a plant, in the stroke of lightning, in the flood, in every manifestation of nature and life.

As to prophecies, intelligent writers gave them up long ago. In all prophecies facts are made to suit the prophecy, or the prophecy was made after the facts, or the events have no relation to the prophecy. Weird and strange and unreasonable interpretations are used to explain simple statements, that a prophecy may be claimed.

Can any rational person believe that the Bible is anything but a human document? We now know pretty well where the various books came from, and about when they were written. We know that they were written by human beings who had no knowledge of science, little knowledge of life, and were influenced by the barbarous morality of primitive times, and were grossly ignorant of most things that men know today. For instance, Genesis says that God made the earth, and he made the sun to light the day and the moon to light the night, and in one clause disposes of the stars by saying that "he made the stars also." This was plainly written by someone who had no conception of the stars. Man, by the aid of his telescope, has looked out into the heavens and found stars whose diameter is as great as the distance between the earth and the sun. We now know that the universe is filled with stars and suns and planets and systems. Every new telescope looking further into the heavens only discovers more and more worlds and suns and systems in the endless reaches of space. The men who wrote Genesis believed, of course, that this tiny speck of mud that we call the earth was the center of the universe, the only world in space, and made for man, who was the only being worth considering. These men believed that the stars were only a little way above the earth, and were set in the firmament for man to look at, and for nothing else. Everyone today knows that this conception is not true.

The origin of the human race is not as blind a subject as it once was. Let alone God creating Adam out of hand, from the dust of the earth, does anyone believe that Eve was made from Adam's rib—that the snake walked and spoke in the Garden of Eden—that he tempted Eve to persuade Adam to eat an apple, and that it is on that account that the whole human race was doomed to hell—that for four thousand years there was no chance for any human to be saved, though none of them had anything whatever to do with temptation; and that finally men were saved only through God's son dying for them, and that unless human beings believed this silly, impossible and wicked story they were doomed to hell? Can anyone with intelligence really believe that a child born today should be doomed because the snake tempted Eve and Eve tempted Adam? To believe that is not God-worship; it is devil-worship.

Can anyone call this scheme of creation and damnation moral? It defies every principle of morality, as man conceives morality. Can anyone believe today that the whole world was destroyed by flood, save only Noah and his family and a male and female of each species of animal that entered the Ark? There are almost a million species of insects alone. How did Noah match these up and make sure of getting male and female to reproduce life in the world after the flood had spent its force? And why should all the lower animals have been destroyed? Were they included in the sinning of man? This is a story which could not beguile a fairly bright child of five years of age today.

Do intelligent people believe that the various languages spoken by man on earth came from the confusion of tongues at the Tower of Babel, some four thousand years ago? Human languages were dispersed all over the face of the earth long before that time. Evidences of civilizations are in existence now that were old long before the date claimed for the flood.

Do Christians believe that Joshua made the sun stand still, so that the day could be lengthened, that a battle might be finished? What kind of person wrote that story, and what did he know about astronomy? It is perfectly plain that the author thought that the earth was the center of the universe and stood still in the heavens, and that the sun either went around it or was pulled across its path each day, and that the stopping of the sun would lengthen the day. We know now that had the sun stopped when Joshua commanded it, and had it stood still until now, it would not have lengthened the day. We know that the day is determined by the rotation of the earth upon its axis, and not by the movement of the sun. Everyone knows that this story simply is not true, and not many even pretend to believe the childish fable.

What of the tale of Balaam's ass speaking to him, probably in Hebrew? Is it true, or is it a fable? Many asses have spoken, and doubtless some in Hebrew, but they have not been that breed of asses. Is salvation to depend on a belief in a monstrosity like this?

Above all the rest, would any human being today believe that a child was born without a father? Yet this story was not at all unreasonable in the ancient world; at least three or four miraculous births are recorded in the Bible, including John the Baptist and Samson. Immaculate conceptions were common in the Roman world at the time and at the place where Christianity really had its nativity. Women were taken to the temples to be inoculated of God so that their sons might be heroes, which meant, generally, wholesale butchers. Julius Caesar was a miraculous conception —indeed, they were common all over the world. How many miraculous-birth stories is a Christian now expected to believe?

In the days of the formation of the Christian religion, disease meant the possession of human beings by devils. Christ cured a sick man by casting out the devils, who ran into the swine, and the swine ran into the sea. Is there any question but what that was simply the attitude and belief of a primitive people? Does anyone believe that sickness means the possession of the body by devils, and that the devils must be cast out of the human being that he may be cured? Does anyone believe that a dead person can come to life? The miracles recorded in the Bible are not the only instances of dead men coming to life. All over the world one finds testimony of such miracles; miracles which no person is expected to believe, unless it is his kind of miracle. Still at Lourdes today, and all over the present world, from New York to Los Angeles and up and down the lands, people believe in miraculous occurrences, and even in the return of the dead. Superstition is everywhere prevalent in the world. It has been so from the beginning, and most likely will be so unto the end.

The reasons for agnosticism are abundant and compelling. Fantastic and foolish and impossible consequences are freely claimed for the belief in religion. All the civilization of any period is put down as a result of religion. All the cruelty and error and ignorance of the period has no relation to religion. The truth is that the origin of what we call civilization is not due to religion but to skepticism. So long as men accepted miracles without question, so long as they believed in original sin and the road to salvation, so long as they believed in a hell where man would be kept for eternity on account of Eve, there was no reason whatever for civilization: life was short, and eternity was long, and the business of life was preparation for eternity.

When every event was a miracle, when there was no order or system or law, there was no occasion for studying any subject, or being interested in anything excepting a religion which took care of the soul. As man doubted the primitive conceptions about religion, and no longer accepted the literal, miraculous teachings of ancient books, he set himself to understand nature. We no longer cure disease by casting out devils. Since that time, men have studied the human body, have built hospitals and treated illness in a scientific way. Science is responsible for the building of railroads and bridges, of steamships, of telegraph lines, of cities, towns, large buildings and small, plumbing and sanitation, of the food supply, and the countless thousands of useful things that we now deem necessary to life. Without skepticism and doubt, none of these things could have been given to the world.

The fear of God is not the beginning of wisdom. The fear of God is the death of wisdom. Skepticism and doubt lead to study and investigation, and investigation is the beginning of wisdom.

The modern world is the child of doubt and inquiry, as the ancient world was the child of fear and faith.

Carl Sagan

This essay, a sermon delivered at Cornell University, is Chapter 23 of Carl Sagan's book *Broca's Brain.* For further information about the author, see page 713.

A Sunday Sermon

Extinguished theologians lie about the cradle of every science as the strangled snakes beside [the cradle] of Hercules.

—T. H. HUXLEY (1860)

We have seen the highest circle of spiraling powers. We have named this circle God. We might have given it any other name we wished: Abyss, Mystery, Absolute Darkness, Absolute Light, Matter, Spirit, Ultimate Hope, Ultimate Despair, Silence.

—NIKOS KAZANTZAKIS (1948)

These days, I often find myself giving scientific talks to popular audiences. Sometimes I am asked to discuss planetary exploration and the nature of the other planets; sometimes, the origin of life or intelligence on Earth;

sometimes, the search for life elsewhere; and sometimes, the grand cosmological perspective. Since I have, more or less, heard these talks before, the question period holds my greatest interest. It reveals the attitudes and concerns of people. The most common questions asked are on unidentified flying objects and ancient astronauts—what I believe are thinly disguised religious queries. Almost as common—particularly after a lecture in which I discuss the evolution of life or intelligence—is: "Do you believe in God?" Because the word "God" means many things to many people, I frequently reply by asking what the questioner means by "God." To my surprise, this response is often considered puzzling or unexpected: "Oh, you know, *God.* Everyone knows who God is." Or "Well, kind of a force that is stronger than we are and that exists everywhere in the universe." There are a number of such forces. One of them is called gravity, but it is not often identified with God. And not everyone does know what is meant by "God." The concept covers a wide range of ideas. Some people think of God as an outsized, light-skinned male with a long white beard, sitting on a throne somewhere up there in the sky, busily tallying the fall of every sparrow. Others—for example, Baruch Spinoza and Albert Einstein—considered God to be essentially the sum total of the physical laws which describe the universe. I do not know of any compelling evidence for anthropomorphic patriarchs controlling human destiny from some hidden celestial vantage point, but it would be madness to deny the existence of physical laws. Whether we believe in God depends very much on what we mean by God.

In the history of the world there have been, probably, tens of thousands of different religions. There is a well-intentioned pious belief that they are all fundamentally identical. In terms of an underlying psychological resonance, there may indeed be important similarities at the cores of many religions, but in the details of ritual and doctrine, and the *apologias* considered to be authenticating, the diversity of organized religions is striking. Human religions are mutually exclusive on such fundamental issues as one god versus many; the origin of evil; reincarnation; idolatry; magic and witchcraft; the role of women; dietary proscriptions; rites of passage; ritual sacrifice; direct or mediated access to deities; slavery; intolerance of other religions; and the community of beings to whom special ethical considerations are due. We do no service to religion in general or to any doctrine in particular if we paper over these differences. Instead, I believe we should understand the world views from which differing religions derive and seek to understand what human needs are fulfilled by those differences.

Bertrand Russell once told of being arrested because he peacefully protested Britain's entry into World War I. The jailer asked—then a routine question for new arrivals—Russell's religion. Russell replied, "Agnostic," which he was asked to spell. The jailer smiled benignly, shook his head and said, "There's many different religions, but I suppose we all worship the same God." Russell commented that the remark cheered him for weeks. And there may not have been much else to cheer him in that prison, although he did manage to write the entire *Introduction to Mathematical Philosophy* and started reading for his work *The Analysis of Mind* within its confines.

Many of the people who ask whether I believe in God are requesting reassurance that their particular belief system, whatever it is, is consistent with modern scientific knowledge. Religion has been scarred in its confrontation with science, and many people—but by no means all—are reluctant to accept a body of theological belief that is too obviously in conflict with what else we know. Apollo 8 accomplished the first manned lunar circumnavigation. In a more or less spontaneous gesture, the Apollo 8 astronauts read from the first verse of the Book of Genesis, in part, I believe, to reassure the taxpayers back in the United States that there were no real inconsistencies between conventional religious outlooks and a manned flight to the Moon. Orthodox Muslims, on the other hand, were outraged after Apollo 11 astronauts accomplished the first manned lunar landing, because the Moon has a special and sacred significance in Islam. In a different religious context, after Yuri Gagarin's first orbital flight, Nikita Khrushchev, the chairman of the Council of Ministers of the USSR, noted that Gagarin had stumbled on no gods or angels up there—that is, Khrushchev reassured his audience that manned orbital flight was not inconsistent with its beliefs.

In the 1950s a Soviet technical journal called *Voprosy Filosofii* (Problems in Philosophy) published an article that argued—very unconvincingly, it seemed to me—that dialectical materialism required there to be life on every planet. Some time later an agonized official rebuttal appeared, decoupling dialectical materialism from exobiology. A clear prediction in an area undergoing vigorous study permits doctrines to be subject to disproof. The last posture a bureaucratic religion wishes to find itself in is vulnerability to disproof, where an experiment can be performed on which the religion stands or falls. And so the fact that life has not been found on the Moon has left the foundations of dialectical materialism unshaken. Doctrines that make no predictions are less compelling than those which make correct predictions; they are in turn more successful than doctrines that make false predictions.

But not always. One prominent American religion confidently predicted that the world would end in 1914. Well, 1914 has come and gone, and—while the events of that year were certainly of some importance— the world does not, at least so far as I can see, seem to have ended. There are at least three responses that an organized religion can make in the face of such a failed and fundamental prophecy. They could have said, "Oh, did we say '1914'? So sorry, we meant '2014.' A slight error in calculation. Hope you weren't inconvenienced in any way." But they did not. They could have said, "Well, the world *would* have ended, except we prayed very hard and interceded with God so He spared the Earth." But they did not. Instead, they did something much more ingenious. They announced that the world *had* in fact ended in 1914, and if the rest of us hadn't noticed, that was our lookout. It is astonishing in the face of such transparent evasions that this religion has any adherents at all. But religions are tough. Either they make no contentions which are subject to disproof or they quickly redesign doctrine after disproof. The fact that religions can be so shamelessly dishonest, so contemptuous of the intelligence of their adherents, and still flourish does not speak very well for the tough-mindedness of the believers. But it does indicate, if a demonstration were needed, that near the core of the religious experience is something remarkably resistant to rational inquiry.

Andrew Dickson White was the intellectual guiding light, founder and first president of Cornell University. He was also the author of an extraordinary book called *The Warfare of Science with Theology in Christendom*, considered so scandalous at the time it was published that his co-author requested his name omitted. White was a man of substantial religious feeling.* But he outlined the long and painful history of erroneous claims which religions had made about the nature of the world, and how, when people directly investigated the nature of the world and discovered it to be different from doctrinal contentions, such people were persecuted and their ideas suppressed. The aged Galileo was threatened by the Catholic hierarchy with torture because he proclaimed the Earth to move. Spinoza was excommunicated by the Jewish hierarchy, and there is hardly an organized religion with a firm body of doctrine which has not at one time or another persecuted people for the crime of open inquiry. Cornell's own devotion to free and non-sectarian inquiry was considered so objectionable in the last quarter of the nineteenth century that ministers advised high school graduates that it was better to receive no college education than to attend so impious an institution. Indeed, this Sage Chapel was constructed in part to placate the pious—although, I am glad to say, it has from time to time made serious efforts at open-minded ecumenicism.

Many of the controversies which White describes are about origins. It used to be believed that every event in the world—the opening of a morning glory, let us say—was due to direct microintervention by the Deity. The flower was unable to open by itself. God had to say, "Hey, flower, open." The application of this idea to human affairs has often had desultory social consequences. For one thing it seems to imply that we are not responsible for our actions. If the play of the world is produced and directed by an omnipotent and omniscient God, does it not follow that every evil that is perpetrated is God's doing? I know this idea is an embar-

---

*White seems also to have been responsible for the exemplary custom of not awarding honorary doctoral degrees at Cornell University: he was concerned about a potential abuse, that honorary degrees would be traded for financial gifts and bequests. White was a man of strong and courageous ethical standards.

rassment in the West, and attempts to avoid it include the contention that what seems to be evil is really part of the Divine Plan, too complex for us to fathom; or that God chose to cloud his own vision about the causality skein when he set out to make the world. There is nothing utterly impossible about these philosophical rescue attempts, but they do seem to have very much the character of propping up a teetering ontological structure.* In addition, the idea of microintervention in the affairs of the world has been used to support the established social, political and economic conventions. There was, for example, the idea of a "Divine Right of Kings," seriously argued by philosophers such as Thomas Hobbes. If you had revolutionary thoughts directed, let us say, toward George III, you were guilty of blasphemy and impiety, religious crimes, as well as such more commonplace political crimes as treason.

There are many legitimate scientific issues relating to origins and ends: What is the origin of the human species? Where did plants and animals come from? How did life arise? the Earth, the planets, the Sun, the stars? Does the universe have an origin, and if so, what? And finally, a still more fundamental and exotic question, which many scientists would say is essentially untestable and therefore meaningless: Why are the laws of nature the way they are? The idea that a God or gods is necessary to effect one or more of these origins has been under repeated attack over the last few thousand years. Because we know something about phototropism and plant hormones, we can understand the opening of the morning glory independent of divine microintervention. It is the same for the entire skein of causality back to the origin of the universe. As we learn more and more about the universe, there seems less and less for God to do. Aristotle's view was of God as an unmoved prime mover, a *roi fainéant,* a do-nothing king who establishes the universe in the first place and then sits back and watches the intricate, intertwined chains of causality course down through the ages. But this seems abstract and removed from everyday experience. It is a little unsettling and pricks at human conceits.

Humans seem to have a natural abhorrence of an infinite regression of causes, and this distaste is at the root of the most famous and most effective demonstrations of the existence of God by Aristotle and Thomas Aquinas. But these thinkers lived before the infinite series was a mathematical commonplace. If the differential and integral calculus or transfinite arith-

*Many statements about God are confidently made by theologians on grounds that today at least sound specious. Thomas Aquinas claimed to prove that God cannot make another God, or commit suicide, or make a man without a soul, or even make a triangle whose interior angles do not equal 180 degrees. But Bolyai and Lobachevsky were able to accomplish this last feat (on a curved surface) in the nineteenth century, and they were not even approximately gods. It is a curious concept this, of an omnipotent God with a long list of things he is forbidden to do by the fiat of the theologians.

metic had been invented in Greece in the fifth century B.C., and not subsequently suppressed, the history of religion in the West might have been very different—or at any rate we would have seen less of the pretension that theological doctrine can be convincingly demonstrated by rational argument to those who reject alleged divine revelation, as Aquinas attempted in the *Summa Contra Gentiles.*

When Newton explained the motion of the planets by the universal theory of gravitation, it no longer was necessary for angels to push and pummel the planets about. When Pierre Simon, the Marquis de Laplace, proposed to explain the origin of the solar system—although not the origin of matter—in terms of physical laws as well, even the necessity for a god involved in the origins of things seemed profoundly challenged. Laplace is said to have presented an edition of his seminal mathematical work *Mécanique céleste* to Napoleon aboard ship in the Mediterranean during the Napoleonic expedition to Egypt, 1798 to 1799. A few days later, so the story goes, Napoleon complained to Laplace that he had found no mention of God in the text.* Laplace's response has been recorded: "Sire, I have no need of that hypothesis." The idea of God as a hypothesis rather than as an obvious truth is by and large a modern idea in the West—although it was certainly discussed seriously and wryly by the Ionian philosophers of 2,400 years ago.

It is often considered that at least the origin of the universe requires a God—indeed, an Aristotelian idea.† This is a point worth looking at in a little more detail. First of all, it is perfectly possible that the universe is infinitely old and therefore requires no Creator. This is consistent with existing knowledge of cosmology, which permits an oscillating universe in which the events since the Big Bang are merely the latest incarnation in an infinite series of creations and destructions of the universe. But secondly, let us consider the idea of a universe created somehow from nothing by God. The question naturally arises—and many ten-year-olds spontaneously think of it before being discouraged by their elders—where

*It is a charming notion that Napoleon actually spent his days aboard ship perusing the highly mathematical *Mécanique céleste.* But he was seriously interested in science and made an earnest attempt to survey the latest findings (see *The Society of Arcueil: A View of French Science at the Time of Napoleon I* by Maurice Crosland, Cambridge, Harvard University Press, 1967). Napoleon did not pretend to read all of the *Mécanique céleste* and wryly wrote to Laplace on another occasion, "The first six months which I can spare will be employed in reading it." But he also remarked, on another of Laplace's books, "Your works contribute to the glory of the nation. The progress and perfection of mathematics are linked closely with the prosperity of the state."

†However, from astronomical arguments Aristotle concluded that there were several dozen unmoved prime movers in the universe. Aristotelian arguments for a prime mover would seem to have polytheistic consequences that might be considered dangerous by contemporary Western theologians.

does God come from? If we answer that God is infinitely old or present simultaneously in all epochs, we have solved nothing, except perhaps verbally. We have merely postponed by one step coming to grips with the problem. A universe that is infinitely old and a God that is infinitely old are, I think, equally deep mysteries. It is not readily apparent why one should be considered more reliably established than the other. Spinoza might have said that the two possibilities are not really different ideas at all.

I think it is wise, when coming face to face with such profound mysteries, to feel a little humility. The idea that scientists or theologians, with our present still puny understanding of this vast and awesome cosmos, can comprehend the origins of the universe is only a little less silly than the idea that Mesopotamian astronomers of 3,000 years ago—from whom the ancient Hebrews borrowed, during the Babylonian captivity, the cosmological accounts in the first chapter of Genesis—could have understood the origins of the universe. We simply do not know. The Hindu holy book, the Rig Veda (X: 129), has a much more realistic view of the matter:

> Who knows for certain? Who shall here declare it?
> Whence was it born, whence came creation?
> The gods are later than this world's formation;
> Who then can know the origins of the world?
> None knows whence creation arose;
> And whether he has or has not made it;
> He who surveys it from the lofty skies,
> Only he knows—or perhaps he knows not.

But the times we live in are very interesting ones. Questions of origins, including some questions relating to the origin of the universe, may in the next few decades be amenable to experimental inquiry. There is no conceivable answer to the grand cosmological questions which will not resonate with the religious sensibilities of human beings. But there is a chance that the answers will discomfit a great many bureaucratic and doctrinal religions. The idea of religion as a body of belief, immune to criticism, fixed forever by some founder is, I think, a prescription for the long-term decay of the religion, especially lately. In questions of origins and ends, the religious and scientific sensibilities have much the same objectives. Human beings are built in such a way that we passionately wish to answer these questions—perhaps because of the mystery of our own individual origins. But our contemporary scientific insights, while limited, are much deeper than those of our Babylonian predecessors of 1,000 B.C. Religions unwilling to accommodate to change, both scientific and social, are, I believe, doomed. A body of belief cannot be alive and relevant, vibrant and growing, unless it is responsive to the most serious criticism that can be mustered against it.

The First Amendment to the United States Constitution encourages a diversity of religions but does not prohibit criticism of religion. In fact it protects and encourages criticism of religion. Religions ought to be subject to at least the same degree of skepticism as, for example, contentions about UFO visitations or Velikovskian catastrophism.⁰ I think it is healthy for the religions themselves to foster skepticism about the fundamental underpinnings of their evidential bases. There is no question that religion provides a solace and support, a bulwark in time of emotional need, and can serve extremely useful social roles. But it by no means follows that religion should be immune from testing, from critical scrutiny, from skepticism. It is striking how little skeptical discussion of religion there is in the nation that Tom Paine, the author of *The Age of Reason*, helped to found. I hold that belief systems that cannot survive scrutiny are probably not worth having. Those that do survive scrutiny probably have at least important kernels of truth within them.

Religion used to provide a generally accepted understanding of our place in the universe. That surely has been one of the major objectives of myth and legend, philosophy and religion, as long as there have been human beings. But the mutual confrontation of differing religions and of religion with science has eroded those traditional views, at least in the minds of many.* The way to find out about our place in the universe is by examining the universe and by examining ourselves—without preconceptions, with as unbiased a mind as we can muster. We cannot begin with an entirely clean slate, since we arrive at this problem with predispositions of hereditary and environmental origin; but, after understanding such built-in biases, is it not possible to pry insights from nature?

Proponents of doctrinal religions—ones in which a particular body of belief is prized and infidels scorned—will be threatened by the courageous pursuit of knowledge. We hear from such people that it may be dangerous

---

*This subject is rich in irony. Augustine was born in Africa in 354 A.D. and in his early years was a Manichean, an adherent of a dualistic view of the universe in which good and evil are in conflict on roughly equal terms, and which was later condemned as a "heresy" by Christian orthodoxy. The possibility that all was not right with Manicheanism occurred to Augustine when he was studying its astronomy. He discovered that even the leading figures in the faith could not justify its murky astronomical notions. This contradiction between theology and science on matters astronomical was the initial impetus moving him toward Catholicism, the religion of his mother, which in later centuries persecuted scientists such as Galileo for trying to improve our understanding of astronomy. Augustine later became Saint Augustine, one of the major intellectual figures in the history of the Roman Catholic church, and his mother became Saint Monica, after whom a suburb of Los Angeles is named. Bertrand Russell wondered what Augustine's view of the conflict between astronomy and theology would have been had he lived in the time of Galileo.

Velikovskian catastrophism Reference to Immanuel Velikovsky (1895–1979), a controversial American physician and historian who argued that spectacular changes in the solar system explain the miraculous events described in the Bible and ancient mythology.

to probe too deeply. Many people have inherited their religion like their eye color: they consider it not a thing to think very deeply about, and in any case beyond our control. But those with a set of beliefs they profess to feel deeply about, which they have selected without an unbiased sifting through the facts and the alternatives, will feel uncomfortably challenged by searching questions. Anger at queries about our beliefs is the body's warning signal: here lies unexamined and probably dangerous doctrinal baggage.

Christianus Huygens wrote a remarkable book around 1670 in which bold and prescient speculations were made about the nature of the other planets in the solar system. Huygens was well aware that there were those who held such speculations and his astronomical observations objectionable: "But perhaps they'll say," Huygens mused, "it does not become us to be so curious and inquisitive in these Things which the Supreme Creator seems to have kept for his own Knowledge: For since he has not been pleased to make any farther Discovery or Revelation of them, it seems little better than presumption to make any inquiry into that which he has thought fit to hide. But these Gentlemen must be told," Huygens then thundered, "that they take too much upon themselves when they pretend to appoint how far and no farther Men shall go in their Searches, and to set bounds to other Mens Industry; as if they knew the Marks that God has placed to Knowledge: or as if Men were able to pass those Marks. If our Forefathers had been at this rate scrupulous, we might have been ignorant still of the Magnitude and Figure of the Earth, or that there was such a place as America."

If we look at the universe in the large, we find something astonishing. First of all, we find a universe that is exceptionally beautiful, intricately and subtly constructed. Whether our appreciation of the universe is because we are a part of that universe—whether, no matter how the universe were put together, we would have found it beautiful—is a proposition to which I do not pretend to have an answer. But there is no question that the elegance of the universe is one of its most remarkable properties. At the same time, there is no question that there are cataclysms and catastrophes occurring regularly in the universe and on the most awesome scale. There are, for example, quasar explosions which probably decimate the nuclei of galaxies. It seems likely that every time a quasar explodes, more than a million worlds are obliterated and countless forms of life, some of them intelligent, are utterly destroyed. This is not the traditional benign universe of conventional religiosity in the West, constructed for the benefit of living and especially of human beings. Indeed, the very scale of the universe—more than a hundred billion galaxies, each containing more than a hundred billion stars—speaks to us of the inconsequentiality of human events in the cosmic context. We see a universe simultaneously very beautiful and very violent. We see a universe that does not exclude a traditional Western or Eastern god, but that does not require one either.

My deeply held belief is that if a god of anything like the traditional sort exists, our curiosity and intelligence are provided by such a god. We would be unappreciative of those gifts (as well as unable to take such a course of action) if we suppressed our passion to explore the universe and ourselves. On the other hand, if such a traditional god does not exist, our curiosity and our intelligence are the essential tools for managing our survival. In either case, the enterprise of knowledge is consistent with both science and religion, and is essential for the welfare of the human species.

Joseph Campbell

Joseph Campbell proposes "comparative mythology" as an academic field in its own right, one encompassing new discoveries in archeology, philology, ethnology, philosophy, art history, folklore, religion, psychology, and Asian studies. Many of his books correlate these disciplines and convey both his enthusiasm and his scholarship to a popular audience.

Campbell was born in New York City in 1904. He attended Dartmouth College and Columbia University, and after receiving his M.A. in 1927, he studied in Paris and Munich. On his return he taught for two years at a private school and then joined the faculty of Sarah Lawrence College. His best-known book is *The Hero with a Thousand Faces* (1949), his reconstruction of the universal "monomyth." This was followed by the series titled *The Masks of God,* four separately published volumes on primitive, Oriental, Occidental, and creative mythology. His latest books are *Myths to Live By* (1972), from which we reprint Part 2 of Chapter 2, *The Mythic Image* (1974), and *Tarot Revelations* (1980).

Mythic Images

In relation to the first books and chapters of the Bible, it used to be the custom of both Jews and Christians to take the narratives literally, as though they were dependable accounts of the origin of the universe and of actual prehistoric events. It was supposed and taught that there had been, quite concretely, a creation of the world in seven days by a god known only to the Jews; that somewhere on this broad new earth there had been a Garden of Eden containing a serpent that could talk; that the first woman, Eve, was formed from the first man's rib, and that the wicked serpent told her of the marvelous properties of the fruits of a certain tree of which God had forbidden the couple to eat; and that, as a consequence of their having eaten of that fruit, there followed a "Fall" of all mankind, death came into the world, and the couple was driven forth from the garden. For there was in the center of that garden a second tree, the fruit of which would have given them eternal life; and their creator, fearing lest they should now take and eat of that too, and so become as knowing and immortal as himself, cursed them, and having driven them out, placed at his garden gate "cherubim and a flaming sword which turned every way to guard the way to the tree of life."

It seems impossible today, but people actually believed all that until as recently as half a century or so ago: clergymen, philosophers, government officers, and all. Today we know—and know right well—that there was never anything of the kind: no Garden of Eden anywhere on this earth, no time when the serpent could talk, no prehistoric "Fall," no exclusion from the garden, no universal Flood, no Noah's Ark. The entire history on which our leading Occidental religions have been founded is an anthology of fictions. But these are fictions of a type that have had—curiously enough —a universal vogue as the founding legends of other religions, too. Their counterparts have turned up everywhere—and yet, there was never such a garden, serpent, tree, or deluge.

How account for such anomalies? Who invents these impossible tales? Where do their images come from? And why—though obviously absurd —are they everywhere so reverently believed?

What I would suggest is that by comparing a number from different parts of the world and differing traditions, one might arrive at an understanding of their force, their source and possible sense. For they are not historical. That much is clear. They speak, therefore, not of outside events but of themes of the imagination. And since they exhibit features that are actually universal, they must in some way represent features of our general racial imagination, permanent features of the human spirit—or, as we say today, of the psyche. They are telling us, therefore, of matters fundamental to ourselves, enduring essential principles about which it would be good for us to know; about which, in fact, it will be necessary for us to know if our conscious minds are to be kept in touch with our own most secret, motivating depths. In short, these holy tales and their images are messages to the conscious mind from quarters of the spirit unknown to normal daylight consciousness, and if read as referring to events in the field of space and time—whether of the future, present, or past—they will have been misread and their force deflected, some secondary thing outside then taking to itself the reference of the symbol, some sanctified stick, stone, or animal, person, event, city or social group.

Let us regard a little more closely the Biblical image of the garden.

Its name, Eden, signifies in Hebrew "delight, a place of delight," and our own English word, Paradise, which is from the Persian, *pairi-*, "around," *daeza*, "a wall," means properly "a walled enclosure." Apparently, then, Eden is a walled garden of delight, and in its center stands the great tree;

or rather, in its center stand two trees, the one of the knowledge of good and evil, the other of immortal life. Four rivers flow, furthermore, from within it as from an inexhaustible source, to refresh the world in the four directions. And when our first parents, having eaten the fruit, were driven forth, two cherubim were stationed (as we have heard) at its eastern gate, to guard the way of return.

Taken as referring not to any geographical scene, but to a landscape of the soul, the Garden of Eden would have to be within us. Yet our conscious minds are unable to enter it and enjoy there the taste of eternal life, since we have already tasted of the knowledge of good and evil. That, in fact, must then be the knowledge that has thrown us out of the garden, pitched us away from our own center, so that we now judge things in those terms and experience only good and evil instead of eternal life—which, since the enclosed garden is within us, must already be ours, even though unknown to our conscious personalities. That would seem to be the meaning of the myth when read, not as prehistory, but as referring to man's inward spiritual state.

Let us turn now from this Bible legend, by which the West has been enchanted, to the Indian, of the Buddha, which has enspelled the entire East; for there too is the mythic image of a tree of immortal life defended by two terrifying guards. That tree is the one beneath which Siddhartha was sitting, facing east, when he wakened to the light of his own immortality in truth and was known thereafter as the Buddha, the Wakened One. There is a serpent in that legend also, but instead of being known as evil, it is thought of as symbolic of the immortal inhabiting energy of all life on earth. For the serpent shedding its skin, to be, as it were, born again, is likened in the Orient to the reincarnating spirit that assumes and throws off bodies as a man puts on and puts off clothes. There is in Indian mythology a great cobra imagined as balancing the tablelike earth on its head: its head being, of course, at the pivotal point, exactly beneath the world tree. And according to the Buddha legend, when the Blessed One, having attained omniscience, continued to sit absorbed for a number of days in absolute meditation, he became endangered by a great storm that arose in the world around him, and this prodigious serpent, coming up from below, wrapped itself protectively around the Buddha, covering his head with its cobra hood.

Thus, whereas in one of these two legends of the tree the service of the serpent is rejected and the animal itself cursed, in the other it is accepted. In both, the serpent is in some way associated with the tree and has apparently enjoyed its fruits, since it can slough its skin and live again; but in the Bible legend our first parents are expelled from the garden of that tree, whereas in the Buddhist tradition we are all invited in. The tree beneath which the Buddha sat corresponds, thus, to the second of the Garden of Eden, which, as already said, is to be thought of not as geographically situated but as a garden of the soul. And so, what then keeps us from returning to it and sitting like the Buddha beneath it? Who or what are those two cherubim? Do the Buddhists know of any such pair?

One of the most important Buddhist centers in the world today is the holy city of Nara, Japan, where there is a great temple sheltering a prodigious bronze image, 53½ feet high, of the Buddha seated cross-legged on a great lotus, holding his right hand lifted in the "fear not" posture; and as one approaches the precincts of this temple, one passes through a gate that is guarded, left and right, by two gigantic, marvelously threatening military figures flourishing swords. These are the Buddhist counterparts of the cherubim stationed by Yahweh at the garden gate. However, here we are not to be intimidated and held off. The fear of death and desire for life that these threatening guardsmen arouse in us are to be left behind as we pass between.

In the Buddhist view, that is to say, what is keeping us out of the garden is not the jealousy or wrath of any god, but our own instinctive attachment to what we take to be our lives. Our senses, outward-directed to the world of space and time, have attached us to that world and to our mortal bodies within it. We are loath to give up what we take to be the goods and pleasures of this physical life, and this attachment is the great fact, the great circumstance or barrier, that is keeping us out of the garden. This, and this alone, is preventing us from recognizing within ourselves that immortal and universal consciousness of which our physical senses, outward-turned, are but the agents.

According to this teaching, no actual cherub with a flaming sword is required to keep us out of our inward garden, since we are keeping ourselves out, through our avid interest in the outward, mortal aspects both of ourselves and of our world. What is symbolized in our passage of the guarded gate is our abandonment of both the world so known and ourselves so known within it: the phenomenal, mere appearance of things seen as born and dying, experienced either as good or as evil, and regarded, consequently, with desire and fear. Of the two big Buddhist cherubim, one has the mouth open, the other, the mouth closed—in token (I have been told) of the way we experience things in this temporal world, in terms always of pairs-of-opposites. Passing between, we are to leave such thinking behind.

But is that not the lesson, finally, of the Bible story as well? Eve and then Adam ate the fruit of the knowledge of good and evil, which is to say, of the pairs-of-opposites, and immediately experienced themselves as different from each other and felt shame. God, therefore, no more than confirmed what already had been accomplished when he drove them from the garden to experience the pains of death and birth and of toil for the goods of this world. Furthermore, they were experiencing God himself now as totally "other," wrathful and dangerous to their purposes, and the cherubim at the garden gate were representations of this way—now theirs —of experiencing both God and themselves. But as we are told also in the

Bible legend, it would actually have been possible for Adam to "put forth his hand and take also of the tree of life, and eat, and live forever." And in the Christian image of the crucified redeemer that is exactly what we are being asked to do. The teaching here is that Christ restored to man immortality. His cross, throughout the Middle Ages, was equated with the tree of immortal life; and the fruit of that tree was the crucified Savior himself, who there offered up his flesh and his blood to be our "meat indeed" and our "drink indeed." He himself had boldly walked, so to say, right on through the guarded gate without fear of the cherubim and that flaming turning sword. And just as the Buddha, five hundred years before, had left behind all ego-oriented desires and fears to come to know himself as the pure, immortal Void, so the Western Savior left his body nailed to the tree and passed in spirit to atonement—at-one-ment—with the Father: to be followed now by ourselves.

The symbolic images of the two traditions are thus formally equivalent, even though the points of view of the two may be difficult to reconcile. In that of the Old and New Testaments, God and man are not one, but opposites, and the reason man was expelled from the garden was that he had disobeyed his creator. The sacrifice on the cross, accordingly, was in the nature not so much of a realization of *at-one-ment* as of penitential *atonement*. On the Buddhist side, on the other hand, man's separation from the source of his being is to be read in psychological terms, as an effect of misdirected consciousness, ignorant of its seat and source, which attributes final reality to merely phenomenal apparitions. Whereas the level of instruction represented in the Bible story is that, pretty much, of a nursery tale of disobedience and its punishment, inculcating an attitude of dependency, fear, and respectful devotion, such as might be thought appropriate for a child in relation to a parent, the Buddhist teaching, in contrast, is for self-responsible adults. And yet the imagery shared by the two is finally older by far than either, older than the Old Testament, much older than Buddhism, older even than India. For we find the symbolism of the serpent, tree, and garden of immortality already in the earliest cuneiform texts, depicted on Old Sumerian cylinder seals, and represented even in the arts and rites of primitive village folk throughout the world.

Nor does it matter from the standpoint of a comparative study of symbolic forms whether Christ or the Buddha ever actually lived and performed the miracles associated with their teachings. The religious literatures of the world abound in counterparts of those two great lives. And what one may learn from them all, finally, is that the savior, the hero, the redeemed one, is the one who has learned to penetrate the protective wall of those fears within, which exclude the rest of us, generally, in our daylight and even our dreamnight thoughts, from all experience of our own and the world's divine ground. The mythologized biographies of such saviors communicate the messages of their world-transcending wisdom in word-transcending symbols—which, ironically, are then generally translated back into such verbalized thoughts as built the interior walls in the first place. I have heard good Christian clergymen admonish young couples at their marriage ceremonies so to live together in this life that in the world to come they may have life everlasting; and I have thought, Alas! The more appropriate mythic admonishment would be, so to live their marriages that in *this* world they may experience life everlasting. For there is indeed a life everlasting, a dimension of enduring human values that inheres in the very act of living itself, and in the simultaneous experience and expression of which men through all time have lived and died. We all embody these unknowingly, the great being simply those who have wakened to their knowledge—as suggested in a saying attributed to Christ in the Gnostic *Gospel According to Thomas:* "The Kingdom of the Father is spread upon the earth and men do not see it."

Mythologies might be defined in this light as poetic expressions of just such transcendental seeing; and if we may take as evidence the antiquity of certain basic mythic forms—the serpent god, for example, and the sacred tree—the beginnings of what we take today to be mystical revelation must have been known to at least a few, even of the primitive teachers of our race, from the very start.

Paul Tillich

A profound and compassionate thinker and one of the great contemporary theologians, Paul Tillich (1886–1965) was born and educated in Germany and was well on his way to a distinguished academic career when he was dismissed from his post as Professor of Philosophy at the University of Frankfurt because of his outspoken criticism of the Nazi movement. In 1933, at the age of forty-seven, he emigrated to the United States at the invitation of Union Theological Seminary in New York, where he taught until 1954. That year he was appointed to the Divinity School Faculty at Harvard, and in 1962 he was named the first Duveen Professor of Theology at the University of Chicago. His books include *The Shaking of the Foundations* (1948) and *The New Being* (1955), two volumes of sermons; *The Protestant Era* (1948); *The Courage to Be* (1952); *Dynamics of Faith* (1957); and *Ultimate Concern: Tillich in Dialogue* (ed. D. M. Brown, 1965), based on tape recordings made during a seminar in the spring of 1964.

Paul Tillich thought of God not as a Being, but as our ultimate concern, the ultimate personal depth and ground of all being. It is this "lost" dimension of depth that he discusses here in an essay first printed in the *Saturday Evening Post,* June 14, 1958.

The Lost Dimension in Religion

Every observer of our Western civilization is aware of the fact that something has happened to religion. It especially strikes the observer of the American scene. Everywhere he finds symptoms of what one has called religious revival, or more modestly, the revival of interest in religion. He finds them in the churches with their rapidly increasing membership. He finds them in the mushroomlike growth of sects. He finds them on college campuses and in the theological faculties of universities. Most conspicuously, he finds them in the tremendous success of men like Billy Graham and Norman Vincent Peale, who attract masses of people Sunday after Sunday, meeting after meeting. The facts cannot be denied, but how should they be interpreted? It is my intention to show that these facts must be seen as expressions of the predicament of Western man in the second half of the twentieth century. But I would even go a step further. I believe that the predicament of man in our period gives us also an important insight into the predicament of man generally—at all times and in all parts of the earth.

There are many analyses of man and society in our time. Most of them show important traits in the picture, but few of them succeed in giving a general key to our present situation. Although it is not easy to find such a key, I shall attempt it and, in so doing, will make an assertion which may be somewhat mystifying at first hearing. The decisive element in the predicament of Western man in our period is his loss of the dimension of depth. Of course, "dimension of depth" is a metaphor. It is taken from the spatial realm and applied to man's spiritual life. What does it mean?

It means that man has lost an answer to the question: What is the meaning of life? Where do we come from, where do we go to? What shall we do, what should we become in the short stretch between birth and death? Such questions are not answered or even asked if the "dimension of depth" is lost. And this is precisely what has happened to man in our period of history. He has lost the courage to ask such questions with an infinite seriousness—as former generations did—and he has lost the courage to receive answers to these questions, wherever they may come from.

I suggest that we call the dimension of depth the religious dimension in man's nature. Being religious means asking passionately the question of the meaning of our existence and being willing to receive answers, even if the answers hurt. Such an idea of religion makes religion universally human, but it certainly differs from what is usually called religion. It does not describe religion as the belief in the existence of gods or one God, and as a set of activities and institutions for the sake of relating oneself to these beings in thought, devotion and obedience. No one can deny that the religions which have appeared in history are religions in this sense. Nevertheless, religion in its innermost nature is more than religion in this narrower sense. It is the state of being concerned about one's own being and being universally.

There are many people who are ultimately concerned in this way who feel far removed, however, from religion in the narrower sense, and therefore from every historical religion. It often happens that such people take the question of the meaning of their life infinitely seriously and reject any historical religion just for this reason. They feel that the concrete religions fail to express their profound concern adequately. They are religious while rejecting the religions. It is this experience which forces us to distinguish the meaning of religion as living in the dimension of depth from particular expressions of one's ultimate concern in the symbols and institutions of a concrete religion. If we now turn to the concrete analysis of the religious situation of our time, it is obvious that our key must be the basic meaning of religion and not any particular religion, not even Christianity. What does this key disclose about the predicament of man in our period?

If we define religion as the state of being grasped by an infinite concern we must say: Man in our time has lost such infinite concern. And the resurgence of religion is nothing but a desperate and mostly futile attempt to regain what has been lost.

How did the dimension of depth become lost? Like any important event, it has many causes, but certainly not the one which one hears often mentioned from ministers' pulpits and evangelists' platforms, namely that a widespread impiety of modern man is responsible. Modern man is neither more pious nor more impious than man in any other period. The loss of the dimension of depth is caused by the relation of man to his world and to himself in our period, the period in which nature is being subjected scientifically and technically to the control of man. In this period, life in the dimension of depth is replaced by life in the horizontal dimension. The driving forces of the industrial society of which we are a part go ahead horizontally and not vertically. In popular terms this is expressed in phrases like "better and better," "bigger and bigger," "more and more." One should not disparage the feeling which lies behind such speech. Man is right in feeling that he is able to know and transform the world he encounters without a foreseeable limit. He can go ahead in all directions without a definite boundary.

A most expressive symbol of this attitude of going ahead in the horizontal dimension is the breaking through of the space which is controlled by the gravitational power of the earth into the world-space. It is interesting that one calls this world-space simply "space" and speaks, for instance, of space travel, as if every trip were not travel into space. Perhaps one feels that the true nature of space has been discovered only through our entering into indefinite world-space. In any case, the predominance of the horizontal dimension over the dimension of depth has been immensely increased by the opening up of the space beyond the space of the earth.

If we now ask what does man do and seek if he goes ahead in the horizontal dimension, the answer is difficult. Sometimes one is inclined to say that the mere movement ahead without an end, the intoxication with speeding forward without limits, is what satisfies him. But this answer is by no means sufficient. For on his way into space and time man changes the world he encounters. And the changes made by him change himself. He transforms everything he encounters into a tool; and in doing so he himself becomes a tool. But if he asks, a tool for what, there is no answer.

One does not need to look far beyond everyone's daily experience in order to find examples to describe this predicament. Indeed our daily life in office and home, in cars and airplanes, at parties and conferences, while reading magazines and watching television, while looking at advertisements and hearing radio, are in themselves continuous examples of a life which has lost the dimension of depth. It runs ahead, every moment is filled with something which must be done or seen or said or planned. But no one can experience depth without stopping and becoming aware of himself. Only if he has moments in which he does not care about what comes next can he experience the meaning of this moment here and now and ask himself about the meaning of his life. As long as the preliminary, transitory concerns are not silenced, no matter how interesting and valuable and important they may be, the voice of the ultimate concern cannot be heard. This is the deepest root of the loss of the dimension of depth in our period—the loss of religion in its basic and universal meaning.

If the dimension of depth is lost, the symbols in which life in this dimension has expressed itself must also disappear. I am speaking of the great symbols of the historical religions in our Western world, of Judaism and Christianity. The reason that the religious symbols became lost is not primarily scientific criticism, but it is a complete misunderstanding of their meaning; and only because of this misunderstanding was scientific critique able, and even justified, in attacking them. The first step toward the nonreligion of the Western world was made by religion itself. When it defended its great symbols, not as symbols, but as literal stories, it had already lost the battle. In doing so the theologians (and today many religious laymen) helped to transfer the powerful expressions of the dimension of depth into objects or happenings on the horizontal plane. There the symbols lose their power and meaning and become an easy prey to physical, biological and historical attack.

If the symbol of creation which points to the divine ground of everything is transferred to the horizontal plane, it becomes a story of events in a removed past for which there is no evidence, but which contradicts every piece of scientific evidence. If the symbol of the Fall of Man, which points to the tragic estrangement of man and his world from their true being is transferred to the horizontal plane, it becomes a story of a human couple a few thousand years ago in what is now present-day Iraq. One of the most profound psychological descriptions of the general human predicament becomes an absurdity on the horizontal plane. If the symbols of the Saviour and the salvation through Him which point to the healing power in history and personal life are transferred to the horizontal plane, they become stories of a half-divine being coming from a heavenly place and returning to it. Obviously, in this form, they have no meaning whatsoever for people whose view of the universe is determined by scientific astronomy.

If the idea of God (and the symbols applied to Him) which expresses man's ultimate concern is transferred to the horizontal plane, God becomes a being among others whose existence or nonexistence is a matter of inquiry. Nothing, perhaps, is more symptomatic of the loss of the dimension of depth than the permanent discussion about the existence or nonexistence of God—a discussion in which both sides are equally wrong, because the discussion itself is wrong and possible only after the loss of the dimension of depth.

When in this way man has deprived himself of the dimension of depth and the symbols expressing it, he then becomes a part of the horizontal plane. He loses his self and becomes a thing among things. He becomes an element in the process of manipulated production and manipulated consumption. This is now a matter of public knowledge. We have become aware of the degree to which everyone in our social structure is managed, even if one knows it and even if one belongs himself to the managing group. The influence of the gang mentality on adolescents, of the corporation's demands on the executives, of the conditioning of everyone by public communication, by propaganda and advertising under the guidance of motivation research, et cetera, have all been described in many books and articles.

Under these pressures, man can hardly escape the fate of becoming a thing among the things he produces, a bundle of conditioned reflexes without a free, deciding and responsible self. The immense mechanism, set up by man to produce objects for his use, transforms man himself into an object used by the same mechanism of production and consumption.

But man has not ceased to be man. He resists this fate anxiously, desperately, courageously. He asks the question, for what? And he realizes that there is no answer. He becomes aware of the emptiness which is covered by the continuous movement ahead and the production of means for ends which become means again without an ultimate end. Without knowing what has happened to him, he feels that he has lost the meaning of life, the dimension of depth.

Out of this awareness the religious question arises and religious answers are received or rejected. Therefore, in order to describe the contemporary attitude toward religion, we must first point to the places where the awareness of the predicament of Western man in our period is most sharply expressed. These places are the great art, literature and partly, at least, the philosophy of our time. It is both the subject matter and the style of these creations which show the passionate and often tragic struggle about the meaning of life in a period in which man has lost the dimension of depth. This art, literature, philosophy is not religious in the narrower sense of the word; but it asks the religious question more radically and more profoundly than most directly religious expressions of our time.

It is the religious question which is asked when the novelist describes a man who tries in vain to reach the only place which could solve the problem of his life, or a man who disintegrates under the memory of a guilt which persecutes him, or a man who never had a real self and is pushed by his fate without resistance to death, or a man who experiences a profound disgust of everything he encounters.

It is the religious question which is asked when the poet opens up the horror and the fascination of the demonic regions of his soul, or if he leads us into the deserts and empty places of our being, or if he shows physical and moral mud under the surface of life, or if he sings the song of transitoriness, giving words to the ever-present anxiety of our hearts.

It is the religious question which is asked when the playwright shows the illusion of a life in a ridiculous symbol, or if he lets the emptiness of a life's work end in self-destruction, or if he confronts us with the inescapable bondage to mutual hate and guilt, or if he leads us into the dark cellar of lost hopes and slow disintegration.

It is the religious question which is asked when the painter breaks the visible surface into pieces, then reunites them into a great picture which has little similarity with the world at which we normally look, but which expresses our anxiety and our courage to face reality.

It is the religious question which is asked when the architect, in creating office buildings or churches, removes the trimmings taken over from past styles because they cannot be considered an honest expression of our own period. He prefers the seeming poverty of a purpose-determined style to the deceptive richness of imitated styles of the past. He knows that he gives no final answer, but he does give an honest answer.

The philosophy of our time shows the same hiddenly religious traits. It is divided into two main schools of thought, the analytic and the existentialist. The former tries to analyze logical and linguistic forms which are always used and which underlie all scientific research. One may compare them with the painters who dissolve the natural forms of bodies into cubes, planes and lines; or with those architects who want the structural "bones" of their buildings to be conspicuously visible and not hidden by covering features. This self-restriction produces the almost monastic poverty and seriousness of this philosophy. It is religious—without any contact with religion in its method—by exercising the humility of "learned ignorance."

In contrast to this school the existentialist philosophers have much to say about the problems of human existence. They bring into rational concepts what the writers and poets, the painters and architects, are expressing in their particular material. What they express is the human predicament in time and space, in anxiety and guilt and the feeling of meaninglessness. From Pascal in the seventeenth century to Heidegger and Sartre in our time, philosophers have emphasized the contrast between human dignity and human misery. And by doing so, they have raised the religious question. Some have tried to answer the question they have asked. But if they did so, they turned back to past traditions and offered to our time that which does not fit our time. Is it possible for our time to receive answers which are born out of our time?

Answers given today are in danger of strengthening the present situation and with it the questions to which they are supposed to be the answers. This refers to some of the previously mentioned major representatives of the so-called resurgence of religion, as for instance the evangelist Billy Graham and the counseling and healing minister, Norman Vincent Peale. Against the validity of the answers given by the former, one must say that, in spite of his personal integrity, his propagandistic methods and his primitive theological fundamentalism fall short of what is needed to give an answer to the religious question of our period. In spite of all his seriousness, he does not take the radical questions of our period seriously.

The effect that Norman Peale has on large groups of people is rooted in the fact that he confirms the situation which he is supposed to help overcome. He heals people with the purpose of making them fit again for the demands of the competitive and conformist society in which we are living. He helps them to become adapted to the situation which is characterized by the loss of the dimension of depth. Therefore, his advice is valid on this level; but it is the validity of this level that is the true religious question of our time. And this question he neither raises nor answers.

In many cases the increase of church membership and interest in religious activities does not mean much more than the religious consecration of a state of things in which the religious dimension has been lost. It is the desire to participate in activities which are socially strongly approved and give internal and a certain amount of external security. This is not necessarily bad, but it certainly is not an answer to the religious question of our period.

Is there an answer? There is always an answer, but the answer may not be available to us. We may be too deeply steeped in the predicament out of which the question arises to be able to answer it. To acknowledge this is certainly a better way toward a real answer than to bar the way to it by deceptive answers. And it may be that in this attitude the real answer (within available limits) is given. The real answer to the question of how to regain the dimension of depth is not given by increased church membership or church attendance, nor by conversion or healing experiences. But it is given by the awareness that we have lost the decisive dimension of life, the dimension of depth, and that there is no easy way of getting it back. Such awareness is in itself a state of being grasped by that which is symbolized in the term, dimension of depth. He who realizes that he is separated from the ultimate source of meaning shows by this realization that he is not only separated but also reunited. And this is just our situation. What we need above all—and partly have—is the radical realization of our predicament, without trying to cover it up by secular or religious ideologies. The revival of religious interest would be a creative power in our culture if it would develop into a movement of search for the lost dimension of depth.

This does not mean that the traditional religious symbols should be dismissed. They certainly have lost their meaning in the literalistic form into which they have been distorted, thus producing the critical reaction against them. But they have not lost their genuine meaning, namely, of answering the question which is implied in man's very existence in powerful, revealing and saving symbols. If the resurgence of religion would produce a new understanding of the symbols of the past and their relevance for our situation, instead of premature and deceptive answers, it would become a creative factor in our culture and a saving factor for many who live in estrangement, anxiety and despair. The religious answer has always the character of "in spite of." In spite of the loss of dimension of depth, its power is present, and most present in those who are aware of the loss and are striving to regain it with ultimate seriousness.

Malcolm Muggeridge

Malcolm Muggeridge, born in 1903 in Surrey, England, was educated at Cambridge. Conservative and iconoclastic, gifted with a sharp eye, a sharp tongue, and a sharp pen, he is difficult to define. He is a journalist; was editor of *Punch,* the British humor magazine, from 1953 to 1957; and is an author of spiritual biography and autobiography. During World War II he served brilliantly in the British Intelligence Corps and received many decorations, but his activities as a spy so depressed him that he considered suicide.

His father was a Fabian socialist, and Muggeridge himself was once a socialist and an avowed atheist. He has gradually moved toward a more conservative position politically, and gradually, too, he has moved toward Christianity. *Jesus Rediscovered* (1969), from which the selection below is taken, was written when Muggeridge had come to a belief in Christ and the Gospels but had not yet come to agreement with organized religion. Among his many other books are *Something Beautiful for God: Mother Teresa of Calcutta* (1971); *A Twentieth-Century Testimony* (1979); and *Like It Was: The Diaries of Malcolm Muggeridge* (1982).

Credo

In trying to formulate what I believe, I have to begin with what I disbelieve. I disbelieve in progress, the pursuit of happiness, and all the concomitant notions and projects for creating a society in which human beings find ever greater contentment by being given in ever greater abundance the means to satisfy their material and bodily hopes and desires. In other words, I consider that the way of life in urbanized, rich countries as it exists today, and as it is likely to go on developing, is probably the most degraded and unillumined ever to come to pass on earth. The half century in which I have been consciously alive seems to me to have been quite exceptionally destructive, murderous, and brutal. More people have been killed and terrorized, more driven from their homes and native places, more of the past's heritage has been destroyed, more lies propagated and base persuasion engaged in, with less compensatory achievement in art, literature, and imaginative understanding, than in any comparable period of history.

Ever since I can remember, the image of earthly power, whether in the guise of schoolmaster, mayor, judge, prime minister, monarch, or any other, has seemed to me derisory. I was enchanted when I first read in the *Pensées* (Pascal being one of the small, sublime band of fellow humans to whom one may turn and say in the deepest humility: "I agree") about how magistrates and rulers had to be garbed in their ridiculous ceremonial robes, crowns, and diadems. Otherwise, who would not see through their threadbare pretensions? I am conscious of having been ruled by buffoons, taught by idiots, preached at by hypocrites, and preyed upon by charlatans in the guise of advertisers and other professional persuaders, as well as by demagogues and ideologues of many opinions, all false.

Nor, as far as I am concerned, is there any recompense in the so-called achievements of science. It is true that in my lifetime more progress has been made in unraveling the composition and mechanism of the material universe than previously in the whole of recorded time. This does not at all excite my mind, or even my curiosity. The atom has been split; the universe has been discovered, and will soon be explored. Neither achievement has any bearing on what alone interests me—why life exists, and what is the significance, if any, of my minute and so transitory part in it. All the world in a grain of sand; all the universe too. If I could understand a grain of sand, I should understand everything. Why, then, should going to the moon and Mars, or spending a holiday along the Milky Way, be expected to advance me further in my quest than going to Manchester and Liverpool, or spending a holiday in Brighton?

Education, the great mumbo-jumbo and fraud of the age, purports to equip us to live, and is prescribed as a universal remedy for everything, from juvenile delinquency to premature senility. For the most part, it only serves to enlarge stupidity, inflate conceit, enhance credulity, and put those subjected to it at the mercy of brainwashers with printing presses, radio, and television at their disposal. I have seen pictures of huge, ungainly, prehistoric monsters who developed such a weight of protective shell that they sank under its burden and became extinct. Our civilization likewise is sinking under the burden of its own wealth, and the necessity to consume it; of its own happiness, and the necessity to provide and sustain the fantasies that embody it; of its own security, and the ever more fabulously destructive nuclear devices considered essential to it. Thus burdened, it, too, may well soon become extinct. As this fact sinks into the collective consciousness, the resort to drugs, dreams, fantasies, and other escapist devices, particularly sex, becomes ever more marked.

Living thus in the twilight of a spent civilization, amidst its ludicrous and frightening shadows, what is there to believe? Curiously enough, these twilight circumstances provide a setting in which, as it seems to me, the purpose that lies behind them stands out with particular clarity. As human love only shines in all its splendor when the last tiny glimmer of desire has been extinguished, so we have to make the world a wilderness to find God in it. The meaning of the universe lies beyond history, as love lies beyond desire. That meaning shines forth in moments of illumination (which come and go so unaccountably; though, I am thankful to say, never quite ceasing —a sound as of music, far, far away, and drowned by other, more tumultuous noises, but still to be faintly and fitfully heard) with an inconceivable clarity and luminosity. It breaks like a crystalline dawn out of darkness, and the deeper the darkness the more crystalline the dawn.

Let me express it, as I have often thought of it, in terms of a stage. In the middle is the workaday world where we live our daily lives, earning a living, reading newspapers, exchanging money, recording votes, chattering and eating and desiring. I call this the Café Limbo. On the left of the stage is an area of darkness, within which shapes and movements can be faintly discerned and inconclusive noises heard; sounds and sweet airs that, as on Caliban's island, give delight and hurt not. I call this Life. The right of the stage is bright with arc lamps, like a television studio. This is where history is unfolded and news is made; this is where we live our public, collective lives, seat and unseat rulers, declare wars and negotiate peace, glow with patriotism and get carried away with revolutionary zeal, enact laws, declaim rhetoric, swear eternal passion, and sink into abysses of desolation. I call this the Legend.

Across this triple stage, between Life, the Café Limbo, and the Legend, a drama is endlessly presented. Two forces shape the play: the Imagination, which belongs to Life, and the Will, which belongs to the Legend. Out of the Imagination comes love, understanding, goodness, self-abnegation; every true synthesis ever grasped or to be grasped. Out of the Will comes lust, hatred, cupidity, adulation, power, oratory; every false antithesis ever propounded or to be propounded. Those who belong exclusively or predominantly to Life are saints, mystics, and artists. In extreme cases

—Christ, for instance—they have to be killed. (This is superbly explained in the famous Grand Inquisitor passage in *The Brothers Karamazov,* Dostoevsky being, like Pascal, of the small, sublime band.) Those who belong exclusively or predominantly to the Legend are power-maniacs, rulers, heroes, demagogues, and liberators. In extreme cases—Hitler, for instance —they bring about their own destruction. In Life there is suffering, deprivation, and sanity; in the Legend, happiness, abundance, and madness.

Most of us spend the greater part of our time in the Café Limbo, casting an occasional glance in the direction of Life, and more than an occasional one in the direction of the Legend. Laughter is our best recourse, with the bar to provide a fillip as and when required. The Café Limbo is licensed. When a character passes from the Legend into Life, he brings some of the light with him, shining like a glowworm, until gradually the light subsides and goes out, swallowed up in the darkness of Life.

This same pattern may be traced more particularly and tragically in a single countenance, as anyone will be aware who has had occasion to watch over a loved face hovering between sanity and madness. (And many have; for as we abolish the ills and pains of the flesh we multiply those of the mind. By the time men are finally delivered from disease and decay —all pasteurized, their genes counted and rearranged, fitted with new, replaceable, plastic organs, able to eat, copulate, and perform other physical functions innocuously and hygienically as and when desired—they will all be mad, and the world one huge psychiatric ward.) You study the loved, distracted face as a scholar might study some ancient manuscript, looking for a key to its incomprehensibility. What you see is a fight to the death between the Will and the Imagination. If the former wins, then the flickering light will be put out forever; if the latter, it will shine again, to burn with a steady radiance, and you can cry out from a full heart: "Oh, beloved, you have come back to me."

I am well aware that, psychiatrically speaking, this is nonsensical. Yet I believe it. I see these two forces struggling for mastery in each individual soul; in mine, in all men's; in each collectivity, throughout our earth and throughout the immeasurable universe. One is of darkness and one of light; one wants to drag us down into the dark trough to rut and gorge there, and the other to raise us up into the azure sky, beyond appetite, where love is all-embracing, all-encompassing, and the dark confusion of life sorts itself out, like an orderly, smiling countryside suddenly glimpsed from a high hill as the mists disperse in the sun's light and warmth. One is the Devil and the other God. I have known both, and I believe in both.

For us Western Europeans, the Christian religion has expressed this ancient and, as I consider, obvious dichotomy in terms of breath-taking simplicity and sublimity. It was not the first word on the subject, nor will it be the last; but it is still *our* word. I accept it. I believe, as is written in the New Testament; if we would save our lives we must lose them; we cannot live by bread alone; we must die in the flesh to be reborn in the spirit; the flesh lusts contrary to the spirit and the spirit contrary to the flesh; God cannot see a sparrow fall to the ground without concern, and has counted the hairs of each head, so that all that lives deserves our respect and reverence, and no one man can conceivably be more important, of greater significance, or in any way more deserving of consideration than any other. God is our father, we are his children and so one family, brothers and sisters together.

It is true that these basic propositions of Christianity have got cluttered up with dogma of various kinds that I find often incomprehensible, irrelevant, and even repugnant. All the same, I should be proud and happy to be able to call myself a Christian; to dare to measure myself against that sublimely high standard of human values and human behavior. In this I take comfort from another saying of Pascal, thrown out like a lifeline to all sceptical minds throughout the ages: whoever looks for God has found him.

At its most obscurantist and debased, the Christian position still seems to me preferable to any scientific-materialist one, however cogent and enlightened. The evangelist with his lurid tract calling upon me to repent, for the Day of Judgment is at hand, is a burning and shining light compared with the eugenist who claims the right to decide in his broiler-house mind which lives should be protracted and which must be put out, or with the colporteurs of sterility who so complacently and self-righteously display their assortment of contraceptives to the so-called "backward" peoples of the world as our civilization's noblest achievement and most precious gift.

The absurdities of the kingdom of heaven, as conceived in the minds of simple believers, are obvious enough—pearly gates, angelic choirs, golden crowns, and shining raiment. But what are we to think of the sheer imbecility of the kingdom of heaven on earth, as envisaged and recommended by the most authoritative and powerful voices of our time? Wealth increasing forevermore, and its beneficiaries, rich in time-payment merchandise, stupefied with television and with sex, comprehensively educated, told by Professor Hoyle[o] how the world began and by Bertrand Russell how it will end; venturing forth on the broad highways, three lanes a side, with laybys to rest in and birth pills to keep them *intacta*,[o] if not *virgo*,[o] blood spattering the Tarmac as an extra thrill; heaven lying about them in the supermarket, the rainbow ending in the nearest bingo hall, leisure burgeoning out in multitudinous shining aerials rising like dreaming spires into the sky; happiness in as many colors as there are pills—green and yellow and blue and

Professor Hoyle Fred Hoyle, astronomer and author of *The Nature of the Universe* (1950).
intacta uninjured, undefiled (Latin).
virgo virgin (Latin).

red and shining white; many mansions, mansions of light and chromium, climbing ever upwards. This kingdom, surely, can only be for posterity an unending source of wry derision—always assuming there is to be any posterity. The backdrop, after all, is the mushroom cloud; as the Gadarene herd[0] frisk and frolic, they draw ever nearer to the edge of the precipice.

I recognize, of course, that this statement of belief is partly governed by the circumstance that I am old, and in at most a decade or so, will be dead. In earlier years I should doubtless have expressed things differently. Now the prospect of death overshadows all others. I am like a man on a sea voyage nearing his destination. When I embarked I worried about having a cabin with a porthole, whether I should be asked to sit at the captain's table, who were the more attractive and important passengers. All such considerations become pointless when I shall so soon be disembarking.

As I do not believe that earthly life can bring any lasting satisfaction, the prospect of death holds no terrors. Those saints who pronounced themselves in love with death displayed, I consider, the best of sense, not a Freudian death wish. The world that I shall soon be leaving seems more than ever beautiful; especially its remoter parts, grass and trees and sea and rivers and little streams and sloping hills, where the image of eternity is more clearly stamped than among streets and houses. Those I love I can love even more, since I have nothing to ask of them but their love; the passion to accumulate possessions, or to be noticed and important, is too evidently absurd to be any longer entertained.

A sense of how extraordinarily happy I have been, and of enormous gratitude to my creator, overwhelms me often. I believe with a passionate, unshakable conviction that in all circumstances and at all times life is a blessed gift; that the spirit that animates it is one of love, not hate or indifference, of light, not darkness, of creativity, not destruction, of order, not chaos; that, since all life—men, creatures, plants, as well as insensate matter—and all that is known about it, now and henceforth, have been benevolently, not malevolently, conceived, when the eyes see no more and the mind thinks no more, and this hand now writing is inert, whatever lies beyond will similarly be benevolently, not malevolently or indifferently, conceived. If it is nothing, then for nothingness I offer thanks; if another mode of existence, with this old, worn-out husk of a body left behind, like a butterfly extricating itself from its chrysalis, and this floundering, muddled mind, now at best seeing through a glass darkly, given a longer range and a new precision, then for that likewise I offer thanks.

Gadarene herd   Herd of swine described in Matthew 8:28–34; possessed by devils, they "ran violently down a steep place into the sea, and perished in the waters."

Thomas Merton

Thomas Merton (1915–1968) was born in France and attended school there and in England. In 1933 he entered Cambridge, where he remembers "breaking my neck trying to get everything out of life that you can get out of it when you are 18. [And] I ran with a pack of hearties who wore multicolored scarves around their necks and would have barked all night. . . ." He refers to those years as his "mental Pompeii," filled with frenetic, empty activity.

Merton then crossed the ocean to attend Columbia University, where he received his B.A. and M.A. degrees; he also taught English, reviewed books, joined a Young Communist Group, and worked in a Harlem settlement house. It was during this time that he attended his first Mass, described below. In 1938 he converted to Roman Catholicism and in 1941 became a Trappist (Cistercian) Monk. He made solemn vows in 1947 and was ordained a priest in 1949.

The vows of a Trappist Monk include the vow of silence, but Merton's taste for solitude was so deep that he became a hermit even in his own monastery, the Abbey of Gethsemani in Kentucky; he lived in a cabin in the woods, where he chopped his own wood and received no visitors. He walked to the monastery only to say Mass and eat his one meal. Yet he continued to study and write. He was an accomplished poet and essayist, as well as a translator and editor. Merton himself felt and said that he had "written too much and published too much." He was dismayed that his early work was sometimes labeled "inspirational" or "spiritual," but he continued to stand behind his "strong criticism of prevailing trends toward global war, totalism, racism, spiritual inertia and crass materialism," and of the "volatile idealism" that is quick to shift ground when the game gets rough. Among his more than thirty volumes are *Selected Poems* (1959), *Gandhi on Non-Violence* (1965), *Conjectures of a Guilty Bystander* (1966), and *Zen and the Birds of Appetite* (1968).

Merton's autobiography, *The Seven Storey Mountain* (1948), tells of his early years of contradiction and confusion with their implied hunger for community and communion, and his gradual awakening to grace. From it, we reprint the passage below.

First Mass, from
The Seven Storey Mountain

. . . . By the time I was ready to begin the actual writing of my thesis, that is, around the beginning of September 1938, the groundwork of conversion was more or less complete. And how easily and sweetly it had all been done, with all the external graces that had been arranged, along my path, by the kind Providence of God! It had taken little more than a year and a half, counting from the time I read Gilson's *The Spirit of Medieval Philosophy* to bring me up from an "atheist"—as I considered myself— to one who accepted all the full range and possibilities of religious experience right up to the highest degree of glory.

I not only accepted all this, intellectually, but now I began to desire it. And not only did I begin to desire it, but I began to do so efficaciously: I began to want to take the necessary means to achieve this union, this peace. I began to desire to dedicate my life to God, to His service. The notion was still vague and obscure, and it was ludicrously impractical in the sense that I was already dreaming of mystical union when I did not even keep the simplest rudiments of the moral law. But nevertheless I was convinced of the reality of the goal, and confident that it could be achieved: and whatever element of presumption was in this confidence I am sure God excused, in His mercy, because of my stupidity and helplessness, and because I was really beginning to be ready to do whatever I thought He wanted me to do to bring me to Him.

But, oh, how blind and weak and sick I was, although I thought I saw where I was going, and half understood the way! How deluded we sometimes are by the clear notions we get out of books. They make us think that we really understand things of which we have no practical knowledge at all. I remember how learnedly and enthusiastically I could talk for hours about mysticism and the experimental knowledge of God, and all the while I was stoking the fires of the argument with Scotch and soda.

That was the way it turned out that Labor Day, for instance. I went to Philadelphia with Joe Roberts, who had a room in the same house as I, and who had been through all the battles on the Fourth Floor of John Jay for the past four years. He had graduated and was working on some trade magazine about women's hats. All one night we sat, with a friend of his, in a big dark roadhouse outside of Philadelphia, arguing and arguing about mysticism, and smoking more and more cigarettes and gradually getting drunk. Eventually, filled with enthusiasm for the purity of heart which begets the vision of God, I went on with them into the city, after the closing of the bars, to a big speak-easy where we completed the work of getting plastered.

My internal contradictions were resolving themselves out, indeed, but still only on the plane of theory, not of practice: not for lack of goodwill, but because I was still so completely chained and fettered by my sins and my attachments.

I think that if there is one truth that people need to learn, in the world, especially today, it is this: the intellect is only theoretically independent of desire and appetite in ordinary, actual practice. It is constantly being blinded and perverted by the ends and aims of passion, and the evidence it presents to us with such a show of impartiality and objectivity is fraught with interest and propaganda. We have become marvelous at self-delusion; all the more so, because we have gone to such trouble to convince ourselves of our own absolute infallibility. The desire of the flesh—and by that I mean not only sinful desires, but even the ordinary, normal appetites for comfort and ease and human respect, are fruitful sources of every kind of error and misjudgement, and because we have these yearnings in us, our intellects (which, if they operated all alone in a vacuum, would indeed register with pure impartiality what they saw) present to us everything distorted and accommodated to the norms of our desire.

And therefore, even when we are acting with the best of intentions, and imagine that we are doing great good, we may be actually doing tremendous material harm and contradicting all our good intentions. There are ways that seem to men to be good, the end whereof is in the depths of hell.

The only answer to the problem is grace, grace, docility to grace. I was still in the precarious position of being my own guide and my own interpreter of grace. It is a wonder I ever got to the harbor at all!

Sometime in August, I finally answered an impulsion that had been working on me for a long time. Every Sunday, I had been going out on Long Island to spend the day with the same girl who had brought me back in such a hurry from Lax's town Olean. But every week, as Sunday came around, I was filled with a growing desire to stay in the city and go to some kind of a church.

At first, I had vaguely thought I might try to find some Quakers, and go and sit with them. There still remained in me something of the favorable notion about Quakers that I had picked up as a child, and which the reading of William Penn had not been able to overcome.

But, naturally enough, with the work I was doing in the library, a stronger drive began to assert itself, and I was drawn much more imperatively to the Catholic Church. Finally the urge became so strong that I could not resist it. I called up my girl and told her that I was not coming out that week-end, and made up my mind to go to Mass for the first time in my life.

The first time in my life! That was true. I had lived for several years on the continent, I had been to Rome, I had been in and out of a thousand Catholic cathedrals and churches, and yet I had never heard Mass. If anything had ever been going on in the churches I visited, I had always fled, in wild Protestant panic.

I will not easily forget how I felt that day. First, there was this sweet, strong, gentle, clean urge in me which said: "Go to Mass! Go to Mass!" It was something quite new and strange, this voice that seemed to prompt me, this firm, growing interior conviction of what I needed to do. It had a suavity, a simplicity about it that I could not easily account for. And when I gave in to it, it did not exult over me, and trample me down in its raging haste to land on its prey, but it carried me forward serenely and with purposeful direction.

That does not mean that my emotions yielded to it altogether quietly. I was really still a little afraid to go to a Catholic church of set purpose, with all the other people, and dispose myself in a pew, and lay myself open to the mysterious perils of that strange and powerful thing they called their "Mass."

God made it a very beautiful Sunday. And since it was the first time I had ever really spent a sober Sunday in New York, I was surprised at the clean, quiet atmosphere of the empty streets uptown. The sun was blazing bright. At the end of the street, as I came out the front door, I could see a burst of green, and the blue river and the hills of Jersey on the other side.

Broadway was empty. A solitary trolley came speeding down in front of Barnard College and past the School of Journalism. Then, from the high, grey, expensive tower of the Rockefeller Church, huge bells began to boom. It served very well for the eleven o'clock Mass at the little brick Church of Corpus Christi, hidden behind Teachers College on 121st Street.

How bright the little building seemed. Indeed, it was quite new. The sun shone on the clean bricks. People were going in the wide open door, into the cool darkness and, all at once, all the churches of Italy and France came back to me. The richness and fulness of the atmosphere of Catholicism that I had not been able to avoid apprehending and loving as a child, came back to me with a rush: but now I was to enter into it fully for the first time. So far, I had known nothing but the outward surface.

It was a gay, clean church, with big plain windows and white columns and pilasters and a well-lighted, simple sanctuary. Its style was a trifle eclectic, but much less perverted with incongruities than the average Catholic church in America. It had a kind of a seventeenth-century, oratorian character about it, though with a sort of American colonial tinge of simplicity. The blend was effective and original: but although all this affected me, without my thinking about it, the thing that impressed me most was that the place was full, absolutely full. It was full not only of old ladies and broken-down gentlemen with one foot in the grave, but of men and women and children young and old—especially young: people of all classes, and all ranks on a solid foundation of workingmen and -women and their families.

I found a place that I hoped would be obscure, over on one side, in the back, and went to it without genuflecting, and knelt down. As I knelt, the first thing I noticed was a young girl, very pretty too, perhaps fifteen or sixteen, kneeling straight up and praying quite seriously. I was very much impressed to see that someone who was young and beautiful could with such simplicity make prayer the real and serious and principal reason for going to church. She was clearly kneeling that way because she meant it, not in order to show off, and she was praying with an absorption which, though not the deep recollection of a saint, was serious enough to show that she was not thinking at all about the other people who were there.

What a revelation it was, to discover so many ordinary people in a place together, more conscious of God than of one another: not there to show off their hats or their clothes, but to pray, or at least to fulfil a religious obligation, not a human one. For even those who might have been there for no better motive than that they were obliged to be, were at least free from any of the self-conscious and human constraint which is never absent from a Protestant church where people are definitely gathered together as people, as neighbors, and always have at least half an eye for one another, if not all of both eyes.

Since it was summer time, the eleven o'clock Mass was a Low Mass: but I had not come expecting to hear music. Before I knew it, the priest was in the sanctuary with the two altar boys, and was busy at the altar with something or other which I could not see very well, but the people were praying by themselves, and I was engrossed and absorbed in the thing as a whole: the business at the altar and the presence of the people. And still I had not got rid of my fear. Seeing the late-comers hastily genuflecting before entering the pew, I realised my omission, and got the idea that people had spotted me for a pagan and were just waiting for me to miss a few more genuflections before throwing me out or, at least, giving me looks of reproof.

Soon we all stood up. I did not know what it was for. The priest was at the other end of the altar, and, as I afterwards learned, he was reading the Gospel. And then the next thing I knew there was someone in the pulpit.

It was a young priest, perhaps not much over thirty-three or -four years old. His face was rather ascetic and thin, and its asceticism was heightened with a note of intellectuality by his horn-rimmed glasses, although he was only one of the assistants, and he did not consider himself an intellectual, nor did anyone else apparently consider him so. But anyway, that was the impression he made on me: and his sermon, which was simple enough, did not belie it.

It was not long: but to me it was very interesting to hear this young man quietly telling the people in language that was plain, yet tinged with scholastic terminology, about a point in Catholic Doctrine. How clear and solid the doctrine was: for behind those words you felt the full force not only of Scripture but of centuries of a unified and continuous and consistent tradition. And above all, it was a vital tradition: there was nothing studied or antique about it. These words, this terminology, this doctrine, and these convictions fell from the lips of the young priest as something that were most intimately part of his own life. What was more, I sensed that the people were familiar with it all, and that it was also, in due proportion, part of their life also: it was just as much integrated into their spiritual organism as the air they breathed or the food they ate worked in to their blood and flesh.

What was he saying? That Christ was the Son of God. That, in Him, the Second Person of the Holy Trinity, God, had assumed a Human Nature, a Human Body and Soul, and had taken Flesh and dwelt amongst us, full of grace and truth: and that this Man, Whom men called the Christ, was

God. He was both Man and God: two Natures hypostatically united in one Person or suppositum, one individual Who was a Divine Person, having assumed to Himself a Human Nature. And His works were the works of God: His acts were the acts of God. He loved us: God, and walked among us: God, and died for us on the Cross, God of God, Light of Light, True God of True God.

Jesus Christ was not simply a man, a good man, a great man, the greatest prophet, a wonderful healer, a saint: He was something that made all such trivial words pale into irrelevance. He was God. But nevertheless He was not merely a spirit without a true body, God hiding under a visionary body: He was also truly a Man, born of the Flesh of the Most Pure Virgin, formed of her Flesh by the Holy Spirit. And what He did, in that Flesh, on earth, He did not only as Man but as God. He loved us as God, He suffered and died for us, God.

And how did we know? Because it was revealed to us in the Scriptures and confirmed by the teaching of the Church and of the powerful unanimity of Catholic Tradition from the First Apostles, from the first Popes and the early Fathers, on down through the Doctors of the Church and the great scholastics, to our own day. *De Fide Divina.* If you believed it, you would receive light to grasp it, to understand it in some measure. If you did not believe it, you would never understand: it would never be anything but scandal or folly.

And no one can believe these things merely by wanting to, of his own volition. Unless he receive grace, an actual light and impulsion of the mind and will from God, he cannot even make an act of living faith. It is God Who gives us faith, and no one cometh to Christ unless the Father draweth him.

I wonder what would have happened in my life if I had been given this grace in the days when I had almost discovered the Divinity of Christ in the ancient mosaics of the churches of Rome. What scores of self-murdering and Christ-murdering sins would have been avoided—all the filth I had plastered upon His image in my soul during those last five years that I had been scourging and crucifying God within me?

It is easy to say, after it all, that God had probably foreseen my infidelities and had never given me the grace in those days because He saw how I would waste and despise it: and perhaps that rejection would have been my ruin. For there is no doubt that one of the reasons why grace is not given to souls is because they have so hardened their wills in greed and cruelty and selfishness that their refusal of it would only harden them more. . . . But now I had been beaten into the semblance of some kind of humility by misery and confusion and perplexity and secret, interior fear, and my ploughed soul was better ground for the reception of good seed.

The sermon was what I most needed to hear that day. When the Mass of the Catechumens was over, I, who was not even a catechumen, but only a blind and deaf and dumb pagan as weak and dirty as anything that ever came out of the darkness of Imperial Rome or Corinth or Ephesus, was not able to understand anything else.

It all became completely mysterious when the attention was refocused on the altar. When the silence grew more and more profound, and little bells began to ring, I got scared again and, finally, genuflecting hastily on my left knee, I hurried out of the church in the middle of the most important part of the Mass. But it was just as well. In a way, I suppose I was responding to a kind of liturgical instinct that told me I did not belong there for the celebration of the Mysteries as such. I had no idea what took place in them: but the fact was that Christ, God, would be visibly present on the altar in the Sacred Species. And although He was there, yes, for love of me: yet He was there in His power and His might, and what was I? What was on my soul? What was I in His sight?

It was liturgically fitting that I should kick myself out at the end of the Mass of the Catechumens, when the ordained *ostiarii* should have been there to do it. Anyway, it was done.

Now I walked leisurely down Broadway in the sun, and my eyes looked about me at a new world. I could not understand what it was that had happened to make me so happy, why I was so much at peace, so content with life for I was not yet used to the clean savor that comes with an actual grace—indeed, there was no impossibility in a person's hearing and believing such a sermon and being justified, that is, receiving sanctifying grace in his soul as a habit, and beginning, from that moment, to live the divine and supernatural life for good and all. But that is something I will not speculate about.

All I know is that I walked in a new world. Even the ugly buildings of Columbia were transfigured in it, and everywhere was peace in these streets designed for violence and noise. Sitting outside the gloomy little Childs restaurant at 111th Street, behind the dirty, boxed bushes, and eating breakfast, was like sitting in the Elysian Fields.

Viktor E. Frankl

Viktor E. Frankl, born in Vienna in 1905, is a psychiatrist and professor of neurology and psychiatry at the University of Vienna. He is best known as the founder of logotherapy, a form of psychotherapy that relates neurotic suffering to a failure to find meaning for one's life. He has lectured at more than 100 colleges and universities in the United States and has written extensively on psychiatry, existentialism, and logotherapy.

Frankl's ideas emerged from his own long experiences in Nazi concentration camps. He and his fellow prisoners suffered the bestial conditions of the

camps, the constant hunger, the humiliations of forced labor, always with fear.
Each prisoner knew that those too weak to work were doomed to the
crematorium. Frankl's mother, father, brother, and his wife died in camps or
were sent to the gas ovens. Frankl was one of the survivors. "It is easy," he
writes, "for the outsider to get the wrong conception of camp life, a conception mingled with sentiment and pity. Little does he know of the hard fight
for existence which raged among the prisoners. This was an unrelenting struggle for daily bread and for life itself, for one's own sake or for that of a good
friend." In his book *Man's Search for Meaning* (1959), he describes his experiences in the camps and then presents the basic concepts of logotherapy. We
print here a self-contained section of Part 1, translated by Ilse Lasch.

from Man's Search for Meaning

In spite of all the enforced physical and mental primitiveness of the life
in a concentration camp, it was possible for spiritual life to deepen. Sensitive people who were used to a rich intellectual life may have suffered
much pain (they were often of a delicate constitution), but the damage to
their inner selves was less. They were able to retreat from their terrible
surroundings to a life of inner riches and spiritual freedom. Only in this
way can one explain the apparent paradox that some prisoners of a less
hardy make-up often seemed to survive camp life better than did those
of a robust nature. In order to make myself clear, I am forced to fall back
on personal experience. Let me tell what happened on those early mornings when we had to march to our work site.

There were shouted commands: "Detachment, forward march! Left-2-
3-4! Left-2-3-4! Left-2-3-4! Left-2-3-4! First man about, left and left and left
and left! Caps off!" These words sound in my ears even now. At the order
"Caps off!" we passed the gate of the camp, and searchlights were trained
upon us. Whoever did not march smartly got a kick. And worse off was the
man who, because of the cold, had pulled his cap back over his ears before
permission was given.

We stumbled on in the darkness, over big stones and through large
puddles, along the one road leading from the camp. The accompanying
guards kept shouting at us and driving us with the butts of their rifles.
Anyone with very sore feet supported himself on his neighbor's arm.
Hardly a word was spoken; the icy wind did not encourage talk. Hiding
his mouth behind his upturned collar, the man marching next to me
whispered suddenly: "If our wives could see us now! I do hope they are
better off in their camps and don't know what is happening to us."

That brought thoughts of my own wife to mind. And as we stumbled on
for miles, slipping on icy spots, supporting each other time and again,
dragging one another up and onward, nothing was said, but we both knew:

each of us was thinking of his wife. Occasionally I looked at the sky, where the stars were fading and the pink light of the morning was beginning to spread behind a dark bank of clouds. But my mind clung to my wife's image, imagining it with an uncanny acuteness. I heard her answering me, saw her smile, her frank and encouraging look. Real or not, her look was then more luminous than the sun which was beginning to rise.

A thought transfixed me: for the first time in my life I saw the truth as it is set into song by so many poets, proclaimed as the final wisdom by so many thinkers. The truth—that love is the ultimate and the highest goal to which man can aspire. Then I grasped the meaning of the greatest secret that human poetry and human thought and belief have to impart: *The salvation of man is through love and in love.* I understood how a man who has nothing left in this world still may know bliss, be it only for a brief moment, in the contemplation of his beloved. In a position of utter desolation, when man cannot express himself in positive action, when his only achievement may consist in enduring his sufferings in the right way—an honorable way—in such a position man can, through loving contemplation of the image he carries of his beloved, achieve fulfillment. For the first time in my life I was able to understand the meaning of the words, "The angels are lost in perpetual contemplation of an infinite glory."

In front of me a man stumbled and those following him fell on top of him. The guard rushed over and used his whip on them all. Thus my thoughts were interrupted for a few minutes. But soon my soul found its way back from the prisoner's existence to another world, and I resumed talk with my loved one: I asked her questions, and she answered; she questioned me in return, and I answered.

"Stop!" We had arrived at our work site. Everybody rushed into the dark hut in the hope of getting a fairly decent tool. Each prisoner got a spade or a pickax.

"Can't you hurry up, you pigs?" Soon we had resumed the previous day's positions in the ditch. The frozen ground cracked under the point of the pickaxes, and sparks flew. The men were silent, their brains numb.

My mind still clung to the image of my wife. A thought crossed my mind: I didn't even know if she were still alive. I knew only one thing—which I have learned well by now: Love goes very far beyond the physical person of the beloved. It finds its deepest meaning in his spiritual being, his inner self. Whether or not he is actually present, whether or not he is still alive at all, ceases somehow to be of importance.

I did not know whether my wife was alive, and I had no means of finding out (during all my prison life there was no outgoing or incoming mail); but at that moment it ceased to matter. There was no need for me to know; nothing could touch the strength of my love, my thoughts, and the image of my beloved. Had I known then that my wife was dead, I think that I would still have given myself, undisturbed by that knowledge, to the contemplation of her image, and that my mental conversation with her would have been just as vivid and just as satisfying. "Set me like a seal upon thy heart, love is as strong as death."

This intensification of inner life helped the prisoner find a refuge from the emptiness, desolation and spiritual poverty of his existence, by letting him escape into the past. When given free rein, his imagination played with past events, often not important ones, but minor happenings and trifling things. His nostalgic memory glorified them and they assumed a strange character. Their world and their existence seemed very distant and the spirit reached out for them longingly: In my mind I took bus rides, unlocked the front door of my apartment, answered my telephone, switched on the electric lights. Our thoughts often centered on such details, and these memories could move one to tears.

As the inner life of the prisoner tended to become more intense, he also experienced the beauty of art and nature as never before. Under their influence he sometimes even forgot his own frightful circumstances. If someone had seen our faces on the journey from Auschwitz to a Bavarian camp as we beheld the mountains of Salzburg with their summits glowing in the sunset, through the little barred windows of the prison carriage, he would never have believed that those were the faces of men who had given up all hope of life and liberty. Despite that factor—or maybe because of it—we were carried away by nature's beauty, which we had missed for so long.

In camp, too, a man might draw the attention of a comrade working next to him to a nice view of the setting sun shining through the tall trees of the Bavarian woods (as in the famous water color by Dürer), the same woods in which we had built an enormous, hidden munitions plant. One evening, when we were already resting on the floor of our hut, dead tired, soup bowls in hand, a fellow prisoner rushed in and asked us to run out to the assembly grounds and see the wonderful sunset. Standing outside we saw sinister clouds glowing in the west and the whole sky alive with clouds of ever-changing shapes and colors, from steel blue to blood red. The desolate gray mud huts provided a sharp contrast, while the puddles on the muddy ground reflected the glowing sky. Then, after minutes of moving silence, one prisoner said to another, "How beautiful the world *could* be!"

Another time we were at work in a trench. The dawn was gray around us; gray was the sky above; gray the snow in the pale light of dawn; gray the rags in which my fellow prisoners were clad, and gray their faces. I was again conversing silently with my wife, or perhaps I was struggling to find the *reason* for my sufferings, my slow dying. In a last violent protest against the hopelessness of imminent death, I sensed my spirit piercing through the enveloping gloom. I felt it transcend that hopeless, meaningless world, and from somewhere I heard a victorious "Yes" in answer to my question of the existence of an ultimate purpose. At that moment a light was lit in a distant farmhouse, which stood on the horizon as if painted there, in the midst of the miserable gray of a dawning morning in Bavaria. *"Et lux in tenebris lucet"*—and the light shineth in the darkness. For hours I stood hacking at the icy ground. The guard passed by, insulting me, and once again I communed with my beloved. More and more I felt that she was present, that she was with me; I had the feeling that I was able to touch her, able to stretch out my hand and grasp hers. The feeling was very strong: she was *there*. Then, at that very moment, a bird flew down silently and perched just in front of me, on the heap of soil which I had dug up from the ditch, and looked steadily at me.

On Death and Dying

The fear of death has found its way into the mythology of nearly every culture. Some admit death, viewing it as part of life, while others try to hide it. Paradoxically, though, the more we hide death, the more we tend to fear it. Today, "the more we are making advancements in science, the more we seem to fear and deny the reality of death. How is this possible?" Elisabeth Kübler-Ross asks this question in response to our growing tendency to separate the dying person from familiar surroundings, to become preoccupied with the technical aspects of the dying body, and to lose sight of the human needs of the dying person. "Is the reason for this increasingly mechanical, depersonalized approach," she wonders, "our own defensiveness?" How many of us, we might ask, have actually seen a dying or dead person?

Paul Jacobs' satire demonstrates the way in which one man, at least, by denying the existence of death, transforms it into a money-making industry. Forest Lawn is not a cemetery but a "Memorial Park" in which to begin a "happy Eternal Life." J. H. Plumb, too, talks of Hubert Eaton's Forest Lawn, but looking at it in a historical context, he has a different attitude. "The urge to obliterate death," he says, "is the urge to extend life." Alice Walker's short story deals with death in the context of loving and does it in a way that exhibits the practical truthfulness of first-rate fiction.

Elisabeth Kübler-Ross

Dr. Elisabeth Kübler-Ross, a psychiatrist, author, and lecturer, has had important influence on our ideas about the care of dying patients and their families. She has said that "whoever has seen the horrifying appearance of the postwar European concentration camps" would share her preoccupation with death. Born in Zurich in 1926, she did relief work in postwar Europe and studied medicine at the University of Zurich. After becoming an M.D. in 1957, she practiced medicine in Switzerland before coming to the United States to do her internship and residency in psychiatry.

Dr. Kübler-Ross, who holds dual American and Swiss citizenship, has taught medicine at the University of Colorado and the University of Chicago, where she instituted a teaching seminar on conversations with the terminally ill. More recently she has been chairman of the board of Shanti-Nilaya near San Diego, a controversial therapeutic and teaching center for dying patients and their families.

Her books include *On Death and Dying* (1969), the first chapter of which is reprinted here; *Questions and Answers on Death and Dying* (1972); *Death: The Final Stage* (1974); *To Live Until We Say Goodbye* (1978); *Working It Through* (1981); *Living with Death and Dying* (1981); and *Remember the Secret* (1981). In addition she has written for professional journals and has contributed chapters to a number of books.

On the Fear of Death

> *Let me not pray to be sheltered from*
> *dangers but to be fearless in facing*
> *them.*
> *Let me not beg for the stilling of*
> *my pain but for the heart to conquer it.*
> *Let me not look for allies in life's*
> *battlefield but to my own strength.*
> *Let me not crave in anxious fear to*
> *be saved but hope for the patience to*
> *win my freedom.*
> *Grant me that I may not be a*
> *coward, feeling your mercy in my*
> *success alone; but let me find the grasp*
> *of your hand in my failure.*

> —RABINDRANATH TAGORE,
> *Fruit-Gathering*

Epidemics have taken a great toll of lives in past generations. Death in infancy and early childhood was frequent and there were few families who didn't lose a member of the family at an early age. Medicine has changed greatly in the last decades. Widespread vaccinations have practically eradicated many illnesses, at least in western Europe and the United States. The use of chemotherapy, especially the antibiotics, has contributed to an ever decreasing number of fatalities in infectious diseases. Better child care and education has effected a low morbidity and mortality among children. The many diseases that have taken an impressive toll among the young and middle-aged have been conquered. The number of old people is on the rise, and with this fact come the number of people with malignancies and chronic diseases associated more with old age.

Pediatricians have less work with acute and life-threatening situations as they have an ever increasing number of patients with psychosomatic disturbances and adjustment and behavior problems. Physicians have more people in their waiting rooms with emotional problems than they have ever had before, but they also have more elderly patients who not only try to live with their decreased physical abilities and limitations but who also face loneliness and isolation with all its pains and anguish. The majority of these people are not seen by a psychiatrist. Their needs have to be elicited and gratified by other professional people, for instance, chaplains and social workers. It is for them that I am trying to outline the changes that have taken place in the last few decades, changes that are ultimately responsible for the increased fear of death, the rising number of emotional problems, and the greater need for understanding of and coping with the problems of death and dying.

When we look back in time and study old cultures and people, we are impressed that death has always been distasteful to man and will probably always be. From a psychiatrist's point of view this is very understandable and can perhaps best be explained by our basic knowledge that, in our unconscious, death is never possible in regard to ourselves. It is inconceivable for our unconscious to imagine an actual ending of our own life here on earth, and if this life of ours has to end, the ending is always attributed to a malicious intervention from the outside by someone else. In simple terms, in our unconscious mind we can only be killed; it is inconceivable to die of a natural cause or of old age. Therefore death in itself is associated with a bad act, a frightening happening, something that in itself calls for retribution and punishment.

One is wise to remember these fundamental facts as they are essential in understanding some of the most important, otherwise unintelligible communications of our patients.

The second fact that we have to comprehend is that in our unconscious mind we cannot distinguish between a wish and a deed. We are all aware of some of our illogical dreams in which two completely opposite statements can exist side by side—very acceptable in our dreams but unthinkable and illogical in our wakening state. Just as our unconscious mind cannot differentiate between the wish to kill somebody in anger and the act of having done so, the young child is unable to make this distinction.

The child who angrily wishes his mother to drop dead for not having gratified his needs will be traumatized greatly by the actual death of his mother—even if this event is not linked closely in time with his destructive wishes. He will always take part or the whole blame for the loss of his mother. He will always say to himself—rarely to others—"I did it, I am responsible, I was bad, therefore Mommy left me." It is well to remember that the child will react in the same manner if he loses a parent by divorce, separation, or desertion. Death is often seen by a child as an impermanent thing and has therefore little distinction from a divorce in which he may have an opportunity to see a parent again.

Many a parent will remember remarks of their children such as, "I will bury my doggy now and next spring when the flowers come up again, he will get up." Maybe it was the same wish that motivated the ancient Egyptians to supply their dead with food and goods to keep them happy and the old American Indians to bury their relatives with their belongings.

When we grow older and begin to realize that our omnipotence is really not so omnipotent, that our strongest wishes are not powerful enough to make the impossible possible, the fear that we have contributed to the death of a loved one diminishes—and with it the guilt. The fear remains diminished, however, only so long as it is not challenged too strongly. Its vestiges can be seen daily in hospital corridors and in people associated with the bereaved.

A husband and wife may have been fighting for years, but when the partner dies, the survivor will pull his hair, whine and cry louder and beat his chest in regret, fear and anguish, and will hence fear his own death more than before, still believing in the law of talion—an eye for an eye, a tooth for a tooth—"I am responsible for her death, I will have to die a pitiful death in retribution."

Maybe this knowledge will help us understand many of the old customs and rituals which have lasted over the centuries and whose purpose is to diminish the anger of the gods or the people as the case may be, thus decreasing the anticipated punishment. I am thinking of the ashes, the torn clothes, the veil, the *Klage Weiber*° of the old days—they are all means to ask you to take pity on them, the mourners, and are expressions of sorrow, grief, and shame. If someone grieves, beats his chest, tears his hair, or refuses to eat, it is an attempt at self-punishment to avoid or reduce the anticipated punishment for the blame that he takes on the death of a loved one.

This grief, shame, and guilt are not very far removed from feelings of anger and rage. The process of grief always includes some qualities of anger. Since none of us likes to admit anger at a deceased person, these emotions are often disguised or repressed and prolong the period of grief or show up in other ways. It is well to remember that it is not up to us to

Klage Weiber   mourning women (German).

judge such feelings as bad or shameful but to understand their true meaning and origin as something very human. In order to illustrate this I will again use the example of the child—and the child in us. The five-year-old who loses his mother is both blaming himself for her disappearance and being angry at her for having deserted him and for no longer gratifying his needs. The dead person then turns into something the child loves and wants very much but also hates with equal intensity for this severe deprivation.

The ancient Hebrews regarded the body of a dead person as something unclean and not to be touched. The early American Indians talked about the evil spirits and shot arrows in the air to drive the spirits away. Many other cultures have rituals to take care of the "bad" dead person, and they all originate in this feeling of anger which still exists in all of us, though we dislike admitting it. The tradition of the tombstone may originate in this wish to keep the bad spirits deep down in the ground, and the pebbles that many mourners put on the grave are left-over symbols of the same wish. Though we call the firing of guns at military funerals a last salute, it is the same symbolic ritual as the Indian used when he shot his spears and arrows into the skies.

I give these examples to emphasize that man has not basically changed. Death is still a fearful, frightening happening, and the fear of death is a universal fear even if we think we have mastered it on many levels.

What has changed is our way of coping and dealing with death and dying and our dying patients.

Having been raised in a country in Europe where science is not so advanced, where modern techniques have just started to find their way into medicine, and where people still live as they did in this country half a century ago, I may have had an opportunity to study a part of the evolution of mankind in a shorter period.

I remember as a child the death of a farmer. He fell from a tree and was not expected to live. He asked simply to die at home, a wish that was granted without questioning. He called his daughters into the bedroom and spoke with each one of them alone for a few minutes. He arranged his affairs quietly, though he was in great pain, and distributed his belongings and his land, none of which was to be split until his wife should follow him in death. He also asked each of his children to share in the work, duties, and tasks that he had carried on until the time of the accident. He asked his friends to visit him once more, to bid good-bye to them. Although I was a small child at the time, he did not exclude me or my siblings. We were allowed to share in the preparations of the family just as we were permitted to grieve with them until he died. When he did die, he was left at home, in his own beloved home which he had built, and among his friends and neighbors who went to take a last look at him where he lay in the midst of flowers in the place he had lived in and loved so much. In that country today there is still no make-believe slumber room, no embalming, no false makeup to pretend sleep. Only the signs of very disfiguring illnesses are covered up with bandages and only infectious cases are removed from the home prior to the burial.

Why do I describe such "old-fashioned" customs? I think they are an indication of our acceptance of a fatal outcome, and they help the dying patient as well as his family to accept the loss of a loved one. If a patient is allowed to terminate his life in the familiar and beloved environment, it requires less adjustment for him. His own family knows him well enough to replace a sedative with a glass of his favorite wine; or the smell of a home-cooked soup may give him the appetite to sip a few spoons of fluid which, I think, is still more enjoyable than an infusion. I will not minimize the need for sedatives and infusions and realize full well from my own experience as a country doctor that they are sometimes life-saving and often unavoidable. But I also know that patience and familiar people and foods could replace many a bottle of intravenous fluids for the simple reason that it fulfills the physiological need without involving too many people and/or individual nursing care.

The fact that children are allowed to stay at home where a fatality has stricken and are included in the talk, discussions, and fears gives them the feeling that they are not alone in the grief and gives them the comfort of shared responsibility and shared mourning. It prepares them gradually and helps them view death as part of life, an experience which may help them grow and mature.

This is in great contrast to a society in which death is viewed as taboo, discussion of it is regarded as morbid, and children are excluded with the presumption and pretext that it would be "too much" for them. They are then sent off to relatives, often accompanied with some unconvincing lies of "Mother has gone on a long trip" or other unbelievable stories. The child senses that something is wrong, and his distrust in adults will only multiply if other relatives add new variations of the story, avoid his questions or suspicions, shower him with gifts as a meager substitute for a loss he is not permitted to deal with. Sooner or later the child will become aware of the changed family situation and, depending on the age and personality of the child, will have an unresolved grief and regard this incident as a frightening, mysterious, in any case very traumatic experience with untrustworthy grownups, which he has no way to cope with.

It is equally unwise to tell a little child who lost her brother that God loved little boys so much that he took little Johnny to heaven. When this little girl grew up to be a woman she never solved her anger at God, which resulted in a psychotic depression when she lost her own little son three decades later.

We would think that our great emancipation, our knowledge of science and of man, has given us better ways and means to prepare ourselves and our families for this inevitable happening. Instead the days are gone when a man was allowed to die in peace and dignity in his own home.

The more we are making advancements in science, the more we seem to fear and deny the reality of death. How is this possible?

We use euphemisms, we make the dead look as if they were asleep, we ship the children off to protect them from the anxiety and turmoil around the house if the patient is fortunate enough to die at home, we don't allow children to visit their dying parents in the hospital, we have long and controversial discussions about whether patients should be told the truth —a question that rarely arises when the dying person is tended by the family physician who has known him from delivery to death and who knows the weaknesses and strengths of each member of the family.

I think there are many reasons for this flight away from facing death calmly. One of the most important facts is that dying nowadays is more gruesome in many ways, namely, more lonely, mechanical, and dehumanized; at times it is even difficult to determine technically when the time of death has occurred.

Dying becomes lonely and impersonal because the patient is often taken out of his familiar environment and rushed to an emergency room. Whoever has been very sick and has required rest and comfort especially may recall his experience of being put on a stretcher and enduring the noise of the ambulance siren and hectic rush until the hospital gates open. Only those who have lived through this may appreciate the discomfort and cold necessity of such transportation which is only the beginning of a long ordeal—hard to endure when you are well, difficult to express in words when noise, light, pumps, and voices are all too much to put up with. It may well be that we might consider more the patient under the sheets and blankets and perhaps stop our well-meant efficiency and rush in order to hold the patient's hand, to smile, or to listen to a question. I include the trip to the hospital as the first episode in dying, as it is for many. I am putting it exaggeratedly in contrast to the sick man who is left at home —not to say that lives should not be saved if they can be saved by a hospitalization but to keep the focus on the patient's experience, his needs and his reactions.

When a patient is severely ill, he is often treated like a person with no right to an opinion. It is often someone else who makes the decision if and when and where a patient should be hospitalized. It would take so little to remember that the sick person too has feelings, has wishes and opinions, and has—most important of all—the right to be heard.

Well, our presumed patient has now reached the emergency room. He will be surrounded by busy nurses, orderlies, interns, residents, a lab technician perhaps who will take some blood, an electrocardiogram technician who takes the cardiogram. He may be moved to X-ray and he will overhear opinions of his condition and discussions and questions to members of the family. He slowly but surely is beginning to be treated like a thing. He is no longer a person. Decisions are made often without his opinion. If he tries to rebel he will be sedated and after hours of waiting and wondering whether he has the strength, he will be wheeled into the operating room or intensive treatment unit and become an object of great concern and great financial investment.

He may cry for rest, peace, and dignity, but he will get infusions, transfusions, a heart machine, or tracheotomy if necessary. He may want one single person to stop for one single minute so that he can ask one single question—but he will get a dozen people around the clock, all busily preoccupied with his heart rate, pulse, electrocardiogram or pulmonary functions, his secretions or excretions but not with him as a human being. He may wish to fight it all but it is going to be a useless fight since all this is done in the fight for his life, and if they can save his life they can consider the person afterwards. Those who consider the person first may lose precious time to save his life! At least this seems to be the rationale or justification behind all this—or is it? Is the reason for this increasingly mechanical, depersonalized approach our own defensiveness? Is this approach our own way to cope with and repress the anxieties that a terminally or critically ill patient evokes in us? Is our concentration on equipment, on blood pressure, our desperate attempt to deny the impending death which is so frightening and discomforting to us that we displace all our knowledge onto machines, since they are less close to us than the suffering face of another human being which would remind us once more of our lack of omnipotence, our own limits and failures, and last but not least perhaps our own mortality?

Maybe the question has to be raised: Are we becoming less human or more human? Though this book is in no way meant to be judgmental, it is clear that whatever the answer may be, the patient is suffering more—not physically, perhaps, but emotionally. And his needs have not changed over the centuries, only our ability to gratify them.

Paul Jacobs

Paul Jacobs, social scientist and writer, was born in New York City in 1918 and attended the City College of New York and the University of Minnesota. He first became active in the union movement as an organizer and later became a labor consultant and copublisher of a labor paper. He was a consultant to the Peace Corps and the War on Poverty program and conducted research and taught journalism at the University of California. He contributed regularly to the *Economist* of London, to many other magazines including *Commentary, Harper's,* and *Newsday,* and was an editor for *Mother Jones.* His books include *The New Radicals* (with S. Landau, 1966); *Prelude to Riot: A View of Urban America from the Bottom* (1967); *Between the Rock and the Hard Place* (1970), about the Middle East conflict; and *The Red, Black and Brown Experience in America* (1971).

Paul Jacobs died of cancer in 1978. He believed that he had been exposed to radiation in 1957 when exploring a site in Nevada that had been declared safe by the Atomic Energy Commission. He was working on a television film on the misuse and mismanagement of nuclear energy in the months before his death.

The essay we print here first appeared in *The Reporter,* September 18, 1958.

The Most Cheerful Graveyard in the World

Along with amassing a comfortable fortune by convincing Los Angelenos that the only fitting way to begin a "happy Eternal Life" is by being laid to rest, in one way or another, at Forest Lawn Memorial Park, the cemetery he founded in 1917, Dr. Hubert Eaton, or "Digger" as he is known in the trade, has also succeeded in almost completely revising the dying industry.

The Digger, whose official title of "Doctor" is purely honorary, accomplished this revision by the simple but profound device of converting the hitherto prosaic act of dying into a gloriously exciting, well-advertised event, somehow intimately and patriotically connected with the American way of life.

Today, thanks to Eaton, dying in Los Angeles is something to be eagerly anticipated, because it is only after death that one can gain permanent tenure at Forest Lawn. Eaton, in one of his earlier roles—that of "the Builder"—described Forest Lawn as "a place where lovers new and old shall love to stroll and watch the sunset's glow, planning for the future or reminiscing of the past; a place where artists study and sketch; where school teachers bring happy children to see the things they read of in books; where little churches invite, triumphant in the knowledge that from their pulpits only words of Love can be spoken; where memorialization of loved ones in sculptured marble and pictorial glass shall be encouraged but controlled by acknowledged artists; a place where the sorrowing will be soothed and strengthened because it will be God's garden. A place that shall be protected by an immense Endowment Care Fund, the principal of which can never be expended—only the income therefrom used to care for and perpetuate this Garden of Memory."

"This is the Builder's Dream; this is the Builder's Creed."

The Builder's Creed is chiseled into a huge, upright stone slab on Forest Lawn's Cathedral Drive, just outside the Great Mausoleum and hard by the Shrine of Love. Viewed, usually in reverent awe, by more than a million visitors each year, Forest Lawn is, along with Disneyland, a favorite tourist attraction in Southern California, far outdrawing the concrete footprints in front of Grauman's Chinese Theatre.

A smaller inscription underneath the Creed points out that on New Year's Day, 1917, Eaton stood on a hilltop overlooking the small country cemetery which had just been placed in his charge. An unemployed mining engineer, Eaton had gone into the cemetery business after a vein of gold in his mine had suddenly vanished.

"A vision came to the man of what this tiny 'God's Acre' might become; and standing there, he made a promise to The Infinite. When he reached home, he put this promise into words and called it 'The Builder's Creed.' Today, Forest Lawn's almost three hundred acres are eloquent witness that The Builder kept faith with his soul."

Indeed, yes. The "almost three hundred acres" also bear eloquent witness to the fact that Eaton, still digging holes in the ground, worked a vein of gold infinitely more reliable than the one that vanished from his mine —the "Science and Art," as he describes it, "of Persuasion." So strongly does Eaton believe the "profession of salesmanship is the greatest of all professions" that he has established The Foundation for the Science and Art of Persuasion at his alma mater, William Jewell College, Liberty, Missouri.

Forest Lawn reflects Eaton's skill in the "Science." The "country cemetery" with only a "scant dozen acres of developed ground" has grown into Forest Lawn Memorial Park, with a permanent "population" of more than 170,000, increasing at the rate of approximately 6,500 a year.

In fact, business has been so good that there are now two additional Forest Lawn "Memorial Parks" in Los Angeles: Forest Lawn-Hollywood Hills, the focus of a bitter political struggle in the city, and adjacent to it Mount Sinai, designed to attract the growing Jewish population of Los Angeles.

Forest Lawn offers the largest religious painting in the United States, displayed in a building, the Hall of the Crucifixion, specially designed for it. There, for a voluntary contribution of twenty-five cents, the visitor sits comfortably in a large theatre, in one of a "broad sweep of seats, richly upholstered in burgundy, rising tier above tier, matching the splendor of the architecture," and watches the three-thousand-pound curtain open on Jesus at Calvary, forty-five feet high and 195 feet long. A lecture about the painting, supplemented with a moving arrow, is delivered by a tape recording in the special kind of rich, organ-toned voice used throughout Forest Lawn.

There are also hundreds of statues, both originals and reproductions, scattered throughout the three hundred acres. Typical of these is an eighteen-figure group depicting Forest Lawn's solution to the "Mystery of Life." Interpretations of the eighteen figures are supplied: "(17) the atheist, the fool, who grinningly cares not at all; while (18) the stoic sits in silent awe and contemplation of that which he believes he knows but cannot explain with any satisfaction."

At the Court of David there is a huge reproduction of Michelangelo's "David"—with a large fig leaf added by Forest Lawn. An exact copy of the sculptor's "Moses" is displayed at the entrance to the Cathedral Corridor in Memorial Terrace, "the only one," according to Forest Lawn, "cast from clay masks placed directly on the original statue in the Church of Saint Peter in Chains at Rome, Italy."

So that the masks could be made, the Church of Saint Peter had to be closed for a day, something that had not happened before. "I gave a lot of dinners and I bought a lot of wine and I sent a lot of cables and St. Peter's was closed," Eaton modestly explains.

Color photos and post cards of the "Moses" statue can be purchased, along with thousands of other items, at Forest Lawn's souvenir shop. There, browsing visitors can choose from showcases displaying money clips, cocktail napkins, book matches, jigsaw puzzles, and charm bracelets —all decorated with Forest Lawn motifs. Prices range from a modest twenty-nine cents for a key chain to $125 for a glass vase etched with a Forest Lawn scene.

There are brown plastic nutshells containing little photos of Forest Lawn, ladies' compacts, cigarette lighters, cufflinks, salt and pepper shakers, picture frames, demitasse spoons, bookmarks, cups and saucers, pen and pencil sets, glass bells, wooden plaques, ashtrays, place mats and doilies, perfume and powder sets, jackknives, and a great variety of other goodies, all with an appropriate Forest Lawn theme. Books like *The Loved One,* Evelyn Waugh's satire of Forest Lawn, are not on sale in the souvenir shop. (Eaton occasionally expresses resentment over the treatment given the cemetery by novelists—especially by one writer to whom he extended free run of the park only to be parodied later. But Eaton also understands that such novels have brought world-wide publicity to Forest Lawn and have not adversely affected his sales, which come not from England but from Los Angeles.)

Among the most popular items at the souvenir shop are those showing reproductions of Forest Lawn's three churches, the Church of the Recessional, the Little Church of the Flowers, and the Wee Kirk o' the Heather.

"Providing a dignified setting for final tribute," the three churches "serve also for the joyous and memorable ceremonies of christening and the exchange of marriage vows." Since the churches have opened, more than 43,000 persons have had "memorable" marriages in them. But Forest Lawn makes no money directly from marrying people, and the profits from the souvenir shop are used for the upkeep of the Hall of the Crucifixion. Forest Lawn's real business is burying people.

"The hardest thing in the world to sell," states one of the organization's top officials, "are 'spaces.' " ("Space" is the euphemism used at Forest Lawn for "grave plot.") The reason for the difficulty is that Forest Lawn's sales organization, which comprises about 175 people, concentrates on sales made "Before Need," another phrase in Forest Lawn's own peculiar language of the flowers. Selling cemetery plots "Before Need" rather than "At Time of Need" or "Post Need," although difficult, is very profitable, since under California law a cemetery pays taxes only on its unsold plots. Once a "space" has been sold, it is removed from the tax rolls. Thus it is to the obvious advantage of Forest Lawn to sell off its land as quickly as possible without waiting for "Need."

There are approximately fifteen hundred individual "spaces" to the acre in Forest Lawn. Prices average $300 per space. There are also rather more elegant neighborhoods at Forest Lawn which are less crowded and therefore more expensive. In the Gardens of Memory, entered only with a special key, there are "memorial sanctuaries designed for families who desire the privacy and protection of crypt interment, but who at the same time long for the open skies and the natural beauty of a verdant garden bathed in sunlight. Under the lawns in the Gardens of Memory have been created a number of monolithically constructed crypts of steel-reinforced concrete."

In the area of ground burial, Forest Lawn has contributed a pleasant innovation. No tombstones are permitted, only markers, set flush with the ground so that there is in fact the pleasant appearance of a park with sweeping green lawns.

But one does not have to be interred to take up permanent residence at Forest Lawn. A number of other arrangements can be made, including being inurned after cremation in the columbarium for as little as $145 or entombed in a mausoleum crypt—which can cost as much $800,000, as in the case of the Irving Thalberg mausoleum. One can also be placed in a large wall out in the open air. Families may be interred, inurned, or entombed as a unit to maintain "togetherness." Should one feel the need for fresh air while spending the "happy Eternal Life" in a crypt, it is possible, at added cost naturally, to have a ventilating system installed. In the mausoleum, tape-recorded music is played as well.

Inurnment is not restricted to a single form of urn. The law in California, which has a strong undertakers' lobby, provides that after cremation ashes must be buried or placed in a columbarium. A wide variety of urn designs can be seen, ranging from books and loving cups to miniature coffins.

The price for the casket or urn sets the approximate amount paid for the funeral itself, but here the range is far greater than for the "space." The least expensive casket, with the metal screw heads showing, is $115; the most expensive goes for $17,500.

Forest Lawn's rich, creamy advertising presentations combine the hard and the soft sell. On radio and television, the same institutional approach is as manifest as at the cemetery itself. Programs of church services and organ music are announced in deep, sonorous tones, and practically no mention is made of the company's product. The institutional approach is also used on billboards picturing stained-glass windows or the "Moses" statue. However, many of Forest Lawn's billboards are given over to the hard, competitive sell, featuring what is Hubert Eaton's original contribution to the American way of death: the concept of combining in one place mortuary functions, such as embalming, with funeral services and burial, thus obviating the necessity for outside undertakers, florists, funeral chapels, and long processions to the cemetery. Forest Lawn successfully undertook the elimination of the undertaking middleman.

Today, Forest Lawn's hard-sell slogans of "Everything In One Beautiful Place" and "Just One Phone Call" are widely copied, as are the ads which usually feature back or side views, sometimes in color, of two dry-eyed, well-groomed people talking to a distinguished-looking, gray-mustached bank-president or diplomat-type man, identified by a discreet sign on his desk as a "Funeral Counselor." Sometimes only the "Counselor" is shown, answering the "Just One Phone Call" with the dedicated air of a statesman. It is clear from the ads that at Forest Lawn, where the concept of death has been abolished, the standards of accepted behavior demand no vulgar signs of outward grief.

But even though its competitors copy Forest Lawn today, Eaton faced a bitter battle when he first attempted to bring a mortuary into the cemetery. Forest Lawn's permit to operate a mortuary was given only after a determined struggle waged against him by some of the undertakers who foresaw disaster for themselves in the new trend of combined services. It was during this period that Forest Lawn began to build up its own political operations, which today make it the most powerful spokesman for the industry in the state.

There have been a number of occasions when, in its self-interest, Forest Lawn has had to do battle, sometimes in ways that might have been frowned on by the dignified gentlemen in their ads. From the 1930's to the early 1950's, Forest Lawn was in a running argument with the county assessor's office over the tax assessments made on its property, with Forest Lawn always claiming that the assessments were too high and almost always getting them reduced, even as much as fifty per cent, by the county board of supervisors. Some supervisors did consistently oppose Forest Lawn's plea for tax reduction and supported the assessor, but when the votes were taken a majority always supported Forest Lawn.

In 1938, in one of its early appearances before the board of supervisors, Forest Lawn requested a tax reduction, claiming that the vacant property in the land it then owned would remain unsold until 1973. At the time, the county assessor pointed out that Forest Lawn had "acquired additional property when they said it was going to take thirty-five years to sell out what they now have, yet they go to work and buy seventy-five acres adjoining at a big price."

Ten years later, in 1948, the issue of how long it would take to fill Forest Lawn's vacant "spaces" became one of the central points in a bitter political hassle within the Los Angeles City Council, and the cemetery completely reversed its argument of ten years earlier. At issue was Forest Lawn's request for a zoning change to permit the use, as a cemetery, of 480 acres of land adjoining Griffith Park, a public park and playground in the Hollywood area.

Forest Lawn's first request to develop this new cemetery was submitted to and rejected by the city planning commission in 1946. When the request was again rejected in 1948, Forest Lawn appealed, claiming, in contrast to its 1938 plea of unsold land, that "by the year 1965 all of the available grave spaces in existing cemeteries will have been exhausted."

The odds against Forest Lawn's gaining approval for its plan to open a new cemetery seemed formidable. The planning commission opposed it, the park department opposed it, the board of health commissioners opposed it, the water and power commission opposed it, the board of public works opposed it, the Hollywood chamber of commerce opposed it, and a variety of community groups opposed it. But the "Builder's Dream" triumphed, and on March 9, 1948, the city council voted 11–3 to permit the opening of the cemetery.

Never an organization to leave stones unturned, within a few hours Forest Lawn had hastily dug six holes in the ground and buried six bodies in them; a move which, under state law, immediately qualified the area as a commercial graveyard that could not then be disturbed or moved except under very specific circumstances.

"We got the bodies we buried through the county hospital or from their next of kin in advance," states Ugene Blalock, vice-president and general counsel of Forest Lawn, "and we made no charge for our services. If the vote in the council had gone against us, we would have given them a free burial elsewhere."

In fact, however, the council vote has rarely gone against Forest Lawn, even when the city fathers were voting on whether to give Beverly Hills the street where Eaton lives, thus providing the Digger with a more distinguished address. Although he hasn't moved, Eaton now lives in Beverly Hills.

No one is quite sure about the exact basis for Eaton's influence; or if they are, they're not willing to talk about it for the record. Blalock states that Forest Lawn as an institution has not made, as far as he knows, any campaign contribution in eighteen years, although he adds, "Individuals may make political contributions." But politics aside, it is Hubert Eaton, master salesman, who is chiefly responsible for Forest Lawn's success.

It is from Eaton's mind that has come the creation of the Council of Regents of the Memorial Court of Honor, twenty-two "outstanding business and professional men" who advise "on all matters concerning the growth of the Memorial Park as a cultural center of religion and fine arts."

Its members, who include the president of Occidental College and the chancellor of the University of Southern California, wear a handsome, flowing red robe, trimmed with velvet, and an elegant round red hat, also trimmed daintily with velvet, while around their necks hangs a kind of Maltese Cross decoration, perhaps the Order of Forest Lawn.

Such touches as these distinguish the imaginative Eaton from his colleagues. Eaton's devotion to salesmanship, as evidenced by his creating special heart-shaped children's sections at Forest Lawn, named Babyland and Lullabyland, began early in life, according to "The Forest Lawn Story," his biography sold at the souvenir shop.

The son of a college professor, Eaton, states the biography, "sat in his little cubbyhole behind his father's bookshelves ostensibly studying but actually eavesdropping on his father's conversations with callers. Invariably they came for advice on one thing or another but more often than not, it was advice on matters affecting money. From these conversations he learned the word salesmanship and what it meant."

It was Eaton, too, who initiated many Forest Lawn public-service activities—the inspirational speaker made available to service clubs, the thirteen half-hour Bible films, and the giving of the Forest Lawn Awards for Persuasive Writing as a "practical service to students and Christian liberal arts colleges."

Long interested in "small, independent, liberal arts colleges" as being "America's last bulwark against the march of Socialism . . ." Eaton believes that "most" college professors are "semi-socialists at heart" who teach young people that salesmanship "smacks of chicanery, demagoguery, of influencing people against their wills . . ."

But Eaton isn't always so serious. Even when he was at college himself, he always had a "good sense of humor." His biography relates that one of his favorite tricks was to persuade a visitor to allow a funnel to be inserted into the top of his trousers and then to make him balance a penny on his chin and try to drop it into the funnel. While the visitor was in this position, young Hubert "or one of his cronies would pour a cup of cold water into the funnel."

Eaton's "good sense of humor changed little in succeeding years," states his biographer, and it certainly hadn't changed much the night when Eaton gave one of his usual huge, lavish parties for a group of friends and guests. It was called "An Enchanted Evening in the South Pacific," of which "Trader" Hubert Eaton was the master of ceremonies. Elaborate Hawaiian acts were presented, and guests received a large, beautifully printed eight-page souvenir program in color, in which Eaton had himself depicted as "Your Happy Planter," jumping from page to page on a golden-shovel pogo stick.

On the cultural level, the printed program carried a large reproduction of the "David" statue, with a fig leaf, a Hawaiian lei, and a girl curled around its neck, all illustrating a poem, "The Secret of Hubie's

David," which described just how it was decided to add a fig leaf to Forest Lawn's copy of Michelangelo's "David" in order not to shock "the ladies of L.A."

But surely the greatest of all the improvements that Eaton has made on the past is Forest Lawn itself. Here, what might have been just an ordinary "country cemetery" has been parlayed into a solemn institution, profitable and widely imitated, looking like Edgar Guest's idea of Heaven° brought to earth, while representing a social level to which all people can aspire after death. And in the future, says Hubert Eaton, "When the place is filled up, my idea, from a financial standpoint, has always been to make Forest Lawn into a museum and charge admission."

J. H. Plumb

J. H. Plumb was born in 1911 and received his Ph.D. in 1936, doing his doctoral research under the social historian G. M. Trevelyan at Christ's College, Cambridge. After serving with the intelligence service of the British Foreign Office during World War II, he began teaching at Cambridge in 1946; he became Master of Christ's College in 1978. He has often served as visiting professor at universities in the United States.

Plumb, noted for his meticulous scholarship and lively prose style, believes that history must use the past to sanctify reason rather than authority or morality. He is a prolific writer, with particular interest in British Renaissance and eighteenth-century history. The essay we reprint here is from *In the Light of History* (1972).

De Mortuis

The British have hilarious fun at the quaint funerary habits of the Americans. The death of Hubert Eaton, the world's greatest entrepreneur of death, and the recent discovery of a funerary home for pets by a wandering British journalist, released another gale of satirical laughter in the English press. The mockery was hearty but sustained, yet was it deserved? Well certainly much of Forest Lawn is hard to take: the wet, nursery language for the hard facts of dying—'the loved one' for the corpse, 'leave

Edgar Guest   American writer (1881–1959) whose verses on friendship, humility, and the value of labor and simple living were printed for years in a nationally syndicated newspaper column.

taking' for burying and 'slumber' for death; the cosmetic treatment—the contortions of death waxed away, replaced by rouge and mascara and fashionably set hair; all of this is good for a gruesome joke. The place names of the Lawn are appalling—Lullabyland, Babyland. The piped guff, the music that flows like oil and the coy fig-leaved art give one goose-flesh. It is hard to repress a sense of nausea, and one turns, almost with relief, to a harsh fifteenth-century representation of the Dance of Death—livid corpses, jangling bones and skulls that haunt. How wholesome, after Hubert Eaton, seem the savage depictions of Bonfigli of the ravages of plague: or even the nightmares of death painted by Hieronymus Bosch. And how salutary in our own age to turn from Forest Lawn to the screaming, dissolving bodies of Francis Bacon, for surely this is how life ends for most of us, in pain, in agony.

And if Forest Lawn nauseates, what of the Pets Parlour?—'Blackie' combed and brushed, stretched out on the hearth rug before a log fire, waits for his sorrowing owners. The budgerigar is naturally wired to its perch. The Ming Room houses the Siamese cats and if you want to do your pussy proud, you can spend three hundred dollars or so on a stately laying out, a goodly coffin (if you're worried about its fun in the after life, you can put an outsize rubber mouse in with it) and naturally a special plot in 'Bide-A-Wee', the memorial park for pets. Certainly it takes some taking, although it seems President Nixon took it, for his dog, Checkers, had the treatment: he lies amongst the immortals in Bide-A-Wee, like Hubert in Forest Lawn.

However, this will become all very cheap, a mere second-class death, if deep freezing really catches on, as it shows every sign of doing. The Life Extension Society is spreading, and the entrepreneurs have smelt the profit in immortality. As soon as the breath goes, get yourself encapsulated in liquid nitrogen and stored in one of the specially constructed freezers that are springing up all over America from Phoenix to New York. And so wait for the day when they can cure what you died of, or replace what gave way—the heart, the brain, the liver or the guts—or simply rejuvenate your cells. Naturally it is not cheap: the capsule costs $4,000 and then there are the freezing costs and who knows what they may be in fifty years, so it would be imprudent not to make ample provision. And then, of course, I cannot imagine the revitalizing process will not dig a big hole into quite a considerable fortune. Forest Lawn may be death for the rich; this is death for the richer, death for the Big Time. And in America there are a lot of very rich, so maybe soon now, outside all the big cities, there will be frigidaires, as huge as pyramids, full of the frozen dead. This surely must be a growth industry. Perhaps, by the year 2000, Hubert Eaton will seem but a modest pioneer of the death industry, for who does not crave to escape oblivion? All rich people have tried to domesticate death, to make death seem like life. The American way of death is not novel, nor, *pace* Hubert Eaton, is it nauseatingly comic: seen in proper historical perspective it reaches back not only down the centuries but down the millennia, for it is a response to a deep human need.

Some of the earliest graves of men, dating from palaeolithic times, contained corpses not only decked out with bits of personal finery but also sprinkled with red ochre, perhaps the symbol of blood and life, maybe in the hope of a future resurrection. After the neolithic revolution, which created much greater resources and very considerable surplus wealth, men went in for death in a very big way. Doubtless the poor were thrown away, burnt or exposed or pushed into obscurity, back to the anonymous mud from which they came.

The rich and the powerful, high priests and kings, could not die, they merely passed from one life to another, and the life hereafter was but a mirror image of life on earth, so they took with them everything they needed—jewels, furniture, food, and, of course, servants. In the royal graves at Ur, some of the earliest and most sumptuous of tombs ever found, a row of handmaidens had been slaughtered at the burial—death's necessities were life's. No one, of course, took this elaboration of funerary activity further than the Egyptians. And the tombs of pharaohs and the high officials of the Egyptian kingdom make Forest Lawn seem like a cheap cemetery for the nation's down and outs. After all, one must use one's imagination. What should we think of vast stone mausoleums outside Washington, stuffed with personal jewellery from Winston's, furniture from Sloanes, tableware by Steuben, food from Bloomingdales, etc., etc., and in the midst of it all the embalmed corpse of a Coolidge or a Dulles? We should roar with laughter. We should regard it as vulgar, ridiculous, absurd.

Pushed back three millennia, such habits acquire not only decorum, but also majesty, grandeur, awe. The Egyptians were as portentous in death as in life, and their grave goods only occasionally give off the breath of life, unlike the Etruscans who domesticated death more completely, more joyously than any other society. A rich caste of princes built tombs of singular magnificence, filling them with amphorae, jewels, and silver. And they adorned their walls with all the gaiety that they had enjoyed alive. There was nothing solemn about their attitude to death. In their tombs they hunted, played games, performed acrobatics, danced, feasted; their amorous dalliance was both wanton and guiltless. Deliberately they banished death with the recollected gusto of life. No society has brought such eroticism, such open and natural behavior to the charnel house. But in the annals of death, Etruscans are rare birds.

How different the grandiose tombs of medieval barons, with their splendid alabaster or marble effigies. There they lie, larger than life, grave, portentous, frozen in death, a wife, sometimes two, rigidly posed beside them, and beneath, sorrowing children, kneeling in filial piety, the whole structure made more pompous with heraldic quarterings. These are yet another attempt to cheat death, to keep alive in stone what was decaying and crumbling below. And even here a breath of life sometimes creeps in.

The Earl and Countess of Arundel lie side by side, dogs beneath the feet, pillows under the head; he in armour, she in her long woollen gown, but, movingly enough, they are holding hands. The sons of Lord Teynham cannot be parted, even in death, with their hawk and hound. Nor were these tombs so cold, so marmoreal, when they were first built to keep the memory of the dead alive. They were painted, the faces as alive with colour as corpses in the parlours of Forest Lawn.

Seen in the context of history, Forest Lawn is neither very vulgar nor very remarkable: and the frigidaires at Phoenix are no more surprising than a pyramid in Palenque or Cairo. If life has been good we, like the rich Etruscans, want it to go on and on and on, or at the least to be remembered. Only a few civilizations have evaded expensive funerary habits for their illustrious rich, and these usually poverty-stricken ones. Even the Hindus, burning bodies and throwing the ashes into the Ganges, austere as they are, have maintained distinction in their pyres. Not only were widows coaxed or thrown on to the flames, but rare and perfumed woods were burnt to sweeten the spirit of the rich Brahman as it escaped from its corrupt carapace. Cremation *à la* Chanel!

What is tasteless and vulgar in one age becomes tender and moving in another. What should we say if we decorated our tombs with scenes from baseball, cocktail bars and the circus, or boasted on the side of our coffins of our amatory prowess, as erect and as unashamed in death as in life. And yet when the Etruscans do just these things, we are moved to a sense of delight that the force of life could be so strong that men and women revelled in it in their graves.

So the next time that you stroll through Forest Lawn, mildly nauseated by its silly sentimentality, think of those Etruscans; you will understand far more easily why seven thousand marriages a year take place in this Californian graveyard. After all, like the Arundels, Eros and Death have gone hand in hand down the ages. The urge to obliterate death is the urge to extend life: and what more natural than that the rich should expect renewal. How right, how proper, that Checkers should be waiting in Slumberland.

Alice Walker

Alice Walker was born in 1944 in Eatonton, Georgia, the eighth child of black sharecroppers. She attended Spelman College for two years, then graduated from Sarah Lawrence in 1965. From 1968 to 1970 she taught writing and black literature at Jackson State and Tougaloo in Mississippi; in 1972 she became lecturer in writing and literature at both Wellesley College and the

University of Massachusetts. She has been a fiction editor of *Ms.* magazine since 1974, on the English faculty at Yale University since 1977, and she has traveled and lived in Africa and the Soviet Union.

Her writings often explore family relationships—the unity and hostility felt within black families because of outside social forces in a racist society. She has written three novels: *The Third Life of Grange Copeland* (1970), *Meridian* (1976), and *The Color Purple,* the 1982 Pulitzer Prize winner for fiction; three books of poems: *Once* (1968), *Revolutionary Petunias* (1973), *Good Night Willie Lee, I'll See You in the Morning* (1979); a biography of Langston Hughes (1973); and she has edited a collection of writings by Zora Neale Hurston. Her two collections of short stories are *You Can't Keep a Good Woman Down* (1981) and *In Love and Trouble: Stories of Black Women* (1973). The latter, from which we print the story below, was awarded the Rosenthal Award by the National Institute for Arts and Letters.

To Hell with Dying

"To hell with dying," my father would say. "These children want Mr. Sweet!"

Mr. Sweet was a diabetic and an alcoholic and a guitar player and lived down the road from us on a neglected cotton farm. My older brothers and sisters got the most benefit from Mr. Sweet, for when they were growing up he had quite a few years ahead of him and so was capable of being called back from the brink of death any number of times—whenever the voice of my father reached him as he lay expiring. "To hell with dying, man," my father would say, pushing the wife away from the bedside (in tears although she knew the death was not necessarily the last one unless Mr. Sweet really wanted it to be). "These children want Mr. Sweet!" And they did want him, for at a signal from Father they would come crowding around the bed and throw themselves on the covers, and whoever was the smallest at the time would kiss him all over his wrinkled brown face and begin to tickle him so that he would laugh all down in his stomach, and his moustache, which was long and sort of straggly, would shake like Spanish moss and was also that color.

Mr. Sweet had been ambitious as a boy, wanted to be a doctor or lawyer or sailor, only to find that black men fare better if they are not. Since he could become none of these things he turned to fishing as his only earnest career and playing the guitar as his only claim to doing anything extraordinarily well. His son, the only one that he and his wife, Miss Mary, had, was shiftless as the day is long and spent money as if he were trying to see the bottom of the mint, which Mr. Sweet would tell him was the clean brown palm of his hand. Miss Mary loved her "baby," however, and worked hard to get him the "li'l necessaries" of life, which turned out mostly to be women.

Mr. Sweet was a tall, thinnish man with thick kinky hair going dead white. He was dark brown, his eyes were very squinty and sort of bluish, and he chewed Brown Mule tobacco. He was constantly on the verge of being blind drunk, for he brewed his own liquor and was not in the least a stingy sort of man, and was always very melancholy and sad, though frequently when he was "feelin' good" he'd dance around the yard with us, usually keeling over just as my mother came to see what the commotion was.

Toward all of us children he was very kind, and had the grace to be shy with us, which is unusual in grown-ups. He had great respect for my mother for she never held his drunkenness against him and would let us play with him even when he was about to fall in the fireplace from drink. Although Mr. Sweet would sometimes lose complete or nearly complete control of his head and neck so that he would loll in his chair, his mind remained strangely acute and his speech not too affected. His ability to be drunk and sober at the same time made him an ideal playmate, for he was as weak as we were and we could usually best him in wrestling, all the while keeping a fairly coherent conversation going.

We never felt anything of Mr. Sweet's age when we played with him. We loved his wrinkles and would draw some on our brows to be like him, and his white hair was my special treasure and he knew it and would never come to visit us just after he had had his hair cut off at the barbershop. Once he came to our house for something, probably to see my father about fertilizer for his crops because, although he never paid the slightest attention to his crops, he liked to know what things would be best to use on them if he ever did. Anyhow, he had not come with his hair since he had just had it shaved off at the barbershop. He wore a huge straw hat to keep off the sun and also to keep his head away from me. But as soon as I saw him I ran up and demanded that he take me up and kiss me with his funny beard which smelled so strongly of tobacco. Looking forward to burying my small fingers into his woolly hair I threw away his hat only to find he had done something to his hair, that it was no longer there! I let out a squall which made my mother think that Mr. Sweet had finally dropped me in the well or something and from that day I've been wary of men in hats. However, not long after, Mr. Sweet showed up with his hair grown out and just as white and kinky and impenetrable as it ever was.

Mr. Sweet used to call me his princess, and I believed it. He made me feel pretty at five and six, and simply outrageously devastating at the blazing age of eight and a half. When he came to our house with his guitar the whole family would stop whatever they were doing to sit around him and listen to him play. He liked to play "Sweet Georgia Brown," that was what he called me sometimes, and also he liked to play "Caldonia" and all sorts of sweet, sad, wonderful songs which he sometimes made up. It was from one of these songs that I learned that he had had to marry Miss Mary when he had in fact loved somebody else (now living in Chi-ca-go, or De-stroy, Michigan). He was not sure that Joe Lee, her "baby," was also his baby. Sometimes he would cry and that was an indication that he was about to die again. And so we would all get prepared, for we were sure to be called upon.

I was seven the first time I remember actually participating in one of Mr. Sweet's "revivals"—my parents told me I had participated before, I had been the one chosen to kiss him and tickle him long before I knew the rite of Mr. Sweet's rehabilitation. He had come to our house, it was a few years after his wife's death, and was very sad, and also, typically, very drunk. He sat on the floor next to me and my older brother, the rest of the children were grown up and lived elsewhere, and began to play his guitar and cry. I held his woolly head in my arms and wished I could have been old enough to have been the woman he loved so much and that I had not been lost years and years ago.

When he was leaving, my mother said to us that we'd better sleep light that night for we'd probably have to go over to Mr. Sweet's before daylight. And we did. For soon after we had gone to bed one of the neighbors knocked on our door and called my father and said that Mr. Sweet was sinking fast and if he wanted to get in a word before the crossover he'd better shake a leg and get over to Mr. Sweet's house. All the neighbors knew to come to our house if something was wrong with Mr. Sweet, but they did not know how we always managed to make him well, or at least stop him from dying, when he was often so near death. As soon as we heard the cry we got up, my brother and I and my mother and father, and put on our clothes. We hurried out of the house and down the road for we were always afraid that we might someday be too late and Mr. Sweet would get tired of dallying.

When we got to the house, a very poor shack really, we found the front room full of neighbors and relatives and someone met us at the door and said that it was all very sad that old Mr. Sweet Little (for Little was his family name, although we mostly ignored it) was about to kick the bucket. My parents were advised not to take my brother and me into the "death room," seeing we were so young and all, but we were so much more accustomed to the death room than he that we ignored him and dashed in without giving his warning a second thought. I was almost in tears, for these deaths upset me fearfully, and the thought of how much depended on me and my brother (who was such a ham most of the time) made me very nervous.

The doctor was bending over the bed and turned back to tell us for at least the tenth time in the history of my family that, alas, old Mr. Sweet Little was dying and that the children had best not see the face of implacable death (I didn't know what "implacable" was, but whatever it was, Mr. Sweet was not!). My father pushed him rather abruptly out of the way saying, as he always did and very loudly for he was saying it to Mr. Sweet, "To hell with dying, man, these children want Mr. Sweet"—which was my cue to throw myself upon the bed and kiss Mr. Sweet all around the whiskers and under the eyes and around the collar of his nightshirt where he smelled so strongly of all sorts of things, mostly liniment.

I was very good at bringing him around, for as soon as I saw that he was struggling to open his eyes I knew he was going to be all right, and so could finish my revival sure of success. As soon as his eyes were open he would begin to smile and that way I knew that I had surely won. Once, though, I got a tremendous scare, for he could not open his eyes and later I learned that he had had a stroke and that one side of his face was stiff and hard to get into motion. When he began to smile I could tickle him in earnest because I was sure that nothing would get in the way of his laughter, although once he began to cough so hard that he almost threw me off his stomach, but that was when I was very small, little more than a baby, and my bushy hair had gotten in his nose.

When we were sure he would listen to us we would ask him why he was in bed and when he was coming to see us again and could we play with his guitar, which more than likely would be leaning against the bed. His eyes would get all misty and he would sometimes cry out loud, but we never let it embarrass us, for he knew that we loved him and that we sometimes cried too for no reason. My parents would leave the room to just the three of us; Mr. Sweet, by that time, would be propped up in bed with a number of pillows behind his head and with me sitting and lying on his shoulder and along his chest. Even when he had trouble breathing he would not ask me to get down. Looking into my eyes he would shake his white head and run a scratchy old finger all around my hairline, which was rather low down, nearly to my eyebrows, and made some people say I looked like a baby monkey.

My brother was very generous in all this, he let me do all the revivaling —he had done it for years before I was born and so was glad to be able to pass it on to someone new. What he would do while I talked to Mr. Sweet was pretend to play the guitar, in fact pretend that he was a young version of Mr. Sweet, and it always made Mr. Sweet glad to think that someone wanted to be like him—of course, we did not know this then, we played the thing by ear, and whatever he seemed to like, we did. We were desperately afraid that he was just going to take off one day and leave us.

It did not occur to us that we were doing anything special; we had not learned that death was final when it did come. We thought nothing of triumphing over it so many times, and in fact became a trifle contemptuous of people who let themselves be carried away. It did not occur to us that if our own father had been dying we could not have stopped it, that Mr. Sweet was the only person over whom we had power.

When Mr. Sweet was in his eighties I was studying in the university many miles from home. I saw him whenever I went home, but he was never on the verge of dying that I could tell and I began to feel that my anxiety for his health and psychological well-being was unnecessary. By this time he not only had a moustache but a long flowing snow-white beard, which I loved and combed and braided for hours. He was very peaceful, fragile, gentle, and the only jarring note about him was his old steel guitar, which he still played in the old sad, sweet, down-home blues way.

On Mr. Sweet's ninetieth birthday I was finishing my doctorate in Massachusetts and had been making arrangements to go home for several weeks' rest. That morning I got a telegram telling me that Mr. Sweet was dying again and could I please drop everything and come home. Of course I could. My dissertation could wait and my teachers would understand when I explained to them when I got back. I ran to the phone, called the airport, and within four hours I was speeding along the dusty road to Mr. Sweet's.

The house was more dilapidated than when I was last there, barely a shack, but it was overgrown with yellow roses which my family had planted many years ago. The air was heavy and sweet and very peaceful. I felt strange walking through the gate and up the old rickety steps. But the strangeness left me as I caught sight of the long white beard I loved so well flowing down the thin body over the familiar quilt coverlet. Mr. Sweet!

His eyes were closed tight and his hands, crossed over his stomach, were thin and delicate, no longer scratchy. I remembered how always before I had run and jumped up on him just anywhere; now I knew he would not be able to support my weight. I looked around at my parents, and was surprised to see that my father and mother also looked old and frail. My father, his own hair very gray, leaned over the quietly sleeping old man, who, incidentally, smelled still of wine and tobacco, and said, as he'd done so many times, "To hell with dying, man! My daughter is home to see Mr. Sweet!" My brother had not been able to come as he was in the war in Asia. I bent down and gently stroked the closed eyes and gradually they began to open. The closed, wine-stained lips twitched a little, then parted in a warm, slightly embarrassed smile. Mr. Sweet could see me and he recognized me and his eyes looked very spry and twinkly for a moment. I put my head down on the pillow next to his and we just looked at each other for a long time. Then he began to trace my peculiar hairline with a thin, smooth finger. I closed my eyes when his finger halted above my ear (he used to rejoice at the dirt in my ears when I was little), his hand stayed cupped around my cheek. When I opened my eyes, sure that I had reached him in time, his were closed.

Even at twenty-four how could I believe that I had failed? that Mr. Sweet was really gone? He had never gone before. But when I looked up at my parents I saw that they were holding back tears. They had loved him dearly. He was like a piece of rare and delicate china which was always being saved from breaking and which finally fell. I looked long at the old face, the wrinkled forehead, the red lips, the hands that still reached out to me. Soon I felt my father pushing something cool into my hands. It was Mr. Sweet's guitar. He had asked them months before to give it to me; he had known that even if I came next time he would not be able to respond in the old way. He did not want me to feel that my trip had been for nothing.

The old guitar! I plucked the strings, hummed "Sweet Georgia Brown." The magic of Mr. Sweet lingered still in the cool steel box. Through the window I could catch the fragrant delicate scent of tender yellow roses. The man on the high old-fashioned bed with the quilt coverlet and the flowing white beard had been my first love.

Rhetorical Index

We indicate below selections that well illustrate some rhetorical and technical procedures traditionally discussed in the study of composition. The listing is meant to be suggestive, not inclusive; most essays employ more than one rhetorical procedure, and many refuse to fit neatly into any traditional genre. We have listed those pieces that particularly illustrate the crucial transition from the more personal to the more analytic or discursive essay as a separate category.

Index of Genres

Following is a list of genres (exclusive of the essay) represented in the book:

Table of Cross-References

We list here, under the heading for each section of the text, titles of essays from other sections that might profitably be studied at the same time.

The Good Life

Race, Racism and Culture

On Women and Men

The Media and Popular Culture

Technology and Human Values

Religion and the Search for Meaning

Author and Title Index

About the Editors

CHARLES MUSCATINE is Professor of English at the University of California at Berkeley, where he has taught since 1948. He received the Ph.D. from Yale University and has served as a Visiting Professor at Wesleyan University and the University of Washington. A distinguished medievalist, Professor Muscatine has received Fulbright and Guggenheim research fellowships; is the author of *Chaucer and the French Tradition, The Book of Geoffrey Chaucer,* and *Poetry and Crisis in the Age of Chaucer;* has published widely in professional journals; and has served as President of the New Chaucer Society. At Berkeley, he has been Chair of the Select Committee on Education, Director of the experimental Collegiate Seminar Program, and Chair of the Committee on Freshman English.

MARLENE GRIFFITH is on the faculty of Laney College in Oakland, California, where she has taught since 1966. She has also taught at Western College for Women, San Francisco State University, and the University of California at Berkeley. She received her B.A. from American International College in Springfield, Mass., and her M.A. from Berkeley. She has contributed articles to *College Composition and Communication, Twentieth Century Literature, Modern Fiction Studies,* and, more recently, *Writing for the Inexperienced Writer: Fluency Shape Correctness* and *Writing to Think* to series published by the Bay Area Writing Project. At Laney, she has directed the Writing Center and been Chair of the English Department.

A Note on the Type

This book was composed in Gael, a computer version of Caledonia designed by W. A. Dwiggins (1880–1956). It belongs to the family of printing types called "modern face" by printers—a term used to mark the change in style of type letters that occurred about 1800. It borders on the general design of Scotch Roman, but is more freely drawn than that letter.